The 9 Competencies and 31 Component Behaviors (EPAS, 2015)	...y, Where Referenced
Competency 6—Engage with Individuals, Families, Groups, Organizations, and Communities:	
a. Apply knowledge of human behavior and the social environment, person-in-environment, and other multidisciplinary theoretical frameworks to engage with clients and constituencies	
b. Use empathy, reflection, and interpersonal skills to effectively engage diverse clients and constituencies	
Competency 7—Assess Individuals, Families, Groups, Organizations, and Communities:	**2, 8, 9, 10, 19**
a. Collect and organize data, and apply critical thinking to interpret information from clients and constituencies	**2, 8, 9, 10, 19**
b. Apply knowledge of human behavior and the social environment, person-in-environment, and other multidisciplinary theoretical frameworks in the analysis of assessment data from clients and constituencies	**2, 21, 22**
c. Develop mutually agreed-on intervention goals and objectives based on the critical assessment of strengths, needs, and challenges within clients and constituencies	**2**
d. Select appropriate intervention strategies based on the assessment, research knowledge, and values and preferences of clients and constituencies	**2, 8, 9, 10, 19**
Competency 8—Intervene with Individuals, Families, Groups, Organizations, and Communities:	**2, 4**
a. Critically choose and implement interventions to achieve practice goals and enhance capacities of clients and constituencies	**2, 4**
b. Apply knowledge of human behavior and the social environment, person-in-environment, and other multidisciplinary theoretical frameworks in interventions with clients and constituencies	
c. Use inter-professional collaboration as appropriate to achieve beneficial practice outcomes	
d. Negotiate, mediate, and advocate with and on behalf of diverse clients and constituencies	
e. Facilitate effective transitions and endings that advance mutually agreed-on goals	
Competency 9—Evaluate Practice with Individuals, Families, Groups, Organizations, and Communities:	**1, 2, 3, 4, 5, 6, 7, 8, 9, 10, 11, 12, 13, 14, 15, 16, 17, 20, 21, 22, 23**
a. Select and use appropriate methods for evaluation of outcomes	**2, 7, 8, 9, 10, 11, 12, 13, 14, 15, 16, 21, 22, 23**
b. Apply knowledge of human behavior and the social environment, person-in-environment, and other multidisciplinary theoretical frameworks in the evaluation of outcomes	**2, 3, 6**
c. Critically analyze, monitor, and evaluate intervention and program processes and outcomes	**2, 4, 5, 7, 8, 9, 10, 11, 12, 13, 14, 15, 16, 17, 21, 22, 23**
d. Apply evaluation findings to improve practice effectiveness at the micro, mezzo, and macro levels	**1, 2, 23**

RESEARCH METHODS FOR SOCIAL WORK

Allen Rubin
University of Houston

Earl R. Babbie
Chapman University

Australia • Brazil • Mexico • Singapore • United Kingdom • United States

Research Methods for Social Work,
Ninth Edition
Allen Rubin and Earl R. Babbie

Product Director: Jon-David Hague

Product Manager: Julie A. Martinez

Content Developer: Theodore Knight

Product Assistant: Stephen A Lagos

Marketing Manager: Margaux Cameron

Art and Cover Direction, Production
Management, and Composition: MPS
Limited

Manufacturing Planner: Judy Inouye

Photo Researcher: Lumina Datamatics Ltd

Text Researcher: Lumina Datamatics Ltd

Cover Image: mihailomilovanovic/
Getty images

For product information and technology assistance, contact us at
Cengage Learning Customer & Sales Support, 1-800-354-9706.

For permission to use material from this text or product,
submit all requests online at **www.cengage.com/permissions**.

Further permissions questions can be e-mailed to
permissionrequest@cengage.com.

Unless otherwise noted all items © Cengage Learning®

Library of Congress Control Number: 2015950165

Student Edition:
ISBN: 978-1-305-63382-7

Loose-leaf Edition:
ISBN: 978-1-305-85961-6

Cengage Learning

20 Channel Center Street

Boston, MA 02210

USA

Cengage Learning is a leading provider of customized learning solutions with employees residing in nearly 40 different countries and sales in more than 125 countries around the world. Find your local representative at **www.cengage.com**.

Cengage Learning products are represented in Canada by Nelson Education, Ltd.

To learn more about Cengage Learning Solutions, visit **www.cengage.com**.

Purchase any of our products at your local college store or at our preferred online store **www.cengagebrain.com**.

Printed in the United States of America
Print Number: 01   Print Year: 2015

To our wives
CHRISTINA RUBIN
SUZANNE BABBIE

CONTENTS IN BRIEF

CONTENTS IN DETAIL

PREFACE

As with previous editions of this text, this ninth edition contains significant improvements to keep up with advances in the field and respond to the excellent suggestions from colleagues. One of the things that hasn't changed is our presentation of boxes to illustrate concepts that bring research content to life and illustrate its relevance to social work and its utility in informing social work practice. In that connection, we have added some new boxes in this edition. Here are some of our other most noteworthy changes to this edition.

CSWE EPAS Core Competencies. As we were writing this new edition, the Council on Social Work Education was in the process of revising its Educational Policy and Accreditation Standards (EPAS) Core Competencies. Accordingly, we have changed the way we show how the contents of our book pertain to those core competencies.

Book Length. In response to reviewer concerns about the length and cost of the book, we strived to shorten this edition in ways that will not sacrifice one of its chief virtues: its comprehensiveness and use of many social work practice examples and illustrations. Although the shortening revisions occurred in many chapters, they are most noteworthy in the content on inferential statistics, in which two chapters were shortened and combined into one (Chapter 22).

Significant Additions. At the same time, we made many additions throughout the book. The most significant additions are as follows:

- Expanded coverage of mixed-methods
- New content on LGBTQ populations in several chapters
- Expanded content on scale development
- New content on criteria for inferring causality in epidemiological research
- More emphasis on how to conduct successful program evaluations

- New, updated content on how advances in technology are affecting surveys and qualitative research
- New content on how to conduct focus group interviewing
- A new Appendix on critically appraising meta-analyses

Below is a chapter-by-chapter description of our most noteworthy changes.

- **Chapter 1.** Several reviewers offered useful recommendations regarding the need to shorten this lengthy chapter. We agreed with and followed their advice. At the same time, however, we managed to add a humorous photo and a new box listing some interventions with strong research support.

- **Chapter 2.** Throughout our discussion of evidence-based practice (EBP), we have increased content showing how EBP applies to the macro and policy levels of social work practice. Also throughout we have replaced wording about EBP *guiding* practice with wording about EBP *informing* practice decisions. We replaced the model of EBP in Figure 2-1 with an updated version of the model. We elaborated our discussion of systematic reviews and meta-analyses and added Figure 2-2 on criteria for critically appraising them. We also updated our box on Google Scholar results.

- **Chapter 3.** In response to suggestions from our reviewers and other colleagues, extensive changes were made to this chapter in an effort to make it less overwhelming and more relevant to social work students. In particular, we have shortened the coverage of philosophical issues, made it less esoteric, and modified it so that instead of dwelling on paradigm wars it puts more emphasis on the flexible use of each paradigm, depending on the research question and study purpose.

In keeping with this new emphasis, we have renamed the chapter, replacing philosophy and theory in the title with "Factors Influencing the Research Process." The philosophical content no longer appears at the beginning of the chapter. Instead, the chapter starts by covering the phases of the research process, moving coverage of philosophical issues from the end of Chapter 4 in the previous edition to the start of Chapter 3 in this one. The previous figure diagraming the research process has been replaced with one that is less cluttered and complex—one that we think students will find more relevant and easier to follow. One of the suggestions we have received from colleagues is to add more LGBTQ content to various parts of the book. In that connection, we have altered the way we cover sex and gender variables in this chapter.

- **Chapter 4.** We have received enthusiastic praise for this chapter from various colleagues, who have added that they'd like to see the content on mixed-methods expanded a bit. So, we have expanded our discussion of mixed-methods, including coverage of additional types of mixed methods designs and a new box providing a case example of a published mixed-methods study of clients and practitioners in a child welfare agency.

- **Chapter 5.** We added content on getting informed consent to videorecord, elaborated on IRB debriefing requirements when deception is involved in the research, added content on federal regulations regarding vulnerable populations, and modified our section on bias and insensitivity to better distinguish the concepts of sex and gender identity and thus make the section more appropriate regarding LGBTQ people. Also bolstering the chapter's attention to research ethics concerning LGBTQ populations, we added a box titled "IRB Imperfections Regarding Research with Lesbian, Gay, and Bisexual Populations." In addition to illustrating mistakes that IRB board members can make, that box shows how best to respond to such mistakes to enhance chances for eventual IRB approval. In response to requests from reviewers, we shortened somewhat the very lengthy section on politics, reducing the amount of attention given to objectivity and ideology. We think that now students will be better able to comprehend and appreciate the relevance of that section.

- **Chapter 6.** We have added substantial content regarding cultural competence with regard to LGBTQ individuals.

- **Chapter 7.** In response to a reviewer's request for more content on research question development we've added a new box illustrating the process of formulating a good research question. In keeping with our overall effort to shorten this book without losing is essential comprehensiveness, we also have implemented reviewer suggestions to make the coverage of units of analysis less extensive and less detailed. In so doing, we think students will find coverage of that topic more relevant and easier to comprehend.

- **Chapter 8.** We clarified what is meant by truisms. We added a box providing more examples of spurious relationships. We simplified somewhat our discussion of conceptions and reality and clarified that the consequences of abstract constructs are real. In response to suggestions from colleagues, we have moved up the section on levels of measurement from Chapter 21 to this chapter. Content on the implications of levels of measurement for statistical analysis remains in Chapter 21.

- **Chapter 9.** We added a brief explanation of the term *correlation* to the section on interrater reliability and a new box to further illustrate the difference between reliability and validity.

- **Chapter 10.** We significantly expanded our discussion of scale development, including a large new section on generating an initial pool of items and how to select items from that pool. We also expanded somewhat our discussion of double-barreled items, partly to enhance reader understanding of some of the nuances involved and partly to compensate for the removal of the outdated box on the subject. In response to reviewer suggestions, and also to try to reduce the length and cost of this edition, we replaced one 3-page long and somewhat outdated figure of a composite illustration with a much shorter (one-half page) figure and replaced the 4.5 page figure displaying excerpts from a lengthy standardized open-ended interview schedule with a brief summary of that schedule and a reproduction of just one item from it.

- **Chapter 11.** We significantly expanded our discussion of criteria for inferring causality, especially in regard to additional criteria used in epidemiological research, such as strength of correlation, plausibility and coherence, and consistency in replication. We also added some comments about ethics and IRB approval in regard to control groups.

- **Chapter 12.** Our colleagues expressed praise for this chapter and had only a few minor suggestions for tweaking it. One found the brief box near the beginning of the chapter to be unnecessary. We agreed and deleted it in keeping with our effort to reduce the length and cost of the book.

- **Chapter 13.** With each new edition of this book we receive consistently positive feedback about this chapter. We found little need to update or otherwise modify this chapter, with one exception. One of our reviewers pointed out the need to address the implications of disagreements among triangulated data gatherers. So we added that for this edition.

- **Chapter 14.** This was one of our more extensively revised chapters. The revisions were primarily in the organization and tone of the chapter, although some new content was added, as well. While keeping most of the previous content on the politics of program evaluation and the difficulties that can pose for evaluators, we wanted to improve the chapter's emphasis on how to conduct successful evaluations. In that connection, we moved most of the politics content toward the back of the chapter, clarified that it pertains mainly to outcome evaluations, and moved other sections closer to the front. Logic models, for example, previously appeared in the penultimate section of the chapter and now appear early in it, right after a moved-up section on planning an evaluation. We also updated and shortened our coverage of the impact of managed care. A section on evidence-based practice was added to our historical overview. It introduces readers to the utility of meta-analyses and effect-size statistics—concepts covered more comprehensively in later chapters. We also expanded our discussion of summative and formative evaluations.

- **Chapter 15.** Our colleagues appear to be relatively pleased with this chapter. We implemented several minor tweaks that they suggested as well as a request by some for a more substantial revision: a shortened and less complex discussion of multistage cluster sampling.

- **Chapter 16.** This chapter received extensive revisions to try to keep pace with new technological advances affecting telephone and online surveys. We also refer readers to sources for keeping abreast of these developments. Four new sections were added regarding: (1) the implications of these advances for telephone surveys; (2) instrument design for online surveys; (3) improving response rates in online surveys; and (4) mixed-mode surveys combining online, telephone, and postal mail methods.

- **Chapter 17.** This is another chapter with new content regarding the ways in which our online world is affecting research. The main change is the addition of a section on online unobtrusive research, which includes examples of studies that monitor social media posts to identify words and phrases that are predictive of actual suicide attempts and other self-harm behaviors.

- **Chapter 18.** Various tweaks were made in this chapter, as suggested by reviewers; however, there were no major additions to it.

- **Chapter 19.** The main revisions to this chapter were as follows: (1) the addition of a section on the types and sequencing of focus group questions, and (2) a new box summarizing a focus group study—published in the *Journal of Gerontological Social Work*—that assessed the psychosocial needs of lesbian and gay elders in long-term care.

- **Chapter 20.** The main revision in this chapter was an expansion of content on open coding.

- **Chapter 21.** We made many significant changes to our chapters on quantitative data analysis in an effort to shorten and simplify this content in ways that better fit how most instructors handle it in their courses. In this chapter, for example, we removed most of the content on levels of measurement in line with requests to move that content up to Chapter 8 (see above). What's left is the content on the implications of those levels for the kinds of descriptive statistics that are appropriate to calculate. As part of our effort to collapse our two inferential data analyses chapters into one chapter and reduce the overall length and complexity of the inferential content, we moved the coverage of measures of association from Chapter 22 into this chapter. We also expanded our coverage of table construction and replaced several tables with ones focusing on illustrations of more direct relevance to social work.

- **Chapter 22**. In keeping with our effort to improve the fit between our coverage of inferential data analysis and how that content is covered in most research methods courses, we removed the content that is much more likely to be covered in statistics courses. In so doing, we were able to collapse and combine our previous two chapters on this content into one chapter. As mentioned above, we moved most of the coverage of measures of association up into Chapter 21, retaining in this chapter only the part dealing with the interpretation of relationship strength. We moved the coverage of statistical power analysis up from Chapter 23 into this chapter. We cut most of the content on tests of significance and moved it up into this chapter, as well, although we added a box that identifies the purpose of some significance tests commonly used in outcome studies relevant to evidence-based practice. Also moved up is our coverage of meta-analyses. We took the content on how to critically appraise meta-analyses out of this chapter and put an expanded version of that content in a new Appendix.
- **Chapter 23**. In this chapter (which used to be Chapter 24), we have added a section comparing large-scale and small-scale RFPs and proposals, including a new box illustrating a small-scale RFP aimed at students who want to conduct research on LGBT family issues.
- **Appendix A**. We've updated the appendix on using the library to make it more consistent with today's online world.

- **Appendix B**. We updated the discussion of selecting random numbers in regard to generating random numbers online.
- **Appendix C**. This new appendix contains expanded coverage on critically appraising meta-analyses.

» ANCILLARY PACKAGE

MindTap

Research Methods for Social Work comes with MindTap, an online learning solution created to harness the power of technology to drive student success. This cloud-based platform integrates a number of learning applications ("apps") into an easy-to-use and easy to access tool that supports a personalized learning experience. MindTap combines student learning tools-readings, multimedia, activities and assessments into a singular Learning Path that guides students through the course. This MindTap includes:

- Entire electronic text
- Additional readings to further explore chapter topics
- Case Studies
- Video Examples
- Quizzing
- Flashcards

Online Instructor's Manual

The Instructor's Manual (IM) contains a variety of resources to aid instructors in preparing and presenting text material in a manner that meets their personal preferences and course needs. It presents chapter-by-chapter suggestions and resources to enhance and facilitate learning.

Cengage Learning Testing Powered by Cognero

Cognero is a flexible, online system that allows you to author, edit, and manage test bank content as well as create multiple test versions in an instant.

You can deliver tests from your school's learning management system, your classroom, or wherever you want.

Online PowerPoint

These vibrant Microsoft® PowerPoint® lecture slides for each chapter assist you with your lecture by providing concept coverage using images, figures, and tables directly from the textbook.

Social Work CourseMate Website for Research Methods for Social Work

Accessible at **http://www.cengagebrain.com**, the text-specific CourseMate website offers chapter-by-chapter online quizzes, chapter outlines, crossword puzzles, flash cards (from the text's glossary), review questions, and exercises (from the ends of chapters in the text) that provide students with an opportunity to apply concepts presented in the text. Students can go to the Companion Site to access a primer for SPSS 17.0.

» ACKNOWLEDGMENTS

We owe special thanks to the following colleagues who made valuable suggestions for improving this edition:

Nikola Alenkin, California State University, Los Angeles

Juan Araque, University of California

Kathleen Bolland, University of Alabama

Annalease Gibson, Albany State University

Susan Grossman, Loyola University

Richard Harris. University of Texas, San Antonio

Mary Jane Taylor, University of Utah

Daniel Weisman, Rhode Island College

Molly Wolf, State University of New York, Buffalo

Allen Rubin
Earl R. Babbie

An Introduction to Scientific Inquiry in Social Work

Science is a word everyone uses. Yet people's images of science vary greatly. For some, science is mathematics; for others, science is white coats and laboratories. The word is often confused with *technology* or equated with challenging high school or college courses.

If you tell strangers that you are taking a course dealing with scientific inquiry and ask them to guess what department it's in, they are a lot more likely to guess something like biology or physics than social work. In fact, many social workers themselves often underestimate the important role that scientific inquiry can play in social work practice. But this is changing. More and more, social workers are learning how taking a scientific approach can enhance their practice effectiveness.

Although scholars can debate philosophical issues in science, for the purposes of this book we will look at it as a method of inquiry—that is, a way of learning and knowing things that can guide the decisions made in social work practice. When contrasted with other ways that social work practitioners can learn and know things, scientific inquiry has some special characteristics—most notably, a search for evidence.

In this opening set of chapters, we'll examine the nature of scientific inquiry and its relevance for social work. We'll explore the fundamental characteristics and issues that make scientific inquiry different from other ways of knowing things in social work.

In Chapter 1, we'll examine the value of scientific inquiry in social work practice and how it helps safeguard against some of the risks inherent in alternative sources of practice knowledge.

Chapter 2 will delve into evidence-based practice—a model of social work practice that emphasizes the use of the scientific method and scientific evidence in making practice decisions.

Chapter 3 will examine the research process in social work and various factors that can influence the way that process is carried out. Chapter 4 will provide an overview of and compare the three contrasting yet complementary overarching models of social work research: one that uses quantitative methods to produce precise and generalizable statistical findings; one that uses more flexible, qualitative methods to delve into deeper understandings of phenomena not easily reduced to numbers; and one that integrates quantitative and qualitative approaches within the same study.

1

Why Study Research?

EPAS Competencies for This Chapter

Competency 1   Demonstrate Ethical and Professional Behavior: You will learn why studying research is part of preparing to be ethical and professional in your social work practice.

Competency 4   Engage in Practice-Informed Research and Research-Informed Practice: As a research text that emphasizes practice applications, all of its chapters address aspects of this competency.

Competency 9   Evaluate Practice with Individuals Families, Groups, Organizations, and Communities: You will learn why studying research is an essential part of evaluating practice.

What You'll Learn in This Chapter

You may be wondering why social work students are required to take a research course. We'll begin to answer that question in this chapter. We'll examine the way social workers learn things and the mistakes they make along the way. We'll also examine what makes scientific inquiry different from other ways of knowing things and its utility in social work practice. We will preface this and the remaining chapters of this book by listing the competencies relevant to each chapter that students are expected to develop according to the Council on Social Work Education Educational Policy and Accreditation Standards (EPAS). Each competency will be accompanied by a brief statement on its relevance to the chapter.

» INTRODUCTION

Social workers—like doctors, lawyers, nurses, or any other type of professional—need to know things that will make their professional practice effective. Although it seems reasonable to suppose that all social workers would agree with that statement, they would not all agree about the *best* ways to go about learning the things they need to know. Some might favor learning things by relying on what most of their teachers, supervisors, and more experienced social workers in general agree to be true. Others might assert that learning things through what they observe and experience in their professional practice is at least as valuable as is learning about what other respected sources agree to be true.

Both of these two ways of knowing things have value not only in guiding social work practice but also in guiding decisions throughout our personal lives. As we grow up, we must rely on what the people we respect tell us to keep us safe and healthy. We shouldn't and don't have to experience the harmful or painful effects of doing unsafe or unhealthy things before we learn not to do them. At the same time, we learn other things through our direct experience and observation.

The two ways of knowing things that we've been discussing are termed *agreement reality* and *experiential reality*. Although each is invaluable in guiding our personal and professional behavior, let's now look at how relying on them exclusively can be risky.

Agreement Reality

Most of what we know is a matter of agreement and belief. Little of it is based on personal experience and discovery. A big part of growing up in any society, in fact, is the process of learning to accept what everybody around you "knows" is so.

You know that it's cold on the planet Mars. How do you know? Unless you've been to Mars lately, you know it's cold there because somebody told you and you believed what you were told. Perhaps your physics or astronomy instructor told you it was cold on Mars, or maybe you read about it somewhere.

However, relying exclusively on agreement reality can be risky because some of the things that everyone agrees on are wrong. For example, at one time everyone "knew" that the world is flat. Throughout the history of the social work profession, there have been things that most social workers and other mental health professionals agreed on that were not only wrong but also harmful.

In the mid-20th century, for example, there was widespread agreement that the main cause of schizophrenia was faulty parenting or other dysfunctional family dynamics. Having what was called a *schizophrenigenic mother* was widely seen as a main reason why a child—perhaps later as an adult—eventually came to have schizophrenia. Such mothers were portrayed as cold, domineering, and overprotective in ways that did not permit their children to develop individual identities. No compelling research evidence supported these concepts, but they were nonetheless widely accepted by mental health practitioners. As a result, social workers and other mental health professionals often dealt with the family as a cause of the problem rather than develop a treatment alliance with the family. Many parents consequently reported feelings of self-recrimination for the illnesses of their offspring. As you can imagine, this was painful for many parents.

Scientific research studies during the 1970s and 1980s debunked the notion that schizophrenia is caused by schizophrenigenic mothers or other dysfunctional family dynamics. Some studies uncovered the biological basis of schizophrenia. Other studies showed how practitioners who were guided by the notion of faulty parenting (or other dysfunctional family dynamics) when treating people with schizophrenia and their families were actually increasing the risk of relapse and unnecessarily exacerbating the burden that such families had to bear when caring for their sick relative (Rubin & Bowker, 1986).

Another example of ineffective or harmful professional practices that were guided by agreement reality includes "Scared Straight" programs. These programs were once popular as an effective way to prevent future violations of the law by juveniles. It was thought that by visiting prisons and interacting with adult inmates, juveniles would be so frightened that their fear would deter them from future criminal behavior. But various scientific research studies found that Scared Straight programs not only were ineffective but actually increased the risk of delinquency (Petrosino, Turpin-Petrosino, & Buehler, 2002).

Experiential Reality

In contrast to knowing things through agreement, we can also know things through direct experience and observation. However, just as relying exclusively on agreement reality can be risky, so can relying exclusively on experiential reality. That's because some of the things that we experience are influenced by our predilections that are based on agreements that may or may not be accurate.

Let's take an example. Imagine you're at a party. It's a high-class affair, and the drinks and food are excellent. You are particularly taken by one type of appetizer the host brings around on a tray. It's breaded, deep-fried, and especially tasty. You have a couple, and they are delicious! You have more. Soon you are subtly moving around the room to be wherever the host arrives with a tray of these nibbles.

Finally, you can't contain yourself any more. "What are they?" you ask. "How can I get the recipe?" The host lets you in on the secret: "You've been eating breaded, deep-fried worms!" Your response is dramatic: Your stomach rebels, and you promptly throw up all over the living room rug. Awful! What a terrible thing to serve guests!

The point of the story is that both feelings about the appetizer would be real. Your initial liking for them, based on your own direct experience, was certainly real, but so was the feeling of disgust you had when you found out that you'd been eating worms. It should be evident, however, that the feeling of disgust was strictly a product of the agreements you have with those around you that worms aren't fit to eat. That's an agreement you began the first time your parents found you sitting in a pile of dirt with half a wriggling worm dangling from your lips. When they pried your mouth open and reached down your throat to find the other half of the worm, you learned that worms are not acceptable food in our society.

Aside from the agreements we have, what's wrong with worms? They're probably high in protein and low in calories. Bite sized and easily packaged, they're a distributor's dream. They are also a delicacy for some people who live in societies that lack our agreement that worms are disgusting. Other people might love the worms but be turned off by the deep-fried bread-crumb crust.

Analogies to this worm example have abounded in the history social work practice (as well as in the practice of other helping professions). Decades ago, for example, practitioners who believed in the schizophrenigenic mother concept were likely to be predisposed to look for, perceive, and interpret maternal behaviors in ways that fit their agreement reality. We have known clinical practitioners who will look for and perceive even fairly inconsequential client behaviors as evidence that their favored treatment approach is being effective while overlooking other behaviors that might raise doubt about their effectiveness. Later in this chapter, we'll discuss this phenomenon in terms of the concept of selective observation, which is one common way in which our agreement reality influences our experiential reality.

Reality, then, is a tricky business. Although when we start out in life or in our professional careers, we must inescapably rely heavily on agreement reality and experiential reality as starting points for "knowing" things, some of the things you "know" may not be true. But how can you really know what's real? People have grappled with that question for thousands of years. Science is one of the strategies that have arisen from that grappling.

» THE SCIENTIFIC METHOD

Science offers an approach to both agreement reality and experiential reality. That approach is called the **scientific method***. When social workers question things and search for evidence as the basis for making practice decisions, they are applying the scientific method. Let's now examine the key features of the scientific method, beginning with a principle that requires keeping an open mind.

All Knowledge Is Tentative and Open to Question

In our quest to understand things, we should strive to keep an *open mind* about everything that we think we know or that we want to believe. In other words, we should consider the things we call "knowledge" to be *tentative* and *subject to refutation*. This feature has no exceptions. No matter how long a particular tradition has been practiced, no

---

*Words in boldface are defined in the glossary at the end of the book.

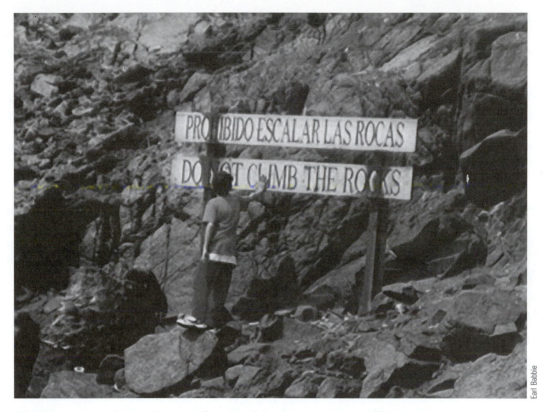

Earl Babbie

We learn some things by experience, others by agreement. This young man seems to be into personal experience.

matter how much power or esteem a particular authority figure may have, no matter how noble a cause may be, no matter how cherished it may be, we can question any belief.

Keeping an open mind is not always easy. Few of us enjoy facts that get in the way of our cherished beliefs. When we think about allowing everything to be open to question, we may think of old-fashioned notions that we ourselves have disputed and thus pat ourselves on the back for being so open-minded. If we have a liberal bent, for example, we may fancy ourselves as scientific for questioning stereotypes of gender roles, laws banning gay marriage, or papal decrees about abortion. But are we also prepared to have an open mind about our own cherished beliefs—to allow them to be questioned and refuted? Only when a belief you cherish is questioned do you face the tougher test of your commitment to scientific notions of the provisional nature of knowledge and keeping everything open to question and refutation.

Replication

However, it is not only our beliefs that are open to question; also tentative and open to question are the findings of scientific studies. Because there are no foolproof ways to guarantee that evidence produced by scientific studies is purely objective, accurate, and generalizable, the scientific method also calls for the replication of studies. *Replication* means duplicating a study to see if the same evidence and conclusions are produced. It also refers to modified replications in which the procedures are changed in certain ways that improve on previous studies or determine if findings hold up with different target populations or under different circumstances.

Observation

Another key feature of the scientific method is the search for *evidence based on observation* as the basis for knowledge. The term *empirical* refers to this valuing of observation-based evidence. As we will see later, one can be empirical in different ways, depending on the nature of the evidence and the way we search for and observe it. For now, remember that the scientific method seeks truth through observed evidence—not through authority, tradition, or ideology—no matter how much social pressure may be connected to particular beliefs and no matter how many people cherish those beliefs or how long they've been proclaimed to be true. It took courage long ago to question fiercely held beliefs that the Earth is flat. Scientifically minded social workers today should find the same courage to inquire as to the observation-based evidence that supports interventions or policies that they are told or taught to believe in.

Social workers should also examine the nature of that evidence. To be truly scientific, the observations that accumulated the evidence should have been *systematic* and *comprehensive*. To avoid overgeneralization and selective observation (errors we will be discussing shortly), the *sample* of observations should have been *large* and *diverse*.

Objectivity

The specified procedures also should be scrutinized for potential bias. The scientific method recognizes that we all have predilections and biases that can distort how we look for or perceive evidence. It therefore emphasizes the *pursuit of objectivity* in the way we seek and observe evidence. None of us may ever be purely objective, no matter how strongly committed we are to the scientific method. No matter how scientifically pristine their research may be, researchers want to discover something important—that is, to have findings that will make a significant contribution to improving human well-being or (less nobly) enhancing their professional stature. The scientific method does not require that researchers deceive themselves into thinking they lack these biases. Instead, recognizing that they may have these biases, they must find ways to gather observations that are not influenced by their own biases.

Suppose, for example, you devise a new intervention for improving the self-esteem of traumatized children. Naturally, you will be biased in wanting to observe improvements in the self-esteem of the children receiving your intervention. It's okay to have that bias and still scientifically inquire whether your intervention really does

improve self-esteem. You would not want to base your inquiry solely on your own subjective clinical impressions. That approach would engender a great deal of skepticism about the objectivity of your judgments that the children's self-esteem improved. Thus, instead of relying exclusively on your clinical impressions, you would devise an observation procedure that was not influenced by your own biases. Perhaps you would ask colleagues who didn't know about your intervention or the nature of your inquiry to interview the children and rate their self-esteem. Or perhaps you would administer an existing paper-and-pencil test of self-esteem that social scientists regard as valid. Although neither alternative can guarantee complete objectivity, each would be more scientific in reflecting your effort to pursue objectivity.

Transparency

Finally, the scientific method requires transparency by researchers in reporting the details of how their studies have been conducted. All *procedural details should be specified* so that others can see the basis for the conclusions that were reached, assess whether overgeneralization and selective observation were truly avoided, and judge whether the conclusions are indeed warranted in light of the evidence and the ways in which it was observed.

The box "Key Features of the Scientific Method" summarizes these features and provides a handy mnemonic for remembering them.

» OTHER WAYS OF KNOWING

The scientific method is not the only way to learn about the world. As we mentioned earlier, for example, we all discover things through our personal experiences from birth on and from the agreed-on knowledge that others give us. Sometimes this knowledge can profoundly influence our lives, such as when we learn that getting an education will affect how much money we earn later in life or how much job satisfaction we'll eventually experience. As students, we learn that studying hard will result in better examination grades.

We also learn that such patterns of cause and effect are probabilistic in nature: The effects occur more often when the causes occur than when they are absent—but not always. Thus, students learn

KEY FEATURES OF THE SCIENTIFIC METHOD

A mnemonic for remembering some of the key features of the scientific method is the word *trout*. Think of catching or eating a delicious trout,[1] and it will help you remember the following key features:

T	Tentative:	Everything we think we know today is open to question and subject to reassessment, modification, or refutation.
R	Replication:	Even the best studies are open to question and need to be replicated.
O	Observation:	Knowledge is grounded in orderly and comprehensive observations.
U	Unbiased:	Observations should be unbiased.
T	Transparency:	All procedural details are openly specified for review and evaluation and to show the basis of conclusions that were reached.

[1] If you are a vegetarian, you might want to just picture how beautiful these fish are and imagine how many of their lives you are saving.

that studying hard produces good grades in most instances but not every time. Social workers learn that being abused as children makes people more likely to become abusive parents later on, but not all parents who were abused as children become abusive themselves. They also learn that severe mental illness makes one vulnerable to becoming homeless, but not all adults with severe mental illnesses become homeless.

We will return to these concepts of causality and probability throughout the book. As we'll see, scientific inquiry makes them more explicit and provides techniques for dealing with them more rigorously than do other ways of learning about the world.

Tradition

One important secondhand way to attempt to learn things is through tradition. We may test a few of these "truths" on our own, but we simply accept the great majority of them. These are the things that "everybody knows." Tradition, in this sense of the term, has clear advantages for human inquiry. By accepting what everybody knows, you are spared the overwhelming task of starting from scratch in your search for regularities and understanding. Knowledge is cumulative, and an inherited body of information and understanding is the jumping-off point for the development of more knowledge. We often speak of "standing on the shoulders of giants"—that is, on the shoulders of previous generations.

At the same time, tradition may be detrimental to human inquiry. If you seek a fresh and different understanding of something that everybody already understands and has always understood, you may be seen as a fool. More to the point, it will probably never occur to you to seek a different understanding of something that is already understood and obvious.

When you enter your first job as a professional social worker, you may learn about your agency's preferred intervention approaches. (If you have begun the field placement component of your professional education, you may have already experienced this phenomenon.) Chances are you will feel good about receiving instructions about "how we do things in this agency." You might be anxious about beginning to work with real cases and might be relieved that you won't have to choose between competing theories to guide what you do with clients. In conforming to agency traditions, you might feel that you have a head start, benefiting from the accumulated practice wisdom of previous generations of practitioners in your new work setting. Indeed you do. After all, how many recently graduated social workers are in a better position than experienced agency staff to determine the best intervention approaches in their agency?

But the downside of conforming to traditional practice wisdom is that you can become too comfortable doing it. You may never think to look for evidence that the traditional approaches are or are not as effective as everyone believes or for evidence concerning whether alternative approaches are more effective. And if you do seek and find such evidence, you may find that agency traditions make your colleagues unreceptive to the new information.

Authority

Despite the power of tradition, new knowledge appears every day. Aside from your personal inquiries, throughout your life you will benefit from others' new discoveries and understandings. Often, acceptance of these new acquisitions will depend on the status of the discoverer. For example, you're more likely to believe the epidemiologist who declares that the common cold can be transmitted through kissing than to believe a layperson who says the same thing.

Like tradition, authority can both assist and hinder human inquiry. Inquiry is hindered when we depend on the authority of experts speaking outside their realm of expertise. The advertising industry plays heavily on this misuse of authority by having popular athletes discuss the nutritional value of breakfast cereals or movie actors evaluate the performance of automobiles, among similar tactics. It is better to trust the judgment of the person who has special training, expertise, and credentials in the matter, especially in the face of contradictory positions on a given question. At the same time, inquiry can be greatly hindered by the legitimate authority who errs within his or her own special province. Biologists, after all, can and do make mistakes in the field of biology. Biological knowledge changes over time. So does social work knowledge, as discussed earlier regarding debunked notions about the cause and treatment of schizophrenia.

Our point is that knowledge accepted on the authority of legitimate and highly regarded experts can be incorrect and perhaps harmful. It is therefore important that social work practitioners be open to new discoveries that might challenge the cherished beliefs of their respected supervisors or favorite theorists.

Also keep an open mind about the new knowledge that displaces the old. It, too, may be flawed, no matter how prestigious its founders. Who knows? Perhaps someday we'll even find evidence that currently out-of-favor ideas about parental causation of schizophrenia had merit after all.

That prospect might seem highly unlikely now given current evidence, but in taking a scientific approach to knowledge, we try to remain objective and open to new discoveries, no matter how much they may conflict with the traditional wisdom or current authorities. Although complete objectivity may be an impossible ideal to attain, we try not to close our minds to new ideas that might conflict with tradition and authority.

Both tradition and authority, then, are two-edged swords in the search for knowledge about the world. They provide us with a starting point for our own inquiry. But they may also lead us to start at the wrong point or push us in the wrong direction.

Common Sense

The notion of *common sense* is often cited as another way to know about the world. Common sense can imply logical reasoning, such as when we reason that it makes no sense to think that rainbows cause rainfall since rainbows appear only after the rain starts falling and only when the sun shines during the storm. Common sense can also imply widely shared beliefs based on tradition and authority. The problem with this sort of common sense is that what "everyone knows" can be wrong. Long ago, everyone "knew" that the Earth was flat. It was just plain common sense since you could see no curvature to the Earth's surface and since hell was below the surface. At one point in our history, a great many people thought that slavery made common sense. Many people think that laws against gays and lesbians marrying or adopting children make common sense. Most social workers think such laws make no common sense whatsoever. Although common sense might seem rational and accurate, it is an insufficient and highly risky alternative to science as a source of knowledge.

Popular Media

Much of what we know about the world is learned from the news media. We first learned about the September 11, 2001, attack on the twin towers of the World Trade Center from watching coverage of that tragic event on television and reading about it in newspapers and magazines and on the Internet. The same sources informed us of the victims and heroes in New York City, Pennsylvania, and Washington, D.C. They provided information on the perpetrators of the attack and a great many related issues and events. We did not have to conduct a scientific study to know about the attack or have strong feelings about it. Neither did we need tradition or authority. We did not have to experience the attack firsthand (although we really did experience it—and probably were at least somewhat traumatized—by what we saw and heard on our television sets).

Although we can learn a lot from the popular media, we can also be misled by them. Witness, for example, disagreements between some cable news networks as to which network is really more trustworthy, fair, and balanced. Although most journalists might strive for accuracy and objectivity, they are still influenced by their own political biases—some more than others. Some also might seek out the most sensational aspects of events and then report them in a biased manner to garner reader interest or appeal to their prejudices (ratings affect profits!).

Even when journalists strive for accuracy in their reportage, the nature of their business can impede their efforts. For example, they have deadlines to meet and word limits as to how much they can write. Thus, when covering testimony at city hall by neighborhood residents, some of whom support a proposed new economic development plan in their neighborhood and some of whom oppose it, their coverage might be dominated not by folks like the majority of residents, who may not be outspoken. Instead, they might unintentionally rely on the least representative but most outspoken and demonstrative supporters or opponents of the proposed development.

Then there are journalists whose jobs are to deliver editorials and opinion pieces, not to report stories factually. What we learn from them is colored by their predilections. The intent of such writing is not to provide a balanced approach but to persuade readers to share their position on the issues.

The popular media also include fictional movies and television shows that can influence what we think we know about the world. Some fictional accounts of history are indeed educational, perhaps informing us about African Americans who fought for the Union during the Civil War or sensitizing us to the horrors of the Holocaust or of slavery. Others, however, can be misleading, such as when most mentally ill people are portrayed as violent or when most welfare recipients are portrayed as African Americans.

More and more these days, many folks get much of their information from the Internet. Despite the wonders of the Internet and the immediate availability of a tremendous array of useful information therein, information available on unscientific sites is not risk free. Perhaps most noteworthy in this regard is the Wikipedia website. Wikipedia is a free online encyclopedia that anyone can edit. A humorous illustration of the risks inherent in allowing anyone to edit the information available at that site was reported by Eve Fairbanks (2008, p. 5). In February 2008, during the heat of the battle between Hillary Clinton and Barack Obama for the Democratic Party's presidential nomination, somebody accessed Clinton's Wikipedia page and replaced her photo with a picture of a walrus. Perhaps in retaliation, the next month, a Clinton supporter altered Obama's bio so that it called him "a Kenyan-American politician." Also that month, somebody replaced Clinton's whole page with "It has been reported that Hillary Rodham Clinton has contracted genital herpes due to sexual intercourse with an orangutan."

Obviously, the above Wikipedia example is extreme, and unless its readers despised Clinton or were imbibing something peculiar when accessing the above website, they would not believe that the walrus was really Clinton or that she had intercourse with an orangutan. But it does illustrate that despite the tremendous value of the Internet and the fact that we can learn many valuable things from popular media, they do not provide an adequate alternative to scientific sources of knowledge.

"Don't believe everything you read on the Internet just because there's a picture with a quote next to it."

—Abraham Lincoln

Library of Congress Prints and Photographs Division [LC-DIG-ppmsca-19305]

» RECOGNIZING FLAWS IN UNSCIENTIFIC SOURCES OF SOCIAL WORK PRACTICE KNOWLEDGE

Scientific inquiry safeguards against the potential dangers of relying exclusively on tradition, authority, common sense, or the popular media as the sources of knowledge to guide social work practice. It also helps safeguard against errors we might make when we attempt to build our practice wisdom primarily through our own practice experiences and unsystematic observations. Scientific inquiry also involves critical thinking so that we can spot fallacies in what others may tell us about their practice wisdom or the interventions they are touting. Let's now look at some common errors and fallacies you should watch out for and at some of the ways science guards against those mistakes.

Overgeneralization

When we look for patterns among the specific things we observe around us, we often assume that a few similar events are evidence of a general pattern. Probably the tendency to overgeneralize is greatest when the pressure is highest to arrive at a general understanding. Yet overgeneralization also occurs casually in the absence of pressure. Whenever it does occur, it can misdirect or impede inquiry.

Imagine you are a community organizer and you just found out that a riot has started in your community. You have a meeting in two hours that you cannot miss, and you need to let others at the meeting know why citizens are rioting. Rushing to the scene, you start interviewing rioters, asking them for their reasons. If the first two rioters tell you they are doing it just to loot some stores, you would probably be wrong in assuming that the other 300 are rioting just for that reason.

To further illustrate overgeneralization, imagine your practice instructor brings in a guest lecturer to talk about a promising new intervention that she is excited about. Although she has a sizable caseload and has been providing the intervention to quite a few clients, suppose her lecture just focuses on an in-depth report of one or two clients who seemed to benefit enormously from the intervention. You might be wrong in assuming the intervention was equally effective—or even effective at all—with her other clients.

Scientists guard against overgeneralization by committing themselves in advance to a sufficiently large sample of observations (see Chapter 15). The replication of inquiry provides another safeguard. As we mentioned earlier, replication basically means repeating a study and then checking to see if the same results are produced each time. Then the study may be repeated under slightly varied conditions. Thus, when a social work researcher discovers that a particular program of service in a particular setting is effective, that is only the beginning. Is the program equally effective for all types of clients? For both men and women? For both old and young? Among all ethnic groups? Would it be just as effective in other agency settings? This extension of the inquiry seeks to find the breadth and the limits of the generalization about the program's effectiveness.

Totally independent replications by other researchers extend the safeguards. Suppose you read a study that shows an intervention to be effective. Later, you might conduct your own study of different clients, perhaps measuring effectiveness somewhat differently. If your independent study produced exactly the same conclusion as the one you first read, then you would feel more confident in the generalizability of the findings. If you obtained somewhat different results or found a subgroup of clients among whom the findings didn't hold at all, you'd have helped to save us from overgeneralizing.

Selective Observation

One danger of overgeneralization is that it may lead to selective observation. Once you have concluded that a particular pattern exists and developed a general understanding of why, then you will be tempted to pay attention to future events and situations that correspond with the pattern. You will most likely ignore those that don't correspond. Figure 1-1 illustrates the circular fashion in which overgeneralization can lead to selective observation and selective observation can lead to overgeneralization. This figure introduces you to a fictitious cartoon character, Dr. Donald Dork, who will reappear in Chapter 9.

Racial and ethnic prejudices depend heavily on selective observation for their persistence. However, selective observation occurs among all of us, not just in people with distasteful prejudices. Social work practitioners who have great compassion for their clients and who do the best they can to help their clients, for example, commonly engage in selective observation in ways that may limit their effectiveness. The practitioner trained to interpret problems in terms of family communication dynamics is apt to look vigilantly for signs of potential communication problems and then magnify the role those problems play in explaining the presenting problem. At the same time, that practitioner is likely to overlook other dynamics or perhaps underestimate their impact.

Recall the overgeneralization example of the practice instructor who brings in a guest lecturer to talk about a promising new intervention that she is excited about and who focuses her lecture on one or two clients who seemed to benefit enormously from the intervention. She may have selectively observed outcome only in those clients who seemed to be benefiting from her work. And even in those clients, she may have selectively observed indicators of positive outcome and overlooked other indicators that might have cast doubt on how much the new intervention was really helping the clients.

Usually, a research design will specify in advance the number and kind of observations to be made as a basis for reaching a conclusion. If we wanted to learn whether women were more likely than men to support the pro-choice position on abortion, we'd commit ourselves to making a specified number of observations on that question in a research project. We might select a thousand people to be interviewed on the issue. Even if the first 10 women supported the pro-choice position and the first 10 men opposed it, we'd interview everyone selected for the study and recognize and record each observation. Then we'd base our conclusion on an analysis of all the observations.

A second safeguard against selective observation in scientific inquiry also works against most of the other pitfalls. If you overlook something that contradicts your conclusion about the way things are, then your colleagues will notice it and

FIGURE 1.1 An Illustration of Overgeneralization and Selective Observation

OVERGENERALIZATION

Ann is Dr. Donald Dork's first recipient of dorkotherapy (his new treatment for depression). She seems happy afterward, so he claims that dorkotherapy is an effective treatment for depression and encourages others to use it.

SELECTIVE OBSERVATION

Dr. Dork next provides dorkotherapy to four more clients: Jan, Dan, Nan, and Van. Three of them remain unhappy, but Dork fails to notice that, only being impressed by Nan's apparent happiness.

OVERGENERALIZATION & SELECTIVE OBSERVATION

Dr. Dork guest lectures in a direct practice elective on the treatment of depression. His lecture discusses only the cases of Ann and Nan, as he extols the wonders of dorkotherapy.

bring it to your attention. That's a service that scientists provide to one another and to the enterprise of science itself.

Ex Post Facto Hypothesizing

Suppose you administer an outreach program for battered women still living with their batterers and you have the idea that if your program is successful, soon after entering treatment a battered woman should start feeling more positive about herself as an individual and about her capacity to be less dependent on the batterer. You might test the program's effectiveness by conducting a brief structured interview with clients several times before and after they enter treatment. In the interview, you'd find out (a) how good they feel about themselves and (b) how capable they feel of living independently away from their batterers. You'd then examine whether they feel better or more capable after entering treatment than before entering it.

But suppose their answers are the opposite of what you expected—that is, suppose they express worse feelings after entering treatment than before. What a disappointment. "Aha!" you might say. "The reason for the negative findings is that before entering treatment, the women were unconsciously protecting themselves with the psychological defense mechanism of denial. They expressed better feelings before treatment because they were refusing to face their dangerous and deplorable situations. Our treatment helped overcome some of this denial and helped them get more in touch with an unpleasant reality they need to face in order to begin trying to change. Therefore, the more 'negative' responses after entering treatment are really more 'positive'! It is good that they are beginning to recognize what bad shape they were in; that's the first step in trying to improve it."

The example we've just described is sometimes called *ex post facto hypothesizing*, and it's perfectly acceptable in science if it doesn't stop there. The argument you proposed clearly suggests that you need to test your hypothesis about the program's effectiveness in new ways among a broader spectrum of people. The line of reasoning doesn't prove that your hypothesis is correct, only that there's still some hope for it. Later observations may prove its accuracy. Thus, scientists often engage in deducing information, and they follow up on their deductions by looking at the facts again.

Ego Involvement in Understanding

Our understanding of events and conditions is often of special psychological significance to us. In countless ways, we link our understandings of how things are to the image of ourselves we present to others. Because of this linkage, any disproof of these understandings tends to make us look stupid, gullible, and generally not okay. So we commit ourselves all the more unshakably to our understanding of how things are and create a formidable barrier to further inquiry and more accurate understanding.

This *ego involvement* in understanding is commonly encountered in social work practice. Naturally, practitioners see it in some of their clients who may blame others or external circumstances beyond their control for their difficulties rather than accept responsibility and face up to the way their own behavior contributes to their problems. Practitioners are less likely to see the way their own ego involvement may impede practice. Rather than scientifically reexamining the effectiveness of our own ways of practicing, which we may like because we are used to them and have special expertise in them, we may tenaciously engage in selective observation, *ex post facto* hypothesizing, and other efforts to explain away evidence that suggests our approach to practice may be ineffective.

Social workers who conduct evaluation research frequently confront this form of ego involvement when their evaluations fail to support the efficacy of the programs they are evaluating. Administrators and other practitioners affiliated with programs undergoing evaluation often don't want to be hassled with elegant evaluation research designs. They may prefer expediency to methodological rigor in the evaluations and would rather leave the work of designing and conducting annoying evaluations to evaluators. The same folks who initially express disinterest and lack of expertise in evaluation design or say that they don't need a methodologically rigorous design, however, can become fanatical critics. They may challenge the methodology of any study whose findings question the efficacy of their program, no matter how rigorous that study might be.

Influenced by their ego involvement and vested interests in the unsupported program, administrators and practitioners are capable of grasping at any straw or magnifying any trivial methodological imperfection in a study in order to undermine the study's methodological credibility. For these same reasons, they are unlikely to notice even glaring methodological imperfections in studies whose results they like; they are apt to tout those studies as proving the value of their programs. Chapter 14, on program evaluation, will examine this phenomenon in more depth.

Administrators and practitioners aren't the only social workers who are vulnerable to ego involvement in understanding. Program evaluators and other social work researchers are just as human. They also run the risk of becoming personally involved in and committed to the conclusions they reach in scientific inquiry. Sometimes it's worse than in nonscientific life. Imagine, for example, that you have discovered an apparent cure for cancer and have been awarded the Nobel Prize. How do you suppose you'd feel if somebody published an article arguing that your cure didn't really work? You might not be totally objective.

A firm commitment to the other norms of science we have examined works against too much ego involvement. But if you lack that commitment, you'll find that your colleagues can evaluate the critical article more objectively than you can. Ultimately, then, although ego involvement is sometimes a problem for individual scientists, it is less a problem for science in general.

Other Forms of Illogical Reasoning

Intelligent humans commonly engage in additional forms of illogical reasoning in their day-to-day lives. One illustration is what statisticians have called the *gambler's fallacy*. A consistent run of either good or bad luck is presumed to foreshadow its opposite. An evening of bad luck at poker may kindle the belief that a winning hand is just around the corner, and many a poker player has lost more money because of that mistaken belief. Or, conversely, an extended period of good weather may lead you to worry that it is certain to rain on the weekend picnic. Even the best of us get a little funny in our reasoning from time to time. Worse yet, we can get defensive when others point out the errors in our logic.

Social workers need to use critical thinking and be vigilant in looking for the flawed reasoning of individuals whose ego involvement or vested interests lead them to make fallacious claims or arguments.

Straw Person Argument One common fallacy is the *straw person argument*, in which someone

attacks a particular position by distorting it in a way that makes it easier to attack. For example, politicians who opposed enactment of the Affordable Care Act (often referred to as *Obamacare*)—as well as those who would like to repeal it—might exaggerate the extent to which it might contain features that have the potential to increase costs or delays in obtaining medical care.

***Ad Hominem* Attack** Another fallacy is the *ad hominem attack*, which tries to discredit the person making an argument rather than addressing the argument itself. In a debate about 20 years ago between two psychologists who had vested interests in competing forms of psychotherapy, for example, one ridiculed the legitimacy of the school from which the other had obtained her professional degree.

Bandwagon Appeal Sometimes new interventions are promoted merely on the basis of their newness or promise. This, too, is a fallacy. When you encounter colleagues making this argument, you might want to remind them that lobotomy was once considered to be a new and promising treatment for mental illness. A somewhat related fallacy is the *bandwagon appeal*, in which a relatively new intervention is touted on the basis of its growing popularity. The implicit assumption is that the sheer number of your professional colleagues jumping on the bandwagon must mean that the intervention is effective. A flier promoting expensive training workshops for a new therapy, for example, once highlighted the fact that more than 25,000 mental health practitioners around the world had already attended the workshops. When you encounter the bandwagon appeal, it may help to recall the various treatment approaches that we have mentioned earlier in this chapter (and others that we will discuss later) whose bandwagon wheels fell off when scientific evidence showed the treatments to be ineffective or harmful.

We are not implying that interventions or policies promoted with fallacious appeals are necessarily ineffective or undesirable. Some might eventually be supported or may have already been supported by sound scientific studies despite the unfortunate ways their proponents have chosen to promote them. The point is not to be swayed one way or the other by appeals based on illogical reasoning. Instead, look for and critically appraise the scientific evidence.

The Premature Closure of Inquiry

Overgeneralization, selective observation, and the defensive uses of illogical reasoning all conspire to close inquiry prematurely. Sometimes this closure of inquiry is a social rather than an individual act. For example, the private foundation or government agency that refuses to support further research on an "already understood" topic effects closure as a social act, as does the denominational college that prohibits scholarship and research that might challenge traditional religious beliefs. Social workers may effect closure by refusing to consider evidence that their favored interventions, programs, or policies are not as effective as they believe. Chapter 5 will examine the ethics of this phenomenon in more depth as well as the effects of politics and ideologies on inquiry.

The danger of premature closure of inquiry is obvious. It halts attempts to understand things before understanding is complete. If you review the history of human knowledge, however, you will reach a startling conclusion: We keep changing the things we know—even the things we know for certain. In an important sense, then, any closure of inquiry is premature.

At its base, science is an open-ended enterprise in which conclusions are constantly being modified. That is an explicit norm of science. Experienced scientists accept it as a fact of life and expect established theories to be overturned eventually. Even if one scientist considers a line of inquiry to be completed forever, others will not. Even if a whole generation of scientists closes inquiry on a given topic, a later generation is likely to set about testing the old ideas and changing many of them.

In part, the reward structure of science supports this openness. Although you may have to overcome a great deal of initial resistance and disparagement, imagine how famous you would be if you could demonstrate persuasively that something people have always believed simply isn't true. What if you could prove that carbon monoxide was really good for people? The potential rewards for astounding discoveries keep everything fair game for inquiry in science.

Pseudoscience

In your social work career, you will probably learn about some practice methods or interventions that are based on the solid foundation of a replicated string of strong research studies. But you'll also probably encounter many claims about the wonders of some interventions based on sloppy and biased research studies or on unscientific sources of knowledge. Some of these claims will be expressed in the form of fliers advertising expensive continuing education training workshops in some "miracle cure." When these claims seem to contain some of the features of scientific inquiry and thus have the surface appearance of being scientific but on careful inspection can be seen to violate one or more principles of the scientific method or contain fallacies against which the scientific method attempts to guard, they are really pseudoscientific.

The preface *pseudo-* means "fake"; thus, pseudoscience is fake science. Some figureheads may espouse an intervention based on pseudoscience because they have a vested interest in the intervention—perhaps gaining fame and fortune from marketing books and workshops on it. Chances are, they really believe in what they are touting. Their followers might also be true believers and might be so ego invested in the intervention they swear by that they won't let facts get in the way of their cherished beliefs.

It's not hard to recognize some purveyors of pseudoscience, such as those peddling miracle cures for obesity or other woes on late-night television infomercials based on the testimonials of a few individuals, some of whom might be celebrities. But other pseudoscientific claims can be harder to recognize, especially when they are based on weak studies that managed to slip by reviewers and get printed in professional journals.

Figure 1-2 displays some common warning signs that should arouse your suspicions as to whether an intervention might be based more on pseudoscience than on science. Most of the signs pertain to flawed ways of knowing that have been discussed earlier in this chapter. The presence of one or more of these signs does not necessarily mean that the intervention is based on pseudoscience. Perhaps the flaws are in the inappropriate way the intervention is touted, not in the quality of the research being cited. For example, perhaps solid scientific research has found an intervention to be moderately effective with certain problems under certain conditions, but the purveyors of the intervention are making it sound like a universal cure-all. However, if you recognize these signs, you should at least beware of the possibility that pseudoscience is in play, and the more warning signs you detect, the more skeptical you should become. Learning about research and the scientific method will help you recognize pseudoscience and

FIGURE 1.2 Common Warning Signs for Detecting the Possibility of Pseudoscience

Pseudoscientific proponents of an intervention will:

- *Make extreme claims about its wonders*
- *Overgeneralize regarding whom it benefits*
- *Concoct unusual, speculative explanations for its effectiveness*
- *Concoct pretentious jargon for aspects of their intervention that sounds scientific but really is not*
- *Base their claims on*
  - *Testimonials and anecdotes*
  - *Authorities or gurus*
  - *Tradition*
  - *Sloppy or biased research*
  - *The popularity of their intervention*
  - *Selective observation of a few cases*
  - *Portrayals of their intervention in the popular media (such as movies or TV shows)*
- *React to disconfirming evidence by*
  - *Ignoring it, citing only those sources that support their intervention*
  - *Explaining it away through ex post facto hypothesizing*
  - *Engaging in an ad hominem attack on those who cite the disconfirming evidence*
  - *Exaggerating the importance of minor flaws in the source of the disconfirming evidence*
  - *Exaggerating the rigor and superiority of the studies that support their intervention*
  - *Engaging in a straw person argument in which they distort the arguments of those who question them so as to make those arguments easier to attack*
  - *Citing a historical scientist (such as Galileo or Freud) whose contemporaries were wrong in questioning them (and thus implicitly comparing themselves to the historical luminary)*
  - *Attributing it to the vested interests of those who are threatened by their intervention and thus engaged in a conspiracy to discredit it*
- *Pursue a premature closure of inquiry by pressuring their minions to refrain from*
  - *Subjecting their claims to rigorous, unbiased research*
  - *Publishing studies that produce disconfirming findings (pointing out flaws in the studies or arguing that publication will prevent those in need of their intervention from benefiting from it)*

In contrast, those employing the scientific method will:

- *Encourage and welcome the pursuit of disconfirming evidence because all knowledge is provisional and subject to refutation*
- *Be cautious in making claims*
- *Avoid overgeneralization*
- *Base their conclusions on*
  - *Observations that are comprehensive, systematic, and unbiased*
  - *Rigorous studies*
  - *Replication, not ignoring or dismissing disconfirming evidence produced by sound research*

be less susceptible to it in your social work practice and your life in general. At the bottom of Figure 1-2 are features of the scientific method that we discussed earlier and that contrast with pseudoscience.

Although it is important to be able to recognize purveyors of pseudoscience, not everything that some people call pseudoscience is fake or without value. Likewise, just because purveyors of a new intervention have a vested interest in it does not necessarily mean that the new intervention is worthless or harmful—even if the research they report or cite is shoddy and biased. Moreover, as noted earlier, some pseudoscience involves interventions that have value and that are based on some solid scientific research but have their effects exaggerated by purveyors of pseudoscience who have vested interests in them. Some things that are now seen as scientifically acceptable were portrayed as pseudoscientific when first introduced. Eye movement desensitization and reprocessing (EMDR), for example, was once depicted as pseudoscience by its various critics, who cited the weaknesses in its early research and some of the pseudoscientific ways that its proponents were touting it. However, after its effectiveness was replicated by many studies with scientifically rigorous designs, it became widely accepted among scientifically oriented experts on psychotherapy research as one of the two most effective treatments for acute PTSD.

» THE UTILITY OF SCIENTIFIC INQUIRY IN SOCIAL WORK

Many social work students wonder why research courses are required in a professional curriculum that is preparing them to become practitioners. They have much to learn about helping people, and they are itching to learn it. Research methodology might be important for academic sociologists and psychologists, but these students might ask, "Why spend time studying research methods when that time could be spent improving my helping skills?"

Some students expect research to be cold, aloof, and mechanistic, qualities that did not attract them to the social work field. Social work tends to be associated with such qualities as warmth, involvement, compassion, humanism, and commitment. These students see many social problems to tackle in the real world, and they are eager to take action. In fact, their unique background may have already led them to identify a problem area they want to deal with. They want to get on with it—but first they must clear the research hurdle.

You might be surprised at the proportion of social work *researchers* who started their careers feeling just that way. Many began their social work

careers not as researchers but as practitioners with a burning commitment to help disadvantaged people and to pursue social justice. With no initial inkling that someday they would become researchers, they discovered during their practice experience that their good intentions were not enough. They realized that our field needs more evidence to guide practitioners about what interventions and policies really help or hinder the attainment of their noble goals. Thus, it was their compassion and commitment to change that spurred them to redirect their efforts to research because it is through research that they could develop the evidence base for practice. Rather than continue to practice with interventions of unknown and untested effects, they decided that they could do more to help disadvantaged people and pursue social justice by conducting research that builds our profession's knowledge base and that consequently results in the delivery of more effective services to clients and the implementation of more effective social change efforts.

Most social work researchers do not fit the traditional stereotypes of academic researchers. They aim not to produce knowledge for knowledge's sake but to provide the practical knowledge that social workers need to solve everyday problems in their practice. Ultimately, they aim to give the field the information it needs to alleviate human suffering and promote social welfare. Thus, social work research seeks to accomplish the same humanistic goals as social work practice; like practice, social work research is a compassionate, problem-solving, and practical endeavor.

Will You Ever Do Research?

At this point you might think, "Okay, that's nice, but the odds that I am going to do research are still slim." But even if you never consider yourself a researcher, you are likely to encounter numerous situations in your career when you'll use your research expertise and perhaps wish you had more of it. For example, you may supervise a clinical program whose continued funding requires you to conduct a scientific evaluation of its effects on clients. You may provide direct services and want to use single-case design methodology to evaluate scientifically your own effectiveness or the effects certain interventions are having on your clients. You may be involved in community organizing or planning and want to conduct a scientific survey to assess a community's greatest needs. You may be administering a program and be required, in order to be accountable to the public, to document scientifically that your program truly is delivering its intended amounts and types of service. You may be engaged in social reform efforts and need scientific data to expose the harmful effects of current welfare policies and thus persuade legislators to enact more humanitarian welfare legislation.

Perhaps you remain skeptical. After all, this is a research text, and its authors may be expected to exaggerate the value of learning the methods of scientific inquiry. You might be thinking, "Even if I accept the notion that social work research is valuable, I still believe that the researchers should do their thing, and I'll do mine." But what will you do? Some agencies provide interventions that research has found to be ineffective. Some day you may even work in such an agency and be expected to provide such interventions. By understanding research and then reading studies that provide new evidence on what is and is not effective, you can increase your own practice effectiveness.

» REVIEWS OF SOCIAL WORK EFFECTIVENESS

Since its inception, various leaders in the social work profession have sought ways to use science to guide social work practice. It was not until the last few decades of the 20th century, however, that a realization of the acute need to improve the evidence base of social work practice began to spread throughout the profession—especially among social work educators.

Early Reviews

During the 1970s, several authors jolted the social work profession with reviews of research indicating that direct social work practice was not effective (Fischer, 1973; Mullen & Dumpson, 1972; Wood, 1978). Many of the studies covered in those reviews did not evaluate specific, clearly described interventions. Because they evaluated the effectiveness of social workers in general, instead of evaluating specific interventions for specific problems, they concluded that social workers in general were not being effective but were unable to identify which particular interventions were more or less effective

than others. The early studies, therefore, provided little guidance to practitioners seeking ways to make their practice more effective.

Studies of Specific Interventions

The early reviews implied that it is unsafe to assume that whatever a trained social worker does will be effective. If you approach your practice with that attitude, then much of what you do might be ineffective. Later studies, however, provided grounds for optimism about the emergence of effective interventions (Gorey, 1996; Kirk & Reid, 2002; Reid, 1997; Reid & Hanrahan, 1982; Rubin, 1985a). An important difference between the studies covered in the earlier reviews and those covered in the later reviews is whether the focus was on the effectiveness of specific, well-explicated interventions applied to specific problems or just the effectiveness of social workers in general. In contrast to the studies covered in the above early reviews, later studies evaluated interventions that were well explicated and highly specific about the problems they sought to resolve, the goals they sought to accomplish, and the procedures used to achieve those goals (Blythe & Briar, 1987; Briar, 1987).

Thus, the particular interventions and procedures you employ to achieve particular objectives with specific types of clientele or problems *do matter*. As the later reviews indicated, mounting scientific evidence supports the effectiveness of a variety of interventions. Consider, for example, the box "Contrasting Interventions: Helpful or Harmful?" Each intervention listed in column A was at one time in vogue among mental health professionals and thought to be effective. Why did they think so? It seemed reasonable in light of the theories they embraced and their clinical intuitions. However, subsequent research found each to be ineffective and perhaps even harmful. In contrast, the interventions in column B, which are geared to the same target populations as their counterparts in column A, have consistently had their effectiveness supported by various research studies.

Research today is identifying more and more interventions that have strong research support for their effectiveness—interventions that you can draw on in your practice. The box "Some Interventions with Strong Research Support" lists some of the ones recognized by the Society of Clinical Psychology as having strong research support regarding their effectiveness.

CONTRASTING INTERVENTIONS: HELPFUL OR HARMFUL?

Column A

Once Popular but Not Supported by Research

- Critical incident stress debriefing for trauma victims
- In-depth, psychodynamic insight-oriented therapy for people suffering from severe and persistent schizophrenia
- Treating dysfunctional family dynamics as the cause of schizophrenia in a family therapy context

Column B

Supported by Research

- Prolonged exposure therapy for trauma victims
- Assertive case management/assertive community treatment for people suffering from severe and persistent schizophrenia
- Psychoeducational support groups for family caregivers of people suffering from severe and persistent schizophrenia

Despite this progress, however, many social workers today continue to use some interventions and procedures that have not yet received adequate testing. Thyer (2002), for example, noted that some problems and fields of practice—such as child abuse and neglect, domestic violence, and political action—have a smaller evidence base than others, particularly when compared to interventions for mental disorders. And some interventions that have been evaluated and have had positive outcomes need more testing before the evidence is sufficient to resolve any lingering doubt as to their effectiveness.

This doubt is not likely to be resolved soon. Moreover, new interventions continually emerge and are promoted without adequate scientific evidence as to their effectiveness. Some will have received no scientific testing whatsoever. Others will have been "tested" in a scientifically unsound manner in which the research design or measurement procedures were biased to produce desired results. Some will have been tested with certain ethnic groups but not with others. Professional social workers commonly are bombarded with fliers promoting expensive continuing education workshops for new interventions that are touted as being effective. Some claims are warranted, but some are not. In the face of this reality, understanding scientific inquiry and research methods becomes practice knowledge, too. If we cannot say with certainty that the actions of trained social workers have demonstrated effectiveness, then learning how to critically appraise whether adequate scientific evidence supports particular interventions in certain practice situations becomes at least as important as learning popular general practice methods that may not always be effective themselves.

SOME OF THE INTERVENTIONS WITH STRONG RESEARCH SUPPORT

- Assertive community treatment (ACT), family psychoeducation, social skills training, and supported employment for schizophrenia
- Cognitive behavioral therapy for various disorders
- Dialectical behavior therapy for borderline personality disorder
- Prolonged exposure therapy, cognitive processing therapy, and EMDR for posttraumatic stress disorder

- Interpersonal therapy and problem-solving therapy for depression
- Motivational interviewing and motivational enhancement therapy for substance abuse/dependence

Source: http://www.div12.org/PsychologicalTreatments/treatments.html

» THE NEED TO CRITIQUE RESEARCH QUALITY

But, you might ask, why can't we just let the researchers produce the needed studies and then tell us practitioners the results? Practitioners would have to focus only on the practice aspects of those interventions that receive adequate scientific support. In an ideal world, that might not be a bad idea, but the real world is a lot messier.

Publication Does Not Guarantee Quality

There is a vast range in the quality of social work research—and of applied research in disciplines that are relevant to social work—that gets produced and published. Some of it is excellent, and some of it probably should never have been published. It is not hard to find studies that violate some of the fundamental principles that you will learn in this book. For example, you may encounter a study in which authors are evaluating a new intervention they have developed by rating client progress. Unfortunately, these ratings are frequently based on their own subjective judgments, which are highly vulnerable to being biased by their desire to see successful results. Or perhaps you will read an advocacy study that improperly defines things so as to exaggerate the need for the policy it is advocating.

The unevenness in the quality of the studies in social work and allied fields has a variety of causes. Biases or varying degrees of competence among researchers are only partial explanations. Many weak studies are produced not because their authors were biased or did not know better but because agency constraints kept them from conducting stronger studies. Later in this book, for example, you will learn the value of assigning clients to experimental and control conditions when the researcher is assessing the effectiveness of interventions. During control conditions, the interventions being tested are withheld from clients. Many agencies will not permit the use of control conditions in clinical research. (There are various practical reasons for this constraint—reasons we'll examine in this text.) Consequently, researchers are faced with a dilemma: either do the study under conditions of weak scientific rigor or forgo the study. Having no better alternative and believing that limited evidence may be better than no evidence, researchers often opt to do the study.

Distinguishing and Facilitating More Useful Studies

This means that if social work practitioners are going to be guided by the findings of social work research studies, then they must understand social work research methods well enough to distinguish studies with adequate scientific methodologies and credible findings from those with weak methodologies and findings of little credibility. It also means that the quality of the social work research produced ultimately depends not just on the researchers' methodological expertise but also on their practice knowledge and on practitioners' research knowledge. Without a partnership between practice-oriented researchers and methodologically informed practitioners, there is not likely to be a climate of support in agencies for the type of research our field needs—research that is responsive to the real needs of agency practitioners under conditions that permit an adequate level of methodological rigor. Even if you never produce any research, an understanding of research methods will help you critically appraise and use research produced by others, communicate with researchers to help ensure that their work is responsive to the needs of practice, and ultimately help foster an agency environment conducive to carrying out good and relevant studies.

» COMPASSION AND PROFESSIONAL ETHICS

Being professional involves several things. For one, we strive to make sure we provide our clients with the most effective services available. How do we do that? Do we just ask our supervisors what they think is best? That may be a starting point, but practitioners who conform only to ongoing practices without keeping abreast of the latest research in their field are not doing everything possible to provide clients with the best possible service. Indeed, well-established, traditional social work services have often been found to be ineffective—as indicated by the previously mentioned reviews of practice effectiveness.

Given how frequently social work services have been found ineffective and the recent emergence of studies that identify new and apparently effective interventions, a failure to keep abreast of the research in the field is a serious failing. With the absence of evidence for the notion that whatever trained social workers do is effective, we cannot justify disregarding research with the rationalization that we are too busy helping people. If our services have not been tested for their effects on clients, then chances are we are not really helping anyone. If so, then who benefits from our blind faith in conventional but untested practice wisdom? Not our clients. Not those who pay for our services. Not society. Do we? In one sense, perhaps. It is less work for us if we unquestioningly perpetuate ongoing practices. That way, we do not make waves. We do not have to think as much. There is one less task—reading research reports—in our daily grind. In the long run, however, practitioners who keep up on the research and know they are doing all they can to provide the best possible services to their clients might experience more job satisfaction and be less vulnerable to burnout.

The main reason to use research, however, is compassion for our clients. We care about helping them, and thus we seek scientific evidence about the effects of the services we are providing and of alternative services that might help them more. If the services we provide are not effective and others are, then we are harming our clients by perpetuating our current services. We are wasting their time (and perhaps money) by allowing their problems to go on without the best possible treatment. Because we are inattentive to the literature, we deny our clients a service opportunity that might better help them.

A shocking example of the value of research in social work practice involves life and death and thus illustrates dramatically why practitioners who critically appraise and use research discriminately may be more compassionate—and ethical—than those who do not. On May 19, 2000, an article in the *Rocky Mountain News* (Crowder and Lowe, 2000) reported the death of a 10-year-old girl who died as a result of a videotaped intervention delivered by a team of adults that included a master's-level social worker. The intervention, called *rebirthing therapy*, did not have a base of evidence supported by research. A psychotherapist and two assistants implemented the now disreputable intervention by balling up the girl in a flannel blanket, covering the blanket with pillows, and pushing against the pillows. The idea was to simulate birth contractions so that she could emerge in a "rebirth" from the womb of her adoptive mother and thus improve

her bond with that mother. The notion was that this controversial procedure would alleviate attachment disorders. The girl remained wrapped up in a fetal position for 70 minutes. During the first 16 minutes she repeatedly said that she was going to die. Two therapists responded, "You want to die? Okay, then die. Go ahead, die right now" (p. 5). When they unbound the girl they found her unconscious in her vomit. The next day she died in the hospital from asphyxiation, and the practitioners were arrested.

» UTILITY OF RESEARCH IN APPLIED SOCIAL WORK SETTINGS

Studies on the effects of social work interventions are just one prominent example of useful social work research. A long list of other examples of completed research studies would also convey the value of research to social work and why students preparing to become practitioners should know research methods so that they can use and contribute to such research. Many of these studies will be cited as illustrations of the methodological concepts addressed throughout this text.

Research Methods You May Someday Use in Your Practice

We also could cite countless examples for additional topics on which you might someday want to see research findings related to policy or administration. Only a few will be cited here. For example, why do so many of your agency's clients terminate treatment prematurely? What types of clients stay with or drop out of treatment? What reasons do they give? What services did they receive? How satisfied were they with those services? What proportion of time do practitioners in your agency spend on different practice roles? Do they spend too much time performing functions that are more highly gratifying and too little time on functions that are less attractive but more needed by clients? What characteristics of social service volunteers best predict how long they will continue to volunteer? What can you do to orient, train, or reward them and reduce volunteer turnover? In what part of your target community or region should you locate your outreach efforts? Where are you most likely to engage hard-to-reach individuals such as the homeless or recent immigrants? Why do so many homeless individuals refuse to stay in shelters, sleeping instead on the streets? What are their experiences when they stay in a shelter, and what is staying in a shelter like from their point of view? What proportion of your target population does not understand English? Why are so few ethnic minorities being served by your agency? What does your agency mean to them? What is the agency atmosphere like from their viewpoint? What happens to the children of unskilled mothers whose welfare benefits have been severed? We could go on and on, but you get the idea: The possibilities are endless.

Learning research methods has value to practitioners beyond just using research studies. They will also be able to use research methods in face-to-face contact with people, especially for treatment planning. During assessment, for example, practitioners collect clinical data from various individuals. Research concepts about such topics as measurement error, reliability, validity, and the principles of sampling will help them evaluate the quality and meaning of the clinical data they collect and help them collect those data in ways that enhance their quality. Practitioners must examine the conditions and situations under which they collect information as part of their practice in the same way and for the same reasons as one systematically collects data for a formal research study.

National Association of Social Workers Code of Ethics

Ethics is one of the most important concerns of social workers as they consider research, and it is a topic that is discussed throughout this book. The Code of Ethics of the National Association of Social Workers (NASW) specifically requires social workers to keep current with and critically examine practice-related research in the professional literature and to include evidence-based knowledge as part of the knowledge base for their practice. When we use research discriminatingly, we help uphold and advance the values and mission of the profession and thus are more ethical in our practice. Still, social work students quite commonly approach research methodology with skepticism about the ethics of many research studies.

We will address those ethical concerns in various chapters of the book, not just in the chapter devoted to ethics. We hope that by the time you finish reading this book, you will have a better understanding not only of the ethical dilemmas involved in social work research but also of the reasons why our professional code of ethics bears on our responsibility to understand, use, and contribute to research.

Perhaps more than ever before, social work research offers all social workers an opportunity to make a difference in the problems they confront. Whether you are a clinical practitioner seeking to maximize the effectiveness of your services, a social activist seeking to promote more humane social welfare legislation, or perhaps both, the success of your efforts to help people is likely to be enhanced by your use of scientific inquiry and research.

MAIN POINTS

- Social work research seeks to provide the practical knowledge that social workers need to solve the problems they confront.
- Social work research seeks to give the field the information it needs to alleviate human suffering and promote social welfare.
- Social work research seeks to accomplish the same humanistic goals as social work practice. Like practice, social work research is a compassionate, problem-solving, and practical endeavor.
- Recognizing when particular interventions for particular practice situations have been supported by adequate scientific evidence is an important guide to social work practice.
- Social work practitioners should understand social work research methods well enough to discriminate between strong and weak studies.
- Compassion for clients is the main reason for social workers to use research.
- Social workers have an ethical responsibility to utilize research and contribute to the development of the profession's knowledge base.
- Much of what we know is by agreement rather than by experience.
- Tradition and authority are important sources of understanding, but relying on them exclusively can be risky.

- When we understand through experience, we make observations and seek patterns of regularities in what we observe.
- In day-to-day inquiry, we often make mistakes. Science offers protection against such mistakes.
- When we use the scientific method, everything is open to question, and we should keep an open mind about everything we think we know or want to believe.
- When we use the scientific method, we should consider the things we call "knowledge" to be provisional and subject to refutation.
- When we use the scientific method, we should search for evidence that is based on observation as the basis for knowledge.
- Scientific observations should be systematic, comprehensive, and as objective as possible.
- Scientific observations should be specified in ways that show the basis for the conclusions that were reached and that allow others to judge whether the evidence warrants those conclusions.
- The scientific method calls for the replication of studies.
- Sometimes we jump to general conclusions on the basis of only a few observations. Researchers and scientific practitioners avoid overgeneralization through replication, or the repeating of studies.
- Once a conclusion has been reached, we sometimes ignore evidence that contradicts the conclusion, paying attention only to evidence that confirms it. Researchers and scientific practitioners commit themselves in advance to a set of observations to be made regardless of whether a pattern seems to be emerging early.
- When confronted with contradictory evidence, all of us make up explanations to account for the contradictions, often making assumptions about facts not actually observed. Researchers and scientific practitioners, however, make further observations to test those assumptions.
- Sometimes people simply reason illogically. Researchers and scientific practitioners avoid this by being as careful and deliberate in their reasoning as in their observations. Moreover, the public nature of science means that scientists have colleagues looking over their shoulders.

- The same support of colleagues helps protect scientists from tying their ego to their conclusions.
- Whereas people often decide they understand something and stop looking for new answers, researchers and scientific practitioners—as a group—ultimately regard all issues as open.
- Pseudoscience has the surface appearance of being scientific but on careful inspection can be seen to violate one or more principles of the scientific method or to contain fallacies against which the scientific method attempts to guard.

REVIEW QUESTIONS AND EXERCISES

1. Review the common errors of human inquiry discussed in this chapter in the section "Recognizing Flaws in Unscientific Sources of Social Work Practice Knowledge." Find a magazine or newspaper article or perhaps a letter to the editor that illustrates one of these errors. Discuss how a scientist would avoid making the error.
2. Examine a few recent issues of the journal *Research on Social Work Practice* or the journal *Social Work Research*. Find an article that reports evidence about the effectiveness of an intervention and thus illustrates the value of research in guiding social work practice. Discuss how a social worker might be guided by the article.
3. Examine several recent issues of a journal in an allied profession such as sociology or psychology. Discuss the similarities and differences you find between the articles in that journal and the ones you examined in exercise 2.

INTERNET EXERCISES

1. Find an example of a research study that offers useful implications for social work practice. After you find a useful research report, write down the bibliographical reference information for the report and briefly describe the report's implications for practice.

2. Search the Internet for controversial interventions that have been depicted as pseudoscientific (you can enter one of the following search terms: "pseudoscientific interventions," "thought field therapy," or "EMDR pseudoscience"). Summarize the arguments and counterarguments you find regarding whether a particular intervention is or is not pseudoscientific. Write down which side has the more persuasive argument and why or why not you are uncertain about the issue.

Visit CengageBrain.com for additional practice and study opportunities including experiential exercises, research tools, glossary, flashcards, and sample test items.

2

Evidence-Based Practice

EPAS Competencies for This Chapter

Competency 1 Demonstrate Ethical and Professional Behavior: The Code of Ethics of the National Association of Social Workers requires social workers to keep current with evidence-based knowledge and to use it as part of what informs their practice decisions. Carrying out this mandate implies engaging in the EBP process, which is the chief focus of this chapter.

Competency 2 Engage Diversity and Difference in Practice: You will learn in this chapter that an important part of EBP involves taking client diversity and differences into account when considering the applicability of research evidence to your client system. This chapter will help you develop the ability to do that.

Competency 4 Engage in Practice-Informed Research and Research-Informed Practice: This competency requires implementing the EPB process, and this chapter will enhance your ability to do so.

Competency 5 Engage in Policy Practice: You will learn in this chapter that EBP applies to all levels of social work practice, not just the clinical level. Your competence for engaging in policy practice will be enhanced by learning how to apply the EBP process to inform the development of and to critically analyze social policies and services.

Competency 7   Assess Individuals, Families, Groups, Organizations, and Communities: Among the things you need to learn to do to meet this competency is how to select appropriate intervention strategies based on research knowledge as integrated with your understanding of the values and preferences of client systems. Doing so is a major part of the EBP process.

Competency 8   Intervene with Individuals, Families, Groups, Organizations, and Communities: This competency specifies that you should be knowledgeable about evidence-informed interventions and understand methods of identifying, analyzing, and implementing evidence-informed interventions to achieve client system goals.

Competency 9   Evaluate Practice with Individuals Families, Groups, Organizations, and Communities: This competency includes learning how to apply evaluation findings to improve practice effectiveness. Doing so is another major part of the EBP process.

What You'll Learn in This Chapter

In Chapter 1, we examined the value of research in social work as well as the risks of not taking a scientific approach in making decisions about social work practice or social policy. In this chapter, we'll examine in depth a comprehensive model to guide social workers in taking a scientific approach to practice. That model is called *evidence-based practice* (EBP).

» INTRODUCTION

Evidence-based practice (EBP) is a process in which practitioners make decisions in light of the best research evidence available. Rather than rigidly constrict practitioner options, the EBP model encourages practitioners to integrate the best available research evidence with the following: their practice expertise and other resources; characteristics, circumstances, needs, values and preferences of their client system or target population; and knowledge of the idiosyncratic circumstances bearing on specific practice decisions. The diagram that appears in Figure 2-1 illustrates the role of EBP in decision making. It shows how EBP implies having research *inform* practice decisions, *not* dictate them. It also recognizes how broader environmental forces and the organizational context can influence the acceptability and feasibility of alternative decisions.

The EBP model applies to decisions at all levels of practice. For example, a clinical practitioner following the EBP model with a newly referred client might attempt to find and use the most scientifically validated diagnostic tools in assessing client problems and treatment needs and then develop a treatment plan in light of the best research evidence available as to what interventions are most likely to be effective in light of that assessment, the practitioner's clinical expertise regarding the client, and the client's idiosyncratic attributes and circumstances. At the level of social policy, the EBP model implies formulating or advocating policies that the best research available suggests are most likely to achieve their desired aims. At the community level, the EBP model implies making practice decisions in light of community-level practice research. Moreover, the EBP process implies that at each level research methods should be used to evaluate the outcomes of practice decisions to see if the chosen course of action is achieving its desired aim. If it is not, then the model implies choosing an alternative course of action—again, in light of the best research evidence available and again evaluating its outcome.

» CRITICAL THINKING IN EBP

In applying the scientific method to practice decisions, EBP is unlike "authority-based practice" (Gambrill, 1999). Rather than automatically accepting everything others with more experience or authority tell them about practice, practitioners engaged in EBP will question things. They will recognize unfounded beliefs and assumptions and think for themselves about the logic and the evidence that supports what others may convey as practice wisdom. Rather than just conform blindly to tradition or authority, they will take into account the best scientific evidence available in deciding how to intervene at micro or macro levels of practice. Doing so requires the use of critical thinking.

The term *critical thinking* has been defined in various overlapping ways, and sometimes in ways that encompass a broad array of components

FIGURE 2.1   Transdisciplinary EBP Model

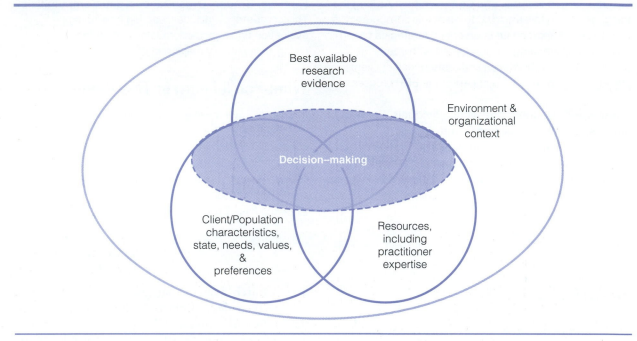

Source: From Satterfield, J., Spring, B., Brownson, R. C., Mullen, E., Newhouse, R., & Walker, B. (2009). Toward a transdisciplinary model of evidence-based practice. *Milbank Quarterly*, 87, 368–390.

unrelated to making social work practice decisions. Most germane to EBP, virtually all of the definitions imply that critical thinkers will do the following:

- Think for themselves.
- Consider whether beliefs or assertions of knowledge are based on sound evidence and logic.
- Think open-mindedly, recognizing and questioning unstated assumptions underlying beliefs and assertions.
- Be willing to test their own beliefs or conclusions and then alter them on the basis of new experiences and evidence.
- Formulate appropriate questions and then gather and appraise evidence as a basis for making decisions.

» EBP IMPLIES CAREER-LONG LEARNING

Before critical thinking practitioners can consider the best scientific evidence as a basis for their practice decisions, they first need to find such evidence.

They cannot be passive in this process, hoping or assuming that the evidence will somehow find its way to them. They need to know how to find relevant evidence and to understand research designs and methods so that they can critically appraise the validity of the evidence they find. Finally, they need to use research methods to evaluate whether the evidence-based actions they take actually result in the outcomes they seek to achieve (Gambrill, 2001).

In recognizing that even evidence-based knowledge is subject to change as newer and perhaps better studies might refute it with better evidence, being an evidence-based practitioner implies engaging in career-long learning. It means recognizing the need to search for and appraise new evidence as an ongoing, "lifelong" part of one's practice.

Engaging in the EBP process does not guarantee that you will find the kind of evidence needed to inform your practice decisions. Sometimes the evidence will be inconclusive, with some valid studies implying one course of action and other valid studies implying a different way to intervene. Sometimes the evidence will indicate what actions *not* to take, such as when studies show certain interventions or policies to be *ineffective*.

Although you will not always find a clear answer on how best to proceed, the important thing is to *look* for those answers. You would not want to miss them if they exist. And even when the evidence is mixed, it will often indicate possibilities you had not considered that are supported by more evidence than another action you were considering. Moreover, you can test one possibility out, and if that doesn't appear to be working, you can try one of the other evidence-based alternatives.

Sometimes the evidence will point toward taking an action that the client does not want. One key step in the EBP process is considering the values and expectations of clients and involving them as informed participants in the decision-making process. Gambrill (2001) reminds us that EBP is primarily a compassionate, client-centered approach to practice. We care about finding the best evidence because we care about maximizing our helpfulness to the client. We should not, therefore, disregard the values and concerns of clients when deciding whether the evidence we find fits the particular client with whom we are working.

Also, even interventions supported by the best evidence are not necessarily effective with every client or situation. An intervention that works with clients of one ethnic group may be less effective with clients of a different ethnicity. An intervention that is effective with females might not work with males or vice versa. You should consider whether the client or situation in question really matches the context in which the intervention was tested. And even if things match, you should remember that interventions supported by the best research are not guaranteed to work with every client or situation.

Studies providing valid evidence that an intervention is effective typically find that the intervention is *more likely* to be effective than some alternative, not that it is effective with every case. (This pertains to the concept of *probabilistic knowledge*, which we will examine more closely in Chapter 3.) These considerations underscore the importance of the client-centered nature of EBP and of taking the final step in the EBP process: using research methods to evaluate whether the decisions you make result in the outcomes you seek. Much of what you learn in this book will help you take this and other steps in the EBP process, which we mentioned earlier—such as finding relevant studies and critically appraising them— and doing so throughout your career.

STEPS IN THE EBP PROCESS

We will now examine more closely the steps of the EBP process. As we do, you may notice the need for you to understand research methods throughout the process. Several authors have provided helpful overviews of the steps in EBP (Cournoyer & Powers, 2002; Gambrill, 2001; Sackett Richardson, Rosenberg, & Haynes, 1997). The steps we describe next are adapted from them.

Step 1. Formulate a Question to Answer Practice Needs

In the first step, you formulate a question on the basis of what is known relevant to a practice decision you must make and what additional information is needed to best inform that decision. Although much of the literature on EBP focuses on questions about the effectiveness of programs, policies, or interventions, there are other types of EBP questions. According to Rubin (2008), four common types of EBP questions are as follows:

1. What intervention, program, or policy has the best effects?

2. What factors best predict desirable or undesirable consequences?

3. What's it like to have had my client's experiences?

4. What assessment tool should be used? (p. 43)

The box "Examples of EBP Questions" illustrates some specific types of EBP questions that can be asked at different levels of social work practice for each of the above general types of EBP questions. In that questions about effectiveness are the most common ones, let's focus on them as we consider the process of formulating an EBP question.

Suppose, for example, that you reside in Alaska and work in a residential treatment facility for girls with emotional and behavioral problems, most of whom are Native Alaskans who have been victims of physical or sexual abuse. Your first question might be, "What interventions have the most research evidence supporting their effectiveness with abused girls with emotional and behavioral problems who reside in residential treatment facilities?" As you search the literature for the answer to that question, you may quickly discover the need to incorporate into your question information about variations in the girls' characteristics.

Interventions that are effective in treating PTSD may not be effective with borderline personality disorder. A particular intervention might be very effective with girls who have had a single trauma but ineffective with girls who have had multiple traumas. That same intervention might even be potentially harmful for girls with dissociative disorders. You might find that some interventions have been found to be effective with older girls but not younger ones. Consequently, you might have to revise your question and perhaps formulate a series of questions. Instead of just asking about abused girls with emotional and behavioral problems, you might need separate questions about the most effective interventions for girls with different diagnoses, different problem histories, different ages, and so on.

You'll also want to incorporate the Native Alaskan ethnicity of the girls into your question. If you do not, you are likely to find many studies relevant to your question but perhaps none that included Native Alaskan participants. Consequently, the interventions you find that were effective with girls of other ethnicities might not be effective with the girls with whom you work. If you do incorporate the Native Alaskan ethnicity of the girls into your question, you will find numerous studies dealing with traumatized youths with substance abuse problems in combination with their other trauma-related disorders and few, if any, studies that focus exclusively on singular disorders that do not include substance abuse. You'll also find studies whose findings suggest that Native Alaskan youths with PTSD may not have a diagnosis of PTSD because cultural factors may influence them to mask their PTSD symptoms. Learning this might lead you to reconsider the diagnosis some of the girls have received and to consider evidence-based interventions for PTSD for some girls who had not previously had that diagnosis in their case record. Thus, including ethnicity in your question can make a huge difference in the evidence you find and the implications of that evidence for your practice.*

The questions we've discussed so far did not specify an intervention in advance. We took an

*We hope you are thinking critically and thus wondering what the evidence is for the assertions made in this paragraph on what you'll find if you incorporate the Native Alaskan ethnicity of the girls into your question. The assertions are based on what one of us (Rubin) found when he conducted a literature search on this question in preparation for a talk on EBP delivered on April 29, 2006, at the University of Alaska Anchorage School of Social Work.

open-ended approach in looking for evidence about whatever interventions have been studied and supported by the best scientific evidence. Sometimes, however, you'll have a good reason to narrow your question to one or more interventions that you specify in advance. Suppose, for example, that the traumatized girls you work with are very young and that your agency tradition is to provide nondirective play therapy as the prime intervention for every girl. As a critically thinking evidence-based practitioner, you might inquire as to the scientific evidence base for this tradition. Suppose that esteemed consultants or supervisors ask you to just trust their authority—or "practice wisdom"—on the matter. As a truly evidence-based practitioner, you'll need the courage to proceed with a search for evidence anyway. If you do, you'd have good reason to formulate a question that specifies play therapy, such as the following: "Will nondirective play therapy be effective in reducing the trauma symptoms of sexually abused Native Alaskan girls aged 8 or less?"

Sometimes it is reasonable to specify one or more alternative interventions in your question as well. Suppose, for example, that a colleague who works in a similar setting and with similar clients informs you that in her agency they prefer directive play therapy approaches that incorporate components of exposure therapy and that a debate rages among play therapy luminaries as to whether her agency's approach or your agency's approach makes more sense on theoretical grounds. Seeking scientific evidence to inform your practice in light of this new information, you might formulate an evidence-based question that specifies both alternative interventions, such as, "If sexually abused Native Alaskan girls aged 8 or less receive nondirective play therapy or directive play therapy, which will result in fewer trauma symptoms?" You might also want to expand the question to include exposure therapy.

The following acronym might come in handy when you want to formulate a question that specifies one or more interventions in advance: CIAO. To help you remember this acronym, in Italian, *ciao* can mean *hello* or *good-bye*. Here's what the acronym stands for:

- **C**lient characteristics
- **I**ntervention being considered
- **A**lternative intervention (if any)
- **O**utcome

EXAMPLES OF EBP QUESTIONS

Questions about Effectiveness

- *Is trauma-focused cognitive-behavioral therapy more effective than nondirective play therapy in reducing the trauma symptoms of children who have been sexually abused?*

- *Is the Housing and Urban Development VA-Supported Housing Program effective in decreasing homelessness among chronically homeless military veterans?*

Questions about Predictors of Desirable or Undesirable Consequences

- *Are child welfare direct service practitioners with social work degrees less likely to turn over or burn out than their counterparts who do not have social work degrees?*

- *What characteristics of foster parent–child matches are most and least likely to result in successful and unsuccessful foster care placements?*

Questions about Understanding Client Experiences

- *What is it like for homeless females to stay in an emergency shelter?*

- *How do multiple overseas deployments of military service members affect the service member's family in regard to family roles, the quality of the marital relationship, and the well-being of their children?*

Questions about Assessment Tools

- *What standardized measure of symptoms of posttraumatic stress disorder (PTSD) is most accurate in assessing for possible PTSD among combat veterans returning from Iraq or Afghanistan?*

- *What measure of children's self-esteem is best able to detect small changes in self-esteem among children who are being treated for low self-esteem and thus will be the best choice for monitoring treatment progress among such children?*

Applying the acronym to our question illustrated above, we get the following:

- **C:** If sexually abused Native Alaskan girls aged 8 or less
- **I:** Receive nondirective play therapy
- **A:** Or directive play therapy incorporating exposure therapy techniques
- **O:** Which will result in fewer trauma symptoms?

Step 2. Search for the Evidence

Later in this book, we will examine in detail how to use the library and your computer to conduct literature reviews to guide research projects. The same principles that we will examine later apply to searching for evidence to inform your practice decisions. However, practitioners rarely have nearly as much time and other resources for conducting exhaustive literature reviews as researchers are likely to have. One option likely to appeal to busy practitioners is the use of online searches of professional literature databases.

To help you search for literature online, your libraries may provide a variety of Internet professional literature database services, such as First-Search, Cambridge Scientific Abstracts, Medline, and OVID. Within these services are choices as to which professional area you'd like to search. For example, Cambridge Scientific Abstracts offers *Social Service Abstracts* and *Sociological Abstracts*. FirstSearch offers *Social Sciences Abstracts*. OVID offers *PsycINFO*. There is considerable overlap in what you'll find across different databases in related areas. For example, if you are looking for literature on child abuse, many of the references you'll find using *Social Service Abstracts* can also be found using *PsycINFO*. You can scan your library's list of online databases to find one (or perhaps a few) that seems most relevant to your topic.

After you enter some search terms, these databases will instantly provide you with a list of relevant books, journal articles, dissertations, and other publications related to your search terms. You can click on the ones that seem most pertinent to view the abstract for that reference. You may even be able to download the entire journal article, book, or dissertation.

What search terms you enter will depend on what you are looking for. If you're interested in a particular book or journal, for example, you can click on "Title" and then enter the title of that book or journal. To find the published works of a particular author, you can click on "Author" and then enter the name of that author. To find references related to a particular subject area, you would follow the same procedure, entering a search term connected to your subject of interest. Search terms that can be used in a search for evidence about the effectiveness of interventions include "treatment outcome," "effectiveness," "evaluation," "intervention," and similar terms. These terms can be used in conjunction with those that are descriptive of the client and situation, such as "residential treatment facility," "posttraumatic stress disorder," "dissociative disorders," "borderline personality disorder," "sexual abuse," and "child abuse" (for the example mentioned in step 1).

Suppose, for example, you want to find literature on support groups for battered women. Then you might enter such search terms as "battered women," "spouse abuse," "domestic violence," or "support groups." You will have options as to how broad or narrow you'd like the search to be. If you want the search to be limited to evaluations of the effectiveness of support groups for battered women, then you could ask for only those references pertaining to an entire set of key words, such as "battered women and evaluation." You might also be able to

limit the search according to other criteria, such as certain years of publication or the English language. If you want a broader search, then you can enter more key words or more broadly worded key words ("domestic violence" will yield more references than "battered wives"), and you would ask for references pertaining to any of your key words instead of the entire set.

If you do not have online access to the professional literature through a specific library, an alternative is to access the Internet directly through your own personal computer's search engine. There are various websites through which you can search for the literature you need. One site is provided by the National Library of Medicine at http://www.nlm .nih.gov. There you can obtain free usage of Medline, a database containing many references relevant to social work and allied fields.

Perhaps the most expedient option, however, is to use a popular search engine, such as Google Scholar. The box "Google Scholar Results for Effective Treatments for Child Abuse" displays four useful references (there were many more) that appeared on our first page of results generated by recently entering the search term "effective treatments for child abuse" in the Google Scholar search box.

Bottom-Up Searches   Two major approaches to searching for evidence have been defined by Mullen (2006) as the *top-down* and *bottom-up* strategies. Using the bottom-up strategy, you would search

GOOGLE SCHOLAR RESULTS FOR EFFECTIVE TREATMENTS FOR CHILD ABUSE

When we recently entered the search term "effective treatments for child abuse" on Google Scholar, over 400,000 links resulted. The first five were as follows:

- Evidence-based treatments in child abuse and neglect
  M Chaffin, B Friedrich - Children and youth services review, 2004 - Elsevier

- Comparison of multisystemic therapy and parent training in the brief treatment of child abuse and neglect.
  MA Brunk, SW Henggeler... - Journal of Consulting and ..., 1987 - psycnet.apa.org

- [PDF] from umc.edu
  Ten-year research update review: Child sexual abuse
  FW Putnam - ... American Academy of Child & Adolescent Psychiatry, 2003 - Elsevier

- [HTML] from nih.gov
  A multisite, randomized controlled trial for children with sexual abuse–related PTSD symptoms
  JA Cohen, E Deblinger, AP Mannarino... - ... Academy of Child & ..., 2004 - Elsevier

the literature looking for any and all sources that provide evidence pertaining to the practice question you formulated. You would then read and critically appraise the quality of the evidence in each source, judge whether it is applicable to your unique practice decision, and ultimately choose a course of action informed by what you deem to be the best applicable evidence available.

Top-Down Searches Using the top-down strategy, instead of starting from scratch to find and appraise all the relevant studies yourself, you would rely on the results of evidence-based searches that others have done. You can find these reports in such sources as books providing practice guidelines for intervening in specific problem areas or diagnostic categories, systematic reviews of the research in particular areas, or meta-analyses.

Systematic Reviews and Meta-Analyses A systematic review will report comprehensive searches for unpublished as well as published studies that address a particular research question. For example, it may examine which interventions have been found to be most (and least) effective in alleviating a specific problem. A good, trustworthy systematic review will indicate whether its authors have a vested interest in the intervention or other focus of the review. It also will critically appraise the rigor of the included studies and will give more weight to the most rigorous studies in developing conclusions and implications for practice.

A meta-analysis is a type of systematic review that pools the statistical results across studies of particular interventions and generates conclusions about which interventions have the strongest impacts on treatment outcome. Understandably, busy practitioners with limited time to search for literature might rely exclusively on the systematic reviews or meta-analyses that they find. However, there are risks in relying exclusively on the *top-down* search approach, as we will discuss in the next section.

Advantages and Risks of Top-Down Searches The prime advantage of the top-down approach is its feasibility. The social work agency where you work may have limited computer access to Internet literature databases, which can be expensive. Universities typically provide their students and faculty with free access to Internet databases that save much time in searching the literature. If you have already used such databases to search the literature

for term papers or other course assignments, you can imagine how much more time it would have taken to go to the library to look for the sources manually. Moreover, even with access to Internet databases, the bottom-up approach can be very time consuming if your search yields a large number of studies that need to be appraised as to the scientific quality of the evidence they provide and the applicability of that evidence to your unique practice decision. Some search terms—such as those looking for effective interventions for child maltreatment, domestic violence, or trauma—can yield more than a hundred studies that you'll need to examine. Reading and appraising those studies, even when you can download them electronically, can take a lot more time than is feasible for busy practitioners with large caseloads. It is much easier to rely on others with advanced expertise in appraising research evidence in particular areas of practice.

The top-down approach, however, has one serious disadvantage—the fallibility of the experts who have conducted the reviews, appraised the evidence, and derived practice guidelines from them. To a certain extent, relying exclusively on a top-down search as an evidence-based way to answer your practice question requires relying on the authority of those experts. Because reliance on authority is inconsistent with the scientific method, using only a top-down approach is therefore paradoxical. Perhaps the "experts" missed many relevant studies in their search. Perhaps other experts with higher methodological standards would disagree with their appraisals as to the scientific quality of the evidence in particular studies and as to which interventions appear to be supported by the *best* evidence. Some "experts" may even be biased in their appraisals—especially if they have a vested interest in the intervention that they claim has the best evidentiary support. If you conduct a top-down search for effective interventions for PTSD, for example, you likely will find experts in exposure therapy and experts in eye movement desensitization and processing (EMDR) therapy arguing over whose reviews are more biased and whose favored treatment approach has the better evidentiary support.

If feasibility obstacles to using the bottom-up approach require practitioners to rely solely on a top-down approach, therefore, they should do so as critical thinkers. They should not rely on just one or a few top-down sources that have been recommended to them or that they find first. They should try to find and appraise all the top-down sources relevant to their practice decision and look for possible disagreements among them. They should try to ascertain whether the authors of the sources have a vested interest in the particular practice approach recommended. Finally, they should examine the evidentiary standards used in the appraisals of studies. Did the studies have to meet certain minimal methodological criteria to qualify for inclusion in the review? What methodological criteria were used to distinguish studies offering the best evidence from those offering weaker evidence? Were those criteria appropriate in light of the information in the rest of this book and in your research courses?

Fortunately, the top-down and bottom-up approaches are not mutually exclusive. Time and access permitting, you can search for and appraise individual studies as well as top-down sources that have already appraised individual studies and developed practice guidelines from them. In fact, a thorough bottom-up search implicitly would find and appraise top-down sources as well as individual studies. It can't hurt to augment your own review of individual studies with the reviews others have provided as long as you critically appraise each source as recommended above. With that in mind, let's now look at two top-down resources that are regarded highly by researchers in social work and allied fields. The box "Some Useful Internet Sites for Reviews and Practice Guidelines" lists the

websites for these two sources as well as some others that you might find useful.

The Cochrane Collaboration and the Campbell Collaboration   The Cochrane Collaboration is an international nonprofit organization that recruits researchers, practitioners, and consumers into review groups that provide reviews of research on the effects of health-care interventions. If you visit the Cochrane Collaboration's website at http://www.cochrane.org, you will find a link to its library, which contains its reviews, comments and criticisms, abstracts of other reviews, bibliographies of studies, reviews regarding methodology, and links that can help you conduct your own review. The Cochrane website also has information that will help you judge the quality of the Cochrane review system.

A sibling of the Cochrane Collaboration is the Campbell Collaboration. Its mission and operations focus on social welfare, education, and criminal justice. Its reviews are written for use by practitioners, the public, policy makers, students, and researchers. If you go to its website at http://www.campbellcollaboration.org, you can find links that are like those of the Cochrane Collaboration but with a focus on topics not limited to health care. For example, you can find reviews of the effectiveness of interventions for domestic violence, sexual abuse, parent training, criminal offenders, juvenile delinquency, personality disorder, conduct disorder

SOME USEFUL INTERNET SITES FOR REVIEWS AND PRACTICE GUIDELINES

- Campbell Collaboration: http://www.campbellcollaboration.org/index.html
- Cochrane Collaboration: http://www.cochrane.org
- American Psychological Association's website on empirically supported treatments: http://www.apa.org/divisions/div12/rev_est
- Center for Substance Abuse Prevention: http://modelprograms.samhsa.gov/template.cfm?page=default
- Crisis Intervention, Comorbidity Assessment, Domestic Violence Intervention, and Suicide Prevention Network: http://www.crisisinterventionnetwork.com

- Expert Consensus Guideline Series: http://www.psychguides.com
- National Guideline Clearinghouse: http://www.guidelines.gov
- National Institute of Drug Abuse: http://www.nida.nih.gov
- Substance Abuse and Mental Health Services Administration: http://www.samhsa.gov/index.aspx
- Additional sites for top-down reviews can be found by entering search terms into a search engine such as Google Scholar or others.

among youths, serious mental illness, substance abuse, welfare reform, housing, foster parent training, eating disorders, and many others.

Step 3. Critically Appraise the Relevant Studies You Find

As we noted in Chapter 1, there is a vast range in the quality of published studies evaluating the effectiveness of various interventions. Many are excellent, but many others violate some of the fundamental principles that you will learn in this book. It would be silly to attempt at this point to explain in depth all the research methods and research design concepts you'll need to know to critically appraise the studies you will find. That's what the rest of this book is for. Moreover, as we mentioned earlier, a good systematic review or meta-analysis (such as those found at the Cochrane Collaboration and Campbell Collaboration sites) will critically appraise the rigor of its included studies and will give more weight to the most rigorous studies in developing conclusions and implications for practice. However, not all systematic reviews and meta-analyses are equally

trustworthy. Therefore, Figure 2-2 lists criteria that can guide you in critically appraising the quality of the systematic reviews and meta-analyses you might want to examine.

Step 4. Determine Which Research-Supported Intervention or Policy Is Most Appropriate for Your Particular Client(s)

Even interventions supported by the best evidence are not necessarily effective with every client or situation. Strong studies providing valid evidence that an intervention is effective typically find that the intervention is *more likely* to be effective than some alternative, not that it is effective with every case. Interventions found to be effective with members of one ethnic group might not be effective with clients with other ethnicities. The intervention supported by the strongest studies might involve procedures that conflict with the values of certain cultures or individual clients. You should use your knowledge of the client system or target population and your cultural competence in making a judgment call.

FIGURE 2.2 Criteria for Critically Appraising Systematic Reviews and Meta-Analyses

- Did the author of the review, or those who sponsored or funded it, have a vested interest at stake in its conclusions?
- Did the study even reveal whether the author of the review, or those who funded or sponsored it, have a conflict of interest regarding any vested interest?
- Are the criteria used for including or excluding studies in the review identified?
- Are those criteria too narrow or restrictive?
- Did the author search for unpublished studies (which may be less likely to have findings supporting the effectiveness of interventions than are published studies)?
- Did the author search for studies written in languages other than English?
- Did the author search multiple literature databases instead of relying on just one or two?
- Did the author examine studies cited in studies already found?
- Did the author search websites related to the research question?
- Did the author contact authors of any studies being reviewed to get further clarification regarding the methodological rigor of the study or the meaning of its findings?
- Does the review critically appraise the methodological rigor of the included studies?
- Does the review sort the evidence from the reviewed studies according to differences in the methodological rigor of studies with contrasting findings?
- Does the review sort the evidence from the reviewed studies according to differences in the types and characteristics of research participants in studies with contrasting findings?
- Did the review use at least two researchers to independently extract findings from the studies and rate their methodological rigor, and did their conclusions agree?
- Does the review report steps that were taken to prevent bias in the review process?

Determining which of the interventions or policies you find is the best fit for your client system or target population involves several considerations. One consideration, of course, is the quality of the evidence that you appraise in step 3. Students commonly ask, "How many good studies do I need to find that support a particular intervention before I can feel confident that I have adequate evidence?" There is no precise answer to that question. One or two methodologically strong studies supporting a particular intervention or policy might offer better research support than a larger number of methodologically weaker studies supporting an alternative. Something supported by one very strong study probably has better evidence than an alternative supported only by various very weak studies.

More important, asking which intervention or policy is "evidence based" is not the right question. It has a ring of finality to it that is not consistent with the provisional nature and refutability of knowledge in the scientific method. Rather than ask whether to consider something to be evidence based, it's better to think in terms of which of the options has the best evidence for the time being. And if the evidence supporting that option emerged from research with clients very unlike yours, it might not be as good as evidence from a study using a somewhat weaker design but with clients who are just like yours.

But what if you find no intervention or policy supported by any study involving clients just like yours, even as you find one supported by a strong study involving clients who are like yours in some important ways but unlike yours in other important ways? Unless the latter option is unacceptable for some reason, it might be worth trying. For example, maybe you'll find no intervention that appears to be effective with 12- and 13-year-old girls in a residential treatment facility who are diagnosed with borderline personality disorder. Perhaps you'll find strong evidence supporting the effectiveness of an intervention for 14- to 16-year-old girls with that disorder but not in a residential facility. If you find no better alternative, you might employ the latter intervention on a trial basis and evaluate (in step 6) what happens.

If it is appropriate and possible to do so before finalizing the selection of any intervention or policy and applying it, you should consider the values and expectations of your client system or target population. You should involve the client or members of the target population in the decision, inform them about the intervention or policy and the evidence about its potential effectiveness and any possible undesirable side effects, and—if in direct practice—obtain the client system's informed consent to participate in the intervention. You'll probably want to avoid a lot of detail when you obtain client system consent and thus merely say something like, "This has the best evidence of effectiveness to date," "This has had a few promising results," or, "We have some beginning evidence that this option may work well for people who have your kinds of concerns." If you are providing direct services to a client, beyond the ethical reasons for obtaining informed consent regarding the choice of intervention, doing so might help the client feel a sense of ownership and responsibility in the intervention process. In turn, the client might be more likely to achieve a successful outcome.

Step 5. Apply the Chosen Intervention

Once the selection of the intervention is finalized, several steps may be needed before applying it. To begin, you may need to obtain training in the intervention through a continuing education workshop or professional conference. Perhaps an elective course is offered on it at a nearby school of social work. You should also obtain readings on how to implement the intervention, including any treatment manuals for it. Try to locate a colleague who has experience providing the intervention and arrange for consultation or supervision. For some relatively new interventions, you may find a support group of professional colleagues who meet regularly to provide each other peer feedback about how they are implementing the new intervention with various cases. If you are unable to obtain sufficient training or supervision, you should try to refer the client to other practitioners who have the requisite training and experience in the intervention.

If you provide the intervention yourself or if you continue working with clients after you've referred them for it, one more step should be taken before the intervention is introduced. You should formulate, in collaboration with the client, treatment goals that can be measured in evaluating whether the selected intervention really helps the client. Chapter 8 will help you define treatment goals in measurable terms. Some of the studies you appraise in step 2 might also identify useful ways to define and measure treatment goals.

Step 6. Provide Evaluation and Feedback

This phase involves measuring and evaluating progress in achieving the goals that have been set for the selected intervention or policy. Several later chapters will help you design the methods for doing that. If in direct practice, for example, you might have the client self-monitor certain behaviors, emotions, or cognitions daily for a while before you apply the intervention, during the course of treatment with the intervention, and perhaps during a follow-up period after you have completed the intervention protocol.

To assess whether the intervention appears to be effective for that particular client, you might graph the daily data and look for the pattern of the graphed data to improve significantly after intervention begins. You and the client can discuss the data in an ongoing fashion, including perhaps the need to modify the intervention if it does not appear to be helpful or if its goals have already been achieved. Some clients like this process—seeing their progress and discussing why symptoms are getting worse or better. Sometimes extraneous important events come up in their lives that affect their progress and that inform the intervention process.

Once your evaluation has finished, you should communicate your findings to relevant colleagues. You might even want to write up your work as a single-case evaluation study for publication. If you choose to do that, Chapter 13 can help you, as can other parts of the text that discuss writing research reports. Cournoyer and Powers (2002) even suggest that you might communicate your findings to the researchers whose studies provided the evidence base for choosing the intervention you applied and evaluated.

But perhaps you are wondering why step 6 is needed in the first place. Why evaluate an intervention if published studies have already provided credible evidence of its effectiveness? There are two answers to this question. The first answer, which we mentioned earlier, is that studies supporting the effectiveness of an intervention typically do not find that the tested intervention is guaranteed to work with every client or situation. Instead, they merely find that it is more likely to be effective than some alternative. Your client or target population may be among the cases for whom the intervention or policy does not work. The second answer

involves the principle of replication. As we discussed in Chapter 1, the scientific method considers all knowledge to be provisional and subject to refutation. The more high-quality studies that replicate a particular outcome for a particular intervention with clients like yours, the more confidence we can have in the evidence about that intervention's effects.

» DISTINGUISHING THE EVIDENCE-BASED PROCESS FROM EVIDENCE-BASED PRACTICES

Many scholars and practitioners commonly use the term *evidence-based practice* when referring to the EBP *process*. However, others commonly use the same term when referring not to the process but rather to specific *interventions* that have been supported by research. Thus, a particular program, policy, or intervention that has received consistent research support might be called *evidence based* and might appear on a list with a plural heading, such as *evidence-based practices*.

Because both the singular and the plural headings can have the same EBP acronym, this often leads to confusion in discussions and debates about EBP. For example, if you probe as to why some clinical practitioners have negative attitudes about EBP, you might find that their attitudes are in reference not to the process definition of EBP but rather to the notion that insurance companies or government agencies will not pay for their services unless they mechanistically provide one of the interventions that appear on the company's list of interventions deemed to be evidence based, regardless of practitioner judgment or client attributes. Keeping in mind the distinction between the *singular* concept of the EBP *process* and the *plural* concept of evidence-based *practices* (which are sometimes called *empirically supported treatments* or *research supported treatments*), the next section discusses some commonly expressed controversies and misconceptions about EBP. Before moving to that section, you may want to examine the box "A Case Example of a Research-Supported Intervention in the EBP Process."

A CASE EXAMPLE OF A RESEARCH-SUPPORTED INTERVENTION (EXPOSURE THERAPY) IN THE EBP PROCESS

Carol is a fictitious social worker who specializes in treating traumatized women and who engages in the EBP process. Through that process, Carol has learned that prolonged exposure therapy (PE) and EMDR have strong scientific evidence as effective treatments for PTSD. Carol also learned that the evidence supporting both PE and EMDR is about equal. She was able to obtain training and supervision in PE and plans to obtain the same in EMDR in the near future.

Carol's new client is Sarah, a young woman who has been diagnosed with PTSD several months after being raped late at night near her car in a dim and remote spot in a large multilevel indoor parking garage. Carol initially had expected to treat Sarah's PTSD symptoms with PE, which engages clients in two forms of exposure therapy: imaginal exposure and *in vivo* exposure, both of which have strong research support and which ideally are used sequentially with the same client. With her other clients, Carol typically has begun PE with the imaginal exposure component first, which involves having the client repeatedly imagine that they are reliving the traumatic event (which in Sarah's case is the rape) and repeatedly describing the event in detail while in the safety of therapeutic environment. This process would be repeated again and again in therapy, with more details coming out during each iteration— details including the client's emotions and various sensual experiences (sights, sounds, smells, and so on) during the trauma.

When clients feel ready, Carol typically moves on to the *in vivo* exposure phase, which begins by asking clients to list things, places, people, and circumstances that—although really safe—tend to remind them of their trauma and therefore trigger their PTSD symptoms. The clients rate each item on the list in terms of the degree of distress that they experience when encountering that item. For Sarah, driving by herself into an indoor parking garage (not the same one where she was raped) at night would be extremely distressful, doing so accompanied by a friend would be somewhat less distressful, doing that with a friend during the day would be even less distressful, and parking outside during the day

not far from such a garage would be distressful but considerably less so (especially if accompanied by a friend). With *in vivo* exposure, Sarah would begin by going somewhere safe with a friend that involves the least amount of distress, discussing the experience in therapy, and then repeating the process with another safe exposure to a situation that had a slightly higher distress rating on her list. This process would be repeated, gradually escalating the distress rating of the safe situation each time.

Underlying both imaginal and *in vivo* exposure is the concept of habituation, in which clients experience success in facing things they used to avoid and thus feel less and less distress as the association is extinguished between the safe triggers and the actual traumatic event. (This, of course, has been a brief and simplified summary of exposure therapy; you can learn more about it by entering it as a search term on the Internet.)

Carol understands the importance of establishing a strong therapeutic alliance with clients as a prerequisite for any research supported treatment to be effective, and as she is establishing that alliance early in treatment (before initiating any discussion of PE with Sarah), she learns that Sarah—a devout Catholic—is having thoughts of suicide connected to her feelings of guilt over recently obtaining an abortion after finding out that her rapist impregnated her. In light of her clinical expertise and this new knowledge of her client's suicidal ideation, Carol decides that Sarah is not yet ready for PE. She realizes that by imaginally reliving the trauma or by encountering even mildly distressful things that remind her of the trauma, Sarah's risk of suicide might increase. Moreover, Carol's clinical judgment dictates that treating Sarah's depressive and suicidal symptoms must be a first priority; the other PTSD symptoms can wait until there is no longer a risk of suicide.

Fortunately, Carol has a good working relationship with a colleague who also engages in the EBP process and who specializes in research supported treatments for depression and suicidality. Her colleague and Sarah agree that a referral to that colleague for treatment of Sarah's depression and suicidal ideation should precede any further trauma therapy with Carol. Once that treatment has been completed, Carol reengages Sarah in treatment for PTSD. However, when explaining imaginal exposure therapy to Sarah, the prospect of imaginally reliving the trauma is unacceptable to Sarah, even after Carol explains why it is really safe and effective and encourages her to try it.

"No how! No way!" Sarah keeps saying. Carol then explains *in vivo* exposure, and Sarah—though apprehensive—is willing to give it a try, finding it less scary to begin by going somewhere safe and only very mildly distressful with a friend than to imagine that she is reliving the rape. Carol hopes that after Sarah successfully completes the *in vivo* component, she will be willing to give the imaginal component a try. Thus, Carol has used her clinical expertise and knowledge of the client's clinical state and preferences—in combination with her knowledge of the research evidence—in intervening with Sarah. In doing so, Carol has employed a research supported intervention as part of the EBP process and has shown how doing so allows room for clinical flexibility and does not require practitioners to operate in a mechanistic, cookbook fashion.

» CONTROVERSIES AND MISCONCEPTIONS ABOUT EBP

A significant early event spurring interest in EBP was a 1995 report by the American Psychological Association's Division 12 Task Force on Promotion and Dissemination of Psychological Procedures (Task Force, 1995) and updates to that report (Chambless et al., 1996, 1998). According to that report, to have its effectiveness be considered "well established," an intervention ideally should have a manual that provides step-by-step specific procedures that practitioners should follow in implementing the intervention. Such manuals are seen as increasing the likelihood that different practitioners will implement the intervention in the intended manner. Likewise, without such manuals, confidence in the effectiveness of the intervention would diminish in light of the increased potential for practitioners to implement it in ways that deviate from the manner in which it was found to be effective.

The impact of the Task Force report led many to equate its recommendations with EBP and to define EBP as the use of interventions that prestigious professional organizations or research reviews deemed to be effective. Moreover, some perceived the use of cookbook-like manualized procedures as a necessary feature of EBP. On the basis of this perception, a number of objections were raised. Let's now examine the most prominent objections to the model and why those criticisms have been deemed misconceptions.

EBP Is Based on Studies of Atypical Clients

One objection concerns the characteristics of clients that have participated in studies providing strong research support for the effectiveness of interventions—specifically, that EBP is based on studies of clients unlike those typically encountered in everyday social work practice. Many such studies have excluded clients with more than one diagnosis, and racial or ethnic minority clients are often underrepresented in them (Messer, 2006; Westen, 2006). This objection is particularly germane to social work since social workers so often work with ethnic minority clients or clients with multiple disorders or with unique concerns that don't fit the formal diagnostic categories required for participation in many studies.

In light of the discrepancies between the kinds of clients participating in evaluations of manualized interventions and the kinds of clients social workers are most likely to encounter in everyday practice, the perception of EBP as requiring practitioners to rigidly follow treatment manuals has been criticized as not allowing them the flexibility to use their expertise to respond to unique client attributes and circumstances.

EBP Is Overly Restrictive

A related objection portrays EBP as an overly restrictive cookbook approach that minimizes professional expertise and applies research supported interventions in the same way to all clients, ignoring client values and preferences. Proponents of EBP have dismissed this objection, as well as the one above, as being based on a misconception of the most prominent definitions of EBP (Gibbs & Gambrill, 2002; Mullen & Streiner, 2004). They argue that these objections overlook components of the EBP process that include the integration of practice expertise, considering the values and expectations of the client, and involving the client in the selection of an intervention, as discussed earlier in this chapter and as illustrated in the box "A Case Example of a Research-Supported Intervention (Exposure Therapy) in the EBP Process."

EBP Is Just a Cost-Cutting Tool

Some critics of EBP have portrayed it as merely a cost-cutting tool that can be exploited by government agencies and managed-care companies that pay for services. Their criticism is based on the notion that third-party payers will only pay for the provision of interventions that have been supported by experimental research and only for the number of sessions that the research results indicate are needed.

Proponents of EBP counter that this is not a criticism of EBP but rather a criticism of the way managed-care companies might distort it. Moreover, they argue that some interventions supported by the best research evidence are more costly than the less-supported alternatives (Gibbs & Gambrill, 2002; Mullen & Streiner, 2004). The aim of EBP is to find the most effective interventions, not to find the cheapest ones.

Evidence Is in Short Supply

Another criticism of EBP is that there are not enough quality research studies to inform practice in social work. Although there is some truth to that assertion, the number of such studies is growing. Moreover, EBP proponents counter this criticism by asserting that a shortage of quality outcome studies is less of an argument against EBP than an argument for it. If practitioners are making decisions on the basis of little or no evidence, all the more reason to "exercise caution and perhaps be even more vigilant in monitoring outcomes" (Mullen & Streiner, 2004, p. 115).

Another counterargument is the piece of mind you can have knowing that you left no stone unturned in trying to find the most effective way to help your clients, even if the evidence you seek does not exist. Imagine the alternative—that is, proceeding to intervene with clients without first thoroughly checking to see whether the way you plan to proceed is the best way to help them. Imagine being treated by a physician who tells you that she hasn't bothered to check to see if the medication she is prescribing is the best thing for you because she does not want to waste her time looking for evidence that *might* not exist.

Furthermore, some interventions that might seem theoretically sound and perhaps might even be in vogue are actually harmful (as discussed in Chapter 1). Imagine how you would feel if you provided a harmful intervention and only later found out that had you examined the research on that intervention, you could have avoided harming your client.

The Therapeutic Alliance Will Be Hindered

Some argue that rigid adherence to treatment manuals associated with many research-supported interventions can inhibit practitioner flexibility in using professional experience and expertise in relationship building, and that this consequently can harm the therapeutic alliance and result in poorer treatment outcomes (Messer, 2006; Reed, 2006; Westen, 2006; Zlotnik and Galambos, 2004). Again, however, proponents of EBP dismiss this objection as ignoring the part of the definition of EBP that emphasizes the integration of practice expertise in the EBP process, as illustrated in Figure 2-1 and in the box "A Case Example of a Research-Supported Intervention (Exposure Therapy) in the EBP Process." Furthermore, this objection overlooks the fact that treatment manuals typically emphasize the importance of the therapeutic relationship as part of the intervention and warn readers that in order for the intervention to be effective, it must be provided in the context of a strong therapeutic alliance. (In fact, every evidence-based treatment manual that we have seen has had that emphasis.)

» COMMON FACTORS AND THE DODO BIRD

If you seek to find an intervention that has the best effects, you should keep in mind that treatment outcome will be influenced by other treatment factors as well, not just selecting the best intervention modality. For example, we already noted the importance of the therapeutic relationship and acknowledged that for any intervention to be effective, it must be provided in the context of a strong therapeutic alliance. Research has consistently identified some common practitioner and treatment characteristics that are likely to influence the strength of the therapeutic alliance and treatment outcome across the gamut of intervention modalities (Hubble, Duncan, & Miller, 2009). Although the empirical literature on such common factors is still evolving, here are some of the practitioner and treatment characteristics that have been supported by rigorous research as having a key influence on treatment outcome:

- Accurate empathy
- Warmth
- Positive regard
- Cultivating hope
- Adapting treatment to the client's stage of change

The research supporting the importance of these common factors should be viewed as an essential part of what should guide practitioners seeking to engage in EBP. That is, if you want to maximize your practice effectiveness in light of research evidence, you will consider not only evidence about intervention modalities but also evidence about common treatment factors. Moreover, you will seek to maximize your skills in the common factors that have the best evidence. Therefore, learning in your practice classes to develop and improve your skills in these common factors is an essential part of learning to intervene effectively with a diverse range of people who have diverse problems and thus learning to engage in EBP.

Some critics of EBP, however, see the importance of these common factors as diminishing the importance of EBP. Citing research studies that found the quality of the therapeutic relationship to have a much greater impact on treatment outcome than does the specific intervention provided, they have deemed the choice of intervention to be irrelevant, arguing that all interventions are equally effective when they are provided by practitioners with good relationship skills (Wampold, 2001). That argument is known as the "dodo bird verdict" because in the *Alice in Wonderland* story the dodo bird declared after a race, "Everyone has won, and all must have prizes" (Luborsky, 1975).

Others, however, have argued against the dodo bird verdict, citing methodological flaws in the studies that support that verdict as well as other studies that found the choice of intervention to have the greater impact (Beutler, 2002; Craighead, Sheets, & Bjornsson, 2005; Lilienfeld, 2007). They have also noted that even if relationship factors have a greater impact on outcome than does the choice of intervention, that does not mean that the choice of intervention is unimportant. Why not emphasize both? they ask. Moreover, the EBP process does emphasize both, as do the treatment manuals for many research-supported interventions.

We do not intend to take sides in the debate over whether relationship factors or intervention choice has a greater impact on treatment outcome. We do, however, suggest that unless and until the controversy becomes resolved in a way that shows that the choice of intervention has no meaningful impact on outcome, then the dodo bird verdict is a false dichotomy. That is, as long as intervention choice can add to the impact of relationship factors in a meaningful way, then even if relationship factors have the greater impact, that is not a compelling argument against engaging in the EBP process. Furthermore, if practitioners base their decision to emphasize relationship factors on the research supporting the dodo bird verdict, then ironically, they are in fact engaging in EBP because they are basing their practice decision on their appraisal of the research evidence.

» REAL-WORLD OBSTACLES TO IMPLEMENTING EBP IN EVERYDAY PRACTICE

Perhaps the most problematic concern about EBP has nothing to do with its desirability and is one that even its proponents find daunting. It has to do with obstacles to implementing it in real-world everyday practice. Social workers commonly work in settings where superiors do not understand or appreciate EBP and do not give practitioners enough time to carry out the EBP process—especially if they follow the bottom-up approach in searching for evidence (as discussed earlier in this chapter). Even in settings where EBP is valued, resources may be insufficient to provide staff with the time, training, publications, and access to Internet databases and search engines needed to carry out the EBP process efficiently and appropriately.

Although some leaders in EBP are formulating and pilot-testing strategies for overcoming these obstacles in agencies, the going is rough. For example, even when it is feasible to find and appraise research—that is, to carry out the EBP *process*—agencies might not be able to afford the costs of the training and supervision practitioners will need to effectively provide the *intervention* that has the best research support.

Alleviating Feasibility Obstacles to EBP

Acknowledging that feasibility concerns perhaps pose the most daunting challenge facing EBP, proponents of EBP have suggested ways to make the EBP process more feasible (Rubin, 2010). One way is to divide the tasks of the EBP process up among a team of practitioners in an agency. The team would focus on one EBP question at a time, with each question addressing a common type of agency client or problem. Each team member would execute one phase of the process. After completing the process for one EBP question of significance to the agency, the team could move on to another. This task could be made even more feasible in agencies that have student field placement interns. Those interns could complete the process as above as part of their fieldwork assignments, thus sparing agency staff members of the burden while learning more about EBP themselves. Furthermore, the students probably would have access to online literature databases through their university library. If that access were not available to the students or to agency practitioners, another option would be to use free governmental literature database sites such as Medline. Also, especially for agencies in urban areas, students or practitioners might be able to get free access to online literature databases through their local public library system.

Mullen et al. (2007) suggested that the burden on practitioners might also be eased by including EBP training in existing agency in-service training sessions or meetings. They also urged schools of social work to train EBP teams within agencies and to provide EBP training to field practicum instructors. Offering continuing education credits for such training would be a good incentive.

Throughout your social career, there may be some times when engaging in the EBP process is more feasible than at other times. But even during those times when the obstacles seem to be the most daunting, we hope that you will do your best to have your practice decisions informed by research

evidence. We also hope that the remaining chapters of this book will facilitate that effort.

MAIN POINTS

- EBP is a process in which practitioners make practice decisions in light of the best research evidence available.
- The EBP model encourages practitioners to integrate scientific evidence with their practice expertise and knowledge of the idiosyncratic circumstances bearing on specific practice decisions.
- Although EBP is most commonly discussed in regard to decisions about what interventions to provide clients, it also applies to decisions about how best to assess the practice problems and decisions practitioners make at all levels of practice.
- EBP involves critical thinking, questioning, recognizing unfounded beliefs and assumptions, thinking independently as to the logic and evidence supporting what others may convey as practice wisdom, and being informed by the best scientific evidence available when making practice decisions.
- Evidence-based practitioners need to track down evidence as an ongoing part of their practice. They need to know how to find relevant studies and understand research designs and methods so that they can critically appraise the validity of the studies they find. In addition, they should use research methods to evaluate whether the actions they take result in the outcomes they seek to achieve.
- In recognizing that even evidence-based knowledge is subject to change as newer and perhaps better studies might refute it with better evidence, being an evidence-based practitioner implies engaging in career-long learning. It means recognizing the need to search for and appraise new evidence as an ongoing, "lifelong" part of one's practice.
- Steps in the EBP process include formulating a question, searching for evidence, critically appraising the studies you find, determining which research-supported intervention or policy is most appropriate for your client(s), applying

the selected option, and evaluating progress and providing feedback.

- EBP questions may be open-ended regarding interventions or policies or may specify one or more of them in advance.
- Perhaps the most expedient way to search for evidence is to use an online search engine or one of your library's online professional literature databases.
- Searching for evidence can employ top-down and bottom-up strategies.
- Using the bottom-up strategy, you would search the literature for sources that provide evidence pertaining to the practice question you formulated. You would then read and critically appraise the quality of the evidence in each source, judge whether it is applicable to your unique practice decision, and ultimately choose a course of action informed by what you deem to be the best applicable evidence available.
- Using the top-down strategy, instead of starting from scratch to find and appraise all the relevant studies yourself, you would rely on the results of evidence-based searches that others have done and that are reported in such sources as books providing practice guidelines, systematic reviews, or meta-analyses.
- Even interventions or policies supported by the best evidence are not necessarily effective with every client or situation. Those found to be effective with members of one ethnic group might not be effective with clients of other ethnicities. Those supported by the strongest studies might involve procedures that conflict with the values of certain cultures or individual clients.
- Various objections have been raised to the call for all practitioners to engage in EBP. Proponents of the model have characterized most of the objections as misconceptions.
- Social workers commonly work in settings where resources might be insufficient to provide staff with the time, training, publications, and access to Internet databases and search engines needed to carry out the EBP process efficiently and appropriately. However, various ways have been suggested to alleviate feasibility obstacles to the EBP process in such settings.
- Some common treatment factors have been supported by research as influencing treatment outcome across the gamut of intervention modalities. Although some have cited the

importance of those common factors as an argument against EBP, proponents of EBP can cite various counterpoints to that argument.

REVIEW QUESTIONS AND EXERCISES

1. Formulate an EBP question to inform your decision about the most effective intervention to employ in the case of a 6-year-old African American boy who witnessed his father severely battering his mother and whose diagnosis includes both conduct disorder and posttraumatic stress disorder.
2. Suppose that your search for evidence to answer your question in exercise 1 yielded no study in which the characteristics of the participants matched those of your client. Discuss the various considerations that would inform your decision about which of several different research supported interventions is most likely to be effective for your client.
3. Discuss how your answer to exercise 2 bears on several objections raised by critics of EBP.
4. Identify what you deem as the most important generic relationship skills that you are learning in your practice courses and discuss how they are part of becoming an evidence-based practitioner.

INTERNET EXERCISES

1. Using an Internet search engine such as Google Scholar or one of the alternative database services mentioned in this chapter, enter a search term for a policy or intervention that interests you. In the search results, click on several links that look most interesting. Briefly describe what you find at those links and how helpful they appear to be in facilitating a search for evidence to inform practice decisions about the intervention or policy you specified in your search term.
2. Using an Internet search engine, enter a search term for a systematic review or meta-analysis regarding the effectiveness of a policy or intervention that interests you. Discuss how relying on reviews such as the one you find represents a top-down search strategy and why using such a strategy would be more expedient than using a

bottom-up search strategy. (An alternative search term might be *systematic reviews in social work*.)

3. Enter the search terms "dodo bird verdict" and "common factors psychotherapy." Go to several sources that discuss the common factors and several sites that argue for or against the dodo bird verdict. Briefly summarize how what you read is likely to influence your outlook regarding EBP.

Visit CengageBrain.com for additional practice and study opportunities including experiential exercises, research tools, glossary, flashcards, and sample test items.

3

Factors Influencing the Research Process

EPAS Competencies for This Chapter

Competency 2 Engage Diversity and Difference in Practice: Part of becoming a culturally competent research practitioner is learning about how cultural diversity can influence the research process.

Competency 3 Advance Human Rights and Social and Economic Justice: In this chapter, you will learn about a research paradigm that uses research procedures to empower oppressed groups.

Competency 4 Engage in Practice-Informed Research and Research-Informed Practice: This competency requires you to understand the principles of scientific inquiry, which implies understanding how various factors covered in this chapter can influence that inquiry.

What You'll Learn in This Chapter

We'll examine the phases in the process of conducting research in social work and begin to look at factors that can influence variations in the way those phases are carried out.

» INTRODUCTION

In this chapter, we shift from a focus on how to use research to inform evidence-based practice to a focus on the way research is carried out. We'll start by diagramming and discussing the phases of the research process. We'll discuss considerations that can affect the sequencing of those phases and begin to look at factors that affect the way each phase is carried out. The factors that we'll examine in this chapter include theories, values, practice models, and paradigms. Additional factors will be addressed in depth in later chapters. These include qualitative and quantitative research approaches, ethics, organizational and political concerns, cultural diversity, research purposes, selecting research questions that have significant utility for practice or policy, and feasibility issues.

» THE PHASES OF THE RESEARCH PROCESS

Social work research has much in common with evidence-based social work practice. Both endeavors follow essentially the same problem-solving process in seeking to resolve social welfare problems. Both begin with the formulation of the problem, which includes recognizing a difficulty, defining it, and specifying it. Researchers and evidence-based practitioners then generate, explore, and select alternative strategies for solving the problem. Finally, they implement the chosen approach, evaluate it, and disseminate their findings. In both practice and research, these phases are contingent on one another. Although the logical order is to go from one phase to the next, insurmountable obstacles encountered in any particular phase will prevent you from moving to the next phase and require you to return to a previous phase.

For example, in evidence-based practice (EBP), if an intervention with the best evidence is unacceptable to your client, you might need to resume your search to find an alternative intervention without as much evidence but that fits your client's values and preferences. Likewise, you would have to do the same if after implementing and evaluating an intervention you find it to be ineffective with your client. As we consider the research process, keep in mind that these same returns to earlier phases apply.

Thus, if after designing an elegant research study we realize that its implementation costs would exceed our resources, we would need to return to earlier phases and come up with a study that would be more feasible to implement.

Despite the occasional need to loop back from later phases of the research process to earlier phases, students often find it helpful to have a diagram of the sequencing process. Figure 3-1 presents a schematic view of that process. To get an idea of the way the phases can deviate from this sequencing, notice the lines at the left on the diagram that point up from later phases to earlier ones.

At the top of the diagram, a problem is identified and a research question is posed, the answer to which it is hoped will provide information that can have implications for decisions about policy or practice. The remaining phases address subsequent steps involved in planning, carrying out, and reporting the research that will be conducted to provide that information. We will not delve into lengthy details about each of the phases here; that is what the rest of this book is for.

Here is an example of the process. Suppose you are working in a group residential facility for children who have behavioral disorders. A problem is perceived about the amount of antisocial behavior that is occurring in the cottages (residential units). You have the idea that some cottages may exhibit more antisocial behavior than others and that this might have something to do with different styles of behavioral management used by parents in different cottages. You find a framework to pursue your idea further in learning theory. On the basis of that theory, you consider conducting a study whose purpose is to test a hypothesis that the cottage parents who use behavioral reinforcement contingencies—such as tokens for good behavior that can be accumulated and cashed in for certain special privileges—are the ones whose cottages experience the fewest antisocial behaviors. (As we will discuss later in this chapter, hypotheses are tentative statements about how variation in one variable is postulated to explain differences in another variable.)

Your next step would be to conceptualize what you mean by *styles of behavioral management, reinforcement contingencies*, and *antisocial behavior*. Then you would need to specify the concrete steps or operations that will be used to measure the concepts. Decisions must be made about whom to study. Will you study all of the residents or cottages in the facility—that is, its population? If not, then how will you go about selecting a sample of them? Or do you wish to draw conclusions about group care facilities in general and thus conceive of your entire facility as a sample that represents a larger population of facilities?

Additional decisions must be made about the choice of a research method. If you want to test your hypothesis you might opt for a quantitative design that compares the number of antisocial behaviors observed in cottages using different behavioral management styles. Or you might choose a different research purpose. Instead of beginning with a hypothesis that you will test, you might opt to use qualitative methods to explore the phenomenon and develop a deeper understanding of it. Thus, you might decide to interview cottage parents in an open-ended manner and observe what goes on in their cottages. (We will discuss quantitative and qualitative methods in depth in the next chapter.)

Whatever you decide, your next step is to determine whether you'll need funding to make your study feasible. If so, you'll want to write and submit a proposal to seek that funding. If you aren't successful in obtaining sufficient funding, you'll need to go back to an earlier phase and formulate a different approach that will be feasible to carry out with your limited resources. Your next phases involve implementing your design, processing the data you collect, and then analyzing the data.

Suppose that in the process of analyzing your data—or perhaps while writing your report—you learn that your facility systematically obtains follow-up information from the community about how well youths adjust to the postdischarge community environment. This information includes data on juvenile court contacts, school attendance, and school academic performance and conduct. Learning about the availability of postdischarge data might make you wonder whether the lower levels of antisocial behavior among children while in the cottages with the most effective behavioral management styles will continue after they are discharged to the community.

Your inquiry might therefore loop back to generate the research process all over again, this time in connection to social adjustment in the community. Suppose you conduct the new study and find that the type of treatment children receive or the gains they make in your program have little or no bearing on their postdischarge adjustment. In other words,

you find no difference in postdischarge adjustment between children who receive certain types of behavior management in your program and those who receive other types or between those who exhibited little antisocial behavior prior to discharge and those who exhibited a lot.

You might again return to the beginning of the research process. You'll have a new problem, one that has been identified in the research you just completed: What happens in your facility seems to have no bearing on postdischarge outcome. Is your program therefore ineffective? Perhaps it is; and if so, that would be a whopper of a problem to begin dealing with. But in thinking about this, you might get another idea. Perhaps your program is effective as far as it goes and given the resources it has; the problem may be that you need to go further—to intervene in the postdischarge environment. Perhaps it is not reasonable to expect your program to do more than demonstrate its ability to enhance the functioning of children while they are in residence and provide them with a healthy environment for as long as they are there. If society expects you to influence their behavior in the community, then it needs to provide your program with the mandate and the resources to intervene in the postdischarge community environment.

Your new idea may be thoughtful and quite plausible, but is it valid? Or is it just a convenient rationalization for the dismal results of your last study? To find out, you begin working on another study. This time your focus will be not on *pre*-discharge factors that are associated with adjustment but rather on factors in the *post*-discharge environment. To what extent are there harmful and beneficial environmental conditions associated with community adjustment—conditions that perhaps can be influenced by *post*-discharge social work intervention? Suppose the results of your new study confirm such an association. Stop reading for a moment at the end of this sentence and ask yourself whether those results would again return you to the start of a new research process and what the next problem or idea might be.

Okay, have you thought about it? If so, then you probably came up with several new problems or ideas. Chances are that one of them is to test whether certain postdischarge interventions can be implemented effectively to influence environmental conditions—and whether those interventions ultimately promote improved community adjustment.

FIGURE 3.1   Phases of the Social Work Research Process

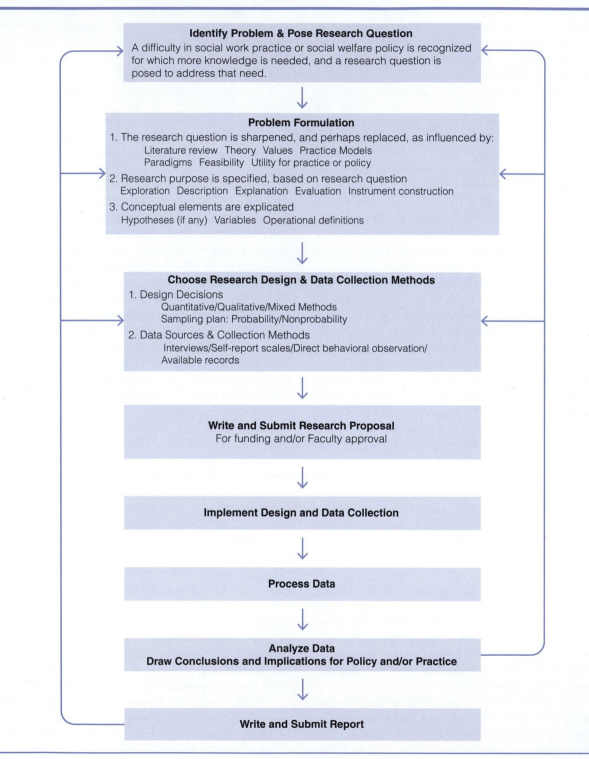

Perhaps this could be done on a small pilot basis if you have funding restraints.

Now that you have an overview of the phases of the research process, let's examine the various factors that can influence that process. We'll begin with a discussion of theory and values.

» THEORY AND VALUES

A theory is a systematic set of interrelated statements intended to explain something. Theory has to do with what is, not with what should be. This means that scientific theory—and, more broadly, science itself—cannot settle debates on value. However, the distinction between theories and values can seem fuzzy when researchers study social programs that reflect values. Suppose we want to evaluate a child welfare program that intervenes with parents referred for abuse or neglect in an effort to prevent future abuse and the consequent need to place the child in foster care. Such programs are often called *family preservation programs.* Some funders and staff connected with these programs might value the preservation of the family as the chief criterion of program success. They would see the placement of an abused child in foster care as an indicator of program failure. Other funders and staff might value the protection of the child as the chief criterion of program success. They would disagree with those who see foster care placement as a sign of failure; instead, their chief indicators of success or failure would pertain to the child's well-being. Although achieving consensus on criteria of success and failure may be difficult, such criteria are essential if research is to tell us anything useful about matters of value.

Another example of this fuzzy distinction involves welfare reform policies. Some researchers might value getting people off welfare and into jobs as the chief criterion of successful social welfare policy. Others might object to that criterion and be concerned more with how welfare reform affects a family's living conditions, their health insurance coverage, and parental ability to meet the needs of their children. Just as a stopwatch cannot tell us if one sprinter is better than another unless we can agree that speed is the critical criterion, research cannot tell us whether one social service program or social policy is better than another unless we agree on what program or policy outcomes we most value.

Utility of Theory in Social Work Practice and Research

Theory plays an important role in social work research, as it does in social work practice. In both practice and research, theory helps us make sense of and see patterns in diverse observations. It helps direct our inquiry into those areas that seem more likely to show useful patterns and explanations. It also helps us distinguish between chance occurrences and observations that have value in anticipating future occurrences.

Imagine that a colleague tells you that she allowed a young boy to play with small toys in a sand tray and nondirectively commented to him on the themes of his play. In this way, she tried to help the boy better cope with the tragic death of his mother and move on with his life. If you had not studied child development theory and learned about the importance of play, then you might respond with bewilderment, wondering how just letting a boy play and talking to him about it could be a powerful professional intervention. In fact, if you asked your colleague to explain why her intervention worked and she could not explain it, then you might be more skeptical about its likelihood of working with your clients than you would be if she could explain it theoretically. Without considering theory, you might flounder around in your practice, trying anything and everything anyone told you in the hopes of stumbling on something that seemed to work. Then, if something did work with one client, you might continue to apply it indiscriminately with other clients for whom it might be inapplicable.

Suppose you decide to test your colleague's sand play idea with one of your clients, a 6-year-old girl who has been depressed and withdrawn after surviving a traffic accident that killed her mother. After several sessions of sand play, the girl's father reports to you that the girl has begun to have angry outbursts and spells of intense sobbing in which she cries out for her mother. Without theory, you might be inclined to stop the sand play, fearing that it was having harmful effects. If, on the other hand, you were aware of theory on child development and grieving, then you might interpret the change in the girl's behavior as a necessary and therefore positive early step in the grieving process, and you would not stop the intervention.

Imagine that you were conducting research on the effectiveness of the sand play intervention in helping other children who survived and were traumatized by similar tragedies. If you were operating without theory, then you would be likely to encounter analogous problems. You might, for example, measure the impact of the intervention prematurely or look for the wrong indicators of success. Without theory, you might be clueless in designing your study. How long should the intervention last? What is the minimum and maximum age for research participants?

Some research studies are conducted in a less structured and more flexible fashion in an attempt to minimize the influence of theoretical expectations on what is being observed; that is, the researchers may not want their theoretical predilections to bias their outlook and narrow what they look for. Theory plays a role in these less structured studies as well. Although these studies may be less guided by theory, they typically seek to identify patterns that will help generate new theory. Also, it may be impossible for professionally trained researchers to put aside completely the theoretical frameworks they have learned. Their prior knowledge of child development theory and theory on the grieving process might help them see patterns in mounds of case record data—patterns suggesting that effective interventions with children who have lost a parent seem to involve a stage when the child acts out his or her anger over the loss. Moreover, the researchers' prior theoretical knowledge can help them make sense out of observations that paradoxically suggest that effective interventions involve a period during which the problem might appear (to a naive observer) to become exacerbated.

Theories also help researchers develop useful implications from their findings for practice and policy. Suppose a researcher finds that single-parent homes produce more delinquency than two-parent homes. Our understanding of why this is so and what we might do about it would be rather limited without the use of theory. Suppose, however, that we have a theoretical understanding of why single-parent homes produce more delinquency and that lack of supervision and the absence of positive role models are two important reasons. This would improve our position to develop effective social programs, such as after-school mentoring programs.

Social Work Practice Models

In social work, we may apply existing social science theories in an effort to alleviate problems in social welfare. But texts on social work practice are less likely to cite social science theories as guides to social work practice than they are to cite something called *practice models*. These models help us organize our views about social work practice and may or may not reflect a synthesis of existing theories.

The social work literature is diverse in terms of which practice models are identified and how they are labeled. If you have taken other social work courses, you may have encountered the following terms for practice models: psychosocial, functionalist, problem solving, cognitive-behavioral, task centered, case management, crisis intervention, ecological perspective, life model, generalist, strength-based, evidence-based practice, and eclectic, among many others.

Over time, particular models tend to expand, encompassing important new areas of research findings and theory. As this happens, distinctions between the models become increasingly blurred. We won't delve into the characteristics of all the various models of social work practice or into the subtleties of how they are similar and different. You can study that in courses on practice or in courses that introduce you to the profession of social work. Instead, we'll simply illustrate how certain models can influence the way we choose to research social work problems.

Consider, for example, an evaluation of the effectiveness of a treatment program for parents at risk of child abuse. The cognitive-behavioral model looks at problems such as child abuse in terms of dysfunctional emotions connected to irrational beliefs and the need to restructure cognitions and learn better coping skills and parenting skills. Rather than focusing on long-term personality change and dealing with unresolved issues stemming from the parents' own childhoods, this model deals in the present with specific skills, cognitions, and behaviors that can be changed in the short term through behavior modification and cognitive therapy techniques.

When researching the outcome of the treatment of at-risk parents, individuals influenced by this model might do the following: administer paper-and-pencil tests that attempt to gauge whether parents have become less angry, have changed their attitudes about normal childhood behaviors that they first perceived as provocative, and have learned new child-rearing techniques (such as using time-outs). These researchers might also directly observe the parents with their children in situations that require parenting skills and count the number of times the parents exhibit desirable (praise, encouragement, and so forth) and undesirable (slapping, threatening, and so forth) parenting behaviors.

In contrast, researchers who are influenced by the psychosocial model might be somewhat skeptical of the adequacy of the preceding approach to researching treatment outcome. In particular, they might doubt whether any observed improvements would last long after treatment ended and whether the parents' ability to give desired test answers or act in an acceptable manner while being observed would really reflect the normal home environment when observers aren't present. They might suggest that a better indicator of outcome would be whether parents were actually court reported for abusive behavior over the longer haul.

Although the foregoing illustration is essentially hypothetical, note that the bulk of actual research with favorable outcomes has evaluated interventions that are associated with the cognitive or behavioral models of practice. Most other models have received less research, and their outcomes have not been as consistently favorable. Proponents of some other models often attribute this to the "superficiality" of outcome indicators used in cognitive-behavioral evaluations and the difficulty of assessing the more complex, longer-range goals of their models. We won't resolve this debate here, and we expect it to continue for quite a while.

Atheoretical Research Studies

Some valuable social work research studies, however, do not involve theory. For example, some studies focus exclusively on methodological issues rather than attempting to explain something. Thus, they might survey published studies, perhaps seeking to identify what types of research methods are used most and least frequently, how often researchers use inappropriate research methods, or the frequency of particular types of findings. Other atheoretical studies might seek to describe something without attempting to explain it. For example, they might assess the average salaries of social workers in various areas, the needs for various services expressed by prospective or current service consumers, and so on.

Some atheoretical studies are agency evaluations that provide a funding source with evidence that agency clients received the types of services the

funders intended them to receive, that the clients felt highly satisfied with those services, and that treatment dropout rates were low. The evidence could be obtained by surveying clients and agency records. The study could be conducted not to test or develop theory but merely to meet the pragmatic purpose of program maintenance. This type of atheoretical study, despite lacking linkages to theory, would have some immediate practical value. Depending on its results, for example, the study could determine whether funding was continued (and perhaps even expanded) or discontinued (or perhaps just reduced).

Although social work research studies can have value without any linkages to theory, their value might be enhanced by such linkages. The above study, for example, might contribute more to the profession's knowledge base if it aimed to go beyond the agency's immediate funding concerns and attempted to build social work practice theory about factors that influence client satisfaction and treatment completion and the consequent implications for what social workers in other agencies can do to improve service delivery. (This is not to suggest that atheoretical studies have no potential value for theory advancement. Related findings in an otherwise unconnected batch of atheoretical studies could, for example, be synthesized and connected to theory in a review of studies.)

Prediction and Explanation

In attempting to explain things, theories inescapably get involved in predicting things. A theory that views being a victim of abuse as a child as a prime factor in explaining later perpetration of child abuse as an adult, for example, would implicitly predict that people victimized as children are more likely than others to become perpetrators as adults. That prediction could be tested, and the credibility of the theory would be affected, depending on whether we found that child victims are more likely to become perpetrators than others.

Although prediction is implicit in explanation, it is important to distinguish between the two. Often we are able to predict without understanding—for example, you may be able to predict rain when your trick knee aches. And often, even if we don't understand why, we are willing to act on the basis of a demonstrated predictive ability. Our ancient ancestors could predict sunrises and sunsets every day and plan their activities accordingly without understanding why the sun rose and set. And even if they thought they understood, with an explanation involving a stationary and flat Earth, they could predict accurately although their explanation was incorrect.

As we examine the components of theory, you will see that a set of predictions is an important part of theory. Consequently, it will be important to remember the distinction between prediction and explanation.

The Components of Theory

Earlier, we defined theory as a systematic set of interrelated statements intended to explain something. The statements that attempt to explain things are called *hypotheses*. A hypothesis predicts something that ought to be observed in the real world if a theory is correct. It is a tentative and testable statement about how changes in one thing are expected to explain changes in something else. For example, a hypothesis in learning theory might be, "The more children are praised, the more self-esteem they will have." The things that hypotheses predict are called variables. The foregoing hypothesis consists of two variables: (a) amount of praise and (b) level of self-esteem. The components of hypotheses are called *variables* because hypotheses predict how they *vary* together. Another term for this is that hypotheses predict *relationships* among variables. By relationship, we simply mean that a change in one variable is likely to be associated with a change in the other variable.

Most hypotheses predict which variable influences the other, in other words, which one is the cause and which one is the effect. A variable that explains or causes something is called the independent variable. It is called *independent* because it is doing the explaining or causing and is not dependent on the other variable. Conversely, the variable being explained or caused—that is, the variable that is the effect—is called the dependent variable. In the foregoing hypothesis, for example, amount of praise is the independent variable, and level of self-esteem is the dependent variable.

A variable—regardless of whether it is independent or dependent—is a concept. A concept is a mental image that symbolizes an idea, an object, an event, or a person. Because variables vary, they are concepts that are themselves composed of other concepts. Some things that concepts symbolize are

abstract and hard to observe, like level of self-esteem. Others might be easier to observe, although perhaps not as simple to observe as some might think. Consider sex and gender, for example. In the past, most researchers measured those concepts simply asking respondents to check whether they were *male* or *female*. More recently, however, we have seen researchers consider asking questions like the following (Bradford, Cahill, et al., 2012).

1. What sex appeared on your original birth certificate? (Check one)
   □ Male
   □ Female

2. What is your current gender identity? (Check all that apply.)
   □ Male
   □ Female
   □ Female-to-Male (FTM)/Transgender Male/ Trans Man
   □ Male-to-Female (MTF)/Transgender Female/ Trans Woman
   □ Genderqueer, neither exclusively male nor female
   □ Additional Gender Category/(or Other), please specify _____
   □ Decline to Answer, please explain why _____

The concepts that make up a variable are called attributes of that variable. Attributes are characteristics or qualities that describe something or somebody. Some examples of attributes include *African American*, *intelligent*, *conservative*, *honest*, *physician*, *homeless*, and so forth. Anything you might say to describe yourself or someone else involves an attribute. Variables, on the other hand, are logical groupings of attributes. Thus, for example, *male* and *female* are attributes of the variable *gender*. Likewise, the variable *occupation* is composed of attributes such as farmer, professor, and *truck driver*. Social class is a variable composed of a set of attributes such as *upper class*, *middle class*, *lower class*, or some similar set of divisions. The box "Illustration of a Hypothesis and Its Components" graphically displays the connections and distinctions between the concepts, independent and dependent variables, and attributes that make up hypotheses.

Thus, theories consist of hypotheses and two kinds of concepts: variables and the attributes that compose those variables. Theories also require observations. Observations are what we experience in the real world that help us build a theory or verify whether it is correct. When our observations are consistent with what we would expect to experience if a theory is correct, we call those observations empirical support for the theory. The credibility of a theory will depend on the extent to which (a) our observations empirically support it and (b) its components are systematically organized in a logical fashion that helps us better understand the world. As a gross generalization, scientific theory deals with the logical aspect of science; research methods deal with the observational aspect. A scientific theory describes the logical relationships that appear to exist among parts of the world, and research offers means for observing whether those relationships actually exist in the real world. The box titled "Components of Scientific Theory" graphically illustrates the bridge between theory and research.

The Relationship between Attributes and Variables

The relationship between attributes and variables lies at the heart of both description and explanation

in science. For example, we might describe a social service agency's caseload in terms of the proportion of clients with each attribute of a variable such as gender or ethnicity. An unemployment rate can be thought of as a description of the variable employment status of a labor force in terms of the attributes *employed* and *unemployed*. Even the report of family income for a city is a summary of attributes composing that variable: $3,124, $10,980, $35,000, and so forth.

The relationship between attributes and variables can be more complicated in the case of explanation. Here's a social work practice example, involving two variables: *use of contracting* and *level of client satisfaction*. For the sake of simplicity, let's assume that the second variable has only two attributes: *satisfied* and *dissatisfied*. Now suppose that 90% of the clients without contracts are dissatisfied and that the other 10% are satisfied. And suppose that 30% of the clients with contracts are dissatisfied and that the other 70% are satisfied. We graphically illustrate this in the first part of Figure 3-2. The relationship or association between the two variables can be seen in the pairings of their attributes. The two predominant pairings are (a) those who have contracts and are satisfied and (b) those who have no contracts and are dissatisfied. Here are two other useful ways of seeing that relationship.

First, let's suppose that we play a game in which we bet on your ability to guess whether a client is satisfied or dissatisfied. We'll pick the

ILLUSTRATION OF A HYPOTHESIS AND ITS COMPONENTS

Concepts	Hypothesis	Variables	Attributes
Student		Independent:	
	Praise by teacher	whether teacher	Praised
Teacher		praises student	
			Not praised
School	will | increase	↓	
Praise	↓		↑ High level of confidence
Confidence	Student confidence at school	Dependent: Student's level of confidence at school	↓ Low level of confidence

COMPONENTS OF SCIENTIFIC THEORY
Michael R. Leming, Department of Sociology, St. Olaf College

According to George Homans, scientific theory is an explanation of a phenomenon by the use of a deductive system of empirical propositions. The three basic components of scientific theory are (1) a conceptual scheme, (2) a set of propositions stating relationships between properties or variables, and (3) a context for verification.

The model of a suspension bridge serves as a good illustration of the relationship between scientific theory's three components. Bridges are constructed out of girders and rivets and tied into both banks of the river. In similar fashion, a theory consists of concepts ("rivets") and propositions ("girders") tied into an empirical base of support. It is the relationship between the components that makes for a bridge or theory. A disorganized pile of girders and rivets are not sufficient components for what we would call a bridge. Likewise concepts, propositions, and observations are not sufficient in themselves for scientific theory.

"Rivets" (concepts)

"Girders" (propositions)

Earth
(ground of
empirical support)

clients one at a time (and will not tell you which one we've picked), and you guess whether the client is satisfied. We'll do it for all 20 clients in part 1 of Figure 3-2. Your best strategy in that case would be to always guess dissatisfied, because 12 of the 20 are categorized that way. Thus, you'll get 12 right and 8 wrong, for a net success of 4.

Now suppose that when we pick a client from the figure, we have to tell you whether the practitioner engaged the client in contracting, and again you guess whether the client is satisfied. Your best strategy now would be to guess dissatisfied for each client without a contract and satisfied for each one with a contract. If you follow that strategy, you'll get 16 right and 4 wrong. Your improvement in guessing level of satisfaction by knowing whether contracting was used is an illustration of what is meant by the variables being related.

Second, by contrast, now consider how the 20 people would be distributed if use of contracting and level of satisfaction were unrelated to one another. This is illustrated in part 2 of Figure 3-2.

Notice that half the clients have contracts and that half do not. Also notice that 12 of the 20 (60%) are dissatisfied. If 6 of the 10 people in each group were dissatisfied, then we would conclude that the two variables were unrelated to each other. Then, knowing whether contracting was used would not be of any value to you in guessing whether that client was satisfied.

We will look at the nature of relationships between variables in some depth in Part 7 of this book. In particular, we'll see some ways in which research analysis can discover and interpret relationships. For now, it is important that you have a general understanding of relationships to appreciate the logic of social scientific theories.

As we mentioned earlier, theories describe the relationships that might logically be expected among variables. Often, the expectation involves the notion of causation. A person's attributes on one variable are expected to cause, predispose, or encourage a particular attribute on another variable. In the example just given, the use of

FIGURE 3.2 Relationships between Two Variables (Two Possibilities)

contracting seemed to possibly help cause clients to be more or less satisfied or dissatisfied. Something about participating in contracting seems to lead clients to be more satisfied than if they do not participate in contracting.

The discussion of Figure 3-2 has involved the interpretation of data. We looked at the distribution of the 20 clients in terms of the two variables. In the construction of a theory, we would derive an expectation about the relationship between the two variables based on what we know about each. We might postulate, for example, that clients with contracts are (a) more likely to agree with their practitioner about the problem to be worked on and (b) more likely to be motivated to work on that problem than are clients without contracts. Because they are more likely to agree with and be motivated to pursue the goals of the services, it follows that clients with contracts would be more likely to be satisfied with those services. We might further postulate that a prerequisite of effective treatment is to deal with problems and pursue objectives on which the client and practitioner agree.

Notice that the theory has to do with the two variables, *use of contracting* and *level of client satisfaction*, not with people per se. People are, as we indicated before, the carriers of those two variables, so the relationship between the variables can be seen only by observing people. Ultimately, however, the theory is constructed using a language of variables. It describes the associations that might logically be expected to exist between particular attributes of different variables.

In this example, *use of contracting* was the independent variable, and *level of client satisfaction* was the dependent variable. That is, we assume that levels of satisfaction are determined or caused by something. Satisfaction depends on something; hence, it is called the dependent variable. That on which the dependent variable depends is called the independent variable; in this case, satisfaction depends on use of contracting. Although the use of contracting with the clients being studied varies, that variation is independent of level of satisfaction.

» TWO LOGICAL SYSTEMS: COMPARING DEDUCTION AND INDUCTION

In Chapter 1, we referred to *the scientific method.* Actually, it might be more accurate to refer to two scientific methods distinguished primarily by the ways in which they use theory in research. One method is based on deductive logic; we'll call it the deductive method. The other is based on inductive logic; we'll call it the inductive method. Let's now examine and contrast these two logical systems, beginning with the deductive method.

In the deductive method, the researcher begins with a theory and then derives one or more hypotheses from it for testing. Next, the researcher defines the variables in each hypothesis and the operations to be used to measure them in specific, observable terms. In the final step, the researcher implements the specified measurements, thus observing the way things really are and seeing if those observations confirm or fail to confirm the hypotheses. Sometimes this final step involves conducting experiments, interviewing people, or visiting and watching the subject of interest.

Figure 3-3 schematically diagrams the deductive model of scientific inquiry, moving from theory to operationalization to observation. We see the researcher beginning with an interest in some problem or an idea about it—say, the problem of adolescent runaways. Next comes the development of a theoretical understanding. The theoretical considerations result in a hypothesis, or an expectation about the way things ought to be in the world if the theoretical expectations are correct.

For example, the researcher might see family dysfunction as explaining why adolescents run away and perhaps use family systems theory to understand family dysfunction and what to do about it. In Figure 3-3, this broadly conceived

FIGURE 3.3 The Deductive Image of Science

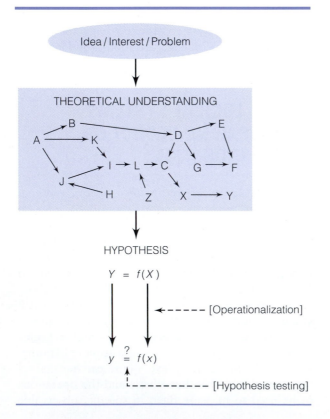

hypothesis is represented by the notation $Y = f(X)$. This is a conventional way of saying that Y (e.g., runaway episodes) is a *function of* (is in some way affected by) X (e.g., family dysfunction). At that level, however, X and Y have general rather than specific meanings. From this theoretical understanding, the researcher derives one or more specific hypotheses—for example, that providing family systems therapy will reduce the likelihood of future runaway episodes. Next, those two general concepts must be translated into specific, observable indicators to make the hypothesis testable. This is done in the operationalization process. The lowercase y and lowercase x, for instance, represent concrete, observable indicators of capital Y and capital X. In the runaway example, y (lowercase) refers to the need to spell out in observable terms exactly what constitutes a runaway episode, and x (lowercase) refers to the need to describe in specific terms the substance and processes that constitute the type of family systems theory being tested. Finally, observations are made to test the hypothesis.

As we already noted, the deductive method uses what is called deductive logic (see *deduction* in the Glossary), which is in contrast to inductive logic (see *induction* in the Glossary). W. I. B. Beveridge (1950), a philosopher of science, describes these two systems of logic as follows:

> Logicians distinguish between inductive reasoning (from particular instances to general principles, from facts to theories) and deductive reasoning (from the general to the particular, applying a theory to a particular case). In induction one starts from observed data and develops a generalization which explains the relationships between the objects observed. On the other hand, in deductive reasoning one starts from some general law and applies it to a particular instance. (p. 113)

The classic illustration of deductive logic is the familiar syllogism: "All men are mortal; Socrates is a man; therefore, Socrates is mortal." This syllogism presents a theory and its operationalization. To prove it, you might perform an empirical test of Socrates' mortality, that is, essentially the approach discussed as the deductive model. Using inductive logic, you might begin by noting that Socrates is mortal and observe other men as well. You might then note that all of the observed men were mortals, thereby arriving at the tentative conclusion that all men are mortal.

Figure 3-4 shows a graphic comparison of the deductive and inductive methods. In both cases, we are interested in the relationship between the number of hours spent studying for an exam and the grade earned on that exam. Using the deductive method, we would begin by examining the matter logically. Doing well on an exam reflects a student's ability to recall and manipulate information. Both abilities should be increased by exposure to the information before the exam. In this fashion, we would arrive at a hypothesis that suggests a positive relationship between the number of hours spent studying and the grade earned on the exam. We say "positive" because we expect grades to

increase as the hours of studying increase. If increased hours produced decreased grades, then that would be called a "negative" relationship. The hypothesis is represented by the line in part I (a) of Figure 3-4.

Our next step, using the deductive method, would be to make observations that are relevant to testing our hypothesis. The shaded area in part I(b) of the figure represents perhaps hundreds of observations of different students, noting how many hours they studied and what grades they got. Finally, in part I(c), we compare the hypothesis and the observations. Because observations in the real world seldom if ever match our expectations perfectly, we must decide whether the match is close enough to consider the hypothesis confirmed. Put differently, can we conclude that the hypothesis

FIGURE 3.4 Deductive and Inductive Methods

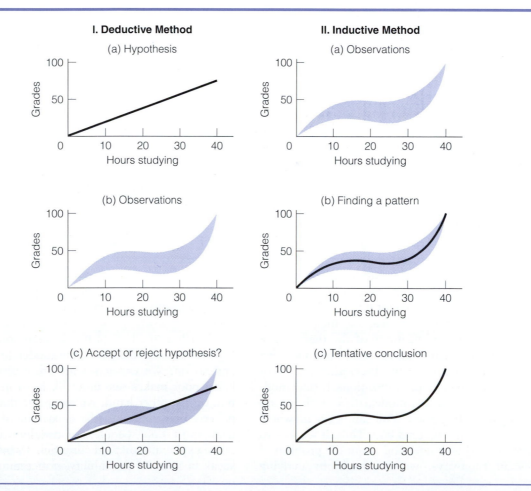

describes the general pattern that exists, granting some variations in real life?

Let's turn to addressing the same research question but now using the inductive method. In this case, we would begin—as in part II(a) of the figure—with a set of observations. Curious about the relationship between hours spent studying and grades earned, we might simply arrange to collect relevant data. Then we'd look for a pattern that best represented or summarized our observations. In part II(b) of the figure, the pattern is shown as a curved line that runs through the center of the curving mass of points.

The pattern found among the points in this case suggests that with 1 to 15 hours of studying, each additional hour generally produces a higher grade on the exam. With 15 to approximately 25 hours, however, more study seems to slightly lower the grade. Studying more than 25 hours, on the other hand, results in a return to the initial pattern: More hours produce higher grades. Using the inductive method, then, we end up with a tentative conclusion about the pattern of the relationship between the two variables. The conclusion is tentative because the observations we have made cannot be taken as a test of the pattern—those observations are the source of the pattern we've created.

What do you suppose would happen next in an actual research project? We'd try to find a logical explanation for the pattern discovered in the data. Eventually, we'd arrive at an explanation—one that would generate further expectations about what should be observed in the real world. Then we'd look again.

In actual practice, then, theory and research interact through a never-ending alternation of deduction, induction, deduction, and so forth. Walter Wallace (1971) has represented this process nicely as a circle, which is presented in modified form in Figure 3-5. In the Wallace model, theories generate hypotheses, hypotheses suggest observations, observations produce generalizations, and those generalizations result in modifications of the theory. The modified theory then suggests somewhat modified hypotheses and a new set of observations that produce somewhat revised generalizations, further modifying the theory. In this model, there is clearly no beginning or ending point. You can begin anywhere in examining what interests you. Thus, if we seek to understand and do something about the problem of adolescent runaways, we can begin by deriving

FIGURE 3.5 The Wheel of Science

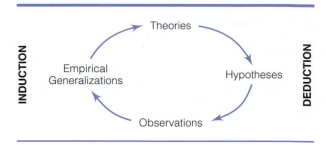

hypotheses from family systems theory (or some other theory) and then making observations to test those hypotheses, or we can begin by immersing ourselves in observations of runaways until we are struck by certain consistent patterns that seem to point us in a particular theoretical direction that, in turn, will lead to hypotheses and observations.

In summary, the scientific norm of logical reasoning provides a bridge between theory and research—a two-way bridge. Scientific inquiry in practice typically involves an alternation between deduction and induction. During the deductive phase, we reason toward observations; during the inductive phase, we reason from observations. Both logic and observation are essential. In practice, both deduction and induction are routes to the construction of social theories.

» PROBABILISTIC KNOWLEDGE

Few things in human behavior can be explained entirely by factors we can identify. Many factors contribute to the explanation of particular phenomena even if we have not yet discovered all of them. Being poor, for example, is a factor that contributes to homelessness, but being poor alone does not cause homelessness. Other factors also come into play, such as the lack of low-income housing, alcoholism or mental disorders, the sudden loss of a job, and so on. We can say with great certainty that being poor makes one more likely to be homeless, but, on the other hand, we recognize that although poverty contributes to the causation of homelessness, most poor people are not homeless. Thus, when explaining or predicting human behavior, we speak in terms of probability, not certainty.

Knowledge based on probability enables us to say that if A occurs, then B is more likely to occur. It does not enable us to say that B *will* occur or even that B will *probably* occur. For example, a research study that finds that intervention A is more likely to be effective than intervention B does not guarantee that intervention A will be effective with your client. Likewise, research into the causation of mental illness has suggested that the offspring of mentally ill parents are about 10 times more likely than the rest of the population to become mentally ill. But most children of mentally ill parents never become mentally ill; only about 10% of them do. Because only some 1% of the rest of the population ever become mentally ill, we can say that having mentally ill parents appears to be one factor that can contribute to mental illness (perhaps through the transmission of certain genetic combinations that make one biologically more vulnerable to other factors that can contribute to mental illness). Our ability to say that parental mental illness is a "cause" of mental illness in their offspring is further restricted by the observation that the parents of many mentally ill people were never mentally ill themselves. (Again, genetics offers a possible explanation here.)

Many "causes" that help "determine" human behavior, therefore, are neither necessary nor sufficient for the "effect" they help to cause. Among many of the homeless, alcoholism may have played a role in causing their homelessness. Yet one can be homeless without ever having been an alcoholic. Alcoholism, therefore, is not a necessary condition for homelessness to occur. Neither is it a sufficient condition, because alcoholism alone does not produce homelessness.

People who crave certainty may be uneasy with probabilistic knowledge and therefore may spurn the findings of social research. They may prefer the comfort of less complex, nonscientific routes to "understanding," such as freewill notions that we simply choose to do what we do. Alternatively, they may prefer narrow explanations proffered with certainty by supervisors and other authorities. In your social work practice, you may find that dealing with uncertainty can be a constant source of uneasiness and anxiety. You may find more relief from this discomfort by latching onto and following unquestioningly the "certain" pronouncements of a guru of a practice dogma than you find in the probabilistic findings of scientific research. In Chapter 1,

we discussed the risks associated with such reliance on authority.

Although escaping from the discomfort of uncertainty may make you feel better, it might lead you further from the truth, which ultimately is not in your clients' best interests. But be forewarned (and therefore hopefully forearmed to better utilize research): Most research studies will not give you the kinds of answers that will bring certainty to your practice.

» TWO CAUSAL MODELS OF EXPLANATION

As we've seen, a multiplicity of reasons can account for a specific behavior. When we try to explain a person's behavior by enumerating the many reasons for it, reasons that might be unique to that individual, we are using the idiographic model of explanation. Of course, we never totally exhaust those reasons in practice. Nevertheless, we must realize that the idiographic model is used frequently in many different contexts.

As an example, let's say we are interested in understanding why a particular young man has become delinquent. If you were his practitioner, you would want to learn everything you could about his family situation, neighborhood, school environment, peers, and anything else that might account for his delinquent behavior. Does he live in a single-parent or dysfunctional family? Does he have delinquent brothers or sisters? Does he belong to a gang? How is he doing in school? Is his family poor? Does he have physical or psychological problems that might contribute to his behavior and your understanding of it? In this instance, your purpose would be to understand this one person as fully as possible, in all his idiosyncratic peculiarities. This is the idiographic model of explanation.

Whereas the idiographic model is often used in daily life and in social work practice, other situations and purposes call for a different approach, one called the nomothetic model of explanation. Rather than seeking to understand a particular person as fully as possible, we try to understand a general phenomenon partially. Following up on the previous example, you might be interested in learning about the causes of juvenile delinquency in general. What factors are most important for explaining delinquency among many young people? Let's consider the role of single-parent homes in causing delinquency.

If you were to study a large number of young people, you would discover a higher incidence of delinquency among those who live in single-parent homes than among those who live with two-parent families. This certainly does not mean that single-parent homes always produce juvenile delinquency or that two-parent homes always prevent it. As a general rule, however, single-parent homes are more likely than two-parent homes to produce delinquency.

Actually, social scientists have discovered the single factor about single-parent homes that increases the likelihood of juvenile delinquency: the lack of adult supervision. Specifically, two-parent families are more likely to have an adult at home when the young person gets home from school; it's the presence of adult supervision that decreases the likelihood of delinquent behavior. In the case of single-parent homes, young people are more likely to be unsupervised after school and thus are more likely to get into trouble.

Whereas the idiographic model seeks to understand everything about a particular case by using as many causative factors as possible, the nomothetic model seeks a partial understanding of a general phenomenon using relatively few variables. The young delinquent we described at the beginning of this discussion may or may not live in a single-parent home; even if he does, that fact may or may not help account for his delinquency. Taking an idiographic tack, we would want to discover all of the particular factors that led that one young man astray. From a nomothetic point of view, we would want to discover those factors, such as lack of adult supervision, that account for many instances of delinquency in general.

The nomothetic model of explanation is inevitably probabilistic in its approach to causation. Being able to name a few causal factors seldom if ever provides a complete explanation. In the best of all practical worlds, the nomothetic model indicates a very high (or very low) probability or likelihood that a given action will occur whenever a limited number of specified considerations are present. Identifying more considerations typically increases the degree of explanation, but the model's basic

simplicity calls for balancing more explanation with fewer identified causal factors.

Use of Nomothetic and Idiographic Research in Social Work Practice

To further illustrate the use of the nomothetic and idiographic models in social work practice, imagine you were a clinical practitioner living in New York City and you volunteered to treat survivors who were experiencing symptoms of post-traumatic stress disorder (PTSD) in the wake of the September 11, 2001, attack on the World Trade Center. In your practice, you regularly kept up with the emerging research literature to make sure you provided the most effective services to your clients, and you recently learned of a promising new intervention for people with PTSD. The intervention has received support in several nomothetic research articles and seemed particularly relevant to a one 9/11 survivor you were treating.

The nomothetic research articles showed that the new intervention appeared more likely to be effective than alternative treatment approaches with people in general who suffer from PTSD. With the new intervention, 70% of clients had their PTSD symptoms disappear within a few weeks as compared to only 30% of those receiving alternative approaches. The new intervention, however, tended to involve more temporary emotional discomfort than alternative approaches because it required that clients call up vivid images of the traumatic incident. You would not want to keep providing the new intervention to your client if it's not working.

The research gave you a nomothetic basis for considering the new intervention; that is, it told you in probabilistic terms that the new intervention is effective in general, but it could not guarantee that it will be effective for your particular client. Perhaps your client was like the 30% who were not helped by the new intervention. The research you've read may give no indication of the variables that make the intervention more or less successful: gender, age, social class, family situation, and so on. Moreover, the research was not done with survivors of the September 11 attack.

As a social work practitioner, you would have been interested in one particular case, and you would have wanted to consider the range of particular characteristics that might influence the intervention's effectiveness. Imagine that your particular case involved a family of two preschool children and their mother, a young woman who recently moved to New York from Puerto Rico and did not speak English fluently. Suppose that her husband was a custodian killed in the 9/11 attack and that she also worked as a custodian in the same tower as her husband but was on a lower floor at the time of the attack and felt guilty that she escaped but her husband didn't. One of her two preschool children had a serious learning disability. The mother was exhibiting PTSD symptoms. So were both of her children, having viewed televised images of the World Trade Center towers being struck and then collapsing. Suppose the mother was abused as a child. To what extent might that have influenced her PTSD symptoms or the likelihood that the new intervention would succeed with her? Would the likelihood of success also be influenced by her minority status, newness to New York, language factors, or socioeconomic stressors? Would it also work with children as young as hers? Would it work with children who had serious learning disabilities? Note, too, that the intervention may not have worked as well with survivors of the 9/11 attack as it did with other kinds of traumas. This is an example of the idiographic model of causation.

Clearly, all of the contextual variables just discussed in this idiographic example could be and often are examined in nomothetic analyses. Thus, we could study whether the new intervention is effective with a large sample of 9/11 survivors. We also could study whether it is more likely to be effective with adults than with children, with children without learning disabilities, or with people who have not previously been victims of other traumas. The key difference is that the nomothetic approach looks for causal patterns that occur in general, whereas the idiographic approach aims at fully explaining a single case.

You could take an idiographic approach in finding out if the intervention is effective with your particular client by conducting a single-case design evaluation. That approach would entail measuring your client's PTSD symptoms each day for a week or two and graphing the results before implementing the new intervention. Then you would continue to graph the symptoms after the new intervention begins. Whether the graphed data show a clear amelioration in PTSD symptoms that coincides with the onset of the intervention will

indicate whether the intervention appears to be effective for your particular client. In Chapter 13, on single-case designs, you will learn more about how to design and conduct idiographic studies like this in your own practice.

The box "Illustration of Idiographic and Nomothetic Tests of a Hypothesis" graphically illustrates the difference between an idiographic and a nomothetic test of a hypothesis regarding a therapy that studies have shown to be effective in alleviating PTSD symptoms. The bottom of the box illustrates a nomothetic test involving 200 research participants. Its results provide probabilistic grounds for deeming the intervention to be effective. At the top of the box, however, an idiographic test shows that the intervention is effective with one client (Jill) but ineffective with another client (Jack). Jack and Jill were not in the nomothetic experiment. But had they received the therapy as part of the nomothetic experiment, Jill would have been among the 70% of recipients whose symptoms were alleviated, and Jack would have been among the 30% of recipients whose symptoms were not alleviated.

>> IDEOLOGIES AND PARADIGMS

When researchers are wedded to a particular system of beliefs and values, those beliefs and values can strongly influence the research process. A closed system of beliefs and values that shapes the understanding and behavior of those who believe in it is called an ideology. Its assumptions are fixed and strong and not open to questioning. To their believers, who may be called *ideologues*, ideologies offer absolute certainty and are immune to contradictory evidence. Ideologues "know" that they are right and don't want to be confused with the facts. To protect their belief systems from contradictory evidence, they will commonly commit some of the errors we discussed in Chapter 1, such as overgeneralization, selective observation, *ex post facto* hypothesizing, and prematurely closing inquiry. You will have difficulty changing the closed mind of an ideologue no matter how sharp your critical thinking and no matter how solid your evidence base.

Ideologies come in many different forms. For example, some social workers can become so rigidly wedded to a particular theory that their theory might seem like an ideology. For example, if a

ILLUSTRATION OF IDIOGRAPHIC AND NOMOTHETIC TESTS OF A HYPOTHESIS

HYPOTHESIS: Exposure therapy is effective in alleviating PTSD symptoms

IDIOGRAPHIC

(Therapy is effective with Jill but not with Jack)

Jill's Level of PTSD symptoms:

High
_____

Low
    Before Exposure Therapy   During Exposure Therapy   After Exposure Therapy

. . . .

Jack's Level of PTSD symptoms:

High
_____   _____   _____

Low
    Before Exposure Therapy   During Exposure Therapy   After Exposure Therapy

. . . .

NOMOTHETIC

(Therapy is effective on *probabilistic* grounds based on results with 200 participants)

PTSD Symptoms	Number of Participants by Treatment Condition	
	Exposure Therapy	No-Treatment Control Group
Alleviated	70	30
	(Jill would be in this group)	
Not Alleviated	30	70
	(Jack would be in this group)	

direct-practice professor taught only a psychoanalytic approach to practice and refused to consider evidence showing that other approaches might be more effective for many of the problems social workers deal with, she might seem to be an ideologue.

Somewhat akin to an ideology, a **paradigm** is a fundamental model or scheme that organizes our observations and makes sense of them. Although it doesn't necessarily answer important questions, it can tell us where to look for the answers. As we'll see repeatedly, where you look largely determines the answers you'll find. Although paradigms share some similarities with ideologies and although some folks can sound rather ideological about the particular paradigms they espouse, paradigms can be viewed as being more open to question and modification than ideologies.

Naturally, we can usually organize or make sense of things in more than one way. Different points of view are likely to yield different explanations. Imagine two people who begin working with emotionally abused wives: one a feminist and the other a firm believer in a conservative Christian view of traditional family values. The two are likely to develop different explanations or select different practice models in their work, particularly in regard to whether the wives should be encouraged to leave their husbands or participate with their husbands in a treatment approach that attempts to preserve the marriage while working on resolving the abuse.

No one ever starts with a completely clean slate to create a practice model or a theory. The concepts that are the building blocks of theory are not created out of nothing. If we suggest juvenile delinquency as an example of a topic to research, you may already have implicit ideas about it. If we ask you to list concepts that would be relevant to a theory of juvenile delinquency, you may be able to make suggestions. We might say that you already have a general point of view or frame of reference.

Thomas Kuhn (1970) referred to paradigms as the fundamental points of view that characterize a science in its search for meaning. Although we sometimes think of science as developing gradually over time and marked by important discoveries and inventions, Kuhn said that it is typical for one paradigm to become entrenched, resisting any substantial change. Eventually, however, as the shortcomings of that paradigm become obvious, a new paradigm emerges to supplant the old one. Thus, the view that the sun revolved around the Earth was supplanted by the view that the Earth revolved around the sun. Kuhn's classic book on the subject is appropriately titled *The Structure of Scientific Revolutions*.

Social scientists have developed several paradigms for use in understanding social behavior. Supplanted paradigms in the social sciences, however, have had a different fate than what Kuhn observed for the natural sciences. Natural scientists generally believe that the succession from one paradigm to another represents progress from a false view to a true view. No modern astronomer, for example, believes that the sun revolves around the Earth.

In the social sciences, on the other hand, paradigms may gain or lose popularity but are seldom discarded altogether. Similar to social work practice models, the paradigms of the social sciences offer a variety of views, each with insights that others lack but also ignoring aspects of social life that other paradigms reveal. The different paradigms in the social sciences sometimes reflect competing philosophical stances about the nature of reality and how to observe it. Let's look at some competing paradigms that influence the process of social work research.

Contemporary Positivism

Researchers who subscribe to the traditional scientific method face a dilemma. Although their task is to observe and understand what is "really" happening, we are all human; as such, we bring along personal orientations that will color what we observe and how we explain it. In other words, we all have our own subjective realities. Ultimately, there is no way we can totally step outside our humanness to see and understand the world as it "really" is.

Applying this dilemma to social work practice, suppose you encounter a case in which wife battering has been reported, but the spouses now deny it. ("I/She just slipped and fell down the stairs. That's what caused all the facial and other bruises.") Perhaps each spouse fears the ramifications of incarceration. Perhaps the wife initially reported the abuse but now fears for her life since her husband threatened her with retaliation if she does not retract her accusation.

Despite the difficulty in being certain about an objective answer to the question of what really happened, you could function within agreed-on standards of evidence to reach a workable conclusion and course of action, such as moving the wife to a shelter. Taking the traditional scientific view, you would acknowledge that although each spouse has his or her own subjective view of reality, although the wife changed her report of her view, and although your investigation into the situation might be influenced by your own prior experiences, it might be possible to ascertain objectively whether wife battering occurred and whether the wife needs to be protected—perhaps in a shelter.

The latter view reflects the paradigm of contemporary positivism. Taking the contemporary positivist view, you might agree that it is virtually impossible to be completely objective and know for sure exactly what happened, but you would nevertheless believe that there is an objective answer to the question of what really happened and that it is worth trying to investigate things as objectively as possible to attempt to maximize the accuracy of your answer to the question.

Positivism, however, has not always been contemporary. Long ago positivist social scientists believed that society could be understood logically and rationally and that it could be studied just as scientifically as biology or physics—with perfect objectivity and the development of universal laws of behavior.

Contemporary positivists, in contrast, recognize that scientists are not as objective as the ideal image of science assumes. Personal feelings can and do influence the problems scientists choose to study, what they choose to observe, and the conclusions they draw from those observations. Although contemporary positivists emphasize objectivity, precision, and generalizability in their inquiries, they recognize that observation and measurement cannot be as purely objective as implied by the ideal image of science. Nevertheless, they still attempt to anticipate and minimize the impact of potentially nonobjective influences. They also seek to verify causality and attempt to sort out what really causes what. They believe that an objective external reality exists, although they recognize its elusive nature. Instead of attempting to verify universal laws, they examine the conditions under which particular ideas and hypotheses are and are not falsified.

Contemporary positivists commonly use highly structured research methods, but they are also likely to employ flexible methods, recognizing that we often are unable to determine in advance the best way to investigate some aspects of social reality. When they use flexible methods, they tend to see their findings as essentially tentative and exploratory in nature, generating new ideas for further testing.

Contemporary positivists are skeptical about the subjective impressions of researchers. Indeed, contemporary positivists tend to be skeptical of the conclusions of any individual research study. They see research as a never-ending and self-correcting quest for knowledge that requires the replication of findings by different investigators. Although

contemporary positivists recognize that research is never entirely free from political and ideological values, they believe that it is possible to use logical arrangements and observational techniques that reduce the influence of one's values on findings.

They also assume that others can judge the validity of one's findings in light of these mechanisms and can test them in later studies. Moreover, they assume that although social reality may remain elusive and that although no one study may be free of distortions, we can continue over the long haul to inch closer to understanding a true objective social reality if many researchers independently conduct rigorous studies using diverse approaches and then communicate about their findings and methodologies with open minds.

Some researchers don't see themselves as positivists, contemporary or otherwise. Those researchers put less emphasis on understanding objective social reality and more on subjective social reality. Thus, their research process is influenced by alternative paradigms. One such paradigm is called interpretivism.

Interpretivism

Interpretive researchers do not focus on isolating and objectively measuring causes or on developing generalizations. Instead, they attempt to gain an empathic understanding of how people feel inside, seeking to interpret individuals' everyday experiences, deeper meanings and feelings, and idiosyncratic reasons for their behaviors.

Interpretive researchers are likely to hang out with people and observe them in their natural settings, where they attempt to develop an in-depth subjective understanding of their lives. Rather than convey statistical probabilities for particular causal processes over a large number of people, interpretive researchers attempt to help readers of their reports sense what it is like to walk in the shoes of the small number of people they study.

Interpretive researchers believe that you cannot adequately learn about people by relying solely on objective measurement instruments that are used in the same standardized manner from person to person—instruments that attempt to remove the observer from the observee to pursue objectivity. Instead, interpretive researchers believe that the best way to learn about people is to be flexible and subjective in one's approach so that the subject's world can be seen through the subject's own eyes. It is not enough simply to measure the subject's external behaviors or questionnaire answers. The subjective meanings and social contexts of an individual's words or deeds must be examined more deeply.

Regardless of their views on the existence of an objective external reality, interpretive researchers are more interested in discovering and understanding how people perceive and experience the world on an internal subjective basis. They further believe that no explanation of social reality will be complete without understanding how people's subjective interpretations of reality influence the creation of their social reality. A contemporary positivist researcher briefly observing each one of a large number of homeless women might note their neglect of personal hygiene and may therefore develop recommendations that are connected to emotional dysfunction or the need for social skills training. An interpretivist researcher, in contrast, would study a small group of homeless women more intensively, probe deeply into their subjective interpretations of their social reality, and conclude perhaps on this basis that their repugnant odor and appearance is a rational strategy for preventing sexual victimization in what they perceive to be a dangerous social context.

Empowerment Paradigm

A third paradigm—the empowerment paradigm—focuses on using research to empower oppressed groups. This paradigm views social life as a struggle among competing individuals and groups and has been labeled in various ways. Some have called it the *critical social science paradigm.* Others have called it a *Marxist paradigm.* Some who focus on using research to empower women have called it a *feminist paradigm.* Because our profession is committed to alleviating human suffering and achieving social reform to empower oppressed groups, we can see this paradigm's features in much of social work research, regardless of what we call it.

Investigators committed to this paradigm might use methods that are typically associated with contemporary positivists, but they are distinguished by their stance toward their findings. Contemporary positivist researchers attempt to minimize the influence of values in interpreting their findings, and they attempt to interpret those findings in a neutral and

factual manner. Empowerment researchers, in contrast, set out to interpret findings through the filter of their empowerment and advocacy aims. To illustrate this point, consider the difference between how a contemporary positivist researcher and a feminist researcher might interpret a finding that, although male social workers tend to earn more than female social workers, this difference diminishes when we compare males and females with the same job responsibilities or years of experience. The contemporary positivist researcher, particularly one who is not well versed in women's issues, might conclude that this finding indicates that the influence of sexism on salaries in social work is less than many assume. The feminist researcher, however, might conclude from the same finding that sexism influences salaries through less pay for "women's work" or by the loss of annual increments during child-rearing years.

When empowerment researchers use interpretivist research methods, they are distinguished from interpretivists by going beyond the subjective meanings of the people they study and by their attempts to connect their observations to their a priori notion of an unjust, broader objective reality that they are seeking to change. Thus, a feminist researcher guided by the empowerment paradigm and taking an interpretive approach in the study of battered women would not stop at seeing reality through the eyes of the battered women but would also address aspects of the feminist's vision of reality that might not be shared by the women being studied. For example, if the battered women deny or minimize the severity of the battering, find excuses for the batterer, or think they cannot leave the batterer, a feminist researcher might note the discrepancy between the women's subjective views and the objective reality as seen by the researcher. A feminist researcher might also raise questions about the reasons for these undesirable discrepancies and attempt to derive recommendations for raising the women's feminist consciousness and empowering them. Figure 3-6 provides an additional example of how different paradigms can influence research.

Paradigmatic Flexibility in Research

As you read about these paradigms, perhaps you find yourself favoring one or disliking another, but you do not have to choose one over another. Individual researchers may find that their investigations resemble one paradigm in one study and a different

FIGURE 3.6 How Might a New Welfare Reform Policy Be Researched Differently from the Perspective of Different Paradigms?

Paradigm	Research Question	Research Design
Contemporary Positivism	Is the new policy effective in reducing poverty?	Conduct an experiment, comparing the proportion of people who move out of poverty in areas that do and do not have the new policy.
Interpretivism	How do welfare recipients experience their lives changing under the new policy?	Conduct in-depth interviews, reporting the impact of the new policy on their lives from the perspectives of the welfare recipients.
Empowerment	Does the new policy really help the poor, or does it keep them oppressed?	Organize poor people to design and carry out their own study about the question as a way to mobilize them and help them gather evidence that they can use to lobby legislators for policy changes that are less oppressive.

paradigm in another study—depending on what they seek to investigate. Moreover, they may find that sometimes they combine elements of more than one paradigm in the same study. For many researchers, the research question and the purpose of the study will determine which paradigm to employ, rather than be wedded to the same paradigm in all of their research.

In this chapter, we examined the research process and various factors that can influence it. Additional factors will be examined in depth in upcoming chapters, including qualitative and quantitative methods in Chapter 4, ethical considerations in Chapter 5, and cultural diversity in Chapter 6.

MAIN POINTS

- The phases of research include problem formulation, designing the study, data collection, data processing, data analysis, interpreting the findings, and writing the research report.
- The sequencing of the phases of the research process varies from study to study, and later phases often loop back to earlier phases.
- A theory is a systematic set of interrelated statements intended to explain some aspect of social life or enrich our sense of how people conduct and find meaning in their daily lives.
- The distinction between theories and values can seem fuzzy when social scientists become involved in studying social programs that reflect ideological points of view.

- In attempting to explain things, theories inescapably get involved in predicting things. Although prediction is implicit in explanation, it is important to distinguish between the two. Often, we are able to predict without understanding.
- Observations that we experience in the real world help us build a theory or verify whether it is correct. When our observations are consistent with what we would expect to experience if a theory is correct, we call those observations empirical support for the theory. The credibility of a theory will depend on the extent to which (a) our observations empirically support it and (b) its components are systematically organized in a logical fashion that helps us better understand the world.
- A hypothesis predicts something that ought to be observed in the real world if a theory is correct. It is a tentative and testable statement about how changes in one thing are expected to explain changes in something else.
- Hypotheses predict relationships among variables—that a change in one variable is likely to be associated with a change in the other variable.
- A variable is a concept, which means it is a mental image that symbolizes an idea, an object, an event, or a person.
- A variable that explains or causes something is called the independent variable. The variable being explained or caused is called the dependent variable.

- The concepts that make up a variable are called attributes of that variable.
- In the deductive method, the researcher begins with a theory and then derives one or more hypotheses from it for testing. In induction, one starts from observed data and develops a hypothesis to explain the specific observations.
- Science is a process that involves an alternating use of deduction and induction.
- Most explanatory social research uses a probabilistic model of causation: X may be said to cause Y if it is seen to have some influence on Y.
- The idiographic model of explanation aims to explain through the enumeration of the many and perhaps unique considerations that lie behind a given action.
- The nomothetic model seeks to understand a general phenomenon partially.
- An ideology is a closed system of beliefs and values that shapes the understanding and behavior of those who believe in it.
- A paradigm is a fundamental model or scheme that organizes our view of something.
- Social work researchers use a variety of paradigms that influence the ways in which research can be done.
- Positivist paradigms emphasize objectivity, precision, and generalizability in research. Contemporary positivist researchers recognize that observation and measurement cannot be as purely objective as the ideal image of science implies, but they still attempt to anticipate and minimize the impact of potential nonobjective influences.
- The interpretivist paradigm emphasizes gaining an empathic understanding of how people feel inside, how they interpret their everyday experiences, and what idiosyncratic reasons they may have for their behaviors.
- The empowerment paradigm focuses on oppression and uses research procedures to empower oppressed groups.

REVIEW QUESTIONS AND EXERCISES

1. Find an article in a social work research journal (such as *Research on Social Work Practice* or *Social Work Research*) that reports a research study. Discuss whether and how the study appeared to be influenced by theory.
2. Examine several recent issues of a social work research journal. Find one article illustrating the idiographic model of explanation and one illustrating the nomothetic model. Discuss the value of each and how they illustrate the contrasting models.

INTERNET EXERCISES

1. Find an article in *Policy Studies Journal* (Spring 1998) by Ann Chih Linn titled "Bridging Positivist and Interpretivist Approaches to Qualitative Methods." Briefly describe Linn's thesis that these two approaches can be combined and are not mutually exclusive.
2. Using a search engine such as Google or Yahoo!, find information on the Internet for at least two of the paradigms discussed in this chapter. Give the web addresses and report on main themes you find in the discussions.

Visit CengageBrain.com for additional practice and study opportunities including experiential exercises, research tools, glossary, flashcards, and sample test items.

4

Quantitative, Qualitative, and Mixed Methods of Inquiry

EPAS Competencies for This Chapter

Competency 4 Engage in Practice-Informed Research and Research-Informed Practice: This competency is enhanced if you are not limited to understanding quantitative methods only or qualitative methods only. Not only should you be able to understand, utilize, and conduct both types of methods, but the same applies to studies that combine both types.

Competency 8 Intervene with Individuals, Families, Groups, Organizations, and Communities: This competency specifies that you should be knowledgeable about evidence-informed interventions and understand methods of identifying, analyzing, and implementing evidence-informed interventions to achieve client system goals. This implies being able to understand qualitative, quantitative, and mixed-methods studies that provide evidence about interventions.

Competency 9 Evaluate Practice with Individuals Families, Groups, Organizations, and Communities: This competency includes understanding and learning how to use all three types of studies discussed in this chapter when evaluating practice.

What You'll Learn in This Chapter

We'll examine three contrasting yet complementary overarching models of social work research: (a) one that emphasizes objectivity in aiming to produce precise and generalizable statistical findings, (b) one that takes a different approach to objectivity and that also is more likely to emphasize subjectivity when attempting to delve into deeper understandings of phenomena not easily reduced to numbers, and (c) one that integrates both of these approaches within the same studies.

» INTRODUCTION

In Chapter 3, we noted that useful social work research studies can differ in the extent to which they emphasize objectivity or subjectivity in their inquiry. An understanding of the complementary nature of these two approaches to inquiry will set the stage for comparing three complementary overarching models of social work research: quantitative methods of inquiry, qualitative methods of inquiry, and mixed methods.

For a long time, scholars have long disagreed about the comparative value of qualitative versus quantitative research methods. In fact, some researchers would be referred to as quantitative researchers (or more briefly as *quants*), while others got branded as qualitative researchers (or *quals*). Proponents of each method of inquiry would argue for the superiority of their approach. During the latter decades of the 20th century, advocates of qualitative methods occasionally objected to what they perceived as the prominence of quantitative methods in the social work research literature while extolling the advantages of qualitative methods.

At the same time and perhaps in part because of the arguments made by advocates of qualitative research, the notion that these two approaches to inquiry were incompatibly lessened, and researchers began to see the approaches as complementary and to use them in conjunction with each other within individual studies. Eventually, this recognition led to the development of a third approach, mixed-methods research, which emphasized the importance of combining qualitative and quantitative research methods within the same studies and included a framework for the different ways of combining them.

This chapter will provide an overview of quantitative and qualitative approaches to inquiry. It will compare the distinguishing features of each approach and their advantages and disadvantages. The chapter will then delve more thoroughly into a third model of inquiry, the mixed-methods model, which, as already noted, integrates both of these approaches within the same studies. Although the mixed-methods model will receive more attention in this chapter, the remaining chapters of this book will describe various specific qualitative and quantitative research methods in more depth.

» OBJECTIVITY AND SUBJECTIVITY IN SCIENTIFIC INQUIRY

When researchers try to be objective, they are trying to observe reality without being influenced by the contents of their own minds. Likewise, when they observe what other people do, they attempt to conduct their observations in ways that will avoid influencing people to do things that they ordinarily would not do when not being observed. When they ask people questions, they attempt to ask the questions in ways that will tap how people really think or feel, not some false impression that people want to convey. It would be misleading, however, to give you the impression that objectivity is easy to achieve or even that its meaning is obvious. As we saw in Chapter 3, even contemporary positivists agree that being completely objective is impossible.

In contrast, many researchers recognize the advantages of subjective inquiry. For example, they might experience something directly themselves (such as being homeless or sleeping in a homeless shelter) and record what that does to the contents of their own minds. Thus, they learn what it feels like to walk in the shoes of the people they seek to understand.

But even when researchers emphasize subjective modes of inquiry, they might paradoxically wonder whether their subjective observations are objective. That is, they might wonder whether other people who observe or experience what they observed or experienced would come up with similar thoughts or feelings. Or did the prior mental and emotional baggage they brought to their experiences and observations influence them to interpret things in ways that yield an inaccurate portrayal of the phenomenon they are trying to understand?

Ultimately, we have no way of proving whether we are observing reality objectively and accurately at any given moment. Nonetheless, the scientific method offers a way to judge whether the conclusions of different research studies are objective and accurate. When different research studies arrive at the same conclusion, then—at least from a contemporary positivist standpoint—we can judge them all to have been objective and to have discovered objective reality. This criterion applies regardless of whether the researchers emphasized objective or subjective modes of inquiry in their studies. Regardless of which approach they emphasize, they may not be proceeding as objectively as they think they are. Being human, they often fall into the errors of human inquiry discussed earlier.

When social workers devise and test a new intervention approach, for instance, the value of their efforts and the recognition they will receive will be far greater when their findings show that their intervention is effective than when it is shown to be ineffective. Sure, a study about an ineffective intervention may be worth publishing so that others can learn from and avoid repeating the "failure," but it is much more gratifying to be able to show the field that you have discovered something that works than it is to discuss why things went wrong.

Because of their vested interests in finding certain results, researchers who emphasize objective methods of inquiry will often devise ways of observing phenomena that attempt to prevent their biases from influencing what is observed. They can do this in many ways, as we will see in later sections of this book. For example, they might employ observers who are not given potentially biasing information about the research. They might use paper-and-pencil self-report scales that respondents complete outside the researcher's presence. Perhaps they'll look at existing information, such as school records, that were collected by others who know nothing of their research.

Researchers who emphasize subjective methods of inquiry need not eschew using objective approaches as well. For example, they can collaborate with coinvestigators, with each of them independently taking a subjective approach and reaching their own independent conclusions unaware of the conclusions their colleagues are reaching. The two sets of conclusions can later be compared, and if they agree, they are deemed to be relatively objective.

These are just a few examples of how researchers can try to be objective regardless of whether they are emphasizing objective or subjective modes of inquiry; we'll examine many more in later chapters. When we do examine these alternatives, we will see that none is foolproof. Every way of observing a phenomenon has some potential for error.

Although we may not know whether one particular observer or observation method is really objective, we assume that objectivity has been achieved when different observers with different vested interests or other possible biases agree on what is observed or when different observational strategies yield essentially the same findings—including those observational strategies that employed subjective methods of inquiry.

A COMPARISON OF QUALITATIVE AND QUANTITATIVE METHODS OF INQUIRY

Quantitative research methods emphasize the production of precise and generalizable statistical findings. When we want to verify whether a cause produces an effect in general, we are likely to use quantitative methods. Quantitative research studies typically attempt to formulate all or most of their research procedures in advance and then try to adhere precisely to those procedures with maximum objectivity as data are collected. Prominent examples of quantitative studies include experiments, quasi experiments, and surveys. Experiments and quasi experiments in social work typically will divide clients into two comparable groups. Each group will receive a different program, policy, or intervention condition. Objective measures are taken to assess whether one program, policy, or intervention appears to be more effective than the other. Surveys will typically administer closed-ended questionnaires to a sample of people in an attempt to develop findings that can be generalized to a larger population than the sample represents. Later in this book separate chapters will be devoted to the foregoing three types of quantitative studies.

Qualitative research methods are more likely to tap the deeper meanings of particular human experiences and generate theoretically richer observations that are not easily reduced to numbers. Qualitative research studies typically begin with a more flexible plan, one that allows the research procedures to evolve as more observations are gathered. Whereas quantitative studies are more likely to seek to generalize precise and objective findings to a larger population, qualitative studies typically permit the use of subjectivity to generate deeper understandings of the meanings of human experiences—often with a much smaller sample of research participants than is typically the case in quantitative studies. This does not imply that quantitative studies are completely inflexible or that qualitative studies have no advanced planned procedures. Likewise, it does not imply that all quantitative studies have larger samples than all qualitative studies. It's more a matter of emphasis, and some studies combine quantitative and qualitative research procedures. Later in this book several chapters will be devoted to various qualitative methods.

ASSESSING THE PSYCHOSOCIAL ASPECTS OF HOSPICE CARE VERSUS STANDARD HOSPITAL CARE

Suppose a medical social worker wants to assess the psychosocial aspects of hospice care versus standard hospital care for terminally ill patients. Put simply, standard hospital care emphasizes using medical technology to fight disease at all costs, even if the technology entails undesirable costs in quality of life and patient discomfort. Hospice care emphasizes minimizing patients' discomfort and maximizing their quality of life during their final days, even if that means eschewing certain technologies that prolong life but hinder its quality.

Suppose the social worker's prime focus in the study is whether and how quality of life differs for patients depending on the form of care they receive. In a quantitative study, the social worker might ask the closest family member of each patient to complete a standardized list of interview questions about the degree of pain the patient expressed feeling, the frequency of undesirable side effects associated with medical technology (e.g., loss of hair due to chemotherapy), the patient's mood, the patient's activities, and so on. An effort would probably be made to find an instrument that scored each question—scores that could be summed to produce an overall quality-of-life score. Ideally, it would be an instrument that had been tested elsewhere and seemed to produce consistent data over repeated administrations and with different interviewers. Thus, it would appear to be a measure that seems unaffected by the investigator's predilections or vested interests. If the scores of the hospice-treated patients turn out to be higher than the scores for patients receiving standard medical care, then the social worker might conclude that hospice care better affects quality of life than does standard medical care.

Perhaps, however, the social worker is skeptical as to whether the instrument really taps all of the complex dimensions of quality of life. The instrument gives only a numerical score—perhaps this is superficial; it tells us little about the ways the two forms of care may differentially affect quality of life, and it provides little understanding of what patients experience and what those experiences mean to them.

As an alternative, the social worker may choose to take a more subjective and qualitative approach to the inquiry. This might entail spending a great deal of time on the standard and hospice wards that care for terminally ill patients in the hospital. There, the social worker might simply observe what goes on and keep a detailed log of the observations. The information in the logs can be analyzed to see what patterns emerge. In Chapter 5, we will examine in depth a study that took this approach (Buckingham, Lack, Mount, MacLean, & Collins, 1976), one in which the investigator actually posed as a terminally ill patient and observed how he was treated differently in the two wards and how this made him feel. Rather than rely on indirect quantitative measures that attempt to avoid his own subjectivity, he decided to experience the phenomenon directly. On the basis of his direct observations and subjective experiences, he was able to discuss in depth how the medical staff members on the hospice ward seemed much more sensitive and empathic than those on the other ward, how family members seemed encouraged to be more involved on the hospice ward and the implications this had for personalized care, and how all of this made the patient feel. By subjectively entering the role of the patient, the investigator was able to propose a deep, empathic understanding of how the two forms of care had different implications for quality of life.

But what are the potential pitfalls of the preceding approach? Some might question whether the investigator's previous ties to hospice care, his predilections, and his desire to obtain important findings may have predisposed him to make observations that would reflect favorably on the relative advantages of hospice care. In short, they would be concerned about whether his observations were sufficiently objective. Which of the two studies is preferable: the quantitative or the qualitative? Actually, both are valuable. Each provides useful information, and each has its own set of advantages and disadvantages in its quest for truth and understanding.

Whether we should emphasize qualitative or quantitative research methods in a particular study—or use both—will depend on the conditions and purposes of our inquiry. Qualitative methods may be more suitable when flexibility is required to study a new phenomenon about which we know very little or when we seek to gain insight into the subjective meanings of complex phenomena to advance our conceptualization of them and build a theory that can be tested in future studies. Qualitative research thus can sometimes pave the way for quantitative studies of the same subject. Other times, qualitative methods produce results that are sufficient in themselves. Each approach is useful and legitimate. Each makes its unique contribution to inquiry. Each has its own advantages and disadvantages. Each is a set of tools, not a dogma. Researchers need to match the tools they use with the research questions and conditions they face—using quantitative methods for some studies, qualitative methods for others, and both methods in combination for still others. These points are illustrated in the box "Assessing the Psychosocial Aspects of Hospice Care Versus Standard Hospital Care."

Although qualitative and quantitative methods are compatible, many studies use one or the other approach exclusively or predominantly, and which one they use or emphasize will significantly influence the nature of the research process. We will be mentioning the terms *qualitative* and *quantitative* research methods throughout this book. At times, we will focus more on qualitative methods; at other times, the focus will be on quantitative methods. Whenever we discuss the strengths or weaknesses of either type of method, you should bear in mind that we are not implying that that particular type is stronger or weaker than the other type. Figure 4-1 lists various attributes of quantitative and qualitative methods of inquiry that tend to differ in emphasis. We have already discussed some of the contrasting attributes. Others may be unfamiliar to you at this point but will be discussed later in this chapter and in subsequent chapters. Keep that in mind as you examine Figure 4-1 so you don't become anxious about any terms you have not yet read about. Also keep in mind that despite their contrasting emphases, qualitative and quantitative methods are compatible (as we discussed earlier and will elaborate in regard to mixed-methods studies). Moreover, although some attributes are more *likely* to apply to one method of inquiry than the other, that doesn't mean they cannot apply to both. For example, some quantitative studies can be inductive, involve small samples, or be conducted early in an investigation for exploratory purposes. Likewise, some qualitative studies might be conducted in an agency instead of the natural environment of the participants. Also, some qualitative studies might be conducted later in an investigation to try to generate a better understanding of quantitative findings from earlier research.

>> MIXED METHODS OF INQUIRY

Many quantitative social work research studies use more than one quantitative research method, and many qualitative studies use more than one qualitative method. A strictly quantitative evaluation of the effectiveness of a child welfare program, for example, might examine whether rates of child mal-treatment in official records decline after the program's onset while also examining whether the program's clients score better after treatment on a test of knowledge of positive parenting. A strictly qualitative inquiry into the experience of being homeless might combine conducting unstructured, open-ended interviews of homeless people with having the researchers live homeless themselves to observe the behaviors of other homeless people with whom they hang out and to get a subjective sense of how it feels to live on the streets.

Although some might portray the above examples as having used mixed methods because one study used more than one quantitative method and the other used more than one qualitative method, the term *mixed-methods research* more commonly has referred to the combination of quantitative and qualitative research methods within the same study. However, as mixed-methods research has become increasingly popular in recent years, it has come to be defined as more than just happening to use both qualitative and quantitative methods in a particular study. It is now seen as a stand-alone type of research design in which a single study not only collects both qualitative and quantitative data but also integrates both sources of data at one or more stages of the research process so as to improve the understanding of the phenomenon being investigated (Hanson, Creswell, Plano Clark, Petska, & Creswell, 2005).

For example, Creswell (2014a) cautions that mixed-methods research is not merely gathering both qualitative and quantitative data. In addition to gathering both forms, it must integrate them in a way that strengthens the study. Likewise, one should not label their study as *mixed-methods* research simply because both forms of data were collected. It is also a mistake to use that label if the different forms of data collected were all quantitative or all qualitative. Both qualitative and quantitative data need to be collected and integrated to merit the *mixed-methods* label. Creswell (2104a) also cautions that mixed-methods research does not imply that the scope or rigor of the qualitative or quantitative approach can be reduced.

Types of Mixed-Methods Designs

Various ways have been suggested for classifying the types of mixed-methods research designs. One way

identifies nine types of designs according to whether qualitative or quantitative methods are emphasized and according to the time sequence in which each set of methods is implemented. According to this way of classifying, there are three possibilities regarding emphasis, as follows:

- Qualitative emphasized
- Quantitative emphasized
- Equal emphasis

There are also three possibilities regarding sequencing:

- Qualitative first
- Quantitative first
- Concurrent (qualitative and quantitative methods implemented at the same time)

The resulting nine possible types of design are displayed in Figure 4-2. In that figure, the type of method that is capitalized is the one that gets priority. Let's now consider some hypothetical illustrations of each of the nine types of mixed-methods designs listed in Figure 4-2.

QUALITATIVE → quantitative   The first design on the list might involve a study that begins with in-depth, open-ended qualitative interviews of military combat veterans who have returned home from the wars in Iraq and Afghanistan. The priority would be on gaining an in-depth understanding of the challenges they experience in returning to and adjusting to civilian life. After collecting and analyzing the data using qualitative data analysis techniques, quantitative methods could be used to examine how many respondents fell into what types of categories generated by the qualitative analysis. The emphasis in the study and its reportage is on the qualitative analysis, and the numbers generated in the quantitative analysis, while not unimportant, are not the study's priority.

quantitative → QUALITATIVE   The second design on the list might begin with a quantitative, structured interview survey of a random sample of military combat veterans in which the veterans complete a checklist indicating what posttraumatic stress symptoms they are experiencing. The purpose of the survey data is *not* the study's priority. Instead, the data are used as the basis for the ensuing qualitative inquiry, in which in-depth,

FIGURE 4.1   Contrasting Emphases in Quantitative and Qualitative Methods of Inquiry

Attribute	Quantitative	Qualitative
Aims	Precision Generalizability Testing hypotheses	Deeper understandings Describing contexts Generating hypotheses Discovery
Structure	Research procedures specified in advance	Flexible procedures evolve as data are gathered
Setting for data gathering	Office, agency, or via mail or Internet	Natural environment of research participants
Theoretical approach most commonly employed	Deductive	Inductive
Sample size likely or preferred	Larger	Smaller
Most likely timing in investigating phenomena	Later, after familiarity with phenomenon has been established	Early, to gain familiarity with phenomenon
Emphasis on objectivity or subjectivity	Objectivity	Subjectivity
Nature of data emphasized	Numbers	Words
Depth and generalizability of findings	More superficial but more generalizable	Deeper but less generalizable
Richness of detail and context	Less contextual detail	Rich descriptions with more contextual detail
Nature of data-gathering methods emphasized	Various but highly structured	Lengthier and less structured observations and interviews
Types of designs and methods commonly used	Experiments Quasi experiments Single-case designs Surveys	Ethnography Case studies Life history Focus groups Participatory action research Grounded theory
Data-gathering instruments emphasized	Closed-ended items in questionnaires and scales	Open-ended items and interviews with probes
Labor intensiveness of data collection for researchers	Less time consuming	More time consuming
Labor intensiveness of data analysis	Less time consuming	More time consuming
Data analysis process	Calculate statistics that describe a population or assess the probability of error in inferences about hypotheses	Search for patterns and meanings in narratives, not numbers
Paradigms emphasized in appraising rigor	Contemporary positivist standards for minimizing bias, maximizing objectivity, and statistically controlling for alternative explanations	Contemporary positivist standards might be used, but standards based on interpretivist, social constructivist, critical social science, and feminist paradigms are commonly used
Ease of replication by other researchers	Easier	Harder

open-ended probing interviews are conducted with a subsample of vets with the most symptoms and a subsample with the least symptoms to try to understand why some vets have worse trauma symptoms than others and to describe what it is like to walk in their shoes.

FIGURE 4.2   Nine Types of Mixed-Methods Designs: Emphasis by Sequence

---

QUALITATIVE EMPHASIS

QUALITATIVE → quantitative	(Qualitative Emphasized with Qualitative Implemented First)
quantitative → QUALITATIVE	(Qualitative Emphasized with Quantitative Implemented First)
QUALITATIVE Emphasized with Concurrent Implementation	

QUANTITATIVE EMPHASIS

QUANTITATIVE → qualitative	(Quantitative Emphasized with Quantitative Implemented First)
qualitative → QUANTITATIVE	(Quantitative Emphasized with Qualitative Implemented First)
QUANTITATIVE Emphasized with Concurrent Implementation	

EQUAL EMPHASIS

Qualitative → Quantitative	(Equal Emphasis with Qualitative Implemented First)
Quantitative → Qualitative	(Equal Emphasis with Quantitative Implemented First)
Equal Emphasis with Concurrent Implementation	

QUALITATIVE Emphasized with Concurrent Implementation The third design on the list might administer the above qualitative interviews and quantitative checklists to the same vets during the same data collection session. (Perhaps half the vets would respond to the qualitative part first, while the other half responds to the quantitative part first.) The priority is on gaining an in-depth understanding of what it's like for the vets to try to readjust to civilian life, and the quantitative data are used for two secondary purposes: (a) to see if they corroborate the qualitative part of the analysis for each vet and (b) to enumerate how many vets are experiencing the various in-depth depictions of the qualitative analysis.

QUANTITATIVE → qualitative The fourth design on the list might have as its priority answering the research question of whether male and female vets differ in the impact of combat on their emotional well-being and in their level of psychosocial readjustment to civilian life. The male and female vets could complete quantitative scales that measure their trauma symptoms and their psychosocial adjustment. Although the priority of the study is to test whether there are statistically significant differences between the genders in their scores on the above measures, after the quantitative data are analyzed, qualitative interviews are conducted with those vets whose scores signify the worst symptoms and adjustment levels. The aim of the qualitative interviews is to augment the quantitative findings

with illustrations that bring the quantitative findings to life and to exemplify how those findings apply in particular cases. An example of a published study using this type of mixed-methods design is summarized in the box "A Mixed-Methods Social Work Research Study with Adult Female Survivors of Childhood Sexual Abuse."

qualitative → QUANTITATIVE The fifth design on the list might begin with qualitative interviews that are conducted as part of a pilot study to generate ideas as to what questions to ask in developing quantitative instruments that will measure psychosocial adjustment to civilian life. The pilot study might also be used to generate hypotheses that could then be tested in a quantitative study. The priority of the mixed-methods study is *not* on the results of the qualitative analysis. Instead, it is on the subsequent use of the instruments in a quantitative study that will test the hypotheses generated in the qualitative study. One such hypothesis might be the postulation that male and female vets differ in their level of psychosocial readjustment to civilian life.

QUANTITATIVE Emphasized with Concurrent Implementation The sixth design on the list might also seek to answer the question of whether male and female vets differ in their level of psychosocial readjustment to civilian life. But instead of administering the qualitative interviews after the quantitative data are analyzed, the vets are divided into two groups. Male and female vets in the larger of the two groups complete the quantitative scales. Their counterparts in the smaller group respond to the in-depth qualitative interviews. The priority is on the quantitative findings, and the qualitative findings are just used to illustrate some of the ways that male and female vets encounter different problems in readjusting to civilian life.

Qualitative → Quantitative The seventh design on the list might place an equal emphasis on answering the question of whether male and female vets differ in their level of psychosocial readjustment to civilian life and on gaining an in-depth understanding of the different kinds of problems they experience and how they try to cope with them as they try to readjust to civilian life. One group of male and female vets might respond to the qualitative interviews, and on the basis of the analysis of those interviews, the quantitative instruments are developed and then implemented with another group of male and female vets. In the report of the study findings, both sets of findings are given equal emphasis.

Quantitative → Qualitative The eighth design on the list also would place an equal emphasis on answering the question of whether male and female vets differ in their level of psychosocial readjustment to civilian life and on gaining an in-depth understanding of the different kinds of problems they experience and how they try to cope with them as they try to readjust to civilian life. However, this design would implement the quantitative part of the study first and then later conduct qualitative interviews with small subsamples of respondents who represent vets with the best, worst, and average adjustment scores. In the report of the study findings, both sets of findings are given equal emphasis.

Equal Emphasis with Concurrent Implementation The ninth design on the list might also seek to answer the question of whether male and female vets differ in their level of psychosocial readjustment to civilian life. But instead of administering the qualitative and quantitative components sequentially, the vets are divided into two groups. Male and female vets in the larger of the two groups complete the quantitative scales. Their counterparts in the smaller group respond to the qualitative interviews. In the report of the study findings, both sets of findings are given equal emphasis. The box providing a case example of a mixed-methods study of

child welfare clients offers an illustration of this ninth design.

Three Basic Mixed-Methods Designs

More recently, Creswell (2014a,b) suggested three basic mixed-methods designs, as illustrated in Figure 4-3. These are the convergent mixed-methods design, the exploratory sequential mixed-methods design, and the explanatory sequential mixed-methods design. We'll now discuss each of those designs, in that order.

Convergent Mixed-Methods Design With this design, quantitative and qualitative data are collected concurrently and then analyzed separately. The results of the separate analyses are then merged for comparison purposes to see if they confirm each other. If they do, then there can be more confidence in the veracity of the set of conclusions derived from the joint findings. For example, suppose a study is undertaken to assess whether there is a difference in the quality of the practitioner–client relationship depending on whether the practitioner follows an evidence-based model of practice. The quantitative data could be collected by having clients complete a written self-report scale regarding the quality of the relationship they have with their practitioner. The qualitative data could delve into the same issue using nondirective, probing interviews with the clients. Both types of data collection would be used because there is uncertainty as to whether either type, alone, would yield accurate, unbiased results. Suppose that after the data are collected and analyzed separately they both agree that there is no difference in the quality of the relationship between those practitioners who do and do not follow an evidence-based model of practice. There would be more confidence in the accuracy of that conclusion than if it had been derived from only quantitative data or only qualitative data.

Even if the results agree for the most part, the qualitative data might shed additional light on the nature of the relationships that the more narrow and structured quantitative data are unable to uncover. For example, they might show that although the clients of both sets of practitioners are on average equally pleased with the quality of the relationship, maybe the clients of the practitioners using the evidence-based model will comment that their practitioners gave them more

A MIXED-METHODS SOCIAL WORK RESEARCH STUDY WITH ADULT FEMALE SURVIVORS OF CHILDHOOD SEXUAL ABUSE

For her doctoral dissertation in social work at the University of Texas at Austin, Tonya Edmond completed a mixed-methods study that emphasized and began with a quantitative experiment evaluating the effectiveness of eye movement desensitization and reprocessing (EMDR) in alleviating the trauma symptoms of adult female survivors of childhood sexual abuse. Although the quantitative part of the study came first, from the outset she conceptualized her research as a mixed-methods investigation in which, after concluding the experimental phase, clients would participate in qualitative interviews about their perceptions of the treatment.

In the experiment (reported in Edmond, Rubin, & Wambach, 1999), 59 adult female survivors of childhood sexual abuse who were experiencing trauma symptoms related to the abuse were assigned randomly to either individual EMDR therapy, individual eclectic therapy, or a delayed treatment control group. Treatment effects were assessed using four standardized measures of different types of trauma-related symptoms that were administered before treatment and then again after treatment. The results of the experiment supported the effectiveness of both the EMDR treatment and the eclectic treatment in that the outcomes for each of these treatments were significantly better than the outcomes for the delayed treatment control group. Although some of the data suggested that the EMDR treatment might have been more effective than the eclectic treatment, those data were not sufficient to conclude that the EMDR treatment was indeed the more effective of the two treatments.

After the experiment ended, Edmond conducted tape-recorded, semistructured qualitative interviews with the research participants who received either the EMDR or the eclectic therapy. (A discussion of this type of interviewing is provided in Chapter 19.) Edmond, Sloan, and McCarty (2004) described the questions she asked as follows:

> How are you doing now as compared to when you entered the study?" "In what way if any was the therapy helpful to you?" "Did it have any effect on the issues that you wanted to address?" If they answered in the affirmative they were asked, "do you think that the benefits gained will be lasting?" "Do you think you will need more therapy to resolve your sexual abuse issues?" "What are your thoughts/feelings about your therapist?" "How did the therapy that you received in the study compare to other therapy or counseling that you have received?" "What did you like or value the most about the therapy you received?" What did you dislike or find least valuable about the therapy you received?" (p. 264)

A qualitative analysis of the interview data (Chapter 20 delves into how to analyze qualitative data) led Edmond and her coauthors to reach two main conclusions: (1) Recipients of EMDR were more likely than recipients of eclectic therapy to perceive a more complete resolution of their trauma symptoms, and (2) recipients of eclectic therapy valued their relationship with their therapist more highly than did recipients of EMDR and were more likely to report having learned effective coping strategies.

Citing the insights gained by the qualitative portion of their study—insights that were unattainable using quantitative methods—Edmond et al. (2004) suggested that "mixed-methods approaches to evaluating interventions have more to offer than either approach can provide individually" (p. 270).

information about the type of intervention to be provided and were more likely to seek their consent to provide the intervention. Likewise, perhaps the clients of the other practitioners will comment that their practitioners were more flexible from session to session regarding the session focus.

Exploratory Sequential Mixed-Methods Design
With this design the qualitative data are collected first, to provide a basis for formulating the quantitative phase. According to Creswell (2014), one aim of this design could be to see if the insights generated from a small sample of people in the qualitative phase can be generalized to a larger, more representative sample of the population in the quantitative phase. Another aim might be to use the qualitative data as a basis for developing a good quantitative data collection instrument. For example, let's return

MIXED-METHODS STUDY OF ENGAGING NONVOLUNTARY CHILD WELFARE CLIENTS IN WORKING RELATIONSHIPS

Many parents entering the child welfare system have a severely limited capacity to engage in healthy relationships. Given this limited capacity, compounded by the fact that their participation in child welfare services in not voluntary, one of the key challenges faced by child welfare practitioners is developing a healthy relationship with the client and enhancing their investment and commitment toward working on resolving the problems that led to their being referred. In light of this problem, Julie Cooper Altman (2008) conducted a mixed-methods study to examine the processes involved in client engagement and whether those processes are related to service outcomes. She collected qualitative and quantitative data concurrently, with both components receiving equal emphasis. The qualitative component of her phenomenological investigation involved interviews with parents and workers in a neighborhood-based family service center provided by a child welfare agency in New York City. The analysis of the qualitative data from those interviews yielded seven main themes perceived to be key in engaging clients. These themes pertained to the need to set mutual goals; to maintain a sense of hopefulness throughout the change process; to

have parents acknowledge understanding of their situation; to remain motivated for change; to respect cultural differences; to have respectful and honest communication; and to maintain persistent and diligent work by all parties in a timely fashion. In the quantitative components of the study, workers and clients completed self-report scales that measured the quality of the worker–client alliance and their degree of satisfaction with the service they were receiving or providing. Quantitative data also were collected from case records to assess whether the case outcome was successful. Unfortunately, however, there was no relationship between the quality of engagement and improved case outcomes. Nevertheless, Altman's findings have value for guiding child welfare practice. Noting that conventional wisdom may be overrating the degree to which the quality of the worker–client relationship impacts case outcomes in child welfare, Altman suggested alternative ways of considering and investigating this service delivery problem.

Source: Altman, J. C. (2008). A study of engagement in neighborhood-based child welfare services. *Research on Social Work Practice, 18*(6), 555–564.

to the fictitious study (discussed above) undertaken to assess whether there is a difference in the quality of the practitioner–client relationship depending on whether the practitioner follows an evidence-based model of practice. If the qualitative phase were conducted first, the researchers might learn to include items in their quantitative scale pertaining to whether the client felt that the practitioner made an adequate effort to explain potential interventions to them and secure their informed consent. They might also learn to include an item or two regarding whether the client felt that the practitioner was too rigid about the focus of each session.

Explanatory Sequential Mixed-Methods Design

According to Creswell, this design is thought to appeal to researchers who are more quantitatively oriented. The quantitative data are collected first, followed by qualitative data collection aimed at

developing a better understanding of the quantitative data. For example, consider a program that brings juvenile offenders into prisons where convicts attempt to scare the youths away from criminal behavior by portraying the sordid nature of prison life. Such a program, known as *Scared Straight*, was implemented in the 1970s and had unexpected, harmful results based on the quantitative crime record data. The juvenile offenders who participated in the program later engaged in much more crime than did a comparable group of offenders who did not participate. Why did this happen? One author speculated that the "tough" juveniles who participated in the program perhaps wanted to prove that they were not scared (Finckenauer, 1979). Although this speculation seems reasonable, following the quantitative data collection with a qualitative approach using in-depth interviews with the juveniles might have made this interpretation less speculative

FIGURE 4.3   Three Basic Mixed-Methods Designs

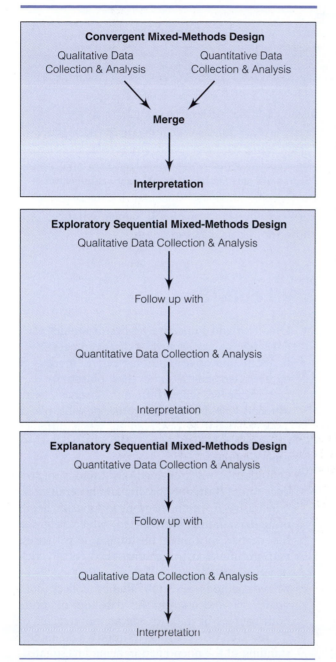

Source: Creswell, 2014a, pp. 37–41; Creswell, 2014b, p. 220.

Three Advanced Mixed-Methods Designs

In addition to the foregoing three *basic* mixed-methods designs, Creswell (2014a) describes three *advanced* ones. The main basis for calling these designs advanced is that a particular research purpose or overarching framework is added to the basic design. For example, the intervention mixed-methods design involves merging a qualitative inquiry with a quantitative evaluation of an intervention's outcome to get a better handle on the meaning of the results. For example, during a large experiment to test the effectiveness of a clinical intervention, a researcher might come to realize that qualitative interviews need to be implemented with clinicians to see if they are enthusiastic and committed to the new intervention.

The second advanced design is the social justice mixed-methods design. What makes this design distinct is not the degree of emphasis or the sequencing of the qualitative and quantitative methods, but rather, that its various methods are based on a social justice theory and aimed at collecting data that will yield a call for action to improve the plight of vulnerable, marginalized or oppressed groups. (This design employs the *empowerment* paradigm that we discussed in Chapter 3.)

The third advanced design is the multiphase mixed-methods design, which also is not distinguished by the sequence or emphasis of the various methods. Instead, it is distinguished by the use of several mixed-methods projects that are implemented in multiple phases over time in a longitudinal study in which the multiple projects focus on a common objective. (We will examine longitudinal studies in Chapter 7.)

Reasons for Using Mixed Methods

As you might surmise from the previous illustrations, there are various reasons for choosing to combine qualitative and quantitative methods. Three broad types of reasons for doing so are as follows: (a) to use one set of methods to illustrate cases or provide numbers for the findings of the other set, (b) to use one set to initiate ideas or techniques that subsequently can be pursued by the other set, and (c) to see if the two sets of findings corroborate each other. These reasons are illustrated in Figure 4-4, with the emphasized type of method in capital letters and with each type

and perhaps would have suggested other explanations for the unexpected findings. (We will return to the *Scared Straight* example in Chapter 14, on program evaluation.)

FIGURE 4.4   Reasons for Using Mixed Methods*

Reason	Sequence	Example
Extend main findings	QUANT → qual	Qual illustrates how QUANT applies in particular cases
	QUAL → quant	Quant indicates the number of cases in the QUAL categories
Generate research questions or techniques	Qual → QUANT	Qual identifies research questions to assess using QUANT or facilitates the development of QUANT measurement instruments
Corroboration	QUANT → qual	Qual used to support the validity of the QUANT findings
	QUAL → quant	Quant used to support the validity of the QUAL findings
	Concurrent	Either of the above of corroboration with both qual and quant findings having an equal emphasis

*The emphasized type of method is in capital letters, and each type is abbreviated (qual = qualitative and quant = quantitative).

abbreviated ("qual" for qualitative and "quant" for quantitative).

For example, in some studies, they are combined so that the qualitative data can provide descriptions of how the quantitative data apply in particular cases. Likewise, some studies might combine them so that the quantitative data can indicate the numbers of cases that fall within the qualitative categories. Those two studies would exemplify the first reason. The second reason would be exemplified by a study in which the qualitative part is used to generate hypotheses to be tested in the quantitative part or a study in which the quantitative part yields perplexing findings that need to be explained by the qualitative part. To illustrate the third reason, perhaps qualitative interviews show that male and female vets are experiencing differences in the types of problems they encounter in trying to readjust to civilian life and differences in their level of adjustment; then those data would corroborate quantitative findings that point to such differences. Alternatively, if the two sets of data contradict each other, then the validity of the findings is in doubt, and the contradictions might have value in implying the need for new avenues of research that might illuminate the meaning of—or resolve—the contradiction.

At this point, we surmise that you might be feeling somewhat overwhelmed with this discussion of qualitative, quantitative, and mixed methods because we have not yet provided a thorough coverage of the various specific kinds of qualitative and quantitative research methods. If you are feeling that way, we encourage you not to worry. Most of your peers are probably feeling like you are. It's only natural that you might feel that way not having

yet read the rest of this book, which will delve into those specific methods in depth.

MAIN POINTS

- Objective and subjective modes of inquiry each have advantages as well as disadvantages.
- In both objective and subjective modes of inquiry, we can assume that objectivity has been achieved when different observers with different vested interests or other possible biases agree on what is observed or when different observational strategies yield essentially the same findings.
- Quantitative research methods attempt to produce findings that are precise and generalizable. Qualitative research methods emphasize depth of understanding, attempt to subjectively tap the deeper meanings of human experiences, and are intended to generate theoretically rich observations.
- Mixed-methods research studies collect both qualitative and quantitative data and integrate both sources of data at one or more stages of the research process so as to improve the understanding of the phenomenon being investigated.
- Nine subtypes of mixed-methods designs can be classified according to whether qualitative or quantitative methods are emphasized and according to the time sequence in which each set of methods is implemented.
- Three basic mixed-methods designs are the convergent parallel mixed-methods design, the exploratory sequential mixed-methods design,

and explanatory sequential mixed-methods design.

- Three advanced mixed-methods designs are the embedded mixed-methods design, the transformative mixed-methods design, and the multiphase mixed-methods design.
- Reasons for choosing to combine qualitative and quantitative methods include (a) to use one set of methods to illustrate cases or provide numbers for the findings of the other set, (b) to use one set to initiate ideas or techniques that subsequently can be pursued by the other set, and (c) to see if the two sets of findings corroborate each other.

PRACTICE-RELATED EXERCISES

1. Examine several recent issues of a social work research journal (such as *Research on Social Work Practice* or *Social Work Research*). Find one article emphasizing quantitative methods and one emphasizing qualitative methods. Discuss the value of each and how they illustrate the contrasting methods.
2. In the same journal, find a recent study that has the term *mixed methods* in the title or abstract and that emphasizes its use of mixed methods. Identify which of the nine mixed-methods designs described in this chapter best matches the approach used in that study and why.
3. Suppose you have been asked to design a research study that evaluates the degree of success of a family preservation program that seeks to prevent out-of-home placements of children

who are at risk of child abuse or neglect by providing intensive in-home social work services. Under what conditions might you opt to emphasize quantitative methods or qualitative methods in your design? What would be the advantages and disadvantages of each approach?
4. Using the family preservation study example in exercise 3, how and why might you choose to combine both types of methods in a mixed-methods design? Provide an example of two alternative mixed-methods designs you might use for that study, as well as their rationale.

INTERNET EXERCISES

1. Go to the website for the online Journal of Mixed-Methods Research (http://mmr.sagepub.com/content/8/2.toc). Click on the prompts for the tables of contents for previous issues until you find the issues published in 2013. Click on the abstracts for each of the articles in those issues to find two articles that report studies that used one or more of the mixed-methods designs discussed in this chapter. For each of the articles, write down the article citation, and identify and describe the type of mixed-methods design used.
2. At the same site and for the same year, find two articles that illustrate the applicability of mixed-methods research to problems of concern to social workers. For each of the articles, write down the article citation, briefly summarize the article, and discuss its applicability to social work.

 Visit CengageBrain.com for additional practice and study opportunities including experiential exercises, research tools, glossary, flashcards, and sample test items.

part 2

The Ethical, Political, and Cultural Context of Social Work Research

5 The Ethics and Politics of Social Work Research

6 Culturally Competent Research

Social work research—like social work practice—is about people. Moreover, it usually involves them as research participants. Consequently, it helps to learn about ethical issues in social work before studying specific research methods and designs. The decisions we can and do make about how we structure and conduct our research are influenced by ethical considerations, as we will see.

Research involving people often has political implications as well. For example, the researcher's own politics and ideology can influence what is studied and how research is carried out. Also, the results of social work research sometimes influence how agency stakeholders view the prospects for securing more funds for their programs. Sometimes research results can influence social policies, perhaps to the liking or disliking of people at different ends of the political spectrum.

Moreover, sometimes research results are reported in ways that offend members of certain cultures, such as when studies of the prevalence of alcohol abuse among the members of that culture are disseminated in ways that reinforce stereotypes about that culture. In addition, research studies can fail to be completed or can produce misleading findings if they are implemented in a culturally incompetent manner.

In Chapter 5, we'll examine special ethical and political considerations that arise in social work research. This chapter will establish an ethical and political context for the discussions of research methods in the remaining chapters.

Chapter 6 will explore how social work researchers can use qualitative and quantitative methods to improve the cultural competence of all phases of the research. We'll see how cultural competence can help researchers obtain and provide information that is relevant and valid for minority and oppressed populations and thus improve practice and policy with those populations.

5

The Ethics and Politics of Social Work Research

EPAS Competencies for This Chapter

Competency 1 Demonstrate Ethical and Professional Behavior: Most of this chapter is devoted to enhancing your competence to engage in ethical behavior when you participate in the conducting of research.

Competency 2 Engage Diversity and Difference in Practice: You will learn in this chapter that ethical research involves employing research procedures that are unbiased regarding sex and culture and that are sensitive to cultural differences.

Competency 4 Engage in Practice-Informed Research and Research-Informed Practice: Engaging in research requires that you adhere to ethical guidelines and being able to obtain approval for your research from panels that examine the ethics of proposed studies.

Competency 9 Evaluate Practice with Individuals Families, Groups, Organizations, and Communities: Using research methods is an essential part of evaluating practice; therefore, you must have competency in research ethics in order to conduct ethical evaluative studies and even to get approval for such studies.

What You'll Learn in This Chapter

In this chapter, you'll see how ethical and political considerations must be taken into account alongside scientific ones in the design and execution of social work research. Often, however, clear-cut answers to thorny ethical and political issues are hard to come by.

» INTRODUCTION

Before they can implement their studies, social workers and other professionals who conduct research that involves human subjects may confront questions about the ethics of their proposed investigations. They must resolve these questions not only to meet their own ethical standards but also to meet the standards of committees that have been set up to review the ethics of proposed studies and to approve or disapprove the studies' implementation from an ethical standpoint.

Concern about the ethics of research that involves human subjects has not always been as intense as it is today. The roots of this concern date back many decades to an era in which studies on human subjects could be conducted with little scrutiny of their ethics—an era in which some research became notorious for its inhumane violations of basic ethical standards. The most flagrant examples were the Nazi atrocities in medical experimentation that were conducted during the Holocaust.

Although the depraved Nazi experiments stand apart as by far the most atrocious examples of inhumane "research," they were not the only studies being done around that time that involved inhumane ethical violations. The most notorious example in the United States was the Tuskegee syphilis study, which started in 1932 in Alabama. In that study, medical researchers diagnosed several hundred poor African American male sharecroppers as suffering from syphilis but did not tell them they had syphilis. Instead, they told the men that they were being treated for "bad blood." The researchers merely studied the disease's progress and had no intentions of treating it. Even after penicillin had been accepted as an effective treatment for syphilis, the study continued without providing penicillin or telling the subjects about it. The subjects were even kept from seeking treatment in the community—since the researchers wanted to observe the full progression of the disease. At times, diagnostic procedures such as spinal taps were falsely presented to subjects as cures for syphilis. Thirteen journal articles reported the study during this time, but it continued uninterrupted. As reported by James Jones (1981) in his book on the Tuskegee experiment, *Bad Blood: The Tuskegee Syphilis Experiment*, "None of the health officers connected with the Tuskegee Study expressed any ethical concern until critics started asking questions" (p. 190). In fact, when a member of the medical profession first objected to the study (in 1965), he got no reply to his letter to the Centers for Disease Control, which read,

> I am utterly astounded by the fact that physicians allow patients with a potentially fatal disease to remain untreated when effective therapy is available. I assume you feel that the information which is extracted from observations of this untreated group is worth their sacrifice. If this is the case, then I suggest that the United States Public Health Service and those physicians associated with it need to reevaluate their moral judgments in this regard. (Jones, 1981, p. 190)

Jones reported that this letter was simply filed away with the following note stapled to it by one of the authors of one of the articles that reported the study: "This is the first letter of this type we have received. I do not plan to answer this letter." In December 1965, Peter Buxtun, who was trained as a social worker while in the U.S. Army, was hired by the Public Health Service as a venereal disease interviewer. Buxtun soon learned of the Tuskegee study from coworkers, and after studying published articles on it, he became relentless in his efforts to intervene. A series of letters to and difficult meetings with high-ranking officials ultimately prompted them to convene a committee to review the experiment, but that committee decided against treating the study's subjects.

Buxtun then went to the press, which exposed the study to the public in 1972. This exposure

Photo from the Tuskegee Syphilis Study.

prompted U.S. Senate hearings on the study. Subsequently, in the mid-1970s, the men were treated with antibiotics, as were their wives, who had contracted the disease, and their children, who had it congenitally (Royse, 1991). According to Jones (1981, p. 203), it was the social worker Peter Buxtun—aided by the press—who deserves the ultimate responsibility for stopping the Tuskegee study.

EP 4, 9

» INSTITUTIONAL REVIEW BOARDS

In response to notoriously unethical research experiments such as the Tuskegee study, federal law now governs research ethics in studies involving humans. Any agency (such as a university or a hospital) wishing to receive federal research support must establish an institutional review board (IRB), a panel of faculty and nonfaculty who review all research proposals involving human subjects and rule on their ethics. Their aim is to protect the subjects' rights and interests. The law applies

specifically to federally funded research, but many universities apply the same standards and procedures to all research, including that funded by nonfederal sources and even research done at no cost, such as student projects.

The chief responsibility of an IRB is to protect the rights and interests of human participants in research and ensure that the risks they face by participating are minimal and justified by the expected benefits of the research. In some cases, the IRB may refuse to approve a study or may ask the researcher to revise the study design. IRBs may continue to oversee studies after they are implemented, and they may decide to suspend or terminate their approval of a study.

The sections that follow describe the key ethical guidelines that IRB panelists consider when reviewing and deciding whether to approve a proposed study. When we consider research such as the Tuskegee study, it is not hard to find the ethical violations and to agree that the research was blatantly unethical. However, some ethical violations in social work research can be subtle, ambiguous, and arguable. Sometimes there is no correct answer to the situation, and people of goodwill can disagree.

Consequently, reasonable people might disagree about whether some studies are ethical—and whether the risks are outweighed by the expected benefits. Thus, there is no guarantee that every IRB decision will be the "correct" or best decision about the ethics of a proposed project. Later in this chapter, after we examine these ethical issues, we'll look at various IRB regulations that researchers must comply with and IRB forms that researchers must complete. We'll also discuss an example of IRB imperfection—in this case, having to do with prejudice and inconsistency regarding research with lesbian, gay, and bisexual populations.

EP 1

Voluntary Participation and Informed Consent

Social work research often—though not always—represents an intrusion into people's lives. The interviewer's knock on the door or the arrival of a questionnaire in the mail signals the beginning of an activity that the respondent has not requested and that may require a significant portion of his or her time and energy. Participation in research disrupts the subject's regular activities.

Social work research, moreover, often requires that people reveal personal information about themselves—information that may be unknown to their friends and associates. And social work research often requires that such information be revealed to strangers. Social work practitioners also require such information, but their requests may be justified on the grounds that the information is required for them to serve the respondent's personal interests. Social work researchers cannot necessarily make this claim, perhaps being able to argue only that their efforts will ultimately help the entire target population of people in need.

A major tenet of research ethics is that participation must be voluntary. No one should be forced to participate. All participants must be aware that they are participating in a study, be informed of all the consequences of the study, and consent to participate in it. This norm might not apply to certain studies. For example, if a community organization measures the amount and speed of automobile traffic at a busy intersection near a school as part of an effort to convince the city to erect a traffic light, it would not need to obtain informed consent from the drivers of every automobile it observes passing through the intersection.

The norm of voluntary participation is far easier to accept in theory than to apply in practice. Again, medical research provides a useful parallel. Many experimental drugs are tested on prisoners. In the most rigorously ethical cases, the prisoners are told the nature—and the possible dangers—of an experiment; that participation is completely voluntary; and, further, that they can expect no special rewards, such as early parole, for participation. Even under these conditions, some volunteers clearly are motivated by the belief that they will personally benefit from their cooperation.

When the instructor in a social work class asks students to fill out a questionnaire that he or she hopes to analyze and publish, students should always be told that their participation in the survey is completely voluntary. Even so, most students will fear that nonparticipation will somehow affect their grade. The instructor should be especially sensitive to such beliefs in implied sanctions and make special provisions to obviate them. For example, the instructor could leave the room while the questionnaires are being completed. Or students could be asked to return the questionnaires by mail or drop them in a box near the door just before the next course meeting.

You should be clear that this norm of voluntary participation goes directly against several scientific concerns we'll be discussing later in this text. One such concern involves the scientific goal of *generalizability*, which is threatened to the extent that the kinds of people who would willingly participate in a particular research study are unlike the people for whom the study seeks generalizations. Suppose that the questionnaire assesses student attitudes about the feminization of poverty and that only a minority of students voluntarily participate—those who care the most deeply about feminism and the poor. With such a small group of respondents, the instructor would have no basis for describing student attitudes in general, and if he or she did generalize the findings to the entire student population, then the generalizations might be seriously misleading.

The need, in some studies, to conceal the nature of the study from those being observed is another scientific concern that is compromised by the norm of voluntary participation and informed consent. This need stems from the fear that participants' knowledge about the study might significantly affect the social processes being studied among those participants. Often, the researcher cannot reveal that a study is even being done. Rosenhan (1973), for example, reported a study in which the research investigators posed as patients in psychiatric hospitals to assess whether hospital clinical staff members, who were unaware of the study, could recognize "normal" individuals (presumably the investigators) who (presumably) did not require continued hospitalization. (The results suggested that they could not.) Had the subjects of that study—that is, the clinical staff members—been given the opportunity to volunteer or refuse to participate, then the study would have been so severely compromised that it would probably not have been worth doing. What point would there be to such a study if the clinical staff was aware that the investigators were posing as patients?

But the fact that the norm of voluntary participation and informed consent may be impossible to follow does not alone justify conducting a study that violates it. Was the study reported by Rosenhan justified? Would it have been more ethical not to conduct the study at all? That depends on whether the long-term good derived from that study—that is, observations and data on the identification, understanding, and possible amelioration of problems in psychiatric diagnosis and care—outweighs the harm done in denying clinical staff the opportunity to volunteer or refuse to participate in the study. The need to judge whether a study's long-term benefits will outweigh its harm from ethically questionable practices also applies to ethical norms beyond voluntary participation, and thus we will return to it later. The norm of voluntary participation and informed consent is important. In cases where you feel ultimately justified in violating it, it is all the more important that you observe the other ethical norms of scientific research, such as bringing no harm to the people under study. Regardless of how you may feel about the norm of voluntary participation and informed consent, if your study involves human subjects, then you will probably have to obtain the approval of its ethics from your IRB, which will probably require participants to sign a consent form before they participate in your study. The consent form should provide full information about the features of the study that might affect their decision to participate, particularly regarding the procedures of the study, potential harm, and anonymity and confidentiality.

IRB consent forms can be quite detailed. Separate forms are required if children are research participants. If you conduct a study involving parents and children, for example, you will probably have to use one consent form for parents that might be several pages long, another form for parents to consent to their child's participation, and a third form for the child to sign. The latter form usually is called an assent form and will be briefer and use simpler language that a child can understand. Likewise, to obtain truly informed consent, you should consider the reading level of prospective research participants and have a translated version if they do not speak English. Figure 5-1 displays a sample consent form (for parents) and an assent form (for children) for a fictitious study. It will give you an idea of the kinds of things that IRBs commonly require in consent forms.

No Harm to the Participants

Research should never injure the people being studied, regardless of whether they volunteer for the study, and your IRB will need to be persuaded that you have minimized the risk that harm will come to participants from your study. Perhaps the clearest instance of this norm in practice concerns the revealing of information that would embarrass them or endanger their home lives, friendships, jobs, and so forth.

Research participants can be harmed psychologically in the course of a study, and the researcher must be aware of the often-subtle dangers and guard against them. Research participants are often asked to reveal deviant behavior, attitudes they feel are unpopular, or personal characteristics they may feel are demeaning, such as low income, the receipt of welfare payments, and the like. Revealing such information is likely to make them feel at least uncomfortable.

Social work research projects may also force participants to face aspects of themselves that they do not normally consider. That can happen even when the information is not revealed directly to the researcher. In retrospect, a certain past behavior may appear unjust or immoral. The project, then, can be the source of a continuing personal agony for the participant. If the study concerns codes of ethical conduct, for example, the participant may begin questioning his or her own morality, and that personal concern may last long after the research has been completed and reported.

Although the fact often goes unrecognized, participants can be harmed by data analysis and reporting. Every now and then, research participants read the books published about the studies in which they have participated. Reasonably sophisticated participants will be able to locate themselves in the various indexes and tables. Having done so, they may find themselves characterized—though not identified by name—as bigoted, abusive, and so forth. At the very least, such characterizations are likely to trouble them and threaten their self-images. Yet the whole purpose of the research project may be to explain why some people are prejudiced and others are not.

By now, you should have realized that just about any research you might conduct runs at least some slight risk of harming people somehow. Like voluntary participation, not harming people is an easy norm to accept in theory but often difficult to ensure in practice. Although there is no way for the researcher to eliminate the possibility of harm, some study designs make harm more likely than others. If a particular research procedure seems likely to produce unpleasant effects for participants—asking survey respondents to report deviant behavior, for example—the researcher should have the firmest of scientific grounds for doing it. If the research design is essential and also likely to be unpleasant for participants, then you will find yourself in an ethical netherworld and may find yourself forced to do some personal agonizing. Although agonizing has little value in itself, it may be a healthy sign that you have become sensitive to the problem. And even if after your agonizing you are convinced that your study's benefits far outweigh its minimal risks of harm, your IRB may disagree with you. Some IRB panelists at times can be overzealous in refusing to approve valuable research projects whose benefits far outweigh their minimal risks of harm. IRB requirements not only guard against unethical research but also can reveal ethical issues that have been overlooked by even the most scrupulous of researchers.

Anonymity and Confidentiality

The protection of participants' identities is the clearest concern in the protection of their interests and well-being in survey research. If revealing their survey responses would injure them in any way, adherence to this norm becomes all the more important. Two techniques—*anonymity* and

confidentiality—will assist you in this regard, although the two are often confused.

Anonymity   A respondent has anonymity when the researcher cannot identify a given response with a given respondent. This means that an interview survey respondent can never be considered anonymous because an interviewer collects the information from an identifiable respondent. (We assume here that standard sampling methods are followed.) An example of anonymity would be a mail survey in which no identification numbers are put on the questionnaires before their return to the research office.

As we will see in Chapter 15 (on survey research), ensuring anonymity makes it difficult to keep track of who has or has not returned the questionnaires. Despite this problem, you may be advised to pay the necessary price in some situations. If you study drug abuse, for example, assuring anonymity may increase the likelihood and accuracy of responses. Also, you can avoid the position of being asked by authorities for the names of drug offenders. When respondents volunteer their names, such information can be immediately obliterated on the questionnaires.

Confidentiality   In a survey that provides confidentiality, the researcher is able to identify a given person's responses but essentially promises not to do so publicly. In an interview survey, for instance, the researcher would be in a position to make public the income reported by a given respondent, but the respondent is assured that this will not be done.

You can use several techniques to ensure better performance on this guarantee. To begin, interviewers and others with access to respondent identifications should be trained in their ethical responsibilities. As soon as possible, all names and addresses should be removed from questionnaires and replaced with identification numbers. A master identification file should be created that links numbers to names to permit the later correction of missing or contradictory information, but this file should not be available to anyone else except for legitimate purposes. Whenever a survey is confidential rather than anonymous, it is the researcher's responsibility to make that fact clear to respondents. Never use the term *anonymous* to mean *confidential*.

As in social work practice, situations can arise in social work research in which ethical considerations dictate that confidentiality not be maintained.

FIGURE 5.1 Sample Informed Consent Forms for a Fictitious Study

[Name of university]

You and your child are being invited to participate in a research study. This form provides you with information about the study. The Principal Investigator (the person in charge of this research) or his/her representative will also describe this study to you and answer all of your questions. Please read the information below and ask questions about anything you don't understand before deciding whether or not to take part. Your participation is entirely voluntary and you can refuse to participate without penalty or loss of benefits to which you are otherwise entitled.

Title of Research Study:

The Effectiveness Of Trauma-Focused Cognitive Behavioral Therapy (TFCBT) in the Treatment of Posttraumatic Stress Disorder (PTSD) in Mexican-American Children Who Have Been Sexually Abused

Name of Principal Investigator (PI):

Funding source:

Purpose of the study:

This study aims to conduct a randomized experimental evaluation of the effectiveness of TFCBT in alleviating the symptoms of Posttraumatic Stress Disorder (PTSD) among 84 Mexican-American children aged 6 to 12 who receive services at the [Name of agency] who had been victims of sexual abuse before entering the center but who are no longer being abused.

What will you be asked to do if you participate in this research study?

If you decide to participate in this study, the Principal Investigator will use a scientific, random process (like a coin toss) that gives you and your child a 50% chance of being assigned to the group that receives TFCBT treatment along with all other Center services and a 50% chance of being assigned to the group that receives all the other Center services as well as therapy without TFCBT. If you are assigned to the group that does not receive TFCBT as part of your therapy, you will be offered TFCBT as part of your therapy three months later. In addition to the therapy services that you will receive, the study also involves you and/or your child completing some forms that will ask questions about the symptoms that are being experienced at the beginning and the end of the therapy. This study will take 12 weeks and will involve one hour sessions with your child, some longer sessions involving both you and your child, and some sessions involving only you. It will include approximately 60 study participants.

What are the possible discomforts and risks involved in this study?

Receiving TFCBT may involve risks that are currently unforeseeable. Possible risks associated with this study may include experiencing emotional discomfort during or after the therapy sessions. TFCBT requires the individual to recall memories that may be upsetting regarding their previous traumatic experiences. Since you are receiving services at an agency that employs mental health personnel, there will be assistance available should you or your child experience any discomfort during treatment. There is also a 24 hour a day, seven day a week call center that may be used if you experience discomfort during times when the agency is closed.

If you wish to discuss the information above or any other risks you may experience, you may ask questions now or call the Principal Investigator listed on the front page of this [form.]

What are the possible benefits of this study?

TFCBT has strong scientific evidence supporting its effectiveness with many sexually abused chiuldren. However, none of the studies so far have been done with Mexican-American children primarily. This study will provide evidence as to how effective TFCBT is with Mexican-American children. Finding this out will help in future decision making about what treatment approaches are most likely to be the most helpful for sexually abused Mexican-American children.

If you choose to take part in this study, will it cost you anything?

No.

Will you receive compensation for your participation in this study?

You will not receive any type of payment for participating in this study.

Do you have to participate?

Your participation is voluntary. You may decide not to participate at all or, if you start the study, you may withdraw at any time. Withdrawal or refusing to participate will not affect your relationship with [Name of university] or [Name of agency] in anyway. You and/or your child's refusal to participate will involve no penalty or loss of benefits to which you or your child are otherwise entitled. You may withdraw your consent, and your child may draw his/her assent, at any time and discontinue participation without penalty.

How can you withdraw from this research study and who should you call if you have questions?

If you wish to stop your participation in this research study for any reason, you should contact: [Name of PI] at [Telephone Number]. You are free to withdraw your consent and stop participation in this research study at any time without penalty or loss of benefits for which you may be entitled. Throughout the study, the researchers will notify you of new information that may become available and that might affect your decision to remain in the study. In addition, if you have questions about your rights as a research participant, please contact [Name and contact information of Institutional Review Board Chairperson].

FIGURE 5.1 *(Continued)*

How will your privacy and the confidentiality of your research records be protected?

Authorized persons from [Name of University] and the Institutional Review Board have the legal right to review your research records and will protect the confidentiality of those records to the extent permitted by law. If the research project is sponsored then the sponsor also has the legal right to review your research records. Otherwise, your research records will not be released without your consent unless required by law or a court order.

If the results of this research are published or presented at scientific meetings, your identity will not be disclosed.

Nine of the children who participate in this study will be selected at random to have one compact disc (CD) recording of one of their TFCBT therapy sessions. The CDs will be coded so that no personally identifying information is visible on them. They will be kept in a locked file cabinet in the PI's office. They will be viewed only for research purposes by the PI and her associates. They will be retained for possible future analysis.

Will the researchers benefit from your participation in this study?

The only ways that the researchers will benefit from your participation in this study is by publishing the results and presenting them at professional meetings.

Videorecording

Some of the TFCBT treatment sessions will be recorded for the purpose of checking to make sure that the TFCBT treatment is being provided as planned. Nobody other than the Principal Investigator and her Co-Principal Investigator will have access to see the videos. One year after completion of the study, all of the videos will be erased. Please check the appropriate box below to indicate whether you agree to have your TFCBT sessions videorecorded during this study. You can still participate in this study if you do not agree to the videorecording.

☐ I agree to the videorecording

☐ I do NOT agree to the videorecording

Signatures:

Your signature below indicates that you have been informed about this study's purpose, procedures, possible benefits and risks, and you have received a copy of this Form. You have been given the opportunity to ask questions before you sign, and you have been told that you can ask other questions at any time. You voluntarily agree to participate in this study. By signing this form, you are not waiving any of your legal rights.

_____

Printed Name of Child

_____   _____

Signature of Parent or Legal Guardian   **Date**

_____   _____

Signature of Child   **Date**

_____   _____

Signature of Principal Investigator   **Date**

ASSENT FORM FOR CHILDREN

The Effectiveness Of Trauma-Focused Cognitive Behavioral Therapy (TFCBT) in the Treatment of Posttraumatic Stress Disorder (PTSD) in Mexican-American Children Who Have Been Sexually Abused

I agree to be in a study about whether a new treatment helps kids like me feel happier and improve their behavior. This study was explained to my parent or guardian and they said that I could be in it. The only people who will know about what I say and do in the study will be the people in charge of the study.

I understand that in the treatment I receive my therapist might ask me to think and talk about things that I might not like to think or talk about. I also understand that if I want to stop doing it all I have to do is raise my hand or say, "Stop," and that nothing bad or wrong will happen to me if I decide to stop my participation in this study at any time.

Writing my name on this page means that the page was read by me or to me and that I agree to be in the study. I know what will happen to me. If I decide to quit the study, all I have to do is tell the person in charge.

_____   _____

Child's Signature   Date

_____   _____

Signature of PI   Date

Suppose that in the course of conducting your interviews, you learn that children are being abused or that respondents are at imminent risk of seriously harming themselves or others. It would be your professional (and perhaps legal) obligation to report this to the proper agency. Participants need to be informed of this possibility as part of the informed consent process before they agree to participate in a study.

There may be other situations in which government agents take legal action to acquire research data that you believe should remain confidential. For example, they may subpoena data on participants' drug use and thus legally force you to report this information. In 2002, the U.S. Department of Health and Human Services announced a program to issue a "Certificate of Confidentiality" to protect the confidentiality of research subject data against forced disclosure by the police and other authorities. Not all research projects qualify for such protection, but it can provide an important support for research ethics in many cases.

Under section 301(d) of the Public Health Service Act (42 U.S.C. 241[d]), the secretary of health and human services may authorize persons engaged in biomedical, behavioral, clinical, or other research to protect the privacy of individuals who are the subjects of that research. This authority has been delegated to the National Institutes of Health (NIH):

Persons authorized by the NIH to protect the privacy of research subjects may not be compelled in any federal, state, or local civil, criminal, administrative, legislative, or other proceedings to identify them by name or other identifying characteristic. (http://grants.nih.gov/grants/policy/coc/index.htm)

The box "Certificates of Confidentiality" provides an example of the language used in these certificates.

EP 9

Deceiving Participants

We've seen that handling participants' identities is an important ethical consideration. Handling your own identity as a researcher can be tricky, also. Sometimes it's useful and even necessary to identify yourself as a researcher to those you want to study. You'd have to be a master con artist to get people to complete a lengthy questionnaire without letting on that you were conducting research.

Even when it's possible and important to conceal your research identity, there is an important ethical dimension to consider. Deceiving people is unethical, and within social research, deception needs to be justified by compelling scientific or administrative concerns. Even then, the justification will be arguable, and your IRB may not buy your justification. The IRB must be convinced that the deception is necessary, presents no more than minimal risk to participants, and will not adversely affect participant rights. In addition, participants must be debriefed after participation regarding pertinent information about the deception and why it was necessary. The IRB might waive the debriefing requirement in rare instances when the debriefing poses more risk of harm to participants than the deception itself, such as when participants were not aware that they were invited to participate in the study because of information that would be very painful for them to learn about.

Sometimes, researchers admit they are doing research but fudge about why they are doing it or for whom. Suppose you've been asked by a public welfare agency to conduct a study of living standards among aid recipients. Even if the agency is looking for ways of improving conditions, the recipient participants are likely to fear a witch hunt for "cheaters." They might be tempted, therefore, to give answers that make themselves seem more destitute than they really are. Unless they provide truthful answers, however, the study will not produce accurate data that will contribute to an effective improvement of living conditions. What do you do? One solution would be to tell participants that you are conducting the study as part of a university research program—concealing your affiliation with the welfare agency. Doing that improves the scientific quality of the study but raises a serious ethical issue in the process.

Analysis and Reporting

As a social work researcher, then, you have several ethical obligations to the participants in your study. At the same time, you have ethical obligations to your professional colleagues. A few comments on those latter obligations are in order.

In any rigorous study, the researcher should be more familiar than anyone else with the study's technical shortcomings and failures. You have an obligation to make them known to your readers. Even though you may feel foolish admitting mistakes, you should do it anyway. Negative findings should be reported if they are at all related to your analysis. There is an unfortunate myth in scientific reporting that only positive discoveries are worth reporting (and journal editors are sometimes guilty of believing that as well). In science, however, it is often just as important to know that two variables are not related as to know that they are. If, for example, an experiment finds no difference in outcome between clients treated and not treated with a tested intervention, then it is important for practitioners to know that they might need to consider alternative interventions—particularly if the same null finding is replicated in other studies. And replication would not be possible if the original experiment were not reported.

The ethical importance of reporting negative findings in studies evaluating the effectiveness of interventions, programs, or policies is particularly apparent in the evidence-based practice (EBP) process (as discussed in Chapter 2). Suppose you are conducting an EBP search looking for interventions with the best evidence supporting their effectiveness for the problem presented by your client and you find a well-designed study supporting the effectiveness of a relevant intervention that we'll call intervention A. If you find no other studies with contradictory findings, you might be tempted to deem intervention A the one with the best evidence base for your client's problem. But suppose several other studies found intervention A to be ineffective for that problem but were not reported because the investigators believed that no one is interested in hearing about interventions that don't work. In reality, then, interventions other than intervention A might have better, more consistent evidence supporting their effectiveness, and if you knew of the studies with negative findings about intervention A, you might propose one of those other interventions to your client. Moreover, suppose that your client is African American or Hispanic and that the one study supporting intervention A involved only Caucasian clients, whereas the other studies—the ones with negative results—involved African American or Hispanic clients. The ethical implications of not reporting those other studies should be apparent to you; not reporting them would mislead you into proposing the wrong, unhelpful intervention to your client.

Researchers should also avoid the temptation to save face by describing their findings as the product of a carefully preplanned analytic strategy when that is not the case. Many findings arrive unexpectedly—even though they may seem obvious in retrospect. So they uncovered an interesting relationship by accident—so what? Embroidering such situations with descriptions of fictitious hypotheses is dishonest and tends to mislead inexperienced researchers into thinking that all scientific inquiry is rigorously preplanned and organized.

In general, science progresses through honesty and openness, and it is retarded by ego defenses and deception. Researchers can serve their fellow researchers—and scientific discovery as a whole—by telling the truth about all the pitfalls and problems they have experienced in a particular line of inquiry. Perhaps that candor will save their colleagues from the same problems.

Weighing Benefits and Costs

We have noted that ethical considerations in the conduct of social work research often pose a dilemma. The most ethical course of action for researchers to take is not always clear-cut. Sometimes it is difficult to judge whether the long-term good to be derived from a study will outweigh the harm done by the ethically questionable practices that may be required for adequate scientific validity. Consider, for example, the study in which a team of researchers deceptively posed as hospitalized mental patients, concealing their identity from direct care staff members to study whether the staff could recognize their normalcy.

Earlier we asked whether the potential benefits of the study—regarding psychiatric diagnosis and care—justified violating the norm of voluntary participation by direct staff. What if the purpose of that study had been to verify whether suspected physical abuse of patients by staff was taking place? Suppose that an appalling amount of staff neglect and abuse of patients really was occurring and that the researchers uncovered it. Would the potential benefits to current and future patients to be derived from exposing and perhaps reforming the quality of care outweigh using deception in the research?

If alternative ways to conduct the research are available—that is, ways that can provide equally valid and useful answers to the research question without engaging in ethically questionable research practices—then the dilemma will be resolved and an alternate methodology can be chosen. Indeed, IRBs can be zealous in identifying a possible alternative methodology and perhaps insisting that it be used

CERTIFICATES OF CONFIDENTIALITY

The following was downloaded from the website of the U.S. Department of Health and Human Services at http://grants.nih.gov/grants/policy/coc/appl_extramural.htm:

> When a researcher obtains a Certificate of Confidentiality, the research subjects must be told about the protections afforded by the certificate and any exceptions to that protection. That information should be included in the informed consent form. Examples of appropriate language follow. Researchers may adapt the language to the needs of the research participants and to the subject matter of the study. However, the language used must cover the basic points.
>
> Researchers should also review the language about confidentiality and data security that is routinely included in consent forms to be certain that it is consistent with the protections of the Certificate of Confidentiality.
>
> Example:
>
> To help us protect your privacy, we have obtained a Certificate of Confidentiality from the National Institutes of Health. With this Certificate, the researchers cannot be forced to disclose information that may identify you, even by a court subpoena, in any federal, state, or local civil, criminal, administrative, legislative, or other proceedings. The researchers will use the Certificate to resist any demands for information that would identify you, except as explained below.
>
> The Certificate cannot be used to resist a demand for information from personnel of the United States Government that is used for auditing or evaluation of Federally funded projects or for information that must be disclosed in order to meet the requirements of the federal Food and Drug Administration (FDA).
>
> You should understand that a Certificate of Confidentiality does not prevent you or a member of your family from voluntarily releasing information about yourself or your involvement in this research. If an insurer, employer, or other person obtains your written consent to receive research information, then the researchers may not use the Certificate to withhold that information.
>
> [The researchers should include language such as the following if they intend to make voluntary disclosure about things such as child abuse, intent to hurt self or others, or other voluntary disclosures.] The Certificate of Confidentiality does not prevent the researchers from disclosing voluntarily, without your consent, information that would identify you as a participant in the research project under the following circumstances. [The researchers should state here the conditions under which voluntary disclosure would be made. If no voluntary disclosures will be made, the researchers should so state.]

even if you think it is much less likely to produce valid and unbiased results.

But sometimes no such alternatives appear. If not, then how researchers resolve this dilemma will depend on the values they attach to the various costs and benefits of the research and whether they believe that some ends can ever justify some means. No objective formula can be applied to this decision; it is inherently subjective. Some individuals would argue that the end never justifies the means. Others might disagree about which particular ends justify which particular means. Even if you resolve this dilemma in your own mind, you will probably find it very difficult to get all the members of your IRB to agree with you.

The box "An Illustration: Living with the Dying—Use of Participant Observation" provides one example of how the long-term good to be derived from a study may have justified violating ethical guidelines. This study, which involved deceiving participants and not obtaining their informed consent to participate, might be of special interest to students who are interested in practicing social work in a medical or hospice setting.

EP 9

Right to Receive Services versus Responsibility to Evaluate Service Effectiveness

Perhaps the most critical ethical dilemma in social work research pertains to the right of clients in need to receive services and whether the benefit of improving the welfare of clients in the long run ever justifies delaying the provision of services to some clients in the short run. Practitioners engaged in the EBP process will search for the best available evidence about the effectiveness of services. As mentioned in Chapter 2, at the top of the EBP research hierarchies for evaluating service effectiveness are studies (and reviews of such studies) with the strongest designs for making inferences about whether the service provided or something else most plausibly explains variations in client outcome. Those designs involve experiments that evaluate the effectiveness of services by comparing the fates of clients who receive the service being evaluated and those from whom the service is withheld. (We will examine experiments in depth in Chapter 12.) Two values are in conflict here: doing something to try to provide immediate help to people in need and the professional's responsibility to ensure that the services clients receive have had their effects—either beneficial or harmful—scientifically tested.

Some researchers argue that individuals in need should never be denied service for any period or for any research purposes. Others counter that the service being delayed is one whose effects, if any, have not yet been scientifically verified—otherwise, there would be no need to test it. How ethical, they ask, is it to provide the same services perennially without ever scientifically verifying whether those services are really helping anyone or are perhaps harmful? And if they are potentially harmful, are those who receive them actually taking a greater risk than those who are temporarily denied them until their effects are gauged? Using another medical parallel, would you think your physician was ethical if he or she treated you with a drug knowing that the beneficial or harmful effects of that drug were as yet untested? If you were being paid to participate in a medical experiment to test the effectiveness of a drug whose benefits and negative side effects were as yet unknown, which group would you feel safer in: the group receiving the drug or the group not receiving it?

The seriousness of the client's problem is one factor that bears on this dilemma. It would be much harder to justify the delay of service to individuals who are experiencing a dangerous crisis or are at risk of seriously harming themselves—suicidal clients, for example—than to those in less critical need. Another factor is the availability of alternative interventions to which the tested intervention can be compared. Perhaps those who are denied the tested service can receive another one that might prove to be no less beneficial.

If alternative interventions are available, then the conflict between the right to service and the responsibility to evaluate can be alleviated. Instead of comparing clients who receive a new service being tested to those who receive no service, we can compare them to those who receive a routine set of services that was in place before the new one was developed. This is a particularly ethical way to proceed when insufficient resources are available to provide the new service to all or most clients who seek service. This way, no one is denied service, and the maximum number that resources permit receives the new service.

Another way to reduce the ethical dilemma when resources don't permit every client to receive the new service is to assign some clients to a waiting list for the new service. As they wait their turn for the new service, they can be compared to the clients currently receiving the new service. Ultimately, everyone is served, and the waiting-list clients should be free to refuse participation in the study without being denied services eventually.

EP 1

National Association of Social Workers Code of Ethics

If decisions about the ethics of research involve subjective value judgments in which we must weigh the potential benefits of the research against its potential costs to research participants and if we must make those decisions in light of various idiosyncratic factors, then those decisions pose dilemmas for which there may be no right or wrong answers. But researchers can do some things to be as ethical as possible. They can obtain collegial feedback as to the ethics of their proposed research. They should carefully consider whether there are ethically superior alternatives and strive to ensure that their research proposal is the most ethical one that they can conceive. And, of course, they must obtain approval from their IRB.

To guide them in this endeavor, various professional associations have created and published formal codes of conduct to cover research ethics. Figure 5-2 shows the codes from the "Evaluation and Research" section of the National Association of Social Workers (NASW) Code of Ethics. Although those codes provide ethical guidelines for conducting research, another section—on social workers' ethical responsibilities as professionals—reminds us that we can violate our ethical responsibilities as professionals not only when we conduct research but also when we refrain from using it to inform our practice. It is worded as follows:

> Social workers should critically examine and keep current with emerging knowledge relevant to social work. Social workers should routinely review the professional literature.... Social workers should base practice on recognized knowledge, including empirically based knowledge, relevant to social work and social work ethics. (NASW, 1999, Section 4.01)

IRB Procedures and Forms

IRBs vary in the amount and format of materials they require to describe the proposed research. In the process of deciding whether to approve a research proposal, an IRB may require certain modifications to make the research acceptable, such as providing additional information to participants before their consent to participate is obtained. For example, some social work research studies might involve situations in which ethical considerations dictate that confidentiality not be maintained, such as when child abuse is unexpectedly encountered or when respondents are at imminent risk of seriously harming themselves or others. You may need to add this contingency to your own consent form and IRB application form. You may also need to assure your participants and your IRB that you will arrange for services to be offered to any participant you encounter who needs them. Because they vary so much, we suggest that you examine your university's IRB forms and procedures, which may be accessible online.

Training Requirement

One regulation that does not vary is the responsibility of IRBs to require education on the protection of human research participants for each individual investigator and research assistant working on studies involving human subjects. Your institution might offer its own educational program on the protection of research participants. Alternatively, you can obtain free online training at the NIH ethics tutorial website at https://phrp.nihtraining.com/.

If you take the online tutorial at this site, you will receive a certificate of completion that some IRBs now require of principal investigators and their research assistants working on studies involving human subjects. This certificate might therefore come in handy later on if you become a research assistant or need IRB approval for your research. You might also ask your instructor if extra credit could be granted for obtaining this certificate.

Expedited Reviews

If you are fortunate enough to have a research instructor who requires that you design and carry out a research project, then you may find that you have to get your study approved by your university's IRB before you can begin collecting data. Moreover, if your research project is to be carried out in an agency that receives federal money, you may have to obtain approval from both your school's IRB and the agency's IRB. Just what you needed, right? Don't panic. Perhaps your study will qualify for an exemption from a full review and you'll be able to obtain approval within a relatively short time (perhaps as short as a few days). Federal regulations allow IRBs to grant exemptions to certain kinds of studies, although institutions vary considerably in interpreting the federal regulations. Exempt studies receive an expedited review. The box "Federal Exemption Categories for Expedited Reviews" lists the guidelines for qualifying for an exemption from a full review. Additional federal regulations, however, exist for members of vulnerable populations such as pregnant women, prisoners, children and minors, cognitively impaired persons, and others. Google the search term "IRB vulnerable population," and you will see links to a variety of sites with lengthier lists and descriptions of vulnerable populations. Although the lists agree regarding the vulnerable populations mentioned above, there is some variation among them regarding additional ones.

Most student research (with the exception of doctoral dissertations) qualifies for at least one exemption. Note that studies that appear to meet one or more exemptions might still require a full review if participants can be identified, if knowledge of their responses could place them at risk of some sort of harm, if the data are sensitive, or if they are part of a vulnerable population. Also, if your study

AN ILLUSTRATION: LIVING WITH THE DYING—USE OF PARTICIPANT OBSERVATION

Buckingham, Lack, Mount, MacLean, and Collins (1976) wanted to compare the value of routine hospital care with hospice care for the terminally ill. (As we mentioned in Chapter 4, the emphasis in hospice care is on minimizing discomfort and maximizing quality of life, and this might entail eschewing medical procedures that prolong life but hinder its quality. Routine hospital care, in contrast, is more likely to emphasize prolonging life at all costs, even if that requires a lower quality of life for the dying patient. The routine approach is less attentive to the psychosocial and other nonmedical needs of the patient and family.)

Buckingham wanted to observe and experience the treatment of a terminally ill patient in two wards of a hospital: the surgical care (nonhospice) ward and the palliative care (hospice) ward. For his observations to be useful, it was necessary that staff members and other patients on his ward not know what he was doing. The steps that he took to carry out his deception are quite remarkable. Before entering the hospital, he lost 22 pounds on a 6-month diet. (He was naturally thin before starting his diet.) He submitted himself to ultraviolet radiation so that he would look as if he had undergone radiation therapy. He had puncture marks from intravenous needles put on his hands and arms so that he would look as if he had undergone chemotherapy. He underwent minor surgery for the sole purpose of producing biopsy scars. He learned how to imitate the behavior of patients dying with pancreatic cancer by reviewing their medical charts and maintaining close contact with them. Finally, for several days before entering the hospital, he grew a patchy beard and abstained from washing.

Buckingham stayed in the hospital 10 days, including 2 days in a holding unit, 4 days in the surgical care unit, and 4 days in the hospice unit. His findings there supported the advantages of hospice care for the terminally ill. For example, on the

surgical care ward, he observed staff communication practices that were insufficient, impersonal, and insensitive. Physicians did not communicate with patients. Staff members in general avoided greeting patients, made little eye contact with them, and often referred to them by the names of their diseases rather than by their personal names. Complacent patients did not receive affection. The negative aspects of the patients' conditions were emphasized.

Buckingham's observations on the hospice ward, however, were quite different. Staff maintained eye contact with patients. They asked questions about what the patients liked to eat and about other preferences. They asked patients how they could be more helpful. They listened to patients accurately, unhurriedly, and empathically. Physicians spent more time communicating with patients and their families. Staff encouraged family involvement in the care process. It is not difficult to see the value of Buckingham's findings in regard to enhancing the care of the terminally ill and their families. In considering whether the benefits of those findings justify Buckingham's particular use of deception, several other aspects of the study might interest you.

Before entering the hospital, Buckingham engaged the hospital's top medical, administrative, and legal staff members in planning and approving the study. (They had no IRB at that time.) The heads of both the surgery ward and the hospice ward also participated in the planning and approved the study. In addition, the personnel of the hospice ward were informed in advance that their unit was going to be evaluated, although the nature of the evaluation was not revealed. Finally, an ad hoc committee was formed to consider the ethics of the study, and the committee approved the study. In light of these procedures and this study's benefits, it may not surprise you to learn that no ethical controversy emerged in response to this study.

involves some controversial procedures—such as pretending to faint every time your instructor mentions statistics so that you can see whether research instructors are capable of exhibiting

compassion or whether this is an effective way to influence exam content—then obtaining IRB approval may be problematic (not to mention what it will do to your grade when the instructor

FIGURE 5.2   NASW Code of Ethics

Section 5.02 Evaluation and Research

(a)   Social workers should monitor and evaluate policies, the implementation of programs, and practice interventions.

(b)   Social workers should promote and facilitate evaluation and research to contribute to the development of knowledge.

(c)   Social workers should critically examine and keep current with emerging knowledge relevant to social work and fully use evaluation and research evidence in their professional practice.

(d)   Social workers engaged in evaluation or research should carefully consider possible consequences and should follow guidelines developed for the protection of evaluation and research participants. Appropriate institutional review boards should be consulted.

(e)   Social workers engaged in evaluation or research should obtain voluntary and written informed consent from participants, when appropriate, without any implied or actual deprivation or penalty for refusal to participate; without undue inducement to participate; and with due regard for participants' well-being, privacy, and dignity. Informed consent should include information about the nature, extent, and duration of the participation requested and disclosure of the risks and benefits of participation in the research.

(f)   When evaluation or research participants are incapable of giving informed consent, social workers should provide an appropriate explanation to the participants, obtain the participants' assent to the extent they are able, and obtain written consent from an appropriate proxy.

(g)   Social workers should never design or conduct evaluation or research that does not use consent procedures, such as certain forms of naturalistic observation and archival research, unless rigorous and responsible review of the research has found it to be justified because of its prospective scientific, educational, or applied value and unless equally effective alternative procedures that do not involve waiver of consent are not feasible.

(h)   Social workers should inform participants of their right to withdraw from evaluation and research at any time without penalty.

(i)   Social workers should take appropriate steps to ensure that participants in evaluation and research have access to appropriate supportive services.

(j)   Social workers engaged in evaluation or research should protect participants from unwarranted physical or mental distress, harm, danger, or deprivation.

(k)   Social workers engaged in the evaluation of services should discuss collected information only for professional purposes and only with people professionally concerned with this information.

(l)   Social workers engaged in evaluation or research should ensure the anonymity or confidentiality of participants and of the data obtained from them. Social workers should inform participants of any limits of confidentiality, the measures that will be taken to ensure confidentiality, and when any records containing research data will be destroyed.

(m)   Social workers who report evaluation and research results should protect participants' confidentiality by omitting identifying information unless proper consent has been obtained authorizing disclosure.

(n)   Social workers should report evaluation and research findings accurately. They should not fabricate or falsify results and should take steps to correct any errors later found in published data using standard publication methods.

(o)   Social workers engaged in evaluation or research should be alert to and avoid conflicts of interest and dual relationships with participants, should inform participants when a real or potential conflict of interest arises, and should take steps to resolve the issue in a manner that makes participants' interests primary.

(p)   Social workers should educate themselves, their students, and their colleagues about responsible research practices.

Source: Copyright © 1999, National Association of Social Workers, Inc. NASW Code of Ethics.

reads your report). Other (more realistic) problematic examples include surveys on sensitive topics, such as drug abuse or sexual practices, or on traumatic events that may be painful for respondents to remember.

Whether or not you seek an expedited review and no matter how sure you are that your proposed research is ethical, it would be prudent to submit your IRB application as early as possible. Suppose

that you hope to complete your data collection before the end of the spring semester—perhaps during the month of May—and your IRB meets to review proposals at the end of each month. Suppose further that it will take you 1 month to complete your data collection. If you submit your application in March and it gets an expedited review, you are probably in the clear. But what if your IRB perceives (or perhaps misperceives) something

FEDERAL EXEMPTION CATEGORIES FOR EXPEDITED REVIEWS

Studies that may qualify for an expedited review are as follows:

1. Research conducted in established or commonly accepted educational settings, involving normal educational practices, such as (a) research on regular and special education instructional strategies or (b) research on the effectiveness of or the comparison among instructional techniques, curricula, or classroom management methods.

2. Research involving the use of educational tests (cognitive, diagnostic, aptitude, or achievement), survey procedures, interview procedures or observation of public behavior, unless (a) information obtained is recorded in such a manner that human subjects can be identified, directly or through identifiers linked to the subjects, and (b) any disclosure of the human subjects' responses outside the research could reasonably place the subjects at risk of criminal or civil liability or be damaging to the subjects' financial standing, employability, or reputation.

3. Research involving the use of educational tests (cognitive, diagnostic, aptitude, or achievement), survey procedures, interview procedures, or observation of public behavior that is not exempt under paragraph (b)(2) of this section if (a) the human subjects are elected or appointed public officials or candidates for public office or (b) federal statute(s) require(s) without exception that the confidentiality of the personally identifiable information will be maintained throughout the research and thereafter.

4. Research involving the collection or study of existing data, documents, records, pathological specimens, or diagnostic specimens if these sources are publicly available or if the information is recorded by the investigator in such a manner that subjects cannot be identified directly or through identifiers linked to the subjects.

5. Research and demonstration projects that are conducted by or subject to the approval of department or agency heads and that are designed to study, evaluate, or otherwise examine (a) public benefit or service programs, (b) procedures for obtaining benefits or services under those programs, (c) possible changes in or alternatives to those programs or procedures, or (d) possible changes in methods or levels of payment for benefits or services under those programs.

6. Taste and food quality evaluation and consumer acceptance studies (a) if wholesome foods without additives are consumed or (b) if a food is consumed that contains a food ingredient at or below the level and for a use found to be safe, or agricultural chemical or environmental contaminant at or below the level found to be safe, by the Food and Drug Administration or approved by the Environmental Protection Agency or the Food Safety and Inspection Service of the US Department of Agriculture.

---

controversial in your proposal and does not grant an expedited review? Suppose further that it gets a full review at the end of March and, rather than approving it, your IRB raises questions and requires you to make significant modifications. Conceivably, that might delay obtaining approval until its next meeting at the end of April or perhaps even later. That might make it impossible to complete your data collection by the end of the spring semester, but had you submitted your IRB proposal a month or more earlier, you would still be able to meet your target date.

EP 2

Overzealous Reviewers

In our experience, we have found most IRB panelists and their support staff to be very reasonable people who make every effort to help investigators (especially students) obtain timely approval for their social work research projects. Occasionally, however, we have run into some IRB panelists who can, at times, be overzealous in their roles as protectors of research participants and in their interpretations of ethical guidelines.

One proposal, for example, included express mailing from Texas a videotape of five 1-hour therapy sessions (with five different clients) to a psychologist in Colorado and another psychologist in New York. The two psychologists were nationally known experts in the particular therapy being evaluated, and their task was to view each therapy session and rate the extent to which the therapist implemented the therapy appropriately. None of the therapy clients were named on the videos. Given that each therapy session was 1 hour long and in light of the busy schedules of the psychologists, it was expected that it might take them a week or more to find the time to rate all the sessions.

On reviewing the proposal, three IRB panelists insisted that the videotape not be express mailed. Instead, they wanted the investigator to carry the video with him on separate trips to Colorado and New York, stay there until the psychologists completed their ratings, and then personally carry the video back to Texas. Their rationale was that the video might get lost in the mail (despite being carefully labeled on the video itself with the researcher's address and so on) and that, if so, mail staff might watch it and recognize one of the clients.

Although far-fetched, such an eventuality was not impossible, and the IRB approval got delayed 1 month—until the next IRB meeting. At that next meeting, the investigator appeared and explained how he was conducting the project without funding as a volunteer at the request of a local residential treatment center (information that was already in the written proposal) and that, in light of that and the potential benefits of the study, it was unreasonable to require him to travel to those two sites and wait there for days instead of using express mail. The chair of the IRB enthusiastically agreed with the investigator and convinced most of the panelists to approve of the study. Nevertheless, in the final vote, the three panelists remained unmoved and voted in the minority against approval.

As illustrated in the foregoing example, although some IRB panelists can be overzealous, we have found most panelists and their support staff to be very reasonable people who make every effort to help investigators obtain timely approval for their social work research projects. But because some IRB members can be overzealous, you should submit your IRB proposal as early as possible and not be cavalier about the prospects for its swift approval. You'll need time to construct a careful, respectful, tactful response to their concerns, including changes to your proposal where appropriate.

Another illustration of these issues is discussed in the box: "IRB Imperfections Regarding Research with Lesbian, Gay, and Bisexual Populations."

»» FOUR ETHICAL CONTROVERSIES

As you may already have guessed, the advent of IRBs and the dissemination of professional codes of ethics have not prevented reasonable people from disagreeing about whether some research projects are ethically justified. In this section, we will describe four research projects that have provoked ethical controversy and discussion. These are not the only controversial projects that have been done, but they illustrate ethical issues in the real world, and we thought you'd find them interesting and perhaps provocative. The first two are from psychology and sociology. They were conducted before the advent of IRBs and are often cited as examples of the need for IRBs. The latter are from social work and were conducted later. As you read each, imagine how you would have responded had you been reviewing their proposals as an IRB member. We'll start with the notorious Milgram study.

Observing Human Obedience

One of the more unsettling rationalizations to come out of World War II was the German soldiers' common excuse for atrocities: "I was only following orders." From the point of view that gave rise to this comment, any behavior—no matter how reprehensible—could be justified if someone else could be assigned responsibility for it. If a superior officer ordered a soldier to kill a baby, then the fact of the order was said to exempt the soldier from personal responsibility for the action.

Although the military tribunals that tried the war crime cases did not accept the excuse, social scientists and others have recognized the extent to which this point of view pervades social life. Often people seem willing to do things they know would be considered wrong by others if they can cite some higher authority as ordering them to do it. Such was the pattern of justification in the My Lai tragedy of Vietnam, when US soldiers killed more than 300 unarmed civilians—some of them young children—simply because their village, My Lai, was believed to be a Vietcong stronghold. This sort of justification appears less dramatically in day-to-day civilian life.

IRB IMPERFECTIONS REGARDING RESEARCH WITH LESBIAN, GAY, AND BISEXUAL POPULATIONS

Several social work researchers (Lea Tufford and her colleagues, 2012) have described case studies that demonstrate how some IRB board members can be simultaneously overprotective and prejudiced in their efforts to protect the safety of lesbian, gay, and bisexual (LGB) research participants. Despite the noble intentions of these board members, their actions can "unwittingly manifest stigma against LGB populations" and present unwarranted obstacles to research of value to those populations (p. 222).

In one case study, the IRB—pertaining to proposed research which involved interviewing LGB MSW students—the board withheld approval because it was concerned that some students might divulge such things as a relationship with an underage partner, criminal activity, or involvement in a same-sex relationship. The investigators were shocked at the prejudicial nature of these concerns, but rather than deal with the board in a confrontational manner, they responded tactfully and asked the board members it would express the same concerns if the interviews were with heterosexual students. Their tactful response resulted in the IRB approving their research.

Another case study involved a research proposal to evaluate a classroom intervention educating social work students about the consequences of heterosexism. Part of the intervention to be evaluated included self-disclosure by gay instructors of their sexual orientation and discussions of the ways they experienced heterosexism. Because the study was to be conducted at two universities, separate IRB approvals had to be obtained by each university's IRB board. One of the boards granted an expedited review and approved the study without expressing any concerns. The other IRB, however, expressed concern that the instructor's self-disclosure might harm the students. As in the first case study, the researchers felt that the board's response reflected heterosexism in that they probably would not have reacted that way if instructors from a different disenfranchised group taught about oppression by discussing their experiences with discrimination. They also wondered if not divulging the instructors' sexual orientation—that is, keeping it a secret—contributed to the perpetuation of heterosexism. Again, however, rather than be confrontational with the IRB, they responded in a tactful, educational manner, resulting in IRB approval.

As Tufford and her colleagues point out, not only do these case studies illustrate inconsistencies between some IRBs and the fact that IRB board members can make mistakes and unwittingly perpetuate harm to the populations that they aim to protect, but also the case studies illustrate the importance of not reacting strongly and defensively to such mistakes. Researchers on the receiving end of mistaken and perhaps prejudicial reviews should not presume IRB members to be hostile or even unsympathetic to their aims. Instead, they should respond in a tactful manner that respects the concerns of the board members, that includes modifications to the research to meet appropriate board member concerns, and tries to explain things to board members as needed regarding elements of the research that need to remain unmodified or about prejudicial issues.

Few would disagree that this reliance on authority exists, yet Stanley Milgram's (1963, 1965) studies of the topic provoked considerable controversy.

To observe people's willingness to harm others when following orders, Milgram brought 40 adult men—from many different walks of life—into a laboratory setting that he designed to create the phenomenon under study. If you had been a subject in the experiment, you would have had something like the following experience.

You would have been informed that you and another subject were about to participate in a learning experiment. As the result of drawing lots, you would have been assigned the job of "teacher" and your fellow subject the job of "pupil." Your pupil then would have been led into another room, strapped into a chair, and had an electrode attached to his wrist. As the teacher, you would have been seated in front of an impressive electrical control panel covered with dials, gauges, and switches. You would have noticed that each switch had a label giving a different number of volts, ranging from 15 to 315. The switches would have had other labels, too, some with the ominous phrases "Extreme-Intensity Shock," "Danger—Severe Shock," and "XXX."

The experiment would run like this. You would read a list of word pairs to the learner and then test his ability to match them. You couldn't see him, but a light on your control panel would indicate his answer. Whenever the learner made a mistake, you would be instructed by the experimenter to throw one of the switches—beginning with the mildest—and administer a shock to your pupil. Through an open door between the two rooms, you'd hear your pupil's response to the shock. Then you'd read another list of word pairs and test him again.

As the experiment progressed, you'd be administering ever more intense shocks until your pupil was screaming for mercy and begging for the experiment to end. You'd be instructed to administer the next shock anyway. After a while, your pupil would begin kicking the wall between the two rooms and screaming. You'd be told to give the next shock. Finally, you'd read a list and ask for the pupil's answer—and there would only be silence from the other room. The experimenter would inform you that no answer was considered an error and instruct you to administer the next higher shock. This process would continue up to the "XXX" shock at the end of the series.

What do you suppose you really would have done when the pupil first began screaming? When he began kicking on the wall? Or, when he became totally silent and gave no indication of life? You'd refuse to continue giving shocks, right? And surely the same would be true of most people.

So we might think—but Milgram found out otherwise. Of the first 40 adult men Milgram tested, nobody refused to continue administering the shocks until they heard the pupil begin kicking the wall between the two rooms. Of the 40, five did so then. Two-thirds of the subjects, 26 of the 40, continued doing as they were told through the entire series—up to and including the administration of the highest shock.

As you've probably guessed, the shocks were phony, and the "pupil" was another experimenter. Only the "teacher" was a real subject in the experiment. You wouldn't have been hurting another person, even though you would have been led to think you were. The experiment was designed to test your willingness to follow orders—presumably to the point of killing someone.

Milgram's experiments have been criticized both methodologically and ethically. On the ethical side, critics particularly cited the effects of the experiment on the subjects. Many seem to have personally experienced about as much pain as they thought they were administering to someone else. They pleaded with the experimenter to let them stop giving the shocks. They became extremely upset and nervous. Some had uncontrollable seizures.

How do you feel about this research? Do you think the topic was important enough to justify such measures? Can you think of other ways in which the researcher might have examined obedience? There is a wealth of discussion regarding the Milgram experiments on the web. Search for "Milgram experiments," "human obedience experiments," or "Stanley Milgram."

Trouble in the Tearoom

The second illustration was conducted by a graduate student and published in a book called *Tearoom Trade: Impersonal Sex in Public Places*. Researcher Laud Humphreys (1970) wanted to study homosexual acts between strangers meeting in public restrooms in parks; the restrooms are called "tearooms" by those who used them for this purpose. Typically, the tearoom encounter involved three people: the two men actually engaged in the homosexual act and a lookout.

To gather observations for his study, Humphreys began showing up at public restrooms and offering to serve as a lookout whenever it seemed appropriate. Humphreys wanted to go beyond his observations as lookout and learn more about the people he was observing. Many of the participants were married men who wanted to keep their homosexuality secret and thus avoid being stigmatized and losing their status in their communities. They probably would not have consented to being interviewed. Instead of asking them for an interview, Humphreys tried to note the license plate numbers of their vehicles and then track down their names and addresses through the police. Then, disguising himself enough to avoid recognition, he visited the men at their homes and announced that he was conducting a survey. In that fashion, he collected the personal information he was unable to get in the restrooms.

Humphreys's research provoked considerable controversy both within and outside the social scientific community. Some critics charged Humphreys with a gross invasion of privacy in the name of science. What men did in public restrooms was their own business and not his. Others were concerned mostly about the deceit involved: Humphreys had lied to the participants by leading them to believe he was only participating as a voyeur. Some were more concerned with Humphreys's follow-up survey than with what he did in public facilities. They felt it was unethical for him to trace the participants to their houses and interview them under false pretenses. Still others justified Humphreys's research. The topic, they said, was worth study and could not be studied any other way. They considered the deceit to be essentially harmless, noting that Humphreys was careful not to harm his subjects by disclosing their tearoom activities.

The tearoom trade controversy, as you might imagine, has never been resolved. It is still debated—and probably will be for a long time—because it stirs emotions and contains ethical issues about which people disagree. What do you think? Was Humphreys ethical in doing what he did? Are there parts of the research you feel were acceptable and other parts that were not? Whatever you feel in the matter, you are sure to find others who disagree with you.

"Welfare Study Withholds Benefits from 800 Texans"

That was the front-page headline that greeted readers of the Sunday, February 11, 1990, edition of the *Dallas Morning News*. Then they read the following: "Thousands of poor people in Texas and several other states are unwitting subjects in a federal experiment that denies some government help to a portion of them to see how well they live without it."

This was pretty strong stuff, and soon the story was covered on one of the national television networks. Let's examine it further for our third illustration.

The Texas Department of Human Services received federal money to test the effectiveness of a pilot program that had been designed to wean people from the state's welfare rolls. The program was targeted to welfare recipients who found jobs or job training. Before the new program was implemented, these recipients received 4 months of free medical care and some child care after they left the welfare rolls. The new program extended these benefits to 1 year of Medicaid coverage and subsidized child care. The rationale was that extending the duration of the benefits would encourage recipients to accept and keep entry-level jobs that were unlikely to offer immediate medical insurance or child care.

The federal agency that granted the money attached an important condition: Receiving states were required to conduct a scientifically rigorous experiment to measure the program's effectiveness in attaining its goal of weaning people from welfare. Some federal officials insisted that this requirement entailed randomly assigning some people to a control group that would be denied the new (extended) program and would instead be kept on the old program (just 4 months of benefits). The point of this was to maximize the likelihood that the recipient group (the experimental group) and the nonrecipient (control) group were equivalent in all relevant ways except for the receipt of the new program. If they were and if the recipient group was weaned from welfare to a greater extent than the nonrecipient group, then it could be safely inferred that the new program and not something else caused the successful outcome. (We will examine this logic further in Chapters 11 and 12.)

If you have read many journal articles reporting on experimental studies, you are probably aware that many of them randomly assign about half of their participants to the experimental group and the other half to the control group. This routine procedure denies the experimental condition to approximately one-half of the participants. The Texas experiment was designed to include all eligible welfare recipients statewide, assigning 90% of them to the experimental group and 10% to the control group. Thus, only 10% of the participants, which in this study amounted to 800 people, would be denied the new benefits if they found jobs. Although this seems more humane than denying benefits to 50% of the participants, the newspaper account characterized the 800 people in the control group as "unlucky Texans" who seemed to be unfairly left out of a program that was extending benefits to everyone else who was eligible statewide and who numbered in the many thousands. Moreover, the newspaper report noted that the 800 control participants would be denied the new program for 2 years to provide ample time to compare outcomes between the two groups. To boot, these 800 "unlucky Texans" were not to be informed of the new program or of the experiment. They were to be told of only the normal 4-month coverage.

Advocates of the experiment defended this design, arguing that the control group would not be denied benefits. They would receive routine benefits, and the new benefits would not have been available for anyone in the first place unless a small group were randomly assigned to the routine policy. In other words, the whole point of the new benefits was to test a new welfare policy, not merely to implement one. The defenders further argued that the design was justified by the need to test for unintended negative effects of the new program, such as the possibility that some businesses might drop their child care or insurance coverage for employees, knowing that the new program was extending these benefits. That, in turn, they argued, could impel low-paid employees in those businesses to quit their jobs and go on welfare. By going on welfare and then getting new jobs, they would become eligible for the government's extended benefits, and this would make the welfare program more expensive.

Critics of the study, on the other hand, argued that it violated federal ethics standards, such as voluntary participation and informed consent. Anyone in the study must be informed about it and all its consequences and must have the option to refuse to participate. One national think-tank expert on ethics likened the experiment to the Tuskegee syphilis study (which we discussed earlier), saying, "It's really not that different." He further asserted, "People ought not to be treated like things, even if what you get is good information."

In the aftermath of such criticism, Texas state officials decided to try to convince the federal government to rescind the control group requirement so that the state could extend the new benefits to the 800 people in the control group. Instead of using a control group design, they wanted to extend benefits to everyone and find statistical procedures that would help ferret out program defects (a design that might have value but that would be less conclusive as to what really causes what, as we will see in later chapters). They also decided to send a letter to the control group members that explained their special status.

Two days after the *Dallas Morning News* broke this story, it published a follow-up article reporting that the secretary of the US Department of Health and Human Services, in response to the first news accounts, instructed his staff to cooperate with Texas welfare officials so that the project design would no longer deny the new program to the 800 control group members. Do you agree with his decision? Did the potential benefits of this experiment justify its controversial ethical practices?

A control group probably could not have been formed had recipients been given the right to refuse to participate. Who would want to be denied extended free medical and child-care benefits? Assuming that it were possible, however, would that influence your opinion of the justification for denying them the new program? Do you agree with the expert who claimed that this study, in its original design, was not that different from the Tuskegee syphilis study? Instead of assigning 90% of the participants to the experimental group, what if the study assigned only 10% to it? That way, the 800 assigned to the experimental group may have been deemed "lucky Texans," and the rest might not have been perceived as a small group of unlucky souls who were being discriminated against. In other words, perhaps there would have been fewer objections if the state had merely a small amount of funds to test out a new program on a lucky few. Do you think that would have changed the reaction? Would that influence your own perception of the ethical justification for the experiment?

Social Worker Submits Bogus Article to Test Journal Bias

Our final illustration is the first well-publicized ethical controversy to involve a social worker's research. National news media ran several stories on it, including two stories in the *New York Times* (September 27, 1988, pp. 21, 25; April 4, 1989, p. 21) and one in the *Chronicle of Higher Education* (November 2, 1988, pp. A1, A7). The information for this illustration was drawn primarily from those three news articles.

The social worker, William Epstein, started with the hypothesis that journal editors were biased in favor of publishing research articles whose findings confirmed the effectiveness of evaluated social work interventions and biased against publishing research articles whose findings failed to support the effectiveness of tested interventions. To test his hypothesis, Epstein fabricated a fictitious study that pretended to evaluate the effectiveness of a social work intervention designed to alleviate the symptoms of asthmatic children. (Some might deem asthma to be a psychosomatic illness.) Epstein concocted two versions of the bogus study. In one version, he fabricated findings that supported the effectiveness of the intervention; in the other version, he fabricated data that found the intervention to be ineffective.

Epstein submitted the fictitious article to 146 journals, including 33 social work journals and 113 journals in allied fields. Half of the journals received the version that supported the effectiveness of the intervention, and half received the other version. Epstein did not enter his own name as author of his fabricated article, instead using a pair of fictitious names.

In his real study, Epstein interpreted his findings as providing some support for his hypothesis: Journal editors were biased in favor of publishing the version of the bogus article with positive findings and against publishing the version with negative findings. Among the social work journals, for example, eight accepted the positive version, and only four accepted the negative version. Nine journals rejected the positive version, and 12 rejected the negative version. Among the journals in allied fields, 53% accepted the positive version, and only 14% accepted the negative version. A statistical analysis indicated that the degree of support these data provided for Epstein's hypothesis was "tentative" and not statistically significant.

After being notified of the acceptance or rejection of his fictitious article, Epstein informed each journal of the real nature of his study. Later, he submitted a true article under his own name that reported his real study to the *Social Service Review*, a prestigious social work journal. That journal rejected publication of his real study, and its editor, John Schuerman, led a small group of editors who filed a formal complaint against Epstein with the NASW. The complaint charged Epstein with unethical conduct on two counts: (a) deceiving the journal editors who reviewed the bogus article and (b) failing to obtain their informed consent to participate voluntarily in the study.

Schuerman, a social work professor at the University of Chicago and an author of some highly regarded research articles, recognized that sometimes the benefits of a study may warrant deceiving subjects and not obtaining their informed consent to

participate. But he argued that in Epstein's (real) study, the benefits did not outweigh the time and money costs incurred for many editors and reviewers to read and critique the bogus article and staff members to process it.

When an article is submitted for publication in a professional social work journal, it is usually assigned to several volunteer reviewers, usually social work faculty members who do not get reimbursed for their review work. The reviewers do not know who the author is so that the review will be fair and unbiased. Each reviewer is expected to read each article carefully (perhaps two or three times), recommend to the journal editor whether the article should be published, and develop specific suggestions to the author for improving the article. The journal editor also is usually a faculty member volunteering his or her own time as an expected part of one's professional duties as an academician. Schuerman noted that, in addition to the time and money costs mentioned, Epstein's experiment had exacted an emotional cost: "the chagrin and embarrassment of those editors who accepted the [bogus] article" (*New York Times*, September 27, 1988, p. 25).

Epstein countered that journal editors are not the ones to judge whether the benefits of his (real) study justified its costs. In his view, the editors are predisposed to value their own costs dearly. Thus, they are unlikely to judge any study that would deceive them as being worth those costs. Epstein argued that the journals are public entities with public responsibilities. Testing whether they are biased in deciding what to publish warranted his deception and the lack of informed consent to participate, actions that were necessary to test for their bias.

One might argue that if journal editors and reviewers are biased against publishing studies that fail to confirm the effectiveness of tested interventions, then the field may not learn that certain worthless interventions in vogue are not helping clients. Moreover, if several studies disagree about the effectiveness of an intervention and only those that confirm its effectiveness get published, then an imbalanced and selective set of replications conceivably might be disseminated to the field. This would mislead the field into believing that an intervention is yielding consistently favorable outcomes when, in fact, it is not. This could hinder the efforts of social workers to provide the most effective services to their clients—and therefore ultimately reduce the degree to which we enhance clients' well-being.

One could argue that Epstein's study could have been done ethically if he had forewarned editors that they might be receiving a bogus paper within a year and obtained their consent to participate in the study without knowing the specifics of the paper. An opposing viewpoint is that such a warning might affect the phenomenon being studied, tipping off the reviewers in a manner that predisposes them to be on guard not to reveal a real bias that actually does influence their publication decisions.

Some scholars who have expressed views somewhat sympathetic of Epstein's thesis have argued that journal editors and reviewers exert great influence on our scientific and professional knowledge base and therefore need to have their policies and procedures investigated. Schuerman, who filed the charges against Epstein, agreed with this view, but he argued that Epstein's study was not an ethical way to conduct such an investigation.

In an editorial in the *Social Service Review*, Schuerman (1989) elaborated his position. He noted that journals have low budgets and small staffs and depend heavily on volunteer reviewers "who see their efforts as a professional responsibility" and receive little personal or professional benefit for their work (p. 3). He also portrayed Epstein's research as "badly conducted," citing several design flaws that he deemed to be so serious that they render the anticipated benefits of the Epstein study as minimal and not worth its aforementioned costs. Schuerman also cited Epstein as admitting to serious statistical limitations in his study and to characterizing his research as only exploratory. "It is at this point that issues of research design and research ethics come together," Schuerman argued (p. 3). In other words, Schuerman's point is that the methodological quality of a study's research design can bear on its justification for violating ethical principles. If the study is so poorly designed that its findings have little value, it becomes more difficult to justify the ethical violations of the study on the grounds that its findings are so beneficial.

The initial ruling of the ethics board of the NASW was that Epstein had indeed violated research rules associated with deception and failure to get informed consent. It could have invoked serious sanctions against Epstein, including permanent revocation of his membership in the professional association and referral of the case to a state licensing board for additional sanctions. But Epstein was permitted to appeal the decision before any disciplinary action was taken. His appeal was upheld by the executive committee of the association, which concluded that his research did not violate its ethical rules. The committee exonerated Epstein, ruling that the case was a "disagreement about proper research methodology," not a breach of ethics. It did not publicize additional details of its rationale for upholding Epstein's appeal and reversing the initial ruling. Epstein speculated that the reversal might have been influenced by the publicity the case received in the press.

If Epstein's speculation is valid, then one might wonder whether the reversal was prompted by the executive committee's sincere judgment that the research really did not violate ethical rules or by expediency considerations, perhaps connected to concerns about potential future publicity or other costs. What do you think? What ideas do you have about the two rulings and about the ethical justification for Epstein's study? Which ruling do you agree with? Do you agree with Schuerman's contention that methodological flaws in the research design can bear on research ethics? Is it possible to agree with Schuerman on that issue and still agree with the executive committee that this case was a disagreement about methodology and not a breach of ethics? If, just for the sake of discussion, you assume that Epstein's study had serious design flaws that prevented the possibility of obtaining conclusive findings, then how would that assumption affect your position on the ethical justification for Epstein's study?

Suppose Epstein had obtained the advance approval of an IRB at his university for his study using a bogus article to test for journal bias. (Epstein told us that his university had no IRB at that time but that he did obtain informal feedback from some of his colleagues, who agreed that his study was ethical.) Had Epstein been able to obtain an IRB approval, even those who later depicted his study as unethical would have had no basis for charging him with unethical conduct. Instead, their complaint would have been with the IRB if it had approved his study. By not making the decision himself—and thus avoiding the chances that his own vested interests or ego involvement, if any, could have influenced his decision—Epstein would have been operating responsibly regardless of how some might later judge the ethics of the research method. Even if we deem Epstein's study to have been ethical, we can say that obtaining IRB approval (had it been possible for him to do so) would have protected Epstein from any ensuing ethical controversy. The case has an epilogue: Epstein completed a replication of his earlier study (Epstein, 2004). This time he obtained permission from his university's IRB to waive informed consent.

EP 1, 2

» BIAS AND INSENSITIVITY REGARDING SEX, GENDER IDENTITY, AND CULTURE

Several chapters of this book discuss examples of how bias and insensitivity regarding sex, gender identity, or culture can hinder the methodological quality of a study and therefore the validity of its findings. Much has been written about these problems in recent years, and some theorists have suggested that when researchers conduct studies in such a manner they are not only committing methodological errors but also going awry ethically.

The question of ethics arises because some studies are perceived to perpetuate harm to individuals who are women minorities, lesbian, gay, bisexual, or transgender. Feminist and minority scholars have suggested a number of ways that such harm can be done. Interviewers who are culturally insensitive can offend minority respondents. If they conduct their studies in culturally insensitive ways, then their findings may yield implications for action that ignore the needs and realities of minorities, may incorrectly (and perhaps stereotypically) portray minorities, or may inappropriately generalize in an unhelpful way. By the same token, studies with sex bias or insensitivity may be seen as perpetuating a male-dominated world or failing to consider the potentially different implications for men and women in one's research.

Various authors have recommended ways to avoid cultural and sex bias and insensitivity in one's research. We will cover these recommendations in greater depth in later chapters on methodology—especially Chapter 6 on culturally competent research—but we'll also mention them here in light of their potential ethical relevance.

Among the more commonly recommended guidelines regarding research on minorities are the following:

- Spend some time immersing yourself directly in the culture of the minority group(s) that will be included in your study (e.g., using qualitative research methods described in Chapters 18 and 19) before finalizing your research design.

- Engage minority scholars and community representatives in the formulation of the research problem and in all the stages of the research to ensure that the research is responsive to the needs and perspectives of minorities.

- Involve representatives of minority groups who will be studied in the development of the research design and measurement instruments.

- Do not automatically assume that instruments successfully used in prior studies of one ethnic group can yield valid information when applied to other ethnic groups.

- Use culturally sensitive language in your measures, perhaps including a non-English translation.

- Use in-depth pretesting of your measures to correct problematic language and flaws in translation.

- Use bilingual interviewers when necessary.

- Be attuned to the potential need to use minority interviewers instead of nonminorities to interview minority respondents.

- In analyzing your data, look for ways in which the findings may differ among different categories of ethnicity.

- Avoid an unwarranted focus exclusively on the deficits of minorities; perhaps focus primarily on their strengths.

- In addition to looking for differences among different ethnic groups, look for differences among varying levels of acculturation within specific minority groups.

- Assess your own cross-cultural competence.

- Look for cross-cultural studies in your literature review.

- Use specialized sampling strategies (discussed in Chapters 6 and 15) that are geared toward adequately representing minority groups.

In her book *Nonsexist Research Methods*, Margrit Eichler (1988) recommended the following feminist guidelines to avoid sex bias and insensitivity in one's research:

- If a study is done on only one of the categories of sex, make that clear in the title and the narrative and do not generalize the findings to the other category.

- Do not use sexist language or concepts (e.g., males referred to as "head of household," and females referred to as "spouses").

- Avoid using a double standard in framing the research question (such as looking at the work–parenthood conflict for mothers but not for fathers).

- Do not overemphasize male-dominated activities in research instruments (such as by assessing social functioning primarily in terms of career activities and neglecting activities in homemaking and child rearing).

- In analyzing your data, look for ways in which the findings might differ for men and women.

- Do not assume that measurement instruments used successfully with males are automatically valid for women.

- Be sure to report the proportion of males and females in your study sample.

>> THE POLITICS OF SOCIAL WORK RESEARCH

The line between ethical issues and politics and values in social work research is extremely fine. People disagree on political aspects of research just as they disagree on ethical ones. Although ethics and politics are often intertwined, the ethics of social work research deals more with the methods employed, whereas political issues are more concerned with the practical costs and use of research. Thus, for example, some social workers raise ethical objections to experiments that evaluate the effectiveness of social work services by providing those services to one group of clients while delaying their provision to another group of clients. Those who voice these objections say that the harm done to clients in delaying service provision outweighs the benefits to be derived from evaluating the effectiveness of those services. A political objection, on the other hand, might be that if the results of the evaluation were to suggest that the services were not effective, then those negative results might hurt agency funding. Another political objection might be that withholding services would reduce the amount of fees for service or third-party payments received, not to mention the bad publicity that would be risked regarding agency "neglect" of people in need.

Another distinction between ethical and political aspects of social work research is the absence of formal codes of accepted political conduct that are comparable to the codes of ethical conduct we discussed earlier. The only partial exception to the lack of political norms is in the generally accepted view that a researcher's personal political orientation should not interfere with or unduly influence his or her scientific research. It would be considered improper for you to use shoddy techniques or lie about your research as a way to further your political views. However, studies are often enough attacked for allegedly violating this norm.

Many scholars do not believe that social work research is ever entirely value-free. For example, researchers of homelessness may be influenced by their values in the way they define homelessness, which in turn influences whom they include in their sample of homeless individuals. Do the homeless include only people living in the streets? Or do they also include people "doubling up" with friends or relatives or living in squalid, temporary quarters who cannot find a decent place they can afford? It is difficult to make such decisions independently of our values. Researchers who have been active in social action efforts to alleviate homelessness may be predisposed to choose the broader definition, which will indicate a greater number of the homeless; researchers who believe social welfare spending is wasteful and incurs too much dependency among the poor may be predisposed to choose the narrower definition.

Scholars who believe that social research is never really value-free typically recommend that we should be aware of our values and describe them in an upfront manner rather than kidding ourselves or others that we are completely objective. Indeed, not all social scientists agree that researchers should try to separate their values from their research activities. Some have argued that social science and social action cannot and should not be separated. Social work has a long tradition of using research as a tool to try to make society more humane. For example, our profession embraced the social survey movement at the turn of the 20th century as a way to convince society to enact environmental reform to alleviate a host of urban problems. More recently, surveys on homelessness have been conducted in the hope that their findings would influence legislators and their tax-averse constituents to spend more public funds to alleviate homelessness.

When we conduct research to alleviate human suffering and promote social welfare, we should not let our humanitarian aims spur us to hide from or distort the truth by biasing the way we conduct our research or interpret its findings. Attempting to be completely objective and value-free in the way we conduct research is an impossible ideal, and it is risky to kid ourselves into thinking that we are completely neutral. This does not mean, however, that we shouldn't *try* to keep our beliefs from distorting our pursuit of truth. Being aware of our biases throughout all phases of our research helps us minimize their impact on our work. And being upfront in describing our predilections to readers better prepares them to evaluate the validity of our findings.

Some social science research studies have stimulated considerable controversy about whether their findings were merely intrusions of a researcher's own political values. Typically, researchers have denied the intrusion, and the denial has been challenged. Let's look at examples of the controversies that have raged and continue to rage over this issue.

EP 2

Social Research and Race

Nowhere have social research and politics been more controversially intertwined than in the area of race relations. For the most part, social scientists during the 20th century supported the cause of African American equality in the United States. Many were actively involved in the civil rights movement, some more radically than others. Thus, social scientists were able to draw research conclusions that support the cause of equality without fear of criticism from colleagues. To recognize the solidity of the general social science position in the matter of equality, we need to examine only a few research

projects that have produced conclusions that disagree with the predominant ideological position.

Most social scientists—overtly at least—supported the end of even de facto school segregation. Thus, an immediate and heated controversy was provoked when James Coleman (1966), a respected sociologist, published the results of a major national study of race and education. Contrary to general agreement, Coleman found little difference in academic performance between African American students attending integrated schools and those attending segregated ones. Indeed, such obvious things as libraries, laboratory facilities, and high expenditures per student made little difference. Instead, Coleman reported that family and neighborhood factors had the most influence on academic achievement. Coleman's findings were not well received by many of the social scientists who had been active in the civil rights movement. Some scholars criticized Coleman's work on methodological grounds, but many others objected hotly on the grounds that the findings would have segregationist political consequences.

Another example of political controversy surrounding social research in connection with race concerns the issue of IQ scores of black and white people. In 1969, Arthur Jensen, a Harvard psychologist, was asked to prepare an article for the *Harvard Educational Review* that would examine the data on racial differences in IQ test results (Jensen, 1969). In the article, Jensen concluded that genetic differences between African Americans and Caucasians accounted for the lower average IQ scores of African Americans. He became so identified with that position that he appeared on college campuses across the country discussing it.

Jensen's position was attacked on numerous methodological bases. It was charged that many of the data on which Jensen's conclusion was based were inadequate and sloppy—there are many IQ tests, some worse than others. Similarly, critics argued that Jensen had not sufficiently accounted for socioenvironmental factors. Other social scientists raised other appropriate methodological objections.

Beyond the scientific critique, however, Jensen was condemned by many as a racist. He was booed, and his public presentations were drowned out by hostile crowds. Jensen's reception by several university audiences was not significantly different from the reception received by abolitionists a century before, when the prevailing opinion favored leaving the institution of slavery intact.

A similar reaction erupted in response to a book titled *The Bell Curve*, published in 1994 and coauthored by Charles Murray, a sociologist known as a leading thinker on the political right, and the late Richard J. Herrnstein, a psychologist and distinguished professor at Harvard University. A small portion of the lengthy book argues that ethnic differences in intelligence can be attributed in part (but not exclusively) to genetic factors.

In their book, Murray and Herrnstein (1994) saw intelligence as a crucial factor that influences whether Americans will prosper or wind up in an underclass culture of poverty and other social ills. Based on the thesis that intelligence is so hard to change, the book recommended against spending money on a variety of social programs, including those aimed at improving the intellectual performance of disadvantaged youths.

Critics have pointed to serious methodological shortcomings in the procedures and conclusions in the Murray and Herrnstein study. But as with the earlier controversy involving Jensen, what is most germane to this chapter is not the methodological critique of *The Bell Curve* but rather its political condemnation. When the book first appeared, its early critics gave more attention to political objections than to the study's serious methodological shortcomings. It was attacked in a *Boston Globe* editorial before it was even published. The *Washington Post* reported that former Education Secretary William Bennett, a politically conservative supporter and friend of Murray, strongly praised the book but was made nervous by the section on race and intelligence. Because of that section, Bennett reportedly characterized Murray as a "marked man."

New Republic magazine devoted its October 31, 1994, issue to the book. The issue contains a 10-page article by Murray and Herrnstein, based on the section of their book that dealt with intelligence and genetics. Preceding that article are 17 pages of editorials by 20 different authors about both *The Bell Curve* and Murray and Herrnstein's *New Republic* article. Some of the editorials debate whether the magazine was ethical in even considering publishing the article, and most sharply attack the article or criticize the magazine's decision to publish it. One editorial depicts Murray and Herrnstein as dishonest. Another portrays them as seeking to justify oppression. Others liken them to racists

trying to justify their racism or to bigots practicing pseudoscientific racism. One harsher editorial, titled "Neo-Nazis," implies that the relevant chapter from Murray and Herrnstein's book is "a chilly synthesis" of the findings of previous works published by neo-Nazis.

In an editorial that justified the decision to publish the Murray and Herrnstein article on grounds of free inquiry, the magazine's editor argued that the burden of proof for suppressing debate on the topic rests with those who seek to suppress the debate. The editorial argues for judging the issue on scientific and logical grounds, not tarring and feathering the authors by impugning their motives or by associating them with Nazis. The editorial also responds to critics who claim that *The Bell Curve* hurts the feelings of African Americans, especially African American children, who don't want to be called genetically inferior. The editor depicts the view that African Americans are vulnerable people who must be shielded from free and open intellectual exchange as itself inherently racist.

Many social scientists limited their objections to the Coleman, Jensen, and Murray and Herrnstein research to scientific and methodological grounds. The purpose of our account, however, is to point out that political ideology often gets involved in matters of social research. Although the abstract model of science is divorced from ideology, the practice of science is not.

When political and ideological forces restrict scientific inquiry in one area, this can have unfortunate spin-off effects that restrict needed inquiry in related areas. For example, in 1991, Lovell Jones, director of Experimental Gynecology–Endocrinology at the University of Texas's M. D. Anderson Cancer Center, expressed concern regarding the dearth of health research about the higher rate of mortality seen in African American women with breast cancer as compared to Caucasian women with breast cancer. Jones postulated that one plausible factor that might contribute to the higher mortality rate among African American women is that they have more breast tumors that are "estrogen receptor negative," which means that those tumors tend to be more aggressive. Jones found it striking that there had been no concrete studies to investigate this possibility; on the basis of feedback he had received from Caucasian research colleagues, he thought he knew why. His colleagues told him that they did not want to pursue this line of inquiry because it would be too controversial politically. They said the research would have to delve into racial differences in genetic predispositions to breast tumors. They feared that they would therefore be accused, like Jensen was, of racial bias—if not for their own findings on breast tumors, then for making it easier for other investigators to study more politically sensitive differences in genetic predispositions between African Americans and whites (e.g., differences connected to intelligence).

Jones also observed that for 10 years (as of 1991), we had known that Caucasian women with a family history of breast cancer have a higher risk of developing breast cancer than do Caucasian women with no family history. Jones reasoned that the field should have quickly followed up this research by investigating whether the same holds true for African American women with and without family histories of breast cancer. But not until 10 years after the research on Caucasian women first appeared did the first study on African American women come out. Jones attributed this time lapse to the political risk that faced researchers in conducting such an investigation; the researchers feared that if they were to find that the risk of African American women getting breast cancer is higher than that of Caucasian women, they would be attacked as racists.

Jones further recounted how he was once told by a staff member of a national news program that a spokesperson for the National Cancer Institute suggested that they would prefer that the word *genetics* not be used in commenting on cancer among African Americans. In a somewhat related incident, Jones recalled how he once wrote an editorial for a prominent newspaper, an editorial that discussed cancer among minority populations. The paper's editor called him to say that the paper could not run the editorial because it would be accused of racial bias if it did. But when the editor learned that Jones was African American, he said, "Well then, we can use it."

Jones's comments* illustrate how politically rooted taboos against certain lines of inquiry may do a disservice to the very people they seek to protect. What is your opinion about such taboos? Are some or all of them justified? Or is the benefit of ensuring that some research findings will not be misused for harmful purposes outweighed by the risk that such taboos will keep others from conducting much-needed research in related areas?

MAIN POINTS

- Social work research projects are likely to be shaped not only by technical scientific considerations but also by administrative, ethical, and political considerations.
- What's ethically "right" and "wrong" in research is ultimately a matter of what people agree is right and wrong.
- Any agency wishing to receive federal research support must establish an IRB to review all research proposals involving human subjects and rule on their ethics.
- Scientists agree that participation in research should, as a general norm, be voluntary. This norm, however, can conflict with the scientific need for generalizability.
- Probably all scientists agree that research should not harm those who participate in it, unless the participants willingly and knowingly accept the risks of harm.
- *Anonymity* refers to the situation in which even the researcher cannot identify an individual by the specific information that has been supplied. *Confidentiality* refers to the situation in which the researcher—although knowing which data describe which participants—agrees to keep that information confidential.
- In some instances, the long-term benefits of a study are thought to outweigh the violation of certain ethical norms. But determining whether a study's ends justify its means is a difficult and often highly subjective process. Today, IRBs make such determinations in approving studies. Certificates of confidentiality protect the confidentiality of research subject data against forced disclosure by the police and other authorities. IRBs require education on the protection of human research participants for each individual investigator and research assistant working on studies involving human subjects.

---

*Lovell Jones's comments were presented in part at the Texas Minority Health Strategic Planning Conference, Austin, Texas, July 18, 1991, in his presentation titled "The Impact of Cancer on the Health Status of Minorities in Texas." Jones elaborated on his conference remarks in a telephone conversation with Allen Rubin on July 25, 1991. Some of the material included in his comments is covered in Wilson (1989, pp. 5–20).

- Federal regulations allow IRBs to grant exemptions to certain kinds of studies. Exempt studies receive an expedited review.
- Different IRBs can respond inconsistently to the same research proposal.
- Some IRB panelists at times can be overzealous in refusing to approve valuable research projects whose benefits far outweigh their minimal risks of harm.
- Obtaining IRB approval can take considerable time if the IRB raises concerns, so responses to those concerns should be prepared carefully and should be respectful and nondefensive.
- Bias and insensitivity about sex and culture have become ethical issues for many social scientists.
- Guidelines have been proposed by feminist and other scholars.
- Although science is neutral on political matters, scientists are not.
- Even though the norms of science cannot force individual scientists to give up their personal values, the use of accepted scientific practices provides a safeguard against "scientific" findings being the product of bias alone.
- Ideological priorities can restrict inquiry out of a fear that certain truths can be misperceived or misused in a manner that will harm certain vulnerable groups; this restriction can lead to incomplete or distorted knowledge building that risks harming the people it seeks to protect.

REVIEW QUESTIONS AND EXERCISES

1. Suppose a social work researcher decides to interview children who were placed for adoption in infancy by their biological parents. The interviewer will focus on their feelings about someday meeting their biological parents. Discuss the ethical problems the researcher would face and how those might be avoided.
2. Suppose a researcher personally opposed to transracial adoption wants to conduct an interview survey to explore the impact of transracial adoption on the self-images of adoptees. Discuss the personal involvement problems he or she would face and how those might be avoided.

3. Consider the following real and hypothetical research situations. Identify the ethical component in each. How do you feel about it? Do you feel the procedures described are ultimately acceptable or unacceptable? It might be useful to discuss some of these with classmates.

   a. A social work professor asks students in a social policy class to complete questionnaires that the instructor will analyze and use in preparing a journal article for publication.
   b. After a field study of a demonstration of civil disobedience, law enforcement officials demand that the researcher identify those people who were observed breaking the law. Rather than risk arrest as an accomplice after the fact, the researcher complies.
   c. After completing the final draft of a book reporting a research project, the researcher and author discovers that 25 of the 2,000 survey interviews were falsified by interviewers, but the author chooses to ignore that fact and publishes the book anyway.
   d. Researchers obtain a list of abusive parents they wish to study. They contact the parents with the explanation that each has been selected at random from among the general population to take a sampling of public opinion.
   e. A social work doctoral student is conducting dissertation research on the disciplinary styles of abusive parents with toddlers. Each parent and his or her child enter a room with toys scattered around it, and the parent is asked to have the child straighten up the toys before playing with them. The parent is told that the researcher will observe the parent–child interactions from behind a one-way mirror.
   f. In a study of sexual behavior, the investigator wants to overcome subjects' reluctance to report what they might regard as deviant behavior. To get past their reluctance, subjects are asked the following question: "Everyone masturbates now and then. About how much do you masturbate?"
   g. A researcher discovers that 85% of the students in a particular university smoke marijuana regularly. Publication of this finding will probably create a furor in the community. Because no extensive analysis of drug use is planned, the researcher decides to ignore the finding and keep it quiet.

h. To test the extent to which social work practitioners might try to save face by expressing clinical views on matters about which they are wholly uninformed, the researcher asks for their clinical opinion about a fictitious practice model.

i. A research questionnaire is circulated among clients as part of their agency's intake forms. Although clients are not told they must complete the questionnaire, the hope is that they will believe they must—thus ensuring a higher completion rate.

j. A participant-observer pretends to join a group that opposes family planning services so she can study it, and she is successfully accepted as a member of the inner planning circle. What should the researcher do if the group makes plans for (a) a peaceful though illegal demonstration against family planning services or (b) the bombing of an abortion clinic during a time when it is sure to be unoccupied?

INTERNET EXERCISES

1. Find an article that discusses ethical issues in social research. (You might enter one of the following search terms: "research ethics," "informed consent," or "institutional review boards.") Read an article that piques your interest. Write down the bibliographical reference information for the article and summarize the article in a few sentences.

2. Repeat exercise 1, this time entering the term "research politics" as the search term.

3. Search for "informed consent" and then narrow your search to "research." Skim the resulting articles and begin to identify groups of people for whom informed consent may be problematic—people who may not be able to give it. Suggest some ways in which the problem might be overcome.

4. Visit the NIH's free course on protecting human research participants and briefly summarize what you learn there. If you take the online tutorial at this site, you will receive a certificate of completion that might come in handy later on if you become a research assistant or need IRB approval for your research. You might also ask your instructor if extra credit could be granted for obtaining this certificate. The site address is: https://phrp.nihtraining.com/.

5. Search for "Tuskegee syphilis study" and visit some of the sites on that topic. Do the same for the search term "Nazi medical experiments."

 Visit CengageBrain.com for additional practice and study opportunities including experiential exercises, research tools, glossary, flashcards, and sample test items.

6

Culturally Competent Research

EPAS Competencies for This Chapter

Competency 1   Demonstrate Ethical and Professional Behavior: This competency requires social workers to avoid cultural bias and insensitivity. This entire chapter, therefore, aims to enhance your ability to demonstrate ethical and professional behavior in any research practice in which you might engage.

Competency 2   Engage Diversity and Difference in Practice: This entire chapter addresses engaging diversity in the practice of research.

Competency 4   Engage in Practice-Informed Research and Research-Informed Practice: Developing your cultural competence in research implies learning about practice with culturally diverse populations and being able to produce research that is better able to inform practice. Thus, this entire chapter aims to build this competency.

Competency 9   Evaluate Practice with Individuals Families, Groups, Organizations, and Communities: Your ability to evaluate practice with culturally diverse individuals, groups, and communities will be enhanced if your research and evaluation methods are more culturally competent. Again, therefore, this entire chapter aims to help build this competency.

What You'll Learn in This Chapter

In Chapter 5, we noted that cultural bias and insensitivity is an ethical issue. Avoiding them requires cultural competence. In this chapter, we will go beyond ethics and examine how cultural competence can influence the success of social work research studies and the validity of their findings. You'll see how researchers can formulate and conceptualize research problems in ways that are responsive to the concerns of minority and oppressed populations, improve the cultural sensitivity of the measurement procedures they use, interpret their findings in a culturally competent manner, and improve the recruitment and retention of minority and oppressed populations as participants in their research.

» INTRODUCTION

Much of social work practice—at the macro as well as the micro level—involves minority and oppressed populations. Consequently, in social work education, a heavy emphasis is placed on helping students learn more about cultural diversity and become more culturally competent practitioners. Cultural competence is also important in the research curriculum. In research, the term cultural competence means being aware of and appropriately responding to the ways in which cultural factors and cultural differences can influence all stages of the research process, including what we investigate, how we investigate, and how we analyze and interpret our findings.

Research Participants

In the sampling phase of the research process, for example, culturally competent researchers will attempt to include a sufficient and representative number of research participants from minority and oppressed populations. Moreover, they will learn how to maximize the likelihood of obtaining such participation. Studies that do not include adequate representation from specific minority and oppressed populations in their samples—no matter how rigorously the studies are designed in other respects—are not generalizable to those populations.

In reviewing this problem, Hohmann and Parron (1996) discussed several studies showing that different cultural groups utilize services differently, have different expectations of services, and interpret and react differently to the problems for which they seek services. Thus, if members of particular minority groups are underrepresented in studies evaluating the effectiveness of interventions, how do we know whether they would benefit from those interventions?

Acknowledging that minority participants historically have not been adequately represented in clinical research, the National Institutes of Health (NIH) in 1994 issued a new policy mandating that all research projects funded by NIH that involve human subjects must include adequate representation of women and members of ethnic minority groups in their samples. Exceptions to this requirement could be justified only with a "clear and compelling" rationale (Miranda, 1996). Moreover, the policy stipulated that research proposals must include detailed plans for how women and minority participants would be recruited and retained in the study. Investigators are required to describe their prior experience in recruiting and retaining such participants, report collaborations with other researchers who have this experience, and provide letters of support for their study from relevant community groups (Hohmann & Parron, 1996).

As implied in the NIH stipulations, just seeking representation of minorities in your study does not guarantee that you will get it. Successfully recruiting and retaining members of minority and oppressed populations in research requires special culturally sensitive knowledge and efforts, which we will discuss in this chapter. One

EP 2

such requirement involves being responsive to the concerns of minority and oppressed communities in the way research problems are formulated. Insensitivity to those concerns can lead not only to problems in recruitment and retention of participants but also to findings that are not relevant to the needs perceived by members of those communities.

Measurement

An additional feature of culturally competent research is the use of measurement procedures that have been shown to be reliable and valid for the minority and oppressed populations participating in the research. (We'll examine the concepts of reliability and validity in measurement in Chapter 9.) If we measure the outcome of our interventions with instruments that are not reliable or valid for some participants from minority and oppressed populations, even interventions that are very effective will yield misleading results for those participants. For example, if we ask questions that respondents do not understand, their answers will be unreliable. If the questions mean something to them other than what we intend them to mean, our information will not be valid. Thus, even if our intervention is helping them attain their goal, our measures might not indicate that attainment because they are not really measuring that goal.

Likewise, if we ask questions in an insensitive way, they might stop participating. For example, suppose one of the variables in your survey is the sex of the respondent. Culturally competent researchers will understand that it is no longer acceptable to use the terms *sex* and *gender* interchangeably and thus to merely ask respondents to check male or female. As mentioned in Chapter 3, sex refers to what appeared on a respondent's birth certificate, referring to the appearance of genitalia at birth. In fact, rather than just asking about sex, it would be even more culturally sensitive to use the term *born-sex*. Gender, in contrast, is a socially constructed term—an "internal experience of maleness, femaleness, both, neither, or somewhere in between (androgyny)" that can evolve over time (Ferguson-Colvin & Maccio, 2012, p. 4). As you might imagine, some LGBT youths might rightfully feel offended and stigmatized and might stop participating in a survey that merely asked: Sex/Gender: ☐ male ☐ female.

EP 1, 2, 4, 9

Data Analysis and Interpretation

Cultural competence can also affect how data are analyzed and interpreted. Culturally competent researchers will not just be interested in whether minority groups differ from the majority group. If they have a sufficiently diverse sample of research participants, rather than combine all minority groups together as one category to compare to the majority group in the data analysis, they will compare the various minority groups to each other. There are two reasons for this. First, it would be

culturally insensitive to be concerned only with how minority groups as a whole compare to the majority group and not with each other. Second, different minority groups differ from the majority group in different ways. For example, Asian Americans on average currently have higher levels of academic achievement than American Caucasians, whereas some other minority groups in the United States on average currently have lower levels of academic achievement than Caucasians. Thus, if the Asian Americans' achievement levels were combined with the levels of one or more of the minority groups with lower levels, their combined (average) level might be close to that of Caucasians. This would mask the real differences as compared to Caucasians and would overlook important differences between the minority groups.

Cultural insensitivity in the data analysis and reporting phases of research can also result in interpreting ethnic differences in a prejudicial manner, focusing too much on the deficits of minorities and too little on their strengths. Miranda (1996), for example, cites studies that interpreted the lower likelihood to delay gratification among inner-city minority children, as compared to middle-class Caucasian children, as innate deficits. Miranda depicts this as a racist interpretation because it overlooked the possibility that the inner-city minority children were merely responding in an adaptive manner to their disadvantaged environment.

Cultural insensitivity in interpreting data can also occur when ethnic minorities are not even included in a study yet that study's findings are generalized as if they had been included. Likewise, studies whose research participants include only one gender should clarify that its results may not generalize to the other gender.

Because minority groups are more likely to be poor than majority populations, culturally competent researchers will include socioeconomic factors in their analyses when they are studying other ways in which minority and majority populations differ. For example, if their findings show that African Americans are less likely than whites to be interested in long-term psychodynamic forms of treatment, rather than considering only cultural factors as the explanation, they will examine whether the difference can be explained by the fact that African Americans are more likely to be poor and therefore more in need of the crisis

EP 1, 2

services to deal with the pressing day-to-day problems confronting poor people of any ethnicity—such as services for problems in finances, unemployment, and housing.

Acculturation[1]

Culturally competent researchers will also consider the *immigration experience* and *acculturation* as factors to include in their research as they study differences between minority and majority populations. Sensitivity to these factors will also alert researchers to study differences within a particular minority group. For example, Latinos or Asians who recently immigrated to the United States are likely to have different needs and problems, have different attitudes about child rearing or marital roles, and respond to social services differently than Latinos or Asians whose parents or grandparents have lived in the United States for several decades or longer. The longer a member of a minority culture has lived amidst a majority culture, the more likely that person is to be acculturated to the majority culture. Acculturation is the process in which a group or individual changes after coming into contact with a majority culture, taking on the language, values, attitudes, and lifestyle preferences of the majority culture. If you want to study factors influencing service utilization patterns or child-rearing attitudes among Korean Americans, for example, level of acculturation is one of the factors you should examine.

The term *level of acculturation* implies that acculturation is not an all-or-nothing phenomenon. For example, suppose a family of five children ages 8 to 18 moved from Mexico to the United States 7 years ago. The eldest child might retain many cultural traditions, values, attitudes, and native language, and the youngest may be the most acculturated, with less knowledge of or interest in cultural traditions, values, or attitudes. The youngest may not even speak Spanish despite understanding it because it is spoken in the home. The siblings in between may be at different levels between these extremes. The parents also might be at different levels between those extremes, with one being more acculturated than the other. The different levels of acculturation among the family might

be vital to assess in some research studies, such as when investigating factors influencing school attendance or attitudes about education.

To illustrate how acculturation factors should be taken into account in the research process, suppose you want to conduct a survey of driving age youths living in the southwestern United States near the Mexico border. The aim of your survey is to assess their attitudes and behaviors regarding driving under the influence of alcohol or illegal drugs—with the ultimate purpose being to use the findings to guide the development of preventive driver educational programs geared to that population. Rather than just ask about their ethnicity, it would behoove you to assess the level of acculturation of the non-Caucasian respondents, especially since you know that so many of them will be Mexican Americans at various levels of acculturation. You might decide that the most feasible way to approximate their level of acculturation is by asking about things like whether they and their parents were born in the United States, how long they have lived continuously in the United States, and whether they prefer to speak in English or Spanish. Not assessing their level of acculturation might result in a failure to detect important differences in which the more and less acculturated youths may differ in how they view and engage in driving while intoxicated and what might be the best way to prevent that problem among them. For example, you might find that the less acculturated youths are less likely to be influenced by peer pressure but more likely to drive after drinking at family celebrations. Their survey answers might indicate the need to focus educational programs on family celebrations—and perhaps to present those programs in Spanish—whereas the answers of the more acculturated youths might point to focusing the programs on peer pressures.

As you can see in the foregoing example, there are various ways to measure level of acculturation. One option is to use one of the existing scales that researchers have developed for that purpose geared to particular ethnic groups. Some of these scales are more feasible to use than others. Some, for example, consist of only a few items, whereas others are much lengthier. In some studies, researchers simply ask respondents to identify their language preference as a proxy for level of acculturation.

In addition to assessing the level of acculturation per se among respondents, researchers should

---

[1]We thank Eden Hernandez Robles, a Mexican American doctoral student in social work at the University of Texas at Austin, for her helpful suggestions about this section on acculturation.

take level of acculturation into account when deciding how to measure other phenomena. For example, suppose you want to measure the extent to which adolescents have experienced stressful life events. Suppose further that a scale already exists to measure that variable and that the scale is commonly used and highly regarded among researchers. In addition, suppose that the scale only asks about stressful life events commonly experienced in the majority culture and does not ask about stressful events associated with the immigration experience. If some of the adolescents who will be completing the scale are immigrants, the information you get from them will be faulty even if you ask them about their level of acculturation. That's because you will not learn about the degree of stress connected to their immigration experience. Moreover, if your scale yields a summated score depicting the extent to which each adolescent has experienced stressful life events, the immigrated adolescents' scores might not depict greater stress than the other adolescents even if—as immigrants—they have had much more stress.

EP 2

Impact of Cultural Insensitivity on Research Climate

Misleading results are not the only harm that can come from culturally insensitive research. In Chapter 5, regarding ethics, we noted that culturally insensitive interviewers can offend minority respondents. Moreover, studies that use culturally insensitive procedures, or that are not responsive to the concerns of minority populations, can poison the climate for future research among those populations. For example, Norton and Manson (1996) discussed the harmful impact of news headlines resulting from press releases put out by investigators in a 1979 study of alcohol use among the Inupiat tribe in Alaska. One headline read, "Alcohol Plagues Eskimos." Another read, "Sudden Wealth Sparks Epidemic of Alcoholism." Overnight, Standard & Poor's dramatically reduced the bond rating of the Inupiat community, which meant that some important municipal projects could no longer be funded. Consequently, some Alaska Native tribes no longer are receptive to research on alcoholism despite the importance of that problem in their communities.

Now that we see the importance of cultural competence in social work research, let's look at how researchers can attempt to make their studies more culturally competent. We'll start with the process of problem formulation.

EP 1

» DEVELOPING CULTURAL COMPETENCE

If you want to conduct research on an ethnic minority or oppressed population, it would behoove you to know quite a bit about that population's culture. Thus, before you begin any investigation, it is crucial that you are well read in the literature on the culture of minority or oppressed populations relevant to your study. This should include readings that describe the culture and its values, as well as research studies dealing with issues bearing on the participation of its members in your study.

In other words, you should develop cultural competence regarding the population you want to include in your study. As discussed by Vonk (2001), cultural competence involves knowledge, attitudes, and skills. You should understand the minority culture's historical experiences—including the effects of prejudice and oppression—and how those experiences influence the ways in which its members live and view members of the dominant culture. You should also understand its traditions, values, family systems, socioeconomic issues, and attitudes about social services and social policies. You should be aware of how your own attitudes are connected to your own cultural background and how they may differ from the worldview of members of the minority culture. You should be aware of and try to avoid ethnocentrism, which is the belief in the superiority of your own culture. You should develop skills in communicating effectively both verbally and nonverbally with members of the minority culture and establishing rapport with them.

Norton and Manson (1996), for example, identified some of the important things you should know to enhance the cultural competence of your research on Native Americans. You should know how Native Americans feel about the loss of their ancestral lands. You should know about the important role played by tribes in their lives and in influencing their participation in research. You should realize that in addition to obtaining the individual's consent to participate in your research, you may have to seek the tribe's permission. You should also be aware of the diversity among tribal cultures and the diversity in where Native Americans reside. You should know that a large minority of Native Americans live on reservations and understand how they feel about that. You should know that many previously living on reservations were forced after World War II to resettle in urban areas. You should know how they feel about that. You might be surprised to learn that according to the 1990 US census, the city with the largest number of Native American residents is New York City. Yet Native Americans who dwell in urban areas are less likely than other ethnic minority populations to concentrate in the same neighborhoods.

Thompson, Neighbors, Munday, and Jackson (1996) identified some important things you should know before implementing studies of mental health services with African Americans. You should know that prior studies that fostered negative images of African Americans or that have been insensitive in other ways have led many African Americans to distrust research, especially research conducted by Caucasians. As is the case with Native Americans, African Americans may see researchers as taking from their community but not giving anything in return. You should be aware of the relatively high degree of stigma that some African Americans attach to the concept of mental illness and how this, coupled with their distrust of research, makes it difficult to obtain their participation in research.

Miranda and her associates (Alvidrez, Azocar, & Miranda, 1996; Miranda, 1996) discuss how misconceptions about Latino attitudes and Latino utilization of mental health services can impede the efforts of psychotherapy researchers to recruit and retain Latinos in their studies. Although the underutilization of mental health services by Latinos has been attributed to their negative attitudes about treatment, many studies have found that Latinos view mental health services positively and often hold more positive views than whites. Another common misconception is that American Latinos prefer family members or *curanderos* (traditional folk healers who dispense herbal medicines and potions for emotional problems) to professional mental health services. But Miranda and associates cite several studies that indicate that the use of traditional folk healers accounts for only a small portion of Latino underutilization of professional mental health services in the United States. If you plan to conduct a study evaluating mental health services in an area where many Latinos reside, it is important that you have accurate knowledge about what influences service utilization among Latinos. Otherwise, you might not undertake appropriate efforts to recruit and retain the participation of Latinos in your study, and you might too readily attribute their lack of participation to negative attitudes rather than to your inadequate efforts to recruit and retain Latinos. For example, Miranda and associates discuss how the individual is valued less among many traditional Latinos than is the family, including extended as well as nuclear family members. Consequently, researchers may need to interact with family members before individuals are permitted or willing to participate in treatment outcome studies.

The above are just some examples of things researchers need to learn about the cultures of ethnic minority groups relevant to their studies and why they need to know those things. Many other examples could be cited, as could the cultures of groups that are disadvantaged or oppressed for reasons other than ethnicity, such as individuals who are homeless or in need of intervention for HIV and AIDS. We will discuss additional examples and additional groups throughout this chapter. Sexual and gender minorities comprise one such group. As we discussed earlier, it is culturally insensitive to ask questions about sex or gender in ways that are limited to heterosexual categories.

More and more is being written these days about cultural sensitivity and competence concerning practice and research with LGBT individuals. For example, in 2005 the Institute for the Advancement of Social Work Research issued a report of a symposium aimed at building a social work research agenda pertaining to LGBT individuals, families and communities (IASWR, 2005). Seven years later the Silberman School of Social Work at Hunter College published a toolkit for practitioners and researchers working with LGBTQ youths (Ferguson-Colvin & Maccio, 2102). (The Q in the acronym was used to refer to the term *queer or questioning*, although these are two very different things.) Part of becoming a culturally competent researcher involves searching for and reading such reports, as well as books and journals articles on cultural competence with this population. Developing this competence is not a simple task, as is illustrated in the box: "LGBTQ Cultural Sensitivity: A Case Example."

LGBTQ CULTURAL SENSITIVITY: A CASE EXAMPLE

Several years ago, a doctoral student submitted an assignment on preparing a questionnaire in which a culturally sensitive item regarding gender included the term *queer* as one of the response options. The much older instructor questioned whether it was advisable to keep that term in a questionnaire that was part of a survey that would go out to people of all gender identities, not only to LGBTQ individuals. His concern was that heterosexual individuals, especially those who are middle age or older, might not realize that that term is no longer considered to be

an insult among LGBTQ individuals. Consequently, even enlightened potential respondents might be offended by the term and therefore refuse to complete a questionnaire that they deemed to be using an egregious epithet. The student disagreed, arguing that the term is now acceptable and insinuating that perhaps the instructor needed to update his cultural sensitivity regarding LGBTQ individuals.

Question to reader: What do you think? Do you agree with the instructor or the student?

Of course, you may already have accumulated considerable experience, knowledge, and sensitivity regarding the culture of interest before even contemplating your research. If so, this might reduce the extent of your basic readings. Nevertheless, you should review the recent literature—especially the research literature—to enhance your assessment of your own cultural competence and to make sure your conceptions are accurate and consistent with the latest findings. Moreover, cultures are not monolithic. They contain diverse subcultures that might be related to differences in factors such as geographic origin, socioeconomic status, and acculturation. In assessing your own cultural competence, therefore, be sure not to overlook the cultural diversity within the culture in which you already have expertise. In this connection, we have observed in-class dialogues between some of our Korean doctoral students in which, despite their own ethnic heritage and expertise in the culture of Korean Americans, they have suggested helpful ways to improve the cultural sensitivity of each other's plans for dissertation research on Korean Americans.

What you learn in other parts of this book can help you learn more about cultures with which you are not already familiar. Chapter 2, for example, provided tips for facilitating literature reviews. Additional tips can be found in Chapter 7 and Appendix A. In addition to the literature review, another helpful early step in seeking to improve the cultural competence of your research involves using the *participant observation* methods described in Chapter 19. These methods will help you

immerse yourself more directly in the culture of interest and enhance your assessment of your own cultural competence.

You should also seek the advice of professional colleagues who are members of the culture or who have a great deal of experience in working with its members. These colleagues should include practitioners as well as scholars whose works have dealt with the culture of interest. Your colleagues can help you not only learn more about the culture but also formulate research questions that are responsive to the needs and perspectives of its members. So too can the input of community members and their leaders. In fact, it is essential that representatives of the minority cultures be included in the formulation of the research questions and in all subsequent stages of the research. Not only will this help you formulate research questions that are responsive to minority group concerns, but it also can help you prevent or deal with culturally related problems that might arise in later stages of the research design and implementation—problems that you might not otherwise have anticipated. Likewise, it can foster a sense of community commitment to the research and more receptivity to future studies.

Using *focus groups*, which we'll discuss in Chapter 18, can aid in learning how community representatives view issues relevant to your study. Alvidrez et al. (1996), for example, mention how conducting a focus group made up of young African American women before initiating investigations about parenting interventions

EP 2

can help researchers. By better understanding attitudes about child rearing among this population, the researchers can be more prepared to develop culturally specific hypotheses about how young African American women might respond to the parenting interventions of concern. Focus groups can also help you to anticipate barriers to recruiting and retaining participants in your study and to identify steps you can take that might enhance recruitment and retention. Let's look now at some of those barriers and steps.

Recruiting and Retaining the Participation of Minority and Oppressed Populations in Research Studies

Recruiting a sufficient and representative sample of research participants from minority and oppressed populations can be a daunting challenge. So can retaining their participation throughout the study after they have been recruited. Many reasons have been postulated to explain difficulties in the recruitment and retention of participants from minority and oppressed populations. Earlier in this chapter, we discussed how the recruitment efforts of current studies can be hampered by the poisoned climate caused by previous studies that were conducted in a culturally insensitive manner. A related barrier is the perception that the research question may have value for the larger society but little value to a particular minority group. Perhaps members of a particular minority group are likely to distrust research in general or members of the majority culture in general.

Some prospective participants can get turned off by *culturally insensitive informed consent procedures*. For example, Norton and Manson (1996) observe, "The sophisticated language required by IRB [institutional review board] protocols may be intimidating to American Indians and Alaska Natives, particularly those for whom English is a second language" (p. 858). They cite an example in which some American Indian Vietnam veterans misinterpreted a consent form, thinking that the words "Clinical Research" in the title meant that they were being asked to participate in a medical procedure rather than an interview.

Another barrier pertains to *not knowing where to look for participants*. Suppose you want to study the impact of parental depression on the child-rearing practices of parents who recently immigrated to the United States from Korea or from Latin America. Because such immigrants have low rates of utilization of traditional mental health services, you may have meager success if you try to recruit participants only through referral sources or advertisements at traditional mental health service providers, where you think they may be in treatment for depression. Locating or identifying prospective participants can be a special challenge when dealing with populations who lack a known residence—such as homeless individuals, migrant workers, or undocumented immigrants. Other hard-to-locate populations consist of people who have some characteristic that is stigmatized by society and therefore risky for them to disclose. People in need of intervention for HIV or AIDS, for example, make up one such "hidden" population (Roffman, Picciano, Wickizer, Bolan, & Ryan, 1998).

What can be done to alleviate or overcome the many barriers to the recruitment and retention of participants from minority and oppressed populations? The literature on this issue is still emerging. A number of potentially useful approaches have been recommended; future inquiries are likely to develop additional recommendations. Not all of the existing recommendations have received adequate empirical testing. Some are based on what various investigators believe they have learned from their experiences in conducting research among certain minority or oppressed populations. With the understanding that some of these recommendations can be viewed more as practice wisdom than as evidence-based procedures, let's look now at what some culturally competent investigators recommend as culturally sensitive approaches for overcoming barriers to the recruitment and retention of participants from minority and oppressed populations.

Obtain Endorsement from Community Leaders

If prospective participants in your study see that it has been endorsed by community leaders whom they respect, their distrust of the researchers or their skepticism about the value of the research to their community may be alleviated. Norton and Manson (1996), for example, discuss the need for investigators who seek to recruit American Indian or Alaskan Natives to obtain permission first from the prospective participant's tribe. They note that the Navajo Nation now has a board staffed by tribal representatives who review, approve, and monitor all health-related research proposed for their community. Tribal governments aggressively evaluate the value of proposed research projects to the tribe. One tribal council even asserted that it had the authority to grant collective consent to participate on behalf of its members.

Seeking consent from community leaders can be a major undertaking. When done in a thorough and careful manner, it involves obtaining their input into the formulation of the research questions as well as into how the study is to be designed and implemented and how its results are to be presented and disseminated. But the effort can pay off not only by enhancing recruitment and retention of participants but also by improving the design of your study or the interpretation of its results. Norton and Manson (1996) cite an example in which their dialogue with a tribal government alerted them to the greater reluctance of study participants in one of their research sites to disclose alcohol consumption to local staff than to clinicians from external communities. Learning this led them to change their plans to use local interviewers, and thus they could obtain responses that were less biased.

Use Culturally Sensitive Approaches Regarding Confidentiality

For those minority groups that value collective identity, it may not be enough to ensure individual confidentiality. They might also require community confidentiality. Norton and Manson (1996) advise that when undertaking research in American Indian and Alaska Native communities, investigators should not identify specific communities when publishing their studies. Press releases should not come from the investigators; instead, they should be initiated by the tribal government. Research findings should be in the form of generalizations; readers should not be able to ascertain the identity of the local communities associated with those findings.

Employ Local Community Members as Research Staff

If you have adequate funding, you can hire local community members to help locate and recruit prospective participants and obtain their informed consent. If the people you hire also happen to be community leaders, all the better since they can enhance your efforts to publicize your research and express their enthusiastic support for it. Employing community members to obtain informed consent also might help overcome any problems in understanding the consent forms or in being intimidated by them since the members can explain the study verbally and answer questions about it in ways that prospective participants may be more likely to understand. Another benefit of employing local community members in your research is that in doing so, your study benefits the community just by providing more jobs. One drawback of employing local community members as research staff is its implications regarding confidentiality. Prospective participants might not want members of their own community interviewing them or knowing of their participation.

Provide Adequate Compensation

People from all backgrounds can be reimbursed for their time and effort in participating in research studies. Compensation for participating in research is particularly applicable to studies of minority and oppressed populations. In light of the high poverty rates in some minority communities, compensation might provide a strong inducement for members to participate. Those same high poverty rates, however, may lead some to view high levels of compensation as coercive and thus unethical. Although you do not want to pay too much, an appropriate level of compensation can be another way your study benefits the local community. Payment should be large enough to provide an incentive yet not so large that it becomes coercive. Norton and Manson (1996) add that compensation need not be limited to individual participants. They cite a request by a Pueblo community that compensation be provided to the tribe as a whole, in keeping with the tribe's emphasis on collective identity.

Money is not the only form of compensation that you can use. If you are studying the homeless, for example, responding quickly to their need for some food or clothing can build trust and reward their participation. A sandwich, some candy, or a cup of coffee can be significant to them. Perhaps you can accompany them to an agency that will give them some shelter, financial assistance, or health care. Food vouchers are a commonly used noncash way researchers can reward homeless or other low-income individuals for their research participation. Perhaps a fast-food chain will be willing to donate vouchers worth about $10 each to your study.

Alleviate Transportation and Child-Care Barriers

Because of the high poverty rates in some minority communities, some barriers to recruitment and retention pertain not to cultural issues per se but, rather, to economic difficulties. For example, suppose you work in a child guidance center and want to evaluate a new, culturally sensitive intervention for an economically disadvantaged minority group in which the parent and child are treated together. Many of the parents you seek to recruit might experience transportation or child-care barriers to coming to your child guidance center for the treatment sessions. A culturally competent approach to your research, therefore, might include the provision of free transportation and child care for their other young children. An alternative to providing free transportation would be to conduct the treatment and data collection sessions at their homes, although many families might still need child care during those sessions.

Choose a Sensitive and Accessible Setting

If your treatment or data collection sessions are not conducted in the participants' homes, you should make sure that the choice of the setting in which they are conducted is sensitive to participant needs, resources, and concerns. Areán and Gallagher-Thompson (1996) have provided some useful insights concerning the culturally sensitive choice of a setting. For example, even if minority group members have transportation and are not dissuaded from participating by economic barriers, some might be reluctant to travel to a particular setting in a different neighborhood out of fear of a racially motivated crime. Or perhaps the setting is in a dangerous section of their own neighborhood. These fears might be particularly salient to elderly minority individuals.

The site you choose, therefore, should be located somewhere that participants will perceive as convenient as well as safe. You should also consider whether some participants might be uncomfortable with the nature of the building you choose. If you choose a community church, for example, some prospective participants who don't belong to that church might be uncomfortable

entering it. Others might not want their neighbors to see them receiving services or participating in a research study. Perhaps a nearby university site, where friends won't know of their participation, would be preferable. If you can implement some of the recommendations we've already mentioned—such as conducting focus groups, involving community leaders in planning your study, and employing local community members as research staff—you should try to ascertain which possible settings are and are not accessible to your prospective participants and be sensitive to their concerns.

Use and Train Culturally Competent Interviewers

It may seem obvious to you that one of the most important ways to enhance the recruitment and retention of minority group participants in your research is to make sure that the research staff who will come into contact with prospective participants are culturally competent. One way to do this, of course, is to employ members of the local community as your research staff, as we mentioned earlier. We also mentioned that in some cases, employing local community members may conflict with confidentiality concerns. What other steps can you take to maximize cultural competence when employing local community members is deemed undesirable or infeasible?

One recommendation commonly found in the literature on culturally competent research is to use interviewers who are of the same ethnicity as the members of the minority population whom you seek to recruit. Thus, if you seek to recruit and retain African American participants in a particular community, you might employ African American interviewers from a different community.

Note, however, that although matching interviewer and participant ethnicity probably won't impede your recruitment efforts, several studies have suggested that successful interviewing depends more on interviewer competence than on racial matching (Jackson & Ivanoff, 1999). In a study by Thompson et al. (1996), for example, racial matching had no effect on the likelihood of African American psychiatric inpatients agreeing to be interviewed. According to the researchers, more important than racial matching is whether the interviewer has adequate previous experience or training in working with members of the target population. Their interviewer training consisted of practicing how to approach participants, practicing how to give them an overview of the study, practicing how best to discuss confidentiality and voluntary participation, and thoroughly learning the intricacies of the survey instruments they were to use. The interviewers had to review every line on every page of the interviewing protocols and of the instructions for introducing the study. Using a script prepared by the research staff, they had to rehearse introducing and explaining the study. They also had to role-play practice interviews with each other and complete two practice interviews with real patients. These practice interviews were reviewed and critiqued.

Although the Thompson study illustrates that with ample interviewer training interviewer–participant matching may not be necessary, we should not overgeneralize their results. They may have had different findings had their subjects not been psychiatric inpatients. What if they had been unable to find interviewers who had ample previous experience working with members of the target population? What if they lacked the resources to train their interviewers so extensively? Under those conditions, matching the ethnicity of interviewers and participants may have made a huge difference.

Use Bilingual Staff

If you are trying to recruit participants from communities where many members have difficulty speaking English, your recruitment staff should be able to communicate in the language with which prospective participants are most comfortable. For example, if your study is to take place in a heavily Latino community, your interviewers should be able to converse in Spanish. If they cannot, your recruitment efforts are unlikely to succeed. Likewise, after recruiting participants, your data collection efforts will need to be conducted in Spanish. And if you are evaluating a treatment, that treatment should be conducted in Spanish. Otherwise, even successful recruitment efforts are likely to be wasted because you will retain so few non-English-speaking participants in the study.

Understand Cultural Factors Influencing Participation

Earlier in this chapter, we discussed the important role played by tribes in the lives of Native

Americans and how many Latinos value the family more than the individual. We noted that researchers might need to interact with tribal leaders or family members before individuals are permitted or willing to participate in a study. Miranda and her associates (Alvidrez et al., 1996; Miranda, 1996) have identified other cultural factors bearing on recruitment and retention of low-income traditional Latinos in research on mental health services. *Familismo* refers to strong, traditional family values among traditional Latinos. *Machismo* refers to the power of the father in decision making, economic and emotional stability, and protecting the family from danger. *Marianismo* refers to the mother's spiritual superiority as she is capable of suffering and self-sacrifice to help her husband and children. *Personalismo* refers to the preferences of many traditional Latinos for a dignified approach when you associate with them, such as by using formal language and formal greetings that convey respect. At the same time, however, recruitment efforts should not be too formal. *Simpatía* refers to the expectation of traditional Latinos that the person treating them with respect will also interact in a warm and friendly manner. To illustrate how sensitivity to these cultural factors can enhance recruitment and retention, Miranda and her associates cite studies whose research staff experienced success in recruiting and retaining Latinos by being warm and personable while using such touches as formal titles (such as *senor* or *señora*), the polite forms of words (such as *usted* for "you"), and remembering the names of participants' children and asking about the children during each interview.

Use Anonymous Enrollment with Stigmatized Populations

Locating and recruiting prospective participants can be a special challenge if your study concerns people who have some characteristic that is stigmatized by society and therefore risky for them to disclose. People in need of intervention for HIV and AIDS constitute one such population. University of Washington social work professor Roger A. Roffman and four associates were honored with an Outstanding Research Award presented by the Society for Social Work and Research for their study of the effectiveness of a telephone group approach to AIDS prevention counseling with gay and bisexual men who had recently engaged in unprotected anal or oral sex with men (Roffman, Downey, Beadnell, Gordon, Craver, & Stephens, 1997; Roffman et al., 1998).

It was not easy for the researchers to find prospective participants for their study. Their recruitment period lasted almost 2 years and included "advertising in the gay press, news coverage in the mainstream press, distributing materials to HIV testing centers and gay/lesbian/bisexual health and social service agencies, and mailing posters to gay bars and baths" (Roffman et al., 1998, p. 9). By implementing both the study and the intervention by telephone, Roffman and his associates were able to assure prospective participants of anonymity if they desired it. Publicizing anonymous enrollment in their recruitment materials enabled prospective participants to feel safer in responding to the recruitment effort and thus helped the research team find a larger pool of prospective participants, many of whom normally would remain hidden because of the societal risk involved in being identified. Beyond making it possible to contact more prospective participants, anonymous enrollment further helped secure their willingness to engage in the study.

Roffman and his associates were creative in their efforts to ensure anonymity and make the prospective applicants feel safe participating in the study. Anonymously enrolled clients were reimbursed (with no name entered on the payee line of the mailed check) for the cost of renting postal boxes in nearby post offices. They used pseudonyms to receive mailed materials from the research staff. The research team succeeded in engaging 548 participants in the study and therefore concluded that anonymous enrollment is an effective way to facilitate participation in research by hidden groups who might otherwise remain unreached. The team also acknowledged, however, that its approach applied only to prospective participants who had telephones and to interventions that can be delivered by telephone. The researchers also acknowledged that although anonymous enrollment appeared to be an important component of identifying and engaging prospective participants in the study, maintaining their participation was facilitated by having a staff that was culturally competent for this population.

Utilize Special Sampling Techniques

Anonymous enrollment is just one way to identify, engage, and maintain hidden groups in your study. The literature on this issue is in its infancy, and future inquiries are likely to identify alternative innovative approaches. Some approaches involve specialized sampling techniques that we will discuss in Chapter 15. One sampling approach commonly associated with this challenge is snowball sampling, which involves asking each research participant you find to help you locate other potential participants. For example, in studying the homeless, you might begin by going to certain areas of town where the homeless are thought most likely to be found. Once you find homeless individuals, you would attempt to expand your snowball sample by asking them for information to help you locate other homeless people whom they know. Another technique would be to recruit relatively large proportions of participants from relatively small minority groups. This is done to ensure that enough cases of certain minority groups are selected to allow for subgroup comparisons within each of those minority groups.

Learn Where to Look

Culturally competent researchers have learned not to rely exclusively on traditional agencies as referral sources in seeking to recruit certain minority group participants or members of hidden and stigmatized populations. But what are the alternatives? The answer to this question will vary, depending on your target population. In their study of people in need of intervention for HIV and AIDS, for example, Roffman and his associates advertised in the gay press, distributed materials at HIV testing centers and gay/lesbian/bisexual health and social service agencies, and mailed posters to gay bars and baths. Homeless participants might be recruited in such places as steam tunnels, loading docks, park benches, bus terminals, missions and flophouses, and abandoned buildings. Culturally competent researchers studying African Americans who have emotional problems have learned that many such individuals do not seek help from traditional mental health services. These researchers therefore seek help in recruiting participants for their studies from ministers, primary care physicians, and informal support networks in addition to traditional service agencies (Thompson et al., 1996). We do not mean to imply that traditional agencies should be ignored, however—just that they should not be relied on exclusively.

Rather than try to identify all the diverse places where you might look to find participants, which will vary greatly depending on the target population of your study, our advice here is that you learn where to look by following some of the other recommendations that we have already discussed. Your literature review on the culture of the target population might offer some important insights. So will advice from key community members or colleagues with expertise about the population of interest. Focus groups (to be discussed in Chapter 19) might offer some additional tips. Of particular value might be what you learn from the involvement of community leaders in the planning of your study or the use of indigenous community members as research staff. As you are learning about the community, you might find it useful to develop a profile of the community. Your profile might list the various organizations and other potential referral sources, as well as additional key community members who can assist in your recruitment efforts (Areán & Gallagher-Thompson, 1996).

Connect with and Nurture Referral Sources

Whether you are relying on traditional or nontraditional organizations for referrals to your study, your success in securing sufficient referrals from those sources will be enhanced if you have established rapport with the individuals working in them. For example, you might attend their meetings and see whether you can volunteer your assistance to them. The more extensive your earlier interactions with key individuals on whom you will rely for referrals and the better your already-established relationship with them, the more helpful they are likely to be when you seek their assistance in recruiting participants for your research. After establishing rapport with referral sources, you should inform them of the benefits your study can provide to the field as well as to individual participants. For example, perhaps the participants will receive a promising new service as well as compensation and other rewards for participating. Perhaps the field will learn whether the promising new service is really effective. Discuss their questions about your study and attempt to assuage their fears about it. You should also nurture your relationship with your referral sources throughout your study. Continue to attend their meetings and assist them. Keep them apprised of how your study is going. Let them know incrementally of any preliminary findings as they emerge.

Use Frequent and Individualized Contacts and Personal Touches

Although many of the techniques we've been discussing so far bear on retention as well as recruitment, much of our discussion has emphasized recruitment more than retention. In studies that involve multiple sessions with participants, however, successful recruitment efforts will be in vain if they are not followed by successful retention efforts. Studies assessing treatment outcome, for example, will need to undertake special efforts to retain clients in treatment. If a no-treatment control group is involved, its members will need to be reminded and motivated to participate in pretesting, posttesting, and perhaps several administrations of follow-up testing.

Miranda and her associates (Alvidrez et al., 1996; Miranda, 1996) recommended some approaches to enhance retention that have been successful in several treatment outcome studies involving low-income Latino participants. We believe that their recommendations might apply to some other low-income minority groups as well. For example, Miranda and her associates advocate the telephoning of no-treatment control group participants regularly, perhaps monthly, by research assistants who are warm and friendly and who ask about the well-being of the participants and their families. The same research assistant should call each time and should remember and discuss the details of the participant's situation and his or her family's situation. This builds rapport and continuity between phone calls. They even recommend sending birthday cards to participants and their children. As we mentioned earlier, transportation to and from each assessment session along with modest cash or food voucher reimbursements to participants after each assessment session will also help. Providing coffee, cold drinks, and perhaps some sandwiches or snacks is also a nice touch. When possible, Miranda and her associates recommend scheduling assessment sessions that coincide with special occasions. For example, you can schedule an assessment during the week of a child's birthday so that you can celebrate at the end of the session with a birthday cake and a small gift. Perhaps you can record the celebrations and give a DVD of the event to participants as a memento of their participation in the study.

In addition to the regular contacts and personal touches that we've just mentioned, there is something else you should always do—something of great importance. Be sure to make reminder calls to participants before their scheduled treatment or assessment sessions. In fact, in addition to calling them a day or two in advance, you should try calling them a week or two in advance. Perhaps they've moved, and you will need time to track them down.

Use Anchor Points

Making reminder calls and other contacts is not easy if your participants are homeless or residentially transient. Hough, Tarke, Renker, Shields, and Glatstein (1996), based on their review of the research on homeless mentally ill people, recommend using anchor points, which are pieces of information about the various places you may be able to find a particular participant. The more anchor points you identify when you first engage an individual in your study, the more likely you will be to find them later. If your participant is a homeless woman, for example, some anchor points might include where she usually sleeps, eats, or hangs out. You might also ask if she has any nearby family or friends and how you can contact them. Are there any social service workers, landlords, or other individuals in the community who might know how to locate her? Is there an address where she goes to pick up her mail, messages, or Supplemental Security Income checks? What, if any, nicknames or aliases does she use? All this information should be recorded systematically on a tracking form. In your subsequent contacts with the participant or others who know of her whereabouts, you should continually update your anchor point information.

Use Tracking Methods

Using your anchor points, Hough et al. (1996) recommend additional techniques for tracking and contacting your participants. If your anchor points include a telephone number, you can use phone tracking. As we already mentioned, you should start calling a week or two in advance of an interview. With a homeless individual, expect to make quite a few calls to the anchor points just to arrange one interview. You should also give homeless participants a toll-free number where they can leave messages about appointment changes, changes in how to locate them, or other relevant information. You might even offer incentives, such as food vouchers,

for leaving such messages. To help participants remember appointments and how to contact the research project, you should give them a card that lists useful information on one side, such as key community resources. On the other side, the card should show appointment times and the research project's address and telephone number.

In addition to phone tracking, you can use mail tracking, in which you mail reminder notices about impending interviews or ask participants to call in to update any changes in how to contact them. Mail tracking might also include sending birthday cards, holiday greetings, and certificates of appreciation for participation. All correspondence should be signed by the research staff member whom the participant knows.

You can also use agency tracking, in which you ask service providers or other community agencies whether they have been in recent contact with participants whom you are unable to locate. Some of these agencies may have been identified in your anchor points. If they are unable to tell you where to locate the participant, you can contact additional agencies, such as social service agencies, hospitals, police, probation and parole officers, substance abuse programs, shelters, public housing staff, Social Security offices, or even the coroner's office. The cooperation you get from these agencies will be enhanced if you follow some of the other recommendations mentioned earlier in this chapter, such as obtaining endorsement for your study from community leaders and connecting with and nurturing your relationships with community agencies relevant to your study.

If your efforts at phone tracking and agency tracking fail to locate a participant, you can resort to field tracking. Field tracking is particularly relevant to research on the homeless and involves talking with people on the streets about where to find the participant. You might go where other homeless people who know the participant hang out and ask them. Offering them small gifts such as coffee or a snack might help. You can also use your anchor points to identify neighbors, friends, family, or previous hangout spots that might help you find the participant.

Regardless of which tracking methods you use, Hough et al. (1996) argue that your persistence is probably the most important factor in obtaining satisfactory retention rates. With some homeless mentally ill participants, for example, you may need to seek out 10 anchor points several times each, make 15 attempts to contact the participant, or show up for a fifth scheduled interview with a participant who has not shown up for the previous four.

These tracking techniques can conflict with the ethical guideline of protecting anonymity and privacy, discussed in Chapter 5. Consequently, before you can use them, you will be required to anticipate them in your informed consent procedures. Participants will need to give you advance permission to seek their whereabouts

EP 2, 4, 9

from the various sources we've been discussing. In addition, you will need to make sure that you do not inadvertently reveal sensitive information about your participant to these sources. The sources should *not*, for example, be informed that your study is on mental illness or AIDS. If these sources are given an address or phone number for the research study, neither should contain anything that would hint at the sensitive nature of the research topic.

» CULTURALLY COMPETENT MEASUREMENT

Earlier in this chapter, we mentioned that culturally insensitive measurement can create problems beyond producing unreliable or invalid information. It can also offend participants, dissuade them from participating in your study or in future studies, and lead to results that they perceive as harmful to their communities. We also discussed how you can attempt to minimize those problems. At this point, we will look more closely at how culturally competent measurement procedures attempt to avoid the problem of producing unreliable or invalid information. Let's begin with culturally competent interviewing.

Culturally Competent Interviewing

As we've noted, using and training culturally competent interviewers is one of the most important ways to enhance the recruitment and retention of minority group participants in research. If interviewing is being used not just to obtain participation in your study but also as one of your data collection methods, whether your interviewers are culturally competent can have a profound impact on the quality of the data you obtain from minority

participants. Three key factors influencing the degree of cultural competence in data collection by interviewers are whether (a) the interviewers speak the same language as the respondent, (b) they are of the same ethnicity as the respondent, and (c) they have had adequate training and experience in interviewing the people of the same ethnicity as the respondent.

The need for your interviewers to speak the language of the people they are interviewing should be self-evident and not require elaboration. If you are an American of European descent who speaks only English, imagine how you would respond to an interview conducted only in Chinese. The influence of matching interviewer and interviewee ethnicity, however, can be more complicated. When people are interviewed by "outsiders," they may have a tendency to exaggerate their views in one direction in an effort to give socially desirable answers. When they are interviewed by someone of their own ethnicity, however, their wish to appear socially desirable may influence them to exaggerate in the other direction. For example, African Americans or Native Americans might deny their true feelings of anger or resentment about racism to a white interviewer. But if they are interviewed by members of their own ethnicity, they might exaggerate their feelings of anger or resentment about racism in an analogous attempt to give answers that they think the interviewer wants to hear.

Although matching interviewer and interviewee ethnicity is not a foolproof guarantee, it is a good rule of thumb to follow whenever possible. Imagine how you would feel, for example, going into a poverty-stricken ethnic neighborhood to interview residents who deem people of your ethnicity as outsiders and perhaps resent them. How much training and experience would it take for you to be as comfortable in the interview as an interviewer who grew up in a neighborhood like that? Even if both of you read the same interview questions verbatim, chances are you would show more discomfort in your posture, eye contact, physical distance from the interviewee, and the naturalness of your tone of voice.

If matching interviewer and interviewee ethnicity is not feasible, you should at least try to use interviewers who have had previous experience in working with members of the target population. Of course, this, too, may not be feasible. But even if you are able to match interviewer and interviewee ethnicity and use interviewers with the desired

CULTURAL ISSUES WHEN INTERVIEWING ASIAN AMERICANS

Nandi (1982) discussed the way various cultural considerations affected an interview survey of Asian Americans. The investigators ruled out the use of mailed questionnaires because of the "astonishingly" high rate of nonresponse they observed in previous studies of Asian Americans. They also noted differences between Indians and Pakistanis, who participated eagerly in the interviews, and members of several other Asian nationalities who were more reluctant to participate. Nandi noted that the interviewees exhibited a high degree of modesty, gratitude for homes and jobs in America, a fear of losing both, and a consequent reluctance to be critical of America.

Consequently, responses to questions about life and work tended to be positive, especially among white interviewers. The researchers tried to alleviate this problem by rechecking each response. For example, after a male Filipino respondent expressed great satisfaction with his job, he expressed a near opposite attitude when the tape recorder was turned off.

The researchers also decided that white males should not be assigned to interview Asian women, because the women are apt to define them as too aggressive, even when, according to majority American norms, those males are not viewed as being aggressive. Similarly, they opted to match female respondents with female interviewers from a different Asian national background. They found that when both interviewer and interviewee shared the same nationality, respondents often feared that confidential information might be divulged. On the other hand, they deemed it unwise to match a female Asian interviewer with a male Asian interviewee because a strong patriarchal feeling among Asian men might bias their responses (perhaps by provoking boastful responses, for example).

Nevertheless, the researchers concluded that no foolproof formula exists to avoid these sorts of problems. Nandi noted that the most intriguing aspect of the in-depth interviews was the apparent inconsistency of responses, sometimes bordering on contradiction. For instance, some Asians simultaneously expressed attraction and repulsion regarding some facet of the same people, value, or system. The researchers attributed this to dualistic philosophical values in some Asian cultures, which unlike Western philosophies can pose a major challenge to conventional techniques in both gathering and interpreting interview data.

previous experience, the need to train them is crucial. Their training should go beyond the general principles for training interviewers, as will be discussed in Chapter 16, and should include a focus on cultural competence through the provision of information and the use of supervised rehearsals, role playing, and practice interviews. The box titled "Cultural Issues When Interviewing Asians" further illustrates measurement problems related to cultural competence in interviewing and how to avoid them.

Language Problems

Regardless of whether we collect data using interviews or alternative techniques, we need to modify our procedures when some of our research participants are not fluent in the majority language. Indeed, IRBs will require translating informed consent forms for such participants before they will approve a proposal. (IRBs were discussed in Chapter 5.) They will also require special provisions for reading informed consent forms to prospective participants who have reading comprehension difficulties. Reading comprehension difficulties are common among many prospective social work research participants, especially those from low-income and/or immigrant populations who may have problems reading even in their primary language.

Three rather obvious steps to be taken to handle language problems are the use of bilingual interviewers, the translating of the informed consent forms and research measures into the language of the respondents, and pretesting the measures in dry runs to see if they are understood as intended. But even these steps will not guarantee success in attaining reliable and valid measurement, or what can be called translation validity. The translation process, for example, is by no means simple.

One problem pertains to the fluency of the bilingual interviewers or translators. Perhaps they are not as fluent in the minority language as we think they are. For example, there may be language differences regarding a particular foreign language between those who can speak only in that language and those who are bilingual. US residents who are bilingual in English and Spanish, for example, might use some English words with a Spanish sound when speaking Spanish—words that might be unintelligible to recent immigrants from Latin America who speak only in Spanish (Grinnell, 1997).

But even if words are accurately translated, that does not guarantee that you have accurately translated the concept being conveyed by those words. That's because the same words can have different meanings to different groups. For example, *the first floor* means different things in different cultures—sometimes the ground floor, sometimes the floor above it. Or consider North American terms such as *feeling blue* (sad or downhearted) that are commonly used in instruments that measure depression. It is difficult to translate these terms into other languages. For example, if you ask Latino or Asian respondents in their own language if they are "feeling blue," they might think you are asking them if they literally have blue skin.

The problem of different words having different meanings to different groups does not only apply to differences between the majority and a minority culture. It also applies to different minority cultures that use the same language. For example, to Puerto Ricans, the word *chavos* means "money." To Mexican Americans, however, the word *chavos* means "men." Thus, a colleague conveyed the following true story to us. Two female professionals were sharing a ride to a conference in the midwestern United States. The less experienced traveler, Carmen, who is Puerto Rican, turned to Rosa, who is Mexican American, and asked her, "How many *chavos* do you have?" The mood changed immediately as Rosa's body language stiffened and her demeanor became distant and cold.

"Sufficiente! (Enough)," Rosa exclaimed.

Carmen did not understand Rosa's sudden mood change but did not pursue the matter. Only some hours later did Carmen learn that Rosa thought Carmen was asking her how many men she had.

Yu, Zhang, et al. (1987) provide the following illustration of some of the complexities involved in translating instruments. They were trying to translate items on self-esteem from English to Chinese for a study being conducted in Shanghai. Their first problem involved whether to translate the instrument into Shanghainese, an unstandardized and unwritten language, or into a standard Chinese language. Another difficulty involved a set of questions that began with the words, "Think of a person who … ," such as "Think of a person who feels that he is a failure generally in life" or "Think of a person who feels he has much to be proud of." They would then ask, "Is this person very much like you, much like you, somewhat like you, very little like you, or not at all like you during the past year?" (p. 78). In their pretesting, Yu and Zhang discovered that most respondents did not understand this form of questioning and frequently asked questions like, "Who is this person?" or "What did you say his name is?" (p. 79).

Yu and Zhang consequently modified the questions but still encountered problems in their continued pretesting. One problematic revised item read, "Have you ever felt that you had something to be proud of?" Yu and Zhang discovered that in the culture they were studying, humility is an important virtue, and therefore they could not use a negative answer to this question as an indicator of self-esteem. Another revised item read, "Have you ever thought that you were a failure in life?" Many poor housewives responded with a blank look, asking, "What is a failure in life?" Living in a society where the communist government then assigned jobs and salaries and where almost no one was ever fired and where income variations were minimal, they previously had not thought of life in terms of competitiveness and success or failure. Yu and Zhang also reported culturally related suspicions that interviewers were part of a surveillance system; such suspicions could impede the validity of the information that respondents provide.

One procedure that has been developed to deal with complexities in translating instruments from one language into another is called *back translation*, which we will discuss a little later in this chapter.

Cultural Bias

A measurement procedure has a **cultural bias** when it is administered to a minority culture without adjusting for the ways in which the minority culture's unique values, attitudes, lifestyles, or limited opportunities alter the accuracy or meaning of what is really being measured. Avoiding cultural bias goes beyond resolving language difficulties. For example, the reluctance among Chinese respondents to acknowledge pride is not a translation problem but rather one of understanding unique cultural values and their implications for social desirability. As another example, asking about sexual issues is extremely taboo in some cultures.

Cultural bias applies not only when administering measurement procedures with people who do not speak the dominant language or who are not assimilated to the dominant culture but also to minorities who are well assimilated to the majority culture. Some may be alienated or perplexed by certain phrases that do not apply to them. Ortega and Richey (1998), for example, discuss how cultural consultants suggested altering some standardized measures to make them more culturally sensitive to African American and Filipino American parents. "I feel like a wallflower when I go out" was changed to "I feel like people don't notice me when I go out." Another change altered "My family gets on my nerves" to "My family upsets me." In a third instance, "My family gives me the moral support I need" was changed to "My family helps me to feel hopeful" (pp. 57–58).

Cultural bias can also occur when the phrases in an instrument are perfectly clear to respondents. Consider, for example, a true/false item on a scale measuring different types of psychopathology worded as follows: "When I leave home I worry about whether the door is locked and the windows are closed." African American youths may be more likely than whites to answer "true," even when they have no more psychopathology than whites. This is because the African American youths are more likely than whites to live in high-crime neighborhoods where an unlocked door is an invitation to burglars (Nichols, Padilla, & Gomez-Maqueo, 2000).

Rogler (1989) provided several additional examples of the influence of cultural bias in connection to research in mental health. One study that Rogler and Hollingshead (1985) conducted in Puerto Rico, for example, examined how one spouse's schizophrenia influences marital decision making. Questions commonly used to evaluate such decision making in the United States—"where to go on vacation, which school the children should attend, the purchasing of insurance policies, and so on"—did not apply to impoverished Puerto Rican families who were "struggling to satisfy their most elementary needs for food, clothing, and housing" (Rogler, 1989, p. 297).

In another example, Rogler discussed findings that indicate that Puerto Ricans who live in the Washington Heights section of Manhattan reported more psychiatric symptoms than did their counterparts in other ethnic groups who share the same social class. Rogler cites other findings that show that the psychiatric symptom statements on the measuring scales were evaluated as less socially undesirable by Puerto Rican respondents than by respondents from other ethnic groups. In other words, the social desirability bias against admitting to psychiatric symptoms seemed to be influencing Puerto Rican respondents less than other respondents. Therefore, the finding of higher rates of psychiatric symptomatology among Puerto Ricans may have been invalid, a measurement error resulting from cultural differences in the social undesirability of particular scale responses.

To anticipate and avoid problems like these, Rogler recommended that researchers spend a period of direct immersion in the culture of the population to be studied before administering measures that were developed on other populations. To assess potential problems in the applicability of the measures, researchers should use various methods that we discussed earlier, such as interviewing knowledgeable informants in the study population and using participant observation methods. When Rogler and his associates did this, for example, they observed spiritualist mediums attempting to control the spirits of patients in a psychiatric hospital in Puerto Rico. This helped sensitize the researchers to the importance of spiritualism in that culture and influenced how they interpreted patient reports of evil spirits in their psychiatric measures.

Rogler's work also illustrates the importance of pretesting your measurement instrument in a dry run to see if your target population will understand it and not find it too unwieldy. We think you can see from this discussion that such pretesting is particularly important when applying an instrument to a population other than the one for whom it was initially developed. It was through pretesting, for example, that Rogler learned of the inapplicability of questions about vacations and insurance policies when studying decision making among impoverished Puerto Rican families. (We will discuss dry run pretesting in Chapters 9 and 10.)

As the literature on culturally competent measurement grows, some traditional concepts for avoiding measurement error are being expanded, questioned, or modified. Ortega and Richey (1998), for example, question the "common practice of rewording or repeating the same questions in an instrument," which is sometimes done to enable researchers to assess an instrument's reliability. Doing this, Ortega and Richey argue, "may be perceived as coercive, cumbersome, and rude by respondents whose culture values reticence and courteousness." Likewise, mixing positively and negatively worded items can present translation and interpretation problems in some cultures that have difficulties with negatively worded items (pp. 59–60). (In Chapter 9, we'll discuss the reasons why researchers like to mix positively and negatively worded items, such as by asking whether respondents love their mother in one item and then asking if they hate her in a later item.)

So far, we have been discussing cultural bias primarily in the context of interviews and measurement instruments. Before leaving this topic, we should point out that cultural bias can also mar data collected using direct observation. Cauce, Coronado, and Watson (1998), for example, cite research showing that when viewing videotaped interactions of African American mothers and daughters, African American observers rated the interactions as having less conflict than did the other observers. The African American raters also rated the mothers as less controlling. Thus, if your study uses observers or raters, it is critical that they be culturally competent.

EP 2, 4, 9

» MEASUREMENT EQUIVALENCE

All of the steps that we have been recommending for developing culturally competent measurement will not guarantee that a measurement instrument that appeared to be valid when tested with one culture will be valid when used with another culture. (We'll discuss measurement validity in depth in Chapter 9.) In the United States, this issue is particularly relevant to the use of instruments that have been tested with whites and then used in research on members of minority groups. Allen and Walsh (2000) point out that most of the

validated personality tests currently used in the United States were validated with samples consisting mainly of Euroamericans. When we modify such instruments, we should assess whether the modified instrument used with the minority culture is really equivalent to the version validated with the dominant culture. We need to do the same when a measure is validated in one country but then applied in another country.

The term measurement equivalence means that a measurement procedure developed in one culture will have the same value and meaning when administered to people in another culture (Burnette, 1998; Moreland, 1996). Three types of measurement equivalence that tend to be of greatest concern are *linguistic equivalence*, *conceptual equivalence*, and *metric equivalence*.

Linguistic Equivalence

Linguistic equivalence, also known as *translation equivalence*, is attained when an instrument has been translated into another language successfully. The back-translation process is perhaps the most commonly used approach to try to attain linguistic equivalence. It begins with a bilingual person translating the instrument and its instructions to a target language. Then another bilingual person translates from the target language back to the original language (not seeing the original version of the instrument). The original instrument is then compared to the back-translated version, and items with discrepancies are modified further.

An alternative approach, forward translation, begins the same way as the back-translation approach—by translating the original instrument into the target language. However, instead of then back-translating it, several bilingual individuals examine both versions to ascertain whether both versions convey the same conceptual meanings.

To illustrate the difference between these two methods, suppose an instrument assessing the quality of relationships between adolescents and their mothers asks, "How often does your mother get on your nerves?" The back-translation approach might correctly translate and back-translate the words *mother* and *nerves* but fail to capture what the sentence really means. In a different culture, the meaning might pertain to the mother putting physical pressure on the adolescent's nerve endings, not to the mother emotionally annoying the adolescent.

Using the forward-translation approach, rather than seeing if the words back-translate correctly, the bilingual individuals would examine the translated version to judge if the translated version still has the emotional annoyance connotation.

Neither the back-translation nor the forward-translation approach, however, is foolproof. Neither guarantees translation validity, the avoidance of cultural bias, or, as we will see next, conceptual equivalence.

Conceptual Equivalence

Conceptual equivalence means that instruments and observed behaviors have the same meanings across cultures. Thus, in the example above, getting on one's nerves might not mean the same thing in non-English-speaking cultures as it does in the United States. Likewise, earlier in this chapter, we discussed how a successful linguistic translation of the term *feeling blue* might not connote feeling sad. Similarly, Moreland (1996) noted that some cultures consider a belch to be a compliment, whereas others consider it to be an insult. If you are observing antisocial behaviors among children, you will not have conceptual equivalence if you count belching as an antisocial behavior among participants from a culture that considers it to be a compliment.

Previously, we noted that forward-translation attempts to attain conceptual equivalence by having bilingual individuals examine the translated version to judge if the translated version still has the intended conceptual connotation. However, what if the bilingual individuals are so acculturated that when they read the translated version, they erroneously interpret it to have the intended meaning? An English-speaking resident of Illinois who is bilingual in Spanish, for example, might read the Spanish version of "I feel blue" (i.e., "Estoy azul," or "Me siento azul") and automatically interpret it in terms of feeling sad because in their culture—despite their proficiency in the Spanish language—it would not occur to them to think it was asking about skin color.

Hurh and Kim (1982) discussed some conceptual equivalence problems in their studies of Korean immigrants. Their interview schedules were translated into Korean by their bilingual, native-born Korean investigators. After the translated version was pretested among some immigrants, a number of questions had to be reworded, added, or eliminated because of conceptual problems. For example, when respondents were asked how often they had been invited to the homes of Americans—or how often they invited Americans to their homes—the question used the Korean term *cho dae*. But in Korea, *cho dae* refers to an invitation to a formal dinner or occasion, often involving well-prepared entertainment. In another study, this one on marital roles in Korean immigrant families, an instrument was used that was developed for American families. After translating it into Korean, some terms had negative connotations for Korean men, who might resist sharing marital roles in chores like grocery shopping or dishwashing.

Metric Equivalence

Metric equivalence, also known as *psychometric equivalence* or *scalar equivalence*, means that scores on a measure are comparable across cultures. To illustrate the difference between conceptual equivalence and metric equivalence, suppose that you devise an instrument that intends to measure the degree of burden experienced by caregivers of frail elderly parents. Some items on the instrument might refer to "objective" burden, such as how much time is spent on caregiving. Other items might refer to "subjective" burden, such as how depressed the caregiver feels about caregiving. At the level of conceptual equivalence, you might be concerned that items about depression, such as "I feel blue," might not have the same meaning across two or more different cultures. At the level of metric equivalence, you might wonder whether in some cultures the amount of time spent in caregiving is really an indicator of burden because some cultures may so esteem their elderly and the caregiving role that the act of caregiving is not seen or experienced as a burden.

An instrument cannot have metric equivalence unless it has linguistic and conceptual equivalence. However, as we have illustrated, linguistic and conceptual equivalence do not guarantee metric equivalence. Accurately understanding the intended meaning of a question about how much time one spends in caregiving does not guarantee that a higher score on time spent indicates more of the concept "burden." Eight hours a day may be perceived in one culture as spending a moderate amount of time on caregiving, whereas in another it may seem huge and more burdensome.

Sue (1996) offers an illustration of problems in metric equivalence in which a study used a scale measuring psychopathology that is widely esteemed for its validity among Caucasians. The scale was administered to Caucasians and to Asian Americans at varying levels of acculturation. The least acculturated Asian Americans had scale scores supposedly indicating the greatest degree of psychopathology, and the Caucasians had scores supposedly indicating the lowest degree of psychopathology. The more acculturated Asian Americans had scores in the middle.

Did these findings indicate that Asian Americans really had more psychopathology than Caucasians and that the least acculturated Asian Americans had the most psychopathology? Possibly. Perhaps the stresses associated with immigration, culture conflict, adjusting to a new environment, language difficulties, prejudice, and so on contributed to higher levels of psychopathology. An alternative possibility, however, is that ethnic differences in the tendency to agree with whatever is being asked makes the scores from the two cultures metrically nonequivalent. Instead of having more psychopathology, perhaps the Asian Americans simply are more likely to agree with statements about psychopathological symptoms in connection with their culture's emphasis on being polite and the notion that disagreeing is impolite.

Suppose the latter explanation in this illustration is the correct one. Would that mean that the scale should not be used to measure psychopathology among Asian Americans because it lacks metric equivalence between the two cultures? Not necessarily. Although the lack of metric equivalence indicates the possibility that the scale is not equally valid for Asian Americans, perhaps some modifications connected to cultural differences can resolve the problem. The problem might also be alleviated by developing unique norms and cutoff scores for Asian Americans. Perhaps a higher score by Asian Americans should be considered indicative of the same level of psychopathology as a lower score by Caucasians. For example, suppose a score of 60 on the scale is considered to indicate the need for mental health treatment, based on studies of the scale with Caucasians. Perhaps analogous studies of the scale with Asian Americans will indicate that a higher score, perhaps around 70 or so, should be considered to indicate the need for mental health treatment by Asian Americans. The foregoing example illustrates the risks you take when you use the same instrument to compare the attributes of two cultural groups. Different scores on the measure indicate only that the two groups *may* differ. Lack of measurement equivalency is the alternative explanation (Sue, 1996).

Assessing Measurement Equivalence

Several procedures can be used to assess the measurement equivalence of an instrument. One approach involves using statistical procedures that we will examine in Chapter 9 to see if items that are answered in similar ways in one culture are answered in similar ways in another culture.

For example, suppose you want to assess caregiver burden among Mexican Americans who are the primary caregivers for their relatives suffering from Alzheimer's disease. Let's assume that you want to use a scale measuring caregiver burden that has been validated with samples that did not include Mexican Americans. Suppose the scale was found to measure three aspects of caregiver burden: objective burden (in which items asking about things like hours spent caregiving and other sacrifices correlated the most with each other), depression (in which items asking about different aspects of depression correlated the most with each other), and physical health (in which items asking about various indicators of the caregiver's physical well-being correlated the most with each other). To assess measurement equivalence with Mexican American caregivers, you would see whether the same items correlate with each other on the same three aspects of caregiver burden. The correspondence need not be perfect. If the discrepancies are small, the results would suggest that the instrument measures the same aspects in both cultures.

Another procedure for assessing measurement equivalence involves assessing whether individuals at different levels of acculturation tend to respond differently to the instrument. Using the previous example, in addition to administering the caregiver burden scale, you might assess the Mexican American caregivers' degree of acculturation and whether they recently emigrated from Mexico. If recent immigrants and others who are less acculturated tend to have the same average burden scores as their more acculturated counterparts, this would support the notion that the scale might be equivalent. If, on the other hand, their average scores are different, that might suggest possible problems in measurement equivalence, since scale scores seem to be influenced by cultural differences.

You should be cautious in making this inference, however. Perhaps the immigration experience and being new and less acculturated in a foreign land actually do make the caregiving role more burdensome. If so, then the differences in average scores would not mean the scale lacked equivalence. To get a better handle on this issue, you might want to explore whether several individual items on the scale each correlated highly with the culture-related factors and whether deleting or modifying those items would sufficiently reduce the differences in average scale scores.

If the foregoing analyses have not convinced you that your scale lacks measurement equivalence, your next step would be to test its validity separately in the different cultures in which you plan to use it, using the various techniques for assessing validity that we discuss in Chapter 9. Assessing the scale's validity is the ultimate test of its measurement equivalence. For example, you might see if a sample of Mexican American caregivers score much higher on the scale than a demographically equivalent sample of Mexican Americans who are not caregivers.

Figure 6-1 depicts the three types of measurement equivalence that we have been discussing. It shows how assessing linguistic equivalence is a prerequisite for assessing conceptual equivalence and how metric equivalence may be assessed once linguistic and conceptual equivalence have been established.

Methods for Improving Measurement Equivalence

Previously, we noted that one way to try to improve measurement equivalence is to use forward translation. However, we also saw how that method is not foolproof. In this section, we'll examine some additional methods to try to improve measurement equivalence.

Selecting Translators   When selecting individuals to serve as back or forward translators, you should remember that language proficiency is only one criterion and that people who speak the same language and are from the same broad culture may differ significantly in dialects and conceptual meanings based on differences in country of origin, in the geographical region of that country, in educational level, and in socioeconomic status. Therefore, Knight, Roosa, and Umana-Taylor (2009)

recommend using a team of translators who vary in those respects.

Pilot Testing   The variability in dialects and conceptual meanings should also be taken into account when pilot testing a translated measurement instrument. If the study's ultimate research sample will contain that kind of variability, then the instrument should be pilot-tested with subgroups of people who represent that variability to see if each subgroup interprets the conceptual meanings of the instrument's items in the same intended manner.

The Value of Qualitative Interviews

Suppose an instrument is developed without adequately detecting and correcting culturally related problems in conceptual equivalence. That predicament is likely to be more severe in a quantitative study than it is if the instrument is being used as an interview guide in a qualitative study. When a standardized instrument is being administered to a relatively large sample of participants in a written self-report format in a quantitative study, there is no opportunity to detect or correct conceptual equivalence problems during the data collection phase of the study. But if the instrument is being used to guide qualitative interviews, then the interviewee has the chance to express puzzlement over what a particular item means. Likewise, the interviewer has the opportunity to notice any verbal or nonverbal cues indicating that interviewees might be perplexed by an item that seems nonsensical to them. For example, if the translated item asks about a relative getting on their nerves, some interviewees might quizzically reply, "No, they never touch me." Or if asked about feeling blue, they might look at their hands and reply, "No, I am always this color." The interviewer then has the opportunity to restate the item in a way that conveys the intended conceptual meaning.

» PROBLEMATIC ISSUES IN MAKING RESEARCH MORE CULTURALLY COMPETENT

Several knotty issues complicate efforts to make research more culturally competent. One involves complexities in defining who qualifies as a member

FIGURE 6.1 Types of Measurement Equivalence

Suppose an instrument measuring the quality of relationships between adolescents and their mothers asks:

How often does your mother get on your nerves?

Almost always   Often   Sometimes   Rarely   Never

Linguistic Equivalence (Translation Equivalence) ↓	Will the non-English versions get translated to words meaning: How often does your mother get on your nerves? Almost always Often Sometimes Rarely Never
Conceptual Equivalence (Assumes linguistic equivalence) ↓	Will non-English speaking adolescents interpret the question in terms of being annoyed? If so, then there is conceptual equivalence. Or will they think they are being asked whether their mother physically puts pressure on their actual nerve endings? If so, then the question lacks conceptual equivalence.
Metric Equivalence (Assumes linguistic and conceptual equivalence)	Will the answer "often" from an adolescent from a culture with less tolerance for disrespect for mothers be more likely to indicate a worse relationship than in the dominant culture? To achieve metric equivalence the extent to which representative samples of adolescents in the two cultures differ in how they respond would have to be assessed. If many more adolescents in one culture respond "often" or "almost always" than in the other culture, then their answers might have to be interpreted differently regarding the severity of the relationship problems that the answers depict.

of a specific ethnic minority group. For example, Norton and Manson (1996) suggest that it is not always easy to answer the question, "Who is an American Indian or Alaskan Native?" What about individuals who seek the benefits of affirmative action as Native Americans merely because their great-great-grandmother was a Cherokee? Beutler, Brown, Crothers, Booker, and Seabrook (1996) point to vagaries and inconsistencies regarding who to classify as Hispanic. Cubans, for example, qualify as Hispanic for "special affirmative action

considerations, whereas Spaniards (the original Hispanics) do not" (p. 893).

A related problem involves the labels we communicate to our research participants to classify their ethnicity. For example, Hispanic/Latino respondents to a questionnaire might be off-put if they must check one of the following three categories to indicate their ethnicity: "white," "Hispanic/Latino," or "black." That is because Hispanics/Latinos can be white or black in addition to being Hispanic/Latino. Therefore, a more culturally competent list of response categories would be "white, non-Hispanic," "black/African American (non-Hispanic/Latino)," and "Hispanic/Latino." You might wonder why we suggest putting black/ African American together, perhaps thinking that doing so is redundant. The reason is that some respondents might be blacks from the Caribbean islands who are not African Americans.

Some less acculturated Hispanic Americans, for example, might prefer the term *Latino*. Many of those who are more acculturated might prefer the term *Hispanic*. Others might resent either term and prefer to be classified according to their nationality, such as *Mexican American*. Which term is preferred varies from person to person and across different geographical regions. If you are planning a study in a particular geographical area where one term is more commonly preferred and another term is likely to be resented, it would behoove you to find this out in advance and make sure that you use the preferred term when communicating with participants to whom that term applies.

Another issue pertains to important subgroup differences within specific ethnic minority groups. No ethnic minority group is homogeneous. As already discussed, each is heterogeneous with regard to such characteristics as culture of origin, socioeconomic status, level of acculturation, whether and how recently individuals or their prior generations immigrated, whether individuals speak the language of the dominant culture, and whether they had traumatic political refugee experiences (Alvidrez et al., 1996). Failing to consider this heterogeneity can result in misleading research conclusions. When we use the term *Hispanic*, it makes a difference whether we are referring to people whose roots are in Mexico, Cuba, Puerto Rico, or elsewhere in Latin America. When we use the term *American Indian* or *Native American*, it makes a difference whether we are referring to people who live in Alaska, on a reservation in New Mexico, or in an apartment in the Bronx. If a study evaluating treatment effectiveness includes only low-income African American participants and only middle-class Caucasians and fails to consider socioeconomic factors, it might end up attributing differences in treatment outcome between the Caucasians and African Americans to ethnicity even if those differences in outcome were really due to socioeconomic differences. To be truly culturally competent, therefore, merely including

ample numbers of minority group participants is not enough. One also has to assess and analyze additional characteristics so as to avoid the following two problems: (1) attributing to ethnicity differences that are really due to other factors; and (2) overgeneralizing to entire minority group conclusions that apply only to subgroups within that minority group.

We end this chapter by noting that there is no foolproof recipe for ensuring that your research will be culturally competent in all respects. Researchers in social work and allied fields are still learning how to make our studies more culturally competent. They also are empirically testing some of the recommendations that are emerging through the practice wisdom of researchers conducting cross-cultural studies. Nevertheless, if you follow the recommendations made in this chapter, we think you will significantly enhance the cultural competence of your research. As with other aspects of research methodology, how much you can do will be influenced by the extent of your resources. Within your feasibility constraints, we hope you will do all you can to maximize the cultural competence of your research, which includes maximizing your cultural competence in general.

EP 2, 4, 9

MAIN POINTS

- Cultural competence means being aware of and appropriately responding to the ways in which cultural factors and cultural differences should influence what we investigate, how we investigate, and how we interpret our findings.
- Studies that do not include adequate representation from specific minority and oppressed populations in their samples are not generalizable to those populations.
- Cultural insensitivity can result in interpreting research findings on ethnic differences in a prejudicial manner, focusing too much on the deficits of minorities and too little on their strengths.
- Culturally competent researchers will include socioeconomic factors in their analyses when they are studying other ways in which minority and majority populations differ.
- Culturally competent researchers will also consider the immigration experience and acculturation

as factors to include in their research as they study differences between minority and majority populations.

- Acculturation is the process in which a group or individual changes after coming into contact with a majority culture, taking on the language, values, attitudes, and lifestyle preferences of the majority culture.

- Studies that use culturally insensitive procedures or that are not responsive to the concerns of minority populations can poison the climate for future research among those populations.

- Before you begin any investigation with minority or oppressed populations, it is crucial that you develop cultural competence regarding those populations, including being well read in the literature on their cultures.

- Representatives of the minority cultures being studied should be included in the formulation of the research questions and in all subsequent stages of the research.

- To alleviate barriers to the recruitment and retention of research participants from minority and oppressed populations, you should obtain endorsement from community leaders, use culturally sensitive approaches regarding confidentiality, employ local community members as research staff, provide adequate compensation, alleviate transportation and child-care barriers, choose a sensitive and accessible setting, use and train culturally competent interviewers, use bilingual staff, understand cultural factors influencing participation, use anonymous enrollment with stigmatized populations, utilize special sampling techniques, learn where to look, connect with and nurture referral sources, use frequent and individualized contacts and personal touches, use anchor points, and use tracking methods.

- Three main threats to culturally competent measurement include (1) the use of interviewers whose personal characteristics or interviewing styles offend or intimidate minority respondents or in other ways make them reluctant to divulge relevant and valid information, (2) the use of language that minority respondents do not understand, and (3) cultural bias.

- When some of your research participants are not fluent in the majority language, you should use bilingual interviewers, translate measures into the language of the respondents, and pretest the measures to see if they are understood as intended.

- Back translation is a commonly used step that is taken to try to attain translation validity. It begins with a bilingual person translating the instrument and its instructions to a target language. Then another bilingual person translates from the target language back to the original language. The original instrument is then compared to the back-translated version, and items with discrepancies are modified further.

- Some researchers use forward translation instead of back translation. Forward translation begins by translating the original instrument into the target language, but then, instead of back-translating it, several bilingual individuals examine both versions to ascertain whether both versions convey the same conceptual meanings.

- Qualitative interviews have more opportunities than self-report quantitative studies for detecting and correcting conceptual equivalence problems in the data collection phase of studies.

- Measurement equivalence means that a measurement procedure developed in one culture will have the same value and meaning when administered to people in another culture.

- Linguistic equivalence is attained when an instrument has been translated successfully.

- Conceptual equivalence means that instruments and observed behaviors have the same meanings across cultures.

- Metric equivalence means that scores on a measure are comparable across cultures. Methods for improving measurement equivalence take into account subgroup differences affecting dialects and conceptual meanings when selecting translators and pilot-testing participants.

- Ways to assess measurement equivalence include assessing whether scores on an instrument are correlated with measures of acculturation and testing the measure's validity separately in the different cultures in which you plan to use it.

- Three issues complicating efforts to make research more culturally competent are (a) complexities in defining who qualifies as a member of a specific ethnic minority group, (b) preferences and resentments regarding the labels communicated to research participants to classify their ethnicity, and (c) important subgroup differences within specific ethnic minority groups (no ethnic minority group is homogeneous).

REVIEW QUESTIONS AND EXERCISES

1. Suppose you want to conduct research whose findings might help improve services or policies affecting migrant farmworkers who recently emigrated from Mexico to the United States.

   a. Contrast how taking a culturally competent approach would differ from a culturally insensitive approach in each of the following phases of the research process: (1) formulating a research question, (2) measurement, (3) recruiting participants, and (4) interpreting findings.

   b. Discuss the steps you would take to recruit and retain the participation of the migrant farmworkers in your study.

2. Interview one or two researchers regarding: (a) how they have incorporated culturally appropriate methods, and (b) any experiences they had in which they realized while implementing their study the need to improve its cultural appropriateness.

3. Examine the tables of contents and abstracts of recent issues of the journal *Research on Social Work Practice* until you find an article reporting on a study assessing the measurement equivalence of a scale. Briefly summarize how that study assessed measurement equivalence and its findings.

INTERNET EXERCISES

1. Using Google or an alternative search engine, enter the search term "culturally sensitive research" to find at least one report of an effort to conduct culturally sensitive research or to improve the cultural sensitivity of a measurement instrument. Briefly summarize and critically appraise what you find.

2. Go to http://www.Treatment.org/Documents/documents.html. There you will find a report titled "Increasing Cultural Sensitivity of the Addiction Severity Index (ASI): An Example With Native Americans in North Dakota." Read the first two chapters of that report, with an emphasis on chapter 2. Critically appraise the steps that were or were not taken to try to improve and assess the cultural sensitivity of the ASI.

3. Find an article titled "Translation of the Rosenberg Self-Esteem Scale Into American Sign Language: A Principal Components Analysis" by Teresa V. Crowe, which appeared in the March 2002 issue of *Social Work Research*. Briefly describe and critically appraise the steps taken in the reported study to achieve and assess measurement equivalence.

4. Find an article titled "Korean Social Work Students' Attitudes Toward Homosexuals" by Sung Lim Hyun and Miriam McNown Johnson, which appeared in the fall 2001 issue of the *Journal of Social Work Education*. Briefly describe how the study reported in this article illustrates the concept of metric equivalence.

5. Find an article titled "Ethnic Pride, Biculturalism, and Drug Use Norms of Urban American Indian Adolescents" by Stephen Kulis, Maria Napoli, and Flavio Francisco Marsiglia, which appeared in the June 2002 issue of *Social Work Research*. Briefly describe and critically appraise how that study illustrates research that is culturally sensitive.

6. Go to the website developed and operated by Dr. Marianne Yoshioka, a social work professor at Columbia University, called "Psychosocial Measures for Asian-American Populations" and located at http://www.columbia.edu/cu/ssw/projects/pmap. Download some of the abstracts of measures you find at that site and briefly describe how they illustrate at least two main points about culturally sensitive measurement discussed in this chapter.

 Visit CengageBrain.com for additional practice and study opportunities including experiential exercises, research tools, glossary, flashcards, and sample test items.

Problem Formulation and Measurement

Posing problems properly is often more difficult than answering them. Indeed, a properly phrased question often seems to answer itself. You may discover the answer to a question just in the process of making the question clear to someone else. Part 3 considers the structuring of inquiry, which involves posing research questions that are proper from a scientific standpoint and useful from a social work and social welfare standpoint.

Chapter 7 addresses the beginnings of research. It examines some of the purposes of inquiry, sources and criteria for selecting a research problem, and common issues and processes to be considered in sharpening the research question and planning a research study.

Chapter 8 deals with specifying what you want to study and the steps or operations for observing the concepts you seek to investigate—a process called *conceptualization and operationalization.* We will look at some of the terms we use quite casually in social work practice—such as *self-esteem, social adjustment,* and *compassion*—and see how essential it is to be clear about what we really mean by such terms. Once we have gotten clear on what we mean when we use certain terms, we are then in a position to create measurements to which those terms refer.

Chapter 9 looks at common sources of measurement error and steps we can take to avoid measurement error and assess the quality of our measurement procedures. Finally, we will look at the process of constructing some measurement instruments that are frequently used in social work research. Chapter 10 will discuss guidelines for asking questions and for the construction of questionnaires and scales.

What you learn in Part 3 will bring you to the verge of making controlled, scientific observations. Learning how to make such observations should enhance your work as a social worker even if you never conduct a research study. Practitioners are constantly engaged in making observations that guide their decision making. The more scientific and valid their observations, the better will be decisions they make on the basis of those observations.

7

Problem Formulation

EPAS Competencies for This Chapter

Competency 1 Demonstrate Ethical and Professional Behavior: The Code of Ethics of the National Association of Social Workers requires social workers to keep current with evidence-based knowledge and to use it as part of what informs their practice decisions. Carrying out this mandate implies competency in reviewing the literature, which we begin to address in this chapter. (We'll cover it in much more depth in Appendix A.)

Competency 4 Engage in Practice-Informed Research and Research-Informed Practice: Engaging in practice-informed research requires understanding how to formulate research questions and studies that will have significant utility for social work practice. Developing that competency is a major focus of this chapter, especially in the sections on research topics and questions.

Competency 9 Evaluate Practice with Individuals Families, Groups, Organizations, and Communities: Just as in other forms of social work research, practice evaluation studies involve a problem formulation stage; thus, this entire chapter pertains to competence in evaluating practice.

What You'll Learn in This Chapter

Here you'll learn about the various purposes of social work research, the beginning of the research process, the methods for planning a research study, and the wide variety of choices to be made concerning who or what is to be studied when, how, and for what purpose.

» INTRODUCTION

The first step in formulating a research problem will vary, depending on such factors as the researcher's prior work on the problem and the existing knowledge base about the problem. For example, researchers embarking on an area of inquiry about which much has been written but who are unsure of what particular aspects they want to study probably should begin with a thorough review of the existing literature on that topic to help them ascertain what new areas of inquiry are most needed. In contrast, researchers who have already done much research on a topic and whose very recently completed studies generated results with specific implications for further research won't have to begin with a comprehensive literature review. But they should make sure that they have kept abreast of the recent works that emerged while they were carrying out their most recent studies.

To set the stage for considering the problem formulation phase of the research process, let's begin by describing and comparing the various purposes of social work research. As you will see, these purposes are not mutually exclusive. Although some studies pursue only one of these purposes, many others pursue multiple purposes.

» PURPOSES OF SOCIAL WORK RESEARCH

Social work research can serve many purposes. Although a given study can have more than one purpose—and most do—we will examine some of the more common purposes separately because each has different implications for other aspects of research design.

Exploration

Much of social work research is conducted to explore a topic—to provide a beginning familiarity with it. This purpose is typical when a researcher is examining a new interest, when the subject of study is relatively new and unstudied, or when a researcher seeks to test the feasibility of undertaking a more careful study or wants to develop the methods to be used in a more careful study. The types of research studies that would fit an exploratory purpose are virtually endless. Here are just a few possible examples:

- Interviewing agency clients who terminated treatment prematurely to develop some preliminary ideas about the reasons why clients drop out of treatment

- Interviewing women who used to reside in a homeless shelter to develop some preliminary ideas about what it is like for them to stay in a shelter and the reasons why so many of them prefer living in the streets

- Interviewing returning combat veterans who have been diagnosed with posttraumatic stress disorder (PTSD) to develop some preliminary ideas about what it is like for them to seek and receive services from community-based practitioners who lack military experience

As already noted, there are many other types of valuable exploratory research in social work. Exploratory studies are essential whenever a researcher is breaking new ground, and they can almost always yield new insights into a topic for research.

Description

Many social work studies aim at a second purpose: to describe phenomena. For example, a descriptive study might assess the extent of homelessness in a community and the proportion of homeless people with various characteristics (such as age, gender, substance abuse, a history of psychiatric hospitalization, and so on). A researcher who computes and reports the number of times individual legislators voted for or against social welfare legislation also serves a descriptive purpose. A descriptive study might assess the career patterns of social work students after they graduate. One of the best-known descriptive studies in social work is the annual canvass of schools of social work conducted by the Council on Social Work Education that identifies a wide variety of characteristics of students and faculty in every school. By following the report of each annual canvass, one can see important trends in social work education, such as increases or decreases in the number of applicants and enrollments at various degree levels, the proportion of women or ethnic minorities enrolled or teaching, and so on.

Quantitative Description All of the preceding examples of descriptive studies are *quantitative* in nature. That is, they focus on counting things. For example, in quantitative studies, *description* typically refers to the characteristics of a population; it is based on quantitative data obtained from a sample of people that is thought to be representative of that population. The data being described in quantitative studies are likely to refer to surface attributes that can be easily quantified, such as age, income, size of family, and so on. In quantitative descriptive studies, the objectivity, precision, and generalizability of the description are paramount concerns.

Qualitative Description Many descriptive studies are qualitative. In qualitative studies, *description* is more likely to refer to a thicker examination of phenomena and their deeper meanings. Qualitative descriptions tend to be concerned more with conveying a sense of what it's like to walk in the shoes of the people being described—providing rich details about their environments, interactions, meanings, and everyday lives—than with generalizing with precision to a larger population. A qualitative descriptive study of mothers receiving welfare in states where the levels of such support are lowest, for example, might describe the effects that the inadequate payments have on the daily lives of a small sample of mothers and their children, how they struggle to survive, how their neighbors and welfare workers interact with them, how that makes them feel, and what things they must do to provide for their families. A quantitative descriptive study of mothers receiving welfare, in contrast, would be likely to select a large, representative sample of these mothers and assess things like how long they require public assistance, their ages and educational levels, and so on.

We will examine methods for qualitative description in more depth in later chapters.

Explanation

A third general purpose of social work research is to explain things. Reporting why some cities have higher child abuse rates than others is a case of explanation, but simply reporting the different child abuse rates is description. A researcher has an explanatory purpose if he or she wishes to know why battered women repeatedly return to live with their batterers rather than simply describing how often they do. Much explanatory research is in the form of testing hypotheses. Reporting the number of agency clients who achieve their treatment goals is a descriptive activity, but testing the hypothesis that a new intervention will increase that number is an explanatory activity. Testing that hypothesis can also have an evaluation purpose, as we will see next.

Evaluation

A fourth purpose of social work research is to evaluate social policies, programs, and interventions. The evaluative purpose of social work research actually encompasses all three of the preceding purposes: exploration, description, and explanation. For example, we might conduct open-ended exploratory interviews with community residents as a first step toward evaluating what services they need. We might conduct a descriptive community survey to evaluate the problems residents report having and the services they say they need. A descriptive study might also evaluate whether services are being implemented as intended, perhaps using both quantitative and qualitative methods. We might conduct an explanatory analysis to evaluate whether factors such as ethnicity or different levels of acculturation explain why some residents are more likely than others to utilize services.

Evaluative studies also commonly ask whether social policies, programs, or services are effective in achieving their stated goals. Evaluations of goal achievement can be done in an exploratory, descriptive, or explanatory way. For example, if we simply ask practitioners in an open-ended fashion to recall techniques they have employed that seemed to be the most or least effective in achieving treatment goals, we would be conducting an exploratory evaluation to generate tentative insights as to what ways of intervening might be worth evaluating further. Suppose we evaluate the proportion of service recipients who achieve treatment goals, such as whether they graduate from high school as opposed to dropping out. That would be a descriptive evaluation. We should not call it *explanatory* unless our study design examines whether it was really our service and not some other factor that explained why the goal was achieved. For example, perhaps the students who were the most motivated to succeed were more likely to seek our services than those who were least motivated. In Part 4 of this text—on the evaluation of policies, programs, and services—we will examine how explanatory studies attempt to rule out such alternative explanations.

Constructing Measurement Instruments

Some studies aim to develop and test measurement instruments that can be used by other researchers or by practitioners as part of the assessment or evaluation aspects of their practice. The research questions implicit in these studies contrast with the types of research questions we've discussed so far. For example, qualitative interviews might be used for the purpose of identifying or refining preliminary items in a measurement instrument. Quantitative methods might be used to assess whether the instrument is reliable and valid. For example, a study might assess whether a 40-item family risk scale accurately predicts whether parents in treatment for child abuse or neglect are likely to be abusive or neglectful again in the future. Or it may assess whether such an instrument that has been accurate with clients from a dominant culture in one country is valid when used with clients of minority ethnicity in that country or with clients residing in other countries. Chapters 9 and 10 of this text will examine the key concepts and methods pertaining to studies that develop and test measurement instruments.

» MULTIPLE PURPOSES

Although it is useful to distinguish the purposes of social work research, we emphasize again that most social work studies have elements of several of these purposes. Because studies can have more than one purpose, sometimes it is difficult to judge how best to characterize a particular study's purpose. This is complicated further by the sometimes-fuzzy distinction between exploratory and explanatory purposes. For example, if we ask homeless people why they are homeless, our ultimate aim is to try to explain the causes of homelessness. However, if we are asking for the purpose of generating new ideas about possible reasons that can be examined later in a more rigorous explanatory study, then our purpose is exploratory.

In attempting to differentiate exploratory and explanatory purposes you might also consider two additional research purposes: *understanding* and *predicting*. If your study is seeking to develop a beginning understanding of a phenomenon, it is more likely to be exploratory than explanatory, even though it might include questions asking respondents to explain why they did something. On the other hand, your study is more likely to be explanatory to the extent that it seeks to rigorously test predictions (hypotheses) implied by tentative explanations derived from previous work on the topic. You will see these several research purposes at work in the various illustrations throughout this book. Figure 7-1 displays the purposes in connection with a study of practitioner views about evidence-based practice, providing quantitative and qualitative examples of each purpose. Now that we've examined these purposes, let's turn to the first phase of the problem formulation process: selecting a topic or problem to research.

» SELECTING TOPICS AND RESEARCH QUESTIONS

Because social work is such a diverse profession, the possible research topics in the field are virtually endless. They can fall in a single problem area or cut across different problem areas, such as health or mental health, child welfare, gerontology, substance abuse, poverty, mental retardation, crime and delinquency, family violence, and many others. Within one or more problem areas, research might focus on individuals, families, groups, communities, organizations, or broader social systems. It might deal with the characteristics of a target population, the services social workers provide, the way social workers are supervised or trained, issues in the administration of social welfare agencies, issues in social policy, assessment of client and community needs for purposes of guiding program development

FIGURE 7.1 Quantitative and Qualitative Illustrations of the Various Purposes of Social Work Research in Investigating Practitioner Views about and Use of Evidence-Based Practice

Purpose	Quantitative Example	Qualitative Example
Exploratory	Administer a close-ended questionnaire to an unrepresentative group of practitioners who are convenient for you to survey, with items that they check to indicate how often they engage in the EBP process and their reasons for doing so or not doing so.	Conduct unstructured, open-ended interviews with a small number of practitioners regarding how often they engage in the EBP process and their reasons for doing so or not doing so.
Descriptive	Administer a structured, close-ended questionnaire to a large, representative sample of practitioners regarding their views of the EBP process and how often they engage in it.	Spend a prolonged period of time (several months or more) hanging out at a child and family service agency. Obtain permission to observe treatment sessions (perhaps by videotape), attending staff meetings and group supervisory sessions, attending in-service trainings, reading practitioner progress notes, and so on. From all of these observations, develop a thick description of the extent and nature of EBP in that agency.
Evaluation	Administer the above scale to practitioners before and after they participate in a continuing education workshop on the EBP process and again six months and one year later to evaluate whether the workshop was effective in improving practitioner knowledge and views regarding the EBP process and in increasing their engagement in that process.	Immediately after practitioners complete a continuing education workshop on the EBP process and again six months later conduct open-ended, probing interviews with them to assess how they experienced the workshop, its value to their practice, whether it influenced their practice and why or why not, suggestions for improving the workshop, and what they perceived to be the most and least helpful aspects of the workshop.
Constructing measurement instruments	After the above scale is finalized, and before it is used in the above descriptive or explanatory studies, administer it to two large groups of practitioners: (1) practitioners who have had extensive training in EBP and who work in agencies that have reputations for their EBP emphases; and (2) practitioners who have had no training in EBP and who work in agencies known not to have any emphasis on EBP. If the average scores of the first group reflect significantly better knowledge and views than the scores of the second group, then the results support the scale's validity.	After developing a preliminary version of the scale to be validated later in a quantitative study, conduct a series of focus groups in several agencies with about five to ten practitioners per agency. Ask the focus group participants to examine the preliminary scale and discuss their reactions to it. For example, what items need to be more clearly worded? Are there any technological terms that they do not understand? Are their views of EBP unlikely to be adequately captured by the scale items, and if so, what additional (or better items) might they suggest for improving the scale?

or treatment planning, the reasons prospective clients don't use services, the dynamics of the problems social workers deal with and their implications for service delivery, how adequately social agencies are responding to certain problems and whether they are reaching the target population in the intended manner, attitudes practitioners have about certain types of clients or services, factors bearing on citizen participation strategies and their outcomes, and a host of other topics.

In social work research, as distinguished from social scientific research in other disciplines, the impetus for selecting a topic should come from decisions that confront social service agencies or the information needed to solve practical problems in social welfare. The researcher's intellectual curiosity and personal interests certainly come into play, as they do in all research, but a study is more likely to have value to the social work field if the topic selected addresses information needed to guide policy, planning, or practice decisions in social welfare. The value of social work research depends more on its applicability to practical social work and social welfare concerns than on whether it builds or tests general social science theories. (The latter are more in the domain of other social scientific disciplines, like sociology, economics, and so on.)

As we discussed in Chapter 3, some useful social work research studies can be carried out without any explicit linkages to general social science theories. Other useful studies do have such linkages. Sometimes, by relating the problem formulation to existing theory, we might enhance the study's potential utility, particularly if that theory provides a framework that helps other researchers comprehend the rationale for and significance of framing the question as we did.

When we say that social work research sets out to solve practical problems in social welfare, the connotation of an "applied" research focus is inescapable. This is in contrast to "pure" research, which connotes the attempt to advance knowledge for its own sake. But this distinction is not as clear as it first may seem. Although social work research may not aim to advance general social science theory, its findings may still have that effect. Polansky (1975), for example, discussed how a social work research study in which he participated—on "behavioral contagion in children's groups"—was cited more frequently in the social psychology literature than in the social work literature (Polansky, Lippitt, & Redl, 1950). By the same token, an applied aim is not necessary in an investigation for it to produce knowledge that is relevant to solving social welfare problems. Social work has always borrowed basic social scientific knowledge advanced by "pure" social research and applied it to practical social welfare concerns.

Some important studies can transcend disciplinary boundaries and still be valuable as social work research. A study to assess the impact of socioenvironmental family stress on whether children drop out of school, for example, could be done by educational psychologists or sociologists. But if the practical need that provided the impetus for selecting that research problem had to do with informing policymakers about the need to employ school social workers to help alleviate family stress as one way to fight the dropout problem, then the study would be of great interest to social workers. The same would apply if the study's main implication was about guiding the practice of school social workers, such as pointing to the need for intensifying interventions to alleviate socioenvironmental sources of family stress or helping families better cope with that stress (as opposed to focusing intervention exclusively on counseling the student). Although research conducted by social workers typically can be considered to be social work research, social work scholars sometimes disagree as to whether a particular study should be deemed social work research or social science research. You might understandably feel that it matters little what we call the research as long as its findings are relevant to social workers.

» NARROWING RESEARCH TOPICS INTO RESEARCH QUESTIONS

Research topics are broad starting points that need to be narrowed down into a research question or research problem. (Because the research question typically deals with needed information to solve practical problems in social welfare, the terms *research question* and *research problem* are often used interchangeably.) Suppose, for example, you want to conduct research on the topic *welfare reform* in the United States. What specific question about welfare reform do you want to research? Do you want to study the similarities and differences among states in the features of their welfare reform legislation? How about factors influencing the legislative process? Perhaps you can compare differential rates of "success" that alternative welfare reform policies have had in removing people from welfare rolls. In contrast, you might want to assess the ways in which policies that aim to remove people from welfare by increasing recipient work requirements have affected the lives of the people who have been moved off of welfare. How do they manage to survive? Do their young children receive adequate supervision, nutrition, and medical care?

As you can see from the previous example, research topics can contain a vast number of diverse alternative research questions, and until you narrow your topic into a specific research question, you can become immobilized, not knowing where to begin. Several criteria can guide you in the narrowing process. Some of these criteria may have already guided your choice of the broader topic. *Personal interest*, for example, may have guided you to choose the topic *sexual abuse of children*. Perhaps you are interested in that topic because you worked for a child welfare agency investigating reported sexual abuse. That experience may have you particularly interested in a research question regarding the validity of a certain investigative procedure for determining whether or not sexual abuse really occurred. Or perhaps you have worked in a treatment center for sexually abused girls and want to study which of several alternative treatment approaches are most effective in alleviating their trauma symptoms. Perhaps you have worked with perpetrators and want to test out the effectiveness of a new treatment for them. Maybe your professional or personal experiences have piqued your curiosity as to whether a close nurturing relationship with a positive adult role model helps prevent the development of severe emotional and behavioral disorders among sexually abused children.

Another criterion for narrowing your topic might be the *information needs of the agency* in which you work or with whom you consult. If you want to conduct your research in a residential treatment center that treats many sexually abused girls who have developed severe impulse control problems, for example, the center staff might advise you that they have a more urgent need to answer the question, "Which is more effective, intervention A or intervention B, in helping these girls develop better impulse control?" than to answer the question, "Does a close nurturing relationship with a positive adult role model help prevent the development of severe emotional and behavioral disorders among sexually abused children?"

When you narrow your topic into a specific research question, you will have to consider the *feasibility* of actually investigating that question. Various resource and other barriers might force you to come up with an alternative question that is more feasible to study. We'll say more about such barriers shortly.

Ultimately, the most important criterion that should guide you in narrowing down your research topic into a research question is that its answer should have significant potential *relevance* for guiding social welfare policy or social work practice. One way to gauge the general utility of a research question is to discuss it with key people who work in the area to which your research question pertains. Another is to conduct a thorough review of the literature relevant to your research question. The literature review is perhaps the most important step in this process. It not only will help you assess the general utility of your research question but will also provide you with an excellent basis for selecting a research question to begin with. Consequently, we'll say more about the literature review a bit later. First, though, let's review the attributes of good research questions.

» ATTRIBUTES OF GOOD RESEARCH QUESTIONS

In discussing the process of narrowing down broad topics into research questions, we have already identified some of the attributes that distinguish good from bad research questions. To begin, we have observed that *a topic is not a research question*. Topics are broad and are not worded as questions. Research questions need to be narrow and worded as questions. Thus, *treatment of sexually abused girls* is a topic and not a research question. In contrast, a good research question might be, "Is play therapy effective in alleviating trauma symptoms among sexually abused girls aged 6 to 8?"

Just wording a broad topic in question form does not guarantee that you will have a good research question. The question needs to be *narrow and specific*. Thus, "Is childhood sexual abuse an important issue in the treatment of depression among women?" would be a better research question if it were worded as, "What proportion of women currently in treatment for major depression report having been sexually abused as a child?"

Research questions need to be *posed in a way that can be answered by observable evidence*. Asking whether criminal sentences for perpetrators of sexual abuse should be stiffer is not a research question. Its answer will depend not on observable evidence but on arguments based largely on value judgments. Of course, it is conceivable that people could marshal known evidence to support their argument in this debate. Perhaps they could mention the high recidivism rate among perpetrators or studies documenting the failure of rehabilitation programs—but that would not make the question being debated a research question. The studies being cited in the debate, however, might have investigated good research questions, such as, "What are the recidivism rates for certain kinds of juvenile sex offenders who have and have not received certain kinds of treatment?"

Previously, we noted that the most important criterion that should guide you in narrowing down your research topic into a research question is that its answer should have significant potential *relevance for guiding social welfare policy or social work practice*. By the same token, a crucial attribute of a good research question is whether it addresses the decision-making needs of agencies or practical problems in social welfare. This does not mean that researchers must ask planners, practitioners, administrators, or other significant social welfare figures to select research questions for them (although getting feedback from those individuals about their needs and priorities is a valuable step in the process). Inspiration for useful research questions can come from many sources. Sometimes it's something you read, something you observe in an agency, or something a colleague says to you. Sometimes a good idea pops into your head from out of the blue.

Whatever the question's source, it's important that before you get carried away—before you invest much of your resources in planning to study the question and before you let your initial enthusiasm or idiosyncratic personal interests wed you too firmly to that question—you take steps to ensure that it passes the "So what?" test. This means that the study you propose to conduct has clear significance and utility for social work practice or social welfare. Assessing in advance whether your study is likely to be useful and significant means skeptically asking what difference the answer to your research question would make to others who are concerned about social work practice or social welfare. For example, a proposed study of the social service needs of family caregivers of relatives Alzheimer's disease might have obvious significance for practice or policy. If you asked your professional colleagues for their reactions about the likely value of such a study, they would probably be enthusiastic immediately. On the other hand, if you were to ask the same colleagues about a study that would assess the leisure-time activities of social service agency directors, they might actually respond by asking, "So what?" and wondering whether you might better use your time by studying a question of greater significance for people in need.

Finally, it is essential that there be more than one possible acceptable answer to the research question. This last requirement can be violated in various ways. One would be by posing a tautological research question: a truism in which the answer is a forgone conclusion. Here's an example of a truism: "Would increasing the proportion of time practitioners spend on certain activities be associated with a decrease in the proportion of time they have left for other activities?" Figure 7-2 illustrates five different research questions—one for each of five research purposes—and shows what type of research design would fit each question and purpose.

Another way in which only one answer might be acceptable would be when feasibility constraints or a system of values make it impossible to implement any changes on the basis of the answer to the research question. Thus, in a fledgling voluntary agency that is constantly struggling to raise enough funds to meet its payroll obligations, there might be little practical value in studying whether increasing the staff–client ratio or travel budget for attending professional conferences would improve staff morale. Feasibility is an attribute of a good research question even when more than one possible answer would be acceptable. If you lack the means or cooperation to conduct the sort of study needed to answer the research question you have posed, then that question won't work for you. You'll need to change it to a question for which you have adequate resources to investigate fully. In light of the great influence it can have on formulating a good research question, let's now look at some of the issues bearing on the feasibility of research.

Feasibility

Experienced and inexperienced researchers alike find it much easier to conceive of rigorous, valuable studies than to figure out how they can actually implement them. One of the most difficult problems that confront researchers is how to make a study feasible without making the research question so narrow that it is no longer worth investigating or without sacrificing too much methodological rigor or inferential capacity. Inexperienced researchers

FIGURE 7.2 How Might an Effort to Provide Culturally Competent Substance Abuse Services in a Border Town Be Researched Differently in Light of Different Research Purposes?

Research Purpose	Research Question	Research Design
Exploration	How do residents—especially those for whom English is not their main language—perceive current substance abuse services, and how do they react to a description of the new services being considered?	Conduct in-depth, qualitative interviews by bilingual and culturally competent interviewers, probing into the perceptions of the residents.
Description	What are the extent and nature of the substance abuse problems in the town—especially among those for whom English is not their main language?	Survey a large representative sample of community residents regarding their substance abuse behaviors, making sure that an adequate proportion of the sample is composed of residents for whom English is not their main language, and using culturally sensitive data collection procedures (as discussed in Chapter 6).
Explanation	What factors are most and least predictive of successful treatment outcomes in current substance abuse services?	Analyze the records of agencies providing the current services, using multivariate statistical procedures to ascertain what client attributes and service provision characteristics are most highly correlated with the degree of treatment outcome success.
Evaluation	Is the new, culturally competent service program more effective than the older approach in reducing the extent and severity of substance abuse?	Conduct an experiment that compares the outcomes of the two approaches when provided to similar groups of service recipients.
Construct a measurement instrument	Is a new self-report paper-and-pencil measurement instrument that attempts to be culturally sensitive more accurate than existing instruments in assessing substance abuse behaviors among border town residents?	Administer each instrument to a sample of residents in treatment for substance abuse and a sample of residents not in treatment for substance abuse and see which instrument depicts greater average differences in the extent of substance abuse between the two groups. Ensure that an adequate proportion of each sample is composed of residents for whom English is not their main language.

commonly formulate idealistic, far-reaching studies and then become immobilized when they find out how much they must scale down their plans if their study is to be feasible. With seasoning, we learn how to strike a happy medium—that is, we learn to formulate and appreciate research questions that are not so narrow that they are no longer worth doing yet are not so grandiose that they are not feasible to investigate.

Common issues in determining the feasibility of a study are its scope, the time it will require, its fiscal costs, ethical considerations, and the cooperation it will require from others. The larger the scope of the study, the more it will cost in time, money, and cooperation. Sometimes, the scope is too large

because the study seeks to assess more variables than can be handled statistically given the available sample size. Ethical issues were examined at length in Chapter 5. A paramount ethical issue that bears on feasibility is whether the value and quality of the research will outweigh any potential discomfort, inconvenience, or risk experienced by those who participate in the study.

The fiscal costs of a study are easily underestimated. Common expenses are personnel costs, travel to collect data, printing and copying expenses, data collection instruments, and postage. Postage costs are easily underestimated. Bulky questionnaires may require more stamps than expected, and nonresponse problems may necessitate multiple mailings. In each mailing, we may also need to enclose a stamped return envelope. Personnel costs commonly involve the hiring of interviewers, coders, and data entry personnel for computer processing.

Time constraints may also turn out to be much worse than anticipated. Inexperienced researchers in particular may underestimate the time required to recruit participants for the study or to make multiple follow-up contacts to urge survey nonrespondents to complete and submit their questionnaires. Scheduled interviews are often missed or canceled, requiring the scheduling of additional ones. Time may be needed to develop and test data collection instruments, perhaps through several dry runs, before actual data collection takes place. A great deal of unanticipated time may be needed to reformulate the problem and revise the study on the basis of unexpected obstacles encountered in trying to implement the research. And, of course, time is needed for each additional phase of the research process: data processing and analysis, writing the report, and so forth.

One time constraint that can be extremely frustrating is obtaining advance authorization for the study. Approval may need to be secured from a variety of sources, such as agency administrators and practitioners, the agency board, and a human subjects review committee that assesses the ethics of the research. Political squabbles in an agency can delay obtaining approval for a study simply because the battling forces will suspect almost anything that its adversaries support. Administrative turnover can also cause frustrating delays. You may have to delay implementing a study when, for example, an executive director moves on to another agency after you have spent considerable time involving him or her in the formulation of your research.

Sometimes, lack of cooperation in one setting forces the researcher to seek a different setting in which to implement a study. Agency members in the original setting may be skeptical about research and refuse to authorize it at all. Perhaps they fear that the research findings will embarrass the agency or certain units or staff. Perhaps in the past they have had bad experiences with other researchers who were insensitive to agency needs and procedures. A common complaint is that researchers exploit agencies so that they can get the data they need for their own intellectual interests and career needs (e.g., doctoral dissertations) and then give nothing back to the agency in useful findings that can help solve agency problems. Some of these agency resistances to research are quite rational, and it is a mistake to treat them lightly or to assume that they result from the insecurity or ignorance of agency members.

» INVOLVING OTHERS IN PROBLEM FORMULATION

Several activities in the problem formulation phase aim to ensure that we ultimately identify an important research problem and articulate a useful research question that is feasible for us to investigate. By engaging in these activities, we progressively sharpen the original research question and its conceptual elements in line with the above criteria. Or we may reject the original question and formulate a new one that better meets these criteria.

Obtaining critical feedback from colleagues and others is an important step in this process, one that helps us more rigorously appraise the study's utility, the clarity of our ideas, alternative ways of looking at the problem, and pragmatic or ethical considerations that pose potential obstacles to the study's feasibility. You must stress to these individuals that you are *not* looking for their approval and that you want them to be critical or skeptical. Otherwise, it may be expedient for them to think that they are currying favor with you by patting you on the back, complimenting you for your initiative and fine mind, and then letting you fall on your face at no cost to themselves.

In Chapter 14 (on program evaluation), we will discuss some of the steps researchers can take to try to overcome or prevent agency resistances to research. One important step is to involve all relevant agency personnel as early as possible in all phases of problem formulation and research design planning. Interact with them and their ideas about what needs to be done. Don't pretend to involve them solely to get their support. Be responsive to what they say, not only in the interaction but also in how you actually formulate the study. If you are responsive to their needs and if they feel they have made a meaningful contribution to the study's design, then chances are better that they will find the study useful and will support it. The dialogue may also build a better, more trusting relationship that can dispel some anxieties about a researcher investigating something in their agency. Moreover, it may help them better understand the purpose and necessity for some of the inconveniences your methodology creates.

One last note before we leave this topic: Lack of cooperation can come not only from agency staff and board members but also from clients or other individuals we hope will be the participants in our research. Perhaps they will refuse to be observed or interviewed or to respond to a survey (particularly when the data collection procedure is cumbersome or threatening). Even if they are willing to participate, will we be able to find them? Suppose you were trying to carry out a longitudinal study of the homeless mentally ill—that is, a study that collects data over a period of years. Imagine how difficult it would be to keep track of them and find them for follow-up interviews (not to mention locating them in the first place for initial interviews). To ensure that your study is sensitive to the needs, lifestyles, and concerns of service consumers, do not overlook representatives of service consumers' groups when involving relevant agency figures in the research planning.

We'll turn now to another important step in the problem formulation phase that will help you identify an important research problem and articulate a useful research question: compiling the literature review.

» LITERATURE REVIEW

One of the most important steps, not only in the problem formulation phase but also in the entire process of designing a study, is the literature review. In view of its importance, we cover the literature review in four places in this book. In this chapter, we'll limit our focus to questions of why, when, and how to review the literature. Appendix A, on using the library, will augment our coverage regarding how to review the literature. In addition, our section in Chapter 2 on searching for evidence in the EBP process dealt with online techniques for finding and reviewing literature (about which we'll say more later). Finally, Chapter 24 will provide in-depth coverage of how to write up a literature review in research proposals and reports. Although we are discussing this step after discussing feasibility issues, the literature review is completed at no one point in the research process. As the research

design evolves, new issues will emerge that require additional investigation of the literature. Be that as it may, usually it is important to initiate a thorough literature review as early as possible in the research process.

Why and When to Review the Literature

Novice researchers commonly make the mistake of putting off their literature reviews until they have sharpened their research question and come up with a design to investigate it. Research can be done that way, but it is not the most efficient use of time. The result may be reinventing the wheel or failing to benefit from the mistakes and experiences of others. Until we review the literature, we have no way of knowing whether the research question has already been adequately answered, of identifying the conceptual and practical obstacles that others have already encountered in this line of research, of learning how those obstacles have been overcome, and of deciding what lines of research can best build on the work that has already been done in a particular problem area.

Another reason to review the literature early: It is a prime source for selecting a research question to begin with. What better way to reduce the chances of selecting an irrelevant or outdated research question than by knowing what has already been done in a particular problem area and the implications of that work for future research? What better way to ensure that your study will be valued as part of a cumulative knowledge-building effort regarding that problem as opposed to being seen as an obscure study that does not seem to address anything that anyone else is addressing or cares about?

Building on prior research does not necessarily imply that your study should never depart radically from previous work or that it should never duplicate a previous study. There may be sound reasons for both. The point is that you make that decision not in ignorance of the prior research but rather in light of it and what your judgment tells you to do. You may wish to repeat a previous study if you think replication is warranted and would be the best contribution you can make. Perhaps your research question has already been answered, but the limitations of the methodologies used to investigate it make you skeptical of the validity of the answer currently in vogue. So you might decide to study the same question with a better methodology.

On the other hand, you may be inspired to look at the problem in a way no one else ever has. You would do this not just to satisfy your own curiosity but also because careful consideration of what has been done before has convinced you that this radical departure is precisely what the field now needs.

There are countless examples of how an early search of the literature can enrich your study and save you from later headaches. Identifying valid measurement instruments, for example, lets you adapt existing measures instead of spending endless hours constructing and testing your own instruments. Another benefit of the literature search is that you can identify alternative conceptions of the problem or variables that had not occurred to you.

Suppose you plan to evaluate the effectiveness of a case management program in helping clients recently discharged from psychiatric hospitals adjust to living in the community. It might seem eminently reasonable to select a reduction in the number of days spent in rehospitalization as the indicator of program effectiveness. But a review of the previous research in this area would inform you that some case management programs paradoxically result in an increase in days of rehospitalization. You would learn that in the face of a woefully inadequate system of community-based resources for the chronically mentally ill, clients commonly need rehospitalization, and effective case managers see that they get what they need.

Had you not done the literature review before implementing your study, you would not have arranged to handle this unforeseen paradox in your design. If your data did indeed show an increase in days of rehospitalization, then you would not be able to conclude that this meant your program was effective because you selected the opposite outcome as the indicator of effectiveness in your problem formulation. But having done the literature review early, you were able to avoid this quandary. You did this by selecting alternative indicators of effectiveness, such as the amount of services (other than case management) clients received while in the community, the quality of their living arrangements, whether they received adequate financial support while in the community, and how well they performed basic activities of daily living in the community. In short, the focus was not on whether the program reduced the amount of time clients spent in the hospital but, rather, on whether it improved their quality of life while in the community.

Some researchers who are using the grounded theory method to construct theory in an inductive fashion (as discussed in Chapter 3) might opt to delay the literature review until they near the end of the research process. Their reason for doing so would be to avoid being influenced by other people's theories in what they observe or how they interpret what they observe. In Chapter 18, we will discuss some logical pitfalls in conducting this kind of research, along with its advantages. We will see that it requires the researcher to make subjective judgments about what is being observed, and this means that what researchers perceive may be influenced in various ways by the orientations they bring to the research. Not everyone agrees with this point of view, and you should know that it is an issue about which reasonable people can disagree. Gilgun (1991) points out that although some grounded theorists delay the literature review, most of them do a thorough literature review before beginning their research. Although they want to conduct their observations with minds as open as possible, they want to start out with an understanding of the current knowledge base and its gaps.

How to Review the Literature

Now that we have established the utility of the literature review, let's briefly examine some common sources for finding the literature that social work researchers typically seek. Appendix A—on using the library—will provide additional information germane to this task, as did the section in Chapter 2 on searching for evidence. Because so many articles and books are always being published, one good way to begin your review is by examining guides to the literature. These guides include abstracts, bibliographies, and indexes.

Abstracts in various fields provide short summaries of published work and indicate where to find the complete publication. You might find relevant material in *Social Work Abstracts* (previously called *Social Work Research & Abstracts*) or abstracts in allied fields such as psychology, sociology, urban studies, or public administration.

Your library's subject guide is another good place to start. Look under several subjects related to your general field of interest. If you are looking for literature pertaining to the problem of child sexual abuse, for example, don't just look under "child sexual abuse." Look also at "child abuse," "child welfare," and so on. While examining the various references, be on the lookout for any bibliographies, particularly those that are annotated, that others have already compiled on your topic; if you find a good one, your search can be expedited a great deal. Also watch for special handbooks that review the literature in an entire field of study.

Searching the Web

As we discussed in Chapter 2 in connection with searching for evidence in the EBP process, your best bet might be to conduct an online search. Your search might involve going to websites that provide information on your research topic as well as professional literature database sites that provide references and abstracts on the topic.

For links to websites providing information, you can enter a search term on a publicly available search engine, such as Google Scholar. Doing so will link you to websites that will vary quite a bit in regard to focus and quality. Whereas some sites will be objective and trustworthy, others will be shoddy or may advocate a particular point of view in a biased manner or be trying to sell something. Some sites will be quite old, while others will be up to date. Some of the more trustworthy sites will be government or university sites.

The box "Some Results of a Google Search for Thought Field Therapy" illustrates the range of links that can come up when searching for websites relevant to your topic. We chose the search term "thought field therapy" for this illustration because it is widely considered to be a debunked pseudoscientific therapy. In the box, you can see that some sites are promoting it, while others are debunking it. You can also see how it is easy to detect some promotional sites because they appear under the "Sponsored Links" column on the right. But other promotional sites are listed in the left column and thus are not separated out as promos.

Although going to various websites for information on your topic can be worthwhile, especially early in your search process, a safer and more efficient way to find scholarly literature on your topic is to search professional literature database sites that provide references and abstracts. Your libraries may provide a variety of Internet professional literature database services, such as *PsycINFO*, PubMed, or Medline. (If you go to the website provided by the National Library of Medicine at

http://www.nlm.nih.gov, you can obtain free usage of Medline.) These services include complete references and abstracts to thousands of journals as well as books. With these services, you identify a list of key words related to your topic and then receive that abstracts of published references associated with those key words.

As we mentioned earlier, Google also provides a useful literature database called *Google Scholar*. You can also take advantage of the "Advanced Scholar Search" to specify a set of words, indicating that all must appear in an article—or just some of them. You can specify a particular author or journal, and you can indicate which scholarly field you are interested in so that the search is limited to articles in that field. The box "Advanced Google Scholar Results for Trauma-Focused Cognitive Behavioral Therapy" illustrates some references that came up when we specified that we wanted to search for publications with all of the words "trauma-focused cognitive behavioral therapy" in the title of the publication.

But don't rely too much on the "magic" of the computer. Some computerized systems will not have some of the references you need, and even if they do have them, there is no guarantee that the key words you select will match theirs. When using these systems, therefore, be sure to use a broad list of key words and to use the noncomputerized guides to the literature as well.

Reference libraries can help you identify the proper computerized abstracting services for your particular research project and compile lists of key words. Keep in mind, however, that such services are not always free. Their use might add to the fiscal costs of your study. (Appendix A provides more detail about these services.)

Be Thorough

No matter how thorough you are in using guides to the literature, you should remember that there may be a time lapse between the publication of a study and its appearance in one of the literature guides, so it is wise to review routinely the tables of contents of recent issues of every professional journal closely related to your topic. This does not take long, assuming that these journals are easily accessible in your library. When you spot a promising title in the table of contents, read the abstract on the first page of the article; it will tell you what you need to

SOME RESULTS OF A GOOGLE SEARCH FOR "THOUGHT FIELD THERAPY"

Search Results

- Thought field therapy for weight loss, anxiety, stress management...
  Includes details on how to get treatment, where to be trained, and collection of self-help articles.
  www.tftrx.com/—15k—Cached—Similar pages www.emotional-health.co.uk

- Thought Field Therapy—Wikipedia, the free encyclopedia
  Thought Field Therapy, or TFT, is fringe psychological treatment developed by an American psychologist, Roger Callahan. [1] Its proponents say that it can...
  en.wikipedia.org/wiki/Thought_Field_Therapy—47k—Cached—Similar pages

- Debunking Thought Field Therapy
  I developed this website to provide mental health consumers and professionals with a more scientific view regarding Thought Field Therapy and its...
  www.geocities.com/pseudoscience_2000/—14k—Cached—Similar pages

- Thought Field Therapy: A Critical Analysis (Skeptical Inquirer...
  Thought Field Therapy is marketed as an extraordinarily fast and effective bodytapping treatment for a number of psychological problems.
  www.csicop.org/si/2000-07/thought-field-therapy.html—41k—Cached—Similar pages by S Inquirer—Related articles

- Thought Field Therapy Training Center
  Thought Field Therapy or TFT is a quick and effective treatment to obtain relief from fear, phobias, trauma, anxiety, depression, stress, addictive urges,...
  www.thoughtfield.com/—8k—Cached—Similar pages

- Evolving Thought Field Therapy: The Clinician's Handbook of ...
  Compare Evolving Thought Field Therapy: The Clinician's Handbook of Diagnoses, Treatment, and Theory ... prices before you buy to make sure you get the best ...
  shopping.msn.com/prices/evolving-thought-field-therapy-the-clinician-s.../ itemid2397567/? ...thought-field-therapy ...—37k—Cached—Similar pages

- Mental Help: Procedures to Avoid
  What is the Callahan Techniques Thought Field Therapy (TFT)?... Hooke W. A review of thought field therapy. Traumatology 3(2), 1998. Swensen DX....
  www.quackwatch.org/01QuackeryRelatedTopics/mentserv.html—29k—Cached—Similar pages

- TFT Suzanne Connolly Workshops—Thought Field Therapy Trainings ...

Sponsored Links

- Learn EFT Therapy on DVD
  The Ultimate Self-Help Technique on Inspirational, Great Value DVDs
  www.emotional-health.co.uk

- Thought field therapy
  Pure Emotional Freedom for You.
  Coaching and Benefits of EFT!
  www.creatingconsciously.com

- Thought Field Therapy
  Compare Products, Prices, & Stores.
  Thought Field. Therapy At Low Prices.
  www.Shopping.Yahoo.com

Suzanne Connolly, LCSW specializes in using Thought Field Therapy to treat Post Traumatic Stress Disorder, PTSD, anxiety, trauma, anger and trains others to...
www.thoughtfieldtherapy.net/—7k—Cached—Similar pages

- Welcome to TFT Worldwide
  This website provides information about Evolving Thought Field Therapy (Tuft), the exciting applications of EvTFT in psychological treatment,...
  www.tftworldwide.com/—12k—Cached—Similar pages

- Thought Field Therapy—Treatment for Traumatic Stress, Phobias
  At the Thought Field Therapy Center of San Diego, Dr. Robert L. Bray uses thirty years of experience as a professional therapist to resolve your individual...
  rlbray.com/—13k—Cached—Similar pages

- Arizona board sanctions psychologist for use of Thought Field Therapy
  APA Monitor article discusses a psychologist placed under probation for practicing thought field therapy, which consists of tapping spots on the body for...
  www.apa.org/monitor/sep99/nl6.html—11k—Cached—Similar pages

- Thought Field Therapy: A Former Insider's Experience—Pignotti ...
  Thought Field Therapy (TFT) is a novel therapy that employs finger tapping on purported acupressure points. Over the past decade, TFT, promoted on the...
  rsw.sagepub.com/cgi/content/abstract/17/3/392—Similar pages by M Pignotti—2007—Cited by 2—Related articles—All 2 versions

- Thought Field Therapy: A Revolutionary Form of Psychotherapy on an... Thought Field
  Therapy is a unique mind-body therapy that capitalizes on the power of the ... Dr. Callahan considers TFT to be a "revolutionary experiment in ...
  www.mercola.com/article/mind_body/thought_field_therapy/overview. htm— 50k—Cached—Similar pages

- Bowen technique*Thought Field Therapy*Energetic
  Healing*Stretching... Learn how the Bowen therapy technique, Thought Field Therapy-energy psychology and other forms of body-centered therapy can address physical, emotional and ...
  www.bowentherapytechnique.com/—7k—Cached—Similar pages

- Thought Field Therapy | Informative Treatment Articles | Casa Palmera
  Thought Field Therapy (TFT) is a non-invasive and effective technique for the elimination of emotional distress. It is believed that TFT gives immediate...
  www.casapalmera.com/articles/thought-field-therapy/—18k—Cached—Similar pages

ADVANCED GOOGLE SCHOLAR RESULTS FOR "TRAUMA-FOCUSED COGNITIVE BEHAVIORAL THERAPY"

- Trauma-focused cognitive behavioral therapy for children and adolescents: An empirical update

  JA Cohen, AP Mannarino, L Berliner, E Deblinger—Journal of Interpersonal Violence, 2000—jiv.sagepub.com

  ... COGNITIVE BEHAVIORAL THERAPY
      This article reviews the four major components of trauma-focused cognitive behavioral therapy (CBT) for children and adolescents ...

  Cited by 53—Related articles—Web Search—BL Direct—All 2 versions

- Comparing the efficacy of EMDR and trauma-focused cognitive behavioral therapy in the treatment of ...
  [PDF]
  GH Seidler, FE Wagner—Psychological Medicine, 2006—Cambridge University Press
  Page 1. REVIEW ARTICLE Comparing the efficacy of EMDR and trauma-focused cognitive-behavioral therapy in the treatment of PTSD: a meta-analytic study ...

  Cited by 18—Related articles—Web Search—BL Direct—All 6 versions

- Trauma-Focused Cognitive Behavioral Therapy: Addressing the Mental Health of Sexually Abused ...

  MD Judith Cohen, E Deblinger, M Charles Wilson, N ...—2007—ncjrs.gov ... NCJ Number: 201247. Title: Trauma-Focused Cognitive Behavioral Therapy: Addressing the Mental Health of Sexually Abused Children....

  Cached—Web Search—All 2 versions

- Jogging the Cogs: Trauma-Focused Art Therapy and Cognitive Behavioral Therapy with Sexually Abused ...

  T Pifalo—Art Therapy: Journal of the American Art Therapy Association, 2007—eric.ed.gov EJ791441—Jogging the Cogs: Trauma-Focused Art Therapy and Cognitive Behavioral Therapy with Sexually Abused - Children....

  Cached—Web Search—BL Direct

know and whether a particular article is sufficiently relevant to your particular focus to warrant reading more. As you read the specific references you have found, make a list of additional relevant references they cite. This way, your bibliography accumulates like a snowball.

Don't just examine journals associated exclusively with social work. Many cross-disciplinary, problem-focused journals are filled with studies that are relevant to the problems dealt with by social workers. For example, if you're interested in studies on the effectiveness of social workers in administering mental health and mental retardation programs, then look also at journals such as *Administration in Mental Health*, the *American Journal of Mental Deficiency*, *Mental Retardation*, and the *Community Mental Health Journal*. Students tend to be unaware of many of these journals, but that

problem is easily remedied by examining the issues of *Social Work Abstracts* from any recent year. Each issue will include a list of the periodicals abstracted for that issue. (The list changes somewhat in each issue.)

How will you know when you have completed your literature review—that you have found all the literature that you need to find? The question has no foolproof answer, one that will guarantee you have not missed any significant work (such as a very recent study in an obscure journal your library doesn't carry). The best answer to this question is that you have probably reviewed enough literature when, having gone through all of the steps delineated here—including the scanning of the recent issues of all relevant journals—you find that you are already familiar with the references cited in the most recently published articles.

>> THE TIME DIMENSION

After you complete your literature review, part of formulating the question and purpose for your research requires considering the time dimension. Research observations may be made more or less at one time, or they may be deliberately stretched over a long period. If, for example, the purpose of your study is to describe the living arrangements of mentally ill patients immediately after their hospital discharge, then you might decide to observe each patient's living arrangements at a predetermined point after their discharge. If, on the other hand, the purpose of your study is to describe how these living arrangements change over time, then you would need to conduct repeated observations of these individuals and their living arrangements over an extended period.

Cross-Sectional Studies

Research studies that examine some phenomenon by taking a cross section of it at one time and analyzing that cross section carefully are called cross-sectional studies. Such a study may have an exploratory, descriptive, or explanatory purpose. A single US census, for example, exemplifies a cross-sectional study for descriptive purposes. If you conducted one open-ended, unstructured interview with each client who prematurely terminated treatment in your agency during a specified period—to generate insights about why your agency's treatment termination rate is so high—you would be conducting a cross-sectional study for exploratory purposes. If you conducted one structured interview with both these clients and those who completed their planned treatment—to test the hypothesis that practitioner–client disagreement about treatment goals is related to whether treatment is completed—then you would be conducting a cross-sectional study for explanatory purposes.

Explanatory cross-sectional studies have an inherent problem. They typically aim to understand causal processes that occur over time, yet their conclusions are based on observations made at only one time. For example, if your cross-sectional study of patients recently discharged from a psychiatric hospital found that those who were living with their families were functioning better and had less symptomatology than those who were not living with their families, then you would not know whether the differences in functioning or symptomatology between the two groups commenced before or after they entered their current living arrangements. In other words, you wouldn't know whether different living arrangements helped cause differences in functioning and symptomatology or whether the latter differences helped to explain placement in particular living arrangements. Although merely finding in a cross-sectional study that such a relationship existed might have significant value, obtaining a better understanding of the causal processes involved in that relationship would require methodological arrangements that we will discuss later in chapters on research designs and statistical analysis.

Longitudinal Studies

Studies that are intended to describe processes occurring over time and thus conduct their observations over an extended period are called longitudinal studies. An example is a researcher who participates in and observes the activities of a support group for battered women or an advocacy group for families of the mentally ill from its beginnings to the present. Analyses of newspaper editorials or US Supreme Court decisions over time on a subject such as abortion or psychiatric commitment are other examples. In the latter instances, the researcher may conduct observations and analyses at one point in time, but because the study's data correspond to events that occur at different chronological points, the study would still be considered longitudinal.

Longitudinal studies can be of great value in assessing whether a particular attribute increases one's risk of developing a later problem. To do this, longitudinal studies might follow over time individuals with and without a particular attribute that might increase their risk of developing that problem. At a later time, the incidence of the problem between the two groups can be compared. For example, children who do and do not have a parent diagnosed with schizophrenia might be followed and compared over many years to see if they become afflicted with schizophrenia. If the incidence of schizophrenia among the children of parents with schizophrenia is significantly higher than it is among the other children, then having a parent with schizophrenia would be deemed a risk factor for developing schizophrenia. Similar longitudinal studies could be conducted to assess the relative risk of contracting HIV or AIDS between groups with and without particular risk factors. By comparing the incidence rates of a problem between two groups, longitudinal studies can calculate the likelihood that individuals with a particular risk factor will develop the problem.

Many qualitative studies that directly observe people over time are naturally longitudinal in nature. Longitudinal studies can be more difficult for quantitative studies, such as large-scale surveys. Nonetheless, they are often undertaken. Three special types of longitudinal studies should be noted here. Trend studies are those that study changes within some general population over time. One example would be a comparison of US censuses over time to show growth in the national population or in specific minority groups. Another example would be an examination of the data generated over the years in the Council on Social Work Education's annual canvass of schools of social work, perhaps to identify fluctuations over time in the number of social work students who specialize in various methods or fields of practice. At the level of a local agency, one could assess whether the types of clients or problems that make up an agency's caseload are changing over time and perhaps use that analysis to make projections as to what these trends imply for future staffing patterns or in-service training needs.

Cohort studies examine more specific subpopulations (cohorts) as they change over time. Typically, a cohort is an age-group, such as the post–World War II baby-boom generation, but it can also be based on some other time grouping, such as people whose first episode of schizophrenia occurred during

a particular time period after deinstitutionalization policies were implemented. For example, we might be interested in what happens to the incidence of substance abuse among young adults with schizophrenia as they age since such abuse is particularly dangerous for this group because of the nature of their illness and the prescribed medications they take. In 2000, we might survey a sample of such persons 20 to 25 years of age and ask them about their use of alcohol or drugs. In 2010, we might survey another sample of such persons 30 to 35 years of age and another sample of those 40 to 45 years of age in 2020. Although the specific set of people would be different, each sample would represent the survivors of the cohort with schizophrenia at the age of 20 to 25 in 2000.

Figure 7-3 offers a graphic illustration of a cohort design. In the example, three studies are being compared: One was conducted in 1980, another in 1990, and the third in 2000. Those who were 20 years old in the 1980 study are compared with those who were 30 in the 1990 study and those who were 40 in the 2000 study. Although the subjects being described in each of the three groups are different, each set of subjects represents the same cohort: those who were born in 1960.

Panel studies examine the same set of people each time. One example would be a follow-up study of people who graduated with a master's degree in social work during a particular year. We might want to see, for example, whether their attitudes about the value of the required research,

FIGURE 7.3 A Cohort Study Design. Each of the Three Groups Shown Here Is a Sample Representing People Who Were Born in 1960

policy, or administration courses change over time. If appreciation of those courses begins to increase dramatically several years after graduation as the alumni move into supervisory and administrative positions, then this information would be useful to both students and faculty as they discuss whether the curriculum should be revised to make it more relevant to the priorities of current students. Or suppose you wanted to learn how teenage mothers from different ethnic groups adapted to their child-rearing responsibilities. You might arrange to observe and interview a sample of such young mothers over time. You would be in a position to see what they learned from other family members, the roles played by their children's fathers, and so on. By getting to know a specific set of young mothers in depth, you would be able to understand a wide range of changes occurring in their lives.

Because the distinctions among trend, cohort, and panel studies are sometimes difficult to grasp at first, we'll contrast the three study designs using the same variable: social work practitioner attitudes about cognitive-behavioral interventions. A trend study might look at shifts over time among direct-service practitioners in their propensity to use cognitive-behavioral interventions. For example, every 5 or 10 years, a new national sample of practitioners could be surveyed.

A cohort study might follow shifts in attitudes among practitioners who earned their social work degrees during a particular era, perhaps between 2010 and 2012. We could study a sample of them in 2013, a new sample of them in 2018 or 2023, and so forth.

A panel study could start with the same sample as the cohort study but return to the same individuals in subsequent surveys rather than draw new samples of practitioners who graduated between 2010 and 2012. Only the panel study would give a full picture of the shifts in attitudes among specific individuals. Cohort and trend studies would uncover only net changes.

Longitudinal studies have an obvious advantage over cross-sectional studies in providing information that describes processes over time. But often this advantage comes at a heavy cost in both time and money, especially in a large-scale survey. Observations may have to be made at the time events are occurring, and the method of observation may require many research workers.

Because panel studies observe the same set of people each time, they offer the most comprehensive

data on changes over time and are generally considered the most powerful and accurate of the three longitudinal approaches. Their chief disadvantage is that they are the most formidable of the three approaches to carry out because of the costs and other difficulties involved in tracking the same individuals over time. A related disadvantage that only affects panel studies is panel attrition: Some respondents who are studied in the first wave of the survey may not participate later. The reasons for this are many. Some respondents move away and cannot be found. Some die. Some lose interest and simply refuse to participate anymore. The danger of such attrition is that those who drop out of the study may not be typical, thereby distorting the study's results. For example, Aneshenshel, Becerra, Fiedler, and Schuler (1989) conducted a panel study of Hispanic and non-Hispanic adolescent girls and looked for and found differences in characteristics of survey dropouts among Hispanics born in the United States and those born in Mexico. Those differences needed to be considered to avoid misleading conclusions about differences between Hispanics and non-Hispanics.

Another potential disadvantage of panel studies is that observing people at an early point may influence what they say or do later. For instance, a teenage gang member who earlier expressed intense enthusiasm for gang membership but who now is having second thoughts about it may not admit to such thoughts to avoid appearing inconsistent and unsure of himself and thus lose face.

You have now seen several purposes that guide social work research and how they relate to the time dimension. To get further clarification of this dimension, we suggest that you examine the box "The Time Dimension and Aging." We turn now to a consideration of who or what you want to study.

» UNITS OF ANALYSIS

Another decision to be made in the problem-formulation phase involves deciding whether you will analyze data on individual people, small groups of people such as families, larger groups of people or entities such as organizations or neighborhoods, or even inanimate things like social artifacts. The latter, for example, could include books, journal articles, houses, and so on. These are called the units of analysis, and the ones you choose for your data analysis are called your units of analysis. If you choose individual people as your units of

THE TIME DIMENSION AND AGING

Joseph J. Leon, Behavioral Science Department, California State Polytechnic University, Pomona

One way to identify the type of time dimension used in a study is to imagine a number of different research projects on growing older in American society. If we studied a sample of individuals in 1990 and compared the different age groups, the design would be termed *cross-sectional*. If we drew another sample of individuals using the same study instrument in the year 2000 and compared the new data with the 1990 data, the design would be termed trend.

Suppose we wished to study only those individuals who were 51 to 60 in the year 2000 and compare them with the 1990 sample of 41- to 50-year-old persons (the 41-to-50 age cohort); this study design would be termed *cohort*. The comparison could be made for the 51-to-60 and 61-to-70 age cohorts as well. Now, if we desired to do a panel study on growing older in America, we would draw a sample in the year 1990 and, using the same sampled individuals in the year 2000, do the study again. Remember, there would be fewer people in the year 2000 study because all the 41- to 50-year-old people in 1990 are 51 to 60 and there would be no 41- to 50-year-old individuals in the year 2000 study. Furthermore, some of the individuals sampled in 1990 would no longer be alive in the year 2000.

	CROSS-SECTIONAL STUDY	
	1990	
	↕ 41–50	
	↕ 51–60	
	↕ 61–70	
	↕ 71–80	

COHORT STUDY

1990	2000
41–50	41–50
51–60	51–60
61–70	61–70
71–80	71–80

TREND STUDY

1990		2000
41–50	↔	41–50
51–60	↔	51–60
61–70	↔	61–70
71–80	↔	71–80

PANEL STUDY

1990	2000
41–50*	41–50
51–60*	51–60*
61–70*	61–70*
71–80*	71–80*
	+81*

↔ Denotes comparison
*Denotes same individuals

analysis, for example, you can make observations to describe the characteristics of each person that you observe. You would then aggregate, or total, the descriptions of the many individuals to provide a descriptive picture of the population made up of those individuals.

For example, you might note the age and gender of each individual client in your agency and then characterize the caseload as a whole as being 53% women and 47% men and having a mean age of 34 years. This is a descriptive analysis of your agency's caseload. Although the final description would be of the agency as a whole, the individual characteristics are aggregated for purposes of describing some larger group. Likewise, if you were to study the members of a street gang to learn about gang members, the individual (gang member) would be the unit of analysis. But if you studied all of the gangs in a city in order to learn the differences, say, between big and small gangs, between "uptown" and "downtown" gangs, and so forth, the unit of analysis would be the *gang*, a social group. Units of analysis, then, are units that we initially describe for the ultimate purpose of aggregating their characteristics in order to describe some larger group or explain some abstract phenomenon.

It is important to understand that you might observe groups of individuals but still use individuals as your units of analysis. For example, you might observe a group of children participating in a group play therapy session. If you are recording the number of antisocial behaviors each of 10 children separately, and later calculating the mean number of anti-social behaviors of the group over

12 sessions, your unit of analysis is individuals. On the other hand, if you are merely recording the number of such behaviors for the group as a whole per session and then charting how that total number increases or decreases over time, your unit of analysis is the group.

Suppose you collect your data from one person—say, the play therapist—regarding what happened in each session. Your unit analysis would still be the group. If, however, you asked the therapist to give you separate information on each child and then entered each child's data separately for your analysis, then your unit of analysis would be individuals.

Many useful studies with valid findings use large groups, such as neighborhoods, as the units of analysis. However, if you use groups as your units of analysis, you should be careful to avoid something called the *ecological fallacy*. Suppose, for example, you find that neighborhoods with the highest proportion of recently arrived immigrants also have the highest crime rates. Without taking into account the fact that group level data do not necessarily reflect individual level data, you might think that your findings mean that certain individuals—in this case, recently arrived immigrants—have the highest crime rates. Perhaps they do, but what if the immigrants have low crime rates but are too poor to live in safer neighborhoods? Then we would make a serious mistake to infer that they have the highest crime rates. That mistake is called the ecological fallacy.

Another concept related to units of analysis is reductionism. Basically, reductionism is an overly strict limitation on the kinds of concepts and variables to be considered as causes in explaining a broad range of human behavior. Sociologists may tend to consider only sociological variables (values, norms, and roles), economists may consider only economic variables (supply and demand and marginal value), or psychologists may consider only psychological variables (personality types and traumas). For example, what causes child abuse? The psychopathology of the perpetrator? Pathological dynamics in family interaction patterns? Socioeconomic stress? Cultural norms? Abnormalities in the child? Scientists from different disciplines tend to look at different types of answers and ignore the others. Explaining all or most human behavior in terms of economic factors is called *economic reductionism*, explaining all or most human behavior in terms of psychological factors is called *psychological*

reductionism, and so forth. Note how this issue relates to the discussion of paradigms in Chapter 3.

Reductionism of any type tends to suggest that particular units of analysis or variables are more relevant than others. A psychologist or psychiatrist might choose perpetrator psychopathology as the cause of child abuse, and thus the unit of analysis would be the individual perpetrator. A family therapist, though, might choose families as units of analysis and examine the interactional dynamics of family systems. A sociologist might also choose families as the unit of analysis to examine the degree of socioenvironmental stress they experience.

Some studies have the purpose of making descriptions or explanations that pertain to more than one unit of analysis. In these cases, the researcher must anticipate what conclusions he or she wishes to draw with regard to what units of analysis. If you read a study in which tentative implications about individuals are derived from group level data, you should not automatically assume that the implications are incorrect and reflect the ecological fallacy. For example, suppose a study finds that crime rates are the highest in communities with the highest levels of adult unemployment. On the one hand, this would not necessarily imply that jobless adults are committing the crimes. On the other hand, we might reasonably surmise that perhaps the poor economic conditions contribute to family disruptions that influence juveniles to commit more crimes. Although the group level data do not permit a conclusion to that effect, they can be useful in stimulating a hypothesis to that effect that can be tested in future research.

This chapter has covered most but not all of the components of the problem formulation phase of the social work research process. The next chapter will examine the latter stage of the problem phase: explicating the conceptual elements of the research. In the chapters that follow, you will learn exactly how to design and execute each specific step of the research process.

MAIN POINTS

- A good research topic should pass the "So what?" test. Also, it should be specific, capable of being answered by observable evidence, feasible to study, and open to doubt and thus answerable in more than one possible way.

- Conducting the literature review is an important step in the problem formulation process. Usually, a thorough grounding in the literature should precede and provide a foundation for the selection of an important topic.
- Anticipating issues in the feasibility of a study is also an important part of problem formulation. Time constraints, fiscal costs, lack of cooperation, and ethical dilemmas are essential things to consider when planning a study.
- The various purposes of social work research studies are not mutually exclusive. Although some studies pursue only one of these purposes, many others pursue multiple purposes.
- Exploration is the attempt to develop an initial rough understanding of some phenomenon.
- Description is the precise measurement and reporting of the characteristics of some population or phenomenon under study.
- Explanation is the discovery and reporting of relationships among different aspects of the phenomenon under study.
- Evaluation studies can be conducted with exploratory, descriptive, and explanatory purposes.
- Cross-sectional studies are those based on observations made at one time.
- Longitudinal studies are those in which observations are made at many times. Such observations may be made of samples drawn from general populations (trend studies), samples drawn from more specific subpopulations (cohort studies), or the same sample of people each time (panel studies).
- Units of analysis are the people or things whose characteristics social researchers observe, describe, and explain. Typically, the unit of analysis in social research is the individual person, but it may also be a social group or a social artifact.
- The ecological fallacy is risked when conclusions about individual behavior are derived from group level data.

REVIEW QUESTIONS AND EXERCISES

1. Consider a problem in social welfare in which you have a special interest (such as child abuse, mental illness, the frail elderly, and so on). Formulate three different research questions about that problem, each of which would be important for the field to answer and might, in your opinion, be of interest to a funding agency. Formulate each question to deal with a different research purpose—one for exploration, one for description, and one for explanation.
2. Look through a social work research journal and find examples of at least three different units of analysis. Identify each unit of analysis and present a quotation from the journal in which that unit of analysis was discussed.

INTERNET EXERCISES

1. Examine several recent issues of a social work research journal (such as *Research on Social Work Practice* or *Social Work Research*). Find articles that report research studies illustrating the purposes of exploration, description, and explanation. Identify which of these three purposes each study illustrates and briefly justify your judgment in that regard.
2. Locate the following longitudinal study from the July 2002 issue of the journal *Social Work*: "Welfare Use as a Life Course Event: Toward a New Understanding of the U.S. Safety Net" by M. R. Rank and T. A. Hirschl. Describe the nature of the study design, its primary findings, and the implications of those findings for social work practice and social welfare policy.

Visit CengageBrain.com for additional practice and study opportunities including experiential exercises, research tools, glossary, flashcards, and sample test items.

8

Conceptualization in Quantitative and Qualitative Inquiry

EPAS Competencies for This Chapter

Competency 4 Engage in Practice-Informed Research and Research-Informed Practice: This competency pertains to this entire chapter because doing practice-informed research requires being able to conceptualize and operationally define variables. The same applies to engaging in research-informed practice because you must understand hypotheses, variables, and operational definitions in order to be able to have research inform your practice.

Competency 7 Assess Individuals, Families, Groups, Organizations, and Communities: Competency to assess requires competency in operationally defining what you want to assess and the utility of existing scales in that process. Thus, this competency pervades the operationalization sections of this chapter.

Competency 9 Evaluate Practice with Individuals Families, Groups, Organizations, and Communities: Evaluating practice requires being able to conceptualize and operationally define the variables to be assessed as part of you evaluation. Thus, this competency pertains to this entire chapter.

What You'll Learn in This Chapter

Many social work terms communicate vague, unspecified meanings. In this chapter, you'll see how quantitative and qualitative studies vary in the conceptualization and definitions of the terms being studied.

» INTRODUCTION

The preceding chapter described various aspects of the problem formulation phase. In quantitative research, explicating the conceptual elements of the research comes at the end of that phase. In qualitative research, the conceptualization process follows a more flexible and emergent pattern. This chapter will discuss the conceptualization process from both a quantitative and a qualitative perspective. After summarizing the contrast between these two approaches to conceptualization, we'll look at each approach separately. We'll begin with the quantitative approach to conceptualization. Because the approach to conceptualization in the problem formulation phase of quantitative studies involves processes that tend to be more specified and complex, it will require a lengthier discussion. However, as you will see, we do not advocate either approach as preferable. Each has its own advantages and disadvantages, and, as we discussed in Chapter 4, the two approaches are not mutually exclusive; mixed-methods studies combine them.

» CONTRASTING QUANTITATIVE AND QUALITATIVE CONCEPTUALIZATION

In purely quantitative studies, conceptualization tends to come at the end stage of problem formulation—when researchers move from vague ideas about what they want to study to being able to recognize and measure what they want to study. It involves refining and specifying abstract concepts (conceptualization) and developing specific research procedures (operationalization) that will result in empirical observations of things that represent those concepts in the real world. This process moves quantitative research closer to concrete measurements because it sets the stage for how concepts will be observed and how data will be collected.

Unlike purely quantitative studies, in purely qualitative studies, variables and indicators tend not to be specified in advance of the observation and data collection process. Instead, qualitative studies emphasize methodological freedom and flexibility so that the most salient variables—and their deeper meanings—will emerge as the researchers immerse themselves in the phenomena they are studying. Despite their greater flexibility, however, even qualitative studies begin with an initial set of anticipated meanings that can be refined during data collection and interpretation. Thus, although the timing and nature of conceptualization tends to differ between qualitative and quantitative studies, it is equally emphasized in both.

A glimpse of the contrast between these two approaches to conceptualization could be found in Figure 7-1 in Chapter 7, which pertained to how quantitative and qualitative studies might differ in investigating practitioner views about evidence-based practice (EBP). In a purely quantitative study, the researchers might—after completing the earlier steps in the problem formulation phase—construct a scale with closed-ended items that can yield a summated score to define the extent to which practitioners view EBP favorably or unfavorably. The scale would list some statements that portray EBP favorably, such as, "Engaging in the EBP process improves practice effectiveness." It would also list some negatively worded statements, such as, "Engaging in the EBP process harms the practitioner–client relationship." Practitioners would indicate their level of agreement or disagreement with each statement by checking whether they strongly agree, somewhat agree, are neutral, somewhat disagree, or strongly disagree with the statement. Each response would get a score from 1 to 5 (or 0 to 4), with the higher score indicating greater agreement with the positively worded statements and greater disagreement with the negatively worded statements. Views about EBP, then, would be defined as the total score on the scale after summating the scores on all of the statements.

The summated score on the above scale would comprise the definition of one variable in the quantitative study, that variable being view of EBP. If the study sought to identify variables that might be related to the scale score, it would define those variables in advance, too. In assessing such variables, the researchers might ask practitioners to enter a number in response to questions about the practitioner's age, how many years of practice experience they have had, how many research courses they took in their professional education, how many EBP continuing education workshops they attended, and so on. They might also ask them closed-ended questions about their sex, ethnicity, whether they work in an agency or in private practice, and so on.

In a purely qualitative study, in contrast, the researchers would not presume that they know enough about practitioner views about EBP to define those views in advance. They would also believe that defining the views in advance would prevent learning important things about those views that were not captured by their a priori definition. Moreover, they would believe that a score on a scale like the one above would be superficial and would fail to capture the deeper meanings and reasons for practitioner views and how those views might be influenced by contextual factors.

For example, some practitioners who answer "neutral" to some statements might really view EBP very favorably as it applies to their own practice and might regularly engage in the EBP process in their own practice. But they answered "neutral" because they believe that for many other practitioners, engaging in the EBP process might not be beneficial. Maybe they believe that many other practitioners would not engage in the EBP process appropriately—for example, perhaps by misconstruing it as a cookbook approach to practice that incorrectly disregards the phase of the process involving integrating research evidence with practitioner expertise and knowledge about client attributes, preferences, and circumstances. Or they might believe that many other practitioners would lack the requisite time and resources to obtain the supervision and training needed to implement the chosen empirically supported intervention properly. Just scoring such respondents as "neutral," therefore, would fail to distinguish them from other "neutral" practitioners whose neutrality is based on a limited or erroneous understanding of EBP or ambivalence about engaging in EBP as part of their own practice.

Consequently, rather than define views about EBP in advance in a quantitative fashion and rather than doing the same regarding other variables that might be associated with those views, qualitative investigators would take a different approach. They might conduct unstructured, open-ended interviews (with neutral probes) with practitioners about their views of EBP. They might spend a prolonged amount of time hanging out with and observing practitioners—or perhaps reading their progress notes in their case records—to develop ideas about whether, why, and how they engage in EBP. They might conduct several focus groups in which practitioners are asked in an open-ended way to discuss their views about EBP. They would let the relevant concepts and definitions pertaining to views about EBP and factors related to those views emerge from these qualitative modes of inquiry.

Keeping in mind the contrast between these two approaches to conceptualization, let's now look at the quantitative approach in detail. After that, we'll return to the qualitative approach.

EP 4

» CONCEPTUAL EXPLICATION IN QUANTITATIVE INQUIRY

Once the foregoing aspects of problem formulation (discussed in Chapter 7) have been handled in quantitative studies, the researchers are ready to specify and operationally define the variables in their study and, if the study is not purely descriptive, to postulate relationships among those variables (i.e., to develop hypotheses). As we discussed in Chapter 3, a *variable* is a concept we are investigating. We defined a *concept* as a mental image that symbolizes an idea, an object, an event, a behavior, a person, and so on. We can also think of concepts as words that people agree on to symbolize something. The words can represent something relatively easy to observe, such as sex, height, residence, or age. Or they can represent something more difficult to observe, such as level of self-esteem, morale of residents in long-term care, level of social functioning, staff burnout, racism, sexism, ageism, homophobia, and so on.

Some concepts are composed of other concepts. Sex (as stated on birth certificate), for example, is a biological concept that for most people consists of the concepts *male* and *female*. As we discussed in Chapter 3, the concepts that make up a broader concept are called attributes. Thus, *male* and *female* are two attributes of the concept *sex*. A third possible attribute for that variable would be *intersex*, which is a concept that applies to people born with a sexual anatomy that does not match typical definitions of female or male.

Not all researchers use the term *attributes*, however, when referring to the categories of their variables. Some might instead use the term *categories*. You should realize that the terms *attributes* and *categories* mean the same thing when researchers are mentioning them in reference to their variables. Other researchers might use the term *values* to mean the same thing as the attributes or categories of their variables. Although that term can be synonymous with the terms *attributes* and *categories*, it is more likely to be used than the other two terms when the categories of the variable in question are numeric, such as with variables such as age, score on a test, and so on.

You may wonder why we use the term *variables* in research. Why don't we just stick with the term *concepts*? One reason is that we investigate things that we think will *vary*. *Male*, for example, is a concept but can't be a variable. It can take on only one value and therefore is only an attribute. Sex, on the other hand, is a concept that can take on more than one value and therefore can be a variable. We could, for example, investigate the relationship between sex and salary. Are salaries for males higher than salaries for females? It would make no sense, however, to investigate the relationship between male and salary. Both *male* and *salary* are concepts, but only the concept *salary* conveys variation and therefore can qualify as a variable.

A concept is a variable if it (1) comprises more than one attribute, or value, and thus is capable of varying and (2) is chosen for investigation in a research study. In quantitative research studies, a third condition must be met before a concept can be called a variable: It must be translated into observable terms. The term *operational definition* refers to that translation: the operations, or indicators, we will use to determine the attribute we observe about a particular concept. Thus, a family's risk of child abuse can be operationally defined as the variable *score on the Family Risk Scale* (a scale completed by child welfare workers

EP 9

that is based on their observations of the family). We will discuss operational definitions in much greater length later in this chapter. First, however, let's examine the development of hypotheses.

Developing a Proper Hypothesis

You may recall from Chapter 3 that a variable that is postulated to explain another variable is called the independent variable. The variable being explained is called the dependent variable. The statement that postulates the relationship between the independent and dependent variables is called the hypothesis. In other words, hypotheses are tentative statements that predict what we expect to find about the way our variables vary together.

A good hypothesis has some of the attributes of a good research question. It should be clear and specific. It should have more than one possible outcome—that is, it should not be a truism. Truisms were discussed briefly in Chapter 7. Here is another example of a truism. Suppose we hypothesized that parents who score better on a measure of child rearing knowledge also score better on a measure of child-rearing attitudes. What would make that a truism is if both measures shared similar items, such as asking parents about harsh corporal punishment, using time-outs, praising, and so on. For example, the knowledge measure might ask the questions in exam-like format, such as true/false or multiple choice, whereas the attitudinal measure might ask parents if they agree or disagree with statements about many of the same child-rearing practices about which the knowledge measure asked. To the extent that the two measures shared items that measure the same thing, then it would be hard to imagine more than one possible outcome for our hypothesis. That is, for most of the parents it would be hard to imagine a parent having an undesirable score on one measure and a desirable score on the other.

A way to have the same hypothesis *not* be a truism would be by having completely different items on the two measures. For example, the attitudinal measure could contain the above agree/disagree statements, whereas the knowledge measure could be restricted to exam like questions about child development, the impact of shaking on an infant's or toddler's brain, the impact of lots of hugging on the development of personality attributes, and so on.

Hypotheses also should be value free and testable. For example, the statement "Welfare reform legislation should be repealed" is not a hypothesis. It is a judgmental recommendation, not a predicted relationship between two variables that is stated in terms that can be verified or refuted. If we modify the statement to read, "Welfare reform is harmful to the children of welfare recipients," we have made it sound more like a hypothesis. But it would still not qualify as a good hypothesis statement. Although it is predicting that a concept, welfare reform, is harming children, it is not clear and specific regarding the nature of the harm—that is, the specific nature of the concept that is meant to be the dependent variable. Moreover, the concept intended as the independent variable, welfare reform, is also vague. What specific aspect of welfare reform are we referring to? We could change the statement into a good hypothesis by being more clear and specific about both variables. One way to do so would be to postulate, "Welfare reform policies that move parents off welfare by increasing recipient work requirements will increase the number of children who lack health insurance coverage." The latter statement predicts a relationship between two clearly stated variables that can be verified or refuted by examining whether increases in the number of children who lack health insurance coverage occur after such policies are implemented or by examining whether states that implement such policies have greater increases in the number of children who lack health insurance coverage than do states not implementing them.

Differences between Hypotheses and Research Questions

Although a good hypothesis has some of the attributes of a good research question and despite the similarity between some hypotheses and some research questions in explanatory studies, hypotheses are not the same as research questions. One way in which the two differ pertains to the purpose of the research. Exploratory and descriptive studies, for example, do not test hypotheses.

Recall the following research question from Figure 7-2 in Chapter 7: "How do residents—especially those for whom English is not their main language—perceive current substance abuse services, and how do they react to a description of the new services being considered?" We mentioned that question in Chapter 7 in connection to a qualitative exploratory study. Notice that it does not

predict a relationship between an independent and a dependent variable. A hypothesis would have to predict such a relationship, and it is conceivable that researchers who are investigating that question might want to formulate and test the following hypothesis: "Residents who do not speak English as their main language are less likely to utilize substance abuse services than are residents whose main language is English." This hypothesis predicts a relationship between main language spoken (the independent variable) and service utilization rate (the dependent variable). Notice also that the same research question could spawn another hypothesis, such as, "Residents who do speak English as their main language are more satisfied with substance abuse services than are residents whose main language is not English."

Also recall another research question from Figure 7-2 in Chapter 7, as follows: "What is the extent and nature of the substance abuse problem in the town—especially among those for whom English is not their main language?" We mentioned this question in Chapter 7 in connection to a quantitative descriptive study. EP 4, 9

Notice that it, too, does not predict a relationship between an independent and dependent variable. Again, however, researchers who are investigating that question could formulate and test several hypotheses, as illustrated in the box "An Illustration of the Differences and Connections Between Research Questions and Hypotheses."

Types of Relationships between Variables

Some hypotheses predict positive, negative (inverse), or curvilinear relationships between variables. In a positive relationship, the dependent variable increases as the independent variable increases (or decreases as the independent variable decreases)—that is, both variables move in the same direction. Thus, we might postulate a positive relationship between the amount of symbolic rewards citizens receive for participating in community organizations and the extent to which they participate. We might also postulate a positive relationship between level of client satisfaction with social services and the extent to which the delivered service focused on the problem or goal for which the client originally sought help (as opposed to a problem or goal that the practitioner chose to work on without

AN ILLUSTRATION OF THE DIFFERENCES AND CONNECTIONS BETWEEN RESEARCH QUESTIONS AND HYPOTHESES

Research Question	Study Purpose	Some Possible Hypotheses
What is the extent and nature of the substance abuse problems in the town—especially among those for whom English is not their main language?	Description	None (no predicted relationship between independent and dependent variables).
	Explanation	Residents whose main language is English have higher rates of substance abuse than other residents.
		Residents whose main language is English are more likely to abuse drugs, whereas other residents are more likely to abuse alcohol.
		Level of acculturation is related to main type of substance abused.
		Parents of recently immigrated teens are less likely to deal drugs than are other parents of teens.

involving the client in the decision). The top graph in Figure 8-1 pictorially represents this hypothesized positive relationship.

A negative (inverse) relationship means that the two variables move in opposite directions—that is, as one increases, the other decreases. We might postulate a negative relationship between the caseload size of direct-service practitioners and their degree of effectiveness because those whose caseloads are too large might be expected to have less time to provide quality services. A negative relationship might also be postulated between family income and level of family stress. The middle graph in Figure 8-1 pictorially represents this hypothesized negative relationship.

A curvilinear relationship is one in which the nature of the relationship changes at certain levels of the variables. For example, some social work educators believe that the students who are most skeptical about the value of published social work research are those who have taken either many research courses or none at all. Those who have never had a research course may not yet have learned to appreciate research's potential utility. Those with a great deal of knowledge about research might be disillusioned by the many serious methodological flaws they detect in much of the published research. Consequently, those with the least skepticism may be the ones in the middle—those who have enough

knowledge to appreciate the value of good research but who have not yet critically scrutinized enough of the literature to realize how many published studies are seriously flawed. Educators who believe this notion might hypothesize a U curve that begins with a negative relationship between the number of courses taken and the degree of skepticism about research and ends with a positive relationship between them. In other words, skepticism decreases as more courses are taken up to a certain number of courses, and then it increases as more courses are taken beyond that. The bottom graph in Figure 8-1 pictorially represents this hypothesized curvilinear relationship.

Extraneous Variables

A third category of variables is termed extraneous variables. These variables represent alternative explanations for relationships that are observed between independent and dependent variables. Suppose, for example, that the economy improves at the same time that a new welfare policy is implemented. If the living standards or employment rates of poor people improve after the policy is implemented, how do we determine whether the improvement is due to the independent variable (the change in policy) or an extraneous variable (the change in the economy)? Suppose that a study finds that the more

FIGURE 8.1 Graphic Display of Types of Hypothetical Relationships between Variables

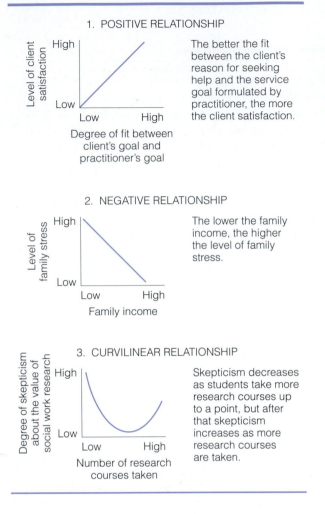

1. POSITIVE RELATIONSHIP

Level of client satisfaction (High / Low)

Degree of fit between client's goal and practitioner's goal (Low / High)

The better the fit between the client's reason for seeking help and the service goal formulated by practitioner, the more the client satisfaction.

2. NEGATIVE RELATIONSHIP

Level of family stress (High / Low)

Family income (Low / High)

The lower the family income, the higher the level of family stress.

3. CURVILINEAR RELATIONSHIP

Degree of skepticism about the value of social work research (High / Low)

Number of research courses taken (Low / High)

Skepticism decreases as students take more research courses up to a point, but after that skepticism increases as more research courses are taken.

social services received by hospital patients, the shorter the patients' life span. That relationship would probably be explained away by the fact that the cases involving the most serious illnesses—particularly terminal illnesses—need to receive more social services. Thus, *severity of illness* might be conceptualized as an extraneous variable that explains the relationship between life span and amount of social services received.

Sometimes our studies check on the possibility that the relationship between our independent and dependent variables (or the apparent lack thereof) is misleading—that it is explained away by other variables. When we do that, the extraneous variables that we seek to control in our design can be called

control variables. In the previous example, we could still conceive of *severity of illness* as an extraneous variable, but because we are controlling for it, we can call it a *control variable* in our study.

Moderating Variables

Sometimes control variables are called moderating variables. Moderating variables can affect the strength or direction of the relationship between the independent and dependent variable. Thus, if we predict that an intervention will be effective only among females and not among males, *sex* would be a moderating variable. Likewise, if we predict that an intervention will be effective only among criminal offenders who committed nonviolent crimes, then *type of crime* would be a moderating variable.

Suppose we want to check on this possibility: The relationship between *life span* and *amount of social services received* is explained by the fact that cases involving the most serious illnesses need to receive more social services. To check this out, we would do the following. First, we would separate all cases into subgroups according to seriousness of illness. For the sake of simplicity, assume that we would divide them into only two groups: (a) those with life-threatening or terminal illnesses and (b) those whose illnesses are not life threatening or not terminal. Next, we would assess the relationship between life span and amount of social services received just for those cases with life-threatening or terminal illnesses. Then we would do the same just for those cases whose illnesses are not life threatening or not terminal. Thus, we would be controlling for seriousness of illness by examining whether the original relationship between our independent and dependent variables changes or stays the same for each level of seriousness of illness.

The term *control* in this context does not mean that the researcher has control over the nature of the illness. It simply means that the researcher examines the hypothesized relationship separately for each category of the control variable. If, when controlling for that variable, the original relationship between the independent and dependent variables disappears, it means that the original relationship was spurious. Thus, a spurious relationship is one that no longer exists when a third variable is controlled. Figure 8-2 provides a pictorial illustration of the type of spurious relationship we have been discussing. To see more examples of spurious relationships,

FIGURE 8.2   Illustration of a Spurious Causal Relationship That Disappears When Controlling for a Third Variable

Spurious Causal Relationship:

Social services in health care increase risk of death

(Arrows indicate incorrect causal interpretation.)

Amount of social services provided to patient and family   Patient death rate

More → Higher

Less → Lower

Actual Causal Relationship:

Severity of illness affects both the amount of social services and the risk of death

(Receiving more social services is associated with a higher death rate only because terminally ill patients receive more social services.)

(Arrows indicate correct causal interpretation.)

Terminal   Severity of Patient's Illness   Not Terminal

More Social Services   Higher Death Rate   Less Social Services   Lower Death Rate

you might want to examine the box "Additional Examples of Spurious Relationships." We will return to the concept of spurious relationships in later chapters of this text when we discuss designs and statistical approaches for ferreting out whether an apparent relationship between two variables really means that one variable causes the other.

Another illustration of how controlling for a moderating variable can affect the relationship between independent and dependent variables is provided in the box "Illustration of How Controlling for a Moderating Variable Can Change Our Understanding of the Relationship between an Independent and Dependent Variable."

Constants

Another way to control for a variable is by including only one of its categories (e.g., only one of its attributes) in a study. In the earlier health-care

spurious relationship, for example, researchers might include only those cases with terminal illnesses in the study and then assess the impact of social services with those cases and no others. Although such a study would *control* for any potentially misleading findings that would result from also including cases with less severe illnesses (such as the spurious finding that recipients of social services are more likely to have shorter life spans), severity of illness would *not* be a control (moderating) variable. It would not be a variable because it would not *vary* in the study since only one of its categories had been included. Nevertheless, the researchers could correctly say that they controlled for that variable by including only one of its categories and thus not letting its variation confound the study results.

Although it is incorrect to call something a variable when only one of its categories is included in a study (and thus when it does not really vary), it is not uncommon to hear researchers correctly say that they *controlled* for a particular variable by including only one of its categories. It is therefore an understandable technical mistake when some refer to such a variable as a control variable. For example, a common mistake is to call sex a control variable in studies that include only males or only females in their samples. Nevertheless, it would be correct to say that such studies control for sex by including men only or females only. Likewise, if an evaluation of the effectiveness of an intervention for posttraumatic stress disorder (PTSD) excludes from its sample clients who are at risk for suicide, it would be correct to depict the study as controlling for the potential impact of suicidality but technically incorrect to call suicidality a control variable.

Mediating Variables

Another type of variable that can affect the relationship between the independent and dependent variables is a *mediating variable*. A mediating variable varies with regard to a mechanism by which an independent variable might affect a dependent variable. If we think that one of the ways by which an intervention reduces recidivism among criminal offenders is by first increasing prisoner empathy for crime victims, then *level of empathy for crime victims* would be our mediating variable. It would come between our independent variable

ADDITIONAL EXAMPLES OF SPURIOUS RELATIONSHIPS

Example 1: When ice-cream sales increase, so do the number of deaths due to drowning, and vice versa. There is, however, no direct link between ice cream and drowning. The third variable at work here is season or temperature. Most drowning deaths occur during summer—the peak period for ice-cream sales.

Example 2: Schoolchildren with larger shoe sizes do better in math. Here, the third variable that explains the puzzling relationship is *age*. Older children have bigger feet and more highly developed math skills, on average, than younger children do.

Example 3: Areas with many storks have high birthrates. Those with few storks have low birthrates. Do storks really deliver babies? Birthrates are higher in the city than in the country; more storks live (in zoos) in the city than the country. The third variable here is urban/rural areas.

Example 4: The more fire trucks that put out a fire, the more damage to the structure. Can you guess what the third variable is? In this case, it is the size of the fire.

(whether prisoners receive the intervention) and our dependent variable (whether they get rearrested for another crime). In other words, we would be conceptualizing a causal chain in which the independent variable affects the mediating variable, which, in turn, affects the dependent variable, as illustrated in Figure 8-3. Because mediating variables come between independent and dependent variables, they can also be called intervening variables. The box "Illustration of the Impact of a Mediating Variable" further illuminates the causal chain. As you examine this box, you should keep in mind that there might be additional mediating variables that can influence the effect of the independent variable on the dependent variable.

Students sometimes confuse the terms *mediating variables* and *moderating variables*. It might help to keep in mind that one definition for the verb *mediate* is to act as a *medium* that occurs between stages and moves something from one stage (the independent variable) to another stage (the dependent variable). In contrast, one definition for the verb *moderate* is to change the extent or severity of something. Thus, moderating variables reside outside the causal chain between the independent and dependent variables but can influence the degree of the relationship between the two. Mediating variables, however, reside in the middle of the causal chain and have no impact on independent variables. In a sense, they are sort of an intermediary dependent variable in that they can be influenced by the independent variable and then, in turn, affect the ultimate and actual dependent variable. Sex, for example, cannot be influenced by an intervention to increase prisoner empathy and thus could not be a mediating variable. It could, however, be a moderating variable in that (as noted above) it might influence the extent of the relationship between an intervention and recidivism.

The Same Concept Can Be a Different Type of Variable in Different Studies

Unlike sex, there is nothing inherent in most concepts that makes them independent, dependent, moderating, or mediating variables in every study in which they are observed. Whether a concept is an independent, dependent, mediating, or moderating variable depends on how it is being conceptualized in a particular study. For example, if one study postulates that increased citizen participation in neighborhood planning is likely to lower resident opposition to locating a homeless shelter at the edge of the neighborhood, then *amount of citizen participation* is the independent variable, and *amount of opposition* is the dependent variable. But another study could reverse the hypothesis, viewing the amount of opposition as predating efforts to increase citizen participation and thus predicting that greater existing opposition motivates citizens to participate more.

You should also realize that whether a variable is independent or dependent does not depend on the sequence in which it is specified in the hypothesis. For example, if we postulate that case management

ILLUSTRATION OF HOW CONTROLLING FOR A MODERATING VARIABLE CAN CHANGE OUR UNDERSTANDING OF THE RELATIONSHIP BETWEEN AN INDEPENDENT AND DEPENDENT VARIABLE

The following two tables show fictitious results of a fictitious evaluation of fictitious intervention A and intervention B that both aimed at preventing future child maltreatment among parents referred for child abuse or neglect. The effects of the two types of treatment were compared in an experiment. Treatment outcome was operationally defined in terms of whether the parents recidivated (were found to have committed further maltreatment by the child welfare agency). The fictitious study controlled for the following moderating variable: whether the parents were substance abusers. We suggest that you examine the two tables to see if you can figure out how controlling for the moderating variable might reveal the otherwise concealed relationship between the independent variable (type of treatment) and the dependent variable (whether the parents recidivated). After that, you can read the narrative that appears below the second table to check on the correctness of your interpretation.

TABLE 1 Recidivism Rate by Type of Treatment

Recidivated?	Intervention A	Intervention B
No	40	40
Yes	40	40
Total	80	80

TABLE 2 Recidivism Rate by Type of Treatment, Controlling for Whether Parents Are Substance Abusers

| Recidivated? | Substance Abusers | | Not Substance Abusers | |
	Intervention A	Intervention B	Intervention A	Intervention B
No	10	30	30	10
Yes	30	10	10	30
Total	40	40	40	40

Table 1 suggests there is no relationship between type of treatment and recidivism rate. Each intervention is shown to have exactly a 50% recidivism rate, because 40 is half of the total number of cases (80) that received each intervention. However, Table 2 shows that the results depicted in Table 1 are misleading in an important way because there really is a relationship between those two variables when the substance abuse variable is controlled (i.e., it is held constant). We can see that for substance abusers, three-fourths (30 out of 40) of the intervention A parents recidivated, while only one-fourth (10 out of 40) of the intervention B parents recidivated. For parents who were not substance abusers, Table 2 shows the opposite results, in which only one-fourth of the intervention A parents recidivated, while three-fourths of the intervention B parents recidivated. Thus, the fictitious intervention A was more effective for parents who were not substance abusers, and the fictitious intervention B was more effective for the substance-abusing parents. To get a further grasp of how controlling for a moderating variable works, you can notice how the numbers in Table 2 correspond to the numbers in Table 1 by combining the two "Intervention A" columns and combining the two "Intervention B" columns, thus yielding a 40/40 split for each intervention when the impact of the moderating variable is withdrawn.

FIGURE 8.3 Illustration of a Mediating Variable

Independent variable:	Mediating (intervening) variable:	Dependent variable:
Type of intervention $\longrightarrow$	Level of empathy $\longrightarrow$	Re-arrested?

intervention is more likely to be provided by practitioners with social work degrees, then *type of intervention* can be the dependent variable even though it is specified first in the hypothesis. This can be confusing because even though the cause must happen before the effect, putting the effect first in the hypothesis does not mean you are saying that it will happen first.

EP 7

» OPERATIONAL DEFINITIONS

Before we implement a quantitative study to collect data on our variables, we must first translate those variables into observable terms. (We will address this issue in qualitative studies later in this chapter.) The term operational definition refers to that translation: the operations, or indicators, we will use to determine the quantity or attribute we observe about a particular variable. Operational definitions differ from nominal definitions. Nominal definitions, like dictionary definitions, use a set of words to help us understand what a term means, but they do not tell us what indicators to use in observing the term in a research study. For example, a nominal definition of *social adjustment* might be "appropriate performance of one's major roles in life"—as parent, student, employee, spouse, and so on. This definition may give us clues about how we might develop an operational definition, but it does

ILLUSTRATION OF THE IMPACT OF A MEDIATING VARIABLE

The following table shows fictitious results of a fictitious evaluation of a fictitious program that tried to prevent recidivism among criminal offenders by first increasing prisoner empathy for crime victims. The table results show that the program was effective in increasing empathy and that it was effective in reducing the rearrest rate among those offenders with greater empathy. Thus, it shows that at least one of the mechanisms by which it prevented recidivism was to increase prisoner empathy. This is evident because the table shows that the empathy scores were higher and the rearrest rates lower among program participants and because the program participants with the higher empathy scores had the lowest rearrest rates. In other words, level of empathy was a mediating variable that was influenced by the independent variable (treatment condition), and that, in turn, influenced the dependent variable (rearrest rate). It is conceivable that there were additional mediating variables—that is, additional ways in which the program affected recidivism—but we have simplified this example by examining just one possible mediating variable.

Treatment Condition	Average Score on an Empathy Measure Administered after the Empathy Program Was Completed	Rearrest Rate
Participated in empathy program*	60 to 80	5%
	40 to 59	15%
Did not participate in empathy program**	30 to 39	30%
	10 to 29	40%

*All program participants had empathy scores between 40 and 80.

**All nonparticipants had empathy scores between 10 and 39.

not specify precisely what indicators we will observe and the exact categories of social adjustment we will note in our research on social adjustment.

We can operationally define abstract variables in many ways. One operational definition of social adjustment might be a score on a scale that measures level of social adjustment. Another operational definition might be whether an individual is receiving social services aimed at restoring social functioning. Those who receive such services might be categorized as having lower levels of social adjustment than others who do not receive such services. Thus, operational definitions point to how a variable will be measured.

Operationally Defining Anything That Exists

You may have reservations about science's ability to operationally define some abstract variables of concern to social workers, such as *love, hate, empathy, feminism, racism, homophobia,* and *spirituality*. You may have read research reports that dealt with something like *spirituality*, and you may have been dissatisfied with the way the researchers measured whatever they were studying. You may have felt they were too superficial, that they missed the aspects that really matter most. Maybe they measured *spirituality* as the number of times a person went to church, or maybe they measured *liberalism* by how people voted in a single election. Your dissatisfaction would surely have been increased if you found yourself being misclassified by the measurement system.

Skepticism about our ability to operationally define some abstract variables is understandable. Most of the variables in social work research don't exist in the same way that rocks exist. Unlike rocks, they seldom have a single, unambiguous meaning. Consider *feminism*, for example. We are not able to observe a feminist in the way we observe a rock. We could attempt to observe whether individuals are feminists by simply asking them if they are. Or we could ask them if they belong to a feminist organization or agree with the position statements of such organizations.

Notice that each of these operational definitions might produce different results. When asked, some people may say that they are feminists even though they disagree with the positions favored by feminist organizations. They may even think that they really are feminists, according to their own idiosyncratic

notion of what that term means. In fact, abstract variables such as *feminism, spirituality,* and the like do not exist in nature like rocks do. They are merely terms that we have made up and assigned specific meanings to for some purpose such as doing research. Yet these terms have *some* reality. After all, there are feminist models of social work practice and research.

Consider, for example, two variables of interest to social workers—racism and homophobia. Throughout our lives, we've observed a lot of things that we connect to racism and homophobia and known they were real through our observations. We've also read or heard reports from other people that seemed real. For example, we heard people say nasty things about people who are gay, lesbian, or members of particular ethnic minority groups. We read about hate crimes against such people. We read about discrimination against them in employment or in other matters. We've heard some people call them ugly names. At some point, some folks made up shorthand terms—such as *racists* and *homophobes*—to portray people who did or approved of some of these things. Even though people cannot directly observe racism and homophobia in the way they observe a rock and even though racism and homophobia don't exist in nature the way rocks exist, we agree to use those made-up terms to represent a collection of apparently related phenomena that we've each observed in the course of life.

Each of these terms exists, but only in terms of our rough agreements to use them in a certain way. Each of us develops our own mental image of real phenomena that we've observed as represented by terms like *racism* and *homophobia*. Some may consider it racist to oppose having lower college admission standards—for affirmative action purposes—for members of minority groups that historically have been discriminated against. Others may hold the opposite view, arguing that the notion that members of those groups need lower standards is racist because it implies that they are somehow inferior.

When we hear or read abstract terms such as *racism*, the mental images we have of those terms are evoked in our minds. It's as though we have file drawers in our minds containing thousands of sheets of paper, and each sheet of paper has a label in the upper right-hand corner. One sheet of paper in your file drawer has the term *racism* on it. On your sheet are all the things you were told about racism and everything you've observed that seemed to be an example of it. Someone else's sheet has what they were told about racism, plus all the things they've observed that seemed to be examples of it.

The technical term for those mental images, those sheets of paper in our mental file drawers, is *conceptions*. Each sheet of paper is a conception. In the big picture, language and communication work only to the extent that we have considerable overlap in the kinds of entries we have on our corresponding mental file sheets. The similarities we have on those sheets represent the agreements existing in the society we occupy. When we were growing up, we were told approximately the same thing when we were first introduced to a particular term. Dictionaries formalize the agreements our society has about such terms. Each of us, then, shapes his or her mental images to correspond with those agreements, but because all of us have different experiences and observations, no two people end up with exactly the same set of entries on any sheet in their file systems.

How can we operationally define variables that exist in terms of our idiosyncratic conceptions of them? Suppose we want to measure whether a boy doing poorly at school is depressed. We can observe, for example, how often he says he dislikes himself and says he has no hope for the future. We can ask his parents how often he isolates himself at home or plays with friends. Perhaps his teacher will tell us he can't concentrate in school and is a loner in the schoolyard. All of those things exist, so we can observe them. But are we really observing *depression*? We can't answer that question. We can't observe depression in that sense because depression doesn't exist the way those things we just described exist. Perhaps his negative self-statements and social isolation are due to low self-esteem, not depression. Perhaps he also has attention-deficit/hyperactivity

disorder, which would explain his inability to concentrate in school. *Depression*, then, is an abstraction—a construct that consists of a "family of conceptions" (Kaplan, 1964, p. 49) that includes your concepts that constitute depression, our concepts that make it up, and the conceptions of all those who have ever used the term. All we can measure are the things we can observe that we think the term *depression* implies. IQ is another example. It is constructed mathematically from observations of the answers given to a large number of questions on an IQ test.

In this context, Kaplan (1964) distinguished three kinds of things that researchers can measure, which are illustrated in the box "Three Classes of Things Social Workers Measure." The first class is *direct observables*: those things we can observe rather simply and directly, like the color of an apple or the check mark made in a questionnaire. The second class is *indirect observables*. If someone puts a check mark beside female in our questionnaire, then we can indirectly observe that person's sex. Minutes of agency board meetings provide indirect observations of past agency actions. Finally, *constructs* are theoretical creations that are based on observations but that themselves cannot be observed directly or indirectly, such as social adjustment or marital satisfaction. Later in this chapter, we'll discuss sources of existing scales that measure various constructs.

Conceptualization

Day-to-day communication usually occurs through a system of vague and general agreements about the use of terms. Usually, people do not understand exactly what we wish to communicate, but they get the general drift of our meaning. Conceptualization

THREE CLASSES OF THINGS SOCIAL WORKERS MEASURE

Classes	Examples
Direct observables	Physical characteristics (sex, skin color) of a person being observed and/or interviewed
Indirect observables	Characteristics (gender, ethnicity, age) of a person as indicated by answers given in a self-administered questionnaire
Constructs	Theoretical abstractions (depression, social adjustment, marital satisfaction, risk of child abuse) as measured by a scale that is created by combining several direct and/or indirect observables

is the process through which we specify precisely what we will mean when we use particular terms. Suppose we want to find out, for example, whether women are more compassionate than men. We can't meaningfully study the question, let alone agree on the answer, without some precise working agreements about the meaning of the term *compassion*. They are working agreements in the sense that they allow us to work on the question. We don't need to agree or even pretend to agree that a particular specification might be worth using.

Indicators and Dimensions

The end product of this conceptualization process is the specification of a set of *indicators* of what we have in mind, markers that indicate the presence or absence of the concept we are studying. Thus, we may agree to use visiting children's hospitals at Christmas as an indicator of compassion. Putting little birds back in their nests may be agreed on as another indicator, and so forth. If the unit of analysis for our study were the individual person, we could then observe the presence or absence of each indicator for each person under study. Going beyond that, we could add the number of indicators of compassion observed for each individual. We might agree on 10 specific indicators, for example, and find six present in Peter, three in Paul, nine for Mary, and so forth.

Returning to our original question, we might calculate that the women we studied had an average of 6.5 indicators of compassion and that the men studied had an average of 3.2. On the basis of that group difference, we might therefore conclude that women are, on the whole, more compassionate than men. Usually, though, it's not that simple.

Let's imagine that you are interested in studying the attitudes of different religious groups about the term *social justice*. To most social work professors and students, a belief in social justice implies politically liberal views about such issues as redistributing wealth, women's reproductive rights, LGBTQ rights, and not imposing the prayers or symbols of a particular religion on students in public schools, among many others. Let's say that one of the groups you study is the membership of a fundamentalist evangelical Christian church.

In the course of your conversations with church members and perhaps in attending religious services, you would have put yourself in a situation where you could come to understand what the members mean by *social justice*. You might learn, for example, that members of the group firmly believe that aborted fetuses are murdered humans and that gays and lesbians, women and doctors who engage in abortions, and non-Christians are sinners who will burn eternally in hell unless they are converted. In fact, they may be so deeply concerned about sinners burning in hell that they are willing to be aggressive, even violent, in making people change their sinful ways. Within this paradigm, then, opposing gay and lesbian rights, imposing Christian prayers in public institutions, and perhaps even blockading abortion clinics might be seen by church members as acts that promote social justice.

Social scientists often focus their attention on the meanings given to words and actions by the people under study. Although this can clarify the behaviors observed, it almost always complicates the concepts in which we are interested.

Whenever we take our concepts seriously and set about specifying what we mean by them, we discover disagreements and inconsistencies. Not only do we disagree, but also each of us is likely to find a good deal of muddiness within our own individual mental images. If you take a moment to look at what *you* mean by *social justice*, you'll probably find that your image contains several kinds of social justice. The entries on your file sheet can be combined into groups and subgroups, and you'll even find several different strategies for making the combinations. For example, you might group the entries into *economic justice* and *civil rights*. The technical term for such a grouping is *dimension*: a specifiable aspect or facet of a concept. Thus, we might speak of the "economic dimension" and the "civil rights dimension" of social justice. Or social justice might be concerned with helping people be and have what we want for them or what they want for themselves. Thus, we could subdivide the concept of social justice according to several sets of dimensions. Both specifying dimensions and identifying the various indicators for each dimension are parts of conceptualization. Specifying the different dimensions of a concept often paves the way for a more sophisticated understanding of what we are studying. We might observe, for example, that law students are more committed to the civil rights dimension of social justice, whereas economics majors are more concerned with the redistribution of wealth. The box "Some Indicators and Dimensions of PTSD" further illustrates this end product of conceptualization.

SOME INDICATORS AND DIMENSIONS OF PTSD

Construct	Self-Report Indicators	Dimensions
PTSD	Intrusive thoughts Flashbacks Dreams of the traumatic event	Reexperiencing symptoms

	Avoiding reminders of the trauma:
	    Places
	    People
	    Social situations
	Avoiding disappointment:
	    Feeling pessimistic
	    Avoiding relationships
	    Distrusting people
		Avoidance symptoms

	Inability to feel love or happiness Loss of sense of humor Loss of interest in formerly enjoyable activities	Numbing symptoms
	Constant state of alert and looking out for danger Easily startled or threatened Difficulty concentrating Irritability Anxiety	Hyperarousal symptoms
	Self-blame Guilt Low self-esteem Feeling powerless	Negative cognitions
	Bodily aches Loss of energy Insomnia	Somatic symptoms

Clarifying Concepts

Reviewing briefly, our concepts are derived from the mental images (conceptions) that summarize collections of seemingly related observations and experiences. Although the observations and experiences are real, the terms associated with concepts are merely devices created for purposes of filing and communication. The word *homophobia* is an example. The consequences of homophobia are real, but we could have as easily and meaningfully created the word *antihomosexualism* to serve the same purpose as the word *homophobia*.

Consequently, the clarification of concepts is an essential and continuing process in social research. In rigorously structured research designs such as surveys and experiments, operationally defining variables is vital at the beginning of study design. In a survey, for example, it results in a commitment to a specific set of questionnaire items that will represent the concepts under study. Without that commitment, the study could not proceed. However, investigators may find themselves still refining the meanings of concepts as they attempt to communicate their findings to others in a final report.

In some forms of qualitative research, concept clarification is an ongoing element in data collection. Suppose you were conducting interviews and observations of a radical political group that is devoted to combating oppression in American society. Imagine how the concept of *oppression* would shift meaning as you delved more and more deeply into the members' experiences and worldviews. In the analysis of textual materials, social researchers sometimes speak of the "hermeneutic circle," a cyclical process of ever-deeper understanding:

> The understanding of a text takes place through a process in which the meaning of the separate parts is determined by the global meaning of the text as it is anticipated. The closer determination of the meaning of the separate parts may eventually change the originally anticipated meaning of the totality, which again influences the meaning of the separate parts, and so on. (Kvale, 1996, p. 47)

Even in less structured forms of qualitative research, however, you must also begin with an initial set of anticipated meanings that can be refined during data collection and interpretation. No one seriously believes it is possible to observe life with no preconceptions; thus, the scientific observer is conscious and explicit about those starting points.

Let's continue the discussion of initial conceptualization as it applies most to structured inquiries such as surveys and experiments. The specification of nominal definitions focuses our observational strategy, but it does not allow us to observe. As a next step, we must specify exactly what we are going to observe, how we will do it, and what interpretations we will place on various possible observations. As we discussed earlier, all of these further specifications make up the operational definition of the concept—a definition that spells out precisely how the concept will be measured. Strictly speaking, an operational definition is a description of the operations that will be undertaken in measuring a concept, as we discussed earlier in this chapter.

Wishing to examine socioeconomic status (SES) in a study, for example, we might decide to ask the people we are studying two questions:

1. What was your total family income during the past 12 months?
2. What is the highest level of school you completed?

Here, we would probably want to specify a system for categorizing the answers people give us. We would specify the way a person's responses to these two questions would be combined in creating a measure of SES, such as into different levels of SES like high, medium or low. Ultimately, we would have created a working and workable definition of SES. Others might disagree with our conceptualization and operationalization, but the definition would have one essential scientific virtue: It would be absolutely specific and unambiguous. Even if someone disagreed with our definition, that person would have a good idea of how to interpret our research results, because what we meant by the term *SES*—reflected in our analyses and conclusions—would be clear.

Here is a diagram that shows the progression of measurement steps from our vague sense of what a term means to specific measurements in a scientific study:

Measurement Step	Simple Example of Social Class
Conceptualization	What are the different meanings and dimensions of the concept social class?
↓	
Nominal Definition	For our study, we will define social class as representing economic differences, specifically income.
↓	
Operational Definition	We will measure economic differences by responses to the survey question, "What was your annual income, before taxes, last year?"
↓	
Measurements in the Real World	Interviewer asks: "What was your annual income, before taxes, last year?"

The Influence of Operational Definitions

How we choose to operationally define a variable can greatly influence our research findings. If our task is to study factors that influence citizen participation in a barrio in Los Angeles, our results may vary, depending on whether we operationally define *citizen participation* as attendance by barrio residents at meetings of a social action organization, their attendance at city government meetings where issues of concern to the barrio are being discussed, contacts they make with governmental officials, or participation in protest demonstrations. The factors that motivate people to attend a protest demonstration might be different than those that motivate them to attend a meeting or write their city council member.

Suppose we want to evaluate a child welfare program aimed at preventing child abuse and preserving families. If we operationally define *child abuse rates* in terms of the number of children placed in foster care and the program reduces that number, the program would be deemed successful. However, what if the rate of abuse actually increases because so many children at great risk for abuse were *not* placed in foster care? Had the operational definition of *child abuse rates* included other indicators of abuse, the same program with the same results might have been deemed a failure.

Suppose we want to study trends over time in the incidence of rape on college campuses. In the past, if a person did not resist sexual intercourse after heavy drinking, generally it was not defined as rape, even if he or she regretted it later and would have resisted had he or she been sober. Today, many would define the same situation as rape if the person later reports regretting the intercourse and feels manipulated through the pressure to drink. The number of rapes that we would find in our study would vary quite a bit, depending on whether our operational definition of rape included a person saying later that he or she regretted and would have resisted intercourse instead of "consenting" after drinking. Suppose we did include that in our operational definition and then reported our findings to the media. Chances are that the media would not consider the difference between our (broader) operational definition of rape and the narrower definitions used in the past. Consequently, a headline might inaccurately portray a shocking jump in the incidence of rape on college campuses.

Sex and Cultural Bias in Operational Definitions

Special care is needed to avoid sex and cultural bias in choosing operational definitions. Suppose we attempt to operationally define *family dysfunction* by including observable indicators of "excessive" contact and dependence between grown children and their parents. What may be considered excessive or pathological dependence in an individualistic culture that emphasizes independence might be quite normal in a culture that values group welfare over individual welfare and that emphasizes the healthy aspects of using the family as a natural support system (Grinnell, 1997).

As to sex bias, suppose we are studying whether the quality of attachment to a parent during childhood influences the resilience of children who were sexually abused by someone other than a parent. Suppose we develop a questionnaire to send to adults who had been sexually abused as children; in asking about early childhood parental attachments, we refer only to the mother and not the father, reflecting a sex bias that only mothers are nurturers of young children. Or maybe we want to study the extent and causes of spouse abuse but inadvertently—because of sex bias—refer to it only as *wife abuse*. Some might argue that asking whether a person remains calm and unemotional in stressful situations as an indicator of social functioning might involve a sex bias. The idea here would be that women might be more inclined to express their emotions and might find that doing so helps them cope.

Another example of sex bias would involve excluding unpaid forms of work that women are more likely than men to do—such as child rearing—in operationally defining concepts such as *occupation* or *work*. Finally, perhaps we want to study whether certain social policies or organizational procedures are effective in alleviating the conflict that employees with young children experience between their roles as parents and as employees. Our operational definition would involve a sex bias if we specified only mothers and not fathers in operationally defining such role conflict, such as by asking whether an agency allows mothers to have flexible work schedules to care for their young children (and not mentioning fathers in the question).

These examples do not mean that every time we refer to only one attribute of sex, our operational definition automatically is biased. If only one category of sex is relevant to our study and if our findings are going to be reported in reference to that category only, then it may be appropriate to include only that category in our operational definition. Male batterers, for example, may need a separate intervention program than female batterers. If we are assessing the men in a group being treated for wife battering, then it would be acceptable to refer to wife abuse instead of spouse abuse. The key here is to be aware of whether defining things in terms of only one category is appropriate rather than letting our definition refer to only one category inadvertently.

» OPERATIONALIZATION CHOICES

As we've indicated, the social work researcher has a wide variety of options available when it comes to measuring a concept. Although the choices are intimately interconnected, we've separated them for purposes of discussion. Realize, however, that operationalization does not proceed through a systematic checklist.

Range of Variation

In operationalizing any concept, you must be clear about the range of variation that interests you in your research. To what extent are you willing to combine attributes in fairly gross categories?

Let's suppose you want to measure people's incomes in a study, collecting the information either from records or in interviews. The highest annual incomes people receive run into the millions of dollars, but not many people get that much. Unless you are studying the very rich, it probably wouldn't be worth much to allow for and track such extremely high categories. Depending on whom you are studying, you'll probably want to establish a highest income category with a much lower floor—maybe $250,000 or more. Although this decision will lead you to throw together people who earn a trillion dollars a year with "paupers" earning only $250,000, they'll survive it, and that mixing probably won't hurt your research any. The same decision faces you at the other end of the income spectrum. In studies of the general American population, a cutoff of $20,000 or less might work just fine.

In the study of attitudes and orientations, the question of range of variation has another dimension. Unless you're careful, you may unintentionally end up measuring only "half an attitude." Here's an example of what we mean.

Suppose you're interested in the views of social work practitioners about transracial adoptions—that is, adoptions of a child, usually of minority ethnicity, by parents of a different ethnicity. You would anticipate in advance that some practitioners consider it a great way to find foster parents for children who otherwise would have little chance of being adopted, whereas other practitioners have never heard of and have no interest in the concept. Given that anticipation, it would seem to make sense to ask people how much they favor expanding the use of transracial adoptions. You might give them answer categories ranging from "Favor it very much" to "Don't favor it at all."

This operationalization, however, conceals half of the spectrum of attitudes toward transracial adoptions. Many practitioners, including minority practitioners concerned about the self-image and stigmatization of minority children raised by white parents in a predominantly white community, have feelings that go beyond simply not favoring it: They are *opposed* to it. In this instance, there is considerable variation on the left side of zero. Some oppose it a little, some quite a bit, and others a great deal. To measure the full range of variation, then, you would want to operationalize attitudes toward transracial adoptions with a range from favoring it very much, through no feelings one way or the other, to opposing it very much.

This consideration applies to many of the variables we study in social science. Virtually any public issue involves both support and opposition, each in varying degrees. Political orientations range from ultraliberal to ultraconservative, and depending on the people you are studying, you may want to allow for radicals on one or both ends. Similarly, people are not just more or less religious—some are antireligious.

We do not mean that you must measure the full range of variation in any given case. You should, however, consider whether such measurement is needed in the light of your research purpose. If the difference between *not religious* and *antireligious* isn't relevant to your research, then forget it. Someone has defined *pragmatism* by saying that "any difference that makes no difference is no difference." Be pragmatic.

Finally, your decision on the range of variation should also be governed by the expected distribution of attributes among your subjects of study. That is what we meant earlier when we said that range depends on whom you are studying. In a study of college professors' attitudes toward the value of higher education, you could probably stop at *no value* and not worry about those who might consider higher education dangerous to students' health. (If you were studying students, however…)

Variations between the Extremes

Precision is a consideration in operationalizing variables. (As we will see in Chapter 9, it also is a criterion of quality in measurement.) What it boils down to is how fine you will make distinctions among the various possible attributes composing a given variable. Does it really matter whether a person is 17 or 18 years old, or could you conduct your inquiry by throwing them together in a group labeled "15 to 19 years old"? Don't answer too quickly. If you wanted to study rates of voter registration and participation, you'd definitely want to know whether the people you studied were old enough to vote.

If you are going to measure age, then, you must look at the purpose and procedures of your study and decide whether fine or gross differences in age are important to you. If you measure political affiliation, will it matter to your inquiry whether a person is a conservative Democrat rather than a liberal Democrat, or is it sufficient to know the party? In measuring religious affiliation, is it enough to know that a person is a Protestant, or do you need to know the denomination? Do you simply need to know whether a person is married, or will it make a difference to know if he or she has never married or is separated, widowed, or divorced?

Of course, there are no general answers to questions like these. The answers come out of the purpose of your study—the purpose you have in making a particular measurement. We can mention a useful guideline, however. Whenever you're not sure how much detail to get in a measurement, get too much rather than too little. During the analysis of data, it will always be possible to combine precise attributes into more general categories, but it will never be possible to separate out the variations that were lumped together during observation and measurement.

A Note on Dimensions

When people get down to the business of creating operational measures of variables, they often discover—or, worse, never notice—that they are not exactly clear about which dimensions of a variable are of real interest. Here's one example to illustrate what we mean.

Let's suppose we are doing in-depth qualitative interviews to determine the attitudes of families toward the long-term care of relatives in nursing homes. Here are just a few of the different dimensions we might examine:

- Do family members think their relative receives adequate care?
- How adequate or inadequate do they think the care is?
- How certain are they in their judgment of the adequacy of care?
- How do they feel about the inadequacy of nursing home care as a problem in society?
- What do they think causes inadequate care?
- Do they think inadequate care is inevitable?
- What do they feel should be done about inadequate care?
- What are they willing to do personally to improve nursing home care?
- How certain are they that they would be willing to do what they say they would do?

The list could go on and on. How people feel about the adequacy of care in nursing homes has many dimensions. It's essential that you be clear about which ones are important in your inquiry and direct the interviews appropriately. Otherwise, you may measure how people feel about it when you really wanted to know how much they think there is or vice versa.

» EXAMPLES OF OPERATIONALIZATION IN SOCIAL WORK

Throughout this chapter, we have discussed how some terms might be operationally defined, as well as some of the complexities involved in operationalization choices. Typically, we have three broad categories of choices for operationalizing variables: self-reports, direct observation, and the examination of available records.

Let's consider the construct *marital satisfaction*. Suppose you are conducting a research study and level of marital satisfaction is one of your variables. Perhaps you want to see if family therapy increases marital satisfaction, in which case it would be your dependent variable. Or maybe you want to see if higher levels of marital satisfaction among foster parents contribute to successful foster placement, in which case level of marital satisfaction would be your independent variable. In either study, what are some of the ways in which you might operationally define level of marital satisfaction? Would you simply define it as a subjective evaluation of the quality of a marital relationship? That nominal definition won't do as an operational definition because it won't bring you any closer to the observable indicators of marital satisfaction. You would merely have substituted one unobservable construct (evaluation of quality of relationship) for another.

However, if you asked your research participants to rate their level of marital satisfaction on a scale from *very dissatisfied* to *very satisfied*, you would have an operational definition. (The same applies if you asked them to rate the quality of their marital relationship from *poor* to *excellent*.) Doing so would mean you were using a self-report approach to operationally defining level of marital satisfaction.

A more thorough self-report option would be an existing scale previously devised to measure level of marital satisfaction. You would ask each person in your study to complete the scale. The higher the score on the scale, the more marital satisfaction. (If both spouses respond, perhaps you will add both scores to get a combined score per couple.) Existing scales that have been constructed to measure certain constructs build the indicators of the construct into the scale. For example, a scale to measure level of marital satisfaction might ask either spouse how often he or she is annoyed with the spouse, has fun with the spouse, feels he or she can rely on the spouse, wants to be with the spouse, is proud of the spouse, feels controlled by the spouse, resents the spouse, and so on. Each scale item gets a score, and the item scores are summed for a total score of marital satisfaction. For instance, an individual might get a score of 5 for each positive item (such as feeling proud of the spouse) to which he or she responds "always" and for each negative item (such as resenting the spouse) to which the response is "never." If there are 20 items on the scale and the individual responds "always" to every positive item and "never" to every negative item, then the total scale score would be 100. That score would indicate that this person had more marital satisfaction than another person who responded "sometimes" to every item, receiving a score of, say, 3 for every item and therefore a total score of 60.

Alternatively, you or your coinvestigators might—from an adjoining room in which you could watch and hear the couples—observe each couple having a conversation and count the number of times that either partner makes a derogatory statement about the marriage or the spouse. This option would be using direct observation. If you go this route, you'll have to grapple with the ground rules for considering a statement derogatory. Perhaps you'll just have to leave that to the judgment of the observer and see if an independent observer (perhaps viewing a videotape of the interview) tends to agree with the original observer's counts. We'll say more about this when we discuss *reliability* in the next chapter.

In addition to (or instead of) counting derogatory statements, you might count the number of times the couples interrupt one another, raise their voices, or make various physical gestures that seem to indicate frustration or dissatisfaction with the other. This can be tricky. If the couple is disagreeing about an intellectual or political issue (such as foreign policy), perhaps the partners actually enjoy having heated, animated debates. Although you have an observable definition, you might wonder whether it is really measuring level of marital satisfaction. We'll get into that issue as well in the next chapter when we discuss *validity*.

Of course, we might attempt to operationally define level of marital satisfaction in many other ways. For example, if we are doing cross-cultural research, we might compare divorce rates in different geographic areas as one operational indicator of marital satisfaction. This illustrates the use of available records.

EP 7

Again, this does not mean that such rates would be a true indicator of the construct, just that they would be operational. Perhaps the culture with the lower divorce rates has no more marital satisfaction, just stricter taboos against divorce. The box "Operationally Defining Level of Positive Parenting: Illustration of Three Sources of Data for Categories of Operationalization Choices" further illustrates alternative ways to operationally define variables and some of the advantages and disadvantages of each alternative.

» EXISTING SCALES

In the foregoing examples, you can see why the use of existing scales can be a popular way to operationally define variables. They spare researchers the costs in time and money of devising their own measures and provide an option that has been used successfully to measure the concept in previous studies. Therefore, let's examine how you find relevant scales and salient information about them.

The most thorough procedure would be to conduct a literature review on the construct you seek to measure. For example, you might review the literature on marital satisfaction to locate materials that report measures of marital satisfaction. Refer to Chapter 7 and Appendix A for information on how to conduct a literature review. Of course, this would be a relatively quick literature review because the purpose is to locate measures of a construct, not review all the research on the construct.

One way to expedite the search for measures is to consult reference volumes that list and describe many existing measures. Figure 8-4 lists volumes that might be useful. Some of them reprint the actual measurement instrument; others describe it and provide additional references. Usually, they will discuss the quality of the instrument (such as its reliability and validity) and tell you how to obtain it and more information about it. You will also be told whether it is copyrighted, which will indicate whether you must purchase it or use it with the author's permission.

Despite the practical advantages of using existing self-report scales to operationally define variables, not everyone would agree that they are the best way to operationally define a particular variable in a particular study, and there can be difficulties in using them. Consider using an existing scale to operationally define social work students' levels of interviewing skill. Which measurement approach would give you more confidence that your data adequately reflected students' interviewing skill: their answers to a paper-and-pencil test about how best to respond to various client statements in varying interviewing scenarios or their actual performance

in a real face-to-face interview with a client? Many of you, we suspect, would prefer the latter as a more realistic test of the interviewer's skill. At the same time, however, you might opt to use an existing self-report scale in an actual study of interviewing skill, not because you think it is the best measure of that concept but because you lack the resources needed to use a preferable measure.

We will further discuss the advantages and disadvantages of using self-report scales in Chapters 9 and 13 and how to construct them in Chapter 10. We'll end this section by identifying some of the issues to consider in choosing an existing scale as an operational definition.

Let's begin on a practical note: How lengthy is the scale? Will it take too long for the subjects in your study to complete? Suppose, for example, that a lengthy scale that takes more than an hour to complete was tested on people who were paid $20 to complete the scale. Its success under those circumstances would not be relevant to a study of busy people who were mailed the scale and asked to volunteer that much time—without pay—to complete and mail back the scale.

Another practical question is whether the scale will be too difficult for your participants to complete. For example, will it be too cumbersome or too complexly worded for them? Suppose you want to study depression among undocumented immigrants from Mexico. Chances are, you would not be able to use a scale that was developed to assess depression among American college students, no matter how successful it proved to be with the latter population.

If your study seeks to measure change over time, perhaps before and after receiving a social work intervention, you will need a scale that is sensitive to small changes over relatively short periods. Some clients, after being treated for low self-esteem, for example, might still have lower self-esteem compared to the rest of the population but have higher self-esteem than they did before the intervention. Some self-esteem scales might be able to detect this movement, while others might not, still simply indicating that these people have much lower self-esteem than the rest of the population.

Two critical issues to consider in choosing a scale are its reliability and validity. In the next chapter, we'll discuss in depth these two terms, which deal with statistical information on the measurement consistency of instruments and whether they

FIGURE 8.4   Reference Volumes for Existing Scales That Can Operationally Define Variables in Social Work

American Psychiatric Association. (2000). *Handbook of psychiatric measures*. Washington, DC: Author.

Anastasi, A. (1988). *Psychological testing*. New York: Macmillan.

Beere, C. A. (1990). *Sex and gender issues: A handbook of tests and measures*. New York: Greenwood Press.

Conoley, J. C., & Kramer, J. J. (1995). *The 12th mental measurements yearbook*. Lincoln, NE: Buros Institute of Mental Measurements.

Corcoran, K. J., & Fischer, J. (2000a). *Measures for clinical practice: Vol. 1. Couples, families, children* (3rd ed.). New York: Free Press.

Corcoran, K. J., & Fischer, J. (2000b). *Measures for clinical practice: Vol. 2. Adults* (3rd ed.). New York: Free Press.

Fredman, N., & Sherman, R. (1987). *Handbook of measurements for marriage and family therapy*. New York: Brunner/Mazel.

Grotevant, H. D., & Carlson, D. I. (Eds.). (1989). *Family assessment: A guide to methods and measures*. New York: Guilford Press.

Hersen, M., & Bellack, A. S. (Eds.). (1988). *Dictionary of behavioral assessment techniques*. Elmsford, NY: Pergamon Press.

Hudson, W. W. (1982). *The clinical measurement package: A field manual*. Homewood, IL: Dorsey Press.

Hudson, W. W. (1992). *The WALMYR Assessment Scales scoring manual*. Tempe, AZ: WALMYR.

Jacob, T., & Tennebaum, D. L. (1988). *Family assessment: Rationale, methods, and future directions*. New York: Plenum Press.

LaGreca, A. M. (1990). *Through the eyes of the child: Obtaining self-reports from children and adolescents*. Boston: Allyn & Bacon.

Magura, S., & Moses, B. S. (1987). *Outcome measures for child welfare services*. Washington, DC: Child Welfare League of America.

Martin, R. P. (1988). *Assessment of personality and behavior problems: Infancy through adolescence*. New York: Guilford Press.

Maruish, M. E. (Ed.). (2000). *Handbook of psychological assessment in primary care settings*. Mahwah, NJ: Lawrence Erlbaum Associates.

Maruish, M. E. (Ed.). (2002). *Psychological testing in the age of managed behavioral health care*. Mahwah, NJ: Lawrence Erlbaum Associates.

Mash, E. J., & Terdal, L. G. (1988). *Behavioral assessment of childhood disorders*. New York: Guilford Press.

McCubbin, H. I., & Thompson, A. I. (Eds.). (1987). *Family assessment inventories for research and practice*. Madison: University of Wisconsin Press.

Mullen, E. J., & Magnabosco, J. L. (Eds.). (1997). *Outcomes measurement in the human services*. Washington, DC: NASW Press.

Ogles, B. M., & Masters, K. S. (1996). *Assessing outcome in clinical practice*. Boston: Allyn & Bacon.

Ollendick, T. H., & Hersen, M. (1992). *Handbook of child and adolescent assessment*. Des Moines, IA: Allyn & Bacon.

Reynolds, C. R., & Kamphaus, R. W. (Eds.). (1990). *Handbook of psychological and educational assessment of children*. New York: Guilford Press.

Rutter, M., Tuma, H. H., & Lann, I. S. (Eds.). (1988). *Assessment and diagnosis in child psychopathology*. New York: Guilford Press.

Sawin, K. J., Harrigan, M. P., & Woog, P. (Eds.). (1995). *Measures of family functioning for research and practice*. New York: Springer.

Suzuki, L., Meller, P. J., & Ponterotto, J. G. (Eds.). (1996). *Handbook of multicultural assessment*. San Francisco: Jossey-Bass.

Touliatos, J., Perlmutter, B. F., & Straus, M. A. (Eds.). (1990). *Handbook of family measurement techniques*. Newbury Park, CA: Sage.

Wetzler, S. (Ed.). (1989). *Measuring mental illness: Psychometric assessment for clinicians*. Washington, DC: American Psychiatric Press.

really measure what they intend to measure. For now, we'll just note that the reference literature on existing scales will usually report whatever reliability and validity figures have been established for a particular scale. But interpret those figures with caution. If they are based on studies that tested the instrument on a population dissimilar to yours or under study conditions unlike those of your study, then they may have no bearing on the instrument's suitability for your particular study. No matter how reliable and valid the reference literature says a scale

may be, you may find that you have to modify it for your particular study or that you cannot use it at all. Moreover, the way an instrument's reliability and validity were assessed may have been seriously flawed from a methodological standpoint, thus limiting the value of those figures, no matter how impressively high they may be. Therefore, you may want to go beyond the reference sourcebook that gives an overview of an existing scale and examine firsthand the studies that reported the development and testing of the scale.

OPERATIONALLY DEFINING LEVEL OF POSITIVE PARENTING: ILLUSTRATION OF THREE SOURCES OF DATA FOR OPERATIONALIZATION CHOICES

Suppose you work in a state child welfare agency that is evaluating an innovative new intervention program to improve positive parenting for parents referred to the agency because of child abuse or neglect. The agency assumes that by improving positive parenting skills, it will reduce the incidence of child neglect and abuse. Several similar counties have been selected for the evaluation. Some counties will implement the new program, and some comparable counties will receive the traditional program. The hypothesis for the evaluation is that parents referred for child abuse or neglect in the counties receiving the innovative program will improve their parenting more than their counterparts in the counties receiving the traditional program.

An important task in designing the evaluation is developing an operational definition of the dependent variable: *level of positive parenting*. You have been given that task. Three sources of data that can be used for the operational definition are illustrated below, along with how each could be used in testing the hypothesis. The illustrations are just some of the ways in which you could operationally define level of positive parenting. You might be able to conceive of superior alternatives.

Source of Data	Operational Definition	Testing the Hypothesis	Some Advantages and Disadvantages
Direct observation	You might begin by making a list of positive parenting behaviors—praising, encouraging, modeling, consistency, use of time-outs, and so on. Another list might specify undesirable parenting behaviors—threatening, slapping, screaming, criticizing, bribing, belittling, and so on. Then you might directly observe the parents or foster parents in a challenging parenting situation (such as getting children to put away their toys) and count the number of times the parents show positive and negative behaviors. Perhaps you will give them 11 for every positive behavior and 21 for every negative behavior and tally the points to get a parenting skill score.	See if the average scores of parents in the counties receiving the innovative program are higher (better) than the average scores of parents in the counties receiving the traditional program.	Advantage: 1. Behaviors are observed firsthand. Disadvantages: 1. Time consuming. 2. Parents will know they are being observed and may not behave the same as when they are not being observed. 3. Possibility of observer bias.

| Self-report | Ask the parents to complete an existing self-report scale that purports to measure knowledge or attitudes about parenting. Such a scale might ask parents questions about what they would do in various child-rearing situations or how they perceive various normal childhood behaviors that some parents misperceive as provocative. | See if the average scale scores of parents in the counties receiving the innovative program are better than the average scale scores of parents in the counties receiving the traditional program. | Advantages: 1. Less costly and less time consuming than direct observation. 2. If scales are completed anonymously, parents might be more likely to reveal undesirable attitudes. Disadvantages: 1. Parents might distort their true attitudes to convey a more socially desirable impression. 2. The scale might not be valid. 3. Knowledge and attitudes may not always reflect actual behaviors. |
| Examination of available records | Examine county records of the number of documented incidents of child abuse and neglect. | See if the number of documented incidents of child abuse and neglect in the counties receiving the innovative program is lower than the number in the counties receiving the traditional program. | Advantages: 1. Less costly and time consuming than either direct observation or self-report. 2. You don't have to assume that positive parenting knowledge and skills translate into less abuse; you measure abuse per se. Disadvantages: 1. Reliance on adequacy of county records. 2. Won't show whether the parents who received your intervention improved their parenting. 3. Possibility of biased reporting. |

You should also realize that existing scales are often used in more than one source of data. For example, children could complete a scale themselves to *self-report* how often they engage in certain behaviors. Alternatively, or in addition to the child's self-report, an adult (such as the child's parent, teacher, or cottage parent) could complete a scale to report how often the child engaged in those behaviors based on their *direct observation* of the child.

» OPERATIONALIZATION GOES ON AND ON

Although we've discussed conceptualization and operationalization in quantitative studies as activities that precede data collection and analysis—you design your operational measures before you observe—you should realize that these two processes continue throughout a research project, even after data have been collected and analyzed. Here's what we mean by that.

We have suggested that you measure a given variable in several different ways in your research. This is essential if the concept lying in the background is at all ambiguous and open to different interpretations and definitions. By measuring the variable in several different ways, you will be in a position to examine alternative operational definitions during your analysis. You will have several single indicators to choose from and many ways to create different composite measures. Thus, you will be able to experiment with different measures—each representing a somewhat different conceptualization and operationalization—to decide which gives the clearest and most useful answers to your research questions.

This doesn't mean that you should select the measurement that confirms your expectations or proves your point. That's clearly not appropriate and doesn't do much to advance our profession's knowledge base. Instead, operationalization is a continuing process, not a blind commitment to a particular measure that may turn out to have been poorly chosen. Suppose, for example, that you decide to measure compassion by asking people whether they give money to charity, and everybody answers, "Yes." Where does that leave you? Nowhere. Your study of why some people are more compassionate than others would be in deep trouble unless you had included other possible measures in designing your observations.

The validity and utility of what you learn in your research doesn't depend on when you first figured out how to look at things any more than it matters whether you got the idea from a learned textbook, a dream, or your brother-in-law.

» LEVELS OF MEASUREMENT

Variables can be operationally defined at one or more of four levels of measurement: nominal, ordinal, interval, and ratio. At the nominal level of measurement, variables are defined in terms of qualitative attributes that are categorical only. For example, defining social adjustment in terms of whether a person is receiving social services (yes or no) is at the nominal level of measurement. So is defining it in terms of whether a person is deemed ready for a sheltered workshop (again, yes or no). Other examples of variables at the nominal level of measurement are ethnicity and birthplace. It makes no sense, for example, to assess how much a person was born in Mexico. They either are or they aren't.

Variables at the ordinal level of measurement can be rank-ordered in that different attributes represent relatively more or less of the variable. But the differences between the attributes are not precise. At the ordinal level, we know only whether one case has more or less of something than another case, but we don't know how much more. For example, we have an ordinal measure if we know that the horse Seabiscuit won the race and the talking TV horse Mr. Ed came in second (he had laryngitis), but we don't know by how much. Likewise, if clients say they are very satisfied with Service A, but only slightly satisfied with Service B, then we have an ordinal measure because we don't know the precise difference in degree of satisfaction.

In contrast, with variables at the interval level of measurement, differences between different levels have the same meanings. Thus, the difference between IQ scores of 95 and 100 is considered to be of the same magnitude as the difference between 100 and 105. If social adjustment is defined in terms of a practitioner's rating of low, medium, and high, it is no longer at the nominal level because the different categories represent higher or lower degrees of adjustment. However, it would not be at the interval level because the differences between low, medium, and high are quite imprecise. It would be at the ordinal level because we cannot assume that the difference between low and medium is the same as the difference between medium and high.

Variables at the ratio level of measurement have the same attributes as interval measures, but in addition have a true zero point. Thus, a person can have no arrests, one arrest, two arrests, and so on. Because there is a true zero point, we know that the person with four arrests has been arrested exactly twice as many times as the person with two arrests. Figure 8-5 presents a graphic illustration of the four levels of measurement.

Earlier in this chapter, we mentioned nominal definitions and contrasted them with operational definitions. Using the term *nominal* in connection to definitions is different than using it in connection to levels of measurement. For example, a nominal definition of income such as the amount of money earned implies a ratio level of measurement (exact amount earned), or at least an ordinal level of measurement (poverty level, middle class, affluent, and so on).

» CONCEPTUALIZATION IN QUALITATIVE INQUIRY

Very often, the specification of reliable operational definitions seems to rob such concepts of their richness of meaning. For example, level of marital satisfaction involves much more than whether a couple is receiving marital counseling. Recognizing the risks inherent in trying to predetermine how to operationally define abstract constructs, we should remember that researchers conducting purely qualitative studies do not restrict their observations to predetermined operational indicators. Instead, they prefer to let the meanings of little-understood phenomena emerge from their observations. How they do this will be discussed in more detail later in this book, but we will elaborate a bit on this issue now.

In qualitative studies, the problem of operationally defining variables in advance is threefold. First, we may not know in advance what all the most salient variables are. Second, limitations in our understanding of the variables we think are important may keep us from anticipating the best way to operationally define those variables. Third, even the best operational definitions are necessarily superficial because they are specified only in terms of observable indicators. Although operational definitions are necessary in quantitative studies, they do not pertain to probing into the deeper meanings of what is observed. These deeper meanings are the purview of qualitative studies.

In a purely quantitative study, we assume that we know enough in advance about a phenomenon to pose a narrow research question about a limited set of variables and to develop precise, objective, observable indicators of those variables that can be counted on to answer the research question. In a purely qualitative study, we assume that we need to develop a deeper understanding of some phenomenon and its subjective meanings as it occurs in its natural environment. We take it for granted that we

FIGURE 8.5 Levels of Measurement

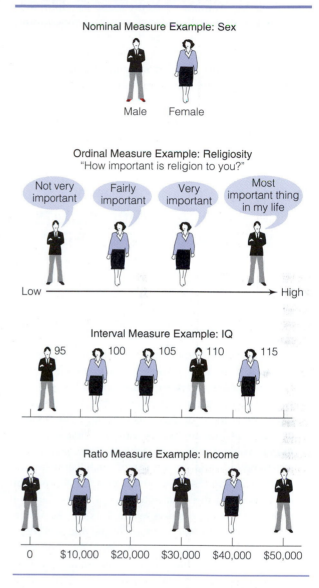

will not be able to develop that richer understanding if we limit ourselves to observable indicators that can be anticipated in advance and counted. In qualitative research, we immerse ourselves in a more subjective fashion in open-ended, flexible observations of phenomena as they occur naturally, and then we try to discern patterns and themes from an immense and relatively unstructured set of observations. Also, in qualitative research, the social context of our observations is emphasized.

To illustrate the importance of social context, as well as the qualitative perspective, imagine a quantitative study that tests the hypothesis that increasing the number of home visits by child welfare practitioners will improve parental functioning and therefore preserve families. Studies like this have been done, and the dependent variable is often operationally defined in quantifiable terms of whether (or for how long) children are placed in foster care. A problem with many of these studies is that the increased home visitation might also increase the practitioner's awareness of neglectful or abusive acts by parents. If so, then it is conceivable that any reductions in foster care placement because of improved parental functioning are canceled out by increases in foster care placement because of increased practitioner monitoring. Thus, the hypothesis might not be supported even though the increased home visits are improving service outcomes.

A qualitative inquiry, in contrast, would probe into the deeper meaning and social context of the

ILLUSTRATIONS OF THE QUALITATIVE PERSPECTIVE ON OPERATIONALIZATION AND ITS COMPLEMENTARITY WITH A QUANTITATIVE PERSPECTIVE

To further illustrate the qualitative perspective on operationalization, as well as its complementarity with a quantitative perspective, let's examine two research questions.

1. *Is burnout among social workers more likely to occur when they work in public welfare agencies or in private family service agencies?*

A qualitative study would not pose this research question. Instead of defining burnout operationally in terms of one or two observable indicators and then looking at it in relationship to a predetermined independent variable (or set of such variables), it might examine the experiences of a small group of social workers in depth and attempt to portray in a richer and deeper sense what it feels like to be burned out and what it means to the social worker. The study might, for example, be in the form of a biography of the career of one or more social workers who are burned out, perhaps contrasted with a biography of one or more who are not burned out. Conceivably, the qualitative study could be done in conjunction with a quantitative study—that is, the quantitative component could look at which of the two types of agencies had more burnout, whereas the qualitative component could try to discover the underlying reasons for the quantitative differences.

2. *Who are the most popular social work instructors: those who teach practice, research, or policy?*

A qualitative study would not pose this research question, either. Instead of using an operational definition of popularity and then seeing if it's related to type of course taught, it might involve observations of all aspects of instructor interactions with students in and out of the classroom, analysis of course materials, and in-depth, open-ended interviews with instructors and students to try to identify what makes instructors popular and what it means to be popular (perhaps popularity does not necessarily imply the most effective instruction).

Identifying instructors who appear to be the most popular could be part of a qualitative study, but the point of the study would be to probe more deeply into the meaning and experience of their popularity, not to see if a particular operational indicator of popularity is quantitatively related to another predetermined variable. Rather than report numbers on how popular one group of instructors is compared to another group, a qualitative study might begin by identifying instructors who students generally agree are the most and least popular. It might then provide a wealth of information about each of those instructors, attempting to discern themes and patterns that appear to distinguish popular from unpopular instructors or to provide the field with ideal or undesirable case study types of instructional patterns to emulate or avoid emulating. As with the previous question, the qualitative component of a study could be done in conjunction with a quantitative component. There is no reason why the hypothesis that popularity will be related to curriculum area taught could not be tested as part of a larger study that looks qualitatively at the deeper meaning of other aspects of popularity.

processes and outcomes in each case. Instead of merely counting the number of placements, it would learn that both a foster care placement in one case and the avoidance of a placement in another case could mean that the practitioner has achieved a valuable outcome. Moreover, a qualitative study would observe in detail what practitioners and clients did, probe into the deeper meanings of what was observed, and attempt to discern patterns that indicated the conditions under which practitioners appear to be more or less effective.

In describing this qualitative perspective on operational definitions, we are not implying that it's a superior perspective (although many qualitatively oriented researchers think so). It's neither superior nor inferior, neither is it mutually exclusive with a quantitative perspective (although some researchers believe the two perspectives are in conflict). In the foregoing family preservation illustration, for example, a qualitative inquiry could be conducted simultaneously with the quantitative inquiry, and both could be part of the same mixed-methods study. The qualitative component could shed light on why the quantitative hypothesis was not supported. The box "Illustrations of the Qualitative Perspective on Operationalization and Its Complementarity with a Quantitative Perspective" provides two additional examples of this issue.

4, 7, 9

MAIN POINTS

- In quantitative research, explicating the conceptual elements of the research comes at the end of the problem formulation phase, whereas in qualitative research the conceptualization process follows a more flexible and emergent pattern.
- Hypotheses consist of independent variables (the postulated explanatory variables) and dependent variables (the variables being explained).
- Relationships between variables can be positive, negative, or curvilinear.
- Extraneous, or control, variables may be examined to see if the observed relationship is misleading.
- A spurious relationship is one that no longer exists when a third variable is controlled.
- Mediating variables refer to intervening mechanisms by which independent variables affect dependent variables.

- Moderating variables influence the strength or direction of relationships between independent and dependent variables.
- Concepts are mental images we use as summary devices for bringing together observations and experiences that seem to have something in common.
- It is possible to measure the things that our concepts summarize.
- Conceptualization is the process of specifying the vague mental imagery of our concepts, sorting out the kinds of observations and measurements that will be appropriate for our research.
- Operationalization is an extension of the conceptualization process.
- In operationalization, concrete empirical procedures that will result in measurements of variables are specified.
- Operationalization is the final specification of how we would recognize the different attributes of a given variable in the real world.
- In determining the range of variation for a variable, be sure to consider the opposite of the concept. Will it be sufficient to measure religiosity from *very much* to *none*, or should you go past *none* to measure antireligiosity as well?
- Operationalization begins in study design and continues throughout the research project, including the analysis of data.
- Existing self-report scales are a popular way to operationally define many social work variables, largely because they have been used successfully by others and provide cost advantages in terms of time and money, but scales need to be selected carefully and are not always the best way to operationally define a variable.
- Additional ways to operationalize variables involve the use of direct behavioral observation, interviews, and available records.
- Qualitative studies, rather than predetermining specific, precise, objective variables and indicators to measure, begin with an initial set of anticipated meanings that can be refined during data collection and interpretation.
- Nominal measures refer to those variables whose attributes are simply different from one another. An example would be gender.
- Ordinal measures refer to those variables whose attributes may be rank ordered along some progression from more to less. An example would be the variable *prejudice* as composed of the

attributes *very prejudiced*, *somewhat preju-diced*, and *not at all prejudiced*.

- Interval measures refer to those variables whose attributes are not only rank ordered but also separated by a uniform distance between them. An example would be IQ.
- Ratio measures are the same as interval measures except that ratio measures are also based on a true zero point. Age would be an example of a ratio measure because that variable contains the attribute *zero years old*.
- A given variable can sometimes be measured at different levels of measurement. Thus, age, which is potentially a ratio measure, may also be treated as interval, ordinal, or even nominal. Quantifying data is necessary when statistical analyses are desired.

REVIEW QUESTIONS AND EXERCISES

1. Pick a social work concept—such as child neglect or abuse, quality of life, or level of informal social support—and specify that concept so that it could be studied in a research project. Be sure to specify the indicators and dimensions you wish to include (and exclude) in your conceptualization.
2. Specify two hypotheses in which a particular concept is the independent variable in one hypothesis and the dependent variable in the other. Try to hypothesize one positive relationship and one negative, or inverse, relationship.
3. Describe how a qualitative researcher and a quantitative researcher might take different approaches regarding operationally defining the level of staff sensitivity to the needs of residents in nursing homes.
4. Another researcher is not sure whether to use self-reports, direct observation, or available records to operationally define the degree of staff sensitivity to the needs of residents in nursing homes. Describe the advantages and disadvantages of each approach and the advice you would give the researcher in light of them.

5. What level of measurement—nominal, ordinal, interval, or ratio—describes each of the following variables?

    a. Agency auspices (public vs. private)
    b. Attitudes about increased social welfare spending (strongly approve, approve, disapprove, strongly disapprove)
    c. Number of students with field placements in social action organizations

INTERNET EXERCISES

1. Find several research articles in the journal *Health and Social Work*. For each study, write down how the main variables in the study were operationally defined. Notice how often existing scales were used as the operational definitions.
2. Using a search engine such as Google or Yahoo!, enter the key word "empathy." Browse through several of the websites on empathy that will appear on your screen. Make a list of the various dimensions of empathy that are described.
3. Find the article titled "Social Justice and the Research Curriculum" by John F. Longres and Edward Scanlon in the fall 2001 issue of the journal *Health and Social Work*. Also examine the reactions to that article in that same issue. Based on what you read, discuss difficulties in operationally defining the term *social justice*. Also discuss how the article illustrates concept clarification as an ongoing element in data collection.
4. Go to a website developed and operated by Dr. Marianne Yoshioka, a social work professor at Columbia University. The site is called "Psychosocial Measures for Asian-American Populations" and is located at http://www.columbia.edu/cu/ssw/projects/pmap. Download three of the abstracts of existing scales you find at that site that operationally define three different concepts. Identify the concepts that are operationally defined by the scales. Also, briefly describe how the scales you find attempt to avoid or alleviate cultural bias in operational definitions.

 Visit CengageBrain.com for additional practice and study opportunities including experiential exercises, research tools, glossary, flashcards, and sample test items.

9

Measurement

EPAS Competencies for This Chapter

Competency 4 Engage in Practice-Informed Research and Research-Informed Practice: This competency pertains to this entire chapter because doing practice-informed research requires being able to measure variables. The same applies to engaging in research-informed practice because you must understand measurement issues and concepts in order to be able to have research inform your practice.

Competency 7 Assess Individuals, Families, Groups, Organizations, and Communities: Competency in assessment implies competency in measurement. Thus, this competency pervades this entire chapter.

Competency 9 Evaluate Practice With Individuals Families, Groups, Organizations, and Communities: Evaluating practice requires being able to measure appropriately the variables to be assessed as part of your evaluation. Thus, this competency pertains to this entire chapter.

What You'll Learn in This Chapter

Now we'll go from conceptualization and operationalization, the first steps in measurement, to a consideration of broader issues in the measurement process. The emphasis in this chapter will be on measurement error, how to avoid it, and assessing how well we are avoiding it.

» INTRODUCTION

Chapter 8 discussed the wide variety of options for operationally defining a concept. We saw that with many variables in social work research, no single indicator will give you the measure that you really want for that variable. Many concepts are subject to varying interpretations, each with several possible indicators. In these cases, you will want to make several observations for a given variable. You can then combine the several pieces of information you've collected to create a *composite* measurement of the variable in question. Chapter 10, on constructing measurement instruments, discusses ways to do that, so we'll give you only a simple illustration at this point.

Consider the concept *school performance*. Some young clients do well in school, and others don't perform well in their courses. It might be useful to study that, perhaps asking what characteristics and experiences are related to high levels of performance, and many researchers have done so. How should we measure overall performance? Each grade in any single course is a potential indicator of school performance, but in using any single grade we run a risk that the one used will not be typical of the student's general performance. The solution to this problem is so firmly established that it is, of course, obvious to you: the *grade-point average*. We assign numerical scores to each letter grade, total the points a student earns, and divide by the number of courses taken to obtain a composite measure. (If the courses vary in number of credits, adjustments are made in that regard.) Creating such composite measures in social research is often appropriate.

No matter how we operationally define abstract concepts, we need to be mindful of the extreme vulnerability of the measurement process to sources of measurement error. This is so, whether we use single or composite indicators and no matter how

we go about collecting data on the indicators we select—whether we use self-report scales, available records, interviews, or direct observation. We must carefully plan to minimize the likelihood that those errors will occur and then take certain steps to check on the adequacy of our measures. How to do that is the focus of this chapter.

EP 4, 7, 9

» COMMON SOURCES OF MEASUREMENT ERROR

Measurement error occurs when we obtain data that do not accurately portray the concept we are attempting to measure. Some inaccuracies may be minor, such as when parents forget about one of the 11 temper tantrums their son had last week and report that he had 10. Other inaccuracies may be serious, such as when a measure portrays an abusive parent as nonabusive. Common sources of measurement error come in two types: systematic error and random error. Let's begin with systematic error.

Systematic Error

Systematic error occurs when the information we collect consistently reflects a false picture of the concept we seek to measure because of either the way we collect the data or the dynamics of those who are providing the data. Sometimes our measures really don't measure what we think they do. For example, measuring what people think is the right thing to do will not necessarily reflect what they themselves usually do. When we try to measure likely behavior by collecting data on attitudes or views, we may be making a big mistake. Words don't always match deeds. Some folks who espouse "liberal" views on issues like school busing end up moving to the suburbs or enrolling their children in private schools when it's their own kids who will be bused. Many people who support the idea of locating residences for the mentally disabled in residential areas would fight efforts to locate one on their block.

Biases Even when measures tap someone's true views, systematic error may occur in thinking that something else (i.e., likely behavior) is being measured. Perhaps the most common way our measures systematically measure something other than what we think they do is when biases are involved in the data collection. Biases can come in various forms. We may ask questions in a way that predisposes individuals to answer the way we want them to, or we may smile excessively or nod our heads in agreement when we get the answers that support our hypotheses. Or individuals may be biased to answer our questions in ways that distort their true views or behaviors. For instance, they may be biased to agree with whatever we say, or they may do or say things that will convey a favorable impression of themselves.

The former bias, agreeing or disagreeing with most or all statements regardless of their content, is called the acquiescent response set. The latter bias, the tendency of people to say or do things that will make them or their reference group look good, is called the social desirability bias. Most researchers recognize the likely effect of a question that begins, "Don't you agree with the Bible that … ," and no reputable researcher would use such an item. Unhappily, the biasing effect of items and terms is far subtler than this example suggests.

The mere identification of an attitude or position with a prestigious person or agency can bias responses. An item such as, "Do you agree or disagree with the statement in our professional code of ethics that …" would have a similar effect. We should make it clear that we are not suggesting that such wording will necessarily produce consensus or even a majority in support of the position identified with the prestigious person or agency, only that support would probably be increased over the support that would have been obtained without such identification. Questionnaire items can be biased negatively as well as positively. "Do you agree or disagree with the position of Adolf Hitler when he stated that …" is an example.

To further illustrate the ways in which different forms of wording questions can have relatively subtle biasing effects, we may consider Rasinski's (1989) analysis of the results of several General Social Survey Studies of attitudes toward government spending. He found that the way programs were identified affected how much public support they received. Here are some comparisons:

MORE SUPPORT	LESS SUPPORT
"Halting rising crime rate"	"Law enforcement"
"Dealing with drug addiction"	"Drug rehabilitation"
"Assistance to the poor"	"Welfare"
"Solving problems of big cities"	"Assistance to big cities"

Asking practitioners about their treatment orientations can involve some subtle biases. Suppose you asked them if they agreed that they should try to motivate people with psychotic disorders who resist taking their psychiatric medications to do so. The practitioners might be predisposed to agree. It sounds right that patients should take the medicine that their physicians have prescribed for them and that social workers ought to help motivate severely ill people to take better care of themselves. But suppose you asked whether they agreed that the principle of self-determination means that they should respect the right of these patients to refuse treatment and should therefore not urge them to take their medications if they don't want to.

As another example of bias, consider the following. In 1989, more than 20 national magazines simultaneously published a questionnaire as part of a survey of opinions on child care and family issues. (We first saw the questionnaire in the February 27, 1989, issue of the *New Republic*.) Readers were encouraged to tear out and complete the questionnaire and return it to "Your Family Matters" at a New York City address. At the top of the questionnaire, readers were informed that the survey was being sponsored by the "nonpartisan advocates Child Care Action Campaign and the Great American Family Tour" and that a national cable television channel underwriting the survey would be airing a special documentary, *Hush Little Baby: The Challenge of Child Care.* Also at the top, in large bold letters, was the heading, "TELL THE PRESIDENT YOUR FAMILY MATTERS." Under this buildup were the questionnaire items, beginning with the following two yes-or-no items:

1. Do you think the federal government pays enough attention to child care and other family concerns?
2. Do you think family issues should be a top priority for the president and Congress?

Some of the subsequent items asked for opinions about whether various levels of government should develop policies to make child care more available and affordable and should set minimum standards for child care centers.

You may note at least three levels of bias in this survey. At one level, it is not hard for readers to discern that the questionnaire's heading shows that the opinions desired by the surveyors are those that call for more government attention to child care and family issues. Indeed, the heading instructs the reader to "tell the president your family matters." The second level of bias concerns the issue of who would bother to complete and mail in the questionnaire. People who care deeply about the issue of child care, especially those who strongly believe that more government attention to it is needed, were probably much more likely to respond than those who feel otherwise. (We will examine the latter level of bias—response rate bias—more closely in Chapter 16, on survey research.) The third level of bias has to do with what segments of the population are likely to see the questionnaire in the first place. Chances are that people who subscribe to and read the selected magazines are not representative of the rest of the population in regard to views on child care and family issues and perhaps are more likely to share the views of the survey sponsors than are the rest of the population. (We will examine that type of bias in Chapter 15, on sampling.)

Social Desirability Bias   Earlier we noted the potential for the *social desirability bias*. Be especially wary of this bias. Whenever you ask people for information, they answer through a filter of concern about what will make them look good. This is especially true if they are being interviewed in a face-to-face situation. Thus, for example, a particular man may feel that things would be a lot better if women were kept in the kitchen, not allowed to vote, forced to be quiet in public, and so forth. Asked whether he supports equal rights for women, however, he may want to avoid looking like a male

chauvinist pig. Recognizing that his views might have been progressive in the 15th century but are out of step with current thinking, he may choose to say yes. The main guidance we can offer you in relation to this problem is to suggest that you imagine how you would feel in giving each of the answers you offered to respondents. If you'd feel embarrassed, perverted, inhumane, stupid, irresponsible, or anything like that, then you should give serious thought to whether others will be willing to give those answers. We will have more to say about the social desirability bias later in this chapter and in forthcoming chapters on data collection methods and on designs for evaluating programs and practice.

Cultural Bias   As we discussed in Chapter 6, another common source of bias stems from cultural disparities. Intelligence tests, for example, have been cited as biased against certain ethnic minority groups. The argument is posed that children growing up in economically disadvantaged environments with different values, opportunities, and speaking patterns are at a disadvantage when they take IQ tests geared to a white, middle-class environment. It is argued, for example, that a minority child may score lower than a white child of equal or lower intelligence simply because the language of the questions is less familiar or because the questions refer to material things that white, middle-class children take for granted but that are unknown to disadvantaged children.

This argument is controversial, but the potential for cultural bias in measurement is not. Suppose, for example, that you are conducting a survey to see whether recent immigrants to the United States from Asia are less likely to utilize social services than are second- or third-generation Asian Americans. If the recent immigrants, because of language difficulties, don't understand your questions as meaning the same as do the other groups, then differences in the data between the groups may have less to do with differences in their views on social service use than with the systematic language bias in your questions.

Monette, Sullivan, and DeJong (1994) illustrated a similar phenomenon in regard to a study of the mental health of Native Americans. In that study, the word *blue* had to be dropped from an instrument that measured depression because *blue* did not mean "sad" among Native Americans.

The same study found that to avoid cultural bias in assessing the use of mental health services, traditional healers (what you may call "faith healers" or "spiritualists") had to be added to the list of professionals from whom Native Americans might seek help.

Random Error

Unlike systematic errors, random errors have no consistent pattern of effects. Random errors do not bias our measures; they make them inconsistent from one measurement to the next. This does not mean that whenever data change over time we have random error. Sometimes things really do change—and when they do, our measures should detect that change. What it does mean is that if the things we are measuring do not change over time but our measures keep coming up with different results, then we have inconsistencies in measurement, or random error.

Random errors can take various forms. Perhaps our measurement procedures are so cumbersome, complex, boring, or fatiguing that our respondents say or do things at random just to get the measurement over with as quickly as possible. For example, halfway through a lengthy questionnaire full of complicated questions, respondents may stop giving much thought to what the questions really mean or how they truly feel about them.

Another example might be when two raters are recording the number of times a social worker gives an empathic response in a videotaped interview with a client. If the raters are not really sure how to recognize an empathic response when they see one, they may disagree substantially about how many empathic responses they observed in the same videotape. Note the difference between this sort of error and systematic error. If one rater was the videotaped social worker's mentor or fiancée and the other rater was the social worker's rival for a promotion, then the differences in the ratings would probably result from systematic error.

For yet another example of random error, suppose clients who have no familiarity with social service jargon are asked whether they have received brokerage, advocacy, or linkage services. Odds are they would have no idea what those terms meant. Not understanding what they were being asked but not wishing to appear ignorant or uncooperative, they might answer yes or no at random, and they might change their answers the next time they were

asked, even though the situation had not changed. That would represent random error. But suppose that even though they had no earthly idea what they were being asked, they suspected that an affirmative response would make them or their social worker look better. If they then responded affirmatively to every question just so they would not appear negativistic or get practitioners in trouble, that would represent systematic error associated with a social desirability bias or acquiescent response set.

Although the term *bias* may sound more insidious than "random error" or "inconsistency in measurement," random error can be a serious problem. Suppose, for example, that an extremely effective school social work intervention to improve the self-esteem of underachieving third graders is being evaluated. Suppose further that the measurement instrument selected for the evaluation was constructed for use with well-educated adults and that the researchers evaluating the intervention were unaware of the fact that underachieving third graders would not understand many of the items on the instrument. This lack of understanding would mean that the children's responses would be largely random and have little to do with their level of self-esteem. Consequently, the likelihood that the instrument would detect significant increases in self-esteem, even after an effective intervention, would be slim. Random error in measurement, therefore, can make a highly effective intervention look ineffective.

Errors in Alternate Forms of Measurement

Earlier we mentioned four alternative options that are commonly used to measure variables in social work research: written self-reports, interviews, direct behavioral observation, and examining available records. We also noted that each option is vulnerable to measurement error. Let's now look at the four options separately and see some of the similarities and differences in the ways each is vulnerable to measurement errors.

Written Self-Reports Having people complete questionnaires or scales is a relatively inexpensive and expedient way to collect data. Consequently, it is perhaps the most commonly used measurement option in social work research. Written self-reports can be used to gather background information about people (their age, sex, ethnicity, and so on) or to measure their knowledge, attitudes, skills, or behavior. Regardless of which of these things we seek to measure, we would want to avoid random errors associated with the difficulty some people may have in understanding how we have worded our items or in the length and complexity of our instrument. We would also want to avoid systematic errors resulting from bias in the way we have worded our items or in respondents' propensity to convey a socially desirable image of themselves.

Even if we completely avoid problems in the way we construct our instruments, however, we should remember that people's words don't necessarily match their deeds. For example, parents referred for abuse or neglect who have completed a mandatory parent education program can learn and check off the desired answers to a written test of their knowledge of, attitudes about, and skills in child rearing without becoming any less likely to neglect or abuse their children. Their written responses about their behavior may be grossly inaccurate because they may want to portray themselves in a socially desirable light. Having them complete the instruments anonymously might alleviate some of this bias, but it does not guarantee the avoidance of such gross inaccuracies because people tend to see themselves in a socially desirable manner.

But even if you were to avoid all of the errors we have mentioned, that would not guarantee that the written answers really measure what you think they measure. Suppose, for example, you develop a self-report scale that you think will measure social workers' orientations about practice. Suppose you are particularly interested in measuring the extent to which they are oriented more toward providing office-based psychotherapy exclusively versus a case management approach that emphasizes—in addition to the therapeutic relationship—such services as home visits, brokerage, advocacy, and helping clients learn social skills and how to manage concrete basic living tasks. Let's further suppose that you word each item by asking how important it is to provide each of these things to clients. It is conceivable that many respondents who provide office-based psychotherapy exclusively and who see the other services as beneath their level of expertise might nevertheless endorse each service as very important because they think that practitioners who are at lower levels than they are would deliver the services other than psychotherapy. Those respondents might be answering in a completely accurate and unbiased manner. They might really believe that those services are very important; they just might not believe that they themselves are the ones who should deliver them. If you interpreted their scale scores as a measure of the way they conduct their own practice, however, your measure would be in error. It would not be measuring what you intend it to measure. The technical term used to convey whether a self-report measure really measures what it is intended to measure is validity. We will discuss *validity* in much greater depth later in this chapter.

Interviews   Another way to collect self-reported information is through interviews. Although interviews are a more time-consuming and costly way to collect data than by using written self-reports, they have several advantages. If a respondent doesn't understand how a question is worded, the interviewer can clarify it. The interviewer can also ensure that the respondent does not skip any items. In addition, interviewers can observe things about the respondent and probe for more information about vague responses to open-ended questions. In qualitative studies that attempt to develop a deeper and more subjective understanding of how people experience things, the use of such open-ended probes can be vital.

Despite their advantages, interviews are susceptible to most of the same sources of error as are written self-reports, particularly regarding social desirability bias. As we noted earlier, the tendency to answer questions in ways that convey a favorable impression of oneself can be greater in an interview than when completing a written instrument. This tendency can be exacerbated when interviewers introduce their own subtle biases, such as by smiling or nodding when respondents answer in ways that support a study's hypothesis. Sometimes interviews can involve biases that are less subtle, such as when a therapist interviews her clients on termination of therapy to ask them how much her therapy has helped them. It's much harder to tell her face-to-face that her therapy did not help than it is to report the same thing by completing a written instrument, especially if the instrument can be completed without the therapist knowing which clients completed which instrument.

Interviews also involve additional sources of random error. Different interviewers, for example, might be inconsistent in the way they ask questions and record answers. Different interviewer characteristics might affect how respondents answer questions. A white interviewer might get different responses than an African American interviewer when interviewing people about their views on race issues. A female interviewer might get different responses than a male interviewer when asking people how they feel about equal rights for women.

Direct Behavioral Observation Rather than rely on what people say as the way to assess their attitudes, skills, or behavior, we can observe their behavior directly. For example, if we want to assess the effects of an intervention program on the parenting behaviors of parents who were referred for abuse or neglect, then we could make home visits and observe how they interact with their children. Or we could have their children play with a bunch of toys in a playroom and then observe through a one-way mirror how the parents handle the challenging task of getting the children to put away their toys.

Although direct behavioral observation can be more time consuming and costly, it has the advantage of seeing behavior for ourselves and not having to wonder whether the way people answer questions reflects how they actually behave. Yet direct observation, too, can be highly vulnerable to systematic error, such as social desirability biases. As we noted earlier, people who know they are being observed may act in a much more socially desirable manner than when they are not being observed or when they do not know they are being observed. In addition, the observers themselves might be biased to perceive behaviors that support their study's hypothesis. Random errors can result from inconsistencies in the way different observers observe and record things, perhaps stemming from differences in how well they understand the phenomena they are looking for and recording.

Examining Available Records Perhaps the least time-consuming and costly measurement option is the examination of available records. Returning to the example of assessing practitioner orientations about their practice, we might want to examine their process notes in their case records, looking to see how often they employ different techniques or provide different services. But some practitioners might exaggerate their records regarding the amount of time they spend on certain activities in the belief that someone might use those records to evaluate their performance. That would be a source of *systematic error*. Maybe they resent all the record keeping that is expected of them and thus aren't careful in documenting their tasks. That would create *random errors*.

» AVOIDING MEASUREMENT ERROR

At this juncture, you may be wondering, "Yikes, is the measurement process so fraught with error that research is hardly worth doing?" We do not intend to imply that. But we are saying that the measurement process is extremely vulnerable to errors, that we need to be aware of the potential for these errors to occur, and that we must take steps to deal with them.

It is virtually impossible to avoid all possible sources of measurement error. Even if all we do is canvass an agency's caseload to describe the proportions of male and female clients of different ages and ethnic groups, chances are we will have some measurement error. For instance, there may be clerical oversights in recording data, coding them, or typing them for computer input. Even relatively concrete concepts such as ethnicity can be misunderstood by survey respondents. During the 1970s, for example, the Council on Social Work Education was asked by some of its Native American constituents to change one item on the questionnaire the council used in its annual canvass of schools of social work. The item pertained to the ethnicity of faculty members, so the council changed the category that previously read *American Indian* to *Native American*. In the first year after that change, there was a large jump in the number of Native American faculty members reported. In fact, some schools that reported having only white faculty members the year before now reported having only Native American faculty members. Fortunately, by comparing the data to the previous year's report from each school, the measurement error was easy to detect and correct. The clerical staff members who had completed the questionnaire in certain schools thought that the term *Native American* referred to anyone born in the United States, regardless of their ethnicity.

No one should be dissuaded from pursuing research simply because of the inevitability of measurement errors. No one expects a study to have perfect measurement, at least not in the field of social scientific research. What matters is that you try to minimize any major measurement errors that would destroy the credibility and utility of your findings and that you assess how well your measures appear to have kept those errors from exceeding a reasonable level.

Because measurement errors can occur countless ways, it's not easy to tell you how to avoid them. The steps you can take depend in large part on your data collection methods. We will discuss some of those steps in Chapter 10, on constructing measurement instruments, and other steps in later chapters. But here is a brief preview of a few of those steps, just to give you an idea of the sorts of things that can be done.

If you are constructing a questionnaire or self-report scale, try to use unbiased wording (to minimize systematic error) and terms that respondents will understand (to minimize random error). Obtain collegial feedback to help spot biases or ambiguities that you may have overlooked. (Because we know what we mean by what we write, it's easy for us to be unaware of ambiguities in our wording.) And be sure to test the questionnaire in a dry run with a handful or two of people like those whom you intend to include in your study to see if they will understand the questionnaire and not find it too unwieldy. (Later in this chapter and some subsequent chapters, we'll discuss administering measurement instruments in pretests with larger samples to collect actual study data regarding the reliability of an instrument or the scores on it before receiving an intervention that is being evaluated. But that is not what we mean by *dry run* here.)

If you're using people to conduct interviews or rate behaviors they observe, be sure to train them carefully and make sure that they are consistent in how they perform their tasks. Also attempt to minimize the extent to which they can be influenced by biases. For example, if they are collecting information on how well clients function before and after an intervention as compared to individuals who receive no intervention, try to keep your data collectors blind as to whether any particular measure is being taken before or after the intervention or on whether any specific individual received the intervention.

If your measurement involves direct observation of behaviors, then try to arrange the situation so that the client is not keenly aware that observations are occurring and is therefore less likely to act out of character in order to look good. This *unobtrusive observation* is used to minimize the social desirability bias. We will return to the concept of unobtrusive observation in several forthcoming chapters.

If your measurement relies on the use of available records, don't assume that they are sufficiently free of error because an agency values them or because they're "official." Talk to agency practitioners and others "in the know" about how carefully or haphazardly records are kept. Probe about any possible reasons why those who enter the data might be influenced by certain biases that reduce your confidence in the validity of what they record.

Several other data collection steps are rather generic in nature, and their use cuts across the many data collection alternatives. One such step involves the principle of triangulation. Triangulation deals with systematic error by using several different research methods to collect the same information. Because there is no one foolproof method for avoiding systematic measurement error, we can use several imperfect measurement alternatives and see if they tend to produce the same findings. If they do, then we can have more confidence (but no guarantee) that measurement error is at an acceptable level. If one method yields data that sharply conflict with the data provided by alternative measures, then we have reason to suspect serious errors somewhere and have clues as to where they may have occurred. Triangulation requires that the different measures have different potential sources of error. If we expect each measure to be vulnerable to the same sources of error, then consistency among the measures would not really tell us whether that source of systematic error was being avoided.

For instance, suppose we assess practitioner responsiveness to chronically mentally disabled clients in three ways, as follows: (1) We assess their self-reported attitudes about treating the disabled; (2) we ask disabled clients about the amount of contact they had with the practitioners and how satisfied they were with the help they received; and (3) we survey case records to tabulate the amount of services practitioners provided to disabled clients. Suppose the practitioners all say that they derive great satisfaction from treating disabled clients but that the case records show that disabled clients usually receive less than three contacts from them and then are no longer followed. Suppose further that the large majority of disabled clients corroborate the case records in terms of the amount of service they received and add that the practitioner seemed impatient with their slowness and disinterested in the problems that they felt were most important. Having triangulated your measures, you would be in a far better position to judge the credibility of your data than if you had used only one of the preceding measures. Moreover, you would be able to avoid the apparent errors inherent in relying on self-reports in measuring practitioner attitudes, errors that seem to be associated with a social desirability bias, which you would not have been able to avoid had you not triangulated your measures.

The other generic steps you can take to minimize measurement error are closely related to triangulation. They involve making sure, before you implement the study, that the measurement procedures you will use have acceptable levels of reliability and validity. Reliability and validity are two of the most important concepts you can learn about research methods. Both concepts will be discussed thoroughly throughout the remainder of this chapter.

» RELIABILITY

In the abstract sense, reliability is a matter of whether a particular technique, applied repeatedly to the same object, would yield the same result each time. Thus, reliability has to do with the amount of random error in a measurement. The more reliable the measure, the less random error in it.

Suppose a large classmate—a tackle on your school's football team—asks you and another classmate to guesstimate how much he weighs. You look him over carefully and guess that he weighs 260 pounds. Your classmate guesstimates 360 pounds. This would suggest that the technique of having people estimate how much other people weigh is not very reliable. Suppose, however, that each of you had used his bathroom scale to measure his weight. The scale would have indicated virtually the same weight each time, indicating that the scale provided a more reliable measure of weight than did your guesstimates.

Reliability, however, does not ensure accuracy. Suppose he set his bathroom scale to shave 10 pounds off his weight just to make him feel better.

Although the scale would (reliably) report the same weight for him each time, both of the weighings you and your classmate performed would be wrong because of systematic error (i.e., a biased scale).

Here's another hypothetical example. Let's suppose we are interested in studying morale among social workers in two different kinds of agencies. One set is composed of public assistance agencies; the other is composed of family service agencies. How should we measure morale? Following one strategy, we could spend some time observing the workers in each agency, noticing such things as whether they joke with one another, whether they smile and laugh a lot, and so forth. We could ask them how they like their work and even ask them whether they think they would prefer their current setting or the other one being studied. By comparing what we observed in the different agencies, we might reach a conclusion about which setting produced the higher morale.

Now let's look at some of the possible reliability problems inherent in this method. First, how we feel when we do the observing is likely to color what we see. We might misinterpret what we see. We might see workers kidding each other and think they are having an argument. Or maybe we'll catch them on an off day. If we were to observe the same group of workers several days in a row, we might arrive at different evaluations on each day. And if several observers evaluated the same behavior, they too might arrive at different conclusions about the workers' morale.

Here's another strategy for assessing morale. Suppose we check the agency records to see how many worker resignations occurred during some fixed period of time. Presumably, that would be an indicator of morale: The more resignations, the lower the morale. This measurement strategy would appear to be more reliable; we could count up the resignations over and over, and we should continue to arrive at the same number.

If you find yourself thinking that the number of resignations doesn't necessarily measure morale, you're worrying about validity, not reliability. We'll discuss validity in a moment. First, let's complete the discussion of reliability.

Reliability problems crop up in many forms in social research. Survey researchers have known for a long time that different interviewers get different answers from respondents as a result of their own attitudes and demeanors. If we were to conduct a study of editorial positions on some public issue, we might assemble a team of coders to take on the job of reading hundreds of editorials and classifying them in terms of the position each takes on the issue. Different coders would code the same editorial differently. Or we might want to classify a few hundred specific occupations in terms of some standard coding scheme—say, a set of categories created by the Department of Labor or by the Census Bureau. Not all of us would code those occupations into the same categories.

Each of these examples illustrates problems of reliability. Similar problems arise whenever we ask people to give us information about themselves. Sometimes we ask questions for which people don't know the answers. (How many times have you been to church?) Sometimes we ask people about things that are totally irrelevant to them. (Are you satisfied with China's current relationship with Albania?) Sometimes people don't understand what our questions mean, such as when we use words that children have not yet learned or terms that have different meanings in different cultures. And sometimes we ask questions that are so complicated that a person who had a clear opinion on the matter might arrive at a different interpretation on being asked the question a second time.

How do you create reliable measures? There are several techniques. First, in asking people for information—if your research design calls for that—be careful to ask only about things the respondents are likely to be able to answer. Ask about things relevant to them and be clear in what you're asking. The danger in these instances is that people will give you answers—reliable or not. People will tell you what they think about China's relationship with Albania even if they haven't the foggiest idea what that relationship is.

Another way to handle the problem of reliability in getting information from people is to use measures that have proven their reliability in previous research. In the case of unreliability generated by research workers, there are several solutions. To guard against interviewer unreliability, it is common practice in surveys to have a supervisor call a subsample of the respondents on the telephone and verify selected pieces of information. Replication works in other situations as well. If you are worried that newspaper editorials or occupations may not be classified reliably, then why not have each editorial or occupation independently coded by several

coders? Those editorials or occupations that generate disagreement should be evaluated more carefully and resolved.

Finally, clarity, specificity, training, and practice will avoid a great deal of unreliability and grief. If we were to spend time with you reaching a clear agreement on how we were going to evaluate editorial positions on an issue—discussing the various positions that might be represented and reading through several together—we'd probably be able to do a good job of classifying them in the same way independently.

Types of Reliability

The type of measurement reliability that is most relevant to a particular study varies according to the study's purpose and design. If the study involves judgments made by observers or raters, for example, then we need to assess the extent of agreement, or consistency, between or among observers or raters. If the study involves using a written self-report scale that respondents complete to measure certain constructs such as self-esteem, depression, job satisfaction, and so on, then reliability is usually measured in one or two ways. If the self-report scale is being used to measure changes in people over time, then we need to assess the *stability* of the scale in providing consistent measurements from one administration to the next. A particularly expedient alternative way to assess a scale's reliability, without concern as to stability over time, is to measure its *internal consistency*. Let's now look at each of these alternatives in more detail.

Interobserver and Interrater Reliability

The term for the degree of agreement or consistency between or among observers or raters is interobserver reliability or interrater reliability. Suppose you are studying whether an in-service training program for paraprofessionals or volunteers increases the level of empathy they express in videotaped role-play situations. To assess interrater reliability, you would train two raters, then you would have them view the same videos and independently rate the level of empathy they observed in each. If they agree approximately 80% or more of the time in their ratings, then you can assume that the amount of random error in measurement is not excessive. Some researchers would argue that even 70% agreement would be acceptable.

Instead of calculating the percentage of agreement, you might want to calculate the correlation between the two sets of ratings. The term *correlation* is a statistical depiction of the extent to which two variables tend to vary together. If there are not many exceptions to a pattern in which social workers who have taken more research courses read more research articles to inform their practice, while those who took fewer research courses read fewer such articles, then there would be a strong *correlation* between number of research courses taken and number of research articles read. Applying correlation to interrater reliability, suppose the ratings are on a scale from 1 to 10 and that although the two raters rarely choose the exact same rating, both tend to give high or low ratings in a consistent fashion; that is, one pair of ratings might be a 9 and an 8, and another pair might be a 2 and a 3. As one rater goes up, the other rater goes up. As one goes down, the other goes down. Although they rarely agree on the exact number, they move up and down together. If so, although the percentage of agreement might be low, the correlation might be high, perhaps above .80. We will discuss correlation later in Part 7. At this point, it is sufficient to know that correlations can range from 0 (meaning no relationship/no correlation) to 1.0 (meaning a perfect relationship with no random error). Later we will also discuss how correlations can be negative, ranging from 0 to –1.0.

Test–Retest Reliability

In studies that seek to assess changes in scale scores over time, it is important to use a stable measure—that is, a scale that provides consistency in measurement over time. If the measurement is not stable over time, then changes that you observe in your study may have less to do with real changes in the phenomenon being observed than with changes in the measurement process. The term for assessing a measure's stability over time is test–retest reliability.

To assess test–retest reliability, simply administer the same measurement instrument to the same individuals on two separate occasions. If the correlation between the two sets of responses to the instrument is above .70 or .80 (the higher the better), then the instrument may be deemed to have acceptable stability. But assessing test–retest reliability can be tricky. What if the individual actually changes between testing and retesting? What if the

EP 4, 7, 9

conditions (time of day and so forth) of the test are different from those of the retest? In assessing test–retest reliability, you must be certain that both tests occur under identical conditions, and the time lapse between test and retest should be long enough that the individuals will not recall their answers from the first testing and yet be short enough to minimize the likelihood that individuals will change significantly between the two testings. Approximately 2 weeks is a common interval between the test and the retest. The box "An Example of Test–Retest Reliability" further illustrates the importance of assessing this form of reliability and how to do it.

Internal Consistency Reliability

Whether or not we plan to assess changes on a measure over time, it is important to assess whether the various items that make up the measure are *internally consistent*. This method, called internal consistency reliability, assumes that the instrument contains multiple items, each of which is scored and combined with the scores of the other items to produce an overall score. Using this method, we simply assess the correlation of the scores on each item with the scores on the rest of the items. Or we might compute the total scores of different subsets of items and then assess the correlations of those subset totals. Using the *split-halves method*, for example, we would assess the correlations of subscores among different subsets of half of the items. Because this method requires administering the measure only one time to a group of respondents, it is the most practical and most commonly used method for assessing reliability.

Before the advent of computers made it easy to calculate internal consistency correlations, research texts commonly mentioned a more time-consuming and more difficult and impractical method for measuring a scale's reliability that was akin to internal consistency reliability. It was called parallel-forms reliability. That method requires constructing a second measuring instrument that is thought to be equivalent to the first. It might be a shorter series of questions, and it always attempts to measure the same thing as the other instrument. Both forms are administered to the same set of individuals, and then we assess whether the two sets of responses are adequately correlated. This reliability assessment

AN EXAMPLE OF TEST–RETEST RELIABILITY

In their research on Health Hazard Appraisal, a part of preventive medicine, Sacks, Krushat, and Newman (1980) wanted to determine the risks associated with various background and lifestyle factors, making it possible for physicians to counsel their patients appropriately. By knowing patients' life situations, physicians could advise them on their potential for survival and on how to improve it. This purpose, of course, depended heavily on the accuracy of the information gathered about each subject in the study.

To test the reliability of their information, Sacks and his colleagues had all 207 subjects complete a baseline questionnaire that asked about their characteristics and behavior. Three months later, a follow-up questionnaire asked the same subjects for the same information, and the results of the two surveys were compared. Overall, only 15% of the subjects reported the same information in both studies.

Sacks et al. (1980) report the following:

Almost 10 percent of subjects reported a different height at follow-up examination. Parental age was changed by over one in three subjects. One parent reportedly aged 20 chronologic years in three months. One in five ex-smokers and ex-drinkers have apparent difficulty in reliably recalling their previous consumption pattern. (p. 730)

Some subjects erased all trace of previously reported heart murmur, diabetes, emphysema, arrest record, and thoughts of suicide. One subject's mother, deceased in the first questionnaire, was apparently alive and well in time for the second. One subject had one ovary missing in the first study but present in the second. In another case, an ovary present in the first study was missing in the second study—and had been for 10 years! One subject was reportedly 55 years old in the first study and 50 years old 3 months later. (You have to wonder whether the physician-counselors could ever have nearly the impact on their patients that their patients' memories did.) Thus, test–retest revealed that this data collection method was not especially reliable.

method is extremely rare in social work research because constructing a second instrument and ensuring its equivalence to the first is both cumbersome and risky. Inconsistent results on the two "parallel" forms might not mean that the main measure is unreliable. The inconsistency might merely result from shortcomings in the effort to make the second instrument truly equivalent to the first.

The most common and powerful method used today for calculating internal consistency reliability is coefficient alpha. The calculation of coefficient alpha is easily done using available computer software. The formula for calculating coefficient alpha is a bit complicated, but in simple terms it involves subdividing all of the items of an instrument into all possible split halves (subsets of half of the items), calculating the total subscore of each possible split half for each subject, and then calculating the correlations of all possible pairs of split-half subscores. Coefficient alpha equals the average of all of these correlations (or is somewhat less than the average after statistically correcting for differences in item standard deviations). When coefficient alpha is at about .90 or above, internal consistency reliability is considered to be excellent. Alphas at around .80 to .89 are considered good, and somewhat lower alphas can be considered acceptable for relatively short instruments. (For statistical reasons that we won't go into, when instruments contain relatively few items, it is harder to get high correlations among the subset scores.) The box "A Hypothetical Illustration of Coefficient Alpha" attempts to clarify this procedure.

We'll return to the issue of reliability more than once in the chapters ahead. For now, however, let's recall that even perfect reliability doesn't ensure that our measures measure what we think they measure. Now let's plunge into the question of validity.

» VALIDITY

In conventional usage, the term *validity* refers to the extent to which an empirical measure adequately reflects the *real meaning* of the concept under consideration. In this section, we look at face validity, content validity, criterion-related validity, construct validity, and factorial validity.

Face Validity

To begin, there's something called face validity. Particular empirical measures may or may not jibe with our common agreements and our individual mental images associated with a particular concept. We might quarrel about the adequacy of measuring worker morale by counting the number of resignations that occurred, but we would surely agree that the number of resignations has *something* to do with morale. If we were to suggest that we measure morale by finding out how many books the workers took out of the library during their off-duty hours, then you'd undoubtedly raise a more serious objection: That measure wouldn't have any face validity.

Face validity is necessary if a measurement is to be deemed worth pursuing—but it is far from sufficient. In fact, some researchers might argue that it is technically misleading to call it a type of validity at all. Whether a measure has face validity is determined by subjective assessments made by the researcher or perhaps by other experts. Having face validity does not mean that a measure really measures what the researcher intends to measure, only that it *appears* to measure what the researcher intended.

To illustrate the limited value of face validity, let's consider the development of the paranoia scale in the Minnesota Multiphasic Personality Inventory (MMPI). The MMPI has long been one of the most widely used and highly regarded personality measures. When it was originally developed for clinical assessment purposes, it contained nine scales. Each scale had items to which one can respond either "true" or "false." One scale measured paranoia. For each item on this scale, a particular answer (either true or false) was scored higher or lower for paranoia. To validate the scale, it was administered to large numbers of people who were and were not diagnosed as paranoid. Items were deemed valid if individuals who were diagnosed as paranoid tended to answer those items differently than did individuals not diagnosed as paranoid.

Below are several of those items on the paranoia scale. Each item differentiated those with paranoia from those not so diagnosed. Examine each item and see if you can determine which answer, "true" or "false," those with paranoia were more likely to select.

"Most people will use somewhat unfair means to gain profit or an advantage rather than lose it."

"I tend to be on my guard with people who are somewhat more friendly than I had expected."

"I think most people would lie to get ahead."

From a face validity standpoint, we expect that you probably chose "true" as the response more likely to be selected by those with paranoia. Indeed, it seems reasonable to suppose that those with paranoia would be more suspicious of the tendencies of others to cheat them, deceive them, or lie to them. But the opposite was the case! Those with paranoia were more likely than normals to answer "false" to the above items (Dahlstrom & Welsh, 1960). In light of this fact, and with 20/20 hindsight, we might be able to construct a rational explanation of why this occurred, perhaps noting that paranoids have unrealistically high expectations of what other people are like and that such overly idealistic expectations lead them to feel betrayed and persecuted when people act less nobly. But without the benefit of hindsight, there is a good chance that we would link the face validity of the preceding items to the likelihood that paranoids would more frequently respond "true." If this were the case and if we relied solely on face validity to determine the scale's quality and its scoring system, then on these items we would be more likely to give a worse (higher) paranoia score to those without paranoia and a better (lower) paranoia score to those with paranoia.

Content Validity

A technically more legitimate type of validity, one that includes elements of face validity, is known as content validity. The term refers to the degree to which a measure covers the range of meanings included within the concept. For example, a test of mathematical ability, Carmines and Zeller (1979) point out, cannot be limited to addition alone but would also need to cover subtraction, multiplication, division, and so forth. Like face validity, however, content validity is established on the basis of judgments; that is, researchers or other experts make judgments about whether the measure covers the universe of facets that make up the concept. Although we must make judgments about face and content validity when we construct a particular measure, it is important to conduct an empirical assessment of the adequacy of those judgments. For no matter how much confidence we may have

A HYPOTHETICAL ILLUSTRATION OF COEFFICIENT ALPHA

Suppose you develop a four-item scale to measure depression among elementary schoolchildren as follows:

	Often	Sometimes	Almost Never
1. I feel sad.	2	1	0
2. I cry.	2	1	0
3. I'm unhappy.	2	1	0
4. I can't sleep.	2	1	0

Suppose you administer the scale to 200 children to test its internal consistency reliability. If the scale is internally consistent, then children who circle 0 on some items should be more likely than other children to circle 0 on the other items as well. Likewise, children who circle 2 on some items should be more likely than other children to circle 2 on the other items. If the scale has excellent internal consistency reliability, then the correlation of each item with each of the other items might look something like this:

Interitem correlation matrix:

	Item 1	Item 2	Item 3	Item 4
Item 1	1.0			
Item 2	.6	1.0		
Item 3	.5	.5	1.0	
Item 4	.4	.5	.6	1.0

In an instant, computer software such as SPSS can produce the above correlation matrix and calculate coefficient alpha. You can see in the above matrix that the four items are strongly correlating with each other. (You can ignore the 1.0 correlations, which simply mean that each item is perfectly correlated with itself.)

Let's suppose the coefficient alpha for this scale is .80 (good). Here's how your computer might have arrived at that figure, which is the average of the correlations of the total scores of all possible split halves of the items:

Correlation of the sum of item 1 + item 2 with the sum of item 3 + item 4	= .85
Correlation of the sum of item 1 + item 3 with the sum of item 2 + item 4	= .80
Correlation of the sum of item 1 + item 4 with the sum of item 2 + item 3	= .75
Sum of the correlations of all three possible split halves of the items	= 2.40

Coefficient alpha = average (mean) of the three correlations = 2.40/3 = .80

It may be helpful to note that the above three split halves exhaust all the possible ways you can divide the four-item scale into two halves. For example, item 1 can be paired with item 2, with item 3, or with item 4. There are no other possible ways to subdivide the scale into two halves, each containing two items. Your computer won't show you any of the split halves or their correlations. It will only tell you the bottom line—that coefficient alpha equals .80 (or whatever else it happens to be for your actual data). We have presented these split halves and their hypothetical correlations just to help take the mystery out of how coefficient alpha gets calculated and what it means.

in those judgments, we need empirical evidence to ascertain whether the measure indeed measures what it's intended to measure. For example, how strongly does the measure correlate with other indicators of the concept it intends to measure? The two most common ways of empirically assessing whether a measure really measures what it's intended to measure are called *criterion-related validity* and *construct validity*.

Criterion-Related Validity

Criterion-related validity is based on some external criterion. When we assess the criterion validity of an instrument, we select an external criterion that we believe is another indicator or measure of the same variable that our instrument intends to measure. For instance, the validity of the college board exam is shown in its ability to predict the students' success in college. The validity of a written driver's test is determined, in this sense, by the relationship between the scores people get on the test and how well they drive. In these examples, success in college and driving ability are the *criteria*. In the MMPI example just cited, the criterion was whether an individual was diagnosed as having paranoia. The validity of paranoia scale of the MMPI was determined by its ability, on the basis of its scores, to distinguish those diagnosed as paranoid from those without that diagnosis.

Two subtypes of criterion-related validity are predictive validity and concurrent validity. The difference between them has to do with whether the measure is being tested according to (a) its ability to predict a criterion that will occur in the future (such as later success in college) or (b) its correspondence to a criterion that is known concurrently. Suppose your introductory practice course instructor devises a multiple-choice test to measure your interviewing skills before you enter your field placement. To assess the concurrent validity of the test, she may see if scores on it correspond to ratings students received on their interviewing skills in videotapes in which they role-played interviewing situations. To assess the predictive validity of the test, she may see if test scores correspond to field instructor evaluations of their interviewing skills after the students complete their fieldwork. The predictive validity might also be assessed by comparing the test scores to client satisfaction ratings of the students' interviews after they graduate.

If you read studies that assess the criterion validity of various instruments, then you'll find many that ascertain whether an instrument accurately differentiates between groups that differ in respect to the variable being measured. For example, the MMPI study discussed above examined whether the test accurately differentiated between groups known to be diagnosed and not diagnosed with paranoia. When the criterion validity of a measure is assessed according to its ability to differentiate between "known groups," the type of validity being assessed may be called known-groups validity, which is simply a subtype of criterion-related validity. Thus, to test the known-groups validity of a scale designed to measure racial prejudice, you might see whether the scores of social work students differ markedly from the scores of Ku Klux Klan members.

Here's another example of known-groups validity. Suppose you devised an instrument to measure the degree of empathy that juvenile sex offenders you were treating developed for their victims while in treatment. To assess the known-groups validity of your instrument, you might compare the scores on it of juvenile sex offenders who haven't been treated with the scores of students attending a nearby high school. If the measure is valid, you would expect the average scores of the offenders to show much less empathy for victims of sex offenses than the average scores of the nonadjudicated students. This would be a reasonable approach to assessing known-groups validity. But what if the purpose for which you developed your instrument was to measure subtle improvements that offenders made in their empathy during the course of their treatment?

Knowing that an instrument can detect extreme differences between groups does not necessarily mean that it will detect more subtle differences between groups with less extreme differences. An ability to detect subtle differences is termed the sensitivity of an instrument. Showing that an instrument can differentiate two extremely different groups that do and do not require treatment for a particular problem does not mean that the instrument will show that the treated group improved somewhat after treatment. Thus, when we select instruments to measure progress in treatment, we need to be mindful of the issue of sensitivity and of whether the instrument's known-groups validity is based on groups whose differences are more extreme than the differences we expect to detect in our own study.

Recognizing that the concept of criterion validity can be somewhat tricky, you may want to test your understanding of it. To begin, see if you can think of behaviors that might be used to validate each of the following attitudinal qualities:

Is very religious

Supports the rights of gays and lesbians to marry

Is concerned about global warming

Now let's see if you can think of ways in which you would assess the concurrent and predictive validity of measures of the following constructs among social work students or practitioners:

Attitude about evidence-based practice

Willingness to engage in social action to advocate for improvements in social justice

Finally, imagine you wanted to assess the known-groups validity of an instrument that intends to measure a sense of hopelessness and despair among the elderly. How might you do so? What would that approach imply about the instrument's potential sensitivity in measuring subtle improvements in hopelessness and despair among extremely frail nursing home residents?

EP 4, 7, 9

Construct Validity

Assuming you are comfortable with the issue of criterion-related validity, let's turn to a more complex form of validity, construct validity. This form is based on the way a measure relates to other variables within a system of theoretical relationships. Let's suppose, for example, that you are interested in studying "marital satisfaction"—its sources and consequences. As part of your research, you develop a measure of marital satisfaction, and you want to assess its validity. In addition to developing your measure, you will also have developed certain theoretical expectations about the way marital satisfaction "behaves" in relation to other variables. For example, you may have concluded that family violence is more likely to occur at lower levels of marital satisfaction. If your measure of marital satisfaction relates to family violence in the expected fashion, then that constitutes evidence of your measure's construct validity. If "satisfied" and "dissatisfied" couples were equally likely to engage in family violence, however, that would challenge the validity of your measure.

In addition to testing whether a measure fits theoretical expectations, construct validation can involve assessing whether the measure has *both* convergent validity and discriminant validity.

A measure has convergent validity when its results correspond to the results of other methods of measuring the same construct. Thus, if the clients whom clinicians identify as having low levels of marital satisfaction tend to score lower on your scale of marital satisfaction than clients who clinicians say have higher levels of marital satisfaction, then your scale would have convergent validity.

A measure has discriminant validity when its results do not correspond as highly with measures of other constructs as they do with other measures of the same construct. Suppose, for example, that

the results of a measure of depression or self-esteem correspond more closely to clinician assessments of maritally satisfied and dissatisfied clients than do the results of your marital satisfaction scale. Then your scale would not have construct validity even if it had established convergent validity. The idea here is that if your scale were really measuring the construct of marital satisfaction, it should correspond more highly to other measures of marital satisfaction than do measures of conceptually distinct concepts. Likewise, if your scale is really measuring marital satisfaction, it should not correspond more highly with measures of self-esteem or depression than it does with measures of marital satisfaction.

It is possible that a scale that intends to measure marital satisfaction will correspond to another measure of marital satisfaction and yet not really be a very good measure of the construct of marital satisfaction. If we assume, for example, that people who have low self-esteem or who are depressed are less likely to be maritally satisfied than other people, then a scale that really has more to do with depression or self-esteem than with marital satisfaction will still probably correspond to a measure of marital satisfaction. The process of assessing discriminant validity checks for that possibility and thus enables us to determine whether a measure really measures the construct it intends to measure and not some other construct that happens to be related to the construct in question.

Let's consider another hypothetical example regarding construct validity. Suppose you conceptualized a construct that you termed "battered women's syndrome" and developed a scale to measure it. Let's further suppose that your scale had items about how often the women felt sad, hopeless, helpless, and undeserving of a better fate and similar items that, although you didn't realize it, all had a lot to do with depression and self-esteem.

You administered your scale to women residing in a battered women's shelter and to those with no reported history of battering and found that the two groups' scores differed as you predicted. Thus, you established the scale's criterion-related validity. Then you administered it to battered women before and after they had completed a long period of intensive intervention in a battered women's program and found that, as you predicted, their scores on your scale improved. This gave you theoretically based confidence in the construct validity of your scale.

At that point, however, you realized that depression and low self-esteem were a big part of what you were conceptualizing as a battered women's syndrome. You began to wonder whether improvement on your scale had more to do with becoming less depressed or having more self-esteem than it did with overcoming your notion of a syndrome. So you decided to test your scale's discriminant validity. You repeated the same studies but this time also had the women complete the best scale that you could find on depression and the best scale you could find on self-esteem. Your results showed that battered women improved more on those scales after treatment than they improved on your scale. Moreover, the differences between battered women and women with no history of battering were greater on those scales than on your scale. In addition, you found that the scores on your scale corresponded more highly with the scales on depression and self-esteem than they did with the women's status regarding battering or treatment. In light of this, you appropriately concluded that although your scale had criterion-related validity, it had more to do with measuring other constructs, such as self-esteem and depression, than it had to do with measuring your conception of a battered women's syndrome. Therefore, it lacked construct validity.

Factorial Validity

One more type of validity that you are likely to encounter in articles reporting social work research studies is called factorial validity. This type of validity can be statistically more complex than the types we have discussed so far, but you don't need to master its statistics to comprehend what it means. Factorial validity refers to how many different constructs a scale measures and whether the number of constructs and the items that make up those constructs are what the researcher intends.

Let's say that you develop a scale to measure the severity of trauma symptoms in abused children. Keeping it simple, let's suppose that you intend the scale to contain an overall symptom severity score as well as subscores for each of the following three constructs: (1) internalizing symptoms (such as depression, withdrawal, anxiety, and so on), (2) externalizing symptoms (such as antisocial behaviors), and (3) somatic symptoms (such as digestive problems, headaches, and so on). When discussing

factorial validity, the subscore constructs are most commonly called *factors* or *dimensions*.

Let's say that your scale contains a total of 15 items, with three sets of five items designed to measure each of the three factors. To assess your scale's factorial validity, you would use a statistical procedure called factor analysis. The results of the factor analysis would indicate which subsets of items correlate more strongly with each other than with the other subsets. Each subset would constitute a factor or dimension. Suppose your factor analysis shows that instead of three factors, you have six factors. Or suppose it shows that you have three factors but that the items making up those three factors are not even close to the ones you intended to correlate most highly with each other. In either case, your scale would lack factorial validity. In contrast, if your results showed that you had three factors and that the items making up each factor were for the most part the ones you intended to correlate most highly with each other, then your scale would have factorial validity.

A scale need not be multidimensional to have factorial validity—that is, it need not contain subscores measuring multiple factors. Perhaps you intend it to be unidimensional—that is, to contain only one overall score measuring one overarching construct. If you intend your scale to be unidimensional and the results of your factor analysis reveal only one factor, then your scale has factorial validity.

As you may have surmised, factorial validity is similar to construct validity. In fact, some researchers consider it to be another way to depict construct validity. To illustrate this point, let's reexamine the items in the box "A Hypothetical Illustration of Coefficient Alpha." The hypothetical scale in that box was intended to be a unidimensional measure of depression with four items: sadness, crying, being unhappy, and not sleeping. Chances are that a factor analysis would confirm that it indeed is unidimensional. However, suppose the scale consisted of the following four additional items:

"I lack confidence."

"I dislike myself."

"I don't like the way I look."

"Other kids are smarter than I am."

Notice that although kids who are depressed may have lower self-esteem than kids who are not depressed, the four additional items appear to have more to do with self-esteem than with depression. A factor analysis would probably show that those four items correlate much more strongly with each other than with the first four items. Likewise, it would probably show that the scale is not a unidimensional measure of depression as intended but, rather, a multidimensional scale in which half the items are measuring depression and half are measuring a different construct. The fact that half the items are measuring a construct other than depression would suggest that the scale lacks factorial validity as a unidimensional measure of depression and that, for the same reasons, it lacks construct validity in that it appears to be measuring a different (albeit related) construct as much as it is measuring its intended construct.

Students often find these differences among the types of validity a bit overwhelming. To get a better grasp on factorial validity and its similarity to construct validity we recommend that you study Figure 9-1. The figure also illustrates the other types of validity we've been discussing. You might also find the following real illustration helpful. It is intended to further clarify the assessment of reliability and validity.

» AN ILLUSTRATION OF RELIABLE AND VALID MEASUREMENT IN SOCIAL WORK: THE CLINICAL MEASUREMENT PACKAGE

During the mid-1970s, Walter Hudson and his associates began to develop and validate a package of nine short, standardized scales that they designed for repeated use by clinical social workers to assess client problems and monitor and evaluate progress in treatment. The nine scales were collectively referred to as the Clinical Measurement Package (Hudson, 1982). Each scale was found to have test–retest reliability and an internal consistency reliability of at least .90, which is quite high. Each scale also was reported to be valid.

Although each scale measures a different construct, the nine scales are similar in format. Each lists 25 statements that refer to how the client feels about things, and the client enters a number from 1 to 5 beside each statement to indicate how often he or she feels that way. The 25 responses are summed (with reverse scoring for positively worded items) to get the client's total score on the scale (the higher the score, the greater the problem with the construct being measured). The nine constructs that the nine scales were designed to measure are (a) depression, (b) self-esteem, (c) marital discord, (d) sexual discord, (e) parental attitudes about child, (f) child's attitude toward father, (g) child's attitude toward mother, (h) intrafamilial stress, and (i) peer relationships.

For a discussion of the entire measurement package, readers are referred to the preceding reference (Hudson, 1982). For our purposes in this text, however, let's consider some of the characteristics of one scale and how its reliability and validity were assessed empirically. The scale we will discuss is called the Child's Attitude Toward Mother (CAM) scale. Its reliability and validity were reported by Giuli and Hudson (1977). Among the 25 statements on the scale were some statements to which the children could admit to often hating their mother, feeling violent toward her, being ashamed of her, and so on. In light of items like these, what source of measurement error would most concern you if you were considering using this scale? You might not be too concerned about the acquiescent response set because some of the items are worded positively and others negatively. But what about a social desirability bias? Would children who hate their mothers or feel violent toward them admit to such feelings? Will differences in scale scores really measure differences in these feelings, or will they instead just measure differences in the propensity of children to admit to their socially undesirable feelings? We can resolve these questions by assessing the scale's criterion-related validity or its construct validity, and we will shortly examine how Giuli and Hudson did so.

But before we consider the validity of the scale, what about its reliability? How vulnerable does the scale appear to be to random error? Will having to select a number from 1 to 5 for each of the 25 items be too cumbersome for children? Are there any words or phrases that they might not understand, such as *embarrasses* in one item, *too demanding* in or *puts too many limits on me* in other items? If the scale is too cumbersome or if it's too difficult to understand, then it will contain too many random errors, meaning that measurement will lack consistency and therefore be unreliable.

Giuli and Hudson administered the scale to 664 high school students. To assess its internal consistency reliability, they computed coefficient alpha, which, as noted earlier in this chapter, is the average

FIGURE 9.1   Types of Validity, Using a Hypothetical Scale as an Illustration

Face validity:

Dork Depression Scale

	Strongly Agree				Strongly Disagree
1. I feel sad	5	4	3	2	1
2. I cry a lot	5	4	3	2	1
3. I worry a lot	5	4	3	2	1
4. I am anxious	5	4	3	2	1
5. I lack confidence	5	4	3	2	1
6. I dislike myself	5	4	3	2	1

Scale developer Dr. Donald Dork thinks, "Hmm; on the face of it, my scale items sure seem to be measuring depression."

Content validity:

A group of experts on depression examines Dr. Dork's 6-item scale and tells him, "We think you need more items on additional indicators of depression; you haven't covered the entire domain of depression yet. In fact, you seem to have as much content on anxiety and self-esteem as on depression."

Criterion validity (known groups):

People in treatment for depression score higher (worse) on Dork Depression Scale

Individual total scale scores:
     22   21   19   18
Group mean score: 20

People not in treatment for depression score lower (better) on Dork Depression Scale

Individual total scale scores:
     12   11   9   8
Group mean score: 10

Ignoring the expert feedback on content validity, Dr. Dork administers his scale to two known groups. The results encourage him that perhaps his scale really is measuring depression. He publishes his results.

Construct validity:
Drs. Rubin and Babbie read Dr. Dork's study and were unimpressed with his criterion validity results. Reasoning that the constructs of depression, anxiety, and self-esteem share some overlapping indicators, they questioned whether Dork's findings were due to such overlap and consequently whether the Dork scale really measures the construct of depression more than it measures the related

FIGURE 9.1   *(Continued)*

constructs of anxiety and self-esteem. To find out, they administered Dork's scale along with other existing scales measuring depression, anxiety, and self-esteem to a large sample of social service recipients. For their first analysis, they analyzed the **factorial validity** of Dork's scale, and found that instead of containing just one factor—depression—it contained three factors: depression, anxiety, and self-esteem. Items 1 and 2 comprised the depression factor. Items 3 and 4 comprised the anxiety factor. And items 5 and 6 comprised the self-esteem factor. These factors are evident in the correlation matrix and the factor analysis results below (as well as in the wording of the items).

Factorial validity?

Interitem correlation matrix: *Factor loadings:*

	Item 1	Item 2	Item 3	Item 4	Item 5	Item 6	Factor 1 Depression	Factor 2 Anxiety	Factor 3 Self-esteem
Item 1	1.0						.7	.2	.2
Item 2	.6	1.0					.7	.2	.2
Item 3	.2	.2	1.0				.2	.7	.2
Item 4	.2	.2	.6	1.0			.2	.7	.2
Item 5	.2	.2	.2	.2	1.0		.2	.2	.7
Item 6	.2	.2	.2	.2	.6	1.0	.2	.2	.7

For their next analysis, Rubin and Babbie assessed the Dork scale's convergent and discriminant validity by examining the correlations between the total scores on the Dork scale and the total scores on the other scales. The results that appear below show that although Dork's scale had convergent validity, it lacked discriminant validity because its correlation was higher with the scales measuring anxiety ($r = .50$) and self-esteem ($r = .50$) than with the existing scale measuring depression ($r = .40$). In their published article they cautioned practitioners against using Dork's scale to diagnose depression—and that a high score on his scale appears to be at least as likely to indicate problems in anxiety or self-esteem as it is to indicate a diagnosis of depression. In that connection, they noted that although depressed people may be more anxious and have less self-esteem than most other people, items 3 and 4 on the Dork scale appear to have more to do with anxiety than with depression, and items 5 and 6 appear to have more to do with self-esteem. In light of their factor analysis results and discriminant validity results, Rubin and Babbie concluded that Dork's scale lacked construct validity; it was not really measuring the construct of depression more than it was measuring other, related constructs.

Convergent validity?

Dork Depression Scale ⟵ $r = .40$ ⟶ An existing depression scale

Discriminant validity?

Dork Depression Scale ⟵ $r = .50$ ⟶ An existing anxiety scale

Dork Depression Scale ⟵ $r = .50$ ⟶ An existing self-esteem scale

of all possible split-half reliabilities. They found a very high *internal consistency reliability*, with a coefficient alpha of .94. To assess the scale's stability over time, they assessed its test–retest reliability. This was done with a sample of adults enrolled in a graduate-level psychology statistics course. The students completed the scale twice, with 1 week between tests. The *test–retest reliability* was .95, which is very high.

To assess the scale's criterion validity, they asked the 664 high school students to indicate whether they were having problems with their mothers. Those who said yes had a mean CAM score of 49.9. Those who said they were not had a mean CAM score of 20.8. This large and significant difference was interpreted by Giuli and Hudson to mean that the scale has excellent *criterion validity* because it does so well at differentiating those who acknowledge a problem with their mother from those who deny having such a problem.

But was the scale really measuring the construct of child's attitude toward mother? Perhaps it was really measuring something else, such as level of depression or self-esteem, that was related to having problems with parents. To assess the scale's *construct validity*, each of the 664 high school students also completed scales (from the Clinical Measurement Package) that measured depression and self-esteem. The strength of the relationship between each measure and whether the student admitted to having problems with his or her mother was then assessed. The CAM score turned out to be much more strongly related to the latter criterion than was either the depression score or the self-esteem score. Giuli and Hudson concluded that these findings supported the construct validity of the CAM scale.

No study in social research is ever perfectly flawless. Even the best ones have some (perhaps unavoidable) limitations. This is just as true for studies assessing measurement reliability and validity as it is for other sorts of studies. Let's consider some possible limitations in the Giuli and Hudson study, for example. Note that reliability was not assessed for children younger than high school age. We cannot fault Giuli and Hudson for that; it's unreasonable to expect them to study every conceivable age group. Finding the resources to do that is extremely difficult. Nevertheless, it would be inappropriate to assume that the same high level of reliability applies to elementary school students, especially those in the lower grades. Perhaps children that young would find the instrument much more difficult to understand or much more cumbersome than did the high school students and therefore would be much less consistent in their responses to it.

Note also the debatable criterion that Giuli and Hudson used to separate the students having

problems with their mothers from those not having such problems. Like the CAM scale itself, that criterion was vulnerable to a social desirability bias because it relied on students' willingness to acknowledge that they were having problems with their mothers. It is conceivable that those not willing to acknowledge such problems on the CAM scale because of a social desirability bias were also unwilling to acknowledge having problems in a general sense when asked because of the same bias. If so, then the construct actually being measured might have less to do with real attitudes toward one's mother than with a willingness to acknowledge socially undesirable attitudes. When selecting a criterion measure of the construct in question, it is essential that the criterion be an *independent* measure of the construct, not just a parallel form of the same measure whose validity you are assessing. If it is not—that is, if it seems just as vulnerable in the same way to the same biases as is the measure in question—then you are really measuring parallel-forms reliability instead of validity.

Giuli and Hudson recognized this problem and conducted a further assessment of the CAM scale's validity. This time they assessed its *known-groups* validity. To do this, they obtained a sample of 38 children who were receiving therapy for a variety of problems. They divided the children into two groups: those known by the therapist to have behaviorally identifiable problems with their mother and those for whom no such problem could be established. The average CAM score for the first group was 54.82, as compared to 14.73 for the latter group. Because the therapists' observations were not vulnerable to the same biases as the CAM scale, the large and significant differences in CAM scores provided stronger grounds for claiming the validity of the CAM scale—that is, for claiming that it really measures attitudes, not just some systematic bias bearing on a person's willingness to acknowledge those attitudes.

» RELATIONSHIP BETWEEN RELIABILITY AND VALIDITY

As we noted earlier, although it is desirable that a measure be reliable, its reliability does not ensure that it's valid. Suppose an abusive mother and father were referred by the courts to family therapy as a precondition for keeping their child. As involuntary clients, they might be reluctant to admit abusive behaviors to the therapist, believing that such admissions would imperil maintaining custody of their child. Even if they continued to abuse their child, they might deny it every time the therapist asked them about it. Thus, the therapist would be getting highly reliable (i.e., consistent) data. No matter how many times and ways the therapist asked about abusive behaviors, the answer would always be the same.

But the data would not be valid: The answer would not really measure the construct in question—the amount of child abuse that was occurring. Instead, what is really being measured is the reluctance of the parents to convey a socially undesirable image to the therapist.

Figure 9-2 graphically portrays the difference between validity and reliability. If you can think of measurement as analogous to hitting the bull's-eye on a target, you'll see that reliability looks like a "tight pattern," regardless of where it hits, because reliability is a function of consistency. Validity, on the other hand, is a function of shots being arranged around the bull's-eye. The failure of reliability in the figure can be seen as random error, whereas the failure of validity is a systematic error. Notice that neither an unreliable nor an invalid measure is likely to be useful. Notice also that you can't have validity without also having reliability.

The box titled "The Difference Between Reliability and Validity" further clarifies these two concepts, this time in relation to follow-up telephone calls to assess whether recipients of a smoking cessation intervention have ever smoked a cigarette again after receiving the intervention. To assess the reliability of the measure, three participants are

called twice, with 2 weeks elapsing between the calls (thus illustrating test–retest reliability). Alas, all three participants have continued smoking despite having received the intervention. Participant 1 admits to having smoked in both phone calls, thus reporting reliable and valid data. Participant 2 denies the smoking at time 1, but admits it at time 2, thus reporting information that is neither reliable (i.e., consistent) nor valid. Participant 3 denies the smoking in both calls, thus reporting information in a way that is reliable but not valid.

A certain tension often exists between the criteria of reliability and validity. Often we seem to face a trade-off between the two. If you'll recall for a moment the earlier example of measuring morale in different work settings, you'll probably see that the strategy of immersing yourself in the day-to-day routine of the agency, observing what went on, and talking to the workers seems to provide a more valid measure of morale than counting resignations. It just seems obvious that we would be able to get a clearer sense of whether the morale was high or low in that fashion than we would from counting the number of resignations.

However, the counting strategy would be more reliable. This situation reflects a more general strain in research measurement. Most of the really interesting concepts that we want to study have many subtle nuances, and it's difficult to specify precisely what we mean by them. Researchers sometimes speak of such concepts as having a "richness of meaning." Scores of books and articles have been written on topics such as depression, self-esteem, and social support, and all of the interesting aspects of those concepts still haven't been exhausted.

Yet science needs to be specific to generate reliable measurements. Very often, then, the

FIGURE 9.2 An Analogy to Validity and Reliability

Reliable but not valid

Neither reliable nor valid

Valid *and* reliable

THE DIFFERENCE BETWEEN RELIABILITY AND VALIDITY

Question: "Have you smoked a cigarette since receiving the smoking cessation intervention?"

Participant 1 (Reliable and valid)

Yes — October 7

Yes — October 21

Participant 2 (Neither reliable nor valid)

No — October 7

Yes — October 21

Participant 3 (Reliable but not valid)

No — October 7

No — October 21

specification of reliable operational definitions and measurements seems to rob such concepts of their richness of meaning. For example, morale is much more than a lack of resignations; depression is much more than five items on a depression scale.

Developing measures that are reliable and still capable of tapping the richness of meaning of concepts is a persistent and inevitable dilemma for the social researcher, and you will be effectively forearmed against it by being forewarned. Be prepared for it and deal with it. If there is no clear agreement on how to measure a concept, then measure it several different ways. If the concept has several different dimensions, then measure them all.

EP 4, 7, 9

» RELIABILITY AND VALIDITY IN QUALITATIVE RESEARCH

Although much of the basic logic about reliability and validity is the same in qualitative and quantitative research, qualitative researchers may approach the issues somewhat differently than quantitative researchers. Let's see what some of those differences might be.

In a quantitative study of adolescent depression, the researcher would conceivably administer a standardized depression scale to a sizable sample of adolescents, perhaps to assess the extent of depression among adolescents or perhaps to see if the extent of depression was related to other variables. In planning the study or in reading about it, a critical issue would be the depression scale's reliability and validity. But we would know that even the best depression scale is not 100% reliable and valid. Even using the best scale, the study would be dealing with probabilistic knowledge—that is, specific scores would indicate a higher or lower probability that the adolescent is depressed. A good clinical scale would be correct about 90% of the time in depicting an adolescent as depressed or not depressed, and it would be important to know how often the scale is accurate and how often it's mistaken. But if all we have on each adolescent are quantitative data from a scale score, then we will not know which adolescents are being accurately depicted and which are among the 10% or so who are not.

In a qualitative study of adolescent depression, the researcher would not rely on a standardized instrument. The researcher would be more likely to study a much smaller sample of adolescents and conduct extensive and varied direct observations and in-depth interviews with each one of them and their significant others. Perhaps the scope would be limited to a biographical case study of the impact of adolescent depression on one family, or perhaps the sample would include several families. In either case, the sample would be small enough to permit the researcher to describe the everyday lives of the subjects in such rich detail that the reader would not question the existence of depression or simply would not care what construct was used to label the observed phenomenon.

Suppose the qualitative report described an adolescent girl whose academic and social functioning began to deteriorate gradually after the onset of puberty. After achieving high grades throughout her previous schooling, she began staying awake all night, sleeping all day, and refusing to go to school. On the days when she did attend school, she was unable to concentrate. Her grades began to fall precipitously. She began to isolate herself from family and friends and refused to leave her room. She began to express feelings of hopelessness about the future and negative thoughts about her looks, intelligence, likability, and worthiness. She no longer had the energy to do things she once did well and started to neglect basic daily tasks associated with cleanliness and grooming. She began to wear the same black clothes every day, refusing to wear any other color. When family or friends reached out to her, she became unresponsive or irritable. She displayed no signs of substance abuse but began to wonder if that might make her feel better. She began to have thoughts of suicide and started to cut herself. She showed no signs of schizophrenia, such as delusions or hallucinations.

A good qualitative report would depict the above clinical deterioration in a format replete with detailed observations and quotations that would be many pages long and would leave the reader with a sense of having walked in the shoes of the girl and her family, sensing the girl's depression and agony as well as the burden placed on the family. The detail of the study and its report would be so rich that if the girl did not score in the depressed range of a standardized scale, the reader would be likely to conclude that this was one of the 10% or so of cases in which the scale got it wrong. The reader might not even care whether the phenomenon described fit best under the rubric of depression or under some other label. Rather than verifying a label for it that could be generalized to others, the study would be geared more to giving the reader a deeper sense of the situation that the girl and her family were struggling with, the ways in which the various family members experienced the situation and the subjective meanings it had for them, and what they felt they needed.

The point of qualitative studies, in other words, is to study and describe things in such depth and detail and from such multiple perspectives and meanings that there is less need to worry about whether one particular measure is really measuring what it's intended to measure. In quantitative studies, on the other hand, we are more likely to rely heavily on one indicator or a few indicators, administered perhaps in a matter of minutes, to determine the degree to which a hypothetical construct applies to a large number of people and with an eye toward generalizing what we find to an even larger number of people. In such studies, it is critical to assess the reliability and validity of the indicators we use. It is thus possible to recognize the critical role of reliability and validity in quantitative studies while at the same time appreciating the need to take a different perspective on the role of reliability and validity in qualitative studies. In fact, without even attempting to quantitatively assess the validity of in-depth qualitative measurement, one could argue that the directness, depth, and detail of its observations often gives it better validity than quantitative measurement.

We are not, however, saying that the concepts of reliability and validity have no role in qualitative studies. Akin to interobserver reliability in quantitative studies, for example, one might assess whether two independent raters arrive at the same interpretation from the same mass of written qualitative field notes. The consistency between the two raters could be calculated through quantitative indicators such as percentages of agreement or correlations. Alternatively, one could merely ask whether the two arrived at the same particular overarching interpretation. Akin to internal consistency reliability, one might examine whether different sources of data fit consistently with the researcher's observations and interpretations. Rather than calculate quantitative reliability coefficients, however, one would attempt to illustrate how, on an overall basis, the different sources were in qualitative agreement. Another approach might compare the qualitative interpretations with data from quantitative measures. To the degree that the quantitative data support the qualitative interpretations, the qualitative material may be seen as more credible (or reliable).

Some researchers use indicators of reliability of a more distinctly qualitative nature. They might, for example, ask the research participants to confirm the accuracy of the researcher's observations. Or the participants might be asked whether the researcher's interpretations ring true and are meaningful to them. Some qualitatively oriented researchers judge reliability according to whether the report indicates ways in which the researcher searched thoroughly for disconfirming evidence, such as by looking for other cases or informants whose data might not fit the researcher's interpretation. They might also ask whether the researcher sufficiently varied the time, place, and context of the observations and whether the interpretations fit consistently across the observations taken at different times, places, and contexts.

Jane Kronick (1989) has proposed four criteria for evaluating the validity of qualitative interpretations of written texts. The first is analogous to internal consistency reliability in quantitative research—that is, the interpretation of parts of the text should be consistent with other parts or with the whole text. Likewise, the "developing argument" should be "internally consistent." Second, Kronick proposed that the interpretation should be complete, taking all of the evidence into account. Her third criterion involves "conviction." This means that the interpretation should be the most compelling one in light of the evidence within the text. Fourth, the interpretation should be meaningful. It should make sense of the text and extend our understanding of it.

As in quantitative research, limitations inhere in some of the qualitative approaches to reliability and validity. For instance, the research participants may not confirm the accuracy of a researcher's observations or interpretations because they do not like the way they are portrayed, may not understand the researcher's theoretical perspective, or may not be aware of patterns that are true but that emerge only from the mass of data. A second rater may not confirm the interpretations of the principal investigator because certain insights might require having conducted the observations or interviews and might not emerge from the written notes alone.

While some qualitative researchers disagree about which of the above types of approaches to reliability and validity to use and how to use them, others reject the whole idea of reliability and validity in keeping with their philosophical rejection of assumptions connected to our ability to be objective. Or they define reliability and validity in terms that are worlds apart from what other researchers mean by those two words. Sometimes, they define reliability and validity in terms that researchers who do not share their philosophical assumptions would perceive as nonscientific or even antiscientific. For instance, some would deem a study valid if a particular group deemed as oppressed or powerless experienced it as liberating or empowering. Thus, rather than define validity in terms of objectivity and accuracy, some define it according to whether findings can be applied toward some social justice or empowerment purpose (Altheide & Johnson, 1994). Others point to writing style as a validity criterion, deeming a study valid if the report is written in a gripping manner that draws the reader into the subjects' worlds so closely that readers feel as though they are walking in the subjects' shoes, recognize what they read to correspond to their own prior experiences, and perceive the report to be internally coherent and plausible (Adler & Adler, 1994).

As you encounter the terms *reliability* and *validity* throughout the remainder of this book, they will be used primarily in reference to their quantitative meanings because these terms are more commonly used in quantitative research. But we will also be discussing qualitative research in the remaining chapters, and we hope you'll keep in mind the distinctive ways in which reliability and validity are considered in qualitative research as you read that material.

EP 4, 7, 9

MAIN POINTS

- Measurement error can be systematic or random. Common systematic errors pertain to social desirability biases and cultural biases. Random errors have no consistent pattern of effects, make measurement inconsistent, and are likely to result from difficulties in understanding or administering measures.

- Alternative forms of measurement include written self-reports, interviews, direct behavioral observation, and examining available records. Each of these options is vulnerable to measurement error.

- Because no form of measurement is foolproof, applying the principle of triangulation—by using several different research methods to

collect the same information—we can use several imperfect measurement alternatives and see if they tend to produce the same findings.

- Reliability concerns the amount of random error in a measure and measurement consistency. It refers to the likelihood that a given measurement procedure will yield the same description of a given phenomenon if that measurement is repeated. For instance, estimating a person's age by asking his or her friends would be less reliable than asking the person or checking the birth certificate.

- Different types of reliability include interobserver reliability or interrater reliability, test–retest reliability, parallel-forms reliability, and internal consistency reliability.

- Validity refers to the extent of systematic error in measurement—the extent to which a specific measurement provides data that relate to commonly accepted meanings of a particular concept. There are numerous yardsticks for determining validity: *face validity*, *content validity*, *criterion-related validity*, *construct validity*, and *factorial validity*. The latter three are empirical forms of validity, whereas the first two are based on expert judgments.

- Two subtypes of criterion-related validity are *predictive validity* and *concurrent validity*. The difference between these subtypes has to do with whether the measure is being tested according to ability to predict a criterion that will occur in the future or its correspondence to a criterion that is known concurrently.

- *Known-groups validity* is another subtype of criterion-related validity. It assesses whether an instrument accurately differentiates between groups known to differ in respect to the variable being measured.

- The ability to detect subtle differences between groups or subtle changes over time within a group is termed the *sensitivity* of an instrument.

- Construct validation involves testing whether a measure relates to other variables according to theoretical expectations. It also involves testing the measure's convergent validity and discriminant validity.

- A measure has *convergent validity* when its results correspond to the results of other methods of measuring the same construct.

- A measure has *discriminant validity* when its results do not correspond as highly with measures of other constructs as they do with other measures of the same construct and when its results correspond more highly with the other measures of the same construct than do measures of alternative constructs.

- *Factorial validity* refers to how many different constructs a scale measures and whether the number of constructs and the items making up those constructs are what the researcher intends.

- The creation of specific, reliable measures often seems to diminish the richness of meaning that our general concepts have. This problem is inevitable. The best solution is to use several different measures to tap the different aspects of the concept.

- Studies that assess the reliability and validity of a measure, just like any other type of study, can be seriously flawed. Ultimately, the degree to which we can call a measure reliable or valid depends not only on the size of its reliability or validity coefficient but also on the methodological credibility of the way those coefficients were assessed. For example, was an appropriate sample selected? Was the criterion of the construct truly independent of the measure being assessed and not vulnerable to the same sources of error as that measure?

- Reliability and validity are defined and handled differently in qualitative research than they are in quantitative research, although some qualitative approaches are analogous to some quantitative approaches.

- Qualitative researchers disagree about definitions and criteria for reliability and validity, and some argue that they are not applicable at all to qualitative research. These disagreements tend to be connected to differing philosophical assumptions about objectivity.

REVIEW QUESTIONS AND EXERCISES

1. In a newspaper or magazine, find an instance of invalid or unreliable measurement. Justify your choice.

2. Suppose a geriatric social worker assesses whether a life history review intervention improves the level of depression among frail nursing home residents by administering a depression measure to them before and after the intervention. Suppose the measure had its validity assessed by comparing scores of frail nursing home residents on it to the scores of healthy elderly folks living independently.

   a. What type (and subtype) of validity was assessed?
   b. Why should the social worker be concerned about the measure's sensitivity?
   c. What more would be needed to establish the measure's construct validity?
   d. If the measure is valid, can we assume it is also reliable? Why?

INTERNET EXERCISES

1. Find several research articles in the journal *Health and Social Work* that utilized existing scales to measure variables. How adequately do the articles report the reliability and validity of the scales they used? What type of reliability and validity do they report? What types of reliability and validity tend to get reported more and less often than others?

2. Using a search engine, enter the search term "cultural bias in IQ tests." Then go to one of the listed websites that intrigues you. (Some of the sites are humorous.) Summarize what you find there and how it illustrates cultural bias in measurement.

3. Return to the website mentioned in Chapter 5, "Psychosocial Measures for Asian-American Populations," at www.columbia.edu/cu/ssw/projects/pmap. Find two abstracts at that site that assessed different forms of reliability and validity. Briefly describe and contrast how each assessed reliability and validity and their results.

 Visit CengageBrain.com for additional practice and study opportunities including experiential exercises, research tools, glossary, flashcards, and sample test items.

10

Constructing Measurement Instruments

EPAS Competencies for This Chapter

Competency 2 Engage Diversity and Difference in Practice: This competency relates to the ability to construct culturally sensitive items in measurement instruments.

Competency 4 Engage in Practice-Informed Research and Research-Informed Practice: This competency pertains to this entire chapter because doing practice-informed research requires being able to design instruments to measure variables.

Competency 7 Assess Individuals, Families, Groups, Organizations, and Communities: Competency to assess requires competency in constructing measurement instruments to use in assessment. Thus, this competency pertains to this entire chapter.

Competency 9 Evaluate Practice With Individuals Families, Groups, Organizations, and Communities: Evaluating practice requires being able to measure appropriately the variables to be assessed as part of your evaluation, which, in turn, requires competency in constructing measurement instruments for measuring variables. Thus, this competency pertains to this entire chapter.

What You'll Learn in This Chapter

Now that you understand measurement error, its common sources, and the concepts of reliability and validity, let's examine the process of constructing some measurement instruments that are commonly used in social work research.

» INTRODUCTION

In this chapter, we will delve further into measurement methodology by examining the construction of measurement instruments widely used in social work research: questionnaires, interview schedules, and scales. Later in this book, we will look at alternative research designs and modes of collecting data. Some of these methodologies will not require the application of the instruments just mentioned, so we will be discussing ways to measure social work variables that don't involve asking people questions or administering written instruments to them. But despite the value of those alternative methodologies, instruments designed to gather data by communicating with people orally or in writing (with questionnaires, interview schedules, and scales) are among the most prominent techniques that social work researchers use to collect data.

As we examine the construction of these types of instruments, bear in mind that the principles guiding their design will vary, depending on whether the research is primarily qualitative or quantitative. Among the most important objectives in designing quantitative instruments is the avoidance of measurement error. Thus, we seek to construct instruments that are reliable and valid. Among the most important objectives in designing qualitative instruments is probing for depth of meaning from the respondent's perspective.

You should also bear in mind that this chapter does not imply that your first impulse in developing the measurement approach for your research should be to construct your *own* instruments. Instead, you should search for *existing* instruments that have already been tested with success and that fit your intended research. Such instruments might include existing scales (as discussed in Chapter 8) known to be reliable and valid or questionnaires or interview schedules that worked well in prior research. If you are fortunate enough to find such instruments, you not only will save yourself a great deal of the time that goes into instrument construction but also may wind up with instruments that are better than the ones you might develop. Of course, you should not use those existing instruments unless they fit your study's aims, variables, intended participants, and so on. But even if they do not fit, examining them can provide ideas that might facilitate your own instrument development efforts. You might even be able to adapt them to fit your study with just minor modifications.

However, before deciding to use an instrument previously developed and used in prior research, you should critically appraise it in light of the principles that you'll read about in this chapter. You might be surprised at how often some of these principles have been violated in the instruments that others have used in their research. We'll begin our consideration of instrument construction by examining some broad guidelines for asking people questions.

» GUIDELINES FOR ASKING QUESTIONS

As we previously implied, one of the most common ways that social work researchers operationalize their variables is by asking people questions as a way to get data for analysis and interpretation. Asking people questions is most commonly associated with survey research, which will be discussed in Chapter 16, but it is also used often in experiments (to be discussed in Chapter 11) and in qualitative research (Chapters 18 and 19). Sometimes an interviewer asks the questions, and the list of questions is referred to as an *interview schedule*. Instead of using an interview schedule, some qualitative studies utilize an *interview guide*, which lists topics to be asked about but not the exact sequence and wording of the questions. Sometimes the questions are written down and given to respondents for completion. In that case, we refer to the sets of questions as *questionnaires* or perhaps as *self-administered questionnaires*.

As we'll see, several general guidelines can assist you in framing and asking questions that serve as excellent operationalizations of variables. There are also pitfalls that can result in useless and even misleading information. This section should assist you in differentiating the two. Let's begin with some of the options available to you in creating questionnaires.

EP 4, 7, 9

Questions and Statements

The term *questionnaire* suggests a collection of questions, but an examination of a typical questionnaire will probably reveal as many statements as questions. That is not without reason. Often, the researcher is interested in determining the extent to which respondents hold a particular attitude or perspective. If you are able to summarize the attitude in a fairly brief statement, then you will often present that statement and ask respondents whether they agree or disagree with it. Rensis Likert formalized this procedure through the creation of the Likert scale response format, in which respondents are asked to strongly agree, agree, disagree, or strongly disagree with brief statements. This format might be used, for example, in a client satisfaction survey questionnaire in which clients indicate the extent to which they agree or disagree with various statements about the quality of the services they received. The same questionnaire might include factual questions about what services they received, their ethnicity, age, and so forth. Both questions and statements may be used profitably. Using both in a given questionnaire gives you more flexibility in the design of items and can make the questionnaire more interesting as well.

Open-Ended and Closed-Ended Questions

In asking questions, researchers have two options. We may ask open-ended questions, in which the respondent is asked to provide his or her own answer to the question. Open-ended questions can be used in interview schedules as well as in self-administered questionnaires. For example, the respondent may be asked, "What do you feel is the most important problem facing your community today?" and be provided with a space to write in the answer or be asked to report it orally to an interviewer.

In an interview schedule, the interviewer may be instructed to probe for more information as needed. For instance, if the respondent replies that the most important problem facing the community

is "urban decay," the interviewer might probe for more clarification by saying, "Could you tell me some more about that problem?" (We'll discuss this process in greater depth in Chapter 16, on survey research.) Because of the opportunity to probe for more information, open-ended questions are used more frequently on interview schedules than on self-administered questionnaires, although they commonly appear in both formats.

With closed-ended questions, the respondent is asked to select an answer from among a list provided by the researcher. Closed-ended questions can be used in self-administered questionnaires as well as interview schedules and are popular because they provide a greater uniformity of responses and are more easily processed. Open-ended responses must be coded before they can be processed for computer analysis, as will be discussed in several later chapters. This coding process often requires that the researcher interpret the meaning of responses, opening the possibility of misunderstanding and researcher bias. There is also a danger that some respondents will give answers that are essentially irrelevant to the researcher's intent. Closed-ended responses, on the other hand, can often be transferred directly into a computer format.

The chief shortcoming of closed-ended questions lies in the researcher's structuring of responses. When the relevant answers to a given question are relatively clear, there should be no problem. In other cases, however, the researcher's structuring of responses may overlook some important responses. In asking about "the most important problem facing your community," for example, your checklist of problems might omit certain ones that respondents would have said were important.

In the construction of closed-ended questions, you should be guided by two structural requirements. The response categories provided should be *exhaustive*: They should include all of the possible responses that might be expected. Often, researchers ensure this by adding a category labeled something like "Other (Please specify:)."

Second, the answer categories must be *mutually exclusive*: The respondent should not feel compelled to select more than one. (In some cases, you may wish to solicit multiple answers, but these may create difficulties in data processing and analysis later on.) To ensure that your categories are mutually exclusive, you should carefully consider each combination of categories, asking yourself whether a person could reasonably choose more than one answer. In addition, it is useful to add an instruction to the question that asks the respondent to select the *one best* answer, but this technique is not a satisfactory substitute for a carefully constructed set of responses.

Make Items Clear

It should go without saying that questionnaire items should be clear and unambiguous, but the broad proliferation of unclear and ambiguous questions in surveys makes the point worth stressing here. Often, you can become so deeply involved in the topic under examination that opinions and perspectives are clear to you but will not be clear to your respondents—many of whom have given little or no attention to the topic. Or if you have only a superficial understanding of the topic, you might fail to specify the intent of your question sufficiently. The question, "What do you think about the proposed residential facility for the developmentally disabled in the community?" may evoke in the respondent a counter question: "*Which* residential facility?" Questionnaire items should be precise so that the respondent knows exactly what question the researcher wants answered.

Avoid Double-Barreled Questions

Frequently, researchers ask respondents for a single answer to a combination of questions. This seems to happen most often when the researcher has personally identified with a complex question. For example, you might ask respondents to agree or disagree with the statement "The state should abandon its community-based services and spend the money on improving institutional care." Although many people would unequivocally agree with the statement and others would unequivocally disagree, still others would be unable to answer. Some would want to abandon community-based services and give the money back to the taxpayers. Others would want to continue community-based services but also put more money into institutions. These latter respondents could neither agree nor disagree without misleading you.

As a general rule, whenever the word *and* appears in a question or questionnaire statement, you should check whether you are asking a double-barreled question. Sometimes it is not easy to judge whether a statement or question is double-barreled,

regardless of whether the word *and* is used. Consider, for example, a client satisfaction survey item asking respondents the extent to which they agree or disagree with the statement "The receptionists at the agency were friendly." There is no *and* in that statement, but maybe one receptionist was friendly and another was not. Or "My case manager was warm and friendly." There is an *and* in that statement, but it seems like almost splitting hairs to call it double-barreled because it is hard to imagine a practitioner being friendly yet cold or warm but unfriendly. Many times we have seen colleagues engaged in questionnaire construction disagree about whether some items are really double-barreled.

We suggest that if you aren't sure about whether an item in a questionnaire that you are constructing is double-barreled—or if it has any other type of wording problems—you might do the following. First, put your questionnaire or scale aside for a day or two and then revisit it and consider how you would answer each item. Perhaps then you will experience more difficulty in answering some items than you did earlier. If you still are uncertain about any particular items, you could ask a few colleagues or friends how they would answer them, also asking them to let you know if the wording of any item seems problematic to them. If you still are uncertain, it is best to play it safe and try to reword the item in a way that you are sure is not double-barreled, not ambiguous, and so on.

Respondents Must Be Competent to Answer

In asking respondents to provide information, you should continually ask yourself whether they are able to do so reliably. In a study of child rearing, you might ask respondents to report the age at which they first talked back to their parents. Aside from the problem of defining *talking back to parents*, it is doubtful whether most respondents would remember with any degree of accuracy. The same difficulty would pertain if researchers asked people entering treatment for alcohol addiction how many alcoholic drinks they consumed during the past 30 days.

Inability to remember accurately is not the only way in which respondents may not be able to answer questions. Another way is that they might not know about the relevant information in the first place. For example, if a survey asks practitioners about their attitudes regarding a new treatment that is so new that most respondents never heard of it, few respondents will be able to provide meaningful answers. Some respondents might be unable to answer certain questions because of psychological or biological impairments. Rather than ask a person with Alzheimer's disease how often he or she gets lost wandering off, for example, it would be better to ask his or her caregiver.

Respondents Must Be Willing to Answer

Often, we would like to learn things from people that they are unwilling to share with us. For example, people living in countries with totalitarian regimes may be very unlikely to admit to any unfavorable attitudes about the living conditions in that country or about the country's rulers. Even in freer countries, respondents may say they are undecided when, in fact, they have an opinion but think they are in a minority or think that their opinion is socially unacceptable. Under that condition, they might be reluctant to tell a stranger (the interviewer) what that opinion is. In a poll on the eve of an election, for example, a prospective voter might say she is undecided rather than admit to planning to vote for an extremist candidate who has been way behind in all the previous polls that were reported. Providing respondents complete anonymity in responding can alleviate this problem.

Questions Should Be Relevant

Similarly, questions asked in a questionnaire should be relevant to most respondents. When attitudes are requested on a topic that few respondents have thought about or really care about, the results are not likely to be useful. Of course, the respondents may express attitudes even though they have never given any thought to the issue and pose the risk of misleading the researcher.

This point is illustrated occasionally when you ask for responses relating to fictitious persons and issues. In a political poll, one of your authors (Babbie) asked respondents whether they were familiar with each of 15 political figures in the community. As a methodological exercise, he made up a name: Tom Sakumoto. In response, 9% of the respondents said they were familiar with him. Of those respondents familiar with him, about half

reported seeing him on television and reading about him in the newspapers.

When you obtain responses to fictitious issues, you can disregard those responses. But when the issue is real, you might have no way of telling which responses genuinely reflect attitudes and which reflect meaningless answers to an irrelevant question.

Short Items Are Best

In the interest of being unambiguous and precise and pointing to the relevance of an issue, the researcher is often led into long and complicated items. That should be avoided. Respondents are often unwilling to study an item to understand it. The respondent should be able to read an item quickly, understand its intent, and select or provide an answer without difficulty. In general, you should assume that respondents will read items quickly and give quick answers; therefore, you should provide clear, short items that will not be misinterpreted under those conditions.

Avoid Words Like *No* or *Not*

The appearance of the word *no* or *not* in a questionnaire item paves the way for easy misinterpretation. Asked to agree or disagree with the statement "The community should not have a residential facility for the developmentally disabled," a sizable portion of the respondents will read over the word *not* and answer on that basis. Thus, some will agree with the statement when they are in favor of the facility, and others will agree when they oppose it. And you may never know which is which.

In a study of civil liberties support, respondents were asked whether they felt "the following kinds of people should be prohibited from teaching in public schools" and were presented with a list including such items as a communist, a Ku Klux Klansman, and so forth. The response categories "yes" and "no" were given beside each entry. A comparison of the responses to this item with other items that reflected support for civil liberties strongly suggested that many respondents answered "no" to indicate willingness for such a person to teach rather than indicate that such a person should be prohibited from teaching. (A later study in the series that gave "permit" and "prohibit" as answer categories produced much clearer results.)

Avoiding words like *no* or *not*, however, does not imply avoiding items with a negative connotation altogether. When constructing a scale, for example, failing to vary positively worded and negatively worded items might encourage respondents to respond favorably (or perhaps unfavorably) to every item. Chapter 9 referred to this potential bias as the *acquiescent response set*. Even if varying positively and negatively worded items does not prevent some respondents from responding favorably (or unfavorably) to every item, their doing so will be reflected in a lower internal reliability coefficient for the scale.

Although it is easier (and thus tempting) to simply insert the word *not* when attempting to vary positively and negatively worded items, you should resist the temptation to do so. For example, consider a scale measuring practitioner attitudes about evidence-based practice (EBP) that is completed by indicating agreement or disagreement with a series of statements about EBP. Suppose the scale has too many positively worded items. It would be easy to change one positively worded item, such as "Engaging in the EBP process will improve one's practice," and make it negatively worded by just inserting the word *not*, as follows: "Engaging in the EBP process will not improve one's practice." It might take a little brainstorming to alter the latter item. One way to improve it might be to word it as follows: "Engaging in the EBP process makes practice too mechanistic" or "Engaging in the EBP process hinders the practitioner–client relationship."

Avoid Biased Items and Terms

The meaning of someone's response to a question depends in large part on the wording of the question that was asked. That is true of every question and answer. Some questions seem to encourage particular responses more than other questions. Questions that encourage respondents to answer in a particular way are called biased. In our discussion of the social desirability bias in Chapter 9, we noted that we need to be especially wary of this bias whenever we ask people for information. This applies to the way questionnaire items are worded. Thus, for example, in assessing the attitudes of community residents about a halfway house proposed for their neighborhood, we would not ask whether residents agreed with prominent clergy in supporting the facility.

Likewise, we would not ask whether they endorsed "humanitarian" proposals to care for the needy in the community.

Questions Should Be Culturally Sensitive

Some of the illustrations just described about problems in asking questions pertain to issues of cultural bias and insensitivity. For example, items that are clear in one culture may not be clear in another. Respondents living in totalitarian societies might be unwilling to answer some questions that respondents in freer societies are willing to answer. Consequently, even if we find that our measurement instruments are reliable and valid when tested with one culture, we cannot assume that they will be reliable and valid when used with other cultures. Chapter 6 discussed the issue of culture competence in measurement extensively, so we won't repeat that material here. The importance of that material, however, bears repeating as we discuss the topics in this chapter. Before moving on to the topic of formatting questionnaires, we'd like to call your attention to the box "Learning from Bad Examples," which illustrates some of the problems in asking questions that we've just discussed.

EP 2

» QUESTIONNAIRE CONSTRUCTION

General Questionnaire Format

The format of a questionnaire is just as important as the nature and wording of the questions asked. An improperly laid out questionnaire can lead respondents to miss questions, confuse them about the nature of the data desired, and, in the worst case, lead them to throw the questionnaire away. Both general and specific guidelines are suggested here.

As a general rule, the questionnaire should be spread out and uncluttered. Inexperienced researchers tend to fear that their questionnaire will look too long and thus squeeze several questions onto a single line, abbreviate questions, and use as few pages as possible. All these efforts are ill advised and even dangerous. Putting more than one question on a line will lead some respondents to miss the second question altogether. Some respondents will misinterpret

LEARNING FROM BAD EXAMPLES
Charles Bonney, Department of Sociology, Eastern Michigan University

Here's a questionnaire I've used to train my students in some of the problems of question construction. These are questions that might be asked in order to test the following hypothesis: "College students from high-status family backgrounds are more tolerant toward persons suffering mental or emotional stress." (Here, *status* has been operationally defined as the combined relative ranking on family income, parents' educational level, and father's occupational prestige—or mother's, *if* father not present or employed.) Each question has one or more flaws in it. See if you can identify these problems. (A critique of the questionnaire appears at the end of the box.)

Questionnaire

1. What is your reaction to crazy people?
   _____
   _____

2. What is your father's income?
   _____

3. As you were growing up, with whom were you living?
   _____ both parents
   _____ mother only
   _____ father only
   _____ other (please specify)

4. What is your father's occupation?
   _____
   (If father is deceased, not living at home, or unemployed or retired, is your mother employed?
   _____ yes _____ no)

5. Did your parents attend college?
   _____ yes _____ no

6. Wouldn't you agree that people with problems should be sympathized with?
   _____ yes _____ no

7. The primary etiology of heterophilic blockage is unmet dependency gratification.
   _____ agree

_____ undecided
_____ disagree

8. If a friend of yours began to exhibit strange and erratic behavior, what do you think your response would be?
   _____

9. Has anyone in your immediate family ever been institutionalized?
   _____ yes _____ no

Critique

The most fundamental critique of any questionnaire is simply, "Does it get the information necessary to test the hypothesis?" While questions can be bad in and of themselves, they can be good only when seen in terms of the needs of the researcher. Good questionnaire construction is probably about as much an art as a science, and even "good" questions may contain hidden pitfalls or may be made even better when the overall context is considered. However, in the examples provided here, the following flaws definitely exist:

1. Derogatory and vague use of a slang term. Because it's the first question, it's even worse: it may contaminate your results either by turning off some people enough to affect your response rate or it may have a "funneling effect" on later responses.

2. The operational definition of status calls for *family* income, not just father's. Also, it's been found that people are more likely to answer a question as personal as income if categories are provided for check-off, rather than this open-ended format.

3. "As you were growing up" is a vague time period. Also, the question is of dubious relevance or utility in the current format, although it *could* have been used to organize questions 2, 4, and 5.

4. The format (asking about mother's employment only if there's no employed father) may well be sexist. Although it follows the operational definition, the operational definition itself may well be

sexist. There are two additional problems. First, a checklist nearly always works better for occupation—open-ended questions often get answers that are too vague to be categorized. Also, in cases where status *will* be measured by mother's occupation, the question only elicits whether or not she's employed at all.

5. Limited measure of educational levels. Also, it's double-barreled: what if one parent attended college and the other didn't?

6. "Wouldn't you agree" is leading the respondent. Also, "sympathized" and "problems" are vague.

7. Technical jargon. No one will know what it means. (In fact, I'm not even sure what it means, and I wrote it! As close as I can translate it, it says, "The main reason you can't get a date is because your folks ignored you.")

8. Asks for speculation regarding a vague, hypothetical situation—which is not always bad, but there's usually a better way. Note, however, that the question is not double-barreled as many have said: it asks only about behavior that is *both* "strange" and "erratic."

9. "Institutionalized" is a vague term. Many types of institutionalization would clearly be irrelevant.

abbreviated questions. And, more generally, respondents who find they have spent considerable time on the first page of what seemed a short questionnaire will be more demoralized than respondents who quickly completed the first several pages of what initially seemed a long form. Moreover, the latter will have made fewer errors and will not have been forced to reread confusing, abbreviated questions. Nor will they have been forced to write a long answer in a tiny space.

The desirability of spreading questions out in the questionnaire cannot be overemphasized. Squeezed-together questionnaires are disastrous, whether they are to be completed by the respondents themselves or administered by trained interviewers, and the processing of such questionnaires is another nightmare. We'll have more to say about this in Chapter 21.

Formats for Respondents

In one of the most common types of questionnaire items, the respondent is expected to check one response from a series. For this purpose, our experience has been that boxes or circles adequately spaced apart are the best format. Some easy examples are provided here.

Rather than providing boxes to be checked, you might print a code number beside each response and ask the respondent to circle the appropriate number (see Figure 10-1). This method has the added advantage of specifying the code number to be entered

later in the processing stage (see Chapter 21). If numbers are to be circled, however, make sure to provide ample space between the numbers so that it is easy to know which number has been circled when entering the data for processing. Also, provide clear and prominent instructions to respondents, because many will be tempted to cross out the appropriate number, making data processing even more difficult. (Note that the technique can be used more safely when interviewers administer the questionnaires because the interviewers themselves record the responses.)

Contingency Questions

Quite often in questionnaires, certain questions will be clearly relevant only to some respondents and irrelevant to others. In a study of birth control methods, for instance, you would probably not want to ask men if they take birth control pills.

Frequently, this situation—in which the topic is relevant only to some respondents—arises when the researcher wishes to ask a series of questions about a certain topic. You might want to ask whether your respondents belong to a particular organization and, if so, how often they attend meetings,

FIGURE 10.1 Circling the Answer

whether they have held office in the organization, and so forth. Or you might want to ask whether respondents have heard anything about a certain community issue and then learn the attitudes of those who have heard of it.

The subsequent questions in series such as these are called contingency questions: Whether they are to be asked and answered is contingent on responses to the first question in the series. The proper use of contingency questions can facilitate the respondents' task in completing the questionnaire because they are not faced with trying to answer questions that are irrelevant to them.

There are several formats for contingency questions. The one shown in Figure 10-2 is probably the clearest and most effective. Note two key elements in this format: (a) The contingency question is set off to the side and enclosed in a box and thus isolated from the other questions; and (b) an arrow connects the contingency question to the answer on which it is contingent. In the illustration, only respondents who answer yes are expected to answer the contingency question. The rest of the respondents should simply skip it.

Note that the questions in Figure 10-2 could have been dealt with by a single question: "How many times, if any, have you smoked marijuana?" The response categories, then, might have read, "Never," "Once," "2 to 5 times," and so forth. Such a single question would apply to all respondents, and each would find an appropriate answer category. Such a question, however, might put some pressure on respondents to report having smoked marijuana because the main question asks how many times they have done so, even though it allows for those who have *never smoked marijuana even once*. (The emphasis used in the previous sentence gives a fair indication of how respondents might read the question.) The contingency question format in Figure 10-2 should reduce the subtle pressure on respondents to report having smoked marijuana.

The foregoing discussion shows how seemingly theoretical issues of validity and reliability are involved in as mundane a matter as putting questions on a piece of paper. Used properly, this technique allows you to construct some rather complex sets of contingency questions without confusing the respondent. Figure 10-3 illustrates a more complicated example.

FIGURE 10.2   Contingency Question Format

Sometimes a set of contingency questions is long enough to extend over several pages. Suppose you are studying the voting behaviors of poor people, and you wish to ask a large number of questions of individuals who had voted in a national, state, or local election. You could separate out the relevant respondents with an initial question, such as, "Have you ever voted in a national, state, or local election?" but it would be confusing to place the contingency questions in a box that stretched over several pages. It would make more sense to enter instructions in parentheses after each answer, telling respondents to answer or skip the contingency questions. Figure 10-4 illustrates this method.

In addition to these instructions, it would be worthwhile to place an instruction at the top of

FIGURE 10.3   Contingency Table

FIGURE 10.4   Instructions to Skip

> 13. Have you ever voted in a national, state, or local election?
>   ☐ Yes (Please answer questions 14–25.)
>   ☐ No   (Please skip questions 14–25. Go directly to question 26 on page 8.)

each page that contains only the contingency questions. For example, you might say, "This page is only for respondents who have voted in a national, state, or local election." Clear instructions such as these spare respondents the frustration of reading and puzzling over questions that are irrelevant to them and also decrease the chance of getting responses from those for whom the questions are not relevant.

Matrix Questions

Quite often, you'll want to ask several questions that have the same set of answer categories. This is typically the case whenever the Likert response categories are used. In such cases, it's often possible to construct a matrix of items and answers, as illustrated in Figure 10-5.

This format has at least three advantages. First, it uses space efficiently. Second, respondents will probably be able to complete a set of questions presented this way more quickly. Third, the format may increase the comparability of responses given to different questions for the respondent as well as for the researcher. Because respondents can quickly

FIGURE 10.5   Matrix Question Format

> 17. Beside *each* of the statements presented below, please indicate whether you Strongly Agree (SA), Agree (A), Disagree (D), Strongly Disagree (SD), or are Undecided (U).
>
> | | SA | A | D | SD | U |
> |--|----|---|---|----|---|
> | a. What this country needs is more law and order. | ☐ | ☐ | ☐ | ☐ | ☐ |
> | b. The police should be disarmed in America. | ☐ | ☐ | ☐ | ☐ | ☐ |
> | c. During riots, looters should be shot on sight. | ☐ | ☐ | ☐ | ☐ | ☐ |
> | *etc.* | | | | | |

review their answers to earlier items in the set, they might choose between, say, "strongly agree" and "agree" on a given statement by comparing their strength of agreement with their earlier responses in the set.

The format also presents some dangers, however. Its advantages may encourage you to structure an item so that the responses fit into the matrix format when a different, more idiosyncratic set of responses might be more appropriate. Also, the matrix question format can foster a response set among some respondents: They may develop a pattern, for example, of agreeing with all of the statements. That would be especially likely if the set of statements began with several that indicated a particular orientation (e.g., a liberal political perspective) with only a few later statements representing a different orientation. Respondents might assume that all the statements represented the same orientation and, reading quickly, misread some of them, thereby giving the wrong answers. Earlier in this chapter and in Chapter 9, we referred briefly to this problem as the *acquiescent response set*. This problem can be reduced somewhat by interspersing positively and negatively worded statements to represent different orientations and by making all statements short and clear. For example, you can handle this problem by interspersing items such as "I resent my mother" and "I dislike my mother" with items such as "I enjoy my mother" and "I am proud of my mother."

Ordering Questions in a Questionnaire

The order in which questions are asked can also affect the answers given. First, the appearance of one question can affect the answers given to later ones. For example, if several questions have been asked about the dangers of terrorism to the United States and then an open-ended question asks respondents to volunteer what they believe to represent problems facing the United States, terrorism will receive more citations than would otherwise be the case. In this situation, it is preferable to ask the open-ended question first.

If respondents are asked to assess their overall religiosity ("How important is your religion to you in general?"), their responses to later questions about specific aspects of religiosity will be aimed at consistency with the prior assessment. The converse would be true as well. If respondents are first asked specific questions about different aspects of their religiosity, their subsequent overall assessment will reflect the earlier answers.

Some researchers attempt to overcome this effect by randomizing the order of questions. This is usually a futile effort. To begin, a randomized set of questions will probably strike respondents as chaotic and worthless. It will be difficult to answer, moreover, because they must continually switch their attention from one topic to another. And, finally, even in a randomized ordering of questions, the appearance of one question can affect the answers given to later ones—except that you will have no control over this effect.

The safest solution is sensitivity to the problem. Although you cannot avoid the effect of question order, you should attempt to estimate the resulting effect and thus be able to interpret results in a meaningful fashion. If the question order seems especially important in a given study, then you might construct more than one version of the questionnaire with different possible orderings of questions. You would then be able to determine the effects. At the very least, you should pretest the different forms of your questionnaire.

The desired ordering of questions differs somewhat between self-administered questionnaires and interviews. In the former, it might be best to begin the questionnaire with the most interesting set of questions. The potential respondents who glance casually over the first few questions should want to answer them. Perhaps the questions will ask for attitudes that they are aching to express. At the same time, however, the initial questions should not be threatening. (Beginning with questions about sexual behavior or drug use is probably a bad idea.) Requests for duller demographic data (age, sex, and the like) might be placed at the end of a self-administered questionnaire. Such questions placed at the beginning, as many inexperienced researchers do, may give the questionnaire the initial appearance of a routine form, and a respondent may not be motivated to complete it.

Just the opposite is generally true for interview surveys. When the potential respondent's door first opens, the interviewer must begin to establish rapport quickly. After a short introduction to the study, the interviewer can best begin by enumerating the members of the household, getting nonthreatening background data about each, such as their age and sex. Such questions are easily answered and are

generally not threatening. Once the initial rapport has been established, the interviewer can move into the area of attitudes and more sensitive matters. An interview that began with the question "Do you believe in God?" would probably end rather quickly. However, an interview might also be aborted if the initial background questions delve into sensitive areas such as income or marital history and thus make respondents feel that their privacy is being invaded.

The impact of item order is not uniform. When Benton and Daly (1991) conducted a local government survey, they found that respondents with less education were more influenced by the order of questionnaire items than were those with more education. In another study, Greene, Murphy, and Snyder (2000) tested alternate versions of a mailed questionnaire: one with items requesting demographic data at the end and another with those items at the beginning. Their results questioned the conventional wisdom, which we mentioned above, that such items are best placed at the end of self-administered questionnaires.

Questionnaire Instructions

Every questionnaire, whether it is to be completed by respondents or administered by interviewers, should contain clear instructions and introductory comments where appropriate. It is useful to begin every self-administered questionnaire with basic instructions to be followed in completing it. Although many people these days are familiar with forms and questionnaires, you should begin by telling them exactly what you want: that they are to indicate their answers to certain questions by placing a check mark or an X in the box beside the appropriate answer or by writing in their answer when asked to do so. If many open-ended questions are used, respondents should be given some guidance about whether brief or lengthy answers are expected. If you wish to encourage your respondents to elaborate on their responses to closed-ended questions, that should be noted.

If a questionnaire is arranged into content subsections—political attitudes, religious attitudes, background data, and so forth—introduce each section with a short statement about its content and purpose, such as, "In this section, we would like to know what people around here consider the most important community problems."

Demographic items at the end of a self-administered questionnaire might be introduced thusly: "Finally, we would like to know just a little about you so we can see how different types of people feel about the issues we have been examining."

Short introductions such as these help make sense out of the questionnaire for the respondent. They make the questionnaire seem less chaotic, especially when it taps a variety of data. And they help put the respondent in the proper frame of mind for answering the questions.

Some questions may require special instructions to facilitate proper answering. That is especially true if a given question varies from the general instructions that pertain to the whole questionnaire. Specific examples will illustrate this situation.

Despite the desirability of mutually exclusive answer categories in closed-ended questions, more than one answer may often apply for respondents. If you want a single answer, then make this clear in the question. An example would be, "From the list below, please check the *primary reason* for your decision to attend college." Often, the main question can be followed by a parenthetical note: "Please check the one best answer." If, on the other hand, you want the respondent to check as many answers as apply, that should be made clear as well.

When answer categories are to be rank ordered by the respondent, then the instructions should indicate as much, and a different type of answer format should be used (e.g., blank spaces instead of boxes). These instructions should indicate how many answers are to be ranked (e.g., all, first and second, first and last, or most important and least important) and the order of ranking (e.g., "Place a 1 beside the most important, a 2 beside the next most important, and so forth."). Rank ordering their responses is often difficult for respondents, however, because they might have to read and reread the list several times, so this technique should be used only when no other method will produce the desired result. If it is used, the list of answer categories to be ranked should be relatively short. Ranking 10 or more categories, for example, may be too difficult for many respondents.

In multiple-part matrix questions, it is helpful to give special instructions unless the same format is used throughout the questionnaire. Sometimes respondents will be expected to check one answer in each *column* of the matrix, and in other questionnaires they will be expected to check one

answer in each *row*. Whenever the questionnaire contains both types, add an instruction to clarify which is expected in each case.

Pretesting the Questionnaire

No matter how carefully researchers design a data collection instrument such as a questionnaire, there is always the possibility—indeed, the certainty—of error. They will always make some mistake: an ambiguous question, a question that people cannot answer, or some other violation of the rules just discussed.

To guard against such errors, pretest the questionnaire in a dry run (as we mentioned in Chapter 9). The pretest sample can be small—perhaps 10 people or less. They should be like the people you intend to include in your study, and you can use your judgment in selecting people whom you think are like those who will participate in your actual study. The ones who participate in the pretest, however, should *not* later participate in the actual study. (As we mentioned in Chapter 9, the dry run that we refer to here is different than administering measurement instruments in pretests with larger samples to collect actual study data regarding the reliability of an instrument or the scores on it before receiving an intervention that is being evaluated.)

When pretesting your instrument, by and large it's better to ask people to complete the questionnaire than to read through it looking for errors. All too often, a question seems to make sense on a first reading but proves impossible to answer.

Cognitive interviewing is a useful tool to use in pretesting. As people complete the questionnaire you can ask them to comment on the questions as they do so. For example, the "thinking aloud" method (Priede & Farrall, 2011) encourages respondents to talk about the questions as they answer them: for example, "I assume here that you wanted to know if I *knew* I was using marijuana."

EP 4, 7, 9

» CONSTRUCTING SCALES

Some variables are too complex or multifaceted to be measured with just one item on a questionnaire. Examples of complex variables that social work researchers may find difficult to tap adequately with a single questionnaire item are level of marital satisfaction, quality of life, level of caregiver burden, level of social functioning, level of client satisfaction with services, practitioner attitudes about a new service or intervention modality, and attitudes about social justice issues—to mention just a few.

The composite or cumulative measures of complex variables are called *scales*. Scales allow us to represent complex variables with scores that provide greater potential for variance than would a single item. Suppose, for example, we are providing play therapy for children who have been abused and have a posttraumatic stress disorder (PTSD) as a result of that abuse. Suppose we want to assess whether their PTSD improves as a result of the play therapy. It is hard to imagine how we could assess that improvement in a reasonable way by just asking one question. Instead, we might want to develop a list of PTSD symptoms, such as having nightmares, difficulties concentrating, worrying about bad things happening, self-blame, hypervigilance (we wouldn't use that term with kids), bad memories, and so on. Beside each symptom, the children (or their parent) might check whether in the past week they've had that symptom.

Excerpts from such a scale appear in Figure 10-6. By adding up the numbers that a parent circles for the items in the scale, we can get a total PTSD score. The higher the score, the worse the PTSD symptoms appear to be. We can assess whether the PTSD symptoms got better (or perhaps worse) after our play therapy by having parents complete the scale before the play therapy treatment commences and at points after the entire play therapy treatment regimen has been completed. We could also administer the scale at weekly intervals during the play therapy treatment period to monitor whether the symptoms are improving, worsening, or staying the same. We would not need to analyze separately the responses to the individual items; instead, we would need only to examine the summated score to represent the multifaceted PTSD variable.

Levels of Measurement

In Chapter 8 we discussed the four levels of measurement: nominal, ordinal, interval, and ratio.

FIGURE 10.6   Condensed Excerpts from Parent Report of Posttraumatic Symptoms Scale*

Please circle a number that best indicates how well each item describes your child **in the past week.** Please do **NOT** skip any item, even if you are not sure.

Not or Rarely True	Somewhat or Sometimes True	Very True or Often True	
0	1	2	Difficulty concentrating
0	1	2	Mood swings
0	1	2	Thinks of bad memories
0	1	2	Sad or depressed
0	1	2	Hyper-alert
0	1	2	Worries
0	1	2	Fearful
0	1	2	Withdrawn
0	1	2	Nervous
0	1	2	Startles easily
0	1	2	Irritable
0	1	2	Difficulty sleeping
0	1	2	Nightmares or bad dreams

*Copies of the full scale can be obtained from Dr. Ricky Greenwald, rg@childtrauma.com, who has the copyright for it. Reproduced by permission.

Scales typically are at the ordinal level. In other words, they rank order people (or other units of analysis) in terms of specific variables, such as attitude toward mother, social functioning, and the like. That rank order is determined by the overall score that combines all of the scale's items.

Although ordinal measures are very useful in quantifying variables, they do not specify the precise degree of quantitative differences. For example, a score of 20 on the scale in Figure 10-6 does not indicate twice as much symptom severity as a score of 10, just as a response of *often true* (scored 2) to an item on the scale does not mean exactly twice as often as a response of *sometimes true* (scored 1). We'll examine the influence of levels of measurement on data analysis in Chapter 21. The important thing to remember for now is that differences in scores on scales at the ordinal level of measurement depict imprecise differences in quantity. We know, for example, that a person scoring 20 on the scale in Figure 10-6 probably has more frequent symptoms than a person scoring 10—and that certainly is valuable information, but it does not mean that one person has twice as much or half as much symptom frequency as the other person.

Some Prominent Scaling Procedures

As you might imagine from the lengthy list of reference volumes for existing scales we presented in Figure 8-4, scales can come in a seemingly endless variety of formats. Some scaling procedures are highly complex and require a tremendous expenditure of labor to develop. Less complex scales can be as simple as one-item scales that may have minimal wording and can be administered in a conversational format. For example, if you want to assess the moods of very young children (perhaps before and after receiving some form of treatment such as play therapy), you might present them with a handful of simple cartoonish faces, with a smiley face at one end of the continuum and a frowning, sad face at the other end. You would then ask them to select the face that best fit how they were feeling. Or you might assess how well your adult clients were responding to your intervention for anxiety by asking them to rate their anxiety on a scale from 1 to 10, with 1 representing no anxiety and 10 representing the worst anxiety imaginable.

One commonly used scaling format is called Likert scaling. Likert scales present respondents with statements followed by response choices for respondents to indicate whether they "strongly agree," "agree," "disagree," "strongly disagree," or are "undecided." Modifications of the wording of the response categories (for example, "approve") may be used, of course. Sometimes there are additional categories, like "strongly agree," "moderately agree," "slightly agree," "slightly disagree," "moderately disagree," "strongly disagree," and so on. Sometimes the respondents are not given the "undecided" choice to avoid having too many respondents duck taking a position. Whether or not to include choices such as "undecided," "uncertain," or "neutral" is usually a judgment call by the researcher; there is no formula or hard-and-fast guideline determining whether to provide the undecided choice. Likewise, whether to include the "moderately" and "slightly" choices also is a judgment call. If the "undecided," "uncertain," or "neutral" choice is included, it would be placed in the middle of the continuum of choices; that is, between the agree choices and the disagree choices.

With five response categories, scores of 1 to 5 might be assigned, taking the direction of the items into account (for instance, assign a score of 5 to "strongly agree" for positive items and to "strongly disagree" for negative items). Each respondent would then be assigned an overall score that represents the summation of the scores he or she received for responses to the individual items. For example, if there are 20 items on the scale, with the respondent getting a score from 1 to 5 for each item, then the respondent's total score can range from 20 (a score of 1 per item) to 100 (a score of 5 per item). With more than five response categories, the maximum total score will be higher. For example, if seven response categories are used (i.e., "strongly agree," "moderately agree," "slightly agree," "undecided," "slightly disagree," "moderately disagree," "strongly disagree") with 20 items, then respondents could get a score of 1 to 7 for each item and a possible total score ranging from 20 to 140 (7 times 20 items).

An alternative to the Likert scale format is the semantic differential format. Here's how that format works.

Suppose we want to assess whether students' level of appreciation of social work research changes after they read this book. Using a semantic differential format, we would ask them to choose between two opposite positions on various indicators of their appreciation of social work research. After developing a comprehensive list of indicators, we would need to choose two *opposite* terms to represent the polar extremes regarding their attitudes about each indicator. Let's suppose one indicator is simply whether respondents find research to be interesting. Two opposite terms in this case could be "interesting" and "boring." Similarly, we might want to know whether they regard research as "valuable" or "useless," "caring" or "uncaring," and so forth.

Once we have determined the relevant indicators and have found terms to represent the polar extremes of each, we might prepare a rating sheet to be completed by each student. Figure 10-7 shows an example of what it might look like.

On each line of the rating sheet, the student would indicate how he or she felt about social work research: whether it is interesting or boring, for instance, and whether it is "somewhat" that way or "very much" so. To avoid creating a biased pattern of responses to such items, it's a good idea to vary the placement of terms that are likely to be related to each other. Notice, for example, that "uncaring" and "useful" are on the left side of the sheet and that "caring" and "useless" are on the right side. It's highly likely that those who select "uncaring" would also choose "useless" as opposed to "useful."

Item Generation and Selection

Regardless of what scaling procedure you use, the first phase in constructing a scale involves generating a large initial pool of items to be considered for inclusion in the scale. The second phase involves deciding which items in that initial pool to include and not to include.

Generate a Large Pool Ideally, the pool of items to be considered for your scale should be very large. There are three reasons for this. First, increasing the pool of items betters your chances of covering the entire domain of indicators of the construct. (Recall our discussion of *content validity* in Chapter 9 and the inadequate content validity of fictional Dr. Dork's depression scale because it did not come close to covering the entire domain of indicators of depression.) Second, a larger pool of items gives you more alternative ways to word items and thus more to choose from in trying to come up with the best possible items. Third, it is often a good idea to use more than one item to get at the same indicator because changes in wording can increase the chances of better detecting a given respondent's actual thoughts feelings or behavior regarding that indicator.

Changes in wording can also increase the chances of distinguishing variations among respondents regarding a particular indicator. For example, a scale developed by Rubin and Parrish (2011) measuring practitioners' attitudes and behaviors about evidence-based practice (EBP) included the following two items with a 5-point response scale from *never* to *very often* (Rubin and Parrish, 2011):

"I read about research to guide my practice decisions."

"I rely on research evidence as the best guide for making practice decisions."

Rubin and Parrish included both of these items in their scale despite recognizing some wording redundancy between them. They did so because they expected that, despite having some

FIGURE 10.7 Semantic Differential

	Very Much	Somewhat	Neither	Somewhat	Very Much	
Interesting	☐	☐	☐	☐	☐	Boring
Simple	☐	☐	☐	☐	☐	Complex
Uncaring	☐	☐	☐	☐	☐	Caring
Useful	☐	☐	☐	☐	☐	Useless
			etc.			

redundancy, including both items instead of just one gave them a better chance of capturing variation among practitioners regarding the construct in question. Suppose they had included only the first of the two items. Then practitioners who read about research very often but do not esteem it as the best guide for their decisions would be indistinguishable from those who read it very often and rely on it as the best guide. In other words, both sets of practitioners would have gotten the same score on the item. On the other hand, suppose they had omitted the first item. Then practitioners who read the research very often but who never rely on it as the best guide would be indistinguishable from practitioners who disdain research and never even read it.

Sources and Procedures for Generating Items

Various procedures and item sources can be used to generate the initial pool of items. One source is your own expertise about the construct you'd like your scale to measure. Suppose you are constructing a scale to measure the level of client satisfaction with your agency's services. Having worked at that agency, you probably would already know a lot regarding the various aspects of service to ask about. You may also have heard colleagues and clients complain about some aspects of service and praise others. Like most scale developers across the gamut of possible constructs to measure, therefore, at some point you'll probably draft some preliminary items derived solely from your own thoughts about the matter.

Additional sources of potential items are your colleagues or others with special expertise in the construct you seek to measure. Yet another is the literature on the construct. Reading that literature has two advantages. First, it can enrich your expertise about the construct, and what you learn might generate ideas about additional items or how to refine the items already in your pool. Second, the literature might contain examples of how others have gone about measuring the construct—or related constructs—and the items that went into their instruments that are relevant to yours. For example, if you dig into the literature on *client satisfaction questionnaires* (or simply Google that term), you are likely to encounter some dos and don'ts about their construction.

Suppose you are considering an item asking about whether the services clients received met their expectations. Examining the literature on client satisfaction questionnaires might prompt you to change that item when you learn that meeting expectations does not necessarily imply satisfaction because the expectations might have been very negative to begin with. For instance, a returning combat veteran with PTSD might have watched a TV exposé characterizing as deplorable how long vets with PTSD have to wait for treatment from the Veterans Administration. If she expects to experience a deplorably long wait, and unfortunately has that expectation met, then agreeing that her expectations were met should not be interpreted as being satisfied.

At some points you might hold focus group discussions with some clients to generate some possible items or to refine or expand your existing pool of items. Focus groups are guided discussions among a small group of people (usually around 8 to 10) that might stimulate some participants to think of or express things that they might not have considered or expressed in an individual interview. Some focus groups might occur early in the item generation and refinement process. Others might take place later, after you have already developed a preliminary version of your scale and you want to see if some members of the population for whom the scale is intended have difficulty with the layout of the scale or with the wording of its instructions or any of its items. (Focus groups are usually considered to be a qualitative method, and we will discuss them in more depth in Chapter 16's coverage of qualitative methods.)

Item Selection Given our discussion of validity in Chapter 9, perhaps it should go without saying that when selecting items from your pool, items should have *face validity*. Recalling our discussion above regarding client satisfaction, you might reject any pool items worded in terms of meeting expectations, as you realize that meeting expectations lacks face validity because for people with negative expectations, having those expectations met is not an indicator of satisfaction.

Likewise, if you want to measure self-esteem, each item should appear on its face to indicate some aspect of self-esteem. You might conceive of concepts related to self-esteem, such as depression, but your self-esteem scale should include items that reflect only self-esteem, not items that reflect depression. Thus, if you are measuring self-esteem, you would not ask people if they feel lonely or blue just because you think that depression is related to self-esteem. Instead, you would reserve that question for a scale that measures depression and restrict the self-esteem scale to items that pertain to the favorability of one's self-image. (You might have items that ask people whether they feel they are smart, attractive, likable, competent, trustworthy, and so on.)

Items should also have adequate *variance*. If everyone gives the same response to a particular item, then that item would have no use in constructing a scale. Suppose, for example, that on a scale that attempts to measure parental child-rearing attitudes, no parents admit to wanting to sexually abuse their children. That item would not be useful in distinguishing parents who are more likely to be abusive from those who are less likely. To find out whether items have adequate variance, you would pretest the scale and then examine the range of responses to each item.

Pretesting the Scale   Earlier in this chapter, we discussed the importance of conducting a dry run with a small group of people to pretest a questionnaire to identify difficulties they might experience in the wording. This can be done individually as well as in a focus group format. Also as mentioned, the people who participate in the pretest should *not* later participate in the actual study. After you think you've corrected any problems identified in the dry run, you'll probably want to conduct additional dry runs as needed until you are convinced the scale has been completely debugged.

Ultimately, which items you select for a scale should depend on how those items influence the scale's reliability and validity, which are determined by using procedures discussed in the previous chapter. For example, you might want to conduct a preliminary, developmental study of the scale's reliability and validity with a small sample before using it in an actual study. Items that have no relationship with other items on the same scale or with an external criterion of the validity of the scale should be discarded or modified. Additional developmental studies might be needed if these modifications are extensive, and you might want to delay using the scale in a larger study until you are satisfied with its reliability and validity. However, in light of the time and resource constraints in most social work settings, not to mention similar constraints confronting many social work researchers

and program evaluators, these additional developmental studies are rarely feasible. Therefore, if you are developing a scale, chances are you might stop the process after your dry runs or perhaps after one developmental study and its indicated modifications, especially if those modifications are neither major nor extensive.

Handling Missing Data

In virtually every study that uses scales, some respondents fail to respond to some items. Sometimes they just leave the item blank; at other times they choose a "don't know" response. You'll need to come up with a way to handle the missing responses because if you don't the summed score on a scale will be misleading.

For example, imagine a client satisfaction scale containing 10 items in which each item is scored on a 5-point scale from 1 (very dissatisfied) to 5 (very satisfied). Suppose Client A gets a 4 on all ten items, giving her a total satisfaction score of 40. Suppose Client B accidentally skips two of the items, answering only eight of them, and gets a 5 on each of those eight items. Multiplying 8 times 5, his total satisfaction score would be 40, the same as Client A's total. It would be improper to conclude that Client B is no more satisfied than Client A because his total score was the same as hers. If skipping two items really was accidental, then in all likelihood he is more satisfied than Client B because he scored 5 on every item to which he responded, and she scored 4.

There are various ways to deal with the problem of missing data. Perhaps the most common way is to assign the respondent's mean score on the items that weren't missing to the ones that were. Thus, Client B above would get a 5 assigned to the two missing items and thus a total score of 50. Alternatively, instead of assigning a value to the missing item, you could calculate a mean item score. In that case, Client B would get a score of 5 (40 divided by 8), and Client A would get a score of 4 (40 divided by 10). Each of these alternatives has the same meaning because the mean item score represents the same thing as a total score when you think of the total in terms of the number of items responded to.

Another common way to deal with this problem is to exclude from the data analysis those few respondents who had missing data on a large number of items. Failing to answer a large number of items raises doubt about how carefully the respondent completed the scale and whether the answered items really are representative of the missing ones. Likewise, if all but a few respondents respond to every item, you might decide to exclude from the data analysis those few respondents whose scale contains just a small amount of missing data. But this should not be done if it looks as if it might bias your remaining sample, such as by excluding most of the people who share a particular characteristic.

Less common, but still often acceptable, is the option of treating missing data as one available response. For instance, if a questionnaire has asked respondents to indicate their participation in a number of activities by checking "yes" or "no" for each, many respondents may have checked some of the activities "yes" and left the remainder blank. In such a case, you might decide that a failure to answer meant "no" and score missing data in this case as though the respondents had checked the "no" space.

EP 4, 7, 9

» CONSTRUCTING QUALITATIVE MEASURES

Although much of the material in this chapter so far has been about quantitative measurement instruments, such as self-administered questionnaires and scales, constructing measurement instruments is also relevant to qualitative research methods. For example, earlier in this chapter we discussed guidelines for asking questions that are just as applicable to gathering information from respondents in qualitative studies as they are in quantitative studies. In either type of study, for instance, one should avoid wording that is biased, too complex, or irrelevant to respondents.

At this point, however, we will examine some of the ways that instrument construction is different in qualitative measurement than in quantitative measurement. Let's begin by noting that, like quantitative research, qualitative research often involves gathering data by directly observing people in addition to asking them questions.

In this chapter, we are limiting the discussion to measures for asking people questions, not instruments used for recording direct observations. The latter types of instruments will be discussed in later chapters.

The chief difference between quantitative and qualitative measures for asking people questions is that quantitative measures are always highly structured, tend to use closed-ended questions primarily, and may be administered in either an interview or questionnaire format, whereas qualitative measures rely on interviews that are often unstructured and that contain mainly open-ended questions with in-depth probes. In Chapter 19, we will discuss qualitative interviewing in greater detail; here, we merely want to illustrate how its measures contrast with quantitative measures.

Qualitative interviews can range from completely unstructured, informal conversational interviews that use no measurement instruments to highly structured, standardized interviews in which interviewers must ask questions in the exact order and with the exact wording in which they are written in advance. Between these two extremes are semistructured interviews that use interview guides that list in outline form the topics and issues the interview should ask about but that allow the interviewer to be flexible, informal, and conversational and to adapt the style of the interview and the sequencing and wording of questions to each particular interviewee.

Ruth McRoy and Harold Grotevant developed a highly structured, standardized open-ended interview schedule that they used in a qualitative study of openness in adoption (McRoy & Grotevant, 1990). Their entire schedule consisted of 179 items that were to be asked in the same order and with the same wording that appeared on the schedule. The items were worded in a neutral manner and sequenced logically. The schedule systematically instructed interviewers to probe for detail and clarification. It provided parenthetical details to help interviewers clarify the point of the question for respondents who may initially have difficulty in answering. It also used contingency questions. Despite being highly structured, it provided interviewers the opportunity afforded by qualitative inquiry to probe for in-depth meanings and subjective perspectives. For example, item 11 on the 179-item interview scheduled appeared as follows:

11. Do any of your friends have adopted children? (Probe: How have they and their experiences influenced your feelings?)

A COMPARISON OF QUANTITATIVE AND QUALITATIVE APPROACHES TO ASKING PEOPLE QUESTIONS

	Quantitative Approaches	Qualitative Approaches
Similarities in measurement principles		
Try to use language that respondents will understand	Always	Always
Ask one question at a time; avoid double-barreled questions	Always	Always
Only ask questions that respondents are capable of answering and that are relevant to them	Always	Always
Avoid biased items and terms	Always	Always
Stylistic differences		
Questionnaires or scale	Often	Rarely
Interviews	Sometimes	Usually
Same wording and sequence of questions for all respondents	Always	Rarely
Interviewer flexibility regarding wording, sequencing, and conversational style	Never	Very often
Open-ended questions	Rarely	Usually
Probes	Rare and brief	Frequent and in depth
Closed-ended questions	Usually	Sometimes
Formality of interview	Relaxed, friendly demeanor but professional tone and not overly casual	More likely to resemble a spontaneous, informal, friendly conversation
Complementary Functions		
Objectivity and consistency versus flexibility and subjective meanings	Develop measures to be administered to many respondents in ways that attempt to minimize random and systematic measurement error but that may be at a superficial level, requiring an investigation of their validity	Develop measures that allow for researcher flexibility and subjectivity in order to pursue deeper, more valid levels of understanding of subjective meanings among fewer respondents
Generalizability versus in-depth, theoretical understanding	Verify, in a precise, statistical fashion, whether understandings emerging from qualitative measurement are generalizable	Develop a deeper theoretical understanding of the meanings of statistical findings emerging from quantitative measurement
Test hypotheses versus generating hypotheses and deeper understandings	Test hypotheses, perhaps generated from qualitative studies, generating new findings that might require further qualitative study to be sufficiently understood	Study phenomena whose meanings are not sufficiently understood, perhaps generating hypotheses for quantitative study

How might the McRoy–Grotevant instrument have appeared had it been in the form of an interview guide for a semistructured interview? Perhaps it would have been a brief outline of questions to ask about, such as the following one, which we have imagined based on examining their entire 179 items:

I. Background regarding adoption

  A. Prior expectations? Counseling?

  B. Adoption process? How it felt?

  C. Discussions with child? Relatives?

  D. Characteristics of child? Similarities and dissimilarities with parents?

  E. Anticipation of life changes and how prepared for?

II. Knowledge about degrees of openness in adoption

  A. Understandings of meanings and options before adoption?

  B. Advantages and disadvantages of each option anticipated?

III. Type of adoption chosen and issues

  A. How discussed and dealt with in family?

  B. Problems? Discomfort discussing? Manipulation? Other siblings?

IV. Issues involving birth parents

  A. Impact of communications on child? On parents? On birth parents? On other children?

  B. Impact of face-to-face meetings? Feelings each set of parents has about the other?

  C. Degree of ongoing contact? Why?

V. Any changes in degree of openness over time?

  A. What type of changes?

  B. Impact?

As we end this chapter, we remind you that, despite pointing out the differences between quantitative and qualitative measures for asking people questions, we've identified commonalities shared by the two approaches. We would also like to reiterate that the same mixed-methods study can use both approaches; they need not be seen as mutually exclusive or in conflict. We summarize these points in the box "A Comparison of Quantitative and Qualitative Approaches to Asking People Questions."

MAIN POINTS

- Questionnaires provide a method of collecting data by (a) asking people questions or (b) asking them to agree or disagree with statements that represent different points of view.

- Questions may be open-ended (respondents supply their own answers) or closed-ended (they select from a list of answers provided them).

- Usually, short items in a questionnaire are better than long ones.

- Negative items and terms should be avoided in questionnaires because they might confuse respondents.

- In questionnaire items, bias is the quality that encourages respondents to answer in a particular way to avoid or support a particular point of view. Avoid it.

- Contingency questions are questions that should be answered only by people giving a particular response to some preceding question. The contingency question format is highly useful because it doesn't ask people questions that have no meaning for them. For example, a question about the number of times a person has been pregnant should be asked only of women.

- Matrix questions are those in which a standardized set of closed-ended response categories are used in answering several questionnaire items. This format can facilitate the presentation and completion of items.

- Single indicators of variables may not have sufficiently clear validity to warrant their use.

- Composite measures, such as scales, solve this problem by including several indicators of a variable in one summary measure.

- Likert scaling is a measurement technique that is based on the use of standardized response categories (e.g., "strongly agree," "agree," "disagree," or "strongly disagree") for several questionnaire items. The Likert format for scale items is popular and extremely useful.

- The semantic differential scaling technique involves asking respondents to choose between two opposite positions on various indicators of the construct being measured.

- Scales that appear to be reliable and valid when tested with one culture may not be reliable and valid when used with other cultures.

- The first step in scale construction involves generating a large preliminary pool of items from which to select for the eventual scale.

- Various procedures and item sources can be used to generate the initial pool of scale items, including the existing literature on the construct to be measured, one's own expertise about it, the expertise of others, and input from some members of the population for whom the scale is intended.
- Items should be selected that have face validity and adequate variance. Some redundancy among items is acceptable if it is not excessive and if it increases a scale's ability to detect differences among respondents regarding the construct being measured.
- Questionnaires and scales should be pretested in dry runs to identify and correct any response problems experienced by some members of the population for whom the instrument is intended.
- If feasible, in addition to dry runs, before finalizing scales, their reliability and validity should be assessed with a small developmental sample of members of the targeted population,
- Several options exist for handling missing data when some respondents don't respond to some scale items.
- Although qualitative and quantitative measurement approaches share certain principles, quantitative measures are always highly structured, tend to use primarily closed-ended questions, and may be administered in either an interview or a questionnaire format, whereas qualitative measures rely on interviews that are often unstructured and contain mainly open-ended questions and in-depth probes.
- Qualitative interviews can range from completely unstructured, informal conversational interviews that use no measurement instruments to highly structured, standardized interviews in which interviewers must ask questions in the exact order and with the exact wording in which they are written in advance. Between these two extremes are semistructured interview guides.

REVIEW QUESTIONS AND EXERCISES

1. Find a questionnaire in a magazine or newspaper (e.g., a reader survey). Bring it to class and critique it.

2. For each of the open-ended questions listed below, construct a closed-ended question that could be used in a questionnaire.

   a. What was your family's total income last year?
   b. How do you feel about increasing public spending on social welfare?
   c. How important is learning theory in your approach to social work practice?
   d. What was your main reason for studying to be a social worker?
   e. What do you feel is the biggest problem that faces this community?

3. Construct a set of contingency questions for use in a self-administered questionnaire that would solicit the following information:

   a. Is the respondent employed?
   b. If unemployed, is the respondent looking for work?
   c. If the unemployed respondent is not looking for work, is he or she retired, a student, or a homemaker?
   d. If the respondent is looking for work, how long has he or she been looking?

4. Using the Likert format, construct a brief scale to measure client satisfaction with service delivery. Next, construct one using the semantic differential format. After that, construct a brief, semistructured qualitative interview guide to assess the same construct.

INTERNET EXERCISES

1. Enter the search term "scaling" to find an article that discusses scale development. Write down the bibliographical reference information for the article and summarize the article in a few sentences. If the article reports the development of a particular scale, critique the scale, its development, or both—either positively or negatively.

2. Find a questionnaire on the web. (Hint: Search for "questionnaire.") Critique at least five of the questions contained in it—either positively or negatively. Be sure to give the Web address for the questionnaire and the exact wording of the questions you critique.

3. Find the article by Robert Greene, Katrina Murphy, and Shelita Snyder, "Should Demographics Be Placed at the End or at the Beginning of Mailed Questionnaires? An Empirical Answer to a Persistent Methodological Question," which appeared in the December 2000 issue of *Social Work Research*. Briefly summarize the main points of the article and give a brief critical appraisal.

 Visit CengageBrain.com for additional practice and study opportunities including experiential exercises, research tools, glossary, flashcards, and sample test items.

Designs for Evaluating Programs and Practice

Whereas the previous two chapters dealt with the validity of measurement, we now turn to a different form of validity. In this section, we'll examine the validity of inferences made about the effectiveness of interventions, policies, and programs. In Chapter 1, we discussed the need to assess the effectiveness of social work practice and programs. We noted that this need stems from such forces as public skepticism about our effectiveness, increasing demands for accountability, and our own professional and humanitarian concerns for the welfare of clients. Implicit in the term *effectiveness* is the notion of causality. Thus, when we discussed evidence-based practice in Chapter 2, we noted that a key question in appraising the quality of the evidence reported in practice effectiveness studies pertains to whether the research design is strong enough to indicate conclusively whether the intervention or something else most plausibly caused the variations we observe in client outcome.

The next four chapters will examine the logic of causal inference and show how different design arrangements bear on our ability to infer cause and effect. They will address these issues primarily from the standpoint of evaluating the effectiveness of social work services.

Chapter 11 will begin by discussing criteria necessary for inferring causality and some common sources of error in causal inference. Then it will examine different experimental designs and how they attempt to enhance our ability to make causal inferences.

Chapter 12 will focus on quasi-experimental designs and ways to strengthen their ability to generate causal inferences. It will also examine some practical pitfalls in attempting to carry out experiments and quasi experiments in social work agencies and some mechanisms for dealing with those pitfalls.

Chapter 13 will discuss single-case evaluation designs. It shows how causal inferences can be made about the effects of a particular intervention on a particular case. Although the generalizability of this approach is limited, Chapter 13 will examine why single-case evaluation designs have great potential utility to practitioners as the final stage in the evidence-based practice process.

Chapter 14 will depart from focusing on logic and methods for making inferences about effectiveness and instead will focus on issues and practical guidelines for conducting program evaluations. It will show how vested interests can influence the ways in which evaluations are conducted and utilized, and how evaluators can deal with those political forces.

What you learn in these chapters should help you appreciate the paradoxical complexities that are involved in selecting a research design and in appraising the evidence you find when engaging in evidence-based practice. On the one hand, using an acute skepticism, you should be prepared to swiftly spot logical arrangements that do not permit sweeping generalizations or causal inferences to be made. On the other hand, you should be aware of the practical obstacles that make ideal logical arrangements infeasible and thus be able to appreciate the utility of findings that may have to be interpreted cautiously.

11

Causal Inference and Experimental Designs

EPAS Competencies for This Chapter

Competency 1 Demonstrate Ethical and Professional Behavior: As you will see in this chapter, if you want to use an experimental design, you'll need competence regarding doing so ethically, especially if you are considering withholding an intervention being tested from some research participants.

Competency 4 Engage in Practice-Informed Research and Research-Informed Practice: This competency pertains to this entire chapter because doing practice-informed research sometimes involves using experimental designs. The same applies to engaging in research-informed practice because you'll need to be able to critically appraise studies that aim to develop causal inferences that can inform your practice.

Competency 9 Evaluate Practice with Individuals Families, Groups, Organizations, and Communities: Evaluating practice sometimes involves using designs that aim to develop causal inferences. Therefore, this competency pertains to this entire chapter.

What You'll Learn in This Chapter

This chapter examines the criteria for drawing causal inferences from research findings and the ways that experimental designs attempt to meet those criteria in the evaluation of the effectiveness of programs, policies, and interventions.

» INTRODUCTION

In this chapter and the next two chapters, we'll look at issues in causal inference and their relationship to various research designs. Let's begin by defining what we mean by the terms *inference*, *causal inference*, and *research design*.

In social work research studies, an inference is a conclusion that can be logically drawn in light of our research design and our findings. A causal inference is one derived from a research design and findings that logically imply that the independent variable really has a *causal* impact on the dependent variable. The term research design can refer to all the decisions made in planning and conducting research, including decisions about measurement, sampling, how to collect data, and logical arrangements designed to permit certain kinds of inferences. Because we'll be focusing on the connection between research design and inference in this chapter, we'll use the term *research design* primarily in connection with logical arrangements.

The kinds of inferences that we seek to make—and legitimately can make—will vary, depending on the purpose of our research. Likewise, the kinds of research designs that are most and least appropriate will depend on our research purposes and the types of inference we seek to make. For example, if our purpose is limited to *description*—such as describing the proportion of homeless people who have severe and persistent mental illnesses—then we don't need a design that will permit us to explain what's *causing* something. Neither would we need such a design if our purpose is limited to *exploring* or *describing* in a pilot study what types of interventions or client problems appear to be associated with what types of service outcomes. That is, we would not be seeking to infer whether certain types of practices or interventions really are the explanations or causes of differences in outcome. However, if our purpose is causal in nature—such as to ascertain whether a particular intervention, program, or policy is effective—then we'll need a design that advances our ability to determine whether variations in policy or service provision really cause variations in the outcomes those policies or services seek to attain.

Shortly, we'll examine some specific types of designs, their strengths and weaknesses regarding causal inference, and how they can use statistical controls to improve the plausibility of the explanations they posit. But first we'll need to examine the criteria that are necessary for inferring causality.

» CRITERIA FOR INFERRING CAUSALITY

Not all causal inferences are persuasive. You probably hear other people making causal inferences quite often. Some of them you probably agree with. Some others might strike you as absurd. Then there may be other causal inferences that seem plausible, but you have some doubts. Even scientific consensus about a causal inference might fail to persuade some people. Witness, for example, the resistance by many to accept the causal inference that humans have contributed to current climate change phenomena such as increases in our planet's temperature, rising sea levels, and melting glaciers.

In your social work career, you are likely to read or hear about many causal inferences relevant to your professional practice. You might dismiss some as mere pseudoscientific claims about the wonders of a new intervention being touted by those with a vested interest in it. Other causal inferences might seem to be more worthy of your consideration, but you're not sure about them. For instance, you are likely to read in professional journals reports of evaluations about the effectiveness of a particular program, policy, or intervention in which the authors of those reports make causal inferences despite acknowledging some methodological limitations inherent in their evaluation design. Where do you draw the line between those inferences that are warranted despite methodological limitations and those that are not warranted?

Fortunately, criteria exist for inferring causality that can help you judge the plausibility of the many causal inferences you will encounter throughout your career. In addition to helping you sort out those inferences that do and do not merit influencing your practice decisions, these criteria are useful in designing any research studies you may someday embark on.

The three most commonly mentioned criteria for inferring causality in social work and allied fields are as follows:

1. Time sequence (The cause must precede the effect in time).

2. Correlation (Changes in the cause are accompanied by changes in the effect).

3. Ruling out alternative explanations

Austin Bradford Hill, a British medical statistician, expands on these three criteria for inferring causality, especially in regard to epidemiological research. Epidemiology is the study of the causes of physical and social disorders and how they spread. Hill (1965) points out that sometimes causal inferences can be persuasive in research on some phenomena for which it is not feasible to employ designs that go beyond establishing time sequence and correlation. Three additional criteria that he proposed that are particularly applicable to causal research in social work are as follows:

4. Strength of correlation

5. Consistency in replication

6. Plausibility and coherence

We'll organize our discussion of criteria around the first three—the ones most commonly mentioned. As we do, we'll incorporate the latter three criteria proposed by Hill to explain why some causal inferences can have important implications for policy or practice even when derived from investigations that are limited to establishing time sequence and correlation only.

Time Sequence

The first requirement in a causal relationship between two variables is that the cause precedes the effect in time. It makes no sense in science to imagine something being caused by something else that happened later on. A bullet leaving the muzzle of a gun does not cause the gunpowder to explode; it works the other way around.

As simple and obvious as this criterion may seem, we will discover endless problems in this regard in the analysis of social work research findings. Often, the time order that connects two variables is simply unclear. Suppose, for example, that a study finds that nuclear families containing a member suffering from schizophrenia are much more likely to be at lower levels of socioeconomic status than are families without such members. Which comes first—the schizophrenia or the lower socioeconomic status? Does socioeconomic stress contribute to the onset of schizophrenia? Or does having a schizophrenic member reduce a family's ability to advance socioeconomically? Even when the time order seems essentially clear, exceptions can often be found. For instance, we would normally assume that the educational level of parents would be a cause of the educational level of their children, yet some parents may return to school as a result of the advanced education of their own children.

Another example of this ambiguity can be found in a study by Rubin (1991) that evaluated the effectiveness of a support group intervention for battered women. One of the group's intervention goals was to help women still living with their batterers to leave them. One of the six women who participated in the study left her abusive husband the day before she attended her first support group meeting. Because the intended effect (leaving the batterer) preceded the hypothesized cause (attending the support group meetings), it would seem at first glance that the intervention could not have caused the intended effect. Indeed, it would seem more logical to suppose that attending the group meeting, rather than being the cause of the separation, was merely one of a variety of ways in which the woman was implementing a decision to separate—a decision that resulted from other forces.

On the other hand, one could argue that this woman's awareness of the support group and her anticipation of being part of it emboldened her to leave. Perhaps she also anticipated being embarrassed by admitting to the group that she continued to live with her batterer, and wanting to make a good impression on the group may have contributed in some way to her decision to leave when she did. If either explanation seems plausible, it follows that without the intervention (i.e., without the presence of the support group), the woman may not have left the batterer, even though she left him before attending the support group.

Because people sometimes change their behavior or cognitions in anticipation of events, such as when our moods improve in anticipation of a joyful event or when our spending increases in anticipation of a bonus or a tax rebate, we must consider potential anticipatory effects when we think about time order and causality.

Correlation

The second requirement in a causal relationship is that the two variables be empirically correlated with one another. Being correlated means that changes in one variable are associated with changes in another variable. (See our discussion of types of relationships between variables in Chapter 8.) It would make no sense to say that a support group helped women leave their batterers if women in the support group were no more likely to leave their batterers than women receiving no support.

Ruling Out Alternative Explanations

The third requirement for a causal relationship is that the observed empirical correlation between two variables cannot be explained away as the result of the influence of some third variable that causes the two under consideration. For instance, you may observe that your left knee generally aches just before it rains, but this does not mean that your joints affect the weather. A third variable, relative humidity, is the cause of both your aching knee and the rain. Likewise, a third variable, preexisting readiness to change, might explain why the women who leave their batterers are more likely to join the support group and leave their batterers. Perhaps the support group really didn't make them any more likely to leave than they were when they joined the group. The box "Correlation and Causality" illustrates the point that correlation does not necessarily point to a particular causal relationship.

Obviously, then, inferring causality from designs that establish time sequence and correlation, only, can be quite risky. As we already mentioned, however, those designs might offer important implications for policy or practice if they meet the additional criteria proposed by Hill. Let's now examine each of those criteria.

Strength of Correlation

The strength of the correlation between heavy smoking and lung cancer is so strong that alternative explanations become implausible. That is, the death rate from lung cancer among heavy smokers is so much higher than it is among nonsmokers that even though we cannot run an experiment to rule out alternative factors, requiring more "proof" regarding such factors before taking action to reduce smoking would be unwarranted and inhumane. The same reasoning perhaps applies to the need to protect the environment from the impact of carbon emissions. Considering the dire consequences that would come about for individual smokers or the world if the above two causal inferences are correct but not acted upon, it can be argued that the burden of "proof" shifts from those making the causal inference to those who want no action until we are absolutely 100% certain about those two inferences.

Likewise, if a study finds that after implementing a new social policy in one geographical area the rate of some undesirable phenomenon drops dramatically, we might not want to wait for alternative explanations to be ruled out before implementing that policy elsewhere. For example, suppose the incidents of police brutality in a city were to drop from a high number to near zero after implementing a new policy requiring all police officers to wear cameras. Maybe it was not the policy that caused the drop. Maybe instead it was a reaction by the police force to all the bad national publicity officers have received after high-profile incidents in which African American men died during interactions with police officers: Did the officers behave better under fear of scrutiny? Did they patrol areas less often or interact with citizens less often? Just knowing time sequence and correlation does not allow us to rule out the possibility of any one explanation, but the likelihood that the police were responding to publicity would seem to be greater if the correlation were not so strong. That is, if the number of unfortunate incidents dropped from about 100 per year before the new policy was implemented to less than 5 in the year after it was implemented, the plausibility of the alternative explanation would be much lower than if the number of such incidents dropped from 100 to 90.

Plausibility and Coherence

The criterion of *plausibility and coherence* requires that the strong correlation should be compatible with existing theory and knowledge. There is, for example, a very strong correlation between the

CORRELATION AND CAUSALITY

Charles Bonney, Department of Sociology, Eastern Michigan University

Having demonstrated a statistical relationship between a hypothesized "cause" and its presumed "effect," many people (sometimes including researchers who should know better) are only too eager to proclaim proof of causation. Let's take an example to see why "it ain't necessarily so."

Imagine you have conducted a study on college students and have found an inverse correlation between marijuana smoking (variable M) and grade-point average (GPA) (variable G)—that is, those who smoke tend to have lower GPAs than those who do not, and the more smoked, the lower the GPA. You might therefore claim that smoking marijuana lowers one's grades (in symbolic form, $M \rightarrow G$), giving as an explanation, perhaps, that marijuana adversely affects memory, which would naturally have detrimental consequences on grades.

However, if an inverse correlation is all the evidence you have, a second possibility exists. Getting poor grades is frustrating; frustration often leads to escapist behavior; getting stoned is a popular means of escape; ergo, low grades cause marijuana smoking ($G \rightarrow M$)! Unless you can establish which came first, smoking or low grades, this explanation is supported by the correlation just as plausibly as the first.

Let's introduce another variable into the picture: the existence and/or extent of emotional problems (variable E). It could certainly be plausibly argued that having emotional problems may lead to escapist behavior, including marijuana smoking. Likewise, it seems reasonable to suggest that emotional problems are likely to adversely affect grades. That correlation of marijuana smoking and low grades may exist for the same reason that runny noses and sore throats tend to go together—neither is the cause of the other, but rather, both are the consequences of some third variable $E_{\rightarrow G}^{\rightarrow M}$. Unless you can rule out such third variables, this explanation, too, is just as well supported by the data as is the first (or the second).

Then again, perhaps students smoke marijuana primarily because they have friends who smoke, and get low grades because they are simply not as bright or well prepared or industrious as their classmates, and the fact that it's the same students in each case in your sample is purely coincidental.

Unless your correlation is so strong and so consistent that mere coincidence becomes highly unlikely, this last possibility, while not supported by your data, is not precluded, either.

Incidentally, this particular example was selected for two reasons. First of all, every one of the above explanations for such an inverse correlation has appeared in a national magazine at one time or another. And second, every one of them is probably doomed to failure because it turns out that, among college students, most studies indicate a direct correlation; that is, it is those with higher GPAs who are more likely to be marijuana smokers! Thus, with tongue firmly in cheek, we may reanalyze this particular finding:

1. Marijuana relaxes a person, clearing away other stresses, thus allowing more effective study; hence, $M \rightarrow G$.

or

2. Marijuana is used as a reward for really hitting the books or doing well ("Wow, man! An 'A'! Let's go get high!"); hence, $G \rightarrow M$.

or

3. A high level of curiosity (E) is definitely an asset to learning and achieving high grades and may also lead one to investigate "taboo" substances; hence, $E_{\rightarrow G}^{\rightarrow M}$.

or

4. Again coincidence, but this time the samples just happened to contain a lot of brighter, more industrious students whose friends smoke marijuana!

The obvious conclusion is this: If *all* of these are possible explanations for a relationship between two variables, then no one of them should be too readily singled out. Establishing that two variables tend to occur together is a necessary condition for demonstrating a causal relationship, but it is not by itself a sufficient condition. It is a fact, for example, that human birthrates are higher in areas of Europe where there are lots of storks, but as to the meaning of that relationship ... !

number of storks in a geographical area and that area's human birthrate. But the notion that storks cause human births is not coherent with our knowledge about births. The opposite is true regarding the correlation between heavy smoking and lung cancer. Thus, not all strong correlations are equally plausible regarding causality. The notion that wearing cameras caused incidents of police brutality to drop to near zero is more coherent than the notion that bad publicity would cause a drop that large. Of course, we cannot entirely rule out the publicity explanation, but the strength and coherence of the camera explanation might be sufficient grounds for implementing the new policy elsewhere.

Consistency in Replication

Suppose the new camera policy is implemented in several cities at different time points. Maybe it is implemented in Cincinnati one month, Los Angeles 6 months later, New York City a year later, and in Dallas 18 months later. Suppose each time the incidents of police brutality drop significantly. Having met the criteria of time sequence and correlation so *consistently*, the notion that something else caused the improvement is no longer plausible, especially if none of the latter three cities experienced bad national publicity just before implementing the new policy.

Suppose you work as a therapist in a residential treatment center for children with behavior problems and you learn of a new intervention that you think might help Johnny, a boy you've been treating for some time with little success. The intervention has not received sufficient testing as to its effectiveness, but it makes sense to you, and besides, nothing else you have tried so far seems to have helped Johnny. So you try the new intervention, and *voila*, Johnny's misbehaviors virtually disappear. But wait! Maybe something else that coincided with the provision of the new intervention was the real cause of his improvement. Maybe he made a new friend who has a good influence on him. Maybe something else nice happened that you don't know about. So you aren't sure.

But several weeks later you implement the same intervention with another child, and see the same positive reaction. And then the same thing happens with a third child several weeks after that. With none of these children were you able to rule out

alternative variables as the real cause. But having met the criteria of time sequence with a strong correlation so *consistently*, the notion that something else caused the improvement is no longer plausible. Why, for example, should some third variable explain improvement at different points in time only when you implement the new intervention? That makes no sense, whereas the new intervention is coherent with your knowledge of childhood behavior problems. Therefore, although you were unable to rule out alternative causal variables, the strength, coherence, and consistency of your observations support your causal inference about the effectiveness of the new intervention and the decision to keep using it until evidence emerges to override your inference.

You can examine Hill's 1965 essay to see six additional criteria of causation that he proposed, but we think the three just mentioned are the most relevant to your current studies and future career. The three we have mentioned are particularly relevant to our discussions of time series designs (in Chapter 12) and single-case evaluation designs (in Chapter 13). The three criteria most relevant to experimental deigns—the main focus of this chapter—are the ones mentioned earlier: time sequence, correlation, and ruling out plausible alternative explanations. The latter of these three criteria—ruling out alternative explanations—pertains to the *internal validity* of a study, which we'll examine next.

EP 4, 9

» INTERNAL VALIDITY

When we consider the extent to which a research study permits causal inferences to be made about relationships between variables, we again encounter the term *validity*. You may recall that when we were discussing measurement validity in Chapter 9, we referred to validity as the extent to which a measure really measures what it intends to measure. When discussing causal inference, however, the term is used differently. Two forms of validity that are important when considering causality are *internal validity* and *external validity*.

Internal validity refers to the confidence we have that the results of a study accurately depict whether one variable is or is not a cause of another.

To the extent that the preceding criteria for inferring causality are met, a study has internal validity. Conversely, to the extent that we have not met these criteria, we are limited in our grounds for concluding that the independent variable does or does not play a causal role in explaining the dependent variable. *External validity* refers to the extent to which we can generalize the findings of a study to settings and populations beyond the study conditions. We will examine external validity later in this chapter after we examine internal validity in some depth. Let's begin that examination by discussing various threats to internal validity.

A threat to internal validity is present whenever anything other than the independent variable can affect the dependent variable. When evaluating the effectiveness of programs or practice, for example, the problem of internal invalidity refers to the possibility that investigators might erroneously conclude that differences in outcome were caused by the evaluated intervention when, in fact, something else really caused the differences. Campbell and Stanley (1963), Cook and Campbell (1979), and Shadish, Cook, and Campbell (2002) have identified various threats to internal validity. Here are seven prominent ones:

1. *History.* During the course of the research, extraneous events may occur that will confound the results. The term *history* is tricky. The extraneous events need not be major news events that one would read about in a history book but simply extraneous events that coincide in time with the manipulation of the independent variable. For example, suppose a study evaluates the effectiveness of social services in improving resident morale in a nursing home merely by measuring the morale of a group of residents before and after they receive social services. Perhaps some extraneous improvement in the nursing home environment—an improvement independent of the social services—was introduced between the before-and-after measures. That possibility threatens the internal validity of the research because the extraneous improvement, rather than the independent variable (social services), might cause the hypothesized improvement in the dependent variable (morale).

2. *Maturation or the passage of time.* People continuously grow and change, whether they are a part of a research study or not, and those changes affect

the results of the research. In the above nursing home illustration, for example, it would be silly to infer that the greater physical frailty of residents several years after receiving social services was caused by the social services. Maturation, through the aging process, would represent a severe threat to the internal validity of such a conclusion. But this threat to internal validity does not require that basic developmental changes occur; it can also refer simply to the effects of the passage of time. Suppose, for example, that a study to evaluate the effectiveness of a crisis-counseling program for victims of rape merely assessed the mood state or social functioning of the victims before and after treatment. We might expect the rape victims' emotional moods or social functioning levels to be at their worst in the immediate aftermath of the trauma. With or without crisis counseling at that point, we might expect the mere passage of time to alleviate some portion of the terrible impact of the trauma, even if we assume that the long-term effects will still be devastating. Likewise, consider bereavement counseling: It would be silly also to conclude that, just because the functioning level or mood of clients whose loved one died immediately before counseling was somewhat better after counseling, the bereavement counseling must have caused the improvement.

3. *Testing.* Often the process of testing by itself will enhance performance on a test without any corresponding improvement in the real construct that the test attempts to measure. Suppose we want to see whether a workshop helps social workers perform better on their state licensure exam. We might construct a test that we think will measure the same sorts of things measured on the licensure exam and then administer that test to social workers before and after they take our workshop. If their scores on the exam improve, then we might wish to attribute the improvement to the effects of our workshop. But suppose the social workers, after taking the first test, looked up answers to test items before our workshop began and remembered those answers the next time they took the same test. They would then score higher on the posttest without even attending our workshop, and we could not claim therefore that taking our workshop caused their scores to improve.

4. *Instrumentation changes.* If we use different measures of the dependent variable at posttest

than we did at pretest, how can we be sure that they are comparable to each other? Suppose that in evaluating the workshop to help social workers perform better on their state licensure exam, we do not want workshop participants to take the same test twice (to avoid testing effects). We might therefore construct two versions of the outcome test—one for the pretest and one for the posttest—that we think are equivalent. Although we would like to conclude that our workshop caused any improvement in scores, it is conceivable that the real reason may have been that, despite our best efforts, the posttest version was an easier exam than the pretest version. And if their scores worsened, rather than indicating that our workshop made them less well prepared for the exam, perhaps the posttest version was more difficult.

Analogous possibilities can occur when the measurement instruments involve ratings made by researchers or practitioners based on interviews with participants or observations of their behavior. Perhaps the researchers or practitioners who provided the posttest ratings were not the same ones who provided the pretest ratings. Perhaps one set of raters had different standards or abilities than the other set. Even if the same raters are used at both pretest and posttest, their standards or their abilities may have changed over the course of the study. Perhaps their skill in observing and recording behaviors improved as they gained more experience in doing so over the course of the study, enabling them to observe and record more behaviors at posttest than at pretest.

A more subtle type of change in instrumentation can occur in experimental studies of children. If a long time passes from pretest to posttest, the child may have outgrown some of the pretest items. For example, if a scale devised to measure the self-esteem of children aged 6 to 12 is administered to children aged 12 at pretest and then, 3 years later, aged 15, the scale items may not have the same meaning to the participants as teenagers as they did to them as 12-year-olds.

5. *Statistical regression.* Sometimes it's appropriate to evaluate the effectiveness of services for clients who were referred because of their extreme scores on the dependent variable. Suppose, for example, that a new social work intervention to alleviate depression among the elderly is being pilot-tested in a nursing home among residents whose scores

on a depression inventory indicate the most severe levels of depression. From a clinical standpoint, it would be quite appropriate to provide the service to the residents who appear most in need of the service. But consider from a methodological standpoint what is likely to happen to the depression scores of the referred residents even without intervention. In considering this, we should be aware that, with repeated testing on almost any assessment inventory, an individual's scores on the inventory are likely to fluctuate somewhat from one administration to the next—not because the individual really changed but because of the random testing factors that prevent instruments from having perfect reliability. For example, some residents who were referred because they had the poorest pretest scores may have had atypically bad days at pretest and may score better on the inventory on an average day. Perhaps they didn't sleep well the night before the pretest, perhaps a chronic illness flared up that day, or perhaps a close friend or relative passed away that week.

When we provide services to only those people with the most extremely problematic pretest scores, the odds are that the proportion of service recipients with atypically bad pretest scores will be higher than the proportion of nonrecipients with atypically bad pretest scores. Conversely, those who were not referred because their pretest scores were better probably include some whose pretest scores were atypically high (i.e., people who were having an unusually good day at pretest). Consequently, even without any intervention, the group of service recipients is more likely to show some improvement in its average depression score over time than is the group that was not referred. There is a danger, then, that changes occurring because subjects started out in extreme positions will be attributed erroneously to the effects of the independent variable.

Statistical regression is a difficult concept to grasp. It might aid your understanding of this term to imagine or actually carry out the following amusing experiment, which we have adapted from Posavac and Carey (1985). Grab a bunch of coins—15 to 20 will suffice. Flip each coin six times and record the number of heads and tails you get for each coin. That number will be the pretest score for each coin. Now, refer each coin that had no more than two heads on the pretest to a social work intervention that combines task-centered and behavioral practice methods. Tell each referred coin (yes, go ahead and speak to it—but first make sure you are truly alone) that tails is an unacceptable behavior and therefore that its task is to try to come up heads more often. After you give each its task, flip it six more times, praising it every time it comes up heads. If it comes up tails, say nothing because you don't want to reward undesirable behavior.

Record, as a posttest, the number of heads and tails each gets. Compare the total number of posttest heads with the total number of pretest heads for the referred coins. The odds are that the posttest is higher. Now flip the nonreferred coins six times and record their posttest scores but say nothing at all to them. We do not want them to receive the intervention; that way we can compare the pretest–posttest change of the coins that received the intervention to what happened among those coins that did not receive the intervention. The odds are that the untreated coins did not show nearly as much of an increase in the number of heads as did the treated coins.

This experiment works almost every time. If you got results other than those described here, odds are that if you replicated the experiment, you would get such results the next time. What do these results mean? Is task-centered and behavioral casework an effective intervention with coins? According to the scientific method, our minds should be open to this possibility—but we doubt it. Rather, we believe that these results illustrate that if we introduce the independent variable only to those referred on the basis of extreme scores, we can expect some improvement in the group solely because those scores will statistically regress to (meaning they will move toward) their true score. In this case, the coins tend to regress to their true score of three (50%) heads and three (50%) tails. When the assessment is done on people, we can imagine their true score as being the mean score they would get if tested many times on many different days.

Of course, human behavior is more complex than that of coins. But this illustration represents a common problem in the evaluation of human services. Because we are most likely to begin interventions for human problems that are inherently variable when those problems are at their most severe levels, we can expect some amelioration of the problem to occur solely because of the natural peaks and valleys in the problem and not necessarily because of the interventions.

6. *Selection biases.* Comparisons don't have any meaning unless the groups being compared are really *comparable*. Suppose we sought to evaluate the effectiveness of an intervention to promote positive parenting skills by comparing the level of improvement in parenting skills of parents who voluntarily agreed to participate in the intervention program with the level of improvement of parents who refused to participate. We would not be able to attribute the greater improvement among program participants to the effects of the intervention—at least not with a great deal of confidence about the internal validity of our conclusion—because other differences between the two groups might explain away the difference in improvement. For example, the participants may have been more motivated than program refusers to improve and thus may have been trying harder, reading more, and doing any number of things unrelated to the intervention that may really explain why they showed greater improvement. Selection biases are a common threat to the internal validity of social service evaluations because groups of service recipients and nonrecipients are often compared on outcome variables in the absence of prior efforts to see that the groups being compared were initially truly equivalent. Perhaps this most typically occurs when individuals who choose to use services are compared with individuals who were not referred to those services or who chose not to utilize them.

7. *Ambiguity about the direction of causal influence.* As we discussed earlier in this chapter, there is a possibility of ambiguity concerning the time order of the independent and dependent variables. Whenever this occurs, the research conclusion that the independent variable caused the changes in the dependent variable can be challenged with the explanation that the "dependent" variable actually caused changes in the "independent" variable.

Suppose, for example, a study finds that clients who completed a substance abuse treatment program are less likely to be abusing substances than those who dropped out of the program. There would be ambiguity as to whether the program influenced participants not

EP 4, 9

to abuse substances or whether the abstinence from substance abuse helped people complete the program.

» PREEXPERIMENTAL PILOT STUDIES

Not all evaluations of social work interventions strive to produce conclusive, causal inferences. Some have an exploratory or descriptive purpose and thus can have considerable value despite having a low degree of internal validity. Thus, when we say that a particular design has low internal validity, we are not saying that you should never use that design or that studies that do so never have value.

Suppose, for example, that your agency has initiated a new, innovative intervention for a small target group about which little is known. It might be quite useful to find out whether clients' posttest scores are better (or perhaps worse) than their pretest scores. If the posttest scores are much better, then it is conceivable that the intervention is the cause of the improvement. However, it would be inappropriate to make a conclusive causal inference to that effect because you haven't controlled for history, passage of time, and various other threats to internal validity. Nevertheless, you have shown a correlation between time (pre- versus posttest) and scores, and you have established time order in that the improved scores came after the intervention. Such results, therefore, would provide a basis for supporting the plausibility that the intervention is effective and for testing its effectiveness further with a stronger (more internally valid) design. Moreover, if you seek funding for a more ambitious study, your credibility to potential funding sources will be enhanced if you can include in your proposal for funding evidence that you were able to successfully carry out a pilot study and that its results were promising.

Sometimes, however, investigators report preexperimental studies as if they were valid tests of the effectiveness of an intervention. Although they usually acknowledge the limitations of their preexperimental designs, they sometimes draw conclusions that suggest to the unwary reader that the evaluated intervention is effective and should be considered evidence based. This is unfortunate, because—despite their value as pilot studies—preexperimental designs rank low on the evidence-based practice research hierarchy because of their negligible degree of internal validity. Let's now examine some common preexperimental designs and consider why they have low internal validity.

One-Shot Case Study

One particularly weak preexperimental design, the one-shot case study, doesn't even establish correlation. The shorthand notation for this design is the following:

$$X \quad O$$

The X in this notation represents the introduction of a stimulus, such as an intervention. The O represents observation, which yields the measurement of the dependent variable. In this design, a single group of research participants is measured on a dependent variable after the introduction of an intervention (or some other stimulus) without comparing the obtained results to anything else.

For instance, a service might be delivered and then the service recipients' social functioning measured. This design offers no way for us to ascertain whether the observed level of social functioning is any higher (or lower) than it was to begin with or any higher (or lower) than it is among comparable individuals who received no service. Thus, this design—in addition to failing to assess correlation—fails to control for any of the threats to internal validity.

One-Group Pretest–Posttest Design

A preexperimental design that establishes both correlation and time order—and which therefore has more value as a pilot study—is the one-group pretest–posttest design. This design assesses the dependent variable before and after the stimulus (intervention) is introduced. Thus, in the evaluation of the effectiveness of social services, the design would assess the outcome variable before and after services are delivered. The shorthand notation for this design is the following:

$$O_1 \quad X \quad O_2$$

The subscripts 1 and 2 in this notation refer to the sequential order of the observations; thus, O_1 is the pretest before the intervention, and O_2 is the posttest after the intervention.

Despite its value as a pilot study, this design does not account for factors other than the independent variable that might have caused the change between pretest and posttest results—factors usually associated with the following threats to internal validity: history, maturation, testing, and statistical regression.

Suppose, for example, that we assess the attitudes of social work students about social action strategies of community organization—strategies that emphasize tactics of confrontation and conflict (protests, boycotts, and so on)—before and at the end of their social work education. Suppose we find that over this time, they became less committed to confrontational social action strategies and more in favor of consensual community development approaches.

Would such a finding permit us to infer that the change in their attitude was *caused* by their social work education? No, it would not. Other factors could have been operating during the same period and caused the change. For instance, perhaps the students matured and became more tolerant of slower, more incremental strategies for change (the threat to internal validity posed by *maturation* or the passage of time). Or perhaps certain events extraneous to their social work education transpired during that period and accounted for their change (the threat of *history*). For example, perhaps a series of protest demonstrations seemed to backfire and contribute to the election of a presidential candidate they abhorred, and their perception of the negative effects of these demonstrations made them more skeptical of social action strategies.

In another example of the one-group pretest–posttest design, suppose we assess whether a three-month cognitive-behavioral intervention with abusive parents results in higher scores on a paper-and-pencil test of parenting skills and cognitions about childhood behaviors. In addition to wondering whether history and maturation might account for the improvement in scores, we would wonder about statistical regression. Perhaps the parents were referred for treatment at a time when their parental functioning and attitudes about their children were at their worst. Even if the parenting skills and cognitions of these parents were quite unacceptable when they were at their best, improvement from pretest to posttest might simply reflect the fact that they were referred for treatment when they were at their worst and that their scores therefore couldn't help

but increase somewhat because of regression toward their true average value before intervention.

Posttest-Only Design with Nonequivalent Groups (Static-Group Comparison Design)

A third preexperimental design is the posttest-only design with nonequivalent groups. The shorthand notation for this design, which has also been termed the static-group comparison design, is the following:

$$X \quad O$$
$$O$$

This design assesses the dependent variable after the stimulus (intervention) is introduced for one group while also assessing the dependent variable for a second group that may not be comparable to the first group and that was not exposed to the independent variable. In the evaluation of the effectiveness of social services, this design would entail assessing clients on an outcome variable only after (not before) they receive the service being evaluated and comparing their performance with a group of clients who did not receive the service and who plausibly may be unlike the treated clients in some meaningful way.

Let's return, for example, to the preceding hypothetical illustration about evaluating the effectiveness of a cognitive-behavioral intervention with abusive parents. Using the posttest-only design with nonequivalent groups rather than comparing the pretest and posttest scores of parents who received the intervention, we might compare their posttest scores to the scores of abusive parents who were not referred or who declined the intervention. We would hope to show that the treated parents scored better than the untreated parents because this would indicate a desired correlation between the independent variable (treatment status) and the dependent variable (test score). But this correlation would not permit us to infer that the difference between the two groups was caused by the intervention. The most important reason for this is the design's failure to control for the threat of *selection biases*. Without pretests, we have no way of knowing whether the scores of the two groups would have differed as much to begin with—that is, before the treated parents began treatment. Moreover, these two groups may not really have been equivalent in certain important respects. The parents who were referred or who chose to participate may have been more motivated to improve or may have had more supportive resources than those who were not referred or who refused treatment.

It is not at all uncommon to encounter program providers who, after their program has been implemented, belatedly realize that it might be useful to get evaluative data on its effectiveness and are therefore attracted to the posttest-only design with nonequivalent groups. In light of the expedience of this type of design and in anticipation of the practical administrative benefits to be derived from positive outcome findings, the providers may not want to hear about selection biases and low internal validity. But we nevertheless hope that you will remember the importance of these issues and tactfully discuss them with others when the situation calls for it.

Figure 11-1 graphically illustrates the three preexperimental research designs just discussed. See if you can visualize where the potentially confounding and misleading factors could intrude into each design.

As we noted earlier, some studies using preexperimental designs can be valuable despite their extremely limited degree of internal validity. What tends to make them valuable is their use as pilot studies purely for one or more of the following purposes: (a) to generate tentative exploratory or descriptive information regarding a new intervention about which little is known, (b) to learn whether it is feasible to provide the new intervention as intended, (c) to identify obstacles in carrying out methodological aspects of a more internally valid design that is planned for the future, and (d) to see if the hypothesis for a more rigorous study remains plausible based on the pilot study results. The box "A Scientific Study and a Pseudoscientific Study Using Preexperimental Designs" provides two examples of published studies that used preexperimental designs. The first illustrates a valuable pilot study that meets all of the foregoing four criteria. The second meets none of them. Now that we've discussed both the utility and the limitations of preexperimental designs, let's examine some designs that have higher levels of internal validity.

EP 4, 9

» EXPERIMENTAL DESIGNS

Experimental designs attempt to provide maximum control for threats to internal validity by first randomly assigning research participants to

FIGURE 11.1 Three Preexperimental Research Designs

1. THE ONE-SHOT CASE STUDY

Administer the experimental stimulus to a single group and measure the dependent variable in that group afterward. Make an intuitive judgment as to whether the posttest result is "high" or "low."

2. THE ONE-GROUP PRETEST–POSTTEST DESIGN

Measure the dependent variable in a single group, administer the experimental stimulus, and then remeasure the dependent variable. Compare pretest and posttest results.

3. THE STATIC-GROUP COMPARISON

Administer the experimental stimulus to one group (the experimental group), then measure the dependent variable in both the experimental group and a comparison group.

experimental and *control groups*. Next, they introduce one category of the independent variable (such as a new program or intervention method) to the experimental group while withholding it from the control group. Then they compare the extent to which the experimental and control groups differ on the dependent variable. The latter comparison, though coming at the end of the sequence, usually involves assessing the experimental and control groups before and after introducing the independent variable.

For example, suppose we wanted to assess the effectiveness of an intervention used by gerontological social workers in nursing home facilities, an intervention that engages clients in a review of their life history in order to alleviate depression and improve morale. Rather than just compare residents who requested the intervention with those who did not—which would be vulnerable to a selection bias because we could not assume that the two groups were equivalent to begin with—our experimental approach would use a random assignment procedure (such as coin tosses). Thus, each resident who agrees to participate and for whom the intervention is deemed appropriate would be randomly assigned to either an experimental group (which would receive the intervention) or a control group (which would not receive it). Observations on one or more indicators of depression and morale (the dependent variables) would be taken before and after the intervention is delivered. To the extent that the experimental group's mood improves more than that of the control group, the findings would support the hypothesis that the intervention causes the improvement.

The preceding example illustrates the *classic experimental design*, also called the pretest–posttest control group design. This design is diagrammed in Figure 11-2. The shorthand notation for this design is the following:

$$R \quad O_1 \quad X \quad O_2$$
$$R \quad O_1 \qquad O_2$$

The R in this design stands for random assignment of research participants to either the experimental group or the control group. O_1 represents pretests, and O_2 represents posttests. The X represents the tested intervention.

Notice how this design controls for many threats to internal validity. If the improvement in mood were caused by history or maturation, then there would be no reason the experimental group should improve any more than the control group. Likewise, because the residents were assigned on a randomized basis, there is no reason to suppose that the experimental group was any more likely to statistically regress to less extreme scores than was the control group. Random assignment also removes any reason for supposing that the two groups were different initially with respect to the dependent variable or to other relevant factors, such as motivation or psychosocial functioning. The box "A Social

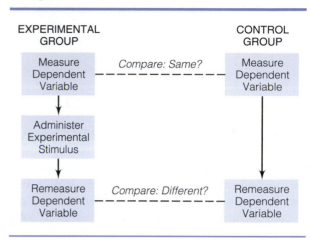

FIGURE 11.2 Diagram of Basic Experimental Design

Work Experiment Evaluating the Effectiveness of a Program to Treat Children at Risk of Serious Conduct Problems" summarizes a published social work experiment study that used a pretest–posttest control group design.

Notice also, however, that the pretest–posttest control group design does not control for the possible effects of testing and retesting. If we think that taking a pretest might have an impact on treatment effects or if we think that it might bias their posttest responses, then we might opt for an experimental design called the posttest-only control group design. Another, more common reason for choosing the posttest-only control group design is that pretesting may not be possible or practical, such as in the evaluation of the effectiveness programs to prevent incidents of child abuse. The shorthand notation for this design is the following:

$$R \quad X \quad O$$
$$R \qquad O$$

This design assumes that the process of random assignment removes any significant initial differences between experimental and control groups. This assumption of initial group equivalence permits the inference that any differences between the two groups at posttest reflect the causal impact of the independent variable. The box "A Social Work Experiment Evaluating Motivational Interviewing" summarizes a published study that used a posttest-only control group experimental design.

If we would like to know the amount of pretest–posttest change but are worried about testing effects, then we could use a fancy design called the Solomon four-group design. The shorthand notation for this design is the following:

$$R \quad O_1 \quad X \quad O_2$$
$$R \quad O_1 \quad \quad O_2$$
$$R \quad \quad X \quad O_2$$
$$R \quad \quad \quad O_2$$

This design, which is highly regarded by research methodologists but rarely used in social work studies, combines the classical experimental design with the posttest-only control group design. It does this simply by randomly assigning research participants to four groups instead of two. Two of the groups are control groups, and two are experimental groups. One control group and one experimental group are pretested and posttested. The other experimental group and control group are posttested only. If special effects are caused by pretesting, then they can be discerned by comparing the two experimental group results with each other and the two control group results with each other.

Sometimes experiments are used to compare the effectiveness of two alternative treatments. Pretests are recommended in such experiments so that the comparative amounts of change produced by each treatment can be assessed. This design is called the alternative treatment design with pretest (Shadish, Cook, & Campbell, 2002). The shorthand notation for this design is the following:

$$R \quad O_1 \quad X_A \quad O_2$$
$$R \quad O_1 \quad X_B \quad O_2$$
$$R \quad O_1 \quad \quad O_2$$

The first row represents the participants randomly assigned to treatment A. The second row represents the participants randomly assigned to treatment B. The third row represents the participants randomly assigned to a control group. To show that treatment A is more effective than treatment B, the first row would need to show more improvement from O_1 to O_2 than both of the other rows. If the first two rows both show approximately the same amounts of improvement and both amounts are more than in the third row, that would indicate that both treatments are approximately equally effective. But if the third row shows the same degree of improvement as in the first two rows, then neither treatment would appear to be effective.

Instead, we would attribute the improvement in all three rows to an alternative explanation, such as history or the passage of time.

Some experiments use the first two rows of this design but not the third row. In other words, they compare the two treatments to each other but not to a control group. Such experiments can have conclusive, valid findings if one group improves significantly more than the other. But suppose that both have roughly the same amount of improvement. The temptation would be to call them equally effective. However, with no control group, we cannot rule out threats to internal validity, such as history or the passage of time, as alternative explanations of the improvement in both groups. An illustrative study is summarized in the box "A Social Work Experiment Comparing the Effectiveness of Two Approaches to Court-Mandated Spouse Abuse Treatment."

A similar type of design can be used to see not only whether an intervention is effective but also which components of the intervention may or may not be necessary to achieve its effects. Experiments using this design are called dismantling studies. The shorthand notation for this design is the following:

$$R \quad O_1 \quad X_{AB} \quad O_2$$
$$R \quad O_1 \quad X_A \quad O_2$$
$$R \quad O_1 \quad X_B \quad O_2$$
$$R \quad O_1 \quad \quad O_2$$

The first row represents the participants randomly assigned to a treatment that contains components A and B. The second row represents the participants randomly assigned to receive component A only. The third row represents the participants randomly assigned to receive component B only. The fourth row represents the participants randomly assigned to a control group. If the first row shows more improvement from O_1 to O_2 than all of the other rows, then that would indicate that the treatment is effective and that both components (A and B) are needed. If either of the next two rows shows as much improvement as the first row shows, then that would indicate that the component signified in that row is all that is needed to achieve the effects shown in the first row and that the other component may not be needed.

Dismantling studies have received considerable attention in recent debates about the comparative effectiveness of two evidence-based interventions

A SCIENTIFIC STUDY AND A PSEUDOSCIENTIFIC STUDY USING PREEXPERIMENTAL DESIGNS

A Scientific Pilot Study

Nancy Grote and her social work faculty colleagues (Grote, Bledsoe, Swartz, & Frank, 2004) wanted to find out if a briefer and more culturally relevant form of interpersonal psychotherapy (IPT)—an evidence-based treatment for depression—would be feasible to provide to depressed pregnant patients on low incomes (most of whom were African American) in an obstetric and gynecological clinic. They postulated that modifying the IPT treatment protocol would help overcome barriers to service use among low-income and minority patients, such as cost, transportation, child care, cultural insensitivity, and so on. Twelve pregnant depressed women were recruited to be in the study, and nine of them completed the eight sessions of treatment. Those nine women displayed significant improvement at post treatment and 6 months later on measures of depression, anxiety, and social functioning. The authors concluded that their preliminary results in treating depression among such patients is sufficiently supported to warrant testing in a subsequent, more internally valid experiment.

One admirable feature of their published study was the way the authors discussed its limitations, noting that their sample was small and perhaps atypical and that they lacked experimental design components that would have controlled for various threats to internal validity. Also admirable was the way they did not go beyond their exploratory pilot study aims in interpreting their outcome data. Unlike some authors who report studies using preexperimental designs, Grote and her colleagues avoided making conclusive causal inferences about the effectiveness of their intervention.

A Pseudoscientific Study

Not all authors of pilot studies interpret their results as cautiously as did Grote and her colleagues. Nor do all reports of studies using preexperimental designs claim to have a pilot study purpose. Authors of such reports often interpret their results inappropriately, making conclusive causal inferences that are unwarranted in light of their design's weak internal validity. Such was the case in an evaluation of the effectiveness of Thought Field Therapy (TFT) by Johnson, Shala, Sedjejaj, Odell, and Dabishevci

(2001). As you read this summary, we suggest that you recall our portrayal of pseudoscience back in Chapter 1. The egregious claims of extravagant treatment success in this one-shot case study have led critics to call it pseudoscience.

TFT is an extremely controversial therapy that uses "mechanical stimulation of points on the body's energy meridians, plus bilateral optical cortical stimulation" in an effort to relieve psychological trauma symptoms (Johnson et al., 2001, p. 1239). In the aftermath of massacre and torture by invading Serbian forces in 1999, TFT was provided to 105 traumatized ethnic Albanian survivors in Kosovo. There was no pretest. Assessment was based on whether recipients of TFT said their trauma was or was not gone after receiving TFT. The report does not specify whether they said this to the TFT therapist or someone else, but in either case the serious potential for social desirability bias in the self-reporting to foreigners who volunteered to help them is compounded by the utter lack of any attempts to control for threats to internal validity. But rather than discuss their results cautiously in terms of assessing the feasibility of their treatment or design protocol or generating hypotheses for future research, the authors claimed that the treatment was "clearly effective" for all but 2 of the 105 patients who received it and all but 2 of their 249 separate traumas. We are not aware of any well-controlled, internally valid evaluation of a psychosocial intervention—including those interventions widely accepted as having the best empirical support and being the most effective—that has had results anywhere near that extreme.

The journal that published this study inserted a footnote on the article's first page. The footnote says that the article was not peer reviewed. Instead, the journal editor agreed to publish it after the discoverer of TFT complained that the journal's review process was biased against TFT. But the editor agreed to publish it only if it was followed by another article that critically appraised the TFT study. The criticism in that accompanying article was scathing.

Source for Scientific Pilot Study: Grote, N. K., Bledsoe, S. E., Swartz, H. A. and Frank, E. 2004. "Feasibility of Providing Culturally-Relevant, Brief Interpersonal Psychotherapy for Antenatal Depression in an Obstetrics Clinic: A Pilot Study." *Research on Social Work Practice, 14*(6), 397–407.

A SOCIAL WORK EXPERIMENT EVALUATING THE EFFECTIVENESS OF A PROGRAM TO TREAT CHILDREN AT RISK OF SERIOUS CONDUCT PROBLEMS

Fraser, Day, Galinsky, Hodges, and Smokowski (2004) evaluated the effectiveness of a multicomponent intervention to treat children referred by teachers for aggressive antisocial behavior and rejection by their prosocial peers. The children were assigned randomly to an experimental group or a wait-list control group. The experimental group children participated in a social skills training program in after-school or school settings, and their parents or caretakers participated in an in-home family intervention program designed to increase parenting skills. The control group children "continued to participate in any routine services they may have [already] been receiving." At the conclusion of the study, the children and parents in the control condition were offered the same intervention package as the experimental group participants received. Outcome was measured by having teachers complete a form at pretest and posttest on which they rated each child's behaviors in classroom and play environments. The results showed that the experimental group children had significantly more improvement than control group children on ratings of prosocial behavior, ability to regulate emotions, and increased social contact with peers.

Source: Fraser, M., Day, S. H., Galinsky, M. J., Hodges, V. G., and Smokowski, P. R. 2004. "Conduct Problems and Peer Rejection in Childhood: A Randomized Trial of the Making Choices and Strong Families Programs," *Research on Social Work Practice, 14*(5), 313–324.

A SOCIAL WORK EXPERIMENT EVALUATING MOTIVATIONAL INTERVIEWING

Schilling, El-Bassel, Finch, Roman, and Hanson (2002) evaluated a motivational interviewing intervention designed to encourage detoxified alcohol users to participate in self-help groups after alcohol detoxification. Ninety-six clients were randomly assigned to either a three-session motivational interviewing condition or a standard care condition. Motivational interviewing is directive but uses client-centered relationship skills (such as being empathic, warm, and genuine) in providing information and feedback to increase client awareness of the problem and consideration of change by helping clients see the discrepancy between their problematic behavior and their broader goals. Outcome was assessed 2 months after discharge from inpatient care via self-reported attendance at self-help meetings and drinking behavior. Although motivational interviewing currently is widely accepted as an evidence-based intervention, this study's results were portrayed by its authors as somewhat disappointing. No differences in drinking behavior were found between the experimental and control groups; however, motivational interviewing recipients averaged twice as many days participating in 12-step self-help groups.

Source: Schilling, R. F., El-bassel, N., Finch, J. B., Roman, R. J., and Hanson, M. 2002. "Motivational Interviewing to Encourage Self-Help Participation Following Alcohol Detoxification," *Research on Social Work Practice, 12*(6), 711–730.

for *posttraumatic stress disorder*. One intervention is *trauma-focused cognitive behavioral therapy* (TFCBT) and the other is *eye movement desensitization and reprocessing* (EMDR). Briefly put, EMDR combines various cognitive-behavioral intervention techniques with a technique involving the bilateral stimulation of rapid eye movements. Many experiments using the pretest–posttest control group design have found EMDR to be effective. However, some dismantling studies found that the same effects could be achieved using the cognitive-behavioral components of EMDR without the eye movements. Some reviewers of the dismantling studies have argued that those dismantling results indicate that EMDR is nothing more than TFCBT with an unnecessary bilateral stimulation gimmick. Leaders in the EMDR field have fiercely criticized the dismantling studies and cited other dismantling studies with results that supported the necessity of the bilateral stimulation component. Perhaps vested interests and ego involvement influence those on both sides of this debate (Rubin, 2002, 2010). The box "A Social Work Experiment Evaluating Cognitive-Behavioral Interventions with Parents at Risk of Child Abuse" illustrates the use of a dismantling study in social work.

Randomization

It should be clear at this point that the cardinal rule of experimental design is that the experimental and control groups must be comparable. Ideally, the control group represents what the experimental group would have been like had it not been exposed to the intervention or other experimental stimulus being evaluated. There is no way to guarantee that the experimental and control groups will be equivalent in all relevant respects. There is no way to guarantee that they will share exactly the same history and maturational processes or will not have relevant differences before the evaluated intervention is introduced. But there *is* a way to avoid biases in the assignment of clients to groups and to guarantee a high mathematical likelihood that their initial, pretreatment group differences will be insignificant: through random assignment to experimental and control groups, a process also known as *randomization*.

Randomization, or random assignment, is not the same as random sampling. The research participants to be randomly assigned are rarely randomly selected from a population. Instead, they are individuals who voluntarily agreed to participate in the experiment, a fact that limits the external validity of the experiment. Unlike random sampling, which pertains to generalizability, randomization is a device for increasing internal validity. It does not seek to ensure that the research participants are representative of a population; instead, it seeks to reduce the risks that experimental group participants are not representative of control group participants.

The principal technique of randomization simply entails using procedures based on probability theory to assign research participants to experimental and control groups. Having recruited, by whatever means, the group of all participants, the researchers might flip a coin to determine to which group each participant is assigned. Alternatively, they may number all of the participants serially and assign them by selecting numbers from a random numbers table (such as the one in Appendix B), or they may put the odd-numbered participants in one group and the even-numbered ones in the other.

In randomization, research participants who make up the study population are randomly divided into two samples. As we will see in Chapter 15, on sampling, if the number of research participants involved is large enough, it is reasonable to expect that the various characteristics of the participants will be distributed in an approximately even manner between the two groups, thus making the two groups comparable.

Matching

Although randomization is the best way to avoid bias in assigning research participants to groups and increasing the likelihood that the two groups will be comparable, it does not guarantee full comparability. One way to further improve the chances of obtaining comparable groups is to combine randomization with matching, in which pairs of participants are matched on the basis of their similarities on one or more variables and one member of the pair is then randomly assigned to the experimental group and the other to the control group. Matching can also be done without randomization, as we will see in Chapter 12 when we discuss quasi experiments, but we have a true experiment only when matching is combined with randomization. Matching without randomization does not control for all possible biases in who gets assigned to which group.

To illustrate matching with randomization, suppose that 12 of your research participants are young white men. You might assign 6 of those at random to the experimental group and the other 6 to the control group. If 14 research participants are middle-aged African American women, you might

A SOCIAL WORK EXPERIMENT COMPARING THE EFFECTIVENESS OF TWO APPROACHES TO COURT-MANDATED SPOUSE ABUSE TREATMENT

Brannen and Rubin (1996) conducted an experiment with intact couples desiring to stay in their current relationship who were referred by a court in San Antonio, Texas, for spouse abuse treatment. The couples were assigned to one of two approaches to group cognitive-behavioral therapy. In one approach, the couples participated together in the group; in the other approach, they participated apart in separate groups for each gender. Outcome was measured using standardized self-report scales that measured the couples' conflict resolution ability, the level of violence in the relationship, the level of communication and marital satisfaction within the relationship, and recidivism. Data were collected from both the victims and the perpetrators of the abuse. Significant pretest-to-posttest gains were found for both groups; however, there was no difference between the groups. Consequently, although the findings were consistent with the notion that both interventions are about equally effective, without a "no treatment" or "routine treatment" control group Brannen and Rubin could not rule out threats like history or the passage of time as possible causes of the improvement.

Source: Brannen, S. J. and Rubin, A. 1996. "Comparing the Effectiveness of Gender-Specific and Couples Groups in a Court-Mandated Spouse Abuse Treatment Program," *Research on Social Work Practice, 6*(4), 405–424.

A SOCIAL WORK EXPERIMENT EVALUATING COGNITIVE-BEHAVIORAL INTERVENTIONS WITH PARENTS AT RISK OF CHILD ABUSE

Whiteman, Fanshel, and Grundy (1987) tested the effectiveness of different aspects of a cognitive-behavioral intervention aimed at reducing parental anger in the face of perceived provocation by children in families in which child abuse had been committed or in families at risk for child abuse. Fifty-five clients were randomly assigned to four intervention groups and a control group that received no experimental intervention but instead continued to receive services from the referral agency. The first intervention group received cognitive-restructuring interventions that dealt with the parents' perceptions, expectations, appraisals, and stresses. The second intervention group was trained in relaxation procedures. The third intervention group worked on problem-solving skills. The fourth intervention group received a treatment package comprising the three interventional modalities delivered separately to the first three intervention groups.

The results revealed no significant differences among the experimental and control groups at pretest. At posttest, however, the treated (experimental group) participants had significantly greater reductions in anger than the untreated (control group) participants. The intervention group with the greatest reduction in anger was the one that received the composite package of interventions delivered separately to the other three intervention groups.

In light of their findings, Whiteman and associates recommended that social workers use the composite intervention package to attempt to reduce anger and promote positive child-rearing attitudes among abusive or potentially abusive parents. Their results also indicated the importance of the problem-solving skills component in reducing anger, the importance of the cognitive-restructuring component in improving child-rearing attitudes, and the relative unimportance of including the relaxation component in the intervention package.

Source: Whiteman, Martin, David Fanshel, and John F. Grundy. 1987. "Cognitive-Behavioral Interventions Aimed at Anger of Parents at Risk of Child Abuse," *Social Work, 32*(6), 469–474.

FIGURE 11.3   Quota Matrix Illustration

	MEN		WOMEN	
	BLACK	WHITE	BLACK	WHITE
UNDER 30 YEARS	8	12	10	16
30 TO 50 YEARS	18	30	14	28
OVER 50 YEARS	12	20	12	22

EXPERIMENTAL   CONTROL
GROUP   GROUP
6   6
7   7
etc.   etc.

randomly assign 7 to each group. The overall matching process could be most efficiently achieved through the creation of a *quota matrix* constructed of all the most relevant characteristics. (Figure 11-3 provides a simplified illustration of such a matrix.) Ideally, the quota matrix would be constructed to result in an even number of research participants in each cell of the matrix. Then, half of the research participants in each cell would randomly go into the experimental group and half into the control group.

Alternatively, you might recruit more research participants than are required by your experimental design. You might then examine many characteristics of the large initial group of research participants. Whenever you discover a pair of highly similar participants, you might assign one at random to the experimental group and the other to the control group. Potential participants who were unlike anyone else in the initial group might be left out of the experiment altogether.

Whatever method is used, the desired result is the same. The overall average description of the experimental group should be the same as that of the control group. For instance, they should have about the same average age, the same gender composition, the same racial composition, and so forth. As a general rule, the two groups should be comparable in terms of those variables that are likely to be related to the dependent variable under study. In a study of gerontological social work, for example, the two groups should be alike in terms of age, gender, ethnicity, and physical and mental health, among

other variables. In some cases, moreover, you may delay assigning research participants to experimental and control groups until you have initially measured the dependent variable. Thus, for instance, you might administer a questionnaire that measures participants' psychosocial functioning and then match the experimental and control groups to assure yourself that the two groups exhibited the same overall level of functioning before intervention.

Providing Services to Control Groups

You may recall reading in Chapter 5 that the withholding of services from people in need raises ethical concerns. It may also be unacceptable to agency administrators who fear bad publicity or the loss of revenues based on service delivery hours. We must therefore point out that when we discuss withholding the intervention being tested from the control group, we do not mean that people in the control group should be denied services. We simply mean that they should not receive the *experimental* intervention that is being tested during the period of the test.

When experiments are feasible to carry out in social work settings, control group participants are likely to receive the usual, routine services provided by an agency. Experimental group participants will receive the new, experimental intervention being tested, perhaps in addition to the usual, routine services. Thus, the experiment may determine whether services that include the new intervention are more effective than routine services rather than attempt to ascertain whether the new intervention is better than no service. Moreover, control group participants may be put at the top of a waiting list to receive the new intervention once the experiment is over. If the results of the experiment show that the tested intervention is effective or at least is not harmful, it can then be offered to control group participants. The researcher may also want to measure whether control group participants change in the desired direction after they receive the intervention. The findings of this measurement can buttress the main findings of the experiment.

However, as discussed in Chapter 5, even if you plan to conduct an experiment that is feasible and ethically justifiable, you'll probably need to obtain approval from an institutional review board before you are permitted to implement it. If your study is funded, the funding body probably will require   EP 1 that approval as a precondition to approving your grant proposal. Even if you don't apply for funding, you'll probably need to get approval for your study from a committee in the setting where you seek to conduct it.

» ADDITIONAL THREATS TO THE VALIDITY OF EXPERIMENTAL FINDINGS

So far, we have seen how the logic of experimental designs can control for most threats to internal validity. Additional threats to the validity of the conclusions we draw from experiments require methodological efforts that go beyond their design logic. Let's now look at each of these additional threats and the steps that can be taken to alleviate them.

Measurement Bias

No matter how well an experiment controls for other threats to internal validity, the credibility of its conclusions can be damaged severely if its measurement procedures appear to have been biased. Suppose, for example, that a clinician develops a new therapy for depression that promises to make her rich and famous and then evaluates her invention in an experiment by using her own subjective clinical judgment to rate improvement among the experimental and control group participants, knowing which group each participant is in. Her own ego involvement and vested interest in wanting the experimental group participants to show more improvement would make her study so vulnerable to measurement bias that her "findings" would have virtually no credibility. Although this example may seem extreme, serious measurement bias is not as rare in experimental evaluations as you might imagine. It is not difficult to find reports of otherwise well-designed experiments in which outcome measures were administered or completed by research assistants who knew the study hypothesis, were aware of the hopes that it would be confirmed, and knew which group each participant was in.

Whenever measurement of the dependent variable involves using research staff to supply ratings (through either direct observation or interviews), the individuals who supply the ratings should not know the experimental status of the participants they are rating. The same principle applies when the people supplying the ratings are practitioners who are not part of the research staff but who still might be biased toward a particular outcome. In other words, they should be "blind" as to whether any given rating refers to someone who has received the experimental stimulus (or service) or someone who has not.

The term *blind ratings* (or *blind raters*) means that the study has controlled for the potential—and perhaps unconscious—bias of raters toward perceiving results that would confirm the hypothesis. Likewise, whenever researchers fail to inform you that such ratings were blind, you should be skeptical about the study's validity. No matter how elegant the rest of a study's design might be, its conclusions are suspect if results favoring the experimental group were provided by raters who might have been biased.

The use of blind raters, unfortunately, is often not feasible in social work research studies. When we are unable to use them, we should look for alternative ways to avoid rater bias. For example, we might use validated self-report scales to measure the dependent variable rather than rely on raters who may be biased. But even

EP 4, 9

when such scales are used, those administering them can bias the outcome. For example, if participants ask questions about scale items that confuse them, biased testers might consciously or unconsciously respond in ways that predispose participants to answer scale items in ways that are consistent with the desired outcome. We have even heard of situations where biased testers—in providing posttest instructions—encouraged experimental group participants to answer "valid" scales in ways that would show how much they improved since the pretest. The term research reactivity refers to changes in outcome data that are caused by researchers or research procedures rather than the independent variable. Let's now look at the various ways in which research reactivity can threaten the validity of experimental findings.

Research Reactivity

Biasing comments by researchers during data collection is just one of many forms of research reactivity. Two related terms that are used to refer to that sort of reactivity are experimental demand characteristics and experimenter expectancies. Research participants learn what experimenters want them to say or do, and then they cooperate with those "demands" or expectations.

Demand characteristics and experimenter expectancies can appear in more subtle ways as well. Some therapists who treat traumatized clients, for example, will repeatedly ask the client at different points during therapy sessions to rate on a scale from 0 to 10 how much distress they are feeling during therapy when they call up a mental image of the traumatic event. Through the therapist's verbal communication as well as nonverbal communication (e.g., smiles or looks of concern), the client can learn that the therapist hopes the rating number will diminish over the course of therapy. Some studies evaluating trauma therapy administer the same 0–10 rating scale at pretest and posttest that the therapist administers throughout treatment. Even if the pretests and posttests are administered by research assistants who are unaware of clients' experimental group status, clients will have learned from the therapist that they are expected to report lower distress scores at posttest than at pretest. Worse yet, in some studies, it is the therapist him or herself who administers the same 0–10 scale at posttest that he or she has been using repeatedly as part of the therapy.

One way to alleviate the influence of experimenter expectancies and demand characteristics is to separate the measurement procedures from the treatment procedures. Another way is to use measurement procedures that are hard for practitioners or researchers to influence. Instead of using the above 0–10 scale at pretest and posttest, for example, a research assistant could administer physiological measures of distress (such as pulse rate) while the client thinks of the traumatic event. It would also help if the assistants administering pretest and posttest scales were blind as to the study's hypothesis or the experimental status of the participants to avoid giving cues about expected outcomes (Shadish, Cook, & Campbell, 2002).

Sometimes we can use raters or scale administrators who are not blind but do not seem likely to be biased. We may, for instance, ask teachers to rate the classroom conduct of children who receive two different forms of social work intervention. The teachers may know which intervention each student is receiving but not have much technical understanding of the interventions or any reason to favor one intervention over another.

A related option is to directly observe and quantify the actual behavior of participants in their natural setting rather than rely on their answers to self-report scales or on someone's ratings. It matters a great deal, however, whether that observation is conducted in an *obtrusive* or an *unobtrusive* manner. Obtrusive observation occurs when the participant is keenly aware of being observed and thus may be predisposed to behave in ways that meet experimenter expectancies. In contrast, unobtrusive observation means that the participant does not notice the observation.

Suppose an experiment is evaluating the effectiveness of a new form of therapy in reducing the frequency of antisocial behaviors among children in a residential treatment center. If the child's therapist or the researcher starts showing up with a pad and pencil to observe the goings-on in the child's classroom or cottage, he or she might stick out like a sore thumb and make the child keenly aware of being observed. That form of observation would be obtrusive, and the child might exhibit atypically good behavior during observation.

A more unobtrusive option would be to have teachers or cottage parents tabulate the number of antisocial behaviors of the child each day. Their observation would be less noticeable to the child because they are part of the natural setting and because being observed by a teacher or cottage parent is part of the daily routine and not obviously connected to the expectations of a research study.

Whenever we are conducting experimental research (or any other type of research) and we are unable to use blind raters, blind scale administrators, unobtrusive observation, or some other measurement alternative that we think is relatively free of bias, we should try to use more than one measurement alternative, relying on the principle of triangulation, as discussed in Chapter 9. If two or more measurement strategies, each vulnerable to different biases, produce the same results, then we can have more confidence in the validity of those results.

Another form of research reactivity can occur not only when the research procedures influence participants to tell us what they think we want to hear in response to our measures but also when the measures themselves produce desired changes. For instance, suppose as part of the research data collection procedures to measure outcome, participants in a parent education intervention self-monitor how much time they spend playing with or holding a friendly conversation with their children. That means that they will keep a running log, recording the duration of every instance that they play with or hold a conversation with their child. Keeping such a log might make some parents realize that they are spending much less quality time with their children than they had previously thought. This realization might influence them to spend more quality time with their children; in fact, it might influence them to do so more than the parent education intervention did.

It is conceivable that desired changes might occur among experimental group participants simply because they sense they are getting special attention or special treatment. To illustrate this form of reactivity, suppose a residential treatment center for children conducts an experiment to see if a new recreational program will reduce the frequency of antisocial behaviors among the children. Being assigned to the experimental group might make some children feel better about themselves and about the center. If this feeling—and not the recreational program per se—causes the desired change in their behavior, then a form of research reactivity will have occurred. This form of reactivity has been termed novelty and disruption effects because introducing an innovation in a setting where little innovation has previously occurred can stimulate excitement, energy, and enthusiasm among recipients of the intervention (Shadish et al., 2001).

A similar form of reactivity is termed *placebo effects.* Placebo effects can be induced by experimenter expectancies. If experimental group participants get the sense that they are about to receive a special new treatment that researchers or practitioners expect to be very effective, then the mere power of suggestion—and not the treatment itself—can bring about the desired improvement.

If we are concerned about potential placebo effects or novelty and disruption effects and wish to control for them, then we could employ an experimental design called the placebo control group design. The shorthand notation for this design is the following:

$$R \quad O_1 \quad X \quad O_2$$
$$R \quad O_1 \quad \quad O_2$$
$$R \quad O_1 \quad P \quad O_2$$

This design randomly assigns clients to three groups: an experimental group and two different control groups. One control group receives no experimental stimulus, but the other receives a placebo (represented by the P in the preceding notation). Placebo group subjects would receive special attention of some sort other than the tested stimulus or intervention. Perhaps practitioners would meet regularly to show special interest in them and listen to them but without applying any of the tested intervention procedures.

Placebo control group designs pose complexities from both a planning and an interpretation standpoint, particularly when experimental interventions contain elements that resemble placebo effects. For example, in some interventions that emphasize constructs such as "empathy" and "unconditional positive regard," intervention effects are difficult to sort from placebo effects. But when they are feasible to use, placebo control group designs provide greater control for threats to the validity of experimental findings than do designs that use only one control group.

Ethical concern about deceiving research participants makes the use of placebos rare in social work experiments. However, sometimes a second control group can receive treatment as usual as a way to compare the outcome of a group receiving a new intervention to the outcome of a group that receives the somewhat special attention of the practitioners providing the less innovative intervention. A study published in a social work research journal that took such an approach is summarized in the box "A Social Work Dissertation That Evaluated the Effectiveness of EMDR."

We do not want to convey the impression that an experiment's findings lack credibility unless the experiment can guarantee the complete absence of any possible research reactivity or measurement bias. It is virtually impossible for experiments in social work or allied fields to meet that unrealistic standard. Instead, the key issue should be whether reasonable efforts were taken to avoid or minimize those problems and whether the potential degree of bias or reactivity seems to be at an egregious level. That said, let's move on to a different type of threat to the validity of experimental findings.

Diffusion or Imitation of Treatments

Sometimes, service providers or service recipients are influenced unexpectedly in ways that tend to diminish the planned differences in the way a tested intervention is implemented among the groups being compared. This phenomenon is termed diffusion, or imitation, of treatments. For instance, suppose that the effects of hospice services that emphasize palliative care and psychosocial support for the terminally ill are being compared to the effects of more traditional health-care providers, who historically have been more attuned to prolonging life and thus less concerned with the unpleasant physical and emotional side effects of certain treatments. Over time, traditional health-care providers have been learning more about hospice care concepts, accepting them, and attempting to implement them in traditional health-care facilities. With all of this diffusion and imitation of hospice care by traditional health-care providers, failure to find differences in outcome between hospice and traditional care providers may have more to do with unanticipated similarities between hospice and traditional providers than with the ineffectiveness of hospice concepts.

A similar problem complicates research that evaluates the effectiveness of case management services. Many social workers who are not called case

managers nevertheless conceptualize and routinely provide case management functions—such as outreach, brokerage, linkage, and advocacy—as an integral part of what they learned to be good and comprehensive direct social work practice. Consequently, when outcomes for clients referred to case managers are compared to the outcomes of clients who receive "traditional" social services, the true effects of case management as a treatment approach may be blurred by the diffusion of that approach among practitioners who are not called case managers. In other words, despite their different labels, the two treatment groups may not be as different in the independent variable as we think they are.

Preventing the diffusion or imitation of treatments can be difficult. Shadish et al. (2001) suggest separating the two treatment conditions as much as possible, either geographically or by using different

A SOCIAL WORK DISSERTATION THAT EVALUATED THE EFFECTIVENESS OF EMDR

As described earlier in this chapter, EMDR combines various cognitive-behavioral intervention techniques with a technique involving the bilateral stimulation of rapid-eye movements. The early research on EMDR suggested that it is extremely effective in treating the posttraumatic stress symptoms of clients who have experienced traumatic events. However, critics of that early research noted the possibility that the EMDR recipients' outcomes might have been due to the placebo aspects of the EMDR intervention. In particular, they cited the fact that during the EMDR treatment protocol, clients are repeatedly asked by the therapist to rate on a scale from 0 to 10 whether the degree of distress they felt when visualizing the traumatic event was dissipating. Most important, that same scale was used on a pretest–posttest basis to measure treatment outcome. Consequently, improved scores on the scale could be due to the placebo effects of the therapist repeatedly conveying the implicit expectation that those ratings should be improving.

To control for the latter possibility, Edmond (Edmond, Rubin, & Wambach, 1999) carried out her social work dissertation research by randomly assigning adult female survivors of childhood sexual abuse to three groups and administering validated

instruments to measure outcome—not basing outcome on the clients' ratings of distress with their therapists. One group received EMDR. A control group was placed on a waiting list to receive EMDR after the research was concluded. A third group received treatment by therapists who were experienced in treating such survivors and who used their usual treatment approaches (which did not include EMDR) in this study. Most notably, during their treatment, they repeatedly asked the clients to do the same rating of distress as is done as part of the EMDR protocol (although those ratings were not used as the outcome measure). Therefore, if the placebo effects of those ratings were the real cause of the superior EMDR outcomes in the previous research, then Edmond's third group should improve as much as her EMDR group. Edmond's results, however, indicated that 3 months after the conclusion of treatment, her EMDR group had improved more than her usual treatment group and that both groups improved more than her wait-list control group.

Source: Tonya Edmond, Allen Rubin, and Kathryn Wambach (1999, June). "The Effectiveness of EMDR with Adult Female Survivors of Childhood Sexual Abuse." *Social Work Research*, 103–116.

practitioners in each. Another possibility is to provide ongoing reminders to practitioners about the need not to imitate the experimental group intervention when seeing control group clients. To monitor the extent to which the imitation of treatment is occurring or has occurred, researchers can utilize qualitative methods (see Chapters 18 and 19) to observe staff meetings, conduct informal conversational interviews with practitioners and clients, and ask them to keep logs summarizing what happened in each treatment session. If these efforts detect imitation while the experiment is still under way, then further communication with practitioners may help alleviate the problem and prevent it from reaching a level that seriously undermines the validity of the experiment.

Compensatory Equalization, Compensatory Rivalry, or Resentful Demoralization

Suppose you conduct an experiment to see if increasing the involvement of families in the treatment of substance abusers improves treatment effectiveness. Suppose the therapists in one unit receive special training in working with families and are instructed to increase the treatment involvement of families of clients in their unit, while the therapists in another unit receive no such training or instructions. Assuming that the staff in the latter unit—and perhaps even their clients and the families of their clients—are aware of the treatment differences, they may seek to offset what they perceive as an inequity in service provision. The staff in the latter unit therefore might decide to compensate for the inequity by providing enhanced services that go beyond the routine treatment regimen for their clients. This is termed compensatory equalization. If compensatory equalization happens, the true effects of increasing family involvement could be blurred, as described above with diffusion or imitation of treatments.

What if the therapists not receiving family therapy training in the above example decide to compete with the therapists in the other unit who do receive the training? Perhaps they will feel that their job security or prestige is threatened by not receiving the special training and will try to show that they can be just as effective without the special training. They may start reading more, attending more continuing education workshops, and increasing their therapeutic contact with clients. This is called compensatory rivalry. The control group therapists' extra efforts might increase their effectiveness as much as the increased family involvement might have increased the effectiveness of the experimental group therapists. If so, this could lead to the erroneous impression that the lack of difference in treatment outcome between the two groups means that increasing family involvement did not improve treatment effectiveness. The same problem could occur if the clients in one group become more motivated to improve because of the rivalry engendered by their awareness that they are not receiving the same treatment benefits as another group.

The converse of compensatory rivalry is resentful demoralization. This occurs when staff or clients become resentful and demoralized because they did not receive the special training or the special treatment. Consequently, their confidence or motivation may decline and may explain their inferior performance on outcome measures. To detect whether compensatory equalization, compensatory rivalry, or resentful demoralization is occurring—and perhaps to intervene to try to minimize the problem—you can use qualitative methods such as participant observation of staff meetings and informal conversational interviews with clients and practitioners.

» ATTRITION (EXPERIMENTAL MORTALITY)

Let's now look at one more threat to the validity of experimental findings, namely, attrition, which is sometimes referred to as *experimental mortality*. Often, participants will drop out of an experiment before it is completed, and the statistical comparisons and conclusions that are drawn can be affected. In a pretest–posttest control group design evaluating the effectiveness of an intervention to alleviate a distressing problem, for example, suppose that experimental group participants who perceive no improvement in their target problem prematurely drop out of treatment and refuse to be posttested. At posttest, the only experimental group participants left would be those who felt they were improving. Suppose that the overall group rate of perceived improvement among control group participants is exactly the same as the overall rate among those assigned to the experimental group (including the dropouts) but that all of the nonrecipients agree to be posttested because none had been disappointed. The experimental group's average posttest score is likely to be higher than the control group's—even if the intervention was ineffective—merely because of the attrition (experimental mortality) of experimental group participants who perceived no improvement.

When the rate of attrition among experimental group participants is disconcerting, researchers can use a technique called *intent-to-treat analysis*. Using intent-to-treat analysis, all participants who originally enrolled in the study—including those who dropped out of treatment—have their outcomes assessed, and those outcomes are included in the data analysis. Including the dropouts in the data analysis is based in part on the notion that an intervention that fails to retain a client in treatment is not being effective with that client. Including the dropouts in the data analysis is also done to avoid the bias that would result from the notion that the participants who are the least motivated or most dysfunctional are the ones most likely to drop out of treatment. For example, if the control condition places few demands on its participants but the intervention being provided to experimental group participants requires placing heavier demands, then the least motivated and most dysfunctional participants are more likely to drop out from the experimental group. If they are not included in the analysis, then despite random assignment, the groups are no longer equivalent. Instead, the deck is stacked in favor of the experimental group because the control group would have a greater proportion of participants who are the least motivated and the most dysfunctional.

A converse attrition problem can occur when participating in the control group protocol is more boring or arduous than participating in the experimental treatment. If so, then the least motivated and most dysfunctional clients might be more likely to drop out of the control group. For example, consider an evaluation that compares the effectiveness of family therapy and discussion groups in the treatment of drug addiction. Shadish et al. (2001) point out that addicts with the worst prognoses are more likely to drop out of discussion groups than they are to drop out of family therapy. Consequently, the family therapy intervention may have poorer results at posttest, not because it is less effective than discussion groups but because the different attrition rates left more difficult cases in the family therapy group at posttest.

Researchers conducting experimental evaluations of the effectiveness of practice or programs should strive to minimize attrition. Here are ways to do that:

1. *Reimbursement.* Reimbursing participants for their participation in research might not only alleviate attrition but also enhance your ability to recruit people to participate in your study at the outset. The level of reimbursement should be sensitive to the time and efforts of participants in pretesting and posttesting. The payment should be large enough to work as an incentive without being so great that it becomes coercive. The amount should fit the difficulties that clients experience in participating and fit their income levels and emotional states. With low-income participants, for example, you should anticipate difficulties in child care and transportation to and from pretesting and posttesting (and perhaps follow-up testing). If feasible, an alternative to extra payments for transportation and child-care costs might be to provide the transportation to the testing site as well as a small child-care service there. Alternatively, it might make sense to conduct the testing at the participant's residence if doing so does not introduce serious measurement biases.

After pretesting, you might want to increase the amount of reimbursement over time at each subsequent measurement point and give a bonus to participants who stay the distance and complete all of the measurements throughout the study. The amount should go beyond the transportation and other costs to the participant and should be enough to acknowledge to participants that their time is valued and that the measurement can be an imposition. The amount should also fit within your research budget. If you can afford it, paying participants $15 to complete pretests, $20 to complete posttests, and perhaps another $15 bonus to stay the distance might be reasonable amounts, but they might have to be adjusted upward, depending on factors such as child-care costs and inflation. (Discount department store gift certificates in the above amounts are commonly used instead of cash payments.)

2. *Avoid intervention or research procedures that disappoint or frustrate participants.* Participants are more likely to drop out of an experiment if they are disappointed or frustrated with the intervention they are receiving as part of the study. Of course, there's not much you can do to prevent disappointment over the fact that the intervention simply is not

effective. But you can try to have the intervention delivered by the most experienced, competent professionals possible. Of particular importance is their experience and ability in developing supportive professional relationships with clients. In contrast, if your intervention is delivered by inexperienced practitioners who are not yet comfortable or confident in building and maintaining treatment alliances with clients, then participants receiving the intervention are more likely to become put off and drop out.

Another way to prevent disappointment and frustration with the intervention is to make sure during the recruitment and orientation of participants that they have accurate expectations of the intervention and that the intervention is a good fit with their treatment objectives and expectations. It also helps if the intervention itself does not contain noxious procedures, such as having participants recall repressed traumatic memories in ways that are like reexperiencing the trauma and then ending sessions without resolving the intense distress that the recalled memory has stimulated. Finally, minimizing the amount of time that elapses between recruitment of participants and the onset of treatment can help avoid attrition because participants assigned to a particular treatment group may become disappointed and frustrated if the wait is much longer than they had expected.

Annoying research procedures can also influence participants to drop out. Common examples are overwhelming participants with measurement procedures that exceed their expectations, stamina, or resources. Researchers should not mislead prospective participants by underestimating the extent of the measurement procedures to which they will be subjected. Neither should researchers mislead participants about issues such as child-care requirements or resources, scheduling difficulties, providing feedback about measurement scores, or protecting confidentiality. Shadish et al. (2001) encourage researchers to conduct preliminary pilot studies to identify causes of attrition that can be anticipated and alleviated when the main experiment begins. For example, research assistants who are not involved in other parts of the pilot study could interview dropouts to ascertain how they experienced the study and why they dropped out.

3. *Utilize tracking methods.* Many recipients of social work interventions are transient or secretive about where they live. Many are unemployed. Some lack telephones. The poor, the homeless, substance abusers, and battered women are prominent examples. Shadish et al. (2001) reviewed the tracking strategies that have been used to find such participants and retain their participation in treatment and measurement. One of their recommendations is to obtain as much location information as possible at the outset of their participation not only from the participants themselves but also from their friends, relatives, and other agencies with which they are involved. (You will need to get the participant's signed permission to contact these sources.) Another recommendation is to develop relationships with staff members at agencies who may later be able to help you find participants. You can also give participants a business card that shows treatment and measurement appointment times and a toll-free number where they can leave messages about appointment changes or changes in how to locate them. If participants have telephones, then research assistants can call them to remind them of each appointment. If they have mailing addresses, you can augment your telephone tracking by mailing them reminder notices of upcoming appointments. (You may recall that we discussed these tracking methods in more depth in Chapter 6, on culturally competent research.)

» EXTERNAL VALIDITY

When a study has a high degree of internal validity, it allows causal inferences to be made about the sample and setting that were studied. But what about other settings and larger populations? Can we generalize the same causal inferences to them?

As we mentioned earlier, external validity refers to the extent to which we can generalize the findings of a study to settings and populations beyond the study conditions. Internal validity is a necessary but not sufficient condition for external validity. Before we can generalize a causal inference beyond the conditions of a particular study, we must have adequate grounds for making the causal inference under the conditions of that study in the first place. But even when internal validity in a particular study is high, several problems may limit its external validity.

A major factor that influences external validity is the representativeness of the study sample, setting, and procedures. Suppose that a deinstitutionalization program is implemented in an urban community. Suppose that community residents strongly support the program, that it's well funded, and that there is a comprehensive range of noninstitutional community support resources accessible to the mentally disabled clients residing in the community. Suppose, in turn, that the well-funded program can afford to hire high-caliber staff members, give them small caseloads, and reward them amply for good work. Finally, suppose that an evaluation with high internal validity finds that the program improves the clients' quality of life.

Would those findings imply that legislators or mental health planners in other localities could logically conclude that a similar deinstitutionalization program would improve the quality of life of mentally disabled individuals in their settings? Not necessarily. It would depend on the degree to which their settings, populations, and procedures matched those of the studied program.

Suppose that their community is rural, has fewer or more geographically dispersed community-based resources for the mentally disabled, or has more neighborhood opposition to residences being located in the community. Suppose that legislators view deinstitutionalization primarily as a cost-saving device and therefore do not allocate enough funds to enable the program to hire or keep high-caliber staff members or give them caseload sizes that are small enough to manage adequately. And what about differences in the characteristics of the mentally disabled target population? Notice that we have said nothing about the attributes of the clients in the tested program. Perhaps they were different in age, diagnosis, ethnicity, average length of previous institutionalization, and degree of social impairment than the intended target population in the communities generalizing from the study findings. To the extent that such differences apply, similar programs implemented in other settings might not have the same effects as did the program in the tested setting.

Would such differences mean that this study had low external validity? Not necessarily. On the one hand, we could say that a study has low external validity if its conditions are far removed from conditions that could reasonably be expected to be replicated in the real world. On the other hand, a study's external validity could be adequate even if it cannot be generalized to many other settings. A study must be generalizable to some real-world

settings, and it must represent that which it intends to represent. It does not have to represent every conceivable population or setting.

For example, a study that evaluates a program of care for the profoundly and chronically disabled in rural settings does not need to be generalizable to the mildly or acutely disabled or to the disabled residing in urban settings in order to have external validity. It just has to be representative of those attributes that it intends to represent, no matter how narrowly it defines them.

Problems in external validity abound in the literature that evaluates social work practice and programs. One common problem that can limit your ability to judge the external validity of a study is ambiguity or brevity in reportage. Many studies do not adequately articulate the specific attributes of the clients who participated in the evaluated service. Many are vague about the practitioners' attributes. Some studies generalize about the effectiveness of *professional* social work practitioners based on findings about the effectiveness of *student* practitioners. Some studies leave out important details about the evaluated clinical setting, such as caseload size and the like. Consequently, although it may be clear that the evaluated intervention did or did not cause the desired change among the studied clients—that is, that the study had high internal validity—it is often not clear to whom those findings can be generalized. Thus, some studies find services to be effective but do not permit the generalization that those services would be effective beyond the study conditions. Likewise, other studies find no support for the effectiveness of services but do not permit the generalization that those services would be ineffective when implemented under other conditions. As we leave this chapter, we hope you can begin to sense how difficult it may be to carry out successfully a well-controlled experiment in a real social work setting. Many practical obstacles, some of which are impossible to foresee, can interfere with our best-laid plans. We have addressed some obstacles in this chapter, such as participant attrition or practitioner imitation of treatments. We will address additional pitfalls in the next chapter, such as improper implementation of the intervention being evaluated, difficulties in recruiting participants, and practitioner resistance to research procedures for assigning cases to experimental and control conditions. In particular, the next chapter will focus on how quasi-experimental designs attempt to achieve a reasonable degree of internal validity when agency obstacles make it impossible to use randomization procedures in assigning participants to experimental and control groups.

MAIN POINTS

- An inference is a conclusion that can be logically drawn in light of our research design and our findings.
- A causal inference is one derived from a research design and findings that logically imply that the independent variable really has a causal impact on the dependent variable.
- The term *research design* can refer to all the decisions made in planning and conducting research, including decisions about measurement, sampling, how to collect data, and logical arrangements designed to permit certain kinds of inferences.
- The three most commonly cited criteria for the determination of causation in social work research include: (a) time sequence (the cause must precede the effect in time); (b) correlation (changes in the cause are accompanied by changes in the effect); and (c) ruling out alternative explanations.
- Three additional criteria for making causal inferences are: (a) strength of correlation; (b) consistency in replication; and (c) plausibility and coherence.
- Internal validity refers to the confidence we have that the results of a study accurately depict whether one variable is or is not a cause of another.
- Common threats to internal validity are history, maturation, testing, instrumentation changes, statistical regression, selection bias, and causal time order.
- Three forms of preexperiments are the one-shot case study, the one-group pretest–posttest design, and the posttest-only design with non-equivalent groups.
- Experiments are an excellent vehicle for the controlled testing of causal processes.
- The classical experiment tests the effect of an experimental stimulus on some dependent variable through the pretesting and posttesting of experimental and control groups.

- The Solomon four-group design and the posttest-only control group design are variations on the classical experiment that attempt to safeguard against problems associated with testing effects.
- Randomization is the generally preferred method for achieving comparability in the experimental and control groups.
- It is generally less important that a group of experimental subjects be representative of some larger population than that experimental and control groups be similar to one another.
- Control group participants in experiments in social work settings need not be denied services. They can receive alternate, routine services or be put on a waiting list to receive the experimental intervention.
- Although the classical experiment with random assignment of subjects guards against most threats to internal validity, additional methodological efforts may be needed to prevent or alleviate the following problems: (a) measurement bias, (b) research reactivity, (c) diffusion or imitation of treatments, (d) compensatory equalization, (e) compensatory rivalry, (f) resentful demoralization, and (g) attrition.
- Techniques for minimizing attrition include reimbursing participants for their participation, avoiding intervention or research procedures that disappoint or frustrate them, and tracking participants.
- Many experimental studies fail to include measurement procedures, such as blind raters, to control for researcher or practitioner bias toward perceiving results that would confirm the hypothesis.
- Experimental demand characteristics and experimenter expectancies can hinder the validity of experimental findings if they influence research participants to cooperate with what experimenters want them to say or do.
- Obtrusive observation occurs when the participant is keenly aware of being observed and thus may be predisposed to behave in ways that meet experimenter expectancies. In contrast, unobtrusive observation means that the participant does not notice the observation.
- External validity refers to the extent to which we can generalize the findings of a study to settings and populations beyond the study conditions.

REVIEW QUESTIONS AND EXERCISES

1. Pick three of the threats to internal validity discussed in this chapter and make up examples (other than those discussed in the chapter) to illustrate each.

2. A director of a prison Bible studies program claims that his program prevents recidivism. His claim is based on data showing that only 14% of the inmates who complete his Bible studies program recidivate, as compared to 41% of the inmates who choose not to participate in his program. Based on what you read in this chapter, explain why his claim is not warranted.

3. What potential threats to the validity of the findings can you detect in the following hypothetical design? In a residential treatment center containing four cottages, the clinical director develops a new intervention to alleviate behavior problems among the children residing in the four cottages. The center has four therapists, each assigned to a separate cottage. The clinical director selects two cottages to receive the new intervention. The other two will receive the routine treatment. To measure outcome, the clinical director assigns a social work student whose field placement is at the center to spend an equal amount of time at each cottage observing and recording the number of antisocial behaviors each child exhibits and the number of antisocial statements each makes.

4. Briefly sketch an experimental design for testing a new intervention in your fieldwork agency or in another social work agency with which you are familiar. Then conduct a qualitative (open-ended, semi-structured) interview with one or two direct-service practitioners and an administrator in that agency, asking them how feasible it would be to carry out your study in their agency.

5. A newspaper article (Perlman, 1982) discussed arguments that linked fluoridation to acquired immune deficiency syndrome (AIDS), citing this evidence: "While half the country's communities have fluoridated water supplies, and half do not, 90% of AIDS cases are coming from fluoridated areas and only 10% are coming from nonfluoridated areas." Discuss this in terms of what you have learned about the criteria of causation, indicating what other variables might be involved.

6. A study with an exceptionally high degree of internal validity conducted with Native Alaskan female adolescents who have recently been sexually abused concludes that an intervention is effective in preventing substance abuse among its participants. Explain how this study can have little external validity from one perspective yet a good deal of external validity from another perspective—depending on the target population of the practitioners who are utilizing the study as a potential guide to their evidence-based practice.

INTERNET EXERCISES

1. Find a study reporting an experiment that evaluated the effectiveness of a social work intervention. How well did the study control for the additional threats to validity discussed in this chapter? What efforts did it make to alleviate attrition? Were its measurement procedures obtrusive or unobtrusive? Do they appear to be free from serious bias? Also critique the study's external validity—either positively or negatively.

2. Find a study that used a preexperimental design to evaluate the outcome of a social work intervention. Critique the study's internal validity and discuss whether it had value despite its preexperimental nature.

3. In this chapter, we looked briefly at the problem of placebo effects. On the web, find a study in which the placebo effect figured importantly. Briefly summarize the study, including the source of your information. (Hint: You might want to do a search using the term "placebo" as a key word.)

 Visit CengageBrain.com for additional practice and study opportunities including experiential exercises, research tools, glossary, flashcards, and sample test items.

12

Quasi-Experimental Designs

EPAS Competencies for This Chapter

Competency 4 Engage in Practice-Informed Research and Research-Informed Practice: This competency pertains to this entire chapter because doing practice-informed research often involves using quasi-experimental designs. The same applies to engaging in research-informed practice because you'll need to be able to critically appraise quasi-experimental studies that might inform your practice.

Competency 9 Evaluate Practice with Individuals Families, Groups, Organizations, and Communities: Evaluating practice often involves using quasi experiments. Therefore, this competency pertains to this entire chapter.

What You'll Learn in This Chapter

Practical constraints in social work agencies often pose obstacles to conducting ideally designed experimental evaluations of the effectiveness of practice and programs. In this chapter, we'll examine what can be done in the face of those obstacles to maximize the degree of validity in the findings of outcome evaluations. Our main focus will be on quasi experiments, which usually resemble experiments but without random assignment. In addition, we'll consider the important role that qualitative research methods can play in assessing how well designs are being carried out and in assessing the meaning of their findings.

» INTRODUCTION

In the previous chapter, we saw the importance of randomly assigning participants to experimental and control groups in order to maximize the chances that the two groups are comparable (thus minimizing the risk of a selectivity bias) in outcome evaluations of the effectiveness of practice and programs. In many social work agencies, however, obtaining a control group is not feasible. And when we can obtain a control group, it is often not feasible to use randomization to determine which participants are assigned to it versus the experimental group.

Agency administrators and practitioners may cite various reasons why it's not acceptable to withhold interventions from clients or prospective clients: Withholding services may seem unethical, it may have unwanted fiscal implications, or it may lead to complaints from consumers who feel deprived. As we already discussed, the ethical concerns are not always warranted. But agency administrators and practitioners who strongly believe in the value of the service being evaluated may not be persuaded of that. They may not agree that perpetually providing untested services may be more questionable ethically than withholding services that might be ineffectual or harmful. No matter how strong a case we may make for random assignment to experimental and control groups, our chances of getting it are usually quite slim. Even if we were able to convince an agency director of the merits of using an experimental design, chances are that we also would have to convince the board members to whom the director reports. It might also be necessary to convince agency practitioners, whom the administrator does not want to alienate and who will refer participants to the experiment.

Rather than forgo any evaluation in such instances, alternative research designs sometimes can be created and executed that have less internal validity than randomized experiments but still provide more support for causal inferences than do preexperimental designs. These designs are called **quasi-experimental designs** and are distinguished from true experiments primarily because they do not randomly assign participants to experimental and control groups.

Despite the lack of random assignment, well-designed quasi experiments can have a high degree of internal validity. Let's now examine three commonly used quasi-experimental designs that, when designed and conducted properly, can attain a reasonable degree of internal validity.

EP 4, 9

» NONEQUIVALENT COMPARISON GROUPS DESIGN

The **nonequivalent comparison groups design** can be used when we are unable to randomly assign participants to groups but can find an existing group that appears similar to the experimental group and thus can be compared to it. Suppose, for example, that we want to evaluate the effects on depression of an intervention that gives pets to nursing home residents. It's unlikely that you would be permitted to randomly select in any nursing home the residents who will and will not receive pets. You can probably imagine the administrative hassles that might erupt because some residents or their relatives feel they are being deprived. As an alternative to a true experimental design, then, you may be able to find two nursing homes that agree to participate in your research and that appear very similar in all of the respects that are relevant to internal validity, such as the same numbers and types of residents and staff, the same level of care, and so on. In particular, you would want to make sure that the resident populations of the two homes were quite similar in terms of age, socioeconomic status, mental and physical disabilities, psychosocial functioning, ethnicity, and so on. You could then introduce the intervention in one home and use the other as a comparison group. (The term *comparison group* is used instead of *control group* when participants are not assigned randomly.)

The two homes could be compared in a pretest to make sure that they really are equivalent on the dependent variable before introducing the independent variable. If their average depression scores are about the same, then it would be reasonable to suppose that differences at posttest represent the effects of the intervention. Of course, such a causal inference would be even more credible had the participants been randomly assigned. But to the extent that you could provide convincing data as to the comparability of the two homes on plausible extraneous variables and if the differences on their average pretest scores are trivial, then your causal inference would be credible, and your study would have value. The shorthand notation for this design is the following:

$$O_1 \quad X \quad O_2$$
$$O_1 \qquad\; O_2$$

You might note that the preceding notation is the same as the pretest–posttest control group design except that it lacks the R for random assignment.

Here's another example of this design, using an excerpt from an actual study in which two junior high schools were selected to evaluate a program that sought to discourage the use of tobacco, alcohol, and drugs. The pairing of the two schools and their assignment to "experimental" and "control" conditions was not random. The local Lung Association had identified the school where we delivered the program as one in which administrators were seeking a solution to admitted problems of smoking, alcohol, and drug abuse. The "control" school was chosen as a convenient and nearby demographic match where administrators were willing to allow our surveying and breath-testing procedures. The principal of that school considered the existing program of health education effective and believed that the onset of smoking was relatively uncommon among his students:

> The communities served by the two schools were very similar. The rate of parental smoking reported by the students was just above 40 percent in both schools. (McAlister, Perry, Killen, Slinkard, & Maccoby, 1980, p. 720)

Without the participants having been randomly assigned to experimental and control groups, we might wonder if the two schools are comparable. It helps to know, however, that in the initial set of observations, the experimental and comparison (control) groups reported virtually the same (low) frequency of smoking. Over the 21 months of the study, smoking increased in both groups but less so in the experimental group than in the control group, supporting the notion that the program did affect students' behavior.

When you read a report of a study that used a nonequivalent comparison groups design, it is important to remember that if selection biases seem highly plausible in that study, then the notion that the groups are really comparable is severely undermined. Unless the researcher can present compelling evidence to document the comparability of the groups on relevant extraneous variables and on pretest scores, then any differences in outcome between the two groups are highly suspect. In other words, depending on how well the researcher documents the comparability of the groups, studies using this design can be strong enough to inform your practice or can be very weak.

Even when much evidence is supplied supporting the notion that the groups are comparable, nagging doubts often remain. Rarely can researchers obtain evidence about every possible extraneous variable that might account for differences in outcome between the groups. For example, the fact that two groups are comparable in their pretest scores and in various background characteristics does not ensure that they are equally motivated to change. Suppose an evaluation is being conducted to see whether a prison Bible studies program reduces rearrest rates after prisoners are released. Suppose further that the prisoners who attend the Bible studies program do so voluntarily and that the study compares the rearrest rates of those prisoners to a matched group of prisoners who share the same background characteristics as the Bible studies group but who chose not to attend the Bible studies program. No matter how many data are provided documenting the background similarities of the two groups, we might remain quite skeptical about their comparability regarding the prisoners' notions of morality, sense of remorse, and motivation to go straight—extraneous variables that might have a greater influence on rearrest rates than many of the background variables on which the groups have been shown to be comparable.

» WAYS TO STRENGTHEN THE INTERNAL VALIDITY OF THE NONEQUIVALENT COMPARISON GROUPS DESIGN

Two design features can help offset some of the doubts about the comparability of nonequivalent comparison groups in the nonequivalent comparison groups design (Shadish, Cook, & Campbell, 2001). One is the use of multiple pretests. The other involves using switching replications. Let's examine each of these features.

Multiple Pretests

One key concern regarding selectivity biases is that the experimental group might be more motivated to change than the control group and therefore was probably already in the process of change before treatment began. By administering multiple pretests—which means administering the same pretest at different time points before intervention begins—we can detect whether one group is already engaged in a change process and the other is not. It can also help us detect whether statistical regression is occurring in one group but not the other. The shorthand notation for adding this design feature to the nonequivalent comparison groups design is the following:

$$O_1 \quad O_2 \quad X \quad O_3$$
$$O_1 \quad O_2 \quad \quad O_3$$

In the top row in this diagram, the experimental group gets the treatment (X). The bottom row represents the comparison group. In each row, O_1 and O_2 signify the first and second pretests. O_3 signifies the posttest.

Suppose two groups of substance abusers have the same mean score of 10 at O_1, indicating how many days during the past month they used illegal substances, as illustrated in part A of Figure 12-1. Also as illustrated in part A, suppose at O_2 that the treatment group mean drops to 6 and that the comparison group mean stays at 10. Suppose at O_3 that the treatment group mean drops further, to 4, and that the comparison group mean stays at 10. Without the second pretest, the difference between 10 and 4 at posttest would appear to indicate that the treatment (X) was effective—that it caused the reduction in substance abuse. But with the second pretest, we can see that the intervention cannot be presumed to be the cause of the drop because the two groups of abusers were not really comparable. That is, we can see a trend toward fewer days of substance abuse in the treatment group before the intervention is implemented. Thus, the treatment group was already engaged in a change process before treatment began (perhaps because of greater motivation to change), and the comparison group was not.

Conversely, if the O_2 scores of both groups had remained at 10, as illustrated in part B of Figure 12-1, we would have more confidence that the drop to 4 at posttest really suggested that the treatment was effective—that it conceivably caused the reduction

FIGURE 12.1 An Illustration of Contrasting Multiple Pretest Results in a Fictitious Substance Abuse Treatment Outcome Evaluation

Part A: Mean pretest scores (days during past month illegal substances used) indicate that the groups are not really comparable: The treatment group is already changing before intervention commences. **The intervention cannot be presumed to be the cause of the improvement in the treatment group,** despite its improvement from pretests to posttest.

Mean Number of Days Illegal Substances Used

	O_1	O_2		O_3
	Pretests			Posttest
Treatment Group	10	6	Intervention	4
Comparison Group	10	10		10

Part B: Mean pretest scores indicate that the groups are comparable: The treatment group is not changing before intervention commences. Therefore, **the difference between the groups at posttest supports the hypothesis that the intervention is effective.**

Mean Number of Days Illegal Substances Used

	Pretests			Posttest
	O_1	O_2		O_3
Treatment Group	10	10	Intervention	4
Comparison Group	10	10		10

in substance abuse. In other words, because the frequency of substance abuse remained the same for both groups prior to intervention in part B, the two groups appear to be equivalent, and the notion that the difference at posttest was due to a selection bias can be ruled out.

Switching Replication

Another way to detect whether a desired outcome might be due to a selection bias is by using a switching replication design feature, which involves administering the treatment to the comparison group after the first posttest. If we replicate in that group—in a second posttest—the improvement made by the experimental group in the first posttest, then we reduce doubt as to whether the improvement at the first posttest was merely a function of a selection bias. If our second posttest results do not replicate the improvement made by the experimental group in the first posttest, then the difference between the groups at the first posttest can be attributed to the lack of comparability between the two groups. The shorthand notation for adding this design feature is the following:

$$O_1 \quad X \quad O_2 \qquad O_3$$
$$O_1 \qquad O_2 \quad X \quad O_3$$

The top row in this diagram represents the experimental group. The bottom row represents the comparison group. In each row, O_1 signifies the pretest.

O_2 and O_3 represent the posttests. The treatment is signified by X.

EP 4, 9

Figure 12-2 returns to our substance abuse treatment example but this time illustrating the use of switching replication. In part A, the two groups of substance abusers have the same mean score of 10 at O_1, indicating how many days during the past month they used illegal substances. At O_2, the experimental group (in the top row) mean drops to 4, and the comparison group mean stays at 10. At O_3, the experimental group mean stays at 4, and the comparison group mean drops to 4. That would suggest that the treatment was effective and that the difference between the O_2 scores of 10 and 4 was not merely due to a selection bias. In contrast, in part B, at O_3, the comparison group mean does *not* improve; that is, despite receiving the intervention, it stays at 10. That would suggest that the treatment was *not* effective and that the difference in improvement between the two groups was merely due to a selection bias.

» SIMPLE TIME-SERIES DESIGNS

Another commonly used set of quasi-experimental designs are called time-series designs. These designs go beyond the use of multiple pretests by additionally emphasizing the use of multiple posttests. A particularly feasible time-series design—feasible

FIGURE 12.2   An Illustration of Contrasting Switching Replication Results in a Fictitious Substance Abuse Treatment Outcome Evaluation

Part A: The Intervention Appears to Be Effective.

Mean Number of Days Illegal Substances Used

	O_1		O_2		O_3
Treatment Group	10	Intervention	4		4
Comparison Group	10		10	Intervention	4

Part B: The Difference between the Groups at Posttest Appears to Be Due to a Selection Bias

Mean Number of Days Illegal Substances Used

	O_1		O_2		O_3
Treatment Group	10	Intervention	4		4
Comparison Group	10		10	Intervention	10

because it does not require a comparison group—is called the simple interrupted time-series design. The shorthand notation for this design is the following:

$$O_1 \quad O_2 \quad O_3 \quad O_4 \quad O_5 \quad X \quad O_6 \quad O_7 \quad O_8 \quad O_9 \quad O_{10}$$

Each O in the notation represents a different observation point for measuring the dependent variable over time. No particular number of measurements is required, although the more, the better. The notation above indicates that the dependent variable was measured at five points in time before the intervention (X) was introduced and another five times after that.

To illustrate the time-series design, we will begin by asking you to assess the meaning of some hypothetical data. Suppose your colleague—a child therapist working in a child guidance center—tells you that she has come up with an effective new technique for reducing hostile antisocial behaviors by children with behavioral disorders during their sessions of group play therapy. To prove her assertion, she tells you about a play therapy group that has had four sessions. During the first two sessions, she noticed that there seemed to be an unusually high number of time-outs required in response to hostile antisocial behaviors, but she did not count them. After the second session, she developed her new technique and decided to test it out. To test it, she counted the number of time-outs in each of the next two sessions, not employing her new technique in the third session and then employing it in the fourth session.

She tells you that during the third session, when she did not employ her technique, there were 10 time-outs, whereas the number of time-outs fell to 4 during the fourth session. In other words, she contends, her new technique cut the number of time-outs by more than half. This simple set of data is presented graphically in Figure 12-3.

Are you persuaded that the new technique employed during session 4 was the cause of the drop in time-outs? You would probably object that her data don't prove the case. Two observations aren't really enough to prove anything. The improvement in time-outs could have resulted from history, maturation, or statistical regression—not to mention the possibility of instrumentation, that is, a change in her own inclination to administer time-outs. Ideally, she should have had two separate play therapy groups with children assigned randomly to each,

FIGURE 12.3 Two Observations of Time-outs: Before and after Using a New Technique

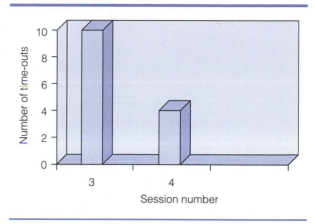

employed the intervention in only one group after one or more pretest sessions, and then compared the two groups in later sessions. But she doesn't have two classes of randomly assigned students. Nor does she have a nonequivalent comparison group. All she has is the one group.

Suppose, however, that instead of counting the time-outs only in sessions 3 and 4, she had been counting them in every session throughout a 10-session treatment period and recording each number in a running log. Suppose further that instead of introducing her new technique during session 4, she introduced it during session 6 and then continued employing it through session 10. Her log would allow you to conduct a time-series evaluation.

Figure 12-4 presents three possible patterns of time-outs over time. In each pattern, the new technique is introduced after the fifth session (i.e., during the sixth session). In each pattern, the vertical line between the fifth and sixth sessions separates the five sessions before the new technique was used and the five sessions during which it was used. Which of these patterns would give you confidence that the new technique had the impact she contends it did?

If the time-series results looked like pattern 1 in Figure 12-4, you would probably conclude that a trend of fewer time-outs with each session had begun well before the new technique was introduced and had continued unaffected after the new technique was introduced. The long-term data suggest that the trend would have occurred even without the new technique. Pattern 1, then, contradicts

FIGURE 12.4 Time-Series Perspective: Three Patterns of Time-outs

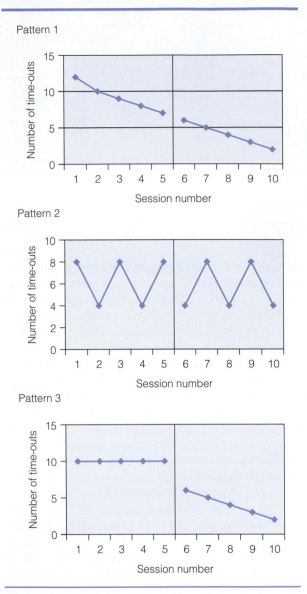

Pattern 1

Pattern 2

Pattern 3

Source: Rajesh Tandon and L. Dave Brown, "Organization-Building for Rural Development: An Experiment in India," *Journal of Applied Behavioral Science* (April–June 1981):182.

the new technique simply was introduced at a point where there would have been a decrease in time-outs anyway. More to the point, we note that during the five sessions when the new technique was used, the number of time-outs kept fluctuating cyclically between increases and decreases in the same way it fluctuated during the first through fifth sessions, or before the new technique was introduced.

Only pattern 3 in Figure 12-4 supports her contention that the new technique mattered. As we see, the number of time-outs before the new technique was introduced had been steady at 10 time-outs per session. Then, beginning immediately with session 6, when the new technique was introduced, the number of time-outs fell to six and continued dropping with each successive session. The data in pattern 3 therefore exclude the possibility that the decrease in time-outs results from a process of maturation indicated in pattern 1 or from regular fluctuations indicated in pattern 2. They also rule out the possibility of statistical regression because the improvement was not based on movement from one extreme and atypical pretest score.

The pattern 3 data do not, however, rule out history as a possible explanation. In other words, it is conceivable that some extraneous event may have caused the change. Perhaps the child guidance center's new psychiatrist started prescribing a new medication for attention deficit/hyperactivity disorder at the same time the new play therapy technique was introduced. Or perhaps a family therapy service for the same children commenced at that time. Nevertheless, the data in pattern 3 do reduce somewhat the *plausibility* of the explanation that history caused the change because the extraneous event would have had to occur at the same time that the new technique was introduced—in a way that could be portrayed as an unlikely coincidence.

One way to further reduce the plausibility of history as an explanation for time-series data like those in pattern 3 would be to find another play therapy group that could serve as a nonequivalent comparison group and assess it at the same points in time as the play therapy group receiving the new technique. If your colleague did that, she would be using a third type of quasi-experimental design—the multiple time-series design. Let's now take a close look at that type of design.

EP 4, 9

the assertion that the new technique decreased the number of time-outs.

Pattern 2 contradicts her assertion also. It indicates that the number of time-outs had been bouncing up and down in a regular pattern throughout the 10 sessions. Sometimes it increases from one session to the next, and sometimes it decreases;

» MULTIPLE TIME-SERIES DESIGNS

Multiple time-series designs are a stronger form of time-series analysis than simple time-series designs (i.e., they have greater internal validity) because they add time-series analysis to the nonequivalent comparison groups design. Probably the most applicable multiple time-series design for social workers is the interrupted time-series design with a nonequivalent comparison group. The shorthand notation for this design is the following:

$$O_1 \; O_2 \; O_3 \; O_4 \; O_5 \; X \; O_6 \; O_7 \; O_8 \; O_9 \; O_{10}$$
$$O_1 \; O_2 \; O_3 \; O_4 \; O_5 \quad O_6 \; O_7 \; O_8 \; O_9 \; O_{10}$$

In this design, both an experimental group and a nonequivalent comparison group (neither assigned randomly) are measured at multiple points in time before and after an intervention is introduced to the experimental group.

Weiss (1972) presented a useful example of this design, one that compared time-series data from an "experimental" state to time-series data from four "control" states:

> An interesting example of multiple time series was the evaluation of the Connecticut crackdown on highway speeding. Evaluators collected reports of traffic fatalities for several periods before and after the new program went into effect. They found that fatalities went down after the crackdown, but since the series had had an unstable up-and-down pattern for many years, it was not certain that the drop was due to the program. They then compared the statistics with time-series data from four neighboring states where there had been no changes in traffic enforcement. Those states registered no equivalent drop in fatalities. The comparison lent credence to the conclusion that the crackdown had had some effect. (p. 69)

Although this study design is not as good as one in which participants are assigned randomly, it is nonetheless an improvement over assessing the experimental group's time-series performance without comparison to a control group. It is also an improvement over comparing an experimental and a nonequivalent comparison group without the added benefit of time-series data. The key in assessing this aspect of evaluation studies is *comparability*, as the following example illustrates.

Rural development is a growing concern in the poor countries of the world and one that has captured the attention and support of many rich countries. Through national foreign assistance programs and international agencies such as the World Bank, the developed countries are in the process of sharing their technological knowledge and skills with the developing countries. Such programs have had mixed results, however. Often, modern techniques do not produce the intended results when applied in traditional societies.

Tandon and Brown (1981) undertook an experiment in which technological training would be accompanied by instruction in village organization. They felt it was important for poor farmers to learn how to organize and exert collective influence within their villages—to get needed action from government officials, for example. Only then would their new technological skills bear fruit.

Both intervention and evaluation were attached to an ongoing program in which 25 villages had been selected for technological training. Two poor farmers from each village had been trained in new agricultural technologies and then sent home to share their new knowledge with their fellow villagers and to organize other farmers into "peer groups" that would help spread that knowledge. Two years later, the authors randomly selected two of the 25 villages for special training and 11 others as comparison groups. A careful comparison of demographic characteristics showed the experimental and comparison groups to be strikingly similar to each other, suggesting that they were sufficiently comparable for the study.

The peer groups from the two experimental villages were brought together for special training in organization building. The participants were given information about organizing and making demands on the government as well as opportunities to act out dramas that were similar to the situations they faced at home. The training took 3 days.

All the outcome variables considered in the evaluation were concerned with the extent to which members of the peer groups initiated group activities that were designed to improve their situation. Six types were studied. "Active initiative," for example, was defined as "active effort to influence persons or events affecting group members versus passive response or withdrawal" (Tandon and Brown, 1981, p. 180). The data for evaluation came from the journals that the peer group leaders had been keeping since their initial technological training. The researchers read through the journals and counted the number of initiatives taken by members of the peer groups. Two researchers coded the journals independently and compared their work to test the reliability of the coding process. Figure 12-5 compares the number of active initiatives by members of the two experimental groups with those coming from the comparison villages. Similar results were found for the other outcome measures.

Notice two things about the graph. First, there is a dramatic difference in the number of initiatives by the two experimental groups as compared with the 11 comparison villages, which seems to confirm the effectiveness of the special training program. Second, notice that the number of initiatives also increased among the comparison villages. The researchers explain this latter pattern as a result of contagion. Because all the villages were near each other, the lessons learned by peer group members

in the experimental groups were communicated in part to members of the comparison villages.

This example illustrates the strengths of multiple time-series designs when true experiments are inappropriate for the program being evaluated. The box "An Illustration of a Quasi Experiment Evaluating a Family Preservation Program" describes another example of an actual quasi experiment—one that combined aspects of nonequivalent comparison groups designs and simple time-series designs.

» CROSS-SECTIONAL STUDIES

A cross-sectional study examines a phenomenon by taking a cross section of it at one point in time. Cross-sectional studies may have exploratory, descriptive, or explanatory purposes. A single U.S. census, for example, exemplifies a cross-sectional study for descriptive purposes. If you conducted one open-ended, unstructured interview with each client who prematurely terminated treatment in your agency during a specified period—to generate insights about why your agency's treatment termination rate is so high—you would be conducting a cross-sectional study for exploratory purposes. If you conducted one structured interview with both these clients and those who completed their planned treatment—to test the hypothesis that practitioner–client disagreement about treatment goals is related to whether treatment is completed—then you would be conducting a cross-sectional study for explanatory purposes.

From the standpoint of internal validity, explanatory cross-sectional studies have an inherent problem. They typically aim to understand causal processes that occur over time, yet their conclusions are based on observations made at only one time. For example, if your cross-sectional study of patients recently discharged from a psychiatric hospital found that those who were living with their families were functioning better and had less symptomatology than those who were not living with their families, then you would not know whether the differences in functioning or symptomatology between the two groups commenced before or after they entered their current living arrangements. In other words, you wouldn't know whether different living arrangements helped cause differences in functioning and symptomatology or whether the latter differences helped to explain placement in particular living arrangements.

FIGURE 12.5 Multiple Time-Series Design: Active Initiatives over Time

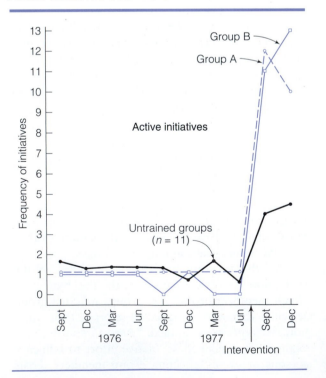

AN ILLUSTRATION OF A QUASI EXPERIMENT EVALUATING A FAMILY PRESERVATION PROGRAM

One of this book's authors (Rubin) contracted with a county child protective service agency to evaluate the effectiveness of one of the agency's programs. The 3-year federally funded demonstration program aimed to prevent foster care placement—and thus preserve families—of children of substance-abusing parents who had been referred for child abuse or neglect. The program sought to achieve its family preservation aims by having its staff provide both intensive case management intervention and direct child welfare services that emphasized things such as role modeling, behavioral techniques, and the use of the relationship between worker and parents.

Although the routine child protective services provided by other agency units were similar to the services in the demonstration program, two things set the demonstration program apart from the routine services: (a) Federal funding enabled the demonstration program practitioners to have much lower caseloads and thus see their clients much more frequently than the practitioners in the other units; and (b) contracts with other agencies were established to improve the prospects that families in the demonstration program would receive a comprehensive spectrum of services to meet their multiple needs. Because random assignment to experimental and control groups was not acceptable to the agency, Rubin devised a quasi-experimental design. One component of the overall evaluation design was called the *overflow design*. The overflow design was a nonequivalent comparison group design because it sought to achieve comparability between groups of clients treated and not treated by the demonstration program without using random assignment to achieve that comparability. Instead of random assignment, the basis for determining which treatment condition each family received was whether the demonstration program's caseloads were full at the time of case assignment.

The demonstration program had far fewer practitioners than the rest of the agency and could serve only 42 active cases at any particular time. Consequently, practitioners expected that many substance-abusing parents would be referred to the demonstration program when its caseloads were full and therefore would have to be referred back to the other units where they would receive the same routine services that all clients received before the demonstration program began.

Despite lacking random assignment, this design would probably possess adequate internal validity because it seemed unlikely that families that happen to be referred when caseloads are full would not be comparable to families that happen to be referred when caseloads are not full. It seemed reasonable to suppose that if demonstration program families had fewer placements of children out of the home than did comparison group families (in the overflow group) that received the routine services, the difference could be attributable to the effects of the program rather than to extraneous differences between the two groups.

Although it seemed unlikely that the two groups would not be comparable, Rubin recognized that this was not the same degree of unlikelihood provided by random assignment. He wondered, for example, whether those practitioners who refer the families would eventually become predisposed to referring only those cases in greater need to the demonstration program. This did not seem to be a far-fetched possibility because the referring practitioners might want to see that the cases with the most need get the most intensive, most comprehensive services. Also, they might tire of having cases referred to the demonstration program referred back to them during overflow periods and therefore might become predisposed to not refer cases to the demonstration program unless those cases were in unusually great need. Another concern was that practitioners in the routine units, who knew about the family preservation aims and methods of the demonstration program, might resent the extra resources and lower caseloads of the demonstration program workers and consequently might copy some of the demonstration program methods to prove that they could be just as effective at preserving families.

In light of these concerns, Rubin added a simple time-series component to the design. It examined agency-wide out-of-home placements of children of referred substance-abusing parents during the four 6-month intervals immediately preceding the demonstration program and four 6-month intervals after it began. He reasoned that if the demonstration program methods were effective and that routine unit practitioners were copying those methods, it would be reflected in a countywide (combining both the demonstration program cases and the routine service unit cases) reduction in out-of-home placements after the onset of the program, and thus no differences might appear in the overflow design. He also reasoned that the same reduction might occur if the demonstration program was effective but its cases were in greater need than the cases in the other units. The results of the non-equivalent comparison group component (overflow design) provided relatively little support for the effectiveness of the demonstration program. Still, the results of the simple time-series design component partially supported the program's effectiveness (Rubin, 1997).

Although cross-sectional studies don't permit definitive, conclusive inferences about what is really causing what, they can have value in building our profession's scientific knowledge base. For example, by showing that two variables are related, cross-sectional studies can support the plausibility of the notion that one might be the cause of the other. Likewise, if they show no relationship between the two variables, then the notion of a causal relationship is less plausible. Suppose that a cross-sectional study examines the plausibility of parent–child discord as a cause of childhood behavioral disorders by administering two measures to children at the same point: One assesses the degree of parent–child discord, and one assesses whether the child has a behavioral disorder. If the two measures are highly and positively correlated—that is, if the probability of behavioral disorder is higher when the amount of parent–child discord is greater—then the results support the plausibility of the supposition that the discord contributes to the causation of behavioral disorders.

Although the results are consistent with the notion that discord helps cause the disorder, they do not themselves demonstrate that the nature of the relationship is indeed causal. For instance, time order is not taken into account. Perhaps the causal order of the relationship is the other way around— that is, perhaps parent–child discord, rather than causing the behavioral disorder, increases as a result of the disorder. Also, the preceding correlation by itself does not rule out alternative variables that might cause both the discord and the behavioral disorder. For example, perhaps stressful life events produce both problems simultaneously.

Recognizing that simple correlations at one point in time do not permit causal inferences, researchers using cross-sectional designs may attempt to rule out the plausibility of rival hypotheses by controlling for alternative variables through multivariate statistical procedures. They do that by collecting data on as many plausible alternative explanatory variables as they can and then analyzing all of the variables simultaneously.

Suppose, for example, that a child guidance center administrator wants to examine whether certain aspects of treatment are associated with better outcomes than other aspects. Does the level and/or type of the clinician's educational degree matter? Do children who receive individual therapy and family therapy in addition to play therapy have better outcomes than those who receive only one or two of those treatment modalities? To simply compare the outcomes without any multivariate controls would be of little value because important differences in factors associated with prognosis could explain why they were referred to a certain type of practitioner or to a certain type of treatment regimen. But suppose that the study controlled for such factors— including every potentially relevant variable in each child's case record—and found that regardless of socioeconomic and other background variables, diagnosis, and so on, there was no difference in outcome between those children treated by psychologists with PhDs and those treated by social workers who either had MSW degrees or were in the field internship of their second year of their MSW program. Those results would not offer as much support for causal inferences as would the results of a well-controlled experiment or of the quasi experiments discussed above, but they would give the administrator some evidentiary grounds for increasing service provision within the agency's limited budget by utilizing more clinicians who are less costly than PhD psychologists. (We are not suggesting that those would be the likely results. As you might imagine, if this were a psychology research text, we might be tempted to alter the results in this fictitious example.)

Although these designs lack the level of internal validity inherent in the designs discussed above in this chapter, they are often stronger from the standpoint of external validity. Their external validity is enhanced if they study a larger and more representative sample of people in the real world than is possible with most experiments or quasi experiments.

EP 4, 9

» CASE CONTROL STUDIES

A type of design that shares some of the internal validity weaknesses and external validity strengths of cross-sectional studies—and that also relies on multivariate statistical procedures to improve the plausibility of its inferences—is called the case control design. The case control design is popular because of its feasibility. As in cross-sectional designs, data can be collected at just one point in time. The case control design compares groups of cases that have had contrasting outcomes and then collects *retrospective* data about past differences that might explain the difference in outcomes.

Suppose we want to learn what interventions may be effective in preventing children who are victims of child abuse from becoming perpetrators of abuse as adults. As will be discussed in the next chapter, we might conduct an experiment that tested one or more particular interventions. But experiments in general are often not feasible, and in this case an additional obstacle to feasibility would be the need to follow and measure the participating children over many years, even after they reach parenthood. Using the case control design as an alternative, we could find a sample of two groups of parents who had been victims of child abuse: one group that had been referred at least once as adults to public child welfare agencies as perpetrators of child abuse and another group that had never been so referred.

We could then collect retrospective data from the adults in each group, asking about their past experiences and seeking to find some intervention that the nonperpetrators were much more likely than the perpetrators to have received earlier in life. (Or perhaps we'll find something harmful

that the perpetrators were more likely to have experienced.) Suppose we find that after controlling statistically for a variety of relevant personal attributes and experiences, the main past experience that distinguishes the two groups is whether a volunteer from a Big Brother or Big Sister agency or some similar program provided them with a long-term, positive, caring relationship that commenced soon after they had been abused as children. That finding would suggest that practitioners intervening with abused children might want to do all they can to secure such a relationship for the children.

But despite their popularity, case control designs can be fraught with problems that limit what can be inferred or generalized from their findings. Cases may need to be selected using sampling procedures that create doubt about how representative they are of the population of people with their outcomes or past experiences. For example, advertisements may be needed to find adults who were abused as children and who did and did not become perpetrators. The people recruited in that fashion may be quite unlike those who cannot be found or who are unwilling to participate in such a study. (We'll examine sampling procedures in Chapter 15.)

Also, perhaps the good relationships children had with caring volunteers are explained more by their preexisting childhood resilience than by the effect of the relationships on the children's resilience. In other words, perhaps the children who were already more resilient were more motivated and better able to utilize and connect with the adult volunteers.

In addition, perhaps adult memories of childhood experiences may be faulty. Forgetting is only one way in which their memories could be faulty. Another way is termed recall bias. Maybe the perpetrators had relationships with adult volunteers that were just as good as the relationships that the nonperpetrators had, but their current recollections of the quality and value of those relationships are tainted by knowing that things didn't work out for them later in life. Likewise, perhaps the adults who are leading happier and more successful lives are more predisposed to attribute their well-being to happy childhood memories while perhaps blocking out the negative ones.

The above are just a few of the problems with the case control design; Shadish et al. (2001) list many more. Despite these problems, studies using case control designs—like cross-sectional designs— can be used in an exploratory fashion to generate hypotheses about the possible effects of interventions. If they use multivariate statistical procedures, the plausibility of the explanations they postulate becomes more tenable. Consequently, they can provide a valuable basis for designing studies using more valid designs to test the effectiveness of those interventions. An example of a valuable case control study is summarized in the box "A Case Control Study of Adverse Childhood Experiences as Risk Factors for Homelessness."

» PRACTICAL PITFALLS IN CARRYING OUT EXPERIMENTS AND QUASI EXPERIMENTS IN SOCIAL WORK AGENCIES

Successfully carrying out valid, useful experimental or quasi-experimental research in social work takes more than developing a rigorous research design. Unlike such studies carried out in other disciplines

A CASE CONTROL STUDY OF ADVERSE CHILDHOOD EXPERIENCES AS RISK FACTORS FOR HOMELESSNESS

Along with three associates, Daniel Herman, a social work professor at Columbia University, conducted a case control study to ascertain whether adult homelessness could be explained in part by certain adverse childhood experiences (Herman, Susser, Struening, & Link, 1997). They began by analyzing available data from an earlier survey of 1,507 adults that was conducted in 1990. They then reinterviewed respondents to that survey, including all 169 who reported having been homeless at some time in their adult lives and a comparable group who had never been homeless but who had attributes typically associated with a higher risk of homelessness (being poor, mentally ill, and so on).

In their follow-up interviews, they used a scale designed to assess respondents' recollections of the quality of parental care during childhood. The answers to various items on the scale enabled the researchers to determine whether the respondent recalled the following types of adverse childhood experiences: lack of parental care, physical abuse, sexual abuse, lack of care plus either type of abuse, and any childhood adversity.

Their initial results indicated that lack of care and physical abuse were each strongly correlated with a greater likelihood of homelessness. The combination of lack of care plus either physical or sexual abuse during childhood was even more strongly correlated with a greater likelihood of adult homelessness.

What made this study particularly valuable, however, was its use of multivariate statistical procedures to control for extraneous variables that might explain away the above findings. Using these procedures, the researchers were able to control for the respondent's gender, age, ethnicity, current residence (urban vs. rural), parental socioeconomic status, whether the family was on welfare during childhood, and the extent of current depressive symptoms. It was important to control for these variables. For example, growing up in poverty might be the real explanation for an increased likelihood of homelessness as an adult and also explain adverse childhood experiences. Parents living in poverty are less likely to be able to care well for their children. Thus, the relationship between adverse parental care and adult homelessness might be spurious—with both attributes being explained by poverty.

A noteworthy strength of this study was its control for the respondent's current emotional well-being. Herman and his colleagues astutely reasoned that a current depressed mood among some respondents might bias them toward recalling more adverse aspects of their childhood experiences. Likewise, respondents who were currently better off emotionally might be biased against recalling adverse childhood experiences.

After controlling for all these variables in their multivariate analyses, Herman and his colleagues found that their initial results changed somewhat. Lack of care and physical abuse continued to be strongly correlated with homelessness, and so did the combination of the two. But the combination of lack of care and sexual abuse was no longer a significant correlate of adult homelessness.

Another nice feature of this study was the way its authors discussed the strengths and limitations of their case control design. It's easy for authors to point out their study's strengths, and indeed there were many in this study. Not so easy yet more impressive is when authors correctly discuss their study's limitations. Thus, Herman and his colleagues point out that people with particularly lengthy homelessness experiences were probably underrepresented in their sample and that despite their control for current level of depression, recall bias is still a potential threat to the validity of their findings because respondents who had been homeless might be predisposed toward recalling more adverse childhood experiences. But recall bias comes with the territory when conducting even the best-case control studies, and this one certainly deserves recognition as among the best in social work.

that tend to take place in laboratory settings or research clinics controlled by researchers, social work experiments tend to take place in agency settings that are controlled by people who are not researchers, who may not understand the requisites of experimental and quasi-experimental designs, and who may even resent and attempt to undermine the demands of the research design. Consequently, if you try to do this kind of research, it won't take you long to learn that in this business the various adages and two-word bumper-sticker warnings about best-laid plans going awry are particularly applicable. Let's now look at four practical pitfalls that are commonly encountered in implementing experimental and quasi-experimental research in service-oriented agencies.

Fidelity of the Intervention

The term intervention fidelity refers to the degree to which the intervention actually delivered to clients was delivered as intended. We often evaluate social work interventions that cannot be spelled out in step-by-step manuals. Instead, we rely on social work practitioners to implement general guidelines in skillful, creative, and idiosyncratic ways with each client. Some practitioners, however, might have better judgment than others. Some might misunderstand or misinterpret the intervention's intent. This means that the intervention that we think we are evaluating may not be the one intended for experimental group participants or that the services received by experimental and control group participants may be more similar than we intended. Related reasons why interventions (the independent variables of experimental and quasi-experimental research) may not be implemented as intended include delays and start-up problems in implementing new programs, the use of staff members who are inexperienced with or untrained in the new intervention, high initial staff turnover in new programs, organizational changes that affect the program, loss of staff enthusiasm over time, and ongoing supervision provided by agency supervisors who may not follow the research protocol.

A good way to assess intervention fidelity is to videorecord several randomly selected treatment sessions from each of your practitioners. Have two experts in the intervention independently view each recorded session and then complete a rating scale assessing their judgment of the degree to which the intervention in the session was implemented appropriately. Calculate the correlation of the two independent sets of ratings. If it is high—say, around .80—then you have good interrater reliability. Hopefully, the raters' scale scores will also indicate that the intervention fidelity was at least adequate. For example, suppose that the rating scale categories, with the corresponding score in parentheses, were *unacceptable* (1), *minimally acceptable* (2), *almost acceptable* (3), *acceptable* (4), and *excellent* (5). If your study's intervention fidelity ratings were consistently at or above a score of 4 (acceptable) but your main findings showed that the intervention was not effective, then it would be difficult for critics to attribute your main findings to a lack of intervention fidelity.

But you do not have to wait until the end of your study to have the tapes rated and utilize the ratings. You could have that done incrementally throughout your study. If you find early in your study that the tapes are receiving low ratings, then you can take steps to try to improve the way the practitioners in your study are implementing the intervention. Better yet, have some ratings done on a pilot basis before your study begins. If there are intervention fidelity problems, then delay the onset of the study until you correct the problem and begin to consistently achieve acceptable ratings.

This would not, however, remove the need to assess fidelity during your study as well.

Contamination of the Control Condition

Even if the experimental group receives the intended intervention at an acceptable level of intervention fidelity, the control condition can be contaminated if control group and experimental group members interact. Suppose, for example, that an experiment in a school social work intervention assigns students in the same school to either an experimental group that receives the new intervention being tested or a control group that receives the routine services. The students in each group will interact in the school setting, and the improvements among the experimental group students may therefore have a beneficial spillover effect on the behavior of the control group students. If this happens, the two groups will not be as different on outcome measures (dependent variables) as was predicted, and we may therefore erroneously conclude that the new intervention did not make a difference. Solomon and Paulson (1995) suggest that contamination of the control condition can even occur if experimental and control group clients share the same agency waiting room.

Resistance to the Case Assignment Protocol

Some practitioners may resent having to assign cases to treatment conditions on the basis of research requirements rather than on the basis of their own professional judgment about the best service match for each client. Practitioners tend to believe that the services they provide are effective, so they may not be committed to adhering to the research protocol in case assignment because they think they already know the answer to the research question. Believing they already know what services work best for what clients, they may feel compelled to violate—perhaps in a covert fashion—the research protocol to make sure that the client receives the service they think the client should receive. Even if they are unsure as to what service works best for what client, they may press to enroll clients in the greatest need into the experimental condition because it's new and innovative or offers more services than does the control condition.

Shadish et al. (2001) reviewed studies that had the following findings about unsuccessful implementation of case assignment protocols: (a) Implementation is less likely to be successful when agency staff implement the case assignment decisions than when outside researchers control them; (b) practitioners seek loopholes to exempt some clients from the case assignment protocol, and when such exemptions are allowed, the successful implementation of the protocol is less likely; (c) implementation is less likely to be successful when several people rather than one person control the case assignment process; and (d) covert manipulation of random assignment occurred often in 30 reviewed criminal justice experiments.

Shadish and his associates offer a number of recommendations to alleviate the above case assignment problems. The following are based on their recommendations and are most relevant to social work evaluations in service-oriented agencies: (a) Carefully explain the purpose and nature of the case assignment protocol to agency staff; (b) provide incentives to them for implementing the protocol properly; (c) pilot-test the randomization procedure in the agency; (d) make sure that you develop clearly worded procedures—in operational terms—for implementing, controlling, and monitoring the case assignment protocol throughout the entire study; (e) have the case assignment protocol controlled by only one person who is part of the research team and not an agency staff member; (f) keep the master list of case assignments in a secure place and a backup copy of it in a different secure place; (g) do not show the master assignment list to agency staff; (h) hold ongoing meetings with agency staff to discuss the case assignment process; (i) have a research staff member continually monitor the implementation of the case assignment protocol throughout the entire study; and (j) keep a log throughout the study of each case assignment and any violations of the case assignment protocol.

Client Recruitment and Retention

Recruiting a sufficient number of clients to participate in the study can be difficult when the research must rely on referrals of clients from outside agencies. This can be particularly problematic when the research design precludes joint involvement by referred clients in the services provided by the referring agencies. This can result in the "dumping" by those agencies of cases they do not want to serve, perhaps because the dumped clients resist services or seem less likely to benefit from services. Moreover, the agencies may be reluctant to refer any clients because that might adversely affect the referring agency's reimbursement when it is based on the amount of services provided directly by the referring agency. Referring agencies also might not understand and may even resent having their referrals assigned to a control condition, particularly if that assignment means referring control clients back to the referral agency.

Moreover, difficulties in client recruitment and retention can arise from the clients' own reactions to case assignment procedures and measurement requirements. Clients may resent the use of randomized procedures to determine which service they receive, and they may therefore not participate. Some clients might first agree to participate and then change their minds after learning that they have not been assigned to the new, innovative, experimental condition. Other clients might take longer to drop out of the control or comparison condition; perhaps after being inconvenienced by completing the pretesting, they will refuse to participate in the posttesting. (Problems in retention are the same as the problems of attrition, discussed in Chapter 11.)

Failing to recruit a sufficient number of clients can also result from overly optimistic estimates or promises by the staff in agencies where a study takes place. Relying on such estimates or promises can be particularly risky when that agency has never before served as a site for an experiment or quasi experiment. For example, a while back the staff at a child guidance center estimated that it could provide more than 100 clients for a 1-year experiment evaluating the effectiveness of a new intervention being delivered by its child therapists. It ended up providing fewer than 20 clients during the first year of the study, and the study had to be extended to 3 years just to obtain 39 participants (Rubin et al., 2001).

If you plan to conduct an experiment or a quasi experiment in an agency that never before served as the main site for such a study, you should be skeptical about staff estimates regarding the number of participants it can provide in a specific time frame. Minimally, you should look for evidence that would assure you that the agency really can deliver the estimated number of participants who would meet your study's eligibility requirements and who would agree to participate. If you cannot obtain that evidence based on the agency's prior experiences or existing data, you probably should conduct a brief pilot test before starting your study in that agency to see if the number of participants provided during that brief time span is consistent with the rate of participation projected for the entire study. For example, if an agency estimates that in 1 year it will provide 100 participants but provides only 3 during your 1-month pilot test, you'll probably want to revise your plans for obtaining a sufficient number of participants before implementing your study.

The foregoing possibilities do not exhaust all of the pitfalls you are likely to encounter if you attempt to carry out experimental or quasi-experimental research. They're simply among the more common ones in a seemingly endless list. The point here is twofold: (a) Be prepared to encounter pitfalls like these; and (b) build mechanisms into your design to prevent, detect, and deal with these pitfalls before they ruin your study.

EP 4, 9

Mechanisms for Avoiding or Alleviating Practical Pitfalls

Solomon and Paulson (1995) recommend several additional mechanisms to help you avoid or alleviate the pitfalls just discussed. One important suggestion is to engage agency staff members in the design of the research and enlist their support from its inception. Although this may help reduce the likelihood or degree of their resistance to the research, it will not guarantee that their resistance is eliminated. You should not assume that agency staff members' support for the research protocol will endure as they begin to encounter daily practice concerns. Instead, you should build into the study ongoing mechanisms in which some research staff members are on-site throughout the project to interact with program staff members and monitor whether they are complying with the research protocol and implementing the experimental and control conditions as intended.

Another suggestion is to locate experimental and control conditions in separate buildings or agencies. This may help avoid contaminating the control condition. You might promote the fidelity of the intervention by developing a treatment manual that clearly and specifically defines the components and steps of both experimental and control interventions. You might anticipate and alleviate client recruitment and retention problems by planning to recruit clients assertively on an ongoing basis throughout your study rather than assume that your initial cohort will be large enough and will remain intact. As we discussed in the section above on attrition, client recruitment and retention might also be enhanced by reimbursing clients for their participation, particularly for their time and efforts in pretesting and posttesting.

Another good idea is to conduct a pilot study before implementing your main study. Above we mentioned conducting a brief pilot test just to see if the agency estimate about the projected number of study participants is accurate. A pilot study can also help you detect additional problems. Do you have intervention fidelity? Is imitation of treatments occurring in the control condition? Are there unanticipated problems in the way instruments are being administered or completed? Are there any other unanticipated data collection problems? Do staff who initially agreed to your protocol for assigning cases to experimental and comparison groups—perhaps because they really didn't understand the protocol and its implications or perhaps because they just weren't paying that much attention and wanted to appear agreeable—start objecting to the protocol and perhaps trying to undermine it when they realize that clients they think should receive the new intervention are being assigned to the control group?

Another good reason for conducting a pilot study is that if you submit a grant application to obtain funding for an experiment or quasi experiment, then showing that you completed a successful pilot study is likely to reassure the funding source that you have detected and resolved any of the above pitfalls likely to undermine your study. In light of all the foregoing reasons, some consider conducting a pilot study not only a good idea but essential as well.

» QUALITATIVE TECHNIQUES FOR AVOIDING OR ALLEVIATING PRACTICAL PITFALLS

Detecting and alleviating practical pitfalls is one place in which techniques commonly employed in qualitative studies can come in handy as a valuable part of a quantitative research study. We've been mentioning qualitative methods throughout this book and will give them much more attention when we get to Chapters 18 through 20. Qualitative methods offer a number of techniques that on-site research staff members can use in attempting to observe research implementation pitfalls.

For example, they can interact formally or informally with agency staff members to identify compliance problems or learn how they are implementing the interventions. They can use videos or practitioner activity logs to assess intervention fidelity. They can also identify implementation problems by following along with (shadowing) practitioners in their daily activities. They can participate in in-service trainings or group supervision to identify discrepancies between the intended intervention and what agency trainers or supervisors are prescribing. The box "Qualitative Techniques for Experimental or Quasi-Experimental Research" summarizes the ways techniques commonly employed in qualitative studies can be used to help avoid or alleviate the many practical pitfalls that can be encountered in trying to carry out quantitative research studies.

As we leave this chapter, we hope you can begin to sense how difficult it may be to carry out successfully a well-controlled experiment or quasi experiment in a real social work setting. You will need to plan carefully and obtain substantial resources to do it well; otherwise, the practical pitfalls we have been discussing are likely to ruin carefully constructed designs that seem to have impeccable internal validity on paper. But even the best-laid plans can encounter practical obstacles that are impossible to foresee. Because of these obstacles, no experiments or quasi experiments in social work agencies are flawless. As an evidence-based practitioner, you should not feel compelled to search for—and be guided by—only those studies that have no flaws. No such studies exist. If you require that a study be flawless before you let it guide your practice, you'll wind up without any evidence to guide you. The critical challenge is to be able to recognize and be guided by those imperfect studies that offer the best evidence, recognize and perhaps be guided by weaker studies whose flaws are more serious but not fatal, and distinguish the foregoing imperfect studies from those whose egregious and fatal flaws render their findings virtually worthless from the standpoint of internal validity and causal inference.

QUALITATIVE TECHNIQUES FOR EXPERIMENTAL OR QUASI-EXPERIMENTAL RESEARCH

It is not uncommon to hear researchers known primarily for their experimental or quasi-experimental quantitative findings say that almost all of their "quantitative" studies have included components that relied on qualitative methods. Here we list some prominent qualitative techniques and the important functions they can serve in experimental and quasi-experimental studies. You can read more about these techniques in Chapters 17, 18 and 19. Many of the ideas here were derived from Solomon and Paulson (1995).

Qualitative Technique	Functions in Experimental and Quasi-Experimental Studies
Ethnographic shadowing (following along and observing practitioners in their daily activities)	• Learn how they actually implement the intervention. • Learn if the interventions and other aspects of the research protocol are being implemented as intended.
Participant observation during training or group supervision	• Identify discrepancies between the intended intervention and what agency trainers or supervisors are actually prescribing.
Participant observation during agency staff meetings	• Determine whether agency staff are complying with the research protocol and identify difficulties they are having with compliance.
Informal conversational interviews with agency staff	• Identify compliance problems with the research protocol. • Learn how they are actually implementing the interventions.
Recording practitioner–client sessions (video or audio)	• Assess the fidelity of the intervention (Is it being implemented in a skillful manner, as intended?).
Practitioner activity logs	• Assess the fidelity of the intervention. • Are the proper amounts and types of services being delivered to the clients for whom they were intended?
Event logs	• Identify major organizational and systems changes that may impede continued compliance with the research protocol.
Focus groups	• Document the process of implementing the research design and interventions and identify implementation problems. • Develop possible explanations for unexpected, puzzling findings.
Snowball sampling	• Recruit subjects from vulnerable or hard-to-find target populations.
Semistructured, open-ended interviews (using interview guides) with prospective clients who refuse services or clients who prematurely terminate services	• Learn why they are unwilling to participate or why they dropped out so as to figure out ways to improve client recruitment and retention.

Qualitative Technique	Functions in Experimental and Quasi-Experimental Studies
Content analysis of agency documents and service delivery manuals	• Identify potential practical pitfalls that need to be planned for in developing the research design.
	• Develop specificity about the services being evaluated.
	• Did the proper amounts and types of services get delivered to the clients for whom they were intended?
Semistructured, open-ended interviews with practitioners or their clients following data analysis	• Develop possible explanations for unexpected, puzzling findings.

MAIN POINTS

• When random assignment to experimental and control groups isn't possible, a nonequivalent comparison groups design can be used in which the experimental group is compared to an existing group that appears similar to it.

• Ways to strengthen the internal validity of nonequivalent comparison groups designs include selecting a comparison group as similar as possible to the experimental group, administering multiple pretests, and switching replications.

• Time-series designs can be used as an alternative to the nonequivalent comparison groups design.

• Time-series designs attempt to attain internal validity through the use of repeated measures before and after the introduction of an intervention.

• Cross-sectional studies are those based on observations made at one time.

• The case control design compares groups of cases that have had contrasting outcomes and then collects retrospective data about past differences that might explain the difference in outcomes.

• A common limitation in case control designs is recall bias. This occurs when a person's current recollections of the quality and value of past experiences are tainted by knowing that things did or did not work out for them later in life.

• Although cross-sectional studies and case control studies do not control for all threats to internal validity, by employing multivariate statistical controls, they can strengthen the plausibility of the notion that the relationships they find are explanatory in nature.

• Many practical pitfalls are likely to be encountered in attempting to implement experiments or quasi experiments in service-oriented agencies. These pitfalls may compromise the fidelity of the interventions being evaluated, contaminate the control condition or the case assignment protocol, or hinder client recruitment and retention.

• One way to detect and alleviate practical pitfalls is by conducting a pilot study of your experiment or quasi experiment before implementing it in full.

• A good way to assess intervention fidelity is to videotape several randomly selected treatment sessions from each of your practitioners. Have two experts in the intervention independently view each recorded session and then complete a rating scale assessing their judgment of the degree to which the intervention in the session was implemented appropriately.

• The inclusion of various qualitative research methods as part of an experiment can aid in detecting and alleviating many of the above problems.

REVIEW QUESTIONS AND EXERCISES

1. Briefly sketch a nonequivalent comparison groups design for evaluating the effectiveness of a parent education program for parents at high risk for child abuse. What would you do to assure the readers of your study that the threat of a selectivity bias seems remote? Include in your sketch a description of the dependent variable and when and how it would be measured.

2. Identify six things you would do to avoid or alleviate practical pitfalls in carrying out the above study.

3. Briefly sketch a multiple time-series design to evaluate the effectiveness of a statewide job-training program for welfare recipients. Explain how it provides adequate control for history, passage of time, statistical regression, and selection biases.

4. Briefly sketch a case control design to generate hypotheses about interventions that may be the most helpful in preventing teen runaways. What are the background variables that would be most important to control for? Identify and explain three uncontrolled threats to the validity of your study that would represent major reasons why the results would be exploratory only.

INTERNET EXERCISES

1. Find a study that used a nonequivalent comparison groups design to evaluate the effectiveness of a social work intervention. How well did it control for selection biases?

2. Find a study that used a simple or multiple time-series design to evaluate the effectiveness of a social work intervention. How well did it control for history, maturation or passage of time, statistical regression, and selection biases?

3. Find a study that used a case control design to test or generate hypotheses about effective social work intervention with some problem. Critically appraise the appropriateness of its conclusions in light of what you've read in this chapter. Include in your appraisal an identification of the study's major strengths and weaknesses. Does the study have value despite its limitations? Explain.

4. Find a study that used a cross-sectional design. Critically appraise the appropriateness of its conclusions in light of what you've read in this chapter. Include in your appraisal an identification of the study's major strengths and weaknesses. Does the study have value despite its limitations? Explain.

 Visit CengageBrain.com for additional practice and study opportunities including experiential exercises, research tools, glossary, flashcards, and sample test items.

13

Single-Case Evaluation Designs

Contents

EPAS Competencies for This Chapter

Competency 4   **Engage in Practice-Informed Research and Research-Informed Practice:** This competency pertains to this entire chapter because doing practice-informed research as well as engaging in research-informed practice requires being able to use single-case designs in research and critically appraise them to inform your practice.

Competency 9   **Evaluate Practice with Individuals Families, Groups, Organizations, and Communities:** This competency pertains to this entire chapter because evaluating practice often can be done using single-case designs.

What You'll Learn in This Chapter

Here you'll see how direct-service practitioners can use the logic of time-series designs with an individual client or client system in order to evaluate their own effectiveness and the effectiveness of particular interventions. These designs, then, are particularly applicable to the final stage of the evidence-based practice process.

» INTRODUCTION

In Chapter 12, we saw that when people cannot be assigned to control groups, time-series designs can help evaluate the impact of programs or interventions on groups of individuals. By taking repeated measures of the dependent variable (the service or policy goal or the target problem that one seeks to change), treated groups can serve as their own controls. These repeated measures attempt to identify stable trends in the target problem. Marked deviations in these trends that coincide with the introduction or withdrawal of the service or intervention can support the plausibility of the hypothesis that changes in the dependent variable were caused by variation in the service or intervention (the independent variable).

Key concepts here are *multiple measurement points* and *unlikely coincidences*. The more measurement points one has and the more stable the trends identified in that measurement, the easier it is to infer whether any changes in the target problem can be attributed to changes in the independent variable or to rival sources of change, such as maturation, history, or statistical regression. In other words, identifying stable trends through many repeated measures enhances the internal validity of evaluations that cannot utilize control groups by enabling the researcher to pinpoint precisely where change in the dependent variable occurs and whether those points coincide with changes in the independent variable. To the extent that changes in the dependent variable consistently occur only after the independent variable is introduced or withdrawn (and not at other times), a pattern of coincidences has been established that makes rival explanations such as maturation and history seem unlikely.

» OVERVIEW OF THE LOGIC OF SINGLE-CASE DESIGNS

Single-case evaluation designs apply the logic of time-series designs to the evaluation of the effect of interventions or policy changes on individual cases or systems. Such designs involve obtaining repeated measures of a client system with regard to particular outcome indicators of a target problem. Repeated measures of the trend in the target problem are obtained before a particular intervention is introduced, and these repeated measures are continued after intervention is introduced to see if a sustained pattern of improvement in the target problem commences shortly after the onset of intervention.

The phase of repeated measures that occurs before intervention is introduced is called the *baseline*. A baseline is a control phase—that is, it serves the same function that a control group does in group experiments. The data patterns collected during the baseline (control) phases are compared to the data patterns collected during the *intervention* (experimental) phases. To infer that an intervention is effective—that is, that improvements in the dependent variable can be attributed to the intervention and not to some rival explanation, such as history or maturation—we look for shifts in the trend or pattern of the data that coincide with shifts between baseline and intervention phases.

Consider the graph in Figure 13-1. We see a shift from a stable pattern of no consistent change in the target problem during baseline to a sustained trend of improvement in the target problem at the start of and throughout the intervention phase. Something other than the intervention may have

FIGURE 13.1 Graph of Hypothetical Single-Case Design Outcome Supporting Effectiveness of Intervention (Basic AB Design)

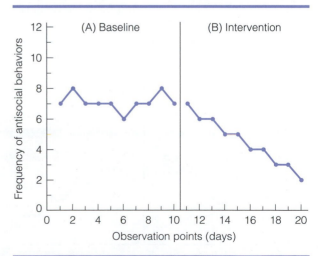

caused that change, but that would be a big coincidence given the large number of repeated measures and the absence of any marked shift in the data pattern at any time other than after intervention begins.

Now, for the sake of contrast, consider the graph in Figure 13-2. Here we see virtually the same intervention data as in Figure 13-1 but after a trend during baseline that shows that the target problem was already improving during baseline at the same rate at which it continued to improve during intervention. Here we would conclude that something other than the intervention, such as maturation or the mere passage of time, was probably causing the improvement. This example illustrates how repeated measures during the baseline and intervention phases enable us to control for threats to internal validity that refer to processes that were under way before treatment begins. Without repeated measures in each phase—that is, with only one preintervention measure and one postintervention measure—we would have no way to detect such ongoing processes (e.g., maturation, reactivity, or regression toward the mean) and thus would need experimental and control groups.

But what about history? Perhaps a big coincidence really did occur regarding the illustration depicted in Figure 13-1. Perhaps a dramatic and helpful change took place in the client's social environment precisely when intervention began. History

cannot be ruled out with results like those in Figure 13-1, but note how history seems less plausible than in simple pretest–posttest group designs that contain only two data points (one before intervention and one after) and in which longer periods of time usually separate the two data points. In single-case designs, we can pinpoint the day or the week when the stable pattern of improvement begins, and we can discuss with the client what significant events or changes occurred at that point (other than the onset of intervention) to get a fairly good idea of whether history seems like a plausible explanation.

Single-case designs can increase their control for history by having more than one baseline and intervention phase. We will examine in depth how that is done later in this chapter. For now, let us consider the following illustration. Suppose a school social worker who seeks to enhance the self-esteem and social functioning of an acting-out adolescent at high risk of dropping out of school monitors the student's disciplinary referrals and administers a standardized self-esteem scale on a weekly basis. Suppose further that the social worker decides to interrupt the intervention phase for a few weeks to see whether the student could maintain the improvement without being dependent on lengthy treatment. If a graph of the student's repeated measures resembles the data patterns displayed in Figure 13-3, then the social worker would have

FIGURE 13.2 Graph of Hypothetical Single-Case Design Outcome Not Supporting Effectiveness of Intervention (Basic AB Design)

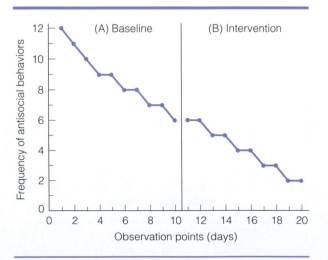

FIGURE 13.3 Graph of Hypothetical Single-Case Design Outcome Supporting Effectiveness of Intervention (ABAB Design)

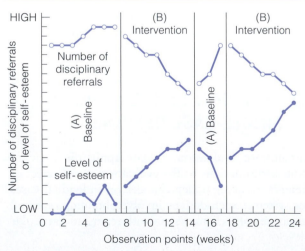

reasonable grounds for inferring that it is probably the intervention and not history that accounts for the student's improved functioning. Such an inference is reasonable because the shifts in the data patterns, or trends, occur on three successive occasions that coincide with the introduction or interruption of intervention and at no other time. With this many successive trend shifts, the odds become extremely slim that other events are producing the desired change in the target problem and simply happen to coincide with variation in the independent variable. Thus, the history hypothesis becomes far-fetched.

» SINGLE-CASE DESIGNS IN SOCIAL WORK

When the preceding logic of time-series analysis is applied to the evaluation of outcome with individual cases, the research designs can be termed *single-subject designs*, *single-case designs*, or *single-system designs*. The latter two terms are favored by those who seek to remind us that client systems need not be individual subjects but can include a family unit, a community, and so on. The term *single-case designs* has become the more commonly used term in social work. Regardless of what we call them, a distinguishing feature of these designs is that the sample size is one. Whether our unit of analysis is one individual, one family, one community, or one organization, the number of sampling elements is one. Consequently, one of the chief limitations of these designs is their dubious external validity. In Chapter 15, we'll discuss the precariousness of generalizing from samples that lack adequate size or selection procedures. What, then, are we to think of a sampling approach that contains only one element? Although some researchers dismiss these designs as little more than idiosyncratic case studies that cannot be generalized, a case can be made for their increased usage in social work.

Those who pooh-pooh single-case designs because of their small sample size perhaps overlook the important role they have played in the history of behavioral research, beginning early in the 20th century with laboratory research on animal behavior. Who, for example, would want to dismiss the importance of Pavlov's dog as a single case in the development of learning theory? As for research on human behavior, single-case designs began to proliferate during the 1960s, when behavior modification studies burgeoned.

Eventually, recognition grew that single-case designs could be used not only in behavioral modification studies but also in the evaluation of any social service intervention for which target problems could be operationally defined in terms that were conducive to multiple, repeated measures. By the late 1970s, a growing cadre of social work researchers and educators was advocating for an increased emphasis on these designs as a way to integrate research and practice, increased amount of practice-oriented research being produced, and ultimately advancement of the empirical base of social work practice. Today, single-case-design evaluations are recognized as the most rigorous way that practitioners can implement the final stage of the evidence-based practice process (as discussed in Chapter 2): assessing whether the intervention they have provided to an individual client appears to be effective in helping that client achieve his or her treatment goals.

As discussed earlier in this book, significant scientific advances do not necessarily require the use of large-scale studies that attempt to verify hypotheses. Important contributions can also be made by exploratory studies that use more flexible methods, including smaller samples, in efforts to discover new insights and generate hypotheses and theories for which generalizability can be tested later in more tightly controlled studies using larger samples.

With a high degree of internal validity, single-case experiments can identify interventions that seem to work in one, perhaps idiosyncratic context and that can be tested for generalizability in subsequent studies. These later studies might include larger-scale experiments that use control groups, or they might be additional single-case experiments that attempt to replicate the original single-case experiment in other contexts. For example, suppose a gerontological social worker finds, on the basis of his or her results in a single-case design, that reviewing life history with a particular client in a long-term care facility significantly improved the client's morale and diminished the client's depression. Gerontological social workers in similar facilities with similar clients could attempt to replicate the intervention and study. To the extent that they also replicate the results, evidence would then accumulate that supported the generalizability of the findings. Ultimately, this evidence may be sufficient to secure the more extensive degree of support needed to make feasible a larger-scale experiment utilizing a control group. But even if a larger control group experiment is never conducted, the accumulation of single-case evidence will advance the scientific basis for continuing to deliver the tested intervention.

Accumulating the findings of single-case experiments has value not only in advancing the scientific basis of particular interventions or of a particular practitioner's effectiveness but also in evaluating an entire agency or program. Suppose, for example, that a funding source calls for a program evaluation to determine whether a family service agency is providing effective services and thus merits continued or perhaps increased levels of support. Suppose further that administrative and ethical considerations rule out the possibility of using a control group in the evaluation. One option might be to conduct a time-series design. But suppose that target problems and service objectives vary substantially from case to case. The objective might be to reduce a child's antisocial behavior in one case, decrease marital conflict in another, prevent abusive parental behavior in yet another, and so on. One option would be to conduct a separate single-case experiment on each case or on a representative subset of cases and to use the idiosyncratic case objectives or target problems as the dependent variable in each experiment. The agency could then report not only the proportion of its cases that attain successful outcomes but also, and more important, the proportion of those outcomes that the logic of time-series analysis shows to have been caused specifically by receiving agency services.

A reverse process also illustrates the value of single-case designs—that is, individual practitioners or agencies may wonder whether interventions supported initially by group experiments in other settings will work as well in their particular and perhaps idiosyncratic context. For instance, suppose a few gerontological social workers first learned about reviewing life histories from an experiment reported in a gerontological social work journal, and they wondered whether they were capable of implementing the reported intervention as effectively and whether their particular clients would be able to benefit from it as much as those in the reported study, whose characteristics may have been inadequately specified or may have differed slightly from those of their clients. They could conduct single-case experiments with one or more clients to answer these questions for themselves. Such experiments would reduce their doubt not only about the effectiveness of particular interventions with particular clients but also about their own effectiveness as clinical practitioners.

EP 4, 9

» USE OF SINGLE-CASE DESIGNS AS PART OF EVIDENCE-BASED PRACTICE

As we noted above and in Chapter 2, single-case designs can be implemented by some practitioners as part of their own clinical practice with individual clients in the final phase of the evidence-based practice process. Because these designs require only one case, the practitioner need not worry about amassing large samples or assigning clients to control groups. Each experiment contains idiosyncratic objectives that are applicable to an individual case—objectives that the practitioner would be helping the client attain as a routine part of practice were no experiment to take place. Likewise, in evidence-based practice, the practitioner would routinely want to monitor the client's progress in attaining those objectives. By taking repeated measures of changes in the target problem, the practitioner both monitors client progress (or lack thereof) and acquires a tool for a more systematic understanding of events or circumstances that may exacerbate or ameliorate the target problem.

For example, suppose a child in a joint-custody arrangement is being treated for explosive and antisocial behaviors. Suppose further that the problematic behaviors tend to occur shortly before the child is about to go into the custody of one or the other parent. Repeated measures of the target behavior might help the practitioner chronologically identify this coincidence during the initial stages of service delivery, in turn helping the practitioner better understand the causes of the target problem and develop an appropriate strategy to deal with it. Practitioners who spend considerable amounts of time unsystematically attempting to record and evaluate their practices might find conducting single-case designs to be one way to make that effort more systematic and valid.

There are, however, practical obstacles to integrating single-case designs as part of direct practice. These constraints make it unrealistic for many practitioners to utilize these designs, particularly when they are working in certain kinds of agency settings or with certain types of target problems. Client crises often do not allow practitioners enough time to take repeated measures to identify baseline trends before implementing the intervention. In some settings, heavy caseloads reduce the amount of time practitioners have to plan or conduct repeated measures during any phase. The practitioner's peers and supervisors in an agency may not recognize the value of researching one's own practice effectiveness and therefore may not support it. Clients may resent the extensive self-monitoring procedures that these designs may require.

Despite these obstacles, practitioners should strive to implement single-case designs whenever they can. Some interventions or services have not yet received adequate scientific testing concerning their beneficial or harmful effects on clients. Others that have been tested and found to be relatively effective are not effective with all clients who receive them. In light of this, the question may be not whether each of us can afford the time needed to use single-case methodology as part of our practices but, rather, whether our profession can afford not to allocate the time. Given our commitment to the social welfare of our clients and our aspiration to call our work truly professional, we can conduct single-case experiments when implementing untested interventions to see whether they are helping clients, harming them, or merely wasting scarce resources that could be put to better use. Likewise, concern for a particular client should prompt us to conduct a single-case evaluation, if feasible, to assess whether even an intervention whose probable effectiveness is supported by prior research is effective for that particular client.

Wasting scarce resources in the social welfare arena is not just a question of efficiency or public accountability; it is also a question of compassion and professional concern for clients. If we are wasting our own and the client's time on ineffectual services, then we are not ameliorating suffering. Nor are we able to use that time to implement alternative services that might really help that client. By conducting single-case designs as part of their practice, social work practitioners can obtain immediate feedback that will indicate whether they should modify the service program to better help (or perhaps stop hindering) specific clients.

Our point is not that practitioners would necessarily become researchers intent on publishing their findings but rather that the use of scientific measurement procedures and single-case design logic can be an important part of evidence-based practice—simply in being a more compassionate, conscientious, and professional practitioner—and requires no aspirations to be a researcher or to publish scientific findings. Suppose, for example, that a new technique is developed for the treatment of trauma symptoms among rape victims, a technique that requires clients to engage in emotionally painful treatment sessions in which they repeatedly recall and retell the details of the rape. Suppose further that although the technique's effectiveness has not yet been adequately tested with well-controlled experiments or quasi experiments, clinical practitioners worldwide are excited about it and using it. Among the practitioners who use this technique and have sufficient time to use single-case methodology, which are the more compassionate and professional—those who use single-case design logic and scientific measurement procedures to monitor whether this intervention is helping clients, harming them, or wasting their time or those who are less systematic about monitoring the technique's effects?

Along the same lines, suppose you had a rare illness that required the use of one or more alternative medical treatments that had not yet been adequately tested. Which physician would you find more humane and want to treat you—one who used single-case principles to monitor the positive and negative effects of each alternative treatment on you or one who simply applied the treatment with which he or she was most comfortable and then didn't burden you with a bunch of scientific testing?

But readers should not be misled by an overly rosy portrayal of the feasibility of conducting single-case designs as part of their own practices, nor should they think that single-case designs offer a panacea for resolving long-standing doubts about the effectiveness of social work practice. As we will see shortly, conducting repeated measures of target problems in a way that provides data that are credible from the standpoint of reliability and validity can be a difficult and complex task. And delaying treatment until a stable trend of baseline measurements has been established (even when it's possible to do so) is a lot easier to recommend in a textbook or classroom lecture than to do when confronted by individuals who are suffering. Also, many client problems do not lend themselves to any sort of repeated measures. It is silly, for example, to conduct repeated measures to see whether a crisis intervention succeeded in helping a family whose house burned down find an emergency shelter. It either did or did not; one need not monitor variation in the degree of goal attainment to find out.

These limitations notwithstanding, single-case designs can be valuable tools for social work researchers, administrators, planners, and practitioners. Because most readers of this text are preparing for careers as social work practitioners, the rest of this chapter will treat the topic of single-case designs primarily from the standpoint of conducting them as part of one's own evidence-based practice. But this treatment will also provide information needed by researchers who seek to conduct single-case designs or by administrators who will use them for agency evaluation, planning, and accountability.

» MEASUREMENT ISSUES

Early decisions in planning a single-case experiment involve identifying the target problem and goals and defining them in operational terms. These decisions influence the next phase of the research plan: developing a measurement and data collection plan.

EP 4, 9

Operationally Defining Target Problems and Goals

Identifying target problems is chiefly a practice consideration and is treated in depth in various texts on practice and assessment. It might involve gathering information from a broad spectrum of individuals who are connected to the client system and carefully considering the reliability and validity of information provided by alternative sources. It might involve the use of standardized assessment instruments, such as self-report scales. It might involve a process of partialization in which problems are prioritized: The most urgent yet easily resolved problems are addressed first, and the thornier, longer-term ones are tackled later. It might also involve establishing a contract in which client and practitioner agree on the problems to be tackled and

how they will be monitored. Readers are referred to practice texts (Compton & Galaway, 1994; Hepworth, Rooney, & Larsen, 2002; Reid & Epstein, 1972) for a thorough treatment of this topic from a practice standpoint.

From a research standpoint, the critical issue is defining the target problems in operational terms (i.e., in precise and observable terms). Operational definitions were discussed at length in Chapter 8, and the same issues discussed there apply to single-case designs. For some reason, however, practitioners seem more likely to dispute the applicability of operational definitions when thinking about individual cases than when thinking about research in general. Some argue that it is impossible to define certain clinical constructs, such as level of social functioning, in specific and observable terms. However, most skeptics ultimately realize that clinicians or clients would never have selected a target problem in the first place if they had no way to observe, at least indirectly, its indicators—that is, they would never choose to work toward improving client functioning in one area or another unless they already had some basis for observing certain indicators that convinced them that the level of functioning was unacceptably low.

Any problem that we would have reason to work on, therefore, could be operationally defined if we simply considered the specific indicators that led us to decide that it needed our attention. Consider the alternative. If it were possible to identify a problem that could not be defined in operational terms, then on what grounds would the practitioner or client have decided that it required intervention? And how in the world would they ever decide whether the problem was or was not adequately resolved? Here we are dealing not just with a research issue but also with a practice issue. Imagine, for example, trying to learn how to do clinical assessment or when to terminate interventions from a practice instructor who taught exclusively via presentations of his or her own cases and was unable to identify for students what he or she observed in each case that led him or her to work on one particular target problem in one case and a different problem in another, or what the instructor observed that led him or her to terminate the intervention in each case.

In considering operational definitions, some students note that practitioners might rely on the client's complaint that a particular problem requires attention. But even here, practitioners are using an operational definition; that is, they are persuaded to work on a problem on the basis of their observation of the extent of the client's expressed difficulty or dissatisfaction with that problem. Thus, they could take repeated measures simply by having clients indicate daily on a brief scale the degree of difficulty they felt they experienced with the problem that day.

But saying that all identified target problems can be operationally defined does not mean that the selection of observable indicators is always a routine or easy decision. We often are confronted with knotty target problems that cannot be observed directly (e.g., anxiety, depression, or self-esteem issues) and that require us to select and observe indirect indicators of the problem. There may be an extensive array of potential indicators, and selecting the wrong one might lead to incorrect conclusions later. Take self-esteem, for example.

Some self-report measures of self-esteem treat level of self-esteem as a fairly permanent personality trait, and consequently, these measures are not sensitive to small, short-term changes. If the operational definition of the target problem were a score on such a scale, then it might be exceedingly difficult to detect changes in self-esteem that represented meaningful improvements from a clinical standpoint.

Among the array of potential observable indicators of a target problem, there may be positive indicators that represent the problem's absence or negative indicators that signify its presence. For instance, if the target problem concerned a client's depression, an operational definition might involve negative indicators, such as the frequency of crying spells or the frequency of self-derogatory remarks. The goal then would be a reduction in the observed indicators. The operational definition might also include positive indicators, such as the amount of time spent in social interaction with friends. If so, then the goal would be to increase those indicators. Practitioners might want to restrict their definition to positive indicators for clinical reasons so that they and the client are not always thinking in negative terms about the problem. They might also choose to monitor several indicators of the problem or goal, perhaps including some that are positive as well as some that are negative.

What to Measure

Because of the need to obtain many repeated observations in single-case experiments, the operational indicators should occur frequently enough to be measured on a regular basis. Direct-service practitioners working in a suicide prevention program, for example, might want to monitor the amount of sleep a client gets each day, the daily number of positive client self-cognitions, or weekly scores on a self-report depression inventory. The practitioners probably would not record an infrequent event, such as the number of suicide attempts each day or week, because it would take too long to establish enough variation in the data pattern. On the other hand, a planner or administrator who uses single-case methodology to evaluate the effectiveness of an entire suicide prevention program could appropriately monitor the number of reported suicides or suicide attempts each week in a populous area served by the program. Likewise, a practitioner who works with an abusive parent might want to monitor the amount of time the parent plays with the child each day or the number of positive statements (praise, encouragement, and so on) from parent to child during weekly observation sessions rather than record the daily or weekly incidence of serious abuse by the parent. But an administrator of a countywide program to prevent child abuse could appropriately monitor the countywide incidence of serious child abuse each week.

No strict rule determines how many operational indicators we should measure. The fewer we measure, the greater the risk that we fail to detect client improvement on indicators other than those being measured. For example, a case manager might be effective in motivating a chronically mentally ill client to take medication as prescribed and in securing more community support services. But if the case manager measured only the client's degree of psychopathology or the client's job-seeking behavior, then he or she might get negative results and erroneously conclude that the intervention was not working. On the other hand, it is unwise to try to measure so many indicators that the data-gathering process becomes unwieldy and overwhelms the client, practitioner, or both. Moreover, the greater the number of indicators that are monitored, the greater the risk that the data pattern of one or more of them will show improvement after intervention solely on the basis of chance fluctuations.

Triangulation

As a rule of thumb, two or three indicators are generally considered appropriate. This is usually a feasible approach on the one hand, and it meets the criterion of triangulation on the other. As discussed in Chapter 9, triangulation is a principle that applies to all types of research designs, not just single-case experiments. It refers to situations in which researchers are confronted with a multiplicity of imperfect measurement options, each having advantages and disadvantages. To maximize the chances that the hypothesized variation in the dependent variable will be detected, the researcher triangulates measures: More than one measurement option is used. Despite its connotation of a triangle, triangulation does not require using three options, only more than one.

In single-case designs, triangulation does not necessarily mean that more than one target problem is to be measured. It means that more than one indicator of the same target problem is to be measured. For instance, a school social worker whose client is underachieving might want to monitor the amount of time the client spends on homework each night and teacher ratings of his or her class attentiveness and participation. Triangulation does not require that the social worker also monitor indicators of other problems, such as antisocial behaviors (fighting, disciplinary referrals, and so on). The practitioner may choose to monitor more than one problem, but the principle of triangulation does not require it. The principle of triangulation applies to all measurement options—not just what to measure—and we will consider it again in our discussion of data gathering.

» DATA GATHERING

The options and decisions to be made in planning measurement and data collection in single-case experiments are not unlike those that confront researchers who are designing other types of studies. Researchers must decide whether the data sources should be available records, interviews, self-report scales, or direct observations of behavior. The advantages and disadvantages of these sources are largely the same in single-case experiments as in other types of research.

Who Should Measure?

One issue involves who should do the measuring. When practitioners make measurements to evaluate their own practice, the risk of observer bias might be heightened, for it is only human to want to obtain findings that support our practice effectiveness and indicate that client suffering is being ameliorated. Perhaps even riskier is relying exclusively on clients to do the measuring themselves. Clients may be biased to perceive positive results, not only to please themselves or to project a socially desirable image to the practitioner but also to avoid disappointing the practitioner. Significant others (teachers, cottage parents, and so on) might be asked to monitor certain behaviors in the hope that they have less invested than the client or practitioner in seeing a positive outcome. But neither their objectivity nor their commitment to the study can be guaranteed. This is particularly important in light of the large amount of time and dedication that might be required to monitor the client's behavior carefully and systematically on a continuous basis.

In light of the repeated measures required by single-case designs and the strong potential for bias, there is no easy answer about who should do the measuring. Here, then, we return to the principle of triangulation and perhaps use all three of the preceding options to gather the data. In this context, we see another advantage of triangulation—the opportunity it provides for assessing measurement reliability. To the extent that different data gatherers agree in their measures, we can have more confidence that the data are accurate.

On the other hand, many disagreements among them might imply inaccuracies in the data. We say *might* because it is conceivable that a client could have different behavior patterns at different parts of the day or in different settings. For example, a child's behavior problems might appear only during the afternoon or only during the evening, and if one cottage parent works during the day and a different one has the evening shift, then their "disagreement" might not reflect unreliability. Instead, it might reflect the need for you to re-conceptualize the nature of the target problem and when and where it should be measured. The advantage of triangulation in that case is that had you only measured during the time when the problems do not appear, your data would have been more problematic than by measuring at both times. That is, by measuring both times, you increased your chances of catching any changes in the problem behavior. And if the day shift and evening shift cottage parents record different frequencies of the problem behavior, you might realize that their differences are not a reliability problem, but, rather, a reflection of when the client has the most trouble. You could then take that into account in your analysis and interpretation of your data. If, however, the disagreement comes from two cottage parents working the same shift in the same setting and with the same opportunity to observe the child's behavior, then that would be more likely to reflect a reliability problem in your data.

Sources of Data

In considering alternative sources of data (available records, interviews, self-report scales, or direct behavioral observations), several issues are particularly salient in single-case designs. Available records, for example, might enable the researcher or practitioner to obtain a retrospective baseline of pretreatment trends and therefore not have to delay treatment while collecting baseline data. This, of course, can occur only when we are fortunate enough to have access to existing records that contain carefully gathered, reliable data that happen to correspond to the way the target problem has been operationally defined in the single-case experiment.

Self-report scales also merit special consideration in single-case designs. On the one hand, they can be quite convenient; repeated measures can be expedited by simply having clients complete a brief self-report scale each day where they reside or each time the practitioner sees them. Self-report scales also ensure that the repeated measures are administered and scored in a uniform fashion.

On the other hand, the use of these scales carries special risks in single-case experiments. For one thing, clients might lose interest in completing them carefully over and over again. Perhaps a more serious risk, however, is the potential for the client to be biased to complete these scales with responses that convey a socially desirable impression. This risk would be greatest when the single-case experiment is being conducted by practitioners to evaluate their own practice because clients might be particularly predisposed to give inaccurate responses in order to please the clinicians about their helpfulness or favorably impress them.

Reliability and Validity

Readers might wonder at this point whether these risks could be avoided by using standardized self-report scales with established high levels of reliability and validity. All other things being equal (such as relevance to the problem or client, sensitivity to change, and instrument length and complexity), of course it is better to use scales whose reliability and validity have been empirically supported if such scales are available for the particular variable one seeks to measure. But the conditions under which the validity of standardized instruments is tested tend to contrast with single-case experimental conditions in critical ways. Standardized instruments tend to be validated in large-scale assessment studies in which (a) the respondent is part of a large group of individuals who have no special, ongoing relationship with the researcher and who are by and large anonymous; (b) the instrument will not be completed more than one or two times by each respondent; and (c) a respondent's score on the instrument has no bearing on whether he or she is benefiting from some service.

In contrast, when clients complete these instruments as part of single-case experiments, they are not anonymous and have a special relationship with a service provider. They may therefore be sensitive about the impression they are conveying and more intent on conveying a favorable impression than in a more anonymous situation. With each repeated completion of the instrument, their answers may become less valid, perhaps because of carelessness or because they remember their previous answers. Finally, and perhaps most important, they may be keenly aware of the difference between nontreatment (baseline) phases and treatment phases; they may know that if the service is being effective, then their scores should improve during the treatment phases. This awareness may predispose them to convey a more positive impression during the treatment phases. In light of these differences, we cannot assume that a particular self-report instrument will adequately avoid social desirability biases in a single-case experiment just because it has empirically been shown in other contexts not to have serious validity problems.

Direct Behavioral Observation

The large number of repeated measures in single-case experiments also complicates the decision to use direct behavioral observations as the data source. This is particularly problematic when the experiment is conducted as part of one's own practice because busy practitioners may lack the time needed to conduct the observations themselves or the resources needed to induce someone else to observe the client. To the extent that observation of the target problem can be limited to office or home visits, the difficulty of practitioner observation is reduced. But many target problems need to be observed on a more continuous basis.

Barring the availability of a significant other (such as a teacher, relative, or cottage parent) who is willing to observe on a regular basis, we are commonly forced to rely on our clients to observe themselves. The term for client self-observation is *self-monitoring*. If the dependent variable is the number of a certain type of thoughts or feelings that a client has during a particular period—phenomena that only the client could observe—then self-monitoring would be the only direct observation option.

The problem with self-monitoring is that, in addition to its vulnerability to measurement bias (as discussed earlier), it is highly vulnerable to the problem of research reactivity. As we discussed in Chapter 12, one way in which reactivity can occur is when the process of observing or recording the data—that is, the self-measurement process itself—brings about change in the target problem. For example, suppose a practitioner encourages a mother who has a conflictual relationship with her son to record each time she praises him and each time she scolds him. Regardless of what else the practitioner does, the mere act of recording may sensitize the mother to her tendency to scold her son too often and praise him too rarely, and this, in turn, may bring her to praise him more and scold him less.

From a clinical standpoint, of course, reactivity might not be such a bad idea—that is, self-monitoring can be used as a clinical tool to help bring about the desired change. Indeed, it's often used that way. But when it's used as the only measurement procedure in research, it clouds the process of inferring whether the intervention alone brought about the change. This problem can be offset somewhat by the realization that if self-monitoring alone is bringing about the desired change, then the change might be detected by noticing an improving trend in a graph of the pretreatment (baseline) data.

You might ask, then, "What's the best way to avoid these problems without sacrificing the use of direct observation?" Answering this question is easy; the problem is getting the resources needed to

do things the best way. First, we would again use the principle of triangulation; that is, we would have more than one person conduct the observations. Second, we would seek to include at least one observer who did not have a vested interest in the outcome of the study or the impression conveyed by the data and who therefore might be relatively unbiased. Third, we would assess the interrater reliability of the observers (how much their observations agree). Finally, we would arrange for at least one observer to conduct the observations in a relatively unobtrusive manner.

Unobtrusive versus Obtrusive Observation

As we discussed in Chapter 11, unobtrusively observing behavior means that the observer blends into the observation setting in such a way that the act of observing and recording is by and large not noticeable to those who are being observed. For example, a group worker who is attempting to reduce the amount of antisocial behavior by boys in a residential facility might ask a colleague who supervises their recreational activities to observe the number of fights, arguments, and so on that the targeted boys get into and to record the numbers in the notebook that he or she always carries while supervising the boys.

The opposite of unobtrusive observation is obtrusive observation. Measurement is obtrusive to the extent that the subject is aware of the observation and therefore vulnerable to research reactivity or to acting in an atypical manner in order to convey a socially desirable impression. Self-monitoring is perhaps the most obtrusive form of observation because the subject is both observed and observer. But many other forms of observation can be so obtrusive that the credibility of the entire study is imperiled. Some of these examples can be deceptive because researchers or practitioners may take steps that at first glance seem to provide some degree of unobtrusiveness.

For example, the researcher or practitioner may observe the client through a one-way mirror, thinking that because the client cannot see him or her, the client is less aware of the observation. To a certain extent this is true. But consider the following wrinkle. After taking pretreatment (baseline) measures through a one-way mirror of a conflictual mother–son dyad interacting, the practitioner introduces a task-centered intervention in which the practitioner and the mother agree that the mother's task will be to try to praise her son more when he acts appropriately. The practitioner continues to monitor the interactions through a one-way mirror to see if the intervention will be effective in increasing the number of statements of praise as compared to the pre-treatment baseline.

Although it is commendable that the practitioner made observations while not visible by the clients, it is wrong to suppose that the observations were truly unobtrusive or that the baseline and intervention phases were really comparable in their degree of obtrusiveness. In both phases, the mother has some degree of awareness that the practitioner is watching from the other side of the mirror. And in the intervention phase, she knows precisely which behavior—praise—the practitioner is watching for, knowledge that she did not have in the earlier, baseline phase.

Thus, the degree of obtrusiveness in both phases is compounded by the increased vulnerability to a social desirability bias during the intervention phase. And because the client is more inclined to provide the socially desirable response during the intervention phase, the problem of obtrusiveness becomes a bigger threat to the credibility of the findings. In other words, the desired increase in praise could easily have nothing to do with the efficacy of the intervention but instead merely reflect the fact that after the intervention was introduced, the client became more predisposed to put on a socially desirable performance—one that might have no correlation whatsoever to the way the mother interacts with her child in a natural setting or when the practitioner is not watching. You might think this example is far-fetched, that no one would conduct single-case research with such obvious potential measurement bias, but studies like this have not only been conducted but also published in our professional literature.

Data Quantification Procedures

Data gathered through direct observation in single-case experiments can be quantified in terms of their *frequency*, *duration*, or *magnitude*. For example, the target problem of temper tantrums could be recorded in terms of the number of temper tantrums observed in a specified period (frequency), how long each tantrum lasted (duration), or how loud or violent it was (magnitude). Using the principle of triangulation, all three quantification procedures could be used simultaneously.

Another procedure—*interval recording*—combines both frequency and duration and may be used when it is impractical to record either frequency or duration alone. This method involves dividing an observation period into equal blocks of short time intervals and then recording whether the target behavior occurred at all during each interval. Suppose, for example, that a target problem of an intervention with conflictual spouses was operationally defined as the degree to which they interrupt each other when conversing. Suppose further that the observer was recording interruptions during a 30-minute period in which the couple was instructed to engage in a typical conversation. (Let's put obtrusiveness aside for now.) The interruptions might occur so rapidly that the observer would be overwhelmed trying to record each one in a frequency count. The interruptions might last so long that duration recording would be too fatiguing. With interval recording, the observer would break the 30-minute session into equal intervals of perhaps 1 minute each. Then all that would be required would be to enter a check mark for each interval that contained at least one interruption.

But the direct observation of behavior does not always require continuous observation during lengthy sessions. *Spot-check recording* can be used to observe target behaviors that occur frequently, last a long time, or are expected to occur during specified periods. For instance, suppose a social worker in a residential treatment facility for distressed adolescents introduces a behavioral modification intervention that seeks to increase the amount of school homework that residents do during specified study periods each evening. The social worker or a cottage parent could briefly glance at the study area each evening, varying the precise time of the observation from day to day, and quickly record whether specified individuals were studying (yes or no) or simply count how many were studying at that particular moment. Spot checks thus have the advantage of being not only less time consuming but also less obtrusive than continuous observation because the observer appears only briefly and at unexpected, intermittent times.

The Baseline Phase

The logic of single-case designs requires taking enough repeated measures to make it unlikely that extraneous factors (such as changes in the client's environment) would account for improvements that take place in the target problem with the onset of intervention. The logic also relies on comparing trends that are identified in the repeated measures to control for factors such as maturation or statistical regression. Based on this logic, the internal validity of single-case designs is enhanced when the baseline period has enough measurement points to show a stable trend in the target problem and enough points to establish the unlikelihood that extraneous events that affect the target problem will coincide only with the onset of intervention. Although the ideal number of baseline measurement points needed will vary depending on how soon a stable trend appears, it is reasonable to plan for somewhere between 5 and 10 baseline measures. With some stable baselines, one can begin to see trends with as few as three to five data points. But the more data points we have, the more confidence we can have in the stability of the observed trend and in the unlikelihood that extraneous events will coincide only with the onset of intervention.

The realities of practice do not always permit us to take an ideal number of baseline measures, however. For example, the client's problem might be too urgent to delay intervention any longer, even though the baseline trend appears unstable or is unclear. When an ideal baseline length is not

feasible, we simply come as close to the ideal as the clinical and administrative realities permit.

A stable trend is one that shows the target problem to be occurring in a predictable and orderly fashion. The trend is identified by plotting the data points chronologically on a graph, drawing a line between each data point, and then observing whether the overall pattern is clearly increasing, as in part A of Figure 13-4, decreasing (part B), relatively flat (part C), or cyclical (part D). By contrast, part E of Figure 13-4 illustrates an unstable baseline without an obvious trend.

The meaning of increasing or decreasing baselines depends on the operational definition of the target problem. If it involves undesirable phenomena such as temper tantrums, then an increasing baseline trend would mean the problem is worsening, and a decreasing baseline would indicate improvement. If the operational definition involves desirable indicators such as doing homework, then an increasing baseline would signify improvement, and a decreasing baseline would signify deterioration.

When the baseline trend signifies improvement, even if it is stable, it may be advisable to continue collecting baseline measures until the improving trend levels off, as illustrated in Figure 13-5. If intervention is introduced at the peak of an improving

FIGURE 13.4 Alternative Baseline Trends

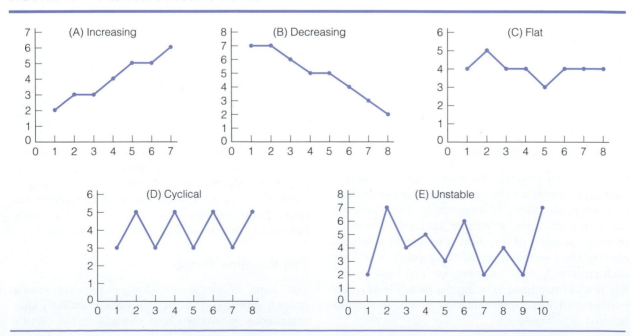

FIGURE 13.5 Graph of Hypothetical Outcome after Extending a Baseline with an Improving Trend (AB Design)

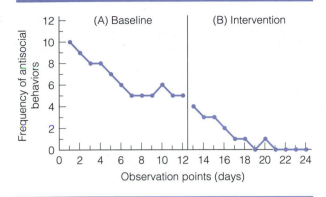

FIGURE 13.6 Graph of Two Hypothetical Outcomes with an Unstable Baseline (AB Design)

baseline trend (before it levels off), it will be difficult to achieve a dramatic improvement in the trend. In other words, the baseline trend would mean that the client was improving so steadily without any intervention that (a) even an effective intervention might not affect the rate of improvement and that (b) perhaps no intervention on that particular indicator was needed in the first place. Introducing an intervention on the heels of an improving baseline introduces the risk of erroneously concluding that an intervention made no difference simply because the ongoing improvement process was already so steady.

We would also want to extend baseline measures beyond the point at which we initially planned to introduce the intervention if the baseline data collected up to that point were unstable (i.e., if they failed to yield a predictable trend). As noted earlier, when we observe an unstable baseline, we ideally would extend the baseline measures until a stable pattern appears. However, it was also noted that the constraints of practice do not always permit us to extend the baseline until a desirable trend is obtained. Other priorities, such as client suffering or endangerment, may take precedence over the internal validity of the research design. If so, then we simply do the best we can with what we have. Perhaps the intervention is so effective that even an unstable or improving baseline pattern will prove to be clearly worse than the intervention data pattern. Figure 13-6 shows an unstable baseline juxtaposed with two alternative intervention data patterns. One pattern illustrates the difficulty

FIGURE 13.7 Graph of a Hypothetical Outcome Supporting Intervention Efficacy with an Improving Baseline (AB Design)

of interpreting outcome with an unstable baseline; the other pattern shows that it is not necessarily impossible to do so. In a similar vein, Figure 13-7 illustrates that even with an improving baseline, it may be possible to obtain results that support the efficacy of the intervention.

We also might want to deviate from the planned time of completion of the baseline phase when, after the design is implemented, we learn that extraneous environmental changes that may have a potentially important effect on the target problem will coincide with the beginning of the intervention period. For example, if the client has a severe hay fever problem and the target behavior is something like interpersonal irritability or school performance, then we would not want to introduce the intervention at the beginning or end of the hay fever season. If we learn of such a situation after the baseline phase has begun, then we might extend the baseline longer than initially planned so that it includes enough data points to identify a stable trend after the relevant environmental conditions have changed. Another option would be to withdraw the intervention for a short time later and then reintroduce it, hoping that the hiatus from treatment would provide a second baseline whose beginning or end would not coincide with important environmental changes. (This latter option is called an ABAB design, and it will be examined in more depth shortly.)

Practitioners can employ single-case practice evaluation procedures even when an adequate baseline is impossible, such as when they cannot obtain more than one or two baseline data points. They can even use these procedures when it is impossible to obtain any baseline data whatsoever. The rationale is that although the lack of an adequate baseline impedes the drawing of causal inferences, the rest of the data collected can enhance practice by providing a more scientific process for monitoring client progress. In light of the previously mentioned practical difficulties in taking repeated measures, especially regarding the practitioner's ability to obtain measures that are not highly vulnerable to various sources of measurement error, you may question whether the likely benefit of these procedures justifies their costs in those instances when it is impossible to obtain an adequate baseline. If you do not think they are justified in such instances, remember that we are referring only to instances when obtaining an adequate baseline is impossible. When you can obtain an adequate baseline, the argument for not using these procedures is much weaker.

Remember also that if you do use these procedures even when you cannot obtain more than a couple of baseline data points, your data do not provide a suitable basis for inferring anything about your efficacy. You may find that these procedures are quite valuable in enhancing your monitoring of client progress, but you should resist the temptation to claim that your data verify the effectiveness of your intervention.

We also remind you that when you cannot delay intervention in order to take baseline measures, you should consider whether it is possible to obtain a useful *retrospective baseline*. Also called a *reconstructed baseline*, a retrospective baseline is constructed from past data. The two primary sources of data for a retrospective baseline are available records or the memory of the client (or significant others). An example of using available records would be obtaining school records on attendance, grades, detentions, and so on for a child who has behavioral problems in school. An example of using memory, provided in a study by Nugent (1991), would be asking clients with anger control problems to recall how many blowups they had during the previous week or two and perhaps triangulating their data with spouse or parent recollections. Bloom, Fischer, and Orme (2006) offer the following two guidelines when relying on memory to reconstruct a baseline: (a) use specific, identifiable events that are easy to recall (such as angry blow-ups, detention referrals, and so on) and therefore less vulnerable to distortion than things that are harder to recall (such as feelings of inadequacy, anxiety, and so on); and (b) for the same reason, use only the immediate past, such as the past week or two, and do not go back more than 1 month.

» ALTERNATIVE SINGLE-CASE DESIGNS

AB: The Basic Single-Case Design

As illustrated in Figures 13-1, 13-2, 13-5, 13-6, and 13-7, a relatively simple single-case design includes one baseline phase (A) and one intervention phase (B): the AB design. This is a popular design among practitioner-researchers because it involves only one baseline phase and therefore poses the less conflict with service delivery priorities than designs with more baseline phases that will be discussed next. But this design is weaker than single-case designs with more baselines. With only one baseline, there is only one point at which the independent variable shifts from baseline to intervention. Consequently, only one unlikely coincidence can occur. Although taking many repeated measures reduces the plausibility that some extraneous event and not the intervention would explain a major shift in the data pattern of the dependent variable that occurs only after the onset of intervention, extraneous events are controlled much better when there are several shifts between baseline and intervention phases.

Despite its relative weakness, the AB design is still quite useful. More rigorous designs may not be feasible in many practice situations, and with enough repeated measures, the AB design can provide some logical and empirical evidence about the effectiveness of interventions for which the impact on clients has not yet received enough scientific testing. Also, AB designs can be replicated, and if the results of various AB studies on the same intervention are consistent, then the evidence about the effectiveness of the intervention is strengthened. For instance, suppose several AB studies at different times and with different clients all find that the same type of target problem begins to improve only shortly after the same intervention is introduced. How credible is the argument that with every client, an extraneous event could have coincided only with the onset of intervention and caused the improvement? AB designs are also useful in that they provide immediate feedback to practitioners, enabling them to monitor variations in the target problem, explore alternative explanations of changes with the client, and modify service delivery if the need for modification is indicated by this information. Thus, AB designs—when feasible—are an excellent way to implement the final stage of the evidence-based practice process.

ABAB: Withdrawal/Reversal Design

To better control for extraneous events, the ABAB withdrawal/reversal design adds a second baseline phase (A) and a second intervention phase (B). The second baseline phase is established by withdrawing the intervention for a while. After a stable trend is identified in the second baseline, the intervention is reintroduced. This design assumes that if the intervention caused the improvement in the target problem during the first intervention period, then the target problem will reverse toward its original baseline level during the second baseline (after the intervention is withdrawn). When the intervention is reintroduced, the target problem should start improving again. The basic inferential principle here is that if shifts in the trend or level of the target problem occur successively each time the intervention is introduced or withdrawn, then it is not

plausible that some extraneous event and not the intervention is causing the change. Because the independent variable is changed three times, there is more causal evidence than in the AB design. In other words, the number of unlikely successive coincidences that would have to occur in an ABAB design is three rather than one, as in the AB design.

The ABAB design has two major problems, although both often can be resolved. One is a practical or ethical problem. Practitioners may feel that withdrawing an intervention that appears to be working is indefensible in light of the suffering or other costs the client may bear if conditions revert to baseline. These concerns would be intensified with clients who had dangerous problems or who were particularly sensitive to setbacks. Practitioners may fear that withdrawal of the intervention would confuse or alienate the client and perhaps hurt the practitioner–client relationship or in other ways impede future efforts when the intervention is reintroduced. These are important and valid concerns, and researchers should not fault practitioners who resist implementing ABAB designs because of these concerns.

Practitioners, however, should not underestimate the opportunities they have for implementing ABAB designs without compromising intervention priorities. Occasionally, there are natural breaks in the intervention phase when the practitioner attends a conference or takes a vacation, and these periods can be exploited to establish a second baseline (provided that the practitioner is not the only one observing and recording the extent of the target problem). Also, it is often consistent with good practice to withdraw an intervention temporarily at a point at which the target problem appears to have been overcome and then monitor whether the client can sustain his or her gains during the hiatus of treatment.

The second major but potentially resolvable problem with ABAB designs is that the assumption that the target problem can revert to baseline conditions may not be valid in many practice situations. Perhaps an intervention has had irreversible effects during the first intervention period. For instance, suppose that the intervention involved social skills training, perhaps training individuals with mild developmental disabilities to interact at social gatherings or in the workplace. Once these skills are learned and the individuals are rewarded in the natural environment for using them, they may not need training to be reintroduced in order to sustain the gains they have made. Or suppose that the intervention was to help an elderly woman become less isolated, lonely, and depressed. Suppose further that the intervention was environmentally oriented and focused on securing a better residence for her, one where she would be among peers with whom she could easily interact and become friends. If this intervention succeeded during the first B period, is it reasonable to suppose that she would lose her new friends or become depressed again because the practitioner withdrew the intervention (i.e., efforts to change her environment, not the new residence)?

To reduce the chances that effects will be irreversible, in some situations we might want to keep the first intervention period relatively short. Then, as soon as the second baseline shows a trend toward reversal, we could reintroduce the intervention and hope to reestablish the improving trend that was briefly interrupted during the second baseline. Irreversible effects also may be less problematic if, despite the failure to obtain a reversal during the second baseline, we observed a new, improving trend during the second intervention period. Suppose, for example, that in the case of the depressed and lonely elderly woman, we reintroduce the environmentally oriented intervention by getting her a pet and that this further alleviates her depression. This possibility is illustrated in Figure 13-8, in which we see a shift in the dependent variable each time the intervention is introduced, but gains made during the first intervention phase are maintained during the second baseline. Despite the absence of a reversal during the second baseline, the data's overall pattern would support the conclusion that it is the intervention and not some extraneous variable that accounts for the improvement and that the intervention's effects simply do not tend to reverse when the intervention is withdrawn.

So what do we conclude when the results of the ABAB design resemble those in Figure 13-9? Was the improvement that occurred only after the first introduction of the intervention caused by some extraneous event that happened to coincide with that introduction? In other words, should we refrain from attributing the improvement to the effects of the intervention because no other changes occurred in the target problem the next two times the intervention was introduced or withdrawn? Or can we

FIGURE 13.8 Graph of Hypothetical Outcome of ABAB Design Supporting Intervention Efficacy Despite Failure to Obtain a Reversal during Second Baseline

FIGURE 13.9 Graph of Hypothetical Outcome of ABAB Design with Unclear Results

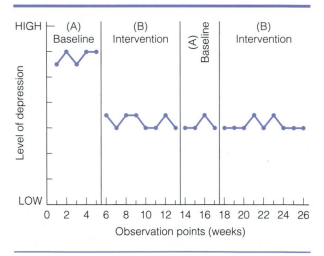

speculate that perhaps the intervention was so effective or the nature of the target problem so irreversible that only one shift in the trend or level of the target problem (i.e., the shift at the onset of the first intervention phase) was possible? Depending on the nature of the target problem and what we learn from the client about extraneous events that coincide with changes in the design phases, it may be possible in some cases to decide which of these rival explanations seems more plausible. Perhaps an even better way to resolve this dilemma is through replication. If results like those depicted in Figure 13-9 tend to be obtained consistently in future ABAB experiments on the same intervention, then the case for powerful or irreversible effects would be strengthened because there is no rational reason why extraneous events that cause shifts in the target problem should occur with every client only at those points at which intervention is first introduced.

Multiple-Baseline Designs

Multiple-baseline designs also attempt to control for extraneous variables by having more than one baseline and intervention phase. But instead of withdrawing the intervention to establish more than one baseline, multiple-baseline designs begin two or more baselines simultaneously. This is done by measuring different target behaviors in each baseline or by measuring the same target behavior in two different settings or across two different individuals. Although each baseline starts simultaneously, the intervention is introduced at a different point for each one. Thus, as the intervention is introduced for the first behavior, setting, or individual, the others are still in their baseline phases. Likewise, when the intervention is introduced for the second behavior, setting, or individual, the third (if there are more than two) is still in its baseline phase.

The main logical principle here is that if some extraneous event, such as a significant improvement in the environment, coincides with the onset of intervention and causes the client's improved functioning, then that improvement will show up in the graph of each behavior, setting, or individual at the same time, even though some might still be in baseline. On the other hand, if the intervention is accountable for the improvement, then that improvement will occur on each graph at a different point that corresponds to the introduction of the intervention.

Figure 13-10 illustrates a hypothetical multiple-baseline design across three nursing home residents who feel an extreme sense of hopelessness. In this illustration, the practitioner read a report of a group experiment by Mercer and Kane (1979), the findings of which supported the efficacy of reducing hopelessness in residents like these by having them care for a houseplant. The practitioner begins taking baseline measures of hopelessness via a self-

FIGURE 13.10 Graph of Hypothetical Outcome of Multiple-Baseline Design across Subjects Supporting Efficacy of Intervention

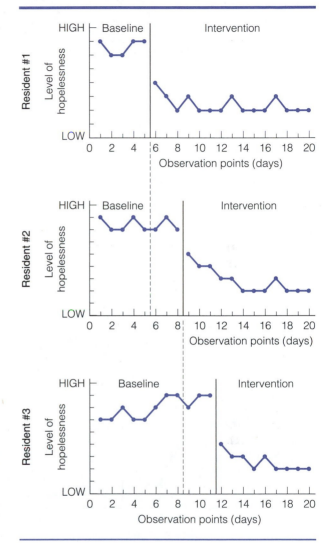

report scale for each resident at the same time. But he or she gives each resident a houseplant, along with instructions about caring for it, at three different times. Each resident's level of hopelessness, as reflected in the self-report scores, begins to decrease steadily only after the intervention is introduced. Therefore, it is not reasonable to suppose that some extraneous event, such as some other improvement in the overall environment of the nursing home, really caused the change.

But suppose the results looked like those in Figure 13-11. There we see that the steady

FIGURE 13.11 Graph of Hypothetical Outcome of Multiple-Baseline Design across Subjects Illustrating Extraneous Variable as Plausible Cause of Improvement

FIGURE 13.12 Graph of Hypothetical Outcome of Multiple-Baseline Design across Target Behaviors with Unclear Results

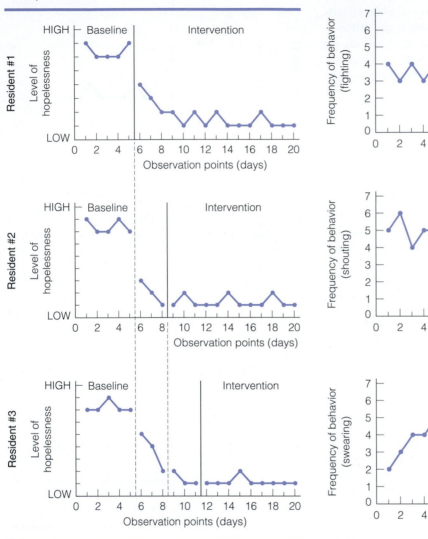

improvement in hopelessness commenced for each resident at the same time that the first intervention (houseplant) was introduced. It is not plausible to infer that the plant was causing the improvement because two of the residents had not yet received theirs. Instead, it is more plausible to suppose that some extraneous improvement in the broader nursing home environment coincided with the onset of the intervention with the first resident and caused the improvement in all three. This illustrates how an AB design (with the first resident) could yield misleading findings because of its

weaker control for history than occurs in multiple-baseline designs.

Figures 13-12 and 13-13 illustrate the same logical principles with multiple-baseline designs across target behaviors or settings. Both figures refer to a hypothetical case that involves a boy referred to a residential treatment center because of his antisocial behaviors. There he participates in a cognitive-behavior modification intervention like the one reported by Taber (1981) that includes teaching him how to say things to himself to help stop him

FIGURE 13.13 Graph of Hypothetical Outcome of Multiple-Baseline Design across Settings with Unclear Results

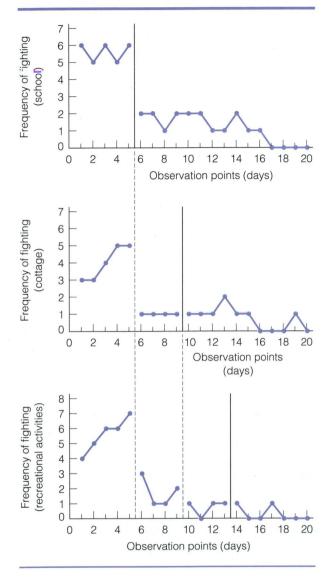

in the data pattern occurs for all three target behaviors at the same time. What caused this? Was it an extraneous event in the residential facility that happened to coincide with the end of the first baseline? Perhaps. But when multiple baselines are applied across different behaviors, a data pattern like this could also be caused by a rival explanation, one termed *generalization of effects*. Generalization of effects occurs when an intervention, although intended to apply to only one behavior or setting at a time, affects other target behaviors or settings that are still in the baseline phase as soon as it is applied to the first behavior or setting. In the current illustration, for instance, the rehearsals regarding fighting perhaps helped the boy simultaneously apply the verbal self-instructions to other behaviors that he knew got him into trouble.

Another way that generalization of effects could occur is when the intervention affects only one target behavior but the change in that behavior changes the other behaviors in turn. In the preceding illustration, for example, the reduction in fighting conceivably gave the boy less to shout and swear about. The reduction in fighting also could have led to more positive feedback from peers and adults, and this improvement in his interpersonal relations (or the rewarding nature of the feedback) could have reduced his need to swear and shout or increased his desire to act appropriately.

The same sort of ambiguity in the data pattern appears in Figure 13-13. Here the three baselines end as the boy rehearses the verbal self-instructions across three different settings. At the end of the first baseline, he rehearses in connection to school. At the end of the second, he rehearses in connection to the cottage. At the end of the third, he rehearses in connection to recreational activities. As in Figure 13-12, we do not know whether the simultaneous improvement in all three settings at the end of the first baseline resulted from an extraneous event or from generalization of effects.

How do we decide which rival explanation—history or generalization of effects—is the more plausible? We may be unable to do so. But, if it is feasible, we might try to replicate the experiment with other clients. If we continue to get results like those in Figures 13-12 and 13-13, then the generalization of effects hypothesis becomes more plausible because it is not reasonable to suppose that some extraneous event would cause improvement in the target problem only at the point where the first

from committing explosive, antisocial behaviors in the situations in which he has been most vulnerable to losing control. In Figure 13-12, the first baseline ends and intervention begins as the client starts to rehearse the verbal self-instructions in connection to fighting. One week later, he begins to rehearse in connection to impulsive, inappropriate shouting. The following week, he starts rehearsing in connection to swearing.

The graphs in Figure 13-12 show that once the client begins rehearsing for fighting, a dramatic shift baseline ends when clients were treated at different times.

With some interventions, it is difficult to conceive how they could possibly be applied to different behaviors or settings at different times. Suppose, for example, that the intervention involves family systems therapy in a case in which a child's poor functioning in various areas is theoretically thought to stem from problems in the parents' relationship with each other. If the practitioner seeks to resolve the target problem in the child by focusing intervention on the parental relationship, then it may not be realistic to try applying the intervention to different behaviors or settings regarding the child. Moreover, to do so might be deemed clinically inappropriate because it would continue to focus the intervention on the child.

Multiple-Component Designs

Several designs can be used to analyze the impact of changes in the intervention. These designs are appropriate when we decide to modify an intervention that does not appear to be helping the client or when we seek to determine which parts of an intervention package really account for the change in the target problem. One such design is called the *changing intensity design*. It includes several phases of the same intervention, but in each phase either the amount of intervention or the level of performance expected of the client is increased. The symbol for this design is $AB^1B^2B^3$. As a hypothetical illustration of this design, suppose a chronically mentally disabled individual is unable to maintain steady employment. The intervention might be social skills training to prepare him for job interviews and appropriate on-the-job behavior. If during B^1 (the first intervention phase) an inadequate degree of improvement is observed, then the amount of time the client spends in social skills training might be increased. Implementing this change marks the beginning of the second intervention phase (B^2). Suppose B^2 results in increased improvement but at a level that still is not acceptable. A third intervention phase, B^3, might be initiated and might involve further increasing the amount of time the client spends in social skills training.

Consider a different approach with this case: When the social skills training yields no improvement in the first intervention phase, it is replaced by a different intervention. Instead of increasing the amount of time the client spends in social skills training, a different behavioral reinforcement intervention is introduced—one that offers a reward for each real job interview the client undergoes or each week he keeps his job. So far, we would have an ABC design, in which B was the social skills training phase and C the reinforcement phase. Suppose there still is no improvement, so a case advocacy phase is initiated to investigate the possibility that we may need to convince prospective employers to consider hiring or be more tolerant of individuals whose illnesses impede their job-seeking skills or on-the-job behavior. The case advocacy phase, then, would add a fourth component to the design, and we would have an ABCD design.

The preceding two designs are flexible; they allow practitioners to change intervention plans as warranted by the data patterns that are observed in each successive phase. But they must be used cautiously because of limitations associated with *carry-over effects*, *order effects*, and *history*.

In the ABCD illustration, suppose that a sustained pattern of improvement was obtained only during the D phase (case advocacy), as illustrated in Figure 13-14. It would be risky to conclude that for future clients like this one, all we need to do is provide the case advocacy and not the other two interventions. It is plausible that had we changed the D phase to the B phase for this client, we may not have had the same positive results. Perhaps the client's social skills improved during the original B phase but those skills were insufficient to help him stay employed because employers were either unwilling to risk hiring someone with a history of

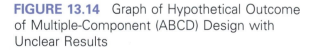

FIGURE 13.14 Graph of Hypothetical Outcome of Multiple-Component (ABCD) Design with Unclear Results

mental illness or unwilling to tolerate any deviance whatsoever from any employee. Conceivably, only with the addition of the case advocacy during the D phase did the improvement in social skills matter. Perhaps the case advocacy would have had no impact had it not been preceded by helping the client attain a level of social functioning that prospective employers could be convinced to tolerate. In other words, the case advocacy might not have worked without the order effects (i.e., in coming after the social skills training, not before it) and the carryover effects of the social skills training on the case advocacy efforts.

History is also a limitation: We must recognize that as we continue to substitute new interventions for those whose data patterns do not adequately differ from baseline, we increase the odds that one of those substitutions eventually will coincide with an extraneous improvement in the client's environment.

One way to sort out the above possibilities would be to replicate the interventions with future clients, introducing them in a different sequence while measuring outcome in the same way. Ultimately, we might find that the intervention that was originally in the D phase produced the desired results only when it was introduced after the interventions in the original B or C phase.

Another option would be to start out with a more complex **multiple-component design** that attempts, in advance, to control for the above limitations. There are a variety of such designs. Because their complexity limits their applicability to real social work practice settings, they will be mentioned only briefly here. One is the *construction design*, A-B-A-C-A-BC-( ), in which the A phases represent baselines and the BC phase combines the B and C interventions. The phase indicated by the parentheses refers to the intervention or combination of interventions that appears to be most effective and is ultimately chosen. Another is the *strip design*, A-BC-A-B-A-C-( ), which is like the construction design but in which the combined intervention (BC) is introduced first. Other possibilities include the *alternating intervention design*, A-(Randomized Alternation of B and C)-(B or C), and the *interaction design*, A-B-A-B-BC-B-BC. We recommend the following texts that deal exclusively with single-case designs to readers who wish to pursue these complex designs in depth: Barlow and

EP 4, 9

Hersen (1984), Bloom et al. (2006), and Jayaratne and Levy (1979).

» DATA ANALYSIS

In analyzing the results of single-case experiments, we ask the following three questions:

1. Is there a *visual* pattern in the graph(s) that depicts a series of coincidences in which the frequency, level, or trend of the target problem changes only after the intervention is introduced or withdrawn?

2. What is the *statistical* probability that the data observed during the intervention phase(s) are merely part of the normal, chance fluctuations in the target problem, fluctuations that we could have expected to occur had the baseline been extended and intervention not introduced?

3. If change in the target problem is associated with the tested intervention, is the amount of change important from a *substantive*, or *clinical*, standpoint?

These three questions refer to the visual, statistical, and substantive significance of the findings.

When we analyzed the meanings of each graph in Figures 13-1 through 13-14, we dealt with *visual significance*. Visual significance is ascertained not through the use of fancy statistics but merely by "eyeballing" the data pattern, as the term *visual* implies. To the extent that shifts in the target problem either do not occur when intervention is introduced or occur just as often at other times, there is less visual significance; that is, in those instances, there is less visual evidence for supposing that the intervention is affecting the target problem. To the extent that shifts in the frequency, level, or trend of the target problem tend to coincide only with shifts in the independent variable as it moves from one phase to another, there is more visual significance and thus more logical support for supposing that the intervention is affecting the target problem.

Sometimes our visual analysis of the data will obviate the need for statistical analysis, particularly when the degree of visual significance (or lack thereof) is dramatic. Indeed, some single-case methodologists cite evidence that suggests that when experienced researchers judge whether an outcome is visually significant, their conclusions are usually supported by subsequent statistical analyses (Jayaratne, Tripodi, & Talsma, 1988). Practitioners who tend to be immobilized by their anxiety about statistics, therefore, can implement single-case designs in the hope that their visual analysis of the data will be sufficient.

Sometimes, however, the changes in the level or trend of the target problem from one phase to the next are subtle or we are not sure whether our visual analysis of the data is being influenced by our desire to see a favorable outcome. At these times, it is helpful to augment our visual analysis with a statistical one.

Statistical and substantive significance mean the same thing in single-case designs as they do in other sorts of research, and they will be discussed in depth, in connection to group designs, in Chapter 22. If you'd like to learn when and how to calculate alternative procedures for estimating statistical significance in single-case design research, we recommend the chapter on that topic in Rubin (2013).

Interpreting Ambiguous Results

Most of this chapter has used illustrations involving clear-cut hypothetical data patterns to simplify conveying the logic of single-case research regarding the differentiation of results that are visually significant from results that are not visually significant. Unfortunately, however, single-case studies in the real world often obtain ambiguous results that are more difficult to interpret. Consider, for example, Figure 13-15, which shows the results from a study by Rubin (1991).

The data in Figure 13-15 were collected from a battered woman who was participating in an intervention geared toward helping battered women live independently from their batterers. The data refer to thoughts, feelings, and behaviors associated with feeling better about oneself and doing things to become more independent. An increase in scores during the intervention phase, therefore, would indicate a desirable outcome.

As you can see, the data in the graph reveal a somewhat unstable baseline, followed by 11 days of intervention without any improvement in scores and then 2 days of dramatic improvement at the end of the study. (This case was part of a larger study involving more clients, and feasibility constraints required that the data collection for this woman end after her 32nd data point.)

FIGURE 13.15   Graph of Outcome of Group Treatment of a Battered Woman

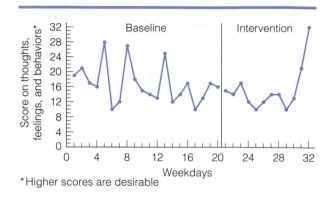

*Higher scores are desirable

Source: Allen Rubin, "The Effectiveness of Outreach Counseling and Support Groups for Battered Women: A Preliminary Evaluation," *Research on Social Work Practice*, 1(4), October 1991, p. 349.

How would you interpret this graph? Do you think it reflects visual significance? One can be tempted to perceive visual significance in this graph, particularly if one is affiliated with the agency and wants the intervention to succeed. One might focus on the dramatic improvement toward the end of the intervention phase and argue that, although it took a while before the intervention started having an effect, it eventually worked. One might further argue that this woman may have been denying her situation and that it therefore stands to reason that the intervention effects would not occur immediately at the onset of treatment. This argument is not unreasonable. Indeed, those who take a psychosocial approach to practice might not expect most clients to begin showing improvement on outcome indicators until intervention has been ongoing for quite a long time because of such factors as resistance, denial, and so on.

We believe, however, that a more compelling argument can be made against perceiving visual significance in this graph, based on two major points. First, the increase in the scores at the end of the intervention period could be nothing more than a random (or perhaps cyclical) temporary blip—just as there were a few upward blips during the unstable baseline. We do not know how short-lived the improvement will be. Second, even if the improvement is permanent, the fact that it did not occur sooner during intervention increases the plausibility that it could be the result of history.

When we argue that this graph is not visually significant, we do not mean to imply that it shows that the intervention could not have caused the improvement. We merely mean that this graph does not provide enough evidence to deem alternative explanations (such as history) much less plausible than the conclusion that the intervention did cause the improvement. We believe it is possible that it simply took a while before the effects of the intervention began to be reflected in the outcome scores. However, saying that this is possible is a far cry from saying that the graph reflects in a visually significant way that this indeed is the most plausible explanation. In other words, saying that a graph is not visually significant does not mean that its interpretation is unambiguously negative. In this case, we believe the interpretation is ambiguous and that the graph lacks visual significance in light of that ambiguity.

The foregoing example illustrates the ambiguity that can occur when intervention goes on for quite a while before any noticeable improvement occurs in the target problem. Sometimes, however, improvement in the target problem coincides nicely with the onset of the intervention but then reverses sharply during the last data point or two. If the intervention and monitoring cannot be continued, then it may be difficult to determine whether the intervention was effective.

Perhaps the undesirable data points at the end of the intervention period indicate that the temporary improvement was merely the result of a honeymoon period or extraneous factors that coincided with the onset of the intervention. On the other hand, perhaps the undesirable data points at the end of the intervention period are themselves merely a result of extraneous forces causing a temporary blip in the context of meaningful, sustainable intervention effects. Ambiguous results can occur in many other ways as well, particularly when there is instability in the data during baseline, the intervention phase, or both.

Aggregating the Results of Single-Case Research Studies

At several points in this chapter, we noted that the interpretation of ambiguous data patterns in single-case research can be enhanced through the replication process. If, for example, improvement occurs late in the intervention phase of one study, then

we cannot rule out history as a plausible explanation. But if improvement occurs roughly at the same late point consistently across studies, then it seems more plausible to argue that the intervention takes a while before showing desired effects than to argue that extraneous events are causing the improvement across different clients who begin intervention at different times. The same logic holds when we don't know whether the data pattern reflects irreversible intervention effects in an ABAB study or the generalization of effects in a multiple-baseline study.

Above and beyond facilitating the interpretation of ambiguous data, replication can serve two additional important purposes in single-case research. One purpose is to reduce doubt about the external validity of our findings. The more we can replicate a particular type of outcome across different clients, settings, and practitioners, the more confidence we develop (inductively) in our ability to generalize that outcome. The other purpose is to evaluate an entire service program. If, for example, an agency conducts a single-case evaluation on a reasonably representative sample of its clients (such as every fifth client entering treatment during a particular time period), then it can assess its overall agency effectiveness by aggregating the results of each individual evaluation.

When we want to aggregate the results of various individual studies, either to deal with ambiguous findings or to generalize about the effectiveness of an intervention or an agency, we need a mechanism for making sense out of the variations in outcome from study to study. One such mechanism is to report the proportion of studies that had each type of outcome in which we are interested. For example, we would want to know the proportion of outcomes that were and were not visually significant, and we might want to know the proportion of studies with the same type of ambiguous data pattern. Thus, we might be able to say that an effective intervention was delivered in, say, 60% of our agency's cases. Or we might be able to say that in, say, 70% of our replications, a data pattern was found that suggests delayed intervention effects.

One problem here is the absence of systematic guidelines as to what specific percentages represent cutoff points regarding alternative interpretations. Should an agency, for example, be happy with a 50% effectiveness rate? A lower rate? Or is a higher effectiveness rate needed before it can claim to be effective in an overall, aggregated sense as a program? If a practitioner replicates an AB study across 10 clients and obtains visually significant results three times, should he or she conclude that the intervention was effective with three cases, or should the practitioner wonder whether some other factor (such as history) accounts for the data pattern in those three cases because the visual significance was not replicated in the remaining seven cases? As the field of single-case research matures, perhaps such guidelines will be developed. For now, however, there may be some value in merely describing the proportion of various outcomes being obtained in connection to a particular intervention, practitioner, or agency. As those outcomes accumulate, one can inductively look for patterns that might suggest hypotheses as to the conditions under which a particular practitioner, intervention, or agency is successful. This accumulation might also establish effectiveness rate norms to which the results of future aggregated evaluations can be compared.

The process of aggregating the results of single-case studies illustrates how this type of research has the potential to go well beyond idiosyncratically evaluating intervention with a single case. Although we have identified a variety of feasibility problems in carrying out single-case research—and we certainly do not see it as a panacea that everyone can use when other designs are not feasible—we hope that you will consider applying what you have learned in this chapter throughout your career as a professional social worker.

» B AND B+ DESIGNS

This chapter has been focusing on the logic of single-case designs in making causal inferences about the effectiveness of an intervention. Thus, the need for ample data points in baseline and the concept of visual significance have been paramount. However, practitioners in the final phase of the evidence-based practice process—in which they measure client progress in achieving treatment goals—can use single-case design techniques without aiming to make causal inferences and thus without the need for ample data points in baseline. Suppose, for example, that you have completed all of the previous steps of the evidence-based practice process with a client suffering from posttraumatic stress disorder (PTSD) and have provided one of

the three interventions for PTSD with the best empirical support—prolonged exposure therapy, cognitive processing therapy, or eye movement desensitization and processing (EMDR) (Rubin & Springer, 2010). Because your chosen intervention has already had sufficient causal evidence replicated in many rigorous experiments, you need not be burdened with generating evidence as to its effectiveness. Instead, your concern is merely to see whether your client's PTSD symptoms are adequately alleviated when you provide the selected intervention. Here's why.

As discussed in Chapter 2, a chief reason for the final phase of the evidence-based practice process is that even the most effective social work interventions with the best empirical support are not guaranteed to work with every client or every situation. Your client may be one of the cases for whom the chosen intervention does not work. Or perhaps you are not delivering the intervention in an ideal way. Consequently, your priority in this phase is merely to monitor your client's progress. If the goals of treatment are achieved as indicated in the B phase of your graph, *voila!* Regardless of what caused the success, it's time to move on. Conversely, if the goals are not achieved, you need to try something else. Although you don't know what's causing or not causing what, your B phase graph can guide your practice decision.

Of course, you would have even more information if you could compare the B phase data to a baseline containing ample data points. However, the constraints of real-world social work practice often make it impossible for practitioners to obtain a baseline with more than one data point. And sometimes it is impossible to obtain even one baseline data point, as with crisis intervention. Rather than eschew using single-case design techniques in such instances, you could start with the B phase or with only one data point in baseline, assuming that you do not intend to make a causal inference.

If your graph consists only of the B phase, then you have used what is called a *B design*. The B design is simpler than the AB design because it has no baseline (A) phase. Often, however, practitioners will have one preintervention data point based on client assessment information. While that one data point won't suffice as a baseline, it does make your graph a tiny bit more than a pure B design. Consequently, we can call it a *B+ design*. Another type of B+ design can eventuate when you start out with a B design but observe no progress during that phase and therefore decide to alter your intervention. If you do so, then the original B phase can turn into a baseline phase for the new intervention phase, which can be called the *C phase*.

Suppose you are unable to obtain even one baseline data point before providing prolonged exposure therapy to reduce PTSD trauma symptoms and your B design data are as depicted in graph 1 in Figure 13-16. Regardless of what caused the resolution of the trauma symptoms, you would have no reason to suppose that prolonged exposure therapy was the wrong choice for your client or that you need to try some alternative intervention. Alternatively, if your data resembled those in graph

2 and continued that way beyond an acceptable time period for your client, you would have reason to suppose that perhaps you better try something else—maybe EMDR. Moreover, your graph 2 results could form the baseline to which the next phase of intervention results could be compared. Thus, if you followed the prolonged exposure therapy with EMDR (or any other intervention) and obtained the results depicted in the B+ design data in graph 3, you would have a visually significant data pattern that—in addition to guiding your practice decision—would offer some support for a causal inference about the effectiveness of the C phase intervention for your client. That support, however, would be limited by the possibility of order effects and carry over effects, as discussed earlier regarding multiple-component designs. That is, perhaps the second intervention (in the C phase) would not have been effective had it not been preceded by prolonged exposure therapy (in the B phase).

» THE ROLE OF QUALITATIVE RESEARCH METHODS IN SINGLE-CASE EVALUATION

In Chapter 12, we saw that some techniques commonly used in qualitative studies can make valuable contributions when incorporated with quantitative methods in experimental and quasi-experimental designs. The same is true of single-case evaluation designs, which are generally considered quantitative. One way these techniques can be helpful is in interpreting ambiguous quantitative results. When instability occurs at a particular point in the data pattern, for instance, we can employ open-ended interviews with the client and significant others to try to learn whether important extraneous events in the client's social environment coincided with the instability. If they did, we might be more inclined to attribute certain changes in the graphed data to extraneous forces rather than consider them reflections of the effectiveness or ineffectiveness of the intervention. If interviewing fails to identify any extraneous forces that may explain the changes observed in the graph, the notion that those changes represent intervention effects becomes more plausible.

Another important role for interviewing in single-case evaluation is in assessment. Open-ended

FIGURE 13.16 Illustration of Contrasting B Design Results

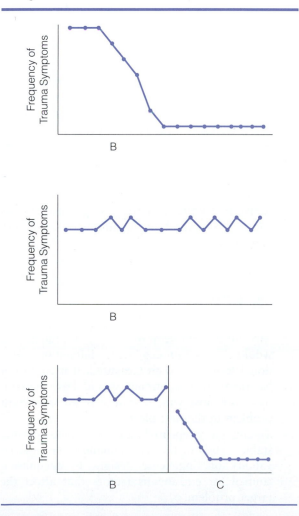

QUALITATIVE TECHNIQUES FOR SINGLE-CASE EVALUATION

As we did for group designs in the previous chapter, in this box we will list some prominent qualitative techniques and the important functions they can serve in single-case design evaluation studies. You can read more about these techniques in Chapters 18 and 19.

Qualitative Technique	Functions in Single-Case Evaluation
Informal conversational interviews with clients or significant others	• Identify extraneous events or forces connected with changes in the graphed data. • Assess target problem and develop measurement and intervention plan. • Assess what parts of the intervention client perceives to be most helpful, and why. • Corroborate the improvement (or lack thereof) that is self-reported or self-monitored by the client or by the significant other.
Video- or audiorecording practitioner–client sessions	• Assess the fidelity of the intervention (Is it being implemented in a skillful manner, as intended?).
Event logs completed by client or significant others	• Assess where and when target problems occur and the circumstances that mediate them. • Identify extraneous events occurring during baseline or intervention phases that might be helpful in interpreting whether changes that occur in the quantitative data are attributable to the intervention.

interviews with the client and with significant others can improve our understanding of the target problem, how to measure it, and how best to intervene. Interviews with significant others can be used to corroborate the improvement (or lack thereof) that is self-reported or self-monitored by the client. Interviews can also assess what parts of the intervention clients perceive to be most helpful and why. In Chapter 19, we will examine additional techniques that are commonly used in qualitative studies and useful in single-case evaluation. Event logs completed by clients or their significant others can also be quite helpful in assessing where and when target problems occur and the circumstances that mediate them. Event logs can also help identify extraneous events occurring during baseline or intervention phases that might be helpful in interpreting whether changes that occur in the quantitative data are attributable to the intervention. The utility of

qualitative techniques as part of single-case designs is summarized in the box "Qualitative Techniques for Single-Case Evaluation."

MAIN POINTS

- Any target problem on which a practitioner would choose to focus can be defined in operational terms and then measured. If it could not be, then the practitioner would have had no basis for observing that it was an important problem in the first place.
- Taking many repeated measures and identifying stable trends in the data enhances the internal validity of single-case designs by facilitating control for extraneous factors that affect the target problem.

- Baselines are control phases of repeated measures taken before an intervention is introduced. Baselines ideally should be extended until a stable trend in the data is evident.
- Single-case designs can be used by practitioners to monitor client progress or their own effectiveness more scientifically and systematically.
- Single-case designs have special measurement problems. Triangulating measures is therefore recommended. This means simultaneously using more than one imperfect measurement option.
- Special caution must be exercised in single-case designs with regard to the measurement problems of reactivity, obtrusiveness, and social desirability bias.
- Including more than one baseline and intervention phase in a single-case experiment strengthens the control of history through the principle of unlikely successive coincidences. This is done in ABAB designs and multiple-baseline designs.
- AB designs have the weakest control for history, but they are the most feasible designs, can provide useful information, and are an excellent way to implement the final stage of the evidence-based practice process.
- When we use designs with more phases than the AB design, we must exercise caution regarding possible carryover effects, order effects, generalization of effects, and the irreversibility of effects.
- The prime weakness of single-case designs is their limited external validity. With a sample of one, we are dealing with idiosyncratic conditions that cannot be generalized to other clients, practitioners, or settings. But this problem can be alleviated through replication.
- Single-case design data should always be analyzed for their visual and practical significance.
- The visual as well as statistical results of single-case research can be ambiguous; the replication process can help resolve this ambiguity.
- The results of various single-case studies can be aggregated by calculating the proportion of studies with specific types of outcomes.

- Practitioners in the final phase of the evidence-based practice process—in which they measure client progress in achieving treatment goals—can use single-case design techniques without aiming to make causal inferences and thus without the need for ample data points in baseline.
- Some prominent qualitative techniques can serve important functions in single-case design evaluation studies.

REVIEW QUESTIONS AND EXERCISES

1. Select some aspect of your own behavior that you would like to improve (e.g., *smoke less*, *eat less*, *exercise more*, *study more*, and so on) and develop a plan to improve it. Conduct a single-case experiment and analyze the data to see if your plan is effective. Try to be aware of the degree to which you experience the measurement problems of reactivity and bias.
2. Think of a particular case or intervention that has piqued your curiosity about practice effectiveness. Design a single-case experiment that is relevant to that case or intervention. Try to design it in a way that would be feasible to implement.

INTERNET EXERCISES

1. Find a study that used a single-case evaluation AB design. Critique the study's design—either positively or negatively—and discuss whether you agree with the way its data were interpreted.
2. Find a study that used a single-case evaluation ABAB design or a multiple-baseline design. Critique the study's design—either positively or negatively—and discuss whether you agree with the way its data were interpreted.

 Visit CengageBrain.com for additional practice and study opportunities including experiential exercises, research tools, glossary, flashcards, and sample test items.

14

Program Evaluation

EPAS Competencies for This Chapter

Competency 4   Engage in Practice-Informed Research and Research-Informed Practice: This competency pertains to this entire chapter because doing practice-informed research as well as engaging in research-informed practice often involves conducting or critically appraising program evaluations.

Competency 9   Evaluate Practice with Individuals Families, Groups, Organizations, and Communities: This competency pertains to this entire chapter because evaluating practice often takes the form of a program evaluation.

What You'll Learn in This Chapter

Whereas the previous three chapters emphasized the logic of research designs in evaluating the effectiveness of interventions, this chapter focuses on the broader picture of evaluating entire programs. It will examine the use of program evaluation not only to assess program effects but also for the purposes of program planning and monitoring processes in program implementation. In addition, you'll see the practical and political obstacles that program evaluators encounter and how evaluators try to deal with them.

» INTRODUCTION

The previous three chapters focused on the logic of methods of different experimental and quasi-experimental designs for evaluating the effectiveness of interventions at various levels of practice. When it comes to evaluating entire programs, however, other research questions arise in addition to whether the program is effective. Experiments and quasi experiments, therefore, are not the only designs used in program evaluation. Many other types of quantitative and qualitative designs and methods can be used. *Program evaluation* refers to the *purpose* of research rather than to any specific research *methods*. Its purpose is to assess and improve the conceptualization, design, planning, administration, implementation, effectiveness, efficiency, and utility of social interventions and human service programs (Rossi & Freeman, 1993).

At the start of this book, we distinguished social work research from basic social scientific research by its purpose, citing the former's focus on practical knowledge that social workers need so they can solve the problems they confront in their practice and that agencies need to guide their efforts to alleviate human suffering and promote social welfare. In light of that focus, program evaluation—when applied to social welfare settings and issues—is conceptually very similar to social work research, and many of the research studies conducted by social workers have a program evaluation purpose. The other chapters of this book are devoted to specific research designs and methods that can be employed in program evaluation (as well as in other research endeavors); this chapter will focus on issues and practical guidelines for conducting program evaluations. We'll start with a historical overview of program evaluation.

EP 4, 9

» HISTORICAL OVERVIEW

Although the growth of program evaluation is a fairly recent phenomenon, planned social evaluation is really quite old. Some authors have traced it back to 2200 B.C. in China and connected it with personnel selection (Shadish, Cook, & Leviton, 1991). Whenever people have instituted a social reform for a specific purpose, they have paid attention to its actual consequences, even if they have not always done so in a conscious, deliberate, or systematic fashion or called what they were doing program evaluation.

In the mid-19th century, for example, the reform movement for more humane care of the mentally ill, led by Dorothea Dix, succeeded in getting states to build more public mental hospitals. Some superintendents of state mental hospitals contributed to such hospitals' growth by citing data that, they contended, indicated that state hospitals were succeeding in curing mental illness (Grob, 1973). Those superintendents were discharging 90% or more of their patients and claiming that this meant that they were achieving 90% to 100% cure rates. At that time, notions of rehospitalization, relapse, and chronicity were not in vogue, and the superintendents therefore temporarily got away with using discharge from the state hospital as an operational definition of recovery from mental illness, although they didn't use the term *operational definition*. (Here we begin to see the importance of the political context of program evaluation, a theme we'll examine in depth later in this chapter.)

More systematic approaches to program evaluation can be traced back to the beginning of the 20th century. Early efforts evaluated schools that used different teaching approaches, comparing educational outcomes by examining student scores on standardized tests. Several decades later, experimental program evaluation studies examined the effects of worker morale on industrial productivity and the impact of public health education programs on hygienic practices. In the 1940s, after New Deal social welfare programs were implemented, studies examined the effects of work relief versus direct relief, the effects of public housing, and the impact of treatment programs on juvenile delinquency. Program evaluation received additional impetus during World War II, with studies on soldier morale and the impact of personnel and propaganda policies on morale.

After the war, large public expenditures were committed to programs that attempted to improve housing, public health, attitudes toward minorities, and international problems in health, family planning, and community development. As expenditures grew, so did interest in data on the results of these programs.

Program evaluation became widespread by the late 1950s as efforts increased to alleviate or prevent social problems, such as juvenile delinquency, and to test innovations in psychotherapy and new psycho-pharmacological discoveries. By the late 1960s, textbooks, professional journals, national conferences, and a professional association on evaluation research emerged. This explosion of interest in program evaluation continued during the 1970s as the public increasingly demanded evidence for a return on its investment in various programs to combat poverty, child abuse, substance abuse, crime and delinquency, mental illness, and so on. But by the late 1970s, after public funding for these programs waned, declines began in the funding of studies to evaluate them. This trend toward reduced funding of program evaluation accelerated during the 1980s as federal evaluation offices were hit hard by the budget cuts of the Reagan administration (Shadish et al., 1991).

The "age of accountability" continued through the 1980s and 1990s, even though the government provided less funding for program evaluation than it did before the 1980s. Liberals and conservatives alike demanded that programs be more accountable to the public and show whether they were really delivering what they promised to deliver. In fact, the need to evaluate may be greater when program funding is scarce than when it is abundant because the scarcity of funds may intensify concerns that meager funding not be wasted on ineffectual programs. In this connection, it is a mistake to assume that only fiscal conservatives—those who are reluctant to spend money on social programs—are the ones who have been expressing skepticism about what "bang the public is getting for its buck." Individuals of all political persuasions have this interest, including human service professionals who fiercely support increased social welfare spending but who are dedicated to finding better ways to help people and who do not want to see scarce welfare resources squandered on programs that don't really help their intended target populations. In fact, a major group that has historically been a force in favor of greater accountability consists of consumer rights advocates who are concerned about whether clients—the consumers of our services—are being served properly.

As a result of these forces and despite governmental funding cuts, by the 1990s program evaluation had become ubiquitous in the planning and administration of social welfare policies and programs. In fact, instead of having a program evaluator position, an agency might assign responsibility for program evaluation activities to personnel called *planners* or *program analysts* (Posavac & Carey, 1985). Funding sources still required both a program evaluation component as a prerequisite for approving grant applications and supportive evaluative data as a basis for renewing funding. But this requirement became a mixed blessing. On the one hand, the requirement that programs evaluate their efforts induced agency personnel to support more research that could help us improve policies and programs and find better ways to help people. On the other hand, this requirement came to mean that agency personnel and others have had vested interests in the findings of that research. (Here again we see the political context of program evaluation, which we'll examine later in this chapter.)

The Impact of Managed Care

The emphasis on program evaluation in health and human service agencies continued to grow because of the impact of "managed care." Defined in various ways, the term *managed care* refers to a variety of arrangements that try to control the costs of health and human services. These arrangements vary in the range of their components and proposed benefits, but the basic idea of managed care is to have a large organization contract with care providers who agree to provide services at reduced costs. Care providers are willing to reduce the costs because the organization pays for the cost of services for a very large number of people. The large organization paying for the care typically is the service recipient's employer or health insurance company. Providers are willing to meet the reduced cost demands of the large organizations so they will be eligible to have the cost of their services covered and thus get more referrals of clients covered under managed care plans. Some common types of managed care organizations are health maintenance organizations (HMOs), preferred provider organizations (PPOs), and employee assistance programs (EAPs). Public social service agencies also may employ managed care techniques to reduce the costs and inefficiencies of service provision.

One way in which managed care companies attempt to reduce costs is by reviewing requests for services by those they cover and approving—that is, agreeing to pay for—only those services they deem to be necessary and effective. This stipulation refers to both the type of service and the amount of service, putting pressure on service providers to come up with brief treatment plans as well as evidence as to how many sessions are needed to achieve certain effects. Suppose two alcohol abuse programs have two markedly different approaches to treating alcohol abuse. Suppose one program does not bother to evaluate the outcomes of treatment for its clients, whereas the other measures outcome from each client and shows that 90% of its clients never again evidence alcohol-related problems while at work after 10 treatment sessions. The latter program is more likely to be approved by a managed care company.

Most pertinent to this chapter is the effect that managed care is having on the way service providers use research methods to evaluate their services. This impact also should be pertinent to you, the reader of this text, because in your social work practice you are likely to experience pressures to use these methods to measure the outcomes of the services you provide.

Evidence-Based Practice

As discussed in Chapter 2, evidence-based practice has emerged as a prominent influence in the helping professions in recent decades. Although it differs from managed care concerns with cost saving, its emphasis on having practice decisions informed by research is consistent with concerns about accountability and effectiveness. Decisions about providing the type of program or intervention with the best chance for successful outcomes are often informed by meta-analyses, which are statistically oriented systematic reviews of research studies. Many meta-analyses aggregate effect-size statistics (to be discussed in Chapter 22) that convey the extent to which particular programs or interventions impact client outcomes. For example, using one type of effect-size statistic, a meta-analysis might show that a particular intervention reduces recidivism rates on average more than do alternative approaches. The implication of this finding for program evaluation would be twofold: (a) assuming the program staff chose to implement that intervention, the program evaluation might focus on assessing the extent to which the intervention is being implemented properly and identifying any implementation problems; and (b) assessing whether its recidivism rate outcome approximates the average outcome reported in the meta-analysis.

As a result of the historical developments, program evaluation has become ubiquitous in the planning and administration of social welfare policies and programs. Let's turn now to the steps involved in planning a program evaluation.

» PLANNING AN EVALUATION AND FOSTERING ITS UTILIZATION

Many things can go wrong in a program evaluation. Program staff might not understand the importance of complying with the research protocol and might resist doing so. Even if they want to comply, busy practitioners whose main priority is service delivery may not have the time to comply adequately or may forget to do so. Some evaluations get completed successfully but then ignored by those for whom its findings and recommendations are intended. To anticipate and attempt to minimize these problems, and foster the eventual utilization of the evaluation recommendations, it is vital that the planning of an evaluation be done carefully and thoroughly.

As a first step in the planning of an evaluation, you should learn as much as possible about the evaluation's *stakeholders*—people who have some interest in the program. Stakeholders can include the program's funders, personnel, service recipients and their families, and board members. Some of these stakeholders might have their beliefs, income, status or careers, or workload affected by the evaluation. Other potential stakeholders—such as residents of the neighborhood where the program is located or the citizens who are concerned about where tax dollars are going—are external to the program but who still could be affected by it in some way. It is essential that key stakeholders be involved in a meaningful way in planning the evaluation. Involving them can increase the chances that the evaluation will study something that is a priority for them, promote their identification with the evaluation, and foster their support of it during the data collection phase and their eventual utilization of its findings and recommendations.

Thus, it is important at the outset to find out who wants the evaluation, why they want it, and who doesn't want it. For example, if program sponsors want the evaluation but program personnel either don't know about it or don't want it, then the evaluator should try to make the program personnel more comfortable with the evaluation to foster their cooperation in collecting and interpreting data. One way to do this, of course, is by involving them as stakeholders and by sharing mutual incremental feedback throughout all phases of the evaluation. Therefore, involvement should begin early in the planning of the evaluation, not after the research design is ready to be implemented. In addition to fostering cooperation with the evaluation, involving personnel in the planning is thought to improve the chances for identifying those daily organizational realities that might pose logistical obstacles to alternative research designs or data collection methodologies.

Planning an evaluation is a two-way street. It should consider not only potential problems posed by stakeholders but also potential problems stemming from mistakes the evaluator might make in designing the evaluation. For example, involving decision makers who are likely to use the research helps ensure that evaluators will address questions that are relevant to their decision-making needs rather than questions that are trivial or of interest only to audiences who are not in a position to act on the research findings. Also, without adequate input from program personnel, evaluators might choose or develop the wrong data collection instruments, such as self-report scales that clients might not understand or be willing to complete. Conceivably, the attainment of program objectives might need to be measured idiosyncratically for each client because each client has unique needs and target problems. If so, practitioners might convince evaluators to assess outcome through an aggregation of single-case designs rather than through a group experiment that assesses all clients with the same outcome measures. Evaluators also might not understand the unrealistic burden that their data collection procedures might place on practitioners who already strain to meet heavy paperwork requirements without sacrificing the quality of service they are providing to their many clients.

The cooperation of program personnel might be fostered further by assuring them that they will get to see and respond to a confidential draft of the evaluation report before it's finalized and disseminated to other stakeholders. They should not be led to think that they will be able to censor the report, but they should be assured that their suggestions will be taken seriously. By meeting with key personnel to discuss the report, evaluators can point out and clarify implications of the findings that personnel might find particularly useful for improving the program. And this should be done in a timely fashion—not after it's too late for certain decisions to be made.

The evaluator can foster the evaluation report's utilization by tailoring its form and style to the needs and preferences of those who are in a position to use it. Clear, succinct, and cohesive composition always helps, as does careful typing and a neat, uncluttered layout. The briefer and neater the report, the more likely that busy administrators and practitioners will read it carefully. When adapting the report to an audience of program personnel, do not present every peripheral finding and do not present negative findings bluntly and tactlessly. If program objectives are not being attained, couch the findings in language that recognizes the yeoman efforts and skills of program personnel and that does not portray them as inadequate. Try not to convey a message of success or failure; rather, provide suggestions for developing new programs or improving existing ones. Alert program personnel in the planning stage that all reports bring both good and bad news and that the focus will be less on judging the program's value than on identifying feasible ways to improve it. Make sure that sufficient attention is given to realistic, practical implications of the findings.

As a final step in engaging program personnel in planning the evaluation, you should obtain their feedback regarding a written proposal that reflects their input. The purpose of presenting them with the proposal is to make certain that they agree with evaluators about the components of the evaluation and the nature of the program being evaluated. In addition, by reconsidering everything in a final, written package, they might see logistical problems that were not apparent in earlier discussions.

EP 4, 9

Logic Models

The evaluation proposal should include a logic model, which is a graphic portrayal that depicts the essential components of a program, shows how those components are linked to short-term process objectives, specifies measurable indicators of success in achieving short-term objectives, conveys how those short-term objectives lead to long-term program outcomes, and identifies measurable indicators of success in achieving long-term outcomes. Logic models are useful tools in guiding evaluations and helping agency administrators and practitioners remain apprised of the program evaluation protocol. They also are useful in helping program planners and administrators conceptualize, develop, and manage their programs. Conrad, Randolph, Kirby, and Bebout (1999) put it this way:

> From a program manager's perspective, the logic model becomes a management tool

that helps the program manager keep the program from deviating from its ideal implementation. For the evaluator, the logic model provides a framework for understanding the extent to which the program as implemented is consistent with the program as intended. (p. 21)

Some federal and private funding sources now require grant applications to include a logic model. The rationale, in part, is that such models help in reviewing the appropriateness of both the evaluation design and the proposed program. Moreover, a good logic model is seen as enhancing the prospects that the program will be managed well, monitored incrementally to assess whether it is being implemented properly, and have its short- and long-range objectives evaluated as planned.

There is no one way to construct a logic model. The W. K. Kellogg Foundation (2004), for example, identifies three different approaches for doing so. One approach emphasizes the underlying theory that influenced decisions about program components and thus explains the reasons for those decisions. Rather than focus on specific program "nuts and bolts," a *theory-based logic model* will begin graphically with boxes identifying underlying program assumptions. It will then show how those assumptions lead to boxes depicting program resources (inputs), how the inputs lead to boxes displaying program processes and activities, how the activities aim to achieve short-term outcomes, how the short-term outcomes intend to lead to longer-term outcomes, and how the longer-term outcomes intend to lead to the ultimate program impact. Unlike other approaches to logic models, the intended short- and long-term program outcomes in the theory approach might be worded in broad terms rather than measurable indicators. Like the other approaches, the columns of boxes will be followed by arrows depicting how they lead to the next column. Thus, the column of boxes depicting assumptions will be followed by arrows pointing to resources, the resource boxes will be followed by arrows pointing to processes and activities, and so on.

Another logic model approach emphasizes outcomes. The boxes in this approach will contain more detail than in the theory approach. Also, the *outcomes approach logic model* is less likely to begin with underlying program assumptions and more likely to begin with program inputs (resources).

A third logic model approach emphasizes the details of the implementation process. It is less likely to include columns of boxes displaying assumptions and inputs and displays less detail regarding outcomes. Instead, the *activities approach logic model* is likely to contain more boxes providing great detail about each activity that must be implemented to keep the program on track.

Which logic model to choose will vary, depending on program needs and what seems to be most helpful for those involved in program management and evaluation. Regardless of which approach you might choose, you should try to find a happy medium between making your logic model so skimpy that it fails to adequately convey the various model components and their logical connections versus packing it with so much detail that the essence is hard to see. Figure 14-1 displays a basic, skeletal format of what an outcomes approach logic model

FIGURE 14.1 Template for Constructing an Outcomes Approach Logic Model for an In-Prison Prerelease Restorative Justice

FIGURE 14.2 Theory-Based Logic Model Used in a Federally Funded Homeless Prevention Program

Source: Mulroy, Elizabeth A., and Helenann Lauber. 2004. "A User-Friendly Approach to Program Evaluation and Effective Community Interventions for Families at Risk of Homelessness," *Social Work*, 49 (4), 573–586. (Figure appears on p. 578.) Copyright © 2004, National Association of Social Workers, Inc. Social Work.

STEPS TO ENHANCE COMPLIANCE WITH AND UTILIZATION OF EVALUATIONS

- Learn about stakeholders.
- Involve stakeholders early in planning the evaluation and in all of its phases.
- Find out who wants the evaluation and why they want it.
- Obtain stakeholders' feedback to a draft of the evaluation proposal that reflects their input.
- Include a logic model in the evaluation proposal.
- Assure program personnel and other stakeholders that they will be able to respond to a draft of the report before it is finalized.

- Tailor the form and style of the report to the needs of stakeholders.
- Present negative findings, if any, tactfully, recognizing the yeoman efforts and skills of program personnel.
- Instead of implying program failure, provide suggestions for developing new programs or improving existing ones.
- Develop implications that are realistic and practical.

might look like. The program involved is an in-prison prerelease restorative justice program in which victims and offenders interact in groups. Figure 14-2 presents a logic model that is more theory based and that was used in the evaluation of a federally funded homeless prevention program.

A note of caution is in order. We are not implying that if you follow all the steps we have proposed in planning an evaluation that you are certain to avoid the various problems we have mentioned. These steps, which are summarized in the box "Steps to Enhance Compliance with and Utilization of Evaluations," are recommended as ways to reduce the likelihood of encountering those problems or the severity of those problems if they do arise. But even if you follow all of the proposed steps, under certain circumstances you may still encounter some of these problems. As we will discuss later in this chapter, various potential political, administrative, and logistical problems can be difficult to avoid. For example, if administrators or practitioners feel their program's funding is threatened by your findings, then they may seek to discredit your evaluation even if you went by the book in dealing with them.

» PURPOSES AND TYPES OF PROGRAM EVALUATION

An early decision to be made in planning an evaluation pertains to the purpose of the evaluation.

A program evaluation might have one or more of the following three broad purposes: (a) to assess the ultimate *success* of programs; (b) to assess problems in how programs are being *implemented*; or (c) to obtain information needed in program *planning* and *development*. Program evaluations can be further classified as *summative* or *formative*.

Summative and Formative Evaluations

Summative evaluations are concerned with the first of the three purposes: involving the ultimate success of a program and decisions about whether it should be continued or chosen in the first place from among alternative options. The results of a summative evaluation convey a sense of finality. Depending on whether the results imply that the program succeeded, the program may or may not survive. Asking whether a program is achieving a successful outcome is perhaps the most significant evaluative question we might ask, and probably the question that immediately comes to mind when we think about program evaluation. It may also be the most politically charged question because it bears so directly on key vested interests, such as those that are associated with funding. But as we noted at the beginning of this chapter, program evaluation can have other purposes and other research questions that, although they may ultimately have some bearing on program outcome, focus on issues in the conceptualization, design, planning, administration, and implementation of interventions and programs.

Formative evaluations, for example, are not concerned with testing the success of a program. They focus instead on obtaining information that is helpful in planning the program and in improving its implementation and performance (Posavac & Carey, 1985). Whereas summative evaluations are usually quantitative in approach, formative evaluations may use quantitative methods, qualitative methods, or both. As you will see, these types or purposes of program evaluation are not mutually exclusive. Rather, they complement one another, and some evaluations can cover more than one of these purposes, such as when an evaluation finds that a program failed to attain its goals because it was never properly implemented in the first place. We'll continue our discussion of the various types of program evaluation by first examining in more depth the use of summative evaluations to evaluate program outcome and efficiency.

Evaluating Outcome and Efficiency

Evaluations of program outcome and efficiency may assess whether the program is effectively attaining its goals, whether it has any unintended harmful effects, whether its success (if any) is being achieved at a reasonable cost, and how the ratio of its benefits to its cost compares with the benefits and costs of other programs with similar objectives.

This approach to evaluation, sometimes called the *goal attainment model* of evaluation, refers to the formal goals and mission of the program— whether it's achieving what its funders or the general public want it to achieve. Typically, in designing goal attainment evaluations, the program's formal goals will be specified as dependent variables and operationally defined in terms of measurable indicators of program success.

The focus is on maximizing the internal validity of the evaluation design to rule out bias and other plausible rival explanations of outcome and to be able to determine whether the particular outcomes observed were really caused by the program. Thus, evaluations of goal attainment ideally should strive to use the most internally valid experimental or quasi-experimental design possible and to use rigorous, objective, quantitative measures. In short, this approach to program evaluation primarily attempts to assess causal connections between program efforts and indicators of program outcome.

No matter how rigorous the assessment of outcome, the evaluation may be deemed incomplete unless it also assesses the costs of obtaining the outcome. In other words, how efficient is the program in achieving its outcome? Suppose, for example, that an evaluation of a case management program to prevent rehospitalization of the severely and persistently mentally ill concludes that the program successfully reduces the number of days patients are hospitalized. Suppose further that the total number of days hospitalized for 50 case-managed patients during the course of the evaluation is 400, as compared to 500 for 50 controls. In other words, the case management program made a difference of 100 fewer hospitalized days.

So far, so good. But suppose the extra cost of providing the case management services during the study period was $50,000. Thus, each day of hospitalization saved by providing case management was costing $500 (which we get by dividing $50,000 by 100). If the cost of hospital care was less than $500 per day per patient, then some might conclude that despite the program's effectiveness, it was not an efficient way to care for the mentally ill.

Such questions of efficiency tend to be purely economic and may not account for important value judgments, such as those dealing with the worth of humanistic benefits reaped by service recipients. The costs of the preceding hypothetical program to the public at large may seem high, but some supporters might believe that those costs are justified by the improved quality of life experienced by patients when they reside in the community.

Thus, once again we see the social and political context of program evaluation. Different stakeholders might disagree about whether a particular benefit of a program is worth the extra cost, depending on which stakeholder is bearing the cost and which is reaping the benefit. And many benefits, such as improved health or an individual's self-esteem, cannot be valued in dollars.

Nevertheless, it's useful to assess program efficiency. Even if humanistic considerations lead us to believe that a less efficient program is still the most desirable option, at least we could make that decision in light of the ratio of costs to benefits. And sometimes assessing efficiency helps us to determine which alternative program provides more humanistic benefits. Suppose, for example, that an alternative type of case management program that costs $25,000 for 50 cases results in 425 hospitalized days for the same study period as the case management program that resulted in 400 hospitalized days. Although the $25,000 program had a slightly worse outcome, its costs were only half that of the $50,000 program. That means that an allocation of $50,000 would enable us to provide the cheaper program to twice as many cases as the more expensive program. Therefore, assuming that a finite level of funding does not permit us to provide the more expensive program to most of the target population, the slightly less effective but much more efficient program might yield greater humanistic benefits.

Cost-Effectiveness and Cost–Benefit Analyses

The two major approaches to assessing the efficiency of a program are called *cost-effectiveness analysis* and *cost–benefit analysis*. In cost-effectiveness analysis, the only monetary considerations are the costs of the program itself; the monetary benefits of the program's effects are not assessed. In cost–benefit analysis, an effort is made to monetize the program's outcome in addition to its costs.

In the foregoing case management example, we would be conducting a cost-effectiveness analysis if we limited our focus to the program cost per day of hospitalization prevented. Thus, if we report that one program costs $500 per hospitalized day prevented and another program costs $300 per hospitalized day prevented, we have reported the findings of a cost-effectiveness analysis. If, on the other hand, we had attempted to monetize outcome by assessing the societal benefits of the program in terms such as the increased economic productivity of the individuals who receive case management, we would have been conducting a cost–benefit analysis. Borrowing from White (1988), we can illustrate the difference between cost–benefit and cost-effectiveness analyses with the following example.

Suppose two alternative-school social work interventions are evaluated, each of which aims to reduce the dropout rate of youths at inner-city high schools. Existing data reported before the study have shown that the graduation rate in the targeted high schools is only 50%. Intervention A costs $50,000 and is used by 100 students; 75 of the 100 students graduate from high school. Intervention B costs $40,000 and is utilized by 100 students; 60 of them graduate from high school. Based on the previously established 50% graduation rate, one would expect 50 of every 100 students to graduate. Because 75 of 100 (75%) who participated in intervention A graduated, a cost-effectiveness analysis would find that intervention A had the effect of adding 25 graduates at a cost of $50,000, or $2,000 per additional graduate. Intervention B was $10,000 cheaper to implement ($40,000 is $10,000 less than the $50,000 cost of intervention A) but had the effect of adding only 10 graduates for the $40,000, which comes to $4,000 per additional graduate. Thus, intervention A is more cost effective because $2,000 per additional graduate is a better cost-effectiveness ratio than $4,000 per additional graduate.

Notice that so far we have not estimated the monetary value of graduating from high school, an estimate that would be required if we were conducting a cost–benefit analysis. Suppose we did conduct such an analysis and found that the projected increased career earnings of the high school graduates was $50,000 per graduate and that the government would have to spend $10,000 less on social services and welfare benefits to each high school graduate as compared to each dropout. Adding those two figures, we could estimate that the monetary benefit per additional graduate is $60,000. Because intervention B had the effect of adding 10 graduates, we could conclude that its monetized outcome was 10 times $60,000, or $600,000. That figure would be far in excess of the intervention's $40,000 cost, so we could argue that the intervention is worth funding—that it is cost beneficial because the dollar value of benefits resulting from the intervention exceeds its dollar value costs.

Note that we could draw this conclusion without ever comparing intervention B to intervention A. Of course, were we to estimate the cost benefit of intervention A, we would find that intervention A's monetized outcome would be even more cost beneficial (with benefits equaling 25 times $60,000, or $1,500,000) than intervention B's. Cost–benefit analyses need not ask whether one program's benefits-to-costs ratio is better than another program's. They may just look at one program and ask whether its monetized benefits exceed its monetary costs.

Assessing the costs of a program can be highly complex. It requires technical expertise in cost accounting and deals with such accounting concepts as variable versus fixed costs, incremental versus sunk costs, recurring versus nonrecurring costs, hidden versus obvious costs, direct versus indirect costs, future costs, opportunity costs, and so forth (Posavac & Carey, 1985). Because program evaluators often lack that expertise, they often do not include cost-effectiveness or cost–benefit analyses as part of their evaluations.

The cost-accounting concepts just mentioned go beyond the scope of this text. Because cost-effectiveness analysis attempts to monetize only program costs and not program outcomes, it involves fewer cost-accounting complexities and fewer questionable monetizing assumptions than does cost–benefit analysis. When we attempt to monetize the outcome of health and welfare programs, we get into difficult value issues, such as attaching a dollar figure to the value of human lives. White (1988) offers the example of neonatal intensive care units to illustrate this point.

Although intensive care units for very low birth-weight babies are not cost beneficial, every major hospital in this country spends hundreds of thousands of dollars providing them. The same point applies to the frail elderly. No matter what the costs are for nursing homes or other programs of care for the frail elderly, the monetized benefits of those programs—such as through increased earning capacity—are not going to exceed the program costs. We do not put a dollar value on the quality-of-life benefits that we seek to provide the frail elderly.

Likewise, when hospice programs attempt to alleviate the pain and suffering of terminally ill people, they cannot monetize that benefit in terms of dollars that the outcome of their care generates through patients' increased earning capacity. Because of the values problem in attempting to analyze benefits in monetary terms, as well as the difficulty in foreseeing and monetizing all of the costs and benefits that might be attributable to a program's outcome, cost-effectiveness analyses are generally considered less controversial and more doable than are cost–benefit analyses.

Problems and Issues in Evaluating Goal Attainment

When people don't like a message they receive, they often blame the messenger. In the same vein, when they don't like the findings of an outcome evaluation,

they often blame the evaluation's methodology. It is commonly perceived that over the years, evaluations of program outcomes have had far more negative findings indicating program failure than positive findings. It is also widely believed that studies with negative findings tend not to be used because of the vested interests at stake. And expectations that rigorous, experimental outcome studies tend to produce negative findings have made administrators wary of such studies and reluctant to authorize them. One common complaint is that the only thing these studies do is tell us that we are failing; they don't show us how to do things better.

One important criticism of the traditional approach to evaluating goal attainment correctly points out that the determination of program goals and their measurable indicators can be hazardous. Sometimes the mission of a program is stated in grandiose terms that no one really takes seriously—terms articulated for political reasons or to convince legislators or others that a program should be funded. Consequently, it's argued that finding negative outcomes in evaluations of the attainment of those goals is a forgone conclusion—that evaluations are doomed to keep coming up with negative findings if they keep taking formally stated goals seriously.

In addition to their grandiosity, formal goals are often stated so vaguely that different evaluators may find it impossible to agree on what they really mean in terms of specific, observable indicators of success. The Head Start program in the War on Poverty is often cited as a case in point. Its formal mission was to offset the effects of poverty and enhance children's opportunities. That's a noble mission, but what are its operational indicators? Evaluative researchers have disagreed over whether the focus of the outcome measures should be on indicators of learning readiness, academic achievement, emotional development and self-esteem, classroom conduct, delinquency later in life, physical health and nutrition, resource redistribution, or something else. The possibilities seem endless, and often program personnel themselves cannot agree on what specific indicators of success are implied by their program's mission statement.

Consequently, when evaluators choose a few operational indicators of success, they risk missing areas in which the program really is succeeding. If so, then their negative findings may be misleading and may endanger the continuation of programs that are succeeding in other, equally important ways. In light of these problems, some argue that the evaluation of outcome ought to be abandoned altogether and replaced by evaluations of program processes. Others argue that, even with these problems, outcome studies at least tell us some things about what is and is not being attained—which is better than having no information at all about program outcomes, particularly if appropriate caution is exercised in acting on the findings.

Some program evaluators suggest keeping the goal attainment model but with some adjustments. One idea has been to ignore the formal goals or mission statement of a program and simply measure every conceivable indicator of outcome that the evaluators think has some potential of being affected by the program. But the feasibility of such undisciplined fishing expeditions for endless potential indicators may be dubious. Also, there is a statistical problem when a large number of dependent variables are assessed independently of one another. An alternative suggestion, therefore, has been to assess official program goals as well as a limited number of additional goals that seem to be the most plausible in light of the social science theories on which the program is based. But this suggestion, too, may be somewhat (albeit less) vulnerable to the same statistical problem, and it offers no guarantee that the most important effects of the program will be detected.

Monitoring Program Implementation

Some programs have unsuccessful outcomes simply because they are not being implemented properly. Suppose an AIDS prevention program develops a public education leaflet and decides to evaluate its effectiveness in a small pilot distribution in a particular high school. Suppose the program personnel deliver the leaflets to the school's vice principal, who agrees to disseminate them to all students. Suppose that for some reason—unanticipated opposition by the principal or the PTA, mere oversight, or whatever—the leaflets never get disseminated. Or perhaps they get disseminated in an undesirable way. Maybe instead of handing them out to every student in a school assembly, the vice principal merely deposits them in teachers' mailboxes with a vague message encouraging them to distribute the leaflets to their students. Maybe some teachers distribute the leaflets but most do not.

Suppose further that the program personnel never learn that the leaflets were not disseminated

as intended. The implications of this turn of events would be quite serious. Because few or no students would have received the leaflet in the first place, the intervention was never implemented as planned and had no chance to succeed. No matter what indicators of outcome were chosen, the leaflet dissemination effort would be doomed to fail. But it would fail not because it was a bad idea or an ineffectual leaflet but because it was never really tried. If the evaluators had merely conducted an outcome study and had not assessed whether and how the program got implemented, they would be in danger of abandoning a public education intervention that, if only implemented properly, might effectively prevent the spread of AIDS.

This example illustrates that no matter how well an outcome evaluation is designed, if it's not supplemented by an evaluation of program implementation, then it risks not identifying or misinterpreting the meaning of negative results. In turn, no matter how highly we value outcome studies, there is a clear need for the evaluation of program implementation. And familiarity with organizational goal theory helps us realize the true importance of implementation evaluations.

Even when we can be sure that we have properly identified the formal, official goals of a program and their operational indicators, we cannot assume that those goals are the real priority of the program personnel who are responsible for attaining them. Program personnel at all levels tend over time to become preoccupied with daily routines and with their own agendas—that is, with unofficial goals pertaining to organizational maintenance, personal prestige and career advancement, bureaucratic rules and procedures, and the like. As these unofficial goals displace official, formal goals, they may result in activities that are either irrelevant to or at odds with the attainment of the official goals.

Thus, for example, administrators of family service agencies may secure federal poverty funds not because they are devoted to fighting poverty but because those funds will help balance agency budgets and enhance the agency board evaluation of the administrators' performance. Suppose the administrators propose to use the funds so that the agencies can reach out to more poverty-stricken individuals and thus try to engage them in receiving the agencies' direct services. Once they've received the funds, however, there is no guarantee that the agencies will try to reach poor clients as diligently as they promised in their grant applications. Even if the administrators sincerely sought to do so, they might run into unanticipated resistance by direct-service practitioners who think that such efforts would be an unrewarding and improper use of their therapeutic talents and who prefer to continue serving the kind of clientele with whom they are familiar and comfortable.

Consider the implications for program evaluation in the foregoing hypothetical example. Suppose a nationwide outcome study were done to see if the federal funding of direct social services to the poor resulted in a reduction in poverty or a reduction in various psychosocial problems among the poor. If the family service agencies never really tried very hard to serve poor clients because of their own internally directed objectives, then the outcome would in all likelihood be negative. But it would be wrong to conclude from such results that the provision of direct services to the poor is an ineffective way to help them deal with the problems of poverty because the services never reached enough poor people in the first place.

For the same reasons, one can see from this example the importance of evaluating program implementation even without any evaluation of program outcome. If an evaluation of agency caseload attributes found that the agencies never implemented the program as planned—that poor people were not being served—then who needs an outcome evaluation? And those results would be quite useful. Instead of simply depicting the program as a success or failure, it would identify what went wrong and could help policymakers consider ways to improve the program's implementation. In addition, simply monitoring program implementation would help keep the agency accountable to its funders. Ultimately, of course, they would want to know the program's outcome. But, in the meantime, just knowing how the program is being implemented is invaluable.

Evaluations of program implementation are not necessarily concerned only with the question of whether a program is being implemented as planned. Many other possible questions might examine how best to implement and maintain the program. Here are just a few of the important questions that can be researched without getting into questions of outcome:

- Which fund-raising strategy yields the most funds?

- What proportion of the target population is being served?

- What types of individuals are not being reached?

- Why are so many targeted individuals refusing services?

- What satellite clinic locations are reaching the most clients?

- What types of practitioners seem to have the best attitudes about working with certain underserved target populations?

- Do practitioners in specialized units have better attitudes than those in multipurpose units?

- How skillful are various types of practitioners in their clinical interventions?

- In what areas do practitioners seem least prepared and in need of continuing education?

- How are staff members reacting to new agency procedures? What difficulties are they experiencing with the procedures?

- Are clients satisfied with services? Why or why not?

- Why do so many clients drop out of treatment prematurely?

Process Evaluation

A term closely aligned with monitoring program implementation is *process evaluation*. Process evaluations (which are an example of formative evaluations, mentioned earlier in this chapter) ask many of the same questions as indicated above in connection with monitoring program implementation, and they focus on identifying strengths and weaknesses in program processes and recommending needed improvements.

Often, agency administrators will ask evaluators to conduct outcome evaluations of their programs while those programs are still in their infancy and have not yet had enough time to identify and resolve start-up bugs and other problematic processes in implementation. These administrators may be in a hurry for outcome data because they are under intense pressure from funding sources to prove their success at goal attainment. Seasoned evaluators, however, may try to persuade them to table any outcome evaluation until a process evaluation has been completed so that outcome data are collected only after the program has been debugged. The administrators may or may not have the time or resources to conduct a process evaluation first and then an outcome evaluation. In contrast, other administrators, perhaps under less external pressure, may be content just to have the process evaluation, asking not whether their program works but how to make it work better.

All of the methodologies covered in this book can be applied to evaluate program implementation. The most appropriate methodology to use depends on the nature of the research question. Experimental or quasi-experimental designs might be used to assess the effectiveness of alternative fund-raising strategies, to measure the impact of different organizational arrangements on staff attitudes, to determine which outreach strategies are most successful in engaging hard-to-reach prospective clients in treatment, and so on. Surveys that use questionnaires or scales might assess staff, client, or community attitudes that affect program implementation decisions. Available records might be analyzed to assess whether the attributes of clients being served match program priorities regarding the intended target population. (We'll be discussing those two methodologies in Chapters 16 and 17.)

Process evaluations, however, tend to rely heavily on qualitative methods, which we've touched on in previous chapters and will be discussing at greater length in the three chapters of Part 6 of this text. Open-ended qualitative interviewing, for instance, might be the best way to learn how staff members are reacting to new agency procedures and the unanticipated difficulties they might be experiencing with them. Qualitative interviewing might also work best for discovering the reasons that clients cite for service dissatisfaction or for refusing or prematurely terminating service delivery. Participant observation might be used to assess how staff members relate to clients or to one another. In some studies, evaluators have posed as clients and observed how staff members behaved and the ways in which their behavior affected clients.

Evaluation for Program Planning: Needs Assessment

Thus far, we have been discussing the evaluation of programs that have already been implemented. But the term *program evaluation* also connotes diagnostic evaluation. Just as clinical practitioners evaluate client problems and needs during a preintervention assessment period to develop the best treatment plan, program evaluators may assess a program's target population in order to enhance program planning. They might assess the extent and location of the problems the program seeks to ameliorate, as well as the target population's characteristics, problems, expressed needs, and desires. This information is then used to guide program planning and development concerning such issues as what services to offer, how to maximize service utilization by targeted subgroups, where to locate services, and so on.

For example, suppose you are planning a new statewide program to help the homeless. What would you need to know to guide your planning? You might want to find out how many homeless people there are in the state. How many are there in specific locations in the state? What are the reasons for each individual's homelessness, and how many people are there for each reason? How many choose to be homeless? How many seem to be homeless because of mental illness or substance abuse? How many are homeless because they lost their jobs and cannot find work? How long have they been homeless? How many of the homeless are in different ethnic groups, and how many are recent immigrants or do not speak English? What proportion of the homeless consists of children and entire family units? What special problems do the children experience in such matters as education, health, nutrition, self-esteem, and so on? What special problems and needs are expressed by the adult homeless, those with emotional disorders, and others? These are just a few of the diagnostic questions you might ask; the answers will help you suggest what interventions to develop, where to locate them, how to staff them, and so on.

The process of systematically researching diagnostic questions like those just mentioned is called *needs assessment*. The term needs assessment is widely used to cover all sorts of techniques for collecting data for program planning purposes, and it has become essentially synonymous with evaluation for program planning.

Before we examine specific alternative techniques of needs assessment, it's important to address a thorny conceptual issue that complicates the definition of needs: whether they're defined in normative terms or in terms of demand. If needs are defined normatively, then a needs assessment would focus on comparing the objective living conditions of the target population with what society—or at least that segment of society that is concerned with helping the target population—deems acceptable or desirable from a humanitarian standpoint. Normatively defining the needs of the homeless, for instance, might lead you to conclude that certain housing or shelter programs need to be developed for individuals who are living in deplorable conditions on the streets, even if those individuals don't express any dissatisfaction with their current homelessness.

If needs are defined in terms of demand, however, only those individuals who indicate that they feel or perceive the need themselves would be considered to be in need of a particular program or intervention. Thus, in this homelessness example, individuals who prefer to be homeless might not be counted as in need of the program. Defining needs in terms of demand can be tricky. Perhaps individuals express no need for a planned program because they don't understand how the planned program will help them or because they have come to expect that every time a social program is provided to them, it is stigmatizing or unacceptable to them in some other way. Thus, in assessing whether the homeless need a new shelter program, many homeless individuals might express no need for the program and might even disdain the idea because they have no reason to believe that the new program really will be more acceptable to them than the filthy, crowded, dangerous shelters they already refuse to use.

How we define *needs* affects the choice of specific techniques to assess them. For example, if we define needs normatively, we might be able to establish the need for a particular program by analyzing existing statistics. Thus, if census data showed a relatively high number of unmarried teenage mothers in a particular area, then we might be predisposed to conclude that more family planning or child-rearing education services are needed in that area. But if we take demand into account, then we might want to supplement the census information by conducting a survey of teenage mothers to determine under what conditions they would actually use the particular services that we are contemplating.

The specific techniques for conducting a needs assessment are usually classified in five categories: (a) the key informants approach, (b) the community forum approach, (c) the rates-under-treatment approach, (d) the social indicators approach, and (e) the community survey approach. Let's look at each one.

Key Informants   The key informants approach utilizes questionnaires or interviews to obtain expert opinions from individuals who are presumed to have special knowledge about the target population's problems and needs as well as about current gaps in service delivery to that population. The key informants selected to be surveyed might include leaders of groups or organizations that are in close contact with the target population and that have special knowledge of its problems. They might also include practitioners who work closely with the target population.

In assessing the needs of the homeless, for instance, key informants might include professionals who work in public shelters or soup kitchens; researchers or other personnel who address homelessness as part of their work for local planning agencies; neighborhood leaders who live in communities where the homeless tend to congregate; administrators and case managers who work in community mental health programs; public officials who advocate legislation to help deal with the problem of homelessness; leaders of citizen advocacy groups who work on behalf of the poor, homeless, or mentally ill; and law enforcement officials who have been dealing with the problem.

The prime advantage of the key informants approach is that a sample can be obtained and surveyed quickly, easily, and inexpensively. Also, conducting the survey can provide the fringe benefits of building connections with key community resources that are concerned about the problem and of giving your program some visibility. The chief disadvantage of this method, however, is that your information is not coming directly from the target population; that information's quality depends on the objectivity and depth of knowledge underlying the expressed opinions.

To illustrate this disadvantage, consider the following possible pitfalls in an assessment of homelessness. Perhaps key informants who are affiliated with public shelters are unaware of those individuals who refuse to use the shelters, their reasons for doing so, and the unique problems they have. Perhaps advocates for poverty legislation will be likely to downplay needs associated with the mentally ill homeless because they see homelessness primarily as an economic problem and do not want to foster the notion that people are homeless because of either defects in character or voluntary preferences. Perhaps mental health officials will be biased toward exaggerating mental illness as the cause of homelessness, or perhaps their bias will be to downplay the problem of homelessness among the mentally ill because that problem may reflect negatively on the mental health policies they have implemented. Perhaps neighborhood leaders where the homeless tend to congregate will be biased toward perceiving the need for services that get the homeless out of their neighborhood. In light of pitfalls like these, it is important that the representativeness of the key informant sample be maximized by using sampling procedures that are as scientific as possible. (We'll discuss such procedures in the next chapter.) But even that is no guarantee that these pitfalls will be sufficiently minimized.

Community Forum   The community forum approach involves holding a meeting in which concerned members of the community can express their views and interact freely about their needs. This approach offers several nonscientific advantages, including its feasibility, its ability to build support and visibility for the sponsoring agency, and its ability to provide an atmosphere in which individuals can consider the problem in depth and be stimulated by what others have said to consider things they might otherwise have overlooked. Still, from a scientific standpoint, this approach is risky.

Those who attend such meetings might not be representative of the people in the best position to know about the needs of the target population and of those whose views are relatively unbiased. Instead, those who have vested interests or particular axes to grind are likely to be overrepresented. The views expressed at such meetings are expressed publicly, and therefore strong social pressures might inhibit certain individuals from speaking at all or from expressing minority viewpoints. In light of these problems, rather than hold an open meeting for anyone to attend, it may be advisable to hold a series of closed meetings, each for a different, preselected, homogeneous group.

Rates under Treatment   Rates under treatment is an approach that attempts to estimate the need for a service and the characteristics of its potential clients on the basis of the number and characteristics of clients who already use that service. This method makes the most sense when the rates under treatment are examined in a community other than but similar to a target community that does not yet

provide the service in question. The assumption is that if the two communities really are comparable, then the size and characteristics of the target population in the community without the service will parallel the size and characteristics of those already being treated in the comparison community.

A prime data collection method in this approach is the secondary analysis of case records from the comparison community. The prime advantages of this approach are its quickness, easiness, inexpensiveness, and unobtrusiveness. Its prime disadvantage is that it assesses only that portion of the target population that is already using services, and thus it pertains primarily to demand and may underestimate normative need. In fact, it may even underestimate demand because the number of individuals who want to utilize the service may exceed the caseload capacity in the comparison community. Moreover, many who want to use that type of service may choose not to use the one offered in the comparison community because of something undesirable in the way it is being provided.

Another disadvantage of this approach is that the records and data in the comparison community may be unreliable or biased. Accurate record keeping may be a low priority in many agencies in the comparison community, particularly if service delivery demands leave little time for it. Also, agencies may exaggerate the number of clients served or their needs for services so that they will look good to funding sources or others to whom they are accountable. One way this can happen is by multiple countings of the same individual across different agencies serving the target population. Another way is by recording one unit of service delivered to a family of four in such a manner that others might think that four units of service were provided to four different members of the target population. These inaccuracies often are not intentional.

Social Indicators   Another type of needs assessment that makes use of existing statistics is the social indicators approach. This approach does not look just at treatment statistics; it examines aggregated statistics that reflect conditions of an entire population. For example, infant mortality rates (the number of infants who die during their first year of life) can be an indicator of the need for prenatal services in a particular community. Such rates could also be examined to identify communities that have the greatest need for these services. Likewise, rates of reported child abuse in a community can be used as an indicator of that community's need for a newly developed abuse prevention program. School dropout rates can indicate the need for a school district to hire school social workers. Using social indicators is unobtrusive and can be done quickly and inexpensively. But those advantages need to be weighed against potential problems in the reliability of a particular existing database. Also, this approach's utility depends on the degree to which the existing indicators can be assumed to reflect future service use patterns accurately.

As we noted, the social indicators approach to needs assessment relies on the utilization of existing statistics. In Chapter 17, we'll discuss the methodological issues involved in using existing statistics as well as prominent sources for finding existing statistics. You may find that material particularly useful if you plan to conduct a needs assessment using the social indicators approach.

Surveys of Communities or Target Groups   The most direct way to assess the characteristics and perceived problems and needs of the target group is to survey its members. This usually involves surveying a sample drawn from the population, although sometimes it's feasible to undertake a census of the entire target group.

Surveying members of target groups to assess their needs involves applying the principles and techniques of sampling and survey research that we'll be discussing in the next two chapters. Ideally, random sampling techniques should be used when we want to maximize the representativeness of the sample. But exceptions to this can be made—for instance, when it's impossible to obtain in advance a list of people from whom to sample, as when attempting to survey the homeless. In such cases, qualitative sampling approaches, which we'll discuss in Chapter 18, may be more appropriate than quantitative ones.

Data collection methods might use highly structured quantitative questionnaires or semistructured qualitative interviews, depending on the nature of the target group and what is already known or not known about its possible needs. For example, in assessing the need for additional day-care facilities for low-income parents, the needs assessment might include questions about the number of preschoolage children living with respondents, current child-care arrangements, whether and when respondents

would use a new day-care facility, what respondents expect it to provide, what respondents would do differently to further their own education or careers were a day-care facility provided, and respondents' demographic attributes.

The advantages and disadvantages of the direct survey approach parallel those of surveys in general. Evaluators ought to be particularly mindful of the potential biases associated with low response rates, social desirability, and acquiescent response sets. Suppose, for example, that the survey is conducted by mail. Those who bother to respond cannot be assumed to represent those who do not respond. In all likelihood, the respondents will feel a greater need for the program than the nonrespondents, and they are likely to differ in other ways as well. Suppose the questions are phrased only in general terms concerning whether a particular service ought to be available. Respondents might be predisposed to agree. Why not agree with the provision of a new service if no mention is made about its costs or whether the respondent would actually use it? But if respondents who agree that a service sounds nice are asked whether they think it's worth specific costs or whether they intend to use it, they might respond negatively.

Thus, the advantages of this method—its directness and its potential for ascertaining how prospective service consumers perceive their need for and likely use of programs—need to be weighed against potential biases in measurement or in response rates. Of course, what you will have learned in this book about sampling, measurement, and surveys might enable you to design a needs assessment survey that adequately minimizes those biases. But doing so would be time consuming and expensive, and feasibility constraints might instead require that you use one or more of the foregoing four approaches to needs assessment.

Like research methods in general, each of the five approaches to needs assessment has its own advantages and disadvantages. Ideally, then, we should combine two or more approaches to needs assessment to get a more complete picture of normative needs, felt needs, and demand for prospective services.

Focus Groups

A relatively speedy and inexpensive qualitative research method often used for needs assessment or for collecting other forms of program evaluation data involves the use of focus groups. We'll give more attention to the use of focus groups in Chapter 19, on qualitative methods. We'll see the advantages and disadvantages of bringing together in the same room a small group of key informants, referral sources, service consumers or potential consumers, or community residents to engage in a guided discussion of community needs or the need to provide a specific program to a particular target population of clients or prospective clients. We'll also see how group dynamics can bring out needs assessment information that might not have emerged in a community survey.

» AN ILLUSTRATION OF A QUALITATIVE APPROACH TO EVALUATION RESEARCH

In several places throughout this text, we have reiterated the view that quantitative and qualitative approaches to empirical inquiry are equally important. In this chapter, we have noted that program evaluations can use both quantitative and qualitative methods. This point is reinforced in the box "Combining Quantitative and Qualitative Methods in Program Evaluation."

Because the emphasis in the previous two chapters was on the use of quantitative methods to evaluate the effectiveness of interventions, we'll provide an illustration of a program evaluation that emphasized qualitative methods. The illustration we'll use was reported by Bogdan and Taylor (1990), two qualitatively oriented researchers who had been conducting evaluation research since the early 1970s on policy issues connected to the institutionalization and deinstitutionalization of people with developmental disabilities. Their work led them to question the policy of institutionalization and to become strong advocates for deinstitutionalization and the integration of people with disabilities into the community. However, their review of qualitative studies that documented the plight of disabled people who have been transferred from dehumanized institutions to dehumanized conditions in the community raised questions about how to improve this target population's integration into the community.

Bogdan and Taylor believed that many quantitatively oriented outcome evaluations on the effects of

deinstitutionalization asked the wrong question—what they called the "Does it work?" question. In their apparent orientation to the stakeholder service model of evaluation practice, Bogdan and Taylor noted that community-based practitioners, like human service practitioners in general, believe in their work. They are not skeptical about what they do and therefore find no value in evaluative studies that merely tell whether a particular program was or was not effective. When "Does it work?" studies produce pessimistic results, they attribute the findings to the unfortunate prevalence of poorly funded, poor-quality community-based programs.

Moreover, they tend to see community integration as a moral question similar to the issue of slavery. Bogdan and Taylor drew an analogy between asking about the effectiveness of policies and programs that free people from institutions and asking about the effectiveness of policies that freed slaves in the Civil War era, pointing out that slavery would not be justified were outcome studies to find that freed slaves were encountering difficulties in community integration. We find this analogy debatable, but we share it with you so that you can see how Bogdan and Taylor's values influenced their work. Even if you disagree with their analogy, you might admire their candor about their values and about how values influenced the questions they asked.

Rather than study whether community integration works, Bogdan and Taylor asked, "What does integration mean?" (notice the qualitative orientation to meanings) and, "How can integration be accomplished?" Bogdan and Taylor saw these questions as more optimistic ones than asking whether community integration works. They also saw these questions as more responsive to practitioner or stakeholder needs, not only because practitioners are optimistic about what they do but also because they are more interested in formative information about how better to accomplish their aims than they are in summative outcome conclusions.

Their focus on discovering insights about what community integration means and how better to achieve it led them to eschew random sampling and to use instead qualitative sampling strategies (which will be discussed in Part 6). Bogdan and Taylor were not interested in studying typical, or average, programs. They were not interested in representativeness. Instead, they sought to identify exemplary programs that were reputed to be doing well in achieving community integration. Their sampling

COMBINING QUANTITATIVE AND QUALITATIVE METHODS IN PROGRAM EVALUATION

Evaluative Function	Quantitative Methods	Qualitative Methods
Planning an evaluation		Open-ended interviews with stakeholders, content analysis of program documents, and participant observation of program activities
Needs assessment	Survey of key informants, target group, or community	Community forum
	Rates under treatment	Focus groups
	Social indicators	
Process evaluation (monitoring program implementation and identifying needed improvements)	Staff and client surveys	Case studies of model programs
	Analysis of agency records on amounts of various types of service delivery and to whom	Focus groups of program staff and service consumers; open-ended interviews with staff about unofficial goals and implementation problems; participant observation of service provision, staff training, and staff meetings; open-ended interviews with service consumers; content analysis of staff meeting documents or practitioner entries in client records; and video- or audiorecording service provision to assess practitioner skill or compliance with recommended procedures
Evaluating goal attainment	Experimental and quasi-experimental designs, combined with process evaluation to determine the nature of the program that did or did not attain its goals	Supplement outcome evaluation with foregoing process evaluation methods to ascertain the nature of the successful program or to learn whether the unsuccessful program was really implemented as intended
Evaluating efficiency	Cost-effectiveness analysis and cost–benefit analysis	

efforts toward identifying exemplary programs used a variety of techniques, "including announcements in professional newsletters, national mailings, and reviews of the professional literature" (Bogdan & Taylor, 1990, p. 187). They also contacted various key informants who could tell them which agencies they felt were doing a good job and who could identify other key informants who might know of other exemplary programs. The key informants included disability rights activists, university-based researchers, and leaders of parent and professional groups.

Bogdan and Taylor conducted in-depth, open-ended phone interviews with officials in each program that was identified in their snowball sample. The purpose of these interviews was to obtain information that would help them whittle the sample down to eight agencies that promised to yield the most comprehensive understanding of what community integration means and how best to achieve it. Their interview questions attempted to probe into what the programs were doing, how well they seemed to be doing it, and how sincere they seemed to be in their efforts. These questions, as well as routine questions about agency characteristics, enabled the researchers to select a sample of agencies that all seemed exemplary but that varied in geographic location, services offered, and administrative arrangements.

The reason for the small sample size was that each agency in the sample was studied intensively, including a series of visits by the researchers over a 3-year period. To gain entry into the agencies and to foster their enthusiastic cooperation with the study, the researchers honestly told agency staff members that their agency had been nominated as innovative or exemplary. This not only flattered administrators but also helped them realize that their participation provided an opportunity to gain national visibility as a model program. Bogdan and Taylor reported that this ironically seemed to lead many officials and staff to talk more openly about their problems than they otherwise might have done.

Each agency site visit lasted several days, during which the researchers employed an approach that involved triangulated qualitative data collection methods, such as direct observation, intensive interviewing, and document analysis. The interviews were conducted with staff members, clients and their family members, and representatives of other local agencies. The site visits yielded thousands of pages of field notes and interview transcripts

(and probably none of the inferential statistics that we'll try to fascinate you with in later chapters).

Bogdan and Taylor's prime approach to data presentation was through *case studies*. The case studies were prepared after each agency visit. They provided an agency overview, described the innovative agency policies that seemed to be fostering community integration, and provided illustrative case examples of how agency innovations are perceived to be affecting people's lives. When applicable, they also reported agency problems and dilemmas. The case study "stories" of the agencies were then disseminated to the field as a whole through short articles in relevant newsletters, articles that focused on the positive aspects of the visited agencies. The articles attempted to disseminate state-of-the-art descriptions to provide readers with new ideas that they might be able to adapt in their efforts to improve community integration in their own agencies.

With this positive, "optimistic," qualitative approach that focused on processes, Bogdan and Taylor believed that they were producing research that would have greater utility to the field and ultimately do more to improve the well-being of disabled individuals than producing quantitative studies of outcome. Although some researchers may disagree as to whether their particular approach is more valuable than other particular approaches to research and evaluation, we think few will fail to appreciate the value of their approach as one of a variety of valuable ways to use research in our efforts to improve practice, alleviate human suffering, and promote social welfare.

» THE POLITICS OF PROGRAM EVALUATION

Because an evaluation of a program's effectiveness can provide ammunition to that program's supporters or opponents, intense political pressure can be introduced into the program evaluation process. Vested interests can impede the atmosphere for free scientific inquiry. Instead of pursuing truth as scientifically as possible to improve human well-being, program evaluation efforts may be implemented in ways that fit perceived program maintenance needs. Sometimes, this means that there will be pressure to design the research or interpret its findings in ways that are likely to make the program look good.

Other times, it may simply mean that the program evaluation is conducted in the cheapest, most convenient way possible, guided by the belief that funding sources don't pay much attention to the quality of the research and just want to be able to say that the programs they fund have been evaluated. Consequently, it is naive to suppose that when administrators hire someone to be responsible for program evaluation activities or to conduct a specific evaluation, they will pick the person most qualified from a scientific research methodology standpoint.

Political considerations—that the evaluation will be done to favor vested interests—may be a much higher priority. Indeed, it probably is not overly cynical to suppose that commitment to conducting the most scientific study possible sometimes will threaten administrators and be perceived as a problem. They are unlikely to admit as much; rather, they may call individuals with a devotion to methodological rigor "too ivory towerish and out of touch with the real world." (And sometimes they are correct—if zeal for methodological rigor blinds researchers and makes them insensitive to realistic feasibility constraints that make some methodological compromises appropriate and unavoidable.)

In-House versus External Evaluators

When program evaluators work for the agency being evaluated, they are called in-house evaluators. Program evaluators who work for external agencies such as government or regulating agencies and private research consultation firms (which often bid for government grants to evaluate programs that receive public funds) are external evaluators. This group also includes university faculty members who have secured research grants to evaluate programs or simply wish to conduct applied research as part of their scholarly duties.

In-house evaluators are often thought to have certain advantages over external evaluators. They may have greater access to program information and personnel, more knowledge about program processes that might bear on the design of an evaluation or the meaning of findings, and more sensitivity to the program's research needs and the realistic obstacles to the feasibility of certain research designs or methods. They might also be more likely to be trusted by program personnel and consequently receive better cooperation and feedback from them. But the flip side of the coin is that

their commitment to the program, their superiors, or the advancement of their own careers might make them less objective and independent than external evaluators.

But it would be naive to suppose that external evaluators are never subjected to the same kinds of political considerations as are in-house evaluators. External evaluators may have strong incentives to get and stay in the good graces of the personnel of the program being evaluated. If they alienate those personnel, then the quality of their evaluation may be imperiled by the lack of cooperation with the research agenda. In fact, one criterion for choosing the recipient of a program evaluation grant might be the quality of the relationship the evaluator has with the program and that relationship's potential for securing cooperation from program participants.

Also, it's incorrect to assume that external sponsors of the evaluation are always more objective than in-house personnel. Perhaps the sponsors of the evaluation want to stop funding the program and need negative evaluation results to justify the cessation of funding to their own constituents. On the other hand, the sponsors might fret that negative results would make them (the sponsors) look bad and, in turn, threaten their own fundraising efforts.

One of the authors of this text (Rubin) has worked on several program evaluations that illustrate these points. In one, the U.S. Congress allocated funds for demonstration programs with the stipulation that the funded programs be evaluated by external evaluators. But Congress did not stipulate anything further about the nature of the evaluation designs or how the external evaluators were to be selected. At a meeting in Washington, the federal bureaucrats—who perhaps were primarily concerned with having Congress continue to fund their programs in the future—encouraged recipients of their funding to use simple preexperimental designs and simplistic measures of program effects that are likely to generate favorable results. For example, they advocated simply assessing whether there was a 10% reduction in out-of-home placements of children from the year before the funded project started to the year after its implementation. They dismissed the need for design controls for threats to internal validity or for statistical controls for chance fluctuations. (Chapter 22 will examine this statistical issue in depth.)

In an informal conversation at the meeting, one external program evaluator whose job security at an agency in the private sector depended on securing contracts from programs to be their external evaluator confided that he would not propose rigorous designs because he believed that such designs would scare off programs whose contracts he needed. Instead, he would propose uncontrolled, preexperimental designs that would use outcome measures to be completed by service providers about their own effectiveness and therefore highly vulnerable to practitioner bias. He seemed to be having great success at the meeting, claiming to have secured "external" evaluation contracts from four program administrators who went to the meeting before selecting an evaluator.

Fiscal concerns not only can affect the evaluation designs employed but also can lead to attempts to influence the way findings are interpreted because administrators may believe that the prospects for future funding are enhanced by obtaining favorable evaluation outcomes. This influence can be exerted in various ways, some more subtle than others. Evaluators can be told, for example, that if the program has a successful outcome, then spinoff programs are likely to be funded, and the evaluator can receive the contract to be the "external" evaluator in those spinoff programs. Assuming additional program development further down the road, external evaluators may realize that staying in the good graces of the people whose programs are being evaluated and producing desired conclusions for those programs can have significant long-term benefits for the evaluator's own job security, income, and career.

Another way to influence evaluators is by criticizing their competence after they have reported findings that program administrators do not like. External evaluators quickly learn, for example, that if they produce reports that reflect favorably on the evaluated program, then program staff members are extremely unlikely to mobilize efforts to discredit the evaluation's credibility or the evaluator's competence. They also learn that if their reports are not as positive as program staff members desire, especially if those members are worried about the impact of the evaluation findings on future funding, such mobilization efforts are likely to ensue, and the evaluator's standing with his or her employing agency might be seriously tarnished. A weak study with positive outcome findings is unlikely to be attacked by program staff members who stand to benefit by those findings. However, a strong study with a few relatively minor flaws is likely to be vilified by staff members who see the findings as a threat to their funding prospects.

Ulterior motives are not the only reason why these things occur. Various stakeholders in an organization often have good intentions in their efforts to influence an evaluation or its findings, believing that they are doing the right thing for the good of the organization. For example, many staff members work hard to secure scarce funding for programs that they believe are helping people. These program staff members may believe that even if we are unsure of the effectiveness of their programs, we should continue investing funds in and working to improve them. Negative findings, they may fear, will simply lead to funding cutbacks with no opportunity to improve on current efforts. Some might argue, from a more cynical perspective, that some staff members are also concerned with enhancing the fiscal well-being of their own agency and the status of their own jobs. There probably is a good deal of truth in both points of view, keeping individual differences in mind. But even if good intentions underlie stakeholder efforts to bias an evaluation or discredit its valid findings, the end result is to undermine the integrity of the program evaluation methods and findings.

Another illustration of these points occurred during the mid-1970s, when the Council on Social Work Education (CSWE) was awarded a research grant by the social work training unit of the National Institute of Mental Health (NIMH) to evaluate the community mental health curricula of schools of social work. A prime purpose of the evaluation was to describe the different ways in which graduate schools of social work were implementing their NIMH training grants. At that time, almost every master's degree program in social work was receiving many thousands of dollars annually to prepare students for practice in the field of community mental health, and the research project sought to identify community mental health curriculum innovations fostered by the NIMH grants.

The researchers were able to identify innovative community mental health curricula in some schools. But based on data gathered over a 2-year period during multiple site visits to participating schools, they concluded that most schools of social work had initiated no curriculum innovations associated specifically with community mental health. Instead, their NIMH grant funds enabled them to expand their traditional curriculum, and they justified that practice on the grounds that everything that has always been taught in a school of social work is related to community mental health.

We might anticipate that faculty members and administrators in schools of social work would be upset with the preceding conclusion, which was included in the report of the evaluation (Rubin, 1979), because school personnel might fear that it would threaten continuation of NIMH funding for programs that used the funds to expand their regular programs without developing any special mental health curriculum. At the same time, we might also anticipate that the NIMH social work training staff would appreciate the candor of the report, thinking that they then could use the report to distinguish schools that appropriately used NIMH funding from those that did not and to influence the latter schools to be more accountable to them. But as it turned out, according to CSWE administrators, the NIMH staff expressed more consternation about the findings than did anyone else.

Their fear was that bureaucrats in other units of NIMH—units that were competing with social work for federal funds—could use the report as ammunition in their efforts to secure a bigger slice of the funding pie for their units at the expense of social work training. If that were to happen, not only would schools of social work receive less funding but also the staff members of the social work training unit would lose status in the bureaucracy and see their own budget reduced.

As you can see, the web of politics in program evaluation can be extensive, and sometimes the external groups that sponsor an evaluation are not as independent and objective as we might suppose. In the foregoing example, the NIMH social work training staff were quite eager to get a report that would portray schools of social work as doing wonderfully innovative things with their NIMH funds, a report that they could then use to justify their own performance in allocating funds and monitoring their usage and in order to argue for more funding for their unit. In choosing CSWE to conduct the evaluation, it is reasonable to suppose that they fully expected that a glowing report would be forthcoming because CSWE is funded and governed by representatives of schools of social work and because one of CSWE's main goals is to lobby for greater funding for social work education. In fact, some CSWE administrative staff expressed

displeasure with the report and tried to influence its author, a CSWE staff member, to modify the interpretation of the findings in order to depict more favorably the public benefits of NIMH funding for schools of social work.

Utilization of Program Evaluation Findings

As the preceding discussion illustrates, the findings of program evaluation studies can affect jobs, programs, and investments. But beliefs and values also are at stake. Consequently, political and ideological forces can influence whether and how program evaluation findings are used.

As president, Richard Nixon appointed a blue ribbon national commission to study the consequences of pornography. After a diligent, multifaceted evaluation, the commission reported that pornography didn't appear to have any of the negative social consequences often attributed to it. Exposure to pornographic materials, for example, didn't increase the likelihood of sex crimes. You might have expected liberalized legislation to follow from the research. Instead, the president said the commission was wrong.

Less dramatic examples of the failure to follow the implications of evaluation research could be listed almost endlessly. Undoubtedly, every evaluation researcher can point to studies that he or she has conducted that were ignored—studies providing clear research results and obvious policy implications.

There are three important reasons why the implications of evaluation research results are not always put into practice. First, the implications may not always be presented in a way that nonresearchers can understand. Second, evaluation results sometimes contradict deeply held beliefs. That was certainly the case with the pornography commission just mentioned. If everybody knows that pornography is bad and that it causes all manner of sexual deviance, then it is likely that research results to the contrary will have little immediate impact. By the same token, people thought Copernicus was crazy when he said the Earth revolved around the sun. Anybody could tell the Earth was standing still.

The third barrier to the use of evaluation results is vested interests. Suppose a group of practitioners in a family service agency, after receiving extensive training (and indoctrination) in a new model of therapy, succeeds in convincing agency colleagues and superiors to let them form a new unit that specializes in service delivery based on that model of therapy. They are convinced that their services will be effective, and forming the new unit has significantly enhanced their prestige and autonomy in the agency. How do you think they are going to feel when your evaluation suggests that their program doesn't work? It is unlikely that they'll fold up their tent, apologize for misleading people, and return willingly to their old routines. It's more likely that they'll point out inescapable limitations in your research, call it misleading or worthless, and begin intense lobbying with colleagues and superiors to have the program continue.

Logistical and Administrative Problems

The social context of program evaluation affects not only the utilization of the outcomes of evaluative studies but also the logistics involved in their implementation. *Logistics* refers to getting research participants to do what they're supposed to do, getting research instruments distributed and returned, and other seemingly unchallenging tasks.

Sometimes, you may find the best-laid plans go awry when unforeseen circumstances influence program personnel to make unanticipated changes that can wreak havoc on an evaluation. If you're lucky, they will discuss in advance the changes they are considering, and this will enable you to learn about these changes in a timely way and interact with program personnel in a way that helps protect the evaluation's viability and utility. This is most likely to occur if you have been allocated enough resources to be on-site at the program on a daily basis. If, however, your resources are insufficient to have a frequent on-site presence and ongoing interaction with program personnel, then you may find out about program changes that wreak havoc on the planned evaluation too late to salvage the evaluation. Do not presume that evaluation plans made months earlier will remain at the forefront of the minds of program personnel as they encounter unexpected difficulties in operating their programs. Moreover, even if they do remember the evaluation plans, they may not realize that the program changes they are considering will impact the evaluation.

For instance, in a family preservation program that one of us (Rubin) evaluated, the program administrator became concerned during the study that parents served by the program did not appear to be improving rapidly enough. Consequently, she decided to extend the treatment duration for each family from 3 months to 1 year, not realizing that this would reduce the evaluation's sample size by 75%. (Instead of having four cohorts each receiving a 3-month treatment during the year, there would be only one 12-month cohort.) Neither did she think to inform the evaluation staff of this decision, which was made several months after the evaluation began and which additionally bore on the timing of the posttests.

Later in the midst of the evaluation, the same administrator decided to start referring comparison group families who seemed to show the most promise for improving their parenting to a comparable family preservation intervention program, not realizing (or perhaps not caring) that this would affect the study design's internal validity. And to make matters worse, the program administrator, who after a lengthy planning discussion had agreed to a careful, detailed plan for ensuring the equivalence of the family preservation group and the comparison group, decided to assign all of the families with the most serious problems to her program and those with the least serious problems to the comparison group. She assigned families on that basis for 3 years and did not inform the evaluator of that until she saw undesirable outcome results at the completion of the evaluation.

When you're in a position in your career to participate in, conduct, or use program evaluations, you should not be naive about the potential influence of vested interests on the integrity or quality of evaluations. Nevertheless, it would be misleading for us to imply that all program evaluation is corrupt. Agency administrators and others who have vested interests often have sufficient integrity and professional concern for learning the best ways to help clients that they are able to put their vested interests aside and act in a manner that fosters the most objective scientific evaluation possible.

Although it may be naive to assume that all (or even most) evaluations will be immune to the political pressures applied by those who have vested interests, it would be cynical to assume that all evaluations are politically biased. Moreover, the political pressures stemming from vested interests pertain primarily to evaluations of program outcome. They are rarer in evaluations conducted for the purpose of program planning.

We could also cite examples of outcome evaluations that were conducted without political pressure and that did not go awry. One such evaluation was conducted by the same coauthor of this book who conducted the politically affected evaluations above. He and his associates conducted a randomized experimental outcome study and found that the practitioners in a Child Guidance Center who were enthusiastic about a new approach to trauma treatment were not achieving any better outcomes with that approach than were being achieved with the preexisting routine service provided by the Center (Rubin, Bischofshausen, et al., 2001). There were no resistances to the research by the Center's administrators or practitioners. Their compliance with the research protocol was exemplary, and they had no problem accepting the disappointing findings. (The same could not be said for some nationally known leaders in that treatment approach, however, who unsuccessfully tried to persuade Rubin to delay publishing the study until other studies with more positive findings about that treatment's effectiveness appeared in print.)

In another successful outcome evaluation, Parrish and Rubin (2011) conducted a quasi-experimental evaluation of the effectiveness of a continuing education workshop to improve practitioner attitudes about and engagement in the evidence-based practice process. The outcome was positive, supporting the effectiveness of the workshop. If you search the literature on program evaluation, you are likely to find other examples of successfully completed outcome evaluations, such as one by Glisson, Thyer, and Fischer (2001) on an effective homeless shelter service.

As we finish this chapter, we hope that your view of the politics of program evaluation is a savvy one—that you will be vigilant about the potential for the corrupting influence of vested interests yet aware that despite this potential, many objective and useful program evaluation studies have been done in the past and are likely to be done in the future.

MAIN POINTS

- Program evaluation applies various research methods and designs in order to assess and improve the conceptualization, design, planning, administration, implementation, effectiveness, efficiency, and utility of social interventions and human service programs.

- Although people have always in some way evaluated the reforms they have instituted, systematic and scientific approaches to program evaluation during the latter half of the 20th century burgeoned as increased social welfare spending spawned an "age of accountability."

- The advent of managed care has intensified pressures on service providers to evaluate the outcomes of their services. But it has also intensified vested interests in obtaining findings that make their services look effective.

- Several steps have been proposed to help evaluators alleviate potential problems in the logistics of their studies as well as to alleviate resistance to them and their utilization. These steps involve learning as much as possible about the stakeholders and their vested interests in the evaluation, involving them in a meaningful way in all phases of planning and performing the evaluation, maintaining ongoing mutual feedback between them and the evaluator, and tailoring the evaluation and its reportage to their needs and preferences as much as possible without sacrificing scientific objectivity.

- Although the evaluation of program outcome is one of the first things that come to mind when people think of program evaluation, other important foci of evaluation research address research questions that are concerned with planning new programs and monitoring their implementation.

- Evaluations of program outcome should strive to enhance causal inference by using the most internally valid experimental or quasi-experimental design possible.

- The assessment of efficiency asks whether program outcomes are being achieved at a reasonable cost and applies the principles of cost accounting to calculate the ratio of program benefits to costs. But deciding whether the benefits of a program justify its costs ultimately means going beyond purely economic considerations and involves making value judgments about humanistic benefits.

- Evaluating program outcome or goal attainment is complicated by ambiguities in determining the specific outcome indicators implied by official organizational goals, by the intentionally grandiose nature of some statements of organizational missions, and by the displacement of official goals by unofficial ones.

- Some programs have unsuccessful outcomes not because they are wrong in theory but because they were never implemented as intended.

- Outcome evaluations ought to be supplemented by evaluations that monitor program implementation. Monitoring implementation can help resolve problems early on, keep agencies accountable, and identify the best ways to implement and maintain programs.

- The most common focus in evaluation for program planning is the assessment of need. Needs can be defined normatively or in terms of demand.

- Five approaches to needs assessment are (a) surveying key informants, (b) holding a community forum, (c) examining rates under treatment, (d) analyzing social indicators, and (e) conducting a direct survey of the community or target group. Each approach is imperfect but offers its own unique advantages and disadvantages. Ideally, a needs assessment will combine more than one approach.

- Evaluation proposals should include a logic model, which is a graphic picture depicting essential program components, their linkage to short-term process objectives, indicators of success in achieving short-term objectives, how those short-term objectives lead to long-term program outcomes, and indicators of success in achieving long-term outcomes.

- Different logic models might emphasize program theory, program activities, or program outcomes. Which logic model to choose will vary, depending on program needs and what seems to be most helpful for those involved in program management and evaluation.

- Various qualitative methods can be useful in program evaluation. One such method useful in needs assessment involves the use of focus groups, which involve people in a guided discussion.

- The importance of program evaluation in funding decisions creates a highly political atmosphere in which stakeholders with vested interests can impede free scientific inquiry.

- Political considerations can affect not only in-house evaluators but also external evaluators who seem to be more independent. Even funding sources and other external sponsors of an evaluation can have a stake in its outcome and may try to influence it for political reasons.

- Political and ideological forces can influence not only the methodology and interpretation of evaluative research but also whether and how its findings are used. We cannot assume that the implications of evaluation research will necessarily be put into practice, especially if they conflict with official interests or points of view.

REVIEW QUESTIONS AND EXERCISES

1. Interview an administrator and some practitioners at a social welfare agency, perhaps the one in which you have your field placement. What evaluations, if any, have been conducted at the agency, and with what outcomes? Were the findings used? Why or why not? Try to identify the stakeholders and their vested interests about those evaluations and findings. If no evaluation has ever been conducted, why not? Are politically or ideologically based resistances involved?

2. In the same or another agency, construct skeletal plans for evaluating program implementation and outcome. What resistances or logistical problems to the evaluation might be anticipated? How would the evaluation be useful to decision makers? What difficulties did you encounter in translating the agency's formal mission statement into observable indicators of outcome?

3. Consider a social problem that is currently receiving a lot of media attention in your community. Design a needs assessment study regarding that problem or a specific service you have in mind for alleviating it. Assume a data collection budget of $5,000 and a 6-month deadline for designing and completing the assessment.

4. Find a research article in a social work journal that describes a study conducted for the purpose of evaluating program outcome. See if you can identify the stakeholders in the research and critique the article from the standpoint of whether it showed how it controlled for potential biases associated with vested interests. Although it is dated, a good example for critiquing purposes would be the study by Boone, Coulton, and Keller (1981).

INTERNET EXERCISES

1. Using a literature database, enter the key words "program evaluation" to find two articles: one that reports a program evaluation study and one that discusses the politics of program evaluation. Write down the bibliographical reference information for each article. For the one reporting a study, briefly identify the strengths and weaknesses of that study. For the other article, summarize its main points about the politics of program evaluation.

2. Using a search engine such as Google or Yahoo!, enter the search term "program evaluation reports." Click on a report that piques your interest. Write down the bibliographical reference information for the report, identify the type of evaluation it illustrates, and briefly identify its methodological strengths and weaknesses.

3. Using a search engine such as Google or Yahoo!, enter the search term "logic models." Browse several of the websites that come up. Write down the most useful sites you examined and briefly summarize at least one thing at each site that you learned about logic models. Also, briefly describe any differences you noticed in the examples of logic models displayed at the different sites.

 Visit CengageBrain.com for additional practice and study opportunities including experiential exercises, research tools, glossary, flashcards, and sample test items.

Data Collection Methods with Large Sources of Data

In earlier chapters, we discussed qualitative and quantitative approaches to inquiry and indicated that social work research studies can have various purposes. The degree to which researchers need to build certain logical arrangements into their studies depends on which purposes guide their work.

For example, if we conduct a nomothetic, quantitative study seeking to describe with precision the characteristics of a population, then it is important to use logical procedures in selecting participants for our study that will maximize the likelihood that the chosen participants are representative of the population to whom we seek to generalize. It is also important that data are collected from those participants in a standardized manner that attempts to maximize objectivity. In contrast, if we are conducting a qualitative study seeking to explore a new area about which little is known or perhaps seeking to develop a tentative, in-depth understanding of a phenomenon, procedures for selecting study participants, as well as the way data are obtained from them, can be more flexible. Trying to structure exploratory studies tightly in order to permit conclusive logical inferences and allow precise generalizations to be made from the findings would be not only unnecessary but also undesirable. An inflexible methodology

in an exploratory or qualitative study would not permit researchers the latitude they need to probe creatively into unanticipated observations or into areas about which they lack the information needed to construct a design that would be logically conclusive.

Although the next three chapters will describe procedures used in both quantitative and qualitative studies, the emphasis will be on quantitative procedures geared toward obtaining findings from large sources of data. For example, we will look at how to select a sample of study participants and collect data from them that can be generalized with accuracy to a larger population. We will also look at how to obtain and analyze data that are already available.

Chapter 15, on sampling, deals with generalizability. As we'll see, it is possible for us to select a few people or things for observation and then apply what we observe to a much larger group of people or things. We'll also look briefly at some of the more flexible methods for obtaining study participants, but we'll save the more in-depth coverage of those more flexible methods for Chapter 18, which focuses exclusively on qualitative research methods.

Chapter 16 will describe survey research, which involves collecting data by asking people questions.

Like Chapter 15, Chapter 16 will discuss some flexible methods for obtaining data but will emphasize methods that attempt to maximize the objectivity, accuracy, and generalizability of the information provided by respondents in self-administered questionnaires or through interviews.

Chapter 17 will examine methods for obtaining and analyzing data in available records. We'll look at both quantitative and qualitative methods for doing so, and we'll see that which method to use depends on the nature of the data and the purpose of our inquiry.

15

Sampling

EPAS Competencies for This Chapter

Competency 4   Engage in Practice-Informed Research and Research-Informed Practice: This competency pertains to this entire chapter because doing practice-informed research requires being able to use sampling methods appropriately. The same applies to engaging in research-informed practice because you must understand sampling methods in order to be able to critically appraise research and distinguish studies that should and should not inform your practice.

Competency 9   Evaluate Practice with Individuals Families, Groups, Organizations, and Communities: This competency pertains to this entire chapter because designing an evaluation requires making decisions about sampling.

What You'll Learn in This Chapter

In this chapter, we'll see how social scientists can select a few hundred or a few thousand people for study—and discover things that apply to hundreds of millions of people not studied.

» INTRODUCTION

Social work research studies, like social scientific research studies in general, typically observe some people or things with the aim of generating tentative new insights about, describing, or testing hypotheses about a larger population of those people or things. The smaller group that the studies observe is called their sample, and the process of selecting this group is called sampling.

In quantitative descriptive and explanatory studies, a key issue is whether the sampling procedures used are likely to yield a study sample that is really representative of the larger population to which the study seeks to generalize. Sampling procedures vary in that likelihood. Two key criteria in judging that likelihood are the size of the sample and whether it was selected in an unbiased manner. Ideally, a sample should be both unbiased and of an adequate size. Some biased sampling procedures can produce unrepresentative findings even with large samples, whereas unbiased sampling procedures can sometimes depict with great accuracy the characteristics of a large population based on observations from a tiny sample.

The history of political polling illustrates how researchers using unbiased sampling procedures can generalize accurately to a large population based on data collected from a tiny fraction of that population. Going into the 2008 presidential elections, pollsters were in agreement as to who would win, in contrast to their experiences in 2000 and 2004, which were closely contested races. Table 15-1 reports polls conducted during the few days preceding the election. Despite some variations, the overall picture they present is amazingly consistent and closely matched the election results.

Now, how many interviews do you suppose it took each of these pollsters to come within a couple of percentage points in estimating the behavior of more than 131 million voters? Often fewer than 2,000. In this chapter, we're going to find out how social researchers can achieve such wizardry.

The foregoing political poll was accurate because it used probability sampling, which involves random sampling. This chapter will show that random sampling is a precise, scientific procedure; there is nothing haphazard about it. Specific sampling techniques can allow us to determine or control the likelihood of specific individuals being selected for study. In the simplest example, flipping a coin to choose between two individuals gives each person exactly the same probability of selection—50%. More complex techniques guarantee an equal probability of selection when substantial samples are selected from large populations.

Although probability sampling is precise, it's not always feasible to use probability sampling techniques. Consequently, social work research studies often use *nonprobability* sampling. Therefore, we'll take some time to examine a variety of nonprobability methods as well. Although not based on random selection, these methods have their own logic and can provide useful samples for social inquiry. We'll examine both the

EP 4, 9

TABLE 15.1 Election Eve Polls Reporting Presidential Voting Plans, 2008

Poll	Date Ended	Obama	McCain
Fox	November 2	54	46
NBC/*Wall Street Journal*	November 2	54	46
Marist College	November 2	55	45
Harris Interactive	November 3	54	46
Reuters/ C-SPAN/Zogby	November 3	56	44
ARG	November 3	54	46
Rasmussen	November 3	53	47
IBD/TIPP	November 3	54	46
DailyKos.com/ Research 2000	November 3	53	47
George Washington University	November 3	53	47
Marist College	November 3	55	45
Actual vote	November 4	54	46

Source: Poll data are adapted from data presented at Pollster .com (http://www.pollster.com/polls/us/08-us-pres-ge-mvo.php) on January 29, 2009. The official election results are from the Federal Election Commission (http://www.fec.gov/pubrec/ fe2008/2008presgeresults.pdf) on the same date. For simplicity, since there were no undecideds in the official results and each of the third-party candidates received less than 1% of the vote, we have apportioned the undecided and other votes according to the percentages saying they were voting for Obama or McCain.

advantages and the shortcomings of such methods, and we'll see where they fit within the social scientific enterprise. To illustrate some of the uses and risks of nonprobability sampling, let's return to some political polling examples.

President Alf Landon

President Alf Landon? Who's he? Did you sleep through an entire presidency in your U.S. history class? No—but Alf Landon would have been president if a famous poll conducted by the *Literary Digest* had proved to be accurate. The *Literary Digest* was a popular newsmagazine published between 1890 and 1938. In 1916, *Digest* editors mailed postcards to people in six states, asking them whom they were planning to vote for in the presidential campaign between Woodrow Wilson and Charles Evans Hughes. Names were selected for the poll from telephone directories and automobile registration lists. Based on the postcards sent back, the *Digest* correctly predicted that Wilson would be elected. In the elections that followed, the *Literary Digest* expanded the size of its poll and made correct predictions in 1920, 1924, 1928, and 1932.

In 1936, the *Digest* conducted its most ambitious poll: Ten million ballots were sent to people listed in telephone directories and in automobile registration lists. More than 2 million responded, giving Republican contender Alf Landon a stunning 57% to 43% landslide over the incumbent, President Franklin Roosevelt. The editors modestly cautioned:

> We make no claim to infallibility. We did not coin the phrase "uncanny accuracy" which has been so freely applied to our Polls. We know only too well the limitations of every straw vote, however enormous the sample gathered, however scientific the method. It would be a miracle if every State of the forty-eight behaved on Election Day exactly as forecast by the Poll. (*Literary Digest*, 1936a, p. 6)

Two weeks later, the *Digest* editors knew the limitations of straw polls even better: Voters gave Roosevelt a third term in office by the largest landslide in history, with 61% of the vote. Landon won only 8 electoral votes to Roosevelt's 523.

The editors were puzzled by their unfortunate turn of luck. A part of the problem surely lay in the poll's 22% return rate. The editors asked:

> Why did only one in five voters in Chicago to whom the *Digest* sent ballots take the trouble to reply? And why was there a preponderance of Republicans in the one-fifth that did reply? … We were getting better cooperation in what we have always regarded as a public service from Republicans than we were getting from Democrats. Do Republicans live nearer to mailboxes? Do Democrats generally disapprove of straw polls? (*Literary Digest*, 1936b, p. 7)

Actually, there was a better explanation—what is technically called the *sampling frame* used by the *Digest*. In this case, the sampling frame consisted of telephone subscribers and automobile owners. In the context of 1936, this design selected a disproportionately wealthy sample of the voting population, especially coming on the tail end of the worst economic depression in the nation's history. The nonprobability sample effectively excluded poor people, and the poor voted predominantly for Roosevelt's New Deal recovery program. The *Digest*'s poll may or may not have correctly represented the voting intentions of telephone subscribers and automobile owners. Unfortunately for the editors, it decidedly did not represent the voting intentions of the population as a whole.

President Thomas E. Dewey

The 1936 election also saw the emergence of a young pollster whose name was to become synonymous with public opinion. In contrast to the *Literary Digest*, George Gallup correctly predicted that Roosevelt would beat Landon. Gallup's success in 1936 hinged on his use of quota sampling, which we'll have more to say about later in the chapter. For now, you need to know only that quota sampling is based on a knowledge of the characteristics of the population being sampled: what proportions

You may be able to find the *Literary Digest* in your library. You can find traces of it by searching the web. As an alternative, go to www.eBay.com and see how many old issues are available for sale.

are men and women and what proportions are of various incomes, ages, and so on. People are selected to match the population characteristics: the right number of poor, white, rural men; the right number of rich, black, urban women; and so on. The quotas are based on those variables that are most relevant to the study. By knowing the numbers of people with various incomes in the nation, Gallup selected his sample to ensure the right proportion of respondents at each income level.

Gallup and his American Institute of Public Opinion used quota sampling to good effect in 1936, 1940, and 1944—correctly picking presidential winners in each year. Then, in 1948, Gallup and most political pollsters suffered the embarrassment of picking New York Governor Thomas Dewey over incumbent President Harry Truman. The pollsters' embarrassing miscue continued right up to election night. A famous photograph shows a jubilant Truman—whose followers' battle cry was "Give 'em hell, Harry!"—holding aloft a newspaper with the banner headline "Dewey Defeats Truman."

Several factors accounted for the pollsters' 1948 failure. First, most of the pollsters stopped polling in early October despite a steady trend toward Truman during the campaign. In addition, many voters were undecided throughout the campaign but went disproportionately for Truman when they stepped into the voting booth. More important for our present purposes, however, is that Gallup's failure rested on the unrepresentativeness of his samples.

Quota sampling—which had been effective in earlier years—was Gallup's undoing in 1948. This technique requires that the researcher know something about the total population (of voters in this instance). For national political polls, such information came primarily from census data. By 1948, however, a world war had already produced a massive movement from country to city and radically changed the character of the U.S. population as described by the 1940 census—whose data Gallup used. City dwellers, moreover, were more likely to vote Democratic; hence, the overrepresentation of rural voters also underestimated the number of Democratic votes.

President John Kerry

Improvements made in political polling enabled election eve polls to accurately predict the outcomes of presidential elections in the decades that followed. Today, probability sampling is the primary method for selecting large, representative samples for social science research. Basically, this technique selects a random sample from a list that contains the names of everyone in the population of study interest. By and large, current probability sampling methods are far more accurate than earlier (nonprobability) sampling techniques.

The value of probability sampling techniques was underscored in the presidential election of 2004. Most election eve polls conducted with probability samples accurately predicted that George Bush would be reelected, beating John Kerry by a small margin. But on election day, various news media and political groups attempted to get an early scoop on the outcome by conducting exit polls, asking voters whom they voted for as the voters left the voting sites. The exit polls did not use rigorous probability sampling. Instead, they were most likely to interview those voters who happened to be near and willing (and perhaps eager) to reveal whom they voted for. As it turned out, Kerry voters were more likely to participate in the exit polls than were Bush voters. Knowing the results of the exit polls, various conservative television pundits looked gloomy throughout the day before the actual results came in, as they anticipated a Kerry presidency and speculated about what went wrong in the Bush campaign. Likewise, various Kerry supporters looked exuberant. Their moods reversed as the actual vote counts came in showing Bush leading in key states predicted in the Kerry column in the exit polls.

» NONPROBABILITY SAMPLING

Despite its advantages, probability sampling is impossible or inappropriate in many of the research situations faced by social workers. Consequently, social work research is often conducted using nonprobability sampling techniques. Suppose you wanted to study homelessness: No list of all homeless individuals is available from which to draw a random sample, and you're not likely to create such a list yourself. Moreover, as we'll see, there are times when probability sampling wouldn't be appropriate even if it were possible. We'll begin now with a discussion of some nonprobability sampling techniques used in social work, and then we'll examine the logic and techniques of probability sampling. We'll examine four types of

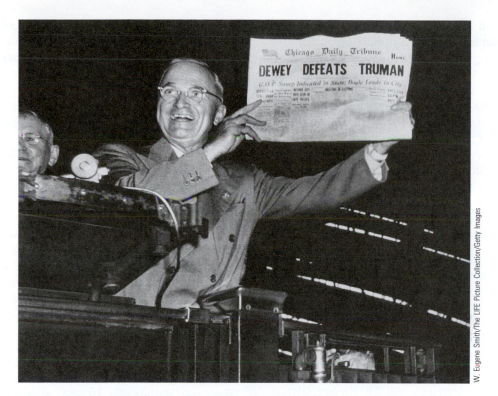

W. Eugene Smith/The LIFE Picture Collection/Getty Images

Based on early political polls that showed Dewey leading Truman, the *Chicago Tribune* sought to scoop the competition with this unfortunate headline.

nonprobability sampling procedures in this section: (a) reliance on available subjects, (b) purposive or judgmental sampling, (c) quota sampling, and (d) snowball sampling. Then we'll examine techniques for selecting informants.

Reliance on Available Subjects

Relying on available subjects—sometimes called availability sampling, *accidental sampling*, or *convenience sampling*—is a frequently used sampling method in social work because it is usually less expensive than other methods and because other methods may not be feasible for a particular type of study or population. As one indicator of the popularity of this sampling method in social work, some form of availability sampling was reported in the majority of research articles published from 1994 through 1999 in the journal *Social Work Research* (Monette, Sullivan, & DeJong, 2002).

Availability sampling can be an extremely risky sampling method. For example, stopping people at a street corner or some other location would be a risky way to assess public opinion about a social issue. Suppose the location was near a suburban

shopping mall and you were polling opinions about proposals to change Social Security or health care policies for the elderly. Your findings would represent the opinions only of people with the characteristics of those passing the sampling point at the specified times. In all likelihood, elderly people and poor people would be underrepresented in your sample. Younger and more affluent people—those who are likely to disagree with the older or poorer people about the policies in question—are likely to be overrepresented in your sample. Even when the use of this method is justified on grounds of feasibility, the researcher must exercise great caution in generalizing from the resulting data and should alert readers to the risks associated with this method.

Suppose several students in a social work research course chose to do a team research project by interviewing students in the course about their attitudes about private practice. The representativeness of the sample would be dubious. Perhaps that research class was the only one whose scheduling did not conflict with an elective on psychotherapy, so students who aspired to become private practitioners of psychotherapy would be more likely to take that research class. It is virtually impossible to anticipate all of the possible biases that might render a particular accidental sample atypical.

University researchers frequently conduct surveys among the students enrolled in large lecture classes. The ease and inexpensiveness of such a method explains its popularity, but it seldom produces data of any general value. This approach may be useful to pretest a questionnaire, but such a sampling method should not be used for a study that purports to describe students as a whole.

Consider this report on the sampling design in an examination of knowledge and opinions about nutrition and cancer among medical students and family physicians:

> The fourth-year medical students of the University of Minnesota Medical School in Minneapolis comprised the student population in this study. The physician population consisted of all physicians attending a "Family Practice Review and Update" course sponsored by the University of Minnesota Department of Continuing Medical Education. (Cooper-Stephenson & Theologides, 1981, p. 472)

After all is said and done, what will the results of this study represent? They do not meaningfully compare medical students and family physicians in the United States or even in Minnesota. Who were the physicians who attended the course? We can guess that they were probably more concerned about their continuing education than other physicians—and we can't say that for sure. Although such studies can be the source of useful insights, care must be taken not to overgeneralize from them.

Despite their risks, however, some studies using availability sampling can provide useful tentative findings, especially when no egregious forms of bias can be detected in the sampling approach taken and when care is taken not to overgeneralize their findings. Suppose, for example, that a local foundation is concerned about a dangerous new drug that recently caused several deaths among teens in the United States. It wants to find out how widely the drug is used among high school students in your midwestern city. The foundation gives you a small grant to survey high school students in your city about whether and how much they've experimented with the new drug. There are 10 high schools in your city, but you manage to obtain

permission to conduct your survey in only 2 of them. One of the high schools is in a poor neighborhood and has a relatively large proportion of African American students. The other high school is in a middle-class neighborhood and has relatively few ethnic minority students.

You conduct your survey by having teachers disseminate your questionnaire about drug use to all the students in each of the two schools. A cover letter asks each student to voluntarily participate in the study by completing the questionnaire and returning it anonymously in a sealed envelope into a large drop box located at the school. Suppose that 50% of the students at each school participate and that the other 50% do not. Suppose further that your findings indicate that exactly 30% of the survey respondents in each school report having experimented with the new drug and that exactly 20% of them say they will continue using it on occasion.

What would be the value of your findings? In considering the answer to this question, we should note that yours is an availability sample because it does not include the 50% of those students who were either unwilling to answer questions about drug use or not motivated to take the time and effort to respond to your survey. Perhaps the students experimenting with drugs were more interested in a drug survey than those not into drugs and thus much more motivated to respond than the other students. Another possibility is that the students experimenting with drugs were more likely to be threatened by your survey and therefore *less* likely to respond. Moreover, not only did your survey not include the nonrespondents in the two schools, but also it did not include the other eight high schools that refused to participate in your survey. Perhaps drug experimentation in those eight schools is greater than or less than it is in the two schools that agreed to participate.

Should the community disregard your findings because they were based on an availability sample? In answering this question, you might note that even if all of the students in the two participating schools who had experimented with the new drug were included among your respondents, your findings would nevertheless mean that 15% of all the students in the two schools say they had experimented with the drug (i.e., 30% of *half* of the students is 15% of *all* the students). Likewise, the findings would mean that 10% of all the students (half of the 20%) in those two schools say they will continue using it on occasion. Moreover, your findings would mean that these figures are minimum estimates because it is conceivable that students experimenting with the new drug were less likely than others to respond to your survey.

Assuming that the students were not lying about experimenting with the dangerous new drug, we think your findings would have significant value. We think your findings would spur the community to implement a program to educate students about the dangers of the new drug and to try in other ways to prevent its usage. Moreover, we think that the community would be concerned not only about the students in the two schools that participated in your survey but also about the remaining schools. In fact, we think your findings would spur the remaining schools to replicate your survey among their students. Although your findings should not be generalized to other schools, they certainly would provide a tentative—but still valuable—basis for concern about the scope of the problem elsewhere, even including other cities.

Another type of research that typically relies on availability samples—and that has immense value to the social work profession and to the public—involves the use of experimental or quasi-experimental designs in evaluating the effectiveness of social work practice or programs, as discussed in Chapters 11 and 12. When you want to evaluate whether or how much your services are helping a particular client or group of clients, it's not like asking people at random to respond to a poll predicting the outcome of a presidential election. You usually must rely on an availability sample of clients who need your services and come to your agency for those services. That's one of the reasons that experimental designs are often characterized as having a relatively low degree of external validity.

Purposive or Judgmental Sampling

Sometimes you may appropriately select your sample on the basis of your own knowledge of the population, its elements, and the nature of your research aims—in short, based on your judgment and the purpose of the study. Especially in the initial design of a questionnaire, you might wish to select the widest variety of respondents to test the broad applicability of questions. Although the study findings would not represent any meaningful population, the test run might effectively uncover any peculiar defects in your questionnaire. This situation would be considered a pretest, however, rather than a final study.

In some instances, you may wish to study a small subset of a larger population in which many members of the subset are easily identified, but enumerating all of them would be nearly impossible. For example, you might want to study the homeless. Many homeless people might be visible in certain areas of town, such as near shelters, a Salvation Army facility, or other social welfare facilities. But it would not be feasible to define and sample all of them. In studying all or a sample of the most visible homeless individuals, you might collect data sufficient for your purposes, particularly if your study is exploratory. Thus, you might ask personnel in those facilities to use their judgment in handpicking cases that they think represent those segments of the homeless population with which they are familiar.

Suppose you are writing a grant proposal to secure funding for new social services to be targeted to the homeless and that the funding source requires that your proposal include an assessment of the social service needs of the homeless in your community. Suppose, given your agency's meager resources and the nearness of the proposal submission deadline, you have neither the time nor the money to conduct a community-wide survey of the homeless using probability sampling. One option would be to select a purposive sample or judgmental sample of community leaders, experts, and professionals known for their work with and expertise on the problem of homelessness in your locality. You could use your knowledge of the community to handpick key people who, in your judgment, represent the range of persons who would best know the needs of the homeless in your community and then survey them as to their estimates of those needs.

Sometimes purposive sampling is used to select not typical cases but atypical ones. This is commonly done when we seek to compare opposite extremes of a phenomenon in order to generate hypotheses about it. For example, in seeking to generate hypotheses about the etiology of mental illness, we might want to study certain children of mentally ill parents, contrasting the life experiences and other attributes of children who became diagnosably mentally ill and those who became extraordinarily healthy. Or, in seeking to gain insights into the attributes of effective practice, we might handpick for intensive study those cases with whom practitioners felt extremely successful and those cases with whom they felt extremely ineffectual.

Researchers conducting qualitative studies are often particularly interested in studying deviant cases—cases that don't fit into fairly regular patterns of attitudes and behaviors—in order to improve their understanding of the more regular pattern. This is called deviant case sampling, and it is another form of purposive sampling. For example, you might gain important tentative insights into the processes of a support group for battered women by interviewing women who remain relatively quiet during support group meetings or by interviewing group members who only rarely attend the meetings. We will discuss deviant case sampling further in Chapter 18, on qualitative research methods.

Quota Sampling

Quota sampling, mentioned earlier, is the method that helped George Gallup avoid disaster in 1936—and set up the disaster of 1948. Like probability sampling, quota sampling addresses the issue of representativeness, although the two methods approach the issue quite differently.

Quota sampling begins with a matrix that describes the target population's characteristics: what proportion of the population is male or female, for example, and, for each sex, what proportions fall into various age categories, educational levels, ethnic groups, and so forth. In establishing a national quota sample, we would need to know what proportion of the national population is urban, eastern, male, under 25, white, working class, and the like and all the other permutations of such a matrix.

Once we have created such a matrix and assigned a relative proportion to each cell in the matrix, we would collect data from people who had all of the characteristics of a given cell. All the people in a given cell are then assigned a weight that is appropriate to their portion of the total population (a process called weighting). When all of the sample elements are so weighted, the overall data should provide a reasonable representation of the total population.

Quota sampling has several inherent problems. First, the quota frame (the proportions that different cells represent) must be accurate, and getting up-to-date information for this purpose is often difficult. The Gallup failure to predict Truman as the presidential victor in 1948 was due partly to this problem. Second, biases may exist in the selection of sample elements within a given cell—even though its proportion of the population is accurately estimated. An interviewer instructed to interview five persons meeting a given complex set of characteristics may still avoid people living at the top of seven-story walk-ups, occupying particularly run-down homes, or owning vicious dogs. Researchers using quota sampling should be aware of potential problems like this and work to prevent them. For example, they should do all they can to obtain an accurate count of the number and characteristics of individuals who make up a particular cell. They should make sure that interviewers are properly trained and supervised to minimize the chances that the interviewers will violate the sampling protocol in order to skip certain undesirable interviews. But there is no guarantee that all potential problems like these will be anticipated or prevented. Therefore, you would be advised to treat quota sampling warily if your purpose is statistical description.

Snowball Sampling

Another nonprobability sampling technique, one that some researchers consider a form of accidental sampling, is called snowball sampling. Snowball sampling is appropriate when the members of a special population are difficult to locate. It might be appropriate, for example, to find a sample of homeless individuals, migrant workers, or undocumented immigrants. This procedure is implemented by collecting data on the few members of the target population whom one is able to locate and then asking those individuals to provide the information needed to locate other members of that population they happen to know. The term *snowball* refers to the process of accumulation as each located subject suggests other subjects. This sampling procedure also results in samples that have questionable representativeness, so it is used primarily for exploratory purposes. Nevertheless, snowball sampling is an important and commonly used technique in qualitative research (as we'll discuss in Chapter 18), and in research on minority and oppressed populations it is often necessary (as we mentioned in Chapter 6).

» SELECTING INFORMANTS IN QUALITATIVE RESEARCH

When qualitative research involves the researcher's attempt to understand some social setting—a juvenile gang or local neighborhood, for example—much of that understanding will come from a collaboration with one or more members of the group being studied. Whereas social researchers speak of "respondents" as people who provide information about themselves and thus allow the researcher to construct a composite picture of the group those respondents represent, informants are members of the group or other people knowledgeable about it who are willing to talk about the group per se.

Potential informants should be evaluated on several criteria. Are they in positions of regular interaction with other members of the group or setting, for example, or are they isolated? Is their information fairly limited to their specific roles, or does it cover many aspects of the group or setting? These and other criteria affect how useful different potential informants might be.

Usually, we want to select informants who are somewhat typical of the groups we are studying; otherwise, their observations and opinions may be misleading. Interviewing administrators alone will not give us a well-rounded view of how a welfare program is working, for example. Along the same lines, we would get a biased view of homelessness if we interviewed only those homeless individuals staying in shelters or those who speak English and not those who refuse to use shelters or who don't speak English.

Because of their willingness to work with outside investigators, it is probably inevitable that informants will be somewhat marginal or atypical within their group. Sometimes, however, you will learn about their marginality only in the course of your research. The marginal status of informants may not only bias the view you get but also limit their access (and hence yours) to the different sectors of the community you wish to study.

These comments should provide some sense of the concerns involved in selecting people to observe and interview in qualitative research projects. Let's shift gears now and look at sampling in large-scale surveys—sampling that aims to produce precise, statistical descriptions of large populations.

» THE LOGIC OF PROBABILITY SAMPLING

If all members of a population were identical in all respects—demographic characteristics, attitudes, experiences, behaviors, and so on—we wouldn't need careful sampling procedures. Any sample would be sufficient. In this extreme case of homogeneity, in fact, one case would be enough of a sample to study the whole population's characteristics.

Of course, the human beings who compose any real population are quite heterogeneous, varying in many ways from one another. Figure 15-1 shows a simplified heterogeneous population. The 100 members of this small population differ by sex and race. We'll use this hypothetical micropopulation to illustrate various aspects of sampling through the chapter.

If a sample of individuals from a population is to provide useful descriptions of the total population, then it must contain essentially the same variations that exist in the population. This is not as simple as it might seem, however.

Let's look at some of the ways in which researchers might go astray. This will help us see how probability sampling provides an efficient method for selecting a sample that should adequately reflect variations in the population.

Conscious and Unconscious Sampling Bias

At first glance, it may look as though sampling is a pretty straightforward matter. To select a sample of 100 university students, you might simply go to campus and interview the first 100 students you find walking around campus. This kind of sampling method is often used by untrained researchers, but it has serious problems.

Figure 15-1 shows what can happen when you simply select people who are convenient for study. Although women are only 50% of our micropopulation, those closest to the researcher (in the upper-right corner) happen to be 70% women, and although the population is 12% African American, not one black individual was selected into the sample.

Beyond the risks inherent in simply studying people who are convenient, we find other potential problems. To begin, our own personal leanings or biases may affect the sample selected in this manner;

FIGURE 15.1 A Sample of Convenience: Easy but Not Representative

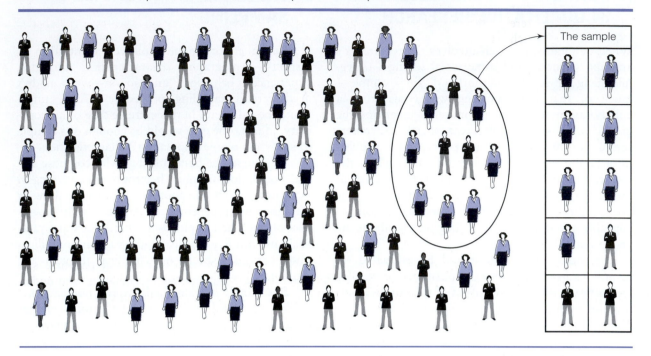

hence, the sample would not truly represent the student population. Suppose you're intimidated by students who look particularly "cool," feeling they might ridicule your research effort. You might consciously or unconsciously avoid interviewing such people. Or you might feel that the attitudes of "super-straight-looking" students would be irrelevant to your research purposes, and you avoid interviewing them.

Even if you sought to interview a balanced group of students, you wouldn't know the exact proportions of different types of students who make up such a balance, and you wouldn't always be able to identify the different types just by watching them walk by. Even if you made a conscientious effort to interview every 10th student who entered the university library, you could not be sure of getting a representative sample because different types of students visit the library with different frequencies. Your sample would overrepresent students who visit the library more often.

When we speak of bias in connection with sampling, this simply means those selected are not typical or representative of the larger populations from which they have been chosen. This kind of bias is virtually inevitable when people are picked by a seat-of-the-pants approach.

Similarly, public opinion call-in polls—in which radio or television stations or newspapers ask people to call specified telephone numbers or use the Internet to register their opinions—cannot be trusted to represent general populations. At the very least, not everyone in the population will be aware of the poll or have Internet access. This problem also invalidates polls by magazines and newspapers that publish coupons for readers to complete and return. Even among readers or viewers who are aware of such polls, not all of them will express opinions, especially if it will cost a stamp, an envelope, or a telephone charge. The possibilities for inadvertent sampling bias are endless and not always obvious. Fortunately, techniques are available that let us avoid bias.

Representativeness and Probability of Selection

Although the term representativeness has no precise, scientific meaning, its commonsense meaning makes it a useful concept in our discussion of sampling. As we use the term here, a sample is representative of its population if the sample's aggregate characteristics closely approximate those same aggregate characteristics in the population. (Samples need not be representative in all respects; representativeness is limited to those characteristics that are relevant to the substantive interests of the study, although you may not know which ones are relevant.) If the population, for example, contains 50% women, then a representative sample would also contain close to 50% women.

A basic principle of probability sampling is that a sample will be representative of its population if all members of that population have an equal chance of being selected in the sample. (We'll see shortly that the size of the sample selected also affects the degree of representativeness.) Samples that have this quality are often labeled EPSEM (equal probability of selection method) samples. We'll discuss variations of this principle later, but it is primary and forms the basis of probability sampling.

Moving beyond this basic principle, we must realize that samples—even carefully selected EPSEM samples—seldom, if ever, perfectly represent the populations from which they are drawn. Nevertheless, probability sampling offers two special advantages.

First, probability samples, even if never perfectly representative, are typically more representative than other types of samples because the biases discussed in the preceding section are avoided. In practice, there is a greater likelihood that a probability sample will be representative of the population from which it is drawn than will a nonprobability sample.

Second, and more important, probability theory permits us to estimate the sample's accuracy or representativeness. Conceivably, an uninformed researcher might, through wholly haphazard means, select a sample that nearly perfectly represents the larger population. The odds are against doing so, however, and we would be unable to estimate the likelihood that he or she has achieved representativeness. The probability sampler, on the other hand, can provide an accurate estimate of success or failure.

As we'll see in a moment, probability sampling rests on the use of a random selection procedure. To develop this idea, though, we need to give more precise meaning to two important terms: *element* and *population*.

An element is that unit about which information is collected and that provides the basis of analysis. Typically, in survey research, elements are people or certain types of people. However, other kinds of units can constitute the elements for social work research—for example, families, social clubs, or corporations might be the elements of a study. (*Note:* Elements and units of analysis are often the same in a given study, though the former refers to sample selection and the latter to data analysis.)

Up to now, we've used the term *population* to mean the group or collection that we're interested in generalizing about. More formally, population is the theoretically specified aggregation of study elements. Whereas the vague term *Americans* might be the target for a study, the delineation of the population would include the definition of the element *Americans* (e.g., citizenship and residence) and the time referent for the study (Americans as of when?). Translating the abstract *adult New Yorkers* into a workable population would require a specification of the age that defines *adult* and the boundaries of New York. Specifying the term *college student* would include a consideration of full- and part-time students, degree and nondegree candidates, and undergraduate and graduate students, among other issues.

A study population is that aggregation of elements from which the sample is actually selected. As a practical matter, you are seldom in a position to guarantee that every element that meets established theoretical definitions actually has a chance of being selected in the sample. Even where lists of elements exist for sampling purposes, the lists are usually somewhat incomplete. Some students are always omitted, inadvertently, from student rosters. Some telephone subscribers request that their names and numbers be unlisted. Thus, the study population from which the sample is taken is likely to be only a part of the population of interest.

Researchers often decide to limit their study populations more severely than indicated in the preceding examples. National polling firms may limit their national samples to the 48 contiguous states, omitting Alaska and Hawaii for practical reasons. A researcher who wishes to sample social work practitioners may limit the study population to those whose names appear on the membership list of the National Association of Social Workers (NASW) or on a list of those licensed by a particular state. (In a sense, we might say that these researchers have redefined their universes and populations, in which case they must make the revisions clear to their readers.)

Random Selection

With these definitions in hand, we can define the ultimate purpose of sampling: to select a set of elements from a population in such a way that descriptions of those elements accurately portray the total population from which the elements are selected. Probability sampling enhances the likelihood of accomplishing this aim and also provides methods for estimating the degree of probable success.

Random selection is the key to this process. In random selection, each element has an equal chance of selection that is independent of any other event in the selection process. Flipping a coin is the most frequently cited example: Provided that the coin is perfect (i.e., not biased in terms of coming up heads or tails), the "selection" of heads or tails is independent of previous selections of heads or tails. No matter how many heads turn up in a row, the chance that the next flip will produce heads is exactly 50:50. Rolling a perfect set of dice is another example.

Such images of random selection, although useful, seldom apply directly to sampling methods in social research. More typically, social researchers use tables of random numbers or computer programs that provide a random selection of sampling units. A sampling unit is that element or set of elements considered for selection in some stage of sampling. In Chapter 16, on survey research, we'll see how computers are used to select random telephone numbers for interviewing, a technique called random-digit dialing.

The reasons for using random selection methods are twofold. First, this procedure serves as a check on conscious or unconscious bias on the part of the researcher. The researcher who selects cases on an intuitive basis might very well select cases that would support his or her research expectations or hypotheses. Random selection erases this danger. More important, random selection offers access to the body of probability theory, which provides the basis for estimating the characteristics of the population as well as estimates of the accuracy of samples.

» CAN SOME RANDOMLY SELECTED SAMPLES BE BIASED?

When discussing probability sampling, students commonly make two mistakes. One mistake is to equate the population with any list of elements

from which a sample is selected. Another is to assume that if the intended sample has been randomly selected, then the sample is random regardless of the nonprobability reasons why many randomly selected elements refuse to participate in the ultimate sample. Both of these mistakes involve the concept of *sampling frames*. Before examining these mistakes further, let's first define the term *sampling frame* and distinguish it from the term *population*.

Sampling Frames and Populations

Simply put, a sampling frame is the list of elements from which a sample is selected. If a sample of students is selected from a student roster, the roster is the sampling frame. If the primary sampling unit for a complex population sample is the census block, the list of census blocks composes the sampling frame—in the form of a printed booklet, a magnetic tape file, or some other computerized record. Here are some reports of sampling frames appearing in research journals:

> The data for this research were obtained from a random sample of *parents of children in the third grade in public and parochial schools in Yakima County, Washington.* (Petersen & Maynard, 1981, p. 92)

> The sample at Time 1 consisted of 160 names drawn randomly from the *telephone directory of Lubbock, Texas.* (Tan, 1980, p. 242)

> The data reported in this paper... were gathered from a probability sample of *adults aged 18 and over residing in households in the 48 contiguous United States.* Personal interviews with 1,914 respondents were conducted by the Survey Research Center of the University of Michigan during the fall of 1975. (Jackman & Senter, 1980, p. 345)

In each example, we've italicized the actual sampling frames.

Properly drawn samples provide information appropriate for describing the population of elements composing the sampling frame—nothing more. It is necessary to make this point in view of the all-too-common tendency for researchers to select samples from a given sampling frame and then make assertions about a population similar but not identical to the study population defined by the sampling frame.

For an example of an overgeneralized sampling frame, take a look at this report, which discusses the drugs most frequently prescribed by American physicians:

> Information on prescription drug sales is not easy to obtain. But Rinaldo V. DeNuzzo, a professor of pharmacy at the Albany College of Pharmacy, Union University, Albany, NY, has been tracking prescription drug sales for 25 years by polling nearby drugstores. He publishes the results in an industry trade magazine, MM & M. DeNuzzo's latest survey, covering 1980, is based on reports from 66 pharmacies in 48 communities in New York and New Jersey. Unless there is something peculiar about that part of the country, his findings can be taken as representative of what happens across the country. (Moskowitz, 1981, p. 33)

The main thing that should strike you is the casual comment about whether there is anything peculiar about New York and New Jersey. There is. The lifestyle in these two states is hardly typical of the other 48. We cannot assume that residents in these large, urbanized, eastern seaboard states necessarily have the same drug use patterns as residents of Mississippi, Utah, New Mexico, and Vermont.

Does the survey even represent prescription patterns in New York and New Jersey? To determine that, we would have to know something about the manner in which the 48 communities and the 66 pharmacies were selected. We should be wary in this regard, in view of the reference to "polling nearby drugstores." As we'll see, there are several methods for selecting samples that ensure representativeness, and unless they are used, we should not generalize from the study findings.

A sampling frame, then, must be consonant with the population we wish to study. In the simplest sample design, the sampling frame is a list of the elements composing the study population. In practice, though, existing sampling frames often define the study population rather than the other way around. In other words, we often begin with a population in mind for our study, then we search for possible sampling frames. Having examined and evaluated the frames available for our use, we decide which frame presents a study population most appropriate to our needs.

Studies of organizations are often the simplest from a sampling standpoint because organizations typically have membership lists. In such cases, the list of members constitutes an excellent sampling frame. If a random sample is selected from a membership list, the data collected from that sample may be taken as representative of all members—if all members are included in the list.

Populations that can be sampled from good organizational lists include elementary school, high school, and university students and faculty; church members; factory workers; fraternity or sorority members; members of social, service, or political clubs; and members of professional associations.

The preceding comments apply primarily to local organizations. Often statewide or national organizations do not have a single, easily available membership list. There is, for example, no single list of Episcopalian church members. However, a slightly more complex sample design could take advantage of local church membership lists by first sampling churches and then subsampling the membership lists of those churches selected. (More about that later.)

Other lists of individuals may be especially relevant to the research needs of a particular study. Government agencies maintain lists of registered voters, for example, that might be used if you wanted to conduct a preelection poll or an in-depth examination of voting behavior—but you must ensure that the list is up to date. Similar lists contain the names of automobile owners, welfare recipients, taxpayers, business permit holders, licensed professionals, and so forth. Although it may be difficult to gain access to some of these lists, they provide excellent sampling frames for specialized research purposes.

Realizing that the sampling elements in a study need not be individual persons, we may note that lists of other types of elements also exist: universities, businesses of various types, cities, academic journals, newspapers, unions, political clubs, professional associations, and so forth.

Telephone directories have been used for "quick-and-dirty" public opinion polls. Undeniably, they are easy and inexpensive to use, and that is no doubt the reason for their popularity. And, if you want to make assertions about landline telephone subscribers, the directory is a fairly good sampling frame. It is not good, however, in representing all telephone users in light of the sizeable portion of the population today that has replaced landlines with cell phones. Moreover, even if the study population consists of landline subscribers, only, a given directory will not include new subscribers or those who have requested unlisted numbers. Other problems are the inclusion in directories of nonresidential listings and the fact that more affluent people may have more than one line.

Street directories and tax maps are often used for easily obtained samples, but they may also suffer from incompleteness and possible bias. For example, in strictly zoned urban regions, illegal housing units are unlikely to appear on official records. As a result, such units would have no chance for selection, and sample findings could not be representative of those units, which are often poorer and more crowded than the average.

Nonresponse Bias

We have just discussed errors in overgeneralization that can occur when sampling frames are not consonant with the population to which we seek to generalize. As we mentioned earlier, another common error occurs when a substantial proportion of people in the randomly selected sample choose not to participate in the study.

Suppose, for example, you want to survey the social workers in your state regarding their views of evidence-based practice and how often they engage in it. You plan to conduct the survey by mailing (through the U.S. Postal Service) each social worker a questionnaire for them to complete and return in the stamped, self-addressed envelope that you enclose with the questionnaire. Your first step would be to obtain a list of all the social workers and their addresses. Let's assume that the only list available to you is the membership roster of your state's chapter of NASW. Let's further suppose that there are 10,000 social worker names on that list and that your limited research budget has only $1,000 for postage. Obviously, you cannot afford to survey all 10,000 members. Let's say you can afford the postage for a sample of 500 social workers, which you randomly select from the list of 10,000.

Your sampling frame is the list of 10,000 names, and you *hope* your sample will be the 500 social workers whose names you randomly selected from that list. We emphasize the word *hope* because many of the 500 randomly selected social workers may choose not to respond to your survey. Suppose only 200 respond. That would not be a probability sample. Why not? Because the reasons for inclusion ultimately were not random. Perhaps most of the 200 who responded are familiar with evidence-based practice and engage in it frequently. Perhaps most of the 300 who did not respond chose not to because they either never heard of evidence-based practice, don't care about it, or dislike it. Perhaps many of them don't engage in it and feel embarrassed about admitting that. Clearly, then, despite choosing the 500 names randomly, your 200 respondents would comprise a nonprobability sample—moreover, a quite biased and unrepresentative one!

Although you used random procedures to generate what you hoped would be your sample, what you really wound up with was a nonprobability sample of 200 available participants—those who for whatever reasons took the trouble to participate. It also bears noting that even if you had 100% participation from all 500 social workers, you might have had some bias in your sample. That's because many social workers in your state might not be current members of NASW. This refers back to our discussion above regarding the distinction between sampling frames and populations. (We used the term *sampling frame* in this illustration and not *study population* because your aim is to generalize to all social workers in your state, not just NASW members.)

In light of the refusal to participate by some randomly selected individuals, many samples that are considered to be random may not be so from a technically pure standpoint. That is, when one or more randomly selected individuals opt not to participate in a study, the randomly selected sample represents only those elements in the population who agree to participate. There might be important differences between those who so choose and those who refuse regarding the variables being assessed. However, when the proportion of the selected elements who refuse to participate is trivial, it is usually reasonable—from a practical standpoint—to call the participants a probability sample. Suppose, for example, that 490 (98%) of the 500 social workers respond to your survey and that 343 (70%) of them express favorable views about evidence-based practice. Even if all 10 of the nonrespondents dislike evidence-based practice, your estimate of the proportion favoring evidence-based practice would be off by less than 2 percentage points. That is, the true percentage favoring evidence-based practice out of the 500 would be 343 divided by 500, or 68.6%—only 1.4 percentage points less than your finding of 70%. But this raises the question of where the cutoff point is for deeming the refusal rate to be too high to still interpret your findings as if they were based on probability sampling. There is no scientific or mathematical answer to this question. Our best guidance on this is to examine whether the proportion of refusals is large enough that their numbers could have changed your findings to a meaningful extent had they participated and been unlike the actual participants in regard to the variables of your study.

Review of Populations and Sampling Frames

Surprisingly little attention has been given to the issues of populations and sampling frames in social research literature. With this in mind, we've devoted special attention to them here. To further emphasize the point, here is a summary of the main guidelines to remember:

1. Findings based on a sample can be taken as representative only of the aggregation of elements that compose the sampling frame.

2. Often, sampling frames do not truly include all the elements that their names might imply. Omissions are almost inevitable. Thus, a first concern of the researcher must be to assess the extent of the omissions and to correct them if possible. (Realize, of course, that the researcher may feel that he or she can safely ignore a small number of omissions that cannot easily be corrected.)

3. Even to generalize to the population composing the sampling frame, it is necessary for all elements to have equal representation in the frame: Typically, each element should appear only once. Elements that appear more than once will have a greater probability of selection, and the sample will, overall, overrepresent those elements.

» SAMPLE SIZE AND SAMPLING ERROR

Probability theory is a branch of statistics that provides the basis for estimating the parameters of a population. A parameter is the summary description of a given variable in a population. The mean income of all families in a city is a parameter, as is the age distribution of the city's population. When researchers generalize from a sample, they're using sample observations to estimate population parameters. Probability theory enables them both to make these estimates and to arrive at a judgment of how likely it is that the estimates will accurately represent the actual parameters in the population. So, for example, probability theory allows pollsters to infer from a sample of 2,000 voters how a population of 100 million voters is likely to vote—and to specify exactly what the probable margin of error in the estimates is.

Estimating the Margin of Sampling Error

Although some complex statistical concepts and formulas are required to specify the exact probable margin of error in probability sampling, we can understand the logic involved without getting into the heavy math. (The mathematical material can be found in Appendix B.) Let's start by imagining that we are tossing a coin to see if it is more likely to come up heads or tails. Suppose we flip it twice, and it comes up heads both times. We would not conclude that the coin always comes up heads or even that it is predisposed to come up heads. We don't need math to recognize that a coin that comes up heads half the time and tails half the time easily can come up heads twice in a row or tails twice in a row. If, on the basis of our two coin flips, we concluded that the coin comes up heads 100% of the time, our estimate of the population of flips of that coin would be off by 50 percentage points. That is, our estimate of 100% heads and 0% tails would be 50 percentage points away from the true population parameter of 50% heads and 50% tails. The difference between the true population parameter (50%) and our estimate (100%) is called sampling error. Thus, our sampling error would be 50 percentage points.

Now imagine that instead of tossing the coin twice, we tossed it 20 times. The likelihood that we would get 100% heads (or 100% tails) would be quite tiny. Thus, because we increased our sample size, we reduced the likelihood that we would have a sampling error of 50 percentage points. And the larger the number of coin tosses, the lower that likelihood becomes. Thus, as sample size increases, the likelihood of random error in sampling decreases. Conversely, the larger the sample size, the greater the likelihood that our estimate will be close to the true population parameter.

To further illustrate this logic, suppose we had the name of every person in the United States written on a tiny piece of paper, had all the pieces crumpled up so that the names were not visible, and put them all in an enormous container. Suppose we shook up the container vigorously and then with eyes closed drew names out of the container at random. Suppose the first two names we drew were female and we therefore concluded that the percentage of females in the population is 100%. Just as with the coins, our sampling error would be close to 50 percentage points. The proportion of females in the U.S. population is 50.8%, according to the *Statistical Abstract of the United States* (U.S. Bureau of the Census, 2006). Next, suppose we had randomly drawn 1,000 slips of paper. The odds are quite high that we would get very close to having 508 (50.8%) females and 492 (49.2%) males. It probably wouldn't be exactly those numbers. We might, for example, get 518 (51.8%) females and 482 (48.2%) males. If we did, our sampling error would be 1 percentage point.

When political polls predict the outcomes of presidential elections, the same logic is involved, and that's why their predictions quite often are so accurate. If you've noticed the results of such polls in the newspaper or on television, you may recall that they come with an estimate of the margin of sampling error. For example, a poll predicting that the vote will be 51% for candidate X and 49% for candidate Y might say that the margin of error is plus or minus 3%. That means that there is a very high probability that the true population parameters are between 48% and 54% for candidate X and 46% and 52% for candidate Y. (That is, 3% is added to and subtracted from the estimates for each candidate to identify the range of likely outcomes in the larger population.) That is why sometimes news reporters will characterize such poll results as a "statistical dead heat." In other words, if the margin of sampling error is 3% but the poll results show only a 2% difference between the two candidates, then it is quite conceivable that the candidate with 49% in the poll might really be favored by 50% or more people in the larger population and that the candidate with 51% in the poll might really be favored by 50% or fewer people in the population.

The same logic applies when we are trying to generalize from a sample to a population about other attributes, such as age, income, ethnicity, educational level, and so on. If a sufficiently large sample is selected randomly, we can estimate those parameters with a small margin of sampling error. When we say "sufficiently large," we do not mean large in the sense of percentage of the population. Accurate presidential polls are conducted with fewer than 2,000 people, much less than 1% of the population of voters.

Probability theory gives us a formula for estimating how closely sample statistics are clustered around a true population value. To put it another way, probability theory enables us to estimate the degree of sampling error to be expected for a given sample design. (This statistical formula is presented in Appendix B.) The formula enables us to be confident (at some level) of being within a certain range of a population parameter and to estimate the expected degree of error on the basis of one sample drawn from a population. Using this formula, for example, a presidential pollster might report that she is 95% confident that between 48% and 54% of the population of voters will vote for candidate X.

The formula also provides a basis for determining the appropriate sample size for a study. Once you have decided on the degree of sampling error you can tolerate, you'll be able to calculate the number of cases needed in your sample. Thus, for example, if a pollster assumes that the election will be close and wants to be 95% confident of predicting the election results within plus or minus 5 percentage points of the actual votes, then she'll need to select a sample of at least 400 people. Although you may not use the formula in any of your own research, Table 15-2 is a convenient guide for estimating the sample size you'll need for the degree of sampling error you can tolerate (at the 95% level of confidence). It also illustrates how, as sample sizes reach a certain point, further increases in sample size would yield diminishing returns in reducing sampling error and perhaps not be worth the additional data-collection costs.

To use Table 15-2, find the intersection between the sample size and the approximate percentage distribution that you anticipate in the population. For example, suppose we assume that roughly 50% of the population intends to vote for candidate X and that 50% intend to vote for candidate Y. Table 15-2 shows that increasing the sample size from 100 to 1,100 will reduce the estimated sampling error by 7 percentage points. But increasing it from 1,100 to 2,000 will reduce it by only another eight-tenths of 1 point.

TABLE 15.2 Estimated Sampling Error

Sample Size	Estimated Percentage Distribution				
	50/50	60/40	70/30	80/20	90/10
100	10	9.8	9.2	8	6
200	7.1	6.9	6.5	5.7	4.2
300	5.8	5.7	5.3	4.6	3.5
400	5	4.9	4.6	4	3
500	4.5	4.4	4.1	3.6	2.7
600	4.1	4	3.7	3.3	2.4
700	3.8	3.7	3.5	3	2.3
800	3.5	3.5	3.2	2.8	2.1
900	3.3	3.3	3.1	2.7	2
1,000	3.2	3.1	2.9	2.5	1.9
1,100	3	3	2.8	2.4	1.8
1,200	2.9	2.8	2.6	2.3	1.7
1,300	2.8	2.7	2.5	2.2	1.7
1,400	2.7	2.6	2.4	2.1	1.6
1,500	2.6	2.5	2.4	2.1	1.5
1,600	2.5	2.4	2.3	2	1.5
1,700	2.4	2.4	2.2	1.9	1.5
1,800	2.4	2.3	2.2	1.9	1.4
1,900	2.3	2.2	2.1	1.8	1.4
2,000	2.2	2.2	2	1.8	1.3

This, then, is the basic logic of probability sampling. Random selection permits the researcher to link findings from a sample to the body of probability theory so as to estimate the accuracy of those findings. The researcher may report that he or she is x% confident that the population parameter is between two specific values.

To further illustrate the difference between the level of confidence and the margin of error, imagine that you are willing to accept a ridiculously high 50% margin of error in predicting the outcome of the next presidential election. If you are willing to be wrong by that much, you can be virtually 100% confident that the eventual outcome of the election will fall within your margin of error. Thus, if you predict that the Democratic candidate will be elected with 54% of the vote, he or she would

have to get less than 4% for the results to be outside of your 50% margin of error.

Conversely, suppose you are willing to accept less than a 3% margin of error. How confident would you be that the Democrat would get between 51% and 57% of the vote? With rigorous probability sampling procedures and a sample size of 2,000, Table 15-2 shows that you could be 95% confident that the actual vote will fall within your predicted range. (It shows that your estimated margin of sampling error for a sample size of 2,000 is exactly 2.2%.) But you would not be 100% confident. Thus, the greater margin of error you are willing to accept, the more confident you can be that the actual result will fall within that margin, and the smaller the margin of error, the less confident you can be. However, as indicated in Table 15-2, with rigorous sampling procedures and an adequate sample size, you can predict a presidential election with a great deal of confidence even with a very small margin of error.

Other Considerations in Determining Sample Size

Another statistical procedure to guide decisions about sample size involves statistical power analysis, which we will address in Chapter 22. At this point, for the sake of simplicity, we can say that statistical power analysis deals with determining how large a sample needs to be in order for researchers to have an adequate probability of obtaining statistically significant findings. Because of the complexities and various factors involved in determining the desired sample size for many studies, you may want to use a statistical software program to help you make this determination. One of the more popular programs available is the Statistical Package for the Social Sciences (SPSS). SPSS offers a feature called SamplePower, which can help you determine your desired sample size on the basis of various aspects of your research design and data analysis plans.

The importance of the foregoing statistical procedures notwithstanding, decisions about sample size in social work research rarely involve estimating sampling error. Often, this is due to practical limitations. It may not be possible to obtain an adequate sampling frame for some populations of concern to social workers, such as homeless people or undocumented recent immigrants. Meager budgets for conducting research or time constraints may preclude conducting preliminary surveys to estimate population parameters. Inadequate resources may also force researchers to simply select the largest sample the budget will permit, knowing in advance that sample size will fall short of the number needed for a desired estimated sampling error.

» TYPES OF PROBABILITY SAMPLING DESIGNS

Up to this point, we have focused on simple random sampling. And, indeed, the body of statistics typically used by social researchers assumes such a sample. As we shall see shortly, however, we have several choices of sampling method, and you will seldom, if ever, choose simple random sampling for two reasons. First, with all but the simplest sampling frame, simple random sampling is not feasible. Second, and probably surprisingly, simple random sampling may not be the most accurate method available. Let's turn now to a discussion of simple random sampling and the other options available.

Simple Random Sampling

Once a sampling frame has been established in accordance with the preceding discussion, to use simple random sampling, the researcher assigns a single number to each element in the sampling frame without skipping any number in the process. The elements can be selected online by a random number generator, which can be found by entering the search term *random number generator*. Alternatively, a table of random numbers can be used to select elements for the sample. Appendix B displays such a table, along with a box explaining its use. It also elaborates on the use of online random number generators.

If your sampling frame is in a computer file, the computer can automatically select a simple random sample. (In effect, the computer program numbers the elements in the sampling frame, generates its own series of random numbers, and prints out the list of elements selected.)

Figure 15-2 illustrates simple random sampling. The members of our hypothetical micropopulation have been numbered from 1 to 100. Using the small table of random numbers included in Figure 15-2 and following the procedures explained in the box

in Appendix B on selecting random numbers, let's decide to use the last two digits of the first column and to begin with the third number from the top. This yields person number 30 as the first one selected into the sample. Number 67 is next, and so forth. (Person 100 would have been selected if "00" had come up in the list.)

Systematic Sampling

Simple random sampling is seldom used in practice. As we shall see, it is not usually the most efficient sampling method, and it can be rather laborious if done manually. Simple random sampling typically requires a list of elements. When such a list is available, researchers usually employ systematic sampling rather than simple random sampling.

In systematic sampling, every *k*th element in the total list is chosen (systematically) for inclusion in the sample. If the list contains 10,000 elements and you want a sample of 1,000, you select every tenth element for your sample. To guard against any possible human bias in using this method, you should select the first element at random. Thus, in the preceding example, you would begin by selecting a random number between 1 and 10. The element having that number is included in the sample, plus every tenth element following it. This method is technically referred to as a systematic sample with a random start. Two terms are frequently used in connection with systematic sampling. The sampling interval is the standard distance between elements selected in the sample: 10 in the preceding sample. The sampling ratio is the proportion of elements in the population that are selected: 1/10 in the example.

$$\text{Sampling interval} = \frac{\text{Population size}}{\text{Sample size}}$$

$$\text{Sampling ratio} = \frac{\text{Sample size}}{\text{Population size}}$$

In practice, systematic sampling is virtually identical to simple random sampling. If the list of elements is indeed randomized before sampling, one might argue that a systematic sample drawn from that list is, in fact, a simple random sample. By now, debates over the relative merits of simple random sampling and systematic sampling have been resolved largely in favor of the simpler method: systematic sampling. Empirically, the results are virtually identical. And, as we shall see

FIGURE 15.2 A Simple Random Sample

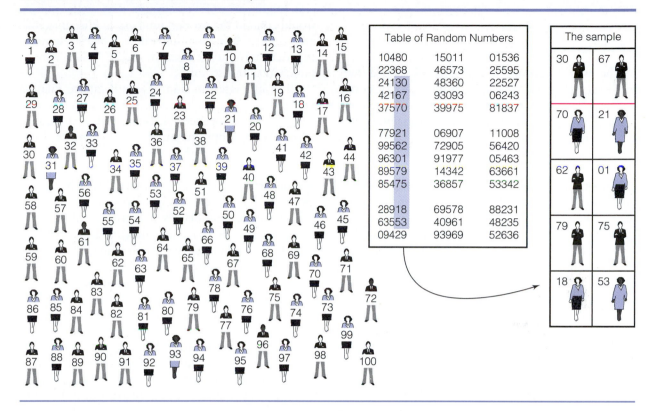

Table of Random Numbers

10480	15011	01536
22368	46573	25595
24130	48360	22527
42167	93093	06243
37570	39975	81837
77921	06907	11008
99562	72905	56420
96301	91977	05463
89579	14342	63661
85475	36857	53342
28918	69578	88231
63553	40961	48235
09429	93969	52636

The sample: 30, 67, 70, 21, 62, 01, 79, 75, 18, 53

in a later section, systematic sampling is slightly more accurate than simple random sampling in some instances.

There is one danger involved in systematic sampling. The arrangement of elements in the list can make systematic sampling unwise. Such an arrangement is usually called *periodicity*. If the list of elements is arranged in a cyclical pattern that coincides with the sampling interval, then a grossly biased sample may be drawn. Two examples will illustrate.

In one study of soldiers during World War II, the researchers selected a systematic sample from unit rosters. Every 10th soldier on the roster was selected for the study. The rosters, however, were arranged in a table of organizations: sergeants first, then corporals and privates, squad by squad. Each squad had 10 members. As a result, every 10th person on the roster was a squad sergeant. The systematic sample selected contained only sergeants. It could, of course, have been the case that no sergeants were selected for the same reason.

As another example, suppose we select a sample of apartments in an apartment building. If the sample is drawn from a list of apartments arranged in numerical order (e.g., 101, 102, 103, 104, 201, 202, and so on), there is a danger of the sampling interval coinciding with the number of apartments on a floor or some multiple thereof. Then, the samples might include only northwest-corner apartments or only apartments near the elevator. If these types of apartments have some other particular characteristic in common (e.g., higher rent), the sample will be biased. The same danger would appear in a systematic sample of houses in a subdivision arranged with the same number of houses on a block.

In considering a systematic sample from a list, then, you should carefully examine the nature of that list. If the elements are arranged in any particular order, you should figure out whether that order will bias the sample to be selected and take steps to counteract any possible bias (e.g., take a simple random sample from cyclical portions).

In summary, systematic sampling is usually superior to simple random sampling—in convenience if nothing else. Problems in the ordering of elements in the sampling frame can usually be remedied quite easily.

Stratified Sampling

In the two preceding sections, we discussed two methods of sample selection from a list: random and systematic. Stratification is not an alternative to these methods, but it represents a possible modification in their use.

Simple random sampling and systematic sampling both ensure a degree of representativeness and permit an estimate of the error present. Stratified sampling is a method for obtaining a greater degree of representativeness—for decreasing the probable sampling error. To understand why that is the case, we must return briefly to the basic theory of sampling distribution.

We recall that sampling error is reduced by two factors in the sample design. First, a large sample produces a smaller sampling error than a small sample. Second, a homogeneous population produces samples with smaller sampling errors than does a heterogeneous population. If 99% of the population agrees with a certain statement, then it is extremely unlikely that any probability sample will greatly misrepresent the extent of agreement. If the population is split 50:50 on the statement, then the sampling error will be much greater.

Stratified sampling is based on this second factor in sampling theory. Rather than selecting a sample from the total population at large, we ensure that appropriate numbers of elements are drawn from homogeneous subsets of that population.

Suppose you seek to obtain a stratified sample of clients in a large social service agency in order to assess client satisfaction with the services they received. You suspect that ethnic minority clients might be relatively dissatisfied with services, and you want to ensure that they are adequately represented in the sample. Consequently, you might first organize your list of cases so that clients of the same ethnicity are grouped together. Then you would draw appropriate numbers from each ethnic group. In a nonstratified sample, representation by ethnicity would be subjected to the same sampling error as other variables. In a sample stratified by ethnicity, the sampling error on this variable is reduced to zero.

Even more complex stratification methods are possible. In addition to stratifying by ethnicity, you might also stratify by age group, type of presenting problem, and so forth. In this fashion, you might be able to ensure that your sample would contain the proper numbers of Hispanic children with behavior disorders, black families experiencing marital discord, elderly Asian American clients, and so forth.

The ultimate function of stratification, then, is to organize the population into homogeneous subsets (with heterogeneity between subsets) and to select the appropriate number of elements from each. To the extent that the subsets are homogeneous on the stratification variables, they may be homogeneous on other variables as well. If age group is related to type of presenting problem, then a sample stratified by age group will be more representative in terms of presenting problem as well. If socioeconomic status is related to ethnicity, then a sample stratified by ethnicity will be more representative in terms of socioeconomic status.

The choice of stratification variables typically depends on what variables are available. Sex can often be determined in a list of names. University lists are typically arranged by class. Lists of faculty members may indicate their departmental affiliation. Government agency files may be arranged by geographical region. Voter registration lists are arranged according to precinct.

In selecting stratification variables from among those available, however, you should be concerned primarily with those that are presumably related to variables that you want to represent accurately. Because sex is related to many variables and is often available for stratification, it is often used. Education is related to many variables, but it is often not available for stratification. Geographical location within a city, state, or nation is related to many things. Within a city, stratification by geographical location usually increases representativeness in social class, ethnic group, and so forth. Within a nation, stratification increases representativeness in a broad range of attitudes as well as in social class and ethnicity.

Methods of stratification in sampling vary. When you are working with a simple list of all elements in the population, two are predominant. One method is to sort the population elements into discrete groups on the basis of whatever stratification variables are being used. On the basis of the relative proportion of the population represented by a given group, you select—randomly or systematically—a number of elements from that group that constitutes the same proportion of your desired sample size. For example, if elderly Hispanics compose 1% of the client population and you desire a sample of 1,000 clients, then you would select 10 elderly Hispanic clients.

The other method is to group cases as just described and then put those groups together in a continuous list. You would then select a systematic sample, with a random start, from the entire list. Given the arrangement of the list, a systematic sample would select proper numbers (within an error range of 1 or 2) from each subgroup. (*Note:* A simple random sample drawn from such a composite list would cancel out the stratification.)

Figure 15-3 offers a graphic illustration of stratified systematic sampling. As you can see, we lined up our micropopulation according to sex and race. Then, beginning with a random start of "3," we've taken every 10th person thereafter: 3, 13, 23, ... , 93.

Stratified sampling ensures the proper representation of the stratification variables to enhance the representation of other variables related to them. Taken as a whole, then, a stratified sample is likely to be more representative on several variables than a simple random sample. Although the simple random sample is still regarded as somewhat sacred, we often can do better.

Recalling our earlier discussion of nonprobability quota sampling, you may be wondering about the difference between it and stratified sampling. That would be understandable since the two methods both identify strata within a population and then select a predetermined proportion within each stratum. The distinction between the two methods is whether the process of selection within each stratum is random. With quota sampling by sex and a sample size of 200, for example, you could stand at a pedestrian-heavy spot on your campus at noon and include in your sample the first 100 men and the first 100 women who walk by. There is nothing random in that haphazard, risky nonprobability procedure for generalizing to your college's population of 5,000 male and 5,000 female enrolled students. In contrast, with stratified random sampling, you would use a list that numbers from 1 to 5,000 all male enrolled students and an identical sort of list for all 5,000 female enrolled students. Then you would use random numbers to select 100 names from each list. As we discussed earlier, the quota sampling

procedure is much riskier. All sorts of biases could make the types of students who walk by your spot on campus at that time of day and who you stop to talk to very different than the ones who don't frequent that spot as often or who are less likely to be talked to.

Implicit Stratification in Systematic Sampling

It was mentioned earlier that systematic sampling can, under certain conditions, be more accurate than simple random sampling. That is the case whenever the arrangement of the list creates an implicit stratification. As already noted, if a list of agency cases is arranged by ethnicity, then a systematic sample provides stratification by ethnicity, whereas a simple random sample would not.

In a study of students at the University of Hawaii, after stratification by school class, the students were arranged by their student identification numbers. These numbers, however, were their Social Security numbers. The first three digits of the Social Security number indicate the state in which the number was issued. As a result, within a class, students were arranged by the state in which they were issued a Social Security number, providing a rough stratification by geographical origins. You should realize, therefore, that an ordered list of elements might be more useful to you than an unordered, randomized list. This point has been stressed here in view of an unfortunate belief that lists should be randomized before systematic sampling. Only if the arrangement presents the problems discussed earlier should the list be rearranged.

Proportionate and Disproportionate Stratified Samples

So far we have been illustrating stratified random sampling with a uniform proportion of cases drawn from each homogeneous grouping. This is called *proportionate stratified sampling*. For example, if our overall sample is to be 10% of the population, then we would draw 10% of each homogeneous group. In some studies, however, it may be advisable to select a larger proportion of cases from some groups than from others. Suppose, for example, that the preceding client satisfaction survey is being conducted in an agency whose 1,000 clients include 600 white clients, 300 African

FIGURE 15.3   A Stratified, Systematic Sample with a Random Start

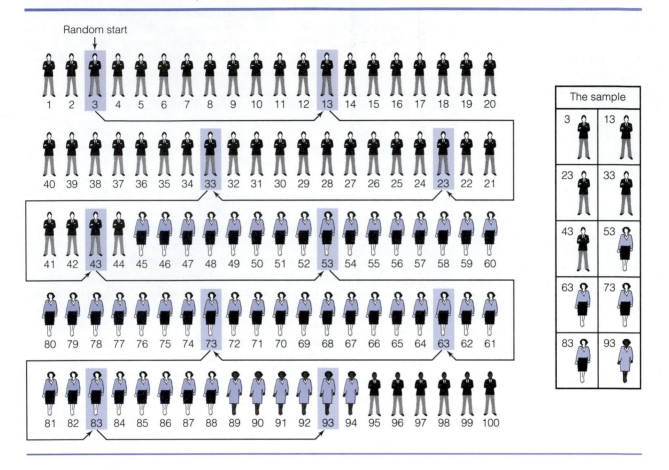

American clients, 40 Hispanic clients, 30 Asian American clients, 20 Native American clients, and 10 clients whose ethnicity falls in a catchall "other" category. We could select 10% of the white and African American clients and have 60 and 30 cases in each group. But if we selected 10% of the clients in the other groups, we would have only 4 Hispanics, 3 Asian Americans, 2 Native Americans, and 1 "other." There would be nothing wrong with this if all we sought to do was to come up with an overall satisfaction rating for the entire agency.

But what if we sought a detailed analysis about each ethnic group or sought to generalize about which ethnic groups were more satisfied or dissatisfied than others? Such an analysis would not be possible for groups represented by only a handful of cases. Therefore, we would have to take a larger proportion of the very small homogeneous

groupings than of the larger ones. This is called disproportionate stratified sampling. This sampling procedure gives cases from specified small subgroups a disproportionately better chance of being selected than cases from larger subgroups.

For example, we might select 10% of the white and African American clients and 50% from each of the remaining groups. That would give us 20 Hispanics, 15 Asian Americans, 10 Native Americans, and 5 "other." This would permit us to undertake our detailed analyses. But if we also wanted to portray an overall agency composite of client satisfaction, then we would have to weight the average satisfaction level of each ethnic group in accordance with its overall proportion in the agency population.

Suppose that on a scale of 1 to 5 ("very dissatisfied" to "very satisfied"), the average rating of each group was as shown in Table 15-3. If the influence

TABLE 15.3 Illustration of Disproportionate Stratified Sampling

Ethnic Group	Number of Cases	Average Rating
White	60	4.0
Black	30	2.0
Hispanic	20	1.0
Asian American	15	3.0
Native American	10	1.0
Other	5	2.0

on the overall mean of the ratings in the 50% selection groups was not adjusted in accordance with the groups' true proportion in the population, then the overall agency average satisfaction rating would be calculated as shown in Equation (1) in Figure 15-4.

But the average rating of 2.75 would underestimate the true overall level of client satisfaction because of the disproportionate influence of the ethnic groups represented by 50% of their cases. To correct for this, we would weight the two 10% groups by multiples (weights) of 5 (to raise their influence to an equivalent 50% representation), as shown in Equation (2) in Figure 15-4.

Thus, the true overall average rating of client satisfaction of 3.17 would be above the midpoint of 3.0 on the 1–5 rating scale, not below it as implied by the misleading 2.75 calculation. This would not negate the accuracy or importance of calculations that show that ethnic minority clientele tend to be far less satisfied with services than is depicted by the overall rating.

» MULTISTAGE CLUSTER SAMPLING

The preceding sections have dealt with reasonably simple procedures for sampling from lists of elements. Such a situation is ideal. Unfortunately, however, much interesting social research requires the selection of samples from populations that cannot be easily listed for sampling purposes. Examples would be the population of a city, state, or nation; all university students in the United States; and so forth. In such cases, the sample design must be much more complex and typically involves the initial sampling of groups of elements—*clusters*—followed by the selection of elements within each selected cluster, a multistage design called cluster sampling.

Cluster sampling may be used when it is either impossible or impractical to compile an exhaustive list of the elements that compose the target population. All church members in the United States would be an example of such a population. It is often the case, however, that the population elements are already grouped into subpopulations, and a list of those subpopulations either exists or can be created practically. Thus, church members in the United States belong to discrete churches, and it would be possible to discover or create a list of those churches. Following a cluster sample format, then, the list of churches would be sampled in some manner as discussed previously (e.g., a stratified systematic sample). Next, you would obtain lists of members from each selected church. Each list would then be sampled to provide samples of church members for study. For an example, see Glock, Ringer, and Babbie (1967).

FIGURE 15.4 Equations for Table 15-3

$$\frac{(60 \times 4) + (30 \times 2) + (20 \times 1) + (15 \times 3) + (10 \times 1) + (5 \times 2)}{60 + 30 + 20 + 15 + 10 + 5}$$
$$= \frac{240 + 60 + 20 + 45 + 10 + 10}{140} = \frac{385}{140} = 2.75 \tag{1}$$

$$\frac{(60 \times 4 \times 5) + (30 \times 2 \times 5) + (20 \times 1) + (15 \times 3) + (10 \times 1) + (5 \times 2)}{(60 \times 5) + (30 \times 5) + 20 + 15 + 10 + 5}$$
$$= \frac{1200 + 300 + 20 + 45 + 10 + 10}{300 + 150 + 20 + 15 + 10 + 5} = \frac{1585}{500} = 3.17 \tag{2}$$

Another typical situation concerns sampling among population areas such as a city. Although there is no single list of a city's population, citizens reside on discrete city blocks or census blocks. We might, therefore, select a sample of blocks initially, create a list of people living on each selected block, and subsample the people on each block.

In a more complex design, you might sample blocks, list the households on each selected block, sample the households, list the persons residing in each household, and, finally, sample persons within each selected household. This multistage sample design would lead to the ultimate selection of a sample of individuals but would not require the initial listing of all individuals in the city's population.

Multistage cluster sampling, then, involves the repetition of two basic steps: listing and sampling. The list of primary sampling units (churches, blocks) is compiled and, perhaps, stratified for sampling. Then a sample of those units is selected. The selected primary sampling units are then listed and perhaps stratified. The list of secondary sampling units is then sampled and so forth.

Multistage Designs and Sampling Error

Although cluster sampling is highly efficient, the price of that efficiency is a less accurate sample. A simple random sample drawn from a population list is subject to a single sampling error, but a two-stage cluster sample is subject to two sampling errors. First, the initial sample of clusters will represent the population of clusters only within a range of sampling error. Second, the sample of elements selected within a given cluster will represent all of the elements in that cluster only within a range of sampling error. Thus, for example, you run a certain risk of selecting a sample of disproportionately wealthy city blocks, plus a sample of disproportionately wealthy households within those blocks. The best solution to this problem lies in the number of clusters initially selected and the number of elements selected within each.

You'll typically be restricted to a total sample size; for example, you may be limited to conducting 2,000 interviews in a city. Given this broad limitation, however, you have several options in designing your cluster sample. At the extremes, you might choose one cluster and select 2,000 elements within that cluster, or you might choose 2,000 clusters and select one element within each. Of course, neither extreme is advisable, but a broad range of choices lies between them. Fortunately, the logic of sampling distributions provides a general guideline to follow.

Recall that sampling error is reduced by two factors: an increase in the sample size and increased homogeneity of the elements being sampled. These factors operate at each level of a multistage sample design. A sample of clusters will best represent all clusters if a large number are selected and if all clusters are very much alike. A sample of elements will best represent all elements in a given cluster if a large number are selected from the cluster and if all elements in the cluster are very similar.

With a given total sample size, however, if the number of clusters is increased, the number of elements within a cluster must be decreased. In this respect, the representativeness of the clusters is increased at the expense of more poorly representing the elements that compose each cluster or vice versa. Fortunately, the factor of homogeneity can be used to ease this dilemma.

Typically, the elements that compose a given natural cluster within a population are more homogeneous than are all elements that compose the total population. The members of a given church are more alike than are all church members, and the residents of a given city block are more alike than are all the residents of an entire city. As a result, relatively fewer elements may be needed to adequately represent a given natural cluster, although a larger number of clusters may be needed to adequately represent the diversity found among the clusters. This fact is most clearly seen in the extreme case of very different clusters that are composed of identical elements within each. In such a situation, a large number of clusters would adequately represent all their members. Although this extreme situation never exists in reality, it is closer to the truth in most cases than its opposite: identical clusters composed of grossly divergent elements.

The general guideline for cluster design, then, is to maximize the number of clusters selected while decreasing the number of elements within each cluster. Note, however, that this scientific guideline must be balanced against an administrative constraint. The efficiency of cluster sampling is based on the ability to minimize the listing of population elements. By initially selecting clusters, you need to list only the elements that compose the selected clusters, not all of the elements in the entire population. Increasing the number of clusters, however, goes directly against this efficiency factor in cluster sampling. A small number of clusters may be listed more quickly and more cheaply than a large number. (Remember that all of the elements in a selected cluster must be listed even if only a few are to be chosen in the sample.)

The final sample design will reflect these two constraints. In effect, you will probably select as many clusters as you can afford. Lest this issue be left too open ended at this point, we present one rule of thumb. Population researchers conventionally aim for the selection of five households per census block. If a total of 2,000 households is to be interviewed, then you would aim at 400 blocks with five household interviews on each. Figure 15-5 graphically portrays this process.

Before moving on, we repeat that cluster sampling almost inevitably involves a loss of accuracy. The manner in which this appears, however, is somewhat complex. First, as noted earlier, a multistage sample design is subject to a sampling error at each stage. Because the sample size is necessarily smaller at each stage than the total sample size, each stage's sampling error will be greater than would be the case for a single-stage random sample of elements. Second, sampling error is estimated on the basis of observed variance among the sample elements. When those elements are drawn from among relatively homogeneous clusters, the estimated sampling error will be too optimistic and must be corrected in light of the cluster sample design.

Stratification in Multistage Cluster Sampling

Thus far, we have looked at cluster sampling as though a simple random sample were selected at each stage of the design. In fact, stratification techniques can be used to refine and improve the sample being selected.

The basic options available are essentially the same as those possible in single-stage sampling from a list. In selecting a national sample of churches, for example, you might initially stratify your list of churches by denomination, geographical region, size, rural or urban location, and perhaps by some measure of social class.

Once the primary sampling units (churches and blocks) have been grouped according to the relevant and available stratification variables, either simple random or systematic sampling techniques can be used to select the sample. You might select a

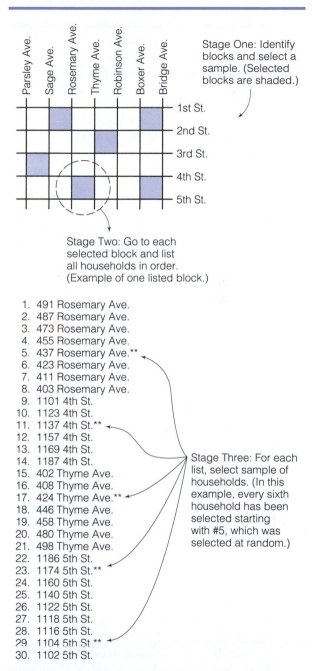

FIGURE 15.5 Multistage Cluster Sampling

specified number of units from each group or stratum, or you might arrange the stratified clusters in a continuous list and systematically sample that list. To the extent that clusters are combined into homogeneous strata, the sampling error at this stage will be reduced. The primary goal of stratification, as before, is homogeneity.

There is no reason why stratification could not take place at each level of sampling. The elements listed within a selected cluster might be stratified before the next stage of sampling. Typically, however, that is not done. (Recall the assumption of relative homogeneity within clusters.)

» ILLUSTRATION: SAMPLING SOCIAL WORK STUDENTS

Now let's use a hypothetical example to see what cluster sampling looks like in practice. Suppose you obtained a large research grant to conduct a longitudinal study of how social work students change their attitudes about cultural diversity during their social work education. To simplify the calculations, suppose there are only 100 graduate programs of social work and 300 undergraduate programs in the United States. You will need to make several repeated site visits to each program selected for the study to collect longitudinal data from the students there. You desire a nationally representative sample of students, but your travel budget limits your site visits to 40 programs.

There is no national list of social work students, so a multistage sampling design is created. In the initial stage of sampling, programs are selected, and then students are selected from each.

Selecting the Programs

The Council on Social Work Education publishes an annual report that lists each social work education program and its enrollment size. This list constitutes the sampling frame for the first stage of sampling. Suppose it shows a nationwide total of approximately 50,000 students, including 25,000 each at both the graduate and the undergraduate level. Consequently, you decide to select 20 programs from each level for your study.

For your data analysis, you desire a sample size of 1,000 students, so you decide to select 25 students from each of the 40 participating programs. To accomplish this, you make two lists of programs: one for graduate programs and one for undergraduate programs. Each list identifies the enrollment size of each program and the cumulative enrollment of the programs on the list, as illustrated in Table 15-4.

The object at this point is to select a sample of 20 programs from each list in such a way that each

TABLE 15.4 Form Used in Listing Social Work Education Programs

Program	Enrollment Size	Cumulative Enrollment
School A	200	200
School B	400	600
School C	100	700

program would have a chance of selection proportionate to its enrollment size. (The term for this is *probability proportion to size sampling*.) To accomplish this, the cumulative totals are used to create ranges of numbers for each program that equal the number of students enrolled in that program. School A in Table 15-4 is assigned the numbers 1 through 200, school B is assigned 201 through 600, school C is assigned 601 through 700, and so forth.

By selecting 20 numbers between 1 and 25,000 for each list, we can select 40 programs for the study. The 20 numbers could be selected in a systematic sample as follows. Set the sampling interval at 1,250 (25,000/20). Select a random start at between 1 and 1,250. Let's say the starting number randomly selected is 563. Because that number falls within the range of numbers assigned to school B (201 through 600), school B is selected.

Increments of 1,250 (the sampling interval) are then added to the random starting number, and every school within whose range one of the resultant numbers appears is selected to participate in the study. In this fashion, each school has a chance of selection that is directly proportionate to its enrollment size. A school that enrolls 400 students has twice the chance of selection as a school with 200 and 10 times the chance of selection as one with only 40 students.

Selecting the Students

Once the sample of programs is selected, a list of the students enrolled is obtained from each selected program. A sampling interval is then computed for each program on the basis of its enrollment size and the number of students desired from each program (25). If a program enrolled 250 students, then the sample interval would be set at 10. A random number is selected and incremented by the sampling interval to select the sample of students from that school. This procedure is repeated for each school.

» PROBABILITY SAMPLING IN REVIEW

The preceding discussions have been devoted to the key sampling method used in controlled survey research: probability sampling. In each examined variation, we have seen that elements are chosen for study from a population on a basis of random selection with known nonzero probabilities. Depending on the field situation, probability sampling can be extremely simple or extremely difficult, time consuming, and expensive. Whatever the situation, however, it remains the most effective method for selecting study elements. There are two reasons for this.

First, probability sampling avoids conscious or unconscious biases in element selection on the part of the researcher. If all elements in the population have an equal (or unequal and subsequently weighted) chance of selection, then there is an excellent chance that the selected sample will closely represent the population of all elements.

Second, probability sampling permits estimates of sampling error. Although no probability sample will be perfectly representative in all respects, controlled selection methods permit the researcher to estimate the degree of expected error.

» AVOIDING SEX BIAS IN SAMPLING

Before leaving this chapter, however, let's look at another form of bias to be avoided in sampling: sex bias. Like cultural bias (discussed in Chapter 6), all aspects of the research process can be affected by sex bias, and sampling is one area in which it can be particularly problematic. It can even affect probability sampling; for example, when we inappropriately decide to exclude a particular sex from our sampling frame. Perhaps the most commonly encountered sex bias problem in sampling is the unwarranted generalization of research findings to the population as a whole when one sex is not adequately represented in the research sample. Campbell (1983) reviewed the occurrence of sex biases in the sex role research literature and identified several illustrations of this problem. For example, she cited studies on achievement motivation and on management and careers whose samples included only white, middle-class male

subjects but that did not specify in their conclusions that their generalizations were limited to individuals with those attributes. She was particularly critical of life cycle research, as follows:

> Nowhere is the effect of bias on sampling more evident than in the popular and growing field of the life cycle or stages. Beginning with Erikson's ... work on the "Eight Stages of Man" to Levinson's *Seasons of a Man's Life* ... the study of life cycles has focused on male subjects. When women are examined, it is in terms of how they fit or don't fit the male model. Without empirical verification, women are said to go through the same cycles as men ... or are said to go through cycles that are antithetical to men's.... Based on a survey of the literature on life cycles, Sangiuliano ... concluded that "Mostly we (researchers) persist in seeing her (woman) in the reflected light of men." (p. 206)

The inadequate representation of a particular sex in a sample can be much subtler than just excluding them entirely or including an insufficient proportion of them. It could also occur because of biased data collection procedures, even when the number of individuals of a particular sex is not the issue. For example, Campbell noted that the Gallup Poll interviewed males beginning at 6 P.M. and conducted most interviews with females between 4 P.M. and 6 P.M. Thus, Campbell argued that most professional women would not be home before 6 P.M. and cannot be adequately represented in the sample. If she was correct, then even if the overall proportion of women in the Gallup Poll seemed to be sufficient, the views expressed by the women in the sample were not adequately representative of the views of the population of women.

As another example, if we wanted to generalize about sex-related differences in job satisfaction, we would not want to select our sample only from those work settings where professional or managerial positions go predominantly to men and where semiprofessional clerical jobs go predominantly to women.

There may be instances, however, when the exclusion of a particular sex from a study's sample is warranted or inescapable—instances where only one sex is relevant and where generalizations will be restricted to that sex. Thus, only one sex would be included in the sample of a survey of client satisfaction in a program whose clientele all happen to be of the same sex—for example, a group support program for battered women or for female rape victims.

We must be on guard not to let sex role biases improperly influence us so that we deem a particular sex irrelevant for a given study. For example, we should not be predisposed to restrict our samples to men when we study topics such as aggression, management, unemployment, or criminal behavior and to women when we study things such as parenting, nurturing, or housekeeping.

In this chapter, we've taken on a basic issue in much social work research: selecting observations that will tell us something more general than the specifics we've actually observed. As we proceed through the rest of this book, we'll see how this issue bears on various designs for collecting and analyzing research data. In the next chapter, for example, we'll examine how different survey methods are vulnerable to sampling bias and how survey researchers can try to avoid it.

MAIN POINTS

- A sample is a special subset of a population that is observed for purposes of making inferences about the nature of the total population itself.
- Purposive sampling is a type of nonprobability sampling method in which the researcher uses his or her own judgment in selecting sample members. It is sometimes called a judgmental sample.
- When informants are used, they should be selected in such a fashion as to provide a broad, diverse view of the group under study.
- In general, nonprobability sampling methods are regarded as less reliable than probability sampling methods. However, they are often easier and cheaper to use.
- The chief criterion of the quality of a sample is the degree to which it is representative—the extent to which the characteristics of the sample are the same as those of the population from which it was selected.
- Probability sampling methods provide one excellent way to select samples that will be quite representative.
- The chief principle of probability sampling is that every member of the total population must have the same known, nonzero probability of being selected into the sample.
- The most carefully selected sample will almost never perfectly represent the population from which it was selected. There will always be some degree of sampling error.
- Probability sampling methods allow us to estimate the amount of sampling error that should be expected in a given sample.
- A sampling frame is a list of the members of a population. It is the resource used in the selection of a sample. A sample's representativeness depends directly on the extent to which a sampling frame contains all the members of the total population that the sample is intended to represent.
- Simple random sampling is logically the most fundamental technique in probability sampling.
- Systematic sampling involves the selection of every kth member from a sampling frame. This method is functionally equivalent to simple random sampling, with a few exceptions.
- Stratification is the process of grouping the members of a population into relatively homogeneous strata before sampling. This practice improves the representativeness of a sample by reducing the degree of sampling error.
- Multistage cluster sampling is a more complex sampling technique that is frequently used in those cases in which a list of all the members of a population does not exist. An initial sample of groups of members (clusters) is selected first, and then all members of the selected cluster are listed, often through direct observation in the field. Finally, the members listed in each selected cluster are subsampled, thereby providing the final sample of members.
- If the members of a population have unequal probabilities of selection into the sample, it is necessary to assign weights to the different observations made in order to provide a representative picture of the total population. Basically, the weight assigned to a particular sample member should be the inverse of its probability of selection.
- Sex bias should be avoided in sampling.

REVIEW QUESTIONS AND EXERCISES

1. Review the discussion of the 1948 Gallup Poll that predicted that Thomas Dewey would defeat Harry Truman for president. Discuss ways in which Gallup could have modified his quota sample design to avoid the error.

2. Using Appendix B of this book, select a simple random sample of 10 numbers in the range from 1 to 9,876. Describe each step in the process.

3. In a paragraph or two, describe the steps involved in selecting a multistage cluster sample of nursing home residents throughout the nation.

INTERNET EXERCISES

1. Find two research articles in the journal Health and Social Work—one that used probability sampling and one that used nonprobability sampling. Critique the sampling procedures used in each—either positively or negatively.

2. Find and examine briefly four additional research articles in the journal Health and Social Work. How many used probability sampling methods? How many relied exclusively on non-probability methods?

3. Browse some of your favorite sites on the Internet until you find one conducting a survey of visitors to that site. For example, certain news media sites typically conduct daily polls about political issues. Discuss the sampling problems connected to the survey you find, addressing issues such as the sampling frame, the representativeness of the sample, and so on.

4. Find the following article in the July 2002 issue of the journal Social Work: "Living on the Edge: Examination of People Attending Food Pantries and Soup Kitchens," by M. A. Biggerstaff, P. M. Morris, and A. Nichols-Casebolt. Critically appraise the multistage cluster sampling procedure used in that study.

Visit CengageBrain.com for additional practice and study opportunities including experiential exercises, research tools, glossary, flashcards, and sample test items.

16

Survey Research

EPAS Competencies for This Chapter

Competency 4 Engage in Practice-Informed Research and Research-Informed Practice: This competency pertains to this entire chapter because doing practice-informed research sometimes involves conducting surveys.

Competency 9 Evaluate Practice with Individuals Families, Groups, Organizations, and Communities: Evaluating practice sometimes involves surveying clients, practitioners, communities, and so on. Thus, this competency pertains to this entire chapter.

What You'll Learn in This Chapter

Researchers have many methods for collecting data through surveys—from mail questionnaires to personal interviews to online surveys conducted over the Internet. Survey data that have been collected by others are also available for analysis. Social work researchers should know how to select an appropriate method and how to implement it effectively.

» INTRODUCTION

Survey research is a very old research technique. In the Old Testament, for example, we find the following:

> After the plague the Lord said to Moses and to Eleazar the son of Aaron, the priest, "Take a census of all the congregation of the people of Israel, from twenty years old and upward." (Numbers 26:1–2)

Ancient Egyptian rulers conducted censuses for the purpose of administering their domains. Jesus was born away from home because Joseph and Mary were journeying to Joseph's ancestral home for a Roman census.

A little-known survey was attempted among French workers in 1880. A German political sociologist mailed some 25,000 questionnaires to workers to determine how much they were exploited by employers. The lengthy questionnaire included items such as these:

> Does your employer or his representative resort to trickery in order to defraud you of a part of your earnings?
>
> If you are paid piece rates, is the quality of the article made a pretext for fraudulent deductions from your wages?

The survey researcher in this case was Karl Marx (1880, p. 208). Although 25,000 questionnaires were mailed out, there is no record of any being returned.

The precursors to surveys in social work were conducted in Europe in the mid-19th century. They focused on the earnings and expenditures of the working poor. Some were conducted to determine appropriate levels of relief grants; others were done to provide evidence for social reform. A prominent influence on the early use of surveys in social work was Charles Booth, a wealthy and politically conservative London shipowner who set out in 1886 to disprove claims by Marxists that one-fourth of the working class lived in severe poverty. Using his own money to fund the research, Booth and his assistants surveyed East London residents about many socioeconomic forces that affected their lives. It took 17 volumes of *The Life and Labour of the People of London* (Booth, 1970) to report

the study. Ironically, instead of disproving the Marxists' claims, Booth concluded that they had underestimated the proportion of people living in poverty. Booth even recommended social welfare measures that he termed *limited socialism*.

Booth's work coincided with the emergence of early social reform efforts in the social work profession. As the 20th century began, muckraking journalists and novelists spurred public interest in surveys such as Booth's, surveys that would document the muckraker's depictions of urban squalor and exploitation. The most famous of the social surveys to follow was the Pittsburgh Survey, which was conducted from 1909 to 1914 by social workers and civic leaders to assess social conditions in that city. Published in several volumes, the Pittsburgh survey exposed the city's deplorable social conditions and stimulated major social reforms.

The Pittsburgh Survey's success demonstrated how survey methods can be used for social reform purposes, and it helped spark what was called the "social survey movement" by social workers in cities throughout the United States. The surveys that were conducted as part of this movement were broad in scope, reporting vast amounts of data on industrial, economic, political, and social factors in one city at a time. The data were amassed to arouse communities to the need for social reform. The surveys thus were often reported in a biased manner and were soon seen as being propagandistic. By the 1920s, their credibility was tarnished, and their popularity waned as the social reform era ended. But the movement had a lasting impact on the use of surveys in social work. Its early successes prompted social agencies to adopt narrower surveys that focused on specialized agency concerns as a regular function. Eventually, the utility of survey methods for a wide range of research purposes was recognized.

Today, survey research is perhaps the most frequently used mode of observation in the social sciences. You probably have been a respondent in a survey more than once, and quite possibly you have done a survey of your own. In a typical survey, the researcher selects a sample of respondents and administers a standardized questionnaire to them. Part of the questionnaire might or might not include a scale that yields a summed score (as discussed in Chapter 10) to assess a particular construct. When a scale is included, the questionnaire might start with the scale items (prefaced by brief scale completion instructions), followed by survey background questions at the end. For example, in a survey of practitioners that included a scale measuring their orientations to evidence-based practice (EBP), the scale items were followed by the following preface to the background questions about respondent characteristics, prior training in EBP, and so on:

BACKGROUND INFORMATION

The remaining items on this questionnaire will provide data that can be analyzed to explore whether differences in practitioner attributes or experiences are associated with differences in how they view or engage in evidence-based practice. (Rubin & Parrish, 2009)

Several of the fundamental elements of survey research have already been covered in detail in this book, so you are already partially trained in this important research method. We examined the logic and techniques of questionnaire and scale construction in Chapter 10, so we won't repeat them here. Also, Chapter 15 covered the topic of sampling, referring most often to survey situations.

Given that you already know how to prepare a questionnaire and select a sample of people to answer it, this chapter will focus on the options available to you for administering the questionnaire. How do you go about getting questionnaires answered?

As you'll see, sometimes it's appropriate to have respondents complete questionnaires themselves, and other times it's more appropriate to have interviewers ask the questions and record the answers. This latter technique can be used in face-to-face interviews or over the telephone. We'll examine each possibility and then compare their relative advantages and disadvantages.

The use of survey results has become an important aspect of survey research in recent years, and it's especially useful for students and others with scarce research funds. Let's begin by looking at the kinds of topics you could study using survey research.

Topics Appropriate to Survey Research

Although survey research can be used for exploratory or explanatory purposes, it is probably the best method for describing a population that is too large to observe directly. Careful probability sampling provides a group of respondents whose characteristics may be taken to reflect those of the larger population, and carefully constructed standardized questionnaires provide data in the same form from all respondents.

For example, surveys can be excellent vehicles for measuring attitudes and orientations in a large population. Public opinion polls are well-known examples of this use. Indeed, polls have become so prevalent that at times the public seems unsure what to think of them. Pollsters are criticized by those who don't think (or don't want to believe) that polls are accurate (candidates who are losing in polls often tell voters not to trust the polls).

The general attitude toward public opinion research is further complicated by scientifically unsound "surveys" that nonetheless capture our attention because of their topics or "findings." For example, cable news programs commonly ask viewers to respond online with their opinion on some controversial political issue. Whom do the respondents represent? Only those people who have the time and inclination to watch the program, have online access, and care enough about the issue to get out of their seats and go to their computers to participate in the poll. Moreover, if the cable news network is reputed to have a political bias, its viewers probably underrepresent people who don't share that bias. And if the broadcasters are biased, their bias may be reflected in the way they word their polling question. "Do you support the pro-abortion view that it's ethical to destroy the lives of unborn, unwanted children?"

Sometimes, people use the pretense of survey research for other, decidedly nonscientific purposes. For example, you may have received a telephone call indicating you've been selected for a survey only to find the first question was, "How would you like to make thousands of dollars a week right there in your own home?" Or you may have been told you could win a prize if you could name the president whose picture is on the penny. (Tell them it's Elvis.) Unfortunately, a few unscrupulous telemarketers try to prey on the general cooperation that people have given to survey researchers.

By the same token, some political parties and charitable organizations conduct phony "surveys." Often under the guise of collecting public opinion about some issue, respondents are ultimately asked to contribute money to support the sender's positions. Some political campaigns have produced another form of bogus survey called the "push poll." Here's what the American Association for

Public Opinion Polling had to say in condemning push polls:

> A "push poll" is a telemarketing technique in which telephone calls are used to canvass potential voters, feeding them false or misleading "information" about a candidate under the pretense of taking a poll to see how this "information" affects voter preferences. In fact, the intent is not to measure public opinion but to manipulate it—to "push" voters away from one candidate and toward the opposing candidate. Such polls defame selected candidates by spreading false or misleading information about them. The intent is to disseminate campaign propaganda under the guise of conducting a legitimate public opinion poll. (Bednarz, 1996)

In short, the labels *survey* and *poll* are sometimes misused. Done properly, however, survey research can be a useful tool of social inquiry. The key task for you is separating the wheat from the chaff. We trust this chapter will help you in that task. Let's turn now to the three major methods for getting responses to questionnaires.

EP 4, 9

» SELF-ADMINISTERED QUESTIONNAIRES

There are three main methods of administering survey questionnaires to a sample of respondents. This section will deal with the method in which respondents are asked to complete the questionnaires themselves—*self-administered questionnaires*—and the following sections will deal with surveys that are administered by staff interviewers in face-to-face encounters or by telephone.

Although the mail survey is the typical method used in self-administered studies, there are several other common methods. In some cases, it may be appropriate to administer the questionnaire to a group of respondents who have gathered at the same place at the same time. A survey of students taking an introductory social work course, for example, might be conducted in this manner during class. High school students might be surveyed during homeroom period.

Some experimentation has been conducted on the home delivery of questionnaires. A research worker delivers the questionnaire to the home of sample respondents and explains the study. The questionnaire is left for the respondent to complete and the researcher to pick up later.

Home delivery and the mail can be used in combination as well. Questionnaires can be mailed to families, and then research workers visit homes to pick up the questionnaires and check them for completeness. In just the opposite method, questionnaires have been hand delivered by research workers with a request that the respondents mail the completed questionnaires to the research office.

On the whole, when a research worker delivers the questionnaire, picks it up, or does both, the completion rate seems higher than for straightforward mail surveys. Additional experimentation with this method is likely to point to other techniques for improving completion while reducing costs.

Mail Distribution and Return

The basic method for collecting data through the mail has been to send a questionnaire accompanied by a letter of explanation and a self-addressed, stamped envelope for returning the questionnaire. The respondent is expected to complete the questionnaire, put it in the envelope, and return it. If, by any chance, you've received such a questionnaire and failed to return it, it would be valuable to recall the reasons you had for not returning it and keep them in mind any time you plan to send questionnaires to others.

A common reason for not returning questionnaires is that it's too much trouble. To overcome this problem, researchers have developed several ways to make returning them easier. For instance, a self-mailing questionnaire requires no return envelope: When the questionnaire is folded a particular way, the return address appears on the outside. The respondent therefore doesn't have to worry about losing the envelope.

More elaborate designs are available also. The university student questionnaire described later in this chapter was bound in a booklet with a special, two-panel back cover. Once the questionnaire was completed, the respondent needed only to fold out the extra panel, wrap it around the booklet, and seal the whole thing with the adhesive strip running along the edge of the panel. The foldout panel contained the return address and postage. The design was improved when the study was repeated a couple of years later. Both the front and the back cover had foldout panels: one for sending the questionnaire out and the other for getting it back—thus avoiding the use of envelopes altogether.

The point here is that anything you can do to make the job of completing and returning the questionnaire easier will improve your study. Imagine receiving a questionnaire that made no provisions for its return to the researcher. Suppose you had to (a) find an envelope, (b) write the address on it, (c) figure out how much postage was required, and (d) put stamps on the envelope. How likely is it that you would return the questionnaire?

A few brief comments are in order here on the postal options available to you. You have choices for mailing questionnaires and getting them returned. For outgoing mail, your choices are essentially between first-class postage and bulk rate. First class is more certain, but bulk rate is far cheaper. (Consult your local post office for rates and procedures.) On return mail, your choice is between postage stamps and business-reply permits. Here, the cost differential is more complicated. If you use stamps, you pay for them whether or not people return their questionnaires. With the business-reply permit, you pay for only those that are used, but you pay an additional surcharge of approximately a nickel per returned piece. This means that stamps are cheaper if a lot of questionnaires are returned, but business-reply permits are cheaper if fewer are returned—and you won't know in advance how many will be.

You will have many other considerations when choosing from among the postal options. Some researchers, for example, feel that stamps communicate more "humanness" and sincerity than bulk rate and business-reply permits. Other surveyors worry that respondents will steam off the stamps and use them for some purpose other than returning the questionnaires. Because both bulk rate and business reply permits require establishing accounts at the post office, you'll probably find stamps much easier in small surveys.

You may be wondering at this point why it's so important to make it easier for people to return their questionnaires? Didn't we say just a while ago that a survey of a smaller grouping of people can accurately portray the characteristics of a larger population? Yes, we said that. But we also said that the accuracy depends on whether the characteristics

of the smaller grouping really represent the characteristics of the population. To the extent that those who choose not to respond to a survey differ from respondents in important ways relevant to the research question, the representativeness of the survey suffers from nonresponse bias.

Imagine a survey of low-income social service recipients to assess their satisfaction with the services they received. Imagine further that a questionnaire is mailed to them with no return envelope or perhaps with an unstamped return envelope. The respondents in all likelihood would be an atypical and tiny proportion of the population whose extreme feelings (perhaps extremely favorable or extremely unfavorable) about the services are so strong that they are willing to go to the trouble and expense of completing and returning the questionnaire. They might also have more money than those who refuse to purchase a stamp. Consequently, the survey results would probably misrepresent the larger population since the folks with less money or less extreme feelings about the services would be much less likely to respond. One of the most important criteria, therefore, in distinguishing useful mailed surveys from misleading ones is whether sufficient steps are taken to maximize the number of people who respond.

Cover Letter

An important factor influencing response rates to mailed surveys is the quality of the cover letter that accompanies the questionnaire. The cover letter is usually what prospective respondents read first, so it should be constructed in a way that will motivate them to respond and alleviate any resistance they may have about participating in the survey.

To motivate individuals to respond, explain the purpose and importance of the survey in terms that the prospective respondent can understand. Obtain an endorsement of or sponsorship for the study from organizations or people who are esteemed by prospective respondents and then identify those organizations or people in the cover letter. Explain why each individual's response is important to the success of the study and to solving a problem that respondents care about. To alleviate resistance to participating, assure potential participants of the anonymity of their responses, explain how the sample was selected, and indicate how long it takes to complete the questionnaire (the quicker, the better).

Figure 16-1 is a cover letter that accompanied a survey of social workers. It illustrates the elements

FIGURE 16.1 A Sample Cover Letter

SCHOOL OF SOCIAL WORK

THE UNIVERSITY OF TEXAS AT AUSTIN

1925 San Jacinto Blvd. • Austin, Texas 78712-1203 • MC D3500 • Fax (512) 471-9600 • email utssw@utxvms.cc.utexas.edu

Dear Colleague,

A critical issue being debated in social work these days involves whether and how the evidence-based practice (EBP) model should be guiding our practice decisions. However, our profession lacks adequate information about the way practitioners view and use EBP and the factors associated with those views. If you would take about 15 to 20 minutes to complete the enclosed questionnaire and return it in the enclosed stamped self-addressed envelope, you will make an important contribution to a survey that seeks to enhance our profession's gathering of such information from practitioners.

The Department of Field Education at the Columbia University School of Social Work (CUSSW) is collaborating with us on the project, and for this reason, you are among 800 licensed clinical social workers selected randomly in four areas (New York, St. Louis, Texas, and Toronto) to be asked to participate in this survey. Your participation is voluntary and your responses are anonymous. Neither I nor anyone else will be able to identify from whom any completed questionnaire came. However, if you would complete and return the enclosed stamped self-addressed postcard, you will help us know whom to contact in follow-up mailings to colleagues who intend to participate but who need to be reminded. By mailing the postcard back separately from the questionnaire, the anonymity of your questionnaire responses will be maintained.

Please return your completed questionnaire and postcard as soon as possible. If you wish to discuss the information above or any concern you may have with this survey, please do not hesitate to contact me, Allen Rubin, Ph.D., at (512) 471-9218. If you have any questions about your rights as a research participant, complaints, concerns, or questions about the research, please contact the Institutional Review Board at Columbia University, 475 Riverside Drive, New York, NY 10115; Phone: (212) 870-3481; E-mail: askirb@columbia.edu.

Your current or future relationship with CUSSW will not be affected whether you choose to participate or not.

Your response is very important to this survey. The value of its results will depend on how many practitioners choose to respond.

Thank you for your attention and time.

Respectfully,

Allen Rubin, Ph.D.

Admissions and Academic Programs (512) 471-5457 • Dean's Office (512) 471-1937 • General Information (512) 471-5456 just discussed for motivating participation and reducing resistance.

Monitoring Returns

The mailing of questionnaires sets up a new research question that may prove valuable to the study. As questionnaires are returned, don't sit idly by; instead, undertake a careful recording of the varying rates of return among respondents.

An invaluable tool in this activity is a return rate graph. The day on which questionnaires were mailed is labeled "Day 1" on the graph, and every day thereafter the number of returned questionnaires is logged on the graph. It's usually best to compile two graphs. One shows the number returned each day—rising, then dropping. The second reports the cumulative number or percentage. In part, this activity is gratifying to the researchers, as they get to draw a picture of their successful data collection. More important, however, it is their guide to how the data collection is going. If follow-up mailings are planned, the graph provides a clue about when such mailings should be launched. (The dates of subsequent mailings should be noted on the graph.)

As completed questionnaires are returned, each should be opened, quickly looked over, and assigned an identification (ID) number. These numbers should be assigned serially as the questionnaires are returned—even if other ID numbers have already been assigned. Two examples should illustrate the important advantages of this procedure.

First, let's assume you're studying attitudes toward day care programs for preschool children. In the middle of your data collection, the news media begin to cover accusations of sexual abuse in day care programs. By knowing the date of that public disclosure and the dates when questionnaires have been received, you will be able to determine the effects of the disclosure.

Second, in a less sensational way, serialized ID numbers can be valuable in estimating nonresponse biases in the survey. Barring more direct tests of bias, you may wish to assume that those who failed to answer the questionnaire will be more like respondents who delayed answering than like those who answered right away. An analysis of questionnaires received at different points in the data collection might then be used to estimate sampling bias. For instance, if the level of client

satisfaction with agency services decreases steadily through the data collection, with those replying right away reporting higher satisfaction and those replying later reporting lower satisfaction, you might tentatively conclude that those who failed to answer at all have even lower satisfaction. Although it would not be advisable to make statistical estimates of bias in this fashion, you could take advantage of approximate estimates.

Follow-Up Mailings

If respondents have been identified for purposes of follow-up mailing, then such mailings should be prepared for as the questionnaires are returned. Follow-up mailings may be administered in several ways. In the simplest, nonrespondents are sent a letter of additional encouragement to participate. A better method, however, is to send a new copy of the survey questionnaire with the follow-up letter. If potential respondents have not returned their questionnaires after 2 or 3 weeks, the questionnaires probably have been lost or misplaced. Receiving a follow-up letter might encourage them to look for the original questionnaire, but if they can't find it easily, the letter may go for naught.

The methodological literature on follow-up mailings strongly suggests that it is an effective method for increasing return rates in mail surveys. In general, the longer a potential respondent delays replying, the less likely he or she is to do so at all. Properly timed follow-up mailings thus stimulate more responses.

The effects of follow-up mailings will be seen in the response rate curves that are recorded during data collection. The initial mailings will be followed by a rise and subsequent subsiding of returns; the follow-up mailings will spur a resurgence of returns, and more follow-ups will do the same. In practice, three mailings (an original and two follow-ups) seem the most efficient.

To reduce the postage costs of follow-up mailings, you can include a stamped, self-addressed postcard with the original mailing and perhaps with each subsequent mailing. The postcard can identify who has responded to the survey and who chooses not to participate in it. The person completing the postcard simply enters their name on it and then mails it back to you separately from the survey questionnaire. That way, the anonymity of the questionnaire is protected, and you will know not to send a follow-up mailing to those whose names are on the postcard. The box "Postcard Contents" shows what you can say on the postcard so that you will know not to send that person another mailing and yet not know whether they chose to participate in your survey.

The timing of follow-up mailings is also important. Here the methodological literature offers less precise guides, but in our experience 2 or 3 weeks is a reasonable interval between mailings. (This period might be increased by a few days if the mailing time—out and in—is more than 2 or 3 days.)

If the individuals in the survey sample are not identified on the questionnaires, it may not be possible to remail only to nonrespondents. In such a case, you should send your follow-up mailing to all members of the sample, thanking those who may have already participated and encouraging the participation of those who have not. (The case study reported in a later section of this chapter describes another method that may be used in an anonymous mail survey.)

Response Rates

A question that new survey researchers frequently ask concerns the response rate that should be achieved in a mail survey. The response rate is the number of people participating in a survey divided by the number of people who were asked to respond in the form of a percentage. The overall response rate is one guide to the representativeness of the sample respondents. If a high response rate is achieved, then there is less chance of significant nonresponse bias than if a low rate is achieved. In the past, response rates of at least 50% were usually considered adequate,

and response rates as high as 60% or 70% were considered good or very good.

Today, however, there is less agreement as to what constitutes an acceptable response rate. Some surveys with lower response rates can have value. For example, suppose an agency mails a questionnaire to all of its clients and on it clients are asked to indicate their level of satisfaction with agency services. Suppose further that the response rate is only 40% and that most respondents indicate that they are very dissatisfied and only a small minority of respondents say they are satisfied. Although agency staff members would not know the exact proportion of very dissatisfied clients, they would know that it is more than 20% (which is half of 40%). They therefore would be able to conclude that even if the nonrespondents are much more satisfied than the respondents (which may or may not be the case), the proportion of dissatisfied clients appears to be an important problem for the agency.

This hypothetical example, however, does not mean that the potential for nonresponse bias should be taken lightly. It is always an important consideration, even when response rates are relatively high. Thus, if the response rate to the above survey were 50% and most respondents indicated high levels of satisfaction, it would be quite risky to conclude that most clients overall were highly satisfied. Maybe the vast majority of the nonrespondents were dissatisfied and because of their dissatisfaction opted not to be bothered by responding to the survey.

When appraising the implications of a survey's response rate, you should bear in mind that a demonstrated lack of response bias is far more important than a high response rate. Suppose in the example with the 40% response rate the researchers had conducted a special follow-up effort with 10%

POSTCARD CONTENTS

Please complete this postcard and return it separately from the questionnaire. Doing so will let us know that you have either responded to the survey or chosen not to participate in it. In turn, that information will let us know not to send you a subsequent follow-up mailing. By mailing this postcard back separately, the anonymity of your questionnaire responses will be maintained.

I,_____, have either responded to the survey or choose not to participate in it.

Thank you!

of the nonrespondents and found that most of them were also very dissatisfied with the agency's services. Moreover, suppose that they found that the personal characteristics (age, ethnicity, presenting problem, and so on) of the nonrespondents were similar to those of the respondents. That follow-up effort and its findings would therefore suggest that although the survey's response rate was not high, its results do not appear to be highly vulnerable to a serious nonresponse bias.

Increasing Response Rates

As you might imagine, one of the more persistent discussions among survey researchers concerns ways to increase response rates and thus reducing the likelihood of nonresponse bias. Survey researchers have developed many techniques addressing this problem. We've already discussed some of them, such as preparing a cover letter that will motivate people to respond and let them know that it won't take much time to respond (10 to 15 minutes *at most* is recommended), making it easy for them to respond, and using follow-up mailings. Offering to share the survey results with those who respond might also help. In addition, some have tried paying people to respond. One problem with paying, of course, is that it can be expensive, but some imaginative alternatives have been used. Some researchers have said, "We want to get your two-cents' worth on some issues, and we're willing to pay"—enclosing two pennies. Another enclosed a quarter, suggesting that the respondent make some little child happy. Still others have enclosed paper money. More commonly, a raffle has been used as an incentive to respond, and the lucky respondent whose name is drawn wins a prize.

From an ethical standpoint, another concern about compensating survey respondents is that such incentives may be somewhat coercive and reduce the voluntary nature of participation. And if some respondents are inspired to participate while others are not, a bias may be introduced in the sample responding. This is not a settled issue for social researchers as a whole, and experimentation with incentives has proceeded. In a review of studies of this topic, Singer, Groves, and Corning (1999) found that with very few exceptions, response rates are increased by the use of incentives in mail surveys, face-to-face interviews, and telephone polls. Also, the authors found no evidence of negative effects on the quality of responses

collected. A decade later, Petrolia and Bhattacharjee (2009) reviewed past experience with incentives and conducted their own study. They confirmed that incentives increase response rates, and they found that prepaid incentives had a greater effect than those introduced later in the process.

A Case Study

The steps involved in the administration of a mail survey are many and can best be appreciated by examining an actual study. We'll thus conclude this section with a detailed description of a student survey conducted by the students in a graduate seminar in survey research methods at the University of Hawaii taught by one of us (Babbie). As you'll see shortly, the study does not represent the theoretical ideal for such studies, but in that regard it serves our purposes here all the better.

Approximately 1,100 students were selected from the computerized university registration list through a stratified, systematic sampling procedure. For each student selected, six self-adhesive mailing labels were printed by a computer.

By the time the questionnaires were ready for distribution, it became apparent that the research funds were inadequate to cover several mailings to the entire sample of 1,100 students (questionnaire printing costs were higher than anticipated). As a result, a systematic two-thirds sample of the mailing labels was chosen.

Earlier, it was decided to keep the survey anonymous to encourage more candid responses to some sensitive questions. (Later surveys of the same issues among the same population indicated that such anonymity was unnecessary.) Thus, the questionnaires would carry no identification of students on them. At the same time, the surveyors hoped to reduce the follow-up mailing costs by mailing only to nonrespondents.

To achieve both aims, a special postcard method was devised. Each student was mailed a questionnaire that carried no identifying marks, plus a postcard that was addressed to the research office—with one of the student's mailing labels affixed to the reverse side of the card. The introductory letter asked the student to complete and return the questionnaire—ensuring anonymity—and to return the postcard simultaneously. Receiving the postcard would reveal that the student had returned his or her questionnaire—without indicating *which* questionnaire it was. This procedure would then facilitate follow-up mailings.

The 32-page questionnaire was printed in booklet form (photo-offset and saddle-stitched). A three-panel cover permitted the questionnaire to be returned without an additional envelope.

A letter that introduced the study and its purposes was printed on the front cover of the booklet. It explained why the study was being conducted (to learn how students feel about a variety of issues), how students had been selected for the study, the importance of each student's responding, and the mechanics of returning the questionnaire.

Students were assured that their responses to the survey would be anonymous, and the postcard method was explained. A statement followed about the auspices under which the study was being conducted, and a telephone number was provided for those who might want more information about the study, although just five students called for such information.

By printing the introductory letter on the questionnaire, the surveyors avoided having to enclose a separate letter in the outgoing envelope, thereby simplifying the task of assembling mailing pieces.

The materials for the initial mailing were assembled in the following steps: (a) One mailing label for each student was stuck on a postcard, (b) another label was stuck on an outgoing manila envelope, and (c) one postcard and one questionnaire were placed in each envelope—with the name on the postcard double-checked with the name on the envelope.

These steps were accomplished with an assembly line procedure that involved several members of the research team. Although the procedure was organized in advance, actual practice determined the best allocation of tasks and people. The entire process was delayed several days while the first manila envelopes were exchanged for larger ones, a delay that could have been avoided if the surveyors had walked through the assembly process in advance.

The distribution of the survey questionnaires had been set up for a bulk rate mailing. Once the questionnaires had been stuffed into envelopes, they were grouped by ZIP codes, tied in bundles, and delivered to the post office.

Shortly after the initial mailing, questionnaires and postcards began arriving at the research office. Questionnaires were opened, looked over, and assigned identification numbers as described earlier

in this chapter. For every postcard received, the remaining labels for that student were destroyed.

After 2 or 3 weeks, all of the remaining mailing labels were used to organize a follow-up mailing. The assembly procedures described previously were repeated with one exception: A special, separate letter of appeal was included in the mailing piece. The new letter indicated that many students had returned their questionnaires already but that it was very important for everyone to do so.

As expected, the follow-up mailing stimulated more returns, and the logging procedures were continued. The returned postcards told the researchers which additional mailing labels to destroy. Unfortunately, time and financial pressures disallowed a third planned mailing, but the first two mailings had resulted in an overall return rate of 62%.

We trust this illustration will give you a fairly good sense of what's involved in the execution of mailed self-administered questionnaires—a very popular survey method. Let's turn now to another method of conducting surveys.

EP 4, 9

»» INTERVIEW SURVEYS

The interview is an alternative method of collecting survey data. Rather than ask respondents to read questionnaires and enter their own answers, researchers send interviewers to ask the questions orally and record respondents' answers. Interviewing is typically done in a face-to-face encounter, but telephone interviewing, as we'll see, follows most of the same guidelines. Also, most interview surveys require more than one interviewer, although you might undertake a small-scale interview survey yourself. Portions of this section will discuss methods for training and supervising a staff of interviewers who will assist you on a survey.

This section deals specifically with survey interviewing. In Chapter 18, we'll talk about the less-structured, in-depth interviews often conducted in qualitative research.

The Role of the Survey Interviewer

Having a questionnaire administered by an interviewer rather than by the respondent has several advantages. To begin, interview surveys typically attain higher response rates than mail surveys. A properly designed and executed interview survey ought to achieve a completion rate of at least 80% to 85%. (Federally funded surveys often require one of these response rates.) Respondents seem more reluctant to turn down an interviewer who is standing on their doorsteps than they are to throw away mail questionnaires.

Within the context of the questionnaire, the presence of an interviewer generally decreases the number of "Don't knows" and "No answers." If minimizing such responses is important to the study, then the interviewer can be instructed to probe for answers—for example, "If you had to pick one of the answers, which do you think would come closest to your feelings?" Interviewers can also provide a guard against confusing questionnaire items. If the respondent clearly misunderstands the intent of a question or indicates that he or she does not understand it, then the interviewer can clarify matters, thereby obtaining relevant responses. (Such clarifications must be strictly controlled, however, through formal specifications. See the section "Coordination and Control" below.)

Finally, the interviewer can observe as well as ask questions. For example, the interviewer can note the respondent's race if this is considered too delicate a question to ask. Similar observations can be made about the quality of the dwelling, the presence of various possessions, the respondent's ability to speak English, the respondent's general reactions to the study, and so forth. In one survey of students, respondents were given a short, self-administered questionnaire to complete—on sexual attitudes and behavior—during the course of the interview. While a student completed the questionnaire, the interviewer made detailed notes on the respondent's dress and grooming.

Before leaving this example, we raise an important ethical issue. Some researchers have objected that such practices violate the spirit of the agreement by which the respondent has allowed the interview. Although ethical issues seldom are open and shut in social research, you should be sensitive to that aspect of research. We have examined ethical issues in detail in Chapter 5.

By necessity, survey research is based on an unrealistic *stimulus–response theory* of cognition and behavior. We must assume that a questionnaire item will mean the same thing to every respondent, and every given response must mean the same when

given by different respondents. Although this is an impossible goal, survey questions are drafted to approximate the ideal as closely as possible.

The interviewer also must fit into this ideal situation. The interviewer's presence should not affect a respondent's perception of a question or the answer given. The interviewer, then, should be a neutral medium through which questions and answers are transmitted.

If this goal is successfully accomplished, then different interviewers will obtain exactly the same responses from a given respondent. (Recall earlier discussions of reliability.) This neutrality has a special importance in area samples. To save time and money, a given interviewer is typically assigned to complete all of the interviews in a particular geographic area—a city block or a group of nearby blocks. If the interviewer does anything to affect the responses obtained, then the bias thus interjected might be interpreted as a characteristic of that area.

Let's suppose that a survey is being done to determine attitudes toward low-cost housing to help in the selection of a site for a new government-sponsored development. An interviewer who is assigned to a given neighborhood might—through word or gesture—communicate his or her own distaste for low-cost housing developments. Respondents might therefore tend to give responses that generally agree with the interviewer's own position. The survey results would indicate that the neighborhood in question strongly resisted construction of the development in its area, although the apparent resistance might only reflect the interviewer's attitudes.

General Guidelines for Survey Interviewing

The manner in which interviews ought to be conducted will vary somewhat by survey population and also be affected somewhat by the nature of the survey content. Nevertheless, we can provide general guidelines that apply to most if not all interviewing situations.

Appearance and Demeanor As a general rule, the interviewer should dress in a fashion that is similar to that of the people who will be interviewed. A richly dressed interviewer will probably have difficulty getting good cooperation and responses from poorer respondents, and a poorly dressed interviewer will have similar difficulties with richer respondents.

To the extent that the interviewer's dress and grooming differ from those of the respondents, it should be in the direction of cleanliness and neatness in modest apparel. If cleanliness is not next to godliness, then it appears to be next to neutrality. Although middle-class neatness and cleanliness may not be accepted by all sectors of American society, they remain the primary norm and are more likely to be acceptable to the largest number of respondents.

Dress and grooming are typically regarded as signals of a person's attitudes and orientations. At the time this is being written, wearing torn jeans, green hair, and a razor-blade earring may communicate—correctly or incorrectly—that you are politically radical, sexually permissive, in favor of drug use, and so forth. Any of these impressions could bias responses or affect the willingness of people to be interviewed.

In demeanor, interviewers should be pleasant if nothing else. Because they will be prying into the respondents' personal lives and attitudes, they must communicate a genuine interest in getting to know each respondent without appearing to spy. They must be relaxed and friendly without being too casual or clinging. Good interviewers also are able to determine quickly the kind of person the respondent will feel most comfortable with and the kind of person with whom the respondent would most enjoy talking. There are two aspects of this. Clearly, the interview will be more successful if the interviewer can become that kind of person. Further, because respondents are asked to volunteer a portion of their time and to divulge personal information about themselves, they deserve the most enjoyable experience the researcher and interviewer can provide.

Familiarity with Questionnaire If an interviewer is unfamiliar with the questionnaire, then the study suffers and an unfair burden is placed on the respondent. The interview is likely to take more time than necessary and be generally unpleasant. Moreover, the interviewer cannot acquire familiarity by skimming through the questionnaire two or three times. It must be studied carefully, question by question, and the interviewer must practice reading it aloud.

Ultimately, the interviewer must be able to read the questionnaire items to respondents without error, without stumbling over words and phrases. A good model for interviewers is the actor who is reading lines in a play or motion picture. The lines must be read as naturally as though they constituted a natural conversation, but that conversation must follow exactly the language set down in the questionnaire.

By the same token, the interviewer must be familiar with the specifications prepared in conjunction with the questionnaire. Inevitably, some questions will not exactly fit a given respondent's situation, and the interviewer must determine how the question should be interpreted in that situation. The specifications provided to the interviewer should give adequate guidance in such cases, but the interviewer must know the organization and contents of the specifications well enough to refer to them efficiently. It would be better for the interviewer to leave a given question unanswered than spend 5 minutes searching through the specifications for clarification or trying to interpret the relevant instructions.

Following Question Wording Exactly Earlier we discussed the significance of question wording for the responses obtained. A slight change in the wording of a given question may lead a respondent to answer "Yes" rather than "No." Even though you have very carefully phrased your questionnaire items to obtain the information you need and to ensure that respondents will interpret items precisely as you intend, all this effort will be wasted if interviewers rephrase questions in their own words.

Recording Responses Exactly Whenever the questionnaire contains open-ended questions—that is, those that solicit the respondent's answer—it is critical that the interviewer record that answer exactly as given. No attempt should be made to summarize, paraphrase, or correct bad grammar.

This exactness is especially important because the interviewer will not know how the responses are to be coded before processing. Indeed, the researchers may not know the coding until they have read a hundred or so responses. For instance, the questionnaire might ask respondents how they feel about the traffic situation in their community. One respondent might answer that there are too many cars on the roads and that something should be done to limit their numbers. Another might say that more roads are needed. If the interviewer recorded these two responses with the same summary—"congested traffic"—the researchers would be unable to take advantage of the important differences in the original responses.

Sometimes, the respondent may be so inarticulate that the verbal response is too ambiguous to permit interpretation. However, the interviewer may be able to understand the respondent's intention through his or her gestures or tone. In such a situation, the exact verbal response should still be recorded, but the interviewer should add marginal comments that give both the interpretation and the reasons for arriving at it.

More generally, researchers can use marginal comments to explain aspects of the response that are not conveyed in the verbal recording, such as the respondent's apparent uncertainty in answering, anger, embarrassment, and so forth. In each case, however, the exact verbal response should also be recorded.

Probing for Responses Sometimes, respondents will answer a question inappropriately. For example, the question may present an attitudinal statement and ask the respondent to strongly agree, agree somewhat, disagree somewhat, or strongly disagree. The respondent, however, may reply, "I think that's true." The interviewer should follow this reply with a probe, a nondirective phrase or question to solicit a more complete answer. An effective one in this example would be, "Would you say you strongly agree or agree somewhat?" If necessary, interviewers can explain that they must check one or the other of the categories provided. If the respondent adamantly refuses to choose, the interviewer should write in the exact response given by the respondent.

Probes are more frequently required in eliciting responses to open-ended questions. For instance, in response to a question about traffic conditions, the respondent might simply reply, "Pretty bad." The interviewer could obtain an elaboration on this response through a variety of probes. Sometimes the best probe is silence; if the interviewer sits quietly with pencil poised, the respondent will probably fill the pause with additional comments. (This technique is used effectively by journalists.) Appropriate verbal probes might be, "How is that?" or "In what ways?" Perhaps the most generally useful probe is, "Anything else?"

Frequently, it is necessary to probe for answers that will be sufficiently informative for analytic purposes. In every case, however, such probes must be completely neutral. The probe cannot affect the nature of the subsequent response in any way. Whenever you anticipate that a given question may require probing for appropriate responses, you should present one or more useful probes next to the question in the questionnaire. This practice has two important advantages. First, you will have more time to devise the best, most neutral probes. Second, all interviewers will use the same probes whenever they are needed. Thus, even if the probe is not perfectly neutral, all respondents will be presented with the same probe. This is the same logical guideline discussed for question wording. Although a question should not be loaded or biased, it is essential that every respondent be presented with the same question, even a biased one.

Coordination and Control

Most interview surveys require the assistance of several interviewers. In the large-scale surveys, of course, such interviewers are hired and paid for their work. As a student researcher, you might find yourself recruiting friends to assist you. Whenever more than one interviewer is involved in a survey, their efforts must be carefully controlled. There are two aspects of this control: training interviewers and supervising them after they begin work.

The interviewer training session should begin with a description of the study. Even though the interviewers may be involved only in the project's data collection phase, they will find it useful to understand what will be done with the interviews they conduct and what purpose will be served. Morale and motivation are usually low when interviewers don't know what's going on.

The training on how to interview should begin with a discussion of general guidelines and procedures, such as those discussed earlier in this chapter. Then you should turn to the questionnaire itself. The whole group should go through the questionnaire together—question by question. Do not simply ask if anyone has questions about the first page of the questionnaire. Read the first question aloud, explain its purpose, and then answer or address the interviewers' questions or comments. Once all of their questions and comments have been handled, go on to the next question in the questionnaire.

It's always a good idea to prepare what are called specifications to accompany an interview questionnaire. Specifications are explanatory and clarifying comments about how to handle difficult or confusing situations that may occur with specific questions in the questionnaire. When you are drafting the questionnaire, try to think of all the problem cases that might arise—the bizarre circumstances that might make a question difficult to answer. The survey specifications should provide detailed guidelines on how to handle such situations. As an example, such a simple matter as age might present problems. Suppose a respondent says that he or she will be 25 next week. The interviewer might not be sure whether to take the respondent's current age or the nearest one. The specifications for that question should explain what should be done. (Probably, you would specify that age as of last birthday should be recorded in all cases.)

If you have prepared a set of specifications, go over them with the interviewers when you go over the individual questions in the questionnaire. Make sure your interviewers fully understand the specifications as well as the questions themselves and the reasons for them.

This portion of the interviewer training is likely to generate many troublesome questions from your interviewers: "What should I do if … ?" Never give a quick answer. If you have specifications, be sure to show how the solution to the problem could be determined from the specifications. If you do not have them prepared, then show how the preferred handling of the situation fits within the general logic of the question and the purpose of the study. Giving offhand, unexplained answers to such questions will only confuse the interviewers, and they will probably not take their work seriously. If you don't know the answer to a question, admit it and ask for time to decide on the best answer. Then think out the situation carefully and be sure to give all of the interviewers your answer and explain your reasons.

Once you have gone through the whole questionnaire, conduct one or two demonstration interviews in front of everyone. Preferably, you should interview someone else. Realize that your interview will be a model for those you are training, so make it good. It would be best, moreover, if the demonstration interview were done as realistically as possible. Do not pause during the demonstration to point out how you have handled a complicated situation: Handle it and then explain later. It's irrelevant if the person you are

interviewing gives real answers or takes on some hypothetical identity for the purpose as long as the answers are consistent.

After the demonstration interviews, pair off your interviewers and have them practice on each other. When they have completed the questionnaire, have them reverse roles and do it over again. Interviewing is the best training for interviewing. As your interviewers practice on each other, wander around and listen in on the practices so that you'll know how well they are doing. Once the practice is completed, everyone in the group should discuss their experiences and ask any other questions they may have.

The final stage of the training for interviewers should involve "real" interviews. Have your interviewers conduct questioning under actual final survey conditions. You may want to assign them people to interview or perhaps allow them to pick people themselves. Do not have them practice on people you have selected in your sample, however. After each interviewer has completed three to five interviews, have him or her check back with you. Look over the completed questionnaires to see if there is any evidence of misunderstanding. Again, answer any questions that individual interviewers may have. Once you are convinced that a given interviewer knows what to do, assign actual interviews—using the sample you have selected for the study.

You must continue to supervise the work of interviewers over the course of the study. Don't let them conduct more than 20 or 30 interviews without seeing you. You might assign an interviewer 20 interviews, have him or her bring back those questionnaires when they are completed, look them over, and assign another 20 or so. Although that may seem overly cautious, you must continually protect yourself against misunderstandings that may not be evident early in the study.

If you are the only interviewer in your study, then these comments may not seem relevant to you—but that's not wholly the case. You would be advised, for example, to prepare specifications for potentially troublesome questions in your questionnaire. Otherwise, you run the risk of making ad hoc decisions during the course of the study that you will later regret or forget. Also, the emphasis that has been placed on practice applies just as much to the one person project as to the complex, funded survey with a large interviewing staff.

» TELEPHONE SURVEYS

For years, telephone surveys had a bad reputation among professional researchers. These surveys are limited by definition to people who have telephones. Years ago, then, this method produced a substantial social class bias by excluding poor people from the surveys. This was vividly demonstrated by the *Literary Digest* fiasco of 1936. Even though voters were contacted by mail, the sample was partially selected from telephone subscribers—who were hardly typical in a nation that was still in the midst of the Great Depression.

Over time, however, that earlier form of class bias substantially diminished, and telephone surveys became very popular. Telephone surveys have many advantages. Probably the greatest advantages are money and time, in that order. In a face-to-face, household interview, you may drive several miles to a respondent's home, find no one there, return to the research office, and drive back the next day—possibly finding no one there again. It's cheaper and quicker to let your fingers make the trips.

When interviewing by telephone, you can dress any way you please without affecting the answers respondents give. And sometimes respondents will be more honest in giving socially disapproved answers if they don't have to look you in the eye. Similarly, it may be possible to probe into more sensitive areas, though that is not necessarily the case. (People are, to some extent, more suspicious when they can't see the person asking them questions—perhaps a consequence of "surveys" aimed at selling magazine subscriptions and time-share condominiums.)

Realize, however, that people can communicate a lot about themselves over the phone, even though they can't be seen. For example, researchers worry about the impact of an interviewer's name (particularly if ethnicity is relevant to the study) and debate the ethics of having all interviewers use vanilla "stage names," such as Smith or Jones. (Female interviewers sometimes ask permission to do this to avoid subsequent harassment from men they interview.)

Telephone surveys can give you greater control over data collection if several interviewers are engaged in the project. If all of the interviewers are calling from the research office, then they can get clarification from the person in charge whenever the inevitable problems occur. Alone in the boondocks, an interviewer may have to wing it between weekly visits with the interviewing supervisor.

Another important factor involved in the use of telephone surveys has to do with personal safety. Dillman (1978) describes the situation this way:

> Interviewers must be able to operate comfortably in a climate in which strangers are viewed with distrust and must successfully counter respondents' objections to being interviewed. Increasingly, interviewers must be willing to work at night to contact residents in many households. In some cases, this necessitates providing protection for interviewers working in areas of a city in which a definite threat to the safety of individuals exists. (p. 4)

Concerns for safety thus hamper face-to-face interviews in two ways. First, potential respondents may refuse to be interviewed, fearing the stranger interviewer. Second, the interviewers themselves may be in danger. All this is made even worse by the possibility of the researchers being sued for huge sums if anything goes wrong.

Telephone interviewing still has problems. As we've already mentioned, the method is hampered by the proliferation of bogus "surveys" that are actually sales campaigns disguised as research. If you have any questions about any such call you receive, by the way, ask the interviewer directly whether you've been selected for a survey only or if a sales "opportunity" is involved. It's also a good idea, if you have any doubts, to get the interviewer's name, phone number, and company. Hang up if they refuse to provide that information.

A related sampling problem involves unlisted numbers. If the survey sample is selected from the pages of a local telephone directory, then it would omit all of those people—typically, folks who only have cell phones and richer people who request that their numbers not be published. This potential bias has been erased through a technique that has advanced telephone sampling substantially: *random-digit dialing*.

Imagine that you were to select a set of seven-digit telephone numbers at random. Even those whose numbers were unlisted would have the same chance of selection as those who were in the directory. However, if you were to start dialing randomly selected numbers, a high proportion of those would turn out to be "not in service," government offices, commercial enterprises, and so on. Fortunately, it is possible to obtain ranges of numbers that are (mostly) active residential numbers. Selecting a set of those numbers at random will provide a representative sample of residential households. As a consequence, random-digit dialing is a standard procedure in telephone surveys.

The ease with which people can hang up, of course, is another shortcoming of telephone surveys. Once you've been let inside someone's home for an interview, they are unlikely to order you out of the house in the middle of the interview. It's much easier to terminate a telephone interview abruptly, saying something like, "Whoops! Someone's at the door. I gotta go," or "OMIGOD! The pigs are eating my Volvo!" (That sort of evasion is much harder to fake when you're sitting in their living room.)

The Influence of Technological Advances

Another potential problem for telephone interviewing is the rapidly changing technology affecting telephone usage. As Dillman (2014) has observed, technological advances have reduced response rates and exacerbated sampling problems in telephone surveys. For example, a variety of mechanisms such as caller ID, answering machines, and voice mail make it easy to avoid answering unknown callers. Also, many households have replaced or supplemented their landlines with cell phones, often with a separate cell phone for each household member. When people move from one area code to another, they often keep the same cell phone number, complicating the process of random digit dialing and obtaining a representative sample from a particular neighborhood, city, state, or other specific geographical area. Moreover, people who use cell phones only, and no landline, tend to be younger, poorer, ethnic minorities and to have different lifestyles than people who still use landlines (Blumberg & Luke, 2013; Christian, Keeter, Purcell, & Smith, 2010).

In addition, the Telephone Consumer Protection Act of 1991 put limitations on telephone solicitations and, because calls to a cell phone may incur an expense to the target of the call (depending on their service plan), the Act made it illegal for automatic dialing systems (e.g., the robocalls alerting you to a special sale on widgets) to call cell phones (FCC, 2012). But where does this leave survey researchers, who aren't selling anything? Although efforts are underway to officially exempt research projects from that ruling, the American Association for Public Opinion Research (AAPOR, 2010) advised members that:

> To ensure compliance with this federal law, in the absence of express prior consent from a sampled cell phone respondent, telephone research call centers should have their interviewers *manually dial cell phone numbers* (i.e., where a human being physically touches the numerals on the telephone to dial the number).

Some technological advances have facilitated telephone interviewing. One such advance is computer-assisted telephone interviewing (CATI). This method is increasingly used by academic, government, and commercial survey researchers. Here's a general example of what using CATI can look like.

Imagine an interviewer wearing a telephone headset, sitting in front of a computer monitor. The central computer has been programmed to select a telephone number at random and dials it. On the video screen is an introduction ("Hello, my name is…") and the first question to be asked ("Could you tell me how many people live at this address?").

When the respondent answers the phone, the interviewer says hello, introduces the study, and asks the first question displayed on the screen. When the respondent answers the question, the interviewer types that answer into the computer terminal—either the verbatim response to an open-ended question or the code category for the appropriate answer to a closed-ended question. The answer is immediately stored in the computer. The second question appears on the video screen and is asked, and the answer is entered into the computer. Thus, the interview continues.

In addition to the obvious advantages in terms of data collection, CATI automatically prepares the data for analysis; in fact, the researcher can begin analyzing the data before the interviewing is complete, thereby gaining an advanced view of how the analysis will turn out.

It is also possible to go a step further than computer-*assisted* interviews. With the innovation of so-called robo-polls, the entire interview is conducted by a programmed recording that can interpret the spoken answers of respondents. This discussion may remind you of the robo-calls in which a recorded voice presents a political or commercial message once you answer your phone. Robo-polls go a step further through the use of *interactive voice recognition (IVR)*. The computer is programmed to interpret the respondent's answers, record them, and determine how to continue the interview appropriately.

Clearly this method is cost-effective by cutting out the labor cost of hiring human beings as interviewers. It has been viewed with suspicion and/or derision by some survey researchers, but in its evaluation of the 2008 primary polling, the American Association of Public Opinion Research (AAPOR) reported no difference in the accuracy of results produced by CATI or IVR (AAPOR, 2009).

Technological changes affecting telephone usage are happening so rapidly that studies of the impact of one technological advance can become outdated upon publication because by that time the advance discussed in the published study has been replaced by another advance. Consequently, if you are considering conducting a telephone survey, we advise you to do an online search to learn of any advances and their implications that emerge in the near future. As we will recommend in regard to online surveys, two excellent sources for staying abreast of these developments are: (a) the American Association for Public Opinion Research (http://www.aapor.org/AAPORKentico/default.aspx); and (b) the online journal *Survey Practice* (www.surveypractice.org).

EP 4, 9

» ONLINE SURVEYS

An increasingly popular method of survey research involves the use of the Internet and the World Wide Web—two of the most far-reaching developments of the late 20th century. Online surveys have the advantage of being quickly and inexpensively sent to very large numbers of prospective respondents anywhere in the world. Moreover, survey response data are automatically entered for computer processing, eliminating the need for manual data entry and making possible a quick online tabulation of results. Online survey tools, such as SurveyMonkey™, can check and verify whether respondents are skipping

an item or in other ways responding inappropriately to it while they are taking the survey and then prompt them to correct any omission or other mistake before proceeding to the next item.

While this section will examine various aspects of online survey research, you should be forewarned that this technique is developing so quickly that new innovations will surely have arisen by the time this book reaches your hands. To stay abreast of these developments, your best single source is the American Association for Public Opinion Research (AAPOR) and two key publications: *Public Opinion Quarterly* (POQ) and the online journal *Survey Practice* (www.surveypractice.org). While neither of these is dedicated to online research solely, an increasing percentage of their articles address that topic. University survey research offices such as those at the University of Michigan, NORC at the University of Chicago, and many other universities around the globe are very active in developing this new technique. Similarly, commercial research firms such as Pew, Harris, and others are equally involved.

One immediate objection that many social researchers make to online surveys concerns representativeness: Will the people who can be surveyed online be representative of meaningful populations, such as all U.S. adults, all voters, and so on? This was the criticism that researchers raised earlier with regard to surveys via fax and telephone. This criticism is particularly relevant to social work surveys of people who are poor or elderly. People who use the Internet and are most apt to respond to online surveys are likely to be younger, more affluent, and more highly educated than the rest of your target population. However, this problem may be waning as more and more people gain access to the Internet and use online devices to do so.

Online Devices

At the outset, online surveys were aimed at users of personal computers, most typically desktop models. More recently, tablets and smartphones have been rapidly gaining in computing power, and increasingly they have been used as vehicles for online surveys. Respondents probably led researchers in this innovation. As respondents attempted, sometimes unsuccessfully, to use smart phones to complete questionnaires designed for desktop computers, survey researchers realized the need and potential for adapting their questionnaires to a variety of devices that may be used by respondents. Screen size, of course, is a major concern, but so are the different navigation systems used by different devices.

Tom Wells, Justin Bailey, and Michael Link (2013) have offered an excellent "state of the art" review of tablet-based surveys at present. Be clear, however, that this aspect of survey research is evolving faster than anyone imagined.

Instrument Design

Over the years, members of industrialized nations have become familiar with the format and process of self-administered questionnaires, but, as just mentioned, the web presents a new challenge for many. The initial temptation, of course, is to simply import a mail questionnaire to a web survey. However, there are two problems with this. First, the mail format doesn't necessarily fit on a computer screen, let alone on a tablet or smartphone. On the other hand, the e-devices offer possibilities unavailable to words on paper. We are unable to list those possibilities for you now, since they are still being developed, but we can connect you with some of the possibilities and challenges currently underway.

For example, researchers like Roger Tourangeau, Mick P. Couper, and Frederick G. Conrad (2013) were concerned about whether the placement of answers in a list would affect respondents' choices. Their conclusion, based on the review of several studies, is that "Up means good." When several opinion choices are arranged vertically, respondents are more likely to choose the top choice.

Husser and Fernandez (2013) examined whether it was better to have an online respondent enter numerical answers by clicking the answer, typing it, or drag along a scale to indicate the answer. With a limited number of responses, clicking radio buttons was fastest, but a long list of possible answers makes dragging the sliding scale more practical.

Those regularly using the Internet are familiar with emoticons such as the "smiley face." While these graphics could be printed in a mail questionnaire, they seem more at home online. Matthias Emde and Marek Fuchs (2012) undertook an experiment to determine the possibility of using a range of faces (sad to happy) in place of radio buttons labeled from bad to good. They concluded that this format change did not affect responses. Thus,

it might be chosen on purely aesthetic grounds. There is no reason not to make surveys appealing.

Malakhoff and Jans (2011) explore some of the more advanced possibilities for online survey research. While the survey interview involves a person showing up on your doorstep or a voice coming over your phone, they suggest an animated avatar might be used to conduct an online interview, and they have begun experimenting with sex and other differences for the animated interviewer. The avatar interviewer can be programmed to change facial expressions based on the respondent's answers. Going one step (or several) further, it would be possible to use the respondents' webcams to monitor their facial expressions and log those data along with the answers provided verbally.

Improving Response Rates

Online surveys appear to have response rates approximately comparable to mail surveys, according to a large-scale study of Michigan State University students (Kaplowitz, Hadlock, and Levine 2004), especially when the online survey is accompanied by a postcard reminder encouraging respondents to participate. While producing a comparable response rate, the cost of an online survey is substantially less than that of a conventional mail survey. The cost of paper, printing, and postage alone can constitute a large expense in the latter.

In another study of ways to improve response rates in online surveys, Stephen Porter and Michael Whitcomb (2003) found that some of the techniques effective in mail surveys, such as personalizing the appeal or varying the apparent status of the researcher, had little or no impact in the new medium. At the same time, specifying that the respondents had been specially selected for the survey and setting a deadline for participation did increase response rates.

The relative youth of online surveys make them a fertile ground for innovation and experimentation. For example, survey researchers have often worried that respondents to self-administered questionnaires might spend more of their attention on the first responses in a list, skipping quickly over those farther down. To test this possibility, Mirta Galesic and colleagues (2008) employed a special eye-tracking computer monitor that unobtrusively followed respondents' eye movements as they completed an online survey. The result: respondents did,

HOW TO DO IT: CONDUCTING AN ONLINE SURVEY

If you're interested in testing the waters of online surveys, Survey Monkey™ gives you one opportunity to try your hand at this emerging technique. At this writing, you can experiment with a limited version of the online survey program at no charge. Visit www.surveymonkey.com/ and click "Take a Tour" and select "Create Surveys" from the drop-down menu to get started.

The program is very user-friendly with regard to designing questionnaire items. Then, after you enter the e-mail addresses of your intended respondents, they'll receive an e-mail invitation to visit the survey web page and participate.

The free, beginner package will also provide you with a basic analysis of the survey results.

You can use Survey Monkey with a limited number of friends to sharpen your survey research skills, and/or you can use it for a full-blown, professional study. In fact, it is sometimes used by professional researchers and research associations.

in fact, spend more time on the early choices, sometimes failing to read the whole list before clicking their choice on the screen.

The years ahead will see many more experiments aimed at improving the effectiveness of online surveys.

You are reading this discussion at an exciting time, when online survey methodology is evolving. For example, in an effort to increase response rates for web surveys, Miller and Dillman (2012) achieved modest increases by sending respondents an email reminder to participate in the survey. Since a large percentage of cell phone owners have smart phones, they were offered the opportunity to complete the survey on those devices instead of going to a computer. As the authors point out, further experimentation with this technique will require tailoring survey formats to accommodate smart phones as discussed earlier. The Pew Center (Smith, 2013) estimates that more than 3 American adults in 5 own a smartphone and as many as 9 in 10 own some kind of cellular phone.

For now, Mick P. Couper's *Designing Effective Web Surveys* (2008) offers a comprehensive guide to this new technique, based on what we have learned about it to date. If you are interested in experimenting with web surveys on your own, see the box "How to Do It: Conducting an Online Survey."

›› MIXED-MODE SURVEYS

In Chapter 4 and elsewhere throughout this book we have extolled the value of mixed methods, primarily focusing on combining quantitative and qualitative methods. That value applies to surveys no less than to other quantitative methods. Surveys can mix different quantitative methods, as well, and when they do they are called mixed-mode surveys. For example, recognizing the limitations inherent in each survey modality—that is, mail, face-to-face, telephone, and online surveys—researchers can combine these modalities. For example, to try to improve response rates, targeted survey recipients can be contacted by more than one modality and given the option of responding via the modality that they choose.

Dillman (2014) identifies three overarching strategies for mixing survey modes:

1. Multiple *contact* modes/one response mode: With this approach, you would use various modes (email, telephone, postal mail, etc.) to contact targeted survey recipients and encourage them to participate in the survey by the single response mode you have chosen (i.e., Internet, mail, telephone). This mode is intended to reduce coverage error, such as when you don't have email addresses for every intended participant.

2. Multiple *response* modes/one contact mode: With this approach, you are less concerned about being able to contact people than with offering the ones whom you do contact the opportunity to choose the mode they prefer for responding. The idea here is that enabling people to respond in the way they prefer might improve response rates.

3. Combined *contact/response* mode: This approach combines the advantages of the above two approaches and thus offers the best chances for increasing response rates and the representativeness of your sample.

In addition to increasing response rates and sample representativeness, Dillman suggests that mixed-mode surveys can lower costs, improve timeliness, and reduce measurement error. Costs can be lowered by using the more expensive modes only for those who don't respond initially to the less expensive mode. Timeliness might be improved if respondents have the option of responding in the way that is most convenient for them. Similarly, enabling people to respond in the way they prefer might enhance the carefulness of their responses and their willingness to be candid and unbiased regarding sensitive questions.

EP 4, 9

» COMPARISON OF DIFFERENT SURVEY METHODS

Now that we've seen several ways to collect survey data, let's take a moment to compare them directly. Self-administered questionnaires are generally cheaper and quicker than face-to-face interview surveys. These considerations are likely to be important for an unfunded student wishing to undertake a survey for a term paper or thesis. Moreover, if you use the self-administered mail format, it costs no more to conduct a national survey than a local one of the same sample size. In contrast, a national interview survey using face-to-face contacts would cost far more than a local one. Also, mail surveys typically require a small staff: One person can conduct a reasonable mail survey alone, although you shouldn't underestimate the work involved. Further, respondents are sometimes reluctant to report controversial or deviant attitudes or behaviors in interviews but are willing to respond to an anonymous self-administered questionnaire.

Interview surveys also have many advantages. For instance, they generally produce fewer incomplete questionnaires. Although respondents may skip questions in a self-administered questionnaire, interviewers are trained not to do so. Computers offer a further check on this in CATI surveys. Interview surveys, moreover, have typically achieved higher completion rates than self-administered ones.

Although self-administered questionnaires may deal with sensitive issues more effectively, interview surveys are definitely more effective in dealing with complicated ones. Prime examples would be the enumeration of household members and the determination of whether a given household address contains more than one housing unit. Although the concept of "housing unit" has been refined and standardized by the Bureau of the Census and interviewers can be trained to deal with the concept, it's extremely difficult to communicate in a self-administered questionnaire. This advantage of interview surveys pertains more generally to all complicated contingency questions.

With interviewers, it is possible to conduct a survey based on a sample of addresses or phone numbers rather than on names. An interviewer can arrive at an assigned address or call the assigned number, introduce the survey, and even—following instructions—choose the appropriate person at that address to respond to the survey. By contrast, self-administered questionnaires addressed to "occupant" receive a notoriously low response.

Finally, interviewers who question respondents face-to-face are able to make important observations aside from responses to questions asked in the interview. In a household interview, they may note the characteristics of the neighborhood, the dwelling unit, and so forth. They may also note characteristics of the respondents or the quality of their interaction with the respondents—whether the respondent had difficulty communicating, was hostile, seemed to be lying, and so forth. Another advantage of face-to-face interviews is that in countries with relatively low literacy rates in some areas people who would not be able to read a self-administered questionnaire can respond to an interview.

The chief advantages of telephone surveys over those conducted face-to-face are a matter of primarily time and money. Telephone interviews are much cheaper and can be mounted and executed quickly. Also, interviewers are safer when interviewing residents in high-crime areas. Moreover, the impact of the interviewers on responses is somewhat lessened when they can't be seen by the respondents.

Online surveys have many of the strengths and weaknesses of mail surveys. Once the available software has been further developed, they are likely to be substantially cheaper. An important weakness, however, lies in the difficulty of assuring that respondents to an online survey will be representative of some more general population.

As respondents become more accustomed to online surveys, they may be able to ease some of the problems that have plagued telephone surveys: allowing for longer and more complex surveys, for example. Online respondents, like those completing mail questionnaires, will have more time to reflect on their responses. Surely, online survey methodology will continue to evolve as previously experienced with other survey techniques.

Clearly, each survey method has its place in social research. Ultimately, you must balance the advantages and disadvantages of the different methods in relation to your research needs and resources, as shown in Table 16-1.

» STRENGTHS AND WEAKNESSES OF SURVEY RESEARCH

Like other modes of observation in social scientific research, surveys have special strengths and weaknesses. It is important to know these in determining whether the survey format is appropriate to your research goals.

Surveys are particularly useful when we describe the characteristics of a large population. A carefully selected probability sample, in combination with a standardized questionnaire, offers the possibility of making refined descriptive assertions about a student body, a city, a nation, or other large population. Surveys determine unemployment rates, voting intentions, and the like with uncanny accuracy. Although examining official documents such as marriage, birth, and death records can provide equal accuracy for a few topics, no other method of observation can provide this general capability.

Surveys—especially the self-administered variety—make very large samples feasible. Surveys of 2,000 people are not unusual. A large number of cases is important for both descriptive and explanatory analyses. Whenever several variables are to be analyzed simultaneously, it is essential to have a large number of cases.

Because surveys make large samples feasible, their findings may be more generalizable than the findings of experiments. (As we mentioned earlier, experiments in social work typically are unable to obtain probability samples.) This advantage in generalizability, however, is offset by the limited ability of surveys to show causality. For example, a survey of the moods of thousands of elderly people can tell us in general whether elderly people with pets have better moods than elderly people without pets. It wouldn't, however, be able to sort out whether having pets caused their moods to improve or whether being less depressed in the first place is what leads to getting a pet.

The survey would also enable us to analyze multiple variables simultaneously; thus, we could see whether the relationship between mood and pets applied to elderly people of different ethnicities, different income levels, different living arrangements, different levels of dependency, and so on. But we would still be uncertain as to causality. By conducting a longitudinal survey—for example, assessing the same elderly folks' moods and pet situations over time—we would be in a better position to speculate about causality. In other words, we could ascertain whether the moods were changing before or after the pets were obtained, although we would still have less confidence regarding causal inferences than in an experiment. Despite the uncertainty about causality, the high level of generalizability of the findings to the population as a whole, as well as to various subgroups of the population in their natural settings, is an advantage of surveys that few experiments can offer.

In one sense, surveys are flexible. Many questions may be asked on a given topic, giving you considerable flexibility in your analyses. Although experimental designs may require you to commit yourself in advance to a particular operational definition of a concept, surveys let you develop operational definitions from actual observations.

Finally, standardized questionnaires have an important strength in regard to measurement generally. Earlier chapters have discussed the ambiguous nature of most concepts. For example, one person's religiosity is quite different from another's. Although you must be able to define concepts in ways that are most relevant to your research goals, you may not find it easy to apply the same definitions uniformly to all respondents. The survey researcher is bound to this requirement by having to ask exactly the same questions of all respondents and having to impute the same intent to all respondents giving a particular response.

Survey research has weaknesses, though. First, the requirement for standardization just mentioned often seems to result in the fitting of round pegs into

TABLE 16.1 Advantages and Disadvantages of Different Survey Methods

Survey Type	Advantages	Disadvantages
Mail surveys	• Cheaper and quicker than interviews • Large samples • Anonymity facilitates responses regarding sensitive areas	• More expensive and time consuming than online surveys • Lower response rates than face-to-face interviews
Online surveys	• Less expensive • Less time consuming • Largest samples • Automatic data entry • Tools to check and correct inappropriate responses • Growth in public use of Internet • Anonymity facilitates responses regarding sensitive areas	• Representativeness (especially the poor and elderly) • Lower response rates than face-to-face interviews • Rapid technological advances in online devices such as smart phones and tablets present challenges regarding instrument design
Face-to-face interviews	• High response rates • Fewer "don't knows" • Fewer missing answers • Opportunity to clarify confusing items • Opportunity to observe • Opportunity to probe	• More expensive and time consuming • Lack of anonymity can impede responses regarding sensitive areas • Interviewer safety
Telephone surveys	• Less expensive and less time consuming than face-to-face interviews • Interviewer's physical appearance won't bias respondents • Fewer "don't knows" • Fewer missing answers • Opportunity to clarify confusing items • Opportunity to probe • Interviewer safety • Opportunity to get supervision during interview • Can be computer assisted	• Unlisted numbers* • Ease of hanging up • Rapid technological advances in cell phone usage, caller ID, and so on present challenges regarding response rates and representativeness of specific geographical areas

*Random-digit dialing can alleviate this problem.

square holes. Standardized questionnaire items often represent the least common denominator in assessing people's attitudes, orientations, circumstances, and experiences. By designing questions that will be at least minimally appropriate to all respondents, you may miss what is most appropriate to many respondents. In this sense, surveys often appear superficial in their coverage of complex topics. Although this problem can be partly offset through sophisticated analyses, it is inherent in survey research.

Similarly, survey research can seldom deal with the *context* of social life. Although questionnaires can provide information in this area, the survey researcher can seldom develop the feel for the total life situation in which respondents are thinking and acting that, say, the participant observer can (see Chapter 19).

Although surveys are flexible in the sense mentioned earlier, they are inflexible in other ways. Studies that use direct observation can be modified as field conditions warrant, but surveys typically require that an initial study design remain unchanged throughout. As a qualitative field researcher, for example, you can become aware of an important new variable operating in the phenomenon you are studying and begin to observe it carefully. The survey researcher would likely be unaware of the new variable's importance and could do nothing about it in any event.

Finally, surveys are subject to artificiality. Finding out that a person gives liberal answers to a questionnaire does not necessarily mean the person is liberal. This shortcoming is especially salient in the realm of action. Surveys cannot measure social action; they can only collect self-reports of recalled past action or of prospective or hypothetical action. This problem has two aspects. First, the topic of study may not be amenable to measurement through questionnaires. Second, the act of studying that topic—an attitude, for instance—may affect it. A survey respondent may have given no thought to whether the governor should be impeached until asked for his or her opinion by an interviewer. He or she may, at that point, form an opinion on the matter.

Survey research is generally weak on validity and strong on reliability. In comparison with qualitative research, for example, the artificiality of the survey format strains validity. As an illustration, people's opinions on issues seldom take the form of strongly agreeing, agreeing, disagreeing, or strongly disagreeing with a specific statement. Their survey responses in such cases, then, must be regarded as approximate indicators of what we first have in mind in framing the questions.

Reliability is a clearer matter. By presenting all respondents with standardized wording, survey research goes a long way toward eliminating unreliability in observations made by the researcher. Moreover, careful wording of the questions can also reduce significantly the respondent's own unreliability.

As with all methods of observation, a full awareness of the inherent or probable weaknesses of survey research can partially resolve them in some cases. Ultimately, though, you are on the safest ground when you can use a number of different research methods in studying a given topic, including combining a survey with qualitative methods as in the Chapter 4 discussion of mixed-methods studies.

MAIN POINTS

- Survey research, a popular social research method, is the administration of questionnaires to a sample of respondents selected from some population.
- Survey research is especially appropriate for making descriptive studies of large populations; survey data may also be used for explanatory purposes.
- Questionnaires may be administered in three basically different ways: (a) self-administered questionnaires can be completed by the respondents themselves; (b) interviewers can administer questionnaires in face-to-face encounters, reading the items to respondents and recording the answers; and (c) interviewers can conduct telephone surveys.
- Follow-up mailings for self-administered questionnaires should be sent to potential respondents who fail to respond to the initial appeal.
- Properly monitoring questionnaire returns will provide a good guide to determining when a follow-up mailing is appropriate.
- The essential characteristic of interviewers is that they be neutral; their presence in the data collection process must not have any effect on the responses given to questionnaire items.
- Interviewers must be carefully trained to be familiar with the questionnaire, to follow the

question wording and question order exactly, and to record responses exactly as they are given.

- A probe is a neutral, nondirective question that is designed to elicit an elaboration on an incomplete or ambiguous response given in an interview to an open-ended question. Examples include "Anything else?" "How is that?" and "In what ways?"

- The advantages of a self-administered questionnaire over an interview survey are economy, speed, lack of interviewer bias, and the possibility of anonymity and privacy to encourage more candid responses on sensitive issues.

- Surveys conducted over the telephone have become more common and more effective in recent years; however, rapid technological advances in cell phone usage have created knotty problems regarding response rate and representativeness of specific geographical areas.

- Some technological advances have facilitated telephone interviewing. One such advance is computer-assisted telephone interviewing (CATI).

- The advantages of an interview survey over a self-administered questionnaire are fewer incomplete questionnaires and fewer misunderstood questions, generally higher return rates, and greater flexibility in terms of sampling and special observations.

- Survey research in general has advantages in terms of economy and the amount of data that can be collected. The standardization of the data collected represents another special strength of survey research.

- Survey research has the weaknesses of being somewhat artificial and potentially superficial. It is not good at fully revealing social processes in their natural settings.

- Online surveys have many of the strengths and weaknesses of mail surveys. Although they are cheaper to conduct, it can be difficult to ensure that the respondents represent a more general population.

- Rapid technological developments, such as the increased use of smartphones and tablets, are posing challenges regarding survey instrument design and response rates.

- Mixed mode surveys can offset the disadvantages associated with relying on only one survey modality.

REVIEW QUESTIONS AND EXERCISES

1. Which of the four survey methods (mailed, face-to-face interview, telephone interview, or online) would you choose to administer a structured questionnaire for each of the following three scenarios? State the reasons for your choice and identify any additional information that would make it easier to choose among those four survey method options.

   a. National survey of parents of children in treatment for psychotic disorders. The parents are members of the National Association for the Mentally Ill. The purpose of the survey is to assess the way the mental health professionals have related to the parents and the parents' satisfaction with the services provided to their children.
   b. National survey of licensed mental health professionals who treat children with psychotic disorders. The purpose of the survey is to assess how the mental health professionals view the causes of childhood psychoses and working with parents.
   c. Survey of the students in your school of social work to assess how they view the causes of childhood psychoses and working with parents of children in treatment for psychosis.

2. If you were to conduct a mail survey for each of the above scenarios, what would you do to maximize the response rate?

3. Locate a survey being conducted on the web. Briefly describe the survey and discuss its strengths and weaknesses.

4. Look at your appearance right now. Identify aspects of your appearance that might create a problem if you were interviewing a general cross section of the public.

INTERNET EXERCISES

1. Find a study in a social work journal (such as *Social Work* or *Health and Social Work*) that used a survey design. Identify the strengths and weaknesses of the survey methods used in the study.

2. Read the following article reporting an online survey: Rubin, A. & Parrish, D. (2007) "Views of Evidence-Based Practice Among Faculty in MSW Programs: A National Survey." *Research on Social Work Practice*, 17(1), 110–122. Briefly identify its main strengths and/or weaknesses and some of the technical difficulties it illustrates regarding trying to conduct an online survey using email. Despite the study's limitations, do you think it provided some useful information? Why or why not?

3. Go to the following site that deals with online survey methodology: http://www.websm.org. Briefly describe something you find there that makes you more optimistic or more skeptical about the likelihood of obtaining representative samples of respondents when using online surveys in social work research.

4. Go to the following site on the Gallup Poll: http://www.gallup.com. Once there, look for information on how various Gallup polling is conducted. (As of this writing, the information can be found in "Methodology Center" near the bottom of the home page.) Briefly summarize what you learn there and why you think the Gallup survey methodology is or is not likely to yield accurate, representative findings.

5. Go to the U.S. Census Bureau website at http://www.census.gov and select QuickFacts. Once there, select your state. Click on the map of your state that appears on your screen. A map with county names will then appear. Click on your county. Find the estimated percentage of all people and of children in your county who live in poverty.

Visit CengageBrain.com for additional practice and study opportunities including experiential exercises, research tools, glossary, flashcards, and sample test items.

17

Analyzing Existing Data: Quantitative and Qualitative Methods

EPAS Competencies for This Chapter

Competency 4   Engage in Practice-Informed Research and Research-Informed Practice: This competency pertains to this entire chapter because doing practice-informed research sometimes involves analyzing existing data. The same applies to engaging in research-informed practice because you might need to critically appraise practice-relevant studies that analyze existing data.

Competency 9   Evaluate Practice with Individuals Families, Groups, Organizations, and Communities: This competency pertains to this entire chapter because analyzing existing data can be part of evaluating practice.

What You'll Learn in This Chapter

This chapter will present overviews of four unobtrusive methods for analyzing existing data: secondary analysis, content analysis, historical and comparative analysis, and unobtrusive online research. Each method allows researchers to study things from afar without influencing them in the process.

» INTRODUCTION

In examining the advantages and disadvantages of alternative modes of measurement, we have confronted problems that are associated with some degree of intrusion by researchers into whatever they are studying. We have discussed, for example, social desirability biases that may influence what people tell us or how they behave when they know we are observing them. Observation is called *obtrusive* when people know we are observing them. Conversely, observation is *unobtrusive* to the extent that those being observed are unaware of it.

The one mode of observation that best avoids being obtrusive is the use of existing data. By *existing data*, we do not mean just compilations of statistical data, although such compilations would be included as a prime example of existing data. The term has a much broader meaning and includes an almost endless array of possible data sources, such as agency case records and practitioner process notes, reports or editorials in newspapers or on television, minutes of board meetings, agency memoranda and annual reports, books or professional journal articles, legal opinions or laws relevant to social welfare, administrative rulings, and online social media.

For example, many social work practitioner-researchers and some social work academics encourage the use of a mixed-methods, practice-based strategy called *clinical data mining* (CDM) to promote greater collaboration between researchers and practitioners in analyzing available quantitative and qualitative clinical and administrative data to derive findings of immediate value to local service providers. The broader implications of some of these findings have been published in several peer-reviewed journals. Its proponents view CDM as a form of *practice-based research* because it emphasizes the participation of practitioners in the research process and the generation of findings that they will find useful. The term *data mining* in CDM should not be confused, however, with how that term is more commonly used outside of social work in connection to advanced computer science methods for extracting information online from gigantic data sets called *big data,* which we will discuss briefly at the end of this chapter. If you want to learn more about CDM, we recommend a book by Irwin Epstein (2010).

Three major advantages associated with the method of using existing data are its unobtrusiveness, its expedience (it usually costs less and takes less time than do other methods of data collection), and our ability to study phenomena that have occurred in the past. In light of these advantages, this chapter will examine four methods of analyzing existing data: secondary analysis, content analysis, historical and comparative analysis, and unobtrusive online research.

To set the stage for our examination of these research methods, we want to draw your attention to an excellent book that should sharpen your senses about the potential for unobtrusive measures in general. It is, among other things, the book from which we take the term *unobtrusive measures*.

» A COMMENT ON UNOBTRUSIVE MEASURES

In 1966, Eugene J. Webb and three colleagues published an ingenious little book on social research (revised in 1981; see Webb, Campbell, Schwartz, & Sechrest, 1981) that has become a classic. It focuses on the idea of *unobtrusive* or *nonreactive research*. Webb and his colleagues have played freely with the task of learning about human behavior by observing what people inadvertently leave behind them. Want to know what exhibits are the most popular at a museum? You could conduct a poll, but people might tell you what they thought you wanted to hear or what might make them look more intellectual and serious. You could stand by different exhibits and count the viewers that came by, but people might come over to see what you were doing. Webb and his colleagues suggest you check the wear and tear on the floor in front of various exhibits. Those where the tiles have been worn down the most are probably the most popular. Want to know which exhibits are popular with little kids? Look for mucus on the glass cases. To get a sense of the most popular radio stations, you could arrange with an auto mechanic to check the radio settings for cars brought in for repair.

The possibilities are limitless. Like an investigative detective, the social researcher looks for clues, and clues of social behavior are all around you. In a sense, everything you see represents the answer to some important social scientific question—all you have to do is think of the question. Although problems of validity and reliability crop up in unobtrusive measures, a little ingenuity can either handle them or put them in perspective. We encourage you to look at Webb's book. It's **EP 4, 9** enjoyable reading and should be a source of stimulation and insight for you in taking on social inquiry through the use of the data that already exist. For now, let's turn our attention to four unobtrusive methods often used by social scientists.

» SECONDARY ANALYSIS

As was evident in Chapter 16, surveys are usually major undertakings. A large-scale survey may take several months or even more than a year to progress from conceptualization to having data in hand. (Smaller-scale surveys, of course, can be done more quickly.) At the same time, however, you can pursue your particular social research interests—analyzing survey data from, say, a national sample of 2,000 respondents—while avoiding the enormous expenditure of time and money that such a survey entails. Secondary analysis makes such work possible.

Secondary analysis is a form of research in which the data collected and processed in one study are reanalyzed in a subsequent study. Often, the subsequent study is conducted by a different researcher and often for a different purpose. Sometimes, however, a different researcher will reanalyze the data for the same purpose, stemming perhaps from doubts about the conclusions derived from the original analysis in the first study. Secondary analyses might also be conducted by the original researcher, perhaps to answer different research questions that require examining different relationships among variables or perhaps to reexamine a modified version of the original research question by controlling for additional variables in the analysis. Moreover, some data sets are so large that not all of their variables (or the vast range of research questions that might pertain to those variables) can feasibly be analyzed in the original study.

The use of secondary analysis is growing among social researchers as more and more data archives become available from agencies and governmental research sources. Also, technological advances have made it easier to access and analyze these archived data sets. Technological advances also have made it easier for social researchers to share their data with one another.

Suppose, for example, that you are concerned about and want to research a potential problem in social work education. Perhaps you have noticed that female faculty members tend to occupy the lower ranks in your school or that they are unlikely to have administrative positions. You might want to assess, on a national basis, whether women and men of equivalent backgrounds differ in regard to such variables as rank, academic responsibilities, salary, and scholarly productivity.

Conducting a nationwide survey of social work faculty members would be quite costly and time consuming. Even if you could get the resources to conduct the survey, you would have to worry about the potential problem of nonresponse. As an alternative to conducting the survey yourself, you could purchase—for far less money than the cost of conducting a survey—a copy of all the data for a given year on the population of social work faculty members already collected by the Council on Social Work Education in its annual statistical canvass, which includes the information you seek to analyze.

The Growth of Secondary Analysis

Beginning in the 1960s, survey researchers became aware of the potential value that lay in archiving survey data for analysis by scholars who had nothing to do with the survey design and data collection. Even when one researcher had conducted a survey and analyzed the data, those same data could be further analyzed by others who had slightly different interests. Thus, if you were interested in the relationship between political views and attitudes toward gender equality, you could examine that research question through the analysis of any data set that happened to contain questions relating to those two variables.

The initial data archives were very much like book libraries, with a couple of differences. First, instead of books, the data archives contained data sets, initially as punched cards, then as magnetic tapes. Today they're typically contained on computer disks, CD-ROMs, or online servers. Second, whereas you're expected to return books to a conventional library, you can keep the data obtained from a data archive.

Sales, Lichtenwalter, and Fevola (2006) depict the growth in the use of secondary analysis as follows:

> Research data have always held the potential for later revisits. The more ambitious the study and the better the quality of the database, the greater the potential for further exploration. Most researchers engaging in large-scale studies, often heavily funded by the federal government, recognized that they have barely skimmed the surface of their data set's potential before the project ends. Funding sources also have become concerned about the limited informational yield compared to the dollar investment that many large-scale research studies entail. In recent years, several federal agencies funding behavioral research have developed new policies to counter this shortfall in study findings. An expanding number of federal agencies, including the National Science Foundation, the National Institute on Alcohol and Alcoholism, and the National Institute of Child Health and Human Development, have issued calls for secondary analyses of existing data sets. More notably, the National Institutes of Health (NIH) now has moved beyond its long-standing general policy of encouraging data sharing … mandating that data from studies they fund be placed in a repository that others may access. It now requires that large-budget research proposals include in their application a plan for data access, storage, and sharing. In addition, several professional organizations … as well as some scientific journals, encourage or require researchers to archive data used for publications or presentations…. These organizations have created pressures on researchers that are rapidly expanding data availability and retrieval options. (pp. 545–546)

Types and Sources of Data Archives

Varied sources collect and provide data to social work researchers. These sources include university research organizations, government and human service agencies, the United Nations, and professional associations. It would take a whole book just to list the sources of data available for analysis. In this section, we'll mention a few and point you in the direction of finding others that are relevant to your research interest.

One type of data archive provides continuing time-series surveys of different samples drawn from the same population. A well-known current example of this type is the General Social Survey (GSS). Every year or two, the federal government commissions the National Opinion Research Center at the University of Chicago to conduct a major national survey to collect data on a large number of social science variables. These surveys are conducted precisely for the purpose of making data available to scholars at little or no cost. You can learn more about the GSS at http://www.icpsr.umich.edu/gss. Another type of archive contains data collected in a national census of an entire population. Data collected in cross-sectional surveys and longitudinal surveys comprise two additional types of archives. Some archives contain more than one of the foregoing types of data sources.

Numerous resources are available for identifying and acquiring existing data for secondary analysis. Here are a few. The National Data Archive on Child Abuse and Neglect (http://www.ndacan.cornell.edu) has data sets on child abuse and neglect. Another source with child welfare data is the Annie E. Casey Foundation (http://www.aecf.org), which has a data set called Kids Count that contains variables relating to the well-being of children. The National Archive of Criminal Justice Data (http://www.icpsr.umich.edu/NACJD) has a data set from a domestic violence research project.

Sales et al. (2006) recommend several additional sources of data. The largest data repository they mention is at the Inter-University Consortium of Political and Social Research (ICPSR) at the University of Michigan. It is available to researchers working at member institutions worldwide. Its archives, which can be accessed at http://www.icpsr.umich.edu, contain social work–related data on aging, substance abuse, mental health, criminal justice, health and medical care, and education. Another useful source mentioned by Sales and her associates is the Sociometrics Social Science Electronic Data Library (http://www.socio.com/edl.htm). Its archive contains more than 200 studies on social work–related topics. For a website that provides links to a broad array of social science data, Sales and her associates recommend the University of California–San Diego Social

Science Data on the Internet (https://libraries.ucsd .edu/info/resources/subjects/social-science-data-services-ssds). The box "Four Useful Sources of Existing Data in Child Welfare" provides further information on some of the above sources as well as some others that might be of particular interest to readers who might like to conduct research in the field of child welfare.

Sources of Existing Statistics

Data sets also can be derived from existing statistics in administrative and public records. Such data are often in aggregate form in agency records. Suppose you wanted to assess the impact of a new statewide program to prevent child abuse. You could examine the existing statistics in the records compiled by the state's human services agency to see whether changes occurred in annual rates of removing children from their homes due to abuse after the program was implemented. When the data are in aggregate form only, they cannot be reanalyzed using the individual as the unit of analysis. Instead, they can be analyzed only in the form of statistics that apply to the aggregate, such as the prevalence of child abuse in different geographic areas, the proportions of different types of services provided in different agencies, and so on.

One valuable book you can buy is the annual *Statistical Abstract of the United States*, which is published by the U.S. Department of Commerce through its Census Bureau. It includes statistics on the individual states and (less extensively) cities as well as on the nation as a whole. You can learn the number of work stoppages in the country year by year, residential property taxes of major cities, the number of water pollution discharges reported around the country, the number of business proprietorships in the nation, and hundreds of other such handy bits of information. You can buy the *Statistical Abstract* on a CD-ROM, making the search for and transfer of data quite easy.

Federal agencies (e.g., the Department of Transportation, the Department of Agriculture, the U.S. Bureau of Labor and Statistics) publish countless data series. To find out what's available, go to your library, find the government documents section, and spend a few hours browsing through the shelves. You can also visit the U.S. Government Printing Office site (http://www.access.gpo.gov) and look around.

The Internet offers many websites that provide access to existing statistics. Table 17-1 illustrates the richness of this resource.

World statistics are available through the United Nations. Its *Demographic Yearbook* presents annual vital statistics (births, deaths, and other data relevant to populations) for the individual nations of the world. The website for the UN databases is listed in Table 17-1. Organizations such as the Population Reference Bureau publish a variety of demographic data, U.S. and international, that a secondary analyst could use. Its *World Population Data Sheet* and *Population Bulletin* are resources heavily used by social scientists. Social indicator data can be found in the journal *SINET: A Quarterly Review of Social Reports and Research on Social Indicators, Social Trends, and the Quality of Life*. Other publications report a variety of other kinds of data. Again, a trip to your library, along with a Web search, is the best introduction to what's available.

The amount of data provided by nongovernment agencies is as staggering as the amount your taxes buy. Chambers of commerce often publish data reports on business, as do private consumer groups. Ralph Nader has information on automobile safety, and Common Cause covers politics and government. And, as mentioned earlier, George Gallup publishes reference volumes on public opinion as tapped by Gallup Polls since 1935.

We're tempted to continue listing data sources, but you probably have already gotten the idea. We suggest you visit the government documents section the next time you're at your college library. You'll be amazed by the data waiting for your analysis. The lack of funds to support expensive data collection is no reason for not doing good and useful research.

Advantages of Secondary Analysis

The advantages of secondary analysis are obvious and enormous: It is cheaper and faster than doing an original survey (or most other types of research). Moreover, the cost savings of this approach enable you to conduct research on very large samples—much larger samples than you would be able to study with typical levels of funding.

Another advantage is that—depending on who did the original study—you may benefit from the work of top-flight professionals. In addition, the

FOUR USEFUL SOURCES OF EXISTING DATA IN CHILD WELFARE

Annie E. Casey's Kids Count
(http://datacenter.kidscount.org)

The Kids Count database is provided by the Annie E. Casey Foundation. It compiles comparative data about the well-being of children state by state across the United States. The well-being indicators pertain to low birthrates, infant mortality, child deaths, teen deaths, teens who are neither attending school nor working, children living in families without a fully employed parent, children living in poverty, children in single-parent families, children in immigrant families, and children without health insurance. In addition to comparing states and cities, it enables analyses to be done within the bounds of a single state, territory, or community. It can create customized state profiles, maps, rankings, and graphs. For example, a bar graph that currently (as we write this book) appears near the top of the site shows the percentage of children who lived in poverty in each of the 50 states as of 2008. Mississippi had the highest percentage (30%), and most of the other states with relatively high rates (above 20%) were in the southern region.

National Data Archive on Child Abuse and Neglect
(http://www.ndacan.cornell.edu/)

This site makes available for secondary analysis high-quality data sets on child abuse and neglect that are acquired from researchers who have investigated this topic. The site also provides technical support for those seeking to conduct secondary analyses of its data sets. The following can give you a sense of the many data sets available at this site: National Family Violence Survey, Family Structure and Functioning in Neglectful Families, National Study of the Incidence of Child Abuse and Neglect,

Runaway and Homeless Youth Management Information, Parenting Among Women Sexually Abused in Childhood, National Survey of Current and Former Foster Parents, Neighborhood and Household Factors in the Etiology of Child Maltreatment, Longitudinal Pathways to Resilience in Maltreated Children, and so on.

United States Children's Bureau Statistics and Research
(http://www.acf.hhs.gov/programs/cb/research-data-technology/statistics-research)

This governmental site provides existing statistics (not databases) on adoption and foster care at the state and national levels. Its Adoption and Foster Care Reporting and Analysis System reports case-level existing statistics on "all children in foster care for whom State child welfare agencies have responsibility for placement, care or supervision, and on children who are adopted under the auspices of the State's public child welfare agency." Among the many useful areas of existing statistics you can find at this site are yearly trends in foster care and adoption, the number of child fatalities, risk factors for child maltreatment, characteristics of perpetrators, child welfare outcomes, and so on.

Child Welfare Dynamic Report System
(http://cssr.berkeley.edu/ucb_childwelfare/)

This site is provided collaboratively by the California Department of Social Services and the University of California at Berkeley. It provides child welfare administrative data about children in California's child welfare system. Charts can be viewed on such topics as the numbers and rates of child abuse referrals, the recurrence of child maltreatment, and so on.

archived data may have been generated by studies that received well-funded federal research grants that made it feasible to implement rigorous sampling approaches and obtain high response rates. Thus, as Sales et al. (2006) point out:

The samples for such studies are therefore likely to be highly representative of the populations from which they are drawn.

Inferences from such studies are likely to have high external validity ... which makes them a powerful and persuasive base for discussions of social needs and social policy. Because social work researchers have only infrequently been recipients of major federal grants, the ability to access high-quality data that inform on key social

TABLE 17.1 Website Sources for Existing Statistics

U.S. Government Websites

Bureau of the Census	http://www.census.gov
Bureau of Labor Statistics	http://www.bls.gov
Central Intelligence Agency	http://www.cia.gov
Centers for Disease Control and Prevention	http://www.cdc.gov/nchs
Data and Statistics	http://www.usa.gov
Department of Housing and Urban Development	portal.hud.gov/hudportal/HUD
Federal Bureau of Investigation	http://www.fbi.gov
Federal Interagency Forum on Child and Family Statistics	http://www.childstats.gov
Government Printing Office	http://www.access.gpo.gov
U.S. House of Representatives	http://www.house.gov
U.S. Senate	http://www.senate.gov
U.S. Whitehouse	http://www.whitehouse.gov

Other Websites for Existing Statistics

Child Welfare League of America	www.cwla.org
National Archive of Computerized Data on Aging	http://www.icpsr.umich.edu/NACDA/index.html
National Association for Welfare Research and Statistics	http://www.nawrs.org
National Data Archive on Child Abuse and Neglect	http://www.ndacan.cornell.edu
UN Databases	http://www.un.org
World Bank	www.worldbank.org

problems may have special advantage for our field. (p. 549)

Well-funded, large-scale studies are also likely to have assessed a much larger number of variables than most original social work research studies can assess. Secondary analysis thus provides the advantage of gathering information on a much larger number of variables. Moreover, in addition to examining information separately for many more variables, a very large sample size makes it possible to employ sophisticated multivariate statistical techniques for analyzing relationships among many variables simultaneously and thus ferreting out the relative explanatory power of each variable when the other variables are controlled.

Another advantage of conducting a secondary analysis of a well-funded study is the likelihood that the original study was methodologically strong in general, not just in the size and representativeness of its sample. For example, to be successful in securing major funding for large-scale studies, research proposals had better reflect well-controlled designs and very strong measurement procedures. Chances are, no matter how well you understand the design and measurement concepts that we've discussed in this book, it will be difficult for you to obtain the level of funding needed to enable you to obtain the resources required to actually implement a study that is as rigorous as you'd like it to be.

Sales et al. (2006) also identify the following additional advantages of secondary analysis:

- **Human Subject Concerns** Proposing to use previously collected data is likely to expedite institutional review board (IRB) approval. (Recall our discussion of IRBs in Chapter 5.) Because you are not collecting the data, you avoid ethical concerns regarding data collection (assuming ample safeguards for protecting identities of respondents).

- **Accessing Hard-to-Identify Populations** Finding and gathering data from members of hidden or hard-to-locate populations (such as those discussed in Chapter 6) can be expensive and beyond the means of most social work researchers. This pertains not only to stigmatized populations but also to people with low-incidence problems. Accessing a data set from a well-funded study whose sample was large enough to include sufficient members from such populations may make more sense than trying to collect original data from those members yourself.

- **Monitoring Trends over Time** As we already mentioned, some data archives contain data gathered in time-series studies or longitudinal studies. Completing such studies probably will require more time and years than you can or want to spend on your research.

- **Comparative Studies** Comparing social problems across different nations is another example of a type of study that—because of its expense—can be conducted much more feasibly in a secondary analysis than in an original study.

- **Technical Support** The federal government encourages the secondary analysis of data archives by providing detailed manuals to help researchers access and analyze the data. In addition, some popular data archives provide workshops offering hands-on training. Some government agencies even reimburse attendee expenses associated with attending their workshops.

Limitations of Secondary Analysis

Secondary analysis can also involve some limitations. If you conduct a secondary analysis or analyze existing statistics in your research (or your practice), you should not assume that the data are free of problems just because they are "official" or because a prestigious agency published them. The data may be outdated by the time they are released. In addition, a key problem is the recurrent question of validity. When one researcher collects data for one particular purpose, you have no assurance that those data will be appropriate to your research interests. Typically, you'll find that the original researcher asked a question that comes close to measuring what you are interested in, but you'll wish the question had been asked just a little

differently—or that another, related question had also been asked. Your question, then, is whether the question that was asked provides a valid measure of the variable you want to analyze. Let's look now at some of the special problems that you might encounter when using this method.

Missing Data Whenever you base your research on an analysis of data that already exist, you are obviously limited to what exists. Before investing a great deal of time in planning a study that will use existing data, you should check the data source to see if the data you need are there at all. If they are there, then you should check to see whether large chunks of the data on certain key variables are missing. If you conduct a national research study using existing data on ethnicity and poverty among retirees in the United States, for example, and states with relatively large numbers of relatively affluent white retirees (such as Florida and Arizona) are missing from the database—or in the database but without reporting ethnicity—then your results might be seriously inaccurate.

Sometimes a variable may have data entered on it, but the lack of variation in the data renders it missing in the sense of being a variable. You may recall from our discussion of variables in Chapters 3 and 8 that, to be a variable, a concept must *vary*. Suppose you want to evaluate the effectiveness of a play therapy intervention for traumatized 6-year-olds by examining its impact on their grades in first grade using school grade records. You should first check the school records to see if sufficient variation exists in grades at that level. Suppose that first-grade teachers give virtually every student an A to avoid discouraging the students or lowering their self-esteem. If that is the case, grades will be missing as a variable in the records because they will not sufficiently vary.

Problems of Validity You will encounter validity problems if the agency that collected the existing statistics you are analyzing defined your variables in ways that don't match your definitions of those variables. Suppose, for example, that a state welfare agency—perhaps seeking to show that its recent welfare reform policy succeeded in getting welfare recipients back to work—defines participation in a government job-training program as being employed. Suppose you, however, are skeptical about how often such training leads to actual paid employment and therefore do not want to count such training in your definition of being employed. Maybe the government data do not distinguish between part-time and full-time employment, and you have defined success in getting welfare recipients back to work to mean full-time employment with wages that match or exceed welfare benefits. If you must rely on the government's existing statistics for your research, you would have a serious validity problem.

Another type of validity problem occurs when existing statistics deal with phenomena that often go unreported but include only reported incidents in the records. Thus, existing statistics may underestimate the number of individuals who have been physically abused by a spouse or a partner or the number of coeds who have been sexually abused on dates because many such incidents go unreported. The actual incidence of these problems can be underestimated even further if the existing statistics include only incidents involving the filing of criminal charges, omitting incidents that were unreported as well as those that were reported but did not lead to criminal charges.

Improper data collection methods can also cause validity problems, such as when survey interviewers make up information so that they can avoid dangerous neighborhoods. Likewise, direct-service practitioners who resent having to spend so much time completing forms on their cases can become careless and sloppy in rushing to complete those forms.

Problems of Reliability The analysis of existing data depends heavily on the quality of the data themselves: Are they accurate reports of what they claim to report? That can be a substantial problem sometimes because the weighty tables of government statistics are sometimes grossly inaccurate.

Because a great deal of the research into crime depends on official crime statistics, this body of data has come under critical evaluation. The results have not been encouraging. Suppose, for purposes of illustration, that you were interested in tracing the long-term trends in marijuana use in the United States predating current trends toward its legalization. Official statistics on the numbers of people arrested for selling or possessing it would seem to be a reasonable measure of use. Right? Not necessarily.

To begin, you face a hefty problem of validity. Before the passage of the Marijuana Tax Act in 1937, marijuana was legal in the United States, so arrest records would not give you a valid measure

of use. But even if you limited your inquiry to the post-1937 era, you would still have problems of reliability that stem from the nature of law enforcement and crime record keeping.

Law enforcement, for example, is subject to various pressures. Crime reports may rise or fall, depending on increases or decreases in the budget for hiring police. A public outcry against marijuana, led perhaps by a vocal citizens' group, can result in a police crackdown on drug trafficking—especially during an election or budget year. A sensational story in the press can have a similar effect. In addition, the volume of other business that faces police affects marijuana arrests.

DeFleur (1975) has traced the pattern of drug arrests in Chicago between 1942 and 1970 and has demonstrated that the official records present a far more accurate history of police practices and political pressure on police than a history of drug use. On a different level of analysis, Black (1970) and others have analyzed the factors that influence whether an offender is actually arrested by police or let off with a warning. Ultimately, official crime statistics are influenced by whether specific offenders are well or poorly dressed, whether they are polite or abusive to police officers, and so forth. Consider unreported crimes, which are sometimes estimated to be as much as 10 times the number of crimes known to police, and the reliability of crime statistics gets even shakier.

These comments concern crime statistics at a local level. Often it's useful to analyze national crime statistics, such as those reported in the Federal Bureau of Investigation's (FBI's) annual *Uniform Crime Reports*. Additional problems are introduced at the national level. Different local jurisdictions define crimes differently. Also, participation in the FBI program is voluntary, so the data are incomplete.

Finally, the process of record keeping affects the records that are kept and reported. Whenever a law enforcement unit improves its record-keeping system—computerizing it, for example—the apparent crime rates always increase dramatically. That can happen even if the number of crimes committed, reported, and investigated does not actually increase.

Similar problems of reliability can occur in existing statistics on many other variables of interest to social work researchers whose definitions or record-keeping methods change over time. Consider child abuse, for example. Some methods of corporal punishment that were deemed acceptable several decades ago are now considered to constitute child abuse. Likewise, statistics on rape may now include incidents of intercourse with a date who did not want it but who was too inebriated to resist, whereas in the past narrower definitions were used to count the incidence of rape.

Awareness is your first protection against the problems of validity and reliability in the analysis of existing data—knowing that the problems may exist. Investigating the nature of the data collection and tabulation may help you assess the nature and degree of these problems so that you can judge their potential impact on your research interest. Replication can also help alleviate the problem.

Inadequate Documentation Often, however, you may not be able to ascertain the nature or appraise the quality of the procedures used to collect and process data in the study that supplied the data for your secondary analysis. For example, information may not be available on such concerns as how well interviewers were trained, whether bias was somehow introduced in data gathering, or how carefully the data were coded (Sales et al., 2006).

Feasibility Issues Although secondary analysis usually is less costly than collecting original data yourself, we should not understate how time consuming this method sometimes is. Some huge data sets, for example, can overwhelm researchers who are not yet accustomed to handling data sets with that many variables or with multiple waves of data collection. When you first encounter such data sets, you may need to make the data sets manageable by extracting only some variables and some waves. You are likely to find this to be necessary despite the vastly expanded capacity of current computers. You also should consider seeking technical assistance if such technical support is available.

Other common feasibility issues pertain to changes in the existing data over time, gaining access to those data, and then maintaining access. As Alexander and Solomon (2006) observe,

> Accessing [government] data sets frequently takes a good deal of negotiation with agencies for permission for use, and often requires compromises and contractual agreements. Generally, it is necessary to work with the producers of the data in order to truly understand the meaning of the existing information. (p. 418)

To illustrate these problems, Alexander and Solomon include in their book a commentary on the challenges that DePanfilis and Zuravin (2002) had to deal with in their study that analyzed existing statistics to assess the effect of services on the recurrence of child maltreatment. They used two sources of available records in Baltimore's public agency for child protective services: case records and a statewide management information system.

One problem involved policy changes over time that resulted in changes in the way the data were formatted. This difficulty was particularly germane because of the longitudinal nature of their study.

Other problems involved difficulties in gaining access to the existing data and then not losing that access over time because of administrative or policy changes. DePanfilis (in Alexander & Solomon, 2006) recommends the following steps for gaining and maintaining access to existing data:

1. **Prepare a short prospectus about the proposed study.**

2. **Schedule face-to-face meetings with agency administrators.** Administrators at state and local levels must approve the study. Approvals must occur prior to submitting a proposal for funding, as a letter that confirms access to the data is required in order to convince a funding source that conducting the study will be feasible in a particular jurisdiction. The researcher is advised to thoroughly understand the state laws about who may have access to existing child welfare data for research purposes before developing the prospectus or planning these meetings.

3. **Gain human research protection approval for the use of archival records in research.**

4. **Develop procedures for access to electronic files.**

5. **Develop procedures for access to case records.** The specific methods for access to hard copies of case records will vary by jurisdiction. It is likely that the researcher must request office space within the local agency for reviewing and coding case records, as the need to protect the confidentiality of the participants' information would usually forbid taking records or copies of records out of the public agency office.

6. **Overcome unanticipated barriers when gaining access to existing records.** It is not uncommon for the agency administrator who wrote the letter of support at the time a proposal was written

to be unavailable at the time a study is implemented.... About a third of the way into our study, a new administrator at the state level was concerned about the number of research studies being undertaken regarding child welfare policies and practices.... The administrator asked for a new Attorney General position about the legality of providing access to child welfare data for research purposes. [This] resulted in our stopping our case-level data collection for nine months. (pp. 435–437)

DePanfilis adds that the prospects for gaining and maintaining access to agency records will be significantly enhanced by developing relationships with agency staff members in charge of operations. For example, she and Zuravin "went out of our way to give people fruit baskets, to participate in local agency programs, and to touch base with administrators on a regular basis" (Alexander & Solomon, 2006, p. 437).

DePanfilis also discusses problems in the databases they were analyzing—problems that took considerable time to reconcile. For example, it took them a year to plan the data collection process. One problem was that they wanted to use both the children and the family as the units of analysis, and the case record data had to be transformed accordingly. In conducting a pilot test, they found discrepancies in 50% of the records between the data self-reported by the client, the statewide management information system data, and the case record data.

Despite the foregoing feasibility issues, analyzing existing statistics is usually less costly and less time consuming than collecting original data. And despite the potential problems that often need to be resolved in the data, the analysis of existing statistics can provide valuable findings for guiding policy and practice.

Illustrations of the Secondary Analysis of Existing Statistics in Research on Social Welfare Policy

Two studies of social welfare policy illustrate the applicability to social work of analyzing existing statistics. They also illustrate some of the problems that have already been discussed in using this method.

In one study, Ozawa (1989) investigated whether the (no longer existing) Aid to Families with Dependent Children (AFDC) welfare program contributed to the dramatic increase in illegitimate births among adolescents. Ozawa hypothesized that a high AFDC payment and a high AFDC acceptance rate increased that birthrate because more generous payments and higher acceptance rates made it easier for the childbearing adolescent to establish her own household and avoid an unwanted marriage. In this connection, Ozawa envisioned positive aspects of the adolescent's decision to raise a child alone rather than to marry. She emphasized that she was not studying the impact of AFDC on the decision to bear a child (she cited prior research showing that adolescents do not bear infants out of wedlock to receive AFDC payments). Instead, she was studying the impact of AFDC on the adolescent's decision whether to marry or raise the child alone.

Ozawa's unit of analysis was the state. Her dependent variable was the state's rate of illegitimacy among women age 19 and under. Her independent variables included the state AFDC benefit level and the state AFDC acceptance rate. (These were not the only independent variables she studied, but to keep this illustration simple, we'll focus on the two primary ones.)

Analyzing data from the U.S. National Center for Health Statistics, Ozawa showed that the national adolescent illegitimacy rate rose 70% between 1970 and 1982. To assess the impact of AFDC on those rates, she obtained government data published by the Bureau of the Census, the House Committee on Ways and Means, and the Social Security Administration. Her results supported her hypothesis: Pregnant adolescents in states with higher AFDC payments and higher acceptance rates were less likely to marry than those in states with lower AFDC payments and lower acceptance rates.

In developing policy implications from her findings, Ozawa (1989) urged policymakers to understand the positive aspects of the decision not to marry and to consider "granting AFDC payments to low-income, unmarried adolescent mothers regardless of the economic backgrounds of their parents" (p. 11).

In another study, Coulton, Pandey, and Chow (1990) were concerned that economic forces in the United States during the 1980s were concentrating poor people in deteriorating central urban neighborhoods where they were becoming further isolated from economic opportunities and increasingly exposed to adverse social and physical conditions associated with extreme poverty. Coulton and her associates postulated that published research that had already documented this trend was based primarily on national census data that might have underestimated the problem because income estimates from the 1980 census were for income earned in 1979 and thus did not reflect the impact of the recession that began late in 1979 and continued into the early 1980s.

To study this phenomenon in depth, as well as several related statistical phenomena that we won't go into here, Coulton and her associates decided to limit their study to one urban area: Cleveland, Ohio. They recognized that this decision would limit the generalizability of their findings but believed that others could replicate their study in other cities to see if the same patterns could be observed.

Coulton and her associates prefaced their study by noting that poverty rates rose sharply in the 1980s and that, to the extent that poverty was becoming more geographically concentrated, it was becoming more difficult for poor people to reach jobs located in the suburbs. Workers who could afford to move closer to suburban jobs were induced to do so, and this further concentrated the poverty of the inner-city neighborhood they left behind and reduced the opportunity of those who were left behind to find jobs close to home (to which they could travel). As the neighborhood deteriorated, the worsening social environment conceivably might have had harmful effects on the individuals left behind—particularly the youths—as they became increasingly exposed to such problems as teen pregnancy, delinquency, school dropout, and so on.

The research team used a variety of sources of existing statistics for Cleveland, including data from the Center for Regional Economic Issues located at Case Western Reserve University, birth and death information reported by the Ohio Department of Health (which provided data on low birth weight, infant death rate, teen birthrate, and illegitimacy rates), crime rate data from the FBI, juvenile delinquency data from the Cuyahoga County Juvenile Court, drug arrest rates from the Cleveland Police Department, and housing value data from the Housing Policy Research Program of Cleveland State University.

The existing statistics analyzed by Coulton and her associates showed that by 1988, nearly 50% of

Cleveland's poor people lived in neighborhoods of concentrated poverty, compared with 21% in 1970. (The researchers defined high-poverty areas as census tracts where more than 40% of the population lives in a household below the poverty threshold.) Thus, poor people were becoming more spatially isolated from the rest of society and less likely to encounter nonpoor people in their neighborhoods. The statistics on poverty-related physical and social problems that Coulton and her associates analyzed indicated that as poor people were becoming more concentrated in high-poverty areas, the social and physical problems to which they were being exposed were deteriorating rapidly, particularly for people who were living in "emerging poverty areas" that lost many blue-collar workers in the early 1980s and consequently became poverty areas after 1980. Noting the importance of the person-in-environment framework for social work practice and the special vulnerability of poor children living in high-poverty neighborhoods, Coulton et al. (1990) recommended that social workers consider interventions at the environmental level:

> Social workers need practice models that combine their traditional approaches to service delivery with economic redevelopment of distressed parts of the city and mechanisms that reestablish connections between central city residents and distant, suburban job locations. Barriers to these connections are geographic but also involve social networks, information channels, and psychological distance. As poor neighborhoods become increasingly adverse environments due to economic and social decline, programs and interventions are needed that will disrupt their growing isolation from the mainstream. (p. 15)

In addition to providing an excellent illustration of the creative analysis of a variety of sources of existing statistics, the study by Coulton and her associates offers a splendid example of the relevance of research (and policy) to social work practice. The foregoing two examples, however, do not imply that secondary analysis is a method that applies to social policy research only. It could apply to any level of social work practice. Rubin and Parrish (2009), for example, more recently conducted a survey of a large sample of social work practitioners and students in four geographical areas. Their findings indicated that their respondents had diverse attitudes about evidence-based practice (EBP) and differed quite a bit in the extent to which they engage in it. Included in the data from their survey is background information from each respondent. Conceivably, someone could conduct a secondary analysis of their data to test hypotheses about possible correlations between certain background variables and practitioner orientations to EBP.

As another example, suppose a large-scale survey were completed 2 years after a traumatic natural disaster and collected data from survivors of that disaster on an extensive list of diverse variables, two of which included the extent of each their current trauma symptoms and what types of posttrauma treatment they received (if any). Another researcher could obtain that study's database and conduct a secondary analysis to see whether—after controlling for various moderating variables—type of treatment was associated with extent of enduring trauma symptoms.

Similarly, suppose a large social service agency conducted a client satisfaction survey that included many other variables in addition to satisfaction level. A secondary analysis could be conducted on the data to assess—after controlling for various mediating variables—whether certain types of clients were more satisfied than others, whether type of client–practitioner dyad was associated with satisfaction level, and whether certain types of service provision or interventions were associated with higher or lower levels of satisfaction.

Distinguishing Secondary Analysis from Other Forms of Analyzing Available Records

At the beginning of this chapter and in Chapter 8, we noted that the terms *existing data* and *available records* refer to much more than just existing or available *statistical* data. As we mentioned, the sources of nonstatistical data are virtually endless. Just a few examples of such sources are agency case records, practitioner process notes, minutes of agency board meetings, professional journal articles, and so on. We also defined secondary analysis as a form of research in which the data collected and processed in one study are reanalyzed in a subsequent study. According to that definition, then, not all studies of available records are secondary analyses. That's because not all forms of available records

consist of data collected in prior research. An illustration of a study of available records that was not a secondary analysis appears in the box "A Content Analysis of Problematic Phrases in Published Research: Implications for EBP." That study used another method for analyzing available records, called *content analysis*, which we'll turn to next.

» CONTENT ANALYSIS

Content analysis is a way of transforming qualitative material into quantitative data. It may be applied to virtually any form of communication, not just available records. It consists primarily of coding and tabulating the occurrences of certain forms of content that are being communicated.

The box "A Content Analysis of Problematic Phrases in Published Research: Implications for EBP" provided an example of a content analysis of published research studies. Another might be to analyze social work course syllabi to see if certain types of faculty members or schools have more content on ethnic minorities than do others. Or we might examine presentations at social work conferences at different times in our profession's history, perhaps counting the number of references to psychoanalytic concepts or to ecological or social reform concepts to see if the popularity of different professional orientations or conceptual frameworks has shifted over time. Or we might tabulate how often various types of issues are mentioned in the minutes of community organization meetings. Is the amount of citizen participation reflected in the minutes related to how frequently certain types of issues appear in the minutes?

Content analysis research can have great applicability to direct social work practice. In his text *Effective Casework Practice*, Fischer (1978) calls the practitioner–client relationship the keystone of casework practice and identifies practitioner empathy, warmth, and genuineness as the three core conditions of an effective helping relationship. The field first learned of the importance of these conditions from an extensive body of content analysis research studies that were reviewed by Marsden (1971). In these studies, written and taped excerpts from therapy sessions were rated according to the degree to which the core relationship conditions were observed. The findings tended to indicate that the

A CONTENT ANALYSIS OF PROBLEMATIC PHRASES IN PUBLISHED RESEARCH: IMPLICATIONS FOR EBP

Based on their routine of keeping current with the research articles published in social work journals, Rubin and Parrish (2007a) seemed to sense a trend in which more and more authors reporting weakly controlled outcome studies were including in their conclusions unwarranted statements (unwarranted because of their weak designs) to the effect that their findings suggested that the program, policy, or intervention that they evaluated was evidence based.

To test out their supposition, they used purposive sampling, examining every issue over 6 years (2000 through 2005) of two prominent research journals in social work: *Research on Social Work Practice* and *Social Work Research*. Although the articles found in those two journals would represent some of the best research in social work, just limiting their sample to them would not represent the range of outcome studies that social work practitioners would find in conducting an Internet search for studies in the EBP process. Consequently, they also searched *PsycINFO*, an electronic database that they deemed likely to yield studies that practitioners would find if they employed the EBP process. They selected "child abuse" and "domestic violence" as search terms given their historical relevance to and interest within social work practice and the consequent likelihood that social work practitioners would attempt to access articles in those areas. All articles reporting an evaluation of an intervention, program, or policy and published between 2000 and 2005 were included in both searches. They found 97 relevant studies published in the two social work research journals and 45 from the *PsycINFO* search. Because four of the studies appeared in both subsamples, they found a total of 138 relevant studies overall.

Each article was assessed regarding the type of research design used and the type of findings and conclusions reported. In particular, they examined whether the conclusions of weakly controlled studies contained any wording in any part of the manuscript that could be misconstrued as implying more empirical support for the evaluated intervention than was warranted. There was a good level of interrater reliability between the two investigators in what they recorded regarding the relevant content of each article. Their results were dramatic and disconcerting. Although more than 70% of the studies used designs that do not warrant making conclusive causal inferences (as discussed in Chapters 11 and 12), almost two-thirds (63%) of those studies contained some wording that could be misconstrued by some readers as implying at least partial evidence-based status for the evaluated intervention, program, or policy.

Rubin and Parrish cautioned that most of the articles in their sample contained comments that described the methodological limitations of the research and signaled the tentative nature of the findings in light of those limitations. Nevertheless, Rubin and Parrish argued that some readers with vested interests in the evaluated intervention might selectively read or remember only the problematic statements in the abstract or discussion and might be inclined to misconstrue or exploit those statements as implying more of a basis for deeming an intervention to be evidence based than the authors intended to imply.

Based on their findings, Rubin and Parrish recommended that journal editors require that articles reporting preexperimental designs or other designs that have significant limitations regarding causal inferences not use any wording (in the abstract or elsewhere) either that conclusively implies that the evaluated intervention, program, or policy was effective or that resembles phrases that can be misinterpreted or exploited to imply evidence-based status for the evaluated intervention, program, or policy. They further suggested that guidelines for authors be developed regarding how best to word the implications or conclusions of weakly controlled studies with positive outcomes. For example, authors of such studies could be instructed to eschew words that might depict the evaluated intervention as "effective" or "evidence based"—even in a tentative sense. Thus, instead of saying, "Preliminary results support the conclusion that the program had positive effects," authors might say, "Although the methodological limitations of our study keep us from drawing causal inferences about program effects, our results provide a basis for further evaluation of the program with more rigorous designs."

more these three conditions were present, the better the clinical process and outcome.

Some topics are more appropriately addressed by content analysis than by any other method of inquiry. Suppose for a moment that you're interested in how mentally ill individuals are portrayed on television. Perhaps the National Alliance for the Mentally Ill plans to mount a campaign to educate the public about the nature of mental illness, alleviate fears about the mentally ill, and offset stereotypes about them. Suppose one facet of the campaign is aimed at the television medium and seeks to reduce the extent to which television programs portray mentally ill individuals as violent or dangerous. Suppose further that you seek to evaluate the impact of that facet of the campaign on television programming and that you will use a time-series design to assess whether the campaign seems to be reducing the extent to which mentally ill individuals are portrayed as violent or dangerous. Content analysis would be the best mode of observation for your time-series study.

Briefly, here's what you would do. First, you would develop an operational definition of your dependent variable: the extent to which mentally ill individuals are portrayed as violent or dangerous. The section on coding later in this chapter will help you do that. Next, you would have to decide what to watch. Probably you would decide (a) what stations to watch, (b) for what days or period, and (c) at what hours. Then, you would stock in some snacks and start watching, classifying, and recording. Once you had completed your observations, you'd be able to analyze the data you collected and determine whether mentally ill individuals were being portrayed less violently after than before the campaign.

Content analysis, then, is particularly well suited to the study of communications and to answering the classic question of communications research: "Who says what, to whom, why, how, and with what effect?" As a mode of observation, content analysis requires a considered handling of the *what*, and the analysis of data collected in this mode, as in others, addresses the *why* and *with what effect*.

Sampling in Content Analysis

In the study of communications, as in the study of people, it is often impossible to observe directly everything in which you are interested. In your study of television portrayals of the mentally ill, for example, we would advise against attempting to watch everything that's broadcast. It wouldn't be possible, and your brain would probably short-circuit before you got close to discovering that for yourself. Usually, then, it's appropriate to sample.

Your first decision would be to decide whether each television show was to be given one overall score, whether each mentally ill person in it would be given a separate score, or perhaps some other option. Next, you would need to establish the universe to be sampled from. In this case, what television stations will you observe? What will be the period of the study—which days and what hours of those days will you observe? Then, how many programs do you want to observe and code for analysis?

Now you're ready to design the sample selection. As a practical matter, you wouldn't have to sample among the different stations if you had assistants—each of you could watch a different channel during the same time period. But let's suppose you are working alone. Your final sampling frame, from which a sample will be selected and watched, might look something like this:

- Jan. 7, channel 2, 7–9 P.M.
- Jan. 7, channel 4, 7–9 P.M.
- Jan. 7, channel 9, 7–9 P.M.
- Jan. 7, channel 2, 9–11 P.M.
- Jan. 7, channel 4, 9–11 P.M.
- Jan. 7, channel 9, 9–11 P.M.
- Jan. 8, channel 2, 7–9 P.M.
- Jan. 8, channel 4, 7–9 P.M.
- Jan. 8, channel 9, 7–9 P.M.
- Jan. 8, channel 2, 9–11 P.M.
- Jan. 8, channel 4, 9–11 P.M.
- Jan. 8, channel 9, 9–11 P.M.
- Jan. 9, channel 2, 7–9 P.M.
- Jan. 9, channel 4, 7–9 P.M.
- … and so on.

Notice that we've made several decisions for you in the illustration. First, we have assumed that channels 2, 4, and 9 are the ones appropriate to your study. We've assumed that you found the 7 to 11 P.M. prime-time hours to be the most relevant and that 2-hour periods would do the job. We picked January 7 out of the hat for a starting date. In practice, of course, all of these decisions should be based on your careful consideration of what would be appropriate to your particular study.

Sampling is simple and straightforward once you have become clear about your units of analysis and the observations that are appropriate to those units and have created a sampling frame like the one we've illustrated. The alternative procedures available to you are the same ones described in Chapter 15: random, systematic, stratified, and so on.

Sampling Techniques

In content analysis of written prose, sampling may occur at any or all of the following levels: words, phrases, sentences, paragraphs, sections, chapters, books, writers, or the contexts relevant to the works. Other forms of communication may also be sampled at any of the conceptual levels appropriate to them.

Any of the conventional sampling techniques discussed in Chapter 15 may be used in content analysis. We might select a *random* or *systematic sample* of agency memoranda, of state laws passed regarding the rights of mental patients, or of the minutes of community organization meetings. We might number all course syllabi in a school of social work and then select a random sample of 25.

Stratified sampling is also appropriate to content analysis. To analyze the editorial policies of American newspapers, for example, we might first group all newspapers by region of the country, size of the community in which they are published, frequency of publication, or average circulation. We might then select a stratified random or systematic sample of newspapers for analysis. Having done so, we might select a sample of editorials from each selected newspaper, perhaps stratified chronologically.

Cluster sampling is equally appropriate to content analysis. Indeed, if individual editorials were to be the unit of analysis in the previous example, then the selection of newspapers at the first stage of sampling would be a cluster sample. In an analysis of political speeches, we might begin by selecting a sample of politicians; each politician would represent a cluster of political speeches. The study of television's portrayal of the mentally ill described previously is another example of cluster sampling.

We repeat: Sampling need not end when we reach the unit of analysis. If novels are the unit of analysis in a study, then we might select a sample of novelists, subsamples of novels written by each selected author, and a sample of paragraphs within each novel. We would then analyze the content of the paragraphs to describe the novels themselves.

Let's turn now to a more direct examination of analysis that has been mentioned frequently in the previous discussions. At this point, *content analysis* will refer to the coding or classification of material being observed. Part 7 will deal with the manipulation of those classifications to draw descriptive and explanatory conclusions.

Coding in Content Analysis

Content analysis is essentially a coding operation. Communications—oral, written, or other—are coded or classified according to some conceptual framework. Newspaper editorials, for example, may be coded as liberal or conservative. Radio broadcasts might be coded as propagandistic or not. Novels might be coded as pro–social welfare or not. Political speeches might be coded as to whether or not they impugn the character of welfare recipients or the homeless. Recall that terms such as these are subject to many interpretations, and the researcher must specify definitions clearly.

Coding in content analysis involves the logic of conceptualization and operationalization as discussed in Chapter 8. In content analysis, as in other research methods, you must refine your conceptual framework and develop specific methods for observing in relation to that framework.

Manifest and Latent Content

Content analysis, like other forms of research, involves choices between *depth* and *specificity* of understanding. Often, this represents a choice between validity and reliability, respectively. Typically, qualitative researchers opt for depth, preferring to base their judgments on a broad range of observations and information, even at the risk that another observer might reach a different judgment of the situation. The choice in content analysis is between coding *manifest content* versus coding *latent content*.

Coding the manifest content—the visible, surface content—of a communication more closely approximates the use of a standardized questionnaire. To determine, for example, how sexist certain books are, you might simply count the number of times male pronouns are used in conjunction with generalized prestigious roles (such as referring to the role of some nonspecified physician as "his" role) or the average number of such uses per page. This strictly quantitative method would have the advantage of ease and reliability in coding and of letting the reader of the research report know precisely how sexist language was measured. It would have a disadvantage, on the other hand, in terms of validity. Surely the term *sexist book* conveys a richer and deeper meaning than the number of times male pronouns are used.

Alternatively, you may take a more qualitative approach by coding the latent content of the communication: its underlying meaning. In the current example, you might read an entire book or a sample of paragraphs or pages and make an overall assessment of how sexist the book is. Although your total assessment might well be influenced by the inappropriate appearance of male pronouns, it would not depend fully on the frequency with which such words appeared.

Clearly, this second method seems better designed for tapping the underlying meaning of communications, but its advantage comes at a cost of reliability and specificity. Somewhat different definitions or standards may be used, especially if more than one person is coding the novel. A passage—perhaps depicting boys as heroes and girls as being rescued—might be deemed sexist by one coder but not another. Even if you do all of the coding yourself, there is no guarantee that your definitions and standards will remain constant throughout the enterprise. Moreover, the reader of your research report would be generally uncertain about the definitions you have used.

Wherever possible, the best solution to this dilemma is to use *both* methods. A given unit of observation should receive the same characterization from both methods to the extent that your coding of manifest and latent content has been reasonably valid and reliable. If the agreement achieved by the two methods is fairly close though imperfect, then the final score might reflect the scores assigned in the two independent methods. If, on the other hand, coding manifest and latent content produces gross disagreement, then you would be well advised to reconsider your theoretical conceptualization.

Conceptualization and the Creation of Code Categories

For all research methods, conceptualization and operationalization typically involve the interaction of theoretical concerns and empirical observations. If, for example, you believe some newspaper editorials to be liberal and others to be conservative, then ask yourself why you think so. Read some editorials, asking yourself which are liberal and which are conservative. Was the political orientation of a particular editorial most clearly indicated by its manifest content or by its tone? Was your decision based on the use of certain terms (e.g., *leftist*, *fascist*, and so on) or on the support or opposition given to a particular issue or political personality?

Both inductive and deductive methods should be used in this activity. If you are testing theoretical propositions, then your theories should suggest empirical indicators of concepts. If you have begun with specific empirical observations, then you should attempt to derive general principles relating to them and then apply those principles to the other empirical observations.

Throughout this activity, you should remember that the operational definition of any variable is composed of the attributes included in it. Such attributes, moreover, should be mutually exclusive and exhaustive. A newspaper editorial, for instance, should not be described as both liberal and conservative, though you should probably allow for some to be middle of the road. It may be sufficient for your purposes to code novels as being erotic or nonerotic, but you might also want to consider that some could be antierotic. Paintings might be classified as representational or not if that satisfied your research purpose, or you might wish to further classify them as impressionistic, abstract, allegorical, and so forth.

Realize further that different levels of measurement may be used in content analysis. You may, for example, simply characterize newspaper editorials as liberal or conservative, or you might wish to use a more refined ranking, ranging from extremely liberal to extremely conservative. Bear in mind, however, that the level of measurement implicit in your coding methods does not necessarily reflect the nature of your variables. If the word *love* appeared 100 times in novel A and 50 times in novel B, then you would be justified in saying that the word *love* appeared twice as often in novel A but not that novel A was twice as erotic as novel B. Similarly, if person A agrees with twice as many anti-Semitic questionnaire statements as person B, that does not make person A twice as anti-Semitic.

No coding scheme should be used in content analysis until it has been carefully pretested. You should decide what manifest or latent contents of communications will be regarded as indicators of the different attributes that compose your research variables and then write down these operational definitions and use them in the actual coding of several units of observation. If you plan to use more than one coder in the final project, each should independently code the same set of observations so that you can determine the extent of agreement produced. In any event, you should take special note of any difficult cases: observations not easily classified using the operational definition. Finally, you should review the overall results of the pretest to ensure that they will be appropriate to your analytic concerns. If, for example, all of the pretest newspaper editorials have been coded as liberal, then you might want to reconsider your definition of that attribute.

As with other types of research, it is not essential that you commit yourself in advance to a specific definition of each concept. Often, you will do better to devise the most appropriate definition of a concept on the basis of your subsequent analyses. In the cases of erotic novels, for example, you might count separately the frequency with which different erotic words appear. This procedure would allow you to determine, during your later analysis, which words or combinations of words provided the most useful indication of your variable.

Counting and Record Keeping

If you plan to evaluate your content analysis data quantitatively, then your coding operation must be amenable to data processing. First, the end product of your coding must be *numerical*. If you are counting the frequency of certain words, phrases, or other manifest content, then that will necessarily be the case. Even if you are coding latent content on the basis of overall judgments, you will need to represent your coding decision numerically: 1 = very liberal, 2 = moderately liberal, 3 = moderately conservative, and so on.

Second, it is essential that your record keeping clearly distinguishes between your units of analysis and your units of observation, especially if they are different. The initial coding, of course, must relate to your units of observation. If novelists are your units of analysis, for instance, and you wish to characterize them through a content analysis of their novels, then your primary records will represent novels. You may then combine your scoring of individual novels to characterize each novelist.

Third, when counting, it normally is important to record the base from which the counting is done. It would tell us little that inappropriate male pronouns appeared 87 times in a book if we did not know about how many words were in the book altogether. The issue of observation base is most easily resolved if every observation is coded in terms of one of the attributes making up a variable. Rather than simply counting the number of liberal editorials in a given collection, for example, code each editorial by its political orientation, even if it must be coded "no apparent orientation."

Let's suppose that we want to study the practice of school social workers. More specifically, suppose we seek to learn whether school social workers today are more likely to intervene with family members and school personnel than in the past and whether in the past they were more likely to restrict their intervention to counseling the troubled student.

One possible approach would be to use school social workers as the units of analysis and to rank the practice orientation reflected in the assessment and process notes in a sample of case records for each social worker sampled. Table 17-2 illustrates a portion of a tally sheet that might utilize a four-point scale to code the orientation of each social worker. In the first column, each social worker in the sample has been assigned an identification number to facilitate mechanized data processing. The second column identifies the number of case records coded for each social worker, important information because it is necessary to calculate the percentage of case records with particular attributes.

The next column in Table 17-2 is for assigning a subjective overall assessment of the social worker's orientation. (Such assignments might later be compared with the several objective measures.) Other columns provide space for recording the number of case records that reflect specific interventions, target problems, or assessment notions. In a real content analysis, there would be spaces for recording additional information in the case records, such as client attributes, dates of service, social worker attributes, and so on.

TABLE 17.2 An Abbreviated Sample Tally Sheet

Social Worker ID	Number of Case Records Evaluated	Subjective Evaluation*	Number of Case Records with Environmental Target Problems	Number of Case Records with Environmental Interventions	Number of Case Records with Assessments Focusing on Student Psychopathology
001	37	2	10	6	25
002	26	4	25	24	2
003	44	3	30	23	14
004	30	1	0	0	30

*1—counseling only; 2—slightly environmental; 3—moderately environmental; 4—very environmental.

As in other forms of social research, there are now computer programs available to assist in content analysis. Here are a couple you might be interested in exploring:

Yoshikoder: http://www.yoshikoder.org

T-LAB: http://www.tlab.it/en

There are many more available programs, however, and German psychologist Matthias Romppel has provided an excellent review of them, as well as other content analysis resources, at http://www.content-analysis.de/category/software/quantitative analysis.

Qualitative Data Analysis

Not all content analysis results in counting. Sometimes a qualitative assessment of the materials is most appropriate. Berg (1989, pp. 123–125) discusses "negative case testing" as a technique for qualitative hypothesis testing. First, in the grounded theory tradition, you begin with an examination of the data that may yield a general hypothesis. Let's say that you're examining the leadership of a new community association by reviewing the minutes of meetings to see who made motions that were subsequently passed. Your initial examination of the data suggests that the wealthier members are the most likely to assume this leadership role.

The second stage in the analysis is to search your data to find all the cases that would contradict the initial hypothesis. In this instance, you would look for poorer members who made successful motions and wealthy members who never did.

Third, you must review each of the disconfirming cases and either (a) give up the hypothesis or (b) see how it needs to be fine-tuned.

Let's say that in your analysis of disconfirming cases, you notice that each of the unwealthy leaders has a graduate degree, whereas each of the wealthy nonleaders has little formal education. You may revise your hypothesis to consider both education and wealth as routes to leadership in the association. Perhaps you'll discover some threshold for leadership (a white-collar job, a level of income, and a college degree) beyond which those with the most money, education, or both are the most active leaders.

This process is an example of what Glaser and Strauss (1967) called *analytic induction*. It is inductive in that it primarily begins with observations, and it is analytic because it goes beyond description to find patterns and relationships among variables.

There are, of course, dangers in this form of analysis, as in all others. The chief risk is misclassifying observations to support an emerging hypothesis. For example, you may erroneously conclude that a nonleader didn't graduate from college, or you may decide that the job of factory foreman is "close enough" to being white collar.

Berg (1989, p. 124) offers techniques for avoiding these errors:

1. If there are sufficient cases, select some at random from each category in order to avoid merely picking those that best support the hypothesis.

2. Give at least three examples in support of every assertion you make about the data.

3. Have your analytic interpretations carefully reviewed by others uninvolved in the research project to see whether they agree.

4. Report whatever inconsistencies you do discover—any cases that simply do not fit your hypotheses. Realize that few social patterns are 100% consistent, so you may have discovered something important even if it doesn't apply to absolutely all of social life. However, you should be honest with your readers in that regard.

There are computer programs now available for qualitative content analysis. For example, you can try out MAXQDA at http://www.maxqda.com. Also, T-LAB, mentioned above, provides for some interesting qualitative analyses, such as mapping word associations in a political speech. Matthias Romppel has provided an excellent review of qualitative content analysis programs at http://www.content-analysis. de/category/software/qualitative-analysis.

Quantitative and Qualitative Examples of Content Analysis

Let's look at two additional examples of content analysis in action in social work. Both involve qualitative material. The first will illustrate the transformation of qualitative material into quantitative data. The second keeps a qualitative focus throughout.

A Quantitative Illustration: The Changing Self-Image of Social Work   Social workers Billups and Julia (1987) wanted to see whether and how the self-image of modern social work has been changing since the formation of the National Association of Social Workers (NASW) in 1955. They decided to study this issue by conducting a content analysis of social work practice position vacancy descriptions that appeared in 1960, 1970, and 1980.

An early task that confronted Billups and Julia was choosing the sources of vacancy descriptions that they would analyze. They thought it would make the most sense to use the publication put out by NASW that carries the most position vacancy descriptions in social work. For the years 1960 and 1970, that source was the journal *Social Casework*. Subsequently, NASW made its *NASW News* the prime source for position vacancy announcements. Accordingly, Billups and Julia decided to use *Social Casework* as their source for 1960 and 1970 and *NASW News* as their source for 1980.

Both publications were issued 10 times per year, and each issue contained a very large number of position vacancy descriptions. Because of their resource constraints, Billups and Julia did not want to analyze every one of the thousands of descriptions that had been published over the 3 years of interest. As explained in Chapter 15, with such a large population it is not necessary to study the entire population of descriptions in order to describe them accurately. Probability sampling techniques enable us to obtain accurate descriptions of a population based on a small fraction of that population. Billups and Julia selected a systematic random sample of 506 position vacancy descriptions, which accounted for 10% of the population of descriptions published in 1960, 1970, and 1980.

Next, Billups and Julia had to formulate a standard definition of dimensions of practice that they would look for in the position vacancy descriptions. They decided that they would examine manifest content only (not latent content). They defined dimensions of practice according to the following four major components: (a) position title (such as administrator, caseworker, clinical social worker, and therapist), (b) principal field of practice where the work would take place (such as family and child welfare and mental health), (c) major practice responsibilities (such as casework, group work, and direct or indirect practice), and (d) required or preferred education and experience. These four components were broken down into mutually exclusive and exhaustive subcategories. Standardized coding instructions were developed that were used by two coders. The intercoder reliability was assessed and found to be acceptable.

Billups and Julia found marked changes in the position vacancy announcements over the years. There was a dramatic drop in the mention of method—specific titles and responsibilities, for example. Whereas almost half of the announcements in 1960 mentioned the term *casework* or *caseworkers*, almost none did in 1980. Replacing the method-specific terms were terms such *as social worker*, *direct practice*, *clinical social workers*, and *therapists*.

Other sizable changes were observed in the fields of practice mentioned in the announcements. Whereas the family and child welfare field was mentioned by almost 60% of the announcements in 1960, in 1980 it was only 21%. The largest growth was observed in the fields of mental health, aging, corrections, rehabilitation, industrial social work, and substance abuse.

In interpreting these changes, Billups and Julia (1987) call attention to two possible contrasting trends. On the one hand, the reduction in the use of method-specific titles such as *casework* and *group work* might signify "a growing expectation that more social work practitioners will need to assume both a holistic view of problems and a broader repertoire of approaches to practice" than in the past (p. 21). On the other hand, decreases in public welfare fields and increases in the use of terms such as *therapist* might signify abandonment of the very poor and a narrower approach to practice imitating the roles of other clinical professions.

A Qualitative Illustration: Adoption Revelation and Communication The foregoing Billups and Julia study illustrates a quantitative approach to content analysis in that it transformed manifest qualitative material into quantitative categories. But some approaches to content analysis keep a strict qualitative focus throughout, reporting qualitative material only in qualitative terms and without transforming the material into quantitative data. An example of this approach in social work is a study by McRoy, Grotevant, Lopez, and Furuta (1990) on adoption revelation.

The researchers thought that the relatively high frequency of psychiatric treatment referrals of adopted children might indicate problems in the process of revealing to children that they were adopted. They decided to explore this issue by looking for patterns among case illustrations of problematic and nonproblematic revelations of adoption. Their nonprobability sample (an availability sample) consisted of 50 adoptive families whose adopted child was in residential treatment facilities and who had been adopted before the age of 2.

Intensive, open-ended interviews were conducted with the parents, adopted child, and caseworker for each family. The interviews were tape recorded and transcribed verbatim. A content analysis was then performed on the information on the tapes. (Thus, this study did not use an unobtrusive content analysis as a way of collecting data; it used intensive interviews for that purpose. The content analysis was applied after the data were collected.)

Like many qualitative research reports, this one did not provide much detail as to methodological procedures—details that would enable the reader to assess the validity of its conclusions. As we will discuss in the next two chapters, qualitative approaches eschew such structure in favor of more flexible approaches that permit deeper probing into subjective meanings—probes that usually seek to generate new insights more than they seek to test hypotheses.

McRoy and her associates presented the results of their content analysis of their interview data primarily in the form of lengthy quotes that they incorporated into composite case illustrations. In one case illustration, for example, a girl was not told by her parents that she was adopted until she was 10 years old. The quotation shows that she refused to believe them and was traumatized by the revelation. In two other case illustrations, boys who learned of being adopted when they were 5 years old reacted with anger or mistrust.

One theme that seemed to cut across the case illustrations was the need for social workers who worked with adoptive families to deal with issues concerning how, when, and by whom children are informed of their adoption. Social workers need to encourage adoptive parents to be the first to inform the child of the adoption.

Another recurrent theme was the need for ongoing communication between parents and the child about the adoption and the need to express empathy and understanding regarding the child's ongoing questions about his or her background and the reasons for being placed for adoption. The evidence for this conclusion is presented in several quotes that illustrate how learning of being adopted seemed to trigger problems in some families but not in others. In one, a daughter describes how she became rebellious against her parents when she found out at age 10 what adoption really means. The problem became exacerbated, in her view, when her parents seemed to have difficulty discussing the adoption with her and were not always truthful with her about aspects of the adoption. Other quotes are provided from cases that involved better communication where the children reported less discomfort with the adoption issue.

These illustrations of content analysis in action should give you a clearer picture of the procedures and potential that characterize this research method. Let's conclude the discussion of content analysis with an overview of its particular strengths and weaknesses.

Strengths and Weaknesses of Content Analysis

Probably the greatest advantage of content analysis is its economy in terms of both time and money. A single college student could undertake a content analysis, whereas undertaking a survey, for example, might not be feasible. There is no requirement for a large research staff; no special equipment is required. As long as you have access to the material to be coded, you can undertake content analysis.

Ease of correcting mistakes is another advantage of content analysis. If you discover you have botched a survey, you may be forced to repeat the whole research project with all its attendant costs in time and money. If you botch your qualitative research, it may be impossible to redo the project; the event under study may no longer exist. In content analysis, it's usually easier to repeat a portion of the study than it is for other research methods. You might be required, moreover, to recode only a portion of your data rather than repeat the entire enterprise.

Importantly, content analysis permits you to study processes that occur over long periods of time. You might focus on the imagery of blacks conveyed in American novels of 1850 to 1860, for example, or you might examine changing imagery from 1850 to the present.

Finally, content analysis has the advantage, mentioned at the outset of the chapter, of being unobtrusive—that is, the content analyst seldom affects the subject being studied. Because the books have already been written, the case records already recorded, and the speeches already presented, content analyses can have no effect on them. Not all research methods have this advantage.

Content analysis has disadvantages as well. For one thing, it's limited to the examination of recorded communications. Such communications may be oral, written, or graphic, but they must be recorded in some fashion to permit analysis.

Content analysis, as we have seen, has both advantages and disadvantages in terms of validity and reliability. For validity, problems are likely unless you happen to be studying communication processes per se. For instance, did the drop in the mention of terms such as *casework* in the Billups and Julia study necessarily mean that practitioners were becoming more holistic in their practice and using a broader repertoire of intervention approaches? Conceivably, the only thing that changed was the labels being used to describe the same forms of practice—that the field was merely using more fashionable terminology for the same old practices.

Although validity is a common problem with content analysis, the concreteness of materials studied in quantitative approaches to content analysis strengthens the likelihood of reliability. You can always code and recode and even recode again if you want, making certain that the coding is consistent. In qualitative research, by contrast, there's probably nothing you can do after the fact to ensure greater reliability in observation and categorization.

» HISTORICAL AND COMPARATIVE ANALYSIS

In this section of the chapter, we examine historical and comparative research, a method that differs substantially from those previously discussed, though it overlaps somewhat with qualitative research, content analysis, and the analysis of existing statistics.

Our examination of research methods to date has focused primarily on studies anchored in one point in time and in one locale, whether a particular small group or a nation. This focus, although accurately portraying the main emphasis of contemporary social work research, conceals the fact that social scientists are also interested in tracing the development of social forms over time and comparing those developmental processes across cultures.

Historical and comparative analysis is usually considered a qualitative method, one in which the researcher attempts to master many subtle details. The main resources for observation and analysis are historical records. Although a historical and comparative analysis might include content analysis, it is not limited to communications. The method's name includes the word *comparative* because most social scientists—in contrast to historians, who may simply describe a particular set of events—seek to discover common patterns that recur in different times and places.

Many historical writings can be found in the social work literature. Biographies of social work pioneers constitute a large segment of these writings. Another segment contains case studies that trace the development of social welfare policies and programs. Less common but perhaps more useful for informing current practice are studies that are more comparative in their efforts to seek recurring patterns that help explain the past and imply possible lessons for the present. An excellent example of the latter type of study, one with particular relevance to social work research, is *Historic Themes and Landmarks in Social Welfare Research* (Zimbalist, 1977).

Based on his analysis of social work research studies published between the late 19th century and the mid-1960s, Zimbalist identified a recurring cycle in which social work researchers exhibited an excessive tendency to go overboard in embracing the latest wave of research. Rather than take a balanced and critical outlook regarding the range of research approaches available, considering both their strengths and weaknesses and the conditions under which each is most appropriate, social work researchers tended to faddishly embrace promising new approaches as a panacea for the profession's research needs.

Zimbalist detected this cycle in early research on the causes of poverty and the measurement of its prevalence, in the embracing of the social survey movement at the beginning of the 20th century, and in the study of the multiproblem family in the mid-1960s. By describing the past, Zimbalist's work gives us a framework for understanding fads in social work research that may emerge today or in the future.

Another excellent example of historical and comparative research that offers lessons for the present is a study by Morrissey and Goldman (1984) on recurrent cycles of reform in the care of the chronic mentally ill. Morrissey and Goldman identify parallels between the deinstitutionalization movement during the 1970s and Dorothea Dix's 19th-century crusade to build state hospitals to provide asylum and sanctuary to individuals too sick to fend for themselves in communities that did not want them. In Dix's era, the reform intended to make care more humane by shifting its locus from the community to the hospital. In the much later era of deinstitutionalization, the reform intended to make care more humane by shifting its locus from the hospital to the community. But today we hear of large numbers of mentally ill individuals who are homeless or in jails and who are living in squalor—many of the same conditions that prompted Dix's crusade.

Morrissey and Goldman show how both reforms failed for the same reason: Each merely shifted the locus of care without garnering enough public fiscal support to ensure that the new locus of care would ultimately be any more humane than the old one. Without adequate financing, Dix's intended humane sanctuaries for the mentally ill too often became overcrowded, inhumane "snake pits" where sick individuals who could not afford expensive private care could be warehoused and forgotten. Without adequate financing, the noble intentions of the deinstitutionalization movement have for too many individuals led to community-based conditions as bad as in the back wards of state hospitals.

One lesson for today from this research is that if we seek to ensure more humane care for the long-term mentally ill, we must go beyond conceptualizing idealized programs or notions about where to provide care; the real issue is convincing the public to allocate adequate fiscal support for that care. Without the latter, our reformist efforts may be doomed to repeat the unintended consequences of previous reforms.

Sources of Historical and Comparative Data

As we saw in the case of existing statistics, there is no end of data available for analysis in historical research. To begin, historians may have already reported on whatever it is you want to examine, and their analyses can give you an initial grounding in the subject, a jumping-off point for more in-depth research. Ultimately, you will usually want to go beyond others' conclusions and examine raw data and draw your own conclusions. These data vary, of course, according to the topic under study. Raw data might, for example, include old letters or diaries, sermons or lectures, and so forth.

In discussing procedures for studying the history of family life, Rothman (1981) points to the following sources:

> In addition to personal sources, there are public records, which are also revealing of family history. Newspapers are especially rich in evidence on the educational, legal, and recreational aspects of family life in the past as seen from a local point of view. Magazines reflect more general patterns of family life; students often find

them interesting to explore for data on perceptions and expectations of mainstream family values. Magazines offer several different kinds of sources at once: visual materials (illustrations and advertisements), commentary (editorial and advice columns), and fiction. Popular periodicals are particularly rich in the last two. Advice on many questions of concern to families—from the proper way to discipline children to the economics of wallpaper—fills magazine columns from the early nineteenth century to the present. Stories that suggest common experiences or perceptions of family life appear with the same continuity. (p. 53)

Organizations generally document themselves, so if you are studying the development of some organization you should examine its official documents: charters, policy statements, speeches by leaders, and so on.

Often, official government documents provide the data needed for analysis. To better appreciate the history of race relations in the United States, Higginbotham (1978) examined 200 years of laws and court cases involving race. Himself the first African American appointed to a federal judgeship, Higginbotham found that the law, rather than protecting blacks, was the embodiment of bigotry and oppression. In the earliest court cases, there was considerable ambiguity over whether blacks were indentured servants or, in fact, slaves. Later court cases and laws clarified the matter—holding blacks to be something less than human.

Many of the source materials for historical research can be found in academic libraries. Specialized librarians may be available to help you locate obscure documents. Skills in using the library, therefore, are essential if you wish to conduct historical research. (We discuss using the library in Appendix A.)

Two broad types of source materials are *primary* sources and *secondary* sources. Primary sources provide firsthand accounts by someone who was present at an event—for example, diaries, letters, organizational bylaws, the minutes of a meeting, the orally reported memory of an eyewitness, and so on. Secondary sources describe past phenomena based on primary sources. Thus, if you cite a book on the history of Lyndon Johnson's Great Society social welfare programs, you are using a

secondary source. But if you go to the LBJ Presidential Library in Austin, Texas, and cite letters, laws, and official documents from that period that you find there, then you are using primary sources.

A danger in working exclusively with secondary sources is that you may merely repeat the mistakes contained in those sources and fail to give yourself the opportunity to provide a new, independent perspective on past events. But primary sources can be flawed as well. For example, an eyewitness could have been biased or may experience faulty memory.

Stuart (1981) argues that people who produce or write primary sources based on events they witnessed probably had a vested interest in those events. He cites an example of bias in the statistical reports of the populations of Native Americans on reservations by Indian agents in the late 19th century. Some agents exaggerated the population size in order to obtain more supplies for their reservations from the federal government's Office of Indian Affairs.

A television biography of Lyndon Johnson, aired by the Public Broadcasting System, relied heavily on primary sources, such as people who worked on Johnson's White House staff. His decision not to run for reelection in 1968 was portrayed largely in terms of his dismay over the tragedy of the war in Vietnam and his desire to find a way to negotiate an end to it. Unmentioned in the historical documentary was the fact that he announced his decision not to run on the eve of the Wisconsin primary election, when political polls there predicted that Senator Eugene McCarthy would beat him by a large margin in that primary and when newspaper articles spoke of the pending humiliation of an incumbent president of Johnson's stature being rejected by the voters of his own party. Was that omission due to overreliance on primary sources who were close to and fond of Lyndon Johnson? We can only surmise.

In conducting historical research, then, keep these cautions in mind. As we saw in the case of existing statistics, you cannot trust the accuracy of records—official or unofficial, primary or secondary. You need always to be wary of bias in your data sources. If all of your data on a pioneer social worker are taken from people who worked for that social worker, you are unlikely to get a well-rounded view of that person. If all of your data on the development of a social movement are taken from activists in the movement itself, then you are unlikely to gain a well-rounded view of the movement. The diaries of affluent, friendly visitors of the Charity Organization Societies of more than a century ago may not give you an accurate view of life among the immigrant poor they visited during those times.

As a final illustration of this point, suppose you conduct historical research in an effort to understand the chief forces at play that led to massive discharges from state hospitals as part of the deinstitutionalization movement in mental health. If you rely only on the reports of the staff of state mental health bureaucracies, you may be led to believe that those discharges were primarily a humanitarian response to advances in psychopharmacology and concern for the civil liberties of the mentally ill. You might not discover that the greatest number of discharges occurred long after the discovery of psychotropic drugs in the mid-1950s. Instead, they came in the mid-1970s, when fiscal crises in state governments

prompted state officials to recognize that by discharging patients from state hospitals to community facilities, the costs of caring for the mentally ill could be passed on from the state to the federal government (Morrissey & Goldman, 1984).

Your protection against these dangers in historical research lies in corroboration. If several sources point to the same set of "facts," your confidence in them might reasonably increase. Thus, when conducting historical research, you should try not to rely on a single source or on one type of source. Try to obtain data from every relevant source you can find and be sure to seek sources that represent different vested interests and different points of view. The box "Reading and Evaluating Documents" provides additional suggestions on how to use historical documents and what to make of them.

The critical review that Aminzade and Laslett urge for the reading of historical documents can

READING AND EVALUATING DOCUMENTS
Ron Aminzade and Barbara Laslett, University of Minnesota

The purpose of the following comments is to give you some sense of the kind of interpretive work that historians do and the critical approach they take toward their sources. It should help you to appreciate some of the skills that historians develop in their efforts to reconstruct the past from residues, to assess the evidentiary status of different types of documents, and to determine the range of permissible inferences and interpretations.

Here are some of the questions historians ask about documents:

1. Who composed the documents? Why were they written? Why have they survived all these years? What methods were used to acquire the information contained in the documents?

2. What are some of the biases in the documents, and how might you go about checking or correcting them? How inclusive or representative is the sample of individuals, events, etc. contained in the document? What were the institutional constraints and the general organizational routines under which the document was prepared? To what extent does the document provide more of an index of institutional activity than of the phenomenon being

studied? What is the time lapse between the observation of the events documented and the witnesses' documentation of them? How confidential or public was the document meant to be? What role did etiquette, convention, and custom play in the presentation of the material contained within the document? If you relied solely on the evidence contained in these documents, how might your vision of the past be distorted? What other kinds of documents might you look at for evidence on the same issues?

3. What are the key categories and concepts used by the writer of the document to organize the information presented? What are the selectivities or silences that result from these categories of thought?

4. What sort of theoretical issues and debates do these documents cast light on? What kinds of historical or sociological questions do they help answer? What sorts of valid inferences can one make from the information contained in these documents? What sorts of generalizations can one make on the basis of the information contained in these documents?

serve you more generally in life and not just in the pursuit of historical and comparative research. Consider applying some of the boxed questions with regard to presidential press conferences, advertising, or—gasp!—college textbooks. None of these offers a direct view of reality; all have human authors and human subjects.

Analytic Techniques

As a qualitative research method, historical and comparative research treats hypotheses differently from the way quantitative methods do when seeking to formulate explanations. Rather than sticking with a hypothesis throughout an entire study that has been rigidly designed in advance to test it, historical researchers are likely to revise and reformulate their hypotheses continually throughout the process of examining, analyzing, and synthesizing the historical documents they encounter.

Whereas the conclusions drawn from quantitative research methods can rest, in part, on numerical calculations—x is either greater than y or it isn't—qualitative conclusions are harder to pin down and more subject to debate. But qualitative conclusions involve more than mere opinions. Albert Einstein (1940) described the foundation of science this way:

> Science is the attempt to make the chaotic diversity of our sense-experience correspond to a logically uniform system of thought. In this system single experiences must be correlated with the theoretic structure in such a way that the resulting coordination is unique and convincing. (p. 487)

The historical and comparative researcher must find patterns among the voluminous details that describe the subject matter of study. Often, the "theoretic structure" that Einstein mentioned takes the form of what Weber called *ideal types*: conceptual models composed of the essential characteristics of social phenomena. Thus, for example, Weber himself did considerable research on bureaucracy. Having observed numerous actual bureaucracies, Weber (1925) detailed those qualities essential to bureaucracies in general: jurisdictional areas, hierarchically structured authority, written files, and so on. Weber did not merely list characteristics common to all the actual bureaucracies he observed. Rather, he needed to understand fully the essentials of bureaucratic

operation to create a theoretical model of the "perfect" (ideal type) bureaucracy.

Often, historical and comparative research is informed by a particular theoretical paradigm. Thus, Marxist scholars may undertake historical analyses of particular situations—such as the history of Hispanic minorities in the United States—to determine whether they can be understood in terms of the Marxist version of conflict theory.

Although historical and comparative research is regarded as a qualitative rather than a quantitative technique, historians often make use of quantitative methods. For example, historical analysts often use time-series data (see Chapter 12) to monitor changing conditions over time, such as data on population, crime rates, unemployment, and infant mortality rates. When historical researchers rely on quantitative data, their reports will rely on numbers, graphs, statistical trends, and the like to support their conclusions. When they rely on qualitative methods, their reports will contain less quantitative data and instead cite narrative material in their sources to illustrate the recurring patterns that they think they have detected.

» UNOBTRUSIVE ONLINE RESEARCH

"Big data" is a term you are likely to hear increasingly in the future. This refers to the gigantic data sets being automatically compiled from online activity. The most notorious of these in recent times has been the National Security Agency's (NSA) compilation and analysis of phone, email, and other communications. Prior to the development of massive data-storage capacities, this would have been unimaginable.

Big data are also in common use by commercial enterprises such as Google and Amazon. Have you ever noticed that after your read an article online about cocker spaniels, you start seeing margin ads on Facebook for dog food? You might begin receiving email advertising pet products, and the marginal ads on websites you visit in the future might feature similar commodities. Social media—Facebook, Pinterest, and Twitter, for example—are another source of big data.

The rise of social media has both impacted society and also opened new avenues for unobtrusive social research. An example of such research relevant to social work is the Durkheim Project, which is summarized in the magazine *Social Work Today* (Coyle, 2014). Named in honor of Emile Durkheim, a sociologist who pioneered studies of suicide more than a century ago, the Durkheim Project studies what words military veterans say in their social media posts that might be predictive of suicide attempts. In light of research suggesting that people intending to kill themselves don't say, "I'm going to kill myself," the project looks for statements pertaining to *being a burden*, others *being better off without me*, and so on. Participation in the study is voluntary. The project employs a methodology that is available on Facebook that uploads into a database the social media and cell phone text content of the participants. You can read more about the project at its website at http://www.durkheimproject.org/news/durkheim-project-will-analyze-opt-in-data/.

In another example of suicide-related social media research, Jashinsky et al. (2014) found that the proportion of Twitter tweets expressing suicidal ideation is strongly correlated with the actual number of suicides in the United States. Both the Jashinsky et al. and the Durkheim Project social media studies have implications not only for research on suicide, but also for clinical practice in that their methodologies enable the real-time monitoring of text content found to be predictive of tendencies toward suicide and other self-harmful behaviors. In that connection, it is important to emphasize that these studies are based on voluntary participation and use privacy protection procedures.

MAIN POINTS

- Unobtrusive measures are ways of studying social behavior without affecting it in the process.
- Secondary analysis is a form of research in which the data collected and processed in one study are reanalyzed in a subsequent study. Often, the subsequent study is conducted by a different researcher and often for a different purpose. Sometimes, however, a different researcher will reanalyze the data for the same purpose, stemming perhaps from doubts about the conclusions derived from the original analysis in the first study.

- Some data sets are in the form of aggregated existing statistics in administrative and public records. When the data are in aggregate form only, they cannot be reanalyzed using the individual as the unit of analysis. Instead, they can be analyzed only in the form of statistics that apply to the aggregate, such as the prevalence of child abuse in different geographic areas, the proportions of different types of services provided in different agencies, and so on.
- Common potential advantages of secondary analysis include cost savings, benefiting from the work of top-flight professionals, analyzing data generated by rigorous sampling approaches with large samples and high response rates, having a large number of variables that makes it possible to conduct a sophisticated multivariate statistical analysis, the likelihood that the original study was methodologically strong in general, facilitating IRB approval, accessing hard-to-identify populations, monitoring trends over time, facilitating cross-national comparisons, and obtaining technical support.
- Common potential limitations of secondary analysis include problems of validity and reliability, missing data, inadequate documentation, and unanticipated feasibility issues.
- A variety of government and nongovernment agencies provide aggregate data for social work research studies.
- Before investing a great deal of time in planning a secondary analysis, you should check the data source to see if the data you need are there at all. If they are there, you should check to see whether large chunks of the data on certain key variables are missing and whether the data contain sufficient variation on your intended variables.
- Content analysis is a social research method that is appropriate for studying human communications. Besides being used to study communication processes, it may be used to study other aspects of social behavior.
- Standard probability sampling techniques are appropriate in content analysis.
- *Manifest content* refers to the directly visible, objectively identifiable characteristics of a communication, such as the specific words in a book, the specific colors used in a painting, and so forth. That is one focus for content analysis.

- *Latent content* refers to the meanings contained within communications. The determination of latent content requires judgments on the part of the researcher.

- Coding is the process of transforming raw data—either manifest or latent content—into standardized, quantitative form.

- Both quantitative and qualitative techniques are appropriate for interpreting content analysis data.

- The advantages of content analysis include economy, ease of correcting mistakes, and the ability to study processes occurring over a long time. Its disadvantages are that it is limited to recorded communications and can raise issues of reliability and validity.

- Social work researchers also use historical and comparative methods to discover common patterns that recur in different times and places. Two broad types of source materials for historical research are primary sources and secondary sources.

- Primary sources provide firsthand accounts by someone who was present at an event—for example, diaries, letters, organizational bylaws, the minutes of a meeting, the orally reported memory of an eyewitness, and so on. Secondary sources describe past phenomena based on primary sources.

- A danger in working exclusively with secondary sources is that you may merely repeat the mistakes contained in those sources and fail to give yourself the opportunity to provide a new, independent perspective on past events. But primary sources can be flawed as well. For example, an eyewitness could have been biased or may experience faulty memory.

- When conducting historical research, you should try not to rely on a single source or on one type of source. Your protection against dangers in using primary and secondary sources lies in corroboration. If several sources point to the same set of "facts," then your confidence in them might reasonably increase. *Hermeneutics* refers to interpreting social life by mentally taking on the circumstances, views, and feelings of the participants.

- An *ideal type* is a conceptual model that is composed of the essential qualities of a social phenomenon.

- The rise of social media has opened new avenues for unobtrusive social research.

REVIEW QUESTIONS AND EXERCISES

1. In two or three paragraphs, outline a content analysis design to determine whether the Republican Party or the Democratic Party is more supportive of public spending on social welfare. Be sure to specify sampling methods and the relevant measurements.

2. Suppose you assess the need for and likely utilization of a suicide prevention program on your campus by conducting a secondary analysis of existing data collected in a recent survey of students asking them about a wide range of issues, including whether they've ever contemplated suicide. Discuss the advantages and disadvantages of basing your needs assessment solely on this secondary analysis.

3. Suppose, in response to managed care pressures, that 5 years ago your child and family services agency dramatically increased the amount of time practitioners had to spend filling out forms on each case, including the provision of details about diagnoses and other information bearing on whether and how long services for each case were eligible for reimbursement from managed care companies. Discuss the specific ways in which this development might create special problems in analyzing existing agency statistics regarding historical trends in the types of diagnoses of clients served by your agency, the nature and amount of services provided, and client background characteristics.

INTERNET EXERCISES

1. Find the following articles that utilized content analysis and were published in the October 2002 issue of the journal *Social Work*:

   "Among the Missing: Content on Lesbian and Gay People in Social Work Journals," by R. V. Voorhis and M. Wagner

   "Client's View of a Successful Helping Relationship," by D. S. Ribner and C. Knei-Paz

Identify each study's methodological strengths and weaknesses, indicate whether it used manifest or latent coding (or both), and indicate whether its methods were quantitative or qualitative. Finally, briefly explain why, in your view, each study's findings did or did not provide important implications for social policy or social work practice.

2. Go to the following website on content analysis: http://www.content-analysis.de/. Once there, find bibliographies on content analysis and lists of software programs for qualitative and quantitative content analyses.

3. Using a search engine such as Google or Yahoo!, enter the search term "existing statistics," then click "Search." Your window will then display a list of various sources of existing statistics. Click on a source that piques your interest. Examine the types of data that are displayed and formulate a research question of general interest that could be answered with the displayed data.

4. Using the Internet, find out how many countries have a higher "expected life expectancy" than the United States. (You might want to try the Population Reference Bureau at www.prb.org.)

Visit CengageBrain.com for additional practice and study opportunities including experiential exercises, research tools, glossary, flashcards, and sample test items.

Qualitative Research Methods

Throughout this text, we have been discussing ways to improve the quality of research data by using qualitative and unobtrusive methods of data collection. For the most part, however, we have examined these methods as a way to complement and strengthen primarily quantitative studies and in the context of other issues such as measurement, sampling, and evaluation. The chapters in Part 6 will be devoted exclusively to qualitative research methods, discussing them in more depth than in previous chapters.

Chapter 18 will focus on general principles in qualitative research, such as appropriate topics, qualitative research paradigms, qualitative sampling, strengths and weaknesses of qualitative research, and ethics in qualitative research. It will show how qualitative studies can sometimes provide deeper understandings and new insights that might escape quantitative studies. It will also address some strategies for strengthening the rigor of qualitative studies.

Chapter 19 will discuss specific types of qualitative research methods, such as participant observation, qualitative interviewing, recording observations, life history, and focus groups. As you read these chapters, you will see how the distinction sometimes can be fuzzy between the general principles and paradigms of qualitative research and the specific methods of qualitative research.

Chapter 20 will examine how to analyze the open-ended data generated by qualitative research studies. We'll look at some conceptual procedures used in searching for meaning among qualitative data and also examine the use of computer software designed for analyzing qualitative data.

18

Qualitative Research: General Principles

EPAS Competencies for This Chapter

Competency 3 **Advance Human Rights and Social and Economic Justice:** In this chapter, you will learn more about participatory action research and standards for evaluating qualitative studies—which pertain to using research to empower oppressed groups.

Competency 4 **Engage in Practice-Informed Research and Research-Informed Practice:** This chapter, as a whole, enhances your preparedness to engage in practice-informed qualitative research and to have qualitative research inform your practice.

What You'll Learn in This Chapter

This chapter discusses general principles for the use of qualitative techniques for conducting social work research in natural settings—where the action is. This type of research can produce a richer understanding of many social phenomena than can be achieved through other observational methods, provided that the researcher observes in a deliberate, well-planned, and active way.

» INTRODUCTION

Many of the research methods discussed so far in this book are designed to produce data that are appropriate for *quantitative* (statistical) analysis. For example, surveys provide data from which to calculate the percentage unemployed in a population, the mean income, and so forth. In contrast, as discussed in Chapter 4, qualitative research methods attempt to tap the deeper meanings of particular human experiences and are intended to generate qualitative data: theoretically richer observations that are not easily reduced to numbers. For example, a qualitative investigation of homelessness might note the "defiant dignity" of homeless people who refuse to use squalid shelters. Likewise, a qualitative investigation might describe the "fatalism" of chronically unemployed men who hang out together. In both cases, the qualitative investigations would not be able to express either the dignity or the fatalism as numerical quantities or degrees.

EP 4

Qualitative research is not only a data-collecting activity but also frequently—and perhaps typically—a theory-generating activity. As a qualitative researcher, you will seldom approach your task with precisely defined hypotheses to be tested. More typically, you will attempt to make sense of an ongoing process that cannot be predicted in advance— making initial observations, developing tentative general conclusions that suggest particular types of further observations, making those observations and thereby revising your conclusions, and so forth. The alternation of induction and deduction discussed in Chapter 3 is perhaps nowhere more evident and essential than in good qualitative research.

» TOPICS APPROPRIATE FOR QUALITATIVE RESEARCH

One of the key strengths of qualitative research is the comprehensiveness of perspective it gives the researcher. By going directly to the social phenomenon under study and observing it as completely as possible, you can develop a deeper understanding of it. This mode of observation, then, is especially, though not exclusively, appropriate to research topics that appear to defy simple quantification.

The qualitative researcher may recognize several nuances of attitude and behavior that might escape researchers using other methods. For example, qualitative research provides a superior method for studying in depth what it feels like to be homeless.

Finally, qualitative research is also a good way to study of social processes over time. Thus, the qualitative researcher might be in a position to examine the rumblings and final explosion of a riot as events actually occur rather than try to reconstruct them afterward.

Other good uses of qualitative research methods would include protest demonstrations, agency board meetings, labor negotiations, public hearings, interactions between social workers and clients, and similar events that take place within a relatively limited area and time. Several such observations must be combined in a more comprehensive examination across time and space.

In *Analyzing Social Settings*, Lofland and Lofland (1995, pp. 101–113) discuss several elements of social life appropriate for qualitative research. They call them *thinking topics*:

1. *Practices*. This refers to various kinds of behavior.

2. *Episodes*. Here the Loflands include a variety of events such as divorce, crime, and illness.

3. *Encounters*. This involves two or more people meeting and interacting in immediate proximity with one another.

4. *Roles*. Qualitative research is also appropriate to the analysis of the positions people occupy and the behavior associated with those positions: occupations, family roles, and ethnic groups.

5. *Relationships*. Much of social life can be examined in terms of the kinds of behavior that are appropriate to pairs or sets of roles: mother–son relationships, friendships, and the like.

6. *Groups*. Moving beyond relationships, qualitative research can also be used to study small groups, such as friendship cliques, athletic teams, and work groups.

7. *Organizations*. Beyond small groups, qualitative researchers also study formal organizations, such as hospitals and schools.

8. *Settlements*. It is difficult to study large societies such as nations, but qualitative researchers

often study smaller-scale societies, such as villages, ghettos, and neighborhoods.

9. *Social worlds*. There are also ambiguous social entities with vague boundaries and populations that are nonetheless proper participants for social scientific study: "the sports world," "Wall Street," and the like.

10. *Lifestyles or subcultures*. Finally, social scientists sometimes focus on ways that large numbers of people adjust to life: groups such as a "ruling class" or an "urban underclass." In all of these social settings, qualitative research can reveal things that would not otherwise be apparent. It does so by probing social life in its natural setting. Although some things can be studied adequately in questionnaires or in the laboratory, others cannot. And direct observation in the field lets you observe subtle communications and other events that might not be anticipated or measured otherwise.

» PROMINENT QUALITATIVE RESEARCH PARADIGMS

There are many different approaches to qualitative research. This section examines four qualitative field research paradigms that are particularly applicable to social work: naturalism, grounded theory, participatory action research, and case studies. Although this survey won't exhaust the variations on the method, it should give you an appreciation of the possibilities. It's important to recognize that specific methods are not attached exclusively to any of these paradigms. The important distinctions of this section are epistemological, having to do with what the data mean, regardless of how they were collected.

Naturalism

Naturalism is an old tradition in qualitative research. It emphasizes observing people in their everyday settings and reporting their stories as they tell them. The earliest field researchers operated on the positivist assumption that social reality was "out there," ready to be naturally observed and reported by the researcher as it "really is" (Gubrium & Holstein, 1997). This tradition started in the 1930s and 1940s at the University of Chicago's sociology department, whose faculty and students fanned out across the city to observe and understand local neighborhoods and communities. The researchers of that era and their research approach are now often referred to as the "Chicago School."

One of the earliest and best-known studies that illustrates this research tradition is Whyte's ethnography of Cornerville, an Italian American neighborhood, in his book *Street Corner Society* (Whyte, 1943). An ethnography is a study that focuses on detailed and accurate description rather than explanation. Like other naturalists, Whyte believed that to fully learn about social life on the streets, he needed to become more of an insider. He made contact with "Doc," his key informant, who appeared to be one of the street-gang leaders. Doc let Whyte enter his world, and Whyte got to participate in the activities of the people of Cornerville. His study offered something that surveys could not: a richly detailed picture of life among the Italian immigrants of Cornerville.

An important feature of Whyte's study is that he reported the reality of the people of Cornerville on their terms. The naturalist approach is based on telling "their" stories the way they "really are," not the way the ethnographer understands them. The narratives collected by Whyte are taken at face value as the social truth of the Cornerville residents. The box "Two Illustrations of Naturalistic, Ethnographic Studies of Homelessness" provides a more detailed illustration of the application of the naturalism paradigm to a problem of great concern to social workers.

While ethnographers seek to discover and understand the patterns of living among those they are studying, Duneier (1999) has warned against what he calls the "ethnographic fallacy." This refers to an overgeneralization and oversimplification of the patterns observed. Despite the existence of patterns within groups, there is also diversity, and you need to be wary of broad assertions suggesting that "the poor," "the French," or "cheerleaders" act or think in certain ways as though all members of the group do so.

Grounded Theory

Grounded theory, a term coined by Glaser and Strauss (1967), was mentioned earlier in connection with the inductive approach to understanding. Grounded theory begins with observations and

TWO ILLUSTRATIONS OF NATURALISTIC, ETHNOGRAPHIC STUDIES OF HOMELESSNESS

As research associates of the Community Service Society of New York City, Baxter and Hopper (1982) embarked in 1979 on an ethnographic investigation of the habitats of homeless individuals in New York City. They originally envisioned their research as part of a larger study of the living conditions of the chronically mentally disabled. Their early observations, however, revealed that the homeless population was far too heterogeneous and the origins of homelessness too diverse to limit their study to the mentally disabled. Displaying the flexibility of field researchers, they modified their focus to include more than the mentally disabled. Their chief concern was "to document how the homeless meet and resolve daily problems of survival in an often hostile environment" (p. 395). They conducted their observations wherever the homeless might sleep, stake out a domain, be fed, or receive services—at

> park benches, street corners, doorways, subways, train stations, bus and ferry terminals, missions and flophouses, publicly and privately operated shelters, food programs, and emergency rooms. The terrain was initially mapped out through interviews with individuals and groups ... serving, researching, or advocating on behalf of the homeless. In the course of our own field work, additional sites were periodically discovered and investigated, including hallways and stairwells in occupied buildings, abandoned buildings, the piers along the East and Hudson rivers, alleyways, and heating vents—often with the homeless serving as guides. (p. 395)

Baxter and Hopper also found some homeless individuals in such out-of-the-way refuges as the steam tunnels running under Park Avenue and loading docks in commercial districts that are unused at night. Had they not used a qualitative approach, they would not have been able to anticipate such locations, and consequently they would not have found as diverse a sample.

They typically began their observations by initiating conversation with the offer of food, coffee, cigarettes, or change, and they introduced themselves as researchers on homelessness. But after encountering resistance, they again displayed flexibility; they began delaying this information awhile and

describing their work in simpler terms, such as that of writers doing a story on homelessness.

In addition to their direct observations and interviews with the homeless, Baxter and Hopper interviewed others who worked with or were connected with homeless people. And on some occasions, they posed as homeless individuals themselves, such as when they entered public shelters to stay overnight. This enabled them to gain insights that would have been difficult to gain from the outside. For example, they were able to discover that from the standpoint of the homeless, their refusal of service has a more rational meaning than it does to professionals or to the public. The latter groups view service refusal as a reflection of defects in character or judgment, a disinterest in being helped, or a preference to live on the street. But Baxter and Hopper's observations indicated that whenever services were offered, they were not adequate to accommodate the number of homeless individuals who sought to use them. Refusal of service seemed rational in light of the deplorable conditions they observed in the public shelters, conditions that sometimes made living in the streets and parks seem more attractive.

In the public shelters, Baxter and Hopper observed overcrowding, lack of sanitation, and inadequate security—conditions that "would not meet federal regulations for prison cells" (p. 398). Among other things, they noted the few toilets and showers, which were often filthy or out of order; louse-infested mattresses and linens; pilfering of clothing; threats of violence; and fears of catching some dread disease.

But despite observing how service refusal can have an element of rationality, Baxter and Hopper also observed the harshness and toll of life on the streets, where the homeless are hungry, cold, socially isolated, and deprived of sleep. They observed how this strain can disorient individuals who were not mentally ill before they became homeless, and they noted that clinicians generally do not understand this because they typically see the homeless only after their desperate straits have taken a toll on their mental health.

Through their immersion with the homeless, they also gained insights about the deeper meanings of other aspects of homelessness. For example, they observed the protective function of appearing bizarre and filthy and of having a noxious odor, which can protect homeless women by repelling men on the prowl. (Baxter and Hopper added, however, that foulness of appearance is virtually unavoidable given the scarcity of toilets and bathing and laundry facilities.)

In light of these insights—insights that have escaped others—Baxter and Hopper concluded that the presumption of incompetence on the part of the homeless was a self-fulfilling prophecy because the homeless are eager to receive decent and humane care in those rare instances when such care is available. Despite the great hardships of living on the streets, that decision can have the deeper meaning of salvaging a sense of defiant dignity and self-determination for the homeless in the face of the deplorable conditions of the shelters available to them. Baxter and Hopper ended their report with several proposals intended to make more and better services available to the homeless, to make it more rational for them to use those services, and to enhance the efforts of social workers to help the homeless.

Several years later, Snow and Anderson (1987) conducted exploratory field research into the lives of homeless people in Austin, Texas. Their major task was to understand how the homeless construct and negotiate their identity while knowing that the society they live in attaches a stigma to homelessness. Snow and Anderson believed that, to achieve this goal, the collection of data had to arise naturally. Like Whyte in *Street Corner Society*, they found key informants whom they followed in their everyday journeys, such as at their day-labor pickup sites or under bridges. Snow and Anderson chose to memorize the conversations they participated in or the "talks" that homeless people had with each other. At the end of the day, the two researchers debriefed and wrote detailed field notes about all the "talks" they encountered. They also taped in-depth interviews with their key informants.

Snow and Anderson reported "hanging out" with homeless people over the course of 12 months for a total of 405 hours in 24 different settings. Out of these rich data, they identified three related patterns in homeless people's conversations. First, the homeless showed an attempt to distance themselves from other homeless people, from the low-status job they currently had, or from the Salvation Army they depended on. Second, they embraced their street-life identity, their group membership, or a certain belief about why they are homeless. Third, they told fictive stories that always contrasted with their everyday life. For example, they would often say that they were making much more money than they really were or even that they were going to be rich.

looks for patterns, themes, or common categories. This does not mean that researchers have no preconceived ideas or expectations. In fact, what has been previously learned will shape the new search for generalities. However, the analysis is not set up to confirm or disconfirm specific hypotheses. By the same token, the openness of the grounded theory approach allows a greater latitude for the discovery of the unexpected, some regularity (or disparity) totally unanticipated by the concepts that might make up a particular theory or hypothesis.

Although grounded theory emphasizes an inductive process, it can also incorporate deductive processes. It does this through the use of constant comparisons. As researchers detect patterns in their inductive observations, they develop concepts and working hypotheses based on those patterns. Then they seek out more cases and conduct more observations and compare those observations against the concepts and hypotheses developed from the earlier observations.

Their selection of new cases is guided by theoretical sampling concepts. Theoretical sampling begins by selecting new cases that seem to be similar to those that generated previously detected concepts and hypotheses. Once the researcher perceives that no new insights are being generated from the observation of similar cases, a different type of case is selected, and the same process is repeated: Additional cases similar to this new type of case are selected until no new insights are being generated. This cycle of exhausting similar cases and then seeking a different category of cases can be repeated until the researcher believes that further seeking of new types of cases will not alter the findings.

Grounded theorists use basically the same methods that are used by other qualitative researchers—methods that we'll discuss in greater depth in Chapter 19, such as participant observation and open-ended interviewing.

To understand the use of constant comparisons in the grounded theory process, imagine that you are seeking to discover the key components of effective community-based social work interventions aimed at forestalling relapse among young adults who have had schizophrenia. You might begin with open-ended interviews of several practitioners who have excellent reputations for their clinical effectiveness in this area. Perhaps you would ask those practitioners to recall their most successful cases and discuss the interventions they used with them.

Let's suppose that you perceive a common pattern across every interview—a pattern in which each practitioner mentions the use of social skills training in the rehabilitation of the young adults and communication skills training in helping their parents cope with them. You might therefore develop a working hypothesis that the use of such behavioral interventions distinguishes effective from ineffective practice in this area.

To better ground your hypothesis in the empirical world, you might interview several additional practitioners with good clinical reputations to see if the same patterns are generated. If those interviews fail to generate new insights, you might reinterview the practitioners but use a different cases sampling approach. This time you might ask them to discuss the interventions they employed with their least successful cases. Suppose a few of them mention the same behavioral interventions that they mentioned with their most successful cases—the same behavioral interventions to which your working hypothesis refers. This would force you to modify your hypothesis. You might probe to uncover other aspects of their practice with their least successful cases—aspects that might help explain why the same interventions that seemed to work well with other cases did not work with these cases.

Let's suppose that these probes generate another common pattern—a pattern in which each of the least successful clients failed or refused to take their prescribed medications. Based on this observation, your modified working hypothesis might combine medication-monitoring interventions with behavioral interventions in distinguishing effective practice.

Continuing the grounded theory process, you would interview additional practitioners and ask about different types of cases. For example, you might learn of parents who did not benefit from the communications skills training because the practitioner did not adequately develop a therapeutic alliance with them before introducing that training. This might lead you to modify your working hypothesis further, perhaps by adding the prerequisite that family intervention be delivered in the context of a supportive relationship with the practitioner, one in which the parents understand that they are not being blamed for their children's illness.

At this point, you might realize that all of your cases have involved clients who live with their parents. Therefore, you might conduct interviews in reference to successful and unsuccessful cases in which the clients did not live with their parents. You might learn that with clients who do not live with their parents, effective practice also requires a lot of attention to securing suitable living arrangements and does not involve family communication skills training. Further sampling might identify many cases that involve dual diagnoses of schizophrenia and substance abuse. You might have to modify your hypothesis to include substance abuse interventions geared for this target population.

By the time you have completed the grounded theory process, you will have interviewed many different practitioners (perhaps including some with poor clinical reputations) and asked about many other types of cases. This additional empirical grounding will probably have led you to add many more modifications to your hypothesis. Some of them might deal with practitioner attributes such as empathy, warmth, and diagnostic skill. Some modifications might deal with client attributes, such as the need for different types of interventions depending on client degree of impairment, social support resources, and so on. Other modifications might deal with the full gamut of case management functions.

Gilgun (1991) sees several parallels between the grounded theory method and what social workers do in direct practice—particularly regarding clinical assessment. Both methods start where the case is and focus on the informant's perceptions. Both try to understand the case in a wider environmental context. Both combine induction and deduction and the constant comparison method in formulating working hypotheses based on observations and then modifying those hypotheses in light of further observations. Both try to avoid imposing preconceived ideas or theories on cases. Both rely heavily on open-ended interviewing and use largely the same interviewing skills (as will be evident later in this chapter when we discuss qualitative interviewing). The process of using notes and memos in grounded theory resembles the social worker's use of process recording and problem-oriented case record keeping. Both attempt "to keep a balance between being in tune with clients and maintaining an analytic stance" (Gilgun, 1991, p. 17). Both like to conduct observations in natural settings, such as in the home or community. The box "An Illustration of Using Grounded Theory in Studying Homelessness" provides an example of a social work investigation based on the grounded theory paradigm.

Participatory Action Research

In the participatory action research paradigm, the researcher's function is to serve as a resource to those being studied—typically, disadvantaged groups—as an opportunity for them to act effectively in their own interest. The disadvantaged participants define their problems, define the remedies desired, and take the lead in designing the research that will help them realize their aims. This paradigm is not exclusively qualitative in that it is distinguished by its empowerment aims, not its methods. We discuss it here, however, because its orientation toward having research participants make decisions about the research process is more akin to qualitative research than quantitative. Moreover, when it does employ quantitative methods, it tends to couple them with qualitative methods in a mixed-methods approach.

This approach began in developing nations research development, but it spread quickly to Europe and North America (Gaventa, 1991). It comes from a vivid critique of classical social science research. According to the participatory action research paradigm, traditional research is perceived as an "elitist model" (Whyte, Greenwood, & Lazes, 1991) that reduces the "subjects" of research to "objects" of research. According to many advocates of this perspective, the distinction between the researcher and the researched should disappear. They argue that the subjects who will be affected by research should also be responsible for its design.

Implicit in this approach is the belief that research functions not only as a means of knowledge production but also as a "tool for the education and development of consciousness as well as mobilization for action" (Gaventa, 1991, pp. 121–122). Advocates of participatory action research equate access to information with power and argue that this power has been kept in the hands of the dominant class, sex, ethnicity, or nation. Once people see themselves as researchers, they automatically regain power over knowledge.

Examples of this approach include community power structure research, corporate research, and "right-to-know" movements (Whyte et al., 1991). Most germane to social work, participatory action research often involves poor people because they are typically less able to influence the policies and actions that affect their lives. Quoss, Cooney, and Longhurst (2000) report a research project involving welfare policy in Wyoming. University students, many of them welfare recipients, undertook research and lobbying efforts aimed at getting Wyoming to accept postsecondary education as "work" under the state's new welfare regulations.

This project began against the backdrop of the 1996 Personal Responsibility and Work Opportunity Reconciliation Act, which eliminated education waivers that had been available under the previous welfare law, the 1988 Family Support Act. These waivers had permitted eligible participants in the cash assistance Aid to Families with Dependent Children program to attend college as an alternative to work training requirements. Empirical studies of welfare participants who received these waivers have provided evidence that education, in general, is the most effective way to stay out of poverty and achieve self-sufficiency (Quoss et al., 2000, p. 47).

The students began by establishing an organization, Empower, and making presentations on campus to enlist broad student and faculty support. They compiled existing research relevant to the issue and established relationships with members of the state legislature. By the time the 1997 legislative session opened, they were actively engaged in the process of modifying state welfare laws to take account of the shift in federal policy.

The students prepared and distributed fact sheets and other research reports that would be relevant to the legislators' deliberations. They attended committee meetings and lobbied legislators on a one-to-one basis. When erroneous or misleading data were introduced into the discussions, the student researchers were on hand to point out the errors and offer corrections.

Ultimately, they were successful. Welfare recipients in Wyoming were allowed to pursue postsecondary education as an effective route out of poverty.

EP 3

Case Studies

A case study is an idiographic examination of a single individual, family, group, organization, community, or society. Its chief purpose is description, although attempts at explanation are also acceptable. Examples would include an in-depth description of a client system and an intervention with it, a depiction of the daily life and folkways of a street gang, an analysis of the organizational dynamics of a social welfare agency and how those dynamics influence the way social services are delivered, and a description of the emergence and experience of a grassroots community organization.

Although case studies are generally seen as a qualitative approach to research, the mode of observation used is not what distinguishes a case study. Instead, case studies are distinguished by their exclusive focus on a particular case (or several cases in a multiple-case study) and their use of a full variety of evidence regarding that case, including, perhaps, evidence gathered by quantitative research methods. Sources of evidence might include existing documents, observations, and interviews. Evidence might also be sought by surveying people about the case or perhaps manipulating some variables (such as when we employ single-case evaluation designs, as described in Chapter 13).

For example, a case study might be conducted to understand why a state decided to close down several of its institutions for the mentally or developmentally disabled, how it implemented that decision, what unanticipated problems occurred in the aftermath of the closings, and so on. Or a case study might focus on a particular client, perhaps employing a single-case evaluation of intervention with that client as part of the case study.

Although case study researchers typically seek an idiographic understanding of the particular case under examination, case studies can form the basis for the development of more general, nomothetic theories. The logical focus in case studies is not on statistical generalization to other cases (or external

validity). Instead, the focus is on connecting case study findings to a particular theory. This is done by showing how the weight of the various sources of evidence gathered in the case study is consistent with a theory. This is not an adequate test of the theory because it is only one case, but the accumulation of consistent results in the replication process can serve as a useful test of the theory in the same way that replications of single-case evaluations or group experiments are utilized.

The rationale for using the case study method typically is the availability of a special case that seems to merit intensive investigation. For example, suppose a particular state is the first to implement a massive program of deinstitutionalization. You might want to conduct a case study of that event and its impact as a way of informing similar policy considerations in other states. Another example might be the first effort to provide case management services in a rural area. A case study might identify implementation problems and the ways they were handled—information that could be of great value to program planners in other rural regions.

Here is one more example. Suppose you theorize that people who volunteer in social service agencies do so primarily to meet egoistic needs that are not being fulfilled in their other life roles, even though they might say they are doing it for altruistic reasons. You might decide to select an agency where your theory might get its stiffest test, with the rationale that if it seems to hold up in that agency, then it would probably hold up anywhere. Maybe, for example, you would study volunteers who work with terminally ill patients in a hospice program, believing that such a program offers the greatest likelihood of finding people whose real underlying motives are truly as altruistic as they claim.

The application of the case study method that is perhaps of greatest interest to social workers is when the case being studied is an individual, group, or family engaged in social work treatment. In the past, much of our profession's practice wisdom was generated by clinical case studies of clients. That method fell out of favor in the 1960s and 1970s as skepticism grew about the objectivity and validity of qualitative case studies about one's own clients, accompanied by a demand for evidence generated from studies with experimental controls for internal validity.

Today, however, a new wave of enthusiasm has emerged for qualitative methods in general as

AN ILLUSTRATION OF USING GROUNDED THEORY IN STUDYING HOMELESSNESS

Another qualitative study of homelessness was reported by Belcher (1991). Belcher was interested in the pathways people travel as they drift from one stage of homelessness to another. Using the grounded theory method, Belcher and two colleagues conducted three rounds of informal conversational interviews over a 3-month period with 40 Baltimore homeless men and women whom they identified using snowball sampling in facilities for the homeless. To gain the trust of respondents and to reduce their anxiety about the interviews, Belcher and his colleagues eschewed carrying paper and pencil, bringing interview guides, or arranging specific interview times. They did not, however, pose as homeless persons, and they told the respondents who they were.

Their interview process began with an initial orienting interview, after which the researchers recorded responses into a case file for the respondent. All the files were then reviewed in an attempt to identify common themes. A second interview was then conducted with the same respondents (after locating them), guided by a set of questions that the researchers developed and kept in mind based on the themes identified from the first set of interviews. After these interviews, responses were again recorded in the case files. Patterns that were detected from responses to both rounds of interviews enabled the researchers to formulate working hypotheses that they checked out with respondents in the third round of interviews. These hypotheses were then revised in light of the responses to the third interview.

The researchers used triangulation in the study by verifying important interview responses with other sources. If, for example, a respondent reported being ejected from a particular shelter, the researchers cross-checked this information with the operator of that shelter.

The process just described led to the postulation that homeless individuals tend to drift downward through three stages of homelessness. In the first stage, they are living below the poverty line and move in and out of intense poverty. Their living arrangements fluctuate episodically in line with fluctuations in their economic plight—sometimes they reside in a tenuous home, and at other times double up with friends or family. They are anxious and fearful, may abuse substances somewhat, have a network of informal supports, and are connected to service providers.

In the second stage, they have been homeless for an extended period but less than a year. They abuse substances more commonly, experience deterioration in their social relationships, are beginning to lose hope, but still do not identify with the community of homeless individuals.

In the third stage, they have been homeless for about a year or more, see themselves as part of the homeless community, have lost hope, abuse substances, stay in shelters, have no social relationships, and are extremely suspicious of and shun members of mainstream society. All their limited energies are focused on surviving on the street; the rest of the world is meaningless to them.

If the preceding hypothesis is true, then homeless individuals drift downward through the stages as they lose income, relationships, and hope. When they drift into the lower two stages, Belcher suggests, it becomes harder to intervene effectively to help them escape homelessness. Consequently, Belcher recommends preventive strategies to deal with homelessness, including social change efforts for long-term prevention and expanding welfare benefits to prevent homelessness, at least temporarily.

well as for the incorporation of qualitative methods into experimental research. Thus, an experiment evaluating the effectiveness of a program or intervention might use qualitative methods to assess problems in the implementation of the program or intervention—information that may help suggest ways to improve future outcomes or that may show that a program or intervention with a negative outcome was never implemented properly in the first place.

Of special interest to practitioners is the trend toward using a mixed-methods case study approach that combines qualitative and quantitative methods while using single-case designs to evaluate one's own practice effectiveness. When we discussed single-case evaluation designs in Chapter 13, for instance, we noted that it is often difficult to detect from the graphed quantitative results whether an improvement in the target behavior was caused by the intervention or by some extraneous event(s). Intensive qualitative (clinical) interviewing of the client, as well as the client's significant others, can help identify what other important changes in the client's social environment may have coincided with changes in the quantitative data on the target behavior. Also helpful in this regard is the use of *client logs*. If the qualitative information indicates that important extraneous events did indeed coincide with the quantitative changes, then the notion that the intervention is responsible for those changes will be less plausible. On the other hand, if intensive interviewing or client logs reveal no such extraneous coincidences, then it becomes more plausible to view changes in the target behavior as intervention effects.

We will take a closer look at qualitative methods involving interviewing in the next chapter. Let's now take a closer look at the use of client logs in case studies.

Client Logs Client logs are journals that clients keep of events that are relevant to their problems. The logs can be utilized to record quantitative data about target behaviors as well as qualitative information about critical incidents. Bloom, Fischer, and Orme (2006) illustrate the use of different logs for different purposes. For example, an exploratory log might be used to obtain beginning assessment information about a problem and therefore involve recording where and when a critical incident occurred, what happened, who was present, the situational context (i.e., at a staff meeting, over dinner, and so on), what the client wanted, and the client's cognitive and behavioral reaction to the incident. A slightly different type of log might be used later in assessment—one that refers to the occurrence of the specified target problem only and that seeks to identify the conditions under which the problem tends to be better or worse.

Client logs can also be useful in recording extraneous events that occur during the baseline and intervention phases of a single-case evaluation when quantitative outcome data are being collected. The information on these logs can help the practitioner determine whether some important extraneous change may have coincided with the improvement in the target problem during the intervention phase, and this determination will illuminate inferences about whether it was really the intervention or something else that produced the change. Although qualitative interviews can also provide this information, a log can help to avoid distortions of memory that might occur in an interview. This may be particularly important with regard to the exact dates when critical incidents occurred; for example, the client might not remember accurately whether an incident occurred during the baseline phase or early during the intervention phase. Likewise, for assessment purposes, knowing whether the improvement began a day or so before the critical incident occurred would be crucial in drawing inferences about that incident's bearing on the target problem.

We refer you to the Bloom et al. (2006) text if you would like to see detailed illustrations of several types of logs. All of these logs are easy to construct. You can head the first column as the date and the next column as the time of day and then have subsequent column headings for the place, the activity, who was present, what happened, events that led up to or followed the problem, the client's cognitive and behavioral reaction, and so on. Alternatively, you can use a simplified version that has fewer columns. It's up to you to judge what best fits the client, the problem, and the log's purpose.

Whatever approach you use, however, make sure that there are lined rows in each column with plenty of open-ended space for the clients to record their qualitative observations. Also, be sure to explain the log carefully to the client, including the log's purpose and value, how it is to be used, the need to restrict entries to brief summaries of critical incidents only, and the importance of recording incidents as soon as possible after they occur (to reduce memory distortions). Bloom and his associates also suggest practicing making entries with the client using hypothetical situations.

» QUALITATIVE SAMPLING METHODS

Chapter 15 discussed the logic and techniques involved in both probability and nonprobability sampling in social research. This section will discuss the matter of sampling as it typically applies in qualitative research. In part, we'll see how the non-probability sampling techniques discussed earlier would apply specifically to qualitative research. But first we should acknowledge that the use of probability sampling techniques in qualitative research is not unheard of. For example, Zippay (2002) reports a longitudinal qualitative interviewing study in which she randomly selected displaced steelworkers, using a sampling frame listing all blue-collar steelworkers at two steel fabrication plants that had closed down.

Although probability sampling is sometimes used in qualitative research, nonprobability techniques are much more common. The reasons for this are many. To begin, the population and the units of analysis in the qualitative research project may be somewhat ambiguous. In studying a community group engaged in social action activities, for example, what exactly are you interested in studying—that group only? the members of the group? social action in general? If you are studying three juvenile gangs in a particular city, are the gangs or the individual juveniles your units of analysis? Are you interested only in describing the gangs, or does your interest extend to juvenile peer relations in general? It is important that you ask yourself what population you wish to make general assertions about when you are finished with your research. The answer to this question will not always be obvious to you, and it may change over the course of your research. A limited initial concern may be expanded later as you conclude that certain of the phenomena you are observing apply well beyond your specific study participants. Although this general issue may not be easy to resolve in practice, sensitivity to it should help clarify your goals and methods.

The concept of sampling in connection with qualitative research is more complicated than for the kinds of research dealt with in the earlier chapters. Many qualitative researchers attempt to observe everything within their field of study; thus, in a sense, they do not sample at all. In reality, of course, it is impossible to observe everything. To the extent that qualitative researchers observe only a portion of what happens, then, what they do observe is a de facto sample of all the possible observations that might have been made. If several people are shouting support for the speaker in a community meeting, those shouts the researcher hears and understands represent a sample of all

such shouts. Or if a researcher observes acts of violence during a riot, the observed acts are a sample of all such acts of violence. You will seldom be able to select a controlled sample of such observations, but you should bear in mind the general principles of representativeness and interpret your observations accordingly.

Sometimes, however, you will be in a position to sample among possible observations. If you are studying the development of a grassroots community organization over time, for instance, you may choose to interview different members of that organization by listing all of the members and then selecting a probability sample. This might not be the best method of sampling for your purposes, however. Three types of nonprobability sampling methods that are specifically appropriate to qualitative research are the quota sample, the snowball sample, and deviant cases.

To begin, if the group or social process under study has clearly defined categories of participants, then some kind of quota sample might be used: Persons representing all different participation categories should be studied. (Review Chapter 15 for a more detailed discussion of quota sampling as a general procedure.) In the study of a formal group, for instance, you might wish to interview both leaders and nonleaders. In studying a community organization, it might be useful to interview both radical and more moderate members of that group. In general, whenever representativeness is desired, you should use quota sampling and interview both men and women, young people and old people, and the like.

Second, the snowball sample is a technique that begins a sample with a few relevant participants you've identified and then expands through referrals. If you wish to learn the pattern of recruitment to a community organization over time, then you might begin by interviewing fairly recent recruits, asking them who introduced them to the group. You might then interview the persons named, asking them who introduced them to the group. You might interview those persons in turn, asking, in part, who introduced them. In studying a loosely structured group, you might ask one of the participants whom he or she believes to be the most influential members of the group. You might interview those people and, in the course of the interviews, ask who they believe to be the most influential.

In each example, your sample would "snowball" as each interviewee suggested others.

Third, there is deviant case sampling, which entails examining cases that do not fit into the regular pattern. Often, our understanding of fairly regular patterns of attitudes and behaviors is further improved by such deviant cases. You might gain important insights into the nature of group morale as exhibited at a meeting by interviewing people who did not appear to be caught up in the emotions of the crowd or by interviewing people who did not attend the meeting at all.

Deviant cases are unusual in some respect. Suppose, for example, you are interested in conducting a case study of several case management programs to describe the diversity of case management practice and generate hypotheses about factors that influence the case management process. If you suspect that the nature of case management may vary considerably depending on the size of the case manager's caseload, you might want to select a couple of programs known for their extremely high caseloads and a couple known for their extremely low caseloads.

For another example, suppose you seek to generate hypotheses about the extent of family involvement in nursing home care. You might want to study intensively several families that are known by nursing home staff as being the most highly involved in the care of their relatives and several that are known to be the least involved.

Perhaps, however, you might suspect that extreme or deviant cases are so unusual that they provide a distorted portrayal of the phenomenon you want to study. If so, Patton (1990) suggests that you consider using *intensity sampling*: select cases that are more or less intense than usual but not so unusual that they would be called deviant. Thus, rather than selecting families that are most and least involved in nursing home care, you might select families that are known to be more or less involved than most families but that are not so involved or uninvolved that they represent aberrations whose information might be misleading or not particularly useful.

Suppose, for example, that you are studying case management processes in a county mental health program where the case managers' average caseload size is 200 cases and in a federally funded model mental health program in a different locality

with an average caseload size of two cases. The former program may be in a state with no real commitment to case management, where funding is abysmally low, and where "case manager" may be a meaningless label used for the sake of appearing to comply with current trends without spending more money. "Case management" in that program would be a misnomer, and the "case managers" in that program would have so little time to spend on any case that studying what they do might not provide a particularly rich source of information about the case management process. The latter program, as well, might not be a rich source of information. It may be so well endowed as a model program that it bears no resemblance to case management programs elsewhere, programs whose caseload sizes tend to range between 20 and 40 cases. Case managers in the model program may have so much time to spend on each case that they perform functions that go far beyond what case managers normally do even in good case management programs. Consequently, rather than select these extreme programs for study, you might select an intensity sample of programs with average caseload sizes of approximately 20 and approximately 40.

Another strategy that can perhaps be viewed as a form of extreme case sampling is *critical incidents sampling*. The critical incidents technique is particularly useful for generating hypotheses about social work practice effectiveness. A critical incident is one in which something of special importance seemed to happen—something either positive or negative—that might offer valuable new insights about how we can improve practice.

One way you could apply this technique would be to ask direct-service practitioners to identify the cases that, in their judgment, turned out to be their best successes or worst failures. Then you could interview them intensively about each case they identify, seeking to detect commonalities in what different practitioners did with their most and least successful cases. From these patterns, you could suggest hypotheses for further study about the attributes that might distinguish successful and unsuccessful practice.

Maximum variation sampling is another option identified by Patton. This strategy aims to capture the diversity of a phenomenon within a small sample to be studied intensively. By observing a phenomenon under heterogeneous conditions, we are likely to generate more useful insights about it. Thus, if you want to study case management processes, you might select programs with high, medium, and low caseload sizes; some in urban, suburban, and rural areas; some that are old and some that are new; and so on.

On the other hand, you might opt for a *homogeneous sample*. Suppose you are interested in studying how case managers attempt to handle role overload. You probably would restrict your sample to programs in which the case managers' caseload sizes were unusually large.

Earlier in this chapter when we discussed grounded theory, we mentioned *theoretical sampling*. We indicated that theoretical sampling begins by selecting new cases that seem to be similar to those that generated previously detected concepts and hypotheses but that once the researcher perceives that no new insights are being generated from observing similar cases, a different type of case is selected, and the same process is repeated until the observation of different types of cases seems to be generating no new insights. Theoretical sampling thus combines elements of homogeneous sampling and deviant case sampling. (In our earlier example of the grounded theory process, we actually combined theoretical sampling with the critical incidents technique.)

The types of nonprobability samples and sampling strategies that we've been discussing can all be called purposive samples, generated by purposive sampling (also discussed in Chapter 15). In purposive sampling—unlike probability sampling—you select a sample of observations that you believe will yield the most comprehensive understanding of your subject of study based on the intuitive feel for the subject that comes from extended observation and reflection. You can use purposive sampling procedures to select deviant cases or critical cases, but you can also use them to try to obtain a fairly representative portrayal of the phenomenon you are studying.

In a study of homelessness, you might wish to observe many different locations in the city. You could pick the sample of locations through standard probability methods, or, more likely, you could use a rough quota system, observing busy areas and deserted ones or including samples from different times of day. In a study of the way nursing home staff and residents interact, you would observe different kinds of nursing homes and different areas of each home, for example. You might even seek to study deviant cases within a representative sample of larger groupings, such as applying the critical incidents technique across a representative sample of agencies. Although controlled probability sampling is seldom used in qualitative research, understanding its principles and logic (as discussed in Chapter 15) is likely to produce more effective intuitive sampling in qualitative research.

In qualitative research, bear in mind two stages of sampling. First, to what extent are the total situations *available* for observation representative of the more general class of phenomena you wish to describe and explain? Are the three juvenile gangs you are observing representative of all gangs? Second, are your *actual* observations within those total situations representative of all *possible* observations? Have you observed a representative sample of the members of the three gangs? Have you observed a representative sample of the interactions that have taken place? Even when controlled probability sampling methods are impossible or inappropriate, the logical link between representativeness and generalizability still holds.

Having discussed specific techniques that may be used for sampling in qualitative research, we conclude with the injunction offered by Lofland and Lofland (1995):

> Your overall goal is to collect the richest possible data. Rich data mean, ideally, a wide and diverse range of information collected over a relatively prolonged period of time. Again, ideally, you achieve this through direct, face-to-face contact with, and prolonged immersion in, some social location or circumstance. (p. 16)

» STRENGTHS AND WEAKNESSES OF QUALITATIVE RESEARCH

Like all research methods, qualitative research has distinctive strengths and weaknesses. Let's take a look at some of them now.

Depth of Understanding

Qualitative research is especially effective for studying subtle nuances in attitudes and behaviors and for examining social processes over time. As such, the chief strength of this method lies in the depth of understanding it permits. Whereas other research methods may be challenged as superficial, this charge is seldom lodged against qualitative research. Let's review a couple of qualitative research examples to see why this is so.

"Being there" is a powerful technique for gaining insights into the nature of human affairs. Listen, for example, to what this nurse reports about the impediments to patients' coping with cancer:

> Common fears that may impede the coping process for the person with cancer can include the following:
>
> —Fear of death—for the patient, and the implications his or her death will have for significant others.
> —Fear of incapacitation—because cancer can be a chronic disease with acute episodes that may result in periodic stressful periods, the variability of the person's ability to cope and constantly adjust may require a dependency upon others for activities of daily living and may consequently become a burden.
> —Fear of alienation—from significant others and health care givers, thereby creating helplessness and hopelessness.
> —Fear of contagion—that cancer is transmissible and/or inherited.
> —Fear of losing one's dignity—losing control of all bodily functions and being totally vulnerable. (Garant, 1980, p. 2167)

Observations and conceptualizations such as these are valuable in their own right. In addition, they can provide the basis for further research—both qualitative and quantitative.

Now listen to what Joseph Howell (1973) has to say about "toughness" as a fundamental ingredient of life on Clay Street, a white, working-class neighborhood in Washington, DC:

> Most of the people on Clay Street saw themselves as fighters in both the figurative and literal sense. They considered themselves strong, independent people who would not let themselves be pushed around. For Bobbi, being a fighter meant battling the welfare department and cussing out social workers and doctors upon occasion. It meant spiking Barry's beer with sleeping pills and bashing him over the head with a broom. For Barry it meant telling off his boss and refusing to hang the door, an act that led to his being fired. It meant going through the ritual of a duel with Al. It meant pushing Bubba around and at times getting rough with Bobbi. June and Sam had less to fight about, though if pressed they both hinted that they, too, would fight. Being a fighter led Ted into near conflict with Peg's brothers, Les into conflict with Lonnie, Arlene into conflict with Phyllis at the bowling alley, etc. (p. 292)

Even though you haven't heard the episodes that Howell refers to in this passage, you have the distinct impression that Clay Street is a tough place to live. That toughness comes through far more powerfully than would a set of statistics on the median number of fistfights occurring during a specified period of time.

These examples point to the greater depth of meaning that qualitative methods can tap into, describing concepts such as *liberal* and *conservative* that is generally unavailable to surveys and experiments. Instead of defining concepts, qualitative researchers will commonly give some detailed illustrations.

Flexibility

Flexibility is another advantage of qualitative research: You may modify your research design at any time, as discussed earlier. Unlike most quantitative research, you often can be prepared to engage in qualitative research whenever the occasion arises, whereas you could not as easily initiate a survey or an experiment. For example, in the Baxter and Hopper (1979) study of homelessness, the researchers expanded their focus from the mentally disabled to homelessness in general after their initial observations revealed the wider heterogeneity of homeless individuals and the diverse origins of homelessness. Likewise, in the Belcher (1991) study of homelessness, a second round of interviews was guided by themes that emerged in the first round of interviews. A third round of interviews followed based on the patterns of homelessness that emerged in the analysis of the data from the second round. (Both of these homelessness studies were discussed in the two boxes that appeared earlier in this chapter.)

Cost

Qualitative research can be relatively inexpensive. Other social scientific research methods may require expensive equipment or an expensive research staff, but qualitative research typically can be undertaken by one researcher with a notebook and pencil or with a good-quality audio or video recorder. This is not to say that qualitative research is never expensive. The nature of the research project, for example, may require a large number of trained observers. Expensive recording equipment may be needed. Or the researcher may wish to undertake participant observation of interactions in expensive Paris nightclubs. Also, the process of conducting in-depth, probing interviews or observing behavior directly tends to take a lot more time than most data-gathering methods using questionnaires or self-report scales. Likewise, as you will see in Chapter 20, processing and interpreting qualitative data can take a lot more time than processing and interpreting quantitative data. (The latter will be discussed in Chapter 21.)

Subjectivity and Generalizability

Qualitative research also has several weaknesses. First, being qualitative rather than quantitative, it seldom yields precise statistical statements about a large population. Observing casual political discussions in Laundromats, for instance, would not yield trustworthy estimates of the future voting behavior of the total electorate. Nevertheless, the study could provide important insights into the process of political attitude formation. Many of the strengths and weaknesses of qualitative research can be understood in terms of subjectivity and generalizability.

Subjectivity   Suppose you were to characterize your best friend's political orientations based on everything you know about him or her. Clearly, your assessment of that person's politics is not superficial. The measurement you arrived at would appear to have considerable validity. We can't be sure, however, that someone else would characterize your friend's politics the same way you did, even with the same amount of observation.

Qualitative research measurements—although in depth—are also often very personal. How others judge your friend's political orientation depends very much on their own orientation, just as your judgment would depend on your political orientation.

Conceivably, then, you would describe your friend as middle of the road, although others might perceive him or her as a fire-breathing radical.

Be wary, therefore, of any purely descriptive measurements in qualitative research. If a researcher reports that the members of a club tend to be conservative, know that such a judgment is unavoidably linked to the researcher's own politics. You can be more trusting, however, of comparative evaluations: identifying who is more conservative than whom, for example. Even if we had different political orientations, we would probably agree pretty much in ranking the relative conservatism of the members of a group.

As we've suggested earlier, those researchers who use qualitative techniques are conscious of this issue and take pains to address it. Not only are individual researchers often able to sort out their own biases and points of view, but also the communal nature of science means that their colleagues will help them in that regard.

In a sense, we've been talking about the issue of generalizability. Let's look at that more directly now.

Generalizability   One of the chief goals of science is generalization. Social scientists study particular situations and events to learn about social life in general. Usually, nobody would be interested in knowing about the specific participants observed by the researcher. Who cares, after all, how George Gallup's sample of 1,500 voters is going to vote? We are interested only if the voters' intentions can be generalized to the total electorate. (This was the key issue in Chapter 15, on sampling.)

Generalizability is a problem for qualitative research. It crops up in three forms. First, as we've already suggested, the personal nature of the observations and measurements made by the researcher can produce results that would not necessarily be replicated by another, independent researcher. If the observation depends in part on the particular observers, then it becomes more valuable as a source of insight than as proof or truth.

Second, because qualitative researchers get a full and in-depth view of their subject matter, they can reach an unusually comprehensive understanding. By its very comprehensiveness, however, this understanding is less generalizable than results based on rigorous sampling and standardized measurements. Let's say you set out to fully understand how your city council operates. You study the members in great depth, learning about their ideological positions, how they came to public life, how they got elected, and who their friends and enemies are. You could learn about their family lives, seeing how personal feelings enter into their public acts. After such an in-depth study, you could probably understand the actions of the council really well. But would you be able to say much about city councils in general? Surely your study would have provided you with some general insights, but you wouldn't be able to carry over everything you learned from the specific to the general. Having mastered the operations of the Dayton City Council, you might not be able to say much about Cleveland's. You should, however, be in a position to organize a great study of the Cleveland City Council.

In reviewing reports of qualitative research projects, you should determine where and to what extent the researcher is generalizing beyond his or her specific observations to other settings. Such generalizations may be in order, but you need to judge that. Nothing in this research method guarantees it.

Finally, there is often a problem of generalizability even within the specific subject matter being observed. As an illustration, let's imagine you were interested in learning about Scientology. Suppose you were particularly interested in the church's recruitment practices: How does it attract new members, what kinds of people are attracted, and so on? One way to find the answers to such questions would be for you to express interest in the church yourself. Talk to members, attend meetings and retreats. In this fashion, you would be able to get a firsthand experience of what you wanted to study. You could observe the way you were treated after expressing interest, and you could observe the treatment of other newcomers. By getting to know the other people who were considering joining the church, you would get an idea of the kinds of people who were joining.

Here's the problem of generalizability. Although you might talk to many church members, you couldn't be sure how typical they were. You might end up talking only to people assigned the job of talking to potential recruits. The potentials for biased sampling are endless. The same would apply to the new recruits you got to know. They might not be typical of new recruits in general.

As we finish discussing the strengths and weaknesses of qualitative research, we should point out that although we did not have a section on the strengths and weaknesses of quantitative research per se in previous chapters, we did devote considerable attention throughout those chapters to the many strengths and weaknesses of quantitative research. With regard to weaknesses, for example, we discussed biases and other flaws in the wording of quantitative measurement instruments, quantitative scales that lack reliability and validity, unrepresentative surveys with inadequate response rates or biased sampling procedures, practice evaluations that lack internal validity or use biased measurement procedures, and so on. Moreover, even in this chapter we have discussed the strengths and limitations of qualitative research in the context of comparing them with the strengths and limitations of quantitative research. Thus, we hope you do not get the impression that qualitative methods are weaker or stronger than quantitative methods. Which line of inquiry is more appropriate will depend on the aim of our research and the nature of the research question we seek to answer.

>> STANDARDS FOR EVALUATING QUALITATIVE STUDIES

As can be seen in this chapter and the next, qualitative inquiry involves a variety of dissimilar research methods and paradigms. This diversity in methods and paradigms is accompanied by different perspectives on how to critically appraise the rigor of qualitative research. Regardless of one's perspective, however, there is general agreement that one key issue in evaluating the rigor of qualitative research is *trustworthiness*. However, one's epistemological paradigm will influence the criteria used to assess trustworthiness as well as whether some other key issues are just as important as trustworthiness.

For those whose epistemological paradigm is oriented mainly toward contemporary positivism (as discussed in Chapter 3), trustworthiness will be the prime focus in evaluating the rigor of a qualitative study. They will be concerned primarily with the extent to which a study can take steps to maximize objectivity and minimize bias. Those who view research through the lens of the critical social science or participatory action research paradigm, however, will additionally ask whether people were empowered by the research. Those with a postmodern or social constructivist paradigm will also use trustworthiness as a key criterion, but they will approach that criterion somewhat differently than contemporary positivists, in keeping with an emphasis on multiple subjective realities. The different criteria that each of these paradigms uses to assess trustworthiness are displayed in Table 18-1. In discussing these criteria, let's begin by examining the criteria used in the contemporary positivist perspective. Then we'll examine the similarities and differences between that approach and those that emphasize alternative paradigms.

Contemporary Positivist Standards

As we already mentioned, for contemporary positivists the key issue in evaluating the rigor of qualitative research is trustworthiness. In her book

Qualitative Methods in Social Work Research, Padgett (1998b) identifies three key threats to trustworthiness: reactivity, researcher biases, and respondent biases. *Reactivity* occurs when the researcher's presence in the field distorts the naturalism of the setting and consequently the things being observed there. As we discussed earlier, *researcher biases* can distort what researchers perceive or how they selectively observe. *Respondent bias* is another concept you may recall from earlier sections; it refers most typically to the need to appear socially desirable.

To minimize the distorting influence of these threats, Padgett recommends six commonly used strategies to enhance the rigor of qualitative studies. Not every strategy is feasible or applicable to every qualitative investigation. You can evaluate the rigor of the qualitative studies you read by asking

TABLE 18.1 Standards Used by Three Different Paradigms for Appraising the Trustworthiness of Qualitative Research

Paradigm	Standards
Contemporary Positivist	Maximize objectivity and minimize the distorting influences of reactivity, researcher biases, and respondent biases, using one or more of the following six strategies: 1. Prolonged engagement 2. Triangulation 3. Peer debriefing and support 4. Negative case analysis 5. Member checking 6. Auditing a paper trail
Social Constructivist	Appraise whether multiple subjective realities are adequately depicted, according to the following criteria: 1. Member checking 2. Fittingness or transferability (provision of thick background information with sufficient detail about the research context, setting and participants) 3. Triangulation not to check for reliability, but to improve chances of detecting the full range of subjective realities
Empowerment	Appraise whether the study empowered research participants. Did it: 1. Evoke action by participants to effect desired change and a redistribution of power? 2. Obtain and report participant testimonials suggesting a change in their views about the need for change and whether the research increased their optimism about the possibility for change?

yourself which of these strategies are applicable to a given study, and, if applicable, were they used?

The first strategy involves prolonged engagement to reduce the impact of reactivity and respondent bias. It assumes that a long and trusting relationship with the researcher gives respondents less opportunity to deceive and makes them less inclined to withhold information or to lie. Lengthy interviews or a series of follow-up interviews with the same respondent might make it easier for the researcher to detect distortion or for the respondent ultimately to disclose socially undesirable truths.

Prolonged engagement also can have a drawback. A lengthy engagement can lead to bias if the researchers over identify with their respondents and lose their objective, analytic stance or their own sense of identity. The term for this phenomenon is going native. Despite this risk, qualitative studies that lack prolonged engagement should be viewed with caution. Some authors, for example, seem to think that because qualitative inquiry emphasizes flexibility, the label *qualitative* means "anything goes." We have seen this in some manuscripts we've reviewed for publication in professional journals. The most common example occurs when an investigator thinks that one brief open-ended interview with each respondent is sufficient. (Conceivably, that may be sufficient in some unusual qualitative studies, but, if so, the author should provide a compelling justification of that as opposed to ignoring the issue.)

The second strategy is triangulation, a term we have used repeatedly throughout this book. Triangulation occurs when researchers seek corroboration between two or more sources for their data and interpretations. Padgett (1998b) describes five types of triangulation in qualitative inquiry. One approach is to have the data analyzed by colleagues who hold contrasting theoretical orientations. Another is to use more than one qualitative method (and perhaps some quantitative methods, too) to collect and analyze data. A third approach is to use multiple observers to collect the data and multiple coders to classify the collected observations. A fourth approach is to use more than one data source (such as direct observations, interviews, and existing records). A fifth type is called *interdisciplinary triangulation*, in which a team of researchers from different fields collaborate. Padgett cautions us, however, not to overreact to inconsistencies in triangulated data. Sometimes disagreement between different data sources simply reveals different perspectives about a phenomenon, such as when two conflicting family members express different versions of family problems.

A third strategy, one that overlaps somewhat with triangulation, is called peer debriefing and support. This occurs when teams of investigators meet regularly to give each other feedback, emotional support, and ideas. They might exchange alternative perspectives and new ideas about how they are collecting data, about problems, and about meanings in the data already collected. The idea here is that the peer debriefing process increases the likelihood of spotting and correcting for biases and other problems in data collection and interpretation.

The next two strategies, negative case analysis and member checking, were discussed in Chapter 9 when we examined how the terms *reliability* and *validity* are sometimes used in qualitative research. Negative case analysis, for example, occurs when researchers show they have searched thoroughly for disconfirming evidence—looking for deviant cases that do not fit the researcher's interpretations. Member checking occurs when researchers ask the participants in their research to confirm or disconfirm the accuracy of the research observations and interpretations. Do the reported observations and interpretations ring true and have meaning to the participants?

The final strategy, auditing, occurs when the researcher leaves a paper trail of field notes, transcripts of interviews, journals, and memos documenting decisions made along the way, and so on. This enables an impartial and qualitatively adept investigator who is not part of the study to scrutinize what was done in order to determine if efforts to control for biases and reactivity were thorough, if the procedures used were justifiable, and if the interpretations fit the data that were collected. Thus, auditing encompasses each of the preceding five strategies because part of the purpose of the audit is to ascertain whether those strategies were appropriately implemented.

Social Constructivist Standards

Social constructivists also emphasize trustworthiness in appraising qualitative research, and they recommend the preceding strategies for enhancing the rigor of qualitative studies. However, they view trustworthiness and these strategies more in terms of capturing multiple subjective realities than ensuring the portrayal of an objective social reality, the objective of contemporary positivists. Thus, for example, minimizing respondent bias becomes less important than making sure that the research participants' multiple subjective realities are revealed as adequately as possible (Krefting, 1991). The point in member checking, then, becomes less concerned with whether the researcher's interpretations were objective and accurate and more concerned with whether participants acknowledge that their subjective realities are being depicted as they see them.

Another criterion is whether the qualitative research report provides enough detail about the study contexts and participants to enable readers in other situations to judge whether the findings seem likely to apply to the context or population with which they are concerned. Guba (1981) referred to this criterion as *fittingness* or *transferability*. Lincoln and Guba (1985) added that this criterion is unlike the external validity or generalizability criteria that we have discussed in connection to quantitative studies. The onus is not on the qualitative researchers to demonstrate that their studies have external validity or to say to whom their findings generalize. Instead, the onus is on the research consumers to make the judgment as to whether the findings seem applicable to their situation or population of concern. To enable the consumer to make that judgment, however, the onus is on the researcher to provide "thick" background information about the research context, setting, and participants.

The constructivist approach also uses triangulation somewhat differently than does the contemporary positivist approach. The contemporary positivist approach would see inconsistencies revealed in triangulation as a reflection of unreliability in the data. It might also reflect researcher bias if two investigators derived contradictory interpretations of the data. In contrast, the constructivist approach would see inconsistencies as a possible reflection of multiple realities. They would want to see the inconsistencies explained; perhaps the explanations of inconsistency in triangulated data would produce a better understanding of the range of subjective realities—especially those that are atypical.

Empowerment Standards

As we previously mentioned, those who take a critical social science or participatory action research approach to qualitative research would add empowerment standards to those mentioned above. Rodwell (1998) discusses empowerment standards for evaluating qualitative research in terms of what she calls *catalytic authenticity* and *tactical authenticity*. According to her paradigm, which actually combines constructivism with empowerment, creating new knowledge is not sufficient in constructivist research. In addition, the research must evoke action by participants to effect desired change and a redistribution of power. She adds that although it will be impossible to prove that the research caused the change, a follow-up should obtain and report participant testimonials suggesting a change in their views about the need for change and whether the research increased their optimism about the possibility for change.

EP 3

» RESEARCH ETHICS IN QUALITATIVE RESEARCH

We introduced the topic of research ethics in Chapter 5 and pointed out that a wide range of ethical issues must be faced in connection with any form of social research. Thus, qualitative research is subject to the same ethical scrutiny as is quantitative research. Yet qualitative field research, by bringing researchers into direct and often intimate contact with their participants, seems to raise these concerns dramatically. Here are some of the issues mentioned by Lofland and Lofland (1995):

- Is it ethical to talk to people when they do not know you will be recording their words?

- Is it ethical to get information for your own purposes from people you hate?

- Is it ethical to see a severe need for help and not respond to it directly?

- Is it ethical to be in a setting or situation but not commit yourself wholeheartedly to it?

- Is it ethical to develop a calculated stance toward other humans, that is, to be strategic in your relations?

- Is it ethical to take sides or to avoid taking sides in a factionalized situation?

- Is it ethical to "pay" people with trade-offs for access to their lives and minds?

- Is it ethical to "use" people as allies or informants in order to gain entree to other people or to elusive understandings? (p. 63)

In light of these issues, it bears stressing that qualitative research studies are required to be reviewed and approved by institutional review boards (see Chapter 5) just as quantitative studies are.

Although we have discussed qualitative inquiry throughout this book, this completes the first chapter that focused exclusively on this important type of research. The next chapter will examine specific types of qualitative research methods. As you read the next chapter, you may notice a fuzzy distinction and considerable overlap between general principles and paradigms of qualitative research and specific methods of qualitative research. After that, Chapter 20 will deal exclusively with the data analysis phase of qualitative research.

MAIN POINTS

- Qualitative research can involve the direct observation of social phenomena in their natural settings.
- Appropriate topics for qualitative research include practices, episodes, encounters, roles, relationships, groups, organizations, settlements, social worlds, lifestyles, and subcultures.
- Qualitative research in social work can be guided by any one of several paradigms, such as naturalism or ethnography, grounded theory, case studies, and participatory action research.
- Ethnography involves naturalistic observations and holistic understandings of cultures or subcultures.
- Grounded theory refers to the attempt to derive theories from an analysis of the patterns, themes, and common categories discovered among observational data.
- A case study is an idiographic examination of a single individual, family, group, organization, community, or society.
- Some case studies combine qualitative methods with single-case experiments to evaluate practice effectiveness.
- Commonly used qualitative methods in case studies involve intensive interviews and client logs.

- Because controlled probability sampling techniques are usually impossible in qualitative research, a rough form of quota sampling may be used in the attempt to achieve better representativeness in observations.
- Snowball sampling is a method through which you develop an ever-increasing set of sample observations. You ask one participant in the event under study to recommend others for interviewing, and each subsequently interviewed participant is asked for further recommendations.
- Often, the careful examination of deviant cases in qualitative research can yield important insights into the normal patterns of social behavior.
- Compared with surveys and experiments, qualitative research measurements generally tap more depth of meaning but have less reliability, and field research results cannot be generalized as safely as those based on rigorous sampling and standardized questionnaires.
- Six strategies for evaluating the rigor of qualitative studies are (a) prolonged engagement, (b) triangulation, (c) peer debriefing and support, (d) negative case analysis, (e) member checking, and (f) auditing.
- Diversity in epistemological paradigms is accompanied by different perspectives on how to critically appraise the rigor of qualitative research.
- The contemporary positivist paradigm emphasizes three key threats to the trustworthiness of qualitative research: reactivity, researcher biases, and respondent biases.
- The social constructivist paradigm views trustworthiness and strategies to enhance rigor more in terms of capturing multiple subjective realities than of ensuring the portrayal of an objective social reality, the objective of contemporary positivists. Thus, minimizing respondent bias is less important than making sure that the research participants' multiple subjective realities are revealed as adequately as possible.
- Those who take a critical social science or participatory action research approach to qualitative research include empowerment standards in critically appraising qualitative research studies.
- Conducting qualitative research responsibly involves confronting several ethical issues that arise from the researcher's direct contact with participants.

REVIEW QUESTIONS AND EXERCISES

1. Choose any two of the paradigms discussed in this chapter. Then describe how a hypothetical qualitative study that you make up might be conducted differently if you followed each paradigm. Compare and contrast the way these paradigms might work in the context of your study.

2. To explore the different strengths and weaknesses of experiments, surveys, and qualitative research, give brief descriptions of two studies especially appropriate to each method. Be sure each study would be most appropriately studied by the method you would choose.

3. Write down the potential threats to the trustworthiness of the findings for each of the following hypothetical scenarios. Compare your answers with those of your classmates and discuss any differences you encounter.

   a. A researcher draws conclusions about the main reasons clients prematurely terminate treatment based on 15-minute interviews with each of the 20 clients who most recently dropped out of treatment (one interview per client).

   b. A researcher who had been a victim of a violent crime interviews other such victims to generate theory about the emotional impact of violent crimes on victims.

   c. A young researcher seeking to understand why youths abuse drugs begins to see the world through the eyes of the youths being observed and draws conclusions based exclusively on their outlook.

4. What strategies could be used to alleviate the threats you identified regarding the scenarios in exercise 3? Discuss your rationale for each strategy. Compare your answers with those of your classmates and discuss any differences you encounter.

INTERNET EXERCISES

1. Find five articles in the journal *Social Work* that debate the goodness of fit between clinical social work practice and qualitative research. The article that sparked the debate, "Does the Glove Really Fit? Qualitative Research and Clinical Social Work Practice," by Deborah K. Padgett, appeared in the July 1998 issue. Three articles that responded to Padgett's article, as well as her response to them, appeared in the May 1999 issue. Briefly describe the main points of each article and discuss your position on this debate.

2. Summarize and critically appraise the methodological strengths and limitations of the following article, and discuss whether and how its use of a qualitative methodology enabled it to provide useful implications for practice that might not have emerged from the use of quantitative methods. Stein, G. L., Beckerman, N. L., & Sherman, P. A. (2010). Lesbian and gay elders and long-term care: Identifying the unique psychosocial perspectives and challenges. *Journal of Gerontological Social Work, 53*, 421–4535.

3. Find one to three articles illustrating the use of ethnography, grounded theory, and participatory action research. (Some articles might report a study using more than one of these paradigms.) Write down the bibliographic reference information for each article and identify its methodological strengths and weaknesses.

Visit CengageBrain.com for additional practice and study opportunities including experiential exercises, research tools, glossary, flashcards, and sample test items.

19

Qualitative Research: Specific Methods

EPAS Competencies for This Chapter

Competency 3 Advance Human Rights and Social and Economic Justice: In this chapter you will learn more about participatory action research and feminist methods—research methods that are used to empower oppressed groups.

Competency 4 Engage in Practice-Informed Research and Research-Informed Practice: This chapter, as a whole, enhances your preparedness to engage in practice-informed qualitative research and to have qualitative research inform your practice.

What You'll Learn in This Chapter

This chapter will continue our discussion of qualitative research and will do so with a greater emphasis on specific types of qualitative research methods, such as participant observation, qualitative interviewing, recording observations, life history, feminist methods, and focus groups. Each method involves principles that were discussed in the previous chapter.

» INTRODUCTION

In the previous chapter, we considered the kinds of topics appropriate to qualitative research, some of the paradigms that direct differ-ent types of qualitative research ef-forts, qualitative sampling methods, the strengths and weaknesses of qualita-tive research, and ethical issues in qual-itative research. Along the way, we saw some examples that illustrate qualitative research in action. To round out the picture, we turn now to specific ideas and techniques for conducting qual-itative research. In qualitative research, the distinc-tion between general principles, paradigms, and specific data collection methods is sometimes fuzzy. For example, grounded theory and ethnography at times are discussed as methods. We hope that you will not let such semantic distinctions stymie you. The main objectives are to see the value in these methods, to recognize how to use these methods in your own research, and to critically appraise studies that report having used them. Let's begin by examining how qualitative research-ers prepare for their contact with the people they plan to study.

EP 4

» PREPARING FOR THE FIELD

Suppose for the moment that you have decided to undertake qualitative research on a grassroots com-munity organization. Let's assume further that you are not a member of that group, that you do not know much about it, and that you will identify yourself to the participants as a researcher. This sec-tion will discuss some of the ways in which you might prepare yourself before undertaking direct observation of the group.

Search the Literature

As is true of all research methods, you would be well advised to begin with a search of the relevant literature, filling in your knowledge of the subject and learning what others have said about it. Because library research is discussed at length in Appendix A, we won't say anything further about it at this point.

Use Key Informants

In the next phase of your research, you may wish to make use of key informants. You might wish to dis-cuss the community group with others who have already studied it or with anyone else who is likely to be familiar with it. In particular, you might find it useful to discuss the group with one of its members. Perhaps you already know a member or can meet one. This aspect of your preparation is likely to be more effective if your relationship with the infor-mant extends beyond your research role. In dealing with members of the group as informants, you should take care that your initial discussions do not compromise or limit later aspects of your research. Realize that the impression you make on the member informant—the role you establish for yourself—may carry over into your later effort. For example, creating the initial impression that you may be a spy for an opposing group is unlikely to facilitate later observations of the group.

You should also be wary about the information you get from informants. Although they may have more direct, personal knowledge of the subject under study than you, what they "know" is proba-bly a mixture of fact and point of view. Members of the community group in our example are unlikely to give you completely unbiased information (neither would members of opposing groups). Before mak-ing your first contact with the group, then, you should be already quite familiar with it, and you should understand the general theoretical context within which it exists.

Establish Initial Contact

You can establish your initial contact with the peo-ple you plan to study in a variety of ways. How you do it will depend, in part, on the role you intend to play. Suppose, for example, you want to take on the role of *complete participant* in the organization as opposed to conspicuously appearing as an outside researcher. (We'll discuss the complete participant and alternative observation roles shortly.) You'll have to find a way to develop an identity with the people to be studied. If you wish to study dish-washers in a restaurant, the most direct method would be to get a job as a dishwasher. In the case of the community organization, you might sim-ply join the group. Many of the social processes that are appropriate to qualitative research are sufficiently open to make your contact with the people to be studied simple and straightforward. If you wish to observe a mass demonstration, just be there. If you wish to observe patterns in jaywalking, hang around busy streets.

Establish Rapport

Whenever you wish to make a more formal contact with the people and identify yourself as a researcher, you must be able to establish a certain rapport with them. You might contact a participant with whom you feel comfortable and gain that person's assistance. If you are studying a formal group, you might approach the group leaders. Or you may find that one of your informants who has studied the group can introduce you.

Although you will probably have many options in making your initial contact with the group, you should realize that your choice can influence your subsequent observations. Suppose, for example, that you are studying a community clinic and begin with high-level administrators. First, your initial impressions of the clinic are going to be shaped by the administrators' views, which will be quite different from those of patients or staff. This initial impression may influence the way you subsequently observe and interpret—even though you are unaware of the influence.

Second, if the administrators approve of your research project and encourage patients and staff to cooperate with you, then the latter groups will probably look on you as somehow aligned with the administration, which can affect what they say to you. Nurses might be reluctant to tell you about their plans to organize through a nurses union, for example.

Explain Your Purpose

In making direct, formal contact with the people you want to study, you will be required to give them some explanation of the purpose of your study. Here again you face an ethical dilemma. Telling them the complete purpose of your research might lose their cooperation altogether or have important effects on their behavior. On the other hand, giving only what you believe would be an acceptable explanation may involve outright deception. Realize in all this that your decisions—in practice—may be determined largely by the purpose of your study, the

nature of what you are studying, the observations you wish to use, and other such factors.

Previous qualitative research offers no fixed rule—methodological or ethical—to follow in this regard. Your appearance as a researcher, regardless of your stated purpose, may result in a warm welcome from people who are flattered that a scientist finds them important enough to study. Or you may end up being ostracized or worse. (Do not, for example, burst into a meeting of an organized crime syndicate and announce that you are writing a term paper on organized crime.)

» THE VARIOUS ROLES OF THE OBSERVER

As we alluded to above, in qualitative research observers can play any of several roles, including participating in what they want to observe. As Marshall and Rossman (1995) point out,

> The researcher may plan a role that entails varying degrees of "participantness"—that is, the degree of actual participation in daily life. At one extreme is the full participant, who goes about ordinary life in a role or set of roles constructed in the setting.
>
> At the other extreme is the complete observer, who engages not at all in social interaction and may even shun involvement in the world being studied. And, of course, all possible complementary mixes along the continuum are available to the researcher. (p. 60)

In the classic work on this subject, Gold (1969, pp. 30–39) discussed four different positions on a continuum of roles that qualitative researchers may play in this regard: *complete participant, participant as observer, observer as participant,* and *complete observer.*

Complete Participant

The complete participant, in this sense, may either be a genuine participant in what he or she is studying (e.g., a participant in a protest demonstration) or pretend to be a genuine participant. In any event, if you are acting as the complete participant, you let people see you only as a participant, not as a researcher.

HOW TO DO IT: ESTABLISHING RAPPORT

In qualitative field research, it is almost always vital that you be able to establish rapport with those you are observing, especially if your observations include in-depth interviews and interactions. **Rapport** might be defined as an open and trusting relationship. But how do you do that?

Let's assume that you will be identifying yourself as a researcher. You will need to be able to explain your research purpose in a way that is nonthreatening. Communicate that you are there to learn about your respondents and understand them, not to judge them or cause them any problems. This will work best if you actually have a genuine interest in understanding the people you are observing and can communicate that interest to them. This gives them a sense of self-worth, which will increase their willingness to open up to you. Pretending to be interested is not the same as really being interested. In fact, if you are not interested in learning what things look like from the point of view of those you are observing, you might consider another activity and not waste their time and your own.

It follows from the above that you will function best as an attentive listener rather than as a talker. You should not remain mute, of course, but you should talk primarily to (a) elicit more information from the other person or (b) answer questions they may have about you and your research. While you don't have to agree with any points of view expressed by your subjects, you should never argue with them or try to change their minds. Keep reminding yourself that your genuine purpose is to understand their world and how it makes sense to them—whether it works for you or not. A little humility may help with this. You will be able to hear and understand people better if you don't start with an implicit feeling of superiority to them.

In doing this, you can apply the skills of active listening that are taught in some basic social work practice methods classes. Thus, if you want to observe direct care staff in a nursing home and while trying to establish rapport with them one says something that demeans the residents, you should avoid the temptation to disagree with them, no matter how inappropriate and perhaps offensive you perceive their comments to be. Instead, you might say something like, "In my research here, I'd like to hear more about that and learn more about what it's like for staff members to work in this setting." Or you might just say, "Can you tell me more about that?"

Be relaxed and appropriate to the setting. Some people are more formal or informal than others, and you will do well to take on their general style. However, find a way to relax with whatever style is most comfortable for them. If you can get them to relax and enjoy the interaction, you will have achieved the rapport you need. And you will probably enjoy the interaction yourself.

Clearly, if you are not a genuine participant in what you are studying, you must learn to behave as though you were. If you are studying a group of uneducated and inarticulate people, it would not be appropriate for you to talk and act like a university professor or student.

Here let us remind you of an ethical issue, one on which social researchers themselves are divided. Is it ethical to deceive the people you are studying in the hope that they will confide in you as they will not confide in an identified researcher? Will the humanitarian value of your study offset such ethical considerations? Although many professional associations have addressed this issue, the norms to be followed remain somewhat ambiguous when applied to specific situations.

Related to this ethical consideration is a scientific one. No researcher deceives his or her participants solely for the purpose of deception. Rather, it is done in the belief that the data will be more valid and reliable and that the participants will be more natural and honest if they do not know the researcher is doing a research project. If the people being studied know they are being studied, they might modify their behavior in a variety of ways. First, they might expel the researcher. Second, they might modify their speech and behavior to appear more respectable than they would otherwise be. Third, the social process itself might be radically changed. Students making plans to burn down the university administration building, for example, might give up the plan altogether once they learn

WHAT DO YOU THINK?

The impact of the observer is a fundamental issue in social research. We've seen that experimenters can influence the way people behave in experiments and that survey researchers can affect how people respond to questionnaires. The problem is also present when participant observers set out to study human behavior in its natural setting. If you participate in the events you are studying, observing them directly and up close and personal, won't your presence change things? How can you observe something as though you aren't actually there observing it? In other words, how close is too close?

Although researchers sometimes conceal their research identity as a way of reducing their impact, anything they do in a social setting will have some impact. Ultimately, the solution to this problem is awareness of it because this allows you to have some control over the impact you have. This approach is coupled with replication by other researchers. Different researchers bring various impacts to different research situations. If they nonetheless discover the same patterns of behavior, our confidence that we've learned something about social life, not just something about our role in it, increases.

Chapman University

that a member of their group is a social scientist conducting a research project.

On the other side of the coin, if you are a complete participant, you might affect what you are studying. To play the role of participant, you must *participate*. Yet your participation might have important effects on the social process you are studying. Suppose, for example, that you are asked for your ideas about what the group should do next. No matter what you say, you will affect the process in some fashion. If the group follows your suggestion, your influence on the process is obvious. If the group decides not to follow your suggestion, the process by which the suggestion is rejected might affect what happens next. Finally, if you indicate that you just don't know what should be done

next, you might be adding to a general feeling of uncertainty and indecisiveness in the group.

Ultimately, *anything* the participant observer does or does not do will have some effect on what is being observed; it is simply inevitable, as discussed in the box "What Do You Think?" More seriously, what you do or do not do may have an *important* effect on what happens. There is no complete protection against this effect, though sensitivity to the issue may provide partial protection.

Participant as Observer

Because of these several considerations, ethical and scientific, the qualitative researcher frequently chooses a different role from that of complete participant. In Gold's terminology, you might choose the role of participant as observer. In this role, you would participate fully with the group under study, but you would make it clear that you were also undertaking research. If you were a member of the volleyball team, for example, you might use that position to launch a study in the sociology of sports, letting your teammates know what you were doing. There are dangers in this role also, however. The people being studied may shift much of their attention to the research project rather than focus on the natural social process, and the process being observed may no longer be typical. Or, conversely, you yourself might come to identify too much with the participants' interests and viewpoints. You might begin to "go native" and lose much of your scientific detachment.

An additional danger has to do with your safety if you are observing or participating in dangerous situations, such as with youth gangs, violent protests, and so on.

Observer as Participant

The observer as participant is one who identifies himself or herself as a researcher and interacts with the participants in the social process but makes no pretense of actually being a participant. A good example of that would be a newspaper reporter learning about a social movement—for instance, the unionization of migrant farmworkers. The reporter might interview leaders and also visit workers where they live, watch strawberry picking, go with an injured worker to the hospital, and so on.

Complete Observer

The complete observer, at the other extreme, observes a social process without becoming a part of it in any way. The participants in a study might not realize that they are being studied because of the researcher's unobtrusiveness. Sitting at a bus stop to observe jaywalking behavior at a nearby intersection would be an example. Although the complete observer is less likely to affect what is being studied and less likely to "go native" than the complete participant, he or she is also less likely to develop a full appreciation of what is being studied. Observations may be more sketchy and transitory.

Davis (1973) characterized the extreme roles that observers might play as "the Martian" and

"the Convert." The latter involves the observer delving deeper and deeper into the phenomenon under study, running the risk that anthropologists refer to as "going native." We'll examine this further in the next section.

On the other hand, you may be able to most fully grasp the "Martian" approach by imagining that you were sent to observe life on Mars (assuming that life forms had been found there). Probably you would feel yourself inescapably separate from the Martians. Some social scientists adopt this degree of separation when observing cultures or social classes different from their own.

Ultimately, different situations require different roles for the researcher. Unfortunately, there are no clear guidelines for making this choice, and you must rely on your understanding of the situation and your own good judgment. In making your decision, however, you must be guided by both methodological and ethical considerations. Because these often conflict with one another, your decision will frequently be a difficult one, and you may find sometimes that your role limits your study.

» RELATIONS TO PARTICIPANTS: ETIC AND EMIC PERSPECTIVES

Having introduced the different roles you might play in connection with your field research observations, we'll now focus more specifically on how you may relate to the participants in your study and to their points of view. In the previous section, we opened the possibility of pretending to occupy social statuses that you don't really occupy. Now let's consider how you would think and feel in such a situation.

Let's suppose you have decided to study a religious cult that has enrolled many people in your own neighborhood or in one for which you have social work responsibilities. You might study the group by joining it or pretending to join it. Take a moment to ask yourself what the difference is between "really" joining and "pretending" to join. The main difference is one of whether you actually take on the beliefs, attitudes, and other points of view shared by the "real" members. If the cult members believe that Jesus will come next Thursday to destroy the world and save the members of the cult, do you believe that, or do you simply pretend to believe it?

Etic Perspective

Traditionally, social scientists have tended to emphasize the importance of "objectivity" in such matters. In this example, that injunction would be to avoid getting swept up in the beliefs of the group. In qualitative research, the term for maintaining your objectivity as an outsider and thus being able to raise questions about the culture you are observing—questions that would not occur to members of that culture—is the etic perspective. Without denying the advantages associated with such objectivity, social scientists today also recognize the benefits to be gained by immersing themselves in the points of view they are studying, gaining what Lofland and Lofland (1995, p. 61) refer to as *insider understanding*. Ultimately, you will not be able to understand the thoughts and actions of the cult members unless you are able to *adopt their points of view as true*—even if you do so only on a temporary basis. In a sense, you need to believe that Jesus is coming next Thursday night to fully appreciate the phenomenon you've set out to study.

Emic Perspective

In contrast to the etic perspective, the emic perspective refers to trying to adopt the beliefs, attitudes, and other points of view shared by the culture being studied. Adopting an alien point of view is an uncomfortable prospect for most people. It's one thing to learn about the strange views that others may hold, and sometimes you probably have difficulty even tolerating those views, but to take them on as your own is 10 times worse. Bellah (1970, 1974) has offered the term *symbolic realism* in this regard, indicating the need for social researchers to treat the beliefs they study as worthy of respect rather than as objects of ridicule. If you seriously entertain this prospect, you may appreciate why Shaffir and Stebbins (1991) concluded that "fieldwork must certainly rank with the more disagreeable activities that humanity has fashioned for itself" (p. 1).

There is, of course, a danger in adopting the points of view of the people you are studying. When you abandon your objectivity in favor of the views you are studying, you lose the possibility of seeing and understanding the phenomenon within frames of reference that are unavailable to your participants. On the one hand, accepting the belief that the world will end Thursday night allows you to appreciate aspects of that belief that are available only to believers; stepping outside that view, however, makes it possible for you to consider some of the reasons why people might adopt such a view. You may discover that some reached that state as a consequence of personal traumas (such as unemployment or divorce), whereas others were brought into the fold through their participation in particular social networks (e.g., their whole bowling team joined the cult). Notice that the cult members might disagree with those "objective" explanations, and you might not come up with those explanations to the extent that you were operating legitimately within the group's views.

Adopting Both Perspectives

The apparent dilemma here is that although the emic and etic perspectives offer important advantages, they also seem mutually exclusive. Yet it is possible (though challenging) to assume both postures. Sometimes you can simply shift viewpoints at will. When appropriate, you can fully assume the beliefs of the cult; later, you can step outside those beliefs (more accurately, you step inside the viewpoints associated with social science). As you become more adept at this kind of research, you may come to hold contradictory viewpoints simultaneously rather than switch back and forth.

›› REFLEXIVITY

Social researchers often refer to the concerns just discussed as a matter of *reflexivity* in the sense of things acting on themselves. Although it has been defined in various ways, reflexivity is a key part of qualitative research. It is applicable not only to qualitative observation methods but also to each of the remaining methods to be discussed in this chapter. According to Gilgun (2010), the core of the idea of reflexivity is "the idea of awareness—that researchers are reflexive when they are aware of the multiple influences they have on research processes and on how research processes affect them" (p. 1).

Being reflexive thus requires that researchers continually reflect on how their own experiences, assumptions, and biases might be influencing what they research, what they or their research participants say or do, and how they interpret what their research participants say or do. Berg (2007) describes the reflexivity process as engaging in an "internal dialogue that repeatedly examines *what the researcher knows* and *how the researcher came to know this*" (p. 179).

Thus, your own characteristics can have an effect on what you see and how you interpret it. The issue is broader than that, however, and applies to the participants as well as to the researcher. Imagine yourself interviewing a homeless person (a) on the street, (b) in a homeless shelter, or (c) in a social welfare office. The research setting could affect the person's responses. In other words, you might get different results, depending on where you conducted the interview. Moreover, you might act differently as a researcher in those different settings. If you reflect on this issue, you'll be able to identify other aspects of the research encounter that complicate the task of "simply observing what's so."

The problem we've just been discussing could be seen as psychological, occurring mostly inside the researchers' or participants' heads. There is a corresponding problem at a social level, however. When you become deeply involved in the lives of the people you're studying, you're likely to be moved by their personal problems and crises. Imagine, for example, that one of the cult members becomes ill and needs a ride to the hospital. Should you provide transportation? Sure. Suppose someone wants to borrow money to buy a stereo. Should you loan it? Probably not. Suppose that person needs the money for food?

There are no black-and-white rules for resolving situations such as these, but you should realize that you will need to deal with them regardless of whether or not you reveal you're a researcher. Such problems do not tend to arise in other types of research—surveys and experiments, for example—but they are part and parcel of qualitative research.

This discussion of reflexivity and the qualitative researcher's relations to participants flies in the face of the conventional view of scientific objectivity. Before concluding this section, let's take the issue one step further.

In the conventional view of science, there are implicit differences of power and status separating the researcher from the participants in research. When we discussed experimental designs in Chapter 11, for example, it was obvious who was in charge: the experimenter. The experimenter organized things, assigned participants to groups, and determined whether each group would receive a particular form of intervention. Something similar might be said about survey research. The person running the survey designs the questions, decides who will be selected for questioning, and is responsible for making sense out of the data collected.

These sorts of relationships can be seen as power or status relationships. In experimental and survey designs, the researcher clearly has more power and a higher status than the people being studied. The researchers have a special knowledge that the participants don't enjoy. They're not so crude as to say they're superior to their participants, but there's a sense in which that's implicitly assumed.

In qualitative research, such assumptions can be problematic. When the early European anthropologists set out to study what were originally called "primitive" societies, the anthropologists thought they knew best. Whereas the natives "believed" in witchcraft, for example, the anthropologists "knew" it wasn't really true. While the natives said that some of their rituals would appease the gods, the anthropologists explained that the "real" functions of these rituals were the creation of social identity, the establishment of group solidarity, and so on. The more social researchers have gone into the field to study their fellow humans face-to-face, however, the more they have become conscious of these implicit assumptions about researcher superiority and the more they have considered alternatives.

EP 4

» QUALITATIVE INTERVIEWING

In part, qualitative research is a matter of going where the action is and simply watching and listening. You can learn a lot merely by being attentive to what's going on. At the same time, as we've already indicated, field research can involve more active inquiry. Sometimes it's appropriate to ask people questions and record their answers. Your on-the-spot observations of a full-blown riot will lack something if you don't know why people are rioting. Ask somebody.

We have already discussed interviewing in Chapter 16, on survey research. The interviewing you will do in connection with qualitative observation, however, is different enough to demand a separate treatment here. In surveys, questionnaires are always structured and commonly use many closed-ended questions, but in qualitative research, interviews will be almost entirely open ended and are likely to be unstructured.

Rubin and Rubin (1995) make this distinction: "Qualitative interviewing design is *flexible, iterative*, and *continuous*, rather than prepared in advance and locked in stone" (p. 43):

> Design in qualitative interviewing is iterative. That means that each time you repeat the basic process of gathering information, analyzing it, winnowing it, and testing it, you come closer to a clear and convincing model of the phenomenon you are studying....
>
> The continuous nature of qualitative interviewing means that the questioning is redesigned throughout the project. (Rubin & Rubin, 1995, pp. 46, 47)

A qualitative interview is an interaction between an interviewer and a respondent in which the interviewer has a general plan of inquiry but not a specific set of questions that must be asked in particular words and in a particular order. A qualitative interview is essentially a conversation in which the interviewer establishes a general direction for the conversation and pursues specific topics raised by the respondent. Ideally, the respondent does most of the talking. If you're talking more than 5% of the time, that's probably too much.

Kvale (1996) offers two metaphors for interviewing: the interviewer as a "miner" and the interviewer as a "traveler." The first model assumes that the subject possesses specific information and that the interviewer's job is to dig it out. By contrast, in the second model, the interviewer

> ... wanders through the landscape and enters into conversations with the people encountered. The traveler explores the many domains of the country, as unknown territory or with maps, roaming freely around the territory.... The interviewer wanders along with the local inhabitants, asks questions that lead the subjects to tell their own stories of their lived world.... (pp. 3–5)

Patton (2015) identifies three forms of qualitative, open-ended interviewing:

1. Informal conversational interview
2. General interview guide approach
3. Standardized open-ended interview

Informal Conversational Interviews

An informal conversational interview is an unplanned and unanticipated interaction between an interviewer and a respondent that occurs naturally during the course of fieldwork observation. It is the most open-ended form of interviewing. When this type of interviewing occurs, the person with whom you are talking may not even think of the interaction as an interview.

When you conduct an informal conversational interview, you should be extremely flexible so that you can pursue relevant information in whatever direction seems appropriate. Your questions should be generated naturally and spontaneously from what you happen to observe at a particular point in a particular setting or from what individuals in that setting happen to say to you. In other words, this is the type of interviewing that will occur spontaneously when you are conducting fieldwork observations and want to maximize your understanding of what you are observing and what the people whom you are observing think about what is happening.

Because you cannot anticipate the situation beforehand, you conduct informal conversational interviews with no predetermined set of questions. Nonetheless, it is important for you to use your skills in asking questions and listening—skills that you probably learned as part of your social work practice training.

Lofland and Lofland (1995, pp. 56–57) suggest that investigators adopt the role of the "socially acceptable incompetent" when interviewing. You should offer yourself as someone who does not understand the situation in which you find yourself and so must be helped to grasp even the most basic and obvious aspects of that situation:

> A naturalistic investigator, almost by definition, is one who does not understand. She or he is "ignorant" and needs to be "taught." This role of watcher and asker of questions is the quintessential *student role*. (Lofland & Lofland, 1995, p. 56)

Asking questions and noting answers is a natural process for all of us, and it seems simple enough to add it to your bag of tricks as a qualitative researcher. Be cautious, however. There is a danger that what you ask is what you get.

As we've already discussed in Chapter 10, question wording is a tricky business. All too often, the way we ask questions subtly biases the answers we get. Sometimes, we put our respondent under pressure to look good. Sometimes we put the question in a particular context that completely precludes the most relevant answers.

Suppose you want to find out why a group of youths in a residential facility for emotionally distressed children is running amok. You might be tempted to focus your questioning on how the youths feel about the disciplinary style of their cottage parents. Although you may collect a great deal of information about their attitudes toward their cottage parents, they may be rioting for some other reason. Or perhaps most are simply joining in for the excitement. Properly done, informal conversational interviewing would enable you to find out.

One of the special strengths of this type of interviewing is its flexibility in the field. It allows you to respond to things you see or hear that you could not anticipate. The answers evoked by your initial questions should shape your subsequent ones. In this situation, merely asking preestablished questions and recording answers doesn't work. You need to ask a question, hear the answer, interpret its meaning for your general inquiry, and frame another question either to dig into the earlier answer in more depth or to redirect the person's attention to an area more relevant to your inquiry. In short, you need to be able to listen, think, and talk almost at the same time.

The discussion of *probes* in Chapter 16 provides a useful guide to getting answers in more depth without biasing later answers. Learn the skills of being a good listener. Be more interested than interesting. Learn to ask such questions as "How is that?," "In what ways?," "How do you mean that?," and "What would be an example of that?" Learn to look and listen expectantly and let the person you are interviewing fill the silence.

At the same time, you can't afford to be a totally passive receiver in the interaction. You'll probably have some general (or specific) questions in mind based on what you are observing, and you will have to learn the skills of subtly directing the flow of conversation.

There's something you can learn here from Asian martial arts. The aikido master never resists an opponent's blow but rather accepts it, joins with it, and then subtly redirects it in a more appropriate direction. You should master a similar skill for interviewing. Don't try to halt your respondent's line of discussion; rather, learn to take what he or she has just said and branch that comment back in a direction that is appropriate to your purposes. Most people love to talk to anyone who's really interested. Stopping their line of conversation tells them you aren't interested; asking them to elaborate in a particular direction tells them you are.

Consider this hypothetical example in which you are interested in why college students chose their majors.

You: What are you majoring in?

Respondent: Engineering.

You: I see. How did you come to choose engineering?

Respondent: I have an uncle who was voted the best engineer in Arizona in 1981.

You: Gee, that's great.

Respondent: Yeah. He was the engineer in charge of developing the new civic center in Tucson. It was written up in most of the engineering journals.

You: I see. Did you talk to him about your becoming an engineer?

Respondent: Yeah. He said that he got into engineering by accident. He needed a job when he graduated from high school, so he went to work as a laborer on a construction job. He spent eight years working his way up from the bottom, until he decided to go to college and come back nearer the top.

You: So is your main interest in civil engineering, like your uncle, or are you more interested in some other branch of engineering?

Respondent: Actually, I'm leaning more toward electrical engineering—computers in particular. I started messing around with microcomputers when I was in high school, and my long-term plan is....

Notice how the interview first begins to wander off into a story about the respondent's uncle. The first attempt to focus things back on the student's own choice of major failed. The second attempt succeeded. Now the student is providing the kind of information you want. It's important for you to develop the ability to "control" conversations in that fashion. At the same time, of course, you need to be on the alert for "distractions" that point to unexpectedly important aspects of your research interest.

Rubin and Rubin (1995) offer several guides to controlling a "guided conversation." For example,

> If you can limit the number of main topics, it is easier to maintain a conversational flow from one topic to another. Transitions should be smooth and logical. "We have been talking about mothers, now let's talk about fathers," sounds abrupt. A smoother transition might be, "You mentioned your mother did not care how you performed in school—was your father more involved?" The more abrupt the transition, the more it sounds like the interviewer has an agenda that he or she wants to get through, rather than wanting to hear what the interviewee has to say. (p. 123)

Because informal conversational interviewing is so much like normal conversations, it is essential that you keep reminding yourself that you are not having a normal conversation. In normal conversations, we want to come across as an interesting, worthwhile person. If you'll watch yourself the next time you are chatting with someone you don't know too well, you may find that much of your attention is spent on thinking up interesting things to say—contributions to the conversation that will make a good impression. Often, we don't really hear each other because we're too busy thinking of what we'll say next. As an interviewer, the desire to appear interesting is counterproductive to your job. You need to make the other person seem interesting—by being interested. (Do this in ordinary conversations, by the way, and people will actually regard you as a great conversationalist.)

Interviewing needs to be an integral part of your whole field research process. Later, we'll stress the need to review your notes every night—making sense out of what you've observed, getting a clearer feel for the situation you're studying, and finding out what you should pay more attention to in further observations.

In this same fashion, you need to review your notes on informal conversational interviews, detecting all of the things you should have asked but didn't. Start asking those things the next time an appropriate informal conversational interview emerges. As with all other aspects of field research, informal conversational interviewing improves with practice. Fortunately, it is something you can practice any time you want. Practice on your friends.

Interview Guide Approach

Besides including the unplanned interviews that emerge spontaneously in the conduct of field observations, qualitative inquiry can include the use of interviews that are planned in advance and that are therefore more structured than informal conversational interviews. Although all qualitative interviewing is open ended and allows respondents to express their own perspectives in their own words, qualitative interviewing strategies can vary in the extent to which the sequencing and wording of the open-ended questions are predetermined.

Highly structured strategies attempt to ensure that all respondents are asked the same questions in the same sequence to maximize the comparability of responses and to ensure that complete data are gathered from each person on all relevant questions. Greater structure can also reduce interviewer biases and inconsistencies in the way different interviewers conduct their interviews. More structure also eases the researcher's task of organizing and analyzing interview data and helps readers of the research report judge the quality of the interviewing methods and instruments used.

The downside to the highly structured approach, however, is that it reduces the natural, conversational nature of the interview and the interviewer's flexibility to follow up on important unanticipated circumstances or responses. Patton (2105) suggests that one way to provide more structure than in the completely unstructured informal conversational interview while maintaining a relatively high degree of flexibility is to use the interview guide strategy.

An interview guide lists in outline form the topics and issues that the interviewer should cover in the interview, but it allows the interviewer to adapt the sequencing and wording of questions to each particular interview. Thus, the interview guide ensures that different interviewers will cover the same material and keep focused on the same predetermined topics and issues while remaining conversational and free to probe into unanticipated circumstances and responses. Interview guides will vary in the extent of detail they provide. How much detail you provide in your guide will depend on the extent to which you are able to anticipate the important topics and issues in advance and how much detail you think your interviewers need to ensure that they will all cover the same material in a thorough fashion (Patton, 2015).

Suppose, for example, that you want to use intensive interviews of social workers in a qualitative evaluation of an in-service training program aimed at improving their own interviewing skills in conducting clinical assessments. A relatively brief interview guide might list a handful or so of broad question areas to ask about, such as the following:

1. What interviewing training activities and assignments did the trainee do in the program?

2. In what areas of interviewing, if any, does the trainee feel more or less skillful as a result of the program?

3. What service functions, if any, does the trainee feel better (or worse) prepared to provide as a result of the training?

4. Has the program influenced the trainee's career plans, and, if so, how?

5. What did the trainee like and dislike most about the program? What are its strengths and weaknesses, and what changes, if any, does the trainee suggest?

A more detailed interview guide for the same type of evaluation might look something like the following rough example:

I. Overall impression of program

   A. Likes? Dislikes?

   B. Strengths? Weaknesses?

   C. Suggested changes?

   D. Perceived influence of program on trainee?

      1. Service functions prepared to provide

      2. Career plans

      3. Interviewing skills, in general

II. Activities in program

   A. Readings?

   B. Written experiential assignments?

   C. Role plays?

   D. Peer or instructor feedback?

   E. Instructor modeling of interview skills?

III. Progress made or not made in specific areas of interviewing

   A. Beginning the interview

      1. Meeting and greeting clients

      2. Making introductions

      3. Putting client at ease

      4. Explaining purpose of interview

      5. Obtaining client's reason for coming

   B. Physical attending

      1. Making eye contact

      2. Using appropriate posture

      3. Using intermittent positive gestures

      4. Being appropriately relaxed and professionally comfortable

   C. Verbal attending

      1. Using nonjudgmental prompts

      2. Making brief pauses before responding

      3. Using appropriate paraphrasing

      4. Encouraging client to talk

      5. Showing sensitivity to differences in culture or ethnicity

      6. Conveying empathy and warmth

      7. Speaking in a natural, spontaneous, genuine manner

   D. Exploring the problem

      1. Taking social histories

      2. Examining problem from different perspectives

      3. Assessing situational and systemic factors

   E. Questioning and probing

      1. Asking clear and succinct questions

      2. Asking questions in an unbiased manner

      3. Asking exploratory questions in an open-ended manner

      4. Interspersing closed- and open-ended questions

      5. Pursuing important details with neutral probes

      6. Knowing not to bombard with too many questions

      7. Using logical sequencing of questions

      8. Being sensitive to privacy concerns

In addition to facilitating your learning about the use of detailed interview guides, we hope this illustrative guide will be useful to you as you think about developing your own skills as a qualitative interviewer and as an interviewer in your social work practice roles.

Regardless of how detailed you make your interview guide, you should make sure that your interviewers are completely familiar with its contents and purposes before they begin any interviews. If they are not, the interview will not flow smoothly, and your efforts to ensure that all of the material is covered in the context of a natural, conversational interview will be imperiled.

Interviewers also have to be prepared to decide when and when not to follow up in a neutral probing manner on unanticipated topics that emerge during the interview, depending on their importance to the respondent and to the purpose of the research. Thus, interviewers should be trained carefully before embarking on any interviews. (See our discussion of coordination and control in Chapter 16 for information on training interviewers.)

Standardized Open-Ended Interviews

As we just mentioned, sometimes you will want to ensure that all interviews are conducted in a consistent, thorough manner, with a minimum of interviewer effects and biases. When this is your aim, the most appropriate strategy is to conduct standardized open-ended interviews. This strategy may also be needed when resource limitations leave you with insufficient time to pursue less structured strategies in a comprehensive way with large numbers of respondents or when you are tracking individuals over time and therefore want to reduce the chances that changes observed over time are being caused by changes in the way interviews are being conducted.

In light of these concerns, in the standardized open-ended interview, "the exact wording and sequence of questions are determined in advance. All interviewees are asked the same basic questions in the same order" Patton (2015, p. 438). Great care goes into the wording of the questions and their sequencing. Probes are to be limited to where they are indicated on the interview schedule, although some studies that use highly skilled interviewers may permit more flexibility in probing than other studies that use this strategy.

Before leaving this topic, we should remind you that the social class issues mentioned in Chapter 16 regarding surveys, such as appearance and demeanor, apply to interviewing in qualitative research as well. So too do the cultural issues that we discussed in Chapter 6.

» LIFE HISTORY

Another method of qualitative interviewing is called life history or life story. Using this method, researchers ask open-ended questions to discover how the participants in a study understand the significant events and meanings in their own lives. Another term sometimes used in connection with this method is *oral history interviews*.

Because life histories provide idiographic examinations of individuals' lives, they can be viewed within the case study paradigm. They are also in keeping with the *naturalist* tradition because their main purpose is to see how the individual subjectively remembers and understands the significant events of their lives—even if the remembrances and interpretations lack objective accuracy. Robinson's (1994) dissertation in social welfare at Brandeis University provides an illustration of the life history method. Robinson sought to give voice to her informants without questioning the veracity of their accounts. Her goal was to describe the significant events in the life stories of delinquent girls as told to her in oral history interviews. In particular, she was interested in life experiences that led to delinquent behaviors resulting in their referral for social services.

She interviewed 30 girls she randomly selected from purposively selected areas thought to be representative of Massachusetts. Robinson embarked on her study with the notion that a history of sexual abuse might be prevalent among this population of girls and that abuse might be a key factor in leading them to delinquent behaviors. Rather than operationally define *sexual abuse*, however, she relied on the girls' own subjective experiences and perceptions. Robinson looked for cues suggestive of possible incidents of sexual abuse, and when she felt there was a cue, she encouraged the girls to elaborate on the nature of the abuse and how they experienced it.

She began each interview with an open-ended request: "Tell me about your family." In addition to observing their verbal responses during the interviews, Robinson took note of the girls' facial expressions, body language, and overall affect. The interviews were unstructured and conversational, although Robinson slowly and gently probed when the girls mentioned or hinted at sensitive events that were difficult for them to talk about. The girls discussed many painful and traumatic life events—including betrayal by parents, miscarriages and abortions, suicide attempts, and others—but Robinson focused on sexual abuse as the key event, noting that 23 of the 30 girls reported having been sexually abused. Ten of the girls reported being victimized by more than one person. Robinson's report cites various excerpts from her interviews, giving readers a sense of the girls' experiences of the abuse in their own voices.

From this information and guided by her theoretical framework and feminist perspective, Robinson concluded that correctional systems and social agencies should begin to view these girls not just as offenders but as victims of horrendous experiences who need services specifically geared to sexual abuse.

» FEMINIST METHODS

Robinson's study illustrates how the different types of qualitative studies we are discussing are not mutually exclusive. For example, her study combined life history interviews with a feminist perspective. We alluded to feminist studies in Chapter 3 as an application of the empowerment paradigm. Many studies using feminist methods aim to generate findings that can be used to improve the well-being of women in a historically male-dominated society. Although feminist studies use both quantitative and qualitative methods, they most commonly use qualitative methods and are most commonly associated with qualitative research. Feminist studies typically employ features of ethnography and oral history in that they attempt to let the voices of women be heard from their own point of view. In this connection, feminist studies typically rest on the assumption that women are different from men in the ways they acquire knowledge and view the world.

EP 3, 4

» FOCUS GROUPS

Our discussions of qualitative research so far have focused on studying or interviewing people in their natural settings. Sometimes, however, researchers bring people into the laboratory to be observed and interviewed as a group. The focus group, which is one type of group interviewing, is usually considered a qualitative method (although it can also be used in a quantitative way, such as by merely counting how many times certain words are expressed). It is based on structured, semistructured, or unstructured interviews. It allows the researcher-interviewer to question several individuals systematically and simultaneously.

Focus groups are often used to assess whether a new social program or social service being considered is really needed in a community. In a focus group, people are brought together in a private, comfortable environment to engage in a guided discussion of a specified topic. The main idea is that the participants in a focus group will be stimulated by each other's comments to think of things that might not have occurred to them in an individual interview. Likewise, what others say may change their views of things they might have expressed differently in an individual interview.

Sampling

Although some focus groups might include a dozen or more people, a smaller number—around 8—is preferred. Participants in focus groups are not likely to be chosen using probability sampling techniques. They are more likely to be selected using purposive sampling based on their relevancy to the topic being discussed. For example, if the topic pertains to prospective consumer utilization of a new service that an agency is considering, then the participants may be community leaders, service providers from other agencies, referral sources, current service consumers, or perhaps a sample of community residents in targeted neighborhoods. If the topic concerns consumer satisfaction with agency services, then the participants may be drawn from current consumers.

It's also common to convene more than one focus group—perhaps three or four; relying on only one group is generally considered too risky because any one particular group may be atypical.

Types and Sequence of Questions

The principles of focus group interviewing are the same as those discussed earlier in this chapter regarding qualitative interviewing in general. Although the focus group interviewer has a general plan of inquiry, the questions are always or almost always open-ended, followed up as needed with neutral probes.

Krueger and Casey (2015) suggest that structured or semistructured focus group interviews might start off with an opening question to which all participants take turns responding and might end asking participants to reflect on the entire discussion or on the interviewer's summary of the discussion. In between are introductory questions, transition questions, and key questions dealing with the various aspects of the phenomenon of concern to the researcher—including unanticipated aspects that arise during the course of the interview.

Opening questions are essentially community-building icebreakers aimed at helping participants feel at ease and in the company of people with whom they have things in common. For example, moderators assessing the unmet needs in a neighborhood might start with an opening question like, "Can you tell us about yourself—for example, your name, where you live, how you like to spend your time, and so on?"

After everyone takes a turn briefly (about 30 seconds) responding to the opening question, the open-ended introductory question is asked. Introductory questions begin the focus on the main topic for the group to address. For example, "What first comes to mind when you think of this neighborhood?" Or, "What is it like to live in this neighborhood?"

Next come transition questions, which provide links between introductory questions and key questions. The key questions are the ones most pertinent to the research focus. A transition question might ask, "How long have you lived in this neighborhood?" Or, "Have you been involved in any neighborhood activities?" Or, "What do you like best about this neighborhood?"

Next come about two to five key questions. The moderator spends the most time on the key questions—perhaps as much as 15 minutes on each one. It is with these questions that the moderator uses the most probes. One key question might be, "In your opinion, what is most needed to make this neighborhood a better place to live?" If the needs assessment has a particular interest in gauging residents' perceptions of needed improvements in police–community relations, the moderator might ask, "How do you feel about police–community relations here?" Or if the potential need for and use of new recreational facilities for youths is being considered, "What do you think of the recreational facilities for youths in this neighborhood?"

Ending questions ask participants to reflect on the discussion. For example, "Of all the neighborhood needs that we've identified, which one or two is/are the most important to you?" Following the ending question is the summary question. For example, the moderator might summarize the main needs expressed in the interview and ask, "Did I miss anything?" Or, "Is my summary accurate?"

An example of a gerontological social work study employing open-ended interview guide questions in a focus group needs assessment is presented in the box "Psychosocial Needs of Lesbian and Gay Elders in Long-Term Care."

Advantages

Despite the risks inherent in generalizing from focus groups, they offer several advantages. They are inexpensive, generate speedy results, and offer flexibility for probing. The group dynamics that occur in focus groups can bring out aspects of the topic that researchers might not have anticipated and that might not have emerged in individual interviews.

Imagine, for example, that you, as a consumer in a social work education program, are being asked about your satisfaction with the program and how it might be improved to offer better services. Suppose you are responding to a structured questionnaire or a structured interview with closed-ended questions about your degree of satisfaction with the classroom course offerings, field practicums, audiovisual or computer resources, quality of the teaching, advisement, instructor accessibility, and so forth. Your responses would be limited to checking off things like "moderately satisfied," "slightly dissatisfied," and so on to program attributes anticipated by those who designed the survey.

Suppose the survey questionnaire also contains open-ended items that ask you to think of anything else you particularly liked or disliked about the program or recommendations you have for improvement. You may or may not give a great deal of

PSYCHOSOCIAL NEEDS OF LESBIAN AND GAY ELDERS IN LONG-TERM CARE

Three social work professors—Gary Stein, Nancy Berkman, and Patricia Sherman (2010)—conducted a focus group assessment of the psychosocial needs of lesbian and gay elders currently living in residential care facilities or anticipating such a move in the future. Using convenience sampling, they convened two focus groups. One was composed of 12 participants at a community-based organization for LGBT seniors in New York City. The other was composed of four residents in a long-term care facility in New Jersey. The interview guide emphasized the following key exploratory questions (p. 427):

1. How comfortable do you feel being openly gay in your neighborhood (or long-term care setting)?

2. What are your thoughts as a gay senior about retirement communities?

3. What thoughts do you have about assisted living residences or nursing homes?

4. Do you think you would be (or are now) comfortable as a gay senior in a residential setting?

5. How can health care providers be more responsive to gay people?

The main themes that emerged in the focus groups pertained to fears of rejection or neglect from health care providers, fears of rejection and lack of respect from other residents, fear of having to return to the closet, and a preference for gay-friendly care. The researchers concluded that long-term care facilities should sensitize their staff members to the needs of gay and lesbian elders and to be respectful of them. They also proposed that ensuring this sensitivity and respect might be to have special "floors, units, or complete facilities that are dedicated to this community" (p. 433).

thought to these open-ended items, and even if you give them considerable thought, you may not think of some things that others may think of and with which you would agree.

Now suppose that you were being asked about these things not in a structured survey format but in a focus group. Instead of asking you to check off your degree of satisfaction with this or that or to come up with your own new ideas for improvements, the focus group leader would ask you and some of your cohorts to engage in a sort of bull-session discussion about your satisfaction or dissatisfaction with the program and how it could be improved. Chances are, if one or more of your colleagues began expressing dissatisfaction with something with which you also were dissatisfied, then you might feel more comfortable in expressing the extent of your own dissatisfaction and its sources. As the members of the focus group interact about these issues, new ideas might be stimulated that would not have occurred to you in an individual interview or in completing a questionnaire.

For instance, someone might say, "Gee, I sure wish the program offered an elective course on interventions connected to death and dying." This might spark someone else to say, "Yeah, and I would have loved to take a course on play therapy." Neither of these ideas may have occurred to you as an individual survey respondent, but on hearing them in a focus group, you might respond, "Wow, I had assumed that the faculty knew best what courses were and were not appropriate to offer in a school of social work, but if those two courses were offered, I sure would have taken them both. They sound like they would have prepared me with specific practice intervention competencies more than a lot of the other electives offered." This might spur other group participants who, like you, may not have thought of these courses in the context of an individual survey, and they might indicate that they also would love to take these two courses. And perhaps a few other prospective elective courses would be identified that students would find highly relevant to practice and that would be fully enrolled. At the same time, these comments might prompt the group members to focus more on preparation for practice competency as their chief source of dissatisfaction with the program, and a rich discussion might ensue identifying issues, potentially popular elective courses, and other ways to improve the program that would not have been anticipated or identified by many respondents in a survey.

Instead of only one or two prospective new elective courses being identified by one or two isolated individuals in a survey, the focus group might identify a larger number of new courses and show which ones would generate the most excitement and the largest potential enrollments.

Disadvantages

That said, however, it's important to remember that focus groups also have disadvantages. As already mentioned, the representativeness of focus group members is questionable. Perhaps those who agree to participate or who are the most vocal are the ones with the biggest axes to grind about the program, the ones most satisfied with it, or those most eager to curry favor with program providers. Although the group dynamics can bring out information that would not have emerged in a survey, those dynamics can also create pressures for people to say things that may not accurately reflect their true feelings or prospective deeds. Whereas some individuals who feel dissatisfied with a program may feel more comfortable about expressing it if others do so first, the same individuals might be less likely to express their dissatisfaction if those who speak up first express great satisfaction with the program.

If a couple of members show enthusiasm for a prospective service, then others may feel group pressure to say that they, too, would utilize the service, even though in reality they would not. In light of these dynamics, special knowledge about group dynamics and special group work skills are needed to moderate focus groups. In a focus group interview, much more than in any other types of interviews, the interviewer has to develop the skills of a moderator. Controlling the dynamic within the group is a major challenge. Letting one interviewee dominate the focus group interview reduces the likelihood that the other participants will express themselves. This can generate the problem of group conformity, or **groupthink**, which is the tendency for people in a group to conform with the opinions and decisions of the most outspoken members of the group. Interviewers need to be aware of this phenomenon and try to get everyone to participate

fully on all the issues brought in the interview. Adding to the challenge, of course, you must resist over-directing the interview and the interviewees, thus bringing your own views into play.

Another disadvantage of focus groups is that the data that emerge are likely to be voluminous and less systematic than structured survey data. Analyzing focus group data, therefore, can be more difficult, tedious, and subject to the biases of the evaluator. The analysis becomes more difficult to the extent that multiple focus groups yield inconsistent open-ended data. Thus, focus groups, like any other qualitative or quantitative research method, have certain advantages and disadvantages and are best used in combination with other research methods.

Although focus group research differs from other forms of qualitative research, it further illustrates the possibilities for doing social research face-to-face with those we wish to understand. In addition, Morgan (1993) suggests that focus groups are an excellent device for generating questionnaire items for a subsequent survey. The box "An Illustration of the Use of Focus Groups and Feminist Methods: The Voices of Battered Women in Japan" describes the use of focus groups in a study conducted by a social worker in the context of using feminist methods as well as the participatory action research paradigm that was discussed in Chapter 17.

EP 3

» RECORDING OBSERVATIONS

Because of the in-depth, open-ended nature of qualitative interviews, recording responses poses quite a challenge to the interviewer. The aims and philosophical roots of qualitative inquiry mandate that the respondent's answers be recorded as fully as possible. Recording them verbatim is ideal. A voice recorder, therefore, is a powerful tool for the qualitative interviewer. It not only ensures verbatim recording but also frees interviewers to keep their full attention focused on respondents, to communicate that they are listening to what is being said, and to probe into important cues. (As you might recall from Chapter 5, audio recording or video recording requires a separate signature line on your IRB consent forms.)

AN ILLUSTRATION OF THE USE OF FOCUS GROUPS AND FEMINIST METHODS: THE VOICES OF BATTERED WOMEN IN JAPAN

Mieko Yoshihama, a social work professor at the University of Michigan, was concerned about the dearth of research that examined the perspectives and experiences of battered women in Japan and the barriers to their seeking and using services. Consequently, she conducted "the first study in Japan to use face-to-face interviews with a community sample of battered women" (Yoshihama, 2002, p. 391). She used focus groups to conduct the interviews because she believed that hearing the experiences and perspectives of other battered women would help alleviate a sense of shame and isolation among study participants, enhance their understanding of their own situation, and make it easier for them to discuss how they perceived and coped with it. She recruited as study participants battered women of various backgrounds by sending fliers to organizations and professionals in Tokyo who come into contact with battered women and by announcing the study in national and local newspapers.

To facilitate the ability of women with diverse backgrounds and time constraints to participate in the study, she scheduled four focus groups during different times of the day, including one weekend group. On-site child care was provided. Participants received small cash reimbursements to partially cover their transportation and other costs of attending. They also received written materials about domestic violence and a list of assistance programs. Sessions were held at convenient and safe sites and lasted 2 hours. To ensure anonymity, participants did not divulge their last names. Some used pseudonyms or nicknames. Each session was audiotaped. The tapes were transcribed, and the meanings or themes expressed by participants in the transcripts were coded. Using the grounded theory method, repeated reviews of the transcripts yielded repeated revisions and improvements of the conceptual and thematic codes. Yoshihama's findings can be best summarized by the following excerpt from the abstract of her article:

Participants' narratives of their experience with their partners' violence suggest a web of entrapment, from which women saw little possibility of escape. The partners' physical violence, interference with the women's social participation, isolation from supportive networks, and degradation and debasement entrapped participants. The victim-blaming attitudes of family, friends, and professionals, as well as the lack of assistance programs and police protection, often reinforced the web. When these women took the risk of exposing what was long considered private and shameful, isolation was broken. (Yoshihama, 2002, p. 389)

In contrast with prevailing views, Yoshihama noted the similarities between the experiences of battered women in Japan and those in Western countries. Despite these similarities, Yoshihama pointed out that the victim-blaming reaction to this problem in Japanese society makes it harder for battered women there to obtain services and protection. Consequently, Yoshihama's study developed various implications for reforming social policy and social work practice in Japan to increase the amount of programs and services for battered women and to make them more sensitive and responsive to the safety needs and rights of battered women instead of blaming them and emphasizing preservation of the marriage. Her study also offered implications for social work practice with battered women emigrants from Japan in the United States who may not be aware of their increased options in the United States and who may need several repeated explanations to understand how things are different than in Japan.

Yoshihama also identified some limitations of her focus group study, specifically its limited generalizability in light of its small sample of self-selected women residing in one city. One of the strengths of the study pertained to its participatory action research function. By participating in the focus groups, the women were able to overcome their sense of shame and isolation, develop a shared understanding of their mutual problem, and obtain information about their legal rights and available assistance programs. Consequently, the participants formed support groups for battered women.

Voice Recording

Despite these advantages of voice recording, interviewers who use voice recorders should take notes while they interview so that they can refer back to something important said earlier in the interview or to occasionally jot down summary points or key phrases to facilitate later analysis of the recording. When done in moderation, that note taking helps pace the interview and lets respondents know that you find what they are saying important.

Voice recorders, however, are not applicable for a great deal of the data gathering in field research, particularly data gathered as a result of observation outside the interview context. And even in interviews, voice recorders cannot capture all of the relevant aspects of social processes. Therefore, other basic tools of field research include a notebook (or field journal) and a pencil. The greatest advantage of the field research method is the presence of an observing, thinking researcher on the scene. If possible, take notes on your observations as you make them. When that's not possible, write down your notes as soon as possible afterward.

Notes

Your notes should include both your empirical observations and your interpretations of them. You should record what you "know" has happened and what you "think" has happened. It is important, however, that these different kinds of notes be identified for what they are. For example, you might note that person X spoke in opposition to a proposal made by a group leader, that you think this represents an attempt by person X to take over leadership of the group, and that you think you heard the leader comment to that effect in response to the opposition.

Just as you cannot hope to observe everything, neither can you record everything you do observe. Just as your observations represent a de facto sample of all possible observations, your notes represent a sample of your observations. Rather than record a random sample of your observations, you should, of course, record the most important ones. The box "Interview Transcript Annotated with Researcher Memos" provides an example given by Sandrine Zerbib from an in-depth interview with a woman film director.

Advance Preparation

Some of the most important observations can be anticipated before the study begins; others will become apparent as your observations progress. Sometimes, your note taking can be made easier if you prepare standardized recording forms in advance. In a study of the homeless, for instance, you might anticipate the characteristics of homeless individuals that are the most likely to be useful for analysis—age, gender, social class, ethnicity, psychiatric history, and so forth—and prepare a form in which actual observations can be recorded easily. Or you might develop a symbolic shorthand in advance to speed up recording. For studying citizen participation at a community meeting, you might want to construct a numbered grid to represent the different sections of the meeting room; then you would be able to record the location of participants easily, quickly, and accurately.

None of this advance preparation should limit your recording of unanticipated events and aspects of the situation. Quite the contrary, speedy handling of anticipated observations can give you more freedom to observe the unanticipated.

Every student is familiar with the process of taking notes. However, good note taking in qualitative research requires more careful and deliberate attention and involves specific skills. Some guidelines follow. You can learn more about this in the book by Lofland and Lofland (1995, pp. 91–96) mentioned earlier in this chapter.

Record Soon

First, don't trust your memory any more than you have to; it's untrustworthy. If this sounds too unkind, try this experiment. Recall the last few movies you saw that you really liked. Now, name five of the actors or actresses. Who had the longest hair? Who was the most likely to start conversations? Who was the most likely to make suggestions that others followed? Now, if you didn't have any trouble answering any of those questions (and think you outsmarted us), how sure are you of your answers? Would you be willing to bet $100 that a panel of impartial judges would observe what you recall? If you are absolutely certain of your answers, what color shoes was your methods instructor wearing three class meetings ago? Gotcha! Even if you pride yourself on having a photographic

INTERVIEW TRANSCRIPT ANNOTATED WITH RESEARCHER MEMOS

Thursday August 26, 12:00–1:00

R: What is challenging for women directors on a daily experience, on a daily life?

J: Surviving.

R: Okay. Could you develop a little bit on that? [I need to work on my interview schedule so that my interviewee answers with more elaboration without having to probe.]

J: Yeah, I mean it's all about trying to get, you know, in, trying to get the job, and try, you know, to do a great job so that you are invited back to the next thing. And particularly since they are so many, you know, difficulties in women directing. It makes it twice as hard to gain into this position where you do an incredible job, because … you can't just do an average job, you have to [347] do this job that just knocks your socks off all the time, and sometimes you don't get the opportunity to do that, because either you don't have a good producer or you have so many pressures that you can't see straight or your script is lousy, and you have to make a silk purse out of sow's hair. You know, you have a lot of extra strikes against you than the average guy who has similar problems, because you are a woman and they look at it, and women are more visible than men … in unique positions.

[It seems that Joy is talking about the particularities of the film industry. There are not that many opportunities, and in order to keep working, she needs to build a certain reputation. It is only by continuing to direct that she can maintain or improve her reputation. She thinks that it is even harder for women but does not explain it.]

R: Hmm … what about on the set—did you experience, did it feel … did people make it clear that you were a woman, and you felt treated differently? [I am trying to get her to speak about more specific and more personal experiences without leading her answer.]

J: Yeah, oh yeah, I mean … a lot of women have commiserated about, you know when you have to walk on the set for the first time, they're all used to working like a well-oiled machine and they say, "Oh, here is the woman, something different," and sometimes they can be horrible, they can resist your directing and they can, they can sabotage you, by taking a long time to light, or to move sets, or to do something … and during that time you're wasting time, and that goes on a report, and the report goes to the front [368] office, and, you know, and so on and so on and so on and so forth. And people upstairs don't know what the circumstances are, and they are not about to fire a cinematographer that is on their show for ever and ever … nor do they want to know that this guy is a real bastard, and making your life a horror. They don't want to know that, so therefore, they go off, because she's a woman let's not hire any more women, since he has problems with women. You know, so, there is that aspect.

I need to review the literature on institutional discrimination. It seems that the challenges that Joy is facing are not a matter of a particular individual. She is in a double bind situation where, whether she complains or not, she will not be treated equal to men. Time seems to be one quantifiable measurement of how well she does her job, and, as observed in other professions, the fact that she is a woman is perceived as a handicap. Review literature on women in high management positions. [I need to keep asking about the dynamics between my interviewees and the crew members on the set. The cinematographer has the highest status on the set under the director. Explore other interviews about reasons for conflict between them.]

[Methods (note to myself for the next interviews): try to avoid phone interviews unless specific request from the interviewee. It is difficult to assess how the interviewee feels with the questions. Need body language because I become more nervous about the interview process.]

Note: A number in square brackets represents a word that was inaudible from the interview. It is the number that appeared on the transcribing machine, with each interview starting at count 0. The numbers help the researcher locate a passage quickly when he or she reviews the interview.

memory, it's a good idea to take notes either during the observation or as soon afterward as possible. If you are taking notes during observation, then do it unobtrusively because people are likely to behave differently if they see you taking down everything they say or do.

Take Notes in Stages

Second, it's usually a good idea to take notes in stages. In the first stage, you may need to take sketchy notes (words and phrases) to keep abreast of what's happening. Then remove yourself and rewrite your notes in more detail. If you do this soon after the events you've observed, the sketchy notes should allow you to recall most of the details. The longer you delay, the less likely it is you'll recall things accurately and fully.

We know this method sounds logical, and you've probably made a mental resolution to do it that way if you're ever involved in qualitative research. Let us warn you, however, that you'll need self-discipline to keep your resolution in practice. Careful observation and note taking can be tiring, especially if they involve excitement or tension and extend over a long period of time. If you've just spent eight hours straight observing and making notes on how people have been coping with a disastrous flood, then your first thought afterward is likely to be directed toward getting some sleep, dry clothes, or a drink. You may need to take some inspiration from newspaper reporters who undergo the same sorts of hardships before writing their stories and meeting their deadlines.

Details Can Be Important

Third, you will inevitably wonder how much you should record. Is it really worth the effort to write out all of the details you can recall right after the observation session? The general guideline here is yes. Generally, in qualitative research you can't be really sure of what is and is not important until you've had a chance to review and analyze a great volume of information, so you should even record things that don't seem important at the outset. They may turn out to be significant after all. Also, the act of recording the details of something "unimportant" may jog your memory on something that is important.

You should realize that most of your field notes will not be reflected in your final report on the project. Put more harshly, most of the notes you take will be "wasted." But take heart: Even the richest gold ore yields only about 30 grams of gold per metric ton, meaning that 99.997% of the ore is wasted. Yet that 30 grams of gold can be hammered out to cover an area 18 square feet—the equivalent of almost 700 book pages. So take a ton of notes and plan to select and use only the gold.

Practice

Like other aspects of qualitative research (and all research for that matter), proficiency comes with practice. The nice thing about qualitative research is you can begin practicing now and can continue practicing in almost any situation. You don't have to be engaged in an organized research project to practice observation and recording. For example, you might start by volunteering to take the minutes at committee meetings.

MAIN POINTS

- You may or may not identify yourself as a researcher to the people you are observing. Identifying yourself as a researcher may have some effect on the nature of what you are observing, but concealing your identity may involve deceit.
- Because qualitative research takes you into close contact with participants, you must negotiate your relationship with them; there are several options.
- You may or may not participate in what you are observing. Participating in the events may make it easier for you to conceal your identity as a researcher, but participation is likely to affect what is being observed.
- Participant observation is a form of qualitative research in which the researcher participates as an actor in the events under study.
- Four different positions on a continuum of participant observation roles are the complete participant, participant as observer, observer as participant, and complete observer.
- Qualitative researchers using the method of participant observation should learn how to simultaneously hold two contradictory perspectives: (a) trying to adopt the beliefs, attitudes,

and other points of view shared by the members of the culture being studied (the emic perspective) while (b) maintaining objectivity as an outsider and raising questions about the culture being observed that wouldn't occur to members of that culture (the etic perspective).

- Reflexivity requires that researchers continually reflect on how their own experiences, assumptions, and biases might be influencing what they research, what they or their research participants say or do, and how they interpret what their research participants say or do. Qualitative researchers often engage in in-depth interviews with the participants—interviews that are far less structured than the interviews conducted in survey research.

- Qualitative interviewing tends to be open-ended and unstructured. Three forms of qualitative, open-ended interviewing are (a) the informal conversational interview, (b) the general interview guide approach, and (c) the standardized open-ended interview.

- An informal conversational interview is an unplanned and unanticipated interaction between an interviewer and a respondent that occurs naturally during the course of fieldwork observation.

- With the interview guide approach to qualitative interviewing, an interview guide lists in outline form the topics and issues that the interviewer should cover in the interview, but it allows the interviewer to adapt the sequencing and wording of questions to each particular interview.

- The standardized open-ended interview consists of questions that are written out in advance exactly the way they are to be asked in the interview.

- Life histories involve asking open-ended questions to discover how the participants in a study understand the significant events and meanings in their own lives.

- To create a focus group, researchers bring participants together and observe their interactions as they explore a specific topic.

- Some key advantages of focus groups are as follows: They are inexpensive, they generate speedy results, and they offer flexibility for probing. The group dynamics that occur in focus groups can bring out aspects of the topic that researchers might not have anticipated and that might not have emerged in individual interviews.

- Among the disadvantages of focus groups are the questionable representativeness of participants, the influence of group dynamics to pressure people to say things that don't accurately reflect what they really believe or do, and the difficulty in analyzing the voluminous data generated.

- The field journal is the backbone of qualitative research because that is where the researcher records his or her observations. Journal entries should be detailed, yet concise.

- Note taking in qualitative research should include both the investigator's empirical observations and the investigator's interpretations of them. You should record what you "know" has happened and what you "think" has happened.

- If possible, observations should be recorded as they are made; otherwise, they should be recorded in stages and as soon as possible (without detracting from your interviewing or observations). Don't trust your memory any more than you have to.

REVIEW QUESTIONS AND EXERCISES

1. Think of some group or activity in which you participate or that you know well. In two or three paragraphs, describe how an outsider might effectively go about studying that group or activity. What should he or she read, what contacts should be made, and so on?

2. Accompanied by one of your classmates, show up 10 minutes early for your next research class session. Each of you should independently observe and take notes on what other classmates say to each other before and after the instructor shows up. Repeat this at the end of class and as students chat outside the classroom. Later on, analyze and interpret your notes as to how communications may or may not differ, depending on the instructor's presence or absence. Have your classmate do the same—but independent of your notes and conclusions. Compare your conclusions with those of your classmate. Write down any disagreements you had in

your conclusions and what you think explains your differences.

3. Together with two other classmates, prepare and carry out the three qualitative interview approaches discussed in this chapter. Each of you should utilize a different approach, and the focus of the interview should be on student attitudes about a topic of your choosing. At three different times, you and your two classmates should separately interview the same student (or perhaps two or three of the same students). Each of you should independently analyze and interpret your own interview data. Compare the similarities and differences in your conclusions and write down why you think you agreed or disagreed.

4. Break down the class into groups of about 8 to 10 students per group. Ask one student in each group to conduct a focus group interview with the group about the strengths and weaknesses of your school's social work curriculum and any revisions they would suggest. Ask another student to be the recorder for the group. Each focus group interview should last approximately 30 minutes, followed by a discussion within each group regarding the strengths and limitations of the process. Reconvene and have the recorders summarize their discussions for the class.

INTERNET EXERCISES

1. Find the following articles in the October 2002 issue of the journal *Social Work* that illustrate the use of focus groups. Briefly identify the similarities and differences in the way these studies used focus groups methodology and critically appraise the strengths and weaknesses of each study.

   "Deciding Who to See: Lesbians Discuss Their Preferences in Health and Mental Health Care Providers," by C. F. Saulnier

   "Work-Family Fit: Voices of Parents of Children With Emotional and Behavioral Disorders," by J. M. Rosenzweig, E. M. Brennan, and A. M. Ogilvie

   "Opportunities and Barriers to Empowering People With Severe Mental Illness Through Participation in Treatment Planning," by D. M. Linhorst, G. Hamilton, E. Young, and A. Eckert

   "The Functions of the Social Worker in Empowering: The Voices of Consumers and Professionals," by A. Boehm and L. H. Staples

   "Voices of African American Families: Perspectives on Residential Treatment," by J. M. Kruzich, B. J. Friesen, T. Williams-Murphy, and M. J. Longley

2. Find one to three articles illustrating the use of participant observation, qualitative interviewing, life history, and feminist methods. (Some articles might report a study using more than one of these methods.) Write down the bibliographic reference information for each article and identify its methodological strengths and weaknesses.

3. Go to the following two websites and discuss two things you learned there about designing or conducting focus group interviews:
   https://assessment.trinity.duke.edu/documents/How_to_Conduct_a_Focus_Group.pdf
   http://www.eiu.edu/~ihec/Krueger-FocusGroup-Interviews.pdf

 Visit CengageBrain.com for additional practice and study opportunities including experiential exercises, research tools, glossary, flashcards, and sample test items.

20

Qualitative Data Analysis

EPAS Competencies for This Chapter

Competency 4   Engage in Practice-Informed Research and Research-Informed Practice: This competency pertains to this entire chapter because doing practice-informed qualitative research requires an understanding of the basics of qualitative data analysis. The same applies to engaging in research-informed practice because understanding the basics of qualitative data analysis will help in understanding qualitative studies and their implications for practice.

Competency 9   Evaluate Practice with Individuals Families, Groups, Organizations, and Communities: This competency pertains to this entire chapter because designing a qualitative evaluation requires understanding the basics of qualitative data analysis.

What You'll Learn in This Chapter

This chapter shows how you can analyze nonnumerical observations made through qualitative research techniques. Although qualitative analysis is an art as much as a science, it has its own logic and techniques, some of which are enhanced by special computer programs.

» INTRODUCTION

As you may have surmised while reading the previous two chapters, data analysis, data collection, and theory are intimately intertwined in qualitative research. Therefore, it is difficult to learn the steps involved in qualitative data analysis in a rote manner. This is unlike the analysis of data generated by quantitative research methods, which we'll examine in the next section of this book. Because qualitative analysis—the nonnumerical examination and interpretation of observations for the purpose of discovering underlying meanings and patterns of relationships—involves a continuing interplay between data collection and theory, understanding must precede practice. In this chapter, we begin with the links between research and theory in qualitative analysis. Then we examine some procedures that have proven useful in pursuing the theoretical aims. After considering some simple manual techniques, we'll take some computer programs out for a spin.

EP 4, 9

» LINKING THEORY AND ANALYSIS

Our discussion of qualitative data analysis will be based on the image of theory offered by Strauss and Corbin (1994) as consisting of "*plausible* relationships proposed among *concepts* and *sets of concepts*" (p. 278). They stress "plausible" to indicate that theories represent our best understanding of how life operates. The more our research confirms a particular set of relationships among particular concepts, however, the more confident we become that our understanding corresponds to social reality.

Although qualitative research is sometimes undertaken for purely descriptive purposes—such as the anthropologist's ethnography detailing ways of life in a previously unknown tribe—this chapter focuses primarily on the search for explanatory patterns. As we'll see, sometimes the patterns occur over time, and sometimes they take the form of causal relations among variables. Let's look at some of the ways qualitative researchers uncover such patterns.

Discovering Patterns

Lofland and Lofland (1995, pp. 127–145) suggest six different ways of looking for patterns in a particular research topic. Let's suppose you're interested in analyzing child abuse in a certain neighborhood. Here are some questions you might ask yourself to make sense out of your data:

1. Frequencies: How often does child abuse occur among families in the neighborhood under study? (Realize that there may be a difference between the frequency and what people are willing to tell you.)

2. Magnitudes: What are the levels of abuse? How brutal are they?

3. Structures: What are the different types of abuse: physical, mental, and sexual? Are they related in any particular manner?

4. Processes: Is there any order among the elements of structure? Do abusers begin with mental abuse and move on to physical and sexual abuse, or does the order of elements vary?

5. Causes: What are the causes of child abuse? Is it more common in particular social classes or among different religious or ethnic groups? Does it occur more often during good times or bad?

6. Consequences: How does child abuse affect the victims in both the short and the long term? What changes does it cause in the abusers?

For the most part, in examining your data you'll look for patterns appearing across several observations that typically represent different cases under study. Miles and Huberman (1994, pp. 435–436) offer two strategies for cross-case analysis: variable-oriented and case-oriented analyses. Variable-oriented analysis is similar to a model we've already discussed from time to time in this book. If we were trying to predict the decision to attend college, Miles and Huberman suggest, we might consider variables such as "gender, socioeconomic status, parental expectations, school performance, peer support, and decision to attend college" (p. 435). Thus, we would determine whether men or women were more likely to attend college. This is a variable-oriented analysis, in which the focus is on interrelations among variables, and the people observed are primarily the carriers of those variables.

Variable-oriented analysis may remind you of the discussion in Chapter 3 that introduced the idea of nomothetic explanation. The aim here is to achieve a partial, overall explanation using a relatively small number of variables. The political pollster who attempts to explain voting intentions on the basis of two or three key variables is using this approach. There is no pretense that the researcher can predict every individual's behavior or even explain any one person's motivations in full. Sometimes, though, it's useful to have even a partial explanation of overall orientations and actions.

You may also recall the Chapter 3 introduction of idiographic explanation, wherein we attempt to understand a particular case fully. This orientation lies at the base of what Miles and Huberman call a case-oriented analysis. In the voting example, we would attempt to learn everything we could about all the factors that came into play in determining one person's decision on how to vote:

> In a case-oriented analysis, we would look more closely into a particular case, say, Case 005, who is female, middle-class, has parents with high expectations, and so on. These are, however, "thin" measures. To do a genuine case analysis, we need to look at a full history of Case 005; Nynke van der Molen, whose mother trained as a social worker but is bitter over the fact that she never worked outside the home, and whose father wants Nynke to work in the family florist shop. Chronology is also important: two years ago, Nynke's closest friend decided to go to college, just before Nynke began work in a stable and just before Nynke's mother showed her a scrapbook from social work school. Nynke then decided to enroll in veterinary studies. (Miles & Huberman, 1994, p. 436)

This abbreviated commentary should give some idea of the detail involved in this type of analysis. Of course, an entire analysis would be more extensive and pursue issues in greater depth. This full, idiographic examination, however, tells us nothing about people in general. It offers nothing in the way of a theory about why people choose to attend college.

Even so, in addition to understanding one person in great depth, the researcher sees the critical elements of the subject's experiences as instances of more general social concepts or variables. For example, Nynke's mother's social work training can also be seen as "mother's education." Her friend's decision can be seen as "peer influence." More specifically, these could be seen as independent variables having an impact on the dependent variable of attending college.

Of course, one case does not a theory make—hence, Miles and Huberman's reference to cross-case analysis, in which the researcher turns to other subjects, looking into the full details of their lives as well but paying special note to the variables that seemed important in the first case. How much and what kind of education did other subjects' mothers have? Is there any evidence of close friends attending college?

Some subsequent cases will closely parallel the first one in the apparent impact of particular variables. Other cases will bear no resemblance to the first. These latter cases may require the identification of other important variables, which may invite the researcher to explore why some cases seem to reflect one pattern while others reflect another.

Grounded Theory Method

The cross-case method just described should sound somewhat familiar. In the discussion of grounded theory in Chapter 18, we saw how qualitative researchers sometimes attempt to establish theories on a purely inductive basis. This approach begins with observations rather than hypotheses and seeks to discover patterns and develop theories from the ground up, with no preconceptions, though some research may build and elaborate on earlier grounded theories.

Grounded theory was first developed by the sociologists Glaser and Strauss (1967) in an attempt to come to grips with their clinical research in medical sociology. Since then, it has evolved as a method, with the cofounders taking it in slightly different directions. The following discussion will deal with the basic concepts and procedures of the grounded theory method (GTM).

In addition to the fundamental, inductive tenet of building theory from data, GTM employs the constant comparative method. As Glaser and Strauss (1967, pp. 105–113) originally described this method, it involved four stages:

1. "Comparing incidents applicable to each category." As Glaser and Strauss researched the reactions of nurses to the possible death of

patients in their care, the researchers found that the nurses were assessing the "social loss" attendant on a patient's death. Once this concept arose in the analysis of one case, they looked for evidence of the same phenomenon in other cases. When they found the concept arising in the cases of several nurses, they compared the different incidents. This process is similar to conceptualization as described in Chapter 8—specifying the nature and dimensions of the many concepts arising from the data.

2. "Integrating categories and their properties." Here the researcher begins to note relationships among concepts. In the assessment of social loss, for example, Glaser and Strauss found that nurses took special notice of a patient's age, education, and family responsibilities. For these relationships to emerge, however, it was necessary for the researchers to have noticed all these concepts.

3. "Delimiting the theory." Eventually, as the patterns of relationships among concepts become clearer, the researcher can ignore some of the concepts initially noted but evidently irrelevant to the inquiry. In addition to the number of categories being reduced, the theory itself may become simpler. In the examination of social loss, for example, Glaser and Strauss found that the assessment processes could be generalized beyond nurses and dying patients: They seemed to apply to the ways all staff dealt with all patients (dying or not).

4. "Writing theory." Finally, the researcher must put his or her findings into words to be shared with others. As you may have already experienced for yourself, the act of communicating your understanding of something actually modifies and even improves your own grasp of the topic. In GTM, the writing stage is regarded as a part of the research process. A later section of this chapter (on memoing) elaborates on this point.

This brief overview should give you an idea of how grounded theory proceeds. The many techniques associated with GTM can be found both in print and on the web. One key publication, *Basics of Qualitative Research* (Straus & Corbin, 1990), elaborates on and extends many of the concepts and techniques found in the original Glaser and Strauss volume.

GTM is only one analytical approach to qualitative data. In the remainder of this section, we'll take a look at some other specialized techniques.

Semiotics

Semiotics is commonly defined as the "science of signs" and has to do with symbols and meanings. It's commonly associated with content analysis, which was discussed in Chapter 17, though it can be applied in a variety of research contexts.

Manning and Cullum-Swan (1994) offer some sense of the applicability of semiotics, as follows: "Although semiotics is based on language, language is but one of the many sign systems of varying degrees of unity, applicability, and complexity. Morse code, etiquette, mathematics, music, and even highway signs are examples of semiotic systems" (p. 466). There is no meaning inherent in any sign, however. Meanings reside in minds, so a particular sign means something to a particular person.

However, the agreements we have about the meanings associated with particular signs make semiotics a *social* science. As Manning and Cullum-Swan (1994) point out,

For example, a lily is an expression linked conventionally to death, Easter, and resurrection as a content. Smoke is linked to cigarettes and to cancer, and Marilyn Monroe to sex. Each of these connections is social and arbitrary, so that many kinds of links exist between expression and content. (p. 466)

To explore this contention, see if you can link the signs with their meanings in Figure 20-1. Most American readers probably know all the "correct" associations. For readers who don't know them, they are 1c, 2a, 3b, 4e, and 5d. The point is this: What do any of these signs have to do with their "meanings"? Draft an e-mail message to a Martian social scientist explaining the logic at work here. (You might want to include some *emoticons*, such as :)—☺, which is another example of semiotics.)

Although there is no doubt a story behind each of the linkages in Figure 20-1, the meanings we "know" today are socially constructed. Semiotic analysis involves a search for the meanings intentionally or unintentionally attached to signs.

FIGURE 20.1   Matching Signs and Their Meanings

SIGN	MEANING
1. Poinsettia	a. Good luck
2. Horseshoe	b. First prize
3. Blue ribbon	c. Christmas
4. "Say cheese"	d. Acting
5. "Break a leg"	e. Smile for a picture

Consider the sign shown in Figure 20-2, from a hotel lobby in Portland, Oregon. What's being communicated by the rather ambiguous sign? The first sentence seems to be saying that the hotel is up to date with the current move away from tobacco in the United States. Guests who want a smoke-free environment need to look no further: This is a healthy place to stay. At the same time, says the second sentence, the hotel would not like to be seen as inhospitable to smokers. There's room for everyone under this roof. No one needs to feel excluded. This sign is more easily understood within a marketing paradigm than one of logic.

The "signs" examined in semiotics, of course, are not limited to this kind of sign. Most are quite different in fact. *Signs* are any things that are assigned special meanings. They can include such things as logos, animals, people, and consumer products. Sometimes the symbolism is a bit subtle.

FIGURE 20.2   Mixed Signals?

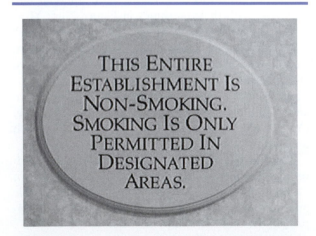

A classic analysis can be found in Goffman (1979). Goffman focused on advertising pictures found in magazines and newspapers. The overt purpose of the ads, of course, was to sell specific products, but Goffman wondered what else was communicated. What in particular did the ads say about men and women?

Analyzing pictures containing both men and women, Goffman was struck by the fact that men were almost always bigger and taller than the women accompanying them. (In many cases, in fact, the picture managed to convey the distinct impression that the women were merely accompanying the men.) Although the most obvious explanation is that men are, on average, heavier and taller than women, Goffman suggested that the pattern had a different meaning: that size and placement implied *status*. Those larger and taller presumably had higher social standing—more power and authority (Goffman, 1979, p. 28). Goffman suggested that the ads communicated that men were more important than women.

In the spirit of Freud's comment that "sometimes a cigar is just a cigar" (he was a smoker), how would you decide whether the ads simply reflected the biological differences in the average sizes of men and women or whether they sent a message about social status? In part, Goffman's conclusion was based on an analysis of the exceptional cases: those in which the women appeared taller than the men. In these cases, the men were typically of a lower social status—the chef beside the society matron, for example. This confirmed Goffman's main point that size and height indicated social status.

The same conclusion was to be drawn from pictures with men of different heights. Those of higher status were taller, whether it was the gentleman speaking to a waiter or the boss guiding the work of his younger assistants. Where actual height was unclear, Goffman noted the placement of heads in the picture. The assistants were crouching down while the boss leaned over them. The servant's head was bowed so that it was lower than that of the master.

The latent message conveyed by the ads, then, was that the higher a person's head appeared in the ad, the more important that person was. And in the great majority of ads containing men and women, the former were clearly portrayed as more important. The subliminal message in the ads, whether intended or not, was that men are more powerful and enjoy a higher status than do women.

Goffman examined several differences in the portrayal of men and women besides physical size. As another example, men were typically portrayed in active roles and women in passive ones. The (male) doctor examined the child while the (female) nurse or mother looked on, often admiringly. A man guided a woman's tennis stroke (all the while keeping his head higher than hers). A man gripped the reins of his galloping horse while a woman rode behind him with her arms wrapped around his waist. A woman held the football while a man kicked it. A man took a photo that contained only women.

Goffman suggested that such pictorial patterns subtly perpetuated a host of gender stereotypes. Even as people spoke publicly about gender equality, these advertising photos established a quiet backdrop of men and women in the "proper roles."

Conversation Analysis

Conversation analysis (CA) seeks to uncover the implicit assumptions and structures in social life through an extremely close scrutiny of the way we converse with one another. Silverman (1993, pp. 435–436), reviewing the work of other CA theorists and researchers, speaks of three fundamental assumptions. First, conversation is a socially structured activity. Like other social structures, it has established rules of behavior. For example, we're expected to take turns, with only one person speaking at a time. In telephone conversations, the person answering the call is expected to speak first (e.g., "Hello"). You can verify the existence of this rule, incidentally, by picking up the phone without speaking.

Second, Silverman points out that conversations must be understood contextually. The same utterance will have totally different meanings in different contexts. For example, notice how the meaning of "Same to you!" varies if preceded by "I don't like your looks," or by, "Have a nice day." Third, CA aims to understand the structure and meaning of conversation through excruciatingly accurate transcripts of conversations. Not only are the exact words recorded, but also all the *uh*s, *er*s, bad grammar, and pauses are noted. Pauses, in fact, are recorded to the nearest tenth of a second.

The practical uses of this type of analysis are many. Kinnell and Maynard (1996), for example, analyzed conversations between staff and clients at an HIV testing clinic to examine how information about safe sex was communicated. Among other things, they found that the staff tended to provide standard information rather than try to speak directly to a client's specific circumstances. Moreover, they seemed reluctant to give direct advice about safe sex, settling for information alone.

These discussions should give you some sense of the variety of qualitative analysis methods available to researchers. Now let's look at some of the data processing and data analysis techniques commonly used in qualitative research.

» QUALITATIVE DATA PROCESSING

Let's begin this section with a warning. The activity we are about to examine is as much art as science. At the very least, there are no cut-and-dried steps that guarantee success.

It's a lot like learning how to paint with watercolors or compose a symphony. Education in such activities is certainly possible, and university courses are offered in both. Each has its own conventions and techniques as well as tips you may find useful as you set out to create art or music. However, instruction can carry you only so far. The final product must come from you. Much the same can be said of qualitative data processing.

At the same time, researchers have developed systematic and rigorous techniques for this type of research. We'll examine some of those here, starting with some ideas relating to the coding of qualitative data. After that, we'll examine ideas for writing memos and graphically mapping concepts. Although far from a "how-to" manual, these ideas give a useful starting point for finding order in qualitative data.

Coding

Whether you've engaged in participant observation, in-depth interviewing, collecting biographical narratives, doing content analysis, or some other form of qualitative research, you will now be in the possession of a growing mass of data—most typically in the form of textual materials. Now what do you do?

The key process in the analysis of qualitative social research data is coding—classifying or categorizing individual pieces of data—coupled with some kind of retrieval system. Together, these procedures allow you to retrieve materials you may later be interested in.

Let's say you're chronicling the growth of a social movement. You recall writing up some notes about the details of the movement's earliest beginnings. Now you need that information. If all your notes have been cataloged by topic, retrieving those you need should be straightforward. As a simple format for coding and retrieval, you might have created a set of file folders labeled with various topics, such as "History." Data retrieval in this case means pulling out the "History" folder and rifling through the notes contained therein until you find what you need.

As you'll see later in this chapter, there are now some very sophisticated computer programs that allow for a faster, more certain, and more precise retrieval process. Rather than looking through a "History" file, you can go directly to notes dealing with the "Earliest History" or the "Founding" of the movement.

Coding has another, even more important purpose. As discussed earlier, the aim of data analysis is the discovery of patterns among the data, patterns that point to theoretical understanding of social life. The coding and relating of concepts is key to this process and requires a more refined system than a set of manila folders. In this section, we'll assume that you'll be doing your coding manually. The concluding section of the chapter will illustrate the use of computer programs for qualitative data analysis.

Coding Units   As you may recall from the earlier discussion of content analysis in Chapter 17, for statistical analysis it's important to identify a standardized unit of analysis prior to coding. If you were comparing American and French novels, for example, you might evaluate and code sentences, paragraphs, chapters, or whole books. It would be important, however, to code the same units for each novel analyzed. This uniformity is necessary in a quantitative analysis, as it allows us to report something like "23% of the paragraphs contained metaphors." This is possible only if we've coded the same unit—paragraphs—in each of the novels.

Coding data for a qualitative analysis, however, is quite different. The *concept* is the organizing principle for qualitative coding. Here the units of text appropriate for coding will vary within a given document. Thus, in a study of organizations, "Size" might require only a few words per coding unit, whereas "Mission" might take a few pages. Or a lengthy description of a heated stockholders meeting might be coded "Internal Dissent."

Realize also that a given code category may be applied to text materials of quite different lengths. For example, some references to the organization's mission may be brief, others lengthy. Whereas standardization is a key principle in quantitative analysis, this is not the case in qualitative analysis.

Coding as a Physical Act   Before continuing with the logic of coding, let's take a moment to see what it actually looks like. Lofland and Lofland (1995) offer this description of manual filing:

> Prior to the widespread availability of personal computers beginning in the late 1980s, coding frequently took the specific physical form of *filing*. The researcher established an expanding set of file folders with code names on the tabs and physically placed either the item of data itself or a note that located it in the appropriate file folder…. Before photocopying was easily available and cheap, some fieldworkers typed their field notes with carbon paper, wrote codes in the margins of the copies of the notes, and cut them up with scissors. They then placed the resulting slips of paper in corresponding file folders. (p. 188)

As the Loflands point out, personal computers have greatly simplified this task. However, the image of slips of paper that contain text and are put in folders representing code categories is useful for understanding the process of coding. In the next section, when we suggest that we code a textual passage with a certain code, imagine that we have the passage typed on a slip of paper and that we place it in a file folder bearing the name of the code. Whenever we assign two codes to a passage, imagine placing duplicate copies of the passage in two different folders representing the two codes.

Creating Codes   So what should your code categories be? Glaser and Strauss (1967, pp. 101–102) allow for the possibility of coding data for the purpose of testing hypotheses that have been generated by prior theory. In that case, then, the codes would be suggested by the theory in the form of variables.

In this section, however, we're going to focus on the more common process of open coding. Strauss and Corbin (1998) define it as follows:

> To uncover, name, and develop concepts, we must open up the text and expose the thoughts, ideas, and meanings contained therein. Without the first analytic step, the rest of the analysis and the communication that follows could not occur. Broadly speaking, during open coding, data are broken down into discrete parts, closely examined, and compared for similarities and differences. Events, happenings, objects, and actions/interactions that are found to be conceptually similar in nature or related in meaning are grouped under more abstract concepts termed "categories." (p. 102)

Open coding is the logical starting point for GTM qualitative coding. Beginning with some body of text (part of an interview, for example), you read and reread a passage, seeking to identify the key concepts contained within it. Any particular piece of data may be given several codes, reflecting as many concepts. For example, notice all the concepts contained in this comment by a student interviewee:

> I thought the professor should have given me at least partial credit for the homework I turned in.

Some obvious codes are "Professor," "Homework," and "Grading." The result of open coding is the identification of numerous concepts relevant to the subject under study. The open coding of more and more text will lengthen the list of codes.

Besides open coding, two other types of coding take place in this method. Axial coding aims at identifying the core concepts in the study. Although axial coding uses the results of open coding, more concepts can be identified through continued open coding after the axial coding has begun. Axial coding involves a regrouping of the data, in which the researcher uses the open-code categories and looks for more-analytic concepts. For example, the passage just given also carries the concept of "Perceptions of Fairness," which might appear frequently in the student interviews, thereby suggesting that it's an important element in understanding students' concerns. Another axial code reflected in the

student comments might be "Power Relationships," because the professor is seen to exercise power over the student.

The last kind of coding, selective coding, seeks to identify the central code in the study: the one that all the other codes relate to. Both of the axial codes just mentioned might be restructured as aspects of a more general concept: "Professor–Student Relationships." Of course, in a real data analysis, decisions such as the ones we've been discussing would arise from masses of textual data, not from a single quotation. The basic notion of the Grounded Theory Method is that patterns of relationships can be teased out of an extensive, in-depth examination of a large body of observations.

Here's a concrete example to illustrate how you might engage in this form of analysis. Suppose you're interested in the religious bases for homophobia. You've interviewed some people opposed to homosexuality who cite a religious basis for their feelings. Specifically, they refer you to these passages in the book of Leviticus (Revised Standard Version):

> 18:22 You shall not lie with a male as with a woman; it is an abomination.
>
> 20:13 If a man lies with a male as with a woman, both of them have committed an abomination; they shall be put to death, their blood is upon them.

Although the point of view expressed here seems unambiguous, you might decide to examine it in more depth. Perhaps a qualitative analysis of Leviticus can yield a fuller understanding of where these injunctions against homosexuality fit into the larger context of Judeo-Christian morality. By gaining this understanding, you hope to be better prepared to develop a social change strategy for combating homophobia.

Let's start our analysis by examining the two passages just quoted. We might begin by coding each passage with the label "Homosexuality." This is clearly a key concept in our analysis. Whenever we focus on the issue of homosexuality in our analysis of Leviticus, we want to consider these two passages.

Because homosexuality is such a key concept, let's look more closely into what it means within the data under study. We first notice the way *homosexuality* is identified: a man lying with a man "as with a woman." Although we can imagine a lawyer seeking admission to heaven saying, "But here's my point; if we didn't actually lie down …" it seems safe to assume the passage refers to having sex, though it is not clear what specific acts might or might not be included.

Notice, however, that the injunctions appear to concern *male* homosexuality only; lesbianism is not mentioned. In our analysis, then, each of these passages might also be coded "Male Homosexuality." This illustrates two more aspects of coding: (a) Each unit can have more than one code; and (b) hierarchical codes (one included within another) can be used. Now each passage has two codes assigned to it.

An even more general code might be introduced at this point: "Prohibited Behavior." This is important for two reasons. First, homosexuality is not inherently wrong from an analytical standpoint. The purpose of the study is to examine the way it's made wrong by the religious texts in question. Second, our study of Leviticus may turn up other behaviors that are prohibited.

There are at least two more critical concepts in the passages: "Abomination" and "Put to Death." Notice that although these are clearly related to "Prohibited Behavior," they are hardly the same. Parking without putting money in the meter is prohibited, but few would call it an abomination, and fewer still would demand the death penalty for that transgression. Let's assign these two new codes to our first two passages.

At this point, we want to branch out from the two key passages and examine the rest of Leviticus. We therefore examine and code each of the remaining chapters and verses. In our subsequent analyses, we'll use the codes we have already and add new ones as appropriate. When we do add new codes, it will be important to review the passages already coded to see whether the new codes apply to any of them.

Here are the passages we decide to code "Abomination." (We've boldfaced the abominations.)

7:18 If any of the flesh of the sacrifice of **his peace offering is eaten on the third day**, he who offers it shall not be accepted, neither shall it be credited to him; it shall be an abomination, and he who eats of it shall bear his iniquity.

7:21 And if any one **touches an unclean thing**, whether the uncleanness of man or an unclean beast or any unclean abomination, **and then eats of the flesh of the sacrifice** of the LORD's

peace offerings, that person shall be cut off from his people.

11:10 But **anything in the seas or the rivers that has not fins and scales**, of the swarming creatures in the waters and of the living creatures that are in the waters, is an abomination to you.

11:11 They shall remain an abomination to you; of their flesh you shall not eat, and their carcasses you shall have in abomination.

11:12 Everything in the waters that has not fins and scales is an abomination to you.

11:13 And these you shall have in abomination among the birds, they **shall not be eaten**, they are an abomination: the **eagle**, the **vulture**, the **osprey**,

11:14 the **kite**, the **falcon** according to its kind,

11:15 every **raven** according to its kind,

11:16 the **ostrich**, the **nighthawk**, the **sea gull**, the **hawk** according to its kind,

11:17 the **owl**, the **cormorant**, the **ibis**,

11:18 the **water hen**, the pelican, the carrion vulture,

11:19 the **stork**, the **heron** according to its kind, the **hoopoe**, and the **bat**.

11:20 All winged insects that go upon all fours are an abomination to you.

11:41 **Every swarming thing** that swarms upon the earth is an abomination; it shall not be eaten.

11:42 Whatever goes on its belly, and whatever goes on all fours, or whatever has many feet, all the **swarming things** that swarm upon the earth, you shall not eat; for they are an abomination.

11:43 You shall not make yourselves abominable with **any swarming thing that swarms**; and you shall not defile yourselves with them, lest you become unclean.

18:22 You shall not **lie with a male as with a woman**; it is an abomination.

19:6 It shall be eaten the same day you offer it, or on the morrow; and anything left over until the third day shall be burned with fire.

19:7 **If it is eaten at all on the third day**, it is an abomination; it will not be accepted,

19:8 and every one who eats it shall bear his iniquity, because he has profaned a holy thing of the

LORD; and that person shall be cut off from his people.

20:13 If a man lies with a male as with a woman, both of them have committed an abomination; they shall be put to death, their blood is upon them.

20:25 You shall therefore make a distinction between the clean beast and the unclean, and between the unclean bird and the clean; **you shall not make yourselves abominable by beast or by bird or by anything with which the ground** teems, which I have set apart for you to hold unclean.

Male homosexuality, then, isn't the only abomination identified in Leviticus. As you compare these passages, looking for similarities and differences, it will become apparent that most of the abominations have to do with dietary rules—specifically those potential foods deemed "unclean." Other abominations flow from the mishandling of ritual sacrifices. "Dietary Rules" and "Ritual Sacrifices" thus represent additional concepts and codes to be used in our analysis.

Earlier, we mentioned the death penalty as another concept to be explored in our analysis. When we take this avenue, we discover that many behaviors besides male homosexuality warrant the death penalty. Among them are these:

20:2 Giving your children to Molech (human sacrifice)

20:9 Cursing your father or mother

20:10 Adultery with your neighbor's wife

20:11 Adultery with your father's wife

20:12 Adultery with your daughter-in-law

20:14 Taking a wife and her mother also

20:15 Men having sex with animals (the animals are to be killed also)

20:16 Women having sex with animals

20:27 Being a medium or wizard

24:16 Blaspheming the name of the Lord

24:17 Killing a man

As you can see, the death penalty is broadly applied in Leviticus: everything from swearing to murder, including male homosexuality somewhere in between.

An extended analysis of prohibited behavior, short of abomination and death, also turns up a lengthy list. Among them are slander, vengeance, grudges, cursing the deaf, and putting stumbling blocks in front of blind people. In chapter 19, verse 19, Leviticus quotes God as ordering, "You shall not let your cattle breed with a different kind; you shall not sow your field with two kinds of seed; nor shall there come upon you a garment of cloth made of two kinds of stuff." Shortly thereafter, he adds, "You shall not eat any flesh with the blood in it. You shall not practice augury or witchcraft. You shall not round off the hair on your temples or mar the edges of your beard." Tattoos were prohibited, though Leviticus is silent on body piercing. References to all of these practices would be coded "Prohibited Acts" and perhaps given additional codes as well (recall "Dietary Rules").

We hope this brief glimpse into a possible analysis will give you some idea of the process by which codes are generated and applied. You should also have begun to see how such coding would allow you to better understand the messages being put forward in a text and to retrieve data appropriately as you need them.

Memoing

In GTM, the coding process involves more than simply categorizing chunks of text. As you code data, you should also be using the technique of memoing—writing memos or notes to yourself and others involved in the project. Some of what you write during analysis may end up in your final report; much of it will at least stimulate what you write.

In GTM, these memos have a special significance. Strauss and Corbin (1990, pp. 197–198) distinguish three kinds of memos: *code notes*, *theoretical notes*, and *operational notes*.

Code notes identify the code labels and their meanings. This is particularly important because, as in all social science research, most of the terms we use with technical meanings also have meanings in everyday language. It's essential, therefore, to write down a clear account of what you mean by the codes used in your analysis. In the Leviticus analysis, for example, you would want a code note regarding the meaning of *abomination* and how you've used that code in your analysis of text.

Theoretical notes cover a variety of topics: reflections of the dimensions and deeper meanings of concepts, relationships among concepts, theoretical propositions, and so on. All of us have times of ruminating over the nature of something, trying to think it out and make sense out of it. In qualitative data analysis, it's vital to write down these thoughts, even those you'll later discard as useless. They will vary greatly in length, though you should limit them to a single main thought so that you can sort and organize them later. In the Leviticus analysis, one theoretical note might discuss the way that most of the injunctions implicitly address the behavior of *men*, with women being mostly incidental.

Operational notes deal primarily with methodological issues. Some will draw attention to data collection circumstances that may be relevant to understanding the data later on. Others will consist of notes directing future data collection.

Writing these memos occurs throughout the data collection and analysis process. Thoughts demanding memos will come to you as you reread notes or transcripts, code chunks of text, or discuss the project with others. It's a good idea to get in the habit of writing out your memos as soon as possible after the thoughts come to you.

Lofland and Lofland (1995) speak of memoing somewhat differently, describing memos that come closer to the final writing stage. The *elemental memo* is:

> a detailed analytic rendering of some relatively specific matter. Depending on the scale of the project, the worker may write from one to several dozen or more of these. Built out of selective codes and codings, these are the most basic prose cannon fodder, as it were, of the project. (p. 194)

The *sorting memo* is based on several elemental memos and presents key themes in the analysis. Whereas we create elemental memos as they come to mind, with no particular rhyme nor reason, we write sorting memos as an attempt to discover or create reason among the data being analyzed. A sorting memo will bring together a set of related elemental memos. A given project may see the creation of several sorting memos dealing with different aspects of the project.

Finally, the *integrating memo* ties together the several sorting memos to bring order to the whole project. It tells a coherent and comprehensive story, casting it in a theoretical context. In any real project, however, there are many different ways of bringing

about this kind of closure. Hence, the data analysis may result in several integrating memos.

Notice that whereas we often think of writing as a linear process, starting at the beginning and moving through to the conclusion, memoing is very different. It might be characterized as a process of creating chaos and then finding order within it.

To explore this process further, refer to the works cited in this discussion and at the end of this chapter. You'll also find a good deal of information on the Web. For Barney Glaser's rules on memoing, for example, you might go to http://gtm.vlsm.org/gnm-gtm3.en.html. Ultimately, the best education in this process comes from practice. Even if you don't have a research project under way, you can practice now on class notes or start a journal and code it.

Concept Mapping

It should be clear by now that analysts of qualitative data spend a lot of time committing thoughts to paper (or to a computer file), but this process is not limited to text alone. Often, we can think out relationships among concepts more clearly by putting the concepts in a graphical format, a process called concept mapping. Some researchers find it useful to put all their major concepts on a single sheet of paper, whereas others spread their thoughts across several sheets of paper, blackboards, magnetic boards, computer pages, or other media. Figure 20-3 shows how we might think out some of the concepts of Goffman's examination of gender and advertising. (This image was created through the use of Inspiration, a concept-mapping computer program.)

Incidentally, many of the topics discussed in this section have useful applications in quantitative as well as qualitative analyses. Certainly, concept mapping is appropriate in both types of analysis. The several types of memos would also be useful in both. And the discussion of coding readily applies to the coding of open-ended questionnaire responses for the purpose of quantification and statistical analysis. (We'll look at coding again in the next chapter, on quantifying data.)

Having noted the overlap of qualitative and quantitative techniques, it seems fitting now to address an instrument that is associated primarily with quantitative research but that is proving very valuable for qualitative analysts as well—the personal computer.

FIGURE 20.3 An Example of Concept Mapping

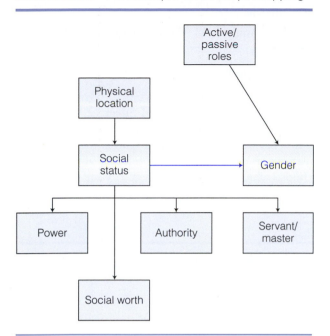

» COMPUTER PROGRAMS FOR QUALITATIVE DATA

Not so many decades ago, the recording and analysis of qualitative research data were paperbound: Interview transcripts, observational notes, official documents, and the like were all compiled and evaluated by hand. The work of writing documents by hand was eventually streamlined by the advent of typewriters. Copying technologies, first carbon paper and, later, photocopying, made it possible to easily reproduce duplicate pages of research information. These printed data could then be cut into slips of paper, with each strip displaying an individual-coded item. This procedure allowed researchers to categorize collected data according to different themes or concepts. Recalling the discussion of Leviticus, one pile of paper slips might contain passages referencing homosexuality, another pile could contain references to abominations, and so forth. And, as our earlier discussion mentioned, a given passage might show up in more than one pile. Once this coding and sorting was done, researchers could manually review all the materials within a particular category, allowing them to look

for and identify common patterns and important distinctions.

As you can imagine, computers changed all that. Once information has been entered into a computer, copying whole documents or pieces is a trivial matter. Simulating the earlier paperbound method, you can copy an interview comment relevant to, say, discrimination against women and paste it into another document created to hold anything relevant to that theme. With nothing but the simplest word processor or text editor, you can streamline the coding process in any number of ways. Imagine that this paragraph was part of textual materials you were analyzing in a study of technological progress. You could augment this document by adding coding notations such as <computer> <qualitative> <coding>.

You could go through this whole chapter, adding these and other notations wherever appropriate. And once you were finished, you could use a simple "Search" function to review all the materials marked <coding>, for example. You could augment this process by searching the chapter for words such as "code," "coding," "category," "classify," or other applicable terms.

We would like these short paragraphs to draw attention and honor to those researchers who could make sense out of social life with little more than paper and pencil. And we hope that a review of past practices will demonstrate what a powerful tool the simplest, bare-bones computer can represent for the analysis of qualitative data.

Now, let's turn 180 degrees from these simple computer manipulations. As you will soon see, those methods may seem like crude tools from the Dark Ages of social research. We are now going to spend some time with a few of the computer programs devised precisely for the analysis of qualitative data.

Qualitative Data Analysis Programs

Today, qualitative data analysis (QDA) programs abound. Whereas the analyst's problem used to be merely finding any such program, the problem now lies in choosing one of so many. Here are a few commonly used QDA programs where you can learn more about them and, in many cases, download demo copies. Because website addresses frequently change, these are not provided. A search of the program will generally reveal the company's home page.

1. AnSWR: Analytic Software for Word-based Records
2. Atlas.ti
3. Ethno: Event Structure Analysis
4. Ethnograph
5. HyperResearch by Researchware Inc.
6. HyperTranscribe by Researchware Inc.
7. MAXQDA
8. N-Vivo
9. QDA Miner by Provalis Research
10. Qualrus
11. Text Analysis Markup System (TAMS)
12. T-LAB
13. Weft QDA

Another excellent resource is *Choosing a CAQ-DAS Package* by Lewins and Silver (2006), which can be found at http://cue.berkeley.edu/qdaarticle.pdf. This will familiarize you with some of the key features in such computer programs and help you choose which one is best suited to your purposes.

FIGURE 20.4   Leviticus Text Displayed in Qualrus

We'll turn now to a couple of illustrations of QDA programs at work. Although the available programs differ somewhat from one another, we think these illustrations will give you a good sense of the general use of computers to analyze qualitative data. We'll begin by returning to the earlier example of the book of Leviticus, with its sexual and other prohibitions. Let's see how a computer analysis might assist the search for patterns.

Leviticus as Seen through Qualrus

We'll first consider one of the programs just listed: Qualrus. Although the text to be coded can be typed directly into Qualrus, usually materials already in existence—such as field notes or, in this case, the verses of Leviticus—are imported into the program. For purposes of this illustration, we simply copied chapter 20 of Leviticus from the Web and pasted it into the document section of the layout.

Figure 20-4 shows how the text is presented within Qualrus. As you can see, although all the

inserted text cannot be displayed in the window at once, you can easily scroll up and down through the document.

One of the themes we discussed earlier concerned the various actions that could result in death, so let's create that as a code in Qualrus. This is most easily done by highlighting it with our cursor to select a passage we wish to code: verse 2, for example. Then click the "Code" button at the top of the page, and you will be presented with another window for creating codes, as illustrated in Figure 20-5.

Click the top, leftmost icon in the window, and you will be asked to enter a new code in the lower left portion of the window, where we have typed "death." This is the first in what will become a list of codes. Notice also that the software has automatically entered the code "death" in the upper-right portion of the window, indicating the designated code for this particular passage. Once you have decided on and inserted additional codes into the program, you will be able to select from that list

FIGURE 20.5 Creating a Code for "Death"

FIGURE 20.6   Displaying the Coding of "Death" Passages

and click the arrow to assign codes to the passage being coded. Once you've assigned the proper code, click "OK" to return to the document.

Having created the code, you can proceed through the text, identifying all the passages that specify the death penalty for some action. Figure 20-6 illustrates what this coding looks like.

As you begin building your coding structure, Qualrus begins to anticipate and suggest appropriate codes for some of the passages you have selected. Figure 20-7 gives an example of this. Qualrus has examined a passage we've selected and has guessed that perhaps it should be coded "death."

The suggested code appears in the upper left panel of the window. If you choose to accept that suggestion, you must select the code and transfer it to the upper-right panel.

FIGURE 20.7 Suggesting a Code

Notice in the Figure 20-7 illustration that we have added several additional codes, which might be useful in our analysis of Leviticus. We've provided for passages that mention adultery, bestiality, homosexuality, incest, the occult, and sex. In addition, in our review of the document, we noticed that some passages specified that God would punish the sinners, while others indicated that the community should mete out the punishment. Figure 20-8 shows what the document looks like when all these codes have been employed.

As you add more codes to your analysis, the display on the right side of the figure may become very complex. However, programs like Qualrus help you make sense of it all. Moreover, as you add more structure to your coding scheme, Qualrus can ease the process. For example, you can tell the program that "adultery," "bestiality," "incest," and "homosexuality" are subsets of the code "sex." Once you have informed Qualrus of that, every time you code a passage for "adultery," for example, it will automatically code that passage as "sex" as well.

The purpose of all this coding is to let you bring together all the instances of a particular topic. For example, let's review all the actions that can result in death. Click the "QTools" button, and you will find yourself in a new window, illustrated in Figure 20-9. We have instructed Qualrus to locate all the passages that were coded "death."

By scrolling up and down through the main panel that contains the passages, you can review all the relevant passages and look for patterns. Let's say that you are particularly interested in

cases where sexual behavior warrants death. Figure 20-10 illustrates that search. Now we have a shorter, more focused set of passages to study.

This has been a brief look into some of the ways you could use the Qualrus program to analyze the prohibitions detailed in book of Leviticus. We have not attempted to offer a theoretical framework for your analysis. We merely want to illustrate the most elementary techniques that could be used in your research into the topic. Moreover, as you can see at the top of the last two figures, the QTools that are available go well beyond the reviewing of one or two codes. To learn more about the additional analytic tools, you should visit the Qualrus website at www.qualrus.com.

At this point, we will shift to another of the listed QDA programs. Although NUD*IST was one of the first such programs to be popularly employed by social researchers, it has evolved through many forms over time. At this writing, QSR International's latest tool is N-Vivo, and it is the program we will discuss next.

N-Vivo

To get started in our introduction to this program for the analysis of qualitative data, Figure 20-11 shows a sample of how N-Vivo might display the data we saw earlier in Figure 20-8 when we were analyzing the book of Leviticus with Qualrus. N-Vivo refers to established codes as *nodes*.

While the formats of different programs vary, of course, the fundamental process of coding and

FIGURE 20.8 Display of Many Codes

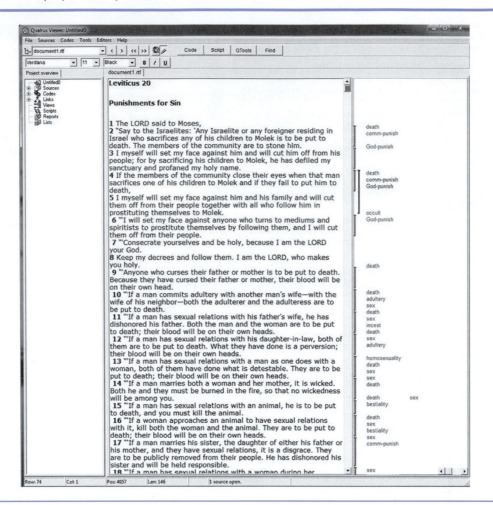

analyzing the coded data is the bedrock of all QDA programs. However, we are going to shift gears at this point.

Thus far, we have limited discussion to the coding of a written document because it offers a clear example of coding. Written documents are hardly the materials appropriate to such an analysis. You've probably already anticipated that these programs would be especially valuable for the analysis of in-depth interviews, and you would be right. At this point, we want to make use of a research example used to introduce N-Vivo on its website at https://www.qsrinternational.com/support_resource-articles_detail.aspx?view=621.

"Environmental Change Down East" is a sample project provided with N-Vivo that explores environmental change in a coastal area of North Carolina. Part of the research for this project involved qualitative interviews with residents of the communities in the area. Figure 20-12 shows a coded portion of one such interview.

Notice the colored coding strips to the right of the interview transcript. The red strip, for example, represents the node "Jobs and cost of living." If you read the passages marked with red strips, you can see why the researchers coded those passages as they did. Note also that a given passage may reflect more than one of the themes being examined, and so it has been assigned more than one node.

Thus far, we have seen that QDA programs can be used to organize documents and interview transcripts in preparation for analysis. That's only the

FIGURE 20.9 Reviewing All the Passages Coded "Death"

beginning, however. Whereas the "Environmental Change Down East" project that we are now examining contains the interviews of a number of residents, the researchers also collected data about physical locations in the study area, such as communities. Figure 20-13 illustrates some of those data.

In a record such as this one, the textual material and/or the photograph (or a portion of the

FIGURE 20.10 Reviewing the Passages Coded "Death" and "Sex"

FIGURE 20.11   Looking at Leviticus with N-Vivo 9

photograph) can be coded by assigning nodes. Later, a review of materials relating to a particular theme will bring together the relevant interviews, documents, photographs, and anything else that has been assigned the node in question.

Visual data for analysis are not limited to photographs. Perhaps your project has collected some of its data in a video format. Figure 20-14 illustrates this possibility.

Once the video files have been imported into the N-Vivo project, they can be coded, retrieved, and played within the program. Audio recording can, of course, be treated similarly.

In these few illustrations, we have intended to give you an idea of the variety of data that can be amassed and organized within N-Vivo. If you have used a bibliographic program such as EndNote, you can import those materials into the project as well. Your own imagination will expand the list of possibilities further.

We'll conclude this discussion by touching on one further element that we mentioned in our earlier discussions of qualitative research: *memos*. At every turn, N-Vivo allows you to record your own notes in the context of other materials—assigning those memos to the appropriate nodes. As you begin to recognize a certain pattern emerging in the intersection of two themes, for example, you can jot down notes about what you've observed so that you don't forget the details.

In the discussion of Qualrus, we saw a couple of examples of preliminary analyses. You'll recall that we retrieved all the passages from Leviticus that dealt with the death penalty; then we searched

FIGURE 20.12   A Coded Interview in N-Vivo 9

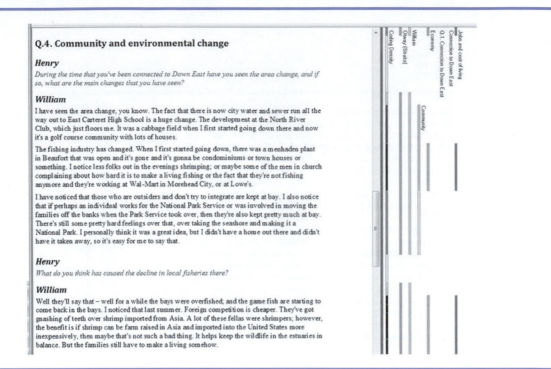

FIGURE 20.13   Data about a Physical Location

FIGURE 20.14 Using Video Data with N-Vivo

Code directly on
the timeline

Add 'see also' links and annotations
to the timeline or to the transcript

A transcript is
optional–you
can import one
or transcribe in
NVivo

Select content and code it at a node

FIGURE 20.15 Attitudes toward Commercial Fishing by Community

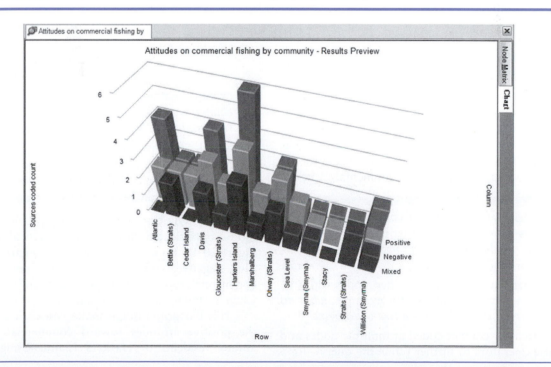

FIGURE 20.16   Mapping "Environmental Change Down East" Concepts

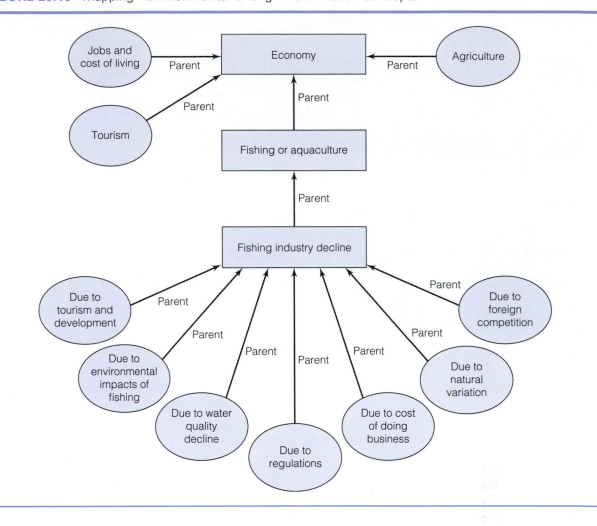

for passages prescribing death for sexual behavior. N-Vivo offers a variety of analytical tools under the heading "Queries." The N-Vivo "Getting Started Guide" is available as a PDF on the QSR website. This guide offers some examples of queries posed in the "Environmental Change Down East" project:

- Gather material coded at combinations of nodes—for example, gather content coded at *water quality* and *recreational fishing* and explore the associations.

- Gather material from classified nodes with specific attribute values—for example, *what do fishermen think about the rise of tourism?*

- Search for content coded at multiple nodes and use operators to further refine the query—for

example, gather content coded at *community change* where it overlaps with content coded at *real estate development.*

- Search for content that is not coded at a specific node—find content coded at *environmental impacts* but not coded at *negative attitude* (QSR International, 2011, p. 31).

Today, QDA programs can also provide for far more sophisticated displays of analytical results. Figure 20-15, for example, offers a summary of positive, negative, and mixed comments made about commercial fishing in the several "Environmental Change Down East" communities.

This bar graph might make you curious about the positive attitudes toward commercial fishing among residents of Harkers Island. Using QDA software, it would be a simple matter to retrieve those specific comments in full.

The QDA programs also offer a graphic presentation of your coding structure, supporting the development of a coherent, theoretical understanding of the subject under study. See Figure 20-16 for an example.

We hope that this brief overview of two QDA programs, Qualrus and N-Vivo, will give you a good idea of the powerful tools available to qualitative data analysts. Realize that we have selected only a few of the features available in the two programs we've illustrated here and also realize that the other programs we listed earlier in this chapter have many of the same or similar capabilities. Most programs provide comprehensive tutorials online, so you can explore, compare, and decide for yourself which program fits your needs.

Finally, you should be warned that such programs may be more expensive than the average student budget can easily accommodate. However, you may find that your school has licensed copies available for your use. The same situation pertains for *quantitative* data analysis programs, such as SPSS.

MAIN POINTS

- Qualitative analysis is the nonnumerical examination and interpretation of observations. Qualitative analysis involves a continual interplay between theory and analysis. In analyzing qualitative data, we seek to discover patterns such as changes over time or possible causal links between variables.
- Examples of approaches to the discovery and explanation of such patterns are grounded theory method (GTM), semiotics, and conversation analysis.
- The processing of qualitative data is as much art as science. Three key tools for preparing data for analysis are coding, memoing, and concept mapping.
- Axial coding identifies the core concepts in a study, regroups the data, and looks for more analytic concepts.
- Selective coding seeks to identify the central code in a study: the one that all the other codes relate to.

- In contrast to the standardized units used in coding for statistical analyses, the units to be coded in qualitative analyses may vary within a document. Although codes may be derived from the theory being explored, more often researchers use open coding, in which codes are suggested by the researchers' examination and questioning of the data.
- Memoing is appropriate at several stages of data processing to capture code meanings, theoretical ideas, preliminary conclusions, and other thoughts that will be useful during analysis.
- Concept mapping uses diagrams to explore relationships in the data graphically.
- Several computer programs, such as Qualrus and N-Vivo, are specifically designed to assist researchers in the analysis of qualitative data.

REVIEW QUESTIONS AND EXERCISES

1. Review Goffman's examination of gender advertising and collect and analyze a set of advertising photos from magazines or newspapers. What is the relationship between gender and status in the materials you found?
2. Review the discussion of homosexuality in the book of Leviticus and suggest ways that the examination might be structured as a cross-case analysis.
3. Imagine you were conducting a cross-case analysis of revolutionary documents, such as the Declaration of Independence and the Declaration of the Rights of Man and of the Citizen (from the French Revolution). Identify the key concepts you might code in the following sentence: "When in the Course of human events, it becomes necessary for one people to dissolve the political bands which have connected them with another, and to assume among the Powers of the earth, the separate and equal station to which the Laws of Nature and of Nature's God entitle them, a decent respect to the opinions of mankind requires that they should declare the causes which impel them to the separation."
4. Write one code note and one theoretical note for exercise 3.

INTERNET EXERCISES

1. Conduct an Internet search using the key term "qualitative data analysis." Briefly describe the data analytic approaches used in two qualitative research studies you find.
2. Conduct an Internet search using the key term "concept mapping." Briefly describe a qualitative research study you find and how it used concept mapping.
3. Conduct an Internet search using the key term "grounded theory." Briefly describe a qualitative research study you find that used GTM and summarize its data analysis approach.
4. Find a research report using conversation analysis. Summarize the main conclusion in your own words.

Visit CengageBrain.com for additional practice and study opportunities including experiential exercises, research tools, glossary, flashcards, and sample test items.

Analysis of Quantitative Data

In this part of the book, we'll discuss the analysis and reportage of data in quantitative research studies. We'll begin by examining how data are prepared for analysis. After that, we'll look at procedures for describing variables separately and then at relationships between variables. Then we'll move on to some more challenging topics in the use of statistics to draw inferences about relationships among variables.

Chapter 21 addresses converting observations into a form that is appropriate for computer analysis, the interpretation of some basic descriptive statistics for analyzing and presenting the data related to a single variable, and then how to construct and read bivariate and multivariate tables that display relationships between and among two or more variables. Then we'll examine ways to measure the strength of those relationships.

Chapter 22 discusses the logic of and how to interpret inferential statistics when making decisions about the implications of the relationships among variables. Both of the chapters in this section put more emphasis on understanding quantitative analysis and its implications for practice than procedures for calculating mathematically complex statistics.

21

Descriptive Data Analysis

EPAS Competencies for This Chapter

Competency 4 Engage in Practice-Informed Research and Research-Informed Practice: This competency pertains to this entire chapter because doing practice-informed quantitative research requires an understanding of the basics of quantitative data analysis. The same applies to engaging in research-informed practice because you must understand the basics of quantitative data analysis in order to be able to critically appraise quantitative studies and the implications of their findings for your practice.

Competency 9 Evaluate Practice with Individuals Families, Groups, Organizations, and Communities: This competency pertains to this entire chapter because designing a quantitative evaluation requires understanding the basics of quantitative data analysis.

What You'll Learn in This Chapter

Often, social work research data are converted to numerical form for statistical analyses. In this chapter, we'll begin with the process of quantifying data and then turn to analysis. Quantitative analysis may be descriptive or inferential and may involve one, two, or more variables. This chapter deals with descriptive data analysis; the next one will cover inferential analysis. We begin our examination of how quantitative analyses are done with some simple but powerful ways of manipulating data in order to arrive at research conclusions.

» INTRODUCTION

In Chapter 20, we saw some of the logic and techniques for analyzing qualitative data. This chapter will examine quantitative analysis, or the techniques by which researchers convert data to a numerical form and subject it to statistical analysis. As was true in qualitative analysis, the first quantitative data analysis step is coding—the process of converting data to a numerical format—and we'll look at that first. After that, we'll look at basic descriptive statistics and tables for analyzing and presenting data about variables and the relationships among them.

» CODING

Today, quantitative analysis is almost always done by computer programs. For these programs to work their magic, they must be able to read the data you've collected in your research. If you've conducted a survey, for example, some of your data are inherently numerical: age or income, for example. Although the writing and checkmarks on a questionnaire are qualitative in nature, a scribbled age is easily converted to quantitative data. Thus, if a respondent reports her age as *sixty-five*, you can just enter *65* into the computer.

Other data are also easily quantified: Transforming *male* and *female* into *1* and *2* is hardly rocket science. Researchers can also easily assign

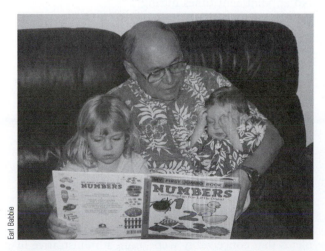

Some students take to statistics more readily than others.

numerical representations to such variables as *religious affiliation*, *ethnicity*, and *region of the country*.

Some data are more challenging, however. If a survey respondent tells you that he or she thinks that the biggest problem facing social service delivery in California today is "immigration from Mexico," the computer can't process that response numerically. You must translate by coding the responses. Answers to open-ended questions might yield many diverse and lengthy responses that need to be collapsed into a smaller list of code categories.

Suppose, for example, that a survey researcher asks respondents, "What is your occupation?" The responses to such a question will vary considerably. Although it will be possible to assign each reported occupation a separate numerical code, this procedure will not facilitate analysis, which typically depends on several subjects having the same attribute.

The *occupation* variable has many preestablished coding schemes. One such scheme distinguishes professional and managerial occupations, clerical occupations, semiskilled occupations, and so forth. Another scheme distinguishes among different sectors of the economy: manufacturing, health, education, commerce, and so on. Still other schemes combine both.

The chosen occupational coding scheme should be appropriate to the theoretical concepts being examined. For some studies, coding all occupations as either *white-collar* or *blue-collar* might be sufficient. For others, *self-employed* and *not self-employed* might be sufficient. Or a peace researcher might wish to know only whether an occupation depended on the defense establishment.

Developing Code Categories

There are two basic approaches to the coding process. First, you may begin with a relatively well-developed coding scheme derived from your research purpose. Thus, as suggested previously, the peace researcher might code occupations in terms of their relationship to the defense establishment. Or you might want to use an existing coding scheme so that you can compare your findings with those of previous research.

The alternative method is to generate codes from your data as discussed in Chapter 20. Let's say we've conducted a self-administered survey of clients who prematurely terminated our agency's services, asking them why they terminated. Here are a few of the answers they might have written in:

Service fees are too high

Not enough parking spaces

Services are not helpful

Have to wait too long to be seen

No appointment times during evenings or weekends

Receptionists are rude

No child-care services provided during appointments

Cannot afford transportation

Did not like my social worker

No bilingual staff

Take a minute to review these responses and see whether you can identify some of the categories represented. There is no right answer, but several coding schemes might be generated from these answers.

Let's start with the first response: "Service fees are too high." What general areas of concern does that response reflect? One obvious possibility is "Financial Concerns." Are there other responses that would fit that category? Table 21-1 shows which of the questionnaire responses could fit.

In more general terms, the first answer can also be seen as reflecting nonstaff concerns. This categorization would be relevant if your research interest included the distinction between staff and nonstaff concerns. If that were the case, then the responses might be coded as shown in Table 21-2.

Notice that we didn't code three of the responses in Table 21-2: (a) *Services are not helpful*, (b) *Have to wait too long to be seen*, and (c) *No appointment times during evenings or weekends*. We did not code them because they could be seen as representing both categories. Services may not be helpful because of ineffectual staff or because the agency doesn't offer the type of services clients feel they really need. Having to wait too long to be seen might be the result either of staff not being punctual or of agency procedures. Inability to get evening or weekend appointments might be the result of staff inflexibility or agency rules.

This signals the need to refine the coding scheme we are developing. Depending on our research purpose, we might be especially interested in identifying any problems that conceivably could

TABLE 21.1 Responses That Can Be Coded "Financial Concerns"

Response	Financial Concerns
Service fees are too high	X
Not enough parking spaces	
Services are not helpful	
Have to wait too long to be seen	
No appointment times during evenings or weekends	X
Receptionists are rude	
No child-care services provided during appointments	X
Cannot afford transportation	X
Did not like my social worker	
No bilingual staff	

TABLE 21.2 Responses Coded as "Staff" and "Nonstaff"

Response	Staff	Nonstaff
Service fees are too high		X
Not enough parking spaces		X
Services are not helpful		
Have to wait too long to be seen		
No appointment times during evenings or weekends		
Receptionists are rude	X	
No child-care services provided during appointments		X
Cannot afford transportation		X
Did not like my social worker	X	
No bilingual staff	X	

have a staffing element; hence, we would code these three responses "Staff." Just as reasonably, however, we might be more interested in identifying problems that conceivably were more administrative in nature and would code the responses accordingly. Or, as another alternative, we might create a separate category for responses that involved both staff and nonstaff matters.

As these examples illustrate, there are many possible schemes for coding a set of data. Your choices should match your research purposes and reflect the logic that emerges from the data themselves. Often, you'll find yourself modifying the code categories as the coding process proceeds. Whenever you change the list of categories, however, you must review the data already coded to see whether changes are in order.

Like the set of attributes composing a variable and like the response categories in a closed-ended questionnaire item, code categories should be both exhaustive and mutually exclusive. Every piece of information being coded should fit into one and only one category. Problems arise whenever a given response appears to fit equally into more than one code category or whenever it fits into no category. Both signal a mismatch between your data and your coding scheme.

If you're fortunate enough to have assistance in the coding process, then you'll need to train your coders in the definitions of code categories and show them how to use those categories properly. To do so, explain the meaning of the code categories and give several examples of each. To make sure your coders fully understand what you have in mind, code several cases ahead of time. Then ask your coders to code the same cases without knowing how you coded them. Finally, compare your coders' work with your own. Any discrepancies will indicate an imperfect communication of your coding scheme to your coders. Even with perfect agreement between you and your coders, however, it's best to check the coding of at least a portion of the cases throughout the coding process.

If you're not fortunate enough to have assistance in coding, then you should still verify your own reliability as a coder. Nobody's perfect, especially a researcher hot on the trail of a finding. Suppose that you're coding the reasons given by runaway adolescents as to why they ran away. Suppose your hunch is that most have run away because they were abused at home. The danger is that you might unconsciously bias your coding to fit your hunch. For example, you might code as *abuse* responses that merely referred to parents being too harsh in their discipline. You might not consider that some adolescents might deem things such as being grounded as harsh discipline. If at all possible, then, get someone else to code some of your cases to see whether that person makes the same assignments you did. Ideally, that person should not have the same predilection you have and should not be aware of the hypothesis you are hoping to support.

» DATA ENTRY

In addition to transforming data into quantitative form, researchers need to convert data into a machine-readable format so that computers can read and manipulate the data. There are many ways of accomplishing this step, depending on the original form of your data and also on the computer program you will use for analyzing the data. We'll simply introduce you to the process here. If you find yourself undertaking this task, you should be able to tailor your work to the particular data source and program you are using.

If your data have been collected by questionnaire, you might do your coding on the questionnaire itself. Then data entry specialists (including yourself) could enter the data into, say, an SPSS data matrix or an Excel spreadsheet and later import it into SPSS.

Sometimes, social researchers use optical scan sheets for data collection. These sheets can be fed into machines that will convert the black marks into data that can be imported into the analysis program. This procedure will work only with research participants who are comfortable using such sheets, and it will usually be limited to closed-ended questions.

Sometimes, data entry occurs in the process of data collection. In computer-assisted telephone interviewing, for example, the interviewer keys responses directly into the computer, where the data are compiled for analysis (see Chapter 16). Even more effortlessly, online surveys can be constructed so that the respondents enter their own answers directly into the accumulating database without the need for an intervening interviewer or data entry person.

» DATA CLEANING

Whichever data-processing method you have used, the next important step is the elimination of errors—that is, "cleaning" the data. No matter how, or how carefully, the data have been entered, errors are inevitable. Depending on the data-processing method, these errors may result from incorrect coding, incorrect reading of written codes, incorrect sensing of black marks, and so forth.

A simple form of data cleaning is called possible-code cleaning. For any given variable, a specified set of legitimate attributes translates into a set of possible codes. In the variable *sex on birth certificate*, for example, there will be perhaps three possible codes: 1 for *male*, 2 for *female*, and 0 for *no answer*. If a case has been coded 7, say, for that variable, then an error clearly has been made.

Possible-code cleaning can be accomplished in two different ways. First, some computer programs can check for errors as the data are entered. If you tried to enter a 7 for sex on birth certificate in such programs, for example, the computer might beep and refuse the erroneous code. Other computer programs are designed to test for illegitimate codes in data files that weren't checked during data entry.

If you don't have access to these kinds of computer programs, then you can achieve a possible-code cleaning by examining the distribution of responses to each item in your data set. Thus, if you find your data set contains 350 people coded 1 on sex on birth certificate (for female), 400 people coded 2 (for male), and 1 person coded 7, then you'll probably suspect that the 7 is an error. Whenever you discover errors, the next step is to locate the appropriate source document (e.g., the questionnaire), determine what code should have been entered, and make the necessary correction.

Although data cleaning is an essential step in data processing, it may be safely avoided in certain cases. Perhaps you will feel you can safely exclude the very few errors that appear in a given item—if the exclusion of those cases will not significantly affect your results. Or some inappropriate contingency responses may be safely ignored. If some men have been given motherhood status, then you can limit your analysis of this variable to women. However, you should not use these comments as rationalizations for sloppy research. "Dirty" data will almost always produce misleading research findings.

Once the above coding and data entry and cleaning steps have been concluded, you are ready to begin your quantitative analysis. Let's look now at some basic descriptive statistics for analyzing and presenting data about a single variable. This is called univariate analysis. Later we'll look at tables and statistics that portray relationships among variables. This is called bivariate analysis or multivariate analysis, depending on how many variables are examined simultaneously.

EP 4, 9

» UNIVARIATE ANALYSIS

Univariate analysis is the examination of the distribution of cases on only one variable at a time. For example, if *sex on birth certificate* were being measured, we would look at how many of the participants were men and how many were women. We'll begin with the logic and formats for the analysis of univariate data.

Distributions

The most basic format for presenting univariate data is to report all individual cases, that is, to list the attribute for each case under study in terms of the variable in question. Suppose you are interested in the ages of clients served by your agency, and suppose hundreds of clients have been served. (Your data might have come from agency records.) The most direct manner of reporting the ages of clients would be to list them: 63, 57, 49, 62, 80, 72, 55, and so forth. Such a report would provide your reader with the fullest details of the data, but it would be too cumbersome for most purposes. You could arrange your data in a somewhat more manageable form without losing any of the detail by reporting that 5 clients were 38 years old, 7 were 39, 18 were 40, and so forth. Such a format would avoid duplicating data on this variable. It provides a frequency distribution, which describes the number of times the various attributes of a variable are observed in a sample.

For an even more manageable format—with a certain loss of detail—you could report clients' ages in frequency distributions of *grouped* data: 246 clients under 45 years of age, 517 between 45 and 50 years of age, and so forth. In this case, your reader would have fewer data to examine and interpret, but he or she would not be able to reproduce fully the original ages of all the clients. Thus, for example, the reader would have no way of knowing how many clients were 41 years of age.

The preceding example presented the grouped data in the form of raw numbers. An alternative form would be the use of percentages. Thus, for example, you could report that $x\%$ of the clients were under 45, $y\%$ were between 45 and 50, and so forth (see Table 21-3). In computing percentages, you frequently must decide from what base to compute—that is, the number that represents 100%. In the most straightforward examples, the base is the total number of cases under study. A problem arises, however, whenever cases have missing data. Let's assume, for example, that you have conducted a survey in which respondents were asked to report their ages. If some respondents failed to answer that question, then you have two alternatives. First, you might still base your percentages on the total number of respondents, reporting those who failed to give their ages as a percentage of the total. Second, you could use the number of persons giving an answer as the base from which to compute the percentages. You should still report the number who did not answer, but they would not figure in the percentages.

The choice of a base depends wholly on the purposes of the analysis. If you wish to compare the age distribution of your survey sample with comparable data that describe the population from which the sample was drawn, then you probably will want to omit the "no answers" from the computation. Your best estimate of the age distribution of all respondents is the distribution for those who answer the question. Because "no answer" is not a meaningful age category, its presence among the base categories would confuse the comparison of sample and population figures. For an example involving 433 respondents who answered and 18 who did not, see Table 21-3.

TABLE 21.3 An Illustration of a Univariate Analysis

Ages of Agency Clients (Hypothetical)	Percentage
Under 35	0.09
36–45	21
46–55	45
56–65	19
66 and older	6
	100% = (433)
No data =	18

Implications of Levels of Measurement

Depending on the level of measurement (nominal, ordinal, interval, or ratio) of the variables you are describing, in addition to frequency distributions you might be able to present your data in the form of summary averages. With a ratio variable like age, for example, we could say that the average age of the clients in a program for children is 10. However, with a nominal variable like sex, calculating an average would not make sense. Even if we assigned numerical codes to the categories—let's say 1 for female and 2 for male—it would not be helpful to report that the average sex was 1.5.

There are, however, "gray-area" situations in the calculation of averages. Suppose, for example, that you were assessing clients' satisfaction with the services they received by asking them to rate those services on a four-point scale: 4 = very satisfied, 3 = satisfied, 2 = dissatisfied, and 1 = very dissatisfied. You should note that this would be an ordinal-level measurement because you would have no reason to believe that the distance from rating 1 (very dissatisfied) to rating 2 (dissatisfied) is the same as the distance between rating 2 and rating 3 (satisfied) and so on. Consequently, calculating the average rating for a large number of clients would be technically questionable because such calculations would treat these ordinal-level ratings as if they were real values.

Yet such technical violations are commonly found and can still be useful. An average score across all clients may not have a precise mathematical meaning in regard to client satisfaction, but it could be useful in comparing large numbers of ratings across client subgroups. For example, suppose the average rating from ethnic minority clients was 1.4, as compared to an average rating of 3.2 from Caucasian clients. Despite its imprecise meaning, this comparison would provide a clear and useful indication that the two groups do not express the same levels of satisfaction and that you ought to assess and deal with the reasons for the difference. (We make similar comparisons all the time, by the way, when we discuss students' grade-point averages.)

The key here is *utility*. You should be somewhat lenient regarding statistics calculated in technically gray areas with ordinal variables if those statistics are useful in informing practice. The other edge of this sword, however, is the danger of being lulled into thinking that the results represent something truly precise. In this case, for example, you might question the utility and appropriateness of carrying the calculations out to three decimal places. Keeping these caveats in mind, let's now look at some prominent descriptive statistics dealing with averages.

Central Tendency

Descriptive statistics in the form of summary averages are measures of *central tendency*. Your options in this regard are the mode (the most frequent attribute, either grouped or ungrouped), the arithmetic mean, and the median (the *middle* attribute in the ranked distribution of observed attributes). Here's how the three averages would be calculated from a set of data.

Suppose that you're analyzing the case records of an adolescent residential facility whose clients range in age from 13 to 19, as indicated in the accompanying table.

AGE	NUMBER
13	3
14	4
15	6
16	8
17	4
18	3
19	3

Now that you've seen the actual ages of the 31 clients, how old would you say they are in general, or on the average? Let's look at three different ways to answer that question.

The easiest average to calculate is the mode, or the most frequent value. As you can see, there were more 16-year-olds (eight of them) than any other age, so the modal age is 16, as indicated in Figure 21-1.

Figure 21-1 also demonstrates how to calculate the mean. There are three steps: (a) multiply each age by the number of clients of that age, (b) total the results of all those multiplications, and (c) divide that total by the number of clients. As indicated in Figure 21-1, the mean age in this illustration is 15.87.

The median represents the "middle" value: Half are above it, half below. If we had the precise ages of each client (e.g., 17 years and 124 days), we would be able to arrange all 31 subjects in order by age, and the median for the whole group would be the age of the middle subject.

As you can see, however, we do not know precise ages; our data constitute grouped data in this regard. For example, three people who are not precisely the same age have been grouped in the category "13 years old."

Figure 21-1 illustrates the logic of calculating a median for grouped data. Because there are 31 clients altogether, the "middle" client would be number 16 if they were arranged by age: 15 would be younger and 17 would be older. Look at the bottom portion of Figure 21-1. The middle person is one of the 16-year-olds. In the enlarged view of that group, we see that number 16 is the third from the left.

Because we do not know the precise ages of the clients in this group, the statistical convention here is to assume that they are evenly spread along the width of the group. In this instance, the possible ages of the clients go from 16 years and no days to 16 years and 364 days. Strictly speaking, the range, then, is 364/365 days. As a practical matter, it's sufficient to call it 1 year.

If the eight clients in this group were evenly spread from one limit to the other, they would be one-eighth of a year apart from each other—a 0.125-year interval. Look at Figure 21-1, and you'll see that if we place the first client half the interval from the lower limit and add a full interval to the age of each successive client, the final one is half an interval from the upper limit.

What we have done, therefore, is to calculate, hypothetically, the precise ages of the eight clients—assuming that their ages were spread out evenly. Having done that, we merely note the age of the middle client—16.31—and that is the median age for the group. Whenever the total number of clients is an even number, of course, there is no middle case. In that case, you merely calculate the mean of the two values it falls between. Suppose there were one more 19-year-old, for example. The midpoint in that case would fall between number 16 and number 17. The mean would then be calculated as $(16.31 + 16.44)/2 = 16.38$.

In the research literature, you'll find both means and medians presented. Whenever means are presented, you should be aware that they are susceptible to extreme values: a few very large or very small numbers. At one time, for example, the (mean) average person in Redmond, Washington, had a net worth in excess of a million dollars. If you had visited Redmond, however, you would have found that

FIGURE 21.1   Three "Averages"

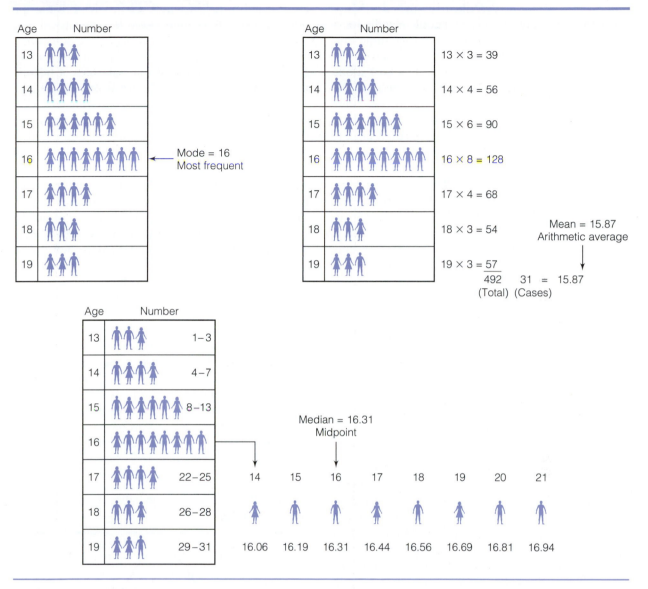

the "average" resident did not live up to your idea of a millionaire. The very high mean reflected the influence of one extreme case among Redmond's 40,000 residents—Bill Gates of Microsoft, who had a net worth in excess of tens of billions of dollars. Clearly, the median wealth would have given you a more accurate picture of the residents of Redmond as a whole.

Here's another example of how extreme values can make the mean misleading, as discussed in a February 10, 2003, editorial in the *New Republic* magazine (p. 9). In President George W. Bush's 2003 State

of the Union Address, he promoted his proposed tax cut of $674 billion as enabling 92 million Americans to "keep an average of almost $1,100 more of their own money." Hearing this, "average" taxpayers easily got the impression that the tax cut would save them nearly $1,100. But according to a study by the Urban–Brookings Tax Policy Center, this was not so. The mean tax cut would be $90,200 for taxpayers whose incomes exceed $1 million and $24,100 for taxpayers whose incomes are in the top 1%. The "average" taxpayer would receive a tax cut of only $256—much less than $1,100.

Nevertheless, one mainstream newspaper, the *Christian Science Monitor*, described the president's tax proposal as making 92 million people eligible for a $1,000-per-person tax cut. A well-known radio talk show host asserted, "Ninety-two million hardworking Americans are going to receive this year alone and then every year thereafter $1,083 because the president is reducing the amount of money they have to pay." Senate Majority Leader Bill Frist argued in favor of the president's proposed tax cut in an appearance on *Fox News Sunday* as follows: "When you say there are 92 million people who are going to be handed a check for $1,000 this year, your viewers right now, is that a tax cut for the rich?" (All of the above quotes are in the *New Republic*, February 10, 2003, p. 9.) This example illustrates the value to you of understanding basic statistical concepts even if you will never do any research yourself. One of those basic concepts, as we discussed above, is how extreme values can make the mean misleading. Let's now turn to another basic statistical concept related to this example—the concept of dispersion.

Dispersion

For the reader, averages have reduced the raw data to the most manageable form: a single number (or attribute) that represents all of the detailed data collected for the variable. This advantage comes at a cost, of course, because the reader cannot reconstruct the original data from an average. This disadvantage of averages can be somewhat alleviated by reporting summaries of the dispersion of responses, the distribution of values around some central value. The simplest measure of dispersion is the *range*: the distance separating the highest from the lowest value. Thus, besides reporting that our clients have a mean age of 15.87, we might also indicate that their ages ranged from 13 to 19.

There are many other measures of dispersion. The one you'll encounter most often is the standard deviation. Its calculation is a bit complex, and if you want to see the formula for it you can examine a statistics book or Google it. With the understanding that its calculation can be done with a statistical software application or at a website (as indicated in the "Internet Exercises" section at the end of this chapter), let's focus on its meaning and utility.

In simple terms, the standard deviation reflects how far away from a variable's mean its individual values are located. The utility of the standard deviation is illustrated in Figure 21-2, which displays a normal curve. A *normal curve* is symmetrical and has a shape that resembles a bell. (It is sometimes called a *bell-shaped curve* or simply a *bell curve*.) When we can assume that our data have a normal distribution (i.e., when they are distributed in the shape of a normal curve), then approximately 34% (0.3413) of our sample data will fall within one standard deviation above the mean, and another 34% will fall within one standard deviation below the mean, as illustrated in Figure 21-2. That leaves almost one-third of the sample values falling more than one standard deviation away from the mean (approximately 16% are more than one standard deviation above the mean, and approximately 16% are more than one standard deviation below the mean). Knowing this, we can get a sense of how far away from the mean the values in our data are falling by calculating the standard deviation.

For example, suppose that a large state mental health department's mean caseload size for its case managers working with people with long-term mental disorders is 28 and that its standard deviation is 2. If we assume a normal distribution of caseload size, then we know that approximately 68% of case managers have caseload sizes between 26 and 30 (with approximately 34% between 26 and 28 and 34% between 28 and 30). We would also know that approximately 16% had caseload sizes

FIGURE 21.2 Standard Deviation Proportions of the Normal Curve

SD = Standard deviation

FIGURE 21.3 High and Low Standard Deviations

A. High standard deviation = spread-out values

B. Low standard deviation = tightly clustered values

FIGURE 21.4 Three Fictional Distributions of Eight Family Incomes Differing in Dispersion but Not Central Tendency

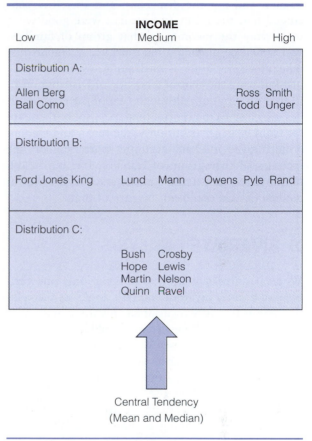

of less than 26 and that some 16% had caseload sizes of more than 30. If the case management research literature tends to recommend that caseload sizes should not much exceed 30, we might portray that state's caseload size as conforming reasonably well to what is recommended.

Suppose that another state reports a mean caseload size of 25, but with a standard deviation of 15. Although that state's mean of 25 is lower than the first state's mean of 28, approximately 16% of its case managers have caseload sizes in excess of 40 (25 plus one standard deviation of 15), and approximately 34% have caseload sizes somewhere between 25 and 40 (as compared to 28 and 30 for the first state). Therefore, despite the lower mean in the second state, we might portray the first state's caseload sizes more favorably because far fewer of its case managers were dispersed far above the mean (or far above the recommended caseload size).

Figure 21-3 further illustrates how a higher standard deviation means that data are more dispersed, whereas a lower standard deviation means that they are more bunched together. Notice that the professional golfer not only has a lower mean score but also is more consistent—represented by the smaller standard deviation. The duffer, on the other hand, has a higher average and is also less consistent, often doing much better or much worse.

Distributions with different degrees of dispersion (and thus different standard deviations) can have the same central tendency, as illustrated in Figure 21-4. That figure also illustrates how reports of descriptive findings that rely exclusively on central tendency can be incomplete and possibly misleading. For example, notice how in Distribution A none of the fictitious families is near the mean and median, whereas in Distribution C all of the families are near the very same mean and median. Thus, for Distribution A if you only knew the mean and median and not the dispersion and therefore concluded that the mean and median were good ways to portray the incomes of that group of families, you would be making a big mistake. A similar mistake, albeit not quite as misleading, would be made just knowing the central tendency of Distribution B. In that distribution, although two of the eight families are close to the central tendency, six of them are far from it. In Distribution C the mean and median would give you an accurate portrayal of the incomes of that group of families, but if you did not have any dispersion statistic (such as the central tendency), you could not be sure of that.

» BIVARIATE ANALYSIS

Whereas univariate analysis looks at only one variable at a time, bivariate analysis looks at the relationship between two variables. Bivariate analysis is different than looking at two variables separately. For example, suppose we are describing our agency's caseload in terms of client age and country of origin. We might say that 50% of our clients are less than 20 years old and that 50% were born in the United States. Although we are quantifying two variables, we are saying nothing about their relationship. They may or may not be related. For example, all of the clients under age 20 may have been born in the United States, some of them may have been, or none of them may have been. If half of the clients under age 20 were born in the United States, and half were born elsewhere, there would be no relationship between the two variables: age and country of origin. At the other extreme, if all of the clients under age 20 were born in the United States, and all those over age 20 were born elsewhere, there would be an extremely strong (indeed, perfect) relationship between the two variables.

When we look at the relationship between two variables, we are conducting a bivariate analysis. Whereas univariate analyses of variables are primarily *descriptive* in purpose, bivariate analysis—in examining *relationships* between two variables— typically does so for *explanatory* purposes. For example, if we find that minority clients are more likely to refuse our services than are Caucasian clients, we may be wondering about deficiencies in

our agency's cultural competence as a plausible *explanation*.

Interpreting Bivariate Tables

Explanatory bivariate tables can be read and interpreted by comparing the independent variable subgroups with one another in terms of a given attribute of the dependent variable. For example, Table 21-4 displays the relationship between ethnicity and service utilization in an imaginary agency. Ethnicity is the independent variable, because we wonder if it explains service refusal. Its categories are spread across the columns. The dependent variable, level of service utilization, is stacked at left in the labels for the rows. The raw numbers are in parentheses. The table shows percentages in the columns with each category of the independent variable summing to 100% in the Total row. That's because we want to compare the service refusal rate among Caucasians to the rate among other clients. We don't care that the number of clients of other ethnicities using the service (80) is the same as the number of Caucasians using the service. That's because the 80 others constitute only 40% of the 200 referred other cases, whereas the 80 Caucasians make up 80% of the 100 referred Caucasian cases. We do care about the percentages, however, because they take into account differences in the total number of cases in each column. Thus, we interpret the table by comparing the dependent variable rates (i.e., the service utilization and refusal rates) for each category of the independent variable.

TABLE 21.4 Bivariate Relationship between Ethnicity and Service Utilization in a Hypothetical Agency

Service Utilization	Ethnicity	
	Caucasian	Minority
Service Utilized	80%	40%
	(80)	(80)
Service Refused	20%	60%
	(20)	(120)
Total	100%	100%
	(100)	(200)

>> INTERPRETING MULTIVARIATE TABLES

Multivariate tables are constructed from several variables. They are constructed using the same logic that we just examined for bivariate tables. Instead of one independent variable and one dependent variable, however, we will have more than one independent variable. Instead of explaining the dependent variable on the basis of a single independent variable, we'll seek an explanation through the use of more than one independent variable.

Consider our imaginary example of ethnicity and service refusal. Suppose we believed that the variable *country of origin* might affect the relationship between ethnicity and service refusal. Maybe it's not the difference in ethnicity that explains the different service refusal rates. Instead, maybe it's the fact that non-Caucasian referrals are more likely to be recent immigrants from another country. For example, if our imaginary agency is in south Florida or south Texas, a large proportion of our referrals may be recent immigrants from Cuba or Mexico. Perhaps the Cuban Americans or Mexican Americans who were born in the United States are no more likely to refuse services than are Caucasian Americans. If that is the case, then language or acculturation factors may have more to do with explaining the different refusal rates than the broader variable of *ethnicity*. Let's examine this possibility by interpreting the imaginary data in the multivariate Table 21-5.

At first glance, the seeming complexity of the multivariate table might overwhelm you. Where on earth to begin?! Let's simplify things. This table is nothing more than two bivariate tables side by side! If you understood how to interpret the bivariate table between ethnicity and service utilization, you should have no trouble interpreting this multivariate table. Just break the process down into two easy steps.

First, we examine the bivariate part of the table pertaining just to those cases born in the United States. There we see no difference whatsoever in the fictional data regarding service utilization and refusal rates for Caucasians and others. Each group had 80 cases born in the United States, with a 12% service refusal rate for each.

Next, we examine the bivariate part on the right side of the table—pertaining just to those cases born in another country. There we see a big difference in the fictional service utilization and refusal rates for Caucasians (50% refusal rate) and others (92% refusal rate). Now we are prepared to summarize the entire table. Here's what we might say (remember that these are fictional data for an imaginary agency):

For referrals born in the United States, there is no difference in service utilization rates between Caucasians and others. However, for referrals who are born in another country, there is a big difference in service utilization rates between Caucasians and others—with other immigrants being much more

TABLE 21.5 Multivariate Relationship between Ethnicity and Service Refusal, Controlling for Country of Origin, in a Hypothetical Agency

	Country of Origin			
	United States		Other Country	
	Caucasian	Minority	Caucasian	Minority
Service Utilized	88%	88%	50%	8%
	(70)	(70)	(10)	(10)
Service Refused	12%	12%	50%	92%
	(10)	(10)	(10)	(110)
Total	100%	100%	100%	100%
	(80)	(80)	(20)	(120)

likely to refuse services than Caucasian immigrants. Moreover, immigrants of either ethnicity are more likely to refuse services than people who were born in the United States. Thus, language and acculturation factors appear to have more to do with service refusal rates than ethnicity, but they appear to have a bigger impact on the service utilization rates of other immigrants than on Caucasian immigrants.

» CONSTRUCTING TABLES

So far we've been examining how to interpret univariate, bivariate, and multivariate tables. Let's turn now to how to construct them. Four common decisions to be made in constructing tables pertain to the following:

- Table titles and variable labels
- How much detail to present in the table
- How to handle missing data
- Whether to calculate percentages by rows or columns

We'll discuss each of these decision areas in the above order.

Table Titles and Labels

Every table, regardless of the number of variables it contains, should be understandable to your readers without having to read your narrative about it. This requires having a succinct yet inclusive table title that identifies the variables in the table, and appropriate labels for each category of each variable. You can see this exemplified in Tables 21-4 and 21-5.

Examining Table 21-5, for example, the title conveys the table's purpose (multivariate relationship), its control variable (country of origin), its control variable categories (United States or other country), the categories of its independent variable (Caucasian or minority), and the categories of its dependent variable (service utilized or service refused).

Comparing that table to Table 21-4, you might notice a difference in the variable labels. In Table 21-4, the independent variable (ethnicity) and the dependent variable (service utilization) each had that variable label above the categories for each

variable. In Table 21-5, however, only the control variable (country of origin) is labeled in the table, while the independent and dependent variable categories are labeled without a variable label above them. The justification for omitting the labels for those two variables in the latter table is as follows: (1) The multivariate table is more complex than the bivariate one, and adding the variable labels would have cluttered it and made it harder for readers to eyeball the table easily and comprehend it; (2) the category labels are self-explanatory; and (3) the table title tells readers all the variable labels.

Thus, you have some flexibility regarding the extent of your labeling in multivariate tables. You should make your decision in light of the best way to help your readers to understand the table just by looking at it. After developing a draft of your table, you should examine it and ask yourself, "Would readers be able to tell what each variable in this table is, and would they be able to interpret the overall meaning of this table, without having to read the narrative text of my report?" If the answer is no, then you'll probably need to make some improvements—perhaps changing the title of the table so that it more clearly portrays what the table contains or perhaps more clearly labeling the table's variables or their attributes.

This does not mean that there is no point in having narrative content about the table. On the one hand, while readers should understand a table just by looking at it, they should not read a narrative that does not reference a table and therefore wonder why a particular table was included in the report.

Moreover, sometimes a table's results can be interpreted in different ways. For example, a table showing that the rate of psychiatric hospitalization among poor people is higher than among affluent people does not tell us whether being poor creates more stress which, in turn, increases the need for hospitalization, whether being psychiatrically impaired makes it harder to attain economic affluence, or whether the rates of psychiatric disorders are the same among poor and affluent people but the latter folks are better able to afford or have better access to alternatives to hospitalization. Various alternative explanations such as these should be discussed in the your report's narrative (in the Discussion section). We will say more about this in Chapter 23 when we discuss writing research reports.

One more principle regarding multivariate table labels should be discussed before we move on to the next section. It pertains to the order of presentation of the control and the independent variables in the table. Notice in Table 21-5 that the control variable (country of origin) label and the labels of its categories appear above the independent variable (ethnicity) category labels. Although we are most concerned with comparing the independent variable categories, we don't enter them at the top because had we done so, it would have been the data for control variable categories that would have been juxtaposed in the table, as appears in Table 21-6. Looking at Table 21-6, it is harder to make the Caucasian/Minority comparison in service utilization for categories of the control variable because the Caucasian/Minority categories are no longer next to each other. In Table 21-5 it was much easier to see that when country of origin is held constant, the service refusal rate among minorities coming from other countries (92%) in these fictitious data is much higher than that rate among Caucasians coming from other countries (50%).

When our students construct multivariate tables, they usually put the independent variable above the control variable. That's an understandable mistake because it seems only natural to want to put the variable of greatest concern first. But as illustrated in Table 21-6, doing that makes it harder to compare the categories of the independent variable, so we hope you'll remember to avoid that tendency if and when you construct multivariate tables.

Detail versus Manageability

If you reexamine the previous three tables, you can notice that the various categories of minority ethnicity were collapsed into one "Minority" category. We did that to simplify our discussion of how to interpret bivariate and multivariate tables; however, in a real study examining the relationship between ethnicity and service utilization you probably would not collapse all the ethnic minority categories into one category. In fact, as we discussed in Chapter 6, doing so might violate culturally competent reportage, especially if there were noteworthy differences in service utilization between some minority categories. If there were no such differences, you might want to mention that in the narrative of your analysis, and mention that as the reason for the collapsed category in your table. If there were noteworthy differences between two categories of ethnicity for which there were a substantial number of clients, while at the same time having various other categories of ethnicity containing very few clients, you'd probably want to report the two categories with a substantial number of clients in separate columns, while collapsing the other categories (those with very few clients) into a column headed "Other." For example, if the data set contained 80 Caucasians, 35 African Americans, 35 Latinos, and 10 others spread across 5 or more additional ethnicity categories in which there were only one or two people per category, you'd probably want your table to look like the one in Table 21-7.

TABLE 21.6 Illustration of Incorrect Positioning of Independent and Control Variables in a Hypothetical Multivariate Relationship

| | Ethnicity | | | |
| | Caucasian | | Minority | |
	USA	Other	USA	Other
Service Utilized	88%	50%	88%	8%
	(70)	(10)	(70)	(10)
Service Refused	12%	50%	12%	92%
	(10)	(10)	(10)	(110)
Total	100%	100%	100%	100%
	(80)	(20)	(80)	(120)

TABLE 21.7 Bivariate Table with Some Collapsed Ethnicity Categories

Service Utilization	Ethnicity			
	Caucasian	African American	Latino	Other
Service Utilized	80% (80)	40% (14)	40% (14)	40% (4)
Service Refused	20% (20)	60% (21)	60% (21)	60% (6)
Total	100% (100)	100% (35)	100% (35)	100% (10)

Handling Missing Data

What if your study had asked the service utilizers to rate the quality of the agency's services from very poor to very good, some of them left the response to that item blank? How would you handle those missing data in your percentage calculations? Suppose there were virtually no differences between your ethnicity categories regarding very small proportions of cases with missing data per category. In that case, you'd probably just want to calculate the percentages with the missing cases excluded. For instance, if out of the 80 Caucasian utilizers and 80 minority utilizers there were 4 missing ratings per category, you'd want to calculate your percentages based on a total of 76 cases per category rather than on 80 cases. Thus, if 38 cases per category rated the services as "very good," that percentage would be 50% (half of 76), and not 47.5% (38 divide by 80).

If, on the other hand, many cases in one category of ethnicity left that item blank, and very few did so in the other category, that might have a potentially meaningful implication regarding client satisfaction. For example, maybe a lot of people refused to respond because they did not want to be negative. There is no hard and fast rule regarding what to do in situations like this. One option is to make a judgment call in an unbiased fashion based on which option seems more reasonable to you and which best facilitates developing implications for improving service delivery. Perhaps a better option is to calculate the percentages both ways—with and without the missing data included—so those who read your report can draw their own conclusions.

With bivariate and multivariate tables, another decision needs to be made about percentages regardless of missing data concerns, as we'll examine next.

Percentaging Bivariate and Multivariate Tables

Students learning to construct bivariate or multivariate tables often ask, "Should I calculate the percentages across the rows or down the columns?" The answer depends on whether the categories of the independent variable appear in the columns or rows. If it is in the columns, then the percentages of the cells in each column should add up to 100% and be calculated based on the total number of cases in that column. If the categories of the independent variable are in the rows, then the same should be done across the rows instead of down the columns. For example, in Table 21-4 the independent variable (ethnicity) was in the columns, and each column's percentages were based on the total number of cases for that column (100 cases for Caucasians and 200 cases for Minorities). This was appropriate in that it enables us to see that the percentage of service utilizers among Caucasians was double (80%) that of Minorities (40%). Had we percentaged across the rows, that would have come to 50% for each category of ethnicity. Not only would that have been misleading, it would have made no sense because service utilization (the dependent variable) cannot affect someone's ethnicity.

Let's turn now to statistical procedures for measuring the strength of the relationships that might be observed in tables.

» MEASURING THE STRENGTH OF RELATIONSHIPS

When we depicted the difference in service utilization and refusal rates in Table 21-5 as "big," we were referring to the *strength of the association between* the variables of concern. Sometimes we can depict that strength merely by eyeballing different percentages in a table. However, it's not always easy to do that. Statistical procedures have been developed to facilitate and make more systematic the interpretation of how strongly variables are related to one another. We'll discuss several commonly used procedures next, beginning with correlation statistics.

Correlation

Correlation statistics measure the strength of association with values that range from zero, which signifies no relationship whatsoever, to 1.0, which signifies a perfect relationship. A value of −1.0 also would signify a perfect relationship. The minus sign in front of this type of relationship magnitude statistic does not mean the relationship is weaker than one with a plus sign. The minus sign only means that the variables are negatively (inversely) related: As one goes up, the other goes down. The closer the value is to zero, the less able we are to predict the relative value of one variable by knowing the other. (Positive and negative relationships were illustrated in Chapter 8.)

For example, if two groups had exactly the same service refusal rate, then knowing whether a particular case was in one group or the other would not affect our calculation of the odds that this case would refuse services. We might be able to predict the odds from the overall service refusal rate for cases in either group, but knowing what group the case was in would not influence our prediction one way or the other. Thus, the relationship magnitude would be zero.

On the other hand, if one group had a 0% service refusal rate and the other group had a 100% service refusal rate, then knowing which group a case was in would enable us to predict with 100% accuracy whether that case would refuse services. The relationship magnitude would be 1.0, a perfect relationship.

Table 21-8 illustrates one two-by-two table that shows a relationship magnitude of zero and two

TABLE 21.8 Illustrations of Relationship Magnitudes of 0, 1.0, and −1.0

Example of a Relationship Magnitude of 0

	U.S. Born	Immigrant
Service Refused	40	40
Service Utilized	60	60

Example of a Relationship Magnitude of 1.0

	U.S. Born	Immigrant
Service Refused	0	100
Service Utilized	100	0

Example of a Relationship Magnitude of −1.0

Case Number	Number of Treatment Sessions Attended	Number of Verbal Abuse Incidents
1	0	7
2	1	6
3	2	5
4	3	4
5	4	3
6	5	2
7	6	1
8	7	0

perfect relationships. The two-by-two table at the top shows no relationship, and the relationship magnitude therefore is zero, because the two groups have exactly the same service refusal rates. The fact that there are fewer service refusers than service utilizers (that is, the service refusal rate is 40%) might be an important descriptive finding. But because each group has the same 40% service refusal rate, knowing what group a case is in offers us nothing to help predict whether that case will refuse services, and therefore the relationship magnitude is zero.

In the second two-by-two table, the relationship magnitude is 1.0 because none of the U.S.-born cases refused services, whereas all of the immigrant cases did. Thus, knowing which group a case was in would be all we needed to know to predict with perfect accuracy whether the case will refuse services.

The same degree of predictability is evident in the third example, but this time there is a minus sign in front of the 1.0 because as one variable increases, the other decreases. The relationship magnitude is −1.0 because each additional session of treatment attended, without exception, reduces the number of incidents of verbal abuse observed by the same amount each time. It is a perfect relationship because the number of sessions a client attends is all we need to know to predict with perfect accuracy the number of incidents of verbal abuse observed. The minus sign is not pejorative and does not signify a weaker relationship; it simply means that an increase in one variable is associated with a decrease in the other.

So far, we have contrasted a perfect relationship (with a magnitude of 1.0 or −1.0) with no relationship (zero magnitude). But what about something in between—for example, a 40% service refusal rate for the U.S.-born group versus a 60% one for the immigrants? In that case, knowing that a referral was in the U.S.-born group would predispose us to predict service utilization, and knowing the referral was in the immigrant group would predispose us to predict service refusal. But if we predicted service refusal for every immigrant referral and service utilization for every U.S.-born referral, then we would be wrong 40% of the time. That's a lot of errors. But with an overall service refusal rate of 50% (which would be the case with an equal number of referrals in the 40% and 60% groups), we would be wrong 50% of the time if we tried to predict recidivism for each referral without knowing which group each referral was in. Thus, knowing which group a referral was in would reduce our percentage of errors from 50% to 40%, or a proportional reduction in error of .20. (The .20 is derived from expressing the .10 reduction from .50 to .40 in proportional terms: .10 is 20%, or .20, of .50.)

In short, if there is some relationship between our variables, it means that knowing the value for one variable will reduce the number of errors we make in predicting the value for the other. And the stronger the relationship is, the more our prediction errors will be reduced.

So far, we have examined correlation measures of association. The type of statistic used to measure a correlation depends on the level of measurement of the variables involved in the relationship. Sometimes the word *correlation* is in the name of the statistic, such as with *Pearson's product-moment correlation (r)*, or the *point-biserial correlation coefficient*. Sometimes it is not, such as with *lambda, Yule's Q, phi, Cramer's V,* or *eta*. You probably won't remember for years to come all the measure of association labels we've just mentioned. That's okay. The important thing is to remember what they mean. (For more information about these measures, we encourage you to examine a statistical text one of us wrote: *Statistics for Evidence-Based Practice and Evaluation.*)

Effect Size

Outcome studies typically refer to strength of association in terms of the size of the effect that an evaluated program, policy, or intervention had on the dependent variable it sought to influence. When they do, the term they commonly use for the measure of association is *effect size*. Sometimes they might use that term in regard to a correlation statistic. More commonly, they will use it to depict how many standard deviations one group's mean was better than another's. The rationale for depicting differences in means in connection to standard deviations is to enable comparisons of strengths of effects across studies that use very different outcome measures.

For example, suppose two different child welfare studies are conducted, each an experimental evaluation of the effectiveness of a different innovative program aimed at preventing further incidents of child maltreatment by parents referred for abuse or neglect. The first study finds that the experimental group parents who received the innovative program averaged one incident of maltreatment during a posttreatment follow-up period, as compared to a mean of four such incidents for control group parents. The second study evaluates outcome not in terms of the number of abusive incidents. Instead, it measures outcome in terms of posttest scores on a self-report scale of parental knowledge and attitudes about child rearing. Its experimental group parents have a mean score of 60, which is 20 points better than the control group mean of 40.

How can we judge which of the two interventions had the stronger effects? Comparing their outcomes as just stated is a bit like comparing apples and oranges because they used different types of outcome indicators. This problem is resolved by dividing the difference between the means by the standard deviation. The most commonly used effect size statistic for this approach is called Cohen's *d*, which we'll examine next.

Cohen's *d*

Cohen's *d* can be used when comparing the means of two groups. It divides the differences between the means by the pooled standard deviation of the two groups combined. Its formula is as follows:

$$d = \frac{\text{Experimental group mean} - \text{Control group mean}}{\text{Pooled standard deviation}}$$

To illustrate the use of the preceding formula, let's return to the hypothetical example of the two child welfare studies mentioned above. In the program that measured outcome in terms of the mean number of incidents of child maltreatment, the difference between the two means of 4 and 1 is 3. If its pooled standard deviation is 1, its Cohen's *d* would be as follows:

$$d = \frac{1-4}{1} = -3.0 \rightarrow +3.0$$

When calculating Cohen's *d*, we interpret the plus or minus sign in the dividend according to whether a reduction in the outcome measure represents a desirable or undesirable effect. In the preceding example, it represents a desirable effect because the program seeks to reduce child maltreatment. It should therefore report the Cohen's *d* as +3.0 (not −3.0), because the minus sign in reporting Cohen's *d* is used only to indicate undesirable effects (in the opposite direction of what was sought). We would interpret this Cohen's *d* of +3.0 by observing that the experimental group's mean was three standard deviations better than the control group's mean. (In the rare occasions when an intervention has a harmful effect, the Cohen's *d* should be preceded by a minus sign.)

In the second study, which measured outcome in terms of a scale measuring knowledge and attitudes about child rearing, its Cohen's *d* would be as follows:

$$d = \frac{60-40}{10} = +2.0$$

Although the two studies quantified outcome in different ways—one dealing with much larger numbers than the other—dividing by the standard deviation makes the results of the two studies comparable. In other words, dividing by the standard deviation showed that the difference of 20 scale points in the second study was a less powerful impact than the difference of 3 maltreatment incidents in the first study.

Odds and Risk Ratios When the independent and dependent variables are both nominal, Cohen's *d* cannot be used. One alternative is to use one of the correlation statistics previously mentioned (like *phi* or Cramer's *V*) to convey the strength of the association, and some outcome studies might refer to a correlation as an effect size. There is nothing wrong with that because, after all, both correlations as well as Cohen's *d* are measures of the strength of relationship between variables. However, when studies seek to learn whether one program is more effective than another in reducing or increasing some nominal outcome variable, they are more likely to refer to their effect size statistic as an *odds ratio* or a *risk ratio*.

The odds ratio shows how much more or less likely a certain nominal dependent variable outcome is for the categories of the independent variable. For example, suppose that 100 parents referred for child maltreatment receive innovative new Intervention A, and another 100 receive treatment as usual (TAU). Suppose further that only 20 (20%) of the 100 Intervention A recipients recidivate after intervention with another maltreatment incident, as compared to 50 (50%) of the 100 TAU recipients. That would mean that the ratio of Intervention A recipients who had a *successful* outcome was 80/20. Because 80 is 4 times 20, the 80/20 ratio means that there were 4 successes for every 1 failure (or 4.0). In contrast, the ratio of TAU recipients with a successful outcome would be only 50/50, or 1 to 1 (or 1.0). Dividing the Intervention A ratio (4.0) by the TAU ratio (1.0) equals 4.0. The odds ratio regarding successful outcomes for Intervention A, therefore, would be 4.0, meaning that its odds of a successful outcome for Intervention A are 4.0 times greater than the odds of a successful outcome for TAU.

Odds ratios also are commonly used in epidemiological studies examining causes of certain desirable or undesirable health or social problems. For example, the odds ratio for developing lung cancer for heavy smokers is in the neighborhood of 10, meaning that the odds of getting lung cancer for heavy smokers is 10 times the odds of non-smokers.

When the outcome in question is undesirable—such as getting a disease or becoming an perpetrator of abuse—some studies calculate the risk ratio. The risk ratio is calculated by dividing the proportion of unsuccessful outcomes in one group by the risk of unsuccessful outcomes in the other group.

Using the previous example of an intervention for child maltreatment, the recidivism proportion for Intervention A is .20 because there were 20 recidivists out of the total of 100 recipients of that intervention. The comparable proportion for TAU is .50 (i.e., 50 divided by 100). The *risk ratio*, therefore, would be .20 divided by .50, which equals .40, meaning that the risk of recidivism for Intervention A recipients was only four-tenths of the risk for TAU recipients.

When a group's risk ratio is less than 1.0, it means that that group has less risk than the other group. If it is greater than 1.0, then it has more risk. If the risk ratio is exactly 1.0, then both groups have the same degree of risk.

» DESCRIPTIVE STATISTICS AND QUALITATIVE RESEARCH

When statistics are reported to *describe* the characteristics of a sample or to *describe* the relationships among variables in a sample, they are called descriptive statistics. In contrast, when statistics go beyond just describing a set of sample observations and attempt to make *inferences* about causal processes or about a larger population, they are called inferential statistics. Both types of statistics apply more to quantitative than to qualitative research. The next chapter will discuss inferential statistics. Before we go there, we'll end this chapter by illustrating the use of descriptive statistics in qualitative research.

The material you have been reading in this chapter clearly applies more to quantitative than to qualitative research, although it is not irrelevant to the latter. It is a mistake to believe that the distinction between qualitative and quantitative research is only about whether counting takes place or statistics are used. Researchers who interpret descriptive statistics often find that some of those statistics imply the need for a qualitative inquiry to understand their meaning better. Researchers who conduct qualitative studies rarely report elaborate statistical analyses, but they

often find that counting some things is an inescapable part of detecting patterns or developing a deeper understanding of the phenomenon they are studying.

Suppose you are conducting a qualitative inquiry to gain a deeper understanding of what it is like to have a sleep disorder. Would your understanding of what it feels like to have the disorder be more or less superficial if, in addition to qualitative observations, you counted things such as the mean number of hours the people you observed slept and the proportion of nights they didn't sleep at all? You wouldn't want to rely on the numbers alone, and you certainly would want to emphasize how the individuals with the disorder subjectively and perhaps idiosyncratically felt about their lack of sleep. At the same time, though, knowing whether we are talking about someone who almost never sleeps versus someone who sleeps on average a handful of hours per night—perhaps with wild swings from night to night (i.e., high dispersion)—gives us a more informed basis to consider their experience. If you tell us that such people's lack of sleep makes it hard for them to concentrate at work, for example, our ability to sense what that must be like for them might be enhanced if we know that they are averaging only about 1 hour of sleep per night.

Here's an example that starts with a quantitative inquiry. Suppose you are administering a child welfare program that aims to improve parenting and preserve families. Your program's funding level is influenced by descriptive statistics about the number of days that children spend in out-of-home placements and scores on a scale that measure risk of child abuse. On both measures, you find that the agency mean is mediocre and that the standard deviation is huge.

This prompts you to examine closely the univariate frequency distribution of each variable, and you find that in each distribution, most cases are not clustered near the mean. Instead, approximately one-third are way above the mean and one-third are way below the mean. You recognize the need to probe into the meaning of these findings to discover what is going on differently with the very successful and terribly unsuccessful cases, realizing that your mean is misleading and that what you find might imply ways to improve outcomes among cases such as those that currently have unsuccessful outcomes.

If you had solid hunches about what was accounting for the difference between the successful and unsuccessful cases, then you might examine additional variables quantitatively. However, you don't have a clue, so you decide to conduct a qualitative investigation, using a couple of social work doctoral students who are seeking hands-on practicum experience in doing qualitative research in an agency setting. They begin by interviewing practitioners qualitatively, probing into their ideas and recollections about what the practitioners did differently with their most and least successful cases. They also pore through case records in an unstructured, open-ended fashion looking for patterns that might distinguish the two sets of cases. Quickly they find that almost all of the cases with the very worst outcomes had been assigned to three particular practitioners and that almost all of the cases with the very best outcomes had been assigned to three other practitioners.

Nobody knows what might explain the differences in outcome between the two sets of practitioners, so the students decide to observe the six practitioners with extreme outcomes in a qualitative fashion in both their office sessions and home visits with clients. After collecting and analyzing a considerable amount of qualitative information, they begin to notice differences in the ways the two sets of practitioners work with parents. The practitioners with the more successful outcomes seem to be more prone toward providing services in the parents' homes, listening to parents empathically and helping them obtain needed resources, educating the parents about child development and child rearing, and teaching specific parenting skills. The ones with less successful outcomes seem to spend less time with parents, make fewer home visits, be less responsive to the concrete needs for resources that parents express, and spend more time moralizing to them.

The students who are conducting the qualitative observations recognize that their insights and report will be more meaningful if they can describe the extent of the differences they so far have been observing qualitatively. For example, to just say one group did something more or less than another group is less meaningful in terms of the qualitative goal of developing a richer understanding of the phenomenon than saying that the successful practitioners averaged three home visits to each client per week as compared to the unsuccessful ones seeing clients only once a month and only in their offices.

So in their qualitative journal log of observational notes, the students begin including such quantitative information as the number and length of home visits versus office sessions, the number of times the practitioner obtains a resource, the number of empathic versus moralizing statements, and the amount of time spent teaching about parenting. We are not saying that these quantitative indicators are the only things or the main things the students will record. They will continue to record qualitative information, such as obtaining the clients' subjective perspectives on how they experience the practitioner's services. Moreover, the quantitative measures will have emerged from an analysis of the qualitative material collected earlier. Eventually, their report might stimulate others to conduct quantitative, hypothesis-testing studies to see if the patterns emerging from this qualitative study can be generalized beyond these six practitioners and their clients. As the never-ending process in the scientific search for understanding continues, those quantitative studies might stimulate future qualitative inquiries to discover the meanings of their findings, and so on.

Now let's consider a hypothetical example of a purely qualitative study. Perhaps you decide to pursue a PhD degree in social work for which you must produce a research dissertation. You decide to conduct a qualitative study like the one that Liebow (1993) conducted to portray the lives of homeless women. Your methodology relies on observation and informal conversational interviews with a small group of homeless women whom you come to know at a shelter and a soup kitchen where you volunteer to help and befriend them.

Perhaps you begin to find, as Liebow did, that what may seem irrational or aimless to most people might be rational and purposeful from the perspective of the homeless women. For example, perhaps you find that a reason they express for neglecting personal hygiene is to make oneself repulsive to men who are abusive and thus prevent victimization while sleeping in dangerous settings. If you begin to detect a pattern regarding this explanation for neglecting personal hygiene, then you might find yourself inescapably wondering how many of the homeless women you meet this explanation applies to. Was the first woman who expressed a rational explanation for neglecting personal hygiene the only one who felt this way? Indeed, it's hard to imagine how you could detect such a pattern in the first

NUMERICAL DESCRIPTIONS IN QUALITATIVE RESEARCH

Unfortunately, some people think in black-and-white or stereotypical ways about quantitative and qualitative studies and the investigators who conduct them. In their most extreme forms, these stereotypes may portray quantitative researchers as inchworms who can do nothing but count and qualitative researchers as never counting anything and perhaps having some kind of math phobia. Those who think qualitative researchers never count anything or never use statistics might find their stereotypes dispelled by reading two compendiums of qualitative studies edited or coedited by social work professors. The two books are *Qualitative Studies in Social Work Research* (Reissman, 1994) and *Qualitative Methods in Family Research* (Gilgun, Daly, & Handel, 1992). In the latter volume, we found that the researchers alluded to doing some counting in 9 of the 16 studies. In four studies, the counting was mentioned only in imprecise terms (which we'll italicize), as exemplified by the following excerpts:

> Participants *often* prescribed to more than one personal theory ... members of couples *frequently* shared the same ... theories (p. 54).

> Caregivers were *often* optimistic.... Weight *loss* or *gain,* sleep disturbances, and *reduced* exercise were characteristic of this phase (p. 75).

> Caregivers *often* spend *a great deal* of time at the bedside of the PWA [person with AIDS] (p. 77).

> ... retirement—*with few exceptions*—has meant husbands' retirement (p. 274).

In five of the studies, the counting clearly involved descriptive statistics, reported in precise terms, usually in connection with describing study participants. Here are some excerpts:

> The average age of the elders was 65, with a range of 48 to 83 ... one-quarter were unsure of their marital status (p. 90).

> The mean age of the sample was 31 for husbands and 30 for wives. The mean length of marriage was 6 years. The couples had experienced a fertility problem for a mean average of 5 years (p. 107).

> The mean age of daughters in the study was 55 years, although there was a range from 33 to 72. More than half (52%) were married, although 21% were widowed and 14% were divorced (p. 204).

In one study, Rank (1992) used qualitative methods to explain quantitative data that indicated that women on welfare have a low fertility rate. The quantitative data are presented in two tables, one of which displays the number and proportion of births in relation to six separate time periods. The other shows the relationship between fertility rates and five demographic variables for different populations.

The Reissman volume contains 10 qualitative studies, four of which report some quantitative data, similarly to the Gilgun book. In one study, Burnette (1994) used a multivariate frequency table to portray her sample of elderly people. Her narrative further described her sample in terms of means and proportions for various demographic characteristics. Later in her report, she referred to a median of 13 years of long-term illness, the proportion of elderly who were cognitively intact, the amount of hours spent watching television, the proportion speaking with friends and relatives at least four times a week, and people in the lowest quartile or quintile of poor health.

The editors of these two volumes have made valuable contributions to the social work research literature. Their work illustrates the diversity in qualitative research, its complementarity with quantitative research, and the ways in which descriptive data are and can be used in qualitative studies.

Here is one more example that demonstrates the special power that can be gained from a combination of qualitative and quantitative approaches. When Silverman (1993) wanted to compare the cancer treatments received by patients in private clinics with those in Britain's National Health Service, he chose primarily in-depth analyses of the interactions between doctors and patients:

> My method of analysis was largely qualitative and ... I used extracts of what doctors and patients had said as well as offering a brief ethnography of the setting and of certain behavioural data. In addition, however, I constructed a coding form which enabled me to collate a number of crude measures of doctor and patient interactions. (p. 163)

Not only did the numerical data fine-tune Silverman's impressions based on his qualitative observations, but his in-depth understanding of the situation allowed him to craft an ever-more appropriate quantitative analysis. Listen to the interaction between qualitative and quantitative approaches in this lengthy discussion:

> My overall impression was that private consultations lasted considerably longer than those held in the NHS clinics. When examined, the data indeed did show that the former were almost twice as long as the latter (20 minutes as against 11 minutes) and that the difference was statistically highly significant. However, I recalled that, for special reasons, one of the NHS clinics had abnormally short consultations. I felt a fairer comparison of consultations in the two sectors should exclude this clinic and should only compare consultations taken by a single doctor in both sectors. This subsample of cases revealed that the difference in length between NHS and private consultations was now reduced to an average of under 3 minutes.
>
> This was still statistically significant, although the significance was reduced. Finally, however, if I compared only new patients seen by the same doctor, NHS patients got 4 minutes more on the average— 34 minutes as against 30 minutes in the private clinic. (Silverman, 1993, pp. 163–164)

place without some awareness of the proportion of your observations that fit the pattern.

In this connection, reports of qualitative studies commonly comment about the proportion of observations that fit various qualitative categories. The researchers may not couch those comments in the context of formal tables of frequency distributions, particularly because they tend to deal with relatively small amounts of numbers. They may couch their quantitative allusions in imprecise terms such as *most*, *few*, or *often*, but if you read many reports of qualitative research, you are likely to find quite a few instances where the researcher obviously counted something. This point—and the more formal use of descriptive statistics in qualitative studies—is elaborated on in the box "Numerical Descriptions in Qualitative Research."

MAIN POINTS

- Data entry can be accomplished in a variety of ways.
- Possible-code cleaning refers to the process of checking to see that only those codes assigned to particular attributes—possible codes—appear in the data files. This process guards against one kind of data-processing error.
- Descriptive statistics is a method for presenting quantitative descriptions in a manageable form.
- Univariate analysis is the analysis of a single variable.
- The full original data collected with regard to a single variable are, in that form, usually impossible to interpret. Data reduction is the process of summarizing the original data to make them more manageable, all the while maintaining as much of the original detail as possible.
- Several techniques allow researchers to summarize their original data to make them more manageable while maintaining as much of the original detail as possible. Frequency distributions, averages, grouped data, and measures of dispersion are all ways of summarizing data concerning a single variable.
- A frequency distribution shows the number of cases that have each attribute of a given variable.
- Grouped data are created through the combination of attributes of a variable.
- A variable's level of measurement influences how it can be analyzed statistically.
- Averages (mean, median, and mode) reduce data to an easily manageable form, but they do not convey the original data's detail.
- Means are susceptible to extreme values; when a small number of extreme values distort the mean, the median can more accurately portray the average.
- Measures of dispersion give a summary indication of the distribution of cases around an average value.
- The standard deviation is one commonly used measure of dispersion.
- In contrast to univariate analysis, bivariate analysis examines relationships between two variables, and it typically does so for explanatory purposes.
- Bivariate analysis (a) divides cases into subgroups in terms of their attributes on some independent variable, (b) describes each subgroup in

terms of some dependent variable, (c) compares the dependent variable descriptions of the subgroups, and (d) interprets any observed differences as a statistical association between the independent and dependent variables.

- Multivariate analysis is a method of analyzing the simultaneous relationships among several variables; it may be used to more fully understand the relationship between two variables.

- Guidelines to follow when constructing tables include (a) giving the table a succinct heading that describes its contents; (b) presenting the original content of the variables in the table itself, if at all possible, or in the text with a paraphrase in the table; (c) clearly indicating the attributes of each variable; (d) indicating the base numbers from which any percentages were computed; and (e) indicating the number of cases omitted from the table because of missing data.

- Readers should be able to tell what each variable in a table is, and they should be able to interpret the overall meaning of the table without having to read the narrative text of the report.

- When constructing tables for the purpose of making subgroup comparisons, attention should be given as to whether and how best to collapse response categories and handle missing data.

- Bivariate and multivariate tables should be percentaged according to the categories of the independent variable. The use of descriptive statistics often can enrich a qualitative study, and it is not uncommon to find quantitative data included in reports of qualitative research. Measures of association such as correlation and effect size statistics assess a relationship's strength.

- Three types of effect size statistics are Cohen's d, odds ratios, and risk ratios.

- Cohen's d divides the difference between the experimental group mean and the control group mean by the pooled standard deviation of the two groups.

- The odds ratio shows how much more or less likely a certain nominal dependent variable outcome is for the nominal categories of the independent variable.

- The risk ratio is calculated by dividing the proportion of unsuccessful outcomes in one group by the risk of unsuccessful outcomes in the other group.

REVIEW QUESTIONS AND EXERCISES

1. You have provided a 15-session outpatient support group intervention for people who recently completed inpatient treatment for substance abuse. Of the 10 clients who were in the group, two attended all 15 sessions, two attended 14 sessions, two attended 13 sessions, two attended 12 sessions, and two attended just 1 session.

   a. Calculate the mean and the median number of sessions attended.
   b. Which measure of central tendency, the mean or the median, do you feel is more appropriate to use in portraying the average number of sessions attended for the above data? Why?

2. Using the hypothetical data in the following table, construct and interpret tables showing the following:

   a. The bivariate relationship between age and attitude toward transracial adoption
   b. The bivariate relationship between ethnicity and attitude toward transracial adoption
   c. The multivariate relationship linking age, ethnicity, and attitude toward transracial adoptionx

AGE	ETHNICITY	ATTITUDE TOWARD TRANSRACIAL ADOPTION	FREQUENCY
Young	White	Favor	90
Young	White	Oppose	10
Young	Minority	Favor	60
Young	Minority	Oppose	40
Old	White	Favor	60
Old	White	Oppose	40
Old	Minority	Favor	20
Old	Minority	Oppose	80

3. Construct multivariate tables that use hypothetical data on a social work research question of interest to you.

INTERNET EXERCISES

1. Find the article below by M. L. McHugh. Briefly summarize what it says about the advantages and disadvantages of the mean, the influence of extreme scores, and the uses of the median and the mode.

   M. L. McHugh. (2003). Descriptive statistics, part II: Most commonly used descriptive statistics (Scientific Inquiry). *Journal for Specialists in Pediatric Nursing*, 8(3), 111–116.

2. Search the term "opinion polls." Alternatively, you might want to expand your search term to include a specific issue, such as opinion polls on abortion, gun control laws, or same sex marriage laws. Surf some sites that pique your interest. Bring to class an example of an interesting bivariate table you find at one of the sites. Briefly state why you think it percentaged the table correctly or incorrectly.

Visit CengageBrain.com for additional practice and study opportunities including experiential exercises, research tools, glossary, flashcards, and sample test items.

22

Inferential Data Analysis

EPAS Competencies for This Chapter

Competency 4 **Engage in Practice-Informed Research and Research-Informed Practice:** This competency pertains to this entire chapter because doing hypothesis testing quantitative research requires an understanding of the basics of inferential data analysis. The same applies to engaging in research-informed practice because you must understand the basics of inferential data analysis in order to be able to critically appraise hypothesis-testing studies and the implications of their findings for your practice.

Competency 9 **Evaluate Practice with Individuals Families, Groups, Organizations, and Communities:** This competency pertains to this entire chapter because designing and interpreting the results of a hypothesis testing evaluation requires understanding the basics of inferential data analysis.

What You'll Learn in This Chapter

Here you'll learn about statistical procedures that are frequently used in social work research to guide decisions about what can be generalized about the relationships we observe in our findings.

» INTRODUCTION

When we analyze data for descriptive purposes, our focus is limited to the data we have collected on our study's sample. Descriptive analysis does not provide a basis for generalizing beyond our particular study or sample. That is okay when our research purpose is descriptive only. But when our purpose is to test one more hypotheses, observing relationships in bivariate or multivariate tables does not provide sufficient grounds for inferring that those relationships exist in general or have any theoretical meaning. This chapter will examine inferential data analysis, which is used for making such inferences.

EP 4, 9

» CHANCE AS A RIVAL HYPOTHESIS

In earlier chapters of this book, we considered in depth many potential sources of error that impinge on our ability to make inferences about the relationships we observe in our findings. For example, we discussed various sorts of bias, threats to internal validity, and the need to control for extraneous variables. If not adequately controlled, these sources of error represent rival hypotheses, or alternative explanations, to the interpretations we seek to draw from our data. Thus, if our data indicate the hypothesized relationship between our independent and dependent variables exists but we haven't controlled for a critical extraneous variable that might plausibly explain as spurious the relationship we think we observe, then a rival hypothesis that contains that extraneous variable represents a plausible alternative explanation of our findings.

Another rival hypothesis, one that we haven't yet discussed, is *chance*. Chance has to do with *sampling error*, a concept covered in Chapter 15 (on sampling theory). It also pertains to the so-called luck of the draw when participants are randomly assigned to groups. No matter how rigorous our random assignment or sampling methods may be, there is always the possibility that, just due to chance, the data we obtain may be a fluke and are not representative of any broader population or causal processes.

For example, suppose we conduct the perfect experiment to evaluate the effectiveness of a social service, an experiment that is flawless in every conceivable way. When we randomly assign individuals to experimental and control groups, no matter how impeccable our random assignment procedures may be, there is always a chance that a large majority of the individuals who are going to improve with or without any treatment will get assigned to the experimental group and that a large majority of those whose problems are the most intransigent will get assigned to the control group. And it can work the other way around, too: The most difficult cases could be assigned to the treatment group and the others to the control group. Although random assignment minimizes the probability of such imbalances, it does not guarantee that they will never occur simply due to chance.

Flukes in random sampling or random assignment need not be dramatic, like an all-or-nothing occurrence, to threaten the validity of our inferences. Suppose you are conducting an experiment to evaluate the effectiveness of an intervention to prevent future incidents of child abuse or neglect by parents who have been referred for being abusive or neglectful. Let's assume that the intervention being evaluated is utterly ineffectual and worthless. Let's further assume that 26 parents will be randomly assigned to the treatment (experimental) group and another 26 to the control group. Thus, your sample size is 52.

Finally, let's assume that with or without receiving the worthless intervention, half of the 52 parents will recidivate and half will not—that is, half will be found to have been abusive or neglectful again during the test period. We will call that half the *recidivists*. What do you suppose the odds are that the 26 recidivists will be divided evenly between your experimental and control groups? Actually, the odds of that happening are far less than 50:50. The chances are much greater that the random assignment will have some other result; perhaps 14 or 15 recidivists will be assigned to one group and 12 or 11 to the other. Or maybe it will even be a split of 16:10, 17:9, and so on. It is even possible, albeit extremely unlikely, to have a 26:0 split.

This does not mean that the 13:13 even split is less likely to occur than any other particular split. To the contrary, no other single split is as likely to occur as the 13:13 split. It just means that the odds are much better than even that one of the other 26 possible splits will occur. In other words, if you add the odds of getting a 14:12 split, a 15:11 split, and so on until all possible splits other than 13:13 are included, then the sum of all those odds will be much greater than the chances of getting a perfectly even 13:13 split.

You can demonstrate this to yourself quickly and easily without any mathematical gymnastics. All you need is a deck of cards. We'll designate each red card as a recidivist and each black one as a nonrecidivist. Begin by shuffling the deck so that the cards are randomly ordered. Next, deal (i.e., randomly assign) the 52 cards alternately into two equal piles of 26 and see whether either pile has exactly 13 red cards and 13 black ones. Finally, repeat this little exercise a couple of times. Did you get a 13:13 split each time? It's possible but not likely. (Of course, in a real study, you wouldn't know who the recidivists would be or how many there would be before random assignment. You would learn that later, toward the end of the study. But in our hypothetical example, because we are assuming that the intervention has no effect whatsoever, we can just designate in advance those who will eventually recidivate for reasons having nothing to do with the intervention.)

Whenever we randomly assign people to groups or randomly select a sample, we use a process that is the same as putting each person's name on a card, shuffling the cards, and then dealing them into one or more piles. The point of this exercise is that when we subsequently collect data from the people (in each "pile"), the odds are that we are going to observe some relationships that are not generalizable or theoretically meaningful—relationships that inescapably result simply from the luck of the draw.

If, for example, you randomly dealt 12 red cards into one pile on your left and 14 into another pile on your right, then you would attribute the difference to luck: You would not infer that the position of the pile (left or right) in a general sense affects the likelihood of its getting red cards. Thus, if in a real study we find that our experimental group of 26 cases had a 46% rate of recidivism (or 12 of 26) and our control group had a 54% rate of recidivism (or 14 of 26), we must take into account the likelihood that the difference had more to do with the luck of the draw in the random assignment, or chance, than with the impact of the tested intervention.

This example illustrates that a study of an independent variable with absolutely no effect on the tested dependent variable has a good chance of obtaining findings that show some relationship—albeit perhaps quite weak—between the two variables. This point applies to all types of explanatory research designs, not just experimental ones. Every time we seek to infer whether the relationships we have observed have some theoretical meaning or can be generalized beyond our sample, we must take into account the role that chance, or sampling error, plays as a potential explanation of our findings.

To further illustrate the need to rule out chance, let's consider a really silly hypothesis. Our point here is to underscore how easy it is to observe relationships in our findings when those relationships occur by chance, only. Our silly hypothesis is one that you can test at the start of your next class session. The hypothesis is as follows: "First-born or only-born children are more likely to have an odd number of letters in their last name than later-borns."

To test this hypothesis, ask all the students in the room whether they were their parents' first-born child and whether their last name has an odd or even number of letters in it. (If they are their parents' only child, count that as first-born.) Most likely, you'll find some relationship between the two variables. For example, maybe 6 of the 10 first-borns will have an odd number of letters in their last names, while 4 of 10 later-borns do.

Although that finding shows a 20% difference between the first- and later-borns, you would not interpret it to mean that first-borns are more likely than later-borns to have an odd number of letters in their last names. That would be ludicrous (as was our hypothesis in the first place), since siblings have the same last names! Yet almost every time we try this experiment in our research classes, we get a difference between first- and later-borns. Sometimes a greater percentage of the first-borns in a classroom have an odd number of letters in their last names, and sometimes the later-borns do. But we almost find some difference due to chance.

Here's another example, this time showing how a finding with a strong correlation could be due to chance if the sample size is very small. Suppose a long time ago a child psychologist who badly needed a vacation came up with the cockamamie idea that if a youth held his hand while reciting the Ten Commandments three times, the youth would grow up to be a humanitarian leader for world peace and social justice. Suppose he decided to test his goofy hypothesis by conducting an experiment in which he would randomly assign youths to either receive his intervention or a control group. As fate would have it, suppose only four youths agreed to participate in his experiment, and they appeared in this order: Mahatma Gandhi, Mother Teresa, Adolph Hitler, and Joseph Stalin.

Suppose that, as each youth arrived, the psychologist flipped a coin for the random assignment. If the coin toss resulted in a head, the youth received the intervention. Once two youths got assigned to one condition, the remaining ones automatically went to the other condition. Now, suppose the first two tosses were heads—so both Mahatma Gandhi and Mother Teresa received the intervention, while Hitler and Stalin served as the control group. As time passed, the psychologist would find the strongest possible relationship in his data. With a 100% success rate for his experimental group, and a 0% success rate for his control group, his correlation would be the maximum possible: 1.0. But how rare is it to flip a coin and get two heads in a row? Not rare at all.

Likewise, it wouldn't have been unusual at all to get two tails in a row, resulting in Hitler and Stalin getting the intervention and therefore giving our psychologist great anguish years later when he saw the havoc he thought he'd wreaked on the world! We can see from these illustrations that the relationships we observe in our findings do not necessarily really exist in the population or in any theoretical sense. Rather than our independent variable (or intervention) being the cause or explanation for differences in our dependent variable, the real explanation may be mere chance—such as the luck of the coin toss or sampling error.

Refuting Chance

In light of what we have said so far in this chapter, it may appear that we face a dilemma whenever we seek to infer whether relationships can be generalized in a theoretical sense or to a population. If any relationship, no matter how dramatic, conceivably could have resulted from the luck of the draw, then how can we decide where to draw the line between findings that can and cannot be generalized? In other words, how are we to decide whether the relationship we have observed verifies our hypothesis or, alternatively, whether it merely resulted from chance?

Suppose, for example, that the recidivism rate in our experimental group is lower than that for our control group. How much lower must it be for us to infer that the intervention, not chance, is probably responsible for the difference? Would a difference of 1% be enough—say, 49% of treated cases recidivate, as compared to 50% of control cases? No? Well, then how about a 2% difference—say, 48% compared to 50%? Still not impressed? Where would *you* draw the line? When asked this question, students often look perplexed. Some say 5%. Others say 10%. Many shrug.

Fortunately, there is a solution to this dilemma, one that enables us to infer, for any particular relationship we observe in our sample, whether that relationship is strong enough to confirm our hypothesis and thus be generalized. That solution involves testing to see if the relationship we have observed is statistically significant.

STATISTICAL SIGNIFICANCE

Testing for statistical significance means calculating the probability, or odds, of finding due to chance a relationship that is at least as strong as the one we have observed in our findings. That probability will fall somewhere between 0 and 1.0. For example, a probability of .05 means that 5 times out of 100, or 1 in 20, we can expect to obtain a relationship at least as strong as the observed one just due to the luck of the draw. If the probability is .10, then we can expect to obtain a relationship that strong 10 times out of 100, or 1 in 10, just due to the luck of the draw and so on.

Statistical significance can be calculated in many alternative ways; the correct method for any given study depends on several considerations that we will address later. But the most important thing to understand here is that all of the methods for calculating statistical significance, no matter how different their mathematical assumptions and formulas, ultimately yield the same thing—a probability between 0 and 1.0 that the observed relationship was obtained simply due to chance.

Theoretical Sampling Distributions

Tests of statistical significance ascertain the probability that observed relationships can be attributed to sampling error, or chance, by using theoretical sampling distributions. When you test your data for statistical significance, you will not have to confront a theoretical sampling distribution; your statistical software program (e.g., SPSS or SAS) will already take that distribution into account and will calculate for you the probability that the relationship in question was obtained due to chance. Nevertheless, you should understand the underlying logic of theoretical sampling distributions in order to truly understand—and take the magic out of—statistical significance.

Just as there are different methods for calculating statistical significance, there are different types of sampling distributions that pertain to different types of data. For example, one type of sampling distribution pertains to sampling error that occurs when drawing a random sample from a population, and another type pertains to the chance variations that occur when using randomization to subdivide a given pool of subjects into subgroups. But the underlying logic of these distributions is similar. For the sake of simplicity, we'll focus our illustrations in this chapter on the latter type of sampling distribution that pertains to random assignment in experimental designs.

The logic of this type of theoretical sampling distribution can be illustrated in an uncomplicated fashion by returning to our hypothetical example of a deck of cards in which the red cards represent recidivists and the black cards represent nonrecidivists. Suppose we have just concluded a real experiment in which 12 (46%) of 26 treated cases recidivated as compared to 14 (54%) of 26 untreated cases. We would want to know the odds that our lower recidivism rate for treated cases was due to the luck of the draw in randomly assigning cases to the two groups. Even though our experiment was real, one way to calculate those odds could involve using a deck of cards. We would begin by writing the name of each of the 26 recidivists, including both the treated and the untreated ones, on a separate red card. Then we would do the same on black cards for the nonrecidivists.

Next, we would shuffle the cards thoroughly, randomly assign (deal) them to two piles of 26 cards each, and record the red:black ratio in each pile. Then we would gather the cards, reshuffle thoroughly, and repeat the entire process, again recording the randomly obtained ratio at the end. We would continue to do this thousands of times, cumulatively tabulating the number of times that

each red:black ratio occurred. At some point, perhaps after days of fanatical shuffling and dealing, we would see that continuing this merriment any further would be pointless; we already would have tabulated so many outcomes that any additional outcomes would not essentially alter the proportions we had already established for each possible outcome.

In other words, if a particular ratio had occurred 100 times after 1,000 deals, then we could say with confidence that the odds of that outcome occurring due to chance were 1 in 10, or .10. Even if we were to continue the process and get that particular ratio on the next two deals, its probability would remain essentially unchanged at 102 divided by 1,002, or .102 (which, with rounding off, would still be .10).

So at that point we would stop our shuffling and calculate the proportion of times that, just due to the luck of the draw, we obtained an outcome that signified a relationship at least as large as the one we observed in our real study; that is, we would add the proportion of 12:14 splits to that of 11:15 splits to that of 10:16 splits and so on. The list of proportions that we calculated for the various outcomes would be our theoretical sampling distribution. Table 22-1 displays the theoretical sampling distribution that we would obtain for this particular example.

Fortunately, the authors did not have to spend days shuffling and dealing cards to obtain this distribution; one of us did it in minutes on a computer using SPSS to calculate the chi-square significance test (corrected for small sample size).

To use Table 22-1, find the row that corresponds to the outcome we happened to obtain in our real experimental findings. We noted earlier that our hypothetical findings had 12 recidivists in the treated group and 14 in the untreated group. By locating that outcome in the theoretical sampling distribution, we can identify the probability associated with it. In Table 22-1, we find that the probability of obtaining that particular outcome due to chance is .377 and that the cumulative probability of finding a difference between the two groups at least as large as the one we found in our experiment is .782. In other words, if we randomly assign 26 recidivists and 26 nonrecidivists into two equally sized groups an infinite number of times, then for every 1,000 assignments, 782 would produce differences between the two groups at least as large as the

TABLE 22.1 Theoretical Sampling Distribution for Randomly Assigning 26 Recidivists and 26 Nonrecidivists in Two Groups of 26 Cases per Group

Outcome (Division of Recidivists between the Two Groups)	Probabilities (Rounded Off to Nearest One-Thousandth)	
	Probability of Each Particular Outcome	Cumulative Probability
26:0 or 0:26	.000	.000
1:25 or 25:1	.000	.000
2:24 or 24:2	.000	.000
3:23 or 23:3	.000	.000
4:22 or 22:4	.000	.000
5:21 or 21:5	.000	.000
6:20 or 20:6	.000	.000
7:19 or 19:7	.002	.002
8:18 or 18:8	.011	.013
9:17 or 17:9	.039	.052
10:16 or 16:10	.114	.166
11:15 or 15:11	.239	.405
12:14 or 14:12	.377	.782
13:13 or 13:13	.218	1.000

difference we found in our experiment, and 377 would produce the exact difference we found. Thus, mere chance produces relationships at least as large as the one we observed in our hypothetically real study 78.2% of the time. That means that we have a 78.2% likelihood of obtaining, just due to the luck of the draw, a difference between the two groups equal to or greater than 12 recidivists out of 26 cases in one group and 14 recidivists out of 26 cases in the other.

This would tell us that the relationship we observed in our actual findings is probably explained by chance and not by the effects of the tested intervention. This does not mean that we have "proven" that the relationship was due to the luck of the draw. Our hypothesis could still be true. Likewise, it is conceivable that if the entire population of abusive or neglectful parents were to receive the tested intervention, then 46% of them would

recidivate as compared to 54% if none received the tested intervention. All we can say at this point, based on our particular results with a sample of 52 people, is that we cannot reasonably rule out chance as a plausible rival hypothesis because findings at least as dramatic as ours occur 78.2% of the time when the only thing that affects the distribution of outcomes in the two groups is the luck of the draw.

As we already mentioned, we fortunately do not have to create a theoretical sampling distribution every time we seek to assess the probability that the relationships we observe in our findings were caused by chance. Statistical procedures called tests of statistical significance handle this for us. Indeed, once we have entered our data into a computer, we can hit a few keys and find out in the batting of an eye the probability that our observed relationship was caused by chance. But it's important to understand that statistical significance tests calculate that probability on the basis of the same theoretical sampling distribution logic that we have just described. Just why that understanding is important should become clearer as we continue our discussion of statistical significance testing.

Significance Levels

Up to now, we have addressed the logic underlying procedures to calculate the odds that a particular relationship we observed in our findings can be attributed to chance and not to the general veracity of our research hypothesis. But we still have not indicated where one draws the line between findings that should and should not be attributed to chance. Obviously, if the probability that chance explains the relationship is very high, say, near or above .50 (i.e., 50:50 odds), it would be unthinkable to rule out chance as a plausible rival explanation. But just how low must its probability be before we can risk ruling out its plausibility? Even if it were as low as .25, would we dare say that a rival hypothesis that is true as often as one out of every four times is not plausible?

No matter where we happen to draw the line between findings that will and will not be attributed to chance, we deem a finding to be of statistical significance when its probability of occurring due to chance is at or below a cutoff point that we select in advance—before we analyze our data. Thus, if we draw the line at .05, then we deem a relationship to be statistically significant if it occurs due to chance no more than 5 times out of 100 randomized trials (or 5 out of 100 deals of the deck). Drawing the line at .05 thus would mean that a relationship with, say, a .06 probability of being caused by chance would be deemed statistically not significant, whereas anything less than .05 would be deemed statistically significant. In short, we call a relationship statistically significant when the probability that it's explained by chance is at or below a point that we have identified in advance as so low that we are willing to risk refuting chance as a plausible rival hypothesis.

In other words, when we call a relationship statistically significant, we say that it can be generalized beyond our sample and that it reflects more than chance covariation. If we assess statistical significance by using a theoretical sampling distribution that pertains to random sampling from a population, then significance refers to generalizing from the sample to the population. On the other hand, if the sampling distribution is based on random assignment of cases, then significance pertains to generalizing about causal processes.

Traditionally, social scientists, including social work researchers, have settled on .05 as the most commonly used cutoff point to separate findings that are not deemed to be significant from those that are. Those findings that fall in the zone beyond the cutoff point and that are therefore considered to be statistically significant make up the critical region of the theoretical sampling distribution. The cutoff point is called the level of significance (or the significance level). When it's set at .05, it's represented by the expression $p \leq .05$. This means that any probability equal to or less than .05 will be deemed statistically significant. Researchers usually just report it as less than .05 ($p < .05$) because the probability rarely equals .05 exactly. A probability that is even a tiny bit above .05—say, at .051—would be considered to be greater than .05, outside of the critical region and therefore statistically not significant.

Returning to the theoretical sampling distribution in Table 22-1, how big a difference in recidivism between our experimental and control groups would we need to have statistical significance at the .05 level? To answer this question, we look at the column of cumulative probabilities until we find the cutoff point between values both above and below .05. Thus, we see that we would need

to have no more than 8 recidivists in one group (and at least 18 in the other) for the difference to be statistically significant. Likewise, we see that any difference that is less extreme than an 8 to 18 split has a probability greater than .05 and would therefore be deemed not significant. Thus, even if our experimental group had a 35% recidivism rate (9 of 26) and our control group's recidivism rate was much higher, at 65% (17 of 26), using the .05 level of significance we would not be able to refute the plausibility of chance as a rival hypothesis. However, had we established in advance .10 as our level of significance, then a 9:17 split would be statistically significant because its cumulative probability of .052 is less than .10.

It is critical to bear in mind that the .05 level of significance is not dictated by mathematical theory. It is not sacred. Not all studies use that level; some use a lower level, perhaps at .01, although that rarely happens in social work research. A strong case can be made for using a higher level, perhaps around .10, under certain conditions, especially when our sample is small (for reasons to be discussed later).

Before moving on, we point out the importance of selecting your significance level (level of significance) before you conduct your data analysis. Doing so after your analysis would put you in the position of deciding the criterion of significance in light of the knowledge of which criteria would make your findings significant or not. Even if you have a great deal of integrity, it would be difficult to rule out the possibility that, perhaps unintentionally, your selection of a significance level was biased by your a priori knowledge of what each significance level would mean for the significance of your findings. Moreover, what if every researcher were in this position? We all may be confident of our own intellectual honesty and capacity to remain unbiased, but we would probably be uncomfortable if everyone else was selecting significance levels in light of whichever level would make their findings "significant."

One-Tailed and Two-Tailed Tests

In the preceding example, you may have wondered why the theoretical sampling distribution illustrated in Table 22-1 lumped together the probability of getting a split of either 12 recidivists in our experimental group and 14 in our control group or 14 recidivists in the experimental group and 12 in the control group. Because we were evaluating the effectiveness of an intervention aimed at preventing recidivism, why would we consider the probability of chance producing a 14:12 or worse split—in which the experimental group's recidivism would be greater (or worse) than the control group's? Why not just limit the probabilities of interest to those for relationships in which the experimental group's outcome (recidivism) is better (or lower) than the control group's?

The positive and negative outcomes were lumped together in our distribution because we did not say that our hypothetical study was interested in finding out only whether the effects of the evaluated intervention are beneficial. We stated that we were evaluating its effectiveness, but we did not foreclose the possibility of finding that it's harmful. And if our findings were to turn out in the harmful direction, we would want to know whether those findings allow us to generalize that the intervention is indeed harmful or whether the results were just a fluke caused by the luck of the draw. Consequently, we would be interested in the probabilities of finding either a positive or negative relationship due to chance.

Hypotheses that do not specify whether the predicted relationship will be positive or negative are called nondirectional hypotheses. When testing nondirectional hypotheses, we use two-tailed tests of significance. For any particular relationship that we find, regardless of whether it is positive or negative, two-tailed tests of significance add the probability of finding a relationship that strong in the positive direction to that of finding one in the negative direction. Using a two-tailed test in our example, we found that the probability of getting a relationship at least as large as a 12:14 or 14:12 split in either direction was .782. That figure adds the probability of getting 12 or fewer recidivists in one group to the probability of getting 12 or fewer recidivists in the other group. Thus, the probability of getting only 12 or fewer recidivists in the experimental group and not including the probability of the reverse results is one-half of .782, or .391.

We say a test has "two tails" because we are interested in extreme, unlikely values in the sampling distribution for both positive and negative relationships. To illustrate this point, we have modified the sampling distribution that appeared in Table 22-1. The revised version appears in Table 22-2. Instead of lumping positive and negative outcomes together, notice how Table 22-2 is symmetrical, with the positive outcomes and their probabilities in the left half and their negative counterparts in the right half. (This is a space-saving format; a computer-generated table would be a long, three-column table, with positive outcomes in the top half and negative ones in the bottom half.) Notice also that each probability is one-half the amount it was in Table 22-1.

The "two tails" in the distribution in Table 22-2 consist of those values at either end (top left or bottom right) of the table that are in our critical region for claiming statistical significance. Because we are using a two-tailed test of significance—that is, because we are interested in both positive and negative outcomes—we would have to add the probabilities we find in each tail to identify our cut-off points. In other words, we would add the two tails together.

Thus, although the probability in this distribution of having 9 or fewer recidivists in the experimental group is less than .05 (at .026), that finding would not be significant because, when added to the probability of having 9 or fewer recidivists in the control group, it exceeds .05 (i.e., .026 + .026 = .052). The figures in Table 22-1, then, reflect the probabilities that pertain to a two-tailed test after adding the two tails together (as shown in Table 22-2). Our significance level in Table 22-2 would still be .05, but two cutoff points—points designating the two tails—would identify the critical region of results that would be deemed statistically significant. One "significant" tail would consist of outcomes with 8 or fewer recidivists in the experimental group, and the other "significant" tail would consist of outcomes with 8 or fewer recidivists in the control group. The probability for each tail would be .0065, but after adding the two tails, the probability becomes .013.

But suppose we had stipulated in advance that we were interested only in whether the intervention's effects were positive. Then we would have formulated a directional hypothesis. Directional hypotheses predict whether a relationship will be positive or negative. When we test a directional hypothesis, we can use a one-tailed test of significance. But this choice restricts our options; that is, we will be able to infer whether the relationship we find can be generalized in the predicted direction only. If our findings turn out to be in the opposite

TABLE 22.2 Theoretical Sampling Distribution (Showing Each Tail) for Randomly Assigning 26 Recidivists and 26 Nonrecidivists into Two Groups of 26 Cases per Group

Outcome (Division of Recidivists and Nonrecidivists between the Two Groups)			Outcome (Division of Recidivists and Nonrecidivists between the Two Groups)		
Experimental Group	Control Group	Cumulative Probability	Experimental Group	Control Group	Cumulative Probability
0:26	26:0	.0000	14:12	12:14	.3910
1:25	25:1	.0000	15:11	11:15	.2025
2:24	24:2	.0000	16:10	10:16	.0830
3:23	23:3	.0000	17:9	9:17	.0260
4:22	22:4	.0000	18:8	8:18	.0065
5:21	21:5	.0000	19:7	7:19	.0010
6:20	20:6	.0002	20:6	6:20	.0002
7:19	19:7	.0010	21:5	5:21	.0000
8:18	18:8	.0065	22:4	4:22	.0000
9:17	17:9	.0260	23:3	3:23	.0000
10:16	16:10	.0830	24:2	2:24	.0000
11:15	15:11	.2025	25:1	1:25	.0000
12:14	14:12	.3910	26:0	0:26	.0000
13:13	13:13	.5000			

direction, then we cannot reverse gears and use a two-tailed test and then claim the same level of significance. Consequently, many social scientists recommend that two-tailed tests should usually be used even when the hypothesis is directional.

To illustrate the use of one-tailed tests, let's apply a one-tailed test of significance to the data in Table 22-2. Because we are interested in generalizing about only positive intervention effects—effects that are associated with lower recidivism in the experimental group—any finding in the opposite direction will simply be interpreted as not supporting the hypothesis and will not be generalized. Consequently, we would establish our cutoff point so that we use the first, positive half of the distribution only; in essence, we would be assessing the probability of getting a certain result or better due to chance. Thus, still using the .05 level of significance, we would now be able to generalize outcomes in which the experimental group had 9 or fewer recidivists because the cumulative probability

for that outcome in the one preselected tail of the distribution is .026 (i.e., $p < .05$).

Suppose, however, that after having planned to use a one-tailed test with our directional hypothesis, we found 17 recidivists in the experimental group and only 9 in the control group. Wanting to alert others to the potentially harmful effects of the tested intervention, suppose we then reversed gears and used a two-tailed test. What would our significance level be if we were to claim this finding as statistically significant? It would not be .05, for we were prepared to call the other tail significant with its cumulative probability of .026. To deem this finding significant, then, our real significance level would have to be at .052 or higher. But if a significance level higher than .05 is acceptable, then why didn't we initially plan to use it in our anticipated one-tailed test? If we choose to use it now, aren't we deceiving ourselves and others and in effect merely manipulating the selection of a significance level to fit our findings?

One way to resolve this dilemma would be to report the two-tailed probability of the finding—calling it not significant—and informing readers that we used a one-tailed test in the other direction with a .05 significance level. If the tested intervention is in widespread use, we might want to alert readers of the unexpected and potentially worrisome direction of this finding and urge them to replicate our evaluation. Readers would then be informed adequately to make their own decision about how to respond to our findings. But it would be inappropriate to cite our findings as a basis for inferring that the tested intervention is indeed harmful.

Figures 22-1 and 22-2 illustrate theoretical sampling distributions with the use of two-tailed and one-tailed tests. Figure 22-1 illustrates a two-tailed test. In it, the .05 level of significance is split between the two tails, forming two critical regions—one in the predicted direction and one in the opposite direction—with each containing 2.5% (half of the randomly generated outcomes that have no more than a 5% probability of occurring due to chance). Figure 22-2 depicts a one-tailed test, with the entire .05 critical region located in the predicted direction.

The Null Hypothesis

Now that you know what directional and nondirectional hypotheses are, let's consider another type of

hypothesis called the *null hypothesis*—a term that you might understandably think was coined by impish statisticians out to make mischief. But you will encounter this term frequently as you produce, use, and participate in research studies, so it is important to understand.

Throughout this chapter, we have been referring to chance as a rival hypothesis. When we refer to that rival hypothesis, we call it the null hypothesis. Simply put, the null hypothesis postulates that the relationship being statistically tested is explained by chance—that it does not really exist in a population or in a theoretical sense—even though it may seem to be related in our particular findings. Thus, when our findings are shown to be statistically significant, we reject the null hypothesis because the probability that it is true—that our results were caused by chance—is less than our level of significance. So, if our results are statistically significant at the .05 level of significance, we would conclude that the null hypothesis has only a .05 probability of being true, and we would therefore reject it. (By reexamining Figures 22-1 and 22-2, you can see pictorial illustrations of when to reject and not reject the null hypothesis.)

What makes this term tricky is that whenever we are rejecting the null hypothesis, we are supporting the plausibility of our research hypothesis (assuming that we are predicting that two variables are related and that we are not seeking to show that

FIGURE 22.1 Theoretical Sampling Distribution Using a Two-Tailed Test of Statistical Significance

FIGURE 22.2 Theoretical Sampling Distribution Using a One-Tailed Test of Statistical Significance

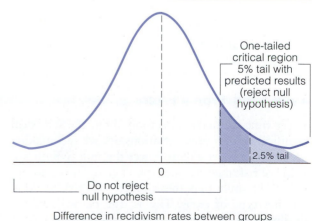

they are unrelated). Conversely, whenever we fail to reject the null hypothesis, we are failing to support our research hypothesis.

So why bother having a null hypothesis? Weren't we managing just fine by referring to chance as a rival hypothesis? Although we could probably get along well enough without this term, it actually does serve one particularly important function: It reminds us that our level of statistical significance does not pertain to the probability that our research hypothesis is true. All it tells us is the probability that the observed relationship was caused by chance—that is, the probability that the null hypothesis is true. Suppose our results are significant at the .05 level. That would indicate that the null hypothesis has only a .05 probability of being true, but it absolutely would not tell us that our research hypothesis therefore has a .95 probability of being true.

Remember, chance is only one of many rival hypotheses that could account for our findings. We mentioned others at the beginning of this chapter: biases, threats to internal validity, extraneous variables, and so on. We need to remain vigilant about this lest we allow low statistical probability levels to lull us into thinking that we can ignore the methodological strengths and weaknesses of a particular study. Indeed, there is no surer way to get statistically significant results than to introduce certain biases into the methodology—for example, rigging the measurement so that you get findings that will support your hypothesis. Thus, by using the term *null hypothesis*, we remind ourselves that the only hypothesis whose likely truth conforms to our significance level is a statistical hypothesis, not our research hypothesis.

The term *null hypothesis* also facilitates our consideration of other potential errors that are connected to statistical significance testing, errors that we will examine next.

Type I and Type II Errors

Every time we make a decision about the statistical significance of a tested relationship, we risk making an error. If we decide to reject the null hypothesis, then we risk making one type of error. If we do not reject the null hypothesis, then we risk making another type of error. This is true because we are dealing with probabilities, not certainties.

Remember that our significance level tells us only the probability that the null hypothesis is false. Although we may reject as implausible a null hypothesis with a probability of .05, we never reject it as impossible. There is always some chance, however slight, that a statistically significant relationship really was caused by chance. In other words, we may have gotten a rare and extremely lucky draw in the random assignment or in random sampling. With a .05 significance level, we can expect to get such a lucky draw once for every 20 tests of statistical significance that we perform.

The error that is risked when we have statistically significant results—and therefore reject the null hypothesis—is called a Type I error. A Type I error occurs if the null hypothesis we have rejected as implausible is really true. When we reject the null hypothesis, we have no way of knowing whether we are actually committing a Type I error; all we know is the probability that we are doing so. That probability is equivalent to our significance level. At the .05 level of significance, therefore, we take a .05 risk of committing a Type I error when we reject the null hypothesis.

The only way we can avoid risking a Type I error is by failing to reject the null hypothesis. However, whenever we do that, we automatically risk making a Type II error. A Type II error occurs if we fail to reject a false null hypothesis. Remember, just because the probability that the tested relationship can be attributed to chance is greater than our significance level does not guarantee that it was caused by chance. If our significance level is .05 and the probability that our result was due to chance is .06, then we fail to reject the null hypothesis—even though the probability that the null hypothesis is true is only .06.

Thus, findings that are not significant do not mean that our research hypothesis has been proven false. They just mean that we lack the level of probability we need to rule out chance as a plausible explanation for our findings. Consequently, if our probability level falls short of being statistically significant but is close to significant, then rather than claim to have disproven our hypothesis, we would probably alert readers to the low albeit nonsignificant probability level and encourage them to replicate our research in this area. It could be that our research hypothesis really is true but we had too small a sample or too unlucky a draw to verify it at a statistically significant level. (We will explain the role of sample size in this issue shortly.)

Table 22-3 summarizes the relationships between Type I errors and Type II errors. It is provided to help you visualize the impossibility of avoiding the risk of both a Type I and Type II error simultaneously. Whenever we lower our significance level to reduce the risk of committing a Type I error, we automatically increase the risk of making a Type II error. Conversely, whenever we raise our significance level to reduce the risk of committing a Type II error, we increase the risk of committing a Type I error.

Social scientists tend to accept a much lower risk of making a Type I error than a Type II error. This probably is connected to their desire to obtain statistically significant results and their consequent wish to offset any biases that might result from that desire. Thus, by taking a .05 or lower risk of incorrectly supporting their own hypotheses, they project an impressive image of scientific caution and objectivity.

But just because so many social scientists conform to this convention does not mean that Type I errors are necessarily more serious than Type II errors—especially when human suffering is at stake. Deciding which type of error is more serious requires making value judgments, and the choice will vary, depending on the nature and context of the research question. To illustrate this point, let's return to our hypothetical example involving the prevention of recidivism among abusive parents, again using the theoretical sampling distribution illustrated in Table 22-2. Recall that a 9:17 split had a probability of .052 with a two-tailed test and therefore was not significant at the .05 level. Consequently, at that significance level, we would decide to risk committing a Type II error and would be unwilling to take a .052 risk of committing a Type I error.

Would we be justified in that decision? Reasonable people might disagree about this issue, but

what if we had little evidence that any alternative interventions effectively prevent child abuse? If nothing else works and there is no evidence that the intervention produces noxious side effects, which error has worse human consequences—recommending an intervention that really has no effect on child abuse or failing to recommend one that really does reduce the incidence of child abuse? As you think about this, realize that if our hypothetical 9:17 results could be generalized, it would mean that the intervention lowers the child abuse rate from 65% (17 out of 26 cases in the untreated control group) to 35% (9 out of 26 treated cases). That's prevention of a substantial amount of suffering and other damage. On the other hand, if the null hypothesis is true, then the use of this intervention by others would result in a lot of wasted resources that could have been spent seeking more effective ways to deal with this serious problem.

Here is another example to illustrate the arbitrariness of the .05 significance level and the need to be mindful of the importance of Type II errors. Suppose 100 people attend a charity event in which each receives one raffle ticket to get a chance for a door prize that will be awarded to one lucky person. Suppose you attend the event, and there you run into a family of seven people in attendance, who are your next-door neighbors. Suppose further that one of them offers to bet you $5 that someone in their family of seven will win the door prize. Assuming that the raffle is on the up-and-up and not rigged for one of them to win, their odds of winning would be only 7 out of 100, or .07. Suppose you ask, "What odds do you want me to give you?" and your neighbor responds, "Odds schmodds, let's make it an even bet. If I win the bet, you give me $5, and if you win, I'll give you $5." Would you take that bet? You betcha! Your odds of winning would be 93 out of 100, one heck of a lot better than their odds of 7 out of 100. You would not need to insist on having only 5 of your neighbor's family members count (thus not needing to insist on reducing their odds to .05) in order to have the deck stacked way in your favor. This example is analogous to discounting the potential value of an outcome with a .07 p-value just because it exceeds .05, which would make no more sense than refusing your neighbor's bet.

One way to resolve the dilemma regarding whether to risk a Type I or Type II error is through

TABLE 22.3 Type of Error Risked as Related to Decision about Null Hypothesis

Type of Error	Decision Regarding Null Hypothesis	
	Reject	Not Reject
Type I	Risked	Not risked
Type II	Not risked	Risked

replication. Another way is to increase our sample size. As we will see next, increasing our sample size provides a way to reduce the risk of committing a Type II error without having to increase the risk of committing a Type I error.

The Influence of Sample Size

As we discussed in Chapter 15, on sampling, the larger our sample, the less sampling error we have. When we reduce sampling error, we reduce the probability that the relationships we observe in our findings can be attributed to it. Consequently, the same relationship that was too weak to be significant with a smaller sample can, without changing in magnitude, become statistically significant with a larger sample. In other words, it is safer to generalize findings from large samples than from small ones, and even a very weak relationship might warrant generalization if it was found in a very large sample.

For example, in a study of the salaries of social work faculty members in 1980, Rubin (1981) found that after controlling for several extraneous variables, the mean salary was $26,638 for men and $26,157 for women. With a very large sample size of 1,067 faculty members, he found that the $481 difference between the mean salaries of men and women was statistically significant at the .01 level.

To illustrate the effects of sample size further, let's return to our hypothetical example on evaluating an intervention to prevent child abuse, but this time we'll vary the sample size, relying in part on examples of hypothetical data presented by Blalock (1972). To begin, suppose that we assigned only 5 cases to each group and found that 2 of the 5 treated parents recidivated as compared to 3 of the 5 untreated controls. Although 3:5 represents a 60% recidivism rate, and 2:5 is only 40%, with these small samples the role of chance is so great that it would be ludicrous to take such percentages seriously. If we were to double our sample size to 10 cases per group and found the same recidivism rates (i.e., 4 out of 10 vs. 6 out of 10), our results still would not be significant at the .05 level.

But if we found the same rates (i.e., the same relationship) with 50 cases in each group (20 out of 50 vs. 30 out of 50), then the probability of the null hypothesis being true would be less than .05, and we would reject it at that level of significance. And if we doubled the sample size to 100 per group

and still found the same 40% versus 60% rates, the probability of the null hypothesis being true would fall to below .01.

To help solidify your understanding of this point, let's compare one more pair of hypothetical results for the preceding example. Suppose we assigned 50 cases to each group and found 24 (48%) treated recidivists and 26 (52%) untreated recidivists. That outcome would not be significant at the .05 level. But suppose we found the exact same relationship with 5,000 cases in each group. That would entail 2,400 (48%) treated recidivists and 2,600 (52%) untreated recidivists. For that finding, the probability of the null hypothesis being true would be less than .001.

» INTERPRETING RELATIONSHIP STRENGTH

When we assess statistical significance, we ask only one question: "Can a relationship be inferred to exist in a theoretical sense or in a broader population?" We do not assess the relationship's strength. It is tempting to treat significance levels as indicators of the relative strength of different relationships—that is, to assume that a relationship that is significant at the .001 level is stronger than one that is significant at the .05 level—but such an assumption would be incorrect.

We just saw how sample size can influence statistical significance. We saw that a 40% recidivism rate among treated cases versus a 60% recidivism rate among controls would be significant at the .05 level for 50 cases per group, whereas a 48% versus a 52% recidivism rate would be significant at the .001 level for 5,000 cases per group. Therefore, the stronger relationship is not necessarily the one with the lower probability of a Type I error.

We may also be tempted to think that because significance testing doesn't tell us how strong a relationship is, it might be okay to bypass significance testing and just deal with measures of the strength of relationships. But that, too, would be inappropriate. Some strong relationships can be caused by chance. If 0% of two treated cases recidivate, as compared to 100% of two untreated cases, then generalizing that strong relationship would be no more appropriate than inferring that two coins were biased if you flipped two heads with one and two tails with the other. In short, significance testing is an essential first step in interpreting a relationship, but it tells us only the probability that a relationship was caused by chance. It does not tell us its strength.

In Chapter 21 we discussed various measures of association, such as correlations and Cohen's *d*. In this section, we'll discuss how to interpret the strength of relationships, particularly in light of the fact that a statistical significant relationship is not necessarily a strong one.

Strong, Medium, and Weak Effect Sizes

It is often useful to interpret relationship strength (or effect size) in terms such as *weak*, *medium*, or *strong* so that they take on added meaning relative to other research findings and other explanations. But such interpretations can be tricky. For example, we may have a reflexive tendency to attach the same meanings to correlations as we attach to exam scores, seeing percentages above 70% or 80% as strong and anything much lower as weak. Although these benchmarks may be applicable to studies of measurement reliability, using them as general guideposts to distinguish strong and weak relationships is incorrect.

As an illustration of this point, consider research on the causes of child abuse. A large, diverse array of factors can influence whether a parent becomes abusive. Whether a parent was abused as a child is one such factor, but there are many others. Many parents who were abused as children do not become abusive parents, and many other factors influence that outcome. Most studies of these factors show that each explains only a tiny percentage of the variation in whether the abused child becomes an abusive parent. If a study were to find that one such factor explained 20% of the variation in whether the abused child becomes an abusive parent, then there would probably be widespread agreement that this was a very strong relationship relative to other findings in this field of study. Indeed, it might be a major discovery.

For another example, suppose we conducted an experiment to evaluate the effectiveness of an intervention to prevent recidivism among parents referred for child abuse. Suppose our experiment found a 40% recidivism rate for 100 treated cases and a 60% recidivism rate for 100 untreated cases. Calculating the *phi*-statistic would show that the

correlation for this relationship equals .20. (You can examine a statistics book if you want to know how this is calculated; in this book we are only concerned with you understanding the meaning of this statistic.) Would we conclude that this was a weak relationship? Although we might not all give the same answer to that question, we probably would agree that there is no one mathematically correct answer to it. Although a correlation of .20 might seem weak at first glance, what about the fact that our intervention reduced the child abuse recidivism rate by 20%, which is a 33% reduction (20% is one-third of 60%)? Also, what if prior experimental research had found that alternative interventions had a weaker effect or even no impact on recidivism rates?

What if our hypothetical experiment were to find a 35% recidivism rate for treated cases versus a 65% recidivism rate for untreated cases? The correlation for that relationship would be .30. Although that might seem small in the context of an exam score or a reliability coefficient, the 65% recidivism rate for untreated cases would nearly double the 35% rate for treated cases.

In this connection, Cohen (1988) argues that a Cohen's *d* of approximately .5 should be considered to be of medium strength, noting that it pertains to the difference in average height if we compare 14- and 18-year-old girls. It also applies to the difference in mean IQ between clerical and semiskilled workers. Cohen also argues that a *d* of .8 should be considered strong, noting that this amount applies to the difference in the mean IQ between college graduates and persons with only a 50:50 chance of passing a high school academic curriculum.

Cohen deems a *d* of about .2, to be weak. There is a mathematical formula for transposing a *d* into its corresponding correlation. We won't go into that formula; instead, we mention it just to point out that a new intervention that improves a treatment success rate from 45% to 55% would have a correlation of only .10. An increase in successful outcomes from .45 to .55 might be very important when the outcome indicator is very important, such as preventing suicide, child abuse recidivism, police brutality, and so on. Therefore, the value of "weak" effect sizes can be underestimated.

Some researchers have developed empirical guidelines for interpreting the relative strength of relationship magnitude statistics, based on their reviews of hundreds of published research studies in the social sciences and helping professions. Their results have, by and large, been close to Cohen's guidelines for weak, medium, and strong relationships. These guidelines can provide approximate benchmarks that can be useful in interpreting effect sizes in future research.

But, as we already mentioned, an intervention's effect size alone does not indicate its value. An intervention with a stronger effect size is not necessarily "better" than one with a weaker effect size. For example, an intervention that reduces the rate of child abuse or school dropout among high-risk individuals from 55% to 45% may be more valuable to society than an intervention that reduces the annual turnover rate among Big Brother or Big Sister volunteers from 60% to 40%. Likewise, an intervention that reduces the rate of extreme physical abuse from 55% to 45% might be deemed more valuable than an intervention that reduces the rate of mild verbal abuse from 65% to 35%. Determining which intervention is "better" or more valuable requires considering the substantive significance of research findings, an issue we shall take up next.

» SUBSTANTIVE SIGNIFICANCE

Measures of the strength of a relationship do not automatically indicate the substantive significance of that relationship. Some researchers might use the term *practical significance*, which is synonymous with substantive significance. In studies of the effectiveness of clinical interventions, the term clinical significance is likely to be used instead of the term *substantive significance*. Both terms mean the same thing. By the substantive significance of a relationship (or its clinical significance), we mean its importance from a practical standpoint. No matter how strong a relationship may be—no matter how well it compares to an average Cohen's *d* or how close to 1.0 its correlation may be—we still can ask whether it constitutes a substantively important or trivial finding.

Let's consider this issue in connection to preventing child abuse. Suppose one intervention makes the difference between a 35% and a 65% recidivism rate. Assuming that the finding was statistically significant, how substantively significant is that finding? In other words, how much practical importance does it have for the field? Suppose

another experiment finds that a different intervention makes a statistically significant difference between a 20% recidivism rate and an 80% rate. Assuming that the two interventions were equal in terms of cost, time, and so on, determining which was the more substantively significant finding would seem to be a fairly straightforward process, and we would choose the one with the 20% recidivism rate. Because everything else but relationship magnitude was of equal importance, the stronger relationship would be the more substantively significant relationship.

But suppose a different experiment finds that after 5 years of daily psychoanalysis costing $600 per week, 80% of treated abusive parents as compared to 20% of untreated parents say they agree with Freud's ideas. Which intervention would you find to be more valuable if you were providing services to that target population: the one that made a 30% difference in child abuse recidivism or the one that made a 60% difference in agreement with Freud's ideas? We hope you would deem the weaker relationship involving the intervention that reduced child abuse by 30% to have more substantive significance than the stronger relationship pertaining to attitudes about a theory. (Not that there is anything wrong with psychoanalysis per se; we would say the same thing about any theory in this practical context.)

The preceding admittedly extreme hypothetical comparison illustrates that no automatic correspondence exists between the strength of a relationship and that relationship's substantive significance. It's important to know how strong a relationship is and how it compares to the findings of other comparable studies that used comparable variables. But not all studies are comparable in practical importance.

Therefore, after we have ascertained the statistical significance of a relationship and measured the strength of the association, we must make subjective value judgments to gauge the substantive significance of that relationship—value judgments that might consider such intangibles as the importance of the variables and problem studied, whether the benefits of implementing the study's implications are worth the costs of that implementation, and what prior knowledge we have about the problem studied and how to alleviate it. If we judge that the study addresses a trivial problem, assesses trivial variables, reports results that imply actions whose costs far outweigh their benefits, or yields findings that add nothing to what is already known, then we might deem observed relationships to be trivial even if they explain a relatively large amount of variation in the dependent variable.

To reiterate, we must consider all three issues: statistical significance, strength of relationship, and substantive significance. We also need to remember the influence of sample size, which was discussed earlier in this chapter. When we take all of these issues into account, we can realize that not only are some weak and unimportant relationships statistically significant because they were calculated with a very large sample size, but conversely some potentially meaningful relationships do not attain statistical significance because they were calculated with a very small sample size. Knowing this, if you were designing a study to test a hypothesis and hoping to obtain statistically significant results, you would want to know in advance how big your sample needs to be to give you a good chance of obtaining such results. Our next section, on statistical power analysis, shows how you could find that out.

EP 4, 9

» STATISTICAL POWER ANALYSIS

Statistical power analysis deals with the probability of avoiding Type II errors. In other words, it assesses the probability of correctly rejecting a null hypothesis that is false. Recall that statistical significance testing tells us only the probability of incorrectly rejecting a null hypothesis that is true. In other words, significance testing tells us only the probability of committing a Type I error, whereas power analysis deals with the probability of committing a Type II error.

Mathematically calculating the risk of committing a Type II error is far too advanced a topic for this book, so we refer you to an outstanding book titled *Statistical Power Analysis for the Behavioral Sciences* by Cohen (1988) if you want to examine the calculations. Fortunately, we can estimate that risk—that is, estimate statistical power—without performing calculations. We can do this simply by examining statistical power tables that Cohen constructed on the basis of the mathematical calculations. What we find in statistical power tables is the power of statistical significance tests for varying levels of significance, sample sizes, and relationship

magnitudes and effect sizes. Cohen's book provides such tables for various types of significance tests.

Drawing from the figures in Cohen's tables, Table 22-4 displays the power of testing the significance of correlations at the .05 and .10 levels of significance for small, medium, and large effect sizes. This table can be used to plan a research study even if your significance test involves measures of association other than correlations; for example, the figures in Cohen's table for the comparison of means are approximately the same as for correlations in Table 22-4. If you desire more precision, you can examine Cohen's book and his more detailed tables.

When using Table 22-4 to plan a research study, you first choose a significance level. (If you choose the .01 level, you will need to examine the tables in Cohen's book.) The next step is to estimate the strength of the correlation between your independent and dependent variables that you expect exists in the population. The columns in the table pertain to small ($r = .10$), medium ($r = .30$), and large ($r = .50$) correlations. The r value depicts the strength of the correlation. (If you want to assess the power for a different correlation—say, .20, .40, or larger than .50—you will need to consult Cohen's book. But you probably will be satisfied using Table 22-4, as you will see.)

Of course, you have no way of knowing before collecting your data the real correlation or effect size in the population or if a relationship exists at all, but you can identify a figure that approximates your expectations. For example, you might choose a correlation and effect size that Cohen deems to be of medium strength. If so, then you would examine the "Medium" ($r = .30$) column in Table 22-4. Alternatively, you might expect that your intervention will have a meaningful effect but with a weak correlation, such as reducing a recidivism rate from 55% to 45%. That would get calculated as a correlation of .10, and therefore you would examine the "Small" column in Table 22-4.

Each figure in each column is the probability (imagine a decimal point before each figure) of correctly rejecting the null hypothesis at different levels of sample size. The different sample sizes are listed in the "Sample Size" column.

Recall our earlier discussion of the effects of sample size on statistical significance. Note how the probability of rejecting the null hypothesis increases as sample size increases. For example, if

TABLE 22.4 Power of Test of Significance of Correlation Coefficient by Level of Significance, Effect Size, and Sample Size[a]

Sample Size[a]	.05 Significance Level			.10 Significance Level[b]			Sample Size[a]
	Effect Size			Effect Size			
	Small	Medium	Medium	Small	Small	Small	
	$r = .10$ $r^2 = .01$	$r = .30$ $r^2 = .09$	$r = .50$ $r^2 = 25$	$r = .10$ $r^2 = .01$	$r = .30$ $r^2 = .09$	$r = .50$ $r^2 = .25$	
10	6	13	33	11	22	46	10
20	7	25	64	13	37	75	20
30	8	37	83	15	50	90	30
40	9	48	92	16	60	96	40
50	11	57	97	18	69	98	50
60	12	65	99	20	76	99	60
70	13	72	*	22	82	*	70
80	14	78		23	86		80
90	16	83		25	90		90
100	17	86		27	92		100
200	29	99		41	*		200
300	41	*		54			300
400	52			64			400
500	61			72			500
600	69			79			600
700	76			84			700
800	81			88			800
900	85			91			900
1,000	89			94			1,000

[a]The figures in this table are approximately the same as for tables on chi-square tests (with a two-by-two table) and *t*-tests. For *t*-tests, the number of cases in each group, added together, would approximate the sample size in this table.

[b]The figures at each level of significance are for a two-tailed test; however, the power figures at the .10 level approximate the power of one-tailed tests at the .05 level.

Note: Power values below the point indicated by an asterisk exceed .995.

Source: The figures for this table were derived from tables in Cohen (1988).

your sample size is only 10 cases, your assumed correlation is .30 (medium), and your significance level is .05, then your probability of correctly rejecting the null hypothesis is only .13; that is, your statistical power would be only .13. That would mean that you would have a probability of 1.00 minus .13, or .87, of incorrectly accepting a false null hypothesis.

The latter probability of .87 would be your probability of committing a Type II error.

But if your sample size is 40 cases, then your power would be .48. Still, however, you would have a .52 probability (1.00 = .48 − .52) of committing a Type II error. To have a .20 probability of committing a Type II error (Cohen recommends

.20 as a maximum), your power would have to be .80 (which we find by subtracting .20 from 1.00). To obtain at least that level of power, your sample size would have to be 90 cases. (More precisely, your power for 90 cases would be .83. If you consult Cohen's book, you will find that 84 cases will give you a power of exactly .80.) If you want your probability of committing a Type II error to equal your probability of committing a Type I error (i.e., to be at .05), then your statistical power will have to be .95, and to obtain that level of power, you will need a sample size of more than 100 cases (140 cases is the precise figure in Cohen's book).

In short, by using this table, you can select a sample size that will provide you with the level of statistical power (i.e., risk of a Type II error) that you desire. But what if it's impossible to obtain a sample that big? Suppose you plan to survey all of the social workers in a rural area where the population of social workers numbers only 50. Table 22-5 indicates that your statistical power is only .57 for a sample size (n) of 50, $r = .30$, and a significance level of .05. Thus, your probability of committing a Type II error would be .43 (1.00 − .57). It might not be worth all the expense and effort to do a study when you know in advance that even if your research hypothesis is true you are taking almost a 50:50 risk of coming up with an incorrect conclusion. In that case, because you cannot increase your sample size, one reasonable alternative would be to lower your risk of committing a Type II error by increasing your risk of committing a Type I error.

For example, you might decide to raise your significance level from .05 to .10 and thus consult the column under the .10 significance level in Table 22-4. In the column for a medium correlation for a sample size of 50 and a .10 significance level, you would find that your power would be .69 (as compared to .57 for the .05 significance level). Thus, by raising the risk of a Type I error to .10, you would reduce the probability of a Type II error to .31 (1.00 − .69). You might still conclude that the risk is too great to warrant doing the study. But if you did decide to pursue it, taking risks of .10 and .31 for the two types of errors might make more sense than taking risks of .05 and .43.

Ideally, of course, you would find some way to increase your sample size—perhaps by including another geographic area in the study—to have an acceptably low risk for both types of errors. Also,

whatever you decided to do about your study and its sample size would be decided in light of the risks involved. It's mind-boggling to imagine that many researchers are implementing studies without taking statistical power analysis into account; consequently, they don't know the odds that they're spinning their wheels trying to confirm hypotheses that, even if true, have a low probability of being supported.

Imagine, for example, that you are evaluating the effectiveness of a school social work program in an inner-city high school. You think it will reduce dropout rates from 55% to 45%, which would correspond to a small correlation of .10. Examining the "Small" column in Table 22-4 shows that to have statistical power of .80 (and therefore a .20 probability of committing a Type II error), you would need a sample size of approximately 800 cases if you chose a .05 significance level or about 600 cases if you chose a .10 significance level.

Although statistical power analysis has its greatest utility when conducted a priori—that is, while your study is still being designed—it also has value on a post-hoc basis after you fail to reject the null hypothesis—that is, after you find that your results are not statistically significant. When reporting null findings, it's important to inform readers of the probability that, in failing to reject the null hypothesis, you are committing a Type II error. This is true regardless of whether your power analysis was conducted before or after your study. Before readers dismiss your hypothesis as one that was not confirmed, they should be informed of the probability that the reason it could not be supported was a Type II error. The importance of this is perhaps most obvious when new interventions are being tested for problems for which we know of no other effective interventions.

Before leaving this topic, let's reiterate a point made earlier to clarify an aspect of statistical power analysis that may seem confusing. How can statistical power analysis tell us in advance the probability of incorrectly failing to reject a false null hypothesis when we have no way of determining ahead of time whether the null hypothesis is false or true? The answer: Statistical power analysis does not tell us in advance the odds that we will reject a false null hypothesis; the probability it gives us tells us only the odds that we will reject the null hypothesis *if it really happens to be* false. In other words, when using statistical power analysis, we begin by saying,

"Suppose the null hypothesis really is false and that a relationship of a certain strength (we also specify the particular strength that we are assuming) really does exist. If that is so, then what is the probability that we will obtain findings that are statistically significant were we to use a given sample size and significance level?"

» SELECTING AND CALCULATING TESTS OF STATISTICAL SIGNIFICANCE

There are many different formulas for calculating statistical significance, which are called *statistical significance tests*. So far, we have been discussing inferential data analysis mainly from a conceptual level. We occasionally mentioned statistical significance tests, but have avoided their calculation formulas. New (often mathematically complex) significance tests are continually being developed, and it is unrealistic to expect researchers to have a deep understanding of all of them. Moreover, if you are planning to be a practitioner who will read research to inform your practice, but not to conduct hypothesis testing research studies, you might be pleased to hear that you do not have know how to calculate statistical significance tests. In fact, it is not

imperative for you to know when to use which significance test.

As we discussed earlier in this chapter, the ultimate aim of every significance test is the same regardless of the formula it uses. That aim is the calculation of the probability (i.e., the *p* value) that an observed relationship between variables can be attributed to chance. In other words, no matter what the significance test is called, no matter how complex its calculations, and no matter what it calls the various statistics involved in those calculations, each test ultimately arrives at the same statistic: the *p* value. That *p* value means the same thing regardless of which test is used, and understanding what it does and does not tell you—as discussed above—is sufficient for you to use research to inform your practice.

So, relax: Despite the heading of this section, we are not going to cover which statistical test to select or how to calculate it. If you are interested in finding out more about those things, you can take a course or read a book that focuses exclusively on statistics. (And preferably both, because reading a book alone would be awfully challenging without the course.) You could also examine the box "Some Tests of Statistical Significance Commonly Used in Outcome Studies" if you want to find out a little more about the purposes of some tests of statistical significance that you may encounter as an evidence-based practitioner.

SOME TESTS OF STATISTICAL SIGNIFICANCE COMMONLY USED IN OUTCOME STUDIES

Name of Test	Purpose
Correlation	Calculate the probability that a correlation statistic measuring the association between two variables can be attributed to chance.
Chi-square	Calculate the probability that the difference in frequencies (or proportions) between two nominal variables can be attributed to chance.
t-test	Calculate the probability that the difference between two means can be attributed to chance.
Analysis of variance (ANOVA)	Calculate the probability that the difference between three or more means can be attributed to chance.
Multiple ANOVA	Calculate the probability that differences between means can be attributable to chance when multiple independent and/or dependent variables are involved.

» META-ANALYSIS

In light of all the concepts discussed in this chapter, you might be wondering whether we can ever be sure about the implications of the inferential data analyses from any particular study. If so, good for you! Such doubt shows that you have gained at least a reasonable level of understanding of these challenging concepts.

Indeed, if you've ever reviewed the research literature on a particular topic (perhaps when preparing a term paper), you know that different studies tend to arrive at different findings about the same topic or research question. One study, for example, might find that Program A has strong effects, whereas a second study might find that it has weak effects. Several studies might find that it has medium effects, and some might find that it has none. Another study might even find that it has harmful effects.

Different studies tend to come up with contrasting findings for a variety of reasons, not all of them statistical. Differences in research design and the ways data are collected constitute one common reason. In studies of intervention efficacy, different studies might come up with contrasting findings because they operationalize the intervention in different ways, differ with respect to the background characteristics of the client groups that make up their samples, or use different ways to measure outcome. Sometimes, studies that seem almost identical come up with different findings simply because of sampling error and chance fluctuations.

Drawing conclusions from a bewildering array of inconsistent findings across different studies on the same topic is not easy, yet it may be of great utility to figure out some way to make some general statement about how effective a program or intervention seems in light of all the studies taken as a whole. Suppose, for example, you are planning a new service delivery program and are torn between emphasizing case management services versus an alternative service delivery approach. You review the research literature evaluating the effectiveness of each approach, hoping to learn whether one by and large tends to be more effective than the other. If you were able to conclude that case management tended to have a Cohen's d of .70 and the alternate approach tended to have a Cohen's d of .25, then you might find that to be an important reason for favoring a case management approach in your planning deliberations.

A method for simplifying the process of drawing conclusions from a bewildering array of inconsistent findings across different studies on the same topic is called *meta-analysis*. Although the term sounds complicated, its underlying meaning is not. Meta-analysis simply involves calculating the mean effect size across previously completed research studies on a particular topic.

Meta-analyses need not be limited to the calculation of mean effect sizes; some statistically complex meta-analytic statistical procedures can be used to calculate the statistical significance of an overall set of results aggregated across various studies. Calculating the overall statistical significance of results across studies has the added advantage of alleviating concerns about the risk of Type II errors in studies with small sample sizes. Whereas each such study by itself might have inconclusive results because of its Type II error risk, that risk can diminish substantially in a meta-analysis that combines the studies and thus yields an aggregated assessment of statistical significance based on the aggregated sample sizes.

Given their obvious utility in synthesizing so many disparate findings across many studies and in alleviating risks of Type II errors, you may not be surprised to learn that hundreds of meta-analyses have been published on many topics of interest to social workers. As we mentioned in Chapter 2, meta-analyses can ease the phases of the evidence-based practice process involved with ascertaining what interventions have the best evidence supporting their effectiveness with a particular target problem. For example, several meta-analyses have reviewed all of the outcome studies done on the treatment of posttraumatic stress disorder and agreed that prolonged exposure therapy, cognitive processing therapy, and eye movement desensitization and reprocessing are the most effective treatments for it—and are about equally effective (Rubin & Springer, 2010). You can find meta-analyses on a vast array of other target problems and interventions, including child welfare programs and treatments for depression, substance abuse, eating disorders, borderline personality disorders—and many others.

Although a good meta-analysis has important benefits, not all meta-analyses are equally trustworthy. As with other types of research, meta-analyses vary with respect to how well they adhere to the methodological principles of this type of analysis. Moreover, some meta-analyses are conducted by folks with a vested interest in whether the results support the effectiveness of a particular program or intervention. Consequently, you should be able to critically appraise the trustworthiness of the meta-analyses that you read as an evidence-based practitioner, and you should understand how to conduct a methodologically rigorous meta-analysis should you ever want to do so.

But this has been a long and perhaps difficult chapter. Therefore, instead of delving at this point into the methodological issues in meta-analyses and how to critically appraise them, we'll refer you to Appendix C, which covers that content. We'll briefly revisit some data analysis concepts in the next chapter, on writing research proposals and reports.

MAIN POINTS

- Inferential statistics help rule out chance as a plausible explanation of our findings; thus, combined with our consideration of design issues, they help us decide whether we can generalize about populations or theoretical processes based on our findings.
- Statistical significance testing identifies the probability that our findings can be attributed to chance. Chance, or sampling error, represents a rival hypothesis for our findings—a purely statistical hypothesis called the *null hypothesis*.
- Tests of statistical significance use theoretical sampling distributions, which show what proportion of random distributions of data would produce relationships at least as strong as the one observed in our findings. The theoretical sampling distribution thus shows the probability that observing the relationship we observed was due to the luck of the draw when and if no such relationship really exists in a population or in a theoretical sense.
- The probability that the observed relationship could have been produced by chance is compared to a preselected level of significance. If the probability is equal to or less than that level of significance, then the finding is deemed

statistically significant, and the plausibility of the null hypothesis (chance) is refuted.
- Social researchers traditionally tend to use .05 as the level of significance, but that is merely a convention. A higher or lower level can be justified, depending on the research context. When .05 is used, a finding that is significant at the .05 level is one that could not be expected to result from the luck of the draw, or sampling error, more than 5 times out of 100.
- When we test directional hypotheses, we can use one-tailed tests of significance. These locate the critical region of significant values at one predicted end of the theoretical sampling distribution.
- When testing nondirectional hypotheses, we must use two-tailed tests of significance. These place the critical regions at both ends of the theoretical sampling distribution.
- Type I errors occur when we reject a true null hypothesis. Type II errors occur when we accept a false null hypothesis. Every decision based on statistical significance testing will risk one error or the other.
- Increasing sample size reduces the risk of a Type II error, but the larger the sample, the greater the likelihood that weak relationships will be statistically significant.
- Statistical significance, relationship strength, and substantive significance (also known as *clinical significance*) must not be confused with one another. Statistically significant relationships are not necessarily strong or substantively meaningful. Strong relationships are not necessarily substantively significant, and some seemingly weak relationships in which only a small percentage of dependent variable variance is explained can have great substantive (or clinical) significance. The substantive (or clinical) significance of a finding pertains to its practical or theoretical value or meaningfulness; it cannot be assessed without making value judgments about the importance of the variables or problem studied, what the finding adds to what is or is not already known about alleviating a problem, and so on.
- Statistical power analysis calculates the probability of avoiding a Type II error. It does so by calculating the probability of committing a Type II error and subtracting that probability from 1.0. The remainder is the statistical

power. By consulting statistical power tables (in which the calculations have already been done for us) in planning our study, we can learn which sample size or significance level will be ideal to effect the level of statistical power we desire. When we test hypotheses without first consulting statistical power tables, we risk having a low likelihood of obtaining findings that would support those hypotheses even if they are true.

- There are many different tests of statistical significance, and the most appropriate one to use will depend primarily on the level of measurement of your variables, the number of variables in the analysis, sampling procedures, and the way the variables are distributed in the population. All of these tests ultimately will tell you the probability of committing a Type I error.

- Meta-analysis is a procedure for calculating the mean effect size across previously completed research studies in a particular field and for aggregating the statistical significance of an overall set of results across various studies.

REVIEW QUESTIONS AND EXERCISES

1. Find several explanatory research articles on a problem area that concerns you in a social work or interdisciplinary journal. Bring them to class and critique them from the following standpoints:

   a. If the null hypothesis was not rejected, did the author adequately address statistical power issues and the probability of committing a Type II error? If correlations are reported, locate in Table 22-4 the closest column heading to each correlation. Then locate the row that corresponds to the sample size used in the study. Then locate the row–column intercept to identify the statistical power for a two-tailed test at the .05 significance level. Was that level of power adequate, in your judgment?

   b. If the null hypothesis was rejected, did the author seem to confuse statistical significance with relationship strength or substantive significance? Was any measure of association

used, or did the author stop the analysis once statistical significance was assessed? How would you interpret the substantive significance of the findings?

2. Deal a deck of cards into two piles of four cards per pile. Do this 20 times, subtracting the number of red cards in the left-hand pile from the number in the right-hand pile each time. After each deal, record the difference in the percentage of red cards between the two piles. Construct a theoretical sampling distribution based on those 20 differences in percentages. Repeat this process, but this time deal 20 cards in each pile. Compare the two sampling distributions. Which has the greater degree of dispersion—that is, the greater degree of sampling error? Suppose each red card represents a student who stayed in school and each black card represents a dropout. If the left-hand pile represents high-risk students who received school social work services and the right-hand pile represents their control group counterparts, then what do these two theoretical sampling distributions illustrate about the influence of sample size on statistical significance? What do they illustrate about the importance of refuting the plausibility of chance?

INTERNET EXERCISES

1. Find two articles on inferential data analysis issues that were discussed in this chapter. Write down the bibliographical reference information for each article and summarize its main points. Two articles worth looking for, both by Bruce Thompson, are as follows:

   Improving research clarity and usefulness with effect size indices as supplements to statistical significance tests. *Exceptional Children*, Spring 1999.
   Why encouraging effect size reporting is not working: The etiology of researcher resistance to changing practices. *Journal of Psychology*, March 1999.

2. Find an article in a social work or social science journal with the words *statistical power* in its title. Write down the bibliographical reference information for the article and summarize its main points.

3. Find two articles in a social work or social science journal with the term *meta-analysis* in their titles. Try to find one article that reports a meta-analytic study on a topic that interests you. Write down the bibliographical reference information for that article and briefly identify its methodological strengths and weakness. Try to find another article that discusses methodological issues in meta-analysis. Write down the bibliographical reference information for that article and summarize its main points.

4. Go to the online statistical power calculator website at http://www.danielsoper.com/statcalc3/calc.aspx?id=47. Once there, calculate power several times after entering various levels of Cohen's *d* and various desired statistical power levels for *p* values of .05, .10, and .01. Notice the different minimal sample sizes you would need for different power levels, different *p* values, and different anticipated effect sizes for one-tailed and two-tailed hypotheses.

 Visit CengageBrain.com for additional practice and study opportunities including experiential exercises, research tools, glossary, flashcards, and sample test items.

part 8
Writing Research Proposals and Reports

This part contains the final chapter of this text. We'll discuss how to communicate the findings of your study as well as all the other aspects of it covered in the previous chapters of the book. We'll begin with the writing of research proposals. You'll see how writing a good proposal is enhanced by comprehension of the material in each of the earlier sections of this text.

23

Writing Research Proposals and Reports

EPAS Competencies for This Chapter

Competency 4   Engage in Practice-Informed Research and Research-Informed Practice: Conducting practice-informed research involves competence in writing research reports and often requires competence in writing proposals seeking funding for the research. Therefore, this entire chapter aims to build this competency.

Competency 9   Evaluate Practice with Individuals Families, Groups, Organizations, and Communities: As with Competency 4, evaluating practice requires competence in writing reports of your evaluation and in writing proposals when funding is needed to make your evaluation feasible.

What You'll Learn in This Chapter

As the title of this chapter implies, here you'll learn how to write proposals to obtain funding for your research and how to report your research once it is completed. We'll also suggest some tips for finding a funding source and some preliminary steps worth taking before you begin writing your proposal. As to the writing of proposals and reports, we'll look at the components of each as well as some general guidelines for how best to communicate with your intended audience.

» INTRODUCTION

You've come a long way. Among other things, you've learned about the value of social work research, the scientific method, research ethics and politics, how to formulate and design a useful and valid research study, alternative ways to measure things and collect data, how to conduct culturally competent research, and how to analyze and interpret your data. Now it's time to take a closer look at how to communicate your work. We'll begin with communicating what you propose to study as you seek approval of your study and perhaps funding for it. Then we'll discuss how to write a report of your completed study. You'll see in both of these endeavors how comprehending the material in the previous chapters of this book will enhance the quality of your research proposal or your research report.

» WRITING RESEARCH PROPOSALS

Quite often, in the design of a research project, you will have to lay out the details of your plan for someone else's review or approval or both. In the case of a course project, for example, your instructor might very well want to see a proposal before you set off to work. Later in your career, if you wanted to undertake a major project, you might need to obtain funding from a foundation or government agency, which would most definitely want a detailed proposal that described how you were going to spend its money.

The guidelines for writing a research proposal will vary depending on its purpose. At one extreme, a relatively lengthy and detailed proposal will be expected when you seek grants to fund your research from federal government agencies, such as the National Institute of Health or the National Institute of Drug Abuse. Research grants from such agencies range from less than $50,000 for a new investigator to conduct a modest study to as high as several hundred thousand dollars per year over several years for more experienced investigators to conduct more ambitious studies. These agencies will evaluate your proposal not only according to how well you write it but also according to the degree of methodological rigor in the proposed

design. Do not expect to be funded, for example, if you seek $250,000 to fund a preexperiment or quasi experiment with weak internal validity or a survey that does not include probability sampling.

At the other extreme are sources that fund much smaller grants, often under $10,000. These might include state or local government agencies seeking a limited evaluation of a program they fund, private foundations, or universities that offer small grants to encourage and facilitate research by faculty members. Although the proposal demands from these sources are likely to be less rigorous than from federal agencies, you should not underestimate them. Your best bet is to learn about the expectations of the funding source before you prepare your proposal and then develop your proposal according to those expectations.

EP 4, 8

» FINDING A FUNDING SOURCE AND RFPS

The process of finding a funding source will vary, depending on your degree of flexibility in what you are willing to research. If you are already committed to a specific research question and design and seek to find funding for that specific study, you will need to find a funding source for which that research question and type of study is a priority. On the other hand, perhaps you are not wedded to any specific line of research and instead want to adapt to the priorities that funding sources have regarding what sorts of research questions and designs *they* seek to fund. In that case, your task will be to stay current in reading various publications and announcements from a wide range of funding sources, looking for a request for proposals (RFP) that piques your interest and fits your area of expertise. An RFP will identify the research questions and types of designs the funding source has in mind, encourage researchers to submit proposals to carry out such research, specify the maximum size of the grants, and provide other information about the source's expectations and funding process.

The most efficient way to find potential funding sources or to be notified of recently issued RFPs is by using the Internet. For example, you might go to the National Institutes of Health website at www.nih.gov to learn about federal funding opportunities. Also, you can search for sites providing information on funding sources, such as the National Institutes of Health Guide for Grants and Contracts and the Grantsmanship Center. At the National Institutes of Health site, for example, you will find useful sections on RFPs, how to apply for a grant, and other helpful topics. A useful resource for identifying foundations that might be interested in the sort of research you have in mind is the Foundation Center. Its website includes a link to the Foundation Directory (http://fconline.fdncenter. org), which provides information on a comprehensive list of foundations—information on the areas of research each foundation is interested in funding, the average range of dollar amounts it typically funds, application procedures, and so on.

You might also be able to obtain e-mail notifications of RFPs and other funding opportunities by joining a professional association connected to your particular research interests. For example, the Research Committee of the Eye Movement Desensitization and Reprocessing International Association regularly e-mails its members about recently issued RFPs that seem potentially related to research on eye movement desensitization and reprocessing (EMDR). If your school of social work has a research center, then it too might be able to provide you with continually updated listings of recently issued RFPs relevant to social work.

You can also enter search terms such as "research grants" in a search engine such as Google or Yahoo! to find funding sources and their RFPs. If you are interested in research grants in a particular area, such as child abuse, you might enter "research grants child abuse." The search engine will then list various sites to click on that might provide what you are looking for. Or you might just enter a particular governmental agency, such as "National Institutes of Health." Websites associated with that agency will then be listed. You can then click on the site or sites that mention funding opportunities.

Because time may elapse between the issuing of an RFP and its posting on some sites or your notification of it via an e-mail list, you may want to regularly examine the *Federal Register*, which is issued daily. Most of its contents deal with government activities and announcements unrelated to social work research. However, because it is the first place in which new RFPs for federal funding will be announced, you may want to wade through it

looking for a relevant RFP so that you will have more time to prepare your proposal before the proposal submission deadline. You can access the *Federal Register* at www.federalregister.gov.

Large-Scale and Small-Scale RFPs and Proposals

As we discussed above, there is a wide variation in the nature of RFPs and their expectations depending on the source of the proposal and the amount of funding involved. Some RFPs and proposals can be characterized as large-scale, others as small-scale.

To illustrate a large-scale RFP and proposal, one of our colleagues recently received a multiyear grant in excess of $1 million from the National Institute on Drug Abuse (NIDA) to conduct an evaluation of the effectiveness of an intervention to prevent drug abuse. Her proposal was more than 100 pages long and was in response to an RFP that was 25 pages long.

To illustrate a small-scale RFP, the box "A Small-Scale RFP for Research on LGBT Family Issues" describes components of an RFP directed at students wanting to research the challenges that LGBT people face in forming, defining, and maintaining families. The full RFP is only two-page long and is for grants not in excess of $15,000. The main part of proposals in response to this RFP is required not to exceed seven pages.

Grants and Contracts

The foregoing section on finding a funding source pertains mainly to research grants. Although a funding source will usually identify some broad priority areas as its funding interests, researchers typically have considerable leeway in the specifics of what they want to investigate within that area and how they want to investigate it. The funding source may not approve the researchers' proposal, but the proposals it does approve can vary significantly. For example, suppose a federal agency issues an RFP in the area of research on the treatment of substance abuse among ethnic minorities in the United States. It might fund one proposal to conduct an experimental evaluation of the effectiveness of a new therapeutic community approach to treating Mexican American cocaine users. At the same time, it might fund another proposal to assess the factors associated with completing versus dropping out of treatment

A SMALL-SCALE RFP FOR RESEARCH ON LGBT FAMILY ISSUES

This box presents excerpts from an RFP from The American Psychological Foundation. It is directed at students wanting to research the challenges that LGBT people face in forming, defining, and maintaining families. The full RFP is only two-page long and is for grants not in excess of $15,000 per year. We have formatted the following excerpts in a way that does not copy the formatting or exactly match all of the wording in the actual RFP, which you can download online at http://www.apa.org/apf/funding/scrivner.aspx. There you can see that students from all fields of the behavioral and social sciences are encouraged to apply for a grant.

RFP Components:

- Overview of the Foundation (3 sentences)
- About the Roy Scrivner Memorial Research Grant (5 sentences)
- Program Goals (4 bullet points, one on each of the following 4 goals)
  - Encourage students to orient their careers toward research on LGBT family issues.
  - Advance the understanding of LGBT family issues.
  - Advance the understanding of coping mechanisms for family members.
  - Advance the understanding of interventions and related issues in this area.
- Amount: $15,000 available per year (one sentence)
- Eligibility Requirements (3 bullet points)
  - Student in good standing endorsed by a supervising professor
  - Demonstrate applicant's ongoing commitment to LGBT issues
  - Receive IRB approval
- Evaluation Criteria (4 bullet points)
  - Conformance with RFP goals
  - Quality of proposed work
  - Applicant's demonstrated scholarship
  - Appropriateness of budget
- Proposal Requirements (6 bullet points)
  - No more than 7 pages describing the project's goal, its relationship to the existing literature, its research plan, and its expected outcomes and impact
  - Timeline
  - Budget and justification
  - CV
  - Faculty advisor recommendation letter
  - Submit as a single PDF document
- Submission Process and Deadline (4 sentences)

among African American heroin users. A third proposal might be funded to conduct a qualitative investigation on how parental substance abuse impacts the lives of Native American children, how they attempt to cope, and their treatment needs.

Unlike research grants, research contracts provide much greater specificity regarding what the funding source wants to have researched and how the research is to be conducted. The research proposal for a research contract will have to conform precisely to those specifications. If a state agency wants to contract for a mailed survey of how satisfied its service consumers are with a new way to provide services that is being pilot-tested, you won't get funded if you propose an experiment or a qualitative investigation utilizing participant observation and unstructured interviews—no matter how methodologically rigorous or theoretically profound your proposal might be.

This does not mean that you have no leeway whatsoever in writing proposals for contracts. After all, the funding source will not have written the proposal for you. If the source wants a mailed survey on consumer satisfaction, then it probably won't stipulate the exact sampling procedures or questionnaire format and contents. You will have to propose many of those technical details. But the degree of leeway you will have in a contract proposal will be much less than in a grant proposal. Also, with governmental research contracts, the size of the proposed budget may be a chief criterion in selecting which proposal to fund.

The process of finding a funding source for research contracts also may differ from the process for research grants. The funding source might seek out a specific researcher or research center and work closely with it in preparing the proposal. Your chances of being awarded a research contract might be greatly influenced by the rapport and credibility you have previously established with key people who are administering or are otherwise connected with the funding source. This also applies to securing grants funded by state governmental agencies.

Before You Start Writing the Proposal

Although research proposals are often conceived and written in response to a specific RFP, your chances of having your proposal funded will be enhanced if you take some preliminary steps before you start to write it. One such step, as we noted above, is to learn about the expectations of the funding source before you prepare your proposal and then develop your proposal according to those expectations. You can learn about those expectations from the funding source's website or by obtaining its written materials.

In addition, you should try to develop a relationship with a staff member at the funding source whose role includes acting as a liaison to prospective grant applicants. Through that relationship, you can better learn of the funding source's potential interest in your research idea. If it is interested, the liaison can suggest how to develop or modify your idea and your proposal to fit the funding source's priorities and funding criteria. With some funding sources, it might be necessary to write a brief preliminary letter summarizing your research idea before you can begin to relate to any of their staff members. If possible, however, it is best to develop a relationship before writing such a letter. Sometimes a liaison can guide you in writing even a preliminary letter and may perhaps advise you regarding the preparation of a brief concept paper (no more than a few pages) that summarizes your preliminary idea. In some instances, the concept paper might be enclosed with the preliminary letter; in others, it should be submitted only after the

funding source expresses a preliminary interest in your idea and encourages you to submit a concept paper. By developing and nurturing a relationship with a liaison from the funding source and following the liaison's advice, you not only increase the degree of fit between your proposal and the source's funding criteria but also increase the chances that the liaison will act as an advocate for your proposal.

You can also get connected with liaisons and other key people who can influence funding by volunteering to be a proposal reviewer at a funding agency. If they accept you as a reviewer, you can network up close and get a firsthand look at the grant review and evaluation process. That can help you in writing future proposals.

Even if you are not a reviewer, you should—as another potentially helpful preliminary step—ask to examine proposals that have previously been funded by the source you are considering. Examining successful proposals might provide additional insights as to the funding source's expectations. Suppose, for example, that every successful proposal included a lengthy section on data analysis plans—not only identifying each statistical procedure that will be used but also providing a rationale for its selection and explaining how the assumptions of each procedure will be checked and what will be done if those assumptions are not met after the actual data are collected. Seeing such a section in every successful proposal will prompt you to emphasize it in your own proposal. It might even prompt you to engage a statistician as a collaborator in your research and in developing your proposal. Some funding sources will provide access to previously funded proposals, perhaps via a website. If a funding source does not, then you can request a list of previous grant recipients whom you can contact. Some of them might be willing to show you their successful proposals. Some might also be willing to give you helpful tips. You might even want to engage one as a collaborator on your project. Your prospects for being funded might be enhanced significantly if the funding source sees that someone with a good track record is collaborating on your project.

By the same token, if you have already established a good track record by having successfully completed previously funded research projects, your chances of being funded will be better, and you may have less need for collaborators with good track records. But if you have not yet established a track record, then you should realize that the process of getting your proposal funded might be a long one. You should not get too discouraged if your first proposal is not funded. Learn from the process. If the funding source provides feedback as to the reasons your proposal was not funded, try not to be defensive in examining those reasons. Based on what you learn, revise the proposal and resubmit it, perhaps to the same funding source. With some federal funding sources, for example, researchers often resubmit improved versions of their proposals several times before eventually being funded.

Finally, you should keep in mind that improving your prospects for getting funded for research involves many of the same grantsmanship principles and strategies that pertain to getting funded for other kinds of projects. Before you write your proposal, it will behoove you to learn about those principles and strategies and begin implementing them. Generic grantsmanship is a large topic that goes beyond the scope of this text. However, if you enter the search term "grantsmanship" on a search engine such as Google or Yahoo!, you will find links to useful websites on that topic. That said, let's now examine common components of a good research proposal.

Research Proposal Components

As we implied earlier, the specific components of your proposal and the guidelines for writing those components will vary, depending on the purpose of your research and the expectations of your funding source. Proposals for primarily qualitative investigations, for example, will differ from primarily quantitative proposals. Proposals for small preliminary pilot projects, for example, might not need to cover the following components as extensively or as rigorously as do more ambitious proposals. We present the following components on the assumption that you need to learn how to prepare an ideal proposal for a major piece of research. Learning how to do that should also prepare you to write less ambitious proposals. In large part, these components will apply to qualitative as well as quantitative research proposals. However, some of the material you are about to read will apply more to quantitative proposals than to qualitative ones. Moreover, preparing a proposal for a qualitative

study can be more challenging than preparing one for a quantitative study. Therefore, after describing the following components, we will discuss similarities and differences between quantitative and qualitative research proposals.

Cover Materials

Before reading your actual proposal, many funding sources will want to see some preliminary materials. A cover letter adapted to the source's expectations regarding cover letters is one rather obvious need. The source might also require a cover page that identifies the title of the proposal, the names and addresses of the people and organization submitting the proposal, and other information, such as the amount of money being requested and the duration of the project. An executive summary statement might also be required. The length of the executive summary will vary. Some sources might expect it to be no more than a paragraph that can fit on the cover page. Others might expect a longer summary that requires a separate page. The preliminary steps that we've discussed above will guide you in determining just how brief the summary should be. Typically, it will supply a sentence or two on each of the proposal's components, highlighting the major features of each component.

Problem and Objectives

What exactly do you want to study? Why is it worth studying? Specify in precise terms the objectives of your proposed study. The objectives should be in the form of a brief list; for example, if you have two objectives, simply indent and number each of them, with a sentence or two after each number. Your objectives likely will be in the form of seeking answers to the research questions of your study, and they should reflect the attributes of good research questions as discussed in Chapter 7. They need to be narrow and specific, answerable by observable evidence, and feasible to investigate and answer. Most important, you need to explain how their answers have significance for practice and policy.

When discussing the importance of the study, cite facts. For instance, if you are proposing to study homelessness, then you might want to cite figures from prior studies that assessed the number of homeless individuals in the nation or in a particular city or state. Or you might describe concrete examples taken from previous case studies so that the subject of your study and its purpose are not vague abstractions. When discussing significant implications for policy or practice, be specific. For example, if you are proposing to study factors that influence school dropout, don't just make vague statements, such as, "By identifying why some children drop out of school and others do not, we can develop new policies and programs to deal with this problem." Spell out in detail what kinds of findings might imply which specific possible policy or program alternatives. Thus, you might say something like, "If we find that the absence of positive male role models is an important factor that contributes to the dropout problem among males of a particular ethnic group, then this may imply the need to hire more male teachers of that ethnicity or to create a special alternative program where such male role models work exclusively with boys on academic material as well as on issues such as what it means to be a man."

As we noted earlier, you should know the funding source's priorities before you prepare or submit your proposal. Try to find a funding source whose priorities come closest to the problem you want to study and to your study's potential significant implications, then word your problem statement in a manner that emphasizes the degree of fit between your proposed study and the funding source's priorities.

Literature Review

What have others said about this topic? What theories address it and what do they say? What research has been done previously? Are there consistent findings, or do past studies disagree? Are there flaws in the body of existing research that you feel you can remedy? How will your study relate to, yet go beyond the previous studies? How has the prior work influenced your proposed study—for example, has it implied the need to examine certain variables or to assess them in new ways? Do not cite monotonous, minute details about every relevant study that has ever been done, especially if the body of existing literature is extensive. If the literature is extensive, concentrate on the most recent findings while also including "classic" studies. Moss (1988, p. 434) recommends that the literature review be "brief enough not to become tedious but

extensive enough to inform proposal reviewers about the study's topic."

You might try to resolve this conflict by sticking to major themes and succinctly summing up groups of related studies, connecting them to a major theme. For instance, you might say something like this (we'll use fictitious references): "Prior studies on the effectiveness of case management with the severely mentally ill have had inconsistent findings. Four studies (Babbie, 1999; Babbie, Rubin, & Freud, 2001; Rubin, 1998; Rubin & Babbie, 2000) found that it is effective. Three studies (Fischer, 2000; Nietzsche, 1998; Scrooge, 1999) found that it is ineffective. The four studies with positive outcomes all used days hospitalized as the dependent variable, whereas the three studies with negative outcomes all used quality of life as the dependent variable...." However, if you have difficulty finding prior studies that are directly relevant to your proposed research, then you should cite studies that are relevant in an indirect way. Thus, if you find no studies on the effectiveness of case management with the mentally ill, then you might look for studies that evaluate its effectiveness with other populations, such as the physically or developmentally disabled.

The importance of avoiding excessive detail in your literature review does not mean that you can safely skip mentioning some relevant studies, especially if the literature is not extensive. Funding source review committees are likely to evaluate your expertise in the topic and your competence as an investigator on the basis of the thoroughness and adequacy of your literature review. They might, for example, ask an expert in your topic to provide an external review of your proposal. That expert might know the literature on your topic as well as or better than you do. If your review has omitted any relevant studies, then your chances of being funded can be significantly diminished, particularly if the reviewer thinks the omitted studies are important. Although you don't want to be tedious in reporting the details of each study, you should cite all the relevant ones and be sure to give adequate attention to those that are most relevant to your line of inquiry.

Also, try to avoid bias in deciding which prior studies to emphasize. Suppose, for example, that you propose to evaluate the effectiveness of a promising new intervention to prevent child abuse among Mexican American teenage parents. Suppose there have been five previous evaluations of the intervention, none with Mexican American parents, and that four of the five studies concluded that the intervention was effective, with the fifth study concluding the opposite. In your eagerness to impress the funding source with the promise of this new intervention, you may be tempted to emphasize the four studies with positive findings and deemphasize or even omit the fifth study. You should resist this temptation. If you do not resist it, reviewers who are aware of that fifth study are likely to interpret your omission or deemphasis of it as an indication that you may lack sufficient competence or objectivity to merit being funded.

You should also avoid writing your literature review in a perfunctory manner—that is, as if it were just a ritualistic list of studies that you are required to provide in a superficial manner without thoughtful organization. Rather than merely providing a summary listing of what other studies have reported, your literature review should show why you chose your particular line of inquiry and why you conceptualized it the way you did. When reviewers read your research questions and hypotheses, they should not perceive them as coming out of thin air. Having read your literature review, they should see where your hypotheses and variables came from. For example, a common mistake students make when proposing studies to evaluate an intervention is to review the literature on the problem the intervention is aimed at alleviating without showing how the literature led them to choose the particular intervention they want to evaluate instead of alternative possibilities. The box "Improving a Weak Literature Review" illustrates some of the points we've been making.

Conceptual Framework

In this section of your proposal, you clearly specify and provide rationales for your research questions, hypotheses, variables, and operational definitions. You should justify why and how you chose to study each item. Your explanation should flow in part from your literature review. It should also show the logic of your own thinking about the inquiry as well as how your study goes beyond and builds on the prior literature. For example, if none of the previous studies supporting an intervention to prevent child abuse included Mexican Americans in their samples, then you could refer to those studies (which should be in your literature review) and the absence of Mexican Americans in their

samples as the rationale for your point of departure. Suppose that all of the previous studies looked only at the reduction of out-of-home placement of children as the sole indicator of success and that none assessed whether the children who were kept in their homes were actually better off than those placed elsewhere. Even if this issue has not been raised in the previous literature, you can raise it yourself in your conceptual framework, explaining your reasoning. You would thus show how your study improves on the methods of prior studies in this regard as well as explain to readers why you chose your particular variables and why you chose to operationally define them the way you did.

Measurement

In this section, you elaborate on how you will measure the variables that you identified and operationally defined in your conceptual framework. This section should flow smoothly from the operational definitions in your conceptual framework, and you should make sure that you are not too redundant and repetitive regarding the specification of your operational definitions and your measurement procedures. For example, if you plan to operationally define child well-being as a score on a validated instrument for assessing the well-being of children in families at risk for abuse, avoid repeating the detail about that scale in both the conceptual framework and the measurement sections of your proposal. Instead, you might simply mention that scores on the scale will be your operational definition; later, in your measurement section, go into detail about the nature of the scale, how it is scored, what subscales it contains, and its reliability and validity.

Regardless of whether you are using existing scales or measurement instruments you may have developed yourself, you should include a copy of each in an appendix to your proposal. If you are using an instrument that has had its reliability and validity tested, then you should not just cite studies that have tested them but should report specific reliability and validity data. For example, you might say that the five studies that have tested the internal consistency reliability of a scale have found coefficient alphas ranging from .87 to .94, all indicating good to excellent internal consistency reliability. In many studies, the investigator can choose from more than one validated instrument to measure a particular construct. There are various validated scales, for example, to measure constructs such as depression and self-esteem. If this is true for your study, then provide a rationale for your choice of scale.

For example, some scales to measure self-esteem are quite valid in distinguishing between people with very low and very high self-esteem but are not sensitive to detecting subtle improvements in self-esteem among people who had very low self-esteem before an intervention and not quite so low self-esteem after the intervention. If you are proposing to evaluate an intervention for people with very low self-esteem, then you might justify choosing an instrument with good reliability and validity and good sensitivity over an alternative instrument with excellent reliability and validity but very low sensitivity. You might also choose to measure a particular variable in more than one way. In previous chapters, we discussed the value of doing this in connection with the principle of *triangulation*. Review committees are likely to be favorably impressed by proposals that incorporate triangulation in their measurement procedures.

Study Participants (Sampling)

Who or what will you study to collect data? First, identify them in general theoretical terms and then ascertain more concretely who is available for study and how you will reach them. Identify any inclusion or exclusion criteria you will use. Will it be appropriate to select a sample? If so, how will you do that? If you will be conducting an exploratory, qualitative study, you will need to use your judgment in identifying and observing variations (e.g., age, ethnicity, and class) among participants as you go along—ensuring that you have tapped into the range of those variations. If your aim is to conduct a survey for purposes of estimating frequencies of characteristics in the population (e.g., determining the unemployment rate), then you will need to select a probability sample. Is there any possibility that your research will significantly affect those you study? If so, how will you ensure that they will not be harmed by the research? That, too, should be addressed in your proposal.

If you must use nonprobability sampling procedures, then you will need to justify that, including attention to the chances that your sample will be biased and unrepresentative of your target population. What efforts will you make to offset or avoid those potential biases? Regardless of whether you use probability or nonprobability sampling procedures, you will need to address issues associated with sample attrition and refusal to participate. What special efforts will you make to enhance recruitment and retention of participants? (We discussed such efforts in Chapter 6 in reference to minority and oppressed populations and in Chapter 11 in reference to experiments.)

You will also need to justify the projected size of your sample. We discussed sample size issues in Chapter 15 on sampling and in Chapter 22. As we mentioned in the latter chapter, a *statistical power analysis* shows whether your sample size is large enough to give you a good chance of supporting your hypothesis if it is indeed true. You should include a statistical power analysis in the sampling section (and perhaps also in the data analysis plans section) of your proposal. You should also tell reviewers why you think it will be feasible for you to obtain the needed sample size. For example, if you are proposing to evaluate an intervention to prevent child abuse among Mexican Americans, provide evidence that child welfare agencies will supply participants for your study in sufficiently large numbers. Such evidence might be letters of support from the agencies as well as data showing how many Mexican American clients who would be eligible for your study have been served by those agencies in recent years.

Design and Data Collection Methods

How will you actually collect the data for your study? Will you conduct an experiment or a survey? Will you undertake field research, conduct a historical study, or focus on reanalyzing statistics already created by others? Regardless of which design you employ, be sure to address the key methodological issues that we discussed previously in the chapter on the design you plan to use.

For example, if you are conducting an experiment or a quasi experiment, describe the logic of your design. Be sure to cover all the important issues discussed in Chapter 11, such as controlling for internal validity and assessing treatment fidelity. Regardless of which design you use, describe when, where, and by whom your data will be collected with each instrument. What expertise and experience qualifications will you seek in your data

IMPROVING A WEAK LITERATURE REVIEW

Following are two literature review sections for a hypothetical proposal seeking funding to evaluate the effectiveness of a cognitive-behavioral therapy in alleviating the behavioral problems of girls residing in a residential treatment center. The girls had been victims of multiple incidents of child abuse before being admitted to the residential treatment center. We suggest that you write down the weaknesses you notice in the first review and how they were improved in the second review. Then you can compare your notes to the points we make at the end of this box in our "Critical Comparison of the Two Reviews."

Example of a Weak Literature Review Section

Child abuse is a tragic problem that can cause many horrific problems for its victims. According to many news media reports, it is a growing epidemic. Its victims commonly experience PTSD. EMDR is an exciting new therapy that has been developed to treat PTSD symptoms and other problems resulting from trauma. Francine Shapiro (described this innovative and promising therapy, in her excellent book *Eye Movement De-Sensitization and Reprocessing: Basic Principles, Protocols, and Procedures*, New York: Guilford Press, 1995). Shapiro shows how this cognitive-behavioral therapy that was developed in 1987 is virtually a miracle cure in desensitizing clients to distressing memories, feelings, and cognitions and in replacing negative cognitions with positive ones. The key component in EMDR is the use of bilateral stimulation. The therapist typically stimulates rapid back-and-forth eye movements or alternates right- and left-hand taps or sounds in the right and left ear while the client visualizes the distressful scene and keeps in mind the related cognitions and feelings.

The optimism about the effectiveness of EMDR is understandable in light of the original experiment by Francine Shapiro (1989), which found that EMDR had very powerful effects in resolving trauma symptoms. Shapiro randomly assigned 22 clients to an experimental group that received EMDR and a control group that received an alternative form of treatment. The clients ranged in age from 11 to 55. They had experienced various types of trauma. She measured

outcome with the Subjective Units of Distress Scale and the Validity of Cognitions Scale. On each measure, the EMDR clients' scores were significantly better than those of the control group clients. The effect sizes were very large. Many mental health therapists who learned of Shapiro's results sought training in EMDR. An intriguing article by Kadet (2002), titled "Good Grief," appeared in *Smart Money* magazine in June 2002. In it, we learn that more than 40,000 mental health practitioners have been trained in EMDR, indicating the promise of this new therapy and how well received it has been among mental health experts.

The research literature evaluating the effectiveness of EMDR with children provides significant additional grounds for optimism about using EMDR to eradicate the devastating effects child abuse has on its victims. For example, Pellicer (1993) used a case study technique in evaluating the effectiveness of one session of EMDR for a 10-year-old girl who had been experiencing nightmares. Pellicer found that that one session of EMDR ended the girl's nightmares. Greenwald (1994) reported five case studies evaluating the effectiveness of EMDR in alleviating trauma symptoms among children who had survived a hurricane. The case studies showed EMDR to be effective. In a quasi experiment, Puffer, Greenwald, and Elrod (1998) concluded that a single session of EMDR reduced trauma symptoms among children and adolescents who had experienced a single trauma or loss.

Chemtob et al. (2002) used a randomized lagged-groups design in examining pre- to post change among two groups of elementary school children who had experienced a hurricane. There were 32 children in their sample. Most of the children met the criteria for disaster-related PTSD. Their ages were 6 to 12. One group received three EMDR sessions. The other group did not. Various standardized psychological measures were used. The study concluded that EMDR was effective in alleviating PTSD symptoms.

Another experiment, this one by Muris et al. (1997), evaluated the effectiveness of EMDR in reducing avoidance behaviors among spider-phobic children. The sample size was 26. One group of the children received one session of EMDR. The other group received an exposure *in vivo* treatment. Different therapists were used for each group. Outcome was measured by direct observation of behavior as well as by self-reports of spider fear by the children. Muris et al. (1997) found positive effects for EMDR.

In another experiment, this one by Muris et al. (1998), the effectiveness of EMDR in reducing avoidance behaviors among spider-phobic children was again evaluated. The sample size was 22. One group of the children received EMDR. The other group received an exposure *in vivo* treatment. Different therapists were used for each group. Muris et al. (1998) found that EMDR produced significant improvement on self-reported spider fear.

The foregoing studies suggest that the prospects are indeed excellent regarding the effectiveness of EMDR in treating children who have been abused and thus underscore the importance of the proposed study, which seeks to evaluate the effectiveness of EMDR in treating children who have been abused.

Example of an Improved Literature Review Section

Eye movement desensitization reprocessing (EMDR) is a cognitive-behavioral therapy that was developed in 1987 to desensitize clients to distressing memories, feelings, and cognitions and to replace negative cognitions with positive ones (Rubin, 2002a). The key component in EMDR is the use of bilateral stimulation. The therapist typically stimulates rapid back-and-forth eye movements or alternates right- and left-hand taps or sounds in the right and left ear while the client visualizes the distressful scene and keeps in mind the related cognitions and feelings. A full description of the eight-phase EMDR protocol can be found in a text written by Shapiro (1995).

Soon after its inception, the popular media depicted EMDR as almost a miracle cure for a wide range of problems, spurring more than 40,000 mental health practitioners to obtain EMDR training (Kadet, 2002). That depiction was fostered by Shapiro's (1989) original study, which found very large effect sizes supporting EMDR's effectiveness. Despite being a randomized experiment, however, Shapiro's study was widely criticized for using measurement procedures that were highly vulnerable to bias and experimenter demand (Herbert et al., 2000; Rosen, 1999). Subsequent studies used less biased

measures, and several reviews have indicated that more controlled studies have been done supporting the effectiveness of EMDR in treating adults with single-trauma posttraumatic stress disorder (PTSD) than has been the case for any other psychotherapy for PTSD (Chambless et al., 1998; Chemtob, Tolin, van der Kolk, & Pitman, 2000; Davidson & Parker, 2001; Spector & Read, 1999; Van Etten & Taylor, 1998).

However, we still do not know whether EMDR is effective with children and adolescents, especially those who have experienced multiple traumas. Moreover, we do not know if it is more effective than alternative exposure treatments. Three pilot studies, which lacked randomized experimental control, supported the effectiveness of EMDR with children who had experienced only a single trauma or loss (Greenwald, 1994; Pellicer, 1993; Puffer, Greenwald, & Elrod, 1998). Only four randomized experiments have assessed EMDR's effectiveness with a sample comprised exclusively of children. Chemtob et al. (2002) used a randomized lagged-groups design and concluded that EMDR was effective in alleviating PTSD symptoms (using standardized measures) with 32 elementary school children (aged 6 to 12) who had experienced a hurricane. Two experiments by Muris and his associates compared EMDR with an exposure treatment for reducing avoidance behaviors among spider-phobic children. In one, Muris et al. (1997) found positive effects for EMDR but superior effects for the exposure treatment. They concluded that EMDR adds nothing of value to the exposure treatment. In the other experiment, the exposure treatment produced significant improvement on behavioral as well as self-report measures, but EMDR produced significant improvement only on self-reported spider fear (Muris et al., 1998). In another randomized experiment, Rubin et al. (2001) found no significant differences in parental reports of emotional and behavioral problems between children in a child guidance center who were treated with EMDR plus routine treatment and children who received routine treatment only. The children had mixed diagnoses. Although some of the children had experienced a single trauma, others had problems connected to multiple traumas or unconnected to any trauma.

Among the studies on children, only those that focused exclusively on PTSD symptoms connected to a single trauma obtained results supporting the efficacy of EMDR. And only one of those studies was a randomized experiment. Nevertheless, EMDR continues to be used by therapists working with children whose problems are not trauma based or whose problems are connected to multiple traumas. And proponents of EMDR continue to tout its effectiveness across a wide array of emotional and behavioral problems among children, including children younger than 2 years old (Tinker & Wilson, 1999). More experimental research is needed to test such claims, particularly regarding the effectiveness of EMDR in treating problems other than single-trauma PTSD symptoms. The proposed study will help meet this need by testing the hypothesis that EMDR will be more effective than an alternative exposure therapy in reducing the frequency of serious incident reports of behavioral problems among girls residing in a residential treatment center.

Critical Comparison of the Two Reviews

Notice how the second review, despite containing some 50 fewer words than the first review, provides more objective information and does so in a more objective manner. The first paragraph of the first review, for example, begins with several sentences of unsubstantiated hyperbole. The acronym PTSD is not spelled out. The citation for Shapiro's book is excessive. Notice how the second review merely refers to it as "Shapiro (1995)" and does so without the hyperbole.

The second paragraph of the first review continues the hype and uses excessive detail in reporting Shapiro's study. Moreover, it reports that study in a biased manner, not mentioning a critical methodological flaw in it. The final two sentences of the paragraph continue the hype and the excessive detail in the Kadet citation. Notice how the second paragraph of the second review comes across as more informed and objective while providing more information in fewer words.

The third paragraph of the first review is less efficient than the second review in describing the pilot studies, and it reports them in a biased fashion, not pointing out the design limitation in these studies that the second review points out. Similar problems can be seen in the remaining paragraphs of the first review, which give excessive detail about the experiments and report their mixed findings in a biased fashion, conveying a more favorable impression of EMDR's effectiveness than is warranted. Moreover, the first review completely omits the Rubin et al. (2001) study, which is mentioned in the second review and which had results questioning the effectiveness of EMDR in treating children with mixed diagnoses who had experienced multiple traumas. Notice also how the second review identifies unresolved issues regarding multiple traumas and comparisons to exposure therapy that are absent in the first review. In that connection, notice how the second review, despite containing fewer words, builds a better foundation for testing the hypothesis in the proposed study than does the first review. If you were on a funding source's review panel, which of these two reviews would make you more predisposed to want to fund the proposed study?

collectors? How will you recruit and train them? What will be done to avoid or minimize bias among them? Will they, for example, be blind as to the hypotheses of your study or the experimental group membership status of the individuals to whom they are administering pretests and posttests? If they are not blind, then will they have vested interests in the outcome of the study? (Hopefully not!) Will you assess their interrater reliability? Will you triangulate data collection methods? (Hopefully, yes!) What is your rationale for collecting your data at the time points and places you specify? What about feasibility issues, such as agency cooperation with your proposed procedures or the amount of time it will take for respondents to complete your instruments or interviews? Are any of your data collection procedures particularly vulnerable to research reactivity (see Chapter 11)?

Data Analysis

Spell out the kind of analysis you plan to conduct. If you anticipate the use of specific statistical analytic techniques—multiple regression, analysis of variance, and so on—identify, describe, and justify your choice. Perhaps your intention is to construct ethnographic ideal types that represent variations in the phenomenon under study. Describe how you will do that. More important, however, is that you spell out the purpose and logic of your analysis. Are you interested in precise description? Do you intend to explain why things are the way they are? Do you plan to account for variations in some quality—for example, why some children are harder to treat than others? What possible explanatory variables will your analysis consider, and how will you know if you've explained variations adequately?

As we noted earlier, different funding sources will have different expectations regarding the length and detail of this section of your proposal. If you are not sure of those expectations, the safe thing to do is to develop this section in detail—providing a detailed rationale for the selection of each data analysis procedure. When using statistical procedures, for example, explain how the assumptions of each procedure will be checked and what will be done if those assumptions are not met after the actual data are collected. Also discuss the statistical power of each procedure in light of your projected sample size. If you must use procedures in which you lack sufficient expertise, then it is advisable to engage a statistician as a collaborator in your research and in writing this section of your proposal.

Schedule

It is often appropriate to provide a schedule for the various stages of research. Even if you don't do this for the proposal, do it for yourself. Unless you have a timeline for accomplishing the several stages of research—and keep in touch with how you're doing—you may end up in trouble. Your proposed timeline should be reasonable. If you project too little or too much time for specific stages of the research, reviewers might question how well prepared you are to carry out the research successfully.

Budget

If you are asking someone to give you money to pay the costs of your research, then you will need to provide a budget that specifies where the money will go. Large, expensive projects include budgetary categories, such as personnel, equipment, supplies, and expenses (e.g., telephones and postage). Even for a more modest project that you will pay for yourself, it is a good idea to spend time anticipating expenses: office supplies, photocopying, transportation, and so on. The costs you specify

in your budget should be reasonable, and you should justify each. You can hurt your chances of being funded by overestimating the costs or by underestimating them. If you overestimate them, funders may fear being "ripped off" or may deem the benefits of the study to be not worth the costs. If you underestimate the costs, you may convey the impression of an inexperienced investigator who does not yet "know the ropes." You may need technical assistance to calculate some expenses, such as pay rates and fringe benefits for personnel. You should inquire as to whether there is a staff member at your school or agency who provides such technical assistance in the preparation of grant applications.

Additional Components

Most funding sources will require additional proposal components, perhaps attached as appendices. For example, you'll probably have to supply materials showing that your proposed study has been approved by an institutional review board regarding its ethics and protection of human subjects. Chapter 5 discussed this process. You may also need to supply attachments that provide evidence of the proposed project's feasibility and your preparedness to carry it out successfully. These attachments might include (a) your resume or a biographical sketch and perhaps the résumés and biographical sketches of your coinvestigators showing how your prior experiences have prepared you to carry out the research successfully, (b) letters of support from administrators of the agencies that will supply you with data or research participants, (c) statements supplying additional evidence as to the potential feasibility of the study regarding recruiting and retaining a sufficient sample and collecting sufficient data in an appropriate manner, and (d) plans for disseminating the results of your research, such as through publication in professional journals and newsletters and through presentations at professional conferences or agency meetings attended by those whose practice or research can be guided by your findings.

As you can see, if you were interested in conducting a social work research project, then it would be a good idea to prepare a research proposal for your own purposes, even if you weren't required to do so by your instructor or a funding agency. If you are going to invest your time and energy in such a project, then you should do what you can to ensure a return on that investment. The degree of difficulty you will encounter in preparing a proposal is likely to vary depending on the type of study you plan to conduct. Preparing a proposal for a qualitative study that you will submit for funding is likely to be particularly challenging, as discussed in the box "Similarities and Differences between Quantitative and Qualitative Research Proposals."

>> WRITING SOCIAL WORK RESEARCH REPORTS

Let's leap forward in time now, from writing your research proposal to writing the report of your completed study. By the time you are ready to write your report, you will have invested a great deal in your research. But unless your research is properly communicated, all the efforts devoted to the various procedures discussed throughout this book will go for naught. This means, first and foremost, that good research reporting requires good English (or Spanish or whatever language you use). Whenever we ask the figures "to speak for themselves," they tend to remain mute. Whenever we use unduly complex terminology or construction, communication is reduced.

Our first advice to you is to read and reread (at approximately 3-month intervals) an excellent small book, *The Elements of Style* by Strunk and White (1999). It is available for free online at http://www .gutenberg.org/ebooks/37134. (Another useful reference on writing is Birchfield [1998].) If you do this faithfully and if even 10% of the contents rub off, you stand a good chance of making yourself understood and your findings appreciated.

Scientific reporting has several functions. First, your report should communicate a body of specific data and ideas. You should provide those specifics clearly and with sufficient detail to permit an informed evaluation by others. Second, you should view your report as a contribution to the general body of scientific knowledge. While remaining appropriately humble, you should always regard your research report as an addition to what we know about social practice or

EP 4, 8

policy. Finally, the report should stimulate and direct further inquiry.

Some Basic Considerations

Despite these general guidelines, different reports serve different purposes. A report appropriate for one purpose might be wholly inappropriate for another. This section deals with some of the basic considerations in this regard.

Audience   Before drafting your report, ask yourself who you hope will read it. Normally, you should make a distinction between professional colleagues and general readers. If the report is written for the former, you may make certain assumptions about their existing knowledge and therefore summarize certain points rather than explaining them in detail. Similarly, you may use more technical language than would be appropriate for a general audience.

At the same time, remain aware that social work, like other professions, is diverse. Terms, assumptions, and special techniques familiar to some of your colleagues might only confuse others. If you report a study on cognitive-behavioral interventions to an audience of colleagues who are not familiar with those interventions, for example, you should explain previous findings in more detail than would be necessary if you were addressing an audience of social workers who specialize in cognitive-behavioral interventions.

Likewise, you should communicate differently depending on the research expertise and professional roles of the colleagues in your intended audience. For example, how you describe the logic of your research design or your data analysis procedures should vary depending on whether your intended audience consists primarily of researchers, administrators, or direct-service practitioners. If your target audience consists primarily of researchers, you'll have less need to explain or avoid using technical research terminology. If your target audience consists primarily of administrators or other practitioners with relatively little advanced technical experience in research, you should keep the terminology as simple as possible and be sure to explain any unavoidable technical terms that they may not yet understand. Also keep in mind that administrators and other practitioners will be far more attentive to executive summaries, visual representations via simple charts and graphs, and implications for practice than to the technical details of your

SIMILARITIES AND DIFFERENCES BETWEEN QUANTITATIVE AND QUALITATIVE RESEARCH PROPOSALS

The elements of research proposals that we've identified in this book are fairly common, regardless of the type of research being proposed. Whether you are proposing a quantitative or qualitative study (or perhaps a mixed-methods study), you will probably need to begin with a statement of the problem or objective and follow that with a literature review, a description of your research methods, and so on. Regardless of which type of study you propose to do, you will have to make a persuasive case as to the importance of the research question and the value of the study. The criteria for a good literature review will also be similar in both types of proposals. Other similarities include the need for a schedule with a realistic timeline, a section covering human subjects review approval, a reasonable budget that anticipates all of the various costs you will encounter, clear and interesting writing, and a neat, professional appearance with laser printing.

Although certain criteria for proposal preparation such as those mentioned above commonly apply to all research proposals, qualitative methodologists have been identifying ways in which proposals for qualitative studies differ from those for quantitative studies. Qualitative proposals are generally agreed to be more difficult to write than quantitative proposals, mainly because of the greater degree of structure and preplanning involved in designing quantitative research. Sandelowski, Holditch-Davis, and Harris (1989), for example, see the preparation of the proposal for a qualitative study as requiring the negotiation of "the paradox of planning what should not be planned in advance" (p. 77). Likewise, Morse (1994) notes the relatively unstructured, unpredictable nature of qualitative research and the difficulty this presents for writing a proposal that promises exciting results or is even specific about the types of alternative conclusions the study is likely to generate. These authors point out that the design of qualitative research tends to be in the form of an open-ended starting point from which methods and truth will emerge through encountering subjects in their natural environment. This is unlike quantitative research, in which the methods and specific alternative findings can be planned and spelled out in detail in advance.

The dilemma for the qualitative researcher, then, is figuring out how to put enough detail about the plan in the proposal to enable potential funders to evaluate the proposal's merits while remaining true to the unstructured, flexible, inductive qualitative approach. In the words of Sandelowski et al. (1989), "The most difficult task in preparing the proposal ... is delineating the method when the investigator can have no definitive method prior to initiating inquiry" (p. 78). This task is even more challenging to the extent that the merits of the proposal will be judged by reviewers who are likely to be more oriented to quantitative research and who expect the precise planning that goes into proposals for quantitative research studies.

One suggestion for those preparing proposals for qualitative studies is to go ahead and describe a plan for sampling and data collection and analysis but indicate that it is only a tentative and initial direction that is open to change as the study proceeds and new insights emerge. Also, the proposal can specify the type of qualitative approach being employed and then describe the general ideas underlying that approach. (Some of the more common qualitative approaches and their orienting guidelines are discussed in Chapters 18 and 19.) Although you will not be able to say in advance exactly what you will do or find, you can convey to reviewers the general principles you will follow in conducting your flexible, emergent inquiry.

The same general idea applies to other qualitative proposal sections that, in a quantitative proposal, would contain a much greater degree of operational specificity. For example, when you discuss sampling, you may not be able to anticipate with the precision of a quantitative proposal the exact number of subjects who will participate in the study and their characteristics. But you can discuss the variety of types of subjects you tentatively think are likely to participate and who you think are likely to supply the most relevant data. You can also describe the general ideas and rationale that underlie the qualitative sampling methods you expect to employ. (These methods were discussed in Chapters 15 and 18.)

Although you may find these suggestions helpful, they won't change the fact that qualitative proposals are more difficult to write and may be reviewed by people who are more accustomed to reading proposals for quantitative research and to judging proposals according to the canons of quantitative research design. Because they may be apt to react to your qualitative proposal with puzzlement, it is particularly important that your proposal demonstrate your expertise about qualitative research and your ability to carry it out. Make sure that every section of your proposal is well written and that your literature review is adequate. (The literature review in qualitative proposals should perhaps be more extensive than in quantitative proposals to demonstrate the investigator's expertise because it may appear as though the funders are being told "Trust me" in qualitative studies more than in quantitative ones.)

Along these lines, it may be helpful to conduct a pilot study on the topic addressed in your proposal and then describe that pilot study in your proposal and submit it as an appendix to the proposal. This will show your commitment and competence. It can also demonstrate how you might go about analyzing the data that might emerge in the proposed study. Of course, being able to refer to previously completed pilot studies will also help your prospects for funding in submitting a proposal for quantitative research, and the two types of proposals are similar in this respect.

Although we do not want to understate the similarities between the two types of proposals or overstate their differences, anyone planning to prepare a proposal for qualitative research should be aware of the special dilemma they face. Reviewers and board members of funding sources should also understand this dilemma and apply different criteria when reviewing the two types of proposals.

research methodology. (For more tips on writing for an audience made up of administrators or other practitioners, you may want to reexamine our comments in Chapter 14, which appear toward the end of the section "Planning an Evaluation and Fostering Its Utilization.")

Even if you are writing your report for submission to a professional journal, you'll need to keep in mind the varying expectations and types of readerships of different professional journals. With some social work journals, such as those with the term *research* in their title, your audience will consist largely of researchers who will understand and value your discussion of methodological issues and who will need less explanation of technical terms. Some other journals might be at the opposite end of the spectrum—with a greater emphasis on practice implications—and still others somewhere in between. Before you write your report for submission to a journal, you should do two things: (a) carefully select a journal whose expectations and audience best match your topic and the type of report you would like to write, and (b) examine the page in that journal where its editor describes the types of articles it is interested in as well as its article format and style expectations. *An Author's Guide to Social Work Journals* (National Association of Social Workers, 2009) might help you select a journal that appears to be the best fit for your report.

Form and Length of the Report   Our comments here apply to both written and oral reports. Each form, however, affects the nature of the report.

It's useful to think about the variety of reports that might result from a research project. To begin, you may wish to prepare a short *research note* for publication in a professional journal. Such reports are approximately one to five pages long (typed and double-spaced) and should be concise and direct. In a small amount of space, you can't present the state of the field in any detail, so your methodological notes must be abbreviated. Basically, you should tell the reader why you feel a brief note is justified by your findings, then tell what those findings are.

Often researchers must prepare reports for the sponsors of their research. These reports may vary greatly in length. In preparing such a report, you should bear in mind its audience—professional or lay—and their reasons for sponsoring the project in the first place. It is both bad politics and bad manners to bore the sponsors with research findings that are of no interest or value to them. At the same time, it may be useful to summarize how the research has advanced social work knowledge (if it has).

Working papers are another form of research reporting. Especially in a large and complex project, you'll find comments on your analysis and the interpretation of your data useful. A working paper constitutes a tentative presentation with an implicit request for comments. Working papers can also vary in length, and they may present all of the research findings of the project or only a portion of them. Because your professional reputation is not at stake in a working paper, feel free to present tentative interpretations that you can't altogether justify—identifying them as such and asking for evaluations.

Many research projects result in papers delivered at professional meetings. Often, these serve the same purpose as working papers. You can present findings and ideas of possible interest to your colleagues and ask for their comments. Although the length of *professional papers* may vary, depending on the organization of the meetings, it's best to say too little rather than too much. Although a working paper may ramble somewhat through tentative conclusions, conference participants should not be forced to sit through an oral unveiling of the same. Interested listeners can always ask for more details later, and uninterested ones can gratefully escape.

Probably the most popular research report is the *article* published in a professional journal. Again, lengths vary, and you should examine the lengths of articles previously published by the journal in question. As a rough guide, however, 20 to 25 typed pages is a good length. A subsequent section on the organization of the report is based primarily on the structure of a journal article, so we shall say no more at this point except to indicate that student term papers should follow this model. As a general rule, a term paper that would make a good journal article also makes a good term paper.

A *book*, of course, is the lengthiest and most detailed form of research report. If your book is published by a prestigious publishing company, some readers may be led to accept your findings uncritically. Consequently, you have a special obligation to your audience.

Aim of the Report Earlier in this book, we considered the different purposes of social work research projects. In preparing your report, you should keep these different purposes in mind.

Some reports may focus primarily on the exploration of a topic. As such, their conclusions are tentative and incomplete. You should clearly indicate to your audience the exploratory aim of the study and point to the shortcomings of the particular project. An exploratory report serves to point the way to more refined research on the topic.

Most research reports have a descriptive element reflecting the descriptive purpose of the studies they document. Carefully distinguish those descriptions that apply only to the sample and those that apply to the population. Give your audience some indication of the probable range of error in any inferential descriptions you make.

Many reports have an explanatory aim: pointing to causal relationships among variables. Depending on your probable audience, carefully delineate the rules of explanation that lie behind your computations and conclusions. Also, as in the case of description, give your readers some guide to the relative certainty of your conclusions.

Regardless of your research purpose, all social work research projects should have the overarching aim of providing information that will be useful in guiding practice or policy. Thus, your report probably will propose implications for action. Be sure that the recommendations you propose are warranted by your data. Thus, you should be especially careful to spell out the logic by which you move from empirical data to proposed action.

Avoiding Plagiarism Whenever you're reporting on the work of others, you must be clear about who said what. That is, you must avoid plagiarism: the theft of another's words or ideas—whether intentional or accidental—and the presentation of those words and ideas as your own. Because this is a common and sometimes unclear problem for students, let's examine it. Here are the ground rules regarding plagiarism:

- You cannot use another writer's exact words without using quotation marks and giving a complete citation that indicates the source of the quotation such that your reader could locate that quotation in its original context. As a general rule, taking a passage of eight or more words without citation is a violation of federal copyright laws.

- It's also not acceptable to edit or paraphrase another's words and present the revised version as your own work.

- Finally, it's not even acceptable to present another's ideas as your own—even if you use totally different words to express those ideas.

The following examples should clarify what is or is not acceptable in the use of another's work:

The Original Work:

Laws of Growth

Systems are like babies: once you get one, you have it. They don't go away. On the contrary, they display the most remarkable persistence. They not only persist; they grow. And as they grow, they encroach. The growth potential of systems was explored in a tentative, preliminary way by Parkinson, who concluded that administrative systems maintain an average growth of 5% to 6% per annum regardless of the work to be done. Parkinson was right so far as he goes, and we must give him full honors for initiating the serious study of this important topic. But what Parkinson failed to perceive, we now enunciate—the general systems analogue of Parkinson's Law.

The System Itself Tends to Grow at 5 to 6 Percent per Annum

Again, this Law is but the preliminary to the most general possible formulation, the Big-Bang Theorem of Systems Cosmology.

Systems Tend to Expand to Fill the Known Universe (Gall, 1975:12–14)

Now let's look at some of the *acceptable* ways you might make use of Gall's work in a term paper:

Acceptable: John Gall, in his work *Systemantics*, draws a humorous parallel between systems and infants: "Systems are like babies: once you get one, you have it. They don't go away. On the contrary, they display the most remarkable persistence. They not only persist; they grow."[2]

Acceptable: John Gall warns that systems are like babies. Create a system and it sticks around. Worse yet, Gall notes, systems keep growing larger and larger.[3]

Acceptable: It has also been suggested that systems have a natural tendency to persist, even grow and encroach (Gall, 1975, p. 12).

Note that the last format requires that you give a complete citation in your bibliography, as we do in this book. Complete footnotes, as shown for the first two examples, or endnotes work as well. See the publication manuals of various organizations such as the American Psychological Association or the American Sociological Association, as well as the *Chicago Manual of Style*, for appropriate citation formats.

Here now are some *unacceptable* uses of the same material, reflecting some common errors:

Unacceptable: In this paper, I want to look at some of the characteristics of the social systems we create in our organizations. First, systems are like babies: once you get one, you have it. They don't go away. On the contrary, they display the most remarkable persistence. They not only persist; they grow. [It is unacceptable to directly quote someone else's materials without using quotation marks and giving a full citation.]

Unacceptable: In this paper, I want to look at some of the characteristics of the social systems we create in our organizations. First, systems are a lot like children: once you get one, it's yours. They don't go away; they persist. They not only persist, in fact: they grow. [It is unacceptable to edit another's work and present it as your own.]

Unacceptable: In this paper, I want to look at some of the characteristics of the social systems we create in our organizations. One thing I've noticed is that once you create a system, it never seems to go away. Just the opposite, in fact: they have a tendency to grow. You might say systems are a lot like children in that respect. [It is unacceptable to paraphrase someone else's ideas and present them as your own.]

Each of the preceding unacceptable examples is an example of plagiarism and represents a serious offense. Admittedly, there are some gray areas. Some ideas are more or less in the public domain, not belonging to any one person. Or you may reach an idea on your own that someone else has already put in writing. If you have a question about a specific situation, discuss it with your instructor in advance.

We've discussed this topic in some detail because, although you must place your research in the context of what others have done and said, the improper use of their materials is a serious offense. Learning to avoid plagiarism is a part of your "coming of age" as a scholar.

» ORGANIZATION OF THE REPORT

Although the organization of reports differs somewhat in terms of form and purpose, a general format for presenting research data can be helpful. The following comments apply most directly to a journal article, but with some modification they apply to most forms of research reports as well.

Title

At this point in your education, you probably don't need to be reminded that your report should have a title. You also probably don't need to be told that your title should closely reflect the main point of your research. Deciding on the best title, however, is not always easy. You should try to give readers enough information without making it too wordy. If it is more than about a dozen words, it probably needs to be shortened. If it has a subtitle, however, it can be a bit longer. Still, it should be as terse as possible.

If possible, you may want to devise a title that is likely to pique the interest of potential readers. A catchy title may be a good idea, but be careful not to go overboard. You don't want your audience to think you are being unscholarly in hyping your report in a misleading manner. This is a judgment call. Certainly, however, the nature of the journal to which you are submitting your report should influence your choice of a title. To be on the safe side, you may want to devise several alternative tentative titles and then seek feedback from your colleagues or any coauthors you have as to their reactions to the various titles. Based on their feedback, you might use one of the titles as currently worded or modify the wording somewhat.

Abstract

Immediately after the title page (which will also list all authors, their degrees, organizational affiliations, and so on), reports will include a separate page containing an abstract that briefly summarizes the study. Different journals vary regarding the maximum length of abstracts, with most maximums falling somewhere between 75 and 150 words. Abstracts typically begin with a sentence identifying the purpose of the research. Next, there is usually a sentence or two that summarizes the main features of the research design and methodology. The main findings are then highlighted in one or two sentences, followed by a brief mention of any major implications. Here is an illustrative abstract:

A randomized experiment tested the effectiveness of adding a psychoeducational group therapy intervention to standard inpatient chemical dependency services for clients dually diagnosed with mental and substance dependence disorders. One hundred clients were randomly assigned to an experimental group and a control group. Outcome variables included drug and alcohol use, incarceration days, psychiatric symptoms, and psychiatric inpatient admissions. No significant treatment effects were found on any of the outcome variables. The tested intervention did not add to the effects of standard treatments for dually diagnosed clients. Practitioners should continue to develop and evaluate alternative treatment approaches that might prove to be more effective than the one tested in this study.

An old forensic dictum says, "Tell them what you're going to tell them; tell them; and tell them what you told them." You would do well to follow this dictum. Your abstract will tell your readers what you are going to tell them. Now let's examine the sections where you go ahead and tell them.

Introduction and Literature Review

The main narrative of your report should begin with an introduction that provides a background to the problem you have investigated. This section of your report should share some of the same features as the problems and objectives and literature review sections of your research proposal. It should, for example, convey the scope of the problem, the objectives and rationale for the study, and the study's importance. It should summarize the previous research as briefly as possible yet provide enough detail to give readers an adequate overview of the topic and to show them how your study is connected to and builds on the prior literature. The entire introductory part of your report—including your problem statement, literature review, objectives, and hypotheses—might appear under one subheading called "Introduction." Or it might be broken up under one or more additional subheadings such as "Literature Review," "Hypotheses," and so on. More important than how many sub-headings you use is whether your introductory material clearly shows the reader the objectives of your research and their rationale, why your study is timely and important, and how your study connects to and builds on the prior literature.

Your review of the literature should bring the reader up to date on the previous research in the area and should point out any general agreements or disagreements among the previous researchers. If you wish to challenge previously accepted ideas, carefully review the studies that have led to the acceptance of those ideas, then indicate the factors that have not been previously considered or the logical fallacies present in the previous research. When you're concerned with resolving a disagreement among previous researchers, you should summarize the research supporting one view, then summarize the research supporting the other, and finally suggest the reasons for the disagreement.

Your review of the literature serves a bibliographical function for readers, indexing the previous research on a given topic. This can be overdone, however, and you should avoid an opening paragraph that runs three pages, mentioning every previous study in the field. The comprehensive bibliographical function can best be served by a bibliography at the end of the report, and the review of the literature should focus only on those studies that have direct relevance to your study. Furthermore, as you focus on the most relevant studies, you should report only the most relevant aspects of those studies. Finally, if multiple studies have had similar findings, rather than discuss each study separately you might simply identify the general finding that they agreed on followed by a citation of the authorship and date of each study in parentheses.

Earlier in this chapter, we presented the box "Improving a Weak Literature Review," which illustrated the points we had made about writing the literature review section of a research proposal. That box also applies to reviewing the literature as part of the introductory material in a report of completed research.

Methods

As we've discussed throughout most of the previous chapters of this book, the worth of the findings of a study depends on the validity of the study's design and data collection procedures. Informed readers will want to read the details of your study's methodological design and execution so that they can judge the value of your findings and decide whether to be guided by them. Readers need to be provided with sufficient detail to enable them to know precisely what was done and to replicate your study.

For some studies, this section will begin with a specification of your hypotheses and variables. For other studies, you might provide that information in the preceding section, showing how your conceptual framework flows from the prior literature. In either case, your "Methods" section should describe in detail how you measured each variable and should give readers enough information to ascertain whether your measurement procedures were reliable and valid. The same sort of detail is needed regarding your data collection procedures, the logical arrangements for drawing causal inferences (if that was your study's purpose), and your sampling procedures.

In reporting the design and execution of a survey, for example, always include the following: the population, the sampling frame, the sampling method, the sample size, the data collection method, the completion rate, and the methods of data processing and analysis. Comparable details should be given if other methods are used. The experienced researcher can report these details in a rather short space without omitting anything required for the reader's evaluation of the study.

Results

Having set the study in the perspective of previous research and having described the design and execution of it, you should then present your data. The presentation of data analyses should provide a maximum of detail without being cluttered. You can accomplish this best by continually examining your report to see whether it achieves the following aims.

If you're using quantitative data, present them so the reader can recompute them. In the case of percentage tables, for example, the reader should be able to collapse categories and recompute the percentages. Readers should receive sufficient information to permit them to compute percentages in the table in the opposite direction from that of your own presentation.

Describe all aspects of a quantitative analysis in sufficient detail to permit a secondary analyst to replicate the analysis from the same body of data. This means that he or she should be able to create the same indexes and scales, produce the same tables, arrive at the same regression equations, obtain the same factors and factor loadings, and so forth. This will seldom be done, of course, but if the report allows for it, the reader will be far better equipped to evaluate the report than if it does not.

Provide details. If you're doing a qualitative analysis, you must provide enough detail that your reader has a sense of having made the observations with you. Presenting only those data that support your interpretations is not sufficient; you must also share those data that conflict with the way you've made sense of things. Ultimately, you should provide enough information that the reader might reach a different conclusion than you did—though you can hope your interpretation will make the most sense. The reader, in fact, should be in a position to replicate the entire study independently, whether it involves participant observation of people who are homeless, an experiment evaluating the effectiveness of an intervention for abused children, or any other kind of study. Recall that replicability is an essential norm of science. A single study does not prove a point; only a series of studies can begin to do so. And unless studies can be replicated, there can be no meaningful series of studies.

Integrate supporting materials. We have previously mentioned the importance of integrating data and interpretations in the report. Here is a more specific guideline for doing this. Tables, charts, and figures, if any, should be integrated into the text of the report—appearing near that portion of the text discussing them. Sometimes students (as well as authors of manuscripts submitted for publication in journals) describe their analyses in the body of the report and place all the tables in an appendix. This procedure can impede the reader, however. As a general rule, it is best to (a) describe the purpose for presenting the table, (b) present it, and (c) review and interpret it.

In published research reports, it is often best to wait until you reach your "Discussion" section, which follows the "Results" section, to present your interpretations of the implications of your results. Interpretations in the "Results" section are usually limited to explaining what the data mean in a technical, factual sense. For example, suppose you have used a relatively new and complex statistical procedure. You would probably want to briefly explain how to interpret that statistic in your "Results" section. Suppose further that your study finds that an intervention for spouse abusers appears to be effective according to the self-reports of the perpetrators but ineffective according to the reports of their spouses. You would factually report each of those findings in your "Results" section but might want to delay trying to explain the discrepancy until your "Discussion" section. On the other hand, your report might be more readable if you integrated the presentation of data, the manipulations of those data, and your interpretations into a logical whole. That is, you would do that all in one section, called "Findings," instead of having separate "Results" and "Discussion" sections. It can frustrate readers to discover a collection of seemingly unrelated analyses and findings in a "Results" section with a promise that all the loose ends will be tied together later in the report. You could prevent such frustration by explaining every step in the analysis at the time it is initially reported. In your "Findings" section, you could present your rationale for each particular analysis, present the data relevant to it, interpret the results, and then indicate where that result leads next.

Discussion and Conclusions

The narrative part of your report should conclude with a section that develops explicit conclusions, draws practical implications on the basis of those conclusions, discusses the methodological limitations of your study, and draws implications for future research.

Many studies have findings that can be interpreted in alternative ways. Reasonable people may disagree about the most appropriate interpretations and conclusions to be drawn. You should acknowledge all of the alternative interpretations that may reasonably be made of your data. Then you should identify which interpretations seem the most warranted and explain why. This is not to imply, however, that you should merely editorialize. The conclusions you draw should be warranted by your data. You should carefully note the specific basis for each conclusion. Otherwise, you may lead your reader into accepting unwarranted conclusions. Point to any qualifications or conditions warranted in the evaluation of conclusions, including the methodological limitations bearing on each conclusion. Typically, you know best the shortcomings and tentativeness of your conclusions, and you should give the reader the advantage of that knowledge.

On the basis of your conclusions, you should draw implications for social work practice or social welfare policy. Some studies may yield implications for social work education. You should also develop implications for future research on the basis of new questions emerging from your findings and perhaps also on any unanticipated practical or methodological pitfalls you encountered in conducting your study. Many journal articles end with the statement, "It is clear that much more research is needed." This conclusion is probably always true, but it has little value unless you can offer pertinent suggestions about the nature of that future research. You should review the particular shortcomings of your own study and suggest ways those shortcomings might be avoided.

Following the forensic dictum mentioned earlier, at the end of your report you may want to tell your readers what you told them. In summarizing your research report, you should avoid reviewing every specific finding, but you should review all the significant ones, pointing once more to their general significance.

References and Appendices

Immediately following the conclusion of the narrative portion of your report should be a list of all the references you cited in the report. Typically, each reference will be indicated in the narrative by putting the authors' last names and the year of publication in parentheses. For example, if we are citing the previous edition of the book you are reading, we would do this as follows: "(Rubin & Babbie, 2014)." We could also cite ourselves as follows: "Rubin and Babbie (2014) suggest that when the author's names that you are citing are a normal part of the sentence, you should just put the date in parentheses." Your list of references at the end of your report will then display each full citation in the alphabetical order of the first author's last name.

An alternative method is to just number each reference with a superscript numeral and then list each full citation in your reference list by number in the order that they appear in the text. Your decision as to which reference format to use should be based on the expectations of those to whom you will be submitting your report. In lieu of such

expectations, it's probably best to use the former method because it is used more widely.

If you have any tables, figures, or graphs that you opted not to integrate into the text of your report, these should be placed immediately after your list of references, followed by any other appendices you may have.

» ADDITIONAL CONSIDERATIONS WHEN WRITING QUALITATIVE REPORTS

Most of our foregoing comments about writing research reports apply to both quantitative and qualitative studies. We have, however, cited some of the ways in which reports of qualitative research may differ from reports of quantitative research. Let's now look at some additional considerations that apply only to qualitative reports—considerations suggested by Neuman (2000).

Because qualitative studies collect data that are harder to condense than the statistics in quantitative studies and because qualitative studies often seek to provide a deeper, empathic understanding of phenomena, qualitative reports tend to be lengthier than quantitative reports. For example, instead of providing summary statistics, qualitative reports may need to present lengthy quotes. They may need to present photographs and very detailed descriptions of the people and circumstances that have been observed. Descriptions of and justifications for less structured, less standardized, and sometimes idiosyncratic data collection methods often need to be longer in qualitative reports than in quantitative ones. More space might also be needed to explain the development of new concepts and new theory that may emerge from a qualitative study. In historical and comparative studies, many detailed footnotes may be needed to describe the sources and evidence for each conclusion. In light of all these factors, it may be difficult to meet the page limitations of many journals that are more accustomed to publishing reports of quantitative studies. Authors of lengthy qualitative reports may need to submit their studies to journals that specialize in qualitative research, such as those with the term *qualitative* in the journal title. Such authors also commonly report their research in book length form.

Whereas quantitative reports typically are written in a formal and succinct style, qualitative reports are more likely to use more creative and varied literary styles in order to convey to readers a deeper, more empathic, more subjective understanding of what it is like to walk in the shoes of the people being portrayed in the report. This is not to imply that anything goes. As we noted earlier, the conclusions being drawn in a qualitative report should be well supported by a wealth of data. Although qualitative researchers have more leeway regarding the style and organization of their reports, each conclusion they draw should be accompanied by sufficient supportive evidence collected in a plausible manner.

We will conclude with a point we mentioned earlier. Research reports should be written in the best possible style. Writing lucidly is easier for some people than for others, and it is always harder than writing poorly. You are again referred to the Strunk and White book. Every researcher would do well to follow this procedure: Write. Read Strunk and White. Revise. Reread Strunk and White. Revise again. After you are satisfied with your report, ask your colleagues to read and criticize it. Based on their criticism, revise yet again. This will be a difficult and time-consuming endeavor, but so is science.

A perfectly designed, carefully executed, and brilliantly analyzed study will be altogether worthless unless you can communicate your findings to others. We have attempted to provide some guidelines toward that end. The best guides are logic, clarity, and honesty. Ultimately, there is no substitute for practice.

MAIN POINTS

- Learn about the expectations of a funding source before preparing a research proposal to it.
- Requests for proposals (RFPs) provide information about the expectations and funding processes of potential research grant funding sources.
- The length and expectations of RFPs will vary across funding sources and depending on the amount of funding involved.
- Various websites on the Internet provide the most efficient way to find potential funding sources for research grants.

- Research grants provide much greater leeway to investigators than do research contracts.
- Before writing your research proposal, you should develop a relationship with a liaison from the funding source and examine proposals that have been funded by that source.
- Proposal components and guidelines will differ depending on the purpose of the research and the expectations of the funding source.
- Preparing a proposal for a qualitative study can be more challenging than preparing one for a quantitative study.
- Research proposals are often prefaced with a cover letter, a cover page, and an executive summary.
- Research proposals should begin with a problem and objectives section specifying exactly what is to be studied and why it is worth studying.
- An important early section of the research proposal is the literature review, which should be both thorough and terse.
- The conceptual framework section of the research proposal specifies and provides rationales for your research questions, hypotheses, variables, and operational definitions.
- The research proposal should contain methodological sections on measurement procedures, sampling procedures, design, and data collection methods.
- Additional components of research proposals often include a schedule for the various stages of the research, a budget, materials showing institutional review board approval, evidence of feasibility, and plans for dissemination of findings.
- Good social research writing begins with good writing. Write to communicate rather than to impress.
- Be mindful of your audience and your purpose in writing the report of your completed research study.
- Avoid plagiarism—that is, presenting someone else's words or thoughts as though they were your own.
- If you use someone else's exact words, be sure to use quotation marks or some other indication that you are quoting.
- If you paraphrase someone else's ideas, be sure to cite them, providing a full bibliographic citation.

- The title of your research report should be as terse as possible yet give readers enough information about the main point of your study.
- Most research reports are prefaced by an abstract summarizing the main purpose of the study, the main features of its design and methods, and the main findings and implications.
- Research reports commonly include the following sections: introduction and literature review, methods, results, discussion and conclusions, references and appendices.
- Compared to reports of quantitative research, reports of qualitative research often have more leeway as to organization and style and require more length in order to provide a deeper understanding of phenomena and to accompany each conclusion with sufficient plausible and supportive evidence.

REVIEW QUESTIONS AND EXERCISES

1. Try to obtain a copy of a funded research grant proposal and a funded research contract proposal in social work or an allied human service field. Begin by asking your instructor whether your school has a center for social work research. If it does not, perhaps individual faculty members have had funded grants or contracts that they can show you. There might also be a university-wide research center that can help you. Local or state social service agencies might also have some funded grants or contracts they can share.

   a. Describe the contrasting degrees of leeway the grant and the contract provide to the investigators.
   b. Describe the ways in which each funded proposal conforms to or deviates from the guidelines for writing research proposals and the components of research proposals discussed in this chapter.

2. Inquiring with the same resources as in exercise 1, try to obtain a copy of a research grant proposal in social work or an allied human service field that was not funded.

   a. Describe the ways in which the nonfunded proposal conforms to or deviates from the

guidelines for writing research proposals and the components of research proposals discussed in this chapter.
   b. Describe how the nonfunded proposal does or does not contain more weaknesses than the funded proposals from the standpoint of the guidelines for writing research proposals and the components of research proposals discussed in this chapter.

3. Try to obtain interviews with authors of one of the nonfunded and one of the funded proposals discussed in exercises 1 and 2. Ask them to describe their experiences in seeking funding for those proposals. Using notes from your interviews, discuss the ways in which their experiences reflect or diverge from the guidelines for writing research proposals and the components of research proposals discussed in this chapter.

INTERNET EXERCISES

1. Using one or more of the websites described in the "Finding a Funding Source" section of this chapter, find an RFP related to a social work research question. After you find the RFP, write down the research question, the funding source, the maximum size of the grants, and the types of designs the funding source has in mind.

2. Find an article whose title or abstract seems to indicate that it contains useful tips for proposal writing. Write down the bibliographical reference information for the article and summarize the article in a few sentences. Identify any tips for proposal writing that are suggested in the article that you think are particularly helpful or that you question.

3. Find two quantitative research articles related to social work. Compare and critique each from the standpoint of the guidelines for writing research reports and components of research reports described in this chapter.

4. Go to http://www.nova.edu/ssss/QR/index.html to find *The Qualitative Report*, an online journal published by Nova Southeastern University. There you can find online copies of articles reporting qualitative research studies. Read an article with a topic related to social work

research. Discuss the similarities and differences between that article and the quantitative studies you found in exercise 3 in regard to the guidelines for writing research reports and components of research reports described in this chapter.

5. Go to http://www.nova.edu/ssss/QR/QR3-1/ heath.html to find Anthony W. Heath, "The

Proposal in Qualitative Research." This article, which is in the online journal *The Qualitative Report* (vol. 3, no. 1, March 1997) provides another guide to proposal writing, this time specifically for qualitative research projects. Briefly summarize how it contrasts with guidelines for writing quantitative research proposals.

Visit CengageBrain.com for additional practice and study opportunities including experiential exercises, research tools, glossary, flashcards, and sample test items.

Using the Library

INTRODUCTION

We live in a world filled with social science research reports. Our daily newspapers, magazines, professional journals, alumni bulletins, and club newsletters—virtually everything you pick up to read—can carry reports that deal with a particular topic. For formal explorations of a topic, of course, the best place to start is still a good college or university library. Today, there are two major approaches to finding library materials: the traditional paper system and the online route. Let's begin with the online method.

ACCESSING AND EXAMINING LIBRARY MATERIALS ONLINE

Most college libraries today provide online access to periodicals, books, and other library materials. Your library's online system should allow you to see which materials are available online and whether paper copies of the materials you seek are available in your library. If your library holds those materials, the system may indicate their call numbers (indicating where in the stacks to find them), whether the books you seek have been checked out, and, if so, the due date for their return. As discussed in Chapters 2 and 7, your library may also provide a variety of Internet professional literature database services to help you search for literature online. (How to use them was discussed in Chapters 2 and 7.)

If you want to examine a book online, you can enter its title as your search term and then see an abstract of that book. Alternatively, you might enter a subject name and see a listing of all the books and articles written on that topic. You could skim through the list and indicate which ones you want to see.

GETTING HELP

When you want to find something in the library, your best friends are the reference librarians, who are specially trained to find things in the library. Some libraries have specialized reference librarians—for the social sciences, humanities, government documents, and so forth. Find the librarian who specializes in your field. Make an appointment. Tell the librarian what you're interested in. He or she will probably put you in touch with some of the many available reference sources.

REFERENCE SOURCES

You've probably heard the expression "information explosion." Your library is one of the main battlefields. Fortunately, a large number of reference volumes offer a guide to the information that's available.

- *Books in Print:* This volume lists all of the books currently in print in the United States, listed separately by author and by title. Out-of-print books often can be found in older editions of *Books in Print*.
- *Readers' Guide to Periodical Literature:* This annual volume with monthly updates lists articles published in many journals and magazines. Because the entries are organized by subject matter, this is an excellent source for organizing your reading on a particular topic.

In addition to these general reference volumes, you'll find a great variety of specialized references. Here are a few examples:

- *Social Work Abstracts*
- *Sociological Abstracts*
- *Psychological Abstracts*
- *Social Science Index*
- *Social Science Citation Index*
- *Popular Guide to Government Publications*
- *New York Times Index*
- *Facts on File*
- *Editorial Research Reports*
- *Monthly Catalog of Government Publications*
- *Public Affairs Information Service Bulletin*
- *Biography Index*
- *Congressional Quarterly Weekly Report*
- *Library Literature*
- *Bibliographic Index*

USING THE STACKS

Once you've identified the call number for a particular book in your subject area, go to the stacks, find that book, and look over the other books on the shelves near it. Because the books are arranged by subject matter, this method will help you locate relevant books you didn't know about. (A book of fiction generally carries no number and is found in alphabetical order by the author's name.)

Alternatively, you might want to go directly to the stacks and look at books in your subject area. In most libraries, books are arranged and numbered according to a subject matter classification system developed by the Library of Congress. (Some follow the Dewey decimal system.) The following is a shortened list of some Library of Congress categories:

Library of Congress Classifications (partial)

A.   General Works

B.   Philosophy, Psychology, Religion

B–BD	*Philosophy*
BF	*Psychology*
BL–BX	*Religion*

C.   History–Auxiliary Sciences

D.   History (Except America)

E–F. History (America)

E	*United States*
E51–99	*Indians of North America*

G.   Geography–Anthropology

GN	*Anthropology*

H.   Social Sciences

HB–HJ	*Economics and Business*
HM–HX	*Sociology*

J.   Political Science

K.   Law

L.   Education

M.   Music

N.   Fine Arts

P.   Language and Literature

Q.   Science

R.   Medicine

RT	*Nursing*

S.   Agriculture—Plant and Animal Industry

T.   Technology

U.   Military Science

V.   Naval Science

Z.   Bibliography and Library Science

ABSTRACTS

Some publications present summaries of books and articles that help you locate a great many references easily and effectively. These summaries, called *abstracts*, are often prepared by the original authors. As you find relevant references, you can track down the original works and see the full details. In social work, the most relevant publication of these abstracts is *Social Work Abstracts* (formerly *Social Work Research & Abstracts*).

The first step in using *Social Work Abstracts* is to look at the subject index to find general subject headings related to your specific topic of interest. Examine the subtopics listed under the relevant general headings and look for topics that appear to be most directly related to your specific topic of interest. Beside each will be one or more numbers.

Because the abstracts are presented in numerical order, you can use the listed numbers to locate the abstracts of potential interest to you. When you read the abstract, you will learn whether the study it summarizes is of sufficient likely relevance to warrant finding and reading the report in its entirety. If it is worth reading, then the abstract will provide the reference information you'll need to find the full report, as well as where you can contact its author.

Let's walk through this process. Suppose you are searching the literature for a valid scale to assess the degree of acculturation of foreign-born Chinese Americans. In using *Social Work Abstracts*, your first step would be to find a subject heading in the Subject Index that fits the focus of your search. If you looked for the heading "acculturation of foreign-born Chinese Americans," you wouldn't find it. It's too specific. But if you looked for the broader heading "Acculturation," you would find it in the alphabetized Subject Index between the two headings, "Accountability" and "Activism," as follows:

Accountability

  and Joint Reviews in England, 1083
  and school choice, 1243

Acculturation

  of Chinese Americans, 1081
  of Hispanic middle school students, 1231
  of Russian immigrants, 1430
  of West Indians, 1387

Activism

  judicial, 1366

Under the heading "Acculturation," you would find four subheadings. The first, "of Chinese Americans," is the one you would want. The number beside it refers to the number of the abstract you would want to examine. Because each issue of *Social Work Abstracts* lists the abstracts it contains in numerical order, you could just flip pages until you found the page that contains abstract number 1081.

Many of the abstracts in *Social Work Abstracts* are referenced under multiple subject headings. Suppose that instead of the heading "Acculturation," you looked for the heading "Chinese Americans." You would find it in the Subject Index between the headings "Children's services" and "Citizen participation" as follows:

Children's services

  vouchers for, 1003

Chinese Americans

  and acculturation, 1081
  psychosocial issues in working with, 1426

Citizen participation

  in advocacy for persons with disabilities, 1219

Under the heading "Chinese Americans," you would find two subheadings. The first subheading, "and acculturation," is the one you would want, and again you would be referred to abstract number 1081.

You can see the names of the article's coauthors, the title of the article, the journal in which it appeared, the volume and issue numbers of that journal, what pages the article appeared on, the date the article was published, a publication code number for that journal, an address for contacting the article's lead author, and a summary of the article.

Social Work Abstracts also provides an Author Index. Suppose you learn the name of an author who had studied the assessment of acculturation of foreign-born Chinese Americans. You could look up her name in the alphabetized Author Index and find the numbers of the abstracts of works written by that author appearing in the volume of *Social Work Abstracts* you happen to be examining. For example, if the author's name were R. Gupta, you would find abstract 1081 by examining the following section of the Author Index of the September 2002 issue of *Social Work Abstracts*:

Gumport, P. J., 1231
Gunther-Kellar, Y., 1003
Gupta, R., 1081
Gupta, R., 1398
Gurnack, A. M., 1122
Guzley, R. M., 1080
H
Hackworth, J., 1359

Gupta's name is listed twice. That's because Gupta authored two of the works abstracted in that issue of *Social Work Abstracts*. You would want to look at all of the abstracts listed for the person you look up in the Author Index; perhaps all of them would be of interest to you.

PROFESSIONAL JOURNALS

Despite the exciting advances occurring in computer-based systems and the great practical value of online database services and publications containing abstracts, you should not rely exclusively on them to locate journal articles that are pertinent to your interests. There is no guarantee that every reference of value to you will be identified in a computer search or a publication of abstracts. You should therefore augment your search by examining the tables of contents in recent issues of professional journals that are the most relevant to your particular interest. For example, if you are searching for studies on interventions for abused children, two of the various journals you may want to examine are *Child Welfare* and *Children and Youth Services Review*.

Examining recent issues of journals is less time consuming than you might imagine. These issues ought to be available in the section of your library that contains unbound current periodicals. Once you locate the recent issues of the relevant journals (the last 2 years or so ought to suffice), it should take only a few minutes to thumb through the tables of contents looking for titles that have some potential bearing on your topic. Once you spot a relevant title, turn to the page on which the article begins. There you will find an abstract of the article; just like the abstracts that appear in publications of abstracts, this one should take only seconds to read and will help you determine if the article is pertinent enough to warrant reading in greater detail.

Your examination of relevant journals can be expedited if your library offers an online service listing the tables of contents of thousands of journals. It might also provide a list of *online journals*—journals whose entire contents can be downloaded and read online.

If you are uncertain about the professional journals that are pertinent to your topic, you might want to examine the list of journals reviewed in several issues of *Social Work Abstracts*. Each issue contains a list of the journals that have been reviewed for that issue. You might also want to get help with this from your reference librarian. Just to start you thinking about some of the journals you might review, here's a beginning list of some of the major journals related to social work, by subject area:

Aging and the Aged

Abstracts in Social Gerontology
Canadian Journal of Aging

Clinical Gerontologist
International Journal of Aging and Human Development
Journal of Aging & Physical Activity
Journal of Aging & Social Policy
Journal of Aging Studies
Journal of Applied Gerontology
Journal of Elder Abuse & Neglect
Journal of Gerontological Social Work
Journal of Gerontology
Journal of Hosing for the Elderly
Journal of Nutrition for the Elderly
Journal of Nutrition, Health and Aging
Journal of Social Work in Long-Term Care
Journal of Women and Aging
Psychology & Aging
Quality in Aging: Policy, Practice, & Research in Social Work
The Gerontologist

Children and Adolescents

Adolescence
Child & Adolescent Social Work Journal
Children & Society
Child & Youth Services
Children and Youth Services Review
Children Today
International Journal of Adolescence & Youth
Journal of Adolescence
Journal of Adolescent & Interpersonal Violence & Trauma
Journal of Child & Adolescent Trauma
Journal of Children & Poverty
Journal of Youth & Adolescence
Residential Treatment for Children & Youth

Child Welfare

Adoption and Fostering
Adoption Quarterly
Child Abuse & Neglect
Child Care Quarterly
Child Maltreatment
Child Survivor of Traumatic Stress
Child Welfare
Family Preservation Journal
Journal of Child Abuse & the Law
Journal of Child Custody
Journal of Child Sexual Abuse

Cognitive or Behavioral Interventions

Behavior Modification
Behavior Research & Therapy

Behavior Therapy
Behavioural & Cognitive Psychotherapy
Child & Family Behavior Therapy
Cognitive & Behavioral Practice
Cognitive Therapy and Research
Journal of Applied Behavior Analysis

Communities

Community Development Journal
Journal of Community and Applied Social
*   Psychology*
Journal of Community Practice
Journal of Jewish Communal Service
Journal of Prevention & Intervention in the
*   Community*
Journal of Social Development in Africa

Crime and Delinquency

Canadian Journal of Criminology
Crime and Delinquency
Journal of Offender Rehabilitation
Journal of Research in Crime & Delinquency
Youth and Society
Youth Violence & Juvenile Justice

Cultural Diversity

Cultural Diversity & Ethnic Minority
*   Psychology*
Hispanic Journal of the Behavioral Sciences
Journal of Black Studies
Journal of Ethnic & Cultural Diversity in
*   Social Work*
Journal of Ethnicity in Substance Abuse
Journal of Immigrant & Refugee Studies

Domestic Violence or Trauma

Family Violence & Sexual Assault Bulletin
Journal of Aggression, Maltreatment &
*   Trauma*
Journal of Emotional Abuse
Journal of Family Violence
Journal of Interpersonal Violence
Journal of Threat Assessment
Journal of Trauma & Dissociation
Journal of Traumatic Stress
Sexual Abuse: A Journal of Research &
*   Treatment*
Stress, Trauma & Crisis
Trauma, Violence & Abuse
Traumatology
Violence Against Women
Violence & Victims

Families

American Journal of Family Therapy
Child & Family Social Work
Conflict Resolution Quarterly
Contemporary Family Therapy
Families in Society
Family Process
Family Relations
Family Therapy
Family Therapy Networker
Journal of Child & Family Studies
Journal of Divorce & Remarriage
Journal of Family Issues
Journal of Family Psychotherapy
Journal of Family Psychology
Journal of Family Therapy
Journal of Family Social Work
Journal of Marital and Family Therapy
Journal of Marriage & the Family
Journal of Sex & Marital Therapy
Marriage & Family Review

Gay, Lesbian, and Transgender Issues and Sexuality

Journal of Bisexuality
Journal of Gay & Lesbian Social Services
Journal of Gay & Lesbian Psychotherapy
Journal of Homosexuality
Journal of Lesbian Studies
Journal of Psychology & Human Sexuality
Sexuality Research & Social Policy

Group Work

Group Dynamics—Theory, Research, and
*   Practice*
Journal for Specialists in Group Work
Social Work with Groups

Health

AIDS & Public Policy Journal
Health and Social Work
Home Health Care Services Quarterly
Hospice Journal
Journal of Behavioral Health Services &
*   Research*
Journal of Health and Social Behavior
Journal of Health & Social Policy
Journal of HIV/AIDS Prevention & Education
Journal of HIV/AIDS & Social Services
Journal of Home Health Care Practice
Journal of Nephrology Social Work
Journal of Occupational Health Psychology

Journal of Psychosocial Oncology
*Journal of Social Work in Disability &
    Rehabilitation*
*Journal of Social Work in Hospice &
    Palliative Care*
Journal of Workplace & Behavioral Health
Social Work in Health Care
Social Work in Public Health

Mental Health

American Journal of Orthopsychiatry
American Journal of Psychotherapy
Archives of General Psychiatry
Clinical Social Work Journal
Community Mental Health
Journal Evidence-Based Mental Health
*Journal of Psychotherapy Practice and
    Research*
Mental Health Services Research
NAMI Advocate
Psychiatric Rehabilitation Journal
Psychoanalytic Social Work
Psychotherapy Networker
Psychotherapy Research
Schizophrenia Bulletin
Social Work in Mental Health

Mental Retardation

American Journal of Mental Deficiency
Journal of Mental Deficiency Research
*Mental Retardation & Developmental
Disabilities Research Reviews*
Retardation

Program Evaluation

Canadian Journal of Program Evaluation
Evaluation
Evaluation Review
New Directions for Evaluation
The American Journal of Evaluation

Qualitative Research

Grounded Theory Review
Qualitative Health Research
Qualitative Inquiry
Qualitative Research
Qualitative Social Work: Research and Practice
Qualitative Sociology

School Social Work

Children & Schools
Journal of School Violence

School Social Work Journal
Social Work in Education

Social Policy

Analyses of Social Issues & Public Policy
Australian Social Policy
Critical Social Policy
Global Social Policy
International Journal of Social Welfare
Journal of Aging & Social Policy
Journal of Children and Poverty
Journal of European Social Policy
Journal of Health & Social Policy
*Journal of Mental Health Policy and
    Economics*
Journal of Policy Analysis & Management
Journal of Policy Practice
Journal of Poverty
Journal of Social Distress and the Homeless
Journal of Sociology and Social Welfare
Policy & Practice of Public Human Service
Public Welfare
Social Policy
Social Policy & Society
Social Policy and Social Work
Social Policy Review
Social Work & Society
Urban Policy and Research

Social Work Research

Journal of Social Service Research
*Journal of Social Work Research and
    Evaluation*
*Journal of the Society for Social Work &
    Research*
Research on Social Work Practice
Social Work Research

Social Work (General)

Advances in Social Work
Australian Social Work
British Journal of Social Work
Canadian Social Work Review
Electronic Journal of Social Work
International Social Work
Irish Social Work
Journal of Baccalaureate Social Work
Journal of Evidence-Based Social Work
Journal of Social Work Practice
Smith College Studies in Social Work
Social Service Review
Social Work

Social Work Abstracts
The European Journal of Social Work
The Hong Kong Journal of Social Work

Spirituality and Religion

Journal of Religion & Abuse
*Journal of Religion & Spirituality in
Social Work*
Social Work & Christianity

Substance Abuse

Advances in Alcohol and Substance Abuse
Alcoholism Treatment Quarterly
American Journal of Drug and Alcohol Abuse
International Journal of the Addictions
Journal of Addictions & Offender Counseling
Journal of Addictive Diseases
Journal of Chemical Dependency Treatment
*Journal of Child & Adolescent Substance
Abuse*
Journal of Drug Education
Journal of Drug Issues
Journal of Ethnicity in Substance Abuse
Journal of Psychoactive Drugs
*Journal of Social Work Practice in the
Addictions*
Journal of Studies on Alcohol
Journal of Substance Abuse Treatment
Substance Abuse

Women's Issues

Affilia
Archives of Women's Mental Health
Australian Feminist Studies
European Journal of Women's Studies
Feminism & Psychology

Feminist Theory
Gender & Society
Indian Journal of Gender Studies
Journal of Feminist Family Therapy
Violence Against Women
Women & Criminal Justice
Women & Trauma

Other

Administration in Social Work
Journal of Applied Behavioral Science
Journal of Forensic Social Work
*Journal of Human Behavior in the Social
Environment*
Journal of Progressive Human Services
Journal of Technology in Human Services
Nonprofit and Voluntary Sector Quarterly
Rural Social Work
Social Work & Social Sciences Review

No matter what approach you take to finding library materials, chances are there will be some documents you miss or that are not available in your library or online. If a document is not available at your particular library or via the web, then you can request an interlibrary loan, which is often free. Many libraries have loan agreements, but it might take some time before the document you need arrives at your library. If the document is located at another library nearby, then you may want to go there yourself to get it directly. The key to a good library search is to become well informed, so remember what we said earlier: *When you want to find something in the library, your best friends are the reference librarians.* Don't be shy about seeking their assistance at various points in your search.

APPENDIX B

Statistics for Estimating Sampling Error

In Chapter 15, we noted that probability theory provides a statistical basis for estimating sampling error and selecting a sample size with an acceptable amount of likely sampling error. We also referred you to this appendix if you wished to examine the more mathematical aspects of how probability theory works. Probability theory enables us to estimate sampling error by way of the concept of sampling distributions. A single sample selected from a population will give an estimate of the population parameter. Other samples would give the same or slightly different estimates. Probability theory tells us about the distribution of estimates that would be produced by a large number of such samples. To see how this works, we'll look at two examples of sampling distributions, beginning with a simple example in which our population consists of just 10 cases.

THE SAMPLING DISTRIBUTION OF 10 CASES

Suppose 10 people are in a group, and each person has a certain amount of money in his or her pocket. To simplify, let's assume that one person has no money, another has one dollar, another has two dollars, and so forth up to the person with nine dollars. Figure B-1 presents the population of 10 people.

Our task is to determine the average amount of money one person has—specifically, the mean number of dollars. If you simply add the money in Figure B-1, you'll find that the total is $45, so the mean is $4.50. Our purpose in the rest of this exercise is to estimate that mean without actually observing all 10 individuals. We'll do that by selecting random samples from the population and using the means

of those samples to estimate the mean of the whole population.

To start, suppose we were to select—at random—a sample of only one person from the 10. Depending on which person we selected, we would estimate the group's mean as anywhere from $0 to $9. Figure B-2

FIGURE B.1 Population of 10 People with $0 to $9

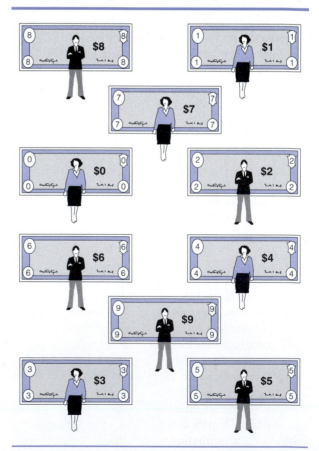

FIGURE B.2   The Sampling Distribution of Samples of 1

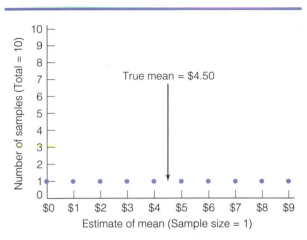

Estimate of mean (Sample size = 1)

FIGURE B.3   The Sampling Distribution of Samples of 2

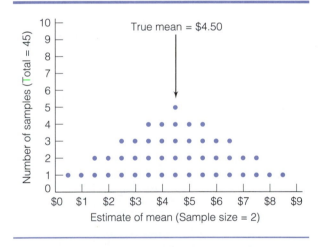

Estimate of mean (Sample size = 2)

displays those 10 possible samples. The 10 dots shown on the graph represent the 10 "sample" means we would get as estimates of the population. The dots' distribution on the graph is called the *sampling distribution*. Obviously, selecting a sample of only one would not be a good idea because we stand a strong chance of missing the true mean of $4.50 by quite a bit.

But what if we take samples of two each? As you can see from Figure B-3, increasing the sample size improves our estimations. We now have 45 possible samples: [$0 $1], [$0 $2], … [$7 $8], [$8 $9]. Moreover, some of those samples produce the same

means. For example, [$0 $6], [$1 $5], and [$2 $4] all produce means of $3. In Figure B-3, the three dots shown above the $3 mean represent those three samples.

The 45 sample means are not evenly distributed, as you can see. Rather, they are somewhat clustered around the true value of $4.50. Only two samples deviate by as much as $4 from the true value ([$0 $1] and [$8 $9]), whereas five of the samples would give the true estimate of $4.50; another eight samples miss the mark by only 50 cents (plus or minus).

Now suppose we select even larger samples. What do you suppose that will do to our estimates of the mean? Figure B-4 presents the sampling distributions of samples of 3, 4, 5, and 6.

The progression of sampling distributions is clear. Every increase in sample size improves the distribution of estimates of the mean. The limiting case in this procedure, of course, is to select a sample of 10: Only one sample of that size is possible—everyone—and it would give us the true mean of $4.50. As we will see shortly, this principle applies to actual sampling of meaningful populations. The larger the sample selected, the more accurate it is as an estimation of the population from which it was drawn.

SAMPLING DISTRIBUTION AND ESTIMATES OF SAMPLING ERROR

Let's turn now to a more realistic sampling situation and see how the notion of sampling distribution applies, using a simple example that involves a population much larger than 10. Let's assume for the moment that we wish to study the adult population of a small town in a rural region. We want to determine whether residents would approve or disapprove of the establishment there of a community-based residential facility for formerly institutionalized, chronically mentally disabled individuals. The study population will be that aggregation of, say, 20,000 adults as identified in the city directory: the sampling frame. (As we discussed in Chapter 15, sampling frames are the lists of elements from which a sample is selected.) The elements will be the town's adult residents. The variable under consideration will be attitudes toward the facility; it is a binomial variable—*approve* and *disapprove*. (The logic of probability sampling applies to the examination of other types of variables, such as mean income, but the

FIGURE B.4 The Sampling Distributions of Samples of 3, 4, 5, and 6

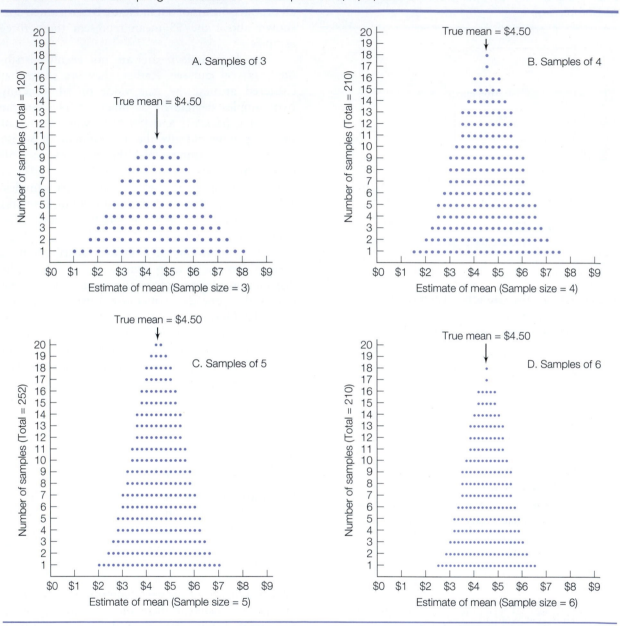

computations are somewhat more complicated. Consequently, this introduction focuses on binomials.) We'll select a random sample of, say, 100 residents to estimate the entire population of the town.

The horizontal axis of Figure B-5 presents all possible values of this parameter in the population—from 0% approval to 100% approval. The midpoint of the axis—50%—represents one-half the residents approving the facility and the other half disapproving.

To choose our sample, we give each resident in the directory a number and select 100 random numbers either online or from a table of random numbers. To do it online, simply enter a search term like *random number generator*, and a variety of links will appear that will let you enter the possible range of random numbers you want and how many you want to select from that range. Then it will choose them randomly for you. If you prefer the old-fashioned way, you can use a table of random

FIGURE B.5 Range of Possible Sample Study Results

Percent of residents approving of the facility

numbers, such as the one in Table B-1, which is explained in the box "Using a Table of Random Numbers."

Then we interview the 100 residents whose numbers have been selected and ask for their attitudes toward the facility: whether they approve or disapprove. Suppose this operation gives us 48 residents who approve of the facility and 52 who disapprove. This summary description of a variable in a sample is called a statistic. We present this statistic by placing a dot on the *x*-axis at the point that represents 48%.

Now let's suppose we select another sample of 100 residents in exactly the same fashion and measure their approval or disapproval of the facility. Perhaps 51 residents in the second sample approve of the facility. We place another dot in the appropriate place on the *x*-axis. Repeating this process once more, we may discover that 52 residents in the third sample approve of the facility.

USING A TABLE OF RANDOM NUMBERS

Suppose you want to select a simple random sample of 100 people (or other units) out of a population totaling 980.

1. To begin, number the members of the population in this case, from 1 to 980. Now the problem is to select 100 random numbers. Once you've done that, your sample will consist of the people having the numbers you've selected. (*Note:* It's not essential to actually number them, as long as you're sure of the total. If you have them in a list, for example, you can always count through the list after you've selected the numbers.)

2. The next step is to determine the number of digits you will need in the random numbers you select. In our example, there are 980 members of the population, so you will need three-digit numbers to give everyone a chance of selection. (If there were 11,825 members of the population, you would need to select five-digit numbers.) Thus, we want to select 100 random numbers in the range from 001 to 980.

3. Now turn to the first page of Table B-1, the table of random numbers. Notice there are several rows and columns of five-digit numbers, and there are two pages. The table represents a series of random numbers in the range from 00001 to 99999. To use the table for your hypothetical sample, you have to answer these questions:

   a. How will you create three-digit numbers out of five-digit numbers?

   b. What pattern will you follow in moving through the table to select your numbers?

   c. Where will you start?

Each of these questions has several satisfactory answers. The key is to create a plan and follow it. Here's an example.

4. To create three-digit numbers from five-digit numbers, let's agree to select five-digit numbers from the table but consider only the left-most three digits in each case. If we picked the first number on the first page—51426—we would only consider the 514. (We could agree to take the digits furthest to the right, 426, or the middle three digits, 142, and any of these plans would work.) The key is to make a plan and stick with it. For convenience, let's use the left-most three digits.

5. We can also choose to progress through the table any way we want: down the columns, up them, across to the right or to the left, or diagonally. Again, any of these plans will work just fine as long as we stick to it. For convenience, let's agree to move down the columns. When we get to the bottom of one column, we'll go to the top of the next; when we exhaust a given page, we'll start at the top of the first column of the next page.

6. Now, where do we start? You can close your eyes and stick a pencil into the table and start wherever the pencil point lands. (We know it doesn't sound scientific, but it works.) Or, if you're afraid you'll hurt the book or miss it altogether, close your

eyes and make up a column number and a row number. ("I'll pick the number in the fifth row of column 2.") Start with that number. If you prefer more methodological purity, you might use the first two numbers on a dollar bill, which are randomly distributed, to determine the row and column on which to start.

7. Let's suppose we decide to start with the fifth number in column 2. If you look on the first page of the table, you'll see that the starting number is 22930. We have selected 229 as our first random number, and we have 99 more to go. Moving down the second column, we select 095, 333, 134, 369, 448, 707, 315, 943, and so forth. At the bottom of column 2, we select number 173 and continue to the top of column 3: 135, 361, and so on.

8. See how easy it is? But trouble lies ahead. When we reach column 5, we are speeding along, selecting 139, 117, 736, 858, 988.... Wait a minute! There are only 980 students in the senior class. How can we pick number 988? The solution is simple: ignore it. Any time you come across a number that lies outside your range, skip it and continue on your way: 551, 177, and so forth. The same solution applies if the same number comes up more than once. If you select 229 again, for example, just ignore it the second time.

9. That's it. You keep up the procedure until you've selected 100 random numbers. Returning to your list, your sample consists of person number 229, person number 95, person number 333, and so forth.

TABLE B.1 Random Numbers

51426	00609	13501	16557	13914	33401	84598	16256	51886	31407	94431	10793	10437	65142
50202	20368	36181	05719	11720	47252	68129	97583	78197	64506	96094	15565	54451	10894
68568	00811	38612	96130	76686	98080	22397	65709	66476	29072	47294	95575	92207	31912
43803	59549	54997	72125	73689	20448	09636	54932	10780	46568	93704	35864	19104	72771
99389	22930	38246	01741	85862	35913	68450	51989	87203	22966	39965	23689	94496	90819
40012	09599	48287	56312	98800	21764	69339	39265	38708	24879	89908	65194	11479	38897
46202	33334	78502	63224	55138	65208	52970	75762	52422	01538	12774	62448	83373	48356
92106	13420	52252	75044	17710	30572	64791	02170	58265	23490	39625	51822	13088	79273
55478	36951	81131	16564	75192	83624	19837	64199	17127	04287	89202	12485	27127	54445
95888	44841	62382	80884	41749	80051	89305	29619	46255	19437	42118	56365	19354	21687
63752	70740	30727	98221	04142	43663	93794	20051	29352	38160	07908	65877	90653	28600
39706	31586	36108	21662	71438	12980	39471	95774	86372	03985	78977	26533	16177	19726
70394	94351	22457	26801	66505	05939	35468	29290	83141	69893	35443	64588	98379	40997
24328	66613	72883	35679	11468	49960	10713	06650	94072	47238	49989	40700	04282	37164
19300	45923	02358	27187	53193	40040	94551	16006	44819	04925	36322	81318	07767	09898
75264	17274	99313	09819	74081	47019	83766	11652	61463	20523	17156	15633	56306	65756
61801	25803	99036	74158	25691	61586	22711	80610	53411	84833	38944	31905	05475	69018
51217	44878	35559	55558	54991	12802	24869	45978	50192	21129	97197	15798	16251	68202
80240	54443	82312	97509	57848	83730	69741	43918	99146	09401	55696	17022	23857	14574
52058	89814	64024	29716	72872	59060	68771	66883	08409	85650	85535	85659	93365	43147
28459	18054	31177	77817	73215	55952	59266	30908	26528	81941	94064	52738	85015	99236
61246	56005	30027	95365	51401	72313	43067	14424	25467	47268	63945	27477	15643	73537
64100	53865	24106	70497	98741	91230	49381	16109	15636	16555	99646	78224	43983	48557
86649	17968	99209	86506	51521	34845	47716	61783	72090	15828	93790	29199	85979	59513
25994	32188	15125	28244	35374	82169	98415	27443	10709	21036	77242	12126	15384	10038
91142	68443	71595	87285	77954	46246	43484	93725	57598	33343	37333	37216	86209	29308
85900	89177	35463	37290	65502	75996	60430	40129	97891	48432	96420	61864	34334	06783
80799	23668	67958	69297	12726	35953	57968	43241	47098	03344	84356	86620	93556	51283
96429	41318	94091	36041	27081	80307	38085	84416	35484	07293	45607	36954	91408	51122
47970	10032	89346	10458	18396	93085	25303	83518	68633	32246	82215	28022	67577	97594
72469	59185	78412	11529	26258	21622	18997	52703	26386	56264	80550	46328	47601	89508
67758	71528	75788	42499	19816	16366	01923	29047	00929	72309	21973	59609	53886	34762
98899	22430	75503	56128	21692	97528	24181	20498	78282	66143	54062	79651	73197	30479
12783	48846	49102	17462	24321	78119	98103	68108	13053	91442	04370	84795	34596	15559
46012	45951	87514	80718	57246	91049	95869	90799	78772	46759	29270	28549	11024	77259
03802	82683	41036	11652	53416	61231	51368	23180	62110	23975	32641	67415	34552	87859
15233	04412	14981	76133	77223	44150	22899	49528	36601	97438	29735	27053	12035	81149
29038	70437	05264	30181	36015	94583	16736	28591	20148	53382	09045	50572	99809	63712
02961	30256	34194	34334	11052	23123	88313	51754	07802	41996	03053	38116	24801	64168
35986	08834	25394	26990	57065	63223	13898	33035	84740	44562	13701	25133	55081	40397

(Continues)

71900	93567	50485	95879	67273	87232	94444	09030	08914	04127	36022	54394	80624	60780
71636	79416	04009	04816	81154	31183	30180	19287	18649	76657	81725	94613	62678	32329
28010	26202	02931	81693	11016	37412	18796	20687	28658	13534	44323	16054	76065	48823
03870	02084	34849	43767	18860	01671	06733	05498	10132	04989	39545	72690	81462	75170
31477	68171	64406	09515	29907	72703	75049	61420	90245	41068	12575	93035	18373	73411
25614	54466	03882	67569	13505	02072	52211	58587	81052	77367	91151	75498	52612	77712
74941	42963	28344	64694	97337	34082	88194	13248	23073	83715	70668	43871	03296	32279
08517	09792	30412	82657	38555	79673	27647	18285	78424	42930	61875	25523	84968	65998
90480	10239	61101	84024	52762	99826	31814	59060	02842	76857	99268	73679	15476	92050
87847	84094	41958	29071	08573	15421	62826	33761	65766	17441	77041	30304	41012	21646
24391	94530	09143	27232	36091	34644	94255	13645	37154	30047	47498	55516	38359	79844
55283	62245	40637	76395	50206	98347	69760	95167	58415	19706	60279	21390	48122	87803
72589	45685	38527	12482	28532	14584	00017	71969	72628	46885	88039	29798	87566	42624
74982	12483	10512	26011	41648	52838	87777	39674	39136	25753	19433	84394	91015	56247
11886	35640	93381	21030	90738	44326	01786	81989	17993	03289	82912	96744	68234	98726
03777	40789	53138	84902	65517	67119	43016	45594	99378	26264	86455	41026	59843	91783
77434	88814	80202	35045	23861	66976	34547	62509	17306	39141	95877	56427	51271	21327
24031	79905	97125	99910	02012	98644	44131	90151	37559	85274	85888	83933	00595	05395
61411	26229	47339	39764	06203	89006	52147	66580	97816	46291	64695	19294	48456	65158
67605	28722	84993	40213	74203	17588	67884	65144	46757	76731	91814	82825	14921	09640
08399	54673	57424	52049	10022	80280	31618	30265	07223	01091	16857	12886	52200	25183
24661	01155	82608	14475	34709	18864	24666	80520	83407	31450	76563	13025	29970	71077
99946	90982	42196	89827	77686	97350	53420	85961	58836	63948	45483	41791	61909	92707
20479	03337	72012	68631	05734	66688	47879	27971	81284	71171	11497	16424	05229	33760
05878	82649	94108	04121	11154	97428	28550	50033	58366	16488	91552	31099	07497	37391
26765	43188	54789	34860	18404	87493	45808	69413	63670	65165	56961	36021	59176	45006
15069	48616	94053	66582	03240	19418	03006	92491	49077	15557	01484	40976	06847	95247
68642	49316	36286	17395	96578	75722	19864	04578	84155	99469	51186	12091	83697	21341
55787	36896	06645	76602	81478	47159	93149	92944	83403	35955	27043	82757	10447	95157
06646	80150	16643	42758	51005	50512	14497	88500	99547	95014	19788	52496	45661	82747
66780	49368	50975	19424	95851	61634	25554	87257	85018	02944	12394	02527	88003	77793
88208	75978	21467	13547	96535	86968	67281	08110	53381	54810	43583	96063	95300	86188
30356	70518	23955	20891	79713	56715	83046	79108	04521	41114	57848	31624	78945	25332
36986	65744	62601	56588	87171	27663	30679	25292	79814	97617	53606	77353	73868	87559
06312	95954	66193	09065	21998	34974	45725	00429	27951	58058	53538	71743	52870	53884
22033	94983	28160	08825	24088	23067	37465	08067	87338	13078	89357	05941	05270	82129
30452	89567	71981	33583	28892	18855	58394	39515	86250	42349	00832	41061	99545	26312
87612	59785	04514	02606	69365	28933	42218	91714	27058	40027	09691	54653	57232	56866
51590	24073	86172	55704	96959	73360	17055	66148	08078	20372	36932	71432	62588	72328
57163	99264	22454	55588	78458	91353	27547	27991	19627	63115	63099	59856	74653	69930
48780	80362	32025	83247	38147	91095	96062	50857	55831	62380	29003	80076	22990	60988
98912	00813	03183	15462	72115	02817	32788	30368	34305	07644	56157	65898	18561	37797
39402	14014	30652	27732	93899	78595	31964	36084	97566	34682	72458	98496	77969	14661
03842	24891	56006	26115	48801	26504	77741	82048	19748	83084	35668	23498	83585	31927
75596	26192	94550	45662	62572	34149	13402	85687	24250	65416	45033	48814	17003	76631
03591	98982	17722	51727	71369	62706	32211	09130	80850	19401	70052	37468	63436	82305
90888	86243	39999	02703	47268	00308	85152	09997	19070	04917	24351	48171	78505	66626
08573	24734	09760	51974	95354	16357	15969	12817	61896	31250	80066	38064	24088	98685
70629	30816	81429	71243	93048	43257	81387	95825	93165	20492	55200	56831	91286	79550
97402	96506	80817	15478	27808	04941	37273	69213	36638	85812	47422	16816	61468	53373
27250	03388	28225	96621	44165	59379	29178	87172	79478	58092	17710	63104	60684	97932
65971	48407	61392	11205	21776	03233	27068	46038	92918	25029	31686	15337	82092	17198
94424	24776	37573	52605	58251	42114	51162	20341	21685	79477	41030	33130	89819	35592
67035	34237	80576	98987	86458	05605	65635	39528	30420	75826	89077	50686	49972	97172
26583	89285	05050	72244	74086	97706	65120	16301	67917	21787	51785	59042	87324	30893
43684	96716	85263	40147	12867	00177	74088	19076	22915	72550	04976	52557	22961	71430
58977	02675	44573	43331	58957	22473	30080	35672	41973	70946	13049	35109	15024	45136
09507	92785	19629	14846	08127	93307	95036	78313	52446	01067	51465	62061	36698	04085
01738	05229	77024	21950	74783	42771	76450	63057	61615	34045	30701	18141	04768	00347
13403	24248	37469	17695	29452	29346	96446	72124	08531	06716	03668	98751	47708	03926
47813	95237	28518	84809	79497	25096	62922	86883	98553	32668	23650	12537	73446	80052
32411	26508	55034	61179	95124	83411	36322	87567	78589	69819	54656	09644	02350	65753
90886	05927	51880	67581	39310	01761	37345	36425	12883	77970	06829	65588	31084	04563
19712	56193	05978	74167	03347	36293	18145	39273	41897	64083	35547	67152	06188	94961
38191	90572	51923	10301	36802	90114	81194	55254	80329	49383	44090	15160	34222	23886
82520	77570	64671	06575	01907	54598	75591	12631	16676	49430	24133	66462	41574	16974
35050	44842	31469	43533	39343	79219	21618	89864	47156	13642	10654	88072	01650	18002
41269	69507	96835	61976	91903	54412	56619	65650	22130	25349	54952	08277	24992	53833
63840	22761	16566	18174	17073	15678	06395	72369	23714	69974	12838	71230	73589	55864
48616	17356	68349	30107	18604	60016	36241	30883	10979	28281	92015	73791	68528	54736

FIGURE B.6 Results Produced by Three Hypothetical Studies

FIGURE B.7 The Sampling Distribution

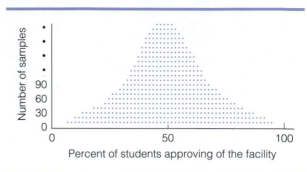

Figure B-6 presents the three different sample statistics that represent the percentages of residents in each of the three random samples who approved of the facility. The basic rule of random sampling is that such samples drawn from a population give estimates of the parameter that pertains in the total population. Each random sample, then, gives us an estimate of the percentage of residents in the town population who approve of the facility. Unhappily, however, we have selected three samples and now have three separate estimates.

To resolve this dilemma, let's draw more and more samples of 100 residents each, question each sample about its approval or disapproval of the facility, and plot the new sample statistics on our summary graph. In drawing many such samples, we discover that some of the new samples provide duplicate estimates, as in Figures B-3 and B-4 for the previous example with a population of 10 cases. Figure B-7 shows the sampling distribution of, say, hundreds of samples. This is often referred to as a *normal curve*.

Note that by increasing the number of samples selected and interviewed, we have also increased the range of estimates that are provided by the sampling operation. In one sense, we have increased our dilemma in attempting to guess the parameter in the population. Probability theory, however, provides certain important rules about the sampling distribution in Figure B-7.

First, if many independent random samples are selected from a population, then the sample statistics provided by those samples will be distributed around the population parameter in a known way. Thus, although Figure B-7 shows a wide range of estimates, more of them are in the vicinity of 50% than elsewhere in the graph. Probability theory tells us, then, that the true value is in the vicinity of 50%.

Second, probability theory gives us a formula for estimating how closely the sample statistics are clustered around the true value. To put it another

way, probability theory enables us to estimate the sampling error—the degree of error to be expected for a given sample design. This formula contains three factors: the parameter, the sample size, and the standard error (a measure of sampling error):

The symbols P and Q in the formula equal the population parameters for the binomial: If 60% of the residents approve of the facility and 40% disapprove, then P and Q are 60% and 40%, respectively, or .6 and .4. Note that $Q = 1 - P$ and $P = 1 - Q$. The symbol n equals the number of cases in each sample, and s is the standard error.

Let's assume that the population parameter in the hypothetical small town is 50% approving of the facility and 50% disapproving. Recall that we have been selecting samples of 100 cases each. When these numbers are put into the formula, we find that the standard error equals .05, or 5%. In probability theory, the standard error is a valuable piece of information because it indicates the extent to which the sample estimates will be distributed around the population parameter. If you are familiar with the standard deviation in statistics, you may recognize that the standard error in this case is the standard deviation of the sampling distribution. (We discussed the meaning of the standard deviation in Chapter 21.)

Specifically, probability theory indicates that certain proportions of the sample estimates will fall within specified increments—each equal to one standard error—from the population parameter. Approximately 34% (.3413) of the sample estimates will fall within one standard error increment above the population parameter, and another 34% will fall within one standard error below the parameter. In our example, the standard error increment is 5%, so we know that 34% of our samples will give estimates of resident approval between 50% (the parameter) and 55% (one standard error above); another 34% of the samples will give estimates between 50% and 45% (one standard error below the parameter). Taken together, then, we know that roughly two-thirds (68%) of the samples will give estimates within 65% of the parameter.

Moreover, probability theory dictates that roughly 95% of the samples will fall within plus or minus two standard errors of the true value and that 99.9% of the samples will fall within plus or minus three standard errors. In our current example, then, we know that only one sample out of a thousand would give an estimate lower than 35% approval or higher than 65%. Figure B-8 graphically illustrates a normal (bell-shaped) curve with the standard deviation proportions that apply to any normal curve. The normal curve represents the sampling distribution—how an infinite number of randomly drawn samples would be distributed. The mean of the curve is the true population parameter.

The proportion of samples that fall within one, two, or three standard errors of the population parameter is constant for any random sampling procedure such as the one just described—if a large number of samples are selected. The size of the standard error in any given case, however, is a function of the population parameter and the sample size. If we return to the formula for a moment, we note that the standard error will increase as a function of an increase in the quantity P times Q. Note further that this quantity reaches its maximum in the situation of an even split in the population:

$$If\ P = .5, PQ = .25$$
$$If\ P = .6, PQ = .24$$
$$If\ P = .8, PQ = .16$$
$$If\ P = .99, PQ = .0099$$

By extension, if P is either 0.0 or 1.0 (either 0% or 100% approve of the facility), then the standard error will be zero. If everyone in the population has the same attitude (no variation), then every sample will give exactly that estimate.

The standard error is also a function of the sample size—and an inverse function. As the sample size increases, the standard error decreases. As the sample size increases, the several samples will cluster closer to the true value. Another rule of thumb is evident in the formula: Because of the square root formula, the standard error is reduced by half if the sample size quadruples. In our current example,

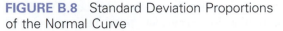

FIGURE B.8 Standard Deviation Proportions of the Normal Curve

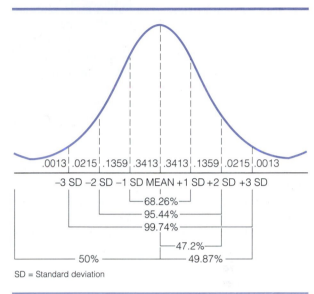

SD = Standard deviation

samples of 100 produce a standard error of 5%; to reduce the standard error to 2.5%, we must increase the sample size to 400.

All of this information is provided by established probability theory as it relates to the selection of large numbers of random samples. (If you've taken a statistics course, you may know this as the *central tendency theorem*.) If the population parameter is known and a large number of random samples are selected, then we can predict how many of the sample estimates will fall within specified intervals from the parameter. Be clear that this discussion illustrates only the logic of probability sampling and does not describe the way research is actually conducted. Usually, we do not know the parameter: We conduct a sample survey to estimate that value. Moreover, we don't actually select large numbers of samples: We select only one sample. Nevertheless, the preceding discussion of probability theory provides the basis for inferences about the typical social research situation. Knowing what it would be like to select thousands of samples allows us to make assumptions about the one sample we do select and study.

CONFIDENCE LEVELS AND CONFIDENCE INTERVALS

Whereas probability theory specifies that 68% of that fictitious large number of samples would produce estimates that fall within one standard error of the parameter, we turn the logic around and infer that any single random sample estimate has a 68% chance of falling within that range. This observation leads us to the two key components of sampling error estimates: confidence level and confidence interval. We express the accuracy of our sample statistics in terms of a *level of confidence* that the statistics fall within a specified *interval* from the parameter. For example, we are 68% confident that our sample estimate is within one standard error of the parameter. Or we may say that we are 95% confident that the sample statistic is within two standard errors of the parameter and so forth. Quite reasonably, our confidence increases as the margin for error is extended. We are virtually positive (99.74%) that we are within three standard errors of the true value.

Although we may be confident (at some level) of being within a certain range of the parameter, we have already noted that we seldom know what the parameter is. To resolve this dilemma, we substitute our sample estimate for the parameter in the formula; lacking the true value, we substitute the best available guess.

The result of these inferences and estimations is that we are able to estimate a population parameter as well as the expected degree of error on the basis of one sample drawn from a population. Beginning with the question, "What percentage of the town population approves of the facility?" we could select a random sample of 100 residents and interview them. We might then report that our best estimate is that 50% of the population approves of the facility and that we are 95% confident that between 40% and 60% (plus or minus two standard errors) approves. The range from 40% to 60% is called the confidence interval. (At the 68% confidence level, the confidence interval would be 45% to 55%.)

The logic of confidence levels and confidence intervals also provides the basis for determining the appropriate sample size for a study. Once you have decided on the degree of sampling error you can tolerate, you'll be able to calculate the number of cases needed in your sample. Thus, for example,

if you want to be 95% confident that your study findings are accurate within plus or minus 5 percentage points of the population parameters, then you should select a sample of at least 400.

The foregoing discussion has considered only one type of statistic: the percentages produced by a binomial or dichotomous variable. The same logic, however, would apply to the examination of other statistics, such as mean income.

Two cautions are in order here. First, the survey uses of probability theory as discussed here are not wholly justified technically. The theory of sampling distribution makes assumptions that almost never apply in survey conditions. The exact proportion of samples contained within specified increments of standard errors, for example, mathematically assumes an infinitely large population, an infinite number of samples, and sampling with replacement—that is, every sampling unit selected is "thrown back into the pot" and could be selected again. Second, our discussion has greatly oversimplified the inferential jump from the distribution of several samples to the probable characteristics of one sample.

These cautions are offered as perspective. Researchers often appear to overestimate the precision of estimates produced by using probability theory. As has been mentioned elsewhere in this appendix and throughout the book, variations in sampling techniques and nonsampling factors may further reduce the legitimacy of such estimates. For example, those selected in a sample who fail or refuse to participate further detract from the representativeness of the sample.

Nevertheless, the calculations discussed in this appendix can be extremely valuable to you in understanding and evaluating your data. Although the calculations do not provide estimates that are as precise as some researchers might assume, they can be quite valid for practical purposes. They are unquestionably more valid than less rigorously derived estimates based on less rigorous sampling methods. Most important, you should be familiar with the basic logic underlying the calculations. If you are so informed, then you will be able to react sensibly to your own data and those reported by others.

Critically Appraising Meta-Analyses

Chapter 22 discussed the benefits of meta-analysis but also noted that, as is the case with any other type of research, some meta-analytical studies are methodologically stronger or weaker than others, and some weak ones can be misleading. This appendix will focus on how to critically appraise the trustworthiness of meta-analyses. We'll begin by discussing some of the key flaws that can weaken a meta-analytical study.

POTENTIAL FLAWS IN META-ANALYSES

Conflicts of Interest

Authors of meta-analyses should have no vested interest in the program or intervention approach being assessed. Otherwise, the meta-analysis might be egregiously biased. A cigarette company, for instance, might conduct a biased meta-analysis to try to refute existing evidence about the harmful effects of tobacco. Likewise, a pharmaceutical company might conduct a biased meta-analysis to support the wonders of its new drug and to minimize its risk of harmful side effects. An inventor of a controversial new type of psychotherapy and his or her disciples—all of whom stand to benefit from marketing it—might conduct a biased meta-analysis of its effectiveness. How, you might wonder, can meta-analyses be biased? Let's look at some of the key ways. As we do, keep in mind that the bias need not be intentional. Some well-meaning researchers, with no conflict of interest, unintentionally make honest mistakes that can lead to biased findings.

Lumping Together Strong and Weak Studies

One way to get biased findings is to include in the analysis various studies with seriously biased research designs and to not separate out their average effect size from the average effect size of more rigorous, unbiased studies. Lumping together studies that are methodologically strong with those that have serious methodological limitations and then treating their results equally in the analysis can lead to dangerously misleading conclusions.

For example, suppose that two studies with weak internal validity both report a *Cohen's d* of 1.0 for a particular intervention and that one strong experiment reports a *d* of 0 for the same intervention. (Chapters 21 and 22 discussed the meaning and calculation of *Cohen's d*.) The mean *d* for the three studies would be .67—two ones and a zero add up to 2, and 2 divided by 3 equals .67. This would be misleading because the finding of the methodologically strong study may be the only one that is valid and therefore the only one that should guide the selection of practice interventions.

An example of this problem once appeared in the social work literature. In a meta-analysis of social work practice effects in treating chronic mentally ill clients, Videka-Sherman (1988) reported that shorter-term treatments produced better effect sizes than did longer-term treatments. This conclusion irked Gerard Hogarty, a social worker who had devoted his career to experimental research on the treatment of individuals with chronic mental illness. Hogarty had pointed out time and again in his research findings and in reviewing the experimental research of his colleagues that chronic mental illness tends to be a lifelong affliction that requires long-term care.

In his critique of Videka-Sherman's meta-analysis, Hogarty (1989) argued that her finding resulted largely from her inclusion of one study whose methodology did not apply to the comparison of short- versus long-term treatment effects. That study used a cross-sectional design and found that service users were much more likely to be rehospitalized than nonusers, with a very large negative d of negative 1.97. As discussed in Chapter 21, a negative d indicates harmful effects. If one study finds a negative d of 1.97 and another study finds a beneficial positive d of 1.97, the mean d of the two studies will be 0 (no effects). Hogarty argued that this finding was due to a selectivity bias in which the treatment users were more impaired than the nonusers and that Videka-Sherman was wrong to view the individuals who had no treatment as having had shorter-term treatment than the more severely impaired individuals who received some treatment.

Hogarty went on to show how Videka-Sherman's meta-analysis would have had the opposite conclusion if it had included only studies with strong experimental controls. In criticizing this and various other findings of the Videka-Sherman meta-analysis, Hogarty (1989) argued that "effect sizes from the better designed studies frequently were overwhelmed [in calculating mean effect sizes] by effect sizes from reports of lower quality that unduly influenced judgments of effective practice" (p. 363). (Despite the apparent flaws in Videka-Sherman's analysis, we know of no reason to suppose that she was intentionally biased in her meta-analysis. Thus, the foregoing example illustrates how biased findings can be produced unintentionally by unbiased researchers who simply make honest mistakes.)

Problems in Ratings of Methodological Quality

In attempting to handle the preceding problem, some meta-analysts rate the methodological quality of studies and then use that rating as a factor in their meta-analyses. For example, they might find no correlation between the rating and the mean effect size and therefore conclude that the studies with weaker methodologies did not skew the overall mean effect size calculation. Or they might calculate the means of the stronger and weaker studies separately and, if they are different, recommend that the mean of the stronger studies hold sway. Another option is to include in the meta-analysis only those studies that meet certain methodological standards, such as having a randomized experimental design with unbiased outcome measures.

All of these approaches are preferable to merely lumping together the strong and weak studies. However, none offers a guarantee of avoiding the reportage of misleading mean effect sizes. That's because there might be errors in judgment regarding the methodological strength of the examined studies. For example, perhaps the meta-analysts overlooked the severe vulnerability to selectivity bias in some of the otherwise strong quasi experiments that got included in the meta-analysis. Perhaps the way measures were administered in a biased manner got overlooked in an otherwise strong randomized experiment. More egregiously, perhaps the meta-analysts had a conflict of interest that (perhaps unconsciously and unintentionally) influenced them to perceive the studies that supported their predilections as stronger than the studies with findings that they did not like.

File Drawer Effect

As you might recall from our Chapter 5 discussion of the ethically controversial Epstein research, there is evidence that studies with findings that support the effectiveness of an intervention are more likely to be published than studies whose findings fail to offer such support. Epstein attributed that phenomenon to bias among journal editorial reviewers. Others have attributed it to a bias on the part of study authors. The latter bias is called the file drawer effect. That term is based on the notion that authors of studies with findings that don't support the effectiveness of an intervention will just file their studies away rather than submit them for publication. They may do this because they suspect (perhaps erroneously) that journals are not interested in studies of interventions that are not effective. Likewise, they might assume that nobody would be interested in reading such studies. Or they might have a vested interest in the intervention they evaluated. Such a vested interest could influence them in more than one way. Most egregiously, perhaps they don't want to publicize the fact that the intervention from which they are benefiting doesn't really work. More innocently, perhaps their bias honestly convinces them that something must have been awry in their study methodology and that rather than "mislead" the field about an intervention they are convinced is wonderful, they should design a better study. (This would exemplify *ex post facto* hypothesizing, as discussed in Chapter 1.)

WHAT TO LOOK FOR WHEN APPRAISING META-ANALYSES

In light of the foregoing potential problems, some meta-analyses are more trustworthy than others. Therefore, it is important that you critically appraise the quality (or trustworthiness) of any meta-analysis that you examine as a potential guide to your practice. What follows are some key things to look for when judging the trustworthiness of a meta-analysis.

Transparency

One of the first things you should look for is whether it included a *conflict-of-interest statement*. Not finding such a statement should make you wary—for two reasons. First, there is the issue of transparency. The better meta-analyses will be transparent about all aspects of their study and thus should include a statement as to whether the authors had a vested interest in any of the interventions examined in their study. Not including such a statement means that there is less transparency and raises questions about the meta-analytical expertise of the authors. Second, its absence might make you wonder whether a conflict of interest is being hidden. And if you do find such a statement and if it reveals a conflict of interest, that too should make you wary even if everything else reported in the study seems to be okay.

Methodologies of Included Studies

Authors also should be transparent about the criteria they used in deciding whether to include or exclude certain studies from their meta-analysis. Did they include only studies with strong randomized designs with unbiased measures? If they included weaker studies too, did they critically appraise the quality of all of the included studies and avoid lumping together the findings of the stronger studies with the findings of the weaker ones? Did they contact the authors of some of the studies they reviewed to obtain more information about their methodologies or findings?

Unpublished Studies

Did the meta-analysis include only published studies? If so, then it might be vulnerable to the file drawer effect. To minimize that effect, it should have included a comprehensive search for unpublished studies, such as by examining dissertations, reports posted only on the Internet, or conference proceedings. Likewise, did the authors try to locate researchers with preliminary findings from ongoing studies?

Comprehensiveness

Aside from the file drawer effect, how comprehensively did the authors search for studies to include in their meta-analysis? What about studies written in languages other than English? How many literature databases did they search? Did they widen their search by examining studies cited in the reports they found? In investigating the effectiveness of an intervention for a particular target problem, did they consider only one type of intervention, or did they take a broader approach by looking at all the interventions that have been evaluated regarding that target population to see which appear to be the most effective ones?

CONCLUSION

Although this appendix has discussed various flaws and the need to critically appraise meta-analyses, we do not want to leave you with the impression that most meta-analyses are methodologically weak. Quite the opposite! Most of the ones being published these days strike us as trustworthy. Moreover, sources like the Cochran Collaboration and Campbell Collaboration do an excellent job in their efforts to ensure that the meta-analyses at their websites are methodologically strong and trustworthy. Nevertheless, you might occasionally encounter a misleading meta-analysis somewhere. And someday you might even want to conduct a meta-analysis yourself. We hope that what you have learned in this appendix will help you in either case.

GLOSSARY

AB design A relatively simple *single-case evaluation design* that includes one *baseline* phase (A) and one intervention phase (B). This is a popular design among practitioners and researchers because it involves only one baseline phase and therefore poses less conflict with service delivery priorities than more complex designs that contain multiple baselines. It has less control for history, however, than most alternative single-case evaluation designs. See Chapter 13.

ABAB withdrawal/reversal design A *single-case evaluation design* that adds a second *baseline* phase (A) and a second intervention phase (B). This design assumes that if the intervention caused the improvement in the target problem during the first intervention period, then the target problem will reverse toward its original baseline level during the second baseline. When the intervention is reintroduced, the target problem should start improving again. The basic inferential principle here is that if shifts in the trend or level of the target problem occur successively each time the intervention is introduced or withdrawn, then it is not plausible that history explains the change. See Chapter 13.

abstract A separate page at the beginning of a research proposal or report that briefly summarizes the proposed or completed study. See Chapter 23.

accidental sampling See *availability sampling*.

acculturation The process in which a group or individual changes after coming into contact with a majority culture, taking on its language, values, attitudes, and lifestyle preferences. See Chapter 6.

acquiescent response set A source of *measurement* error in which people agree or disagree with most or all statements regardless of their content. See Chapter 9.

agency tracking Asking service providers or other community agencies whether they have been in recent contact with research participants—particularly those who are transient or homeless—whom you are unable to locate and whom you need to contact for further sessions or interviews. See Chapter 6.

alternative treatment design with pretest An experiment that compares the effectiveness of two alternative treatments. Participants are assigned randomly to two *experimental groups*, each of which receives a different intervention being evaluated, and to a *control group* that does not receive any intervention. Each group is tested on the *dependent variable* before and after the experimental groups receive the intervention. See Chapter 11.

analysis of variance A form of data analysis in which the variance of a *dependent variable* is examined for the whole sample and for separate subgroups created on the basis of one or more *independent variables*. See Chapter 22.

anchor points Pieces of information about the various places you may be able to find particular research participants—particularly transient or homeless participants—for future follow-up sessions or interviews. See Chapter 6.

anonymity An arrangement that makes it impossible for a researcher to link any research data with a given research participant. Distinguished from *confidentiality*, in which the researcher is able to identify a given person's responses but essentially promises not to do so publicly. See Chapter 5.

anonymous enrollment A method of recruiting members of hidden and oppressed populations to participate in research studies; the method emphasizes techniques that enable prospective participants to feel safer in responding to recruitment efforts and participating in studies. See Chapter 6.

area probability sample A form of multistage *cluster sample* in which geographic areas such as census blocks or tracts serve as the first-stage sampling unit. Units selected in the first stage of sampling are then listed—all the households on each selected block would be written down after a trip to the block—and such lists would be subsampled. See Chapter 15.

assent form A brief *consent form* that a child can understand and sign before participating in a study;

it uses simpler language than consent forms for adults about the features of the study that might affect their decision about whether they want to participate in it. See *consent form* and Chapter 5.

attributes   Characteristics of persons or things. See *variables* and Chapters 3 and 8.

attrition   A threat to the validity of an experiment that occurs when participants drop out of an experiment before it is completed. Also called *experimental mortality*. See Chapter 11.

auditing   A strategy for improving the trustworthiness of qualitative research findings in which the researcher leaves a paper trail of field notes, transcripts of interviews, journals, and memos documenting decisions made along the way and so on. This enables an impartial and qualitatively adept investigator who is not part of the study to scrutinize what was done in order to determine if efforts to control for *bias* and *reactivity* were thorough, if the procedures used were justifiable, and if the interpretations fit the data that were collected. See Chapter 18.

availability sampling   A sampling method that selects elements simply because of their ready availability and convenience. Frequently used in social work because it is usually less expensive than other methods and because other methods may not be feasible for a particular type of study or population. See Chapter 15.

available records   A source of data for a study in which the information of concern has already been gathered by others. For example, an evaluation of a statewide dropout prevention program may use available school records on dropout rates. See Chapters 8 and 17.

average   An ambiguous term that generally suggests typical or normal. *Mean*, *median*, and *mode* are specific examples of mathematical averages, or measures of central tendency. See Chapter 21.

axial coding   A type of coding in qualitative data analysis that identifies the core concepts in a study, regroups the data, and looks for more analytic concepts. See Chapter 20.

back translation   A method used when translating instruments from one language into another. The steps are (a) a bilingual person translates the instrument and its instructions to a target language, (b) another bilingual person translates from the target language back to the original language (not seeing the original version of the instrument), (c) the original instrument is compared to the back-translated version, and (d) items with discrepancies are further modified. See Chapter 6.

baseline   The phase of a *single-case evaluation design* that consists of repeated measures before a new intervention or policy is introduced. See Chapter 13.

B design   The simplest *single-case evaluation design* that includes only an intervention phase (B). Although this design does not permit causal inferences, it can be used to monitor client progress. It is especially valuable when there is no need to make causal inferences because the intervention has already had sufficient causal evidence as found in the earlier phases of the evidence-based practice process. See Chapter 13.

B+ design   This is a B design that contains one preintervention data point or that contains a C phase that eventuates after observing no progress during the B phase. When there is a C phase, causal inferences might become possible because the B phase can serve as a baseline for the C phase. See Chapter 13.

bias   (1) That quality of a measurement device that tends to result in a misrepresentation of what is being measured in a particular direction. For example, the questionnaire item "Don't you agree that the president is doing a good job?" would be biased because it would generally encourage more favorable responses. See Chapters 9 and 10 for more on this topic. (2) The thing inside a person that makes other people or groups seem consistently better or worse than they really are.

binomial variable   A variable that has only two attributes is binomial. "Gender" would be an example, having the attributes "male" and "female."

bivariate analysis   The analysis of two variables simultaneously to determine the empirical relationship between them. The construction of a simple percentage table or the computation of a simple correlation coefficient would be examples of bivariate analyses. See Chapter 21.

CA   See *conversation analysis*.

case control design   A design for evaluating interventions that compares groups of cases that have had contrasting outcomes and then collects retrospective data about past differences that might explain the difference in outcomes. It relies on *multivariate statistical procedures*. See Chapter 12.

case-oriented analysis   An *idiographic* qualitative data analysis method that focuses on attempting to understand a particular case fully. See Chapter 20.

case study An *idiographic* examination of a single individual, family, group, organization, community, or society using a full variety of evidence regarding that case. See Chapter 18.

causal inference An inference derived from a research design and findings that logically imply that the independent variable really has a causal impact on the dependent variable. See Chapter 11.

census An enumeration of the characteristics of some population. A census is often similar to a *survey*, with the difference that the census collects data from all members of the population and the survey is limited to a sample. See Chapter 16.

chi-square A *statistical significance* test used when both the independent and dependent variables are *nominal level*. See Chapter 22.

client logs A *qualitative* or *quantitative* method that can be used as part of *case studies* or *single-case evaluations* in which clients keep journals of events that are relevant to their problems. See Chapter 18.

clinical significance The term used for substantive significance in clinical outcome studies. See also *substantive significance* and Chapter 22.

closed-ended questions Unlike in *open-ended questions,* the respondent is asked to select an answer from among a list provided by the researcher. See Chapter 10.

cluster sample A sample drawn using *cluster sampling* procedures. See Chapter 15.

cluster sampling A *multistage sampling* procedure in which natural groups (clusters) are sampled initially, with the members of each selected group being subsampled afterward. For example, we might select a sample of U.S. colleges and universities from a directory, get lists of the students at all the selected schools, and then draw samples of students from each. This procedure is discussed in Chapter 15.

codebook The document used in data processing and analysis that tells the location of different data items in a data file. Typically, the codebook identifies the locations of data items and the meaning of the codes used to represent different attributes of variables. See Chapter 21.

coding The process whereby raw data are transformed into a standardized form that is suitable for machine processing and analysis. See Chapters 20 and 21.

coefficient alpha A statistic for depicting the *internal consistency reliability* of an instrument; it represents the average of the correlations between the subscores of all possible subsets of half of the items on the instrument. See Chapter 9.

cognitive interviewing A useful tool to use in pretesting in which participants can comment as they are completing the questionnaire. See Chapter 10.

cohort study A study in which some specific group is studied over time, although data may be collected from different members in each set of observations. For example, a study of the professional careers of students earning their social work degrees in 1990, in which questionnaires were sent every five years, would be a cohort study. See Chapter 7.

community forum An approach to needs assessment that involves holding a meeting where concerned members of the community can express their views and interact freely about their needs. See Chapter 14.

compensatory equalization A threat to the validity of an evaluation of an intervention's effectiveness that occurs when practitioners in the comparison routine-treatment condition compensate for the differences in treatment between their group and the *experimental group* by providing enhanced services that go beyond the routine-treatment regimen for their clients, thus potentially blurring the true effects of the tested intervention. See Chapter 11.

compensatory rivalry A threat to the validity of an evaluation of an intervention's effectiveness that occurs when practitioners in the comparison routine-treatment condition decide to compete with the therapists in the other unit. They may start reading more, attending more continuing education workshops, and increasing their therapeutic contact with clients. Their extra efforts might improve their effectiveness and thus blur the true effects of the tested intervention. See Chapter 11.

complete observer One who observes a social process without becoming a part of it in any way. See Chapter 19.

complete participant Either a genuine participant in what he or she is studying (e.g., a participant in a protest demonstration) or someone pretending to be a genuine participant. See Chapter 19.

computer-assisted telephone interviewing (CATI) Interviewing over the phone by reading questions from a computer screen and immediately entering responses into the computer. See Chapter 16.

concept   A mental image that symbolizes an idea, an object, an event, or a person. See Chapter 3.

concept mapping   A qualitative data analysis method in which relationships among concepts are examined and diagrammed in a graphical format. See Chapter 20.

conceptual equivalence   Instruments and observed behaviors having the same meanings across cultures. See Chapter 6.

conceptualization   The mental process whereby fuzzy and imprecise notions (*concepts*) are made more specific and precise. So you want to study prejudice. What do you mean by "prejudice"? Are there different kinds? What are they? See Chapter 8.

concurrent validity   A form of *criterion-related validity* examining a measure's correspondence to a criterion that is known concurrently. See Chapter 9.

confidence interval   The range of values within which a population parameter is estimated to lie. A survey, for example, may show 40% of a sample favoring candidate A (poor devil). Although the best estimate of the support existing among all voters would also be 40%, we would not expect it to be exactly that. We might, therefore, compute a *confidence interval* (e.g., from 35% to 45%) within which the actual percentage of the population probably lies. Note that it's necessary to specify a *confidence level* in connection with every confidence interval. See Appendix B.

confidence level   The estimated probability that a population parameter lies within a given *confidence interval*. Thus, we might be 95% confident that between 35% and 45% of all voters favor candidate A. See Appendix B.

confidentiality   A promise by the researcher not to publicly identify a given research participant's data. Distinguished from *anonymity*, which makes it impossible for a researcher to link any research data with a given research participant. See Chapter 5.

consent form   A form that human subjects sign before participating in a study that provides full information about the features of the study that might affect their decision about whether to participate—particularly regarding its procedures, potential harm, and *anonymity* and *confidentiality*. See Chapter 5.

constant comparative method   A qualitative data analysis method in which the researcher looks for patterns in inductive observations, develops concepts and working hypotheses based on those patterns, seeks out more cases and conducts more observations, and then compares those observations against the concepts and hypotheses developed from the earlier observations. The selection of new cases is guided by theoretical sampling concepts in which new cases are selected that seem to be similar to those generated by previously detected concepts and hypotheses. Once the researcher perceives that no new insights are being generated from the observation of similar cases, a different type of case is selected, and the same process is repeated. Additional cases similar to this new type of case are selected until no new insights are being generated. This cycle of exhausting similar cases and then seeking a different category of cases is repeated until the researcher believes that further seeking of new types of cases will not alter the findings. See Chapter 20.

construct validity   The degree to which a measure relates to other variables as expected within a system of theoretical relationships and as reflected by the degree of its convergent validity and discriminant validity. See also *convergent validity*, *discriminant validity*, and Chapter 9.

contemporary positivism   A *paradigm* that recognizes the virtual impossibility of being completely objective yet assumes that there is an objective answer to research questions and that it is worth trying to investigate things as objectively as possible to attempt to maximize the accuracy of answers to research questions. See Chapter 3.

content analysis   A research method for studying virtually any form of communication, consisting primarily of *coding* and tabulating the occurrences of certain forms of content that are being communicated. See Chapter 17.

content validity   The degree to which a measure covers the range of meanings included within the concept. See Chapter 9.

contingency question   A survey question that is to be asked of only some of the respondents, depending on their responses to some other question. For example, all respondents might be asked whether they belong to the Cosa Nostra, and only those who said yes would be asked how often they go to company meetings and picnics. The latter would be a contingency question. See Chapter 10 for illustrations of this topic.

contingency table   Any table format for presenting the relationships among variables in the form of percentage distributions. See Chapter 21.

control group   In experimentation, a group of participants who do *not* receive the intervention being evaluated and who should resemble the *experimental* group in all other respects. The comparison of the control and experimental groups at the end of the experiment points to the effect of the tested intervention. See Chapter 11.

control variable   A *variable* that is held constant in an attempt to further clarify the relationship between two other variables. Having discovered a relationship between education and prejudice, for example, we might hold gender constant by examining the relationship between education and prejudice among men only and then among women only. In this example, "gender" would be the control variable. See Chapter 8 and also Chapter 11 to see the importance of the proper use of control variables in analysis.

convenience sampling   See *availability sampling*.

convergent parallel mixed methods design   With this design quantitative and qualitative data are collected concurrently and then analyzed separately. The results of the separate analyses are then compared to see if they confirm each other. See Chapter 4.

convergent validity   The degree to which scores on a measure correspond to scores on other measures of the same construct. See also *construct validity*, *discriminant validity*, and Chapter 9.

conversation analysis (CA)   A qualitative data analysis approach that aims to uncover the implicit assumptions and structures in social life through an extremely close scrutiny of the way we converse with one another. See Chapter 20.

cost–benefit analysis   An assessment of program efficiency in which an attempt is made to monetize the benefits associated with a program's outcome and thus see if those monetary benefits exceed program costs. See Chapter 14.

cost-effectiveness analysis   An assessment of program efficiency in which the only monetary considerations are the costs of the program; the monetary benefits of the program's effects are not assessed. Cost-effectiveness analysis looks at the cost per unit of outcome without monetizing the outcome. See Chapter 14.

criterion validity   The degree to which a measure relates with some external criterion. For example, the validity of the college board exam is shown in its ability to predict the college success of students. See *known-groups validity*, *concurrent validity*, *predictive validity*, and Chapter 9.

critical region   Those values in the statistically significant zone of a theoretical sampling distribution. See Chapter 22.

critical social science   A *paradigm* distinguished by its focus on oppression and its commitment to use research procedures to empower oppressed groups. See Chapter 3.

cross-case analysis   A qualitative data analysis method that is an extension of *case-oriented analysis* in which the researcher turns to other subjects, looking into the full details of their lives as well but paying special note to the variables that seemed important in the first case. Some subsequent cases will closely parallel the first one in the apparent impact of particular variables. Other cases will bear no resemblance to the first. These latter cases may require the identification of other important variables, which may invite the researcher to explore why some cases seem to reflect one pattern whereas others reflect another. See *case-oriented analysis* and Chapter 20.

cross-sectional study   A study based on observations that represent a single point in time. Contrasted with a *longitudinal study*. See Chapters 7 and 12.

cultural bias   A source of measurement error or *sampling error* stemming from researcher ignorance or insensitivity regarding how cultural differences can influence measurement or generalizations made to the entire population when certain minority groups are inadequately represented in the sample. A measurement procedure is culturally biased when it is administered to a minority culture without adjusting for the ways in which the minority culture's unique values, attitudes, lifestyles, or limited opportunities alter the accuracy or meaning of what is really being measured. See Chapters 6 and 9.

cultural competence   A researcher's ability to obtain and provide information that is relevant, useful, and valid for minority and oppressed populations. Cultural competence involves knowledge about the minority culture's historical experiences, traditions, values, family systems, socioeconomic issues, and attitudes about social services and social policies; awareness of how one's own attitudes are connected to one's own cultural background and how they may differ from the worldview of members of the minority culture; and skills in communicating effectively both verbally and nonverbally with members of the minority culture and establishing rapport with them. See Chapter 6.

culturally competent research   Being aware of and appropriately responding to the ways in which cultural factors and cultural differences should influence what we investigate, how we investigate, and how we interpret our findings—thus resulting in studies that are useful and valid for minority and oppressed populations. See Chapter 6.

curvilinear relationship A *relationship* between two *variables* that changes in nature at different values of the variables. For example, a curvilinear relationship might exist between amount of social work practice experience and practice effectiveness, particularly if we assume that practitioners with a moderate amount of experience are more effective than those with none and at least as effective as those nearing retirement. See Chapter 8.

deduction The logical model in which specific expectations of *hypotheses* are developed on the basis of general principles. Starting from the general principle that all deans are meanies, you might anticipate that Dean Moe won't let you change courses. That anticipation would be the result of deduction. See also *induction* and Chapter 3.

dependent variable That variable that is assumed to depend on, or be caused by, another (called the *independent variable*). If you find that income is partly a function of amount of formal education, then income is being treated as a dependent variable. See Chapters 3 and 8.

descriptive statistics Statistical computations that describe either the characteristics of a sample or the relationship among variables in a sample. Descriptive statistics merely summarize a set of sample observations, whereas *inferential statistics* move beyond the description of specific observations to make inferences about the larger *population* from which the sample observations were drawn. See Chapter 21.

deviant case sampling A type of *nonprobability sampling* in which cases selected for observation are those that are not thought to fit the regular pattern. For example, the deviant cases might exhibit a much greater or lesser extent of something. See Chapters 15 and 18.

dichotomous variable A variable that has only two categories. See also *binomial variable*.

diffusion (or imitation) of treatments A threat to the validity of an evaluation of an intervention's effectiveness that occurs when practitioners who are supposed to provide routine services to a comparison group implement aspects of the experimental group's intervention in ways that tend to diminish the planned differences in the interventions received by the groups being compared. See Chapter 11.

dimension A specifiable aspect or facet of a *concept*.

direct behavioral observation A source of data, or type of data collection, in which researchers watch what people do rather than rely on what they say about themselves or what others say about them. See Chapters 8 and 9.

direct observation A way to operationally define variables based on observing actual behavior. See also *direct behavioral observation* and Chapters 8 and 9.

discriminant validity The degree to which scores on an instrument correspond more highly to measures of the same construct than they do to scores on measures of other constructs. See also *convergent validity*, *construct validity*, and Chapter 9.

dismantling studies Experiments designed to test not only whether an intervention is effective but also which components of the intervention may or may not be necessary to achieve its effects. Participants are assigned randomly to groups that either receive the entire intervention package, separate components of it, or a control condition and are tested on a *dependent variable* before and after the intervention components are provided. See Chapter 11.

dispersion The distribution of values around some central value such as an *average*. The *range* is a simple example of a measure of *dispersion*. Thus, we may report that the mean age of a group is 37.9, and the range is from 12 to 89. See Chapter 21.

disproportionate stratified sampling A sampling method aimed at ensuring that enough cases of certain minority groups are selected to allow for subgroup comparisons within each of those minority groups. See Chapters 6 and 15.

double-barreled question Asking for a single answer to a question that really contains multiple questions; for example, "Should taxes be raised so welfare funding can be increased?" See Chapter 10.

ecological fallacy Erroneously drawing conclusions about individuals based solely on the observation of groups. See Chapter 7.

effect size A statistic that portrays the strength of association between variables. Effect-size statistics might refer to various measures of proportion of dependent variable variation explained or specifically to the difference between the means of two groups divided by the *standard deviation*. The latter is usually called the effect size, ES, or Cohen's *d*. See Chapter 22.

element   That unit in a sample about which information is collected and that provides the basis of analysis. Typically, in survey research, elements are people or certain types of people. See Chapter 15.

emic perspective   Trying to adopt the beliefs, attitudes, and other points of view shared by the members of the culture being studied. See Chapter 19.

empirical support   Observations that are consistent with what we would expect to experience if a theory is correct or an intervention is effective. See Chapters 1, 2, and 3.

empowerment paradigm   A research paradigm that focuses on using research to empower oppressed groups. See Chapters 3 and 18.

Epidemiology   The study of the causes of physical and social disorders and how they spread.

equal probability of selection method (EPSEM)   A sample design in which each member of a population has the same chance of being selected into the sample. See Chapter 15.

ES   See *effect size*.

ethnocentrism   The belief in the superiority of one's own culture. See Chapter 6.

ethnography   A *qualitative research* approach that focuses on providing a detailed and accurate description of a culture from the viewpoint of an insider rather than the way the researcher understands things. See Chapter 18.

etic perspective   Maintaining objectivity as an outsider and raising questions about the culture being observed that wouldn't occur to members of that culture. See Chapter 19.

evidence-based practice   Using the best scientific evidence available in deciding how to intervene with individuals, families, groups, or communities. See Chapter 2.

existing statistics analysis   Research involving the analysis of statistical information in official government or agency documents and reports. See Chapter 17.

experimental demand characteristics   Research participants learn what experimenters want them to say or do, and then they cooperate with those "demands" or expectations. See Chapter 12.

experimental design   A research method that attempts to provide maximum control for threats to *internal validity* by (a) randomly assigning individuals to experimental and control groups, (b) introducing the *independent variable* (which typically is a program or intervention method) to the experimental group while withholding it from the control group, and (c) comparing the amount of experimental and control group change on the *dependent variable*. See Chapter 11.

experimental group   In experiments, a group of participants who receive the intervention being evaluated and who should resemble the control group in all other respects. The comparison of the experimental group and the *control group* at the end of the experiment points to the effect of the tested intervention. See Chapter 11.

experimental mortality   A threat to the validity of an experiment that occurs when participants drop out of an experiment before it is completed. Also called *attrition*. See Chapter 12.

experimenter expectancies   Research participants learn what experimenters want them to say or do, and then they cooperate with those "demands" or expectations. See Chapter 11.

explanatory sequential mixed methods design   This design is thought to appeal to researchers who are more quantitatively oriented. The quantitative data are collected first, followed by qualitative data collection aimed at developing a better understanding of the quantitative data. See Chapter 4.

exploratory sequential mixed methods design   With this design the qualitative data are collected first, to provide a basis for formulating the quantitative phase. One aim of this design could be to see if the insights generated from a small sample of people in the qualitative phase can be generalized to a larger, more representative sample of the population in the quantitative phase. Another aim might be to use the qualitative data as a basis for developing a good quantitative data collection instrument. See Chapter 4.

external evaluators   Program evaluators who do not work for the agency being evaluated but instead work for external agencies such as government or regulating agencies, private research consultation firms, or universities. See Chapter 14.

external validity   Refers to the extent to which we can generalize the findings of a study to settings and populations beyond the study conditions. See Chapter 11.

extraneous variable A variable that represents an alternative explanation for a relationship that is observed between an independent and dependent variable. See Chapter 8.

face validity That quality of an indicator that makes it seem a reasonable measure of some variable. That the frequency of church attendance is some indication of a person's religiosity seems to make sense without a lot of explanation: It has face validity. See Chapter 9.

factor analysis A statistical procedure that identifies which subsets of variables or items on a scale correlate with each other more than with other subsets. In so doing, it identifies how many *dimensions* a scale contains and which items cluster on which dimensions. See Chapter 9.

factorial validity Whether the number of constructs and the items that make up those constructs on a measurement scale are what the researcher intends. See Chapter 9.

field tracking Talking with people on the streets about where to find research participants—particularly those who are homeless—to secure their participation in future sessions or interviews. See Chapter 6.

file drawer effect A term based on the notion that authors of studies with findings that don't support the effectiveness of an intervention will just file their studies away rather than submit them for publication. See Chapter 23.

focus groups An approach to needs assessment in which a small group of people are brought together to engage in a guided discussion of a specified topic. See Chapters 10, 14, and 19.

formative evaluation A type of program evaluation not concerned with testing the success of a program but focusing instead on obtaining information that is helpful in planning the program and improving its implementation and performance. See Chapter 14.

forward translation A method used when translating instruments from one language into another that begins by translating the original instrument into the target language, but then, instead of back-translating it, several bilingual individuals examine both versions to ascertain whether both versions convey the same conceptual meanings. See Chapter 6.

frequency distribution A description of the number of times the various attributes of a variable are observed in a sample. The report that 53% of a sample were men and 47% were women would be a simple example of a frequency distribution. Another example would be the report that 15 of the cities studied had populations under 10,000, 23 had populations between 10,000 and 25,000, and so forth. See Chapter 21.

gender bias The unwarranted generalization of research findings to the population as a whole when one gender is not adequately represented in the research sample. See Chapter 15.

generalizability That quality of a research finding that justifies the inference that it represents something more than the specific observations on which it was based. Sometimes, this involves the generalization of findings from a sample to a population. Other times it is a matter of concepts: If you are able to discover why people commit burglaries, can you generalize that discovery to other crimes as well? See Chapter 18.

generalization of effects A rival explanation in a *multiple-baseline design* that occurs when an intervention that is intended to apply to only one behavior or setting affects other behaviors or settings that are still in baseline. See Chapter 13.

generalize To infer that the findings of a particular study represent causal processes or apply to settings or populations beyond the study conditions. See Chapter 18.

going native A risk in qualitative field research that occurs when researchers overidentify with their respondents and lose their objective, analytic stance or their own sense of identity. See Chapters 18 and 19.

grounded theory A *qualitative research* approach that begins with observations and looks for patterns, themes, or common categories. See Chapters 18, 19, and 20.

grounded theory method (GTM) A *qualitative* methodology for building theory from data by beginning with observations and looking for patterns, themes, or common categories in those observations. See Chapters 18 and 20.

groupthink The tendency for people in a group to conform with the opinions and decisions of the most outspoken members of the group. See Chapter 19.

GTM See *grounded theory method*.

hermeneutics A *qualitative research* approach in which the researcher mentally tries to take on the circumstances, views, and feelings of those being studied in order to interpret their actions appropriately. See Chapter 17.

historical and comparative research A research method that traces the development of social forms over time and compares those developmental processes across cultures, seeking to discover common patterns that recur in different times and places. See Chapter 17.

history A threat to *internal validity* referring to extraneous events that coincide in time with the manipulation of the *independent variable*. See Chapters 11 and 13.

hypothesis A tentative and testable prediction about how changes in one thing are expected to explain and be accompanied by changes in something else. A statement of something that ought to be observed in the real world if a theory is correct. See *deduction* and also Chapters 3, 7, and 8.

hypothesis testing The determination of whether the expectations that a *hypothesis* represents are actually found to exist in the real world. See Chapters 3 and 7.

ideology A closed system of beliefs and values that shapes the understanding and behavior of those who believe in it. See Chapter 3.

idiographic model An approach to explanation in which we attempt to explain a single case fully, using as many idiosyncratic, explanatory factors as may be necessary. We might explain why Uncle Ed is such a bigot by talking about what happened to him that summer at the beach, what his college roommate did to him, and so on. This kind of explanation won't necessarily help us understand bigotry in general, but we'd feel we really understood Uncle Ed. By contrast, see *nomothetic*. See Chapter 3.

independent variable A variable whose values are not problematical in an analysis but are taken as simply given. An independent variable is presumed to cause or explain a *dependent variable*. If we discover that religiosity is partly a function of gender—women are more religious than men—gender is the independent variable and religiosity is the dependent variable. Note that any given variable might be treated as independent in one part of an analysis and dependent in another part of the analysis. Religiosity might become an *independent variable* in the explanation of crime. See Chapters 3 and 8.

index A type of composite measure that summarizes several specific observations and represents some more general dimension. See Chapter 10.

induction The logical model in which general principles are developed from specific observations. Having noted that Jews and Catholics are more likely to vote Democratic than are Protestants, you might conclude that religious minorities in the United States are more affiliated with the Democratic Party and explain why. That would be an example of induction. See also *deduction* and Chapter 3.

inference A conclusion that can be logically drawn in light of a research design and findings. See Chapter 11.

inferential data analysis The use of inferential statistics to judge whether relationships exist in general or have any theoretical meaning. See Chapter 22.

inferential statistics The body of statistical computations that is relevant to making inferences from findings based on sample observations to some larger *population*. See also *descriptive statistics* and Chapters 21 and 22.

informal conversational interview An unplanned and unanticipated interaction between an interviewer and a *respondent* that occurs naturally during the course of fieldwork observation. It is the most open-ended form of interviewing, and the interviewee might not think of the interaction as an interview. Flexibility to pursue relevant information in whatever direction seems appropriate is emphasized, and questions should be generated naturally and spontaneously from what is observed at a particular point in a particular setting or from what individuals in that setting happen to say. See Chapter 19.

informant Someone who is well versed in the social phenomenon that you wish to study and willing to tell you what he or she knows. If you were planning participant observation among the members of a religious sect, then you would do well to make friends with someone who already knows about the members— possibly even a sect member—who could give you background information about them. Not to be confused with a *respondent*. See Chapters 15 and 19.

in-house evaluators Program evaluators who work for the agency being evaluated and therefore may be under pressure to produce biased studies or results that portray the agency favorably. See Chapter 14.

institutional review board (IRB) An independent panel of professionals that is required to approve the ethics of research involving human subjects. See Chapter 5.

intent-to-treat analysis A technique in which all participants who originally enrolled in an evaluation of treatment outcome—including those who dropped out of treatment—are included in the data analysis. See Chapter 11.

internal consistency reliability   A practical and commonly used approach to assessing *reliability* that examines the homogeneity of a measurement instrument by dividing the instrument into equivalent halves and then calculating the correlation of the scores of the two halves. See Chapter 9.

internal invalidity   Refers to the possibility that the conclusions drawn from experimental results may not accurately reflect what went on in the experiment itself. See Chapter 11 and also *external invalidity*.

internal validity   The degree to which an effect observed in an experiment was actually produced by the experimental stimulus and not the result of other factors. See Chapter 11 and *external validity*.

interobserver reliability   See *interrater reliability*.

interpretation   A technical term used in connection with the *elaboration model*. It represents the research outcome in which a *control variable* is discovered to be the mediating factor through which an *independent variable* affects a *dependent variable*. See Chapter 11.

interpretivism   An approach to social research that focuses on gaining an empathic understanding of how people feel inside, seeking to interpret individuals' everyday experiences, deeper meanings and feelings, and idiosyncratic reasons for their behaviors. See Chapter 3.

interrater reliability   The extent of consistency among different observers in their judgments, as reflected in the percentage of agreement or degree of correlation in their independent ratings. See Chapter 9.

interrupted time-series design with a nonequivalent comparison group   The most common form of *multiple time-series design* in which an *experimental group* and a *control group* are measured at multiple points in time before and after an intervention is introduced to the control group. See Chapter 12.

interval measure   A level of measurement that describes a variable whose attributes are rank ordered and have equal distances between adjacent attributes. The Fahrenheit temperature scale is an example of this because the distance between 17° and 18° is the same as that between 89° and 90°. See also *nominal measure*, *ordinal measure*, *ratio measure*, and Chapter 21.

intervening variable   See *mediating variable*.

intervention fidelity   The degree to which an intervention being evaluated is actually delivered to clients as intended. See Chapter 12.

intervention mixed-methods design   A qualitative inquiry is merged with a quantitative evaluation of an intervention's outcome to get a better handle on the meaning of the results. See Chapter 4.

interview   A data collection encounter in which one person (an interviewer) asks questions of another (a *respondent*). Interviews may be conducted face-to-face or by telephone. See Chapters 16 and 19 for more information on interviewing.

interview guide approach   A semistructured form of *qualitative interviewing* that lists in outline form the topics and issues that the interviewer should cover in the interview but allows the interviewer to adapt the sequencing and wording of questions to each particular interview. See Chapter 19.

inverse relationship   See *negative relationship*.

IRB   See *institutional review board*.

judgmental sample   A type of *nonprobability sample* in which we select the units to be observed on the basis of our own judgment about which ones will be the most useful or representative. Another name for this is *purposive sample*. See Chapter 15 for more details.

key informants   An approach to needs assessment that is based on expert opinions of individuals who are presumed to have special knowledge about a target population's problems or needs. See Chapter 14.

known-groups validity   A form of *criterion* that pertains to the degree to which an instrument accurately differentiates between groups that are known to differ in respect to the variable being measured. See Chapter 9.

latent content   As used in connection with content analysis, the underlying meaning of communications as distinguished from their *manifest content*. See Chapter 17.

level of significance   See *significance level*.

life history (or life story or oral history interviews)   A qualitative research method in which researchers ask *open-ended questions* to discover how the participants in a study understand the significant events and meanings in their own lives. See Chapter 19.

life story   See *life history*.

Likert scale   A type of composite measure developed by Rensis Likert in an attempt to improve the levels of measurement in social research through the use of standardized response categories in survey *questionnaires*. "Likert items" use such response categories as strongly agree, agree, disagree, and strongly disagree. Such items may be used in the construction of true Likert scales and also be used in the construction of other types of composite measures. See Chapter 10.

linguistic equivalence (*or* translation equivalence) The result of a successful translation and *back translation* of an instrument that was originally developed for the majority language but that will be used with research participants who don't speak the majority language. See Chapter 6.

logic model A graphic portrayal that depicts the essential components of a program, shows how those components are linked to short-term process objectives, specifies measurable indicators of success in achieving short-term objectives, conveys how those short-term objectives lead to long-term program outcomes, and identifies measurable indicators of success in achieving long-term outcomes. See Chapter 14.

longitudinal study A study design that involves the collection of data at different points in time, as contrasted with a *cross-sectional study*. See Chapter 7.

mail tracking A method of locating and contacting research participants by mailing reminder notices about impending interviews or about the need to call in to update any changes in how they can be contacted. It might also include sending birthday cards, holiday greetings, and certificates of appreciation for participation. See Chapter 6.

managed care A variety of arrangements that try to control the costs of health and human services by having a large organization that pays for the cost of services for many people contract with care providers who agree to provide that care at reduced costs. Managed care is thought to have contributed to the growth of program evaluation. See Chapter 14.

manifest content In connection with content analysis, the concrete terms contained in a communication, as distinguished from *latent content*. See Chapter 17.

matching In connection with experiments, the procedure whereby pairs of subjects are matched on the basis of their similarities on one or more variables, and one member of the pair is assigned to the *experimental group* and the other to the *control group*. See Chapter 12.

maturation A threat to internal validity referring to aging effects or developmental changes that influence the *dependent variable*. See Chapters 11 and 12.

mean An *average*, computed by summing the values of several observations and dividing by the number of observations. If you now have a grade-point average of 4.0 based on 10 courses and you get an F in this course, then your new grade-point average (the mean) will be 3.6. See Chapter 21.

measurement bias A threat to the validity of outcome studies that can occur when participants are influenced by practitioners or researchers to respond in ways that reflect the desired outcome. See Chapter 11.

measurement equivalence The degree to which instruments or observed behaviors have the same meaning across cultures, relate to referent theoretical constructs in the same way across cultures, and have the same causal linkages across cultures. See Chapter 6.

median Another *average*; it represents the value of the "middle" case in a rank-ordered set of observations. If the ages of five men are 16, 17, 20, 54, and 88, then the median would be 20 (the *mean* would be 39). See Chapter 21.

mediating variable (*or* intervening variable) The mechanism by which an *independent variable* affects a *dependent variable*. See Chapter 8.

member checking A strategy for improving the trustworthiness of qualitative research findings in which researchers ask the participants in their research to confirm or disconfirm the accuracy of the research observations and interpretations. Do the reported observations and interpretations ring true and have meaning to the participants? See Chapter 18.

memoing A qualitative data analysis technique used at several stages of data processing to capture code meanings, theoretical ideas, preliminary conclusions, and other thoughts that will be useful during analysis. See Chapter 20.

meta-analysis A procedure for calculating the average strength of association between variables (i.e., the mean *effect size*) across previously completed research studies in a particular field. See Chapter 22.

metric equivalence (*or* psychometric equivalence *or* scalar equivalence) Scores on a measure being comparable across cultures. See Chapter 6.

mixed-methods research A stand-alone research design in which a single study not only collects both qualitative and quantitative data but also integrates both sources of data at one or more stages of the research process so as to improve the understanding of the phenomenon being investigated. See Chapter 4.

mixed-mode surveys Surveys that mix different quantitative methods. See Chapter 16.

mode The most frequently observed value or attribute. If a sample contains 1,000 Protestants, 275 Catholics, and 33 Jews, then Protestant is the modal category. See Chapter 21.

moderating variable A variable that influences the strength or direction of a relationship between *independent* and *dependent variables*. See Chapter 8.

multiphase mixed-methods design This design is distinguished by the use of several mixed methods projects that are implemented in multiple phases over time in a longitudinal study in which the multiple projects focus on a common objective. See Chapter 4.

multiple-baseline design A type of *single-case evaluation* design that attempts to control for extraneous variables by having more than one *baseline* and intervention phase. See Chapter 13.

multiple-component design A type of *single-case evaluation design* that attempts to determine which parts of an intervention package really account for the change in the target problem. See Chapter 13.

multiple pretests Administering the same pretest at different time points before intervention begins. See Chapter 12.

multiple regression analysis A multivariate statistical procedure that shows the overall correlation between a set (or sets) of *independent variables* and an *interval- or ratio-level dependent variable*. See Chapter 22.

multiple time-series designs A form of time-series analysis in which both an *experimental group* and a *nonequivalent comparison group* are measured at multiple points in time before and after an intervention is introduced to the experimental group. See Chapter 12.

multivariate analysis The analysis of the simultaneous relationships among several variables. Examining simultaneously the effects of age, sex, and social class on religiosity would be an example of multivariate analysis. See Chapters 11, 21, and 22.

naturalism A qualitative research paradigm that emphasizes observing people in their natural, everyday social settings and on reporting their stories the way they tell them. See Chapter 18.

needs assessment Systematically researching diagnostic questions for program planning purposes. For example, community residents might be surveyed to

assess their need for new child care services. See Chapter 14.

negative case analysis A strategy for improving the trustworthiness of qualitative research findings in which researchers show they have searched thoroughly for disconfirming evidence—looking for deviant cases that do not fit the researcher's interpretations. See Chapter 18.

negative relationship A *relationship* between two *variables* in which one variable increases in value as the other variable decreases. For example, we might expect to find a negative relationship between the level of utilization of community-based aftercare services and rehospitalization rates. See Chapter 8.

nominal measure A level of measurement that describes a variable whose different attributes differ only categorically and not metrically, as distinguished from *ordinal*, *interval*, or *ratio measures*. Gender would be an example of a nominal measure. See Chapters 10 and 21.

nomothetic model An approach to explanation in which we attempt to discover factors that can offer a general, though imperfect, explanation of some phenomenon. For example, we might note that education seems to reduce prejudice in general. Even though we recognize that some educated people are prejudiced and some uneducated people are not, we have learned some of what causes prejudice or tolerance in general. By contrast, see *idiographic*. See Chapter 3.

nondirectional hypotheses Predicted relationships between variables that do not specify whether the predicted relationship will be positive or negative. See Chapter 22.

nonequivalent comparison groups design A *quasi-experimental design* in which the researcher finds two existing groups that appear to be similar and measures change on a *dependent variable* before and after an intervention is introduced to one of the groups. See Chapter 12.

nonparametric tests *Tests of statistical* significance that have been created for use when not all of the assumptions of *parametric* statistics can be met. *Chi-square* is the most commonly used nonparametric test. See Chapter 22.

nonprobability sampling Selecting a sample in some fashion other than those suggested by probability theory. Examples include *judgmental (purposive)*, *quota*, and *snowball sampling*. See Chapters 15 and 18.

nonresponse bias   A threat to the representativeness of survey findings, the seriousness of which depends on the extent to which survey respondents differ from nonrespondents in important ways relevant to the research question. See Chapter 16.

novelty and disruption effects   A form of *research reactivity* in experiments in which the sense of excitement, energy, and enthusiasm among recipients of an evaluated intervention—and not the intervention itself—causes the desired change in their behavior. See Chapter 11.

NVivo   A computer program designed to assist researchers in the analysis of qualitative data. See Chapter 21.

null hypothesis   In connection with *hypothesis testing* and *tests of statistical significance*, the *hypothesis* that suggests there is no relationship between the variables under study. You may conclude that the two variables are related after having statistically rejected the null hypothesis. See Chapters 21 and 22.

number needed to treat (NNT)   The number of people necessary to treat in order to reduce the number of undesirable outcomes by one. See Chapter 22.

observations   Information we gather by experience in the real world that helps us build a *theory* or verify whether it is correct when testing *hypotheses*. See Chapter 3.

observer as participant   One who identifies himself or herself as a researcher and interacts with the participants in the social process but makes no pretense of actually being a participant. See Chapter 19.

obtrusive observation   Occurs when the participant is keenly aware of being observed and thus may be predisposed to behave in socially desirable ways and in ways that meet *experimenter expectancies*. See Chapters 11, 12, 13, and 17.

odds ratio   How much more or less likely a certain dichotomous dependent variable outcome is for the dichotomous categories of the independent variable. See Chapter 21.

one-group pretest–posttest design   A *preexperimental design*, with low *internal validity*, that assesses a *dependent variable* before and after a stimulus is introduced but does not attempt to control for alternative explanations of any changes in scores that are observed. See Chapters 11 and 12.

one-shot case study   A *preexperimental research design*, with low *internal validity*, that simply measures a single group of subjects on a *dependent variable* at one point in time after they have been exposed to a stimulus. See Chapters 11 and 12.

one-tailed test of significance   *Statistical significance tests* that place the entire *critical region* at the predicted end of the *theoretical sampling distribution* and thus limit the inference of *statistical significance* to findings that are only in the critical region of the predicted direction. See Chapter 22.

online surveys   Surveys conducted via the Internet—either by e-mail or through a website. See Chapter 16.

open coding   A qualitative data-processing method in which, instead of starting out with a list of code categories derived from theory, one develops code categories through close examination of qualitative data. During *open coding*, the data are broken down into discrete parts, closely examined, and compared for similarities and differences. Questions are asked about the phenomena as reflected in the data. Through this process, one's own and others' assumptions about phenomena are questioned or explored, leading to new discoveries. See Chapter 20.

open-ended questions   Questions for which respondents are asked to provide their own answer rather than selecting from among a list of possible responses provided by the researcher as for *closed-ended questions*. See Chapter 10.

operational definition   The concrete and specific *definition* of something in terms of the *operations* by which observations are to be categorized. The *operational definition* of "earning an A in this course" might be "correctly answering at least 90% of the final exam questions." See Chapters 8 and 13.

operationalization   One step beyond *conceptualization*. Operationalization is the process of developing *operational definitions*. See Chapter 8.

oral history interviews   See *life history*.

ordinal measure   A level of measurement describing a variable whose attributes may be rank ordered along some dimension. An example would be measuring "socioeconomic status" by the *attributes* high, medium, and low. See also *nominal measure*, *interval measure*, and *ratio measure* and Chapters 10 and 21.

panel attrition   A problem facing *panel studies*, based on the fact that some respondents who are studied in the first wave of the survey may not participate later. See Chapter 7.

panel studies   *Longitudinal studies* in which data are collected from the same *sample* (the panel) at several points in time. See Chapter 7.

PAR   See *participatory action research*.

paradigm   (1) A model or frame of reference that shapes our observations and understandings. For example, "functionalism" leads us to examine society in terms of the functions served by its constituent parts, whereas "interactionism" leads us to focus attention on the ways people deal with each other face-to-face and arrive at shared meanings for things. (2) Almost a quarter. See Chapter 3.

parallel-forms reliability   Consistency of measurement between two equivalent measurement instruments. See Chapter 9.

parameter   A summary statistic describing a given variable in a population, such as the mean income of all families in a city or the age distribution of the city's *population*. See Chapter 15 and Appendix B.

parametric tests   Tests of statistical significance that assume that at least one variable being studied has an interval or ratio level of measurement, that the sample distribution of the relevant parameters of those variables is normal, and that the different groups being compared have been randomly selected and are independent of one another. Commonly used parametric tests are the t-*test*, *analysis of variance*, and *Pearson product-moment correlation*. See Chapter 22.

participant as observer   In this role, you would participate fully with the group under study, but you would make it clear that you were also undertaking research. See Chapter 19.

participatory action research (PAR)   A qualitative research paradigm in which the researcher's function is to serve as a resource to those being studied—typically, disadvantaged groups—as an opportunity for them to act effectively in their own interest. The disadvantaged participants define their problems, define the remedies desired, and take the lead in designing the research that will help them realize their aims. See Chapter 18.

passage of time   A threat to *internal validity* referring to changes in a *dependent variable* that occur naturally as time passes and not because of the *independent variable*. See Chapters 11 and 12.

path analysis   A statistical procedure, based on *regression analysis*, that provides a graphic picture of a causal model for understanding relationships between variables. See Chapter 23.

Pearson product-moment correlation (*r*)   A *parametric* measure of association, ranging from −1.0 to +1.0, used when both the *independent* and *dependent variables* are at the *interval* or *ratio level* of measurement. See Chapter 22.

peer debriefing and support   A strategy for improving the trustworthiness of qualitative research findings in which teams of investigators meet regularly to give each other feedback, emotional support, alternative perspectives, and new ideas about how they are collecting data or about problems and about meanings in the data already collected. See Chapter 18.

phone tracking   A method of locating and contacting research participants—particularly those who are transient or homeless—to secure their participation in future sessions or interviews. This method involves repeated telephoning of *anchor points* in advance to schedule an interview and providing participants a toll-free number where they can leave messages about appointment changes or changes in how to locate them, incentives for leaving such messages, and a card that lists appointment times and the research project's address and telephone number. See Chapter 6.

placebo control group design   An experimental design that controls for *placebo effects* by randomly assigning subjects to an *experimental group* and two *control groups* and exposing one of the control groups to a stimulus that is designed to resemble the special attention received by subjects in the experimental group. See *placebo effects* and Chapter 11.

placebo effects   Changes in a *dependent variable* that are caused by the power of suggestion among participants in an *experimental group* that they are receiving something special that is expected to help them. These changes would not occur if they received the experimental intervention without that awareness. See Chapter 11.

plagiarism   Presenting someone else's words or thoughts as though they were your own; constitutes intellectual theft. See Chapter 23.

population   The group or collection that a researcher is interested in generalizing about. More formally, it is the theoretically specified aggregation of study elements. See Chapter 15.

positive relationship   A *relationship* between two *variables* in which one variable increases in value as the other variable also increases in value (or one decreases as the other decreases). For example, we might expect to find a positive relationship between rate of unemployment and extent of homelessness. See Chapter 8.

positivism A paradigm introduced by August Comte that held that social behavior could be studied and understood in a rational, scientific manner—in contrast to explanations based in religion or superstition. See Chapter 3.

possible-code cleaning Examining the distribution of responses to each item in a data set to check for errors in data entered into a computer by looking for impossible code categories that have some responses and then correcting the errors. See Chapter 21.

postmodernism A *paradigm* that rejects the notion of a knowable objective social reality. See Chapter 3.

posttest-only control group design A variation of the classical *experimental design* that avoids the possible testing effects associated with pretesting by testing only after the *experimental group* receives the intervention, based on the assumption that the process of *random assignment* provides for equivalence between the experimental and control groups on the *dependent variable* before the exposure to the intervention. See also *pretest–posttest control group design*. See Chapter 11.

posttest-only design with nonequivalent groups A *preexperimental design* that involves two groups that may not be comparable in which the *dependent variable* is assessed after the *independent variable* is introduced for one of the groups. See Chapter 12.

PPS See *probability proportionate to size*.

practice models Guides to help us organize our views about social work practice that may reflect a synthesis of existing theories. See Chapter 3.

PRE See *proportionate reduction of error*.

predictive validity A form of *criterion-related validity* involving a measure's ability to predict a criterion that will occur in the future. See Chapter 9.

preexperimental designs Pilot study designs for evaluating the effectiveness of interventions; they do not control for threats to *internal validity*. See Chapters 11 and 12.

pretest–posttest control group design The classical *experimental design* in which subjects are assigned randomly to an *experimental group* that receives an intervention being evaluated and to a *control group* that does not receive it. Each group is tested on the *dependent variable* before and after the experimental group receives the intervention. See Chapter 11.

pretesting Testing out a scale or questionnaire in a dry run to see if the target population will understand it and not find it too unwieldy as well as to identify any needed modifications. See Chapters 6 and 10.

probabilistic knowledge Knowledge based on probability that enables us to say that if A occurs, then B is more likely to occur. It does not enable us to say that B will occur or even that B will probably occur. See Chapter 3.

probability proportionate to size (PPS) This refers to a type of multistage *cluster sample* in which clusters are selected, not with equal probabilities (see *equal probability of selection method*) but with probabilities proportionate to their sizes—as measured by the number of units to be subsampled. See Chapter 15.

probability sample The general term for a sample selected in accord with probability theory, typically involving some *random selection* mechanism. Specific types of *probability samples* include *area probability sample, EPSEM, PPS, simple random sample*, and *systematic sample*. See Chapter 15.

probability sampling The use of *random sampling* techniques that allow a researcher to make relatively few observations and generalize from those observations to a much wider population. See Chapter 15.

probe A technique employed in interviewing to solicit a more complete answer to a question, this nondirective phrase or question is used to encourage a respondent to elaborate on an answer. Examples include "Anything more?" and "How is that?" See Chapters 16 and 19 for discussions of interviewing.

prolonged engagement A strategy for improving the trustworthiness of qualitative research findings that attempts to reduce the impact of *reactivity* and respondent *bias* by forming a long and trusting relationship with respondents and by conducting lengthy interviews or a series of follow-up interviews with the same respondent. This improves the likelihood that the respondent ultimately will disclose socially undesirable truths and improves the researcher's ability to detect distortion. See Chapter 18.

proportionate reduction of error (PRE) The proportion of errors reduced in predicting the value for one variable based on knowing the value for the other. The stronger the relationship is, the more our prediction errors will be reduced. See Chapter 22.

pseudoscience Fake science about an area of inquiry or practice that has the surface appearance of being scientific but on careful inspection can be seen to violate one or more principles of the scientific method or contain fallacies against which the scientific method attempts to guard. See Chapter 1.

psychometric equivalence See *metric equivalence* and Chapter 6.

purposive sample See *judgmental sample* and Chapters 15 and 18.

purposive sampling Selecting a sample of observations that the researcher believes will yield the most comprehensive understanding of the subject of study, based on the researcher's intuitive feel for the subject that comes from extended observation and reflection. See Chapters 15 and 18.

qualitative analysis The nonnumerical examination and interpretation of observations for the purpose of discovering underlying meanings and patterns of relationships. This is most typical of field research and historical research. See Chapter 20.

qualitative interview An interaction between an interviewer and a *respondent* in which the interviewer usually has a general plan of inquiry but not a specific set of questions that must be asked in particular words and in a particular order. Ideally, the respondent does most of the talking. See Chapter 19.

qualitative research methods Research methods that emphasize depth of understanding and the deeper meanings of human experience and that aim to generate theoretically richer albeit more tentative observations. Commonly used qualitative methods include participant observation, direct observation, and unstructured or intensive interviewing. See Chapters 4, 18, 19, and 20.

quantitative analysis The numerical representation and manipulation of observations for the purpose of describing and explaining the phenomena that those observations reflect. See especially Chapter 21 and also the remainder of Part 7.

quantitative research methods Research methods that typically seek to produce precise and generalizable findings. Studies using quantitative methods typically attempt to formulate all or most of their research procedures in advance and then try to adhere precisely to those procedures with maximum objectivity as data are collected. See Chapter 4.

quasi-experimental design Design that attempts to control for threats to *internal validity* and thus permits causal inferences but is distinguished from true experiments primarily by the lack of *random assignment* of subjects. See Chapter 12.

questionnaire A document that contains questions and other types of items that are designed to solicit information appropriate to analysis. Questionnaires are used primarily in survey research and also in experiments, field research, and other modes of observation. See Chapters 10 and 16.

quota sampling A type of *nonprobability sample* in which units are selected into the sample on the basis of prespecified characteristics so that the total sample will have the same distribution of characteristics as are assumed to exist in the population being studied. See Chapters 15 and 18.

r^2 The proportion of variation in the *dependent variable* that is explained by the *independent variable*. See Chapter 22.

random error A measurement error that has no consistent pattern of effects and that reduces the reliability of measurement. For example, asking questions that respondents do not understand will yield inconsistent (random) answers. See Chapter 9.

random selection A *probability* sampling procedure in which each element has an equal chance of selection independent of any other event in the selection process. See Chapter 15.

randomization A technique for assigning experimental participants to *experimental groups* and *control groups* at random. See Chapter 11 and Appendix B.

randomized clinical trials (RCTs) Experiments that use random means (such as a coin toss) to assign clients who share similar problems or diagnoses into groups that receive different interventions. If the predicted difference in outcome is found between the groups, it is not plausible to attribute the difference to a priori differences between two incomparable groups. See Chapters 2 and 12.

range A measure of *dispersion* that is composed of the highest and lowest values of a variable in some set of observations. In your class, for example, the range of ages might be from 20 to 37. See Chapter 21.

rapport An open and trusting relationship. See Chapter 19.

rates under treatment An approach to needs assessment based on the number and characteristics of clients already using a service in a similar community. See Chapter 14.

ratio measure A level of measurement that describes a variable whose attributes have all the qualities of *nominal, ordinal,* and *interval measures* and also are based on a "true zero" point. Age would be an example of a ratio measure. See Chapters 10 and 21.

reactivity   A process in which change in a *dependent variable* is induced by research procedures. See Chapters 12 and 13.

recall bias   A common limitation in case control designs that occurs when a person's current recollections of the quality and value of past experiences are tainted by knowing that things didn't work out for them later in life. See Chapter 12.

reductionism   A fault of some researchers: a strict limitation (reduction) of the kinds of concepts to be considered relevant to the phenomenon under study. See Chapter 6.

reflexivity   A key part of all qualitative research methods that requires that researchers continually reflect on how their own experiences, assumptions, and biases might be influencing what they research, what they or their research participants say or do, and how they interpret what their research participants say or do. See Chapter 19.

reification   The process of regarding as real things that are not real. See Chapter 8.

relationship   *Variables* that change together in a consistent, predictable fashion. See Chapters 3 and 8.

reliability   That quality of a measurement method that suggests that the same data would have been collected each time in repeated observations of the same phenomenon. In the context of a survey, we would expect that the question "Did you attend church last week?" would have higher reliability than the question "About how many times have you attended church in your life?" This is not to be confused with *validity*. See Chapter 9.

reminder calls   Telephoning research participants to remind them of their scheduled treatment or assessment sessions in a study. See Chapter 6.

replication   Generally, the duplication of a study to expose or reduce error or the reintroduction or withdrawal of an intervention to increase the internal validity of a quasi-experiment or single-case design evaluation. See Chapters 1, 3, 12, and 13.

representativeness   That quality of a sample of having the same distribution of characteristics as the population from which it was selected. By implication, descriptions and explanations derived from an analysis of the sample may be assumed to represent similar ones in the population. *Representativeness* is enhanced

by *probability sampling* and provides for *generalizability* and the use of *inferential statistics*. See Chapter 15.

request for proposals (RFP)   An announcement put out by funding sources that identifies the research questions and types of designs the funding source would like to fund, encourages researchers to submit proposals to carry out such research, specifies the maximum size of the *research grant*, and provides other information about the source's expectations and funding process. See Chapter 23.

research contract   Type of funding that provides great specificity regarding what the funding source wants to have researched and how the research is to be conducted. Unlike a *research grant*, a research contract requires that the research proposal conform precisely to the funding source's *specifications*. See Chapter 23.

research design   A term often used in connection with whether logical arrangements permit causal inferences; also refers to all the decisions made in planning and conducting research. See Chapter 11.

research grant   Type of funding that usually identifies some broad priority areas the funding source has and provides researchers considerable leeway in the specifics of what they want to investigate within that area and how they want to investigate it. See Chapter 23.

research reactivity   A process in which change in a *dependent variable* is induced by research procedures. See Chapters 11, 12, and 13.

resentful demoralization   A threat to the validity of an evaluation of an intervention's effectiveness that occurs when practitioners or clients in the comparison routine-treatment condition become resentful and demoralized because they did not receive the special training or the special treatment. Consequently, their confidence or motivation may decline and may explain their inferior performance on outcome measures. See Chapter 11.

respondent   A person who provides data for analysis by responding to a survey *questionnaire* or to an interview. See Chapters 16 and 19.

response rate   The number of persons who participate in a survey divided by the number selected in the sample, in the form of a percentage. This is also called the "completion rate" or, in self-administered surveys, the "return rate"—the percentage of *questionnaires* sent out that are returned. See Chapter 16.

risk ratio   The proportion of unsuccessful outcomes in one group divided by the risk of unsuccessful outcomes in the other group. See Chapter 21.

sample   That part of a population from which we have data. See Chapter 15.

sampling   The process of selecting a sample. See Chapter 15.

sampling error   The degree of error to be expected for a given sample design, as estimated according to probability theory. See Chapter 15 and Appendix B.

sampling frame   That list or quasi list of units that compose a population from which a sample is selected. If the sample is to be *representative* of the population, then it's essential that the sampling frame include all (or nearly all) members of the population. See Chapter 15.

sampling interval   The standard distance between elements selected from a population for a sample. See Chapter 15.

sampling ratio   The proportion of elements in the population that are selected to be in a sample. See Chapter 15.

sampling unit   That element or set of elements considered for selection in some stage of sampling. See Chapter 15.

scalar equivalence   See *metric equivalence* and Chapter 6.

scale   A type of composite measure composed of several items that have a logical or empirical structure among them. See Chapter 10.

scientific method   An approach to inquiry that attempts to safeguard against errors commonly made in casual human inquiry. Chief features include viewing all knowledge as provisional and subject to refutation, searching for evidence based on systematic and comprehensive observation, pursuing objectivity in observation, and replication. See Chapter 1.

secondary analysis   A form of research in which the data collected and processed by one researcher are reanalyzed—often for a different purpose—by another. This is especially appropriate in the case of survey data. Data archives are repositories or libraries for the storage and distribution of data for secondary analysis. See Chapter 16.

selection bias   A threat to *internal validity* referring to the assignment of research participants to groups in a way that does not maximize their comparability regarding the *dependent variable*. See Chapters 11 and 12.

Selective coding   A type of coding in qualitative data analysis that seeks to identify the central code in a study: the one that all the other codes relate to. See Chapter 20.

self-mailing questionnaire   A mailed *questionnaire* that requires no return envelope: When the questionnaire is folded a particular way, the return address appears on the outside. The respondent therefore doesn't have to worry about losing the envelope. See Chapter 16.

self-report scales   A source of data in which research subjects all respond in writing to the same list of written questions or statements that has been devised to measure a particular construct. For example, a self-report scale to measure marital satisfaction might ask how often one is annoyed with one's spouse, is proud of the spouse, has fun with the spouse, and so on. See Chapters 8, 9, and 13.

self-reports   A way to operationally define *variables* according to what people say about their own thoughts, views, or behaviors. See Chapters 8 and 9.

semantic differential   A scaling format that asks respondents to choose between two opposite positions. See Chapter 10.

semiotics   The science of symbols and meanings, commonly associated with *content analysis* and based on language, that examines the agreements we have about the meanings associated with particular signs. See Chapter 20.

sensitivity   The ability of an instrument to detect subtle differences. See Chapter 9.

sex bias   The unwarranted generalization of research findings to the population as a whole when one wither males or females are not adequately represented in the research sample. See Chapter 15.

significance level   The probability level that is selected in advance to serve as a cutoff point to separate findings that will and will not be attributed to chance. Findings at or below the selected probability level are deemed to be *statistically significant*. See Chapter 22.

simple interrupted time-series design   A *quasi-experimental design* in which no comparison group is utilized and that attempts to develop causal inferences based on a comparison of trends over multiple measurements before and after an intervention is introduced. See Chapter 12.

simple random sample (SRS)   A type of *probability sample* in which the units that compose a population are assigned numbers. A set of *random* numbers is then generated, and the units having those numbers are included in the sample. Although probability theory and the calculations it provides assume this basic sampling method, it's seldom used for practical reasons. An equivalent alternative is the *systematic sample* (with a random start). See Chapter 15.

single-case evaluation design   A *time-series design* used to evaluate the impact of an intervention or a policy change on individual cases or systems. See Chapter 13.

snowball sample   A *nonprobability sample* that is obtained by asking each person interviewed to suggest additional people for interviewing. See Chapters 15 and 18.

snowball sampling   A *nonprobability* sampling method often employed in *qualitative research*. Each person interviewed may be asked to suggest additional people for interviewing. See Chapters 6, 15, and 18.

social desirability bias   A source of *systematic measurement error* involving the tendency of people to say or do things that will make them or their reference group look good. See Chapter 9.

social indicators   An approach to needs assessment based on aggregated statistics that reflect conditions of an entire population. See Chapter 14.

social justice mixed methods design   This design is distinguished by the use of various methods that are based on a social justice theory and aimed at collecting data that will yield a call for action to improve the plight of vulnerable, marginalized, or oppressed groups. See Chapter 4.

Solomon four-group design   An *experimental design* that assesses testing effects by randomly assigning subjects to four groups, introducing the intervention being evaluated to two of them, conducting both pretesting and posttesting on one group that receives the intervention and one group that does not, and conducting posttesting only on the other two groups. See Chapter 11.

specifications   Explanatory and clarifying comments about how to handle difficult or confusing situations that may occur with specific questions in the questionnaire. See Chapter 16.

spurious relationship   A relationship between two *variables* that are no longer related when a third variable is controlled; the third variable explains away the original relationship. Thus, the relationship between number of storks and number of human births in geographic areas is spurious because it is explained away

by the fact that areas with more humans are more likely to have a zoo or a larger zoo. See Chapters 8 and 11.

stakeholders   People who have some interest in a program being evaluated. See Chapter 14.

standard deviation   A descriptive statistic that portrays the dispersion of values around the *mean*. It's the square root of the averaged squared differences between each value and the mean. See Chapter 21.

standardized open-ended interviews   The most highly structured form of *qualitative interviews*, which are conducted in a consistent, thorough manner. Questions are written out in advance exactly the way they are to be asked in the interview, reducing the chances that variations in responses are being caused by changes in the way interviews are being conducted. See Chapter 19.

static-group comparison design   A *cross-sectional design* for comparing different groups on a *dependent variable* at one point in time. The *validity* of this design will be influenced by the extent to which it contains multivariate controls for alternative explanations for differences among the groups. See Chapters 11 and 12.

statistic   A summary description of a *variable* in a *sample*. See Appendix B.

statistical power analysis   Assessment of the probability of avoiding *Type II errors*. See Chapter 22.

statistical regression   A threat to *internal validity* referring to the tendency for extreme scores at pretest to become less extreme at posttest. See Chapter 11.

statistical significance   A general term that refers to the unlikelihood that relationships observed in a sample could be attributed to sampling error alone. See *tests of statistical significance* and Chapter 22.

stratification   The grouping of the units that compose a population into homogeneous groups (or "strata") before sampling. This procedure, which may be used in conjunction with *simple random*, *systematic*, or *cluster sampling*, improves the *representativeness* of a sample, at least in terms of the stratification variables. See Chapter 15.

stratified sampling   A probability sampling procedure that uses *stratification* to ensure that appropriate numbers of elements are drawn from homogeneous subsets of that population. See *stratification* and Chapter 15.

study population   The aggregation of elements from which the sample is actually selected. See Chapter 15.

substantive significance   The importance, or meaningfulness, of a finding from a practical standpoint. See Chapter 22.

summative evaluation   A type of program evaluation focusing on the ultimate success of a program and decisions about whether it should be continued or chosen from among alternative options. See Chapter 14.

switching replication   A way to detect selection bias in a quasi experiment that involves administering the treatment to the comparison group after the first posttest. If we replicate in that group—in a second posttest—the improvement made by the experimental group in the first posttest, then we reduce doubt as to whether the improvement at the first posttest was merely a function of a selection bias. If our second posttest results do not replicate the improvement made by the experimental group in the first posttest, then the difference between the groups at the first posttest can be attributed to the lack of comparability between the two groups. See Chapter 12.

systematic error   An error in measurement with a consistent pattern of effects. For example, when child welfare workers ask abusive parents whether they have been abusing their children, they may get biased answers that are consistently untrue because parents do not want to admit to abusive behavior. Contrast this to *random error*, which has no consistent pattern of effects. See Chapter 9.

systematic review   A report of a comprehensive search for unpublished as well as published studies that address a particular research question. See Chapter 2.

systematic sample   A type of *probability sample* in which every kth unit in a list is selected for inclusion in the sample—for example, every 25th student in the college directory of students. We compute k by dividing the size of the population by the desired sample size; the result is called the *sampling interval*. Within certain constraints, systematic sampling is a functional equivalent of *simple random sampling* and usually easier to do. Typically, the first unit is selected at random. See Chapter 15.

***t*-test**   A test of the *statistical significance* of the difference between the *means* of two groups. See Chapter 23.

test–retest reliability   Consistency, or stability, of measurement over time. See Chapter 9.

tests of statistical significance   A class of statistical computations that indicate the likelihood that the relationship observed between variables in a sample can be attributed to sampling error only. See *inferential statistics* and Chapter 22.

theoretical sampling distribution   The distribution of outcomes produced by an infinite number of randomly drawn samples or random subdivisions of a sample. This distribution identifies the proportion of times that each outcome of a study could be expected to occur as a result of chance. See Chapter 22.

theory   A systematic set of interrelated statements intended to explain some aspect of social life or enrich our sense of how people conduct and find meaning in their daily lives. See Chapter 3.

time-series designs   A set of *quasi-experimental designs* in which multiple observations of a *dependent variable* are conducted before and after an intervention is introduced. See Chapter 12.

translation equivalence   See *linguistic equivalence*, *translation validity*, and Chapter 6.

translation validity   Successful translation of a measure into the language of respondents who are not fluent in the majority language, thus attaining *linguistic equivalence*. See Chapter 6.

trend studies   *Longitudinal studies* that monitor a given characteristic of some population over time. An example would be annual canvasses of schools of social work to identify trends over time in the number of students who specialize in direct practice, generalist practice, and administration and planning. See Chapter 7.

triangulation   The use of more than one imperfect data collection alternative in which each option is vulnerable to different potential sources of error. For example, instead of relying exclusively on a client's *self-report* of how often a particular target behavior occurred during a specified period, a significant other (teacher, cottage parent, and so on) is asked to monitor the behavior as well. See Chapters 9, 13, and 18.

two-tailed tests of significance   Statistical significance tests that divide the *critical region* at both ends of the *theoretical sampling distribution* and add the probability at both ends when calculating the *level of significance*. See Chapter 22.

Type I error   An error we risk committing whenever we reject the *null hypothesis*. It occurs when we reject a true null hypothesis. See Chapter 22.

Type II error   An error we risk committing whenever we fail to reject the *null hypothesis*. It occurs when we fail to reject a false null hypothesis. See Chapters 21 and 23.

units of analysis   The "what" or "whom" being studied. In social science research, the most typical units of analysis are individual people. See Chapter 7.

univariate analysis   The analysis of a single variable for purposes of description. *Frequency distributions*, *averages*, and measures of *dispersion* would be examples of *univariate analysis*, as distinguished from *bivariate* and *multivariate analysis*. See Chapter 21.

unobtrusive observation   Unlike in *obtrusive observation*, the participant does not notice the observation and is therefore less influenced to behave in socially desirable ways and ways that meet *experimenter expectancies*. See Chapters 11, 12, 13, and 17.

validity   A descriptive term used of a measure that accurately reflects the concept that it's intended to measure. For example, your IQ would seem a more valid measure of your intelligence than would the number of hours you spend in the library. Realize that the ultimate validity of a measure can never be proven, but we may still agree to its *relative validity*, *content validity*, *construct validity*, *internal validation*, and *external validation*. This must not be confused with *reliability*. See Chapter 9.

variable-oriented analysis   A *qualitative data analysis* method that focuses on interrelations among variables, with the people observed being the primary carriers of those variables. See Chapter 20.

variables   Logical groupings of *attributes*. The variable "gender" contains the attributes "male" and "female." See Chapters 3 and 8.

verstehen   The German word meaning "understanding," used in qualitative research in connection to *hermeneutics*, in which the researcher tries mentally to take on the circumstances, views, and feelings of those being studied to interpret their actions appropriately. See Chapter 17.

weighting   A procedure employed in connection with sampling whereby units selected with unequal probabilities are assigned weights in such a manner as to make the sample representative of the population from which it was selected. See Chapter 15.

withdrawal/reversal design   See *ABAB withdrawal/reversal design*.

AAPOR Cell Phone Task Force. (2010). New considerations for survey researchers when planning and conducting RDD telephone surveys in the U.S. with respondents reached via cell phone numbers. Online at http://www.aapor.org/AM/Template.cfm?Section=Cell_Phone_Task_Force_Report&Template=/CM/ContentDisplay.cfm&ContentID=3179#.UrCkt5Fe3PQ.

Abramovitz, R., Ivanoff, A., Mosseri, R., & O'Sullivan, A. (1997). Comments on outcomes measurement in mental and behavioral health. In E. J. Mullen & J. L. Magnabosco (Eds.), *Outcomes measurement in the human services: Cross-cutting issues and methods* (pp. 293–296). Washington, DC: NASW Press.

Acker, J., Barry, K., & Esseveld, J. (1983). Objectivity and truth: Problems in doing feminist research. *Women's Studies International Forum, 6,* 423–435.

Adler, P. A., & Adler, P. (1994). Observational techniques. In N. K. Denzin & Y. S. Lincoln (Eds.), *Handbook of qualitative research* (pp. 377–392). Thousand Oaks, CA: Sage.

Aiken, L. R. 1985. *Psychological testing and assessment*. Rockleigh, NJ: Allyn & Bacon.

Alexander, L. B., & Solomon, P. (Eds.). (2006). *The research process in the human services: Behind the scenes*. Belmont, CA: Thomson Brooks/Cole.

Allen, J., & Walsh, J. A. (2000). A construct-based approach to equivalence: Methodologies for cross-cultural/multicultural personality assessment research. In R. Dana (Ed.), *Handbook of cross-cultural personality assessment* (pp. 63–85). Mahwah, NJ: Lawrence Erlbaum Associates.

Allen, K. R., & Walker, A. J. (1992). A feminist analysis of interviews with elderly mothers and their daughters. In J. Gilgun, K. Daly, & G. Handel (Eds.), *Qualitative Methods in Family Research* (pp. 63–85). Thousand Oaks, CA: Sage.

Altheide, D. L., & Johnson, J. M. (1994). Criteria for assessing interpretive validity in qualitative research. In N. K. Denzin & Y. S. Lincoln (Eds.), *Handbook of qualitative research* (pp. 485–499). Thousand Oaks, CA: Sage.

Altman, J. C. (2008). A study of engagement in neighborhood-based child welfare services. *Research on Social Work Practice, 18*(6), 555–564.

Alvidrez, J., Azocar, F., & Miranda, J. (1996). Demystifying the concept of ethnicity for psychotherapy researchers. *Journal of Consulting and Clinical Psychology, 64*(5), 903–908.

American Psychiatric Association Task Force for the Handbook of Psychiatric Measures. (2000). *Handbook of psychiatric measures*. Washington, DC: American Psychiatric Association.

Anastasi, A. (1988). *Psychological testing*. New York: Macmillan.

Andrulis, R. S. (1977). *Adult assessment: A source book of tests and measures of human behavior*. Springfield, IL: Thomas.

Aneshenshel, C. S., Becerra, R. M., Fiedler, E. P., & Schuler, R. A. (1989). Participation of Mexican American female adolescents in a longitudinal panel survey. *Public Opinion Quarterly, 53*(Winter), 548–562.

Areán, P. A., & Gallagher-Thompson, D. (1996). Issues and recommendations for the recruitment and retention of older ethnic minority adults into clinical research. *Journal of Consulting and Clinical Psychology, 64*(5), 875–880.

Arnold, B. R., & Matus, Y. E. (2000). Test translation and cultural equivalence methodologies for use with diverse populations. In I. Cuéllar & F. A. Paniagua (Eds.), *Handbook of multicultural mental health: Assessment and treatment of diverse populations* (pp. 121–135). San Diego: Academic Press.

Asch, S. E. (1958). Effects of group pressure upon the modification and distortion of judgments. In E. E. Maccoby, T. M. Newcomb, & E. L. Hartley (Eds.), *Readings in social psychology* (3rd ed., pp. 174–183). New York: Holt, Rinehart and Winston.

Asher, R. M., & Fine, G. A. (1991). Fragile ties: Sharing research relationships with women married to alcoholics. In W. B. Shaffir & R. A. Stebbins (Eds.), *Experiencing fieldwork: An inside view of qualitative research* (pp. 196–205). Newbury Park, CA: Sage.

Babbie, E. R. (1966). The third civilization. *Review of Religious Research* (Winter), 101–102.

Babbie, E. R. (1985). *You can make a difference.* New York: St. Martin's Press.

Babbie, E. R. (1986). *Observing ourselves: Essays in social research.* Belmont, CA: Wadsworth.

Babbie, E. R. (1990). *Survey research methods.* Belmont, CA: Wadsworth.

Babbie, E. R., Halley, F., & Zaino, J. (2000). *Adventures in social research.* Newbury Park, CA: Pine Forge Press.

Baker, V., & Lambert, C. (1990). The National Collegiate Athletic Association and the governance of higher education. *Sociological Quarterly, 31*(3), 403–421.

Banfield, E. (1968). *The unheavenly city: The nature and future of our urban crisis.* Boston: Little, Brown.

Barlow, D. H., & Hersen, M. (1984). *Single case experimental designs: Strategies for studying behavior change* (2nd ed.). New York: Pergamon Press.

Bartko, J. J., Carpenter, W. T., & McGlashan, T. H. (1988). Statistical issues in long-term follow-up studies. *Schizophrenia Bulletin, 14*(4), 575–587.

Baxter, E., & Hopper, K. (1982). The new mendicancy: Homeless in New York City. *American Journal of Orthopsychiatry, 52*(3), 393–407.

Bednarz, M. (1996, April 5). Push polls statement. Report to the AAPORnet listserv. Available: mbednarz@umich.edu.

Beebe, L. (1993). *Professional writing for the human services.* Washington, DC: NASW Press.

Beere, C. A. (1979). *Women and women's issues: A handbook of tests and measures.* San Francisco: Jossey-Bass.

Beere, C. A. (1990). *Sex and gender issues: A handbook of tests and measures.* New York: Greenwood Press.

Belcher, J. (1991). Understanding the process of social drift among the homeless: A qualitative analysis. Paper presented at the Research Conference on Qualitative Methods in Social Work Practice Research, Nelson A. Rockefeller Institute of Government, State University of New York at Albany, August 24.

Bellah, R. N. (1970). Christianity and symbolic realism. *Journal for the Scientific Study of Religion, 9,* 89–96.

Bellah, R. N. (1974). Comment on the limits of symbolic realism. *Journal for the Scientific Study of Religion, 13,* 487–489.

Bennet, C. A., & Lumsdaine, A. A. (Eds.). (1975). *Evaluation and experiment.* New York: Academic Press.

Benton, J. E., & Daly, J. (1991). A question order effect in a local government survey. *Public Opinion Quarterly, 55,* 640–642.

Berg, B. L. (1989). *Qualitative research methods for the social sciences.* Boston: Allyn & Bacon.

Berg, B. L. (1998). *Qualitative research methods for the social sciences* (3rd ed.). Boston: Allyn & Bacon.

Berg, B. L. (2007). *Qualitative research methods for the social sciences* (6th ed.). Boston: Allyn & Bacon.

Bernstein, I. H., & Havig, P. (1999). *Computer literacy: Getting the most from your PC.* Thousand Oaks, CA: Sage.

Beutler, L. E., Brown, M. T., Crothers, L., Booker, K., & Seabrook, M. K. (1996). The dilemma of factitious demographic distinctions in psychological research. *Journal of Consulting and Clinical Psychology, 64*(5), 892–902.

Beveridge, W. I. B. (1950). *The art of scientific investigation.* New York: Vintage Books.

Bian, Y. (1994). *Work and inequality in urban China.* Albany: State University of New York Press.

Biggerstaff, M. A., Morris, P. M., & Nichols-Casebolt, A. (2002). Living on the edge: Examination of people attending food pantries and soup kitchens. *Social Work, 47*(3), 267–277.

Billups, J. O., & Julia, M. C. (1987). Changing profile of social work practice: A content analysis. *Social Work Research and Abstracts, 23*(4), 17–22.

Birchfield, R. W. (1998). *The new Fowler's modern English usage* (3rd ed.). New York: Oxford University Press.

Black, D. (1970). Production of crime rates. *American Sociological Review, 35*(August), 733–748.

Blair, J., Zhao, S., Bickart, B., & Kuhn, R. (1995). *Sample design for household telephone surveys: A bibliography 1949–1995.* College Park: Survey Research Center, University of Maryland.

Blalock, H. M. (1972). *Social statistics.* New York: McGraw-Hill.

Blaunstein, A., & Zangrando, R. (Eds.). (1970). *Civil rights and the black American.* New York: Washington Square Press.

Blood, R. O., & Wolfe, W. (1960). *Husbands and wives: The dynamics of married living.* New York: Free Press.

Bloom, M., Fischer, J., & Orme, J. G. (2006). *Evaluating practice: Guidelines for the accountable professional* (5th ed.). Boston: Allyn & Bacon.

Blumberg, S. J., & Luke, J. (2013). *Wireless substitution: Early release of estimates from the National Health Interview Survey, January–June, 2013.* National Center for Health Statistics. Retrieved from http://www.cdc.gov/nchs/data/nhis/earlyrelease/wireless201312.pdf.

Blythe, B. J., & Briar, S. (1987). Direct practice effectiveness. In *Encyclopedia of social work* (18th ed., Vol. 1, pp. 399–408). Silver Spring, MD: National Association of Social Workers.

Bogdan, R., & Taylor, S. J. (1990). Looking at the bright side: A positive approach to qualitative policy and evaluation research. *Qualitative Sociology, 13*(2), 183–192.

Bohrnstedt, G. W. (1983). Measurement. In P. H. Rossi, J. D. Wright, & A. B. Anderson (Eds.), *Handbook of survey research* (pp. 70–121). New York: Academic Press.

Boone, C. R., Coulton, C. J., & Keller, S. M. (1981). The impact of early and comprehensive social work services on length of stay. *Social Work in Health Care (Fall)*, 1–9.

Booth, C. (1970). *The life and labour of the people of London*. New York: AMS Press. (Original work published 1891–1903).

Botein, B. (1965). The Manhattan Bail Project: Its impact in criminology and the criminal law process. *Texas Law Review, 43*, 319–331.

Boyd, L., Hylton, J., & Price, S. (1978). Computers in social work practice: A review. *Social Work, 23*(5), 368–371.

Bradburn, N. M., & Sudman, S. (1988). *Polls and surveys: Understanding what they tell us*. San Francisco: Jossey-Bass.

Bradford, J., Cahill, S., Grasso, C., & Makadon, H. (2012). *How to ask about sexual orientation and gender identity in clinical settings*. Boston: The Fenway Institute.

Brannen, S. J., & Rubin, A. (1996). Comparing the effectiveness of gender-specific and couples groups in a court-mandated spouse abuse treatment program. *Research on Social Work Practice, 6*(4), 405–424.

Briar, S. (1973). Effective social work intervention in direct practice: Implications for education. In *Facing the challenge: Plenary session papers from the 19th annual program meeting* (pp. 17–30). Alexandria, VA: Council on Social Work Education.

Briar, S. (1987). Direct practice: Trends and issues. In *Encyclopedia of social work* (18th ed., Vol. 1, pp. 393–398). Silver Spring, MD: National Association of Social Workers.

Briggs, H. E., & Rzepnicki, T. L. (Eds.). (2004). *Using evidence in social work practice: Behavioral perspectives*. Chicago: Lyceum Books.

Brodsky, S. L., & Smitherman, H. O. (1983). *Handbook of scales for research in crime and delinquency*. New York: Plenum Press.

Brownlee, K. A. (1975). A note on the effects of nonresponse on surveys. *Journal of the American Statistical Association, 52*(227), 29–32.

Buckingham, R., Lack, S., Mount, B., MacLean, L., & Collins, J. (1976). Living with the dying. *Canadian Medical Association Journal, 115*, 1211–1215.

Burnette, D. (1994). Managing chronic illness alone in late life: Sisyphus at work. In C. Reissman (Ed.), *Qualitative studies in social work research* (pp. 5–27). Thousand Oaks, CA: Sage.

Burnette, D. (1998). Conceptual and methodological considerations in research with non-white ethnic elders. In M. Potocky & A. Y. Rodgers-Farmer (Eds.), *Social work research with minority and oppressed populations: Methodological issues and innovations* (pp. 71–91). New York: Haworth Press.

Buros, O. (1978). *Eighth mental measurements yearbook*. Highland Park, NJ: Gryphon Press.

Campbell, D. T. (1971). Methods for the experimenting society. Paper presented at the meeting of the Eastern Psychological Association, New York, and at the meeting of the American Psychological Association, Washington, DC.

Campbell, D. T., & Stanley, J. (1963). *Experimental and quasi-experimental designs for research*. Chicago: Rand McNally.

Campbell, P. B. (1983). The impact of societal biases on research methods. In B. L. Richardson & J. Wirtenberg (Eds.), *Sex role research* (pp. 197–213). New York: Praeger.

Carmines, E. G., & Zeller, R. A. (1979). *Reliability and validity assessment*. Beverly Hills, CA: Sage.

Cauce, A. M., Coronado, N., & Watson, J. (1998). Conceptual, methodological, and statistical issues in culturally competent research. In M. Hernandez & M. R. Isaacs (Eds.), *Promoting cultural competence in children's mental health services* (pp. 305–329). Baltimore: Paul H. Brookes.

Cautela, J. R. (1981). *Behavior analysis forms for clinical intervention* (Vol. 2). Champaign, IL: Research Press.

Chaffee, S., & Choe, S. Y. (1980). Time of decision and media use during the Ford-Carter campaign. *Public Opinion Quarterly (Spring)*, 53–69.

Chambless, C. M., Baker, M. J., Baucom, D. H., Beutler, L. E., Calhoun, K. S., Crits-Christoph, P., et al. (1998). Update on empirically validated therapies II. *Clinical Psychologist, 51*, 3–16.

Chambless, D. L., Sanderson, W. C., Shoham, V., Johnson, S. B., Pope, K. S., Crits-Christoph, P., et al. (1996). An update on empirically validated therapies. *Clinical Psychologist, 49*, 5–18.

Chemtob, C. M., Nakashima J., & Carlson J. G. (2002). Brief treatment for elementary school children with disaster-related posttraumatic stress disorder: a field study. *Journal of Clinical Psychology, 58,* 99–112.

Chemtob, C. M., Tolin, D. F., van der Kolk, B. A., & Pitman, R. K. (2000). Eye movement desensitization and reprocessing. In E. B. Foa, T. M. Keane, & M. J. Friedman (Eds.), *Effective treatments for PTSD: Practice guidelines from the International Society for Traumatic Stress Studies.* New York: Guilford Press, 139–154.

Christian, L. M., Keeter, S., Purcell, K., & Smith, A. (2010). *Accessing the cell phone challenge.* Paper presented at the annual conference of the American Association for Public Opinion Research, Chicago, IL. Available at http://www.pewresearch.org/2010/05/20/assessing-the-cell-phone-challenge/.

Chronicle of Higher Education. (1988, November 2). Scholar who submitted bogus article to journals may be disciplined, pp. A1, A7.

Chun, K.-T., Cobb, S., & French, J. R. (1975). *Measures for psychological assessment: A guide to 3,000 original sources and their applications.* Ann Arbor, MI: Institute for Social Research.

Ciarlo, J. A., Brown, T. R., Edwards, D. W., Kiresuk, T. J., & Newman, F. L. (1986). *Assessing mental health treatment outcome measurement techniques.* DHHS Publication No. (ADM) 86–1301. Rockville, MD: National Institute of Mental Health.

Cohen, J. (1977). *Statistical power analysis for the behavioral sciences.* New York: Academic Press.

Cohen, J. (1988). *Statistical power analysis for the behavioral sciences* (2nd ed.). New York: Lawrence Erlbaum Associates.

Coleman, J. (1966). *Equality of educational opportunity.* Washington, DC: U.S. Government Printing Office.

Compton, B. R., & Galaway, B. (1994). *Social work processes.* Homewood, IL: Dorsey Press.

Comrey, A., Barker, T., & Glaser, E. (1975). *A sourcebook for mental health measures.* Los Angeles: Human Interaction Research Institute.

Comstock, D. (1980). Dimensions of influence in organizations. *Pacific Sociological Review* (January), 67–84.

Conoley, J. C., & Kramer, J. J. (1995). *The 12th mental measurements yearbook.* Lincoln, NE: Buros Institute of Mental Measurements.

Conrad, K. J., Randolph, F. L., Kirby, M. W., & Bebout R. R. (1999). Creating and using logic models: Four perspectives. *Alcoholism Treatment Quarterly, 17*(1/2), 17–31.

Cook, E. (1995, April 25). Communication to the METHODS listserv from Michel de Seve (T120@music.ulaval.ca) to Cook (EC1645A@american.edu)@Online.

Cook, T. D., & Campbell, D. T. (1979). *Quasi-experimentation: Design and analysis issues for field settings.* Chicago: Rand McNally.

Cooper, H. M. (1989). *Integrating research: A guide for literature reviews.* Newbury Park, CA: Sage.

Cooper-Stephenson, C., & Theologides, A. (1981). Nutrition in cancer: Physicians' knowledge, opinions, and educational needs. *Journal of the American Dietetic Association* (May), 472–476.

Corcoran, J. (2000). *Evidence-based social work practice with families: A lifespan approach.* New York: Springer.

Corcoran, J. (2003). *Clinical applications of evidence-based family interventions.* Oxford: Oxford University Press.

Corcoran, K. J., & Fischer, J. (2000a). *Measures for clinical practice: Vol. 1. Couples, families, children (3rd ed.).* New York: Free Press.

Corcoran, K. J., & Fischer, J. (2000b). *Measures for clinical practice: Vol. 2. Adults (3rd ed.).* New York: Free Press.

Corcoran, K., & Gingerich, W. J. (1994). Practice evaluation in the context of managed care: Case-recording methods for quality assurance reviews. *Research on Social Work Practice, 4*(3), 326–337.

Coulton, C., Pandey, S., & Chow, J. (1990). Concentration of poverty and the changing ecology of low-income, urban neighborhoods: An analysis of the Cleveland area. *Social Work Research and Abstracts, 26*(4), 5–16.

Couper, M. P. (2001). Web surveys: A review of issues and approaches. *Public Opinion Quarterly, 64*(4), 464–494.

Couper, M. P. (2008). *Designing effective web surveys.* New York: Cambridge University Press.

Cournoyer, B., & Powers, G. T. (2002). Evidence-based social work: The quiet revolution continues. In A. R. Roberts & G. J. Greene (Eds.), *Social workers' desk reference* (pp. 798–807). New York: Oxford University Press.

Cowger, C. D. (1984). Statistical significance tests: Scientific ritualism or scientific method? *Social Service Review, 58*(3), 358–372.

Cowger, C. D. (1985). Author's reply. *Social Service Review, 59*(3), 520–522.

Cowger, C. D. (1987). Correcting misuse is the best defense of statistical tests of significance. *Social Service Review, 61*(1), 170–172.

Coyle, S. (2014). Social media and suicide prevention. *Social Work Today*, Vol. 14, No. 1 (January/February), p. 8. Retrieved from http://www.socialworktoday.com/archive/012014p8.shtml.

Crawford, K. S., Thomas, E. D., & Fink, J. J. (1980, October–December). Pygmalion at sea: Improving the work effectiveness of low performers. *Journal of Applied Behavioral Science*, 482–505.

Creswell, J. (2014a). *A concise introduction to mixed methods research*. Thousand Oaks, CA: Sage.

Creswell, J. (2014b). *Research design: Qualitative, quantitative, and mixed methods approaches*. Thousand Oaks, CA: Sage.

Crowe, T. V. (2002). Translation of the Rosenberg Self-Esteem Scale into American Sign Language: A principal components analysis. *Social Work Research*, 26(1), 57–63.

Cuéllar, I., & Paniagua, F. A. (Eds.). (2000). *Handbook of multicultural mental health: Assessment and treatment of diverse populations*. San Diego: Academic Press.

Cummerton, J. (1983). A feminist perspective on research: What does it help us to see? Paper presented at the annual program meeting of the Council on Social Work Education, Fort Worth, TX.

Curtin, R., Presser, S., & Singer, E. (2005a). Changes in telephone survey nonresponse over the past quarter century. *Public Opinion Quarterly*, 69(1), 87–98.

Curtin, R., Presser, S., & Singer, E. (2005b). The effects of response rate changes on the index of consumer sentiment. *Public Opinion Quarterly*, 64(4), 413–428.

Dahlstrom, W. Grant, & Welsh, G. S. (1960). *An MMPI handbook*. Minneapolis: University of Minnesota Press.

Dallas Morning News. (1990, February 11). Welfare study withholds benefits from 800 Texans, p. 1.

Daly, K. (1992). The fit between qualitative research and characteristics of families. In J. Gilgun, K. Daly, & G. Handel (Eds.), *Qualitative methods in family research* (pp. 3–11). Thousand Oaks, CA: Sage.

Dana, R. (Ed.). (2000). *Handbook of cross-cultural personality assessment*. Mahwah, NJ: Lawrence Erlbaum Associates.

Davidson, P. R., & Parker, K. C. H. (2001). Eye movement desensitization and reprocessing (EMDR): A meta-analysis. *Journal of Consulting and Clinical Psychology*, 69, 305–316.

Davis, F. (1973). The Martian and the convert: Ontological polarities in social research. *Urban Life*, 2(3), 333–343.

DeFleur, L. (1975). Biasing influences on drug arrest records: Implications for deviance research. *American Sociological Review* (February), 88–103.

De Maria, W. (1981). Empiricism: An impoverished philosophy for social work research. *Australian Social Work*, 34, 3–8.

Denzin, N. K., & Lincoln, Y. S. (1994). *Handbook of qualitative research*. Thousand Oaks, CA: Sage.

DePanfilis, D., & Zuravin, S. J. (2002). The effect of services on the recurrence of child maltreatment. *Child Abuse and Neglect*, 26, 187–205.

Dillman, D. A. (1978). *Mail and telephone surveys: The total design method*. New York: John Wiley & Sons.

Dillman, D. A. (2000). *Mail and Internet surveys: The tailored design method* (2nd ed.). New York: John Wiley & Sons.

Dillman, D. A. (2014). *Internet, phone, mail and mixed-mode surveys: The tailored design method* (2nd ed.). Hoboken, NJ: John Wiley & Sons.

Donald, M. N. (1960). Implications of nonresponse for the interpretation of mail questionnaire data. *Public Opinion Quarterly*, 24(1), 99–114.

Draguns, J. G. (2000). Multicultural and cross-cultural assessment: Dilemmas and decisions. In G. R. Sodowsky & J. C. Impara (Eds.), *Multicultural assessment in counseling and clinical psychology* (pp. 37–84). Lincoln, NE: Buros Institute of Mental Measurements.

DuBois, B. (1983). Passionate scholarship: Notes on values, knowing and method in feminist social science. In G. Bowles & R. Duelli-Klein (Eds.), *Theories of women's studies* (pp. 105–116). London: Routledge & Kegan Paul.

Duelli-Klein, R. (1983). How to do what we want to do: Thoughts about feminist methodology. In G. Bowles & R. Duelli-Klein (Eds.), *Theories in women's studies* (pp. 88–104). London: Routledge & Kegan Paul.

Duneier, M. (1999). *Sidewalk*. New York: Farrar, Straus & Giroux.

Edmond, T., Rubin, A., & Wambach, K. (1999). The effectiveness of EMDR with adult female survivors of childhood sexual abuse. *Social Work Research* (June), 103–116.

Edmond, T., Sloan, L., & McCarty, D. (2004). Sexual abuse survivors' perceptions of the effectiveness of EMDR and eclectic therapy. *Research on Social Work Practice*, 14(4), 259–272.

Eichler, M. (1988). *Nonsexist research methods*. Boston: Allen & Unwin.

Einstein, A. (1940, May 24). The fundamentals of theoretical physics. *Science*, 487.

Elder, G. H., Jr., Pavalko, E. K., & Clipp, E. C. (1993). *Working with archival data: Studying lives*. Newbury Park, CA: Sage.

Emde, M., & Fuchs, M. (2012). Exploring animated faces scales in web surveys: Drawbacks and prospects. *Survey Practice*, 5(1). Available at http://www.surveypractice.org/index.php/SurveyPractice/article/view/60.

Emerson, R. M. (Ed.). 1988. *Contemporary field research*. Boston: Little, Brown.

England, S. E. (1994). Modeling theory from fiction and autobiography. In C. K. Reissman (Ed.), *Qualitative studies in social work research* (pp. 190–213). Thousand Oaks, CA: Sage.

Epstein, I. (1985). Quantitative and qualitative methods. In R. M. Grinnell (Ed.), *Social work research and evaluation* (pp. 263–274). Itasca, IL: Peacock.

Epstein, W. M. (2004). Confirmational response bias and the quality of the editorial processes among American social work journals. *Research on Social Work Practice*, 14(6), 450–458.

Evans, W. (1996). Computer-supported content analysis: Trends, tools, and techniques. *Social Science Computer Review*, 14(3), 269–279.

Fairbanks, E. (2008). Wiki woman: The battle to define Hilary online. *The New Republic*. Available: http://www.tnr.com/article/wiki-woman.

Federal Communications Commission (FCC). (2012, May 24). Truth About Wireless Phones and the National Do-Not-Call List, May 24, 2011, online at http://www.fcc.gov/guides/truth-about-wireless-phones-and-national-do-not-call-list.

Feick, L. F. (1989). Latent class analysis of survey questions that include don't know responses. *Public Opinion Quarterly*, 53, 525–547.

Ferguson-Colvin, K. M., & Maccio, E. M. (2102). *Toolkit for practitioners/researchers working with lesbian, gay, bisexual, transgender, and queer/questioning (LGBTQ) runaway and homeless youth (RHY)*. National Resource Center for Permanency and Family Connections, Silberman School of Social Work.

Festinger, L., Reicker, H. W., & Schachter, S. (1956). *When prophecy fails*. Minneapolis: University of Minnesota Press.

Finckenauer, J. (1979). *Evaluation of juvenile awareness project: Reports 1 and 2*. Newark, NJ: Rutgers School of Criminal Justice.

Fischer, J. (1973). Is social work effective: A review. *Social Work*, 18(1), 5–20.

Fischer, J. (1978). *Effective casework practice: An eclectic approach*. New York: McGraw-Hill.

Fischer, J. (1990). Problems and issues in meta-analysis. In L. Videka-Sherman & W. J. Reid (Eds.), *Advances in clinical social work research* (pp. 297–325). Silver Spring, MD: NASW Press.

Foa, E. B., Keane, T. M., & Friedman, M. J. (2000). *Effective treatments for PTSD*. New York: Guilford Press.

Fong, R., & Furuto, S. (Eds.). (2001). *Culturally competent practice: Skills, interventions, and evaluations*. Boston: Allyn & Bacon.

Fowler, F. J., Jr. (1995). *Improving survey questions: Design and evaluation*. Thousand Oaks, CA: Sage.

Frankfort-Nachmias, C., & Leon-Guerrero, A. (1997). *Social statistics for a diverse society*. Thousand Oaks, CA: Pine Forge Press.

Franklin, C., & Nurius, P. (1998). *Constructivism in practice: Methods and challenges*. Milwaukee, WI: Families International.

Fraser, M., Day, S. H., Galinsky, M. J., Hodges, V. G., & Smokowski, P. R. (2004). Conduct problems and peer rejection in childhood: A randomized trial of the making choices and strong families programs. *Research on Social Work Practice*, 14(5), 313–324.

Fredman, N., & Sherman, R. (1987). *Handbook of measurements for marriage and family therapy*. New York: Brunner/Mazel.

Gage, N. (1989). The paradigm wars and their aftermath: A "historical" sketch of research and teaching since 1989. *Educational Research*, 18, 4–10.

Galesic, M., Tourangeau, R., Couper, M. P., & Conrad, F. G. (2008). Eye-tracking data: New insights on response order effects and other cognitive shortcuts in survey responding. *Public Opinion Quarterly*, 72, 892–913.

Gall, J. (1975). *Systemantics: How systems work and especially how they fail*. New York: Quadrangle.

Gallup, G. (1984, December 13). Where parents go wrong. *San Francisco Chronicle*, p. 7.

Gambrill, E. (1999). Evidence-based practice: An alternative to authority-based practice. *Families in Society*, 80, 341–350.

Gambrill, E. (2001). Educational policy and accreditation standards: Do they work for clients? *Journal of Social Work Education*, 37, 226–239.

Garant, C. (1980). Stalls in the therapeutic process. *American Journal of Nursing (December)*, 2166–2167.

Gaventa, J. (1991). Towards a knowledge democracy: Viewpoints on participatory research in North America. In O. Fals-Borda & M. A. Rahman (Eds.), *Action and knowledge: Breaking the monopoly with participatory action-research* (pp. 121–131). New York: Apex Press.

Gibbs, L., & Gambrill, E. (1999). *Critical thinking for social workers: Exercises for the helping professions*. Thousand Oaks, CA: Pine Forge Press.

Gibbs, L., & Gambrill, E. (2002). Evidence-based practice: Counterarguments to objections. *Research on Social Work Practice*, 12, 452–476.

Gilgun, J. (1991). Hand into glove: The grounded theory approach and social work practice research. Paper presented at the Research Conference on Qualitative Methods in Social Work Practice Research, Nelson A. Rockefeller Institute of Government, State University of New York at Albany, August 24.

Gilgun, J. (2010). Reflexivity and qualitative research. *Current Issues in Qualitative Research*, 1(2), 1–8.

Gilgun, J., Daly, K., & Handel, G. (Eds.). (1992). *Qualitative methods in family research*. Thousand Oaks, CA: Sage.

Ginsberg, L. (1995). *Social work almanac* (2nd ed.). Washington, DC: NASW Press.

Giuli, C. A., & Hudson, W. W. (1977). Assessing parent–child relationship disorders in clinical practice: The child's point of view. *Journal of Social Service Research*, 1(1), 77–92.

Glaser, B., & Strauss, A. (1967). *The discovery of grounded theory: Strategies for qualitative research*. Chicago: Aldine.

Glisson, C. (1987). Author's reply. *Social Service Review*, 61(1), 172–176.

Glisson, G. M., Thyer, B. A., & Fischer, R. L. (2001). Serving the homeless: Evaluating the effectiveness of homeless shelter services. *Journal of Sociology and Social Welfare*, 28, 89–97.

Glock, C. Y., Ringer, B. B., & Babbie, E. R. (1967). *To comfort and to challenge*. Berkeley: University of California Press.

Goffman, E. (1961). *Asylums: Essays on the social situation of mental patients and other inmates*. Chicago: Aldine.

Goffman, E. (1963). *Stigma: Notes on the management of a spoiled identity*. Englewood Cliffs, NJ: Prentice Hall.

Goffman, E. (1974). *Frame analysis*. Cambridge, MA: Harvard University Press.

Goffman, E. (1979). *Gender advertisements*. New York: Harper & Row.

Gold, R. L. (1969). Roles in sociological field observation. In G. J. McCall & J. L. Simmons (Eds.), *Issues in participant observation* (pp. 30–39). Reading, MA: Addison-Wesley.

Goldberg, W., & Tomlanovich, M. (1984). Domestic violence victims in the emergency department. *Journal of the American Medical Association*, 32, 59–64.

Goldman, B. A., & Busch, J. C. (1982). *Directory of unpublished experimental measures* (Vol. 3). New York: Human Sciences Press.

Goldstein, E. G. (1995). Psychosocial approach. In *Encyclopedia of social work* (19th ed., Vol. 3, pp. 1948–1954). Washington, DC: National Association of Social Workers.

Gorey, K. M. (1996). Effectiveness of social work intervention research: Internal versus external evaluations. *Social Work Research*, 20, 119–128.

Gottlieb, N., & Bombyk, M. (1987). Strategies for strengthening feminist research. *Affilia* (*Summer*), 23–35.

Goyder, J. (1985). Face-to-face interviews and mailed questionnaires: The net difference in response rate. *Public Opinion Quarterly*, 49, 234–252.

Graham, L., & Hogan, R. (1990). Social class and tactics: Neighborhood opposition to group homes. *Sociological Quarterly*, 31(4), 513–529.

Graham, M. (1989). One toke over the line. *The New Republic*, 200(16), 20–21.

Greene, R., Murphy, K., & Snyder, S. (2000). Should demographics be placed at the end or at the beginning of mailed questionnaires? An empirical answer to a persistent methodological question. *Social Work Research*, 24(4), 237–241.

Greenwald, R. (1994). Applying eye movement desensitization and reprocessing (EMDR) to the treatment of traumatized children: Five case studies. *Anxiety Disorders Practice Journal*, 1, 83–97.

Grinnell, R. M., Jr. (1997). *Social work research and evaluation: Quantitative and qualitative approaches*. Itasca, IL: Peacock.

Grob, G. N. (1973). *Mental institutions in America*. New York: Free Press.

Grote, N. K., Bledsoe, S. E., Swartz, H. A., & Frank, E. (2004). Feasibility of providing culturally relevant, brief interpersonal psychotherapy for antenatal depression in an obstetrics clinic: A pilot study. *Research on Social Work Practice*, 14(6), 397–407.

Grotevant, H. D., & Carlson, D. I. (Eds.). (1989). *Family assessment: A guide to methods and measures*. New York: Guilford Press.

Groves, R. M. (1990). Theories and methods of telephone surveys. In W. R. Scott & J. Blake (Eds.), *Annual review of sociology* (Vol. 16, pp. 221–240). Palo Alto, CA: Annual Reviews.

Guba, E. G. (1981). Criteria for assessing the trustworthiness of naturalistic inquiries. *Educational Resources Information Center Annual Review Paper*, 29, 75–91.

Gubrium, J. F., & Holstein, J. A. (1997). *The new language of qualitative method*. New York: Oxford University Press.

Haase, R. F., Waechter, D. M., & Solomon, G. S. (1982). How significant is a significant difference?

Average effect size of research in counseling psychology. *Journal of Counseling Psychology, 29*(2), 59–63.

Habermas, J. (1971). *Knowledge and human interests.* Boston: Beacon Press.

Hamblin, R. L. (1971). Mathematical experimentation and sociological theory: A critical analysis. *Sociometry, 34,* 4.

Hanson, W. E., Creswell, J. W., Plano Clark, V. L., Petska, K. S., & Creswell, J. D. (2005). Mixed methods research designs in counseling psychology. *Journal of Counseling Psychology, 52*(2), 224–235.

Harrington, R. G. (Ed.). (1986). *Testing adolescents: A reference guide for comprehensive psychological assessment techniques.* Elmsford, NY: Pergamon Press.

Healey, J. F. (1999). *Statistics: A tool for social research.* Belmont, CA: Wadsworth.

Heath, A. W. (1997). The proposal in qualitative research. *Qualitative Report* [Online serial], *3*(1). Available: http://www.nova.edu/ssss/QR/QR3-1/heath.html.

Heineman, M. B. (1981). The obsolete scientific imperative in social work research. *Social Service Review, 55,* 371–397.

Hempel, C. G. (1952). *Fundamentals of concept formation in empirical science* (*International encyclopedia of unified science,* Vol. 2, No. 7). Chicago: University of Chicago Press.

Hepworth, D. H., Rooney, R., & Larsen, J. A. (2002). *Direct social work practice: Theory and skills* (6th ed.). Belmont, CA: Wadsworth.

Herbert, J. D., Lilienfeld, S. O., Lohr, J. M., Montgomery, R. W., O'Donohue, W. T., Rosen, G. M., & Tolin, D. F. (2000). Science and pseudoscience in the development of eye movement desensitization and reprocessing: Implications for clinical psychology. *Clinical Psychology Review, 20,* 945–971.

Herman, D. B., Susser, E. S., Struening, E. L., & Link, B. L. (1997). Adverse childhood experiences: Are they risk factors for adult homelessness? *American Journal of Public Health, 87,* 249–255.

Hernandez, M., & Isaacs, M. R. (Eds.). (1998). *Promoting cultural competence in children's mental health services.* Baltimore: Paul H. Brookes.

Hersen, M., & Bellack, A. S. (Eds.). (1988). *Dictionary of behavioral assessment techniques.* Elmsford, NY: Pergamon Press.

Higginbotham, A. L., Jr. (1978). *In the matter of color: Race and the American legal process.* New York: Oxford University Press.

Hill, A. B. (1965). "The Environment and Disease: Association or Causation?" *Proceedings of the Royal Society of Medicine, 58,* 295–300.

Hill, R. R. (1978). Social work research on minorities: Impediments and opportunities. Paper presented at the National Conference on the Future of Social Work Research, San Antonio, TX, October.

Hirschi, T., & Selvin, H. (1973). *Principles of survey analysis.* New York: Free Press.

Hogarty, G. (1979). Aftercare treatment of schizophrenia: Current status and future direction. In H. M. Pragg (Ed.), *Management of schizophrenia* (pp. 19–36). Assen: Van Gorcum.

Hogarty, G. (1989). Meta-analysis of the effects of practice with the chronically mentally ill: A critique and reappraisal of the literature. *Social Work, 34* (4), 363–373.

Hohmann, A. A., & Parron, D. L. (1996). How the NIH guidelines on inclusion of women and minorities apply: Efficacy trials, effectiveness trials, and validity. *Journal of Consulting and Clinical Psychology, 64*(5), 851–855.

Homans, G. C. (1971, Winter). Reply to Blain. *Sociological Inquiry, 41,* 23.

Hough, R. L., Tarke, H., Renker, V., Shields, P., & Glatstein, J. (1996). Recruitment and retention of homeless mentally ill participants in research. *Journal of Consulting and Clinical Psychology, 64*(5), 881–891.

Howell, J. T. (1973). *Hard living on Clay Street.* Garden City, NY: Doubleday Anchor.

Hudson, W. W. (1982). *The clinical measurement package: A field manual.* Homewood, IL: Dorsey Press.

Hudson, W. W. (1992). *The WALMYR Assessment Scales scoring manual.* Tempe, AZ: WALMYR.

Hudson, W. W. (1997). Assessment tools as outcomes measures in social work. In E. J. Mullen & J. L. Magnabosco (Eds.), *Outcomes measurement in the human services: Cross-cutting issues and methods* (pp. 68–80). Washington, DC: NASW Press.

Hughes, M. (1980). The fruits of cultivation analysis: A reexamination of some effects of television watching. *Public Opinion Quarterly* (*Fall*), 287–302.

Humphreys, L. (1970). *Tearoom trade: Impersonal sex in public places.* Chicago: Aldine.

Husser, J. A., & Fernandez, K. E. (2013). To click, type, or drag? Evaluating speed of survey data input methods. *Survey Practice, 6*(2). Available at http://www.surveypractice.org/index.php/SurveyPractice/article/view/40.

Hutchby, I., & Wooffitt, R. (1998). *Conversation analysis: Principles, practices and applications*. Cambridge: Polity Press.

Hyun, S. L., & Johnson, M. M. (2001). Korean social work students' attitudes toward homosexuals. *Journal of Social Work Education, 37*(3), 545–554.

IASWR (2005). Enhancing the health and well-being of LGBT individuals, families and communities: Building a social work research agenda. Institute for the Advancement of Social Work Research. Available at http://www.socialworkpolicy.org/wp-content/uploads/2007/06/3-LGBT-SW-Res-Ag-2005.pdf.

Jackman, M. R., & Senter, M. S. (1980). Images of social groups: Categorical or qualified? *Public Opinion Quarterly, 44*, 340–361.

Jackson, A. P., & Ivanoff, A. (1999). Reduction of low response rates in interview surveys of poor African-American families. *Journal of Social Service Research, 25*(1–2), 41–60.

Jacob, T., & Tennebaum, D. L. (1988). *Family assessment: Rationale, methods, and future directions*. New York: Plenum Press.

Jashinsky, J., Burton, S. H., Hanson, C. L., West, J., Giraud-Carrier, C., Barnes, M. D., et al. (2014). Tracking suicide risk factors through Twitter in the US. *Crisis, 35*(1), 51–59. http://www.ncbi.nlm.nih.gov/pubmed/24121153.

Jayaratne, S., & Levy, R. L. (1979). *Empirical clinical practice*. New York: Columbia University Press.

Jayaratne, S., Tripodi, T., & Talsma, E. (1988). The comparative analysis and aggregation of single case data. *Journal of Applied Behavioral Science, 1*(24), 119–128.

Jensen, A. (1969). How much can we boost IQ and scholastic achievement? *Harvard Educational Review, 39*, 273–274.

Johnson, C., Shala, M., Sedjejaj, X., Odell, R., & Dabishevci, K. (2001). Thought field therapy—Soothing the bad moments of Kosovo. *Journal of Clinical Psychology, 57*(10), 1237–1240.

Johnson, J. C. (1990). *Selecting ethnographic informants*. Newbury Park, CA: Sage.

Johnston, H. (1980). The marketed social movement: A case study of the rapid growth of TM. *Pacific Sociological Review (July)*, 333–354.

Jones, J. H. (1981). *Bad blood: The Tuskegee syphilis experiment*. New York: Free Press.

Jones, L. (1991). The impact of cancer on the health status of minorities in Texas. Paper presented at the Texas Minority Health Strategic Planning Conference, Austin, TX, July.

Kadet, A. (2002). Good grief! *Smart Money, 11*, 108–114.

Kahane, H. (1992). *Logic and contemporary rhetoric* (2nd ed.). Belmont, CA: Wadsworth.

Kalton, G. (1983). *Introduction to survey sampling*. Newbury Park, CA: Sage.

Kaplan, A. (1964). *The conduct of inquiry*. San Francisco: Chandler.

Kaplowitz, M. D., Hadlock, T. D., & Levine, R. (2004). A comparison of Web and mail survey response rates. *Public Opinion Quarterly, 68*(1), 94–101.

Keeter, S. (2006). The impact of cell phone noncoverage bias on polling in the 2004 presidential election. *Public Opinion Quarterly, 70*(1), 88–98.

Keeter, S., Dimock, M., Christian, L., & Kennedy, C. (2008, January 31). The impact of "cell-onlys" on public opinion polls: Ways of coping with a growing population segment. Pew Research Center Publications. Available at http://pewresearch.org/pubs/714/the-impact-of-cell-onlys-on-public-opinion-polls.

Keitel, M. A., Kopala, M., & Adamson, W. S. (1996). Ethical issues in multicultural assessment. In L. Suzuki, P. J. Meller, & J. G. Ponterotto (Eds.), *Handbook of multicultural assessment* (pp. 29–50). San Francisco: Jossey-Bass.

Kelly, A. 1978. Feminism and research. *Women's Studies International Quarterly, 1*, 226.

Kendall, P. L., & Lazarsfeld, P. F. (1950). Problems of survey analysis. In R. K. Merton & P. F. Lazarsfeld (Eds.), *Continuities in social research: Studies in the scope and method of "The American Soldier."* New York: Free Press, 160–176.

Kestenbaum, C. J., & Williams, D. T. (Eds.). (1988). *Handbook of clinical assessment of children and adolescents*. Austin, TX: PRO-ED.

Kinnell, A. M., & Maynard, D. W. (1996). The delivery and receipt of safer sex advice in pretest counseling sessions for HIV and AIDS. *Journal of Contemporary Ethnography, 24*, 405–437.

Kirk, S. A., & Reid, W. J. (2002). *Science and social work*. New York: Columbia University Press.

Kish, L. (1965). *Survey sampling*. New York: John Wiley & Sons.

Knight, G. P., Roosa, M. W., & Umana-Taylor, A. J. (2009). *Studying ethnic minority and economically disadvantaged populations: Methodological challenges and best practice*. Washington, DC: American Psychological Association.

Knoff, H. M. (1986). *The assessment of child and adolescent personality*. New York: Guilford Press.

Krefting, L. (1991). Rigor in qualitative research: The assessment of trustworthiness. *American Journal of Occupational Therapy, 45*(3), 214–222.

Kronick, J. C. (1989). Toward a formal methodology of document analysis in the interpretive tradition. Paper presented at the meeting of the Eastern Sociological Society, Baltimore, MD.

Krueger, R. A., & Casey, M. A. (2015). *Focus groups: A practical guide for applied research* (5th ed.). Thousand Oaks, CA: Sage Publications, Inc.

Kuhn, T. (1970). *The structure of scientific revolutions* (2nd ed.). Chicago: University of Chicago Press.

Kulis, S., Napoli, M., & Marsiglia, F. F. (2002). Ethnic pride, biculturalism, and drug use norms of urban American Indian adolescents. *Social Work Research (June)*, 101–112.

Kvale, S. (1996). *InterViews: An introduction to qualitative research interviewing.* Thousand Oaks, CA: Sage.

Ladd, E. C., & Ferree, G. D. (1981). Were the pollsters really wrong? *Public Opinion* (December/January), 13–20.

LaGreca, A. M. (1990). *Through the eyes of the child: Obtaining self-reports from children and adolescents.* Boston: Allyn & Bacon.

Lake, D. G., Miles, M. B., & Earle, R. B., Jr. (1973). *Measuring human behavior: Tools for the assessment of social functioning.* New York: Teachers College Press.

Lasch, C. (1977). *Haven in a heartless world.* New York: Basic Books.

Lazarsfeld, P. (1959). Problems in methodology. In R. K. Merton (Ed.), *Sociology today.* New York: Basic Books, 39–78.

Lazarsfeld, P., Pasanella, A., & Rosenberg, M. (Eds.). (1972). *Continuities in the language of social research.* New York: Free Press.

Lee, R. (1993). *Doing research on sensitive topics.* Newbury Park, CA: Sage.

Lewins, A., & Silver, C. (2006), *Choosing a CAQ-DAS Package.* Available online at: http://cue.berkeley.edu/qdaarticle.pdf.

Lewis-Beck, M. (1995). *Quantitative application in the social sciences: Vol. 103. Data analysis: An introduction.* Thousand Oaks, CA: Sage.

Liebow, E. (1967). *Tally's corner.* Boston: Little, Brown.

Liebow, E. (1993). *Tell them who I am: The lives of homeless women.* New York: Free Press.

Lincoln, Y. S., & Guba, E. A. (1985). *Naturalistic inquiry.* Beverly Hills, CA: Sage.

Lipsey, M. W. (1990). *Design sensitivity: Statistical power for experimental research.* Newbury Park, CA: Sage.

Literary Digest. (1936a, October 31). Landon, 1,293,669: Roosevelt, 972,897, pp. 5–6.

Literary Digest. (1936b, November 14). What went wrong with the polls?, pp. 7–8.

Lofland, J. (1995). Analytic ethnography: Features, failings, and futures. *Journal of Contemporary Ethnography, 24*(1), 30–67.

Lofland, J., & Lofland, L. H. (1995). *Analyzing social settings* (3rd ed.). Belmont, CA: Wadsworth.

Longres, J. F., & Scanlon, E. (2001). Social justice and the research curriculum. *Health and Social Work, 37*(3), 447–463.

Luborsky, L., Singer, B., & Luborsky, L. (1975). Comparative studies of psychotherapies: Is it true that "Everyone has won and all must have prizes"? *Archives of General Psychiatry, 32,* 995–1008.

Luker, K. (1984). *Abortion and the politics of motherhood.* Berkeley: University of California Press.

Magura, S., & Moses, B. S. (1987). *Outcome measures for child welfare services.* Washington, DC: Child Welfare League of America.

Malakhoff, L. A., & Jans, M. (2011). Towards usage of avatar interviewers in web surveys. Survey Practie. 4, Retrieved online at: http://surveypractice.org/index.php/SurveyPractice/article/view/104/html

Manning, P. K., & Cullum-Swan, B. (1994). Narrative, content, and semiotic analysis. In N. K. Denzin & Y. S. Lincoln (Eds.), *Handbook of qualitative research* (pp. 463–477). Thousand Oaks, CA: Sage.

Marsden, G. (1971). Content analysis studies of psychotherapy: 1954 through 1968. In A. E. Bergin & S. L. Garfield (Eds.), *Handbook of psychotherapy and behavior change: An empirical analysis.* New York: John Wiley & Sons.

Marshall, C., & Rossman, G. B. (1995). *Designing qualitative research.* Thousand Oaks, CA: Sage.

Martin, R. P. (1988). *Assessment of personality and behavior problems: Infancy through adolescence.* New York: Guilford Press.

Maruish, M. E. (Ed.). (2000). *Handbook of psychological assessment in primary care settings.* Mahwah, NJ: Lawrence Erlbaum Associates.

Maruish, M. E. (Ed.). (2002). *Psychological testing in the age of managed behavioral health care.* Mahwah, NJ: Lawrence Erlbaum Associates.

Marx, K. (1867). *Capital.* New York: International Publishers. (Reprinted 1967).

Marx, K. (1880, July 5). *Revue socialist.* Reprinted in T. B. Bottomore & M. Rubel (Eds.), *Karl Marx: Selected writings in sociology and social philosophy.* New York: McGraw-Hill, 1956, 204–212.

Mash, E. J., & Terdal, L. G. (1988). *Behavioral assessment of childhood disorders*. New York: Guilford Press.

Matocha, L. K. (1992). Case study interviews: Caring for persons with AIDS. In J. Gilgun, K. Daly, & G. Handel (Eds.), *Qualitative methods in family research* (pp. 66–84). Thousand Oaks, CA: Sage.

Maxwell, J. A. (1996). *Qualitative research design: An interactive approach*. Thousand Oaks, CA: Sage.

McAlister, A., Perry, C., Killen, J., Slinkard, L. A., & and Maccoby, N. (1980). Pilot study of smoking, alcohol, and drug abuse prevention. *American Journal of Public Health (July)*, 719–721.

McCall, G. J., & Simmons, J. L. (Eds.). (1969). *Issues in participant observation*. Reading, MA: Addison-Wesley.

McCubbin, H. I., & Thompson, A. I. (Eds.). (1987). *Family assessment inventories for research and practice*. Madison: University of Wisconsin Press.

McRoy, R. G. (1981). A comparative study of the self-concept of transracially and in racially adopted black children. Dissertation, University of Texas at Austin.

McRoy, R. G., Grotevant, H. D., Lopez, S. A., & Furuta, A. (1990). Adoption revelation and communication issues: Implications for practice. *Families in Society, 71*(9), 550–557.

McWirter, N. (1980). *The Guinness book of records*. New York: Bantam.

Mehta, A. (1978). *Perception of Asian personality*. Calcutta: S. Chand.

Menard, S. (1991). *Longitudinal research*. Newbury Park, CA: Sage.

Mercer, S., & Kane, R. A. (1979). Helplessness and hopelessness among the institutionalized aged. *Health and Social Work, 4*(1), 91–116.

Messer, S. B. (2006). What qualifies as evidence in effective practice? Patient values and preferences. In J. C. Norcross, L. E. Beutler, & R. F. Levant (Eds.), *Evidence-based practices in mental health: Debate and dialogue on the fundamental questions* (pp. 31–40). Washington, DC: American Psychological Association.

Mies, M. (1983). Toward a methodology for feminist research. In G. Bowles & R. Duelli-Klein (Eds.), *Theories of women's studies* (pp. 117–139). London: Routledge & Kegan Paul.

Miles, M. B., & Huberman, A. M. (1994). *Qualitative data analysis* (2nd ed.). Thousand Oaks, CA: Sage.

Milgram, S. (1963). Behavioral study of obedience. *Journal of Abnormal and Social Psychology, 67*, 371–378.

Milgram, S. (1965). Some conditions of obedience and disobedience to authority. *Human Relations, 18*, 57–76.

Millar, M. M., & Dillman, D. A. (2012). "Encouraging survey response via smartphones: Effects on respondents' use of mobile devices and survey response rates." *Survey Practice, 5*(3). Available at: http://www.surveypractice.org/index.php/SurveyPractice/article/view/19.

Miller, D. C. (1983). *Handbook of research design and social measurement* (4th ed.). New York: Longman.

Miller, D. C. (1991). *Handbook of research design and social measurement* (5th ed.). New York: Longman.

Miller, W. L., & Crabtree, B. F. (1994). Clinical research. In N. K. Denzin & Y. S. Lincoln (Eds.), *Handbook of qualitative research* (pp. 340–352). Thousand Oaks, CA: Sage.

Miranda, J. (1996). Introduction to the special section of recruiting and retaining minorities in psychotherapy research. *Journal of Consulting and Clinical Psychology, 64*(5), 848–850.

Mitchell, J. V. (1983). *Tests in print* III. Lincoln, NE: Buros Institute of Mental Measurements.

Mitchell, J. V. (Ed.). (1985). *The ninth mental measurements yearbook*. Lincoln: University of Nebraska Press.

Mitchell, R. G., Jr. (1991). Secrecy and disclosure in field work. In W. B. Shaffir & R. A. Stebbins (Eds.), *Experiencing fieldwork: An inside view of qualitative research* (pp. 97–108). Newbury Park, CA: Sage.

Mitofsky, W. J. (1999). Miscalls likely in 2000. *Public Perspective, 10*(5), 42–43.

Monette, D. R., Sullivan, T. J., & DeJong, C. R. (1994). *Applied social research: Tool for the human services* (3rd ed.). Fort Worth, TX: Harcourt Brace.

Monette, D. R., Sullivan, T. J., & DeJong, C. R. (2002). *Applied social research: Tool for the human services* (5th ed.). Fort Worth, TX: Harcourt Brace.

Moore, D. W. (2002). Measuring new types of question-order effects: Additive and subtractive. *Public Opinion Quarterly, 66*, 80–91.

Moreland, K. L. (1996). Persistent issues in multicultural assessment of social and emotional functioning. In L. Suzuki, P. J. Meller, & J. G. Ponterotto (Eds.), *Handbook of multicultural assessment* (pp. 51–76). San Francisco: Jossey-Bass.

Morgan, D. L. (1993). *Successful focus groups: Advancing the state of the art*. Newbury Park, CA: Sage.

Morgan, L. H. (1870). *Systems of consanguinity and affinity*. Washington, DC: Smithsonian Institution.

Morrison, D., & Henkel, R. (Eds.). (1970). *The significance test controversy: A reader*. Chicago: Aldine-Atherton.

Morrissey, J., & Goldman, H. (1984). Cycles of reform in the care of the chronically mentally ill. *Hospital and Community Psychiatry*, 35(8), 785–793.

Morse, J. M. (1994). Designing funded qualitative research. In N. K. Denzin & Y. S. Lincoln (Eds.), *Handbook of qualitative research*. Thousand Oaks, CA: Sage, 220–235.

Moskowitz, M. (1981, May 23). The drugs that doctors order. *San Francisco Chronicle*, p. 33.

Moss, K. E. (1988). Writing research proposals. In R. M. Grinnell, Jr. (Ed.), *Social work research and evaluation* (3rd ed., pp. 429–445). Itasca, IL: Peacock.

Mowbray, C. T., Jordan, L. C., Ribisl, K. M., Kewalramani, A., Luke, D., Herman, S., et al. (1999). Analysis of post-discharge change in a dual diagnosis population. *Health and Social Work*, 4(2), 91–101.

Moynihan, D. (1965). *The Negro family: The case for national action*. Washington, DC: U.S. Government Printing Office.

Mullen, E. J. (2006). Facilitating practitioner use of evidence-based practice. In A. R. Roberts & K. R. Yeager (Eds.), *Foundations of evidence-based social work practice* (pp. 152–159). New York: Oxford University Press.

Mullen, E. J., & Bacon, W. B. (2004). Implementation of practice guidelines and evidence-based treatment: A survey of psychiatrists, psychologists, and social workers. In A. R. Roberts & K. Yeager (Eds.), *Evidence-based practice manual: Research and outcome measures in health and human services* (pp. 210–218). New York: Oxford University Press.

Mullen, E. J., & Dumpson, J. R. (Eds.). (1972). *Evaluation of social intervention*. San Francisco: Jossey-Bass.

Mullen, E. J., & Magnabosco, J. L. (Eds.). (1997). *Outcomes measurement in the human services: Cross-cutting issues and methods*. Washington, DC: NASW Press.

Mullen, E. J., & Streiner, D. L. (2004). The evidence for and against evidence-based practice. *Brief Treatment and Crisis Intervention*, 4, 111–121.

Murray, C. (1984). *Losing ground*. New York: Basic Books.

Muris, P., Merckelbach, H., van Haaften, H., & Mayer, B. (1997). Eyemovement desensitization and reprocessing versus exposure in vivo: A single-session crossover study of spider-phobic children. *British Journal of Psychiatry*, 171, 82–86.

Muris, P., Merckelbach, H., Holdrinet, I., & Sijsenaar, M. (1998). Treating phobic children: Effects of EMDR versus exposure. *Journal of Consulting and Clinical Psychology*, 66, 193–198.

Murray, C., & Herrnstein, R. J. (1994). *The bell curve*. New York: Free Press.

Nandi, P. K. (1982). Surveying Asian minorities in the middle-sized city. In W. T. Liu (Ed.), *Methodological problems in minority research* (81–92). Chicago: Pacific/Asian American Mental Health Research.

National Association of Social Workers. (2009). *An author's guide to social work journals* (5th ed.). Washington, DC: NASW Press.

National Association of Social Workers. (1999). *NASW Code of Ethics*. Washington, DC: NASW Press.

Neuman, W. L. (1994). *Social research methods: Qualitative and quantitative approaches*. Needham Heights, MA: Allyn & Bacon.

Neuman, W. L. (2000). *Social research methods: Qualitative and quantitative approaches* (4th ed.). Boston: Allyn & Bacon.

Newton, R. R., & Rudestam, K. E. (1999). *Your statistical consultant: Answers to your data analysis questions*. Thousand Oaks, CA: Sage.

New York Times. (1984, June 6). Method of polls in two states, p. 12.

New York Times. (1988, September 27). Test of journals is criticized as unethical, pp. 21, 25.

New York Times. (1989, April 4). Charges dropped on bogus work, p. 21.

Nicholls, W. L., II, Baker, R. P., & Martin, J. (1996). The effect of new data collection technology on survey data quality. In L. Lyberg, P. Biemer, M. Collins, C. Dippo, N. Schwartz, & D. Trewin (Eds.), *Survey measurement and process quality*. New York: John Wiley & Sons, 221–248.

Nichols, D. S., Padilla, J., & Gomez-Maqueo, E. L. (2000). Issues in the cross-cultural adaptation and use of the MMPI-2. In R. Dana (Ed.), *Handbook of cross-cultural personality assessment* (pp. 247–266). Mahwah, NJ: Lawrence Erlbaum Associates.

Nie, N. H., Hadlai Hull, C., Jenkins, J. G., Steinbrenner, K., & Bent, D. H. (1975). *Statistical Package for the Social Sciences*. New York: McGraw-Hill.

Norton, I. M., & Manson, S. M. (1996). Research in American Indian and Alaska Native communities: Navigating the cultural universe of values and process. *Journal of Consulting and Clinical Psychology*, 64(5), 856–860.

Nugent, W. R. (1991). An experimental and qualitative analysis of a cognitive-behavioral intervention for anger. *Social Work Research and Abstracts, 27*(3), 3–8.

Nurius, P. S., & Hudson, W. W. (1988). Computer-based practice: Future dream or current technology? *Social Work, 33*(4), 357–362.

Oakley, A. (1981). Interviewing women: A contradiction in terms. In H. Roberts (Ed.), *Doing feminist research*. London: Routledge & Kegan Paul, 221–242.

Ogles, B. M., & Masters, K. S. (1996). *Assessing outcome in clinical practice*. Boston: Allyn & Bacon.

O'Hare, T. (2005). *Evidence-based practices for social workers: An interdisciplinary approach*. Chicago: Lyceum Books.

Ollendick, T. H., & Hersen, M. (1992). *Handbook of child and adolescent assessment*. Des Moines, IA: Allyn & Bacon.

Orme, J. G., & Combs-Orme, T. D. (1986). Statistical power and type II errors in social work research. *Social Work Research and Abstracts, 22*(3), 3–10.

Ortega, D. M., & Richey, C. A. (1998). Methodological issues in social work research with depressed women of color. In M. Potocky & A. Y. Rodgers-Farmer (Eds.), *Social work research with minority and oppressed populations: Methodological issues and innovations* (pp. 47–70). New York: Haworth Press.

Øyen, E. (Ed.). (1990). *Comparative methodology: Theory and practice in international social research*. Newbury Park, CA: Sage.

Ozawa, M. N. (1989). Welfare policies and illegitimate birth rates among adolescents: Analysis of state-by-state data. *Social Work Research and Abstracts, 24*(2), 5–11.

Padgett, D. K. (1998a). Does the glove really fit? Qualitative research and clinical social work practice. *Social Work, 43*(4), 373–381.

Padgett, D. K. (1998b). *Qualitative methods in social work research*. Thousand Oaks, CA: Sage.

Padilla, A. M., & Medina, A. (1996). Cross-cultural sensitivity in assessment. In L. Suzuki, P. J. Meller, & J. G. Ponterotto (Eds.), *Handbook of multicultural assessment* (pp. 3–28). San Francisco: Jossey-Bass.

Parrish, D. E. (2008). Evaluation of the impact of a full-day continuing education training on how practitioners learn about, view, and engage in evidence-based practice. Dissertation. The University of Texas at Austin, 3341945.

Parrish, D. E., & Rubin, A. (2011). An effective model for continuing education training in evidence-based practice. *Research on Social Work Practice, 21*, 77–87.

Parsons, T., & Shils, E. A. (1951). *Toward a general theory of action*. Cambridge, MA: Harvard University Press.

Patton, M. Q. (2015). *Qualitative research and evaluation methods* (4th ed.). Newbury Park, CA: Sage.

Payne, C. M. (1995). I've got the light of freedom: The organizing tradition and the Mississippi freedom struggle. Berkeley: University of California Press.

Pellicer, X. (1993). Eye movement desensitization treatment of a child's nightmares: A case report. *Journal of Behavior Therapy & Experimental Psychiatry, 24*, 73–75.

Perinelli, P. J. (1986, February 14). No unsuspecting public in TV call-in polls [Letter to the editor]. *New York Times*.

Perlman, D. (1982, September 6). Fluoride, AIDS experts scoff at Nelder's idea. *San Francisco Chronicle*, p. 1.

Petersen, L. R., & Maynard, J. L. (1981). Income, equity, and wives' housekeeping role expectations. *Pacific Sociological Review (January)*, 87–105.

Petrolia, D. R., & Bhattacharjee, S. (2009). Revisiting incentive effects: Evidence from a random-sample mail survey on consumer preferences for fuel ethanol. *Public Opinion Quarterly, 73*, 537–550.

Petrosino, A., Turpin-Petrosino, C., & Buehler, J. (2002). "Scared Straight" and other juvenile awareness programs for preventing juvenile delinquency. *Cochrane Database of Systematic Reviews, 2*, CD002796.

Polansky, N. A. (1975). *Social work research*. Chicago: University of Chicago Press.

Polansky, N. A., Lippitt, R., & Redl, F. (1950). An investigation of behavioral contagion in groups. *Human Relations, 3*, 319–348.

Polster, R. A., & Lynch, M. A. (1985). Single-subject designs. In R. M. Grinnell (Ed.), *Social work research and evaluation* (pp. 381–431). Itasca, IL: Peacock.

Population Reference Bureau. (1980). 1980 world population data sheet. Poster prepared by Carl Haub & Douglas W. Heisler. Washington, DC: Author.

Porter, S. R., & Whitcomb, M. E. (2003). The impact of contact type on Web survey response rates. *Public Opinion Quarterly, 67*, 579–588.

Posavac, E. J., & Carey, R. G. (1985). *Program evaluation: Methods and case studies*. Englewood Cliffs, NJ: Prentice Hall.

Potocky, M., & Rodgers-Farmer, A. Y. (Eds.). (1998). *Social work research with minority and oppressed populations*. New York: Haworth Press.

Presser, S., & Blair, J. (1994). Survey pretesting: Do different methods produce different results? In P. Marsden (Ed.), *Sociological methodology* (pp. 73–104). San Francisco: Jossey-Bass.

Priede, C., & Farrall, S. (2011). Comparing results from different styles of cognitive interviewing: "'verbal probing' vs 'thinking aloud.'" *International Journal of Social Research Methodology*, 14(4), 271–287.

Public Opinion. (1984, October–November). See how they ran, pp. 38–40.

Puffer, M. K., Greenwald, R., & Elrod, D. E. (1998). A single session EMDR study with twenty traumatized children and adolescents. *Traumatology*, 3, 171–177.

QSR International. (2011). NVivo 9: Getting started. Available: http://download.qsrinternational.com/Document/NVivo9/NVivo9-Getting-Started-Guide.pdf.

Quay, H. C., & Werry, J. S. (1972). *Psychopathological disorders of childhood*. New York: John Wiley & Sons.

Quoss, B., Cooney, M., & Longhurst, T. (2000). Academics and advocates: Using participatory action research to influence welfare policy. *Journal of Consumer Affairs*, 34(1), 47.

Rank, M. (1992). The blending of qualitative and quantitative methods in understanding childbearing among welfare recipients. In J. Gilgun, K. Daly, & G. Handel (Eds.), *Qualitative methods in family research* (pp. 281–300). Thousand Oaks, CA: Sage.

Rank, M., & Hirschl, T. A. (2002). Welfare use as a life course event: Toward a new understanding of the U.S. safety net. *Social Work*, 47(3), 237–248.

Ransford, H. E. (1968). Isolation, powerlessness, and violence: A study of attitudes and participants in the Watts riots. *American Journal of Sociology*, 73, 581–591.

Rasinski, K. A. (1989). The effect of question wording on public support for government spending. *Public Opinion Quarterly*, 53, 388–394.

Ray, W., & Ravizza, R. (1993). *Methods toward a science of behavior and experience*. Belmont, CA: Wadsworth.

Reed, G. M. (2006). What qualifies as evidence of effective practice? Clinical expertise. In J. C. Norcross, L. E. Beutler, & R. F. Levant (Eds.), *Evidence-based practices in mental health: Debate and dialogue on the fundamental questions* (pp. 13–23). Washington, DC: American Psychological Association.

Reid, W. J. (1997). Evaluating the dodo's verdict: Do all evaluations have equivalent outcomes? *Social Work Research*, 21, 5–18.

Reid, W. J., & Epstein, L. (1972). *Task-centered casework*. New York: Columbia University Press.

Reid, W. J., & Hanrahan, P. (1982). Recent evaluations of social work: Grounds for optimism. *Social Work*, 27(4), 328–340.

Reinharz, S. (1992). *Feminist methods in social research*. New York: Oxford University Press.

Reissman, C. (Ed.). (1994). *Qualitative studies in social work research*. Thousand Oaks, CA: Sage.

Reynolds, C. R., & Kamphaus, R. W. (Eds.). (1990). *Handbook of psychological and educational assessment of children*. New York: Guilford Press.

Richmond, M. (1917). *Social diagnosis*. New York: Russell Sage Foundation.

Roberts, A. R., & Greene, G. J. (Eds.). (2002). *Social workers' desk reference*. New York: Oxford University Press.

Roberts, A. R., & Yeager, K. R. (Eds.). (2004). *Evidence-based practice manual: Research and outcome measures in health and human services*. New York: Oxford University Press.

Roberts, A. R., & Yeager, K. R. (Eds.). (2006). *Foundations of evidence-based social work practice*. New York: Oxford University Press.

Roberts, M. C., & Hurley, L. K. (1997). *Managing managed care*. New York: Plenum Press.

Robinson, R. A. (1994). Private pain and public behaviors: Sexual abuse and delinquent girls. In C. Reissman (Ed.), *Qualitative studies in social work research* (pp. 73–94). Thousand Oaks, CA: Sage.

Rodwell, M. K. (1987). Naturalistic inquiry: An alternative model for social work assessment. *Social Service Review*, 61(2), 232–246.

Rodwell, M. K. (1998). *Social work constructivist research*. New York: Garland.

Roethlisberger, F. J., & Dickson, W. J. (1939). *Management and the worker*. Cambridge, MA: Harvard University Press.

Roffman, R. A., Downey, L., Beadnell, B., Gordon, J. R., Craver, J. N., & Stephens, R. S. (1997). Cognitive-behavioral group counseling to prevent HIV transmission in gay and bisexual men: Factors contributing to successful risk reduction. *Research on Social Work Practice*, 7, 165–186.

Roffman, R. A., Picciano, J., Wickizer, L., Bolan, M., & Ryan, R. (1998). Anonymous enrollment in AIDS prevention telephone group counseling: Facilitating the participation of gay and bisexual men in intervention and research. In M. Potocky & A. Y. Rodgers-Farmer (Eds.), *Social work research with minority and oppressed populations: Methodological issues and innovations* (pp. 5–22). New York: Haworth Press.

Rogler, L. H. (1989). The meaning of culturally sensitive research in mental health. *American Journal of Psychiatry, 146*(3), 296–303.

Rogler, L. H., & Hollingshead, A. B. (1985). *Trapped: Puerto Rican families and schizophrenia*. Maplewood, NJ: Waterfront Press.

Rose, S., Bisson, J., & Wessely, S. (2001). Psychological debriefing for preventing post traumatic stress disorder (PTSD). *Cochrane Database of Systematic Reviews, 3*, CD000560.

Rosenberg, M. (1965). *Society and the adolescent self-image*. Princeton, NJ: Princeton University Press.

Rosenberg, M. (1968). *The logic of survey analysis*. New York: Basic Books.

Rosenhan, D. L. (1973). On being sane in insane places. *Science, 179*, 240–248.

Rosenthal, R., & Rubin, D. (1982). A simple, general-purpose display of magnitude of experimental effect. *Journal of Educational Psychology, 74*(2), 166–169.

Rosenthal, R. N. (2006). Overview of evidence-based practice. In A. R. Roberts & K. Yeager (Eds.), *Foundations of evidence-based social work practice* (pp. 67–80). New York: Oxford University Press.

Rossi, P. H., & Freeman, H. E. (1982). *Evaluation: A systematic approach*. Beverly Hills, CA: Sage.

Rossi, P. H., & Freeman, H. E. (1993). *Evaluation: A systematic approach* (5th ed.). Newbury Park, CA: Sage.

Rothman, E. K. (1981). The written record. *Journal of Family History* (Spring), 47–56.

Rowntree, D. (1981). *Statistics without tears: A primer for non-mathematicians*. New York: Charles Scribner's Sons.

Royse, D. (1988). Voter support for human services. *ARETE, 13*(2), 26–34.

Royse, D. (1991). *Research methods in social work*. Chicago: Nelson-Hall.

Rubin, A. (1979). *Community mental health in the social work curriculum*. New York: Council on Social Work Education.

Rubin, A. (1981). Reexamining the impact of sex on salary: The limits of statistical significance. *Social Work Research and Abstracts, 17*(3), 19–24.

Rubin, A. (1983). Engaging families as support resources in nursing home care: Ambiguity in the subdivision of tasks. *Gerontologist, 23*(6), 632–636.

Rubin, A. (1985a). Practice effectiveness: More grounds for optimism. *Social Work, 30*(6), 469–476.

Rubin, A. (1985b). Significance testing with population data. *Social Service Review, 59*(3), 518–520.

Rubin, A. (1987). Case management. In *Encyclopedia of social work* (18th ed., Vol. 1, pp. 212–222).

Silver Spring, MD: National Association of Social Work.

Rubin, A. (1990). Cable TV as a resource in preventive mental health programming for children: An illustration of the importance of coupling implementation and outcome evaluation. *ARETE, 15*(2), 26–31.

Rubin, A. (1991). The effectiveness of outreach counseling and support groups for battered women: A preliminary evaluation. *Research on Social Work Practice, 1*(4), 332–357.

Rubin, A. (1992). Is case management effective for people with serious mental illness? A research review. *Health and Social Work, 17*(2), 138–150.

Rubin, A. (1997). The family preservation evaluation from hell: Implications for program evaluation fidelity. *Children and Youth Services Review, 19*(1–2), 77–99.

Rubin, A. (2002a). Eye movement desensitization and reprocessing. In A. R. Roberts & G. J. Greene (Eds.), *Social Worker's Desk Reference*. New York: Oxford University Press, 412–417.

Rubin, A. (2002b). Is EMDR an evidence-based practice for treating PTSD? Unanswered questions. Paper presented at the annual conference of the Society for Social Work and Research, San Diego, January 18.

Rubin, A. (2008). *Practitioner's guide to using research for evidence-based practice*. Hoboken, NJ: John Wiley & Sons.

Rubin, A. (2010). Research for providing the evidence-base for interventions in this volume. In A. Rubin & D. W. Springer (Eds.), *Treatment of traumatized adults and children: Vol. 1. The clinician's guide to evidence-based practice*. Hoboken, NJ: John Wiley & Sons, 423–429.

Rubin, A. (2010). Teaching EBP in social work: Retrospective and prospective. *Journal of Social Work, 11*(1), 64–79.

Rubin, A. (2013). *Statistics for evidence-based practice and evaluation* (3rd ed.). Belmont, CA: Brooks/Cole Cengage Learning.

Rubin, A., Bischofshausen, S., Conroy-Moore, K., Dennis, B., Hastie, M., L. Melnick, L., et al. (2001). The effectiveness of EMDR in a child guidance center. *Research on Social Work Practice, 11*(4), 435–457.

Rubin, A., & Bowker, J. (Eds.). (1986). *Studies on chronic mental illness: A new horizon for social work researchers*. New York: Council on Social Work Education.

Rubin, A., Cardenas, J., Warren, K., Pike, C. K., & Wambach, K. (1998). Outdated practitioner views about family culpability and severe mental disorders. *Social Work* (September), 412–422.

Rubin, A., & Conway, P. G. (1985). Standards for determining the magnitude of relationships in social work research. *Social Work Research and Abstracts, 21*(1), 34–39.

Rubin, A., Conway, P. G., Patterson, J. K., & Spence, R. T. (1983). Sources of variation in rate of decline to MSW programs. *Journal of Education for Social Work, 19*(3), 48–58.

Rubin, A., & Johnson, P. J. (1982). Practitioner orientations toward the chronically disabled: Prospects for policy implementation. *Administration in Mental Health, 10*, 3–12.

Rubin, A., & Johnson, P. J. (1984). Direct practice interests of entering MSW students. *Journal of Education for Social Work, 20*(2), 5–16.

Rubin, A., & Parrish, D. (2007a). Problematic phrases in the conclusions of published outcome studies: Implications for evidence-based practice. *Research on Social Work Practice, 17*(3), 334–347.

Rubin, A., & Parrish, D. (2007b). Views of evidence-based practice among faculty in MSW programs: A national survey. *Research on Social Work Practice, 17*(1), 110–122.

Rubin, A., & Parrish, D. (2009). Development and validation of the EBP process assessment scale: Preliminary findings. *Research on Social Work Practice, 20*(6), 629–640.

Rubin, A., & Shuttlesworth, G. E. (1982). Assessing role expectations in nursing home care. *ARETE, 7*(2), 37–48.

Rubin, A., & Springer, D. W. (Eds.). (2010). *The clinician's guide to evidence-based practice*. Hoboken, NJ: John Wiley & Sons.

Rubin, A., & Thorelli, I. (1984). Egoistic motives and longevity of participation by social service volunteers. *Journal of Applied Behavioral Science, 20*(3), 223–235.

Rubin, H. J., & Rubin, R. S. (1995). *Qualitative interviewing: The art of hearing data*. Thousand Oaks, CA: Sage.

Ruckdeschel, R. A., & Faris, B. E. (1981). Assessing practice: A critical look at the single-case design. *Social Casework, 62*, 413–419.

Rutter, M., Tuma, H. H., & Lann, I. S. (Eds.). (1988). *Assessment and diagnosis in child psychopathology*. New York: Guilford Press.

Sackett, D. L., Richardson, W. S., Rosenberg, W., & Haynes, R. B. (1997). *Evidence-based medicine: How to practice and teach EBM*. New York: Churchill Livingstone.

Sackett, D. L., Richardson, W. S., Rosenberg, W., & Haynes, R. B. (2000). *Evidence-based medicine: How to practice and teach EBM* (2nd ed.). New York: Churchill Livingstone.

Sacks, J. J., Krushat, W. M., & Newman, J. (1980). Reliability of the health hazard appraisal. *American Journal of Public Health* (July), 730–732.

Sales, E., Lichtenwalter, S., & Fevola, A. (2006). Secondary analysis in social work research education: Past, present, and future promise. *Journal of Social Work Education, 42*(3), 543–558.

Saletan, W., & Watzman, N. (1989). Marcus Welby, J. D. *New Republic, 200*(16), 22.

Sandelowski, M., Holditch-Davis, D. H., & Harris, B. G. (1989). Artful design: Writing the proposal for research in the naturalistic paradigm. *Research in Nursing and Health, 12*, 77–84.

Sarnoff, S. K. (1999). "Sanctified snake oil": Ideology, junk science, and social work practice. *Families in Society, 80*, 396–408.

Satterfield, J., Spring, B., Brownson, R. C., Mullen, E., Newhouse, R., & Walker, B. (2009). Toward a transdisciplinary model of evidence-based practice. *Milbank Quarterly, 87*, 368–390.

Sattler, J. M. (1988). *Assessment of children* (3rd ed.). Brandon, VT: Clinical Psychology Publishing.

Sawin, K. J., Harrigan, M. P., & Woog, P. (Eds.). (1995). *Measures of family functioning for research and practice*. New York: Springer.

Schilling, R. F., El-Bassel, N., Finch, J. B., Roman, R. J., & Hanson, M. (2002). Motivational interviewing to encourage self-help participation following alcohol detoxification. *Research on Social Work Practice, 12*(6), 711–730.

Scholl, G., & Schnur, R. (1976). *Measures of psychological, vocational, and educational functioning in the blind and visually handicapped*. New York: American Foundation for the Blind.

Schuerman, J. (1989). Editorial. *Social Service Review, 63*(1), 3.

Selltiz, C., Wrightsman, L. S., & Cook, S. W. (1976). *Research methods in social relations*. New York: Holt, Rinehart and Winston.

Shadish, W. R., Cook, T. D., & Campbell, D. T. (2002). *Experimental and quasi-experimental designs for generalized causal inference*. Boston: Houghton Mifflin.

Shadish, W. R., Cook, T. D., & Leviton, L. C. (1991). *Foundations of program evaluation*. Newbury Park, CA: Sage.

Shaffir, W. B., & Stebbins, R. A. (Eds.). (1991). *Experiencing fieldwork: An inside view of qualitative research*. Newbury Park, CA: Sage.

Shanks, J. M., & Tortora, R. D. (1985). Beyond CATI: Generalized and distributed systems for computer-assisted surveys. Paper presented at the First Annual Research Conference, Bureau of the Census, Reston, VA, March 20–23.

Shapiro, F. (1989). Efficacy of the eye movement desensitization procedure in the treatment of traumatic memories. *Journal of Traumatic Stress*, 2, 199–223.

Shapiro, F. (1995). *Eye movement de-sensitization and reprocessing: Basic principles, protocols, and procedures*. New York: Guilford Press.

Shea, C. (2000). Don't talk to the humans: The crackdown on social science research. *Lingua Franca*, 10(6), 27–34.

Shlonsky, A., & Gibbs, L. (2004). Will the real evidence-based practice please stand up? Teaching the process of evidence-based practice to the helping professions. *Brief Treatment and Crisis Intervention*, 4(2), 137–153.

Silverman, D. (1993). *Interpreting qualitative data: Methods for analyzing talk, text, and interaction*. Newbury Park, CA: Sage.

Silverman, D. (1999). *Doing qualitative research: A practical handbook*. Thousand Oaks, CA: Sage.

Simon, C. E., McNeil, J. S., Franklin, C., & Cooperman, A. (1991). The family and schizophrenia: Toward a psychoeducational approach. *Families in Society*, 72(6), 323–333.

Singer, E., Groves, R. M., & Corning, A. D. (1999). Differential incentives: Beliefs about practices, perceptions of equity, and effects on survey participation. *Public Opinion Quarterly*, 63, 251–260.

Smith, A. (2013). "Smartphone ownership." Report from the Pew Research Center's Internet and American Life Project (Jun 5, 2013). Report available at www.pewinternet.org/reports/2013/Smaartphone-Ownership-2013.aspx.

Smith, A. E., & Bishop, G. F. (1992). The Gallup secret ballot experiments: 1944–1988. Paper presented at the annual conference of the American Association for Public Opinion Research, St. Petersburg, FL, May.

Smith, E. R. A. N., & Squire, P. (1990). The effects of prestige names in question wording. *Public Opinion Quarterly*, 54, 97–116.

Smith, J. (1991). A methodology for twenty-first century sociology. *Social Forces*, 70(1), 117.

Smith, M. L., & Glass, G. V. (1977). Meta-analysis of psychotherapy outcome studies. *American Psychologist*, 32(9), 752–760.

Smith, T. W. (1988, Spring). The first straw? A study of the origins of election polls. *Public Opinion Quarterly*, 54, 21–36.

Smith, T. W. (2001). Are representative Internet surveys possible? In *Proceedings of Statistics Canada symposium, 2001, Achieving data quality in a statistical agency: A methodological perspective*.

Snow, D. A., & Anderson, L. (1987). Identity work among the homeless: The verbal construction and avowal of personal identities. *Journal of Sociology*, 92(6), 1336–1371.

Sodowsky, G. R., & Impara, J. C. (Eds.). (1996). *Multicultural assessment in counseling and clinical psychology*. Lincoln, NE: Buros Institute of Mental Measurements.

Solomon, P., & Paulson, R. I. (1995). Issues in designing and conducting randomized human service trials. Paper presented at the national conference of the Society for Social Work and Research, Washington, DC, January.

Spector, J., & Read, J. (1999). The current status of eye movement desensitization and reprocessing (EMDR). *Clinical Psychology & Psychotherapy*, 6(3), 165–174.

Srole, L. (1956). Social integration and certain corollaries: An exploratory study. *American Sociological Review*, 21, 709–716.

Stein, G. L., Beckerman, N. L., & Sherman, P. A. (2010). Lesbian and gay elders and long-term care: Identifying the unique psychosocial perspectives and challenges. *Journal of Gerontological Social Work*, 53, 421–435.

Stouffer, S. (1962). *Social research to test ideas*. New York: Free Press of Glencoe.

Strachan, A. M. (1986). Family intervention for the rehabilitation of schizophrenia: Toward protection and coping. *Schizophrenia Bulletin*, 12(4), 678–698.

Straus, M., & Brown, B. (1978). *Family measurement techniques: Abstracts of published instruments*. Minneapolis: University of Minnesota Press.

Strauss, A., & Corbin, J. (1990). *Basics of qualitative research: Grounded theory procedures and techniques*. Newbury Park, CA: Sage.

Strauss, A., & Corbin, J. (1998). *Basics of qualitative research: Grounded theory procedures and techniques* (2nd ed.). Newbury Park, CA: Sage.

Strauss, A., & Corbin, J. (1994). Grounded theory methodology: An overview. In N. K. Denzin & Y. S. Lincoln (Eds.), *Handbook of qualitative research* (pp. 273–285). Thousand Oaks, CA: Sage.

Strunk, W., Jr., & and White, E. B. (1999). *The elements of style* (4th ed.). New York: Macmillan.

Stuart, P. (1981). Historical research. In R. M. Grinnell (Ed.), *Social work research and evaluation* (pp. 316–332). Itasca, IL: Peacock.

Sudman, S. (1983). Applied sampling. In P. H. Rossi, J. D. Wright, & A. B. Anderson (Eds.), *Handbook of survey research* (pp. 145–194). New York: Academic Press.

Sue, S. (1996). Measurement, testing, and ethnic bias: Can solutions be found? In G. R. Sodowsky & J. C. Impara (Eds.), *Multicultural assessment in counseling and clinical psychology* (pp. 7–36). Lincoln, NE: Buros Institute of Mental Measurements.

Suzuki, L. A., Meller, P. J., & Ponterotto, J. G. (Eds.). (1996). *Handbook of multicultural assessment*. San Francisco: Jossey-Bass.

Sweet, S. (1999, January). Using a mock institutional review board to teach ethics in sociological research. *Teaching Sociology, 27,* 55–59.

Taber, S. M. (1981). Cognitive-behavior modification treatment of an aggressive 11-year-old boy. *Social Work Research and Abstracts, 17*(2), 13–23.

Takeuchi, D. (1974). Grass in Hawaii: A structural constraints approach. MA thesis, University of Hawaii.

Tan, A. S. (1980). Mass media use, issue knowledge and political involvement. *Public Opinion Quarterly, 44,* 241–248.

Tandon, R., & Brown, L. D. (1981, April–June). Organization-building for rural development: An experiment in India. *Journal of Applied Behavioral Science,* 172–189.

Task Force on the Promotion and Dissemination of Psychological Procedures. (1995). Training in and dissemination of empirically validated psychosocial treatments: Report and recommendations. *Clinical Psychologist, 48,* 3–23.

Taylor, J. B. (1977). Toward alternative forms of social work research: The case for naturalistic methods. *Journal of Social Welfare, 4,* 119–126.

Taylor, H., & Terhanian, G. (1999). Heady days are here again: Online polling is rapidly coming of age. *Public Perspective, 10*(4), 20–23.

Thomas, W. I., & Znaniecki, F. (1918). *The Polish peasant in Europe and America*. Chicago: University of Chicago Press.

Thompson, B. (1999a). Improving research clarity and usefulness with effect size indices as supplements to statistical significance tests. *Exceptional Children, 65*(3), 329–337.

Thompson, B. (1999b). Why encouraging effect size reporting is not working: The etiology of researcher resistance to changing practices. *Journal of Psychology, 133*(2), 133–140.

Thompson, E. E., Neighbors, H. W., Munday, C., & Jackson, J. S. (1996). Recruitment and retention of African American patients for clinical research: An exploration of response rates in an urban psychiatric hospital. *Journal of Consulting and Clinical Psychology, 64*(5), 861–867.

Thomson, B. (1996, May 29). Letter on push polling. AAPOR-net listserv. Available: billt@pos.org.

Thyer, B. (2001). Evidence-based approaches to community practice. In H. E. Briggs & K. Corcoran (Eds.), *Social work practice: Treating common client problems* (pp. 54–65). Chicago: Lyceum Books.

Thyer, B. (2002). Principles of evidence-based practice and treatment development. In A. R. Roberts & G. J. Greene (Eds.), *Social workers' desk reference* (pp. 738–742). New York: Oxford University Press.

Tinker, R. H., & Wilson, S. A. (1999). Through the eyes of a child: EMDR with children. New York: Norton.

Tobler, N. S. (1986). Meta-analysis of 143 adolescent drug prevention programs: Quantitative outcome results of program participants compared to a control or comparison group. *Journal of Drug Issues, 4,* 537–567.

Todd, T. (1998). Co-constructing your business relationship. In C. Franklin & P. Nurius (Eds.), *Constructivism in practice: Methods and challenges* (pp. 323–347). Milwaukee, WI: Families International.

Touliatos, J., Perlmutter, B. F., & Straus, M. A. (Eds.). (1990). *Handbook of family measurement techniques*. Newbury Park, CA: Sage.

Tourangeau, R., Couper, M. P., & Conrad, F. G. (2013). Up means good: The effect of screen position on evaluative ratings in web surveys. *Public Opinion Quarterly, 77,* Special issue, 69–88.

Tuckel, P. S., & Feinberg, B. M. (1991). The answering machine poses many questions for telephone survey researchers. *Public Opinion Quarterly, 55,* 200–217.

Tuckel, P. S., & O'Neill, H. (2002, September/October). The vanishing respondent in telephone surveys. *Journal of Advertising Research,* 26–48.

Tufford, L., Newman, P. A., Brannan, D. J., Craig, S. L., & Woodford, M. R. (2012). Conducting research with lesbian, gay, and bisexual populations: Navigating Ethics Board Reviews. *Journal of Gay and Lesbian Social Services, 24*(3), 221–240.

Turk, T. G. (1980). Hospital support: Urban correlates of allocation based on organizational prestige. *Pacific Sociological Review (July),* 315–332.

Turner, J. (1974). *The structure of sociological theory*. Homewood, IL: Dorsey Press.

U.S. Bureau of the Census. (1979). *Statistical abstract of the United States*. Washington, DC: U.S. Government Printing Office.

U.S. Bureau of the Census. (1992). *Statistical abstract of the United States*. Washington, DC: U.S. Government Printing Office.

U.S. Bureau of the Census. (1995). *Statistical abstract of the United States*. Washington, DC: U.S. Government Printing Office.

U.S. Bureau of the Census. (1996). *Statistical abstract of the United States, 1996, National Data Book and Guide to Sources*. Washington, DC: U.S. Government Printing Office.

U.S. Bureau of the Census. (2006). *Statistical abstract of the United States, 2006, National Data Book and Guide to Sources*. Washington, DC: U.S. Government Printing Office.

U.S. Department of Health and Human Services. (1992). *Survey measurement of drug use*. Washington, DC: U.S. Government Printing Office.

U.S. Department of Labor, Bureau of Labor Statistics. (1978). *The consumer price index: Concepts and content over the years*. Report 517. Washington, DC: U.S. Government Printing Office.

van Etten, M., & Taylor, S. (1998). Comparative efficacy of treatments for posttraumatic stress disorder: A meta-analysis. *Clinical Psychology and Psychotherapy*, 5, 126–145.

Videka-Sherman, L. (1988). Meta-analysis of research on social work practice in mental health. *Social Work*, 33(4), 325–338.

Vonk, M. E. (2001). Cultural competence for transracial adoptive parents. *Social Work*, 46(3), 246–255.

Votaw, C. D. (1979). *Women's rights in the United States*. Washington, DC: Clearinghouse Publications.

Wagner-Pacifici, R. (1995). *Discourse and destruction: The city of Philadelphia versus MOVE*. Chicago: University of Chicago Press.

Walker, D. K. (1973). *Socioemotional measure for preschool and kindergarten children*. San Francisco: Jossey-Bass.

Walker, J. R., & Taylor, T. (1998). *The Columbia guide to online style*. New York: Columbia University Press.

Walker, J. T. (1994). Fax machines and social surveys: Teaching an old dog new tricks. *Journal of Quantitative Criminology*, 10(2), 181–188.

Walker Research. (1988). *Industry image study* (8th ed.). Indianapolis: Author.

Wallace, W. (1971). *The logic of science in sociology*. Chicago: Aldine-Atherton.

Walster, E., Piliavian, J., & Walster, G. W. (1973). The hard-to-get woman. *Psychology Today* (September), 80–83.

Webb, E., Campbell, D. T., Schwartz, R. D., & Sechrest, L. (1981). *Nonreactive research in the social sciences*. Chicago: Rand McNally.

Webb, E., Campbell, D. T., Schwartz, R. D., & Sechrest, L. (2000). *Unobtrusive measures*. Thousand Oaks, CA: Sage.

Weber, M. (1925). Science as a vocation. In H. Gerth & C. Wright Mills (Trans. & Eds.), *From Max Weber: Essays in sociology*. New York: Oxford University Press.

Weber, R. P. (1990). *Basic content analysis*. Newbury Park, CA: Sage.

Weinbach, R., & Grinnell, R. (1998). *Statistics for social workers* (4th ed.). New York: Longman.

Weisbrod, B. A., Test, M. A., & Stein, L. I. (1980). Alternative to mental hospital treatment: II. Economic benefit-cost analysis. *Archives of General Psychiatry*, 37(4), 400–408.

Weiss, C. H. (1972). *Evaluation research*. Englewood Cliffs, NJ: Prentice Hall.

Weisz, A. N., & Black, B. M. (2001). Evaluating a sexual assault and dating violence prevention program for urban youths. *Social Work Research*, 25(2), 89–99.

Wells, T., Bailey, J. T., & Link, M. W. (2013). Filling the Void: Gaining a Better Understanding of Tablet-based Surveys. *Survey Practice*, 6(1). Available at http://www.surveypractice.org/index.php/SurveyPractice/article/view/25.

Westen, D. I. (2006). Patients and treatments in clinical trials are not adequately representative of clinical practice. In J. C. Norcross, L. E. Beutler, & R. F. Levant (Eds.), *Evidence-based practices in mental health: Debate and dialogue on the fundamental questions* (pp. 161–171). Washington, DC: American Psychological Association.

Wetzler, S. (Ed.). (1989). *Measuring mental illness: Psychometric assessment for clinicians*. Washington, DC: American Psychiatric Press.

White, K. R. (1988). Cost analyses in family support programs. In H. B. Weiss & F. H. Jacobs (Eds.), *Evaluating family programs* (pp. 429–443). New York: Aldine de Gruyter.

White, R. (1951). *Value-analysis: The nature and use of the method*. New York: Society for the Psychological Study of Social Issues.

Whiteman, M., Fanshel, D., & Grundy, J. F. (1987). Cognitive-behavioral interventions aimed at anger of parents at risk of child abuse. *Social Work*, 32(6), 469–474.

Whittaker, J. K. (1987). Group care for children. In *Encyclopedia of social work* (18th ed., Vol. 1, pp. 672–682). Silver Spring, MD: National Association of Social Workers.

Whyte, W. F. (1943). *Street corner society*. Chicago: University of Chicago Press.

Whyte, W. F., Greenwood, D. J., & Lazes, P. (1991). Participatory action research: Through practice to science in social research. In W. F. Whyte (Ed.), *Participatory action research* (pp. 19–55). New York: Sage.

Williams, J., & Ell, K. (1998). *Advances in mental health research: Implications for practice*. Washington, DC: NASW Press.

Wilson, J. (1989). Cancer incidence and mortality differences of black and white Americans: A role for biomarkers. In L. Jones (Ed.), *Minorities and cancer*. New York: Springer-Verlag.

W. K. Kellogg Foundation. (2004). *W. K. Kellogg Foundation logic model development guide*. Battle Creek, MI: Author.

Wood, K. M. (1978). Casework effectiveness: A new look at the research evidence. *Social Work, 23*(6), 437–458.

Yin, R. K. (1984). *Case study research: Design and methods*. Beverly Hills, CA: Sage.

Yinger, J. M., Ikeda, K., Laycock, F., & Cutler, S. J. (1977). *Middle start: An experiment in the educational enrichment of young adolescents*. London: Cambridge University Press.

York, J., & Persigehl, E. (1981). Productivity trends in the ball and roller bearing industry. *Monthly Labor Review (January)*, 40–43.

Yoshihama, M. (2002). Breaking the web of abuse and silence: Voices of battered women in Japan. *Social Work, 47*(4), 389–400.

Yu, E. S. H., Zhang, M.-Y., Xia, Z.-Y., & Liu, W. T. (1987). Translation of instruments: Procedures, issues, and dilemmas. In W. T. Liu (Ed.), *A decade review of mental health research, training, and services* (pp. 75–83). Chicago: Pacific/Asian American Mental Health Research Center.

Ziesel, H. (1957). *Say it with figures*. New York: Harper & Row.

Zimbalist, S. E. (1977). *Historic themes and landmarks in social welfare research*. New York: Harper & Row.

Zippay, A. (2002). Dynamics of income packaging: A 10-year longitudinal study. *Social Work, 47*, 291–300.

Zlotnik, J. L., & Galambos, C. (2004). Evidence-based practices in health care: Social work possibilities. *Health and Social Work, 29*, 259–261.